D1486781

HUNGARIAN BALLADS
AND THE
EUROPEAN
BALLAD TRADITION
II.

HUNGARIAN BALLADS
AND THE
EUROPEAN
BALLAD TRADITION

II.

BY

LAJOS VARGYAS

AKADÉMIAI KIADÓ · BUDAPEST 1983

THIS IS THE ENGLISH VERSION OF THE AUTHOR'S

A MAGYAR NÉPBALLADA ÉS EURÓPA I–II.
Zeneműkiadó, Budapest

Translated
by
IMRE GOMBOS

ISBN 963 05 2990 4. Vols. I–II
ISBN 963 05 2991 2. Vol. I
ISBN 963 05 2992 0. Vol. II

Printed in Hungary

CONTENTS

New ballads. Types 121–134.

Appendix

SPECIAL PART

Hungarian Ballads
with Comparative Studies by Types

———

OLD STYLE BALLADS

1. THE UNFAITHFUL WIFE BURNT TO DEATH

1.

1. Go, husband, rise and go to Kolozsvár,
   Go to Kolozsvár, to my father's mansion,
   Go and fetch, fetch me the broad sheets of linen,
   The broad sheets of linen, the gift of cambric.
5. Do not go, father, do not go, aye, do not leave the house,
   For mother is in love with Barcsai!
   Do you hear, wife, do you hear what the child is prattling?
   Pay no attention, husband dear, the child is drunk.
   So off he went at his wife's bidding.
10. At his wife's bidding, aye, he set out to Kolozsvár.
    When he was half-way there,
    He remembered his youngest child's words.
    He turned at once and started for home,
    Started for home and arrived at his place.
15. Open the door, open the door, my wedded wife!
    I'll open it at once, my dear, kind husband,
    Just let me put on my workday skirt,
    Just let me put on my apron!
    Open the door, open the door, my wedded wife!
20. I'll open it at once, my dear, kind husband.
    Just let me put on my long boots,
    Just let me tie up my head-kerchief!
    Open the door, open the door, my wedded wife!
    Aye, what could she do? She had to open the door.
25. Give me, give me the key to the big chest!
    I will not give, I will not give you the key to the big chest:
    I went to see the neighbour and, when crossing the fence,
    I lost the key to the big chest.
    But we shall find it at crimson dawn,
30. At crimson dawn, at the bright day-break.
    At once he kicked the side of the bright, painted chest in,
    And when he split off one of its sides,
    Barcsai rolled out of it.
    Aye, he took his sword and cut off Barcsai's head.
35. Do you hear, wife, do you hear, wife, do you hear?
    Which one will you choose of the three deaths?
    Have your choice now: shall I take your head?
    Or shall I sweep the house with your silk hair?
    Or would you prefer to sit up till morn,

40. And bear candle to the entertainment of seven guests at table?
Of the three deaths I choose
To bear candle to the entertainment of seven guests at table.
My foot-page, my foot-page, my little foot-page,
Bring here, bring here the broad sheets of linen,
45. The broad sheets of linen, the gift of cambric!
Start at her head, wrap her in it down to the heel,
Wrap all the gift of cambric at her head!
Start at the head, put pitch down to her heel,
Start at the heel, light it and burn it up to her head!
50. Let a Vlach flutist stand at her head,
Let a Gipsy fiddler stand at her feet!
Blow, Vlach, blow the Vlach flute,
Play, Gipsy, play the gipsy fiddle!
Blow it loud, play it at once:
55. Let my wife find her heart's pleasure!

Udvarhelyszék, Sándor Gálfi = MNGY I, 149.

2.

Parlando ♩= 60

1. É - des a - pám - u - ram,

É - des - a - nyám - asz - szony Bar - csa - it sze - - re - ti!

1. Father dear, father dear,
   Mother is in love with Barcsai.

2. Pay no attention, my kind husband, pay no attention, my kind husband,
   For the child is wandering, he does not know what he is saying!...

3. Then he set out on his long way about the country,
   But he returned from half-way and went to the window of his house.

4. Open the door, open the door, my dear wife!
   I'll open it at once, I'll open it, dear husband.

5. Just let me put on my skirt embroidered with gold,
   Just let me put on my red, long boots with the heel iron.

6. He could not wait so long, he kicked the door in.
   He could not wait so long, he kicked the door in.

7. What have we to eat, wife? What have we to eat, wife?
   In the large window there is a dish of pork seasoned with pepper.

8. I don't want to have, I don't want to have anyone's leavings,
   But I want to have walnuts and hazelnuts from the big chest.

9. Dearest heart, kind husband, I have been busy in the kitchen
   And I lost, and I lost the key to the big chest.

10. He could not wait so long: he kicked the side of the big chest in.
    Barcsai rolled out, Barcsai rolled out.

11. Seizing him by the hair, he dragged him to the threshold,
    He dragged him to the threshold and cut his throat.

12. Dearest wife, dearest wife!
    Which one of the three deaths will you choose?

13. Will you be a butcher's block? Will you be a woodcutter's block?
    Or will you bear candle to the entertainment of twelve guests at table?

14. I will bear candle to the entertainment, I will bear candle to the
    entertainment.
    Boys, bring the waxed cloth!

15. We'll start at her feet and wrap her in it up to her head;
    We'll light it at the head and burn her at the entertainment,

16. Let all take a lesson from this on how a whore ends!
    Let all take a lesson from this on how a whoremonger ends!

Kibéd (Maros-Torda) Seprődi = SZND 34.

3.

1. Father, father, father, my dear father!
   I say, mother is in love with Barcsai.
   Do you hear, wife, do you hear what the child is saying?
   I hear it, husband, I hear it, my dearest heart, my gentle mate!
5. But the child is wandering, he does not know what he is saying.
   At once he started out, aye, he started for Kolozsvár.
   When he was half-way there he turned and went back home.
   And he reached his home.
   Open the door, open the door, wife!
10. I open it up, dearest husband, dear heart, my gentle mate!
    Just let me put on my gold-embroidered skirt,
    Just let me put on my dress of cambric,
    Just let me put on my beautiful red long-boots!
    He kicked the door of the house in at once.
15. Give me, give me the key to the big chest!
    I have been to the neighbour's and while crossing the fence

13

I dropped the key to the big chest.
But we shall find it at beautiful, crimson dawn.
Then he kicked the side of the big chest in.
20. Barcsai rolled out of it.
Aye, he seized him and struck off his head at once.
Come here, come here, wife!
Which one of the three deaths will you choose?
Shall I blow out your brains or shall I strike off your head?
25. Or shall you bear candle to the entertainment of seven guests at table?
My choice of the three deaths is
To bear candle to the entertainment of seven guests at table.
I say, maid, bring here the sheet of linen,
And bring here the big barrel of pitch!
30. Start at her head and wrap her in it down to her heel,
Start it at her heel and burn it up to her head!
My God, my God, what have I done!
I have killed Barcsai and my dear wife!

Marosszék, Nyárád-riverine, Kriza=MNGY XI. No. 381.

Cf. Leader, 250.

Variant readings:

(a) Instead of Barcsai's execution: "Wife, my dearest, dearest wife, Don't you see the little child said the truth!" In the end: "Wife, my dearest, dearest wife, Of the three deaths you have chosen this!"
(b) Having asked his wife for something to eat, he goes down to the basement and breaks down the door with an axe. "Why do you cry, wife?... I have burnt oak...", etc. "Will you be my woodcutter's block?" "Will you be my kettle for distilling brandy?" "No... I wish to be your true wife." "Set her on flame, the infamous whore!"

Earliest provenience: 1853

Dissemination: Maros-Torda county (Jobbágytelke, Kibéd, "Marosszék, Nyárád-riverine", Csittszentiván); Udvarhely county ("Udvarhelyszék"); "Székely area"; Bukovina (Istensegíts). Total: 7.

Textual relationships with other ballads:

Comic variant with the wife's lover escaped: No. **78**. Burning the live body: No. **28**. Phrases uttered in an attempt at delaying the opening up of the door: Nos **20, 21, 25** and **78**. Reference to smoke of burnt oak as an excuse for crying: No. **20**.
Apart from the published variant, two tunes of the ballad have been recorded:

In the second variant some of the lines are expanded to include as many as sixteen syllables. This form is not exceptional at all, see for example No. **17.** In connection with this Bartók remarked that "the performer was drunk"; in spite of this we should not regard the form as corrupt; the technique of expansion does not undermine the tune's four-line structure (four-section construction) which is clearly detectable.

Partial parallels in foreign-language areas:

SPANISH-PORTUGUESE-CATALAN: *1–7. Cossio-Solano* I, 215–227 27/120–122; Nos 125–6, 128–9. *8. Geibel-Schack* 350. *9. Braga* II, 87. *10. Amades*, 428 No. 2322.

MONGOLIAN: *11. Potanin* No. 117. *12. Verbickij* 151, 2. par.

SOUTHERN SLAV: *13. Vuk* II, No. 31. *14.* Ib. III, No. 7, 149. *15.* HNP V, 389. No. 217. *16–41.* HNP V, 610. Supplement to No. 217, 26 excerpt. *42–43.* HNP V, Nos 354 205 and 595. Supplement to No. 205, excerpt. *44. Geseman* 166 No. 117. *45. Stojanović-Vitezica*, 418. *46.* Istarske p. I, 69. No. XXV. *47. Žganec* 1950, 460 Note to No. 375.

BULGARIAN: *48–49. Stoin* 1939. Nos 1057–8. *50–51. Stoin* 1931, Nos 2358–60. *52–54. Arnaudov* 1913, Nos 113–5. *55. Miladinovi* No. 163. *56–58. Shapkarev* III, Nos 334, 395, 426. *59.* SbNU 1, Nos 294, 251. *60–61.* SbNU 9, No. 11. 3. and 78. No. 1. *62.* SbNU 13, 103, No. 11. *63–65.* SbNU 14, 57 No. 21, 57 No. 60 and 75 No. 8. *66.* SbNU 16, 171 No.1. *67–68.* SbNU 38. *Burmov* No. 50 and No. 138. *69–70.* SbNU 43 *Vatev* No. 90 and No. 140. *71–72.* SbNU *Ivanov* No. 49 and No. 52. *73–74.* SbNU 46. I. Tsitselkova No. 201–202. *75. Dozon* 1875 No. 35. = *Stoilov* 1916–18. 886. *76.* Izv. Ethn. Muz. VI, 118–121. *77. Kachanovskij* 443, No. 182.

ROMANIAN: *78.* Ethn. 1897, 189. *79. Papahagi*, 1925. No. 382. (= Anna Molnár). *80. Brăiloiu*, 94. *81. Amzulescu* 291.

The Hungarian ballad about the unfaithful wife burnt to death has parallels in the distant Iberian peninsula and also in the still more distant Altai mountains in the East.

In the Spanish, Portuguese and Catalan ballads the husband leaves his home and goes to hunting or war while his wife reciprocates the advances of a knight. The husband returns unexpectedly. He bangs the door—in some versions he has to break it down because the wife has lost the key to the corridor where the knight is hiding. The process of discovery, however, is not so simple as in the Hungarian ballad for in the western parallels the knight's horse is neighing in the stable at the critical moment and a series of questions on the part of the husband are followed by as many evasive answers on the wife's part, like in the Hungarian ballad of The Beguiled Husband **((129.)** concerning the owner of the clothes, sword, etc. Apparently the ballad is an amalgamation of two. (As a separate comic ballad the story of Beguiled Husband is known in the French-speaking territories, therefore it is likely that the Iberian parallel's elements, amalgamated from two different ballads are borrowed from the French, although I have not been able to trace so far the French text corresponding to the serious portion.) Additional evidence of the secondary nature of the amalgamation lies in the fact that one of the Portuguese texts omit the continuation, in which case the burning is involved only in the form of an allusion: "A woman who speaks like this deserves to be burnt. Thirty full cartloads and as many branches of tree." Another convincing proof of the self-evident amalgamation is that also the Romanians have melded the ballad with the Hungarian version of the same type *(81.)*.

The Altaic song contains other portions to complement the ballad. *(11.–12.)*. The hero's mother and sister ally themselves with a foreign warrior, and then they send the hero to get the heart of a magic serpent or to fetch meerschaum from the sea, hoping he will perish on the way. The hero, however, warned by his *magic horse,* returns and fights the enemy. He cannot defeat the warrior whom the women hide in the big chest of the family. Returning once from hunting, the hero asks the women for his father's bowl, from which he wishes to eat a dish. (The motif of asking for the bowl occurs in many songs.) "You will find it in the chest of your father."—answer the women. When he opens the chest, his enemy jumps out of it— to conquer this time. Nevertheless, the hero is restored to life by his magic horse, and succeeds in destroying his enemy. Then he offers the women their choice: either they fill eighty ditches with dung or they milk eighty mares. They chose the latter and were trodden to death by the wild mares.

The scene of asking for food in combination with the rival that is to appear from the chest is so characteristic as to preclude the possibility of a chance occurrence in two distant places; and if this correlation is granted, then the other agreements become meaningful, such as the sending of the husband on errand, the warning of the child or of the magic horse, and the choice among the different kinds of death made more conspicuous by the same idea, notably that the choice of the seemingly milder form of punishment leads to the most painful death. What is more, even the method of execution may originate from the epic songs. Gyula László calls attention to the representation of Saint Ladislas of Hungary in a legendary now in the Vatican: before striking off the Kuman warrior's head, Ladislas is dragging him on the ground by his hair, just like the husband is dragging Barcsai. In any case, it is the corresponding elements of epic songs about an act of treachery that have coagulated into a a ballad—following perhaps the model of a western, possibly French ballad of adultery. The amalgamation has been highly successful, no break of style occurs anywhere, so that the Hungarian ballad may be considered the prototype of the genre.

The most impressing scene, in which the unfaithful woman is wrapt in tarred linen and so burnt has had greatest impact on the peoples of the Balkan peninsula. Southern Slavs, Bulgars and Romanians have incorporated this scene into their epic songs speaking about treacherous women. (Among the Transylvanian Romanians the full story of Barcsai comes up, although in a not quite authentic recording.)

2. THE WALLED-UP WIFE

4.

Parlando

1. El - in - dult, el - in - dult ti - zen-két kő - mí - ves,

A ti - zen - har - ma - dik Ke - le - men Kő - mi - ves.

É - pí - te - ni kezd ték ma - gas Dé - va vá - rát,

A - mit es - tig rak - tak, reg - ge - lig le om - lott.

1. Twelve masons set out, set out to walk,
   The thirteenth was Kelemen the Mason.
   They began to build the high castle of Déva.
   What they built by day fell down by night.

2. They took counsel together, the twelve masons,
   The thirteenth was Kelemen the Mason:
   Whoever's wife happens to come here first,
   She shall be burnt, she shall be thrown into the fire.

3. The ashes of the burnt body shall be gathered,
   And shall be thrown to the last into the slaked lime,
   In this way we may build the high castle of Déva safely,
   By means of a beautiful woman's ashes.

4. That night Kelemen's wife had a dream:
   A well of blood spurted out in her courtyard.
   Coachman, coachman, my dearest coachman,
   Bring out the coach, and harness the horses!

5. Kelemen the Mason saw her from afar,
   And he began to pray: God, my God,
   Send a shower so that the coach should break down,
   So that it should miss the way never to reach here!

18

6. But God did not pay heed to him,
   And his wife was nearing.
   Good day, good day to you, twelve masons,
   And to the thirteenth, Kelemen the Mason.

7. I have greeted you the second time, and you do not answer me.
   Well, what is the matter with you, will you tell me?
   Here is our answer, here is our answer, my dear wife:

8. We have made a strong agreement, and you must die.
   My dear wife,—aye, my dear, bonny child,
   How can you fare when your mother is dead?

9. Seize her tenderly, throw her into the fire,
   Gather her ashes and mix them into the lime.
   With this we shall be able to build up the high castle of Déva,
   With this we shall be able to stop the ruining of the walls.

10. Good evening, good evening, my dear father,
    Where is dear mother, why is she so long to come home?
    Don't cry, my dear son, she will arrive by night,
    And if she is not come by night, she will come by morning.

11. Night has come, yet she is not come home,
    Morning has come, yet she is not come home.
    Tell me, father, where is my dear mother,
    Why is she so late to come?

12. Dearest son, I cannot endure it any longer,
    Your mother has died because she has been burnt.
    And with her ashes we have built up the high castle of Déva.

13. Curse on you, high castle of Déva!
    Even the sun may not shine on you!
    Because of you I have lost my dear wife,
    And my only child has been left orphan.

Zsére (Nyitra county), Tibor Ág = AP 4407/b.

5.

1. Lo, twelve masons set out to walk,
   They set out to walk to the high castle of Déva.
   They begin to build the high castle of Déva.
   What they built by night fell down by day,
5. What they built by day fell down by night...
   Kelemen the Mason made the rule:
   Whichever wife should be the first
   To bring her husband's dinner basket,
   She must be walled up among the stones and burnt alive there!

10. She must be built into the pile of the high castle of Déva!
Lo! his own wife set out,
Carrying the dinner basket on her head,
And carrying her little child on her arm.
Her husband saw her from afar:
15. O God, my God, send two wild beasts before her,
Perhaps they will make her turn back!
But she escaped them...
My God, my God,
Send a black cloud before her,
20. Make pebbles rain down before them,
Perhaps it will make her turn back!
But she escaped that, too.
Good day, good day to you, twelve masons!
My God, my God, what is the matter:
25. To greet them three times without a reply!...
Your dear husband has made the rule:
Whichever wife should be the first
To bring her husband's dinner basket
She must be walled up among the stones and burnt alive there!
30. She must be built in the pile of high Déva castle.
I care not if you have come
To loathe your life with me...
They took the dinner basket off her head,
They took her little child off her arm.
35. When they built up as far as her knee, she took it only as a joke.
When they built up as far as her waist, she took it as a jest.
When they built up as far as her breast, she took it in earnest:
Don't cry, my little son,
There are kind women who will give you the breast;
40. There are kind children who will rock you to sleep.
The birds of heaven hop from branch to branch,
They will chirrup to you to send you to sleep!
Father, dear father, where is my dear mother?
Don't cry, little son, for she will come home this evening!
He waited till evening, and his mother was not back.
Father, dear father, where is my dear mother?
Don't cry, little son, for she will come home in the morning!
He waited till morning, too, and his mother was not back.
Both mother and child died!...

Nyárád-riverine, Székelyföld= MNGY I., p. 174.

6.

1. Ho - vá mégy, hová mégy Ti - zen - két kő - mi - es?

El - me- nyünk, elmenyünk, Hogyha dolgot kapnánk,

1. Where are you going, where are you going, twelve masons?
   We are going, we are going to seek a job.

2. Come, I will hire you, come, I will hire you,
   To build up the high castle of Déva.

3. For one bushel of gold, for two bushels of silver,
   For two bushels of silver, three bushels of copper!

4. They began to build the high castle of Déva:
   What they built in the forenoon fell down in the afternoon,

5. What they built in the afternoon fell down at night,
   What they built in the afternoon fell down at night.

6. The twelve masons took counsel together:
   Whichever of the wives comes first here,

7. She must be seized, she must be burnt,
   She must be seized, she must be burnt,

8. Her beautiful white ashes must be mixed into the lime,
   So that we may build up with it the high castle of Déva!

9. My God, my God, raise a dark wood,
   So that my wedded wife should turn back!

10. God granted it, yet she did not turn back,
    God granted it, yet she did not turn back.

11. Good day, good day, Kelemen the Mason!
    Welcome, welcome, my wedded wife!

12. I have come, I have come to see you!
    You have come, you have come to lose your head!

13. Aye, I know your ways very well,
    You kill people and so you make money!

14. Aye, they then seized her, they cut her throat,
    They burnt her in the fire, they burnt her in the fire,

15. They mixed her beautiful white ashes into the lime,
They mixed her beautiful white ashes into the lime.

16. So they built up the high castle of Déva,
So they built up the high castle of Déva.

17. Thereupon they were paid one bushel of gold,
One bushel of gold, two bushels of silver.

18. Two bushels of silver, three bushels of copper,
Two bushels of silver, three bushels of copper.

19. Kelemen the Mason started home.
His daughter asked him: Father, dear father,

20. Father, dear father, where is my dear mother?
She is gone far away, she will come home in the evening.

21. Evening has come, yet she has not come home,
Evening has come, yet she has not come home.

22. His next daughter asked him: Father, dear father,
Father, dear father, where is my dear mother?

23. Your dear mother is standing in the high wall of stone,
Your dear mother is standing in the high wall of stone...

Gyergyóalfalu (Csík county), 1910. a woman of 65, Kodály = Sz. Nd. No. 56.

7.

1. They are building, they are building the high castle of Déva,
They are building, they are building the high castle of Déva.

2. What they build by day, they pull down by night,
What they build by day, they pull down by night.

3. The greatest master made the rule:
Whichever of the wives comes first here in the morning,

4. She must be taken at once, her blood must be drawn,
Her tender bones must be built in the wall of stone.

5. Her tender bones must be built in the wall of stone,
Her red blood must be mixed into the lime.

22

6. The master's wife had a dream:
   In the middle of her courtyard there was a stream of blood flowing.

7. My coachman, my coachman, my dearest coachman,
   Prepare my coach for the way, harness my six horses!

8. The horses are the dogs', the way is the Lord's,
   Drive, coachman, drive towards high Déva!

9. Good morning, good mornig, dearest husband!
   Good morning, good morning, dearest wife!

10. My dear wife, why did you come here now,
    Why did you come here now, when you must lose your head?!

11. They took her at once, they had her blood drawn,
    And they built her tender bones in the wall of stone.

12. They built her tender bones in the wall of stone,
    They mixed her red blood into the lime.

13. My God, my God! What befalls my little son?
    My God, my God! What befalls my little son?

14. There are cradles to rock him to sleep,
    There are kind women to give him the breast!

15. My God, my God! Where is my dear mother?
    My God, my God, where is my dear mother?

16. Don't cry, my little son, she will come home in the evening,
    And if not in the evening, she will come home in the morning.

17. And if she is not come in the morning, she is lost for ever,
    And if she is not come in the morning, she is lost for ever! . . .

18. Curse be then on the high castle of Déva,
    May the bright sun not shine on it!

19. I have lost for it my dear wife,
    And my dear child has been left orphan!

Kászonaltíz (Csík county) 1912. A woman of 50,
Kodály = Sz. Nd. No. 122.

8.

Kit éj - jen fel - rak - nak,   e nappal mind le - hull.

Isz - te - nem, Isz - te - nem,   hogy te -gyünk egy törvényt!

1. They are building, they are building the high castle of Dio,
   What they build by day, falls down by night,
   What they build by night, falls down by day.
   My God, my God, let us make a rule,

2. Perhaps we shall be able to erect the high castle of Dio!
   The greatest mason made the rule:
   Whichever of the wives
   Comes first here, she must be killed.

3. The greatest mason's wife had a dream
   That came true on Sunday morning.
   Get up, servant, get up, harness the horses,
   While I prepare my little son for the road.

4. The greatest mason stood out on the hill,
   He waved with his hand and spoke with his mouth:
   My God, my God, my beloved God,
   Make a terrible thunderstorm fall before them!

5. God granted it, yet they did not turn back.
   I say the second time: My God, my God,
   My God, my God, my beloved God,
   Send three wicked wolves before them,

6. Perhaps they will turn back, perhaps they will turn back.
   God granted it, yet they did not turn back.
   I say the third time: My God, my God,
   My God, my God, my beloved God,

7. Make a big windstorm fall before them,
   Perhaps they will turn back, perhaps they will turn back.
   God granted it as well, yet they did not turn back.
   God granted it as well, yet they did not turn back.

8. They were going, they were going on,
   Until they arrived at the high castle of Dio.
   The greatest mason made a rule,
   Whichever of the wives

24

9. First comes here,
   She must be killed, she must be walled up,
   She must be killed, she must be walled up.—

10. When they built up as far as her knee: Is it in earnest, or is it a joke?
    Is it in earnest or is it a joke, twelve masons?
    It is in earnest, madam, your husband made a rule,
    It is in earnest, madam, your husband made a rule.

11. When they built up as far as her waist; Is it in earnest or is it a joke?
    Is it in earnest or is it a joke, twelve masons?
    It is in earnest, madam, your husband made a rule,
    It is in earnest, madam, your husband made a rule.

12. If it is in earnest, place this little son of mine
    Place this little son of mine beside me!
    They placed her little son beside her,
    Streams of water sprang from her breasts.

Trunk (Moldavia), 1930. A woman of 58.
Sándor Veress = MF. 2489/a-2490/a.

The 1–2. lines of the third stanza are borrowed from a lyrical song.

A prose version of the ballad was recorded at Zenta (Bács-Bodrog county) in 1970. A month after the recording, the informant produced a more detailed version of the story. The latter variant is published here; the more interesting parts of the former are added in brackets.

"Well, I know it like this, I heard the story about the building of Bálványos Castle like this: Once upon a time they began to build the castle of Bálványos. When they were building—nine men were working on it—what they built up one day, fell down the next day. Then the men thought that it won't be good unless they make something by way of sacrifice. Then the nine men swore, saying: Whichever wife should be the first to bring her husband's dinner, she must be built up in the castle. And they began to work in the morning. The men were all together at the castle of Bálványos. They saw what they had built the previous day fell down by night. Well then, today we'll continue. All men felt uneasy, because they did not know whose wife should be the first to come. One of them was particularly anxious, because he had three children. My wife will be certainly late to come with my dinner, since she has to do things in order about my three children. About ten or eleven o'clock each of the nine men was restless: Which one of our wives? ...Alas, were it not mine! The other man: Aye, were it not mine! ... And the one, the father of the three children, grew very sad: what if his Julis were the first to come? Alas, it would be very sad to think of her coming! Even though she has always been quick, she should not come first this time! Would she leave the children all right. What will befall my three children? At about half past eleven he looks at the corner of the street, towards the city: lo, there comes his Julis with the dinner. (Then the man began to

25

shout: turn back, turn back! But the woman did not hear him shouting, she was glad to bring him food: I have come first with the dinner!) Arriving there, the woman greets him decently: Dearest heart, my husband, I have come with the dinner. Alas, I wish you did not come! The woman grew angry: Why? You received me gladly on other occasions. Why are you so angry now?—She has no idea what happened to her man. Tell me, dearest heart, what's the matter. Is it that I've brought the dinner? Is it the matter?—It is not that! If only you knew what is in store for you!—What is it?—Then he tells her: You see, what we have built so far has fallen down to the last piece of stone, and the nine of us swore that whichever wife should be the first to bring her husband's dinner must be walled up. Then the woman burst out crying: Did you not think of your three children?—Well, I thought of them, although I did not think you would come first.—Well, if you had decided to erect a monument of the world, building up the castle of Bálványos, wall me up—says she—three orphans of mine will be raised somehow!"

On questioning, the performer stated that he had heard the story from old people who related it as a tale while working. The name Bálványosvár (the castle of Bálványos) was known to him from a book of tales which he had read and which he had referred to, although in connection with some other story. (The story was a sort of legend, closely connected to the ballad story according to the performer who therefore recited it as a sequel.) On the first occasion, the story went on without any mention of the name, only the case of walling-up was important.) *(Katona-Tripolyszky)*

The use of the numerical adjective nine instead of twelve is probably due to its prevalence in the poetry on outlaws from where it got into the mind of the performer.

The text's spread is not confined to this single locality in the region. *Kálmány* wrote the following: "I succeeded in noting down at Török-Becse (Torontál county) a few lines of Kőmives Kelemenné (The Wife of Kelemen the Mason) listed under No. 314 in Kriza's collection Vadrózsák." (Szeged Népe II, p. 167.) "It would be interesting to know to what extent the Great-Plain variant differs from the Székely variants; I have made attempts at finding out it, although to no avail, because the board of school at Török-Becse... raised obstacles." Unfortunately, he fails to publish the "few lines" which—as can be inferred from Kálmány's information—may have been a fragment in verse from the other side of the Tisza, the Trans-Tisza Region.

Divergences in the sung variants

The texts here published represent the most common incipit motifs of the ballad. Especially widespread is the formula "They are building..." as incipit. But there is another starting formula which does not come up in the given examples: "Twelve masons made counsel together That they would build up the high castle of Déva." This incipit is always associated with a reference to material incentive: "That they would build it up for half a bushel of silver, For half a bushel of silver, half a bushel of gold", in the light of which the sacrifice of the wife seems even more condemnable. On seeing the wall falling down, it is the master mason who makes the decision; in other instances the twelve masons make an agreement which is sometimes brought out in an implied, impersonal statement: "Therefore they say, This castle won't stand, This castle won't stand, It wants someone to be sacrificed." (Pürkerec). Two variants from the Moldavian Klézse takes over the solution of the Romanian Manole-song in that the master learns what to do from a dream. This adoption has been facilitated by the dream motif occurring in the major part of the Hungarian variants, which attribute it to either the wife or the coachman. The vision of the blood stream welling up in the courtyard of the master and that of the child falling into it, makes the wife to hurry to her husband. When this is the case, the wife possessed with fear of some impending danger always goes by coach to see her husband, and also the coachman is called, but such variants constituting the major bloc of the ballad type never contain allusion to the wife's bringing dinner to her husband. That is to say, the majority of the Hungarian versions have resorted to a solution which develops the tragic plot not from some incidence but from the disposition of a worrying wife eager to see her man. Therefore she arrives first. In such instances another motif will also regularly present itself: the woman urges the coachman—and accelerates thereby the dénouement—asking him not to spare horses and coach: "The horses are not yours, nor is the coach yours, Whip the horses, let us go faster!" This motif occurs in numerous different formulations. And when it simply announces that the woman wishes to see her man, without referring to a dream, then there follows another formula speaking about bad weather, strom and wind, and the coachman making efforts to turn the woman back because he had a bad dream.

Number 5 offers a more seldom solution which, however, seems to be older as it survives only in fragments, including the earliest record of the ballad in the Almásy MS. We know of five such variants in all. (In point of fact, Number 5 is also a fragment: it ends abruptly with sketchy closing sentence.) In this group the victim is invariably the woman that first brings his man's *dinner basket*. But in such cases the coach is never mentioned (in some variants not even the dinner is involved).

Exceptional is the turn in an isolated variant in which the master is sending home his apprentice in order to delay his wife's coming, although to no avail for the apprentice bids her make haste. This is certainly a secondary development as shown by one of the texts in which the motif of delaying—mostly linked up with the coachman—is associated with the apprentice who foresees the danger and wishes to have the woman turn back. A strange innovation is when the master shoots the unfaithful servant arriving at the castle; a similarly individual development occurs in another variant that adds eight more stanzas to the ballad telling about the master mason applying to the Town Council with his complaint, actually after the story had been closed.

Seeing the wife approach, the master utters an oath praying God to set some obstacle in the way. A less poetic representation of the psychological situation is the one in which he does not speak, he only waves with his hand, whereby he only speeds up the dénouement. Another solution giving up the endeavour to depict the psychic condition introduces the storm and other obstacles not in consequence of a prayer but as a chance occurrence, and the coachman wants to turn back, but the wife persists. This development is of a secondary nature because it cannot be reasonably supposed that the storm should turn subsequently into a psychologically substantiated, although naive, wish. Also on the point of arrival two parallel formulations are seen to concur in the variants, though the two do never blend: in the one, which is more effective from the psychological point of view, the wife's greeting is left unanswered; the other, in which the woman's greeting is returned with the following sentence: "Why did you come here now when you must lose your head?!" usually continues by repeating the decision, and if reference had been made in the beginning to "winning the big payment" then here, after the completion of the construction, the motif often recurs, lending a greater emphasis on the material motive of the murder. Thereby the motif of punishment expressed in the scene of encounter with the orphan child is effectively prepared. Some of the text variants incorporate other motifs to reinforce the tragic effect: during the walling-up, the wife's hopeful questions are answered by the masons asserting: "This is in earnest...your husband has made the rule"; and in some of the variants it is the master mason that sums up the lesson: "I made the rule, And it falls back on my pow". (As can be inferred from the perfect rhyme *(törvényt-történt)*, this formulation must be a later development, added by somebody with a view to underlining the moral teaching, which is apparent and which has been always known to everybody.

A very important difference manifests itself in the manner of building in: in some of the variants the woman is built in alive, in others first her head is taken and her blood spilled. Obvious is the walling-up alive in those scenes in which—like in No. 5—the wife is taking the thing as a jest, or at least would like to believe that the men are only playing. One of the fairly complete formulations of the scene reads like this:

Well, now that you came here, to the place of your death,
Stand among the stones, let us build you in lime!
When they raised the wall up to her knees, She asked her husband:
My husband, my dear husband, is it a jest or is it in earnest?
I say, this is not a jest, My darling wife,
The decision has been made, and it must be fulfilled.
When they raised the wall up to her waist, She asked her husband (cont. as before)
When they raised the wall up to her neck (cont. as before)
Well, then, if this is not in jest, Kelemen the Mason...

Borszék, Csík county.

The variant with the woman's blood mixed into lime comes up more frequently. The influence of this device is to be felt even when the corresponding scene speaks about walling-up alive, although the masons decided beforehand to kill the wife and take her blood, or possibly the master mason makes an announcement to this end subsequently. Conversely, survivals of walling up alive are met with in such variants which speak consistently about spilling her blood and mixing it in lime, for example, towards the end of No. 6: "Your dear mother is standing in the high wall of stone." In a fragment originating from Válaszút (a

28

village in Transylvania) the woman asks: "Is it in earnest or is it in jest that I should climb the wall? "Sometimes the child walks to the castle and calls his mother who answers him. This last-mentioned solution is obviously a survival from the older version of walling-up alive, although its most intact formulation comes up in such variants in which the basic idea of erecting the wall with blood mixed in lime prevails throughout the ballad (for instance, in the variant of *Kriza*).

Before the walling-up commences, the woman utters the most moving diction characterizing both her state of mind and the fate of the child left orphan (see No. 5, 39–43; and No. 7, Stanza 14). Some of the variants are worth-while to be quoted here:

Place my little child into a rocking cradle!
Beautiful women will come to give it the breast,
Mild rains will fall to wash it,
Gentle breezes will blow to send it to sleep.

(Lisznyó, Háromszék county)

Don't be frightened, darling, don't be frightened
Warm rains will fall to wash you,
Mild winds will come to rock you to sleep,
Beautiful birds will come to give you to eat.

(Bogdánfalva, Moldavia)

I have a little child, put him in a cradle,
Put him in a cradle, in the middle of the courtyard!
Kind women will come to give him the breast,
Mild rains will fall to wash him,
Gentle breezes will blow to rock him to sleep.

Alsórákos, Nagyküküllő county.

It is undoubtedly a later development when the wife asks for permit to walk home and to take leave of her son and her neighbours. (Kibéd, Enlaka, Fehér-Nyikó riverine = *Kriza*, Szentegyházasfalu, Gyimes, Józseffalva; being fairly similar in the different portions of texts, these places may well have been secondary developments that came into existence under the influence of the renowned *Kriza* variant.)

The plot is completed with the scene in which the man arrives at home and the child's inquiry brings into prominence all dreadful consequences of the murder. Some of the variants, however, continue by the child's walking up to the castle, calling his mother, upon whose answer the hearts of both child and mother break. See, for instance, the version of *Kriza* from the Fehér-Nyikó riverine.

Go, son, go and walk up to high castle of Déva,
There you'll find your mother built in the wall!
Thrice he called at the high castle of Déva:
Mother, my dear mother, say a word at least to me!
I cannot say a word, my son, for the wall of stone is heavy on me.
I am walled up here in big stones.

His heart broke, and also the ground broke beneath,
And her little son fell into the crevice.

According to *Vikár*'s recording from Enlaka:
Where are you, mother dear? Say a word to me!
(She spoke in the wall)

Here I am, though you cannot see me, my dearest heart, my little son.
His heart broke, and also the ground broke beneath,
And her little son fell and died in the crevice.

A variant from Gyimes includes a continuation in prose. The child decides to look up his mother. Therefore he walks to the castle of Déva. Arriving there, he calls his mother crying with tears. The woman relates the story and so sad are her words that the son's heart breaks. Altogether five variants preserved the dialogue between the walled-up mother and her son. (In certain additional ones, the child's death is developed from this scene.)

Some of the variants add in prose what we have read in No. *8* about the wells of milk or water springing from the breasts of the woman. For example, at Alsórákos "the old woman completed the story with the following remark: Her two teats were left unwalled, Two clear springs burst out from them." At Pürkerec the following version was recorded: "Her dear husband did not work any longer, and while the castle was standing, the two children sucked her two teats, because wells of milk came out of the wall, although nowadays only wells of water are found there." From the same place, the following version has been recorded: "Well then, I beg your pardon, his wife was walled up to her breast, and a well of milk sprang out of it."

In 1968 a forty-seven-year-old Gipsy woman of Szilice (Gömör county) performed an incoherent prose narrative which included several elements of the ballad under discussion. György Martin's recording of the narrative contains the following elements: Mentioning the names of the castle of Déva and the wife of Kelemen the Mason; the walls falling down in the morning; the masons's agreement concerning the walling up of the wife that first comes with her husband's dinner; the woman's taking leave of her child; the opening through which the woman could give the breast to her child. In addition to these Hungarian elements the same informant's narrative contained a typical Balkan motif which does not come up in any of the Hungarian versions, to wit: the master mason goes home and sets various tasks to his wife in order to delay her trip to the castle. Although the Gipsies of Szilice have been living in the mentioned village for several generations' time back, and they can speak only Hungarian, the occurrence of this otherwise isolated motif may well preserve memories of their former migrations, or of their encounter with migrant Gipsies; therefore no further conclusions can be deduced from their narrative in regard of the development of the Hungarian ballad.

It should be mentioned, by way of conclusion, that three versions of the Klézse (Moldavia) Csángós mention the name of Manole, the hero of the Romanian version of the ballad about the walled-up wife, what is more, they add a stanza in Romanian to the story; besides, one of them embeds also a known motif of the Transcarpathian Romanian versions into the context of the final stanzas, according to which the masons make wings from the shingles used at the building, with the aid of which they fly down from the top of the wall and so they go home. There is no reference to punishment, neither do they die in consequence of their attempt at flying; all this clearly indicates that the insertion is a later development upon Romanian influence.

There is a very important remark in a letter Dániel Berzsenyi wrote to Ferenc Kazinczy: "I am wrestling with many of my writings as Béla the Blind was with the castle he wanted to build on the top of Ság; what I do in the day-time falls down in the night-time." (Nikla, 25 November 1809. See Dániel Berzsenyi: Collected Works, 1956, p. 527.) Not a single written record of the ballad under discussion was known at that time in Hungary or abroad, thus the possibility of a literary information is absolutely out of question. Unfortunately, it does not transpire from this note whether it refers to a legend in prose or a verse, further whether the legend had anything to do with the building sacrifice.

Earliest provenience: 1823–48 (the *Almásy* MS. published by *Erdélyi*).

Dissemination: Nyitra county *(Zsére);* Gömör county (Szilice, prose variant, gipsy informant); Heves county (Bodony, uncertain data); Bács-Bodrog county (Zenta, legend in prose); Torontál county (Törökbecse, data); Kolozs county (Vajdakamarás, Válaszút, Visa); Maros-Torda county (Kibéd, Nyomát); "Székely land"; Udvarhely county (Etéd, Enlaka, Fehér-Nyikó riverine, Siklód, Kisbacon, Szentegyházfalu 2); Nagyküküllő county (Alsórákos); Csík county (Ajnád, Borszék, Csíkmenaság, Csíkverebes, Gyergyóalfalu, Gyergyóditró, Gyergyóremete 2, Gyergyószárhegy, Gyimes, Kászonaltíz, Kászonimpér, Kászonjakabfalva); Háromszék county (Lisznyó); Brassó county (Pürkerec 4); Transylvania without closer specification; Bukovina (Józseffalva-Bátaszék, Tolna county); Moldavia (Bogdánfalva 2, Klézse 2, Lészped, Trunk 2+1 prose variant). Total: 45, and two data.

Textual relationships with other ballads:

Urging the coachman ("The horse belongs to dogs...") : **10., 39.;** the fate of the foresaken child "There are warm showers...") : **4.** and **5.;** at the farewell scene ("For three chimes are tolled for the dead, But no bell will be rung for my orphan head"): **20.,** and in several variants of other types; the well of blood as an omen coming in dream: **19., 23., 51.** My coatchman, my coatchman... **16.**

Tunes:

9.

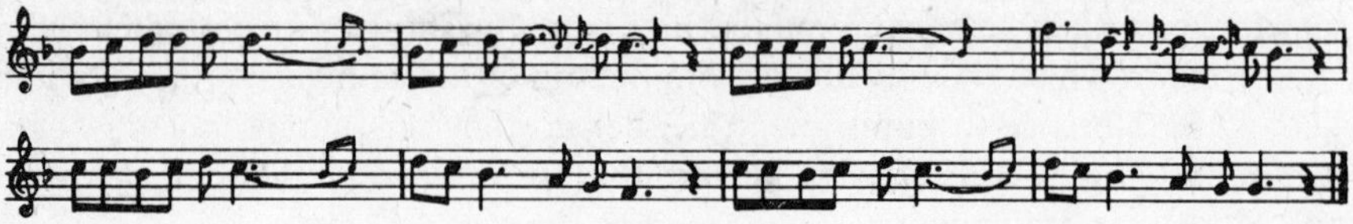

10.

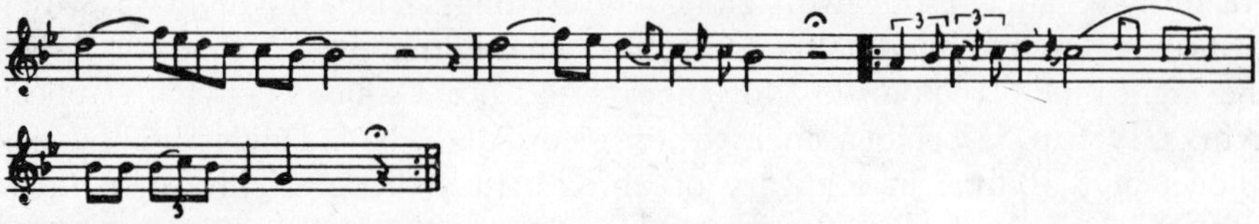

11.

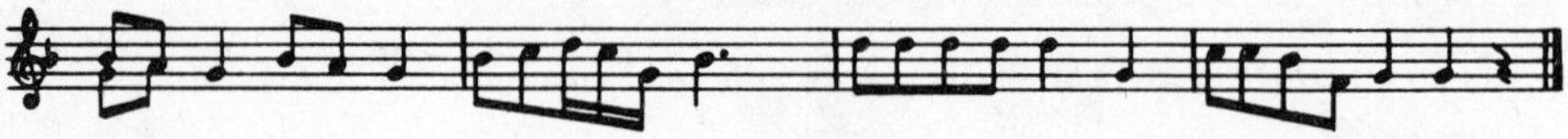

12.

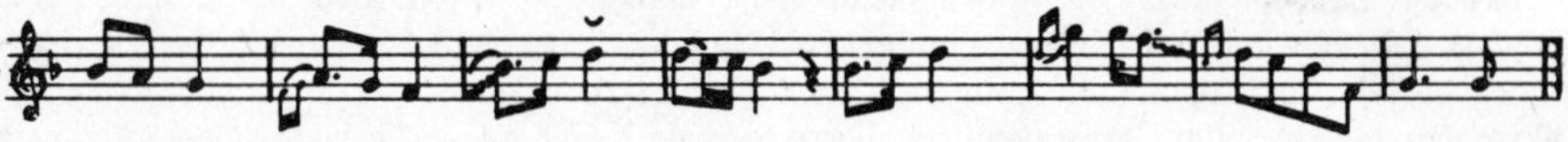

13.

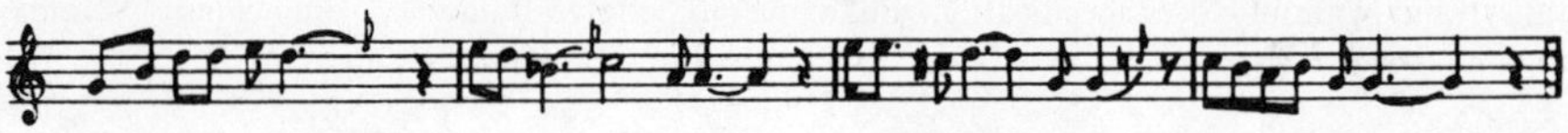

14.

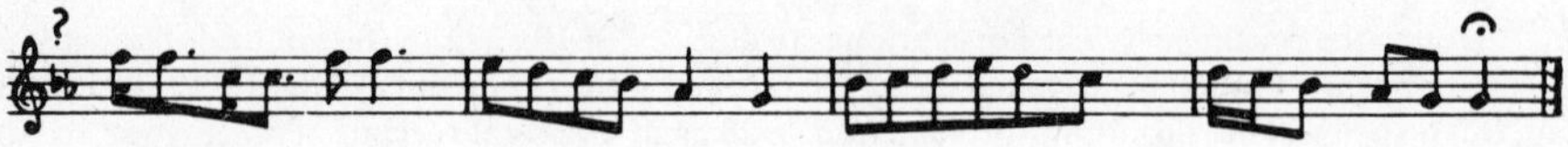

15.

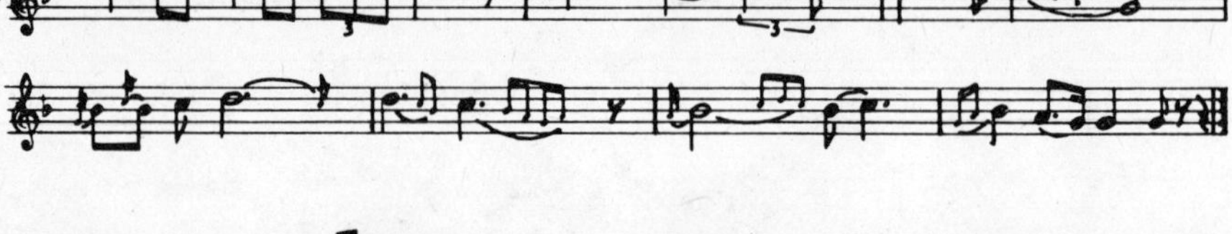

16.

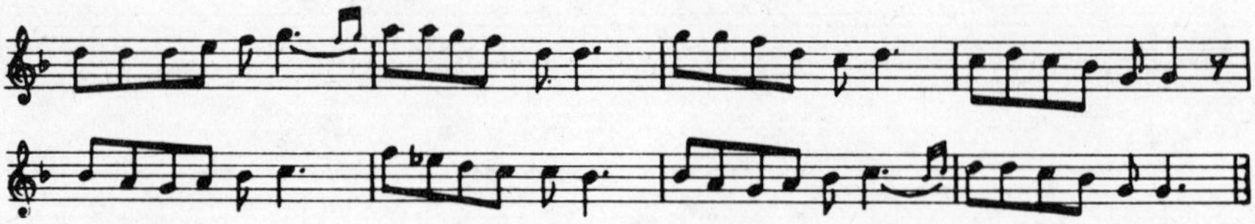

17.

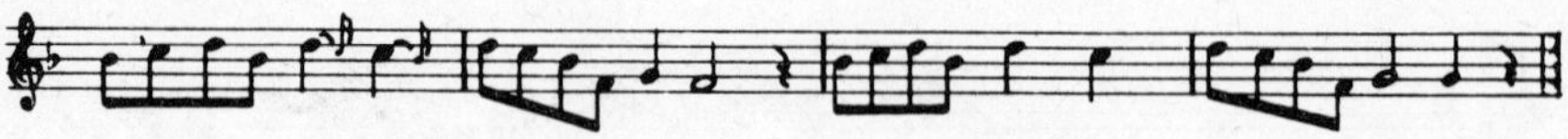

1. = the tune of No. 4, occurring in other three variants as well. **2.** = the tune of No. 6, and in two further variants. **3.** = the tune of No. 7 in three further variants. **4.** = the tune of No. **8**. Further 5–19. (cf. tune examples). Tune **8** occurs in a further two variants; **9** and **13** in an additional one example. The sectional distribution on Tune **7** in the stanza shows the following pattern: ab ab b.

Versions in languages other than Hungarian

BULGARIAN: 1–57. Arnaudov 1920 (57 texts, respectively their abstacts, of which many have been known to me in full variants from other publications: cf. the lists in my former studies.) *58–59. Idem* 1930, 1A and variants. *60–65. Stoin* 1928 Nos 14, 37, 38, 140, 358, 3631. *66–70. Idem* 1931 Nos 9, 43, 44, 46, 47. *71–78. Idem* 1939, 12, 33–39, 79. *Vatev* 126. *80. Ivanov* 1949, 120. *81–82.* SbNU 14, 34 No. 5, and 46, 52 No. 76. *83.* A–V 26. *84. Stoilov* 1924, 4. *85–87. Syrku* (three texts).

ROMANIAN: *88. Alecsandri* 186, No. 18. *89. Teodorescu*, 460. *90. Pamfile*, 72. *91–92. Giuglea* 177, 183. *93. Wellmer* 36. *94–96. Tocilescu*, 18, 21, 25. *97. Păsculescu*, 188. *98. Mailand*. *99. Mateescu** 13. *100. Sandu-Timoc**, 135. *101. Diaconu* 1930, 254. *102. Idem* 1934, 40. *103.* Monografia*, 455. *104–134. Taloş* 1–31. *135–136. Pop*, 433, 437.

AROMOUN: *137. Petrescu* 84*, 138. *Papahagi* 1922, 67.

SERBO-CROAT: *139–140. Karadžić* II, 25 and I², 175. *141–162.* HNP I, 30, + abstracts of 14 variants, V 90–92, + abstracts of 3 variants on pages 459–60, and X, 163. *163. Petranović* III, 52. *164. Hörmann I*, 68. 165. *Djordjević* 1931, 567. *166–167. Žganets* 1950 No. 374 and variant on page 458. *168. Raić* 15. *169. Krauss*, 19. *170. Syrku*, 155. *171–175.* INU MSS.

ALBANIAN: *Dozon* 1884, 255*. *177.* Zt. f. Vkde I, 143. *178.* Bosnische Post 1912*. *179. Kind*, 205. *180. Strauss* 1895, 512. *181. Hequard*, 17*. *182. Belloja**. *183. Mihačević* 67*. *184.* The Chronicle of Barleti*), *Sansovino*, 657. *185–189.* MS. variants from the collection of *E. Stockmann* and *W. Fiedler*.

GREEK: *190.* Ho en Konstant., 82*. *191. Iatrides*, 208*.*Zampelios**. *193. Tommaseo* III, 178. *194. Passow*, 512. *195–196.* Deltion I, 55, 716*. *197. Jeannaraki* 271. *198. Rouse* 184*. *199. Dietrich* 291. *200. Arnaudov* 1920, 396. *201. Joakimov*, 19. *202–203. Lagarde* 43, 44.* *204–485.* Photocopies of the Archives of the Academy of Athens, variants from the entire Greek area.

GIPSY: *486–487.* Ethn. 1903, 458 (Serbia and Greece).

GEORGIAN-ABKHAZIAN: *488–493. Chikovani*, 830, 831. *494. Haxthausen* I, 136*. *495–501. Istvánovits* 1958, 124.

MORDVINIAN: *502.* Ethn. 1928, 52. *503–504. Paasonen* 12, 13. *505. Erdélyi I.*

This famous ballad has a wide currency in five language areas of the Balkan peninsula, and it is not the Hungarian version that gained international recognition but rather the Southern Slav text on the building of the castle of Skadar (Scutari) and later the Greek ballad about the construction of the bridge of Arta had come to be known as typical products of Balkan balladry. (The former through the mediation of Vuk Karadžić's collection.) Later on also Romanian, Bulgarian and Albanian versions have come into the focus of interest.

The Romanian version speaks about the building of the monastery of Argeş. Negru the Voivod is seeking a place for the monastery he plans to build. The site is shown by a young shepherd, and on the ruins of an old building the voivod has the monastery built up. Before starting the operation, he promises either a generous pay or a severe punishment to the builders, dependent on the success of their work. But what they build by day falls down by night, and conversely. Negru the Voivod threatens them with death. Partly under the influence of a dream partly as a result of a consultation, the masons decide to wall up the wife that first comes to bring dinner to her man. The head master Manole's wife happens to come first. In several variants the head master entrusts her with different tasks in order to delay her arrival, while the other masons warn their wives well in advance of the danger. Manole sees his wife coming on the way from afar, and he prays much in the same way as Kelemen the Mason of the Hungarian versions, asking God turn back the woman, who nevertheless arrives. She is being walled up. Until they reach up to her knees, then to her breast, she thinks they are joking; finally she realizes that they are walling her up in earnest and starts to cry, speaks about the sad lot of her child; her loud bewailing is heard even from the walls. Then comes Negru the Voivod to take a look at the building. He asks the masters if they would be able to erect a still more beautiful edifice. Upon the masons' boastful words he grows angry and has the scaffolds pulled down so that the masons should perish on top of the walls. So he wants to prevent them from building another monastery. The masons construct wings from shingles, and make an attempt to fly down, which however turns out to be a failure: they meet the same fate as Icarus in the Greek myths. A well springs from the spot where Manole crushed himself to death.

The Romanian texts of the ballad are usually very long, extending to as many as eight hundred lines sometimes and rarely contenting themselves with fewer than three hundred. It follows from this that their style is characterized by a tendency to minuteously detailed narrative performance. After the publication of my first study on the ballad in word large-scale collection was started also in Transylvania from where then only one or two recordings of doubtful authenticity had been known. It appeared from the new collection that the ballad is sung as a colinda song in the Romanian regions of Transylvania, and that the Transylvanian texts show a marked difference compared with these of the Transcarpathian areas: no reference is found in them to Negru the Voivod or the name of the monastery of Argeş; instead they speak about various castles which have to be built up; neither do they know about the punishment of the masons by the cruel voivod, nor about their attempt to escape by means of wings; at the same time they are short (varying between forty-two and one hundred and thirty-seven lines, and averaging around seventy to eighty lines); also the motifs of the head master setting different tasks to his wife and the parallel breach of agreement on the part of the other masons are absent in the Transylvanian versions which follow, on the whole, the plot development of the Hungarian ballad.

With the Bulgars briefer variants are encountered, although the story also there finds an extensive form of performance sometimes. A high degree of variability of details is also characteristic of them: bridge, castle and even church will come up with three brothers or a great number of masons, journeymen and apprentices as builders; the head mason is mostly called Manoil, but not always, because many other names are attributed to him. It is a general feature in them that the master builders go home after the decision has been made; therefore they make a solemn oath not to let out their secret, which they all betray except for the head master; if this is not the case, they send message home to their wives asking them to be late with the dinner; here again it is a frequent occurrence that the master mason entrusts his wife with different tasks so that she may not arrive too early, and also the oath comes up when the head master perceives his wife on the way and asks God to set some obstacle to her; the motif of taking the walling-up in jest on the part of the wife occurs as well. Finally, some of the Bulgarian variants also know about the well of milk trickling from the breast of the woman.

In the Serbo-Croat regions not the variability of details but the ramification of the story into several directions can be spoken of. In the wake of the Bulgar variants the story about the building of Skadra as well as some other similar texts mention three brother princes who wish to have the edifice raised; the masons are told by a fairy in these variants that the walls will fall as long as the wife bringing first her husband's dinner is not walled up. The brothers, go home in these variants as well, and let out the plan, with the exception of the youngest. The rest of the story also runs much in the same route, with the walling up carried out in three steps, the woman thinking the men are playing, and asking them in the end to leave a hole through which she may be able to see her child. What makes a difference in the story is the introduction in which the elf first demands two brothers of identical names to be walled up, and only after the king had his servant search in vain for such twins throughout the whole of his domain does the elf give a different order. This heading is actually another version of the story about the walling-up which can be traced as an independent song, in whose variants the twins of identical names are found indeed, and also walled up, though no mention is made in them of the mason's wife. One of the variants continues the plot even after the twins have been walled up: Mehmed the Pasha is frightened to see that the bridge he had built is banged by a trunk of fir-tree which the storm has driven there; he tries to save the bridge by throwing part of his treasure into the water but to no avail; then he drives his axe into the fir that returns the blow by sprinkling blood; eventually the Pasha learns that he has been punished for having exacted tolls from those crossing the bridge. Another story attributes the plan of building to a giaour governor (kaur ban) and stands the wall by the walling up of a boy who first walks that way. The mother of the sacrificed boy detects traces of blood on the wall, everything is made clear and the governor is ordered to be beheaded by the pasha.

Still more striking is the divergence in the song telling about the building of a dzhami by Dervish Pasha. The mosque is built in seven years, the masons go home, but at night the storm demolishes it. It is rebuilt seven times and so many times it is overthrown by the storm. The Pasha then prays to Allah, and in a dream he learns that his own son is required as sacrifice. He steals the son away from the mother whose heart breaks. The mosque is built and the woman buried. There is a still further variation in which the original story is reduced to a lovers' tragedy: a girl is walled up by her brothers who want to sever her from her beloved one; she entreats them to leave an opening in the wall through which to see her lover.

But even those variants which follow by and large the thread of the plot of the prototype show marked differences. In one of the version of the story that has many variants in Croatia and Slavonia the walled-up wife escapes at last: upon order from God, elf or a saint lightning comes to bring down the wall, the woman is set free; she goes home and reproaches her husband because she did not betray the decision to her; eventually she kills him for his having walled her up. Sometimes her child walks to the castle where he drinks milk from the stream flowing from the breast of his mother; he recognizes his mother and God ruins the wall with lightning. Finally, we may mention a variant in which the builder has the elf torn to pieces by armed men, or wolves or falcons and so he prevents the development of the tragic plot. But apart from the version referred to in the foregoing there are many other versions which turn the trend of the story in the most diverse directions. It would seem as if each story had been relating a different case of walling-up and that the stories are connected only by similarities of certain details.

Also in the Albanian language area parallels of the skeletal tale of the Skadra castle are encountered (without the introductory part about the twins). Besides, however, the story has another Albanian variant which is remarkable just on account of its being closely linked up with the building of the castle of Skadra: the builder learns that the wall which falls down from time to time cannot be stopped unless a woman is sacrificed. His younger sister happens to walk there, the masons seize her and wall her up. It is held that the girl's name, Rosafa, has been transferred to the hill on which the castle was built.

The story of the walled-up wife of the head mason assumed a new form with the Greeks. The masons engaged in building the Arta bridge cannot complete their work because the walls always fall down. The master masons weep until the ghost under one of the arches tells them to wall up the wife of the head master. That is, here it is known from the very beginning who is to be sacrificed. In spite of this, the head mason sends his wife a letter by a bird instructing her not to put on her best dress and delay her arrival as long as she can. The bird misunderstands the message, flies off and asks the woman to hurry. She appears in a gorgeous dress. Then follows the scene built on the ring motif well known also with the Bulgars: the head mason pretends to have dropped his ring in the vault and asks his wife to bring it out. When the woman is amidst the stones, they pour lime on her, throw stones on her, and so they wall her in. She is wailing: they had been three sisters, and all three were to see the same fate, one supporting the bridge of the Danube, the other that of Avlon, and now she must hold the bridge of Arta. Next she lays a curse on the bridge so that the first person that happens to cross it may die. But they bid her to withdraw the curse, saying that it may affect her brother. Apart from this, there is another variant in which the ghost insists on the act of sacrifice, without specifying the victim. A long dialogue follows as to whom the head mason should offer; in the end he thinks that he may get another wife although he may not get another mother or sister, etc., therefore his choice falls on his wife. It is also worthy of mention that the majority of the variants do not speak about a real bridge but about the so-called *Trihas bridge* which souls have to cross on their way to the world beyond, according to the Moslem belief.

Now, if we single out from the national versions those elements which occur at least in two different language areas, we find that the Bulgarian variants play a central role in a certain sense. The order passed by the ruler and influencing the masons's decision comes up in the Romanian, Bulgarian and Serbian variants. The prayer "My God, may you raise a storm", further the formula "They built her up to the knees but she took it in jest", and the woman's words concerning the child who will be left orphan: "There come warm rains to bathe him..." connect the Hungarian, Bulgarian and Romanian versions. Monastery or church are to be built in the Bulgarian and the Romanian variants; building the castle and milk flowing from the walls, and the implication of the child at the end feature the Hungarian,

Bulgarian, Serbian and Albanian variants. Betrayal of the decision and the manifold tasks set by the head mason to his wife are common traits in the Romanian, Bulgarian, Albanian and Serbian ballads. The woman being told her fate upon her arrival: is a turn typical of Hungarian, Bulgarian and Serbian variants; agreement as to the nature of sacrifice through the head mason's decision or counsel with the other master masons come up as a common motif in the Hungarian and Bulgarian versions; sending the wife to bring up the ring, three brothers engaged in building the edifice, and the variable numbers of the master masons are encountered in the Bulgarian, Greek, Albanian and Serbian versions. Window is opened for the *eyes* in the Bulgarian and Serbian, for the breast in the Bulgarian, Albanian and Serbian ballads. Sending message to the wife occurs in the Bulgarian and Greek variants.

As can be seen, the Bulgarian variants are involved in each set of motifs.

It seems, therefore, that the Bulgars must have some central role in the spread of the ballad. Even this assumed, the question of origin is not yet settled, as a matter of course, only a point of orientation concerning the trend of spread can be inferred. As regards questions of donors and adaptors, we have more reliable points of approach. For instance,

1. moments typical of a language area occur in another, while the latter's do not come up in the former;

2. misinterpreted or confused motifs devoid of any sense are incorporated into the story;

3. motifs divested of their original character occur in the performance;

4. a plot uniformly applied by all the nations concerned shows a marked divergence in one of the language areas.

On the basis of the last-mentioned criterion, which is of extraordinary significance, we may state that the Serbo-Croat versions cannot be regarded as points of origin, rather they ought to be considered to be in a stage of final dissolution. Skeletal frames of the plot developed in so many diverse directions could not have provided grounds for bringing about a uniform story among the neighbouring peoples. But on the same basis we may leave out of consideration also the Romanian version. The characteristic details of the texts from Old Romania (the Regat), such as the scene of Negru the Voivod, or the punishment of the masons, never occur in the neighbouring language areas (disregarding such ethnic groups which came under the influence of the surrounding Romanian population, like the Csángós of Moldavia who really have got variants with the mentioned elements, unknown in the Hungarian versions). This observation is further supported by the existence of Romanian variants in Transylvania. Whether the Transylvanian or the Old Romanian variants are considered original, there is no reason that two so different versions should be developed with so marked territorial differentiation within one and the same language area. At the same time it may be readily surmised that the ballad had been mediated by the Bulgars to the Old Romanian parts and the Hungarians to the Transylvanian Romanians.

The Albanian area can be precluded on much the same grounds: had the ballad of the master mason's wife come into existence in that territory, the Rosafa legend connected with the sister of the prince would certainly not have been associated with it. At the same time, the existence of an aetiological legend with the Albanians may be supposed in relation of the Rosafa hill, on the one hand, and the Bulgarian transmission of the common Balkan ballad, on the other. Thus, the Albanian version may be regarded as a combination of the two.

Accordingly, the place where the ballad was handed over, or taken over, has to be determined somewhere in the Greek, Bulgarian or Hungarian language areas. The fact of borrowing is well brought out in the case of the Greek version by the figuring of the message the master mason sends to his wife asking her to be late, whereas it had been made certain at the very beginning that she would be sacrificed; further, there is no question of walling up that wife that happens to arrive first. With the Bulgars, on the other hand, it is quite reasonable that the decision to this end has been agreed upon between the masons, and indeed there are many variants of their ballad to inform us about their stratagem. Another decisive moment is the scene of the ring. Where the building operation is connected with a castle, it is understandable that the woman is sent down to bring forth the ring (as is the case with the majority of the Bulgarian variants). But the Greek versions know exclusively about the building of a bridge, which render it difficult to surmise the application of the trick. Therefore the Greek variants (and also some of the Bulgarian ones) make the woman swim in the river in order to meet the point. The original meaning is similarly overshadowed in the variant with the Trihas bridge, which cannot possibly provide the basis for a story telling about building sacrifice. And it should be noted that the Greek variants go with this motif in the southern and eastern parts of the language area, only the northern regions adjacent to the Bulgarian frontiers have developed ballads about the building of a real bridge.

In relation to the Hungarian and Bulgarian variants, there are five motifs to supply points of orientation in respect of the trend of spread: (1) the master mason's prayer for obstacles, (2) the woman's farewell to her child, (3) the gradation of walling-up, accompanied by the woman's astonishment ("is it in jest or in earnest?"), (4) the spring spurting from the wall, and finally (5) the master mason's decision or the counsel taken together to the effect of sacrificing a woman. Since the Romanian variants come into consideration in connection with all the five motifs, and therefore are of significant importance for the process of dissemination, they deserve to be examined parallel with the Hungarian and the Bulgarian versions.

In addition to the texts given above as examples, the master mason's prayer comes up in the following formulations.

(1) Hungarian:

— My God, my God, send a heavy shower,
Send a heavy shower so that my wife may not arrive here,
So that the coach may break and she may not arrive here!
Good day...

— My God, my God, send a heavy shower,
Send a shower so that she may not come here.
The faster the shower was pouring, the more she made haste,
And when she arrived....

— Send a round cloud, a big shower,
   So that my wife may turn back!
   God has granted it, yet she did not turn back...

— My Lord, my God, take her somewhere else!
   May my four chesnut horses break their legs,
   May the wheels of my coach break to pieces,
   May God's lightning strike the road,
   And may my horses turn back snorting!
   But no ill befell either horse of coach.
— ..... *(after the prayer)*
   God does not hear the pleas of Kelemen,
   But helps his dear wife to approach.

In other variants he asks for wind, or for a wolf to eat the horse's leg, and immediately after comes the wife's greeting. In the Moldavian Csángó variants he asks, in addition to bad weather, for wild wolves, and the summit of reality is reached at the turn: God sent those, too, but still they did not return.

It appears that the Hungarian variants stick to the stylized description of the psychological state even when the moment of reality is involved by the phrase: God gave it, but still they did not turn back. But this again is a stylized formula which does not raise the sense of reality; further it mainly occurs in Moldavia where the ballad style has somewhat faded in the common mind. In addition, there are seven variants in which the master mason warns his wife to turn back by a wave, of course in vain, and some of the variants do not include the prayer, only "bad weather" and storm are spoken of which similarly fail to make the woman turn back. These are obviously paler versions of the original motif of psychological desription, although the story is still kept within the original frame of a stylized character.

(2) Bulgarian:

The motif occurs in seven variants with the Bulgars.

My God, sent dark clouds,
From the dark clouds, thick rain!
So that my love should slip,
Spill the dinner and turn back.

God does not hear the prayer of Manojlo, his love arrives.

This turn with the slip and the spilling of the food degrades the formula from the height of stylization by inserting a casual detail into the general picture; but even so, it maintains the character of a wish. In another variant the master mason asks much in the same way for rain and wind, his wife to spill the dinner and turn back, which all come true except that the woman does not turn back but arrives at the castle. In this case the picture becomes more realistic and deviates considerably from the stylized form. And when the prayer is omitted and only the bad weather remains, as in certain Hungarian variants, the wife starts three times, but returns twice to her aunts and arrives only the third time at the place where her husband is waiting for her. This is a realistic augmentation of the situation, which, however, does not mean a gradation of the psychological condition. In one of the variants the rain soaks the dinner and the woman turns back to consult her aunts, who tell her in turn why they do not go out with the dinner. In this instance the original formula is utterly corrupted. (Finally, in some of the variants the master mason waves his hand only, or else fragmentary texts are found which fail to inform us whether the prayer has or has not been heard.)

(3) Romanian:

In the Romanian texts the "realistic description" of the scene is fully replaced by an unreal, fantastic, representation. Closest affinity with the Hungarian version can be seen in the text of *Alecsandri,* in which God raises a storm, which is depicted, together with the master mason's psychological state, in thirty-nine lines. In another variant she is obstacled by a bush, a wolf standing in her way and threatening her with its bloody tongue, and by a scorpion. On two occasions she gets frightened and spills the soup, but when the scorpion appears, she makes a short cut and so she arrives. In another variant, this device is combined with the motif of the master mason setting tasks to his wife in order to delay her arrival. First the husband asks for a shower, then for darkness to fall down so that the wife may spill the food, and for a divine suggestion to set out and search for the lost oxen. All this happens, the dinner is spilt, but she finds the ox and prepares a fresh food from it, with which she arrives. In the rest of the variants the woman meets with a dragon, a wolf, a bear, a serpent, and sometimes she is held up by a thistle or flock of sheep guarded by wild hounds; triple repetition and turning back being constant features in every case. Apparently the psychological description's transformation into a realistic picture, which appears only as a moderate tendency in the Bulgarian variants, assumes such proportions which far exceed the ballad style, approximating the fields of fantastically detailed unrealistic images.

The formula "Is it in jest or is it in earnest" has been presented in its most explicit forms in the sample ballads given above. With the Bulgars it comes up almost in the same way as in the Hungarian language area:

> As they build the wall up to her knees,
> She is laughing, laughing.
> As they build her up to the waist,
> She is laughing, laughing.
> As they raise the wall up to her breast,
> She gets frightened and begins to weep.

But this again is not depicting a stylized psychological state of a woman who is making desperate effort not to recognize the situation. The woman in the Bulgarian ballads simply refuses to take it in earnest. In another variant we find the following formulation:

> Then they built the wall up to her knees,
> But she was laughing with loud laughter.
> Then they built the wall up to her waist,
> But she was crying with loud cries.

They built the wall up to her knees,
Radka did not take it in earnest.
They built the wall up to her breast,
Her white milk spurted out.
This Radka took already in earnest.

They built the wall up to her knees,
She did not drop a tear.
They built up the wall to her throat,
Then she was shedding tears.

They built the wall up to her waist,
But she was looking to and fro, laughing.
Then she asked: are you joking with me?
The masons continued. They placed stone on her breast,
They placed brick on her head.
Pavlica burst into tears.

In the last instance the formula is broadened out into a narrative. A still more detailed variation is the following:

They build her in, but she, oh, Lord, only laughs.
They built half-way up, and she still laughed
When they had built up to her head,
Then she understood that they were going
To leave her as a human sacrifice in the tower.

They build, one after the other,
The young wife does not realize the truth,
She calls to the masons to let her go home to her child,
And tells them the things she has to do.
They build the wall up to her waist,
Then she realizes the truth and prays for her child.

It is obvious that the formula has lost the clear outlines: first it is rather concise, though it is not a description of a soul in utter despair. Later it turns gradually into a narrative form, indulging in details.

The process is being carried still farther with the Romanians, not only because the motif is expanded to form an amply detailed scene but also because certain portions of the formula are omitted in a random way. The content of the scene contained in the excessively long variant recorded by *Teodorescu* can be summed up as follows: Caplea was only smiling as she was being built in, and took fright only when she was hardly able to peep over the wall: If this is a joke, it is not a good one! They paid no attention to her; but continued to pour the lime, lay the bricks, while she was wailing: Manole, if this is a joke, . . . the wall is very heavy on me . . . etc. This repeated several times, as the wall is raised up to her mouth, her husband answers.

In the variant recorded by *Pamfile* the master masons pretend to wall her up for fun's sake. "This is not a good joke!" says the woman. Manole does not answer, the wall is rising. It rose from her leg to her knees, from her knees to her breast, from her breast to her eyes. The masons were making speed, while she kept on saying: "Manole, my husband, my dear man, the wall is pressing me...". In another variant we have the following formulation: "While she was being built in, the woman was laughing, because she thought they were playing a joke on her. The building rose to her waist, then up to her breast. And what did she do? She wanted to break out and she cried in a low voice: Manoles, Manoles!" Then the husband's accusation follows, then again the woman's wailing complaint that she had come to the place, upon which the head mason repeats his command: "Make haste, don't stop building...from her waist up to her breast, so that one looking at her teats should think they are made of marble!", and the like.

Let us now examine the woman's prayer we have read in the Hungarian variants quoted. There are two fragmentary examples which are rather laconic on this point: "Kind women will give you the nipple, there are kind girls to do the washing.", and "Sleep, sleep, Kind women will give you the breast, wash your clothes and dry them in the sun." In a more complete form:

Put him into the cradle and the middle of the yard,
Kind women will come to suckle him,
Gentle breezes will come to rock him.

My God, my God, what will become of my little son?
There are rocking cradles to send him to sleep,
There are kind women to give him the breast.

Put my rocking cradle before me,
Put my child into it.
There will be soft rains to wash him,
There will be gentle breezes to rock him to sleep.

Put my child in the rocking cradle,
Beautiful women will come to suckle him,
Soft rains will come to wash him,
Gentle breezes will blow to send him to sleep.

Who will bathe my son?
There are soft rains to bathe him,
Who will wrap my son?
There are kind women who will wrap him up.
Who will give my son his dinner?
There are kind little birds who will bring him food.

Who will rock my son to sleep?
There are gentle breezes to rock him to sleep.

This formula is a commonplace in Hungarian ballads which occurs in two other types as well (Types 4 and 5). The mother in the ballad of The Enticed Wife Forsaking Her Child (Csanád county) addresses her children when placing them under a tree:

..... When the birds
Flap their wings, just imagine
That your mother is speaking to you.

42

> When the rain falls, just imagine
> That it is I, your mother, that is bathing you.

Similar is the address of Ilona Budai to her child:

> Kind women will come to suckle you,
> Soft rains will come to bathe you,
> Gentle breezes will come to rock you to sleep.
>
> Warm rains will come to bathe you,
> Warm winds will come to rock you to sleep.

The formula comes up with the Bulgars, even though not very frequently. At the wife's question "Have you no pity on your son?", the husband, to console her, says that the cradle will be brought and that *it will be walled in too*. "And when the wind blows, it will rock the child to sleep; when the rain falls, it will bathe him; when the birds fly thither, they will feed him, too." In another variant the original image is worn away, although the textual connection with the foregoing is obvious: "Who will feed my little baby? My sister will feed him. And who will feed my child? The wild birds will feed him."

It is worth-while to cast a cursory glance at the Bulgarian parallels of the Hungarian ballad of The Enticed Wife Forsaking her Child, in which the motif also comes up in a somewhat modified formulation. The woman taken prisoner by the Turks puts her little son down under a tree or at the foot of the mountains, placing him under the protection of the Stara Planina. Then comes the above motif transformed into a realistic scene and modified in a way that young hinds passing there suckle him. The child grows up, and sometimes he will be the rescuer of his imprisoned mother. (Cf. No. **5**.) Let me quote a portion of the song: "Then Todorka said: Sleep, my son, Damyanka, when winds blow, they will rock your cradle, when the hinds go past, they will suckle you, when the soft rain falls, it will wash you, so that you will grow up and free your mother from the Turks." (*Stoin* 1931 No. 181.)

Also the Romanian versions contain some detail which is apt to reinterpret, in a realistic way, this poetic turn originally contemplated to flash up the motherly feelings and the fate of the child separated from his mother. The woman keeps on wailing as the building proceeds, and her child is weeping. In the end she is walled up to her mouth, and then Manole replies: "God will look after your child, as you left it in its bed. Fairies will go to it and suckle it; when it snows it will be anointed; when it rains it will be bathed, and when the wind blows it will be rocked to sleep, and that is how your child *will be brought up.*" Besides one or two formula-like solutions we find such ones as in No. **10**, for example: "When you have finished with me, put a tower on top of the building, and a cradle on top of it, and put Ivanka in it. He is still very tiny, poor little thing, the wind will rock him, if snow falls it will anoint him, if rain falls it will bathe him."

A similar course of development can be documented in relation of the spring of milk. The motif is rather economically referred to by the Hungarian variants which just mention that a well of milk or water spurted out from the place where the woman was walled up. Very often the Bulgars develop this motif to grow into a scene of suckling: "They walk to the stone bridge, and they awake Manoilitsa in the bridge: Manoilitsa, your little child is weeping! Then a tiny stream of milk spurts from the bridge, it flows into the mouth of Pavel, the little lad; And the white milk starts to flow as many times as Pavel, the little lad, cries." More general is the form in which an opening is left—sometimes at the woman's request—for her breast. In the Albanian a fantastic tube appears that conveys the milk down to the child's mouth, while the Croatian variants have a stream of milk from which the child can drink. The motif is utterly deprived of its original meaning when a window is left to the *eyes* of the woman; this formula becomes prevalent in the Serbian versions. Finally it is turned into a fully corrupted form—which is quite incompatible with the basic conception of human sacrifice—in which the wife asks the masons to leave an opening so that she may breath fresh air. This is the case in two Romanian versions in Yugoslavia.

These examples clearly indicate that the original form, which corresponds to the ballad style, has been preserved by the Hungarian formulation, and that the Bulgarian, Romanian and Serbian versions followed a course of development quite contrary to the nature of popular ballads. Therefore only the Hungarian can be the original. This is further confirmed by the rest of the Hungarian and Bulgarian parallelisms in which the differences appear much in the same way: in the Hungarian the application of the motifs is always in line with the special requirements of the ballad genre, while in the Bulgarian these are more or less ingnored or blurred.

There still remains a possibility for comparison, which I did not think it proper to exploit before the relation between Hungarian and Bulgarian variants is not made clear on, so to say, self-supplied evidence. To wit, here the Caucasian and Mordvin versions offer themselves for examination. These again corroborate the result of comparison of Hungarian with the Balkan ballads, and further clarify the early history of the former. Notably, a legend in verse speaking about building sacrifice has been recorded also from the Georgians. The story is about the walling-in of a child instead of a woman. There survive several variants, sometimes in verbatim recording, sometimes only abstracts are given. It can be ascertained that what we have here is a summary in prose of a poetic composition whose decisive scene, the dialogue of mother and child, still retains its verse form. In the story of the Suram Castle what is built by day falls down by night. On the advice of a priest the only son of a widow, Zurab is walled up, or victimized by drawing the lots. His mother runs to the wall and calls out her son: How do you feel, my child, are you still alive? He replies from the wall: Alas, mother, the wall has reached up to my knees (then, in succession, up to the waist, breast and neck), and finally he says: Alas, mother, I am dying! The wall never dries but always remains wet from the boy's tears (or from those of the mother, which is obviously erroneous). This dialogue is rather uniformly represented by the variants.

Apparently the Georgian song must have been based on some common European tradition for a much-quoted German legend in prose has preserved similar *gradations*: In order to make a castle impregnable, the builders buy a child and wall it up. The child is given cakes to eat while the wall is being raised, and the child munching on it cries to the mother: Mother, I can still see you! Mother I can still see you a little. When the last stone was put in place: Mother, I can no longer see you! Here again we have a rendering in prose of what has been formulated in verse form in Georgian.

It is undeniable that the Hungarian ballad is close to the Georgian song in two places: in the gradual walling-up of the victim, together with the pertaining duologue, and the final scene with the duologue between mother and son. In one respect the Hungarian is further away: the roles are reversed, with the mother walled up and the child speaking to her from outside, and the gradation of the duologue between husband and wife. In the latter case, however, the formulation: when she was walled up to the knees, when she was walled up to the waist, etc. shows nearly the same gradation in the two language areas, so much so that a *textual* correspondence may be established.

One cannot imagine that motifs so closely related as these should develop independently of each other in so distant places. One is struck already by the fact that it is only two places in the world where the legends of building sacrifice have developed into verse compositions in the folklore character, notably in the contiguous Hungarian and Balkan areas, and in the Caucasus. The more striking is that the two elaborations are related by strong textual affinities. If the possibility of a connection is not contradicted by historical considerations, then it is also obvious that the one had developed from the other.

But such a historical possibility is only granted in the one-time connections of the Hungarian people with those of the Caucasus. We do not think solely of the linguistic contacts that have been definitely proved in relation of Hungarians and the Alans of the Caucasus region; we have in mind also the association of certain Caucasian ethnic groups with the early Hungarians, for instance a fragmentary group of the Alans, named Varshans (*Varsányok*) joined the Hungarians in the Conquest Period, later the Yases (*Jászok,* also an Alanic tribe) migrated into Hungary together with the Cumans, leaving even a linguistic record of their idiom from the fourteenth century.

But apart from historical evidence, the text themselves argue for an undeniable relationship. Closest similarity in the scene of gradual walling up, accompanied with the duologue, is to be found in the Hungarian versions, in which the original stereotype formulation clearly survives while in the other nations' tradition it has been gradually beclouded. It is another question, of course, that in Hungarian the story has been transformed according to the special requirements of the genre so as to enhance the vigour of the psychological characterization. It is in the Hungarian variants that the duologue between the walled-up victim and the relative—mother and child—is placed at the end of the ballad,—a scene which always appears in a more or less distorted form with the other nations. It is only in the Hungarian versions that the spring of water on the wall is just mentioned—or transformed into a spring of milk, being the walled-up one a young mother—which scene finds a self-contained formulation in the Balkan areas, in a sharp contrast to the Caucasian version. It is also interesting to note in this connection that the Greek version knows very little—and the Trebizond Greek variants practically nothing—of all this, although these are closest territorially to the Caucasian areas.

How far the traditional material spread from the Caucasus may be well realized from the song variants of it among the Mordvins living in the vicinity of the Volga Bend. Their songs relating to the building of the Kazan Castle or a village church show several points of agreement with the Hungarian variants: what they build by day falls down by night; their opening formula: What shall we do, what shall we think of it? Let us go and build the castle of Kazan! reminds one of the incipit of the Hungarian ballads: "Twelve masons started out, started out to build the high castle of Déva"; and "Twelve stonemasons took counsel together how they should build the high castle of Déva," etc. With the Mordvins, however, a maid has to be sacrificed; in one of the variants she is walled up alive while in others her bones are broken (as sometimes the bones of Kelemen's wife), and she is even quartered up in one of the variants. In spite of these differences, the duologue between the mother and the child always follows much in the same way as in the Georgian versions, which clearly indicates that the murder before the walling-up takes place has been a secondary development, just as in Hungarian. The *mother* goes to the wall on three consecutive days and asks: Are you still alive, my child? The answer is: It is tight round my breast... and the like, but on the third occasion the victimized girl is silent. That is to say, the duologue is still exactly like the Georgian: a mother speaks to the walled-up child, with the difference that the victim is already a *woman,* a grown-up maid. And this is what we have in the Hungarian ballad as well.

After the translation of my manuscript was finished *Pál Szalmási* read a paper at a session of the Hungarian Ethnographical Society about "The Caucasian antecedents of the ballad of Kelemen Kőmives" (The Walled-up Wife), exposing Armenian variants closely related to the Georgian texts.

(1) As the masons were laying the foundations of the old bridge of Astarakh, the river carried away the stones. All their attempts at restoring the pillars were frustrated by the river. Old people in the village advised them to put the foundation at some other place, and that they should wall up an orphan girl alive. The masons bought an orphan girl from her stepmother and built her in the walls of the bridge. The girl subjected herself to the builders' will without saying a word of protest. When the wall reached up to her knees, she spoke up mournfully:

"They walled me up, mother, they walled me up
Right to my knees..."

(As the wall reached up to her breast:)

"They walled me up, mother, they walled me up
Right to my breast..."

(As the wall reached up to her throat:)

"They walled me up, mother, they walled me up
Right to my throat..."

No more word of the girl was heard, and the bridge was successfully finished.

(2) The foundations of the bridge at the village of Koter were repeatedly destroyed by the waves of the Euphrates. The master mason is near to commit suicide. The spirit of the water imparts to his sixteen-year-old daughter that the bridge would not be finished until a maid or a lad below eighteen has been

sacrificed. The girl decides to sacrifice herself. In spite of her father's protest, she stands in the vault of the bridge. The masons begin to lay the bricks around her. As the wall is raised, the girl is singing:

"They walled me up, father, they walled me up
Right to my knees...
They walled me up, father, they walled me up
Right to my breast.
They walled me up, father, they walled me up
Right to my eyes."

(3) Five masons, who were brothers, began to build the bridge. As they laid the foundations of the five pillars, the waves of the river Sakaria carried away the stones. This occurs several times. The masters are told that a man has to be sacrificed. The brothers decide to sacrifice the first person who happens to go there. Soon the wife of the youngest brother arrives, bringing food to the builders. (It was her turn that day.) By force of their counsel, they sacrifice the woman. Thus the bridge was completed. In the evening the mother-in-law of the youngest brother asks the man: Where is my daughter? Where have you left her? Learning what has happened she runs down to the bridge, mad with grief, calling to the by-passers: Give me back my daughter!

(4) Master Batman is building a bridge. The foundations are carried away by the river several times. Once he has a dream: an old man advises him to build in a man or an animal. Any living creature that may first arrive in the morning. Next day the master sees his wife and his hunting dog approaching. The woman who is bringing food, stumbles at a stone and drops the jug from which the dog gulps down the dish. The wife arrives, and Batman grows very sad. The wife asks him why he has grown so sad. The mason relates his dream. The woman answers: Well, let it be if it must. Wall me up so that the bridge should not collapse. The bridge is constructed, and the master carves his wife's figure in stone. It is said that two wells of milk have spurted from the breasts of the woman. Travellers drink from it.

(5) As the Armenians were building the castle of Akhaltsikhe, the walls collapsed half-built from time to time. They make inquiries for the reason. Finally they learn that four (?) girls have to be built in the wall. A woman sells them the orphan daughter of her late sister for a bushel of gold. The girl is placed on the foundation and walled up gradually. The girl addresses her aunt weeping:

"They walled me up, aunt, they walled me up
Right to my knees."

(Her aunt answers:)

"Let them wall you up, Soghik, let them wall you up,
Let them wall you up to your waist!"

(As she is walled up to her waist, the girl says:)

"They walled me up, aunt, they walled me up
Right to my waist."

(From the other side her aunt says:)

"Let them wall you up, Soghik, let them wall you up
Right to your breast!"

(The girl says again:)

"They walled me up, aunt, they walled me up
Right to my breast!"
"Let them wall you up, Soghik, let them wall you up
To your throat!"

At this, the girl dies. Therefore the walls of the castle are shedding tears to this day.

(6) While they are building the castle of Bitlis the gods ruin their work. They cannot make it ready. A soothsayer tells them to wall up a beautiful girl. They follow his advise and succeed in completing the construction. An almond-tree grows from the girl's tears on the rock, which is a frequented goal of pilgrimage even today.

(7) In order to prevent the castle of Alashkert under construction from collapsing, the masons wall up a girl. Later, when the castle was a ruin, many people saw the girl's locks hanging down from the stones.

(8) The masons are under obligation to finish the construction of the castle of Sparkert in a year. But what they build in the day-time falls down in the night-time. A woman says to the master mason: Amira, if you find a boy who is the dear son (not stepson) of a married couple, and put him in the walls of the castle, it will not collapse. They started out to look for one. A woman sold them a twelve-year-old shepherd boy who was her nephew. As they are walling him up, the boy begins to blow his shepherd's pipe. As they walled him up to the knees, he said:

"Wall me up, aunt, wall me up,
The stones have reached my knees already..."

(As they rose to his heart:)

"Wall me up, aunt, wall me up,
The stones have reached to my heart already..."

(As they rose to his head:)

"Wall me up, aunt, wall me up,
The stones have covered my head already...
You have destroyed me, aunt, you have destroyed me.
You have destroyed the dear son
Whom God had sent to his father and mother!"

As can be seen, in this case the figure of the wife who arrives first to bring food for his man appears as a motif. At the same time, we witness variations of the legends connected with building sacrifice influencing the texts which are in a stage of development where the most impressive solution is being sought for.

Of all the motifs occurring in the above texts it is only the figure of the master mason's wife that is common to every national version. None of the rest come up in the Greek poems, one or two appear now in the Bulgarian, now in the Romanian or Southern Slav ballads, at the same time, all of them can be found in the

48

Hungarian version. And what is very meaningful: they show the closest affinity to the Caucasian formulation.

It follows from the foregoing that the legend in verse about the building sacrifice had been brought either by the Hungarian settlers or by such Caucasian ethnic groups which have subsequently joined them (Varshans, Yases). In any case, the original form must have contained elements from which the parable of the walled-up wife of the master mason could have been developed at a time when the ballad style became known to the Hungarian population, from which the story made its way towards the peoples of the Balkans. The trend of transformations shows the following way: first the Bulgars took it over from the Hungarians. But the Bulgars may not have been contented with the psychological evidence of the punishment afflicting the master mason only, but they wanted to reduce his responsibility by introducing the motif of treason on the part of the other masons, thus making them more culpable and the master mason almost a victim. At the same time, holding in view not the method of parables but the psychology of quotidian mind, they also attributed certain stratagems to the master mason, such as the various tasks he set to his wife in order to delay her arrival. All this, however, truthful in reality as it may be, becomes irrealistic in a way: if there is a possibility of treason, then the role of fate coming into play in the decision-making is void of sense and the ballad is deprived of the catharsis element, that is of its tragic beauty. Thus transformed, the ballad reached the Trans-Carpathian Romanians who further developed the story by adding to it the punishment by the Voivod of the master mason; furthermore, it reached the Albanians and the Serbians as well. The Greeks, who had also got the ballad through Bulgarian mediation, go even farther as concerns the transformation of the tragic feature. They start out from the beginning from the fact that fate had appointed the chief mason's wife; consequently, his responsibility comes to nothing, or almost to nothing, and the song loses its intensity; so much of the latter is retained only as is concomitant with an anticipated fulfilment of the tragic event.

Besides, many other details of the story are transformed. The modification is largely due to traditional conceptions showing a great diversity in regard of building sacrifice. To wit, the belief that the local ghost *(genius loci)* disturbed by the building operation should be appeased by human sacrifice has not only produced numberless legends all over the world, from Mexico to Japan and from the Estonians to Black Africa, but it can also be demonstrated as a living practice from earliest records to the most recent excavations, in fact up to the seventeenth or eighteenth centuries. These legends and recorded cases include all the variation possibilities which can be discovered in the Balkan form of the ballad, as well as in its Caucasian and Mordvinian counterparts: the burying of the victim alive, sometimes a boy and a girl together, or a boy who happens to walk there, a maid or the master mason's son; the mixing of blood with lime and the sprinkling of blood on the foundation of the building; not infrequently the victim undertakes to be sacrificed out of his own will, thinking it to be a glorious feat, as presented in some of the Southern Slavic texts; even the name of the victims are specified in some instances, for example in certain Serbian variants; the stipulation that "it should not be a passenger or a beggar" in the Greek texts refers to more recent practice when only such victims could be taken into consideration; with the Bulgars we encounter with the walling-up of the shadow of a man or woman, which is tantamount to the utter degeneration of a one-time lively custom (survival). On the other hand it is interesting to note that it is just the topic of the ballad under discussion—the walling-up of the master builder's wife—that is missing in the legends relating to the practice of building sacrifice (except the Armenian). It is more likely that the explanation lies in the very nature of the ballad genre indulging in psychological conflicts in domestic life; it may have been in the wake of such western domestic ballads that the narrative in verse brought from the East had been transformed, since it originally contained ballad-like elements in the duologue depicting the psychic condition of mother and son. The transfer of the son's role onto the mother may have been made easier by the circumstance that the Hungarians had got knowledge of walled-up women while staying in the East: the Mordvinian stories speak about a maid, those of the Abkhazes about a woman, one Armenian text about a wife and what is more, a report from west of Lake Baikal describes the remains of a female corpse, buried alive beside an earthen fort in a twisted position, whose cramped fingers—as if scratching the face—testified to the terrible custom of burial alive.

Assuming the ballad form, the story first reached then the Bulgars somewhere in the area of the Banate of Szörény and in the adjacent Bulgarian banate; from there it spread towards the Transcarpathian Romanians. It should be remarked that the area of the one-time Banate of Szörény used to be inhabited by considerable Hungarian populations whose memory still survive in a number of topographical names, and even in the names of rivers. (*Lükő* 1935, *Kniezsa* 1938, p. 388). The map below, drafted by *Lükő,* shows settlements of Hungarian settlers that used to be bordering on Romanian as well as Bulgarian language areas. The Transylvanian Romanians must have learned the ballad from Hungarians with whom they lived together; through Bulgarian mediation it reached the Greeks, Albanians and Serbians. Further, the Croats came in contact with the Hungarians at the juncture of the rivers Danube and Sava, somewhere on the border of the Hungarian, Bulgarian and Croatian language areas, in the vicinity of the Banate of Szörény, and so the ballad followed its route toward the West, in the Drava–Sava interfluve, according to the evidence of the modified variants. The most conspicuous differences are shown just in the final sections of the mentioned routes.

We have still to establish the approximate period when the ballad was tranferred. Apart from the times of the Great Hungarian Conquest, it was only in the period of the Angevins (Louis the Great reigning from 1342 to 1382) that Hungarians maintained close connections with the Bulgars, notably when the King established the Bulgarian Banate headed first by Stratsimir, then by Hungarian barons. At that time the towns of Viddin, Fehérvár (Belogradchik) and Laganj were packed with garrisons under whose protection perhaps also Hungarian settlers were living in the foreign lands; the Banate of Szörény was similarly inhabited by Hungarians, the area of the two banates having been divided by a long frontier. At latest the transfer of the Hungarian ballad can be dated to those times. As late as 1377 Louis the Great was able to celebrate a victory he had won over the Turks in Bulgaria, but later on the Turkish troops flooded the Northern territories of the

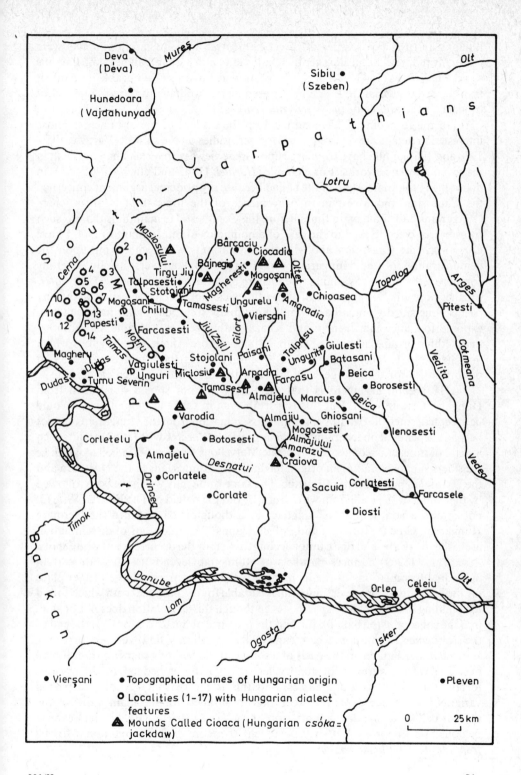

Deva
(Déva)

Mureş

Sibiu
(Szeben)

Carpathians

Olt

Hunedoara
(Vajdahunyad)

South

Lotru

Cerna

Maşosului

2
1

Bârcaciu

Ciocadia

Oltet

Topolog

Arges

Pitesti

4 3
5 6 7
10 9 8
11 12 13
14

Talpasesti
Stotojani
Mogosani
Chiliu

Tirgu Jiu

Bajnegi

Magheresti

Mogoşani

Tamasesti

Ungurelu

Amaradia

Chioasea

Jiu(Zsil)

Gilort

Viersani

Farcasesti

Talpasu

Giulesti

Stojolani

Paisani

Unguriti

Batasani

Cotmeana

Vedita

Magheru

Tamas

Mofru

Dudas

Vagiulesti

Miclosiu

Arpadia

Farcasu

Beica

Dudas

Unguri

Turnu Severin

Tamasesti

Almajelu

Marcus

Beica

Borosesti

Varodia

Almajiu

Ghiosani

Ienosesti

Corletelu

Almajelu

Botosesti

Mogosesti
Almajului
Amarazu
Craiova

Desnatui

Dranceq

Corlatele

Sacuia

Corlatesti

Farcasele

Timok

Corlate

Diosti

Balkan

Danube

Lom

Ogosta

Orleq

Celeiu

Olt

Isker

Vedea

Pleven

Balkans and the possibilities of direct Hungarian and Bulgarian contacts were gradually reduced. In the next century János Hunyadi led campaigns in the Balkans against the Turks (1443–48), but those years were no longer favourable for a direct transfer of Hungarian folk poetry. Consequently, we have to date the period of transfer to the *middle of the fourteenth century*.

In the foregoing, I have summed up the essence of my arguments. Those interested in details are referred to my former studies on the subject (Vargyas 1956, 1960 and 1967). Still I have to enlarge upon some views with which I had not dealt in the given reference works. For example, *Horálek* (1963 and chiefly 1965) calls in doubt the Hungarian origin of the ballad because my principal argument concerned the Caucasian and Mordvinian provenience of the topic, that is areas where Hungarians had come up in times before the Conquest. He maintains that no such transfer can be conceived in the case of a nomadic nation. In point of fact, I have *disregarded* the Caucasian and Mordvinian variants when embarking upon the demonstration of the Hungarian origin of the Balkan versions by carefully comparing the national variants; the Eastern material has been involved only *later*. Furthermore, the Hungarians of those times cannot be characterized as having been so one-sidedly nomadic as would hold many still today. They had been long exposed to Caucasian, Iranian and Khazar influences, even Alanic and Khorezmian ethnic groups had joined them, let alone those Alanic (Yas) groups which migrated into Hungary in the twelfth century. Thus there had been plenty of opportunities for them to get acquainted with the Caucasian saga elements.

His second argument is that the ballad did not spread northward from Hungary. Certainly not. But this is a truth even in case the Balkan origin would be accepted, since the ballad's route and dissemination from the Hungarians cannot be made dependent on its origin! And it is precisely *Horálek* who (1963) admits such a trend of transfer in connection with The Marvellous Corpse **(68)**, a ballad which he considers similarly Balkan in origin, mediated by Hungarians to the Northern and the Ukrainian populations of Europe. The same route may well have been followed by the ballad of the walled-up wife! But why did the ballad of The Enticed Wife **(3)** not enter the Southern Slavs' language area though it has reached the German, Hungarian, Czech, Moravian and Polish regions? The questions of dissemination are rather intricate, and one cannot account as yet for the occurrence of white spots.

Taloş (1969) adduces parallels of Romanian legends to illustrate certain individual formulations of the Romanian ballad: they are seeking a proper place for the building; only one definite ruin is suitable for the purpose (with which found the building sacrifice can be spared—even though this speculation does not fit at all into the concept of the ballad), further, the presence of the Icarus motif at the end of the story when the masters seek escape by flying. All this, however, reinforces my statement that I made on the basis of a survey of the building sacrifice tradition all over the world; variants of sundry legends will be embedded in the various formulations with various peoples, and this is the reason why diverse partial variants arise. Since *Taloş* fails to bring up parallels for the main motif of the present ballad, to wit the victimization of the *head mason's wife*, his data cannot demonstrate the *origin* but they document the Romanian formulation *differing from all other national versions*.

52

Taloş refers to a diary of travel from 1654–58 which recorded a method of building of the monastery of Argeş quite different from what is usually found in the ballad. He concludes that the Regat version introducing Negru voda and Manole had not been extant at that time, and that only the Transylvanian variants may have existed. Although this is irrelevant for the question of origin, evidencing at most a later development of the Romanian variant, I do not believe that the fact that a foreigner had heard a legend somewhere should be interpreted in a way that another legend or ballad did not exist at the time.

Megas (1971), summing up what he had advanced in 1969–70, gives a detailed answer to my study which he promised to do as early as 1960. From the variants he infers a basic type that should have developed in Epirus and preserved in Greek areas more to the South. He omits from this all such traits which may testify to the borrowed nature of the Greek formulation (although he himself acknowledges that these traits are generally known throughout the entire Greek region). The pristine text included the following motives in his opinion: a number of masons want to build a bridge, and what they build by day falls down by night; a ghost voice appoints the victim in the person of the master mason's wife; the master mason calls his wife; she is suspicious of her man's intention, rocks her child to sleep and bids farewell to her home; the actual construction completed is made known by the woman's lamenting her own and her sisters' fate; finally she lays a curse on the bridge which she withdraws later. According to *Megas*, the same area of Epirus which gave birth to the "primitive form" had developed the additional motifs as well: message to warn the would-be victim to come late; the woman's questioning the messenger if he had come to bring good news or bad news; the ring scene and the duologue between man and wife. But he gives no explanation whatever as to why these contradictory elements were added later; he rests content with stating that they must have been added at an early date because they range over the whole of the Greek areas. This argumentation, however, undermines the authenticity of an "inferred primitive form". In all likelihood, his conclusion has been based on certain motifs which are missing in some of the variants (forgetting that each story contains such elements which cannot be omitted without annihilating the story itself). The contradiction is not eliminated by the supposition of a possible primitive form but is referred to a later Greek form; therefore *Megas*'s central argument does not alter the facts. He has only one comment on the utterly senseless message to delay the woman's arrival: "Das Motiv selbst, nach dem der Frau aufgetragen wird, ihre Ankunft zu verzögern, ist als Sinnesänderung des Helden, bevor es sich der schrecklichen Notwendigkeit fügt, zu verstehen." He certainly fails to explain why this motif—which is well fitted into the plot with the Bulgars—finds such unreasonable application with the Greeks. What kind of change of intention can be surmised after the master mason had accepted the decision to build in his own wife into the bridge; how can he then reasonably send word to her to come late? Could she not be built in later? And above all, may we suppose at all that this change of intention should have been the origin of the motif of betrayal, and of the message, occurring throughout the Balkans as organic parts of the plot?

He tries to mitigate the senselessness of the ring scene by arguing that the woman is sent down into the "watery base" though more often than not she has to walk into the river. Anyway, he attributes this scene to the influence of another Greek song in which a demon disguised as a beautiful girl is sending a young man into a well to bring up the ring that has fallen off from his finger. But the fact that water and ring are involved in this story does not mean at all that it is related in any way with the ring scene in the ballad of The Walled-up Wife. With the Bulgars and the neighbouring nations, the master mason induces his wife to descend into the depth of the wall pretending that he had dropped his wedding ring there, this being the reason of his sadness. In any case I can see no point in bringing this scene in connection with a bridge and a descent into a river.

Megas does not pay any attention to the contradiction that presents itself in the spread of the "drawing of lots" motif. This mainly occurs in Kappadocia and in some islands of the Dodecanessos (sporadically also elsewhere). In the northern neighbouring areas this is an organic part of the plot. It is inconceivable that this motif should have reached the Bulgars without passing the Middle Greek areas, and conversely, from the Bulgars it could not penetrate the southern and eastern regions. It follows, therefore, that his motif must have existed in wider areas, and that it was ousted to the peripheral stretches by the intruding of another motif, that of the decision of a superhuman being typical of the Greek tradition, and consequently more suitable to the Greek.

From the fact that the ballad is known throughout the entire Greek-inhabited area including Minor Asia and the southern archipelagos it would follow that it originates from Byzantine antecedents, since later the "political unity" was broken by the Frank conquer in 1204, and even before that by the Seljuks gaining foot as early as 1071 in Asia Minor.

The French and the Venetian rule, however, could hardly prevented the Greeks in maintaining connections and exchanging their songs between their various groups, since in feudal Europe the political frontiers were no obstacles to such contacts. As to the Seljuks, it is not necessary perhaps to go back to so early times and think of the incessant warfares, rather credit should be given in this respect to the argument brought up by the mentioned author in connection with the further spread of the ballad: "Zu dieser Verbreitung trug die Tatsache bei, dass diese Länder früher jahrhundertelang unter der gleichen politischen Verwaltung Roms und Byzanz und später unter der der Türken-Sultane befanden, was auch den geistigen Austausch der zusammenlebenden Völker begünstigte." (p. 52.)

Well, if the Turkish rule had had any role to play in the spread of the ballad through the Greek, Bulgar, Romanian and Hungarian territories—Rome may be perhaps neglected in this respect—then there may have been no obstacle to its transmission between the Greeks themselves. The ballad may well have found its way to the remote Greek ethnic groups even under the Turkish occupation.

Megas attributes the ballad's dissemination in Hungary to Greek settlers who used to play an important part in the cultural affairs of those countries in which they found refuge. But Greeks came as merchant to Hungary, and we have no knowledge of any considerable influence of them on this countries culture. He rejects the possibility of a direct connection between the Hungarian and the Bulgarian ballads—in spite of many word-for-word agreements of both content and form—by the following statement: "Sein Versuch, einen engen Zusammen-

54

hang zwischen den ungarischen und bulgarischen Versionen zu beweisen, ist meiner Meinung nach als verfehlt zu bezeichnen." He, however, fails to support this statement by any reasoning.

He originates the Hungarian ballad from the Romanian version because he discovers close relationships between the Transylvanian Romanian and Hungarian texts and because he does not take into consideration the existence of the Nyitra variant—that is to say, he ignores the Hungarian versions outside the mixed Romanian and Hungarian areas of Transylvania. Then he refutes the conclusions of *Taloş* and *Pop* saying that the Romanian is not the primary formulation, and that the hypothesis of a double generation of the same ballad in two different places is not possible, being the Greek area the starting point. He argues as follows: the kolindas of *Taloş* are sung by children in Transylvania and therefore there "handelt es sich offensichtlich um eine verkürzte Version, die zu einem Kinderlied... umgestaltet und aus praktischen Gründen abgekürzt wurde." (p. 53.) The Hungarian shows a very close resemblance with this shortened "children song": "Die ungarische Fassung zeigt im Gegenteil eine grössere Ähnlichkeit mit der einfacheren Version des rumänischen Liedes." *(Ibid.)* Before this, however, he declares that the Hungarian is essentially similar in construction to the ancient Greek variant inferred by him. "Es sei hier auch noch bemerkt, dass auch die ungarische Ballade von der Eingemauerten Frau, was den Verlauf der Handlung betrifft, ebenso einfach und hart (?) wie die griechischen ist." (Although he only presents a skeletal sketch of the ballad!) That is to say, the version abridged in the practice of Romanian children have been taken over by the Hungarians, and eventually the plot thus curtailed may provide a proof of the ballad-like construction of the Greek "prototype".

His summary based on three hundred and thirty Greek variants contains no one single argument which would provide me ground for altering my opinion formed on the basis of two hundred and ninety-seven Greek, two hundred and seven other, and forty-five Hungarian variants. There is only one novel point in it: the rejection of a Romanian origin. So far the Romanian researchers challenging me, namely *Taloş, Pop* and *Vrabie* have readily referred to *Megas's* review of 1960, in which he refuted my statements. Tacitly it was implied that they, *Megas* and the mentioned Romanians, took a uniform stand against me. Now it appears that they are of the same opinion as long as they are engaged in debate with me, and this is what they mostly did so far; nevertheless, they refute each others' statements as soon as it comes to the gist of the question. That is to say, there are not two standpoints, one against my conception, but there are three different opinions which mutually preclude each other. One is always at variance with the other two.

Literature: including only the more important references from times before 1967: *Grozescu* 1864: the Hungarian is a counterfeit of the Romanian; *Mailand* 1885: Greek > Serbian > Romanian > Hungarian; *Syrku* 1890: either the Romanian or the Serbian is original, the Greek being "underdeveloped"; *Schladebach* 1894: the Romanian or the Serbian is original: *Alexics* 1897: the Hungarian originates from the Romanian: *Sarudy* 1899: on the basis of Albanian, Serbian, Romanian, Bulgarian and Greek versions, the Greek or perhaps the Albanian seems to be original, the Hungarian having been borrowed from the Romanians; *Sainean* 1902: in the wake of Syrku he thinks either the Serbian or the Romanian to be original, the Hungarian having come from the Romanian; *Dietrich* 1902:

the Greek is original; *Stoilov* 1902: the Greek is original since Greek culture had influenced the whole of the Balkans; *Horger* 1902: the Hungarian originates from the Romanian; *Szegedy* 1910: translated Serbian versions, the Hungarian shows Serbian and Romanian influences; in his opinion the ballad can be dated to the age of the Hunyadis; *Sebestyén* 1911: the Hungarian originated from the Balkans; *Arnaudov* 1920: Greek is original, from which Albanian, Serbian and Aromun variants developed (these mutually influencing each other), Serbian and Romanian variants developed from the Bulgarian, the Hungarian from the latter; *Solymossy* 1923: the Greek is original (he refers to a Greek bridge and to the name of Manole surviving from 1659; the Hungarian came from the Serbian, the Romanian being a prose version; *Gragger* 1926 accepts Solymossy; *Skok* 1929: the ballad ows its spread to Aromun masons; *Stefanović* 1931: (and 1937): *Karadžić* version is original, it blended the story with the legend of the sacrificed child; *Stefanović* 1934: the Greek and the Bosnian versions are original, from which the *Karadžić* variant developed in the twelth and the thirteenth centuries; *Stefanović* 1935: the Hungarian forms a separate group, being related not with the Serbian but the Slavonian and Macedon variants; *Baud-Bovy* 1936: the Greek is original; *Ortutay* 1936: accepts *Solymossy; Entwistle* 1939: spread from the Greeks to the Balkans; *Kázmér* 1942: Balkan origin; *Caracostea* 1942: the Romanians borrowed it from the Balkan nations; *Ortutay* 1948: association with the earlier material of the Mordvinian legend; *Entwistle* 1949: the Greek being very old, even though not "Akritic", gave rise to the Serbian and Romanian versions, as well as to "London Bridge is Falling down", *Cocchiara* 1950: the Greek is the ancient version because it is most archaic; *Csanádi* and *Vargyas* 1954: accepts *Solymossy; Ortutay* 1955: accepts *Solymossy; Comişel* 1956: the Romanians have many versions of the ballad; *Chikovani* 1955: Georgian, Hungarian and Serbian parallelisms; *Istvánovits* 1958: new and more exact Caucasian data; *Erdélyi, I.* 1958: New Mordvinian examples; *Megas* 1960: reviews the works by *Cocchiara* and *Vargyas*, rejecting the latter for ignorance of two hundred and fifty Greek versions in manuscript; *Hadžis* 1960: the Greek is original, having been spread by Greek emigrants; *Maskaev* 1964: (pp 79—112) discussing the Mordvinian songs, and Hungarian parallels on the basis of *Vargyas* 1960; *Taloş* 1962: publishes thirty-one Transylvanian variants and quotes a further twenty-seven; *Pop* 1963: the Transylvanian Romanian is original from which the Hungarian and the Regat—completely different—forms developed, as well as all other national versions; *Vargyas* is a representative of the old school of Hungarian folklorists who always sought to demonstrate the superiority of Hungarians. (NB. those belonging to the "old school" invariably demonstrated a Romanian or Serbian primacy: *Mailand, Alexics, Sarudy, Horger, Szegedy, Sebestyén, Solymossy, Gragger, Ortutay, Kázmér*, and even myself in the volume *Csanádi* and *Vargyas* 1954 before surveying the vast material of variants in their national idioms; as against this, the Romanian researchers—from *Grozescu* and *Saineanu* to *Pop* and *Vrabie* mostly derived the ballad from Romanian tradition all over the spread area.) *Horálek* 1963: the ballad came from the South to the Hungarians and Romanians but it did not penetrate the Slovak language area; *Amzulescu* 1964: enumerates the published variants, leaving out the Transylvanian kolinda versions; *Horálek* 1965: contests my conception; *Vrabie* 1966 (pp. 67—107): no "Hungarian variant" can be spoken of because only Székely and Moldavian variants exist, these being mere "reflections" of the Romanian; *Taloş* 1969: Romanian legends connected with the ballad; *Megas* 1969—70: the Greek is original: *Megas* 1971: repeats his former statement on the basis of a detailed examination of the Greek variants; *Suliţeanu* 1971: analyzes the tune of the Romanian ballad which is non-strophic but an epic construction of variable tune elements; *Taloş* 1973: topically the ballad is a Balkan product. Contesting the Caucasian origin put forward by *Vargyas*, he thinks that there is no explanation for the interchange of the child's role with that of the mother. He ignores the large number of similar transfers' role in the course of transmitting variants: Type **26**. The Girl Danced to Death—Tristes noces: the young man is poor; in the French the girl is poor. Type **13**. The Bride Dying in the Wedding Procession: in the English ballad the brother stabs the girl; in the Italian, the brother protects her. Type **16**. The Mother's Curse: the Italian mother curses the girl, who wishes to marry, while in *Child* 25: she curses her son because he goes to see his sweetheart. Type **3**. The French and Polish forms of The Enticed Wife: the girl pushes the knight in the water—in Polish version inversely; French Type 62. Germine—*Child* Type 76. the man gives signs—the girl does it; Type **9**. The Two Chapel Flowers (in the Hungarian the child curses his mother while in the Slovak version the mother curses herself; in the Hungarian a young aristocrat falls in love with a serf's daughter, in the Spanish version the King's daughter with a poor nobleman); Type **18**. The Knight and the Damsel (the French young man tries to appease the girl while in the East European versions he makes her sing); Type **20**. The Brigand's Wife (in the Transdanubian regions the wife has her husband, who is a robber, executed while in Transylvanian and Romanian ballads it is the brigand that has his wife killed; Type **65.** The Speaking Corpse (in the French the dead girl speaks to her bridegroom while in the Hungarian the dead young man to his bride); Type **71.** The Coward Lover (in the Hungarian the girl calls the young man who raises objections while in the Spanish the young man asks the woman for admission and the woman raises objections). In this context we should refer to such parallels as are: Type **63.** The Wicked Wife and Type **64.** The Incredulous Husband, in which the topic is the same but the characters change in function. Besides, *Taloş* completely ignores the agreement in the formula of walling-up by gradation and declares the Hungarian version of Nyitra to be a revival.

3. THE ENTICED WIFE

9.

A soldier was luring a young wife
To go away into a foreign land;
He kept on luring
Until he succeeded in luring her away.
5. They were going, they were going in a small wood,
In a small wood, in a small field;
They arrived at a beautiful tree,
And cool moss under the beautiful tree.
Sit down here, beautiful young woman,
10. Look in my head for a little while.
(While searching in his head, the young woman was
thinking of how she could escape. When the soldier
fall asleep, she drew his sword and cut his head. Then:)
She dressed in his clothes.
She galloped back and reached her home.
Good day, kind sheriff, my goodman!
Will you let me pass the night under your roof?
15. I cannot take you in, brave soldier,
For I have no wife
To cook you a supper.
I don't need your supper,
I need only your warm room.
(He was shown into a warm room and given a supper, too. Before going to bed, the
guest spoke up once more:)
20. Take off, sheriff, my boots,
Dry my foot-cloth.
Take off, my daughter, his boots,
Dry his foot-cloth!
Father, father, my dear father,
25. It is my mother that has been here!
Shut up, son of a bitch!
Your mother has gone with the soldier.
Father, father, my dear father,
It is my mother that has been here!
30. I knew her by her feet,
And by her slender waist,
By her two rocking arms.

She unbuttoned her mantle,
She suckled her son,
35. She entreated her kind husband.

Köveskálla (Zala county). Gyula Sebestyén, 1906. MNGY VIII, 180.

10.

1. Come with me, Anna Molnár
   Into the forest, far, far away,
   Into the forest, far, far away.

2. I cannot go, Márton Jajgó,
   For I have a wedded spouse
   And a little son sitting in my arms.

3. After much luring and cajoling
   He took her onto his horse and ran away with her,
   He took her onto his horse and ran away with her.

4. They started on the long way
   Into the forest, up to the snowy mountains,
   Into the forest, up to the snowy mountains.

5. They arrived at a branched tree,
   They sat down in its shade,
   They sat down in its shade.

6. Anna Molnár, my dearest heart,
   Will you look in my head for a little while!
   Will you look in my head for a little while!

7. She was looking in his head,
   And he fell asleep in her lap.
   He fell asleep in her lap.

8. Anna Molnár was looking high and low,
   And on the branches of the branched tree
   She saw six beautiful girls hanged!

9. Aye, she thought,
   I am going to be the seventh today,
   I am going to be the seventh today.

10. The tears were pouring from her eyes,
    And they poured down on Márton Jajgó's face,
    And they poured down on Márton Jajgó's face.

11. Why are you crying, why are you crying, Anna Molnár?
    I am not crying, Márton Jajgó,
    It's only dew from the branch of the tree.

12. How could it be dew,
    When it is just noon,
    When it is just noon!

13. Prepare, prepare, Anna Molnár!
    Climb the branched tree,
    Climb the branched tree!

14. I cannot climb, Márton Jajgó,
    I am not used to climbing trees,
    I am not used to climbing trees.

15. But you must go before me, showing me an example
    So that I may learn from you how to climb,
    So that I may learn from you how to climb.

16. He started to climb the branched tree,
    His sharp sword fell back,
    His sharp sword fell back.

17. Throw it up, throw it up, Anna Molnár!
    Just a moment, just a moment, brave soldier,
    Just a moment, just a moment, brave soldier.

18. She threw up his sharp sword
    And so she cut his tender neck,
    And so she cut his tender neck.

19. You have served to it, Márton Jajgó,
    For you have cheated me out of my country,
    For you have cheated me out of my country.

20. She put on his mantle,
    And his gown that reached down to the heels,
    And his gown that reached down to the heels.

21. She jumped on his horse
    And rode back to her country,
    To the gate of her kind husband.

22. I say, my goodman,
    Can you put me up for the night?
    Can you put me up for the night?

23. I can put you up for the night,
    Although my son is crying,
    Although my son is crying.

24. Aye, it does not matter if he is crying,
    For I have heard a child crying,
    For I have heard a child crying.

25. Well, then you may come in
    And we manage to spend a night somehow,
    And we manage to spend a night somehow.

26. I say, my goodman,
    Can you have good wine in the village,
    Can you have good wine in the village?

27. There is good wine to be had here,
    But my son is crying, who shall I leave him to,
    But my son is crying, who shall I leave him to?

28. While the goodman has been out fetching the wine
    She was tending the child,
    She was tending the child.

29. She unbuttoned her mantle
    And suckled her crying son,
    And suckled her crying son.

30. She suckled him, she kissed him,
    She rocked him to sleep by the fireplace,
    She rocked him to sleep by the fireplace.

31. I say, my goodman,
    What if your wife were alive,
    What if she came home alive?

32. Would you then scold her, would you beat her,
    Would you reproach her in this life,
    Would you reproach her in this life?

33. I should not scold her, I should not beat her,
    Nor should I reproach her in this life,
    Nor should I reproach her in this life.

34. I am your wife
    With whom yon swore to live,
    With whom you swore to live.

35. And they flung themselves into each other's arms,
    And they lived together to death,
    And they lived together to death.

Kibéd ("Marosszék", Maros-Torda county). Seprődi 1908 = Erdélyi Múzeum, cylinder XX/1. = Ethn. 1913, 38.

11

Come with me, Anna Molnár,
Come with me to a foreign land.
I will not go, my gallant sire;
For I have a little child,
5. A little child and a kind husband,
With whom I have no rest
Either in the night or in the day.
Come, come, Anna Molnár;
For I have got six palaces
10. And I shall place you in the seventh!
He was cajoling her with many words,
And in the end he cheated her out of her home.
They are going, they are going in a strange land,
And they arrived in the middle of a green wood.
15. Sit down here, Anna Molnár,
Sit down in the shade of the branched tree
So that I my lie in your lap;
Look in my head for a little while!
Anna Molnár, Anna Molnár,
20. Anna Molnár, Anna Molnár,
Do not look up into the branched tree!
I shall not look up, my gallant sire.
My gallant sire went asleep.
And Anna Molnár looked up
25. And raised her eyes up to the top of the branched tree.
There she beheld six beautiful maidens,
Six beautiful maidens hanged!
She thought
She would be the seventh to be hanged!
30. Her tender heart throbbed,
Her warm tears began to flow,
And they flew onto the face of the gallant sire,
And my gallant sire woke up.
Why are you crying, why are you crying, Anna Molnár?
35. You have looked up into the oak-tree,
Up to the top of the branched tree!
I did not look up, my gallant sire;
Three orphan children have been passing here,
And I thought of my little child!
40. I thought of my little child, of my kind husband
With whom I have had no rest
Either in the night or in the day.
Climb before me, Anna Molnár,
Climb up to the top of the branched tree!

45. I will not climb, my gallant sire,
    For I am not used to go before anyone.
    My gallant sire began to climb the tree before her.
    She suddenly drew out his bright sword
    And cut off the gallant sire's head!
50. She clad in his clothes,
    She put on his scarlet gown;
    Then she jumped on the steed
    And started home,
    To the gate of her kind husband.
55. Kind goodman, kind goodman,
    Can you put me up for the night?
    I cannot put you up for the night, my gallant sire,
    For I have a little child
    With whom I have no rest.
60. I have no rest either in the night or in the day.
    Kind goodman, kind goodman,
    I am used to such things!
    Kind goodman, kind goodman,
    Is there good wine to be had in the village?
65. It is to be had with the neighbour's as well.
    Go, go, kind goodman,
    Go and fetch a cup of it for supper!
    Go, go, you kind servant,
    Go and fetch some shavings for the night!
70. She unbuttoned her mantle,
    Her scarlet gown that reached down to the heels,
    And she suckled her little child,
    And her little child fell asleep.
    The kind goodman has come back:
75. My gallant sire, my gallant sire,
    What is the reason
    That my little child has fallen asleep;
    It is three weeks and three days
    That he has not slept!
80. Kind goodman, kind goodman,
    What if your wife came home?
    Should you beat her, should you scold her?
    Or should you reproach her to her last day?
    I should not beat her, I should not scold her
85. And I should not reproach her to the last of her day.
    She unbuttoned her mantle,
    Her scarlet gown reaching down to the heels;
    She kissed her little child,
    Her little child,—and her kind husband.

"Székelyföld", Samu Szabó, 1872 = MNGY I, 141.

12.

1. Gye-re ve-lem   Mó-nár An-na   Ren-ge - teg-re, hosz-szú/út -ra!

Nem   më-gyëk én, Aj- gő   Már-ton.   Va-gyon ne - këm hi - tes tár - sam.

Sí -ró gyermökëm

1. Come with me, Anna Mónár,
   Let's go into the forest, far, far away!
   I will not go, Márton Ajgó,
   For I have a wedded spouse,

2. A wedded spouse, a kind husband,
   A little child sitting in my arms.
   He was luring, he was cheating her,
   Finally he raised her on the horse and ran away with her.

3. They started out and kept on going, going
   On their long way to the forest.
   There they found a branched tree,
   And sat down in its shade.

4. Anna Mónár, my dearest heart,
   Will you look in my head for a little while!
   She was looking in his head
   And he fell asleep in her lap.

5. Anna Mónár, looked over her shoulder,
   And she looked up to the branches of the tree.
   And lo! there are six beautiful maidens
   Hanged one after the other in a line.
   Aye, she thought,
   I shall be the seventh today!

6. Tears fell from her eyes
   Onto the face of Márton Ajgó.
   What made you weep, what made you weep, Anna Mónár?
   I am not weeping, Márton Ajgó,
   There is dew on the branches of the tree,
   And dew has dropped on your cheeks.

7. How could dew be dropping now
   When the day is at noon?
   Prepare, prepare, Anna Mónár,
   Climb the oak-tree!

64

8. I will not climb, Márton Ajgó
   For I am not used to climb a tree!
   But show me how I could, go ahead of me,
   So that I may learn from you how to climb!

9. Márton Ajgó started to climb,
   His sharp sword fell back.
   Pass it to me, pass it to me, Anna Mónár!
   Wait a minute, wait a minute, galant soldier!

10. She flung up his sword with such strength
    That she cut his tender neck.
    You have served to it, Márton Ajgó,
    For you have cheated me out of my home!

11. Anna Mónár clad in his clothes,
    And put on his scarlet gown reaching down to the heels.
    Then she jumped on his swift horse
    And galloped back to her country,
    There she stopped at the gate of her home,
    And called into the courtyard:

12. I say, kind goodman,
    Will you put me up for the night?
    I could put you up for the night, brave soldier,
    But I have a child crying at the hearth.

13. My wife has forsaken me,
    And there is a child crying at my hearth.
    If it's only for that, you may put me up,
    For it is not the first time I have heard a child cry.

14. I say, kind goodman,
    Is there good wine to be had in the village?
    If there is good wine to be had in the village
    Go and fetch me a cup of it for supper!

15. Aye, it's a long way to the place where good wine is to be had,
    And whom shall I leave my crying child to?
    While you are out fetching the wine
    I shall take care of your child.

16. No sooner the goodman started out,
    The goodman started out,
    Than she unbuttoned her mantle
    And suckled her crying child.

17. She suckled him, she kissed him,
    And she rocked him to sleep by the fire-side.
    The father of the child returned
    And wondered why the child was not crying.
    Maybe, the child is silent
    Because there is a stranger in the house.

18. They set to table to have supper.
    The guest spoke up, addressing the goodman:
    I say, kind goodman,
    There's a question for you to answer!

19. Suppose, your wife were alive,
    And came home alive,
    Should you scold her, should you beat her,
    Or should you reproach her in this life?
    I should not scold her, I should not beat her
    Nor should I reproach her in this life.

20. I am your wife
    With whom you swore to live.
    They recognized each other,
    And they also embraced each other.
    They spent the supper merrily
    And lived together to their death.

Gyimesfelsőlok-Sántatelek (Csík county), a 34-year-old woman, Kallós-Martin-Pesovár, F. 1962 = AP 5200/a.

Divergences: The variants of Regions I–III are more or less abridged and more incomplete versions of No. 9 published here. Sometimes even the motif of enticement is missing: the hero and heroine meet in a forest and when the soldier wants to kiss the wife she draws out his sword and slashes his neck. At the same time, the scene of suckling the child, and the subsequent reunion, recur in every variant. One of the texts, however, is interpreted in a way that the wife leaves the house, because upon the child's words the father's reply reads as follows: "Had I known that she was your mother, I should not have let her go for sixteen thousand forints!". Not infrequently the smallest fragments preserve very important details. In the variant of Béd the "Old man" is Carrying Fair Ilona *(Szép Ilona)* through hills and dales, Through hills and dales, and thorns and bushes. Stop now, stop now, you Old Man! ... *We shall stop when we arrive at the tree which I have cut at the top: There I have nine castles, And I shall close you up in the tenth"*. Boasting of having castles, being an element of enticement, occurs in some of the texts: Come with me, Anna Molnár, I have six houses made of stone—sometimes castles—I am just building the seventh—or I shall give you the seventh. The fragment of Tamásfalva contains only thus much: "I have six castles of stone, And I am just building the seventh". The informant adds that the fragment originates from the story of Anna Mónár which had been sung in his village when he was yet a child. (By courtesy of *Sándor Bálint.*) The castle motif occurs in nine variants. Further variants of the enticement motif are the following: "Come, let's go, Anna Molnár On a long way, into the forest. To the place that floods with milk and honey! I will not go, ...Anna Molnár could not withstand, And she started on the long way, To the place that floods with milk and honey." (MNGY I. 146, *Kriza*): "Come with me, Anna Molnár, For I shall buy you holiday clothes!"; in two Moldavian variants the soldier asks the wife to go to walk: "Come with me, Anna Mónár! Come on the long way, let us have a walk"! In several variants: the soldier *walking* in the street asks Anna Molnár: "Come with me, Anna Mónár!". As to the the rest of the motifs, there are no considerable divergences; and the differences are rather due to curtailments of the text by omission.

First mentioned: 1840–41 (Klézse, *Rokonföld*).

Dissemination: Sine loco (supposedly Transdanubian), Moson county (Cikolasziget 2), Sopron county (the Csepreg region), Vas county (Ikervár), Zala county (Keszthely, Köveskálla, Újudvar), Veszprém county (the environment of Somló, Borzavár), Nyitra county (Béd—fragment embedded in the ballad of the Murderer of the Old Husband, Type 131), Bars county (Lédec 2), Hont county (Garamsalló), Ung county *(sine loco)*, Torontál county (Tamásfalva, a fragment of two lines), Csanád county (Mezőkovácsháza), Torda-Aranyos county (Aranyosrákos), Maros-Torda county (Kibéd, Nyárádköszvényes, a fragment of two lines, Szabéd, Szováta 2, "Marosszék"), Udvarhely county (Atyha, Lengyelfalva 2, Rugonfalva, Szombatfalva, Udvarhelyszék, "Székelyföld" = probably Udvarhely 3), Csík county (Borszék, Csíkmadaras, Ditró, Gyergyószentmiklós, Gyimesfelsőlok, Gyimesfelsőlok-Sántatelek 2, Gyimesközéplok-Bükkhavaspataka, Gyimesközéplok-Háromkút 2, Gyimesközéplok-Jávordipataka, Gyimesvölgye-Hidegség, Gyimesvölgye-Récepatak, Gyimesvölgye-Magyarsügés, Szárhegy, Tekerőpatak), Háromszék county ("Alsóháromszék", Sepsiköröspatak)? Bukovina (Andrásfalva-Kakasd, Tolna county, Fogadjisten, Istensegíts, "Bukovina" prose text added to the ballad about The Brigand's Wife), Moldava (Bogdánfalva 3, Gerlén, Klézse 4, Külső-Rekecsin, Lészped 6, Magyarfalu 2, Nicolae Balcescu, Pusztina 2, Somoska, Trunk 3). Total 78. I–III: 17, IV: 37, V: 24.

Rejected: the text described as having been recorded at Ipolyföldémes and Ipolyszakállas, which shows a word-for-word agreement, apart from three minor deviations, with a variant formerly recorded in Ung county: furthermore, the piece AP 5173/i, recorded from a fifteen-years-old girl at Bélzerind, Arad county, which is apparently a variant of the Transylvanian text that the informant had learned from a printed book.

Textual relationships with other ballads: **5, 30**; in respect of the "looking-in-the-head" motif: **40, 41.**

Tunes: 1 = No. *10, 2* = No. *12.* The numbers of tune variants are given in brackets *7* (2), *10* (3), *13* (2), *14* (4), *15* (2), *17* (3), *18* (2), *19* (2), *25* (4), *27* (5).

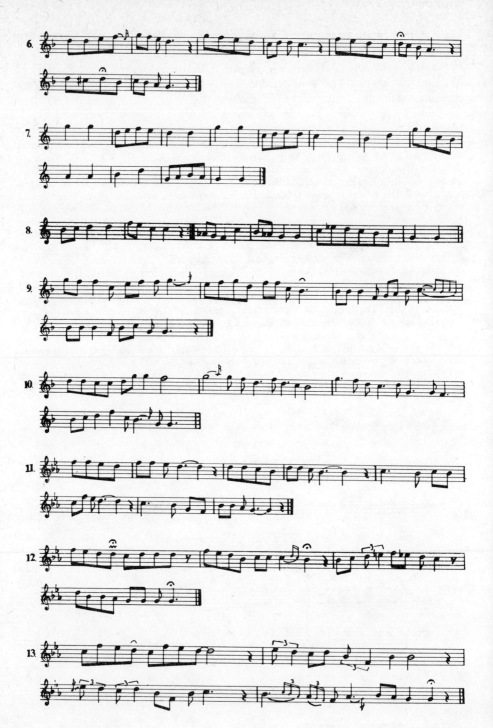

Versions in languages other than Hungarian:

FRENCH: **1.** *Simon* 1900 Wallonia 8, 82. **2.** *Canteloube* IV, 46. *3. Puymaigre* 1865, 98. *4. Davenson* 7. *5. Barbeau-Sapir* 25. *6. Barbeau* 1962, 143 (reconstruction). *7–9. Barbeau* MS. *10. Decombe* 92. *11.* Rev. Trad. Pop. 1894, 406[+]. *12—25. Millien* 1906, 113—117A–D + 10 variants. *26–29. Rossat* 1917 11A–D. *30. Guillon*, 85.[+] *31. Smith* 1881, 149. *32.* Champfleury-Weckerlin, 172. *33. Bujeaud* II, 237. *34. Ampère*, 256. *35. Simon* 1926, 169. *36. Tiersot* 1903, 142. (*Nygard* 1958 enumerates 36 MS. variants from Canada.)

ITALIAN: *37–42. Nigra* 13A–F. *43. Ferraro* 1870, 4 3. *44. Giannini* 1889, 143 4. *45. Pergoli* 13 7.

46. Ferraro 1877, 14 2. *47–48. Widter–Wolf* 73A–B. *49. Bernoni* 1872 Punt. V. 2.

PORTUGUESE: *50–52. Braga I,* 152–153 (= *Hardung* 61 and 63), 154.

SPANISH: *53. Wolf–Hoffmann* II, 22 119. *54–55. Cossio–Solane* II, 21–233 275–276. *56.* JB.f. Romanische u. Englische Lit. 1861, 285. *57–58. Armistead–Silverman* 1971/I, 17 and 54, A2 and B15. 59. Id. 1971/II 18.

ENGLISH: *60–66. Child* 4. *67–207. Bronson* 4. *208. Greig* 2. *209–216. Belden* 4A–H.

DUTCH: *217: Hoffmann* v. F. 10. *218.* MS.[+] *219.* D. Vlr. 41/1b = Souterliedekens 2. *220.* E–B 41k. *221. Lootens–Feys* 37. *222.* MS[+] *223–225. Lambrechts* 156–158. 226. D. Vlr. 41/10. *227.* MS.[+]

GERMAN: *228–400.* D. Vlr. 41/12–231 (including the recently published *Parisius* 5–6, 88, 340, 431/a, 550 and 682).

DANISH: *441–473.* DgF 183 (11 MS. and broadside and 22 traditional variants).

SWEDISH: *474–475, Geijer–Afzelius* 66–67. *476–478. Nygard* 1958 A–B, E.

NORWEGIAN: *479–496. Nygard* 1958, A–R.

POLISH: *497–548. Kolberg* 1857 5a–bbb (a = *Czernik,* 294, d = ibid., 298, bbb = *Karlowicz* 4, 407 = *Czernik* 300). *549–550. Kolberg* 1871–84, 6, 112 208 and 169 336. *551.* ibid. 12, 63 131. *552–553.* ibid. 16, 289–290 473–474. *554.* ibid. 19, 148 453*. *555–569. Karlowicz* 4 f. 18A, 25, 51, 51A, 53,58A, 66A, 76, 78, 79, 408–409 + var. and 9 f. 121, 124, 667–668, 669. (129 + 1 variants are enumerated and discussed, but only the mentioned ones are published with full texts.) *570–576. Ligęza–Sbiński*[+] 5A–E, H, J.

SLOVAK–MORAVIAN: *577. Národop. Vestn. Česk.* 1906, 277. *578.* Sl. Sp. IH. 513. *579–585. Sušil* 179/360–361, 189//405–408. *586–587. Bartoš* 1901 46 and 104. (D. Vlr. quotes the Czech variants under *Erben*[3] 1864 15–16., see also *Burlasova* 21.)

ROMANIAN: *588–590. Papahagi* 1925 374, 382 and 395. *591. Tiplea* 3. *592. Amzulescu* 288/II. (Rejected: Marienescu 22 and the translation thereof in Ethn 1897, 185, *Vulcanu* 57, because of unmistakable signs of their having been transcriptions; further the data "from the collection of *A. Hermann,* Bihar county", Ethn 1897 and *Moldován* 6 and 46 should be handled with utmost reservation, these being free translations without the originals added and the provenience specified.)

SOUTHERN SLAV: (partially relevant) *593–598. Štrekelj* 133–138. *599.* HNP V/2, 158 99. *600.* TALVJ II, 172 = ? *Kapper* II, 318. (Translated from the Vuk Collection.)

The Ballad of The Enticed Wife survives in the traditions of fifteen nations, and is known to all peoples in Western and Middle Europe; therefore the fact of a common origin cannot be called into doubt, neither its trend of spread from west to east. Consequently, it was generally held earlier that it reached Hungary through German mediation. This statement, however, is contradicted by a closer analysis of the facts. Notably, the story has four fairly different formulations in the German-speaking territories. The first has western borders of the mentioned areas as its field of dissemination, stretching roughly along the Rhine up to the Dutch frontier. This version does not include the scene under the tree with the hanged women, at most fragments of it occur in some of the variants; for example, hanged girls are seen by the riders on their way. The story runs as follows: The knight lifts the girl on the horse and they ride three days in desolate fields; finally the girl asks the knight for food and drink. "Wait till we arrive at the lime-tree or the spring", answers the knight. When they reach the place, the knight owns that he has killed several girls before at the very place; in one or two variants they see hanged girls indeed, their sight being the cause of the knight's intimation. He also imparts to the girl that she has to die. She is offered to have her choice between three deaths: to be hanged on a pine-tree, to be drowned in water, or slain by the sword. The girl chooses the sword, but warns the knight to take off his clothes because maiden blood will spray far. The knight turns away to undress, and the girl draws out his sword and cuts his head. Then she jumps on the knight's steed; at this moment the severed head asks her to blow his horn hanging from the saddle. The girl, however, escapes the trap and rides away. Meeting with the knight's mother on the way, she tells her that she has left her son at the tree where he had slain already seven girls, and that she should have been the eighth.

The Dutch version amplifies the story by sending the girl first to her father, then to the mother and her brothers, whom she asks one after the other if she may go on a ride with the knight; apart from this, however, the story runs much the same as in the German version. In one of the variants the girl returns home bringing the seducer's severed head with her, and the father gives a feat to celebrate the glorious escape of his daughter.

The next German version which has been recorded from the German-speaking populations of Southern Germany, Switzerland, Bohemia and pre-wars Hungary presents the following formulation of the same story. The magic song of a knight is heard from outside the palace. The girl wishes to go with him so that he can teach her his song. She collects her valuables and selects the best of the horses from the stable, and they gallop off. At the edge of a forest, a turtle-dove warns the girl not to believe the knight, for he has trapped eleven already and she is to be the twelfth. She asks what the turtle-dove said, but the knight explains it away. In the forest he spreads his cloak on the ground and asks the girl to search his head for lice. For every lock of his hair she goes through she drops a tear. "Why are you weeping?"—asks the knight. "—Are you perhaps lamenting your proud, youthful spirit, or your father's wealth, or your honour which you shall never regain? Or is it perhaps because of the pine-tree?" The girl admits that it is the pine-tree that makes her weep, because she sees eleven girls hanged on it. "Don't cry, Anneli, for you will be the twelfth!" Yet the girl asks him to let her cry out three times, and he grants the request since there is no one to hear her in the forest. But her brother does hear her, sets off after them and kills the seducer.

More towards the East and North, in the territories of Saxony, Brandenburg, Mecklenburg, Pomerania and the East-Prussian provinces, the brother arrives too late to rescue the girl, he can only revenge her death. This is the third type which shows a manifold contamination with motifs of other ballads. (For instance: "What blood stained your sword (or clothes) red?", asks the brother. "I have slain a dove", answers the seducer.) Nevertheless, the three cries form a strong link between this and the former type. As can be seen, proceeding from the West to the East, the figure of a determined, self-rescuing girl gradually changes into a passive victim who has to be saved, or revenged. The fourth version, similarly of the western areas, occurs alternating with the first. There are no previous victims in it, the knight kills the girl, and the text seems to justify him doing so, and even permits him to marry another girl in the end.

Had the ballad been transmitted by the Germans to the Hungarians, it ought to have been from the areas of the second type discussed, this being characteristic of the German populations living within and in the neighbourhood of Hungary. As against this, we have a Hungarian heroine who rescues herself, just as in the westernmost type. On the other hand, as regards the scene under the tree, there are closer similarities with the second type than with the first in which the motif comes up only in a fragmentary form.

72

1. Golden mounting of a sword sheath. Eremitage (Siberia, ca. 300 B.C.—400 A.D.)

2. Mural painting in 14th-century church of Bántornya (Muraköz). (Water-colour reproduction.)

3. Mural painting in the 14th-century church of Zsegra (Szepes county). (Strongly repainted in the 17th century. Water-colour reproduction.)

5. Mural painting in the church of Maksa (Háromszék county), from the 14th century. (Water-colour reproduction.)

4. Mural painting in the church of Vitfalva (Szepes county), from the turn of the 14th—15th centuries

6. Mural painting in the church of Székelyderzs (Háromszék county), from the 15th century

7. Vatican Legendary (a series of pictures of Hungarian origin from 1357—70). Representing a scene of the St: Ladislas legend

8. The title-page of the Thúróczi Chronicle from 1488

9. Illuminated Chronicle detail (after 1358). St. Ladislas's fight with the Cumanian warrior

Before drawing conclusions, let us examine the other western versions. The French, being concise and remarkably uniform of presentation, can be outlined as follows: The knight carries the girl on a long journey (for many miles) without a word passing between them. At last the girl asks for food and drink. "Eat your own flesh and drink your own blood, because you are not going to get any proper food", says the knight. They reach a fish-pond. Here he admits that he has already drowned thirteen women and that she is to be the fourteenth, and tells her to undress. She asks him to turn his back because it is not meet that a knight should see a girl undress. When he does so, she pushes him into the water. He catches hold of a branch but she cuts it off with his sword. In vain he begs her to save him: whatever people will say if she returns home without her bridegroom? "I shall tell them—says the girl—that I did to you what you intended to me." And with this the ballad ends.

This story spread, practically without alteration, to the Italians (Spanish), and with changes in detail, but essentially unaltered, to the English. (There the scene of rescue is placed on the seashore, and the girl arriving at home has a dialogue with her parrot and asks the bird not to betray her.) Some of its particular elements, however, penetrated also into the Dutch and West German territories and reached even the Middle German and Austrian provinces.

At the same time, the scene under the tree shows an opposite trend. This appears in the four German sub-types in differing forms and with differing frequency. It is most persistent in the second, South-German type. But even this type fails to combine all the elements which are present in the Hungarian. For if we take into parallel consideration all the details of the different German types, together with those of the Dutch and Danish versions, disregarding the Hungarian variants for the time being, then the following phases can be brought together in the scene: the man puts his head into the woman's lap, he has the woman search his head, and falls asleep; the woman begins to weep (mainly because she has seen the previous victims hanged on the tree). But it is only the Hungarian variants that have all these five motifs *together*, and what is more, they are to be found together in most of the variants. In no other language areas do we find all five coming up in one and the same ballad. In the South-German type, which bears nearest resemblance to the Hungarian, mostly the head-searching and the tears of the girl figure, after she catches sight of the hanged victims. But the knight does not go asleep, nor does he put his head in her lap, but invites her to take her place beside him on the outspread cloak. One group of variants, however, has the motif of the head bent in her lap without the head-searching: such texts occur in the areas stretching from the juncture of the Saxon-Silesian and the Czech-German territories northward to Brandenburg and along the Oder. (Remarkably enough, only one single Moravian text *(5.)* has been found, to my knowledge, in this region—of course, not German—in which the head-searching motif is formulated with the following words: "jiškaj mi v moju hlave".) The Danish ballads have no hanged victims; the man is digging a grave and so the girl learns what fate is in store for her, although the head-searching comes up in ten variants—it is the girl that asks leave to do that, after she had heard what fate awaits her; in three other variants only traces of it remain, while in one the knight asks the girl to do the favour. In this case, in turn, he puts his head into the lap of the maid and also falls asleep, and what is more, in one of the texts he is sent to sleep by a magic song, which is also explanation for the girl's escape. Sometimes the scene is further complicated inasmuch as the man had informed the girl about her fate before he goes to sleep in her lap, but to make this seem credible, he takes her promise well in advance that she will not kill him as he sleeps. (Faded memory of this solution is encountered in northern Scottish variants of doubtful authenticity.) The Swedes and the Norwegians have either the sleeping or the head-searching, and sometimes they speak explicitly about witchcraft.

Among the northeastern Germans: in East-Prussian, Pomeranian, Mecklenburg and Polish German territories, the whole of the scene is missing. It is also missing among the Poles, whereas they have, in an obscure form though, the motif of the brother hearing the cry for help, which shows that the third German type found its way and spread its influence to this area. In the fourth German type the whole scene is missing, as a rule. (If it is contained in some form or other, it has been adapted from the first type, which contaminated with it in the western border region.) The first—western—variant knows only the tree with the girls hanged on it, but the scene under it is lacking; what is more, the tree motif itself often figures only in the choice between the three deaths, and in such cases the hanged girls are never seen. But in the Rhine area the different types have mixed in a mosaic pattern, and here the motif of head-searching has also penetrated into some of the western-type texts. Among the Dutch, on the other hand, no traces of the scene are to be found, only the hanged girls emerge though not in a forest but in a field where the girls are hanged on gallows. Half of the variants, however, have no memory of the scene at all, only the choice between the three deaths is vaguely remembered, one being death by hanging.

As can be seen from the foregoing, the scene becomes more and more vague and fragmentary the further west and north we go, which makes the spread of the tree-scene from the southeast probable.

Admittedly, in Hungary, too, there are areas in which only isolated details now remain of the coherent scene, for example, in Transdanubian and one or two northern counties. This seems to permit the conclusion as if we were faced with a process of erosion that has set in gradually in the tradition, only the process has reached a more advanced stage with the Germans than the Hungarians. But among the Hungarian-speaking population of Transdanubia various details of the scene have been noted from a relatively narrow area, therefore it can be assumed that all the motifs were once present together in all the texts. Among the Germans, however, there are large areas in which one or another motif is consistantly missing, while in other areas other motifs are also consistently missing (or present). And what is even more surprising, in Germany it is the most backward, eastern regions where the scene is completely lacking and the more developed peasant populations of the Rhine region and the south German territories have preserved most of the details; at the same time, in Hungary the more developed Transdanubian regions have preserved only fragments of the scene, while in the traditional regions of Transylvania and Moldavia, much more backward as regards urbanization, the scene survives in its full integrity. That amounts to say that among the Hungarians the case is really one of deterioration of the scene in the Transdanubian parts. With

74

the Germans, however, the differences are such features which have been existing from the very beginning. This is well substantiated by those sixteenth-century broadside variants which show a complete agreement with the actual situation.

In contrast to the scene under the tree which migrated from east to west, details of the French formulation spread from west to east, and at the points of juncture they bring about mixed forms. It is a common feature of the French and Italian versions that the couple travel for miles without a word being spoken, until the girl asks for food and drink and from the knight's answer learns in advance what her fate is to be. This motif also occurs in the west-German Type 1, and here and there even in the south German territories in Type 2, spreading as far as Austria, the western frontier of Bohemia, and towards the North to the line of Nuremberg and Cologne. The French scene—drowning in the water—appears in the variants in which the murder takes place at a spring: "You will eat when we reach the spring", says the seducer, and later the spring gives forth blood as evil omen. But an opposite trend is indicated by the formulation: "We shall eat when we reach the linden-tree", as well as by the vague reminiscence of the scene under the tree. What is more, a contamination of the two scenes is apparent in one of the earliest recorded forms already, that of Augsburg, published as broadside around 1560: the hanged women are seen at the spring. It is more confused in the Nuremberg broadside of 1550–65, in which they settle at the spring first, the girl searches the head, and she weeps, then they continue their journey, and it is after all this that the hanged girls come into display. Another betraying sign is that the victim is a *girl* also in this version, like in the whole of the European tradition, yet the knight asks: "Are you perhaps lamenting your *husband?*" Only the Hungarian ballad has a woman as its heroine who forsakes her husband in favour of the knight. Revealing for the trend of spreading is the motif of the choice between three kinds of deaths in the Dutch and West German form which practically combines the motif of drowning in the water, characteristic of the French, and that of the hanging, together with the cutting off of the head, typical of the Hungarian variants. A similarly revealing contamination is the one observable in the south German variants which are containing a somewhat far-fetched formulation of the scene inasmuch as the girl asks the knight to hang her in her clothes but he insists on her undressing because he thinks the clothes will be welcome to his young sister. In the French version the knight's wish to undress the girl before drowning her in the water—naive as it is—is not fully nonsensical. Final erosion has been manifest in the text originating from the neighbourhood of Bonn where the seducer first cuts off the girl's head, throws it into the *spring* and then announce that he will hang himself on the nearby lime-tree. It is more than evident from all this that the scene under the tree had spread from the Hungarians to the Germans, and further to the Danes and the Dutch population, and that it contaminated with elements of the French formulation in the west. There remain two questions to be answered: where did the Hungarians got the ballad from, and where does the scene under the tree originate from?

The first question can be answered from two portions of the ballad, to wit, the beginning and the ending parts. The motif of return receives particular emphasis in the Hungarian versions, later development tends to culminate in this scene as shown by the gradual expansion of the story just at this part. More or less curtailed forms of the scene are to be found everywhere in the West. The French variant refers to it by the words of the knight drowning in the water; the English have further developed the scene: the girl is received by her parrot at home and the girl promises to give a golden cage to the bird in case it will not let out where she has been during the night. The Dutch heroine returns home gloriously with the severed head, and she occupies the first place at the feast arranged in honour of her victory. (It is on this basis that the whole of the ballad has been brought into correlation with the biblical story of Judith and Holophernes and that the Dutch variant has been made the starting point.) In another Dutch variant the girl meets with the knight's relatives and tells them what has happened to her bridegroom. It is only the German variants that fail to give an explanation of the return in the Hungarian version: they bring the girl's brother into the forest and that is the end of the story. Self-rescue and return of the heroine as dénouement link the ballad to the western type. Once these given, the opening formula will decide to which one of the western types. As against this, the Hungarian variants stubbornly and consistently reiterate one and the same beginning formula: "Come with me, Anna Molnár, let us go to foreign lands", and in some of the Csángó and Székely variants unceremoniously speak about "a walk" to be taken. Fragmentary variants in other parts of Hungarian-inhabited areas have sometimes the eroded formula: "The soldier kept on calling, kept on luring the young wife until she...". And this is the beginning formula of the early French variants: "My sweetheart, let us go to walk along the seashore, sweetheart, let us go, let us go!" ("Belle, allons nous épromener Tout le long de la mer coulante, Belle, allons-y, allons-y donc"; or "Veux-tu venir, bell'Jeanneton, Le long de la mer coulante, Nous épromener tout au long"; or "Allons-y, bell' nous promener tout le long de la mer coulante, Allons-y bell' nous promener", and so on). At least half the variants start with this formula, in the case of those of the Canadian emigrants, twenty-four out of thirty-six. At the same time, the German beginning formulas are the following: "Wel will met Gert Olbert utriden gon, De mot sick kleiden in Samt un Seiden"; "Als Odilia ein klein Kind war, ... Sie wuchs dem Reiter wol in den Schooss"; and the most frequent south German formula bearing closest territorial affinity to the Hungarian reads: "Es ritt guet Reuter durch das Ried, er sang ein schönes Tagelied, Er sang von heller stymme, das in der Bürg erklinget"; sometimes instead of "in heller" there stands "dreierlei".

It cannot, therefore, be called in doubt that the Hungarians had borrowed the ballad of "blue beard" from the French. Nevertheless, the borrowed theme of the plot has undergone substantial changes in the Hungarian territories, to wit, a new series of scenes has been incorporated into the ballad, that of the tree motif, and so amplified it re-migrated to become widespread in remote areas. Possible traces of the transmission can be detected in the fact that the name Anna—Anneli, Ännchen, etc.—often emerge in the southern and northeastern German regions, and that, remarkably enough, the girl enticed is the daughter of a *miller* (= *molnár* in Hungarian) in one of the Swiss variants, unlike the rest of the German variants that invariably select the heroine from the aristocratic world. Furthermore, there is a west German text that seems to be a reverberation of the Hungarian, almost as a translation: "Wilst du umklimmen den hohen Baum? ..." "Ich kann nicht klimmen den hohen Baum...".

There had been French settlers in East Europe who transmitted their ballad to the Polish as well. With them, namely, other characteristic features of the French formulation survive; the travelling through miles without a word being spoken, the seducer pushed into the water trying to catch hold of a branch of tree, his entreating the girl to save him, and finally the cutting off of the branch with the sword; although all this turned to the opposite—as in the fourth GermanType—inasmuch as it is the young man that kills the girl who in turn begs the seducer to save her.

Research has failed so far to explain these agreements; At the same time, the clue of the question is to be found in the one-time role of a populous Walloon bloc that used to live along the Polish frontier in the region called *Szepesség*; and one might justifiedly think of the four villages of French settlers in the Polish areas stretching along the Silesian borders, too; further the intensive wine trade that used to be going on between Walloons of the Hegyalja region (the traditional country of Tokay wine) and Cracow. Annual comings and going of caravans of carts, regular contacts of popular elements, such as drivers, attendents of the shipments transported, their convivial drinking together, and their common singing may have offered ample opportunities of transmission of their songs as well. Consequently, the abridged starting formula of the French ballad comes up in the Polish version: "He persuaded Kasia to go with him"; and in one or two texts even the duologue shows a fair agreement: "Set out, Kasiu, set out to wander, let us go together!". Accordingly, also the east Prussian texts contain such beginning formulas which deviate from the other German forms: "Ullrich wollt spazieren gehn, Redinchen wollte mit ihm gehen"; and rarely: "Ach, Änchen, schönstes Änchen, Komm mit mir in den Walde härein". Here only the Polish may be the transmitters for the formula of this kind has a wide spread in their areas while it occurs only in isolation among the Germans living along the Polish borders. The presence of this formula in the Polish area can well be accounted for by the French mediation, but in cannot in the Prussian territory. By the involvement of the French settlements in Hungary, therefore, a compass is found with which one can readily orientate oneself in the medley experienced in connection with the North-European variants of the ballad under discussion.

Now we arrive at the point where we have to answer the stirring question: where did the Hungarians get the tree scene from?

As early as 1944, the question was adequately answered by *Gyula László* in his book entitled *A honfoglaló magyar nép élete* (The life of the Hungarians in the Conquest Period), pp. 416–421. After a thorough analysis of a Siberian gold relief, originating from somewhere around the beginning of our era, further of certain sixteenth-century Persian miniatures and fourteenth- and fifteenth-century Hungarian representations of St. László (King Ladislas I of Hungary, 1077–1095 canonized 1192), he declared the scene under the tree to be a motif of the Conquest Period. Before him, *Géza Nagy* called attention to the fact that the Hungarian representations of St. László's legends contained a scene which agreed with the Siberian gold relief preserved in the Ermitage. This scene does not come up in the known version of the text of the legend. Therefore already *Géza Nagy* announced that the Hungarian legend of St. László absorbed some saga elements originating from the pagan stage. *Tibor Kardos* (pp. 100–101) arrived at the same conclusion in connection of the Gesta Hungarorum, independently of *Nagy*. The gold relief shows a woman sitting under a tree, a warrior sleeping with his head in the lap of the woman, and beside them another warrior in sitting posture, holding two horses on reins. The sleeping warrior's quiver and bow are hung on the tree.

In the St. László frescoes and miniatures either this is represented, or the scene is modified by showing not St. László in the picture but the Kuman warrior that raped the girl, and by transferring the scene of the resting knight with his head in the girl's lap into a room, in a lordly bed, finally, what is most decisive, the gesture of the girl's hand clearly shows in every instance that she is searching in his head. This movement of the hand was interpreted in this sense by *Nándor Fettich* in connection with the Siberian gold relief. And it was this movement that suggested the idea to *Gyula László* that there must be a connection between the series of the St. László legend's representations in pictures and the ballad of Anna Molnár. According to him, the whole of the story is remnant of a heroic song into which the legend of Blue Beard was embedded at a later date. Nevertheless, as has been made clear in the foregoing, it is the western framework of this ballad into which the Hungarians incorporated elements of their ancient heroic song of eastern origin.

In Fig. 2, the Kuman warrior is seen to rest his head in the lap of the abducted girl whose hand is searching in his hair; beside him stands his horse; also the tree is shown, although the warrior's weapons are not hung on it. NB. In the same series of frescoes the scene is also represented with St. László. (By courtesy of *Gyula László*.) Fig. 3 shows St. László resting his head in the girl's lap; his helmet and iron gauntlet, that is parts of his armour, are hung on the tree. In Fig. 4 St. László is shown lying on a bed in a room with his head in the girl's lap; she is searching his head. In Fig. 5 St. László (lying in a room?) rests his head in the lap of the girl who is searching his head. In Fig. 6 St. László rests his head in the girl's lap; his sword and shield are seen beside him. Also here the girl places her hand on the hero's head. In Fig. 7 there is a stylized tree under which St. László is resting with his head in the girl's lap, and the girl is busy with her fingers in his hair. Here the trees seem to be mere decorations.

Gyula László directed attention to another scene in the St. László frescoes, which is also paralleled by some Siberian and other eastern pictures: St. László and the Kuman warrior, dismounted, wrestle with each other; behind them there stands the abducted girl, looking at them or helping the rescuer.

It is obvious from the pictures that the Hungarians modifed the story acquired from the French by adding a motif originating in an eastern epic song. There remains now only one more step to be taken to complete the course of demonstration: we have to produce the text parallels of the representations in pictures.

To achieve this, the Siberian epic material had to be examined. For it seemed to us more than natural that the representations of a legend that survive in vast territories extending from Central Asia through Iran to Hungary from the first centuries A. D. or even earlier in the form of eastern gold reliefs and otherwise, including the Hungarian ballad scenes, must have had their textual counterparts also in the Siberian regions which can be traced up even in our days. And we have not been mistaken in this assumption.

Let us quote a characteristic detail from an Abakan epic song. A foreign warrior kills the father and the mother of two children and drives off their men and cattle; he also tries to kill the children, but their magic horses pick them up in their mouths and there begins a chase through regions of heaven and earth. At last they reach a gold and a silver poplar standing in the middle of a white plain. "O, golden-poplar-father"—says the girl—"O, silver-poplar-mother",—I am fleeing before an enemy. A mighty warrior is chasing me. Help me, golden poplar!" A door opens in the side of the tree and the girl enters with her young brother. They behold there "a different region with different sun and moon" open before them—that is the world beyond—where she finds food and drink. Then she goes to sleep and when she awakes she finds her head is resting in the lap of a damsel who is searching her head.

There is another magic tree mentioned in the same song, "the branchy iron larch", to the trunk of which the hero tethered his horse. The tree is usually nine-branched; this, as well as the golden poplar, is encountered at the turning points of the epic song: before the decisive battle or at the place where the chased one finds rescue, in any case, under the tree, a very significant event takes place which determines the further fate of either the person who flees or the enemy. Not infrequently there stands beside the iron larch a nine-cornered iron house. In an Altaic song, for instance, the mythical hero ties his horse to the iron poplar and enters the house standing by it, asking: "Why did you kill my brother?" The two trees are really one and the same tree: the mythical world-tree whose golden part is the earth's axis reaching up to the sky while its iron part reaches down to the nether world where Erlik Khan and his people are living in an iron house, lording it over the nether regions. The adventures and struggles of the mythical heroes always take place here, that is in places inaccessible to common people. In a Kachints song the younger sister of the hero has been raped. Her brother is looking for her in the upper as well as the lower world and arrives at the nine-cornered iron house. The hero enters it and there he finds his adversary. "The bold warrior Töngüsh Khan sleeping on a golden bed. Seven yellow maidens were holding his head and searching for lice." A fierce fight begins, and the hero kills his enemy, although he himself nearly perishes in the fight. He is rescued by his magic horse "who" gets to another tree "standing at the foot of a hill with its golden leaves and silver bark". Here the magic horse receives help from the heavenly Kudais and rescues his hero-master. In an epic song of the Shor Tartars (living in the Abakan Basin of the Altai-Sayan Mountains), the hero goes to meet with his dreadful adversary, Kara Mükü. After frightful adventures he reaches the iron house. "Having passed through forty rooms, Mergen Khan saw Kara Mükü, with his nine wives, lying on a golden bed, asleep and snoring. Six women were busy stroking his soles and seven women were searching his head for lice, lulling him to sleep. The hero strikes his enemy such a blow that Erlik Khan's whole underworld realm rings with it, then he kills him in a terrible struggle (wrestling!). In one of the Abakan songs recorded by *Radloff* the hero pursuing his enemy finds a terrible monster in the iron house: "A maiden with seven ears and seven ear-rings is lying there. Three girls are fanning her with a kerchief, three girls are searching his head for lice, and three girls are licking her soles."

But, as we saw in the first song referred to above as an example, the head-searching comes up in connection not only with the adversary but also with the hero of the song. Thus, for example, the wife of Yoloi Khan, the Karakirghiz hero, meets her son whom she has not seen for a long time. "Ak Shaikal embraced him and pulled him off his horse; she was so weak that she could not greet him, being at a loss for words. Ak Shaikal was scratching his black head with her nails." What we have here is head-searching as a sign of affection. And its lulling character comes out clearly in parallel details of other heroic songs. For instance, in a fragmentary Soyon song (in Chinese territory) a khan's daughter is looking after the herd of horses when a young hero meets her. The girl says to him: "Look in my head!", and when he does, she falls asleep. Then he puts a foal into her belly (a symbol of mythical, totemic fecundation), thus forcing her to be his wife. In a Buryat-Mongolian tale adversaries, during a desperate race, try to hinder the hero's express messenger—who has magic powers—by the following trick: "When he had reached the appointed place, there was an old woman sitting on the road, who invited him to rest: She began to search in his head, and he fell asleep." And when he awoke, his adversaries were already half-way along the road.

The significance of the magic tree can be made clear from some of the texts in a similar way. In a Karakirghiz legend the struggle with the demon takes place under a poplar; on his way from the nether world to the upper world "the hero reached the *middle of the world,* and there he found a high poplar with its tip reaching to the sky." (He is taken up to the human world by a gryphon, as in the Hungarian folk-tales.) In a heroic song of the Minusinsk region, a girl in search of the head of her murdered brother goes down into the nether world and finds there an iron house in which dwell the Irle Khans. "Nine tall larches grow in front of the door of this house out of one stock—these are the posts to which the nine Irle Khans tether their horses, right down there . . . At the time when Kudai created the earth and the heavens, he shaped this larch, too. None has ever reached this tree alive, neither man nor beast, except the Irle Khans."

Precisely for this reason the bodies of the great heroes are buried in this tree. In another song of the Minusinsk Basin the hero says to his son: "When I die, you must never bury me in the womb of the earth, but tie the tips of the nine larches together and put the coffin on the top". In the Shor-Tartar song of the Minusinsk Basin, too, the hero's bones are put "on the tip of nine larches", "beyond sixty layers of heaven." This is why the destruction of the mythical hero takes place near the magic tree. In an Altaic song, a child stolen out of a woman's body is found "nailed to the tip of an iron larch with iron nails". Nor is it surprising, then, that the "end of the world" threatens mankind from the *iron mountains.* "Where the moon and the sun sunk to rest, in the far distance flows the sea, and there stands a mountain reaching nearly up to the sky, and on this iron mountain grow seven tall larches that lift their peaks right up to the sky."

The place where the death of the mythical hero takes place may be, on the other hand, also the place where his life begins. According to an Altaic tale, "Kizil Tash was born at the foot of the iron larch". In another text "on the slope of a black hill there stands a thick poplar . . .", and the fugitive parents put their child down there: . . . "at the place of death he became a living being".

80

The young heroes often receive their weapons from this miraculous tree. In one of the Altaic texts, for instance, Radloff found the following data: "Outside stands, under the iron poplar, a steel-grey steed, tethered with a golden saddle and a golden bit. He saw the horse champing its bit, wallking round the iron poplar. Leaning against the black post he saw a splendid black bow." In a Sayan Shor Tartar song, again, the hero passes the night under a wonderful birch on the seashore. After a sleep under the tree, by the morning there are saddle and bridle on the horse and the hero is given also food and drink. Before he goes further, on back of the horse, a white-bearded old man speaks from the top of the tree and gives the hero a name. (This name-giving is always of a magical significance for without a name thus gained the hero cannot be a full-blown warrior.) When the young man asks the old man who he is, he replies: "I am God the Creator." In another Buryat-Mongolian story, hazy as it is, the same feature is to be found in a form that the hero receives a letter from the girl destined to him by Heaven, telling him his weapons are buried under the golden poplar.

Nevertheless, these mythical scenes come up, even in the Altai-Sayan region, only in the most ancient traditions, primarily among the peoples of the Minusinsk Basin, the Abakans and Shor Tartars, further in the songs of the Karakirghizes. The latter people is thought to have swarmed out from the Abakan region, too. In turn, the Abakan valley is the region, the artistic taste of which had left its marks on the clothing and weapons of the Hungarians of the Conquest period. (*Fettich* 39–40.)

These scenes can be easily brought into connection with the Siberian as well as Hungarian representations. By a closer examination one can see that the tree on the golden plate is a picture of a larch-tree with nine branches: counting the branches we find them to be exactly nine, and the clusters of leaves at the ends of the branches are clear signs of a stylized larch. The quiver and the bow hanging from the tree may refer either to the scene where the hero receives his weapons (the moustache has no relevance in this case, since the heroes of heroic songs are often full-grown men even at three years of age), or—giving credit to a more recent interpretation by Gyula László—the armament hung on the tree may indicate that the hero being with a woman does not want to be disturbed. (Although those things are usually fixed on the door of the house on such occasions, so in this case the armament placed on a tree may rather involve the first explanation.) The woman, whose headgear suggests a princess, is fingering the man's hair also in this scene, as well as in the mural paintings and miniatures representing St. László in a similar situation. Since in the various representation of St. László the scene is now under a tree with the weapons hanging from it, now on bed within a house, and the girl is either fingering the hair of the Kuman warrior that raped the girl or that of St. László, the saviour, it is obvious that the legend presented in several variations, but always in such ones whose parallels may be found in the Siberian epic songs as well, it is indisputable, that this legend of Siberian origin must have lived in many variants applied to St. László in the fourteenth and fifteenth centuries; otherwise it could not have been represented in so different and numerous paintings in so distant churches, as well as in the miniaturists' shop of the royal palace.

Our conclusion expounded in the foregoing is further confirmed by another type of representation analyzed by *Gyula László,* to wit, the one in which St. László and the Kuman warrior are shown engaged in wrestling. (*László* 1970, 113, 1944.) This form of struggle between the dismounted heroes is represented with a remarkable consistency on metal objects of the Eastern Migration Period, in Iranian miniatures and in the frescoes and miniatures relating to the St. László legend in Hungary (and the Vatican). (Cf. Figs 8 and 9.)

Let us adduce a text in demonstration of this statement: in the territories of older traditions mentioned above the fight between the heroes takes place much in the same way. "They leap off their horses, throw off their armour and wrestle. They seize each other by the waist, bending this way and that way as they struggle, neighing like wild colts. They bend forward and backward as they struggle, bellowing like young bulls. Where their hands grip, they tear out each other's flesh.—They struggled for seven days and never fell to the ground. They struggled for nine days and never dropped into the dust. They kicked each other. The side of the iron mountain that leaned against the sky fell down and made a flat plain. The winged bird under the tent of the heavens could no longer stay in its nest, the clawed beast on the black earth could not stay in its cave." Years pass, and the heroes grow thin. Finally the adversary begins to weaken: "Now he was rarely on feet and often supported himself on his hands... (finally the hero) seizes him, lifts him up so that he cannot hold on to the tabilgi bush, nor lean against the lentil tree, he lifts him right up to the sky and then dashes him down upon the ground"; usually he stamps his backbone apart in six places. There is also a wrestling scene in which, while the three-year-old child called in to help by the celestial Kudais struggles against the frightful Swan Woman, the whole universe is shaken: the celestial Kudais hold up the fight for three days while they strengthen the heaven and the earth. The mythical struggle shaking the whole universe must have been represented in the pictures showing St. László wrestling with the Kuman warrior.

Now let us see how all this is connected with the ballad of Anna Molnár. If the Hungarians had a miraculous tree closely connected with death—on which the monsters nailed their victims; on which the dead bodies of the heroes were put; which usually appeared in the decisive moments in the stories as the scene of the great danger, the great battles but also of the great escapes—,then, it is clear why, at the critical point in the story of the girl-murderer, this tree should replace the fish pond of the western versions, and why the bodies of the previously killed women are hanging from it. And that such a tree had existed in the tradition of the fourteenth-century Hungarians is substantiated, besides the artistic representations mentioned before, also by a more recent folklore data. *Sándor Szűcs* recorded from the lips of an eighty-nine-old shepherd in 1921 the following: the old shepherd had heard from a crane-hunter that "There is somewhere in the world a miraculous tree with nine forking branches, each big enough to be a forest. When these begin to stir and wave, the wind begins to blow. It is such a wondrous great tree that not only the moon can pass between its branches but the sun too. This tree, however, can be found only by someone who was born with teeth. ...." It is therefore no wonder that in the fourteenth century the epic traditions associated with this tree were still alive. (It is not irrelevant to note here that the *burkus* tree is explained by collectors, obviously relying on what they heard from their informants, as a shady, branchy, spreading tree. The variant of the attribute "burkus" being "bukros" in some of the ballads, the explanation can be readily accepted, since *bukros~ burkus* (= *bokros* 'branchy') allows of a case of metathesis phonetically.).

Thus the scene under the tree as the most impressive detail of the heroic songs and their late descendents, the St. László legends, has been passed down to the ballads; wherever it seemed appropriate, it was incorporated into the plot. How successful the amalgamation was is shown by the spread of the motif over exceedingly vast areas.

The Hungarian transformation of the western story, however, contains another significant element which is not to be found in other language areas: the return and reunion, that is the motif of reconciliation. Since this can only be applicable in relation of a wife and a mother, the possibility of adaptation of this motif was out of question in the western spheres where the female character was invariably a damsel. The chances of transmission to the German areas were still more restricted since the Germans—the first adopters—always end the story in a forest, where the girl had met her brother, the rescuer. Again, to the French the modification could not find its way back, because it was later inserted into what the Hungarians had borrowed from them. (Nor can such a transmission of the Hungarian development be imagined in the case of the English, or Italian ballads since they are similarly French in origin.) Thus the Hungarian innovation was destined to remain within the boundaries of the Hungarian-speaking areas. Although in this instance the story of the ballad has become much more emphatic as regards its poetic value. Admittedly, the story has been expanded after the *point,* the dramatic culmination of the plot was reached, that is from the two sentences of the French ballad referring to the girl's return. A further sign of adopting is that the original nucleus of the story has been shortened gradually so as to become completely eliminated from some of the Transdanubian variants. What we have here is a typical case of the deterioration of a ballad, which always is indicative of borrowing. Yet, in this instance, the usual procedure of an adopting nation has brought about a new value, and what is more, it lent a deeper meaning to the original story. The wife's return to her husband and the reconciliation of the married couple involved another centre of gravity in the psychological sense which happily balances the motif of the murderous adventure. The western ballad relates the story of a girl escaped or rescued from a dangerous adventure. With the Hungarians, it is telling about a woman who let herself to be seduced, who got into a difficult situation, into life danger, and who escaped and regained her sober mind which induced her to return to her home. Indeed, the ballad is a psychological representation of the return to the domestic hearth. True to say, the adventure is an "amorous" one, and the community of the ballad may well have realized something revealing, some primitive-humane problem of instincts in the figure of the woman-murderer seducer; still it is evident from the various attempts of the various nations to find the true interpretation of the ballad that here lies the vulnerable point of the story: notably, the hero of the ballad cannot be a murderer of girls, and a looser in the game, but the abducted woman, the victim who escapes—to return home again. The motif of return formulated in different ways places, subsequently, into different lights the whole body of the story. The English girl's talk to the parrot reduces the story to the level of a plain, frivolous adventure. The Dutch tried to elevate the narrative to the heights of a heroic deed—which again is seriously contradicted by the preliminaries. The various methods of solution with the Germans can also be accounted for by the unreassuring dénouement. And it is this weak point of the story that has been made into a new centre of gravity in the Hungarian transformation, developing the basic story towards the psychic conflicts of balladry.

For more details, the reader is referred to Ethn 1960, 479 (in Hungarian); Acta Ethn. 1961, 241 (in German); *Vargyas* 1967, 129 (in English).

Literature: Grozescu 1864: the Hungarian is a fake translated from Romanian; *Grundtvig* 1869 (Note 10 Dgf 183): surveying the Scandinavian, Dutch, English, Italian, Wendish, Serbian, Finnish and Estonian variants, concludes that the ballad derives from the Danish song on Oldemor, originally a magic chant: *Abafi* 1876d: German, Dutch, French, Scottish and Spanish variants compared with the Hungarian version; *Bugge* 1879* developed from the story of Judith and Holophernes, the Dutch is the original; *Child* 1882: surveying, in addition to the above-mentioned variants, the Hungarian, Czech, Polish, Southern Slavic and Portuguese versions, rejects the origin from the tale of Judith and Holophernes (the biblical story may have influenced certain Dutch variants subsequently), and states that the German and the Hungarian variants show a fair degree of agreement; *Nigra* 1888: presents a survey of the Neo-Latin (Romanic) versions chiefly, concluding that the ballad originated from Scandinavia, from where it proceeded, through Dutch mediation, towards the South; *Karlowicz* 1890: presents variants from Poland and describes the English and Northern Slavic variants; E–B 1893: numerous German variants published, with reference to English and Scandinavian versions, on the basis of *Grundtvig* he thinks the ballad is a hazy version of the "Elfenlied"; *Karlowicz* 1895: further Polish variants; *Vikár* 1910: the ballad originates from the time of Székely—Hungarian coexistence; *Solymossy* 1924: distinguishes two separate groups in the German-speaking territories, (1) being based on the motif of self-rescue, (2) on that of applying for help, which arrives *late,* this type is the original; the Hungarian belongs to the former group and the Romanians acquired the ballad from the Hungarians; *Gragger* 1926: accepts *Solymossy,* saying that the ballad was brought by western minstrels into Hungary; *Ortutay* 1936, 1948: accepts *Solymossy; J. Meier* (D. Vlr. 41) 1937: on the basis of several thousand variants surveys the full area of dissemination, the Dutch is original coming down from the years around 1300, rejects the biblical source and the Elfenlied theory of *Grundtvig,* as well as the Blue Beard connection; the Hungarian is related with the German; *Dános* 1938: quotes *Solymossy* and *Gragger; Entwistle* 1939: the Dutch is the original, being a chant with traces of biblical influence, spread from Dutch areas to German, Hungarian, Scandinavian, Scottish, French, Italian, Spanish and Portuguese territories; *László* 1944: the basic tale is of Siberian origin; *Seemann* 1951: comparing Lithuanian variants with German, Polish and Nortern Slavic correspondences; *Nygard* 1952: the demonic element is the original nucleus (441), which gradually transformed during its spread towards East in the German areas to change the motif of self-rescue into applying for help; *Kemppinen* 1954: written by a Dutch minstrel about 1100 and 1200, originally a mythical song intertwined with Christian counter-spell; *Nygard* 1958: Dutch origin, spread to Scandinavia and France; detailed quotation and discussion of the Scandinavian material (English, Dutch, German and French variants also examined); *Wilgus* 1959, 308–10: sums up the result of researches, reviews *Kemppinen* and *Nygard* in particular: "... but so different are their methods and concepts that one is never sure that the two scholars are studying the same material"; *Vargyas* 1960: French origin, with an episode borrowed from an epic song; *Taylor* 1964: rejects connection with tale; *Vargyas* 1967 = 1960; *Seemann, Strömbäck* and *Jonsson* 1967: survey the major monographs up to *Vargyas* 1967 inclusive.

4. THE HEARTLESS MOTHER

13.

Ilona Budai was leaning out of her window.
She receives news of enemy looting in the neighbourhood.
She thinks at once of her jewel case,
She takes her jewel case under her arm,
5. She led her pretty daughter on her right hand,
She took her bonny son on her left hand.
She is walking, walking, walking through a thick pine forest,
Along a desolate path in a dark forest.
Aye, she thinks she hears the drumming of horses' hoofs,
10. And forthwith she puts down her little daughter.
Her pretty daughter spoke up, weeping:
Mother, dear mother, do not leave me back on the way,
Let your heart take pity on me, do not leave me here!
I do leave you here, my daughter,
15. For God gives me daughter instead of a daughter,
But God does not restore my money for nothing!
She is walking, she is walking through the thick pine forest,
Along the desolate path in the dark forest.
Aye, she thinks she hears the drumming of horses' hoofs.
20. And forthwith she puts down her little son.
Her bonny son spoke up, weeping:
Mother, dear mother, do not leave me back on the way,
Let your heart take pity on me, do not leave me here!
I do leave you here, my son,
25. For God gives me son instead of a son,
But God does not restore my money for nothing!
She is walking, she is walking through the thick pine forest,
On the desolate path in the dark forest,
And she arrives at a beautiful, spacious meadow.
30. Aye, there was a cow-buffalo coming down there,
Carrying her this year's calf between her horns,
And mooing to her last year's calf to follow.
This beholding, Ilona Budai
Cast herself down upon the ground and began to weep with bitter tears,
Weeping with bitter tears, she blamed herself:
A callous beast will not forsake her calf,
My God, my God, my dear God,
How could I, a soulful creature, forsake my child?!
With this, she turned back on her way in the thick pine forest,

40. On the desolate path in the dark forest.
    She soon reached the place and extending her hand
    She began to call her bonny son.
    Aye, I will not go, for you have not been a true mother to me!
    Had you been a true mother, you would not have left me here!
45. She is walking, she is walking through the thick pine forest,
    On the desolate path through the dark forest.
    She soon reached the place and extending her hand,
    She began to call her pretty daughter with many a kind word.
    Aye, I will not go for you have not been a true mother to me,
50. Had you been a true mother, you would not have left me here!
    When she heard these words, she began to cry:
    I am like a tree by the road,
    Anyone passing may break down my twigs,
    Anyone may break my twigs and tread them into the mud!

(Székelyszentmihály (Udvarhely county), Kriza=MNGY XI 585.)

14.

1. Úd më - nën, úd më - nën Sze - gien ár - va asz - szon
   Ed nad hosz-szu ú - ton Sz ed nad ré - gi ú - ton.

1. Speeding along the long, long way,
   The broad, old way, goes the poor woman.

2. On her right side she takes her little, weeping daughter,
   On her left side she takes her little weeping son.

3. My Lord, my Lord, my beloved Lord,
   Which of the two shall I put down and which shall I lift?

4. Sit down, daughter, in this field of roses,
   To pick cornflowers, to make a wreath,

5. Warm rains will come to wash you,
   Warm winds will blow to rock you to sleep.

6. Speeding along the long way, the poor woman goes,
   And finds an animal, and a beast it was,

7. That has been carrying her two-year-old calf on her right side
And her little calf she was carrying between her horns.

8. My Lord, my Lord, my beloved Lord,
This is a beast, and an animate beast that I am,

9. How was I able to put down my little crying daughter?
She turned on her way and went back.

10. Aye, the little girl was surrounded by three dreadful wolves.
The biggest dreadful wolf spoke:

11. Let us tear her in three, let us tear her in three.
The middle dreadful wolf spoke:

12. Well, I don't mind if we do, I don't mind if we do.
The youngest dreadful wolf spoke:

13. O don't do that to the poor soul, don't do that, don't do that to the poor soul, don't.
Rather let us take her to our thicket,

14. And let us raise her in our thicket,
Giving her tender mutton and tender pork to eat.

15. Mother, my dear mother, my dear wolf-mother!
Let me go to take a walk in the woods,

16. To take a walk in the woods and to take a rest in the field.
Don't you go, daughter, don't you go, for many hunters are walking about

17. And they will strike off your head, they will strike off your head!
Father, my dear father, my dear wolf-father!

18. Let me go to take a walk in the woods,
To take a walk in the woods and to take a rest in the field.

19. Speeding along the long way her dear mother goes,
Speeding along the long way her dear mother goes,

20. Where are you walking, daughter, where are you, where are you walking, daughter, where are you?
Hold your tongue, mother, hold your tongue, hold your tongue, mother, hold your tongue!
(To the third and fourth metodic sections.)
Had you been a mother to me, you would not have left me.

Trunk (Moldavia), 1929. Performed by a woman. Domokos 1941, 11.

Cf. Leader 297–298.

Divergences: The starting formula of the Székely variant—introducing the mother fleeing before the enemy—comes up in one more variant, to wit in the Moldavian variant recorded earliest by *Rokonföldi:* "The poor woman, Wishing to escape the bitter imprisonment, The captivity with the Tartars, Took her on her right arm...". This motif has been worn out of the other Udvarhely variant to be quoted below in full extent. Obviously, the flight motif was originally part of the plot, without this the woman's behaviour in the woods would be unmotivated in respect of her children. The mentioned variant is incomplete, strongly abridged at the end, and also its rhythm is faulty, still it is interesting and revealing.

> The mournful Belle Dame
> Took her jewel case in her right hand,
> She took her bonny little son on her left arm.
> She started out on the broad, old long way.
> My Lord, my Lord, am I to leave my money?
> If I leave my money, God will not give me more money,
> But if I leave my son, God will give me another son.
> Lo, she seated her son under a tree,
> She put a golden wand in his right hand,
> And in his left hand she put a golden apple:
> Kind women will come to suckle you,
> Gentle rains will fall to wash you,
> Soft breezes will blow to send you to sleep.
> So saying, she took her jewel case and went off.
> Aye, there was a cow going with a calf in her mouth,
> And another calf was mooing behind her.
> Alas, my Lord, this is but a callous beast,
> Yet she does not forsake her calf!
> How could I forsake my little one?
> She threw her jewel case into the bush,
> And as she reached the place, she saw
> Two black ravens fetching the bowels of her son.
> She fell back and died a dreadful death.

Rugonfalva (Udvarhely county), 1902–3, Vikár.

The formula of consoling the child is also expressed in a fuller form in Klézse (Moldavia): "Beautiful little birds will come To give you to eat, Warm rains will fall To wash you, Gentle breezes will blow To rock you to sleep." This beautiful motif is applied in four variants. A further six contain a somewhat modified version of the woman's speech: "May the beasts of the woods be your fathers, May the birds of the air be your mothers!" Upon this, the child answers: "Do not lay curse on me!...". It is mostly these variants that usually end as the next variant of Lészped: 20. When she went back To take up her son, She did not find her son, Her little son was nowhere to be seen! 21. The beasts ate him, Her little son, Casting from branch to branch His tender bones. 22. The birds of the air are bathing in his blood. My God, my God..." These and the story of Ilona Budai mentioned first have only a cow-buffalo to give the mother a lesson. Eight Moldavian variants add to it the wolf motif of No. *14*, too. But this motif occurs already with *Rokonföldi*, namely in his first Moldavian collection made in 1841–42.

Earliest notation: 1841–42.

   Dissemination: Udvarhely county 2 (the Fehér-Nyikó riverine and Rugonfalva); Kisküküllő county (Magyarsáros); Moldavia 14 (Gerlén, Klézse 3, Lészped 4, Rácsila, Somoska 2, Trunk 3); total 17.
   Textual interrelationships with other ballads: the motif of the child put and left under a tree: **5.** "Warm rains will fall": **2., 5.** The birds are bathing in his blood, and only the bones of the child remain: **5!** (This is a remarkable agreement of the Moldavian texts with the isolated Great-Plain text variants; and obviously, a very old element which two similar Hungarian ballads have in common.) "God will give me son instead of a son...": **52, 69.** The contrasted role of the two older wolves and the youngest one: **19.**
   Tunes: 1. = 14. in three notations. Further tunes: 2.–6., 3. in two variants.

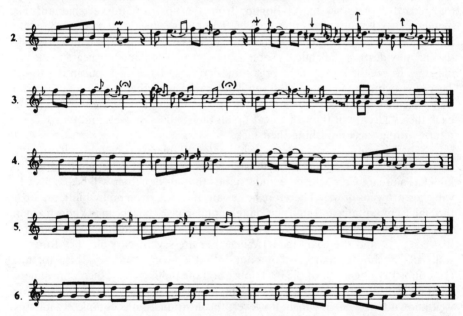

   European parallels: non-existing. What had been earlier mentioned as such by *Gragger* and, in his wake, by *Ortutay* and *Dános* is not corresponding to this ballad but to The Unmarried Mother Who Killed Her Child (Type **23.**) to be discussed below.
   The motif of fleeing from the enemy should neccessarily be included in the plot subjected to comparative examination since otherwise the story would make no sense and also because the earliest Székely and Moldavian variants have this motif. In regard of the wolf motif, however, we may not be so positive in our standpoint. To wit, the variants ending with the motif of birds bathing in the blood of the child—which naturally precludes the wolf-scene—maintain a close relationship with Type **5** and are therefore very old. On the other hand, the ending formula of the

Ilona Budai text cannot be derived from these, since in this text the child while still alive replies to this mother much in the same way as in the variants with the wolf motif, thereby causing the moral collapse of the mother. Dénouements ramifying in several direction are not contrary to the practice followed in ballad poetry (Cf. Types **20.** and **21.**) But if the variant with the destroyed child had been from the very beginning paralleled by another variant in which the child remained alive to make his mother ashamed, then it may be surmised that the wolf motif was not a secondary gradation added, but it was a genuine element of the plot.

In looking for parallelisms, we may certainly exclude the partial agreement with a fairly modern Greek song which has nothing in common with the Hungarian, except the beast motif that makes the heartless mother feel ashamed: an unmarried mother is about to kill her baby, but she is given a lesson by a partridge and consequently decides to raise the child (*Lüdecke* and *Megas* 24). East of Hungary, on the other hand, we find partial agreements in different stories. *Potanin* (59) recorded the story of An-Bogdor from the lips of a Buryat shaman: The daughter of a khan is expecting a child. The khan fears the arrival of the child, thinking it will try to kill him. He therefore has his daughter thrown into prison so that he may destroy the child as soon as it is born. The daughter bears twins and manages to get them out of the prison in secret and have them put into a forest. There the twins are adopted by seven wolves who tend them and bring them up. Later on, their grandfather hears of this and sends soldiers to the forest to bring back the children, but the wolves eat up all the soldiers' horses, and they have to return without accomplishing their task.

The beginning of the story is readily identifiable with the fable recorded by *Merényi* (pp. 81–84) telling the circumstances of the birth of Peter and Paul Vizi. A king has a dream from which he understands that his daughter will bear sons who will overthrow his power. Therefore he has an enormous iron house built, on top of the highest mountain, and shuts his daughter up in it so that she may know no man. The girl, however, conceives by the spring that rises in the earth on which the iron house stands, and she bears twins. When they are seven years old they force the walls of the house apart and go out into the world and try their fortune. (Undoubtedly, the motif of the iron house and the pulling down thereof originates from the world of heroic songs.) From this onward, the story changes over into a well-known tale type, in which, however, this introduction is completely missing. The voluminous monograph of *Ranke* (Die zwei Brüder, FFC 114, Helsinki 1934) while listing seven other opening formulas fails to mention anything like the type of the Hungarian variant. It follows, therefore, that no such motif is known in Europe. On the other hand, it fully corresponds to the Mongolian song right down to the involvement of the wolves—what is lacking in it but exist in the Moldavian ballad. The latter and the Moldavian songs have in common the motif of wolves offering patronage to the children against the cruel relative. At the same time, the Mongolian song does not speak about the flight from the enemy, unless we consider the grandfather and his armed men to be enemies. Nevertheless, this motif occurs in another Mongolian song just in the same form as in the ballad Ilona Budai. An elderly khan and his wife are threatened by a foreign warrior. They hide their new-born child in the forest before they are taken prisoners together with their people

90

and livestock. An aged shepherd and his wife are left behind and they bring up the child. But wolves come and demand that they hand over the child. The old people will not do so, but the child, overhearing what is being discussed, goes among the wolves and kills them all. (*Potanin* 109, *Verbitsky* 140, the latter being fragmentary.) In this instance, we are closer to the other text: the child is hidden from the enemy, he gets among wolves in the forest which, however, behave as enemies.

The existence of the fable of Peter and Paul Vizi makes it absolutely certain that the Hungarians must have known a story like that of An-Bodgor, and this circumstance well answers for the hazy agreement of the wolf motif. But we may imagine another contact with the heroic song that may have come about in the following way: first a ballad developed about a heartless woman who, fleeing from the enemy, leaves her children in the forest; at this point the similarity between the two stories offered an opportunity for the wolf motif to be incorporated—and to receive a psychological significance in the given context. The hazy character of the agreement is readily explained by the usual course of transformation into a ballad, and at the same time, the plausibility of an agreement is reinforced by the technique of transformation typical of the genre.

To wit, instead of a mythical adventure, a parable was held in view. The mother forsakes her children instead of her jewel case. Even beasts know better than that. Therefore she is denied by her children. Here is the motivation of the moral collapse. Such a difference of the poetical content affords only certain useful motifs to be retained so as to fit into the context and different atmosphere of the new genre. The Székely ballad does not even resort to the wolf motif: this is the maturest formulation of the story in the Hungarian-speaking areas, and we do not know how many similar specimens have been lost for ever in the Székely and other regions of Hungary, where the ballad style has been flourishing for centuries and brought about similar masterpieces; in any case, this variant is one of those successful formulations which can be placed among the best representatives of the genre.

On the ground of all these considerations, as well as for its ancient elements which possibly come down from the Conquest Period, and finally on the basis of its agreement with portions of 5 of the Szeged region, we list this piece along with the earliest, fourteenth-century Hungarian ballads.

Literature: *Vargyas* 1959–62/II, 1967.

5. THE ENTICED WIFE FORSAKING HER CHILD

15.

Come on, come on, Beautiful Kata Bán,
Come to our land, to fair Turkey!
I will not go, I will not go, Black Pétör Rác,
For I have a son, a little running son,
5. A daughter sitting on my arm, and a kind wedded spouse.
Never mind, don't you think of them!
Come on, come on, Beautiful Kata Bán,
Come to our land, to Fair Turkey.
Even dogs bark in a different way in fair Turkey
10. Than in Hungary.
I will not go, I will not go, Black Pétör Rác,
For I have a son, a little running son,
A daughter sitting on my arm, and a kind wedded spouse.
Come on, come on, Beautiful Kata Bán,
15. Come to our land, to fair Turkey,
For two hundred silver coins, sixty-six thalers
17. Three hundred gold coins!

(Upon this, she was willing to go with him.)

18. They reached the forest,—she left her son there,
Her little running son, her daughter sitting on her arm.
20. I leave you here by this poplar,
When birds are clapping their wings,
You must think
That your mother is speaking to you.
When it rains, you must think
25. That I am bathing you, I, your dear mother!

(She put them up in the tree.)

Eagles tore their hearts, ravens picked their eyes,
Cleaving the sad hearts of the poor orphan souls.
They were going ahead, going ahead, then they sat down to rest.
Beautiful Kata Bán was searching the Turk's head.
30. How is that, how is that, Beautiful Kata Bán:
It is not raining, not even a cloud is seen,
Yet my head is soaking with water?
There has been a black cloud rising just above us,
And a few drops of rain have fallen from it.

(She looked up and saw a bird giving her young to eat; therefore she was weeping.)

35. Let us start, let us start, Beautiful Kata Bán,
    Let us start, let us start, for it is growing dark!
    As they arrived in the Turk's home,
    As they took a rest in the Turk's room,
    Black Pétör Rác said to the woman:
40. Cook a dish, cook a dish, Beautiful Kata Bán!
    Beautiful Kata Bán went into the kitchen,
    And she spat right in the middle of the kitchen:
    Now, my dear little spit, when the Turk says:
    Cook a dish, cook a dish, Beautiful Kata Bán,
45. You must answer: It will be soon made ready!
    Dish up, dish up, Beatutiful Kata Bán!
    I shall dish up soon, Black Pétör Rác!
    Dish up, dish up, Beautiful Kata Bán!
    I shall dish up soon, Black Pétör Rác!
50. Dish up, dish up, Beautiful Kata Bán!
    I shall dish up soon, Black Pétör Rác!
    Black Pétör Rác could not wait any longer,
    He went into the kitchen
    But he did not find Beautiful Kata Bán there.
55. Beautiful Kata Bán started out on the way.
    Anon Black Pétör Rác harnessed
    His best palfrey.
    He galloped after her through many a forest
    But he did not find her anywhere.
60. Black Pétör Rác, then, galloped home.

(Reaching the place where she had left her little ones, Beautiful Kata Bán did not find anything, except bones.)

61. She took some of the bones home, to her mother's place.
    Open, mother, open your locked door!
    It is me, your daughter, your daughter Kata!
    Go away, fiend, go away, and do not tempt me,
    For I have no daughter!
65. Nine weeks have passed, and it turned into the tenth
    That the fishermen are searching for her with their nets,
    But they have not found her!
    Open, mother, open your locked door!
    It is me, your daughter, your daughter Kata!
70. Go away, fiend, go away and do not tempt me,
    For I have no daughter!
    Nine weeks have passed, and it turned into the tenth
    That the fishermen are searching for her with their nets,
    But they have not found her!
75. Open, mother, open your locked door,
    For if you do not open it, my heart will break!

I do not open it, I do not open it, for I have no daughter!
Nine weeks have passed, and it turned into the tenth
80. That the fishermen are searching for her with their nets,
But they do not find her!

(When her mother opened the door, there was Kata Bán lying face to the ground beside the bones of the small children.)

Apátfalva (Csanád county) = Kálmány 1882, 162. Cf. Leader 300.

The story of the ballad is known only from the above variant, although fragments of texts have come up in two Transdanubian places:

Come with me, come with me, Beautiful Kata Bán,
Come to my land!
There wheat is harvested twice a year, wine is vintaged three times,
All kinds of flowers blossom thrice.

Alsónyék (Tolna county), from a 70-year old female informant.

The other prose fragment was found embedded in a legend:
"Éva Bán, a great-grand-mother on the maternal lineage, was driven away by the Turks. She was roped together with a child, and so they were driven by a janizary who held the end of the chain. Well, the janizary fell asleep on back of his horse. The two of them fled. Walking into a pond, they hid under the large leaves of water-pumpkins. The janizary was searching for them everywhere, although not in the water. It grew dark, and they started on their way home. In the day time they found refuge under the vaults of bridges; finally they reached a village where they were rid of the chains. But this Éva Bán did not dare to come down the loft in the rest of her life, even her food was brought up, for fear of the Turks who would have killed her if they had taken her as a refugee. And this I was told not only by one single man, but by several old people. Also a song is sung about her. One of the old men related the story of the song to me. The Turk said to her that he would take her to a country where *wheat is harvested twice a year and wine is vintaged three times.* So Éva Bán had been cajoled, because she had been a very beautiful girl, and as she refused to go on her own will, she had been taken by force."—*Margit Luby.* EA N. XVI. 12/1954. Madocsa (Tolna county).

As can be seen, only the motif of enticement to go into a wonderful country survives in this fragment. Nevertheless, the name and the manner of rendering the story indicate clearly that the ballad used to flourish in South Transdanubia, too.

While preparing my work for the press, I learned that a prose variant, with sung details, had been recorded among the Hungarians in Yugoslavia. The words read as follows: "It occurred in the years over eighteen hundred, at Gombos, in the big forest situated between Gombos and Doroszló. A very handsome young man, called Black Péter Rác enticed the woman called Kata: would she come to the forest where she would be fairly treated (bathed in milk and butter). The widow gave credit to his words. She wrapped her children in linen and started out with him. While they were walking to the forest, the gang spoiled all her fortune at home. They were going, the woman got tired, and begged him:

94

Poco rubato

Jaj ke - zem, jaj lá - bam, jaj de el - fá - rad - tam!

Fe - ke - te Rác Pé - ter,   Köss hin - tát,   köss hin - tát!
                              men - jünk hát,   men - jünk hát!

Jaj Ka - ta,   nem kö - tök,   nem kö - tök.

Alas, my hands, alas, my feet, alas, I am tired!
Black Péter Rác, make a swing, make a swing!
Alas, I cannot make a swing, I cannot make a swing.

They continued, and Kata spoke up again, begging him:

Alas, my hands, alas, my feet, alas, I am tired!
Black Péter Rác, make a swing, make a swing!

Thereupon Péter made a swing, put her children in it, and then the woman bade farewell to her children, saying:

Ha a szél fúj, gon-dol-já - tok: rin-gat - gat-lak.

Ha az e -ső e - sik, gon-dol-já - tok: si - rat - gat-lak.

Ha a le-vél hul-lik,   gon-dol-já - tok: ta - kar - gat-lak.

Fe-ke-te Rác Pé - ter, mit tet-tem, mit tet -tem!

El-vesz-tët-tem drá - ga,   két, kis gyer-më-ke-met.

Jaj ke-zem, jaj lá-bam, jaj ho-va   is   men-tem!

Fe-ke-te Rác Pé - ter, mit   tet-tem, mit tet - tem!

95

When wind is blowing, you must think I am rocking you.
When rain is falling, you must think I am lamenting you.
When leaves of trees are falling, you must think I am covering you with a blanket.

Setting out again, they went on. Once again she spoke up:

Alas, my hands, alas, my feet, alas, I am tired! They went on and on, and just when the woman thought of stifling the children, gendarms arrived. So they ran away. As they returned, the children were devoured by wolves. The woman was weeping:

Black Péter Rác, what have I done, what have I done?!
I have lost my two dear little children!
Alas, my hands, alas, my feet, alas, where have I gone?
Black Péter Rác, what have I done, what have I done?

This is how the story of yore ended."

Gombos–Bogojevo, 1971, Ilona Garai, 54 years of age. *Ilona Kovács* and *Lajos Matijevics:* Folk Ballads from Gombos.

Dissolved beyond comprehension, the story still preserves the outlines of the plot, the names of the characters, and two characteristic details, the act of abduction to a land of wonders, and the fate of the forsaken children ("There are warm showers..."). Also the melody is vaguely reminiscent of the original, which had been, in all likelihood, composed of four sections. The tune seems to be nearest to that of No. *4,* although it may be related in some portions with other tunes as well.

Earliest notation: 1882.

Dissemination:
Csanád county (Apátfalva), Tolna county (Alsónyék, Madocsa), Bács-Bodrog county (Gombos).
Textual relationships with other ballads:
The whole of the story, together with the motif of searching the head, the enticement to go to a wonderful country: Type **3.,** the placing of the children under a tree and the relating formula: **4.,** only the formula: **2.,** the chase and the mother's words: **30.,** searching the head: **3., 40, 41.**
Tune one fragment.
Versions in non-Hungarian language areas:
MORAVIAN *1–4. Sušil* 144/300–303, *5. Bartoš* 1901 16, *6. Bartoš* 1953 189.
SLOVAK *7. Horák* 1958, 177 No. 59.
BULGARIAN *8–10.* A–V 147–149. *11–16. Stoin* 1931 181–186. *17–25. Idem* 1928 Nos 2885–2886, 2889, 2892–2897. *26–28.Idem* 1939 Nos 115, 118–119. *29. Ivanov* 1949 178. *30–32. Idem* 1936 162–164. *33–34. Tsitsélkova* 168–169.
Partial variants DANISH *35–45.* DgF 82 (only MS variants, see further DgF 249 and *ibid. Jonsson). 46–55. Ibid.* 249.
UKRAINIAN *56–58. Golovackij* III/1, 54 13, I, 72, 116, 117.
RUSSIAN *60. Chernyshev 3. 61. Sobolevsky* 218†.
LITHUANIAN cf. *Seemann* 1951, 188 78.
POLISH *ibid.*

96

The plot of this ballad can be found in two more language areas, viz. the Moravian and the Bulgarian. In the Moravian song, a brief introductory part is followed by the story of the miller's widow who is asked to go on a journey by three young men or a Turk. (Sometimes perhaps an innkeeper's wife is involved because she is asked about the price of her wine.) The woman refers to her children whom she cannot leave by themselves; the young men suggest to send one of them to school, the next to the prince, while the third to a peasant, and so on, so that they may learn various trades. There occur such variants as well in which the woman agrees at once, asking the young men to wait until she rocks her child to sleep and suckles the smallest baby. In every case she takes the youngest son with her, but on the way she puts him under a tree, and while binding him to the tree she recites the well-known formula: My little son, when the wind blows you will think that your mother is rocking you; my little son, when it is raining you will think that your mother is washing you; my little son, when the leaves of trees are falling you will think that your mother is clothing you. My little son, when a star is shining you will think that your mother is coming; my little son, when the moon is shining you will think that your father is coming. (In some of the variants, the formula is omitted.) Later, in such variants which have the story in its full extent, it occurs to her—or it is the Turk who reminds her—that she had committed a crime, and her heart breaks with sorrow. This story is known to me in one single Slovak variant.

With the Bulgars the Turk is not a seducer but a kidnapper of the woman and her child. She puts down him, saying the following words of dedication to Stara Planina (the Balkan Mountains): "When the wind blows, it will rock you to sleep, when it is raining, it will wash you, when the does come to pass here, they will suckle you . . ." But in this instance all this is understood in face value, for the continuation either has it that the child has been really raised to rescue his mother from the Turkish captivity or else the mother adds: "grow up and release your mother" (whereupon the Turk sometimes flies into a passion and destroys both of them). That is to say, the words describing the child's fate in a figurative way will be transformed to assume a real meaning, which is an unmistakable sign of a secondary, revaluated adaptation of what was originally meant to be a poetic symbol.

But the Moravian (Slovak) form is similarly indicative of the transformation, because the number of children is increased, of whom the mother takes care in advance—obviously with a view to mitigating the mother's cruel deportment—and also because a *widow* is selected to be the hero of the story, which again is contrived to render the motif of enticement more plausible—; all the same, the mother carries the smallest child on the journey and leaves him under a tree—a somewhat exaggerated solution which can by no means be regarded as original. An intention of mitigating the genuine action of the plot and yet to preserve the most effective portion of it led here to an intrinsic contradiction; apart from this, also the expansion of the preliminaries is telling about the fact of adoption, since it well corresponds to the psychology of adaptation.

It is interesting to note, on the other hand, that neither of the two nations that had taken over the full plot did preserve the enticer's words about the land of wonder (the Moravian version speaks about a strange ["čizy"] land). At the same time, this motive has been taken over by the northeastern neighbours, the Ukrainians. For instance, in *56.* the formula is as follows: "Wander, wander with us, pretty girl, with us who are Kossacks and young! With us the wand of willow bears pears, with us the girls are clad in gold, with us the hills are gold coloured, with us the rivers are flooding with honey." The same formula emerges in the Russian ballads as well: "Let us start, pretty maid, to our place by the Don. With us, on the banks of the Don, everything is different than with you: they do not spin and weave there, still they are well clad." *(60.)* (Nevertheless, the Russian story is completely different: three lads are enticing a girl who retails wine in an inn; they take her into a forest, tie her to a pine-tree and burn her there.) Or in another variant: "They do not spin and weave, still they wear silk dresses; they do not plough and sow, still they eat white bread." *(61.)* The same formula occurs almost word-for-word in the Lithuanian texts, and *Seemann* mentions similar ones in connection with the Polish material. At the same time he states that these texts cannot be brought into correlation with the German variants, for enticement in the German ballads come up in another form: the young man boasts of his seven mills which grind sugar, clove, nutmeg, and other spices. (The question has been discussed in a different context in connection with the mills of The Marvellous Corpse (Type **68**).

Nevertheless, it seems as if the motif of enticement in the above formulation should have come from the West. This is brought out by the fact that it has been preserved in many variants of two types with the Danes. The Danish ballads have a fairly uniform wording of the formula in the various texts: "Gulldborre, Guldborre, be my true love! I shall take you into a rich land. So rich is the land I take you to that no sorrow ever reaches there; no birds, except the owl, sing there, no grass, except onions, grows there, no water, except wine, flows there . . ." (DgF 82 A.) And what is the weightiest: "there you shall live and never die!" Characteristically enough, in some of the variants also the promise of gold is added—substituting for the formula sometimes—not unlike the Hungarian text.

The Danish ballads have a different plot: the one is a story of a girl and her lover prosecuted by her brothers, while the other speaks about a young man who puts to test the enticed girl by pretending to be poor. On the other hand, the formula is tied up with the Danish type of The Enticed Wife in more than one way. Consequently, the motif may have reached Hungary through the intermediation of some other ballad, possibly of The Enticed Wife. This is the more likely since in all indication the Hungarians had relied on the plot of this ballad when shaping the story of their new ballad. As to the time of its generation, we may suppose that the ballad discussed is contemporaneous with the earliest Hungarian borrowings from the French.

Literature: Vargyas 1959–62/III, 1967, 218–19.

6. THREE ORPHANS

16.

Parlando

1. Somogyszo-bi te-me-tő-be Fűz-fa van a kö-ze-pé - be.

Há-rom ár-va *j* ül a-lat-ta, *j* É-dës-anyját si-rat - gat-ja.

1. In the graveyard of Somogyszob
   There stands a willow, right in the middle.
   Three orphans are sitting under the tree,
   Lamenting their dear mother.

2. Rise, dear mother,
   Because our clothes are torn!
   I cannot rise, three orphans,
   Because I am dug deep in the earth.

3. You have got a stepmother
   That can take care of you.
   As she combs your hair,
   She stains your faces with blood.

4. She cooks the supper as well,
   But the three orphans can look at it from afar.
   Let us go to the shed,
   Let us embrace each other,
   Let us lament our dear mother,
   Our kind nurse who raised us.

Somogyszob (Somogy county). Performed by a male informant in 1898.
Vikár = MNGY VI. 6. = MP 33/c.

17.

Poco rubato

1. Ho - vá mégy te, há-rom ár - va? Ko-má-rom-ba, szol-gá - lat - ra.

Ne menj o - da, há - rom ár - va, Ko-má-rom-ba, szol-gá - lat -ra.

1. Where are you going, you three orphans?
   We are going to Komárom to look for a job.
   Do not go there, three orphans,
   Do not go to Komárom to look for a job!

2. I give you an iron switch.
   Strike the graveyard with it!
   Rise up, dear, kind mother,
   For my clothes are worm to rags!

3. I cannot rise, my son,
   For my eyes have sunk in.
   I cannot rise, my son,
   For my arms have lost flesh.

4. But you have got a stepmother already,
   Who gives you white shirts to put on.
   When she is combing our hair,
   Red blood is flooding down to our heels.

Ziliz (Borsod county). Performed by a female informant of 58, 1955. László Vikár.

18.

1. Where are you going, you three orphans?
   We are going to Komárom, to find a job.
   Do not go there, three orphans,
   For you are not going to find a kind master there!

2. I give you a switch of willow,
   Strike the graveyard with it...
   Rise, rise, dear mother,
   For our clothes are torn to rags.

3. I cannot rise, my sons,
   For my eyes have sunk in,
   My feet have withered,
   My tears are flooding on my face.

4. You have got a stepmother
   To look after you...
   We do have a step mother
   But she is not looking after us.

5. If we ask her for a piece of bread,
   She puts a piece of stone in our hands.
   When she gives us clean underwears to put on,
   She causes us to bleed.

6. When she is combing our head,
   There is blood running down onto our heels.
   She never stops tormenting us,
   Dear mother, do rise up!

Nagyszalonta (Bihar county), performed by a female informant of 67, 1918
Kodály = MNGY XIV. 21.

19.

1. Three orphans started out and went
   To the churchyard gate,
   To the grave of their dear mother,
   There stood the Virgin Mary.

2. I give these three switches to you,
   Strike the graveyard with them!
   Strike the grave of your dear mother,
   Strike the grave of your dear mother!

3. Rise, our dear mother, rise up!
   Our mourning clothes are torn to rags.
   Comb our head,
   Mend our clothes!

4. I cannot rise, my sons,
   My bones have fallen apart,
   My sinews are snapped,
   My eyes are sunk and withering away,
   But you have got a step mother
   To take care of you!

5. A stepmother is only a stepmother,
   She is not like a dear mother:
   Iron is her comb, and iron is the food she gives,
   Iron is the towel she dries us with.
   When she combs our hair,
   Blood is running down to our heels!

6. Their dear mother rose up,
   She rose up and went to the edge of the grave.
   She mended their clothes
   And combed their hair.

7. Now, my sons, you must go home,
   Your stepmother will ask
   Who combed your hair,
   Who mended your clothes?

8. A kind neighbour woman
   Combed our hair,
   She mended our clothes,
   And she washed our clothes!

(The tale goes on in prose): The stepmother went there and scolded her for having combed their hair. The second time they went to the graveyard, they said their godmother had mended their clothes. When they went the third time, their mother said: My sons, when you go home do not come here again, because the Blessed Virgin Mary has allowed me to rise three times, but no more. And tell your stepmother that your real mother combed your hair and mended your clothes. The stepmother went to the graveyard and scolded the dead woman for having combed their hair. Finally, however, she disappeared. Alas, there was only one kind stepmother, and even that was taken away by the devil.

Kövegy (Csanád county) = Kálmány 1954 5/b.

20.

Rubato, lento

1. El - in - du-la há - rom ár - va Hosz-szú út - ra, buj - do - sás - ra.

Azt kérd - te a szép Szűz Már-ja: Ho-vá mën-tëk há - rom ár - va?

1. Three orphans set out
   On a long way, in exile.
   The beautiful Virgin Mary asked them:
   Where are you going, three orphans?

2. We are going in exile,
   Walking from door to door.
   Do not go, come back,
   Do not go, come back!

3. I give you three switsches,
   Strike the graveyard with it.
   Rise, rise, dear mother,
   For our mourning clothes are torn!

4. I cannot rise up, my son,
   For my sinews are snapped,
   My legs have rotted,
   My arms are numb.

5. Pray, dear mother,
   Give me the key to the lock,
   Let me open your coffin,
   Let me kiss your face!

6. Let me kiss your face!
   Your two arms that earned clothes to me,
   Your feet that walked after me,
   Your feet that walked after me.

Gyergyóalfalu (Csík county), 1910. Kodály.

21.

1. Three orphans are walking along
   The Virgin Mary asks them:
   Where are you going, three orphans,
   Where are you going, three orphans?

2. Stop, three orphans,
   I will give you a golden switch.
   Strike the graveyard with it,
   Strike the graveyard with it!

3. Rise up, rise up, dear mother,
   Because our mourning clothes are torn!
   I cannot rise, my dear son,
   Because my sinews have rotted.

4. My sinews have rotted,
   So have my arms and my legs.
   Also my blood has streamed from me,
   And my soul, too, has left me.

5. Dear mother, give me
   The key to your coffin,
   So that I may unlock your coffin,
   And kiss your hand and feet.

6. A young wife is walking along,
   Both of her cheeks are painted.
   She is now to be your stepmother,
   And she will dress you in white clothes.

7. When she dresses you in white clothes,
   Your backs will be blossoming with blood,
   When she gives you bread to eat,
   Your tears will pour into your bosom.

8. My God, don't wait long
   To behold the fate of the orphan,
   So that he may not be an outcast,
   Begging from door to door.

(To the third and fourth melodic sections:)
   If he is pitied at one door,
   He is abused at the other.

Gyergyótölgyes (Csík county), 1907. Bartók = MF 1033/c.

22.

1. There is a poplar [*var.* birch] in my hay-field,
   Three orphans are sitting under it.
1954 Three orphans are sitting under it,
   All three are clad in full mourning clothes.
1932 All three are clad in full mourning clothes,
   All three are clad in full mourning clothes.

2. Where are you going, three orphans?
   Where are you going, three orphans?
   We have started on the long way,
   On the long way, seeking service.

3. I will cut a golden switch for you,
   Strike the graveyard with it!
   Rise up, rise up, our dear mother,
   For our mourning clothes are torn!

4. I cannot rise up, my dear son,
   Because I am covered with the moss of the earth.
   Then take your key to the lock
   And open up your coffin!

5. Let us kiss her hands and feet,
   Besides also her two cheeks!
   Let us kiss her hands and feet,
   Besides also her two cheeks.

6. My son, my son, my dear son,
   Go home now!
   You have a stepmother
   To take care of you.

7. We have a father, but he is silly,
   We have a mother, but she is a stepmother.
   When she is combing our heads,
   She tears out all our thin hair.

8. When she gives you white clothes to put on,
   Your backs are foaming with blood.
   When she gives your white clothes to put on,
   Your backs are foaming with blood.

9. Shall we complain to a strange one?
   He is sure to let it out at once.
   Shall we complain to the grass and to the tree?
   So that everybody may look into our mourn?

10. Rather let us complain to the broom,
    Because it will not let it out to anyone.
    It will not let it out to anyone,
    Except the dust-pan.

Lészped (Moldavia)–Szárász (Baranya county). Performed by a 57-year-old woman. 1932–1952–1954 = Gr 201/A = Domokos and Rajeczky, No. 51.

Cf. Leader, 82

   Divergences: Instead of the Virgin Mary, once an *old man* is encountered. In one of the texts, *two* orphans are spoken of. Different formulations:

The nut-tree has three branches,
Three orphans are sitting beneath them.

Don't you go, three orphans,
For you will not find a good master anywhere!

The Virgin Mary walked to them,
Asking them: Why do you weep, three orphans?
We have every reason to weep, Virgin Mary,
Because our mother has been wrapt in earth.
Take this switch in your hand
And strike the graveyard with it!

It is regarded as a major deviation that at the beginning of 23 texts, from Transylvania, and mainly Moldavia, the following motif appears:

The youngest son says loudly:
Take out my heart,
Take out my liver,
Put them into a copper plate,
Wash them with wormwood wine,
Wrap them in fine linen,
Send them down to Barassó,
Place them in the gate of the castle!
Let everyone take an example of me:
Such is the lot of an orphan!

(Each line is repeated.)
Take out my heart,
Cut it in five or six,
Wash it with wormwood wine.

(Only in one variant.)
Sometimes:
Wrap it in fine linen,
So place it into the coffin.

Or:
Close it up in a green chest.
Sometimes the ballad begins like this:
Let us not go in exile,
Rather take out... (etc.)

In Transylvania, the elder son says, although in rare instances: Kill the youngest one, Take out..., or: I don't mind...Take out....

Earliest mentioned: 1840.
Dissemination: Hungary, without specification as to locality: 1 (from 1859).

I. Transdanubia: Moson county (Pozsonyligetfalu), Sopron county (Egyházashetye 3, Kemenes-Mihályfa, Rábakovácsi), Zala county (Balatonederics, Csapi, Dergecs, Kiskomárom 2, Resznek), Somogy county (Hetes, Somogyszob), Baranya county (Hirics), Fejér county (Csákvár); total 17.

106

II. Northern region: Komárom county (Guta), Nyitra county (Berencs) from 1840, Bars county (Mohi), Hont county (Kisgyarmat), Pest county (Aszód), Nógrád county (Karancsberény, Kishartyán, Salgóvidék), Heves county (Füzesgyarmat, Parád 2), Borsod county (Borsodszentiván, Gesztely, Mezőkövesd, Zsiliz), Gömör county (Balogpádár, Deresk, Perjése), Abaúj county (Cekeháza), Ung county (Csap); total 20.

III. Great Hungarian Plain: Bács-Bodrog county (Nagybaracska), Csongrád county (Hódmezővásárhely 4, Szeged-felsőváros), Békés county (Békésszentandrás 2, Doboz, Endrőd, Kötegyán, Mezőgyán), *Sine loco* from the Szeged region, Torontál county (Szaján), Csanád county (Kövegy 3), Arad county (Magyarszentmárton 2, Nagyzerénd, Pécska 2, Zsigmondháza), Bihar county (Gálospetri, Nagyszalonta 7), Szabolcs county (Paszab), Szatmár county (Kérsemlyén); total 33.

IV. Transylvania and Bukovina: Kolozs county (Kolozsvár, Körösfő, Mákófalva, Méra, Visa 2, Vista, Zentelke), Maros-Torda county (Deményháza, Jobbágytelke, Kibéd 2, Nyárádköszvényes), Szolnok-Doboka county (Vice), Udvarhely county (Boldogasszonyfalva, Bögöz, Enlaka, Kadicsfalva, Kisbacon, Lengyelfalva, Mádéfalva, Martonos, Rugonfalva, Siklód 2, Szentegyházasoláhfalu, Székelyudvarhely, "Udvarhely"), Alsófehér county (Miriszló), Csík county ("Csík", Csíkgyimes, Csíkszentsimon, Csíkvacsárcsi, Gyergyóalfalu, Gyergyótekerőpatak, Gyimes, Gyimesfelsőlok 4, Gyimesközéplok 2, Kászonújfalu), Háromszék county (Árkos, Bükszád, Erdővidék, Kovászna, Nagykadácsi, Zágon), Bukovina (Andrásfalva 3 + 3 from Hertelendifalva, Hadikfalva 6, Istensegíts 4, Józseffalva 2); total 67.

V. Moldavia: (Bogdánfalva 4, Diószeg, Frumosza, Gajcsána 2, Gerlén 2, Klézse 7, Lábnik, Lészped 13, Máriafalva, Nicolae Balcescu, Rácsila 2, Templomfalva, Trunk, Újfalu); total 38. Hungary total: 71. Transylvania, Bukovina and Moldavia total: 105. All-Hungarian total: 176 variants.

Textual relationship with other ballads: Take out my heart: **20, 25, 31, 38, 57;** The corpse speaking up from the grave: **65.**

Tunes: 1 = No. 16, 2 = No. 17, 3 = No. 18, 4 = No. 20, 5 = No. 21 (in four variants), 6 = No. 22 (in two variants). The numbers of tune variants are given in brackets: 9 (2), 13 (2), 14 (2), 16 (5), 20 (2), 26 (2), 32 (4), 33 (4), 35 (3), 36 (5), 37 (2), 40 (3), 41 (3), 44 (2), 46 (2), 48 (2), 51 (2), 53 (5), 55 (3), 62 (2), 65 (2), 69 (2), 74 (2).

110

41. 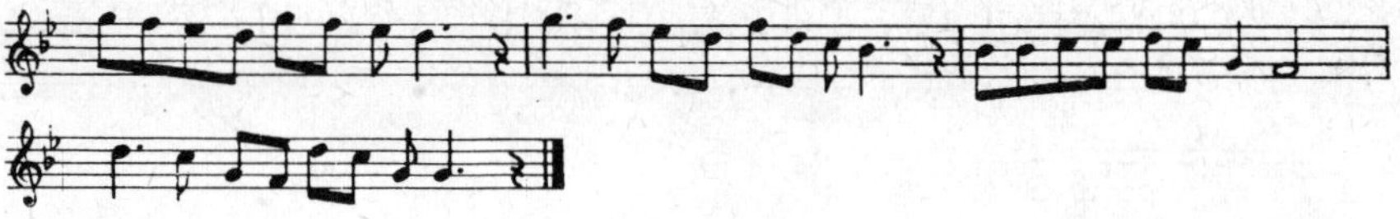

42. 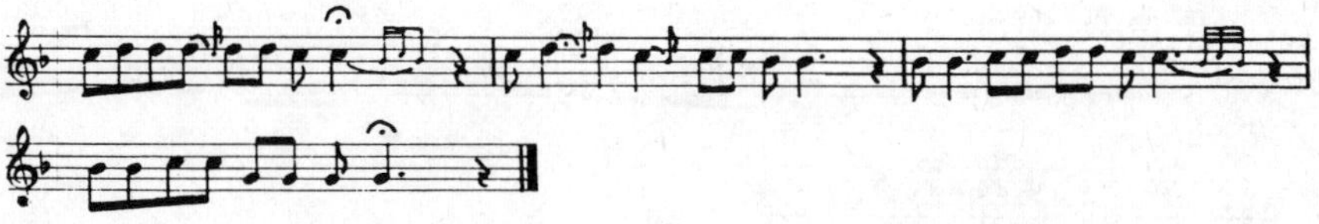

43 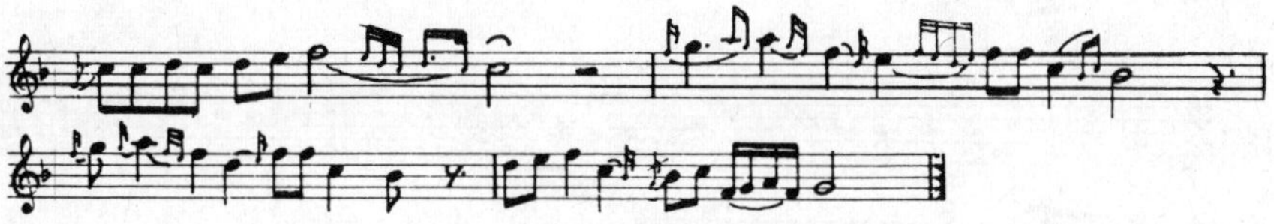

44. 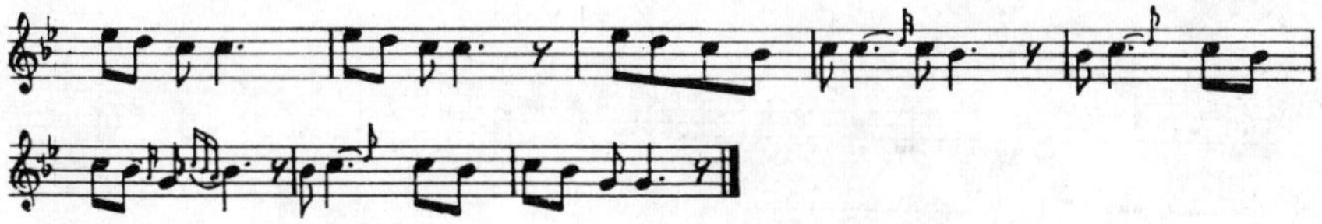

45. 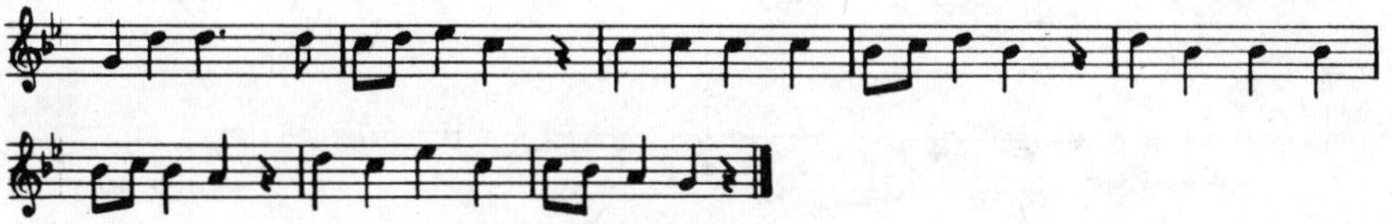

46. 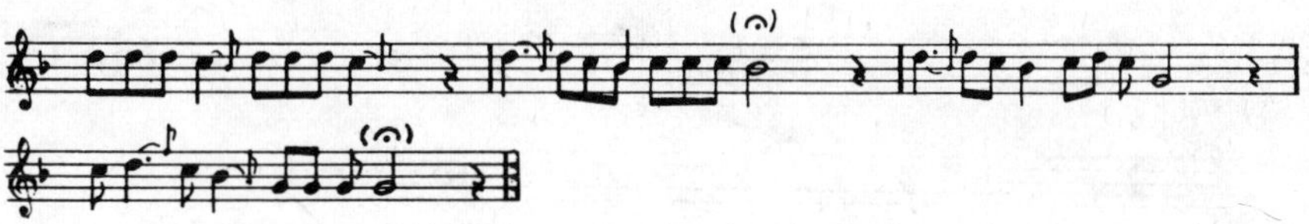

47. 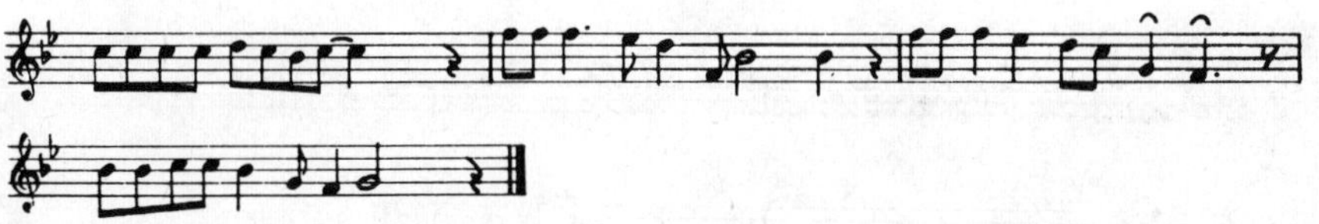

48. 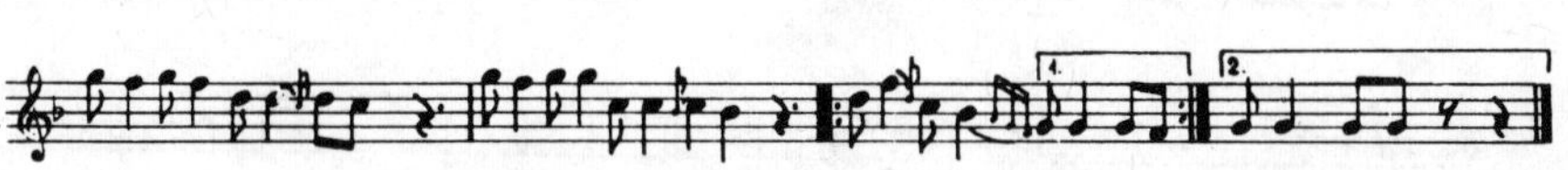

49. 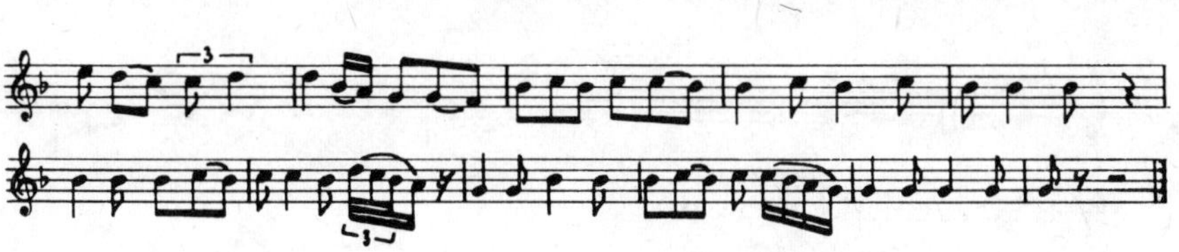

112

Versions in languages other than Hungarian:

FRENCH: *1–13*. Walloon variants from Belgium received through courtesy of Roger *Pinon* who had kindly sent me copies of them actually available either in manuscripts or in journals, including *Senny-Pinon* 33 and Wallonia 1913, 262 No. 16. *14. Puymaigre* 1885, 117 = *Rolland* III 178c *(Walloon)*. *15. Rolland* III 178. *16–17. Barbeau* 1962, 269, 273. *18. Decombe* 99. *19. Rolland* III 178b. *20–23. Millien* 50–53A–D. *24–27. Rossat* 1917 III 67A–D. *28–30. Smith* Romania 1875, 108–118. *31. Rolland* III 178d. *32. Arbaud* I, 73 = *Puymaigre* 1885, 118 = *Udry* 215. *33–34. Tiersot* 1903, 96. *35. Sébillot* 1892, 232† (fragment).

ITALIAN: *36. Nigra* 39. *37. Ferraro* 1870, 22.

NETHERLANDISH: *38. Canteloube* IV, 15. Flanders, France *39. Lootens and Feys* 55 = *Puymaigre* 1885, 114. *40. Coussemaker* 58 = *Puymaigre* 1885, 105 = *E–B* 202c. *41. E–B* 202d.

GERMAN: *42–183*. D. Vlr. 116.

DANISH–SWEDISH: *184–210*. DgF 89 (= Olrik II, 7 transcribed). Further variants and comparisons: DgF III, 860.

SLOVAK: *211. Horák* 1958 44 = *Medvecky* 1906, 256. *212–213. Medvecky* 1906, 257 I–II. *214.* Sb. sl. n. p. I, 31. *215–217. Kolečány* 61–63. *218. Dobšinsky* 1874 14†. *219. Dobšinsky:* Prostonárodny I, 89. *220.* Sb. sl. n. p. II, 91 13. *221–222.* Slov. Sp. I. 188 and 226. *223–225. Bartók* 1959, 45a–b, 61b.

MORAVIAN: *226–230. Sušil* 159/337–341.

CZECH: *231. Holas* 1†. *232. Erben* 1864, 467 2†. *233. Erben* 1842 1. *234. Erben* 1852 1*. *235. Erben* manuscript (cf, *Horák* 1917). *236. Swoboda* 9†. *237. Waldau* 1.

POLISH: *238–244. Kolberg* 1871–84/17 14, 18 347*, 19 446*, 21 181–183*, 22 293*. *245. Pauli* 3*. *246. Kozlowski* 23. *247–252. Kolberg* 1885, II, 353*, III, 563–565*, IV, 438*.

UKRAINIAN: *253–254. Golovatsky* III/1, 272–277 4–5. *255–256. Kolberg* 1882–89 II. 358–359. *257. Lintur* 1959, 83 (Trans-Carpathian Ukraine). *Horák* 1917 quotes seven further variants.

WHITE RUSSIA: *258–261. Shejn* I/1, 516–519†. *262. Karsky,* 328†.

LITHUANIAN: *263–264. Seemann* 1951 79–80.

SOUTHERN SLAV: *265–266. Kurelac* 306 and 486 (North-western Transdanubia). *267. Žganec* 1924 109. *268. Žganec* 1950 333. *269–275. Žganec* 1950–52 98, 345a, 346ab, 511, 512a, 516b. *276.* HNP I. 28. *277.* HNP V. 44. *278. Blažinčić* 94†. (*279–286. Štrekelj* I. 344–351, pointing to relationships with new German versions). *Kumer* 507 (+415?).

BULGARIAN: *287–290. Stoin* 1928 1641 (= A–V 66), 1642–1643, 3638. *291. Bukoreshliev* 233. *292–302. Stoin* 1931 1620–1630. *303–304. Tsitselkova* 74 and 81. *305. Ivanov* 1949 72†. *306. Arnaudov* 1930 8. *307–311.* SbNU 42, *Ivanov* 1936 61–62, 64–65, 72. *312.* SbNU 42, *Marionov* 20. *313.* SbNU 16–17, Materialy, 94, 11.

The Hungarian ballad type shows closest affinity with the French formulation that has a wide spread in a fairly uniform shape. Let us take a variant from the Paris area *(18.)*;

I know a plaintive song about three children, whose mother died, and their father married again. He took a bad wife who beat the children. The youngest asked for a piece of bread. He was floored by a kick in the stomach. The eldest raised him: "Get up, dear brother! Come, both of you, and let us go to the graveyard to find our mother!" On the way they met with our Lord Jesus Christ. "Where are you going to, three little angels?" "We are going to the graveyard to look for our mother." Do not weep, three little angels!" "Rise up, poor soul, from Paradise! I will let you live fifteen years *(elsewhere seven)* for bringing up your children." There came the fifteenth year. She began to weep. The children asked her: "Why are you weeping?" "I must go back to the graveyard today." "Do not weep, mother, we will go with you!"

Instead of Jesus, it is often Saint Michael, Peter or John who helps, and even the *dear Virgin Mary* among the Flemings and Walloons in northern France. If to this we add that one southern French variant has: "Go and touch your mother's grave!", *(34.)*, then there remains little doubt that the connection is very close. Further similarities are found in the Walloon variants: the mother emerges from the grave and instructs the children how to behave; and if their stepmother asks them who tought them, they must say their mother, rotting in the grave. Among the Flemings in France, they say, after their mother has risen and suckled the youngest: "O, mother, we are very hungry! Get up and come begging with us!" "Children, how I get up, my body is locked in the ground, and what you see is my soul." (The latter explanation seems to be a subsequent addition made in order to raise a realistic effect.) In German variants from France—Lorraine and Moselle—there is no meeting with the sainted. The oldest says to the youngest: "Let us three little children go and find our mother." When they reach the graveyard and their mother's grave, they say: "O mother, dear mother, if only we could be with you!" "You cannot be with me, children, my bones are so heavily weighed down with soil." Then an angel descends from Heaven and brings a chair for the mother so that she can sit on it and teach the children how to take off their caps when they meet people. And if they are asked who taught them this, they are to say their mother lying deep in the grave. Thus here, the motif of resurrection is combined with the other solution, in which the mother does not rise up but speaks up from the grave, telling about her helplessness.

The French ballad also made its way to the Italians in the Piedmont. In most of the details there is a close agreement between the Italian and the French versions, but there is an essential point in which they sharply differ from one another: the Italian variants do not mention the meeting with the sainted characters,—a feature that contrasts them with the Hungarian variants, too.

In spite of very substantial transformations, the Danish, Swedish and Norwegian versions can be readily derived from the French. In the northern countries we have a lengthy introduction: Husband and wife are leading a happy life, until the woman falls victim to an epidemic. The man marries again. When he takes home the new wife, the children go out to greet her, but she kicks them. She has them sleep on straw and starves them. Upon their cries, their mother awakes; she goes before Jesus Christ and asks him for leave to go down to see her children on the earth. She is granted a short visit. With her coffin on her back, she appears before her daughter, who can hardly recognize her. Then she has them sit on a chair and combs their golden locks. She is weeping, while the youngest child is sitting in her lap. Then she calls the man and the stepmother to account because of her children who have to sleep on straw instead of gold and blue cushons she had left to them. Finally she threatens them with a painful death in case she finds the children in the same condition when she next comes to see them. Next day the children are playing with pieces of gold.

The meeting with the heavenly being takes place in Heaven here. The mother here again is granted a short—that is, definite—term; she is tending her children, as in the southern variants; but the story is finished with a "happy ending" typical of the North, inasmuch as the stepmother changes her attitude towards the children, in consequence of the mother's threating words.

The western set of variants might well have proceeded through the German-speaking areas towards Hungary and the East-European countries. There is the rub, however, inasmuch as no German formulation of the ballad survives from mediaeval times. Of the German elaborations of this topic, perhaps D. Vlr. 116 shows closest affinity with the narrative of the Hungarian ballad, and of the French ballad at the same time, but the mentioned German variant is a fairly recent development, bearing traces either of literary influences, or of borrowing from the Czechs of the nineteenth century. *Seemann* writes: The German orphan-ballads—Nos 116–120—are unexceptionally songs of the nineteenth century, showing, as they do, after-lives of earlier existing ballads. In contrast, the traditional forms of orphan ballads outside Germany are highly varied and also remarkable for their numerical weight. "Bei den deutschen Waisenballaden Nr 116 Nr 120 handelt es sich durchweg um jüngere Lieder des 19. Jahrhunderts, die nur noch einen Nachklang wohl einst vorhandener älterer Balladen darstellen. Die ausserdeutsche Überlieferung der Waisenlieder is dagegen reicher und vielgestaltiger". (D. Vlr. V, 291.) He establishes that variants 1 and 2 of No. 116 had developed along the Czech frontier in the nineteenth century through immediate popular mediation, while the rest of the variants owe their existence at a folklore level to the text published in 1857 by *Joseph Wenzig* who had translated the poem from the Czech original. "Wenzigs Übertragung hat im gesamten deutschen Sprachgebiet traditionsbildend gewirkt. Die in der Überlieferungsliste genannten deutschsprachigen Aufzeichnungen gehen sämtlich auf den von *Wenzig* geschaffenen Text zurück, mit Ausnahme von 1. und 2., deren Entstehung aus direkter Berührung mit tschechischen bzw. polnischen Liedgut in Kontaktzone aufgezeigt wurde."

These recent transmissions and the development of still more recent variants among the Germans may be attributed to the fact that they did not have a widespread mediaeval formulation of the topic. Consequently, the German areas could not be the scenes of mediation of the French ballad to Hungary.

It follows from what has been said so far that—omitting the possibility of a German or Italian mediation—we must suspect of the French-Walloon settlers as intermediaries between the Western and the Eastern European areas, separated by the German territories from each other. Another proof of this can be found if the Hungarian version is compared with the versions of the neighbouring nations.

Among the Slovaks there are hardly two forms that are uniform. The only common feature is that it is not three orphan boys that appear in them but one girl. In some variants the girl asks her mother to make her bridal garland, to let her marry, and in some there is no stepmother mentioned at all. Elsewhere she says: "Get up, get up, mother dear", and also the complaint is heard that the stepmother throws bread to her roughly, beats her when she washes her, and that when she combs the girl's hair, blood flows. Sometimes there is the amplification that the stepmother treats her own child differently. The motif of striking the grave also appears, and in one variant three times: the first time, the earth shakes, at the second, blood flows, and at the third, the mother begins to speak. There is a recurrence of the motif that the mother refers her daughter to the stepmother ("you have a new mother"), and what is more, we also have a faint echo of the mother's words about her helplessness: "Dear daughter, I should be happy if I could rise, but I am buried deep beneath the earth". There are, however, new elements, too: an angel takes the girl to Heaven, and a devil carries the stepmother to Hell, furthermore, her father, mother, elder brother and sister all die, and the stepmother gives her stone instead of bread.

However, these elements do not figure together, as in the Hungarian, but one here and one there, or at most two, appear amidst lyrical lines, and sometimes none is present. For this reason, the text are shorter than the Hungarian average. But they all include the mother's answer to the orphan's complaint. None of them do mention, however, the meeting with the Virgin Mary.

But the latter motif occurs in the Moravian texts, which bear more closer resemblances to the Hungarian variants than to those of the Slovak ethnic blocks living within the Carpathian Basin, in the old Hungarian Kingdom. The orphan girl goes to visit her mother. On the way she meets an old man—sometimes this old man is the Lord God—, in other cases the girl goes to the gravedigger. The old man asks where she is going to, shows her her mother's grave and advises her to break off a switch and strike the graveyard. At this the mother speaks from the grave; "Who is knocking on my grave?" From here onwards, the texts agree with the Slovak texts. There appears the motif of blood flowing after combing, as well as of the washing with beating; sometimes even further details are added, like: "When it is dinnertime, she sends us to draw water; when it is suppertime, she sends us outside the door", and similar things. Here, too, angels carry the child to Heaven, while devils take the stepmother to Hell. The Czech variants follow the Moravian ones with the exception that the encounter with the heavenly being and the beating of the grave are omitted. By contrast, the ending is amplified: the child goes home from the grave and dies there, or the mother rises from the grave and kills the stepmother.

In the Polish texts, too, occur the poetic lines "When she combs our hair, our blood flows",—indeed, the motif even reaches the Lithuanians, and similarly to the Slovak texts, there is mention of how the stepmother changes the children's shirts (cf. the Hungarian: "When she puts white clothes on us..."), and also the meeting with Jesus occurs, with the advice to break a switch and strike the grave with it. Finally, two angels come for her and carry her up to Heaven, while the Devil takes the stepmother to Hell. The Ukrainian versions run much in the same way, only they go into greater detail about the punishment, and with them the child does in fact die. In Polish and Ukrainian areas the carriers of the orphans' ballad were singing beggars, and consequently their versions end with lengthy moralizations. The Lithuanian version had been borrowed from the Polish, while among the White Russians only debris of the common tale is to be found.

In connection with the motif of the meeting with the heavenly beings, *Seemann* (1951) quotes *Horák* who holds that it was of Polish origin, and that Moravian and Croat pilgrims may have heard it in Częstochowa and carried it to their lands. This view, however, fully ignores the Hungarian and French correspondences.

Two very much eroded versions of the European ballad have been recorded from isolated Croatian settlements in western Hungary. In the one (*266.*) three orphans meet Saint Peter who shows them the way to their mother's grave; but there is no mention whatever of the switch or other details described above. The mother begs her sons, in order of their age, to raise her head, body and legs; however, they cannot, for her head has become a white stone, her body black earth, her legs two tree-trunks. In the other (*265.*) not even so much of the common elements are found; there is only a long complaint of the orphan saying that the mother's mouth, in the earth, is unable to speak, and that her hair is dissolved in the black soil, and bewailing the stepmother's wicked ill-treatment. (But nothing is heard about blood gushing in the wake of the comb or the other motifs characteristic of the Hungarian variants.) Consequently, we must regard these two variants, in the knowledge of the entire variant series, as dim reflections of the common story in the final stage of erosion. In any case, it is striking to see how far they are separated from the neighbouring Hungarian variants.

On the other hand, the versions recorded from Croatia proper and Slovenia show closer relationships with the Hungarian ballad; and in each of them we can find the characteristic traits of the market-singers. The majority of them begins with market-place appeal for attention: "Poslušajte vi ljudi (or: kristjani), Kak žene tak i muži. Što se jeste zgodilo U 'noj zemlji Madžarskoj!" (Listen, you people or: Christians both men and women, to what happened on Hungarian soil!) Instead of Hungary, they sometimes refer to Croatia or to "our land". The collector of one or another variant added the note that he obtained the song from some blind beggar or that it was "blind men's song". It is beyond doubt that the Croat or Slovene singers acquired the song from their Hungarian colleagues who in turn must have learned it from Hungarian folk-ballad singers. The first records referring to singing performers of the ballad in Croatia and Slovenia were published in 1859, and these songs are not unlike the Hungarian ballad, as far as their texts are concerned. A hundred years later one of the market singers reported on by *Lajos Takács* as one who sold out most of the song of "the orphans" performed the piece in a so diffuse manner that it had already little to do with the ballad construction. As against this, the Southern Slav song differs from the Hungarian only in so far as the former assembles the happenings in order, that is not jumbled, beginning with the words of the orphans and their starting out to wander, as in the Hungarian: a mother has died and the husband taken another wife, and the stepmother has been ill-treating the children, and so on, much in the same way as the French version. And finally the mother sends her children to the Blessed Virgin (mostly the one in Bistrica). In this last turn something has been preserved of the main features of the Hungarian ballad, the meeting with the heavenly being. Otherwise, in the southern Slav songs it is the bell-ringer that shows the children their mother's grave, which deviation indicates that the memory of the common narrative has already faded in them. In spite of this, they undoubtedly originate from the more recent Hungarian versions, while the two Croat texts recorded in the Transdanubian regions are strongly eroded remains of earlier adopted versions.

There are two Bulgarian texts (*290.* and *307.*) that might perhaps be brought in correlation with the Hungarian. A girl is weeping at her mother's grave asking her to rise up. The mother answers that she cannot because the black earth is heavy on her body. The duologue refers to the stepmother as well. Other Bulgarian variants strongly deviate from the common topic: a shepherd is playing his pipe beside the grave from which comes the voice of his master's dead wife, asking whether her man has married again, and whether the new wife is treating the children well. When she hears the contrary, she asks the shepherd to besprinkle the grave and light candles. This done, the grave opens, and the mother takes the children with her into the grave. If in fact there is a connection, the theme may have reached them directly from the Hungarians, for I know of no intermediate Serbian variants to connect them with the Croatians, from which, anyway, they differ considerably.

Literature: Greguss 1865 and 1886: refers, without specifying the place, to Danish and Norwegian parallels. *Haraszti* 1896: quotes a French version. *Horák* 1917: comparing the Slav area of dissemination (mentions, besides German, Danish, Piedmontan versions a French ballad from foreign source and a Hungarian from German translation). He regards the Polish as original. *Ortutay* 1936: quotes *Greguss* and *Haraszti*. *Dános:* the Dutch version is of Hungarian origin. *Entwistle* 1939: the Scandinavian, Faroese, Provençal and German versions originate from "northern mythology". *Seemann* 1951: discusses Lithuanian and northern Slav versions comparing them with the Germans. *Csanádi and Vargyas* 1954: mention Danish and Norwegian versions. *Vargyas* 1960 and 1967: *French origin*, D. Vlr. 116—119 (1967): survey of the European versions; determination of the origin of German versions.

7. JESUS SEEKING LODGING

23.

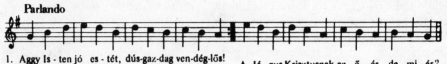

Parlando

1. Aggy Is - ten jó es - tét, dús-gaz-dag ven-dég-lős!
Ad - ná - ɛ tɛ szál-lást a Jé - zus Krisztus-nak
A Jé - zus Krisztusnak az ő ér -de - mi - ér?

1. Good evening, rich innkeeper!
   Will you give lodging to Jesus Christ,
   To Jesus Christ for all his merits?

2. I cannot give lodging to Jesus Christ,
   For I am waiting for rich guests to come today,
   And they would make mock of him.

3. Go, Peter, go to the outskirts of the town,
   You will find a poor widow living there,
   You will find a poor widow living there...

4. Good evening, Widow Veronika!
   Will you give lodging to Jesus Christ,
   Will you give lodging to Jesus Christ?

5. Why should I not give lodging to Jesus Christ,
   To Jesus Christ for all his merits,
   To Jesus Christ for all his merits?..

6. I have a little bower and three beds made up,
   He can sleep in whichever He likes,
   He can sleep in whichever He likes.

7. Jesus laid himself in one of the beautiful beds,
   Saint Peter waited for him to go to sleep,
   Saint Peter waited for Him to go to sleep.

8. At His head rose a bright sun,
   At His feet rose a sparkling moon,
   At His feet rose a sparkling moon.

Pécs (Baranya county), 1933. Performed by a 63-years-old woman. = Berze Nagy J,
334.

Cf. Leader, 331.

The rest of the variants have the following incipit:

When our Lord Jesus Christ walked on this earth,
He could not find a lodging in Jerusalem.
He went in a house, into an inn,
He went in a house, into an inn.

In the Komárom version the picture of the rising sun and moon is replaced by the words of Jesus:

Widow Veronika, for all this you will be given
A sparkling crown in the high heavens,
A sparkling crown and a richly laid table.

Anyway, this is the only variant in which Jesus is not recognized but called a "poor wayfarer".

Earliest mentioned: 1906. *Berze Nagy* adds a note to his publication of the ballad, according to which his informant had learned it from a broadside originating from the 1860s.

Dissemination: Vas county (Alsóőr) Zala county (Kiskomárom), Somogy county (the Balaton region, Tapsony) Baranya county (Bánfa, Kiskőszeg, Mohács, Pécs), Komárom county (Komárom) Győr county (Nagybaráti), Bács-Bodrog county (Gombos). Total: 11. (Omitted as irrelevant are the data published by *Sebestyén* and *Berze Nagy* on the Sainted Family seeking lodging before Jesus was born.)

Textual relationships with other ballads: the motif of refusal of characters seeking lodging occurs in Type **17**, "The Two Captives" (NB., in the French correspondence, refusal is given with reference to a conviviality, a wedding feast!) Further: Types **22, 41,** and **43:** Refusal of a nonrecognized relative or lover.

Tunes: seven notations are known, all being variants of the melody given above.

Versions in languages other than Hungarian:
FRENCH: *1—2.* Wallonia XIII, 24, 56, 1905. *3. Canteloube* IV, 86. *4. Canteloube* II, 91. *5. D'Harcourt* 12. *6. Barbeau* 1962, 241. *7. Barbeau* and *Sapir,* 73. *8. Beauquier,* 175. *9—11. Millien* 1906, 17A-C. *12. Rossat* 1917 II, 2. *13. Rossat* 1907, 433. *14. Bladé* 1879, 21. *15. Arbaud* I, 59. *16. Tiersot* 1903, 92. *17. Champfleury* and *Weckerlin,* 5. *18.* JAF 1919/123, 19*. *19.* Romania, 467 1873*. *20.* La Chanson Française I, 6 1908, 13*. *21. Guillon,* 9*. *22. Trébucq* II, 198*. *23. Weckerlin* 1903 I, 38.

Parallels of this Hungarian ballad are only known from the French-speaking areas. There a rather uniformly shaped song tells about Jesus begging from door to door in beggar's clothing. "Give me the crumbs left over from the meal!" The master of the house, a rich man, will not give even the crumbs, for they are needed for his dogs which catch hares for him, while the poor man is of no use to him. The master's wife, however, takes pity on the poor beggar, gives him food, then takes him to her own room to offer him a resting place. She finds the room bathed in light. Jesus makes Himself known, and explains that the light is the light of her good deeds (in other variants: the effulgence from angels). Sometimes the sun and the moon are mentioned: "En entrant dans la chambre se forme un' grand' clarté. Dites moi donc, le pauvre, Qu'est-ce qui reluit ici: C'est le jour qui donne Ou bien la lune qui luit? C'est ni le jour qui donne Ni la lune qui luit: ce sont vos bon's aumones Qui ouvr'nt le Paradis." Then He fortells that she will die in three days' time and will go to Heaven, but her husband will incur damnation.

The French ballad is obviously the original, with the Saviour in disguise meeting with bad and good treatment, and with punishment and reward being delivered correspondingly, and not the Hungarian where they know from the start that they are dealing with Jesus, and yet turn him away, and moreover the moral teaching of a parable is also omitted. As against this, the Hungarian versions have given new meaning to the radiance and the sun and moon references, by applying a highly effective poetic picture: At the head of Jesus the sun rises, at His feet, the moon. On the basis of certain correspondences demonstrated by *Berze Nagy* and my own researches this motif points back to eastern heroic-song traditions. The sun often appears at the head of the hero, and the moon at his feet, in the Siberian and Caucasian songs. In one of the songs published by *Radloff* (I, 31), the sun rises on one side of the hero, the moon on the other, while the evening star can be seen on his forehead; in another song recorded by *Radloff,* the moon rises at the head, the sun at the feet of the hero, and the star comes up at his heart. A Caucasian tale places the sun on one of the hero's feet, the moon on the other, and the star on his hand. When the hero of a Shor Tartar song gets the girl destined to him, "the old Khan Altün bended their heads together, and the moon sparkled before them, and the sun shone behind them". (*Dyrenkova* 14, p. 171.) In a Mongolian heroic song the hero marries a girl on whose neck the sun, and on whose nape the moon are shining. (*Potanin,* p. 117.) A Karakirghiz song contains the following lines: "On my right side the sun can be seen, on my left, the moon. The evening star can be seen on my forehead, so he spoke. The father told his elder sons: you must kill the one who is distinguished by such signs and bring his dead body here." (*Radloff* II, lines 32—35.)

This is another proof of the fact that the Hungarians of the mediaeval times tried to fit, whenever a possibility arose, their ancient traditions in the proper places of the new poetic composition. In result, however, the ending had to be changed of necessity; the glorification of the merciful woman was omitted and replaced by that of Jesus. In spite of this, there are correspondences with the contrasted callous rich husband and the merciful wife: Jesus in the role of a beggar and the radiance in the room.

This ballad may be considered as belonging among the earliest borrowings from the French, that is dating to the early fourteenth century.

Literature: Berze Nagy J, 335—6; *Vargyas* 1959—62 I, 1967.

8. THE GIRL TAKEN TO HEAVEN

24.

Fair Damsel Julia went out one day
To pick corn-flowers in the corn-field,
To pick corn-flowers, to make them into a wreath,
To make them into a wreath, to entertain herself.
5. She looked up to the high sky, —
Aye, a beautiful path was coming down from there,
A crispy, white lamb was lowering on it,
Bringing the sun and the moon between its horns;
It was bringing the bright star on its forehead,
10. Aye, two beautiful golden rings were on its two horns!
Aye, on both its sides there were two beautiful burning candles,
And as many stars were on it as many were its hairs!
The crispy, white lamb told her, speaking:
Do not get fright of me, Fair Damsel Julia!
15. For there is a want in the host of the maidens,
If you were willing to come with me, I would take you up there,
Into the heavenly choir, among the sainted maidens,
So as to fill with you their saintly order.
I would give you the key to Heaven,
20. At the cock's first crow I would come to see you,
At the cock's second crow I would sue for you,
At the cock's third crow I would take you with me.
Fair Damsel Julia turns to her mother,
She tells her, speaking: Mother, dear mother!
25. I went out to pick corn-flowers,
To pick corn-flowers, to make them into a wreath,
To make them into a wreath, to entertain myself.
I looked up to the high sky,
Aye, a beautiful path was coming down from there,
30. A crispy, white lamb was lowering on it,
Bringing the sun and the moon between its horns;
It was bringing the bright star on its forehead,
Aye, two beautiful golden rings were on its two horns!
Aye, on both its sides there were two beautiful burning candles,
35. And as many stars were on it as many were its hairs!
The crispy, white lamb told me, speaking:
Do not get fright of me, Fair Damsel Julia!
For there is a want in the host of the maidens,
If I were willing to go with it, it would take me up there,

40. Into the heavenly choir, among the sainted maidens,
So as to fill with me their saintly order.
It would give me the key to Heaven,
At the cock's first crow they will come to see me,
At the cock's second crow they will sue for me,

45. At the cock's third crow they will take me with them.—
Lament, mother, lament, let me hear while I am alive,
How you will lament me when I am dead!
My daughter, my daughter! You, who has been in my flower-garden
The tender honeycomb of my first swarm of bees,

50. The wax of the tender honeycomb turning yellow,
The smoke of the yellow wax spreading over the earth.
Smoke spreading over the earth and flame reaching up to the sky!
The heavenly bell chimed without being tolled,
The heavenly door opened without being opened,

55. Alas! my daughter was led in there!

Korond (Udvarhely county, the riverine of the Fehér-Nyikó). Kriza=MNGY XI, 270.

25.

1. Ot - tan ke - re - ke-dik Egy ke - rek dom - becs- ka.

Ar - ra ne - vel - ke - dik Egy é - des al - ma - fa.

1. There arises
A roundish hillock,
And a sweet apple-tree
Is growing on it.

2. Its apples are sweet,
Its leaves grow in bunches.
Its apples are sweet,
Its leaves grow in bunches.

3. Under it there sits
Fair Ilona Márton.
Under it there sits
Fair Ilona Márton.

4. She is making her wreath
Of white and crimson.
She is making her wreath
Of white and crimson.

5. And where she is short of flowers,
   She fills the room.
   And where she is short of flowers,
   She fills the room,

6. She fills the room
   With her flooding tears,
   She fills the room
   With her flooding tears.

7. Aye, there is coming
   A crispy, white lamb.
   Aye, there is coming
   A crispy, white lamb.

8. At the peaks of its two horns
   There are two beautiful burning candles.
   At the peaks of its two horns
   There are two beautiful burning candles.

9. At its two ears
   There are two beautiful golden rings.
   At its two ears
   There are two beautiful golden rings.

10. It spoke with words, saying:
    Don't you be frightened, don't be frightened,
    Don't be frightened, don't be frightened,
    Fair Ilona Márton!

11. For I am not a devil,
    Nor am I a ghost.
    I am neither a devil,
    Nor am I a ghost.

12. From the host of God,
    A messenger, that's what I am.
    From the host of God,
    A messenger, that's what I am.

13. In the host of God
    Someone is missing.
    In the host of God
    Someone is missing.

14. If you came with me,
    You would make up for the loss.
    If you came with me,
    You would make up for the loss.

15. The Kingdom of Heaven
    Will be complete with you.
    The Kingdom of Heaven
    Will be complete with you.

16. And she started on the way
    To the Kingdom of Heaven,
    To the Kingdom of Heaven,
    To the seventh chamber.

17. She was dressed
    In pilgrims' clothes.
    She was dressed
    In pilgrims' clothes.

18. She took in her right hand
    Her rosary of seven ells.
    She took in her right hand
    Her rosary of seven ells.

19. She took in her left hand
    Her pilgrim's rod.
    She took in her left hand
    Her pilgrim's rod.

20. She spoke with words, saying,
    Thus spoke Fair Ilona Márton,
    She spoke with words, saying,
    Thus spoke Fair Ilona Márton:

21. Lament, mother, lament,
    Lament with loud bewails!
    Lament, mother, lament,
    Lament with loud bewails!

22. Let me hear while I am alive
    How you will lament me, when I am dead.
    Let me hear while I am alive
    How you will lament me, when I am dead.

23. Don't go, child, don't go,
    Fair Ilona Márton.
    Don't go, child, don't go,
    Fair Ilona Márton,

24. On the long, long way,
    On those untrodden paths.
    On the long, long way,
    On those untrodden paths!

25. Stop. mother, stop,
    Don't lament me any longer!
    Stop, mother, stop,
    Don't lament me any longer!

26. For I heard while I was alive
    How you lament me when I am dead.
    For I heard while I was alive
    How you lament me, when I am dead.

27. Then she started on the way
    To the blessed Kingdom of Heaven.
    Then she started on the way
    To the blessed Kingdom of Heaven.

28. When she was approaching
    The gate of Heaven,
    When she was approaching
    The gate of Heaven,

29. The heavenly gates
    Sprang open without being opened.
    The heavenly gates
    Sprang open without being opened.

30. And the heavenly candles
    Burnt without being lit.
    And the heavenly candles
    Burnt without being lit.

31. The heavenly bells
    Chimed without being tolled.
    The heavenly bells
    Chimed without being tolled.

32. She was asked with words:
    What are you looking for, what are you looking for,
    What are you looking for, what are you looking for,
    Fair Ilona Márton?

33. In behalf of my father and mother
    I am looking for room.
    In behalf of my father and mother
    I am looking for room.

34. Alas, it is a great thing you ask for,
    Yet, it will be granted.
    Alas, it is a great thing you ask for,
    Yet, it will be granted.

35. My God, my God,
    How shall I die!
    My God, my God,
    How shall I die!

36. Before the Great God,
    How shall I answer!
    Before the Great God,
    How shall I answer!

37. How shall I die,
    How shall I share the life of the sainted!
    How shall I die,
    How shall I share the life of the sainted!

Pusztina (Moldava), 1956. Performed by a 22-years-old girl. Kallós = M. Sz. 6743.

Cf. Leader, 56.

The following variant starts with the incipit formula common to several European ballads (for example, Pernette, 98 and almost all the German texts from Gottschee), notably with the motif of rising up in the early morning:

> Fair Damsel Zsuzsanna got up early in the morning,
> And she walked out to the rose-field,
> There she lay down at the stem of a rose-tree;
> She began to tidy her golden locks,
> She began to wash her rosy cheeks.
> A path was coming down from Heaven,
> A crispy-haired lamb was walking down on it.
> "Don't be frightened, don't be frightened, Fair Damsel Zsuzsanna,
> I am not a ghost, I am a messenger from Heaven:
> Our Lord Jesus Christ has sent me to you
> Because there is one single soul missing in the host of maidens,
> And if you come with me, the place will be filled with you!"
> "I shall go, I shall go, but first let me go home
> To take leave of my father and mother."

They go to the girl's place, then at the second crow of the cock:

> ......The heavenly door opens without being opened,
> The heavenly bell chimes without being tolled,
> And the key to Heaven is given in her hand.
> Take care of this, Fair Damsel Zsuzsanna,
> Take care of this, for ever, Amen!"

Karácsonyfalva, Marosszék (Maros-Torda county), Nyr 7, 143 1878.

The mother's words of farewell have been preserved in an almost identical form by another variant:

> "... She goes into the little bower,
> She begins to lower her golden hair.
> Mother, dear mother, lament me,
> Let me hear while I am alive, how you will lament me, when I am dead!

"You, who have been white honeycomb of my first bee-swarm,
Yellow, strained wax of the white honeycomb,
White candle from the yellow, strained wax,
Flame of the white candle reaching up to the sky,
Smoke going to Heaven from the flame reaching up to the sky.
At the cock's first crow, she was sued for,
At the cock's second crow, she was given away,
At the cock's third crow, she departed from this world.
The heavenly doors opened by themselves,
They gave the heavenly key in her hand,
Of this, Fair Damsel Márta took care!"
Stop, mother, mother, my dearest heart,
For I heard while I was alive, how you lament me, when I am dead.

EA. Sövényfalva (Kisküküllő county). Mailand legacy, No. 5.

In a variant recorded from Diószeg, and in two more from Klézse, the girl says
farewell to her mother:

May God reward you,
Mother, dearest heart,
For the nine months's time
When you carried me in your womb,
For the nine months' time
When you carried me in your womb.
As the nine months were over
You brought me into this world,
As the nine months were over
You brought me into this world,
By the rocking cradle
You sat up so many nights!"

Details of the miraculous vision survive in Hungarian folk tradition even
outside the sphere of balladry, and what is more, outside the dissemination area of
the ballad under discussion. The most conspicuous and most frequently quoted
parallelism is contained in the Transdanubian *regös* songs (chant connected with
winter-solstice masquarade). The initial picture is the following:

There is a round lawn developing there,
And there is a wonder-doing deer grazing on it...

MNGY IV, 16.

There is a long, splendid road rising there
Beside it a fish-pond is taking shape,

Refrain.

It is overgrown with tiny sedge,
The wonder-son-deer gets to graze there...

MNGY IV, 2.

Refrain.
There is a branchy oak-tree there,
The ground under it has been overgrown with tiny, beautiful grass;
Our Lady Mary is sitting on a chair,
Our Lord God is lying in the cradle...
(Each line is followed by a couplet of refrain.)

MNGY IV, 1.

The image of the wonder-son-deer is still closer to that of the crispy, white lamb in the following variant of the *regös* song:

I have the bright rising sun on my forehead,
I have the beautiful moon (of Transylvania?) on my side,
I have the heavenly stars on my right kidney,
I have antlers, a thousand of them,
On the peaks of my antlers I have a hundred thousand torches,
They burn without being lit, they burn out without being blown out...

MNGY IV, p. 43, No. 2. (Many variants are to be found in the mentioned volume.)

A bridal farewell song, traditionally performed at wedding ceremonies among the Palots population of County Nógrád, preserves faded fragments of this initial image and the meeting with the heavenly messenger:

There is a round .... tree growing there,
Beside the .... tree, the beautiful carrying girl is sitting.
The beautiful carrying girl, do not wonder at it!
I am not a wonder, but you are the wonder.
Alas, my pal Márta, my loveable flower,
Are you not sorry to part with your dear mother?
With your dear mother, and all your girl friends?
Alas, I am very sorry to part with them, I am near to die.

Őrhalom MNT III/A, Nos 240 and 241.

The counterpart of the path lowering from the sky and the image of the splendid wide road of the *regös* songs was demonstrated bv *Fettich* (1959, 67) among the "charming prayers", that is spells, published by *Péter Bornemisza* in the sixteenth century. The spell reads as follows:

"My Lord, Almighty God! There was a wide *regös* way, Our Hallowed Lord, the God was walking on it; He met with seventy-seven kinds of red gout. Our Hallowed Lord, the God, said: Where are you going on this old, wide *regös* way?..." "My Lord, Almighty God, there was a wide *regös* way, Our Lord, the Almighty God was walking on it together with His loving Saints, and with Saint John the Baptist. They met with seventy-seven kinds of stomach-ache that make people feeble. Our Lord, the God, said the following words: Where are you going on this wide *regös* way?..."

130

Obviously the vision conveyed by the ballad had developed from a multiplicity of Hungarian traditions which had been blended with memories of the *Agnus Dei* representations of churches. Apparently, the ballad thus formed used to have a dissemination area much larger than it has nowadays.

First mentioned: 1862.

Dissemination: Marostorda (Nyárádkarácsonfalva), Kisküküllő county (Sövényfalva), Udvarhely county (the riverine of Fehér-Nyikó), Háromszék county (Erdővidék), Moldavia (Diószeg, Forrófalva, Klézse 10, Lészped, Pokolpatak, Pusztina, Trunk 3).

Total: 22 variants.

Textual relationships with other ballads: The beginning of the ballad of The Test of Faithfulness (**43.**) and the formula "She was sewing in the window" show similarities to the description of the girl making a wreath: "She is binding her garland of white and crimson, And where she is short of flowers, she fills up the want with her pouring tears, And she smoothes it even with her many sighs", and so on. The motif "At the first ... second ... third crow of the cock..." comes up in **79**.

Tunes: have all been recorded from Moldavia. *1* = No. 25 published above; the same occurs in twelve more notations. *2–3* occur in one variant only, *4* in two. (NB. A further three texts published without music also have tunes, which, however, are not available to me momentarily.)

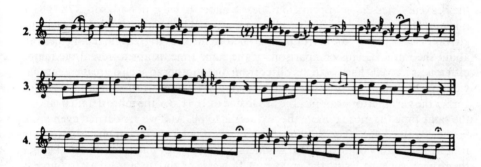

: *Variants (partly relevant) in languages other than Hungarian:*

GERMAN: *1–7.* E–B 2120–2126. *8. Hermann* and *Pogatschnigg,* 31 ("Regina". Further variants quoted by *Domokos* 1959.)

DANISH (SWEDISH): *9–17.* DgF 103. *18–27.* DgF 104 (*†Jonsson*).

Of dubious relevance:

SPANISH *28–29. Menéndez Pidal* 68–69.

GERMAN: *30–31.* E–B 2127–2128. *32. Parisius* 639 (The Sultan's Daughter. Further variants are quoted by *Domokos* 1935). *33.* E–B 2129. *34–36. Parisius* 640, 662, 774. (The Daughter of the Captain of Nagyvárad.)

Although the question of origin of this ballad has received much attention in the literature, it has not yet been settled in a reassuring way. *Domokos* has brought forth many parallelisms, but even he failed to find a doubtless correspondence. What has been brought in correlation mostly referred to the loose outlines of the theme, but by no means to the whole, not even to details, of the formulation. For instance, the Type "Regina" (*1–8.*) presents the story of the girl taken to Heaven in the following manner (4):

Regine gieng in Garte, wollt breche Röseli ab,
die feinen und die zarte, wo i dem Garte stan.
Regine lueget ume, Sah einen jungen Knab:
Wo bist du ine kume? 's ist Alles wohl vermacht.
Kei Mur Ist mir zu hoche, Kei Schloss ist mir zu stark:
Ich bin der Herr Jesus selber, Der Alles erschaffe hat.
Bist du der Herr Jesus selber, So gheiss mich mit dir cho,
So will ich mit dir reise In's ebige Himelreich.
Willst du denn mit mir reise In's ebige Himelreich,
So muesst du dich schneeweise kleide, Dass du bist dent Engle glich.
Wüsst das min Vater und Muetter, Dass ich im Himel bi,
Si würded mi nit lang suche, Sie chämed au dohi.
Herr Jesus schrieb es Briefli, Schrieb nu drü einzige Wort:
D'Regine sei im Himel, Sei a me schönen Ort.

As can be seen, a certain degree of similarity can be established between the two songs: Here the girl is picking flowers in a garden; there she walks out to the corn-field to take a wreath for herself; here Jesus appears in a miraculous way, there the heavenly messenger appears in no less wonderful way; in both songs the girl is taken to Heaven; here the girl's parents are advised by a letter, there, however, the girl takes leave of her parents (or mother) before she goes to Heaven, telling them all about the miracle. This comparison, at the same time, is apt to reveal the major differences as well. The two texts differ from one another to such a great extent that we have to regard as precluded their having originated from one another. The earlier the variant (for example, the broadside of 1631, 3.), the more detailed, and at the same time the more remote the text seems to be. And we are carried even more farther by the Type "The Sultan's Daughter", in which a pagan girl admires in a rapture the beauty of flowers and wonders by whom they might have been shaped; then there appears Jesus, the creator of flowers: at this turn a long discourse is initiated on certain theological questions; the girl goes with Jesus to the kingdom of Heaven, where she fails to receive admittance until it is made clear that she is the bride of Jesus; finally she gets into the kingdom of Heaven. A remote variant of this story is the one in which a simple pagan girl is the heroine, who does not reach Heaven but is taken by the Saviour, after a wonderful flight, into a nunnery, where eventually she joins the sisters.

In this story the motif of "miraculous time" comes up already, inasmuch as the flight takes place in no time; this motif appears in combination with other miraculous events in the ballad about the "Daughter of the Captain of Nagyvárad". The girl taken to Haven is allowed to gaze at the delight of Paradise for three days and three hours; then she is told by Jesus to go home; and when she arrives at home, she finds everything altered, she herself is not recognized either. We learn that she had left home a hundred and twenty years before. As soon as she touches earthly dish, she changes in colour and dies. The theme of visiting the world beyond come up also in the *Exemplum mirabile* of the Érdy-codex of Hungary (a young man is taken up to Heaven by the Lord God), as well as in many mediaeval legends. In the final analysis, this motif is of eastern, more precisely Indian origin. How deeply it had got embedded into Hungarian tradition is shown by the fact that the latter parable can be traced back, in all probability, to eleventh-century preliminaries. This is reflected also in the folk tradition: they are known to occur in several folk-tales (cf. *Faragó*). It is not mere chance, perhaps, that the German story about the "Daughter of the Captain of Nagyvárad" brings the legend into correlation with the Hungarian land. Market-singers must be responsible for its spread. *Puigmaigre* (1885, 161–166) states that among the German-speaking population of France market-singers used to sing this story, illustrating their performance by means of pictures. ("Celle qui est intitulée 'La Fiancée hongroise' est très connue dans la partie allemande du département de la Moselle. Jadis les chanteurs ambulants la redisaient en montrant sur une grande toile grossièrement peinte les diverses scènes qui en font le sujet." "In Ungerland, zu Grosswardein, Was Neues da geschehen sey...") But this origin is clearly indicated by the text itself; In Ungarland in Grosswardein Soll neulich was geschehen sein. Das will ich itzo zeigen an, Merkt es mit Fleiss, ihr Fraun und Mann." (*34*.) E–B also refers to broadside variants, and *Parisius* publishes one of them under No. 774. It is interesting that the variants registered in the DVA show the following distribution area: seven variants originate from Lorraine, two from the Rhine province, further variants from Upper Silesia, Egerland (Bohemia), and from the Germans of Vértesacsa (Hungary). In addition, there are also broadside variants of sundry publications. Finally, the Altmark texts published by *Parisius* from the environment of Berlin may be mentioned. The point of gravity of dissemination is—in spite of the intermediary role of broadsides—the French–German border region, with which the Hungarian-speaking areas had maintained the best developed connections, owing to Hungarian pilgrimages, in mediaeval times.

All this means, however, no more than a ramification in popular verse form of the legend. The Hungarian ballad does not contain two of their most essential motifs, namely those of the return to the earth, and the time-wonder.

Nor do we get nearer to the Hungarian ballad by examination of the Spanish variants. The King's daughter is sought in marriage in vain, because she had dedicated herself to the Virgin Mary. While she is absorbed in prayers, the Blessed Virgin appears before her: "I have come for you, come with me on a pilgrimage." But she cannot go without her father's consent. Reluctantly though, he gives his consent finally. The Holy Virgin leads her to an olive-tree where she has to stay for seven years without being given anything to eat or to drink, except the odour of a flower which a pigeon carries there. After seven years, the Virgin Mary appears again, asking her if she wants to get married or to be a nun. The girl chooses to be a nun. In fact, this story has already nothing to do with the Hungarian ballad.

Of all the texts, the Danish versions show closest semblance to the Hungarian. Admittedly, the first version (variant) is not unlike the German "Regina" type (*9–17*): Maiden Thorelille walks into the garden to water the flowers and do other works; God's angel appears before her, asking if she wishes to go with him to Heaven. The girls falls on her knees and prays for the kings, the peasants, the school-boys, the orphans, sailors, prisoners, and so on. The second variant, however, contains one or two motifs that allows of comparison with the Hungarian ballad (*18–27*.). God sends down His angel to fetch Him the girl. The heavenly herald assumes the shape of a bird, and so he lights on a branch of a tree, singing.

The girl walks out of the palace and goes to the tree, sighing: Would Jesus Christ grant it that she might possess the bird! She takes it in her hands, whereupon it addresses the girl in a sweet voice: "In the morning you will be in Heaven." "And then I shall see my Saviour." answers the girl. She went out of the house in good health and returned with death in her mouth. She asks her sister to make her bed, her mother to call a priest, her father to stay by her, and her ancestors to gather together in Heaven. Upon the fourth or fifth stroke of the bell she was seen to bed, upon the eighth and ninth, she was dead—and happy. An angel showed her the way to Heaven.

As can be seen, there is a degree of similarity in the gradation with the strokes of the bell, as well as in the animal-shaped heavenly messenger, recalling the vision of Fair Damsel Júlia. This, however, is still not sufficient to authorize us to set up a theory of some common origin. The similarities, again, imply serious dissimilarities, too, and we think the theme as it is may involve such remote agreements in remote areas, independently of each other.

Nevertheless, the remote correspondences of certain motifs of the story are indicative of the fact that they are rooted in common mediaeval legends, and also in folk-tales and popular versions, sometimes versified variants, of these legends which had developed in every language area and owe their spread mainly to the intermediary role of pious broadsheets. But the songs of the Székely and Csángó populations were formulated in the ballad style, and the scene of the miraculous vision was developed in them from ancient, heathen poetic traditions. Consequently, in the chant about Fair Damsel Júlia, this particularly attractive linguistic achievement of Hungarian balladry, the rare, mature and exquisite poetic beauty is due precisely to its ancient origin.

Literature: Sebestyén 1902: points to similar traits connecting the wonder-son-deer of the *regös* songs with the crispy, white lamb of the ballad. *Katona* 1909: compares the ballad with the *Exemplum mirabile*. *Gragger* 1926: rejecting the connection with the *regös* songs, derives the ballad from the "Daughter of the Sultan" and "The Daughter of the Captain of Nagyvárad". *Dános* 1938: accepts *Gragger*. *Ortutay* 1936–1948: accepts *Gragger:* The Hungarian ballad is not preserving some pagan tradition, but is a very beautiful tradition of the pious disposition of the Székely population." *Csanádi and Vargyas* 1954: accepts the parallelism with the *regös* songs, rejecting the German parallelisms. *Domokos* 1959, I: surveying the international relationships, maintains that the Hungarian ballad originated from the German legend. *Fettich* 1959: explains the ballad from parallelisms given between the *regös* songs, spells, mediaeval and even earlier symbols of fine arts. *Faragó* 1968: publishes more recent ballad texts and folk-tale parallels.

9. THE TWO CHAPEL FLOWERS

26.

Mother, mother, my dear mother,
Lady Gyulai, my dear mother,
I shall marry Kata Kádár,
The beautiful daughter of our serf.
5. I won't let it, my dear son,
Márton Gyula.
Instead, marry some big lord's
Beautiful daughter!
I don't want any big lord's
10. Beautiful daughter,
I want only Kata Kádár,
The beautiful daughter of our serf!
Then you may go, my dear son
Márton Gyula,
15. I disown you, you are not my son,
Either now or in the future!
Groom, groom, my best groom,
Prepare my coach and harness my horses!
They harnessed the horses and started on the way.
20. Kata Kádár gave him a handkerchief:
When this handkerchief turns red,
Then you will know that my life has also changed.
Márton Gyula rides over hills and dales,
Until he sees the embroidered handkerchief has changed its colour.
25. Groom, groom, my best groom:
The earth is God's, the horses are the dogs',
Let us turn back for the handkerchief has turned red,
A fatal thing must have befallen Kata Kádár!
At the end of the village he met the swincherd.
30. I say, kind shepherd, what's news in your country?
As for us, everything's all right, though there are bad news for you,
Because Kata Kádár has met her end.
Your mother had her taken away.
And thrown into the fathomless lake.
35. Kind shepherd, show me the way to that lake!
Yours shall be all my gold, my horse and my coach!
They went to the edge of the lake:
Kata Kádár, dearest heart, say a word, are you here?
From the depth of the lake Kata Kádár called to him.

40. Márton Gyula plunged into the water.
His mother sent divers to fish him out,
They found them dead, embracing each other.
The one was buried before the altar,
The other was buried behind the altar.

45. Two chapel flowers grew out of the two bodies
And they interwined above the altar.
The mother went there and broke them off.
The chapel flower said to her:
Curse on you, curse on you,

50. My mother, Lady Gyulai!
You were wicked to me while I was alive
And even now you have killed me!

Udvarhelyszék. Kriza, 1865 = MNGY XI, 11.

27.

1. Lady Gyulai, my dear mother,
Grant me a favour, pray:
Let me seek in marriage Kata Kádár,
The beautiful daughter of our serf!

2. I will not let it, my dear son,
That you seek in marriage Kata Kádár.
You can find in this village
A king's daughter, a baron's daughter!

3. I don't want a king's daughter,
I don't want a baron's daughter,
Rather I go in exile,
In exile, and a long way from here.

4. He started on the long way,
On the long way, in exile.
And he was going, he was going,
Until he arrived at a mill.

5. I say, master miller,
What's news in the village?
I have heard of no news, except that
Kata Kádár had been taken by force.

136

6. Kata Kádár has been taken by force
   And thrown into a bottomless lake.
   Kata Kádár has been taken by force
   And thrown into a bottomless lake.

7. As Márton Gyula heard this,
   He went to the shore of the lake:
   Are you alive, sweetheart, or are you dead,
   Or are you thinking of me?

8. I am not alive, nor am I dead,
   But I am thinking of you all the time.
   He crossed himself
   And plunged into the deep lake.

9. From the one there grew a gillyflower,
   From the other there grew a rosemary.
   They grew and grew
   Until they intertwined.

10. Hearing of this, Lady Gyulai
    Went to the shore of the lake,
    She went to the shore of the lake
    And tore off both of them.

11. You did not let me in peace while I was alive,
    And I have no peace now when I am dead.
    May the Lord of Heaven punish those
    Who forbid love!

Csíkjenőfalva (Csík county). Performed by a 50-year-old man. Sárosi, 1958 = AP 2506/b.

28.

1. Let me, dear mother,
   Dear mother, Lady Gyulai,
   Let me marry Kata Kádár,
   Mrs. Kádár's beautiful daughter.

2. I will not let it, my dear son,
   My dear son, Márton Gyula.
   The big lords have daughters enough,
   You can marry one of them as well.

3. I do not want, dear mother,
   Any of the daughters of big lords.
   I want only Kata Kádár,
   Mrs. Kádár's beautiful daughter.

4. Where are you, where are you my brave groom?
   Saddle my palfrey!
   He mounts the grey horse
   And starts out on the long way.

5. Kata Kádár saw all this,
   Kata Kádár opened him her gate.
   Don't open your gate, Kata Kádár,
   For it is not that that I have come for today.

6. It is not that that I have come for today,
   I do not want to entertain myself with you;
   But I have come today
   To bid farewell to you for good.

7. Wait, wait, Márton Gyulai,
   Let me give you a white cloth!
   This white cloth will be blood-stained,
   And then you shall know that I am dead.

8. He put it into his bag,
   And so he started on the long way.
   Once he looked in his bag,
   And, lo, the white cloth was blood-stained.

9. At once he turned back,
   And he met with a vineyard-guard.
   Good day to you, vineyard-guard!
   God has brought you, Márton Gyulai!

10. Tell me, vineyard-guard,
    What news is there in the village!
    I have heard no bad news,
    Though there is one rather bad for you.

11. Kata Kádár has been perished,
    That beautiful daughter of Mrs. Kádár;
    She has been thrown into the big lake,
    Into the bottomless big lake.

12. Come with me, vineyard-guard,
    To the shore of that bottomless lake!
    I give you my grey horse,
    My grey horse, my palfrey!

13. They went to the big lake,
    To the shore of the bottomless lake.
    Are you there, say a word, Kata Kádár!
    Mrs. Kádár's beautiful daughter!

14. Here am I, Márton Gyulai,
    Here am I, but I am dying.
    He jumped into the big lake,
    Into the big, bottomless lake.

15. Lady Gyulai heard of this
    And sent divers to fish him out.
    She had both of them laid out
    On the coast of the bottomless lake.

16. For the one, she had
    A coffin of white marble made,
    For the other, she had
    A coffin of yellow marble made.

17. The one, she had buried
    Before the altar,
    The other, she had buried
    Behind the altar.

18. On the one, there arose
    A leafless rosemary,
    On the other, there arose
    A stemless pink.

19. They grew and grew
    Until they intertwined.
    Lady Gyulai behold this
    And broke off both of them.

20. Her son Márton said with words:
    Curse upon you, mother!
    You did not leave us in peace while we were alive,
    And you do not leave us in peace when we are dead!

21. May the water flood before you,
    May the mud well forth after you,
    May you see no bliss of Heaven,
    May you see no bliss of Heaven!

22. May your bread turn into stone,
    May your wash-water turn into blood,
    May your towel burst into flame,
    May your cheeks catch fire of it!

Kadicsfalva (Udvarhely county) = Bartalus III, 7.

Divergences: Instead of "The beautiful daughter of our serf" sometimes we have "The beautiful daughter of my cottar", or of "Mrs. Kádár", the latter referring to craftsmanship. The mother's words: "Instead of consenting to it, son, I will perish Kata Kádár" are supplemented in one single instance with the following lines: "Kata Kádár is a poor girl, She is no match to you". In another instance, the young man says: "I don't want a daughter of a lord, I want only Kata Kádár." The young man going in exile is called sometimes "Clerk Márton". In eight cases he hears the news from a miller, in five texts from a Romanian shepherd, sometimes from a vineyard-guard, a little shepherd, a Hungarian young man, and in two instances from Esq. János Gál. In exchange for the news he gives all he has: "My bay palfrey shall be yours, And so shall all my fine clothes". But sometimes only the horse and the harness are mentioned, or the horse alone. The divers come up in five instances, twice the mother has the corpse fished out by means of an iron hook; flowers growing out of the water figure three times; these are immediately destroyed by the mother, if not later, after the burial is over. Particularly interesting is the description of the flower when not a plant but something else is involved: "White stalk of lily" or "Red marble stalk of lily", the latter in three cases; "Leafless marjoram", "Rootless marjoram", "White marble scion" or "Red marble scion". With reference to these *Nándor Fettich* stated (1959) that the motif of marble flower can be brought into correlation with the carved, floral ornamentations of churches built in the Romanesque or Gothic periods, indeed the image of white marble flower alternating with red can be readily explained from the flower symbols carved either in red or in white marble in mediaeval churches, since the lovers were buried either beside the church or the altar. (Of course, the genuine symbol referred to living flowers growing out of the lovers graves.) The curse laid on the mother applies three times the motif characteristic of the ballad about "The Sister of the Man Condemned to Death" **(27.):** the water for washing turning into blood, bread into stone, the towel emanating flame, etc. This motif comes up in the earliest recording from the last century when the mentioned ballad was not yet entered into the Transylvanian collections. (That is to say, either the ballad had existed in earlier days escaping the collectors's notice or the curse was a mediaeval commonplace shared by several ballads in common.)

First mentioned: 1861. It should be noted, however, that the story found its way, through literary adaptation, to the romance *Telamon* published as early as 1578.

Dissemination: Kolozs county (Kolozsvár, Magyargyerőmonostor, Vajdakamarás, Visa). Udvarhely county (Etéd, Kadicsfalva 2, Nagygalambfalva, "Udvarhelyszék" 2), Torda-Aranyos county (Kercsed), Csík county (Borszék, Csíkjenőfalva, Csíkmenaság 3, Gyergyóditró 2, Gyergyótekerőpatak 4, Gyergyótölgyes, Gyergyóújfalu, Kászonaltíz), Háromszék county (Karatna), "Székelyföld", Moldavia (Lábnik, Ploszkucén).

Total: 29 variants.

Textual relationships with other ballads: **48.,** chapel-flower: **10., 28., 37., 38.;** "Show me the place and you shall have my horse...": **19.;** the lovers die for each other: **21.;** asking a miller, a shepherd, a beggar or an old man to show the way: **10;** "Groom, groom, prepare the coach... Lash the horse ...": **2., 10., 11., 13., 16., 21., 27., 39.;** "Are you still alive...": **10.**

Tunes: 1 = No. 27 (7 variants), *2* = No 28, *3* (3 variants), *4* = (2 variants).

Versions in languages other than Hungarian:

PORTUGUESE: *1–16. Braga* I, 263 (= *Geibel and Schack*, 339 = *Wolf*, 92), 265, 267, 268, 272 (= *Hardung*, 220), 273 (= *Hardung*, 221), 275 (= *Hardung*, 223), "Conde Nillo"; *ibid.* 277, 283, 286, 290, 293, 297 (= *Hardung*, 225), 301 (= *Hardung*, 229), 305 (= *Geibel and Schack*, 357), "Prinzesa peregrina".

SPANISH: *17–28. Cossio* and *Solano* I 13/35–46. *29–31. Menéndez* and *Pidal* 1885 24–26. *32–33. Armistead* and *Silverman* 1971 B/2 and C/6.

ITALIAN: *34. Ferraro* 1888 10a.

ENGLISH: *35–42. Child* 17A–H. *43–51. Child* 75A–I. (For the chapel flower, see *ibid.* 7, 64, 73, 74, 76, 86, 87, 222.) *52.* JAF 1954/265, 252. *53–56. Sharp* and *Karpeles* 21A–E. *57–71. Greig,* 10 (15 variants). *72. Belden* 50/C. *73–89. Bronson* 17 (a further 17 variants). *90–159. ibid.* 75.

DANISH: *160–175.* DgF 446.

SOUTHERN SLAV: *176–177.* HNP VI 174–175 (175 = Hungarian translation by *Vujičić,* 8). *178–237. ibid.* Dodatak (= addenda), 175. *238. ibid.* 61. *239. Raič,* 38 3. *240. Tordinac* 1. *241.* Vuk I 341 (Hungarian translation by *Vujičić*), 7). *242. ibid.* 342. *243. Osvetnik,* 49 8. *244. Bugarinović,* 24. *245.* Bilten, 113 36. *246–268. Štrekelj* I. *246.* 726–747.

GERMAN: *269–270. Hauffen* 59–60. Gottschee, Slovenia (partly relevant E–B 92).

BULGARIAN: *271–276. Stoin* 1928 366–367, 481, 2602–2604. *277–279. idem* 1931 2162–2164. *280. idem* 1939 1425. *281. idem* 1934 652. *282. Verković* 137. *283–284. Miladinovi* 288 and 497. *285.* SbNU 44 *Ivanov* 144. *286–287. Tsitselkova* 71 and 101. *288–291.* A–V 50–53. *292.* Izv. Ethn. Muz. 8, 133 7. *293.* SbNU *Burmov* 68. *294.* SbNU 42 *Ivanov* 103.

ROMANIAN: *295–297. Alexics,* 286–287. *298. Marienescu,* 50. *299. Candrea–D.* 42 = *Ţiplea,* 19. *300. Ţiplea,* 31, 23. *301. Moldovan,* 64. *302.* Bud, 4. *303–305. Amzulescu* 269–271 (= Subtypes I–III of Type *305.;* under *305.* enumerates 16 variants, excusively from the territories of pre-wars Hungary.)

SLOVAK: *306. Horák* 1958 14 = Sl. Sp. I 216 = *Medveczky* 1923 1. *307. Kolečány* 16.

RUSSIAN: *308–309. Bezsonov* I 167. 168.* *310–311. Chubinsky V,* 711 309 and V, 1208 50.* *312–313. Balashov,* 50–51. (The ballad is known among the Trans-Carpathian Ukrainians as well. *By courtesy of Lintur.)*

VOTYAK: *314.* Ethn 1904, 238 = *Vasilev,* 129.

Partial variants:

BRETON: *315. Villemarqué,* 61.

GERMAN: *316–325.* D. Vlr. 65, Die Bernauerin.

Of the western relations of the ballad under discussion, two English ballads should be mentioned first of all. In one of them Lord Lovel (*Child* 75) bids farewell to his wife, because he wants to travel in foreign lands. But later he is assailed by dark misgivings, and returns home. The bell is just being tolled for a burial. On his questioning the people he is told that it is his wife they are burying, who incidentally is called by a name in the French style, Nancy Belle. The lord has the coffin opened, kisses the corpse and dies. One of them is buried in the apsis, the other in the chancel. (Elsewhere beside the church, in the chancel, or in the nave and the chancel, and so on.) Flowers (red rose and white brier) grow out of their bodies, which reaching the top of the church, intertwine in a true lovers' knot. A typical example of this motif is found in *Child* 75/A, which ends like this: "Lady Ouncebell was buried in the high chancel, Lord Lovill in the choir; Lady Ouncebell's breast sprang out a sweet rose, Lord Lovill's a bunch of sweet brier. They grew till they grew to the top of the church, And then they could grow no higher. They grew till they grew to a true lovers' knot, And then they tyed both together. An old woman coming by that way, And a blessing she did crave, To cut off a bunch of that true lovers' knot, and buried them both in one grave." In another ballad (*Child* 74A) the clerk of the parish happens to go there and cuts the flowers by misfortune.

The second English parallel (*Child* 17) contains other details of Kata Kádár, embedded in the story of a husband arriving to find his wife getting married to another man. The husband had received a ring from his wife when he left; when it changes colour it signifies that her love has changed, too. Returning home on seeing the sign, the husband meets with a beggar. (This beggar must be connected in a way or other with the *mill*: in variant A and in *Bronson* 3: "the auld beggar man was bound for the mill".) "What news, what news? said young Hind Horn. No news, said the old beggar man. No news, said the beggar, no news at a'. But there is a wedding in the king's ha'." At this he exchanges his scarlet coat and his horse for the beggars clothes, and goes in disguise to the wedding where his wife recognizes him by the ring. Here there is, of course, no grave-flower.)

Let us compare the corresponding scene of the Hungarian ballad Kata Kádár: the young man meets a miller or a (Romanian) shepherd. " Master miller, what's news in the village?" "No news at all, but Kata Kádár has been lost . . . Take me to the lake . . . I'll give you my palfrey, and all my rich embroidered clothes."

142

If we want to discover the real connections underlying these striking similarities, we must start from the fact that the most characteristic motif of the Hungarian ballad, that of the *grave-flower, is unknown in German territory*. Admittedly, there is something similar at the end of some of the German ballads: out of the grave of the heroine in some cases grows a lily bearing the inscription that she was innocent, or that her soul has gone to Heaven. But the image of the intertwining flowers or trees growing out of the dust of the dead lovers is lacking. This circumstance is pointed out by the complete German edition in connection with the text of Gottschee, Slavonia, in which this motif occurs, borrowed from the Slovene much in the same form as in the Hungarian ballad (D. Vlr. I, 83.). In English, however, we find it in many variants of nine different ballads, indeed, in one or two of them even the subsequent breaking off appears, though not always motivated by the revenge of the cruel parent or enemy, as has been seen in the examples quoted above. The motif is rather typical of the Danish versions as well: DgF 305, 415/B, 446, 448, 473. Even the representation of the scene is similar to the Hungarian, as in DgF 305 Ff 11th–15th stanzas: "They laid down (buried) Fredensborg before the church, and they laid down little Kirstin behind the church (that is on the northern side). Lilies arose from their mouths, lilies grew out of their hearts, And lilies arose from their breasts, and they grew and grew throughout the summer and autumn. And lilies arose from their graves, and they grew and grew until they reached the top of the church. And they grew above the church, so high as to be able to intertwine on top of the roof." What is more, the Danish correspondences may be extended to cover a similar story, too (DgF 446): A knight marries a beautiful girl, then he has to travel far away, into foreign lands. There comes an epidemic which carries away the woman. She sends word by a dove to her husband, then she dies. The husband rides home with the speed of wind, on the way he hears the ill news from a skylark, to which the knight gives no credit. Finally he sees the corpse. His brother-in-law says to him that it is his wife. He takes the ring off his finger and has it buried with her, then stabs himself in the heart. A golden lily grows from one of them, and a green lily from the other. Above the top of the church they intertwine, and they stay there until God allows the church to stand. (Of the fifteen related variants the motif of the chapel flower occurs in A, D and E.) As can be seen, the Danish ballad is blended from the elements of the two English Types discussed before.

In the French ballads, however, the motif occurs rather rarely and in a rather corrupt form: it is more likely to be a case of flowers *planted* on the graves of the lovers, which then twine together. Yet the earliest appearance of the complete picture is to be found in the French Tristan legend, created before the development of the ballad genre. Consequently, what we have in the French ballads must be an eroded form of the original. But on the other hand, no details concerning the story of The Two Chapel Flowers can be demonstrated from the French version. We do, however, meet with them again in the Portuguese and Spanish folk poetry.

In the Portuguese, Conde Nillo falls in love with the king's daughter, but the king will not let them marry; they die, intertwining flowers grow out of their graves, and the father has them torn down. In another type, the Prinzesa peregrina, the story becomes more complicated in that a poor knight brought up in the royal court flees from the wrath of the king and takes another wife. The princess follows him and, on learning of her lover's marriage, dies. The young man follows her into the grave, and the grave-flower is destroyed by the jealous wife—in any case a woman, if not the mother. The contrast between noble and serf of the Hungarian ballad takes the form of the contrast beween royal offspring and a minor noble, only the roles are reversed: it is the girl who is the more exalted figure. The grave-flower motif corresponds exactly to the Hungarian: here too one is buried behind the altar, the other at the door of the church. "Out of the one grows a cypress, out of the other an orange-tree (there are several other variations). "One grew, the other grew, too, until they intertwined. The king heard of this and had them out down at once. Out of the one flowed blood, out of the other, royal blood."

Nevertheless, at this point in most of the Portuguese ballads a new element is joined in, which is not known in English: Out of the cut-down flowers two doves appear, or a dove from the girl and an eagle from the young man. These sometimes fly onto the shoulder of the king and whisper in his ears that they will not part even in death, or they fly, kissing each other, up to the skies. In other instances the role of the birds is less distinct, while that of the flower is quite similar to the Hungarian: the two lovers are buried beside the church, and out of the girl grows a *white* jasmine, out of the young man a *red* one; they leaned towards each other and intertwined, growing so high that they reached the sky. All the birds of the world lighted on them to sing and to mate.

These birds are familiar in the Hungarian tradition, too, though they are not found in the Transylvanian texts of The Two Chapel Flowers (Kata Kádár), but in those of The Disgraced Girl in Hungary proper **(10.)** in which the grave-flower is fairly common. Here the Portuguese motif appears as follows: "One of them was buried towards the east, the other towards the west. On the grave of one of them two rosemary flowers grew, on the other's grave two pairs of turtle-doves cooed." "On the one there appeared a white dove, and on the other, the young man, a white cockerel." And they cooed and crowed the lesson to be drawn: lovers must not be parted. (Further examples see there.) Here again, therefore, we have the combined image of flowers and birds, though not one after the other but brought into play simultaneously; and this is without doubt a corruption for the two rosemary flowers and the two doves are indicative of their arising not from one grave but from two. These motifs go hand in hand with the chapel flower motif, which in this ballad shows a close resemblance to the parallel scene in the Transylvanian ballad Kata Kádár. Of the Kata Kádár story, then, at least the motif of the grave-flowers were generally known in Hungary, too, while a motif was preserved by the Portuguese which was lost in Transylvanian tradition, that of the birds figuring together with the flowers. And that the same motif may have existed not only in the Iberian Peninsula but also in France, is well brought out by the ending of a song in the Breton language: "It was a marvellous sight at night, after the lady had been buried in one grave with her husband; out of their new grave-mounds two oaks grew, in their branches two doves hopping about so merrily! They sang till dawn, then took wing up into the sky." Since this motif is lacking in the numerous English stories of the grave-flowers, it could have reached the Bretons only from the French.

In the Italian version this motif is so sparsely and so vaguely represented that we can ignore it. The more variegated are the southern Slav forms, though embedded in quite different stories. The young man is married off by his mother to a girl whom he does not love (there is no mention made about rich and poor, or high and low-born lovers); the young man dies during the wedding ceremony, sometimes commits suicide, and his sweetheart dies after him. Out of their grave two pine-trees, or a pine and a flower arise, and entwine round one another. Among the Slovenes, instead of the forced marriage, we have the young man going to be a priest. Then there are stories in which the young man, after the engagement is settled, does not go to bed with the girl, therefore the mother forces him to marry another; and still other stories occur, in which the separation of the lovers is told very briefly. Only the Hungarian—Portuguese version of the story motivated with social differences is missing, together with the parts which these and the English versions have in common (the kerchief with the omen, the sweetheart dying while the young man is away, his return home and inquiry "what news is there in the village?", and the scene related to it, and that he dies after the girl). Indeed, the graveflower itself is much simpler in the Yugoslav versions than in the Portuguese and the Hungarian: there are no birds, no breaking down of the flowers, and no wicked parent's hatred surviving the grave. In several cases the motif is completely missing from the narrative.

Those researchers who have tried to explain the ballad of Kata Kádár as coming from Italian short stories through southern Slav mediation ignored all these facts, because they could not conceive any other route between Italian and Hungarian communication. But the Italian novelle resemble the story of the Hungarian ballad only in a broad general way, and they also lack the details common to the Portuguese and English ballads. Moreover, the southern Slav plots differ so much from the Hungarian that if they had not the ending constructed with the grave-flower, there would be nothing to connect them. And if this motif is left out, all resemblance ceases.

The plot of the relevant Bulgarian songs is even more remote. They contain at most two or three lines to say that the lovers could not be united; anyway, the girl either dies from a snake-bite, or her stepmother poisons her. But in the grave-flower we have a closer link, showing an unquestionable connection with the Hungarian. The two lovers are buried in front or behind the church (but often only at the upper and lower end of the village). Lady Gyulai's cruelty also appears in a changed form in the Bulgarian songs: the mother pours hot water on the flower growing out of the girl's remains. In one of the variants, birds fly up from the flower to the heavens, but sometimes they turn into stars and ascend into the sky.

Similar is the connection with the Slovak ballad. The story of the Slovak version agrees with Kata Kádár only in that the two lovers cannot be united, and therefore they die. A mother will not let her daughter marry her sweetheart: the text says: "she has her walled up". But later on the girl is still living, and the mother will not let her go to see the body of the young man on the bier when he dies of sorrow. But at last she manages to do so and dies over his body. Then follows a story of the grave flowers similar to the Hungarian: one of the lovers is buried on one side of the church, the other on the other side. A rosemary flower and a golden tulip grow out of their remains and intertwine above the church. The girl's mother cuts them down with a sickle, and blood drips from the stems. The mother regrets her action and curses herself. Here, too, the connection with the Hungarian is obvious in the scene relating to the two grave-flowers, in spite of the preliminary story, which is based on a quite different plot. As to the Russian songs, they bear only a very remote relationship in their preliminary plot to the Hungarian ballad, although the motif of the grave-flower connects them to a certain extent.

It appears that the northern and southern Slavs' ballads acquired the grave-flower motif from the Hungarian ballads only, while they use as a preliminary story either simply the bare basic idea, or resort to various plots of their own devices. The process could not have happened in reverse, for in every case precisely those elements are missing or appear only in defective, eroded forms, which connect the Hungarian to the Portuguese and the English versions.

Of all the neighbouring peoples it is the Romanian whose corresponding songs contain more of the plot of The Two Chapel Flowers. They, too, have the kerchief that changes colour (the gold on it melts), and they also have the girl drowned in the lake; here, too, the man returns from soldiering when he sees the sign; he also discovers from a shepherd outside the village that his sweetheart has been killed on order of her father; and he also jumps into the lake. It is underlined that they both are buried beside the monastery, and that the grave-flowers growing out of their remains intertwine above the monastery. There is, however, a significant difference: here the couple are husband and wife, and the husband has to go to war. Sometimes the mother-in-law does away with the young bride, in which case the story really begins with the incipit of The Cruel Mother-in-Law. The father's behaviour is not given any sort of motivation, and it is the emperor that has the bodies fished out of the lake upon the sepherd's information. There is no social antagonism in this narrative—for the lovers had been united—consequently the story cannot go on to relate how the flowers were cut down and destroyed; for the same reason, there is no mention of the birds either. These are very weighty characteristic features, which sharply distinguish the Romanian versions from the western formulations. As against this, the similarities mentioned clearly link them to the Hungarian ballad; and among the similar elements the drowning in the lake and the recovery of the bodies occur only in the Hungarian variants of the ballad (beside the romance of Telamon mentioned before). Accordingly, the Romanian form must be regarded as derived from the Hungarian, especially as the relating variants have come up in the Transylvanian regions.

Thus all these variants found among the neighbouring peoples can only be explained by reference to the Hungarian, and do not form a link between the Hungarian, Portuguese and English ballads. There must, therefore, have been a French ballad which passed on to the southern and western regions—and to Hungary—the various elements of the plot, and in which there were the social antagonism as the obstacle to the lovers, as in the Hungarian and the Portuguese (in one Romanian variant—*Amzulescu* II—this motif also occurs, similarly borrowed from the Hungarian); the young man's exile, as in the Hungarian, English and—in a different form—the Portuguese; the young man's inquiry on his return and his giving away (or exchange) of clothes, as in the English and Hungarian; the grave-

146

flowers with the birds and the vengeful mother (father, wife), which have been preserved by the Portuguese, English and Breton with varying elements. The drowning in the lake may well be regarded, as suggested by earlier research, as a continuation of the motif of the Bernauer legend. German chronicles contain the story about Prince Albert of Bavaria who married secretly Agnes Bernauer, the daughter of a bath attendant. While the Prince was away, his father had the hangman of the place destroy her: he bound her hands and feet together and threw her into the Danube. The young woman get out of the water somehow, but the hangman threw her back again. Since the sixteenth-century Reformed Church's books of sermons often quoted this story, it may have influenced the ballad of The Two Chapel Flowers in Hungary; but the drowning into the lake occurs in the Transdanubian variant of The Cruel Mother-in-Law, too, therefore it may be considered to be a common tradition of Hungarian balladry. (The German summary edition attaches the following note to the ballad of Agnes Bernauer: "Das Lied ist in seiner Überlieferung auf Deutschland beschränkt"; that is it does not bring the German song into correlation with the Hungarian ballad.)

Another evidence that makes the one-time existence of the French ballad plausible is provided by the English ballads referred to, in which the scene describing the clothes-exchange with the beggar agrees almost word for word with the Hungarian, and also agrees with a story of literary origin (gest or romance) which was preserved among both the English and the French in the thirteenth-fourteenth-century manuscripts (see *Child* 17, I, 188–193). The scene survives in French, too. Obviously, it is from some such lengthy adventure story in verse that provided material for a short French ballad whose structure and details have been preserved by the Hungarian ballad of Kata Kádár, while the original passed out of mind among the French. Among the English, however, its details have been preserved till today in ballads with related themes, and a reminder of it is the French name of the heroine: Nancy Bell.

Literature: Abafi 1876/a: the grave-flower. International distribution; *Child* 1882–1892: grave flower, international distribution; *Bászel* 1906: reviews the Bernauer legend; *Reichard* 1910: the connection between the Bernauer legend, the Telamon romance and the Hungarian ballad; *Király* 1924: the Hungarian ballad originated from Italian novella and arrived in Hungary through southern Slav mediation; *Gragger* 1926: accepts preceding results in the literature and lists Romanian and Yugoslav versions; D. Vlr. I, 83 and 101–2 1935: on the German form of the grave-flower and international connections of the "Heimkehr des Ehemannes"; *Ortutay* 1936: accepts *Király*, the Hungarian ballad belongs to the southeastern European group, the western ones deviate in structure; *Solymossy* 1937: international connections of the Hungarian ballad on the basis of previous publications; *Dános* 1938: accepts the views of earlier publications; *Kardos* 1941; 246: the Hungarian ballad originated from Telamon; "... the Hungarian version is nearest of all the variants to the tale of Tristan and Iseut."; *Ortutay*[3] 1948 = *Ortutay* 1936 with additional literature; *Csanádi* and *Vargyas* 1954: various connections of the Hungarian ballad on the basis of publications hitherto; *Vargyas* 1960: the Hungarian ballad originated from the French, the eastern European versions developed from the Hungarian; *Amzulescu* 1964: enumerates Romanian published variants, and presents the text of one; *Vargyas* 1967 = *Vargyas* 1960; *Truţa* 1972 (published after my manuscript was closed): a survey of the entire Romanian data on the grave-flower.

10. THE DISGRACED GIRL

29.

Tempo giusto

1. An - go -li Bor -bá - la Kis szok-nyát var - ra - tott.

É -lül kur -táb - bo -dott, Há - tul hosz - szab - bo - dott.

1. Borbála Angoli
   Has a short skirt sewed for herself,
   It was getting short at the front,
   It was getting long at the back.

2. It was getting short at the front,
   It was getting long at the back.
   Her beautiful, slender waist
   Was getting thicker and thicker.

3. Daughter, daughter, daughter,
   Borbála Angoli,
   What is the matter with you;
   Your round skirt

4. Is getting short at the front,
   It is getting long at the back,
   Your beautiful, slender waist
   Is getting thicker and thicker!

5. The tailor did not cut it properly,
   The seamstress did not sew it properly,
   This chamber-maid
   Did not help me into it properly.

6. Daughter, daughter, daughter,
   Borbála Angoli,
   What is the matter with you:
   Your round skirt

7. Is getting short at the front,
   It is getting long at the back,
   Your beautiful, slender waist
   Is getting thicker and thicker!

148

8. Mother, mother, mother,
Kati Vándorvári,
I drank river water,
It makes me get thick.

9. Daughter, daughter, daughter,
Borbála Angoli,
What is the matter with you:
Your round skirt

10. Is getting short at the front,
It is getting long at the back,
Your beautiful, slender waist
Is getting thicker and thicker.

11. In vain should it be denied,
For I have to own up to it in the end:
It is master Gyöngyvári
Who has made me get thicker.

12. Pandours, come here
And take her, carry her away from here,
Take her, carry her away from here,
Cast her into the prison!

13. For thirteen days
She shall get nothing to eat, nothing to drink,
She shall get nothing to eat, nothing to drink,
Nor shall she be let sleep!

14. On the thirteenth day
Her mother comes:
Do you eat, do you drink,
Or are you sleeping?

15. I do not eat, I do not drink,
Nor am I sleeping.
Give me only an hour's time
To write my letter,

16. To write my letter
To master Gyöngyvári,
To master Gyöngyvári,
My dearest sweetheart!

17. Good evening, good evening
Unknown mother!
Where can I find, where can I find
My dearest darling?

18. She has gone into the flower garden
    To pick lilies-of-the-valley,
    To make a mourning wreath
    And to wear it on her head.

19. She is not there, she is not there,
    Unknown mother.
    Tell me, where she is,
    Where is my dearest darling!

20. In vain should it be denied,
    I have to own it up in the end:
    She is in the room
    Lying on a black bench.

21. In the bridegroom goes,
    In he goes in a haste,
    He takes his big knife
    And turns it against his heart.

22. Let my blood flow together with yours,
    In one and the same stream.
    Let my heart lie with your heart
    In one and the same grave!

23. Let my heart lie with yours
    In one and the same grave,
    Let my soul worship
    One God with yours.

*Vésztő (Békés county). Performed by an 18-year-old girl and a 34-year-old woman.
Bartók 1918 = Bartók 1924 34a.*

30.

1. A widow
   Had twelve daughters.
   The twelfth of them was
   Ilonka Londonvári.

150

2. Ilonka Londonvári,
   What is the reason
   That your green silken skirt
   Is getting long at the back?

3. The tailor did not cut it properly,
   The seamstress did not sew it properly,
   May the Lord punish her,
   She has spoiled it very much.

4. Hangmen, hangmen,
   Take my daughter,
   Take my daughter
   Hang her on the gallows!

5. Kind mother, kind mother,
   Wait half an hour,
   Wait half an hour,
   Or a minute at least!

6. Swallow, my little swallow,
   Take my letter,
   Take my letter
   To young Miklós Király!

7. If you find him at lunch,
   You will place this on his table.
   If you find him at supper,
   You will place this by his plate.

8. Coachman, my coachman,
   Harness six horses,
   Harness six horses,
   The finest ones, the best ones!

9. Let us drive, as swift as wind,
   As swift as thought!
   Perhaps we shall find
   Ilonka Londonvári alive.

10. Kind mother, kind mother,
    My unknown mother,
    Where is my sweetheart
    Ilonka Londonvári?

11. She has gone down to the brook
    To wash her feet,
    To wash her feet,
    To comfort herself.

12. She is not there, she is not there,
    My unknown mother.
    Where is my sweetheart
    Ilonka Londonvári?

13. She has gone to her flower garden
    To pick flowers,
    To pick flowers
    And to make a wreath of them.

14. She is not there, she is not there
    My unknown mother.
    Where is my sweetheart
    Ilonka Londonvári?

15. She has gone to the neighbour's
    To see her gossip,
    To see her gossip,
    To her girl friend.

16. She is not there, she is not there,
    My unknown mother.
    Where is my sweetheart
    Ilonka Londonvári?

17. There is no more word to waste,
    She is in the room,
    And she is laid out
    On a beautiful, green cushion.

18. The bridegroom went in,
    Mad with sorrow,
    Mad with sorrow,
    He drove a knife into his heart.

Újszász (Pest county). Performed by a 12-year-old girl. Bartók 1918 = Bartók 1924 161.

31.

Poco rubato

1. Lá-nyom, é-des lá-nyom, Fo-dor Ka-ta-li-na,

Mi-cso-da do-log az,   A te rá-sa-szoknyád
E-lül rö-vi-de-dik,   Há-tul hosszab-bo-dik?

152

1. Daughter, my dear daughter
   Katalina Fodor,
   What is the matter with you,
   That your skirt of fine cloth

(To the 3rd and 4th melodic sections:)

   Is getting short at the front,
   And getting long at the back?

2. Mother, my dear mother,
   Mistress Péter Sárfodor:
   The tailor did not cut it properly,
   The seamstress did not sew it properly.

3. Daughter, my dear daughter,
   Katalina Fodor,
   The tailor has cut it properly,
   The seamstress has sewed it properly.

4. Mother, dear mother,
   Mistress Péter Sárfodor,
   I should in vain deny it,
   I must own it up,

(To the 3rd and 4th melodic sections:)

   That I have been lusty
   For six months.

5. My servants, my servants,
   My kind servants,
   Seize her, take her,
   Throw Katalina Fodor

(To the 4th melodic section:)

   Into the deep prison!

6. Daughter, my dear daughter,
   Katalina Fodor,
   Are you alive or are you dead already
   In the deep prison?

7. Mother, my dear mother,
   Mistress Péter Sárfodor,
   I am neither alive nor dead,
   But I am praying to God.

8. Mother, my dear mother,
   Mistress Péter Sárfodor,
   Last night I had a dream,
   And saw a vision:

(To the third and fourth melodic sections:)

> I had my fine scarlet gown
> Cast over my shoulders,
> I had my yellow shoes
> On my feet,
> I had a scourge of two tails
> In my hand.

9. Daughter, my dear daughter
   Katalina Fodor,
   Your fine, scarlet gown
   Means your red blood.

10. Your yellow shoes
    Mean your yellow complexion,
    The scourge of two tails
    Means the hangmen to come for you.

11. My God, my God,
    Send down your angel
    In the image of a bird,
    So that I may write a letter

(To the third and fourth melodic sections:)

> To György Hédervári,
> To János Györgyvári.

12. My little bird, my little bird,
    Take my letter!
    If you meet him at lunch,
    Put it on his table,

(To the third and fourth melodic sections:)

> If you meet him asleep,
> Put it on his pillow.

13. Grooms, my grooms,
    My faithful grooms!
    Don't mind if dogs will devour
    My six palfreys fed on oats,

(To the third and fourth melodic sections:)

> We must get alive
> Katalina Fodor.

14. Mother, my dear mother,
    Mistress Péter Sárfodor,
    Where is your daughter
    Katalina Fodor?

15. I sent her down to the well
    To fetch drinking-water.
    In the mirror of the water
    She is looking at her own face.

16. Mother, my dear mother,
    Mistress Péter Sárfodor,
    Where is your daughter
    Katalina Fodor?

17. I do not deny it any more,
    I have to own it up:
    I have passed her
    Into the hangman's hands.

18. Let my blood flow with your blood
    In one and the same torrent,
    Let my body rest with your body
    In one and the same grave!

19. One of them was buried
    On the eastern side.
    The other was buried
    On the western side.

20. On the grave-mound of one of them
    There arose a beautiful walnut-tree.
    On the grave-mound of the other
    There nested a pair of turtle-doves, hatching the eggs.

21. The sad turtle-dove
    Is cooing and says:
    Cursed be the father,
    Still more the mother

(To the third and fourth melodic sections:)

    Who bid two lovers
    Part with each other!

Ghymes (Nyitra county). Performed by a 68-years-old woman. L. Vikár 1958 = AP 3467/d.

32.

Poco rubato

1. Lá - nyom, é - des lá - nyom, Mi lel - te ru - há - dat?

E -lől rö - vi - de - dik, Há - tul hosz - szab - bo - dik!

155

1. Daughter, my dear daughter,
   What is the matter with your dress?
   It is getting short at the front,
   It is getting long at the back!

2. The tailor did not cut it properly,
   The seamstress did not sew it properly,
   May God punish her,
   Alas, she has marred it for good!

3. Take her, devils,
   To the scaffold!
   Take my daughter
   To the scaffold!

4. Mother, my dear mother,
   Wait, pray, for an hour's time only,
   Wait, pray, only for an hour's time,
   Till I write my letter.

5. Swallow, my little swallow,
   Take my letter,
   Take my letter
   To master Gyöngyvári!

6. If you arrive there at noon,
   Put it on his plate,
   If you arrive there evening,
   Put it on his pillow.

7. I know, he will read it,
   He will soak it with his tears.
   Because of his flooding tears
   He will not be able to see the letters.

8. Coachman, my coachman,
   My fastest coachman,
   Harness six horses,
   The best of the horses!

9. You shall be the thunderbolt,
   I shall be its lightning,
   We must find
   Boriska Hangoli alive!

10. Good day, good day
    Unknown mother!
    Where can I find, where can I find
    Boriska Hangoli?

11. She has gone down to the Tisza
    To wash her handkerchiefs.

She wants to present them
To master Gyöngyvári.

12. I have been looking high, looking low,
Yet I have not found her.
Where can I find, where can I find
Boriska Hangoli?

13. She went into the flower garden
To pick lilies-of-the-valley.
She wants to present them
To master Gyöngyvári.

14. I have been looking high, looking low,
Yet I have not found her.
Where can I find, where can I find
Boriska Hangoli?

15. She went into the room
To lay the table,
To lay the table,
To arrange the plates.

16. I have been looking there, too,
Yet I could not find her.
Where can I find, where can I find
Boriska Hangoli?

17. Why should I deny any longer
If I have to own up to it in the end!
She is sleeping in her room,
She is resting in her bed.

18. The bridegroom enters,
Out of the pocket of his mantle
He draws a big knife
And drives it into his heart.

19. If I could not be yours
I shall not be someone else's!
Let my blood blind with yours
In one stream.

20. Let my body rest with yours
In one grave.
Let my soul worship
One God with yours!

21. Bury my body
In the middle of the church,
Bury our little babe
In front of the altar!

Bárna (Nógrád county). Performed by a team of girls. Kodály 1906.

33.

Parlando

1. Lá-nyom,é-des lá-nyom,Fo-dor Ka-ta-li-na,

Mi lé-te szok-nyá-dat? E-lü rö-vi-dö-dik, Há-tu hosz-szab-bo-dik!

1. Daughter, my dear daughter!
   Katalina Fodor!
   What's the matter with your skirt?
   It's getting short at the front
   It's getting long at the back!

2. Mother, dear mother,
   The tailor did not cut it properly,
   The tailor did not cut it properly,
   The seamstress did not sew it properly,
   The seamstress did not sew it properly.

3. Daughter, dear daughter,
   The tailor has cut it properly,
   The tailor has cut it properly,
   The seamstress has sewed it properly,
   The seamstress has sewed it properly.

4. Mother, dear mother,
   In vain should I deny,
   In vain should I deny,
   For I must own up to it in the end,
   For I must own up to it in the end:

5. János Gyöngyvári's,
   János Gyöngyvári's
   Child it is for eight months back,
   János Gyöngyvári's
   Child it is for eight months back.

6. Seize her and take her
   To the deepest prison,
   To the deepest prison,
   For fifteen days
   She shall be there in shackles of rough iron!

7. On the fifteenth day
   Her elder brother went there.
   Her elder brother went there,
   Onto the door of the prison,
   Onto the door of the prison.

8. Sister, my dear sister,
   Katalina Fodor,
   Are you alive or are you dead?
   Sister, my dear sister,
   Are you alive or are you dead?

9. Brother, my dear brother,
   I am neither alive nor dead,
   I am neither alive nor dead,
   But I am wailing here,
   I am wailing here!

10. Sister, my dear sister,
    Katalina Fodor,
    Write a letter
    To János Gyöngyvári,
    Who is your sweetheart.

11. Brother, my dear brother,
    I have not even a pen,
    I have not even a pen!
    Let then be pen for you
    The tips of your fingers.

12. Brother, my dear brother,
    I have not ink either,
    I have not ink either!
    Let then be ink for you
    Your pouring tears!

13. Brother, dear brother,
    But I have no one to carry the letter,
    I have no one to carry the letter!
    Let your letter be taken
    By the twittering swallow!

14. Brother, my dear brother,
    I am writing the letter,
    I am writing the letter
    To János Gyöngyvári,
    Who is my sweetheart.

15. My God, my God,
    I am taken to the scaffold,
    I am taken to the scaffold,
    In the field of Simeon,
    In the field of Simeon!

16. Swallow, my dear swallow,
    Carry my letter,
    Carry my letter

To János Gyöngyvári,
Who is my sweetheart!

17. If you get there in the morning,
Light on his bedstead,
Light on his bedstead!
If you get there by noon,
Light on his plate!

18. If you get there in the evening,
If you get there in the evening,
Light on his table,
If you get there in the evening,
Light on his table:

19. It got there by noon,
And lighted on his plate,
It lighted on the plate
And János Gyöngyvári
Dropped his spoon,

20. János Gyöngyvári
Mounted his horse at once,
Mounted his horse at once,
And rode to the field of Simeon
Without waisting time.

21. He was waving from afar
A red Viennese kerchief,
He was waving from afar
Thus he saved her sweetheart
From the gallows.

22. Dearest heart, my only love,
Katalina Fodor!
Come, then, nearer now!
Come, then, nearer now!
Let me embrace you on my heart!

23. She went close to him,
He took her in his arms,
He took her in his arms.
But the beautiful loving pair
Still lost their lives.

24. One of them was buried
Before the altar,
Before the altar,
The other was buried
Behind the altar.

25. On their grave there arose
    Two beautiful stems of rosemary-flower,
    Two beautiful stems of rosemary-flower,
    Even these leaned together,
    Even these leaned together.

26. The mother went there,
    The mother went there
    To lament her daughter,
    The mother went there
    To lament her daughter.

27. Of the rosemary flower
    She broke off a branch,
    She broke off a branch.
    A drop of blood
    Spurted out from it at once.

28. Daughter, my dear daughter,
    Katalina Fodor,
    Rise up from your grave,
    Rise up, my dear daughter,
    Rise up from your grave!

29. Mother, dear mother,
    Let my body rest in peace,
    Let my body rest in peace!
    Even though you did not let me live,
    Let my body rest in peace!

Magyaregregy (Baranya county). Performed by a 69-year-old woman. 1936 = Berze Nagy, 165.

Divergences: a) Regions I–III in Hungary

In the western and northern parts of the country the following names occur with highest frequency: Dorka Londonvári, mostly in the form of Idorka Londonvári (14), since the Christian name "Dorka" is not currently used in the regions: sometimes Dolka or Dajka Londonvari also come up. Further variants are: Ilona Londonvári (5), Ibolya, Ilonka of the Londonváris, Idol Londonvár (14), Idol Londonvár, Dorka Landorvári (12), Madam Londonvári, Mrs. Landorvárai, Dorka Lendorvári (3), Idol Londolvár, Ridolba Londonba, Dorka Nándorvári (Dajka Nándorvári) (5), Idorka Nándorgó (in the same environment, however, they speak about twelve daughters of the count Londonvári), Dorka Londoványi (2), Idorka Nándorvári or Idorka Gondorvár, (2), Kati Hédervári (3), Kata Szedervári (2), Katica Szegvári (4).

Names of this type are territorially alternating with the rarer Katalina Fodor (10).

In eastern Hungary we encounter more frequently with the name of Borbála Angoli (or Mistress Angoli) (5) and its variants: Borbála Angoldi (9), Borbála Angola (2), Mrs. Angolvári, Borbála Angora (2), Borbella Angora (1), Boriska Angodi (6), Zsuzsánna Angodi (2), Borbála Hangodi (3), Borbála Ungodi (3), Ilonka Ungvári, Borbála Amboli (2), Borbála Angyalon, Boriska Hamvadi, Noble Lady Hollódi, Borbála Andorla and Borbála Andale.

The mother is sometimes called "Princess of Ujbécs" (Újbécs = a mediaeval Hungarian village near Pest!) (3), and the girl "Young Lady of Vienna". The bridegroom is usually called Király Kis Miklós (Prince Miklós the King's son), or Master Gyöngyvári and János Gyöngyvári. Still other names come up occasionally, and not infrequently the characters are called by their Christian names.

The ballad is often begun with a borrowed formula: for instance, the head of the ballad contains a fairly recent folksong about a girl put in the family way: "Good evening, brown girl, what has happened to you, Perhaps your supper did not taste good to you?" The continuation mentions the girl hardly being able to bind the belt at her waist, then a curse is said, sometimes in an extremely rude language, which is common in the folksong but mostly omitted when portions of the song are incorporated in the ballad (22 time, details in 7 instances). Another song beginning with the line: "You can see the white tower of the black town" (8), and further the initial formula of the song about the "Murdered spinning girl" are also used as the head of the ballad. In five instances a variant of a lyrical folksong is involved for the purpose: "I go up the hill and look down into the valley, There I see a mother clad in black from head to heel." When this is the starting formula, the bridegroom appears immediately in the continuation. Many a variant has preserved only this portion of the original ballad, rounding out the story with senseless additional details (49).

The variant entitled "Gyurica Görögfi" represent, one of the successful solutions by incorporating alien bodies into the text of the ballad (*Kallós* 1970 No. 102), which, however, is on the verge of becoming a new type or a self-contained branch of Hungarian balladry. The two inserted stanzas read as follows:

"Mother, mother, mother, dearest, kindest mother,
I see there, far away, a big, swarning camp,
I know the name of their captain:
Gyurica Görögfi, son of the Turkish emperor.

Grant me, mother, grant me at least a quarter of an hour,
So that I may go to see Gyurica Görögfi!
I will not grant, daughter, even the half of the half of that time,
Lest your should die and leave me for ever!

Then the story continues as usual: the bridegroom arrives and is sent hither and thither on wild goose chases. (The name being Mrs. Almádi.) The insertion echoes the beginning formula of the ballad about "The Bride Forced to Marry" **(12–13),** with the difference that here it is the girl that wants to marry and the mother that opposes the marriage, while in the mentioned ballad their roles are reversed. It is not impossible either that in this case we are dealing with the remains of some old story which had sunk in oblivion as a separate narrative.

162

The overwhelming majority, however, maintained the beginning formula of the motif of shortening of the skirt at the front. (There is one text which adds that the girl's face has become spotty.) A further detail of the girl's confession is the following: "The one who has sued for me seven times during the last Carneval, Has put me in the family way seven months ago."—"For Prince Miklós the King's Son I laid the green bed, I laid the green bed, And I fell in love with him."—"I have been walking in my flower-garden, And I fell in love With János Gyöngyvári, My sweetheart, Under a rose-tree". (Elsewhere: Under an apple-tree).

Before sending the letter, she asks for leave to say farewell to her flowers and clothes: "My flowers, my flowers, may you wither away to your roots, My clothes, my clothes, may you fall down from the peg.", and the like (20). She trusts the letter to the care of a swallow, sometimes a stork, a turtledove: in some instances she first precludes the possibility of a crow or a magpie to conclude on a swallow. Often enough she writes the letter with her tears, and once we have the following variation:

I have neither ink
Nor pen to write with.
You will have for ink
Your red blood,
For pen to write with
You will have your tiny, white nail."

(Baracska, Fejér county.)

The writing of the letter is sometimes preceded, or even replaced, by the scene in which the girl recounts her dream to her mother: she had her scarlet gown on her shoulders, her yellow shoes on her feet, a scourge of two tails in her hand, the red colour meaning her red blood, the yellow colour the two hangmen. (It should be noted that in mediaeval times disgraced women were branded with some sort of symbol of yellow colour.) It is also interesting to observe that the instruction given to the bird is mostly built up by means of alliteration:

Ha délben találod,
Tedd a tányérjára,

Ha ebéden éred
Tedd a tányérjára,
Ha vacsorán éred,
Tedd a vánkosára,

Ha früstökön éred,
Vesd a findzsájára.

When the lover receives the letter, we read the following stereotyped lines:

He is reading, reading it,
Shedding his tears,
Dropping the silver spoon
Out of his hand.

Coachman, my coachman,
My fastest coachman,
Prepare me
The lightest coach!
Drive, coachman, drive,
Even though each of them will die,
Never mind,
Even if they will be devoured by dogs!

This scene well known from the "Walled-up Wife" appears sometimes in combination with the scenes of "The Two Chapel Flowers" (in any case, in the text it comes up together with the grave-flower). For instance:

Harness, coachman,
Harness six black horses
To the black coach!
Load the coach
With three bags
Of silver and gold!

(*In prose:* When the young gentleman occupied his seat in his coach, he said to the coachman:)

Drive, coachman, drive!
And I drove, and I drove
Until an old beggar man
Crossed my path.
I asked the old beggar man:
Why are people crowding over there?
It is Kati Szedervári
That is taken to be hanged.
Drive, coachman, drive!
The faster you drive
The surer you will get my coach
And the six black horses.
By the time they got there
Two of the horses had died.

(This formula is repeated twice, after several subsequent stanzas.)

"Coachman, my coachman,
Drive, my dear coachman!
You shall have the two horses
And the coach with the glass-windows."

"Coachman, my coachman,
Drive, my dear coachman!
You shall have my six horses
And the silver-mounted harness!"

164

Instead thunderbolt and lightning, some variants use other formulas, to express the plea to drive fast:

> Let us run like the wind-storm,
> Or like the thought,
> So that we may find alive
> My dearest sweetheart!

Occasionally the meeting with the old man is represented in a different way, for example:

> Grand-dad, grand-dad,
> Elderly grand-dad,
> What are those white creatures
> Around the gallows?
> Are those white things geese,
> Or perhaps sheep grazing?
> Those white things are neither geese
> Nor sheep grazing,
> But they are busy with hanging
> Kata Szedervári,
> Kata Szedervári,
> Who is a dame of fame.

(The old man received a box on the ear; another old man came, saying "Who was a beautiful girl", and got a hundred pengős.)

> Dear sirs, dear sirs,
> My dear sirs of Gyöngyvár!
> May I ask a favour?
> May I say a word or two?
> Aye, you may say not one and not two
> But twelve words, if you please!

(He went to the girl and embraced and kissed her.) Then follows the formula "May my blood flow with yours..." In several texts he kisses the hanged girl and then both of them die. (This scene is misunderstood in No. *33*, in which we read: "By this he rescued her", though the continuation reports on the death of the two lovers.) Another speech delivered at the gallows field reads as follows:

> My sirs and young gentlemen,
> Do stay your decree,
> Do stay your decree,
> Your dire decree!
> Let me say
> The Lord's prayer three times!
> One for my own sake,
> Another for my Dorka,
> And the third for our little babe!

There is only one variant, recorded from Gyimes region, in which the bridegroom rescues his sweetheart.

The final motif of the grave flower that is broken off and made to speak occurs in counties Zala, Somogy, Baranya (once in each), Veszprém (2), Nyitra, Bars, Hont, Nógrád (2), Esztergom (2), Heves and Torontál. (That is, in a total of fourteen instances we have the mentioned motif.) Beside the grave-flower, the birds come up in additional variants, like:

> On the grave of one of them
> There arose two rosemary flowers,
> On the grave of the other
> There appeared two sad turtledoves.
> The sad turtledoves
> Kept on cooing:
> Cursed be the father,
> And seven-times cursed be the mother.

(Ricse, Zemplén county)

> On the grave of one of them there arose
> A white dove,
> On that of the young man
> A white cockerel.
> The little white dove
> Keeps on cooing:
> Cursed be, cursed be
> The mother
> Who denies her daughter
> To marry to her sweetheart!
> The white cockerel
> Keeps on crowing:
> Cursed be the father...

(Ószentiván, Torontál county.)

Further examples recorded from Kisbér, Hédervár, Gyimes (3). The curse sometimes ends with the words of the Sister of the Man Condemned to Death.

It is interesting to note that the informant in one fragmentary variant, which starts with the arrival of the bridegroom, tries to explain his confused story by stating that "The Fair Mariska happened to meet with a richer suitor, and this is why the murder had to take place". Another informant insists, on the basis of what he had heard from his mother, that the event took place at a farmstead in the vicinity of Tarpa.

b) IV. Transylvania, Bukovina; V. Moldavia

We find a separate group of variants in the Transylvanian regions. There the following names occur: Zsuzsánna Homlódi (7), (variations: Komlódi, Omlódi, Homlódi), Zsuzsánna Hollódi, Young Maid Zsuzsánna, Mihály Holmódi, Mrs. Székvári; rather frequently they have simply Aranyos Bözsikém (Darling Betty); in one single example also the Lord of Gyöngyvár appears. Another characteristic

166

feature, beside the fairly uniform use of personal names, consists in a similarly uniform fragmentary state of the variants. The beginning formula here tends to amalgamate with the song "Good evening, brown girl" in a still higher percentage. (This occurs in 26 instances, that is in fifty per cent of the variants.) Instead of the sending of the letter, we mostly have the lengthy farewell speech of the girl, which she says to her clothes, flowers, girl friends, etc. (33). With this done, the majority of the variants are ended, that is the dénouement proper is missing. (24). As against these, a smaller portion of the variants start with the bridegroom's arrival (7), which is equally detrimental to the development of the story. Apart from these, there exist what might be called real fragments, so that in the final issue there are but two variants that might be regarded as complete in themselves, and even in these the motif of the bird bringing the bride's message is wanting. Furthermore, we have come across a complete variant at Bardóc, which cannot be aligned with the rest of the variants because it is a mere echo of *Bartók's* text collected at Újszász, indeed, even the names of Ibolya Londorvár and Miklós Kiskirály are sufficient to arouse our suspicion, since they are unknown in Transylvania. Someone may have learned this variant in Hungary at a more recent time, or perhaps from a book; by no means can it be considered an old Transylvanian tradition. (Nor can be considered as such the text of *Jób Sebesi* which contains all the details known from the first version described from Hungary, even though in strongly transcribed forms and attached to "Küküllővár".) Still further to the east, in Moldavia, only broken fragments of the ballad can be discovered, contaminated with the story of "The Emperor of Hungary" and of "The Miraculous Mill", and even these begin with the arrival of the bridegroom.

Earliest provenience: 1872, details: 1857.
Dissemination: Without mentioning the place: 3.

I. Sopron country (Bősárkány), Vas county (Csörötnek, Katafa), Zala county (Balatonederics, Csácsbozsok, Cserespuszta, Hahót, Kávás, Kerkakutas 2, Murarátka, Nova, Oltárc 2, Orosztony, Rédics 3, Resznek, Szentgyörgyvölgy, Szombatfa 2, Zalacsány, Zalagalsa), Somogy county (Berzence, Mosdós, Nagyatád, Öreglak, Riticspuszta, Szöllősgyörök), Verőce county (Haraszti, Lacháza, Lászlófalva, Szentlászló 2), Baranya county (Hegyszentmárton, Kiskőszeg, Kopács, Magyaregregy, Mohács, Pécsarányos, Püspökszenterzsébet, Szaporca, Téseny), Tolna county (Miszla, Mőcsény, Ozora, Szekszárd), Fejér county (Alap, Baracska, Cece, Ercsi, Pákozd, Pusztaforma), Veszprém county (Bakonyszentlászló, Csögle, Réde, Rezi, Rigács, "Somlóvidék", Szentgál, Veszprém, Veszprémhidegkút [Germans performing in Hungarian]), Komárom county (Ászár, Császár, Kisbér, Tata), Győr county (Hédervár, Szemere, Támlánypuszta). Total in Region I: 71.

II. Pozsony, county (Martos), Nyitra county (Bodok, Csitár, 2, Ghymes 7, Kolon, Mocsonok, Pográny, Tardoskedd, Vicsápapáti, Zsére 2), Trencsén county (Trencsénteplic), Bars county (Lédec), Hont county (Füzesgyarmat, Ipolyszög, Kemence, Perőcsény), Esztergom county (Bajna, Libád, Nagysáp, Pilismarót), Nógrád county (Bárna, Bernecebaráti, Bocsárlapujtő 2, Buják, Dejtár, Héhalom, Mihálygerge, Nógrádmegyer, Szanda, Szandaváralja 2, Szécsény, Tereske 3, Uppony), Heves county (Besenyőtelek, Bükkszenterzsébet, Eger, Erdőkövesd, Erdőtelke, Fedémes 2, Feldebrő, Füzesabony, Gyöngyös 2, Hevesaranyos, Istenmezeje, Nagyvisnyó, Ostoros, Recsk, Tarnalelesz, Visznek), Borsod county (Edelény, Mezőkövesd, Szentistván 2), Abaúj county (Cekeháza, Fóny, Göncruszka, Kéked, Nagyszalánc), Zemplén county (Bodrogkeresztúr, Gesztely, Ricse 3, Sárospatak 2, Tőketerebes), Bereg county (Lónya 2, Tarpa, "Tiszahát"), Máramaros county (Hosszúmező). Total in Region II: 85.

III. Pest county (Abony, Alpár, Isaszeg, Kiskunfélegyháza, Kiskunmajsa, Kunszentmiklós, Újszász 2, Vácszentlászló), Jász-Nagykun-Szolnok county (Jánoshida, Jásztelek, Karcag, Ókécske,

Tiszasas), Bácsbodrog county (Bácskertes 2, Pince), Torontál county (Csóka, Egyházaskér 2, Ószentiván, Szaján 2, Tiszahegyes), Csongrád county (Algyő, Ásotthalom, Csongrád, "Csongrád county", Hódmezővásárhely 3, Horgos, Nagymágocs, Röszke, Szeged), Csanád county (Apáca, Magyarbánhegyes) Békés county (Békésszentandrás, Bélmegyer 3, Dévaványa, Doboz 3, Endrőd, Körösladány, Mezőgyán, Orosháza 2, Pusztaföldvár 2, Sarkadkeresztúr 3, Újkígyós 2, Vésztő), from the Lower Tisza Region, *s. l.* 4, Arad county (Gyorok), Bihar county (Biharkeresztes, Biharugra, Csökmő, Értarcsa, Körösnagyharsány 4, Nagyszalonta 2), Hajdú county (Hajdúdorog), Szabolcs county (Nyírbátor 2, Nyírlugos, Nyírmada, Nyírtura, Nyírvaja, Rétközberencs, Tiszakarád), Szatmár county (Avasújváros, Gebe, Vállaj). Total in Region III: 85.

IV. Kolozs county (Kötelend, Válaszút 2, Visa 5, Vista) Torda-Aranyos county (Bágyon, Sinfalva, Torda 3), Maros-Torda county (Jobbágytelke, Kibéd 2, Szabéd, Szentgerice 3), Alsó-Fehér county (Lőrincréve, Nagyenyed), Udvarhely county (Etéd, "the riverine of the Fehér-Nyikó", Homoródújfalu, Kénos, Szombatfalva, Tarcsafalva, Tordátfalva, Zetelaka 2), Csík county (Borszék, "Csík county", Gyergyóalfalu, Gyergyóditró, Gyergyógilyénfalva, Gyergyótekerőpatak, Gyimesközéplok, Gyimesvölgye-Ugrapataka, Karcafalva), Háromszék county (Bardóc, Bereck, Sepsibükszád), "Székelyföld" 3, Bukovina (Hadikfalva 4, Józseffalva), Moldavia (Gerlén, Lészped 2). Total in Region IV–V: 55. *Sum total:* 299, *sine loco:* 3, I–III: 241, IV: 55.

Textual relationships with other ballads: Dream foreboding evil: **23;** "My flowers, my flowers"... : **11–13., 15., 29., 31.;** "Coachman, my dear coachman, harness my coach of six...": **2., 9., 21., 39.;** Questioning an old beggar, miller or shepherd: **9.;** Graveflower: **9., 28., 37., 38., 48. (68.);** "Let my blood flow with yours...": **11., 19., 21.;** sending here and there; **12., 28.**

Tunes: 1 = No. *29,* in 11 variants; *2* = No. 30; *3* = No 31, in 11 variants; *4* = No. 32, in 22 variants, mostly with the incipit of *s s m, s s m; 5* = No 33; *6* (16 variants) *7* (35 variants); *8* (13 variants); *10* (3 variants); *12* (2 variants); *14* (6 variants); *16* (3 variants); *22* (3 variants); *23* (25 variants); *28* (3 variants); (*7, 8, 12* and *14* are branching off from the same melody).

Versions in languages other than Hungarian:

PORTUGUESE: *1–24. Braga* I, 309–417 (356 = *Geibel–Schack* 83) II, 222. *25. Hardung,* 195. *26. Wolf,* 109.

CATALAN: *27 Amades* 3263.

Spanish: *28–31. Wolf* and *Hofmann* II, 191–192, 158 (=*Geibel* and *Schack* 407), 138. *32–35. Cossio* and *Solano* I, 18/58–61. *36. Cossio* 14, (Further Iberian variants enumerated by *Armistead* and *Silverman* 1971, 82–92, Note 7.)

ENGLISH: *37–44. Child* 65/A–H. *45–46. Sharp·K* 17A–B. *47–57. Bronson* 65/1–11 (12–13 = *Sharp-K.*).

GERMAN: *58–60.* D. Vlr 67 (*58.* = The Upper Black Forest, *59.* = environs of Zurich, *60.* = Volga colony, originally environs of Zweibrücken).

RUSSIAN: Lintur reports that the ballad is known in the Trans-Carpathian Ukraine.

Partial variants:

(a) Shortening of the skirt:

ENGLISH: *61–64. Child* 100A, D, 101, 66A + 269C.

GERMAN: *65–394.* D. Vlr. 55. *395–454.* D. Vlr. 73 (certain variants).

GREEK: cf. D. Vlr. III, 47–49.

FRENCH: *455. Legrand* 25.

(b) "You have died for me...", or "Let my blood flow with yours in one stream..."

FRENCH: *456. Decombe* 96.

SLOVAK–MORAVIAN: *457. Sušil* 89/181. *458. Šrežnevskij* VII. *459. Kolečány* 13. *460. Medveczky* 1906, 253. *461.* Sl. Pohl. 1897, 497. *462. Sušil* 92/193. *463. Bartók* 1959 No. 324. (*458–463.* in the Cruel Mother-in-Law).

UKRAINIAN: *464. Golovatski* II, 710 No. 13.

SIBERIAN: *465* Radloff II. No. 2, lines 57–9. *466.* Ibid. No. 5, lines 1194–6. *467.* Ibid. No. 6, line 434. *468.* Ibid. No. 19, lines 1416–9. *469.* Ibid. No. 14, around line 2800. *470,* Ibid. No. 21, lines 739–40. *471.* Dyrenkova, 15 para 3 line 3.

The name of the heroine (Borbála Angoli = Barbara of England, or Dorka Londonvári = Dolly of London Castle) in itself suggests French or Netherlandish origin; personal names of this type refer to foreign origin, always indicating that the hero or heroine belongs to a *neighbouring* nation: in the Hungarian-speaking areas, the same practice prevails inasmuch as German or Turkish origin is indicated in Hungary proper, Moldavian in Transylvania, Polish in Moldavia. With the French, on the same principle, Spanish or *English* names are involved. (For example, in the ballad *Le mariage anglais* the foreign bridegroom is an English man.) Thus the

170

names in the Hungarian ballad point to the French or Dutch areas as the origin of the ballad. Let us see what lessons can be drawn from this circumstance regarding the dissemination of the ballad.

Among the Germans the plot and the formulas are divided into three different types. One of them, called the "König von Mailand" (The King of Milan), is a story known in three variants, which has been found only along the French frontiers between Zweibrücken and Zurich, at three points along the Rhine. The second known as the "Ritter und Magd" is found throughout Germany, and the third is the "Schwabentöchterlein". The story of the first ballad is as follows: A king is entertaining a large crowd of guests; One of them makes love to the King's daughter and then departs. The girl gives birth to the child and her brother helps to keep the matter secret. But the mother finds out, and persuades the King to have his daughter executed. The girl writes a letter to her lover, in one variant with blood from her finger, and her brother goes to deliver it to the knight, but he finds the latter has gone out riding. When the knight returns and sees the letter, his eyes fill with tears so that he can hardly read it. He has his horse saddled, and hurries with his knights to rescue the girl. Before she is to be hanged, the girl asks them to wait, for she can hear the hoofbeats of her darling's steed. The hangman takes pity on her, and the knight arrives in time to save her. He stabs the mother to death and carries his sweetheart off to his home. The father later visits them and is reconciled with the young couple.

Although the story shows considerable agreements with the Hungarian, the differences are still more significant. Instead of the discovery of the girls gravidity, the narrative starts from the preliminaries and relates the developments in the chronological order; the child is born but there is no tragic consequence in the end. At the same time, the typical motif of the girl's skirt getting shorter at the front is missing.

But the other two German ballads contain the formula of the shortening skirt, though embedded in a different plot. The "Ritter und Magd" tells about a knight who has spent a night with a peasant girl and tries to pay her off in the morning (in some variants he offers her to his servant). The girl rejects the offer and sadly sets off for home. The mother calls to her from afar: "How have you fared, daughter? I see your skirt is long at the back and too short at the front!" The girl dies in childbirth. The knight has a dream in which the girl appears to him; he rises and goes to see her. But on his arrival sees only the funeral procession. He plunges his dagger into his own breast. The "Schwabentöchterlein", too, has but the shortening of the skirt in common with the Hungarian ballad, similarly embedded in a completely different story.

The heroine of the corresponding English ballad is besieged by suitors in vain. Finally the girl imparts to her brother that she is with child to a knight. Her parents discover this, and her father examines her condition and determines to have her executed. "O where will I get a bonny boy to carry my letter!" cries the girl. A page undertakes the mission. The knight at once has his horse saddled, and rides to the rescue. The girl, now at the stake, hears the approaching hoofbeats but in vain does she asks her brother to put out the flames; and the lover arriving too late wreaks vengeance on the girl's family.

In one variant the girl's brother exposes her condition with the following words: What's come o a' your long claithing, was aince for you too tite?" What is more, a vague reflection also seems to be made by the girl concerning the person who has spoiled her dress: "O he that made my claithing short, I hope he'll make them side; And he that made my stays narrow, I hope he'll make them wide"; although these words refer to the child to be born, and are rather a confession than concealment of the matter (with a duplicity of meaning typical of balladry, as well as of stage plays). But here, too, this motif has been incorporated into other ballad types, just like with the Germans: the pregnant girl's father, the king, bids the girl undress so that he can see whether she is still a maid, "her petticoats they were short, her face it was pale and wan, and her haunches were round". Or: "Her petticoats they were so short, she was full nine months gone." (Cf. the partial variants enumerated above, nearer to the Hungarian version in so far at least that one variant contains, even though in a faded form, the motif of the badly fitting clothes; on the other hand, there is no actual birth, and the ending is likewise tragic, for here, too, the lover arrives too late to rescue his sweetheart.)

A still closer relationship can be discovered in the corresponding Spanish–Portuguese ballad. This is introduced by several differing preliminaries, relating how the lovers spent the night together, the young man's vow to seduce her, and the way the secret comes out; in fact, there are such texts, too, in which the girl conceives from the water of a particular spring, which beginning has nothing to do with the further development of the story. The introduction, however, is often omitted, and this shows that the sundry preliminary stories are later developments. Where the introduction is omitted, the plot begins at once with the scene where the shortening of the dress is discovered, and in such instances not only the spoilt shape of the dress appears in the texts but also the girl's excuses about how the tailor has spoilt it. She was sitting with her father at a table, and her father was looking hard at her: "Donna Areira, it seems to me that you are with child." "The tailors are at fault, they cut my skirt badly." He called the tailors to him behind closed doors. They looked at one another, then said: "There is nothing wrong with the skirt, in nine months' time it will again reach to the ground." (In other variants the king begins like this: "How ugly your dress is!", or "after a few months were gone, her dress began to heave.") The father has his daughter detained and the pile of faggots prepared. The girl sends a page to her lover with a letter. "If he is asleep, wake him, if you find him awake, give him the letter", or "If you find him at dinner, make him leave the table; if he is walking about, give him the letter at once.", "If you find him at the window, hand it over to him", and so on, as in the Hungarian variations. As he reads the letter, he breaks down and weeps. He has his horses saddled and shod. Then follows the Iberian deviation: he dresses in friar's clothes and appears at the place of execution to shrive the girl, and this manages to escape with her; this scene is given much colourful detail. Thus we have again a happy ending in place of the tragic one. In some Catalan variants we find the letter, too, written with blood in place of ink; this motif is commented on in the complete German edition as a wandering motif not particularly attached to any definite type of ballad, because it does not at all acknowledge the possibility of a relationship between the enumerated ballads for reasons of hardly conceivable territorial interconnections.

172

Yet, this connection is substantiated by the existence of the Hungarian ballad Borbála Angoli. To wit, this contains all the elements which are to be found scattered here and there, one by one, in the Portuguese–Spanish, the English, and the three separate German types. Even the motif of the message sent by the bird is understandable, if we bear in mind what a commonplace this is in the French lyrical songs and ballads. It follows, therefore, that there must have been once a French ballad, now lost, which contained every element found in the Hungarian ballad, and even its structure might have been identical with the Hungarian, that is it started at once with the shortening skirt. This supposition is the more plausible because the French ballads know best of all how to reduce the plot to the essential elements, and how to exploit the facility of beginning the story *in medias res*. The story passed from them to the neighbouring peoples, with more or less alterations, omissions and amplifications, and from the French, too, it came directly to Hungary, where it has been able to survive in a broadly similar form without omissions, till today.

A Hungarian formulation of the ballad under discussion, including all the essential motifs, cannot be imagined without an intervening French version. The Hungarians could not have picked the various elements from so many places, to reunite them into a new story. Had it been otherwise, then the Hungarian ballad should have borrowed the framework of the story from the Rhine area, or even from the more remote English-speaking territories; further, it should have dropped the preliminary tale, so as to begin at once with the shortening skirt, which motif again ought to have been taken over from another German variant (where it is found in a form closest to the Hungarian), and then to continue by inserting the Iberian motif of the girl's excuses, blaming the tailors for the bad shape of her skirt, and the similarly Iberian formula of sending the message (If you find him at table...); to apply a tragic ending borrowed from the English and to contrive a formula in which the bridegroom is sent here and there on wilde-goose chases: all this would seem impossible, indeed. On the other hand, all this can be readily explained by the assumption that there used to be an intermediary French ballad which the Hungarians acquired from French settlers within the boundaries of Hungary.

Anyway, the existence of a multiplicity of mosaic-like fragments around a void space ought to have directed attention to the French area, where eroded remains of the ballad discussed still survive. To mention a few examples, we may refer, first of all, to the motif of the shortening skirt occurring, now in a quite indistinct form, in one of the French songs (*455.*); the parents have a dress made for their daughter "which is short at the back and long at the front". This, of course, makes no sense, but shows clearly that the motif used to exist in the French-speaking areas. This is confirmed by the occurrence of the motif in the Greek language area, too, where it may have arrived together with other stories of French origin. Still more interesting from this point of view is *Verrier's* article (1937) bringing into correlation a Danish ballad with a mediaeval French text in which a possible literary antecedent of the ballad of "The Disgraced Girl" can be detected. The French text speaking about "Belle Aiglentine" had been inserted into the epic poem of Jean Renart who, according to *Verrier,* must have found it among the people as a popular, short, possibly strophic song. Fair Aiglentine is sitting in the bower of her dame (mother?) and is sewing a shirt in her presence, but she does the work somewhat differently from her usual way, and pricks her finger. The dame (mother) notices it and asks her to undress so that she may see her "noble body". The girl says she is cold and refuses to undress. The dame (mother) continues her questioning: why is she so pale and why is she getting thicker and thicker? "My dear mother (dame), I cannot deny it any longer, I fell in love and have lain with Knight Henry. If ever you have been in love, show mercy to me!" The mother persuades her to go and see the Knight, whom she succeeds in convincing that their marriage has to be concluded. Indeed, he marries the girl. The opening scene is a commonplace occurring in many Danish ballads: the heroine always appears sewing in her bower, distraught and pricking her finger; this scene answers exactly to the common European formula: "She has been sewing in the window..." *Verrier* discovers the mentioned poem in the beginning scene of some of the Danish variants. The "clumsy manner" in which they are fitted together betrays in DgF 83 and 265 (and in some other type) that a borrowed scene has been applied as a preliminary to certain other stories which are recited without this introduction in other instances. In my opinion, however, this text could not be their preliminary story, rather we may think of a popular ballad developed from it because the discovery involves a tragic ending in the Danish versions as well, and there are still other partial correspondences with the common European ballad formula which are absent in the literary text.

The motif of sending the bridegroom to and fro under various pretexts and the recognition of the irrevocable fatal act is known in many places in Europe. We shall enter into this question in more detail when we deal with the type "The Bride Found Dead". (Type **12.**)

The strong erosion and the eighteenth-century revival of the French ballads in a different formulation make it understandable that a French ballad had gone into oblivion in its own country but survived in Hungary and several other countries. Thus here is one more ballad which the Hungarians had borrowed from the French, together with the others whose original are still extant in French-speaking areas.

In practically every variant of this ballad, and occasionally in other ballads too, there occurs the following closing formula: "May my blood flow in one stream with yours, my body rest in one grave with yours, my soul worship one God with yours." In a recently discovered variant from the Mezőség, after "my blood with yours" follows "my bones with yours". This formula is in our ballad put into the mouth of the bridegroom who killed himself over the body of his dead bride, and is unique in Western Europe. The French and German formula used in a similar situation is different: "Puisqu' elle est morte pour moi, je veux mourir pour elle", "Hast du gelitten den bittern Tod, so will ich leiden Schmerzen", which is also used sometimes by the Hungarians before the formula above.

Berze Nagy established long ago (1940 I, 219) that passages corresponding to our formula figure in Abakan heroic songs as a form of ceremony for making the formation of friendship. *463.* "When we die, may our souls be together, if our blood flows, may it flow together" they said, and so saying they became friends. *464.* "Like two ears is how we wish to be friends, when we die, may our bones be together, if our blood flows, may it flow together." *465.* "When we die, may our bones be together, if our blood flows, may it be together, let us all three be friends". *466.* "Come to me, if things go ill with me, and if things go ill with you, I will come to you. May our bones make one heap, our outpoured blood one stream." *467.* "We wish to be friends always, like the two horns of a cow, we wish to see our dead bodies, we will follow our destroyed souls." *468.* "When we die, may our bones make one hill, if our blood flows, may it make one river." *469.* "When the immortal, indestructible Kartyga Pergen dies, may my blood and his be together, if he walks alive, may our souls be together."

The correspondence appears in places to be quite literal; no doubt they would be even closer if the Turkish text were compared with the Hungarian.

Moreover similar formulas appear among our neighbours, too, corresponding to the Hungarian formulation. Slovak: "Neh tam leži telo s telom, A dve duši s Pánom Bógom" (*452.*) "Nak tu leži duša s dušou . . ." (*460.*) Similarly in *463.* "Leži tady s tělo s tělom, dve dušicky s Pánem Bohem" (*457.*) "Zostavaj tu tělo s tělem a dušičky s Panem Bohem" (*462.*) *458–463.* in The Cruel Mother-in-law. Ukrainian: "A tak edno telo leglo s drugim telom, Dushi spochivayut s milym panom Bogom". (*464.* variant of the Speaking Corpse.)

This ballad belongs to the earliest borrowings in the fourteenth century.

Literature: Gragger 1926: related to the "Ritter und Magd". *Zhirmunsky* 1928: "König aus Mailand", and parallel English and Iberian variants; *Ortutay* 1936: "The ballad has a general spread and is known practically all over Europe", quotes *Child* 63 (?), 65 and 101 (partial variants of the shortening skirt), E–B 97 and 110 (Ritter und Magd), and the German variants published by *Zhirmunsky; Verrier* 1937: compares the Danish ballads with a French poem from the thirteenth century; *Dános* 1938: quotes *Ortutay. Meier* 1941: connects the German variants with Fleur et Blanchefleur and three other ballads; *Ortutay* 1948: = 1936; D. Vlr. 67, 1954: rejects *Zhirmunsky*'s view that the English and Iberian variants are connected with the German; *Csanádi and Vargyas* 1954: ballad-subject known throughout Europe; mentions *Meier*'s view on the Blanchefleur connection; *Vargyas* 1960 and 1967: French origin; *Armistead–Silverman* 1971: full survey of the Iberian variants, together with the comparative material.

11. THE BRIDE DRAGGED TO DEATH

34.

Poco rubato ♪= 140

1. Rá - kó - ci kocs - má - bo Két ka - raj - cár a bor,

Ar - ra mén, ar - ra mén Sze - gény öz - vegy asz - szony.

1. In the inn of Rákóc
   Wine is to be had for two coppers.
   That way, that way
   A poor old woman is walking.

2. Come in, come in
   You poor old woman!
   Drink a pint of wine,
   Though you may drink two as well.

3. It is not at your cost,
   Nor is it at your son's,
   But at your maiden daughter's
   Katalina Bodor!

4. Daughter, my dear daughter,
   Katalina Bodor,
   I have sold you away*
   In the inn of Rákóc
   To the little lord of Rákóc!

5. Mother, my dear mother,
   My dear mother who gave birth to me and nursed me,
   Why did you give me away to a murderer,
   Which the little lord of Rákóc is,
   Sleeping in the day-time
   And going about murdering in the night-time?

6. Mother, my dear mother
   Who gave birth to me and nursed me,
   What troop is coming there,

That black troop:
Coming from the east
And going towards west?

7. Daughter, my dear daughter,
   Katalina Bodor,
   They are coming for you,
   The black troop.

8. Good morning, good morning to you,
   My dear mother-in-law!
   May God grant us one,
   Husband of my dear daughter!

9. Where can I find, where can I find
   My betrothed sweetheart?
   She is in the first room
   Tidying herself.

10. Good morning, good morning to you,
    My betrothed sweetheart!
    May God grant us one,
    Little lord of Rákóc!

11. Then he picks her up,
    Ties her to the tail of his horse
    And so he drags her through thistle and briar,
    And through bush.

12. Go slowly, go slowly,
    Young lord of Rákóc,
    For my red boots swim
    To the heels with blood!

13. Then he picks her up,
    And shortens the stirrup,
    And so he drags her through thistle and briar,
    And through bush.

14. Go slowly, go slowly,
    Young lord of Rákóc,
    For my beautiful silken dress swims
    To the waist with blood!

15. Then he picks her up,
    And shortens the stirrup,
    And so he drags her through thistle and briar,
    And through bush.

16. Go slowly, go slowly,
    My betrothed sweetheart!
    For my golden wreath
    Is half covered with blood!

17. Then he picks her up,
    Pressing her against his breast:
    What would you eat, what would you drink
    My betrothed sweetheart?

18. I wish neither to eat nor to drink,
    I only wish to lie in bed.
    I wish neither to eat nor to drink,
    I only wish to lie in bed.

19. What would you eat, what would you drink,
    My betrothed sweetheart?
    From my mother's table
    I would like to eat nice bird's wing,
    From my father's window
    I would like to drink good white wine.

20. Open, mother, open
    Your green gate,
    Make up, mother, make up
    A gay death-bed for me!

*The Hungarian phrase *eladni* (sell away) has a connotation (to give a girl in marriage) originating from ancient times when girls were sold in marriage for money or other objects of value (fur, for instance).

Törökkoppány (Somogy county). Performed by a 69-year-old woman. Lajtha 1938 = Gr. 21–22.

35.

1. Lá-nyom, é-dös lá-nyom, Mönj el a kis kert-be,
Bú-csuzz el vi-rág-tól, Vi-rág bim-ba-já tól.

1. Daughter, my dear daughter,
   Go down to the flower garden,
   Say farewell to the flowers,
   To the buds of flowers!

2. Mother, my dear mother,
   Shall I say farewell to them so soon?
   I have planted them with my own hands,
   I have watered them with my own hands.

3. Daughter, my dear daughter,
   Go into the chamber,
   Change your clothes
   And put on your mourning dress!

178

4. Mother, my dear mother,
   Why should I change clothes?
   I have cut this with my own hands,
   I have sewed this with my own hands.

5. Daughter, my dear daughter,
   Open your gate!
   For they are coming for you
   With a coach of six.

6. Mother, my dear mother,
   Who is coming for me
   With a coach of six?

7. Pár Vidrai's son,
   Who is to be your dear wedded spouse.
   And a spouse of the devil,
   But never mine while I am alive!

8. Pár Vidrai's son,
   Tie her to the tail of your horse,
   Drag her through thistle and bush,
   Drag her as long
   As she does not call you
   Her dear wedded spouse!

9. Drive slower, coachman,
   My dear postilion!
   For my flapping shirt of fine linen
   Is soaked with my tears,
   And my two little shoes
   Are filled with my blood!

10. Pár Vidrai's son
    Jumped off the coach,
    And he takes Katica Gyöngyvári
    In his arms.

11. Katica Gyöngyvári,
    My dear wedded spouse,
    What would you drink, what would you eat?
    What would taste good to you?
    O, tender wing of a jay,
    O, tender wing of a jay.

(By this time they reached the man's place.)

12. Pár Vidrai's son
    Takes his gun
    And goes into the woods

To get a jay.
He bagged the jay
And started for home, taking the bird.

13. Taking the bird
He hears the bell chiming.
Boys, boys,
For whom are they tolling the bell?

14. For Kati Gyöngyvári
Who is your wedded spouse.
I cannot believe it!
I cannot believe it!

15. Women, women,
For whom are you sewing this?
For Kati Gyöngyvári,
Who is your wedded spouse.
I cannot believe it!
I cannot believe it!

16. Men, men,
For whom are you making this?
For Kati Gyöngyvári,
Who is your wedded spouse.

17. Pár Vidrai's son
Jumps off the coach.
Cursed be the father,
And so be the mother
Who give away their own child to live
In a far away land!

18. Men, men,
Dig a grave deep and wide,
So that my body and her body
Can be laid in one grave!

19. Let my blood with her blood
Flow in one stream,
Let my soul and her soul
Worship one God!

20. Masters, masters,
Sing a chant
So that on my grave
There should grow a vine,
And on her grave
There should grow a tulip!

Gáborjaháza (Zala county). Performed by a woman. Vikár = Ethn 1910, 207. = MF 646. Notation by Bartók.

36.

1. Pes - ten csi - nál - tat - tam Egy a - ra - nyos há - zat,

Ab - la - kot is rá - ja Ép - pen há - rom - szá - zat.

1. In the town of Pest
   I had a golden house made.
   And it had windows no fewer
   And no more than just three hundred.

2. In one of the windows
   Fair Ilona Horvát is leaning on her elbow.
   In another window
   Gyula Szalontai is leaning on his elbow.

3. My Fair Ilona Horváth,
   Will you call me your husband!
   Will you call me your husband,
   Or your wedded spouse!

4. I would rather call you
   A shepherd's dog a thousand times,
   But not once my husband,
   Or my wedded spouse.

5. Coachman, coachman,
   Harness my horse and put it to the cart,
   Harness my horse and put it to the cart,
   And see that it is the swiftest one!

6. Tie Fair Ilona Horvát
   To the horse's tail.
   And so drag her
   Along the longest street!

7. First she called
   When she could not endure it any longer:
   Stop, stop, and let it be enough of that,
   Gyula Szalontai!

8. The second time she said
   When she could not endure it any longer:
   Stop, stop, and let it be enough of that,
   Gyula Szalontai!

9. The third time she said
   When she could not endure it any longer:
   I have neither hands nor feet,
   My dear wedded spouse!

10. He jerked the rein
    And picked up Ilona.
    He took her into the palace,
    And laid her in a studded bed.

11. What would you eat, what would you drink,
    Fair Ilona Horvát?
    A jackdaw's tongue,
    Its flapping wings.

12. They are tearing off the jackdaw's
    Tongue and flapping wings;
    But Ilona Horvát
    Is going to die in a short time.

Gesztely (Zemplén county). Performed by a 38-years-old woman. L. Vikár 1955 = AP 1203/b.

Divergences: The motif of selling away (in marriage) of the girl is overdetailed in some of the variants (cf. No. 34); sometimes, however, we learn about the fact from the mother's laconic words: Daughter, my dear daughter, I have sold you away. In some of the variants the girl does not even let the bridegroom enter her room, and eventually the door has to be broken up. Such texts also are known in which the bridegroom complains of the girl's behaviour: „Noble Lady Fodori, She will not accept me as her spouse; rather as her murderer!—Tie her to the horse's tail and drag her until she accepts you as your spouse!" In one instance the girl looks out of the window and sees first a cart of two oxen then a cart of four oxen approaching, finally the bridegroom is seen to arrive in a coach of four. An early recording tells about the girl dropping her fork during supper: leaning down to lift it she sees the bridegroom's hoofs; that means that he is the devil in person. A prose variant recorded from Baranya county combines the story with the tale of the infant sold to the devil while the mother was carrying it in her womb. But still there are fragmentary *portions in verse* -telling about the devil who arrives in the guise of the bridegroom—which clearly reveal the original ballad form. It is a subsequent development that the cruel acts are explained by the devil involved; the other variants explicitly speak about the reluctance and breaking of the girl sold away in marriage in a strange country. This is well brought out by the texts here published, and even more by the following lines of a variant not given among the examples: „Cursed be the mother, Cursed be the father, Who give away their own child To be brought into a distant land, Into a distant land, To live with strange people!" In another variant the mother comes to lament her daughter, but the latter repels her saying: „Even the soil is cursed In which I laid."—At the end of a variant from Arad county the husband asks his wife, already dying, what she is going to bequeath to him, whereupon the answer is: "The gallows!"

Earliest provenience: 1887.

Dissemination: point of gravity falling to southern Transdanubia. Vas county (the Őrség), Zala county (Balatonederics, Dergecs, Gáborjaháza, Resznek, Rigyác) Somogy county (Somogyacsa, Mosdóc, Törökkoppány), Baranya county (Sásd), Nógrád county (Bánk), Heves county (Bükkszenterzsébet, Hevesaranyos, Mikófalva), Zemplén county (Gesztely), Arad county (Szentpál). Total: 19 recordings.

Textual relationships with other ballads: There are obvious interconnections between this ballad and that of "The bride Found Dead" (Type **12,** further Types **13** and **15**), these being well brought out by the introductory duologue taking place between the mother and the daughter, further the girl's farewell speech to the flowers and dresses, as well as by some other details. The connection is so strong that we have a text recorded in Baranya county which seems to be an amalgamation of the two ballads. The story of this variant mainly reminds of the story of "The Girl Danced to Death", although the beginning scene containing the motif of inviting the girl for a dance, and also the tune to which the variant is sung refer unequivocally to the type of "The Bride Dragged to Death". The tune is never applied to other ballad texts. For the sake of comparison, I think it appropriate to present here the text in its full extent:

1. Katica Szalai
   Was driving the pigs
   Into the woods where there was a brothel,
   Into the woods where there was a brothel.

2. There was revelling
   Ferenc Győri Horvát,
   Ferenc Győri Horvát.

3. Come in, come in,
   Katica Szalai,
   For a dance or two,
   For a dance or two!

4. I shall not go in, I shall not go in,
   Because I am afraid of you,
   Ferenc Győri Horváth,
   Ferenc Győri Horvát.

5. Come in, come in,
   Katica Szalai,
   For a dance or two,
   For a dance or two!

6. I shall not go in, I shall not go in,
   Because I am afraid of you,
   Ferenc Győri Horvát,
   Ferenc Győri Horvát.

7. Go, friend, go and take in
   Katica Szalai
   For a dance or two,
   For a dance or two!

8. Play, gipsy, play your violin,
   Play it from early dawn (when the swineherd drives out the pigs)
   Till evening (when the cowboy drives in the cattle)!

9. Let me go, let me go,
   Ferenc Győri Horvát,
   For my round skirt
   Is covered with blood!

10. I will not let you go,
    For it is not five times,
    Not five times nor twice
    But twelve times that I have sued for you!

11. Let me go, let me go,
    Ferenc Győri Horvát,
    For my garland of fine canvas
    Is covered with blood!

12. You may go now, you may go now,
    Because I don't want you any longer;
    You are not wanted either by me or by anyone else,
    Not even by your mother!

13. Open, mother, open
    Your gate of green posts;
    Lay my bed, mother, lay
    My cold bed!

17. My women friends,
    My girl friend,
    You may learn from my example
    That you must not give a kiss (sung to the third section)
    To a villain!

"Who sleeps in the day-time": **20**; "Coachman... harness my horse": **2., 9., 10., 13., 16., 21., 27., 39.**;
"Let my blood flow with yours...": **10.**

Tunes: 1. = No. 34.; performed with two text-variants in Somogy county, and with one in Baranya county, the latter showing a greater deviation. 2. = 35.; this and 4. and 5. are different ramifications of 1. The completest form is represented by 1. and two other recordings from Somogy county, these being probably closest to the mediaeval tune of the ballad. Nearly related to the tune is the French melody of Roi Renaud (cf. NÉ 1958, 155 = AE 1960, 397). For more detail see the chapter on the tunes (p. 237). 3. = 36. in three further variants. (A more remote variant of the latter is represented by 6.)

Versions in languages other than Hungarian:

FRENCH: *1. Weckerlin* 1887, 303 (from 1763); *2. Haupt,* 99 (1799); *3. Davenson* 2. *4. Beaurepaire,* 167. *5. Legrand,* 376. *6. Decombe* 91. *7. Gagnon,* 158 = *D'Harcourt* 4. *8. Barbeau* 1962, 133 (reconstructed). *9. Millien* 1906, 183 (in prose). *10. Arbaud* II, 82 (*Doncieux* 15 lists seven variants, some of which are not available for me).
ITALIAN: *11–14. Nigra* 6A–D. *15. Ferraro* 1870, No. 9.
DANISH (SWEDISH): *16–104.* DgF 311. (Ibid. *Jonsson.*)

The fiendish revenge the rejected lover takes on the girl by dragging her to death is the leading motif of a very famous French ballad entitled Les anneaux de Marianson in the various collections. The story runs as follows: Marianson's

184

admirer has a copy of her ring made in her husband's absence, and used this to make him jealous. In a rage the husband rides home and when his wife shows him her new-born babe, he dashes it on the ground. One of the text continues as follows: He seized her by her hair and tied her to his horse's tail, dragging her from Paris to Saint Denis. Not a hedge, not a briar along the way but caught the blood of Marianson. "My handsome Renaud, my sweetheart, let us stay a little!" "And if I stop, it is not for you but for my horse which is tired out. Say, harlot, where are your three rings?" At this point the mistake comes to light. "My Marianson, noble lady, what shall I give you to make you well? Is it bread, is it wine you need, a silken or a linen sheet?" In another variant: "I will kill a goose, a capon to make my Marianson well again." *(9.)* "I want neither bread nor wine, neither silk nor linen sheet. Only a needle and thread are needed, and a fine linen for shroud." *(5.)*

The agreement in the text is unmistakable, even though the story itself shows great divergences. Starting from the point of issue, the Hungarian ballad agrees to some extent with the French in every motif, (only the construction deviates somewhat). The tying to the horse's tail, the dragging from bush to briar, then the plea to stop—in the Hungarian this scene is given an extraordinary tension by the application of gradation in three steps, making the narrative more ballad-like—the stop at which it transpires that the torture was unnecessary (in the Hungarian it is here that the torture of the woman becomes unnecessary because it is here that her resistance is broken; in any case, it is here that the man begins trying to save her from death); the question as to what she will eat or drink, even the offer of a table-bird are the same, only the Hungarian representation is more stylized: and finally the woman's last words referring to her nearing death. It is evident that the part related is the essence of the ballad, which the Hungarians introduced with the story of "The Girl Married against Her Will", developed here in many different ways, justifying that essence with the anger of the rejected suitor, while the French based the story on the motif of the revenge of the husband who thought he had been deceived. Both developments of the plot are equally effective from the psychological point of view, and of equal poetic merit at the same time.

Anyway, the question of priority cannot be settled on considerations like these; more consequential is the fact that the French ballad is a self-contained, homogeneous type, while in the Hungarian the part which agrees is only one continuation of a story developed in four different ways. The girl given in marriage to a strange man, against her will, either wishes to die, bids farewell to her home and dies indeed as soon as the bridegroom comes to fetch her; or she dies on the way, in the bridal procession, or else she is unable to avoid being taken away (Nos 12–15.). These variants are linked up with each other by different threads of the formulation, as a matter of course. If beside these the fairly divergent fifth variant had developed on Hungarian soil,—to wit, that she refuses to accept the man as spouse, and therefore she is dragged to death by him—it would be difficult to imagine why this one solution had reached France, and why is it that precisely the most general element of the Hungarian version is missing from the French. On the other hand, the route in the reverse can be easily understood, as also the transformation of the story can be readily explained. In all likelihood, the two basic plots of "The Girl Married against Her Will" (Types 12–13.) derive from French mediaeval antecedents. It will be shown below that there are traces to indicate their French origin. In the final analysis, in this case the Hungarians have amalgamated two French ballads into one single, though very effective story.

The French masterpiece is not known anywhere else, expect in Piedmont, where even the French name was preserved in the form of Mariansun, together with French place-names, for instance, the rival seeks the husband from Lyon to Paris. The only deviation is in the more detailed opening and the slightly different formulation of the punishment. For in the Italian the wife, tied to the horse's tail, is dragged twice round the castle. "In every stream and on every bush Mariansun's blood flowed." (NB. the bush remained with less justification!) "The lady groans: O why do you so torture me? What have your pretty little son done to you, that you should send me to my death?" And the closing runs: "I can never get well again, because I shall not see my little son alive again. I want to die with him!" At this the husband kills himself with the words: "Because of a treachorous tongue the three of us must die!" This deviation which appears *uniformly* in the Piedmont variants, draws a certain boundary between the Italian and the Hungarian variants; pecisely those details are missing from which the Hungarian version developed, notably the equivalents to the dragging through bush and briar, the phrases "slow down, my betrothed sweetheart", "what would you eat, what would you drink?", and the short ending: "mother, make my gay death-bed!"

Among the Danes the story has gone still farther from the one developed in Hungary; nevertheless, the characteristic motif of dragging to death clearly betrays the French origin. Adelbrand asks Lenelil (Kristen or Cecilia) in marriage, but meets with a flat refusal on the girl's part, who says: I have less trust in Adelbrand's faithfulness than in one of my father's worn shoes. In other variants he is unable to get a ring from the girl, therefore he applies force. Rumour is spreading that Abelbrand has died. The girl rides out in a coach and meets with the young man's dog. She gets frightened that she might meet him as well. Indeed, the man comes and draws the girl out of the coach, ties her to his saddle by her hair and so drags her through stubble-fields and logged-lands. There was not a green spot, but caught her blood, not a tiny twig but stained with blood spurting from Lenelil's breast. They arrive at a water they stay a little. The girl imparts her last will: she leaves her sundry valuables to her father and mother, and a knife to Abelbrand, to be fixed in his heart. Abelbrand orders two of his maids to comb the girl's hair, another two to put a garland on her head, still another two place her in her bed. The next day there are three dead bodies: the girl, the young man and his mother who dies of sorrow for her son. It is interesting to note that the Danes, too, motivate the terrible revenge by the anger of the rejected suitor, instead of the motif of jealousy known from the French versions. As against this, however, there are remarkable deviations as compared with either the French or the Hungarian ballads. It is only the formulation of the act of dragging to death that connect the three types.

On the evidence of exact partial agreements, the Hungarian ballad can have reached Hungary only from the French.

The Hungarian ballad belongs to the class of earliest French borrowings, probably of the fourteenth century.

186

Literature: Moór 1925: the initial formula comes from the German *Graf Friedrich*, the continuation consists in the Hungarian motif of dragging to death; *Gragger* 1926: accepts *Moór*, minstrels brought the ballad into Hungary; *Dános* 1938: accept *Gragger*, adding incorrect German, Danish (DgF 38) and Norwegian parallels; *Ortutay* 1934 and 1948: accepts *Moór*, on the basis of *Gragger; Dégh* 1952: accepts *Moór*, on the basis of *Ortutay; Csanádi and Vargyas:* Hungarian origin, the beginning distantly related to some German versions; *Vargyas* 1966 and 1967: French origin.

12. THE BRIDE FOUND DEAD

37.

1. The Miss went out and sat on a golden chair,
   She sat on a golden chair and began to sew a golden shirt.
   She rested her feet on a small golden stall,
   And lo, a pair of golden rings clinked in her lap.

2. Mother, mother, mother, what does it mean
   That a pair of golden rings clinked in my lap?
   Daughter, my dear daughter, it means
   That I have given you into the hands of the young heir.

3. Mother, mother, mother, why did you give me to him?
   I wish you had given me to a turkey-herd.
   My groom, my groom, who gives food in my hand,
   Go up to the hill and climb the high tower.

4. Scan, scan the plains towards Vienna,
   And tell me if you can see someone, if you can see someone!
   Miss, Miss, I can see nobody,
   I can see nobody, I can see nothing.

5. My turkeys, my turkeys, that I have fed with my own hands,
   Throw yourselves down upon the ground and lament for me;
   My clothes, my clothes, who sheltered my body,
   Fall off the pegs and lament for me!

6. My groom, my groom, who gives food in my hand,
   Go up the hill and climb the high tower;
   Scan, scan the plains towards Vienna
   And tell me if you can see someone, if you can see something!

7. Miss, Miss, now I can see somebody,
   And he has an escort of twelve coaches and forty men.
   May the Lord grant me that sooner than they arrive,
   Sooner than they arrive here, I should be laid out!

8. Good morning, good morning, my unknown mother!
   Where can I find, where can I find Erzsébet, my beautiful betrothed one?
   She has gone, she has gone down to the Tisza to wash,
   To wash handkerschiefs to present young masters with.

9. I cannot find her there, my unknown mother,
   Where can I find, where can I find Erzsébet, my beautiful betrothed one?
   She has gone down to the garden to pick flowers,
   To make a wreath to present young masters with.

10. {I cannot find her there,
    {Good morning, she is not there, my unknown mother,
    Where can I find, where can I find then
                Erzsébet, my beautiful betrothed one?
    I should deny it in vain, for I must own up to it in the end,
    She is laid on bier in the big dining-room.

11. Will you have a coffin made for me?
    I shall have, sweetheart, a coffin of marble made.
    Will you have it wrapped with canvas?
    I shall have it, sweetheart, wrapped in black veil.

12. Will you have it studded with nails?
    I shall have it studded, sweetheart, with gold and silver.
    Will you hire gipsy musicians to see me to the churchyard?
    I shall have, sweetheart, princes to see you to the churchyard.

13. Will you have the triple bells tolled?
    I shall have, sweetheart, all the sixteen bells tolled.
    Will you see me out, sweetheart, at least as far as the gate?
    I shall see you, sweetheart, as far as the realm of eternal rest.

Szirénfalva (Ung county). = EA. 4535/1905. Vikár B. = MNGY I, 180.

38.

1. Bá - tyám, kedves bá - tyám, u - gyan mi do - log az: Ab - la - ko - mon ű - lék,

fe - hér hi - met var - rék.

1. Brother, my dear brother, what does it mean*
   That two beautiful white doves set on my shoulders?

2. Two beautiful white doves set on my shoulders,
   Two beautiful golden rings clinked in my apron?

3. Sister, my dear younger sister, stand up onto the stone bench,
   Stand up onto the stone bench, and look to the left.

4. Brother, my dear brother, I see they are coming from Turkey,
   They are coming with joy, with loud merry-making.
   There are three white coaches, there are three red flags.

5. Sister, my dear younger sister, why should I deny,
   Why should I deny, I have to own up to it in the end:
   I have sold you away to be brought to Turkey,

6. Into the hands of a heathen, for two helmet-ful of silver,
   For two helmet-ful of silver, two helmet-ful of gold.

189

7. Brother, my dear brother, why did you sell me
   To be brought to Turkey, into the hands of a heathen?
   I wish you had given me to the humblest of your servants,
   To the humblest of your servants, or to your postilion!

8. She went into her chamber where she swooned anon.
   My clothes, my clothes, fall off the pegs,
   Fall off the pegs, down upon the ground,
   So that my brother may see how you mourn for me!

9. She went to the flower-garden, where she swooned anon,
   My flowers, my flowers, wither away at the root,
   Wither away at the root, fall down upon the ground,
   So that my brother may see how you mourn for me!

10. She went into the palace, and there she died at anon.
    Her eyes are closed, her mouth is closed,
    Her two beautiful arms are bent on her breast.
    Her two beautiful arms are bent on her breast,
    Many a beautiful young girl-friend is lamenting over her.

11. Brother-in-law, brother-in-law, my unsought-for-brother-in-law,
    Open your iron gate, hand over my beautiful betrothed one!
    My fiancée, my ringed one, Kalára Bátori!

12. You have no fiancée, your fiancée has died,
    Her eyes are closed, her mouth is clothed,
    Her beautiful two arms are bent on her breast,
    Many a beautiful young girl-friend is lamenting over her.

13. I don't believe you, I don't believe you, until I see it with my own eyes!
    He kicked in the iron gate, and it shattered to pieces.
    He went into the palace, where he swooned anon.

14. My coachman, my groom, my dear postilions,
    Go and have mourning clothes cut for every man!
    The coach belongs to the road, the horses belong to the fire,
    But what they carry belongs to me, her husband!

15. My son, my dear son, what does it mean
    That you started in red and returned in black?

16. Mother, my dear mother, we have brought a daughter-in-law to you,
    To whom you need not to give to drink or to eat any more.

17. Show her in, son, show her in, I'll meet her pleasure,
    Take her, son take her into the dining-room,
    Whenever you go out, you will kiss her,
    Whenever you return, you will mourn her.

18. We shall have a golden coffin made for her,
    The lid will be made of diamond, its cross of silver.
    We shall toll sixty-six bells for her,
    We shall bury her with sixty-six of our clan.

*The beginning formula in the 1959 recording runs as follows:

"I was sitting at my window, working on my white embroidery,
Two beautiful white doves set on my shoulders,
Two beautiful golden rings fell clinking in my lap."

Nyírvasvári (Szabolcs county). Performed by a 67-year-old woman. Vargyas = AP 7346/g (= 1959 Erdész = Ethn. 1938, 373, Ortutay: prose without tune).

39.

1. Mother, my dear mother,
   What does this mean:
   The golden ring
   Is turning on my finger,
   And two beautiful white doves
   Set on my shoulders?

2. Daughter, my dear daughter,
   I have sold you
   To be brought to Turkey,
   For the use of young lords.

3. Mother, my dear mother,
   Why did you sell me away?
   I wish you had sold me
   To someone in our village,
   In our own country,
   Even though to a turkey-herd!

4. My groom, my groom,
   Go up to the tower
   And scan, and scan
   The plains of Buda!

5. My groom, my groom,
   What have you seen, my groom?
   Alas, my dear Miss,
   I have not seen anything.

6. My groom, my groom,
   It is the second time I tell you
   To go up to the tower,
   Scan, scan,
   Scan, scan
   The plains of Buda!

7. My groom, my groom,
   What have you seen?
   Alas, my dear Miss,
   I have not seen anything.

8. My groom, my groom,
   I tell you the third time
   To go up to the tower,
   Scan, scan,
   Scan, scan
   The plains of Buda!

9. My groom, my groom,
   What have you seen?
   Alas, my dear Miss,
   Now I have seen three people.

10. One was clad in black clothes,
    The other in white,
    While the third was clad
    In pink silk.

11. Mother, my dear mother,
    My unknown mother,
    Where can I find, where can I find
    My beautiful betrothed Kalára?

12. She has gone to the shop
    To buy ribbons.
    He went after her to the shop,
    But he could not find her.

13. Mother, my unknown mother,
    Where can I find, where can I find
    My beautiful betrothed Kalára?

14. She has gone down to the flower-garden
    To pick red roses,
    To you, my son,
    She will make a beautiful wreath.

15. He went after her to the garden,
    But he could not find her.
    Once more he went to the house
    And once more be asked:

16. Mother, my dear mother,
    My unknown mother,
    Where can I find, where can I find
    My beautiful betrothed Kalára?

17. Why should I deny,
    I have to own up to it in the end:
    In the dining-hall
    You will find her laid on the bier.

18. He went there as well,
    And he found her there.
    He embraced her, kissed her,
    And lamented her with much bewailing.

19. Will you have a coffin
    Made to her?
    Alas, I shall have a coffin of marble
    Made for her.

20. Will you nail it
    With iron nails?
    Alas, I shall nail it
    With pure gold nails.

21. Will you have a grave-post
    Made for her?
    Alas, I shall have a pure brass grave-post
    Made for her.

22. Will you see her
    To the gate?
    Alas, I shall see her
    To the eternal house.

Magyargyerőmonostor (Kolozs county). 1958. Performed by a 63-year-old woman. Folklore Institute, Kolozsvár, No. 15619 = Almási 1963, 109–10.

40.

Boriska, Boriska, we have come for your beautiful daughter,
Hand your beautiful daughter over to the Turks!
Stand up, daughter, stand up, stand up onto the stone bench,
Look out of the window if you can see anything underneath.
5. I see three coaches of glass and nine flags of gold.
   Aye, did you not have a piece of bread,
   A piece of bread and a glass of wine,
   To save me from the hands of the Turks?
   She walks into the garden and throws herself down upon the lawn,
10. And cries, sobbing with tears: My flowers, my flowers,
    Wither away at the root, decay down to the ground,

So that everybody may see you are mourning for me!
She walks into the house, and throws herself down upon her bed,
And cries sobbing with tears: My clothes, my clothes,
15. Fall off the pegs and get rotten on the ground,
So that my stepmother may see you are mourning for me!

Gyalu (Kolozs county). Pál Gyulai 1872. 2 = MNGY I, 148.

41.
István Fogarasi is leaning on his elbow in the window,
His younger sister is leaning on her elbow beside him.
My dear younger sister, have you heard the latest news:
I have pledged you to be taken to Turkey,
5. As a would-be betrothed to the great Turkish emperor.
I have heard nothing about it, my dear brother!
May God grant me a good and merry supper,
After the good and merry supper a light disease,
And departure from this world at a beautiful, crimson dawn!
10. God gave an ear to her wish
And granted her a good, merry supper,
After the good, merry supper a light disease,
And departure from this world at a beautiful, crimson dawn.
There arrived, there arrived the great Turkish emperor
15. And asks: Where can I find my ringed betrothed?
She is setting flowers in her flower-garden.
The great Turkish emperor walks into the garden;
Aye, all the flowers have withered away,
And his sweetheart was not to be found anywhere.
20. The great Turkish emperor comes back
And asks: Where can I find my ringed betrothed?
She is putting on her clothes with the help of her maids in the maidens' house.
The great Turkish emperor walks into the maidens' house,
Aye, all the girls were clad in mourning clothes,
25. And his sweetheart is lying on the bier.
Give me, give me, brother-in-law Fogarasi,
Give me the body of my ringed betrothed!
I will have a coffin of marble made for her
Covered with black cloth down to the ground,
30. And I shall have it studded with golden nails,
And I shall order sixty soldiers to lament her.
I will not give, I will not give her body to you, great Turkish emperor,
For I myself want to have a coffin of marble made for her,
I shall have it covered with black cloth down to the ground,
35. And I shall order sixty soldiers to lament her,
Let her rest here together with her father and her mother,
With her father and her mother, in the land where she was born.

1863 Kriza = MNGY III, 3.

Divergences Most often the ballad starts with the following formula: "Kalára Bátori, My sweetest-kindest daughter, Stand up onto the stone bench and look out of the window If you can see someone coming...". One of the variants collected at Szucság clearly shows that the Turkish suitor is regarded not so much as an enemy but rather as a stranger: "Aye, did I not have a piece of bread, A piece of bread and a glass of water or two? Why did you give me in the hands of the Turks, In the hands of the Turks, in *foreign land?*". The self-curse of the girl in one of the Moldavian variants recalls the ballad of The Bride Dying in the Wedding Procession: "Mother, my dear mother, May God grant me: When they start out I shall be lying in my sick-bed, When they are on half-way I shall be lying on the bier!" (Each line repeated. Cf. the end of Note to Type 14.)

Earliest provenience: 1863.

Dissemination: Heves county (Mikófalva, a fragment of three stanzas); Bereg county (Oroszi); Ung county (one "Ung county", the other Szirénfalva); Arad county (Vadász); Bihar county (Nagyszalonta 8, Nagyvárad); Szabolcs county (Nyírvasvári); Kolozs county (Gyalu, Kide—fragment—Magyargyerőmonostor 6, Szucság 2, Válaszút); Udvarhely county (Udvarhely?, Oroszhegy); Moldavia (Gajcsán). Total: Hungary: 15, Transylvania and Moldavia 14, All-Hungarian-speaking areas: 29. In this case the point of gravity of dissemination falls onto the northeastern—eastern parts of Hungary and the western—non-Székely—regions of Transylvania.

Textual relationships with other ballads:

Plot: **11., 13–15., 20.;** farewell to the flowers: **10., 11., 13., 15., 29.,** and **31.;** "Hand your daughter over!": **14., 31.;** "Will you have a coffin made?": **65.,** "May God grant me a disease and departure from this world!": **79.;** "She was sewing in the window (I was sewing a golden shirt)": **14., 21., 31., (43.), 49;** sending here and there: **9., 28.**

Tunes: 1. = No. 38; fragment of a melody generally known in eastern Hungary. For the sake of comparison I present here the true form of the tune, as well as a mutilated variant of it, reduced to three melodic sections.

2. = No. 39. There is one more recorded variant of the tune. Further tunes (*4.* and *5.* in three each, and *6.* in two recordings).

Versions in languages other than Hungarian:

SLOVAK: *1. Slov. Sp.* I, 157 (418).

MORAVIAN: *2.* and *3. Sušil* 128/269–270. *4.* and *5. Bartoš* 1901 18a–b. *6. Bartoš* 1889 I, 135. var.

CZECH: *7.* Česky lid 1905, 149. *8. Waldau* 89 CXVI.

UKRAINIAN: *9.–11. Golovatsky* 37–41, Nos 1–3. (*9.* = *Pauli* 173–177 VII. [+]*11.* belongs to the type of "The Bride Dying in the Wedding Procession", although for the major part agrees with the other two variants.) *12.–18. Antonovich* and *Dragomanov* 65A–B–V–66A–B–V67.[+] *19. Lukašević* 11.[+]

GERMAN: I. Die Todesbraut *20.–26.* D. Vlr. 49, II. Erzwungene Ehe. *27–29.* D. Vlr. 50/1–3.

SOUTHERN SLAV: *30. Vuk* I, 551. *31. Kuhač* II 746. *32–33. Štrekelj* 224–225. *34–37.* HNP V 178 and four supplements in the form of an excerpt. *38. Kurelac* 462 (Milistrof, Transdanubia). *39. Raić* 4. (Subotica). *40.* Istarske pj. II, 65 LXVIII. *Kumer* 418 (?).

ROMANIAN: *41. Amzulescu* 247 (+ 14 vars).

BULGARIAN: *42.–43. Arnaudov* 1913, 72–73. (72 = A–V 76). *44. Stoin* 1928 2596. *45. Idem* 1934 618. *46. Idem* 1939 140. *47.* SbNU 4, 17.[+] *48.* SbNU 44. *Ivanov* 303. *49–50. Tsitselkova* I, 234–235.

GREEK: *51. Passov* 418 (Transl. by *Lüdeke;* cf. D. Vlr. 49.var. 48). *52. Lübke* 256. *53. Firmenrich* 6–9. *54. Lüdeke* 215 (D. Vlr. 49 describes 142 variants).

BRETON: *55. Villemarqué* XXVIII.

Doubtful correlation:

SLOVAK: *56. Kolečány* 32.

LITHUANIAN: *57.* cf. *Seemann* 1951, 74.

196

The story of MORAVIAN 2. runs as follows:

The doorkeeper at the Turkish frontier has a beautiful daughter. The Turk sends a letter to the court in which he asks for the hand of the girl, Katsenka. The father is standing at the window, sighing. The girl, hearing his deep sighs, asks her father what his trouble is. He confesses that he has given her away to a Turk. (Up to this point the story agrees in formulation with the next type, The Girl Dying in the Wedding Procession.) The girl orders a coffin, knowing that by the time the Turk arrives she will die. The Turk comes and learns of the death of the girl. First he does not give credit to the statement, but when he sees her dead, he laments over her with loud bewailing (anyway the lamentation makes up the major part of the ballad). He orders his men to make a marble grave, coffin of gold and silver, further to toll the bells so that their sound may be heard as far as Turkey. Then he leaves the place. "Had you been mine, you would have been entertained among fine young men." (?) Several Moravian and Czech variants interpret the death-scene in a way that as soon as the Turk leaves the house, the girl steps out of the chamber, and calls: "May God be with you till you arrive in Turkey!" By this turn the story changes into one in which the outwitting of the enemy plays the leading motif.

In the UKRAINIAN versions (*9–10.*) Romansko goes to the fair of Suchava where a Turk gives him a horse and silver in exchange for his young sister. In some of the variants, at home, in others at the inn, he leans his head on the table, pondering whether he should sell the girl. When he arrives home, his sister asks him where he got the horse from? He tells her that a Turk gave him the horse, and in addition a great deal of gold. Then he tells the girl to clean the courtyard, the house, whereupon she expresses her wonder since it is neither Sunday nor Christmas or Easter. Then the man orders her to tidy up her hair, because he expects guests to come the next day. The girl looks out of the window: "What smoke is seen there, is it eagles or shepherds with their flocks?" Then he confesses that Turks, Tartars and their vassals are coming. The girl asks the cook for a knife which she stabs in her heart: I sooner die than become a Turk's wife." (Variant 10. ends at this point.) Arriving the Turks learn from the cook all that had happened. They drag the corpse out of the house and cut it to pieces in the courtyard. As can be seen, they appear here as enemies.

The narrative of the GERMAN Type I (Todesbraut *20.*) runs as follows: At dawn, before the sun rises, a beautiful bride goes to fetch water. As she arrives at the well in the courtyard, a sharp root pierces her foot. The root was poisonous. Her father was a joiner (rather a quack just engaged in making a chest). "O father, my dear, kind father, for whom are you making this chest?—For my youngest daughter.—O father, dear, kind father, I don't need a chest. I would prefer you making a coffin painted black!—O mother, my dear, kind mother, for whom are you stripping the feathers?—For my youngest daughter.—O mother, my dear, kind mother, I don't need any feather, rather make up my snow-white bed! Make it up by the wall, for my life has come to an end."—In the morning, when the sun rose, the courtyard was full of people. The bridegroom's father was among them. He asked where his daughter-in-law was.—"She is in the kitchen gathering together her kerchiefs and skirts."—The brother of the bridegroom was among them, too. He asked where her sister-in-law was.—"She is in the kitchen picking up the vessels, pails and strainers for she is milking the cows."—Also the bridegroom's mother is among them. She asked where her daughter-in-law was.—"She is in the chamber assembling her cushions and pillows."—The bridegroom's young sister was also among them and asked where her sister in law was.—"She is in the chamber collecting her cross and book."—Also the bridegroom is among them and asks where his sweetheart is.—"She is about to die."—When the bridegroom hears this, he kicks in the door of the chamber whith such force that it sprang out of its hinge. He lifts the white shroud and looks in the eyes of his sweetheart. . . . They arrived with joy and returned to their homes in full mourn. (Five variants and a few contaminated forms. Three from the Sudeten, one from the Lower Danube riverine, two and the contaminated variants from Gottschee.) Here the cause of the death is a chance event, nevertheless the indirect answers given in order to delay the confession of the fact are still recognizable elements of the plot of the Hungarian ballad.

The story of GERMAN II (Erzwungene Ehe 27.) runs as follows: "Get up, Anneli, they are come for the bride!"—"I shall not get up and I shall not go to sleep, I do not want him, I do not want to marry."—Entering the kitchen, Anneli greets her mother by wishing good day to her: "I wish no more good day to you, for nobody can force me to marry!"—Entering the room, Anneli greets her father wishing good day to him: "I wish no more good day to you, for nobody can force me to marry!"—They lift Anneli catching her by her apron, and they seat her on back of a tall horse. As they reach the house, her mother-in-law steps out of the door: "Welcome, welcome, pretty bride, be my dear daughter!"—They seat Anneli at the head of the table, and give her steak and fish to eat. They open the small window so that she may take a last glimpse of her father's house.—"As I look at my father's house, I feel that my happy days are over." "They are by no means over, on the contrary, they are just beginning, because you have got a kind husband!"—Anneli is caught by death pains, her red cheeks turn white as snow. The bridegroom takes her in his arm, and she is cold in her body, may God have mercy on her. Today a bride, the next day she died, and on the third day she is up in the Kingdom of Heaven. The bridegroom runs up and down the path, he casts himself down and throws away his life.—"We thought we were going to celebrate a wedding, and now we may partake of a burial feast! We thought we were bringing a bed and a chest into the house, and lo, we are taking two dead bodies out of it." (Three variants from Switzerland, Württemberg and Rhine Province, one from each, further some contaminated variants from Switzerland, Lorrain and Württemberg.) In this case a reluctant girl dies because she is given in marriage to a man in a strange land; in other respects, this version is reminiscent of the next type, The Bride Dying in the Wedding Procession, in which it is similarly the mother-in-law that receives the bride, who is already dead.

CROATIAN 34. has the following tale: Janko Ugrijanin (János Hunyadi, father of Matthias Corvinus) is about to marry. On the first day he asked for the danak, on the second day he brought his presents, on the third day the girl grew ill, complained of sickness to her mother, and died bequeathing her embroidered shirt to her beloved Janko. Ignorant of all this, Janko gathers together his men and starts on the wedding procession. He sees omens of evil portent on the way: his flags turn in the wrong way and so they float in the wind, his horses step aside. "Perhaps my pretty maid has died?"—he asks, but his men reassure him. As he reaches the place, he finds the windows closed and meets his mother-in-law in mourning clothes in the courtyard. She imparts the truth to him, but he does not want to believe it before he is shown to the grave. The bridegroom is mourning over the grave. A letter arrives with the following message: "Mild dews, do not fall thickly, do not marr my sweetheart's face. And you, small birds, do not sing too early, Do not wake my sweetheart Fatima!" The bridegroom orders his men to turn back. His mother meets him in the courtyard at home and wonders where the bride is.—Here again the last scene reminds us of The Bride Dying in the Wedding Procession.

No. *38*. (from the AUSTRIAN frontier of Transdanubia) contains the following plot: The German Knight sends an ultimatum to Ivo Karlovič, saying: "You have nine castles, Ivo, and they are all white, and in those nine castles you have one girl who is like a rose. If you refuse to give me the girl who is like a rose, I shall ruin all your nine castles and rob the girl who is like a rose!"—Ivo returns the following answer: "Come, then, and take Jela, my beautiful young sister!"—The girl was walking in the white castle and says to her brother: "Don't marry me to the German Knight because I cannot understand his language!"—He tries to appease her: "Never mind, for I give twelve interpreters with you!" "What use are the twelve interpreters to me if I cannot speak with him without their aid?" Then she looks out of the window, and calls her brother to follow her up to the upper hall. There she asks him what he sees: is it crows or ravens? "It is neither crows nor ravens but a wedding procession." She asks him with much bewail to let her go to see her girl friends. "Pray to God and the Holy Virgin Mary that I should not spend a night with the German Knight!" She walked then round twice, the third time she was dead. While dying she ordered the girls to bring her clothes to Celje and offer them to be preserved in the treasure house of the Holy Virgin.

No. *39*. (SUBOTICA). The girl is sleeping on the balcony. Her mother says: "Sleep, my dear child, for you have no idea of whom your father gave you to!" Mara hears this: To whom? To Prince Stipan in exchange for treasures, horses and the like (detailed according to the members of the family mentioned). Then she curses them, again one after the other, except her brother. "When you hold glimpse of the wedding procession, take me out to the courtyard and lay me up as if I were dead!" Her wish is fulfilled. The wedding procession arrives. The bridegroom tells his servants to put live coals on her heart; nothing happens in result. Then he tells them to put a snake on her neck, finally he himself lays his hand on the girl's body to see if he can make her laugh. All this is to no avail. They leave bewailing, and the girl rises singing. Her mother asks her if the test was hard to endure.

In this instance the suitor is not a Turk; the stranger is represented by a German. An aristocratic girl, the daughter of a feudal lord living in a castle is asked for in marriage, like in the Hungarian, and she is sold away by her brother; the girl protests against marrying to a foreigner. The nearer we are here to the Hungarian area, the more common traits are found; the motif of looking out of the window occurs (though the persons addressed are interchanged), the appearance of a cloud on the horizon gives rise to query, and finally in this case, too, the girl dies before the arrival of the bridegroom, but in some texts during the wedding procession, as is usual in the second type.

The Slovenes living still farther away either did not know or did not understand the cause of the girl's death; therefore they found a different motivation. Let us examine the following examples.

SLOVENIAN *32*. A girl is sewing her bridal shirt singing. The Holy Virgin comes: "Why are you singing?" "Why not? I am going to marry tomorrow." "You will die tomorrow." "Why?" "When she was pregnant with you, your mother made a promise to give you to the nuns." The bestmen come, sit to table and began to eat. "Is there no bride here?" "She is preparing her clothes." "We have enough to eat and drink, but where is the bride?" "She is driving out the oxen which she wants to take with her dowry." "But now we must see, mother, what the bride is doing?" The mother shows them into the chamber and there they see the bride dead. "O, what have I committed?"—and once more the statement made by the Holy Virgin is heard. The bridegroom says: "If you had died for me, let me die for you!" He presses his hands to his head and casts himself down upon the white bed. "You shall be buried in a beautiful sunny place, and I shall be buried in a gloomy, cold place. A beautiful white lily will grow out of your grave, and a beautiful rose will grow out of mine. Both flowers will rise up to Heaven, to the seat of our Heavenly Father."

ROMANIAN *41*. In the tavern of Chiva young men are drinking wine, entertaining themselves by singing songs. They ask for the hand of Chiva's daughter. They ask for her on Thursday and Friday, but by Friday noon the girl grows sick an dies on Saturday. On Sunday, in the forenoon, they dress her in silken clothes and seat her at table in the bride's chair. Her mother goes out of the house to see the bestmen come on iron-shod black horses. Their shoes leave glowing embers behind them, and sparkles burst out of the horses' bodies. The mother addresses them: "Please, forgive me asking you not to come in because Fair Chivuca has fallen asleep after lunch and is resting now on the bride's seat clad in silken clothes." The bridegroom does not give an ear to her words and enters the house. He takes the girl in his arms and kisses her lips. Then he says: "Mother, my dear little mother, please cut two pieces of fine linen from our clothes and bury us as a brother and a sister under a rosemary bush at the gate of Rusalin, so that the branches it bears may tie us together from branches; let the world admire how pure love developed between a young man and a girl!" (Maros Province, 1907, *Popovici*.) The Romanian formulation connects the ballad to the Southern Slav and Bulgarian versions on account of several reasons, like death unmotivated, the events taking place between Thursday and Sunday, the love of bride and bridegroom, the absence of the motif of sending the bridegroom here and there. In all probability the story had been borrowed from one of the neighbouring peoples in the Balkans.

BULGARIAN *46*. Radica is confined to bed. She is ill. Her mother, ignorant of her disease, betrothed her to a young man. The bridegroom collects many people in the wedding procession. As they stop to rest under a tree, they find an inscription on its trunk: "Go back, because the bride has died! The mother had her body carried out of the house, covered it with a red kerchief and distributes presents among gipsy women and sundry wayfarers." Everybody believes that the girl is dead, except the bridegroom. He rides on and finds his betrothed dead, and her mother distributing presents. The bridegroom gets the bridal garland.—As can be seen, this story has hardly anything of the original plot, apart from the basic idea of the bride found dead.

GREEK *51*. Over there, in the neighbour's place, there in the street, the robber Charos has failed so far to pay a visit, although once, at Easter time, he procured a betrothed girl there, who was dearly loved by her mother. Her mother stood weeping at the head of her bed: "Get up, Maudia, my child, get up, for the host of your father-in-law is nearing!" "Let them come, God forbid them, and offer them bread and dishes of fish for the burial feast... etc."—So much about the bride's death. Soon the wedding procession arrives with loud music and flags. The bridegroom is among them. A bird lights on their way and makes them know that there are many people come together in the bride's home. "Perhaps my father-in-law has died, or my brothers-in-law have, or maybe one of my brothers-in-law has left for Byzantium?" "None of them, but your sweetheart has been carried away by the wild stream. They put an end to music. The house-people are making preparations for the burial ceremony. The bridegroom has the grave dug wide enough to receive both of them. Then he pierces his dagger in his heart. A slender reed and a cyprus-tree grow out of their grave and twine over it. They could not kiss each other while they were alive but they are united in death. *53*. A beautiful girl slights death, pretending that she has no of it, because she has nine brothers and Constantine, her bridegroom possesses many houses and four palaces. At this moment death changes into a bird and appears in the shape of a black swallow to shoot its arrow into the girl's heart. Her mother mourns her with loud bewails: "Death, you have brought a great sorrow on me, O my only daughter, my only one, my beautiful daughter!" And lo, there arrives Constantine followed by sixty musicians and four hundred men. "Stop your merry-making, your sporting and singing! I see a cross on the door of my brother-in-law. Perhaps one of my brothers-in-law has died..." etc. From this forth the story runs parallel to the preceding one.

It is impossible not to see that there is hardly any motivation for the occurrence of death in this latter variant, nor can we take the Charos motif as a substantially motivated tragic event, it can be regarded at best as a chance variation of the theme marked by unexpected death.

LITHUANIAN (according to No. 74 of *Seemann* 1951). "Saddle my horse for I am bound to go to my young sweetheart!" As I was riding through the forest, birds were singing, as I arrived at home, I went to sleep. I saw a dream: my heart trembled. Quickly I got up and mounted on my horse. As I reached the courtyard, I found the whole family in deep mourn. I entered the chamber and there I saw my dearest one lying on the bier, with her arms hanging down, her eyes closed.

The international relationship of the ballad discussed can be traced in two distinct channels; one including versions more or less related to the so-called "Todesbraut" Type *49*. in the all-German edition, the other to Type *50*. entitled "Erzwungene Ehe" in the same edition. The mentioned collection lists a vast number of the first type, proceeding from the Greek to the Lithuanians; the second type, mainly restricted to a fairly narrow German-speaking area adjacent to the French frontiers, is brought into correlation—on rather doubtful grounds—with a few Italian, Rhaeto-Romanic and Slovenian versions. In the present work only such variants have been entered which have been considered proper for our purposes. Indirect references are made to the variants enumerated in D. Vlr. Although the interrelationships of the national versions and the spreading of the theme has been mapped as a result of evaluation of a very rich series of variants in the last-mentioned collection, we had to draw other materials into the sphere of our comparative analysis—mainly the Hungarian versions and the foreign variants of these, provided their relationship could be clearly established—furthermore we had to interpret in a different way even the samples found there.

Complications of the elaboration of the material according to the German concept are due to the fact that the two thematically related ballads, which are multilaterally intertwined in the international material as well, namely the two branches of "The Girl Forced to Marry against Her Will", "The Bride Found Dead" and "The Bride Dying in the Wedding Procession" maintain only a very blurred correlation with each other in the German variants, because the Germans invented some peculiar motivation for the bride's death in their formulation of "The Bride Dying in the Wedding Procession", known under the name of Graf Friedrich. Consequently, the intertwined variants of the two ballads received a uniform treatment in the German elaboration—mostly in connection with the Todesbraut ballad, while no attention was paid to the circumstance that the two German ballads stem from one and the same root. True to say, there exist significant differences between them, the reason for which is—in my opinion—that they may have developed, indeed, from two different trends, the first being a derivate of a Hungarian—East-European formulation, while the second, of a French version which is no more or not yet known.

The difference is caused by the fact that in the relationship of the "Todesbraut", i.e. in the overwhelming majority of The Bride Found Dead type, it is not made known—especially with the Southern Slavs—why the bride is bound to die, or if so, various explanations are given in order to fill up the gap. Nevertheless, something still remains of the other elements of the plot here and there, at least in certain variants, to indicate the correlation existing between the members of the variant series: the bride is prepared to receive the approaching wedding procession, the arrival of the suitor's bestmen, the arrival of the wedding procession, evasive answers to the questions concerning the whereabouts of the bride and attempts at concealing the fact of death, what is more, even the sending of the bridegroom to and fro after the bride, and finally the bridegroom's sadness or his suicide, together (rarely) with the motif of the intertwining grave-flowers.

The basic plot can be recognized over large areas from the Greek through the Slav and Hungarian-speaking territories, as far as the Lithuanians. Having dealt with the theme in two studies, *Seemann* (D. Vlr. *49.* and *Seeman* 1951, No. 74) derives the ballad from the Greek because among them the bride's death is motivated by an ancient popular belief: the heroine slights the strength of Charon stating that he has no power over her. Another argument he adduces in support of the Greek origin is the enormous number of variants collected from the very extensive Greek areas: he listed some 142 variants. Anyway he states that this motif is fully absent from the Balkanian tradition, explaining the phenomenon by the fact that the mentioned folklore element is unknown in the popular beliefs of other nations, therefore they omitted it from the text, thus leaving the bride's death unmotivated.

In this connection attention should be drawn to the circumstance that the Charon motif does not enjoy an exclusive preponderance in the Greek tradition either. Admittedly, the variants including this motif represent the majority, but these are, for the most part, built up with a faulty logic: their central character is a *wife* whose boastful behaviour evokes the wrath of the Lord of the Dead, yet the bridegroom comes, at the head of the wedding procession, to fetch her, much in the same way as in the other, minor group. In the latter group, however, Charon is not involved, and there is no contradiction either: simply a bride is spoken of, for whom the wedding procession arrives. The sending of the bridegroom on wild-goose chase, as well as the suicide he commits when he learns the truth, relates this group with the Hungarian and other East-European versions, while the Charon motif occurs in many other stories, too, and therefore the variants with this motif show a number of further divergences in the contaminated stories. Considering all this, we think it highly doubtful that the series of variants has its origin in the Charon motif. Rather would it seem its final distortion.

One thing remains beyond doubt, however. Namely, the motivation of the occurence of death is left out either fully or to a considerable part from the various national formulations. On the other hand, it is precisely from the German "Erzwungene Ehe" that Seemann succeeded in demonstrating the presence of a sound explanation inasmuch as the death is elicited by the horror of parting with the native land, of being married to a stranger. "Hier wie dort (i.e. in the Italian variants) bangt das Mädchen vor der Ehe, zu der sie gezwungen wird, weil sie darüber Eltern und Heimat verlassen muss, und geht in der Fremde zugrunde . . ." (D. Vlr. II, 248.) But even this he inferred from one single variant only, the other ones showing no trace whatever of this motif. It would seem as if the other nations were not convinced of the psychological value of this motivation—the Hungarian ballad does not speak openly of the cause of death but resorts to some sort of innuendo embedded in the dialogue—and this is the reason why they stand baffled in the face of the girl's death, leaving it unmotivated as a possible chance occurrence, if not trying to find some other reasonable solution. Such is the solution applied by the Slovenes who make the mother denounce her former promise to give her daughter to the nuns. Already Seemann was aware that the element in this form cannot be the original motivation of a ballad theme, but must be a secondary development replacing the genuine one. A similar reasoning may have given rise—in my opinion—to the Greek versions' Charon motif, that is the variants motivated with the vengeance of Charon. But apart from this, unmotivated variants come up everywhere in the areas from the Greek to the Lithuanians. In such instances the other part of the ballad tries to make the story interesting for the audience, the bridegroom's arrival at the scene when the bride is already dead, delaying of the confession by false accounts, finally the bridegroom's response to the death of his bride. In this case the last-mentioned motif is the more significant since there is no explicit indication of the circumstance that the girl did not love the young man, consequently an opportunity is open for incorporating the obligatory dénouement of the separated lovers: the young man dies after the girl, and even grave-flowers may grow out of their dust.

In the vast area of dissemination, it is only the Hungarian ballad in which the girl protests—unconditionally and exclusively—against her being carried into a foreign land as soon as the plan is brought to her knowledge; further, she foretells her death, takes leave of her environment—this being the central portion of the plot—and it is only after this that the bridegroom arrives who, of course, does not commit suicide, being the story not about true lovers, at most he laments over the frustrated family relation. At the same time, the motifs of concealment of the death case and his sending about in search of the bride are to be found in a highly explicit form in the Hungarian variants.

It cannot be called in doubt that the other German ballad, the "Erzwungene Ehe", closely attaches to this Hungarian solution. It is almost beyond comprehension why the relationship of the Hungarian ballad with the Todesbraut has not attracted attention before. The East-European ballads here quoted and discussed may well have given rise to such consideration, because in these, particularly in the Hungarian variants, emphasis is always laid on the motif of protest against the forced marriage and the girl's being given away to a foreigner, and the plot is always based on this motif. It is precisely this that Seemann infers as the cause of the girl's death in his analysis of the ballad about the Forced Marriage. True, the formulations of the two German ballads are so divergent that it is difficult to reduce them to a common source, the more so since the Todesbraut version receives precisely among the Germans a peculiar motivation by involvement of a poisonous root, a snake or a spit which pierces into the girl's foot. Making departure from the Hungarian, it becomes obvious that the difference consists in that each of the two versions retained different elements of the common theme.

Nevertheless, the fact that the two methods of formulation are differentiated territorially permits further conclusions to be deduced. While the Todesbraut occurs exclusively, though sporadically, in the eastern and southeastern border regions ("die in Deutschland nur spärlich und nur im Süden und Südosten überlieferte Ballade", *Seemann* 1951 74), the Erzwungene Ehe comes up similarly sporadically, but in the western regions stretching along the French frontiers. ("Die Belege der nur spärlich und dazu mehrfach bloss bruchstückhaft überlieferten Ballade stammen ausnahmlos aus einem verhältnissmässig kleinen Bereich der deutschen Sprachgebieten, der sich von der Schweiz einerseite nach Württemberg, andererseite über Lothringen bis in die Eifel erstreckt." *Seemann D*. Vlr. II, 244.) That is to say, one and the same theme occurring in two different formulations, one in a narrow western the other in an equally narrow eastern area allows of the conclusion that the Germans received the ballad from two opposite sides, i. e. from the French and from the Hungarians. (In the latter case through Slav mediation.) If the theme is supposed to have existed once among the French, then its wide spread among the Greek can be readily explained, as well as the absence of the Greek traits in the Balkan formulations: namely, the Greek may have borrowed it directly from the French, while the rest of the Balkan peoples acquired it probably from the Hungarians, as has been the case with many other ballads when the Balkan and Greek traditions preserved identical western ballad types.

The quondam existence of the French ballad may be substantiated by a Breton song—of doubtful authenticity, unfortunately, being published in the strongly transcribed *Villemarqué* collection. (For more detail see p. 228 in Notes to the next type.) Like so many of the texts mentioned by *Seemann,* the Breton song refers to the girl's death as one that did not take place at her own home but in the bridegroom's house. At the same time the motif of the forced marriage and the concomitant despair of the girl being afraid of the foreign environment find unmistakable expression in it.

The fact of transcription is evident in the extensively detailed presentation, as well as in the application of magic elements. For example, the girl asks the "heads" of the family, one after the other, if she is really married to a stranger. Her father and mother seem to know nothing, send her to her brother who eventually imparts the full truth to the girl. Obviously, there were several possible solutions in the original formulations—like in the Hungarian where sometimes the brother, sometimes the mother come up in the variants—and these have been amalgated by the Bretons. The embellishment of the story by incorporating dead bodies clad in white clothes and the like may be attributed to the transcriber's literary predilections. But in spite of the lengthy representation, the nucleus of the theme can be clearly discovered, and it proves to be identical with that of the Hungarian ballad about The Bride Dying in the Wedding Procession. Here again the two related themes are interlocked, like in the entire area of dissemination, as has been shown above.

Another argument in support of the French origin is that the Hungarians had melded the story of The Bride Dragged to Death, which is undisputedly French of origin, precisely with the story of The Bride Forced to Marry against Her Will. The adaptor people always makes such amalgamation from two texts of the same donor nation.

There is every indication therefore that both variants of the Forced Bride (those of The Bride Found Dead and The Bride Dying in the Wedding Procession) derived and disseminated from one, or two, French antecedents, no longer extant, to prevail throughout Greek, German and Hungarian territories, as well as among the neighbouring peoples both towards the north and the south.

Literature: see the next chapter.

13. THE BRIDE DYING IN THE WEDDING PROCESSION

42.

1. I have given you away in marriage,
   Fair, pink-faced Örzsébet.
   I have married you to a white-faced young man,
   Whose face is as white
   As a white swan,
   And even whiter,
   As white as the wool of lambs.

2. Örzsébet walks out and goes
   To the chamber in the cemetery.
   She is dressed gorgeously,
   Wearing her green silken dress.
   She has filled her pockets
   With numberless coins,
   And so she goes round and round
   The house of the poor.

3. Poor, poor,
   You who are the poor of the Lord God!
   Pray to God so
   That He should put an end to my life!
   When I go to the wedding service
   Let me shiver with cold,
   When I take my oath,
   Let me die of cold shiver.

4. Coachman, my coachman,
   My best coachman!
   Whip the horses,
   Let them run with triple leaps!
   Coachman, my coachman,
   My best coachman,
   Give me a glass of water!
   I am dying of thirst!

5. But I don't give you water to drink,
   I rather give you red wine to drink!
   My Mikula, my Mikula,
   Give me a glass of water to drink!
   I am dying of thirst.
   But I don't give you water to drink,
   I rather give you red wine to drink.

6. My son, my dear son,
   My dear German Mikula,
   What kind of bride have you brought?
   She does not say a word to me.
   She does not extend her hand,
   Nor does she utter a word,
   Nor does she move a leg.

7. Daughter-in-law, my dear daughter-in-law
   Fair pink-faced Örzsébet!
   Before I knew you
   I took a liking of you.
   And now you made my many, nice guests
   Dress in morning clothes,
   And you have thrown both myself and my son
   Into bitter sorrow!

Salgó region (Nógrád county) = Pap No. 1.

43.

1. May God grant us a good day,
   Wife of the mayor of Szeged!
   Give me your daughter,
   Your beautiful daughter, marriageable daughter,
   In exchange for a glass of wine,
   And my beautiful greeting words!

2. I have no daughter,
   Except the one I am rocking in the cradle!
   But you have got a daughter,
   A pink-faced, crispy daughter,
   In the market of Szöged
   She was selling red apples.

3. I have bought some from her,
   And I have also tasted them.
   I have shown a deep love
   Towards your daughter Téra!

4. Daughter, my dear daughter,
   I have sold you
   In exchange for a glass of wine,
   And the beautiful words of greetings of a young man!

5. Mother, my dear mother,
   To whom did you sell me?
   To young János Török,
   I have married you, my daughter!

6. Cursed be the father,
   A thousand-times more the mother,
   Who drinks away their child
   In the inn!

7. Girls, my girl friends,
   Pray to God,
   When they are coming to fetch me,
   Let me shiver with cold;
   When they take me half way,
   Let me lay out dead!

8. The daughter looks out,
   She looks out of the glass window:
   Look, mother, look out of the window!
   What is that outdoors?

9. There is a black cloud,
   In the middle of it
   There is a raven of yellow feet!
   The black cloud there,
   The black raven there,
   The raven with yellow feet:
   And the golden coach there;
   Perhaps they are coming for you!

10. When they reached the place,
    She was shivering with cold,
    When they took her half way from the place,
    She was shivering with deathly cold.

11. The bridesmaid
    Shouts with loud words:
    Slow down, slow down
    Young János Török,
    For our bride
    Is near dying!

12. The second time the bridesmaid
    Shouts with loud words:
    Slow down, slow down,
    Young János Török,
    For our bride
    Is near dying!

13. The third time the bridesmaid
    Shouts with loud words:
    Slow down, slow down,
    Young János Török,
    For our bride
    Has died already!

208

14. Coachman, my coachman,
    Take my horse,
    The swiftest one,
    Go and tell my mother
    Not to prepare
    For a wedding feast,
    But to come as if she were invited
    To a burial feast!

15. As they arrive at home
    She begins to lament over her:
    Daughter-in-law, my dear daughter-in-law,
    Had you been kind to me,
    I would have given honey to you.
    Had you been wicked to me,
    I would have given poison to you!

16. Her mother went there,
    Her own dear mother,
    She begins to lament over her:
    Son-in-law, my dear son-in-law,
    Are you going to have
    A coffin of walnut wood made for her?
    I am going to have, mother,
    A coffin of marble made for her!

17. Are you going, then, to have
    Six bells tolled?
    I am going to have, mother,
    All the sixteen bells tolled!

18. Are you going, then, to have
    Her body buried in the ditch of the graveyard?
    I am going, mother, to have
    Her body buried in the corner of the rose-garden

19. Are you going, then, to lament her
    When nobody can see you?
    I am going to lament her, mother,
    Before the eyes of all!

20. Are you going to see her out
    To the threshold of the kitchen?
    I am going to see her out, mother.
    To the mound of her grave!

Szaján (Torontál county) = *Kálmány 1882, No. 5.*

44.

1. Daughter, my dear daughter,
   My fair daughter Örzsébet!
   Perhaps you don't know yet
   That I have married you to a man!

2. Mother, my dear mother,
   My dearest one, who nursed me!
   What sort of man, what sort of man
   Is he you have sold me to?

3. Daughter, my dear daughter,
   My fair daughter Örzsébet!
   He is not unlike
   A white dove;

4. He is not unlike
   A white swan,
   Only he is still whiter,
   Like the wool of lambs!

5. Örzsébet walks out and goes
   To the chamber in the cemetery.
   She is dressed gorgeously
   In her green silken dress.

6. Mother, my dear mother,
   My dearest, kindest mother!
   Give me, give me
   A good deal of small coins!

7. Let me throw alms
   To the Lord's poor!
   So that they may pray
   That I shall die!

8. She fills her pockets
   With numberless coins.
   Then she walks round and round
   The house of the poor.

9. Poor, poor,
   You, who are the Lord's poor!
   Pray to God
   So that He may put an end to my life!

10. When they come to fetch me,
    May I shiver with cold,
    When they seat me in the coach,
    May I be shaken with cold shiver,
    When we reach the border of his land,
    May I be taken by cold shiver!

11. When they seat me in the coach,
    May I shiver with cold,
    When they reach the border of his land,
    May I die a terrible death!

12. Mother, my dear mother,
    My dearest one, who nursed me,
    He is not the sort of man, not the sort of man
    You had told me he was!

13. Mother, my dear mother,
    My dearest one, who nursed me,
    Give me, give me
    A good deal of small coins!

14. So that I may throw alms
    To the Lord's poor,
    So that they may pray
    That I shall not die!

15. When they come to fetch me,
    Let me not shiver with cold,
    When they seat me in the coach,
    Let me not be shaken with cold shiver.
    For He is not the like
    You had told me he was!

16. When they came to fetch her,
    She was shivering with cold,
    When she was seated in the coach,
    She was taken with cold shiver.

17. My groom, my groom,
    My dear bridegroom!
    Give me, give me a drop of water!
    But I don't give you water,
    Rather I give you red wine!

18. My coachman, my coachman,
    My best coachman,
    Whip the horses
    So that they should run with triple leaps!

19. My groom, my groom,
    My dear bridegroom,
    Is it still a long way
    Till we reach the border of Újbécs?

20. Cast up, cast up,
    Your eyes
    You can see, you can see
    The border of Újbécs!

21. She caught a glimpse, she caught a glimpse
    Of the border of Újbécs.
    Further, she caught a glimpse
    Of the bridegroom's green gate.
    As she beheld this,
    She died a terrible death.

22. My bestman, my bestman,
    My dear bestman,
    Take, take
    My swift bay horse!

23. Order them, order them to open
    The gate of Újbécs;
    Call out, call out
    The young priest of Győr!

24. We have not brought a bride here,
    But we brought a dead body.
    My son, my dear son,
    My dearest, kindest son,

25. What kind of bride have you brought?
    She does not speak a word to me,
    She does not extend her arms,
    Nor does she utter a word.

26. Mother, my dear mother,
    My dearest, kindest mother!
    I did not bring a bride,
    But I brought a dead body.

27. Daughter-in-law, my dear daughter-in-law,
    Fair Örzsébet, my daughter-in-law!
    I did not know you,
    Yet I loved you.

28. My many fine guests
    Have clothed in mourning clothes for you,
    My son and myself
    Are filled with bitter sorrow for you!

Pécska (Arad county) = *Kálmány 1877, No. 18.*

The chamber in the cemetery *(ossarium)* and the "house of the poor" beside it recall mediaeval conditions. In the vicinity of the mediaeval parish there stood the buildings of the school, the hospital, that is the "house of the poor", these being belongings of the church. (By courtesy of *László Mezey*.) The meaning of the "chamber in the cemetery" having gone into oblivion, people interpreted the expression as the bower or dressing chamber of the daughter of the family; in all likelihood, the original formulation must have spoken first about the dressing of the

212

girl, and only after that may she have gone to the "chamber in the cemetery" and to the "house of the poor" to distribute alms (farthings) among the beggars and invalids staying there.

"White as a swan" contrasted with "Fair pink-faced Örzsébet" is used with a connotation of strangeness of the person to whom the phrase is applied. In a similar way the Danish use the attribute "black" when raising the impression of unpleasant strangeness of a foreigner. (Sorte Törning, Iver, DgF 364–365.)

Újbécs: a mediaeval village in the vicinity of Pest (no more extant). "I do not give you water, Rather I give you red wine" seems to be adoption of a tale motif, according to which the girl remains alive only in case she gets water to drink. (Aa Th 408.)

Divergences in the variants not published here:

Mihálygerge: The bride is married to *Mikula Német* (Nicolas German) who is living in the castle of *Német (German) Újbécs. Feldebrő:* When it is made clear to whom the girl is married, she says: "You might have given me the crust of your bread to eat, You might have given me swill to drink, Rather than to give me to that bad one!" During the wedding procession, after the words telling about the misfortune, the following lines can be read: "The bride will not die, Only women are false.—Nuts are good when broken, women are good when beaten." As the bridegroom arrives at his mother's place, bringing the bride, the mother says the following: "Wait and I shall give you your father's little scourge, Just strike at her only once, and she will look you in the eyes..." (which is to say that inimical mother-in-law is involved in this version). The variant ends with the curse formulated like this: "Cursed be the father... Who sells his only daughter for a glass of wine..."

Magyarbánhegyes: after the girl has cursed herself three times, the mother says: "Daughter, my dear daughter, Fair pink-faced Örzsébet, Stand on the bench of stone, Look onto the yard, What do you see outdoors?" The request is voiced three times, finally the girl says: "I cannot see anything else But there are coming far away Three glassed coaches and a silver flag." The mother-in-law addresses the dead bride: "My God, my God, I wish I had seen only once The leaping of your feet, The winking of your eyes, The smiling of your mouth! Son, my dear son, Will you have then A coffin of walnut wood made?..." etc. (lengthily, as in the parallel place of the ballad about The Speaking Corpse). NB., It is surprisingly little what *Kálmány* was able to collect of The Speaking Corpse in his field; he succeeded to pick up no more than two. At the same time, the final dialogue characteristic of The Speaking Corpse comes up rather frequently and in a fairly detailed form in this rare ballad.

Pusztaföldvár: At the beginning: "Go my Ilonka, go out And stand up on the dust heap (!), Look around from the heap Right to Hungary..." (Later on, towards Turkey.) János Török, the bridegroom says when he arrives: "Erzsébet Bátori, open your iron gate, Hand over your beautiful daughter! Wait, János Török, She is just putting on Her beautiful silken dress! I tell you the second time: Open your iron gate, And hand over your beautiful daughter! Wait, János Török! She is just putting on her golden Embroidered shoes, She is just taking leave Of her silken dresses. My fine silken dresses, Fall off the pegs, Turn your colour into mourning black, Lament for me! This is the third time I tell you: Open your iron gate, Hand over your beautiful daughter! Wait, János Török, She is just taking leave Of her beautiful flowers. She has picked three of them: My flowers, my flowers, Turn into dry stalks, Fall onto the ground, Lament for me!" The continuation proceeds like this: "My Ilona Bátori, When can I expect You coming home? You may expect My coming home, When you see blue violet Grow in your window!" -etc. in three gradation. During the procession the following is heard: "Stop, coachman, stop, For the bride is ill! Perhaps she is sleeping."

Ószentiván: "My flowers, my flowers, Wither away all of you..." etc. *Egyházaskér: Mikola Német* "buys the girl" while he is drinking in a wine-cellar in Buda. "I have sold you, daughter, To Mikola Német, Who is *king of the country!* Mother...you have not sold me But you have killed me!" Then follows an inserted passage borrowed from a lyrical song: "If only I knew Which way they will be coming, I should wrap it at once With black veils, With black veils, Black velvet." At the end: "Will you, then, have a coffin of walnut wood made ..." and so on. *Magyarszentmárton:* "Young János *Török* Went into the inn..." In the ninth stanza: "Curse upon the mother, Upon the dear mother, Who does not refrain to drink away Her child in the inn, And sells her to the *Turk!*" This version ends in prose: As she was placed in the grave, he fell on his sword, and he was placed beside her in the grave.

A recording of dubious authenticity informs of the following (contributed by *Gábor Kovács* to *Jó Barát,* 1867, 107, cf. EA 92, a study by Oszkár Elek NB. no place of the collecting is mentioned): Gyulafi sold his daughter to the Turk. Katalin, the girl, refuses to go away with the hangman. But the Turk forces her to step into the black coach. They arrive at a black forest, then he binds the girl lying on her back on top of a hill. Katalin sends message to her mother by way of a swan. "At the first crow of the cock They arrived there; At the second crow of the cock They released the girl; At the third crow of the cock They arrived at home; At the fourth crow of the cock The girl passed away."

Whether or not the ballad belongs here, as suggested by the opening formula, is an intricate question because the continuation contains divergent, obscure and unrelated portions. The part related in verse resembles The Girl Brought to Heaven.

It is worthy of attention how long and with what tenacity the original trait of the ballad survives among the Hungarian population of the Szeged region—a region that had been exposed to adversities of Turkish occupation lasting for a hundred and fifty years.

The bridegroom coming from a foreign country is not an enemy: Mikola Német is the king of the country; and when the "Turkish" bridegroom is the suitor, he falls on his sword; the reference to the "white" colour probably has something to do with the *Germans* contrasted with the *Hungarians* who are described as "red-faced". In addition, we have the solution which lends quite a different turn to the psychological development of the story, inasmuch as the girl eventually falls in love with the stranger, whom she abhorred before she had seen him, although she is no longer able to avert death which she had so eagerly desired before; all this provides clear evidence of the fact that the basic idea of the ballad does not concern the story of "the girl kidnapped by the enemy", not even that of "the girl surrendered to the

214

enemy", but the ballad is basically one of a girl married without being asked to a stranger, in other words: one expressing opposition against the idea of forced marriage. Therefore we think that *Putilov* (1965) is fully mistaken when stating that the song of the girl robbed (?) by the Turks or Tartars stems from real grounds in each Slavic nation (?), to wit, from the memories of fights against the Turks and Tartar oppressors. Such a supposition had been refuted already by *Sirovátka* (1968 II), on the basis of the Slovak–Moravian material adducing arguments not unlike those of mine. In the light of the latter study, the nature of literary transcription in the variant of *Kollár* (24) comes into still more emphatic relief. (Concerning the authenticity of his texts, see *Horálek* 1959, p. 193.)

Earliest provenience: 1865.

Dissemination: Nógrád county (Salgó region, Mihálygerge), Heves county (Feldebrő), Csanád county (Magyarbánhegyes), Békés county (Pusztaföldvár), Arad county (Pécska), Torontál county (Szaján, Ószentiván, Egyházaskér, Magyarszentmárton), Total: 10 variants. Seven of these are due to the field work of *Kálmány*.)

Textual relationships with other ballads: the development of the narrative and the plot: **11–12., 14–15.**, with reversed parts of the characters: **16.** (the girl would like to marry and the mother would like to detain her); portions of text agree in the same variants: "I have sold you, daughter . . . for a glass of wine", "When I go to say my wedding oath . . .", "Slow down . . .", "My flowers, my flowers . . ." (also in **31.**), "Tell mother not to come as if she were coming to her wedding feast. . .". **(65):** "Are you going to have . . . . made. . .?; **2., 9., 10., 16., 21., 27., 39.**: "Coachman, my coachman, whip the horses. . ."

Tunes: none of the variants has been recorded with tune.

Versions in languages other than Hungarian:

ITALIAN: *1. Marcoaldi* 11. *2–4. Ferraro* 1888, pp. 11–14. No. V. *Idem.* 1870 No. 35. *6. Widter and Wolf* No. 83. *7–11. Nigra* 37A–E.

RHAETO-ROMANIC *12.* 18th-cent. manuscript.† *13. Fluigi* No. 18.†

GERMAN: *14–22.* D. Vlr. 48 Graf Friedrich (*1–9.* complete publication, furthermore discussion of the 84 extant German variants which I have perused in the original copies of the DVA, including *Parisius* 2., 244., and 597.)

SLOVAK–MORAVIAN: *23. Kolečány,* 28 7. *24–25. Kollár* II. 6–7. *26–27.* Slov. sp. I 418 (= *Horák* 29) and II, 737. *28. Bartoš* 1882 135. *29. Idem* 1889 41. *30–32.* Idem 1901 17, 19 and 20. *33–38. Sušil* 89/183–184, 147/310–313. *39. Bartók* 1959 186/a. *40.* SL'P II, 66 87. (*41.* Slov. sp. II, 395: the bridegroom stabs to death the reluctant bride; *42. ibidem,* III 145. *43. Medveczky* 1905, 253). *44. Manga* 1956, 246–249 (*Burlasova* 10a).

UKRAINIAN: *45. Fincicky* 294 (= Figyelő 18; p. 33, Hungarian translation with some deviation). *46. Golovatsky* 41 3. *47–49. Chodzko,* 89, 93, 94 (French translation).

ROMANIAN: *50. Chodzko,* 248 (three variants). See further Nos 54 and 70 on The Girl Abducted by the Turks.

SOUTHERN SLAV: *51. VUK* III 78 (= *Csuka,* 124, Hungarian translation = *Cronia* 146–147). *52–53. Žganec* 1950 364 and Note on page 449. *54. Idem* 1950–52 96/b I. *55.* Ist.pj. II, 124 CXXVIII. *56. Bogišić,* 95 = *Stojanović* and *Vitezica,* 674. *57. Prodanović* 105 = *Petranović* 156. *58. Vuk* I, 551 756. *59–64. Štrekelj* 102–107.

BULGARIAN: *65–66.* A–V 75 plus var. *67. Bukoreshliev* 407. *68–69. Stoin* 1928 2761 and 3753. *70–72. Idem* 1939 736–738. *73. Idem* 1934 340. *74–75. Shapkarev* 317 and 325. *76–77. Verkovič* 8 and 205. *78. Dozon* 1875 49. *79. Miladinovi* 241. *80. Stoilov* 333.

BRETON: *81. Villemarqué* XXVIII.

ENGLISH: *82–92. Child* 11. *93–100. Bronson* 11.

Let us survey first the versions of the nations neighbouring the Hungarian. It seems most appropriate to begin with the northern versions, because the Slovak–Moravian texts show the highest number of variants.

The toll-collector or gate-keeper of the town of Preshporok (Bratislava) has a very beautiful daughter. She is sitting in the window, sewing and singing in a fascinating voice. The Turkish pasha hears her singing: What is it? Is it the sound of bells or the humming of bees? He sends the father a letter: he will either have the girl in marriage or occupy Preshporok. (*39*. begins like this: A war is in progress against Sir Melicher. He offers peace: I shall give you Hungary if you give me your daughter Barbara. Several other variants begin with relating that the father can be redeemed from the Turkish captivity at the cost of his daughter given in exchange.) The father reads the letter—or he is sitting at the table covering his face with his hands—breathing with deep sighs. His daughter asks him if he has a head-ache or a stomach-ache. He admits that he has promised her to the Turks. (Thus far the ballad agrees with most of the variants of The Bride Found Dead.) The girl looking out of the window, asks: What caused that dust cloud float there? Are they driving a flock of sheep or are they coming for me? (Or: Why do they beat the drum, why do they play music?) Postilions arrive. The girl is dressed and her hair combed. She gets in a coach, thanks her mother for having kept her well so far, her father for her being forced into a bad marriage. (D'akujem vám, mamko, za dobre chovanie, Vám, tat'ik d'akujem za zlé vidávanie." *24–25., 27., 37.,* and *39.*) When the bridal procession reaches the Danube, she asks for water. She is offered wine to drink from a golden cup. "I have not been taught to drink from golden cup, I have only been taught to drink from the Danube." In some variants she addresses the fish in the Danube with the following words: "Eat me up, little fish in the Danube, so that my bridemaids should not be Turks; eat me up together with the crabs so that my best-men should not be Turks!" Or variants of this. For more details see the ballad of The Girl Abducted by the Turks. (Type **29**). In *35.* she first throws her garland into the water saying: "Swim, swim, my garland, swim to my father and tell him that I have married the swift-flowing Danube!" ("Plyň, ty můj vínečku, az k mému tatíčku a povežty jim tam, že sem sa vydala bystrému Dunaju.") This strongly reminds us of the monologue of "The Brigand's Wife" (Type **20**), and will occur in a still closer formulation in the southern Slav variants. Then she kills herself by drowning in the Danube. In *38.* she asks for a knife to cut an apple in two, but instead she drives it into her own heart. In *39.* the same motif appears after the address to the fish, as an obvious subsequent insertion. The Turk mourns his bride, stating that he would have her walk on gold and silver. In *39.* the Turk's mother receives the bridal procession, asking why they are coming so sad; have they been deceived, have they not got the bride? "We have not been deceived, and the bride was handed over to us, and we have buried her by the tall tower." The mother-in-law laments the girl: My dear daughter, why were you afraid of me, of my gold, my kindness? At home you wore silk and velvet, with me you might have worn gold and silver all over your body." In *23–24.* the Turk orders fishermen to search for the girl. On two occasions they haul fish, the third time the girl. The Turk's words agree with the text of a Transdanubian variant of The Cruel Mother-in-Law (**28.**): This is not the fish I dearly love! ("Ach, nie je to ryba mojmu srdcu l'úba"—"Toto je tá ryba, mojmu srdcu l'úba.")

As appears from the details adduced, the northern neighbours of Hungary preserve the various elements of the stories of "The Bride Dying in the Wedding Procession" and "The Girl Abducted by the Turks" in one single ballad. Sometimes even portions of "The Brigand's Wife" and the Transdanubian variant of "The Cruel Mother-in-law" are also mingled in the ballad. (See the girl's thanking for her mother's kind treatment and father's forcing her into a bad marriage, further the part beginning with the words: "Swim, my garland...", and the Turk's lament when the bride is fished out of the water.

Similar phenomena are encountered among the other northern neighbours of Hungary, viz. the Ukrainians. Let us take a cursory look at some of the variants. *45.* The mother sells her daughter to the Turk at a village fair and then she goes home. "Put on your finest clothes!"—she says to her daughter. "Why, it is not Sunday today?" "Just go out and see who is coming there!" The girl goes out, then returns frightened: "Alas, mother, I am afraid the Turks are coming for me!" She asks them to put her clothes on the servant maid. The Turks set to table and have the daughter appear before them. They send the girl away, recognizing that she is not the one they want to have, only her clothes. Finally they take away the real object of the bargain. During the journey she asks for a knife to cut an apple with. But she pierces her heart with it. The bridal procession continues to the gate of the mother-in-law, who expresses surprise about the haughtiness of the girl: she does not speak a word to her! "She is not haughty, mother, only she is dead!" *35.* The father returns home after a carousal of three days (or simply he drinks away his daughter). He has her daughter fetch water to him. The girl asks him what kind of smoke is clouding there afar, is it the smoke of shepherds' fire or perhaps Tartars are marauding and kidnapping?—"Neither the one, nor the other, but they are coming for you. It is a bridal procession, because I have sold you to a man living *a hundred miles away* from here." In two days mounted men come and bang the door. "Bring out your daughter!" They show them the servant maid. "This is only her clothes! "There is no excuse, you either surrender the daughter or we destroy your house!" The girl takes leave of all the members of the family, except her father. The next day she beholds a tree in full blossom by the road and asks for leave to cut a branch of it. She covers herself with the branch and stabs herself to the heart. A cuckoo betrays to the Turk what has happened. "I wish I had been drowned before I gave her the knife!" *48.* A man sells his sister Mary for 7,000 pieces of gold. He announces to his sister that the first Turk that comes to see them will be her bridegroom. The girl is sewing, working over her embroidery, and looks out of the window. She asks her brother to hire one of the kitchen-maids and let herself be walled up by the masons. The Turks and Tartars arrive and summon the girl to open the gate. The kitchen-maid goes to meet them, she makes a low bow. "This is not the gait of our Mary." They threaten her brother with the gallows. He admits that the girl is walled up in the mason's wall beside the Danube. *49* Beyond the blue sea Anulka is sewing a shirt. As she looks out of the window, she addresses her brother: "O brother, will you tell me what lights are flashing there? It is harvesters working or perhaps oxen feeding on the grass?" "It is neither the one nor the other, but the Turks coming for you." "Go

217

brother, select a kitchen-maid, for I won't go with them, rather I lock myself behind ten gates, under ten locks." The Turks arrive and demand the girl. "This girl is not the one we have come for, only the head-dress is hers, but the face, is not hers, the string of beads is hers but the neck is not hers (and so on)." The kitchen-maid tells them where the girl is. The Turks break in all ten doors and carry her away. They place her on a cart, wrap her in tent-cloth, and their sword pierces Anulka's heart so that her blood flows in streams.

The relationship with the Hungarian ballad, or ballads, is obvious in this instance as well. The motifs of the girl sewing at the window, the brother's admission that he had sold her to the Turks, the girl looking out of the window and asking questions about the cloud of dust,—are all well known from Hungarian balladry. Only the girl dying of sorrow has been replaced by a girl committing suicide: instead of drowning in the Danube after a speech addressed to the fish, she stabs a dagger in her heart. (In the last variant this motif has changed into the vengeance of the Turks.)

Proceeding towards the southeastern neighbours, that is the Romanians, we find two types related to the Hungarian ballad. In 50. the parts of the characters in the story known so far have been reversed: the bridal procession is approaching the bridegroom's place. The bridegroom goes ahead of the rest and dies, so that the mother receives the members of the family with the bad tidings. Evidently, this is a very remote and a wellnigh independent solution whose meagre narrative is hardly more than an excerpt of the original. The second type (Amzulescu 50, and ramifications) will be discussed in detail in the chapter about The Girl Abducted by the Turks, since elements characteristic of this ballad preponderate in it. To wit, it is not explicitly stated that the girl has been married to a Turk, she only sees a troop nearing to their home; the girl hides but the Turks insist and finally take her with them: therefore, what we have here is a plain kidnapping, and the girl abducted commits suicide at the banks of the Danube.

Among the southern and southwestern neighbours fairly wide deviations are found between the individual variants. For example, the story survives not only in the form of a ballad song, but also in one of a heroic-song-like formulation, which follows from the nature of the theme: the marriage feast of the hero, the detailed description of the bridal procession are favourite themes of the heroic songs. A solution according to which the bride dies of some—mainly supernatural—reason well fits in this sphere of themes. Such one is the Vuk variant (51.) which relates the story in the manner of the epic singers, that is to say, by embellishing the story with many colourful details. Standard-bearer Milič cannot find a girl beautiful enough to match him. People recommend Vid's daughter who is a renowned beauty. He goes to marry her, followed by a fine bridal procession. He meets a proper reception, gets the girl, although the mother of the girl is weeping because so far all her eight daughters witnessed some mischance during the wedding ceremony, owing to some evil spell. The same fate awaits the ninth girl, too: she is getting ill during the procession; upon her request the music is stopped and so is the whole bridal procession. But all this is done in vain, for the bride dies, and is buried. Then they go home where the mother-in-law sees the guests in. When she learns what had happened, she recites a long lament for her daughter-in-law, whom she had never known.

The ballad-like variants of the story can be met with among the so-called "women's songs". *52–53*. Mara is married by her mother to Yovan, a man living in the Danube riverine. The girl receives information from her girl-friends that the man has married nine times already, though he could not spend a night with any of his brides, because they all died before the wedding ceremony had come to an end. The girl imparts the tidings to her mother, who advises her to kindle the dry willow on top of a hill as they arrive there. The bridal procession arrives for to fetch the bride. But she cannot take a step. She shouts to someone to unfasten her green garland. The bridegroom wants to help her, draws his knife from his belt and cuts the bride's red face. Her blood is spilling. (Variant *53.* contains some further lines: the bridegroom asks: "Dearest heart, does it hurt you very much?" O you have not struck me, so it does not hurt me." Walking in the mountains, she picked leaves of trees to stop bleeding the wound, walking through the plain, she picked roots to stop bleeding the wound.) During the way the girl asks if the young man's place is still very far? "It is neither very far nor very near." They reach the place. The bridegroom sits to table while the girl goes into the chamber. The bridegroom sends his mother after her to see what she is doing there. "My daughter-in-law is just washing her white face." He does not believe it, therefore he sends her sister after the bride. "The bride is combing her yellow hair." He does not believe her either, and sends his brother to see what she is doing. He returns with news of her death. Thereupon he breaks his sword in two, and his mother's heart breaks.

Here again certain typical Hungarian motifs can be discovered: the question of the bride, asking if the bridegroom' place is still very far; the evasive answers given in order to conceal the death of the bride (well known from The Bride Found Dead); the motif of sending away, in this case, of the different members of the family. Also the southern Slavs refer to some curse as the motivation of what is supported by psychological and social motives in the Hungarian. The bride's horror of the marriage is not due to the strangeness of her bridegroom, she is rather afraid of the cruel experiences which are in store for her in the foreign land. Similar is the narrative and the motivation of the tragic event in *55.* The Fair Maid Mara is stitching with minute stitches. As she is sewing, she looks out of the window. Three finely clad young men are approaching in the field. "Whichever of you reaches the branch of the almond-tree shall have my Mara." The first young man reached the branch of the almond-tree and demanded the bride. "I shall not give her to you, I give you my three chests of gold instead." "I don't want your gold, give me the bride you have promised!" "I shall not give her to you, I give my three golden coins instead." "I don't want your money, give me the bride you have promised to give to me!" Eventually he had to give him the Fair Maid Mara. The girl said to her mother: Don't sew a long and wide dress for me, because I shall not tear it! Ivan had loved nine girls, but he did not spend a night with anyone of them. Nor will he spend one with me, who am his tenth bride. Good-bye, dear old mother, bind a black kerchief on my eyes so that I may not see my mother's face when I leave her. As they arrived at a flat meadow, she beheld three green willows. Two intertwined branches of the tree obstacled their progress in the way, therefore Ivan pulled them apart.

219

One of the branches hit Mara on the head. "My dear Jela, does it hurt you?" "Not only did it hurt me, but it beat me to death. Stop the wound if you want me to arrive at your mansion alive. For heaven's sake, Ivan, is it a long way to your mansion?" "There it is where the sun is setting." They reach the white castle, people gather around them asking where the bride is. The mother-in-law asks the same, too. "There, you see, she is sitting on the horse; she is tall, slender, black-eyed and white-faced. Make her bed without delay, because she has travelled a long way, and she is very young!" Afterwards the members of the family go one after the other to wake her for the supper, but she does not even open her eyes. Finally they discover that her ring is swimming with blood. "Swim, my ring, swim across three flooding waters, and let them toll the bells for me!" The mother of the girl hears this and says: "I bore my daughter for the sake of Ivan, but her soul has departed."

In this variant again the familiar scenes and motifs of the Hungarian ballad occur: the girl sewing at the window and beholding her suitor, the question the dying girl asking if the place is still far away, the sending of the relatives on wide-goose chase (of course, with quite a different purport, yet in order to delay the final development), and towards the end we hear reverberating the characteristic phrases of complaint uttered by "The Brigand's Wife": "My God, my God, make the river flood, let it take me to the gate of my father's house. ...", although the water is changed into blood in this instance, but still retaining memories of the original image inasmuch as the ring swimming in blood reaches the mother's place through the flooding water. The connection with the ballad of "The Brigand's Wife" presents itself in some further details, too: *54.* Jelka is sleeping at the Danube. Her mother calls her because the suitor has arrived with his family filling two carts. Haughty Pavel, the suitor, is sitting in the third. "Don't give me, mother, to haughty Pavel who is a wicked *thief!*" "Why should I not give you to him? He has brought valuable presents, silken dresses to me and a hat of marten-skin to your father!" She is set in the coach. The bridegroom shouts: "Turn pale, moon, as you can, drive, coachman, drive the horses as swift as you can! Lest Jelka should know the way back to her mother!" They reach the courtyard of Pavel's home; as Jelka gets out of the coach, she turns into a hare. Pavel takes his gun and shoots the hare. At this, the hare resumes the shape of Jelka: "Flow, my blood, flow, flow, till you arrive at my mother's courtyard; let she know to whom she has given me, for the haughty Pavel is a wicked thief!" The man takes the gun to the blacksmith: "Hey, blacksmith, you have not made a good gun for me. I have killed nine of my sweethearts with it, and now I have killed Jelka in my own courtyard!"

Similarly to *51.*, *56.* starts in the courtyard of the bridegroom. Pavel is sent by his own sister to sue for a girl who lives beyond three pine forests and three hills covered with maples: people are dancing kolo before the mansion, and among them he will find the girl's mother. The young man collects the participants of the bridal procession and sets out to ask the girl in marriage. The mother is leading the dance, but she is wiping her tears at the same time: she announces to the young man that her daughter has died. He asks them to show him the place the girl was buried in, because he wants to dig her up to see her dead if he had not seen her alive. "With us the custom is not to bury a young girl in the earth but to throw her dead body into the sea." "Show me, where she was thrown, I am a diver and I shall bring up her body. Let me see her dead if I could not see her alive." Now the aunt of the girl admits—against a rich reward—that the girl has not died, she only had a quarrel with her mother and retired in her bower. The young man goes in, and the girl entreats him to let her alone because she does not want to cross the mountains. All in vain! Finally she takes leave of her mother, begging her once again not to take her out of the white courtyard, because she will die a painful death if she is carried away. While she is being carried accross the hills, she complains anew. Seeing her growing paler and paler, the bridegroom takes the girl of the palfrey. The girl reproaches him, repeating that she had told him well in advance not to take her out of her mother's court. She dies and is buried; a church is built beside her grave. Further, a rose-tree is planted on the grave and a well dug for wayfarers passing by.—In this case the girl's death on the way to the bridegroom's place shows a closer resemblance to the Hungarian version, because of the absence of manipulations with a knife, curse, beating, and the like; only the girl's grief of leaving the paternal house is emphasized; further parallelisms are manifest in the words spoken in order to delay the dénouement, the denial of the girl's death, but the rest of the plot proceeds in a quite different direction, ever more farther from the Hungarian. The girl's dispair finds motivation by involvement of an aged bridegroom in *57.* The girl is married to a man whose white beard reaches down to his waist. On seeing him first in the bridal procession, the girl asks one of the maids for a knife to cut an apple in two, and she drives it into her heart. In *58.* the scene is made even more effective by the presence of a young man in the bridal procession whom the bride would be willing to accept much more readily than her bridegroom with the long white beard. In this instance she does not commit suicide during the way but dies in the house of the bridegroom. Typical Hungarian traits come up again in *59.* The girl has a dream: she sees three suns of different colours rise. Her mother explains the meaning of her dream: she has received skirts of three different colours from her father. The girl climbs a hill, looks down and asks what things are emerging in the field below: are they ears of corn, are they pearls and gold or perhaps a strong army? "They are your suitors." As they reach the white castle, the girl wants to know which one of them is her bridegroom. Then she is carried away. They arrive at a spring, at which the girl grows thirsty and asks leave to get off the horse to drink, while doing so a sword wounds her heart. She asks her maids to cut the ribbons off her hair to make a bandage on her heart. The young man says it would be a pity to cut her ribbons. "Never mind, it is not you but my father that bought them." On their arrival the mother-in-law asks why her daughter-in-law is so pale. The answer is that she has lost much blood during the way. She wants to go to bed. The bridegroom asks when it is allowed to go to her at night. The answer is: at three after midnight. Then she casts off her ring, saying: "Go, go my ring, tell my mother how I fare! Had she not married me to this man, I should not part with the world." When going to her, the bridegroom finds a dead bride. "You have died because of me, and I die because of you." And he himself dies after his bride. *60.* The heroine gets up and goes out into the courtyard, climbs up a ladder and looks around asking her mother what she sees in the distant field: is it mist rising from the water, from the hills, or is it a storm cloud? None of them, explains the mother, but they are the Turks coming for her. The girl turns pale. She asks her mother not to give her to the

Turk whose mother has killed nine of her daughters-in-law. She offers wine to drink and bread to eat to her son's bride. The girl's mother advises the girl to pour away the wine and give the cakes to the hounds. The girl tells her to give the Turks wine till they are drunk and keep her hiding place in secret. She is refused, and carried away by the Turks. On the way her horse stumbles, its saddle slips aside and a sharp tool hidden in the saddle pricks the girl. The bridegroom exclaims: "This is the work of my mother!" The girl complains, saying that the news was true: the Turk's mother has killed eight brides so far. She puts right the saddle and they proceed. The girl asks if they are to ride a long way till they reach the castle. It is rather near already, one can even see its silver gate. The mother-in-law goes out to meet them. She states, she has heard many words in praise of the girl's beauty, and offers her wine, which the girl spills, and bread, which she gives to the hounds. Where is she to go to bed, asks the girl. According to the mother-in-law, it is not customary to view the place in advance with the Turks. Finally the bride goes to bed, removes the bandage from the wound and says: "Flow, my blood, for my mother will not see me again, and I send her my blood to remind her of me!" Then she dies. The bridegroom curses his mother, then exclaims: I don't want to part with her, I shall sleep by her side." And this exclamation betokens his own death as well. Death comes as if by chance again in *61*. Anica walking on the porch looks at the high road. "Father, dear father, what mist is there in the field?" "It is no mist but the youngest son of the Turkish emperor, it is the dust his palfrey leaves behind!" "Don't give me to him, father!" "Don't be afraid, daughter, you will walk in a castle, you will have your choice in gold and silver." "Let the Turk perish with all the yellow gold of his castle!" The coach stopped in front of the gate, and the suitor is offered wine. "Hey, father, my dear father, you have given me your little Anica." The bridegroom bows, his bright sword slips out of its sheath, the young woman reaches after it and stabs herself to death. This may serve as an example to fathers and mothers who marry their daughters to strange men living in distant lands.—The last sentence indicates that the memory of the real cause of death still lingered in the mind of the community; it follows, therefore, that the motivation by an accident is a secondary development, inconsistent with the real explanation. The original idea comes once again in *62*. The Turkish emperor asks in marriage the daughter of a noble man. In case he fails to get the girl, he will deprive the nobleman of all his property and slaughters all his men. The girl sits in a coach and prays to God that she may die before leaving the province of Carinthia and be not taken to the land of the Turks. After a short ride she has a head-ache and a sore heart; the Turkish emperor asks her what the matter is with her. The girl soon passes away.

By courtesy of *Zmaga Kumer* we have at hand exact translations of two variants which we publish in the following. *63*. Over beyond, over beyond there stretches a flat meadow. On the flat meadow there courses a narrow path. By the narrow path there stands a white palace. A nobleman lives in the palace, A nobleman and a noble lady. The lady gets up early in the morning, She washes her white body. Then she looks at the flat meadow. There was something twinkling in the flat meadow. "Alas, what is it? Is it white soldiers, Or the bridal procession of Židanko that comes there? Hey, hey, noble lord, Noble lord and noble lady! Give me your Brajdica in marriage, You promised her to give to us long ago When you rocked her in the cradle!" The nobleman calls her daughter: Hey, hey, Brajdica, Will you marry Židanko?" "Alas, alas, my dear father, My dear father my dear mother, Don't give me, don't give me to Židanko! Židanko has three sweethearts, And a son by each of them. But if you give me to Židanko, Fill up the bridal chest With two layers of white linen sheets, With three layers of sorrow."—They were going on, they were going on their way, At once Židanko stabs Brajdica in the flank with his sword. They took the linen sheets To bandage Braidica's wound with. They were going on, they were going on Towards the residence of Židanko. "Alas, alas, mother, Where is the light bower, And where is my little, white bed?" "It is not customary with us to ask where the light bower is, Either the light bower or the white little bed. With us it is the custom to ask where the smoky kitchen is, and where the stable of horses is?" At the first crow of the cock Židanko went to see his Brajda: "Alas, my little Brajdica, Have you a head-ache?" At the second crow of the cock Židanko went to see his Brajda: Her blood was flooding towards the threshold, It flooded to the ninth country, To the house of her dear old mother. Let this serve as a lesson to each mother Who gives her daughter in marriage to a strange man in a distant land.

64. Do you want to be a distinguished young lady, The wife of the Spanish king?—I don't want anybody, Not even the Spanish king! When did you promise me to him, When did you agree upon my marriage without my consent?—We promised you in marriage When we pledged the white palace; But look, daughter, look at your bridegroom: he is coming for you over there.—Look, mother, I say to you, I have no mind to marry any man. I shall go into my light bower, And you will tell him: Alas, the girl is ill!—How can a girl be ill Whose face is red as blood? This is only an excuse. But listen, mother! When they put my chest on the cart, Cover it with my finest veil, So that I may take hold of it first. The mother had the chest put on the cart, And covered it with her finest veil. They started out and proceeded along the Donava (Danube). As the bride got there, As she got at the river Donava, Her shoe fell off her feet And sank in the deep water. Listen, my youngest bestman, Go and bring here my shoe!—Let him bring your shoe Who will sleep with you tonight! The bestman jumped off his horse, His bright sword swang. And it drove into the body of the young lady. Blood was flooding from her heart.—Listen, my youngest bestman! Make speed and fetch me the veil on the chest! I shall bandage the wound, I shall stop bleeding my red blood.—The bestman went to the painted chest To fetch the veil, And the young lady dressed her wound with it. They are riding on, And they reach the ninth country. The mother addresses the bride: Everybody wondered at you Who visited your country, Everybody extolled your beauty, Although I think everybody is blind, Because there is nothing beautiful in you.—Listen, mother, aye, listen, Where is the light bower, And where is the little white bed In which I can have a rest?—It is not the bride's duty To care for the bed; See the cutlery be clean And entertain us with a good feast!—The young lady goes in the bower, She goes to bed, Her wound re-opens, Her red blood spills away. The bridegroom enters the bower And beholds the white little bed, And the dead bride in it. The unfortunate man says: May the Lord have mercy on me a hundred times! I have gone nine times to bring a bride to the house, Yet I have no wife!—And he collapsed dead.

As appears from the examples, the southern Slav tradition has preserved, in part at least, memory of the girl dying of sorrow, although the majority of their formulations of the story rejects this solution; yet the death is not due to suicide— except for one or two cases—but it occurs owing to a wound received in consequence of an accident, or through the intrigue of the mother-in-law, if not a curse. Anyway, the plot forks into two branches in so far as the major part of the ballads relate the beginning of the story from the bride's point of view, while the smaller portion treats the events from the angle of the bridegroom, like the Bulgarian ballad of "The Bride Found Dead".

With the Bulgarians the ballad under discussion begins with the description of the bridal procession nearing the bridegroom's place. *89*. They proceed through a forest. A hind appears which the men began to chase. The bridegroom remains with the girl and wants to kiss her (or to remove the veil from her face which he has not seen during the three years' time of their engagement). His knife or dagger slips from his belt and hurts the girl's heart. They dress the bleeding wound, and the procession goes on. (In *79*. the bride questions whether the village is still afar. She is appeased by the bridegroom's brothers and the bestmen. When they reach the village, she asks again if the house is far. She is once more calmed.) Arriving at the house, the mother-in-law asks her why she is so green and yellow like a green apple and a lemon. The girl cannot make a bow, therefore she asks the mother-in-law to take out of her bosom the gold apple she has got from the bridegroom. The mother-in-law removes the bandage soaked with blood and the bride dies. This formulation is widest spread among the Bulgarians. Apparently, one of the southern Slav conception had reached them, which they complemented with the hind motif. Less frequently also other southern Slav solutions are met with. *73*. The girl forced to marry a Turk asks for a knife while on the way towards the bridegroom's home, pretending she wants to cut an apple in two, and she drives it into her heart. *77*. The girls asks for water to drink on the way and expires.

At this point I think it necessary to dwell at some length on the manner of suicide the bride commits under the pretext of cutting apple. Scattered among the Moravians, Slovaks and Ukrainians in the north, and the southern Slavs and Bulgarians in the south, we find this motif occurring in separation, owing to the intervening Hungarian language area, much in the same way as some other elements known from the Hungarian ballads. At the same time this motif appears in one of the French ballads that may be brought into correlation with The Girl Abducted by the Turks. This motif must have existed in the Hungarian areas connecting the western and the southeastern territories, notably either in the form of various Hungarian variants (one should not forget that the ballad of The Girl Abducted by the Turks is known from *one extant* Hungarian variant only!) or in that of the French population living in Hungary, in which case it must have disseminated in both direction from Hungary.

Similarly to the Bulgarian ballad, the German version entitled Graf Friedrich begins *in medias res,* that is with the bridal procession. The traditions of the western and the southern Slav populations supposedly failed to meet the German tastes, or else from the very beginning they received a mutilated form of the ballad, deprived of its initial scenes. In any case, in the second belt,—that is beyond the sphere of the

224

borrowing nations—the story begins with the introduction of the wedding procession, and that in both directions. Furthermore, the tragic development is caused by a chance occurrence resulting in the girl being wounded throughout the German territories, and without an exception at that.

The German summary edition (D. Vlr.) discerns four main groups among the variants. The first group includes eighteen variants—eleven of which are broadsides from the years 1552–1584 up to the end of the seventeenth century, further variants recorded from modern oral tradition, too. But even in these longest variants we can find hardly one or two stánzas to relate the actual catastrophe which represents the gist of the ballad. The Graf is bringing his bride in the middle of the bridal procession; while descending on a steep slope, his sword slips from the sheath and hurts the girl. (Out of the thirty-eight stanzas of D. Vlr. 48/1. = *14.*, the first three stanzas are devoted to the event; the girl is hurt in the heart.) The bridegroom makes desperate efforts to bandage the girl's wound and to comfort her, then gives instruction to the people in the wedding procession to drive slowly because the sun shines hot, and the bride cannot endure it. At home the mother-in-law wonders why she is so pale; is she perhaps in the family way? Her son ticks her off. Then they sit to table, but the girl wants to go to bed. The mother-in-law exclaims indignantly that she has never heard of such a thing. The young man does not explain that the girl is about to die. During the night the girl asks the bridegroom to leave her maiden for one more night (till daybreak), and this granted she dies. In the morning the relatives of the bride arrive. The Graf admits to the father that he is to blame for the girl's death, whereupon the father cuts off the Graf's head and buries it in the swamp. But there comes an angel from heaven to witness to his having been innocent (in other variants a lily grows out of his grave bearing an inscription to the same effect) and finally the young man receives a proper burial. Seemingly, the performers of the ballad try to make good for the loss arising from the omission of the original conflict, that is the curtailment of the original plot, by broadening out the aftermath of the catastrophe by incorporating an additional tragic event into the story. The second group consisting of sixteen ballads relates the narrative in a somewhat shorter form, but at the arrival of the relatives the admission of death is delayed by evasive answers; nevertheless the bridegroom is killed in this group, too. According to *Seemann*, the motif of retardation is a borrowing from the Todesbraut; variants of this kind of both ballads have been collected in the Sudeten. The third group (including 23 variants) agrees with part of the Slav variants inasmuch as the bridegroom commits suicide after the girl's death. As against this, the fourth version presents the story in so brief a form that the theme proper in half of the variants ignore the girl's getting wounded during the wedding procession, retaining only the scene at table where the girl does not want to stay, dies, and the bridegroom follows her into the realm of death.

It is understandable that the German singers tend to depict the girl's agony and the bridegroom's fate after he has died, for the wound received by a chance occurrence during the travel cannot provide ground for a real conflict, indeed it is not quite credible, not even in the stylized world of ballads. It is for this reason that one of the variants tries to render the plot more reasonable by the mother-in-law having poisoned the bridegroom's sword in advance so that the blade slipping out as if *by chance* should wound the girl's leg, thus causing her death. What the singers may have felt a deficiency—as can be inferred from the trend of further variation—has been stated in an explicit form by *John Meier,* the elaborator of the ballad; therefore he tries to restore the "original" and more closely motivated solution. First of all, he considered the sword poisoned by the mother-in-law an original trait, as well as the circumstance—referred to by some of the variants much in the same way as in the surveyed southern Slav ballads that the Graf had in vain betrothed his former brides because they all had died. The motivation is original in his view, because "wir haben für ihre Urfassung keine Zufälligkeit der Verwundung vorauszusetzen, wie sie bei freier dichterischen Gestaltung auch kaum tragbar war". Apparently it would have required a long way to go to discover among the misty paths of origin the one which concerns the girl's despair at her being forced to marry a stranger in a distant land and the suicide that ensued as the original solution which came to be substituted subsequently for the chance event of wounding the girl. Thus he emphasizes the hind motif of the Bulgarian ballads. Similar solutions occur in the Scandinavian material as well. In the Scandinavian ballads, too, the participants of the wedding procession abandon the bride when they catch glimpse of the hind, and the bride left unguarded falls from the bridge and drowns in the river. Since this ballad is a northern parallel of another German ballad, called the Rheinbraut, *Meier* supposes that the same may have existed in the pristine form of the Graf Friedrich ballad, as well as in the Rheinbraut, from which it is similarly missing, but the motif may have gone into oblivion in the course of time, surviving only in two fringe areas, namely among the Scandinavians and the Bulgarians. (D. Vlr. II, 211.) (And we may add that it has disappeared also in the southern Slav territories which are otherwise rich in tradition.)

In spite of all his efforts, *Meier* fails to notice that the motif of the chance wounding cannot be eliminated by an involvement of the hind scene. What is more, the mother's intrigue and the hind motif are practically inconsistent with each other.

And there are still further vulnerable points in his theoretical reconstruction of the original form. Notably, such a supposition can be hardly maintained in the case of a ballad that has been collected in a rich variant series from the entire German-speaking area, and what is more, in addition to oral tradition early written records from the middle of the sixteenth century show also the uniformly current form, with the chance wounding and without the slightest traces of the hind motif. It cannot be postulated, of course, that every ballad in each nation should be perfectly built up. Only so much holds true that a series of variants passing through a broad area must have had once and somewhere a complete and coherent, that is intelligible and sound formulation, no matter how many obscure and senseless elements it may actually carry. The sound and sensible ballad in this instance is to be found in the Hungarian version of The Girl Dying in the Wedding Procession, and in the related versions of the neighbouring peoples. The gradually dissolving parts of the Hungarian ballad—and even the mosaic-like portions contaminated with fractions of other Hungarian ballads—appear here and there around the Hungarian language area, losing gradually their psychological motivations, and reaching eventually the German areas, too, probably through southern, possibly

226

Western Slav, mediation. A trend in the reverse is absolutely inconceivable. If the German were taken for the starting point, then an inadequately motivated, short beginning ought to have been developed into a more soundly motivated story to assume the final and most reassuring formulation in the Hungarian territories. In principle, such a trend is not precluded either, provided the development can be followed in a series of variants proceeding along a well defined route and in logical gradation. But as has been shown, the details agreeing with the Hungarian formulation, or bearing reminiscences of the same, come up in a mosaic-pattern scattered in every possible direction, in the north as well as south, embedded in a medley of other solutions. These, however, always abridge and alter the Hungarian and West-European formulation, and cannot therefore be brought into correlation with the more extensive western texts. Can it be reasonably supposed that various solutions, similar in nature but independent of each other should have proceeded from the most diverse directions, yet yielding to a common law, into a centre where to become united in the most satisfactory form which at the same time would have been best in accordance with the western ballad style? Let us think, for example, of the motif "She was sitting at the window sewing...".

But such an assumption would make no sense whatever. A trend in the reverse, however, can be well imagined and is substantiated by every experience: a logically formulated ballad loses its original consistency in a gradual process of disintegration as it proceeds ever farther from the place of origin, retaining certain elements yet changing to such an extent that eventually the original story, the genuine conflict is eroded or replaced, if not left as it is in its incoherent form, by a new plot. Manifold experience shows at the same time that those parts tend to be swelled into enormous dimensions which had *followed* the original conflict; indeed, it seems to be a rule that when the original formulation had lost its meaning, its transpiring clarity, then the community tries to lend significance to the mutilated or obscured story by adding further details and a different dénouement to it.

Owing to the position of German settlers wedged in between various peoples the "final stage" had got back to such areas in which a more complete form standing closer to the "original" used to exist in a large number of variants. An abridged variant of the story of Graf Friedrich has appeared in recent Slovak collections. (40.) A girl is sitting under a tree. Her lover comes, his broad sword slips out of its sheath and hurts the heart of the girl. Yet they go to the wedding feast, although the girl asks for a (funeral) garland instead of a headdress. Receiving this, she stops breathing.

If now we survey the texts of farther nations, for instance of the Italians, we find once again complete and well-motivated stories, which however do not include details typical of the Hungarian formulation. It is made known at the outset in the manner of a narrator that the girl is forced to marry against her will. She flares up and tells her father to say "yes" instead of herself. But the father entreats her not to put him to shame. The girl's brothers promise to escort her to the new country and bring her back if she did not like it. During the way she looks back at her father's castle, and wishes to turn back (in some variants she falls on her knees to pray to God not to let her reach the bridegroom's village alive). Yet she is taken there and is received by the mother-in-law. The variants make us realize the grief of the bride in various ways: she is not glad of the jewels offered to her, saying that she has more of them at home. Or she complains that she will never see her father's castle again. In one of the variants the bridegroom asks her on the wedding night why she shows so little care for him, whereupon the girl answers that he ought to have asked her about the feeling of her heart before he had applied to her father and mother. At this point the young man stabs her to death. But it is the general solution that the girl dies of sorrow, and the brothers return home with news of her death which they tell to their mother.

The Rhaeto-Romanic people, a small Neo-Latin ethnic group in Switzerland, also called Ladin, supports the motivation of the girl's despair by speaking about a former engagement of the girl with a young man. Now she takes a sad leave of her family, being forced to another man. On the way she meets her true lover whom she invites to the wedding festival, asking him to bury her when she is dead. The mother-in-law greets her as her own daughter, which she refuses, saying she would never be her daughter. At table she does not touch food, and eventually she asks leave to go to her room. According to her mother-in-law it is not customary to voice such a wish in the village. But when she is in her room, the plate turns round three times on the table, from which her brother learns of the nearing disaster. He goes to the room and hears her last words of farewell, after which the girl expires. The bridegroom dies after her, and intertwining grave-flowers grow out of their bodies (which is out of place here, since the case is not one of separated true lovers but on the contrary, one of a girl forced to marry an unwanted-for man). Apparently, this small nation wedged between the Italian and the German language areas blended portions of formulation borrowed from both neighbouring nations.

The Italian formulation is separated from the Hungarian by a zone of Slav variants. The latter invariably display traces of the Hungarian formulation, whereas the Italian version has none of them. The Slav versions collected precisely in regions situated nearest to the Italian language area show the most marked deviation from the basic idea preserved by the Italians. All this bears to the fact that both the Italians and the Hungarians have inherited the basic idea from one and the same source. As a common source, again the French may come into consideration, which however is again represented by a rather conspicuously transcribed text of the Bretons. (84.) For comparison's sake we give here the excerpt of its translation.

As I was washing by the river, I heard the death-bird sigh: Little Tina, don't you know that you have been sold to the Baron Jauioz?—Is it true, mother, that you have sold me to old Jauioz?—My dear daughter, I know nothing of it, ask your father! He does not know of it either, sends her to her brother. Dear brother Lanik, tell me, am I sold away to that lord?—Yes, we have sold you to the Baron, and you must start at once without any delay, for we have already received the price: fifty white silver and as many bright gold.—Dear mother, which one of my dresses shall I put on? The red one, the white one which my sister sewed for me, or the black velvet one?—Put on what you will, for it is quite the same, daughter, for a black horse is before the gate waiting for it to open in the night. They had hardly left the farmstead, the girl heard the sound of bells. She burst into tears: Good-bye St. Anne, bells of my country, bells of my parish! [As they reached the Lake of Anguish, she saw a host of corpses, all in white robes, in a bark. She saw the crowd of the dead clapping their jaws at the breast of the girl. As they reached the Valley of Blood, she saw the dead bodies all running after her. Her heart was filled with sorrow, her eyes were shut, she lost conscience.]—Take a seat and wait for the feast to begin. The lord was standing at the fire-place, he was black as raven, his beard and hair white as snow, his two eyes like glowing ember. — Here is, then, the girl I have been yearning for so long. Come with me and let us count my gold and silver in the room.—Rather I wish I were with my mother counting the shavings with which we feed the fire!—Let us go down into the cellar and taste the wine which is sweet as honey! Rather than that, I would drink the water of meadows where my father's horses are feeding!—Let us go and buy a sunday coat for you!—Rather than that I would have a pettycoat of canvas which my mother sewed for me! ... (and so on). I can make out from your words that you do not love me... Then the girl asks the bird to greet all the members of her family (enumerating them one after the other). At home all were asleep at midnight when a mild tapping was heard at the door, and a low voice saying: Father, mother, for heaven's sake, pray for me: your daughter is being taken to the graveyard!

As appears from the excerpt, we have to deal with a literary transcription in this case. It is particularly the parts put in square brackets where the fantasy of the transcriber was decisively governed by mythological reminiscences. Nevertheless, the nucleus of the theme might be the same as has been made clear from the survey of the whole European material; the girl forced to marry against her will dies of sorrow during the bridal procession on the way to the bridegroom's mansion, or after she is taken there. Since at the time when *Villemarqué* published his collection there was hardly anything known of the variants of the diverse nations (at best the version of Nigra may have been available to him), we may surmise that he had worked up an original Breton popular ballad in the manner of the literary forgery of the nineteenth century. If this be the case, we may justifiedly suspect that the Breton text was of French origin; the more so since the same conclusion has been drawn in many other instances. This supposition is further supported by the circumstance that also the English have such ballads in which the bride finds her death during the way to her bridegroom. But there the girl is not married against her will, only the suitor whom she loves dearly has failed to ask her hand from her brother, too, and therefore the brother stabs her to death with his dagger when she is just about to leave (*82—100:* The Cruel Brother). The girl is bleeding during the ride. It is no sooner that they perceive her trouble. Stanza 19 runs like this:

Ride softly on, say the best young man,
For I think our bonny bride looks pale and wan!

Or in gradation (B/12—15):

Ride up, ride up, said the foremost man;
I think our bride comes hooly on.
Ride up, ride up, said the second man,
I think our bride looks pale and wan!
Up then cam the gay bridegroom,
And straught unto the bride he came.

Variants I and J are similar. The bridegroom asks what the matter is with her. Is it the saddle pressing her, the horse jerking, or the rain soaking her gloves; and so on. The girl asks them to take her to a spring, and there imparts to them her last will, in the manner of ballad heroines. Thus here the scene of dying finds a very similar formulation, while the motivation is closer to certain variants of the Balkan ballads: vengeance and dagger are involved. This transformation seems to have been more acceptable in many places than the solution with the bride's dying of sorrow.

It appears from this survey that there is an Italian, and there is a Breton ballad built up on the same scheme as the Hungarian but formulated widely differently; there is an English ballad which is based on a different conflict but the details of which are formulated much in the same way as those of the Hungarian; furthermore there is a series of variants among the Germans and the Slavs which may be derived from the Hungarian version. All this indicates, with a high degree of probability, that there used to exist a French ballad of which the Breton, Italian and Hungarian have preserved the basic conflict, while the English moulded a new one by means of transformation in a way that it retained its most effective scene, that of the gradation in the agony of the bride riding in the wedding procession.

If the French origin is once accepted, we find explanation also to the question why the motivation of this ballad (and of the related 12.) has been applied as an introduction to "The Bride Dragged to Death", replacing the dramatic plot of jealousy of the "Les anneaux de Marianson" version. In this instance it is the Hungarians that amalgamated two French ballads, just as the Hungarians' neighbours have combined two Hungarian ballads, namely the one under discussion and "The Girl Abducted by the Turks"; the method is the same which may be observed in the interconnections of many other nations in the field of balladry (Cf. Notes to 63. and 68.).

Literature: Moór 1925: derived from the German Graf Friedrich; Gragger 1926: accepts Moór, German Spielleute brought it to Hungary (partial modification of the system of Moór's classification into types); Ortutay 1936—49: quotes Moór on the basis of Gragger; Csanádi and Vargyas 1954: only German parallels are extant, either an independent Hungarian development or a survival of a lost German ballad which influenced some of the Hungarian variants; Putilov 1965, II/2: all-Slavic development, typological agreements, manifestation of struggle against Turkish-Tartar oppression; Hungarian and western parallelisms left unmentioned; Sirovátka 1966–67: the ballads of Turkish themes spread as far as the frontier between Moravia and Bohemia; Idem: 196ﻮ II refutes Putilov, the ballad is a western story of the short-story (novella) type; the Turks have been involved in it as a secondary development.

14. THE BRIDE GIVEN IN MARRIAGE TO POLAND

45.

Parlando ♩ = 126

1. Ud szir ud ke - sze - reg Szep-rő - di Bor - bá - ra
Ke - rek ud - va - rá - bo, pi - lo - ta á - gyá - bo.
Ab - lak - ba varr va - la Szep-rő - di Bor - bá - ra,
Ő esz varr - ja va - la az é gyász-ru - vá - ját

1. Borbára Szeprődi is weeping and moaning
   In her round courtyard, in her bed covered with eiderdown.
   Borbára Szeprődi is sewing at the window,
   And she is sewing her mourning dress.

2. She is sewing it with black silk yarn,
   She is embroidering it with her pouring tears.
   Why are you weeping, why are you mourning, Borbára Szeprődi?
   Alas, I have good reason to weep, alas, I have good reason to mourn:

3. I have been sold by father to be brought to Poland,
   To be brought to Poland, to the great king of Poland;
   And not even to him, but to his bastard son,
   And not even to him, but to his bastard son...

4. They are coming, they are coming in a coach of six,
   Escorted by sixty soldiers and a shabby servant.
   Even the drums are beat to dance,
   Even the horses are all made to prance.

5. They arrived at János Szeprődi's
   At the barred gate of János Szeprődi.
   Do you hear me, do you hear me, Sir János Szeprédi?
   Hand over to us your beautiful daughter Borbára Szeprédi!

6. I don't give you Borbára Szeprédi,
   For I have seen lords bigger than you in my father's house,
   And I did not let them lord it over me, nor will I let you lord it over me,
   I did not let them lord it over me, nor will I let you lord it over me!

7. Do you hear me, do you hear me, Sir János Szeprédi?
   Hand over to us your beautiful daughter Borbára Szeprédi,
   For if you don't, give her to us, we shall levy on you,
   We shall levy on you the emperor's tax!

8. Finally he had to give her to them, there was no other choice for him,
   There was no other choice for Sir János Szeprédi.
   And they carried away, they carried away Borbára Szeprédi,
   Borbára Szeprédi, seated in the coach of six.

9. Seated in the coach of six, escorted by sixty soldiers,
   Escorted by sixty soldiers and a shabby servant.
   Even the drums were beat to dance,
   Even the horses were all made to prance.

Forrófalva (Moldavia), performed by a male informant, 1932 = Domokos 1940, No. 24.

The text published here is the only extant variant that has clearly preserved the basic idea of the ballad about the girl forced to marry under unalterable conditions to a man in a foreign land.

Divergences: Obviously, the concise formulation of the story was found unsatisfactory for the singers of the other variants, therefore attempts were made at rounding it off by incorporating series of events borrowed from different ballads. In the text to follow the first twelve stanzas contain the story proper, while stanzas 13–23 are additions in the above sense.

13. They arrived in Poland,
    They reached the court of the good Polish King,
    Not even his, but that of his bastard son.
    My dearest heart, my wife, will you call me your lord!

14. I will never call you so, never in my life,
    For I have seen bigger lords at my father's house,
    And I did not let them lord it over me, nor will I let you!
    My dearest heart, my wife, will you call me your lord!

15. I will never call you so, never in my life,
    For I have seen bigger lords at my father's house,
    Bigger lords, indeed, and I did not let them lord it over me,
    I did not let them lord it over me, nor will I let you!

16. For the third time I say, call me your lord!
    I will never call you so, never in my life!
    Servant, my dear servant, go to town
    And buy a guilt saddle and a guilt bridle,

232

17. A guilt bridle and a Tartar scourge.
    I know that they will ask you what do you buy those things for.
    This shall be your answer: We have bought a palfrey,
    That is untamed, and we want to break it in!

18. He started out and returned home
    With the guilt saddle and the guilt bridle,
    With the guilt bridle, and the Tartar scourge.
    Placing them on the table, he said: Will you call me your lord!

19. Dearest heart, my wife, will you call me your lord!
    I will never call you my lord, never in my life!
    He saddled her, he bridled her,
    And began to whip and spur her slender waist.

20. Enough of that, enough, enough, my dear lord and master,
    Sunshine went in at one of my sides,
    Sunshine went out at the other side,
    Enough of that, enough, enough, my dear lord and master!

21. Once she heard the voice of her father by the gate:
    Are you at home, are you in, my dearest heart, my daughter?
    Ah, I am at home, and I am in, my dearest heart, my father!
    But when I gave you away to be brought to Poland,

22. These two beautiful cheeks of yours were different,
    They were as beautiful as two red roses,
    And now they are like two white linen cloths.
    What is the matter, what is the matter, my dearest heart, my daughter?

23. There is nothing the matter, nothing the matter, my dearest heart, father,
    I have been in the kitchen, I have burnt oak,
    I have burnt oak, I have rocked my child in the cradle,
    And the smoke of oak has brought out my tears.

As can be seen, the basic idea of the ballad of "The Haughty Wife" (66.) and various portions of its formulation were introduced into the text, though with a quite different interpretation. Maybe, the similar formulas of Stanza 6 had given the incentive for that. The husband's reproaching and punishing his wife show transformed motifs of "The Wife Kicked to Death" (39.), as the scene known from "The Brigand's Wife" (20.) was also applied, in a transformed shape, so as to make the father acquainted with the girl's sufferings in her married life. Unfortunately, the result is not satisfactory: in a plot lacking all convincing force heterogeneous elements have been thrown together. The two complemented variants came to light from one village, Klézse, in 1956 and 1963, that is some twenty or thirty years after first recording is the span of time during which the attempt at expansion took place. It can by no means be assumed that a formerly more extensive story was abridged by the performer in 1932. On the one hand, the inserted portions of text remain what they are, to wit, clumsy and incidental attempts at innovation, and on the other hand the first, independent part seems to have been deeply rooted in earlier tradition because elements of its formulas are to be found in the text of "Fair Ilona Langos" (Type **49**), as well as in the variants of "Katalina Bíró" presented below. (In these, the plot felt to be meagre is rendered more meaningful by means of gradation.)

1. Katalina Bíró is sitting in the window,
   She is sewing her dress with black silk,
2. She is filling the middle of it with her shedding tears,
   She is filling the middle of it with her shedding tears.
3. As she looks at the corn-field
   Aye, they are coming with loud shooting: the son of the Turkish emperor is nearing!
4. He is coming in a coach of six and with sixty soldiers.
   At once the son of the Turkish emperor asks at the door:
5. Are you at home, are you at home, my would-be mother?
   I am at home, I am at home, my would-be son.
6. Is your daughter at home, whom you promised to me?
   She is at home, she is at home, confined to bed.
7. Katalina Bíró is sitting in the windcw...

(repetition of the former scene word for word, only the pretext is changing at the end of the formula: She is laid on the bier; and for the third time: She is buried deep in the earth. At this, the bridegroom bursts out in threating words: Mother, my dear mother, If you did not give your daughter into my hands, Give your soul to God and give your body into my hands!—The mother is scared and changes the tone: Come, my son-in-law, Take my daughter, Let her be yours till death!—Other variants say even more at the end: Come, Kati, come, so that they should take you, So that they should take you To the foreign land! Alas, Katalina Bíró must go away. She kisses her mother, Shedding her tears. Mother, my dear mother, How could you promise me to the son of the Turkish emperor? In a foreign country! So that you may have no longer a daughter in your home To take care of you! Or: Mother, my dear mother, To whom did you promise me in a foreign land? Shall I have no longer a mother?—I shall be your mother Son of the Turkish emperor.— Katalina Bíró burst out crying, She got in the big coach. Katalina Bíró was taken away, Katalina Bíró was taken to a foreign country.

The improvized, not quite mature text speaks of a relatively recent origin, especially in the closing part of the ballad, in other words precisely in the place where a "novel" motif comes into play in this ramification of "The Bride Forced to Marry against Her Will", although the solution falls short of expressing in an adequate manner the tragic moment inherent in the theme.

Dissemination: Moldavia (a) Borbála Seprődi—(Szeklédi): For-rófalva, Klézse 2; (b) Katalina Bíró: Lészped 3. Total: 6.

Textual relationship with other ballads: the basic plot represents a ramification of **12.** and **13.** (viz. **11.** and **15.**). The tragic fate of the girl forced

234

to marry in a foreign land is brought out by the failure of the girl's afforts to gainsay, that is by her being carried away inevitably. The formula "She is sewing in her window..." occurs in Types **12, 21, 31, (43)** and **49**.

Tunes: (a) Borbála Seprődi has three variants all sung to the tune published. (b) Katalina Bíró: has one melody in two variants.

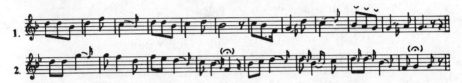

At this point we have to mention some isolated texts which are ramifications of the theme of "The Bride Forced to Marry in a Foreign Country". These texts show that the popular theme has been applied in various ways, all preserving close realtionships of the individual details. The texts can be arranged in the following geographical pattern:

1.Resznek (Zala county):

Make speed, daughter, make speed and go to your private bower,
Change your clothes and put on your funeral attire!
For they have come to carry you away in a coach of six,
In a coach of six, and the horses are harnessed in gold!
Thank you, thank you, mother, my dear mother
For all the care you showed in raising me, and for all your instructions!
Although I do not thank you for your marrying me,
For you did not marry me to the one I have loved long,
But you gave me to one whom I have hated long.
I have fallen apart from whom I have loved long,
And I have fallen in bed with him whom I have hated long.
(Recorded without melody.)

2. Válaszút (Kolozs county):

Mother, mother, mother, my dear mother,
There over I see a big camp, a crowded camp.
I know, I know who is their captain,
It is Gyurica Görögfi, son of the Turkish emperor.
Let me, mother, let me go for a quarter of an hour at least!
I will not let you, daughter, not even for a moment!
Because sooner than I would let you go you should die,
Because sooner than I would let you go you should die!
Good morning, good morning, Mistress Almádi!
Where can I find, where can I find my bride?

And so on: changes into the story of "The Disgraced Girl", characterized by the motif of sending the bridegroom on wide-goose chase. (The continuation see there.)
= *Kallós* 1970 No. 102.

235

Tune:

Fine   D.C al
                                                           Fine

3. Parajd (Udvarhely county):

My Ilona, my Ilona, my tender, fair violet,
Go to the gate, stand up on the gate
And see, see who comes to visit you!
My dear lady mother, twelve young men are coming,
All from Szentmiklós, coming with twelve flags.
Mother, my dear mother, maybe, you have sold me?
In vain should I deny, I have sold you, to be sure!
Mother, my dear mother, grant me a favour:
Let me go down into my flower garden to take a look at my flowers!
My flowers, my flowers, have you, too, got bore of me?
May you wither away, all of you, when I am being taken away,
May you turn into dry stalks, may you dry down to dust,
Let my mother see that you have taken pity on me!
Mother, my dear mother, grant me a favour:
Let me go to my room to take a look at my clothes.
My clothes, my clothes, have you got bore of me?
May you fall off your pegs, may you cast yourself down upon the ground,
Let my mother see that you too have taken pity on me!
Mother, my dear mother, grant me a favour:
Let me go to my room to write a letter there!
I am writing my short letter, carry it my little swallow!
If you find him asleep, put it on his eiderdown,
If he is walking in his room, put it in his window!

Apparently this variant, too, changes into the turns of "The Disgraced Girl" in the continuation. (= MNGY VII, 9.)

4. Istensegíts (Bukovina):

They are coming with such a loud shooting through the field.
Prepare, daughter, prepare, for I have promised to give you
To the Turkish emperor.
And not even to him, but to his son.
Daughter, my daughter, flower of my garden,
Will you ever come back here?
I shall come back, mother, when a grain of wheat,
When a grain of wheat yields a hundred stooks!
(Rep.) You see, I shall never come back here again.

Further examples:

When a pennyless market will be held in front of your gate.
Or: When broad-cloth sells at nine farthings by the ell.

236

Tune:

5. Gajcsána (Moldavia):

Make ready, daughter, make ready, for I have sold you!
To whom, mother, to whom have you sold me? To the Turkish army.
May God grant me, mother, my dear mother:
When they start out, may I lie in my sick-bed,
When they are half-way, may I lie on the bier,
When they reach here, may I be laid in deep earth!

Tune:

5. Gajcsána (Moldavia):

Prepare, daughter, prepare, for I have sold you!
To whom, mother, to whom have you sold me?
To a big mountain brigand.
When they start out, may I be in my sick-bed,
When they are half-way, may I be on the bier,
When they reach here, may I lie in the deep earth!
Finally they arrived. He sent in, he sent in his youngest servant.
Good morning, good morning, my dear old mother!
Can we have, can we have the girl you promised to give to us?
You can see her, you can see her, she is in her sick-bed.
He went in a very glad man and came out a very sad man.
He sent in, he sent in his second servant

(etc. the answer is: "She lies on the bier", and for the third time: "She lies deep in the earth.")

He crossed himself and died a painful death.
(= *Domokos* No. 13.)

Tune:

This text shows a word-for-word agreement with a more recent variant recorded at Zágon (Háromszék county). It seems very likely that the informant had learnt the ballad from Domokos's book.

15. THE BRIDE AND THE ROOSTER

46.

1. Prepare, make haste
   Fair maid Anna!
   Your father promised you to us
   While you were in your mother's womb!

2. I make haste, I make haste
   My dear suitors!
   Wait a little,
   Wait till I warm my washing water!

3. She runs out, she runs out,
   And runs to the roost:
   My roosters, my roosters,
   My black roosters!

4. My dear black roosters,
   Crow, do crow
   Because they are going to carry me away from here,
   God knows, where!

5. The white one answers:
   Let the black one reply!
   The black one answers:
   We have time enough yet!

6. Make haste, make haste
   Fair maid Anna!
   Your father promised you to us
   While you were in your mother's womb!

7. Wait, wait
   My dear suitors!
   Wait till I put on
   My red skirt!

8. My skirts, my skirts,
   My beautiful, red skirts!
   Fall off your pegs,
   Wrap yourself in mourn!

9. Then she ran out again
   And she ran to the roost;
   My roosters, my roosters,
   My black roosters!

10. My dear little rooster,
    Crow,
    Because they are going to carry me away from here,
    God knows, where!

11. The white one answers:
    Let the black one reply!
    The black one answers:
    We have time enough yet!

12. Make haste, make haste
    Fair maid Anna!
    Your father promised you to us
    While you were in your mother's womb!

13. Wait, wait
    My dear suitors!
    Let me take leave
    Of my flowers!

14. My flowers, my flowers,
    My beautiful, red flowers,
    Turn into dry stalks,
    Wrap yourself in mourn!

15. She ran out again
    And she ran to the roost:
    My roosters, my roosters,
    My beautiful, white roosters!

16. My beautiful white roosters,
    Crow!
    Because they are going to carry me away from here,
    God knows, where!

17. We will not crow,
    Because you did not give us to eat!
    You gave to the others
    And chased us away!

(The white roosters were orphan children.)

Szőreg (Torontál county) = Kálmány 1891, 1.

This ballad was recorded in one single variant, without a tune added, in 1891. The collector *Kálmány* attached the following note: "An extremely precious data from which we may realize how close connection is between parts of the ballad and folk tales.—Anna has been sold while in her mother's womb to the devil, although the fact is not expressly stated, in any case either the devil or a similar being is involved, as can be inferred from the traits of the poem: notably, Anna wants to expel the suitors by the cocks' crowing, which is a common feature of Hungarian folk tales connected with the devil.—The father usually sells to the devil the thing of whose existence at his home he has no knowledge; and the thing, as can be seen in this ballad as well, is usually the child yet in the womb of the mother.—Another trait the ballad in word has in common with Hungarian folk tales is that the animals refuse to assist Anna, who has been maltreating them, and therefore the girl falls victim to the evil creatures." *Kálmány* may be right in his statement, for there is another type of "The Bride Forced to Marry against Her Will", in which the cruelty of the bridegroom can be explained from the story of the child sold to the devil while it was still in the mother's womb. In both cases the motif got into the ballad as a secondary development at a time when similar acts of mediaeval cruelty were already unimaginable. At the same time, however, the sale of the unborn child may well be a reminiscence of aristocratic marriages of the mediaeval times, in which case the transformation of the story has been due to its relationship with the folk-tale motif. But neither interpretation can explain the fact that the cocks were "orphan children", as the informant would have it. The story is obscure and fragmentary in many ways, complemented with fabulous motifs. But the diction addressed to clothes and flowers, further the rejection of the suitors and the attempt at delaying the dénouement brings the ballad in correlation with Types **12., 13., (11, 29. and 31.).** The phrase "God knows, where" also bears evidence to the fact that originally the story spoke about the bride forced to marry in a *foreign land*. It is doubtless, therefore, that we are dealing with a special ramification of the two main solutions.

16. THE MOTHER'S CURSE

47.

Tempo giusto ♪ = 150-175

1. A kál - la - i j asz - tal   Kö- rül   van kar-szék - vel.

Kö - ze-pi - be le - vél   Fe-ke - te pe - csét-tel,   Fe - ke - te pe - csét-tel.

1. The table in Kálló is surrounded with chairs.
   In the middle of it there is a letter sealed with black seal, sealed with black seal.

2. Mother, my dear mother, it's time for me to marry!
   Don't, don't marry, daughter, don't leave me alone, don't leave me alone!

3. Her daughter paid no heed to her words, and she married.
   The mother cursed her with eternal imprisonment, eternal imprisonment.

4. When you go to the wedding, let cold shiver catch you,
   When you sit at table in the evening, let your soul part with you, let your soul part with you!

5. When she went to the wedding, the bride grew sad,
   The mournful garland fell from her head, the mournful garland.

6. First the youngest bestman spoke up:
   Woman, cook, the bride is growing paler and paler, the bride is growing paler and paler!

7. For the second time the second bestman spoke up:
   Woman, cook, the bride is withering away, the bride is withering away!

8. For the third time the oldest bestman spoke up:
   Woman, cook, the bride is growing paler and paler, the bride is growing paler and paler!

9. Coachmen, coachmen, put the horses to the coach,
   Go and fetch her mother from the town of David, from the town of David!

10. Tell her to come to the ball,
    To come to the ball, for her daughter is dying, her daughter is dying!

11. She came to the ball to see her daughter dying.
    Daughter, my dear daughter, what is the matter with you, the matter with you?

12. Daughter, my dear daughter, what is the matter with you, my dear?
    Perhaps the supper did not taste you good, that did not taste you good?
    good?

13. The supper did taste me good,
    It is my mother's curse that fulfilled on me, that fulfilled on me!

14. Fall off, you leaves of trees, hide me from the eyes of the world,
    Because I have pushed my only daughter into her grave, I pushed her into her
    grave!

Fornos (Bereg county). Performed by a girl, 1912. Bartók = MF 1638/e
48.

1. This little brown girl wants to marry
   But her mother will not let her to do so.

2. She pays no heed to her mother's words, she marries.
   But, aye, the mother's curse is heavy on her.

3. When you go to bed, may you be taken with cold shiver,
   When you eat your supper, may you die of cold shiver!

4. First the younger bestman spoke up:
   My dear aunt, the bride is swooning!

5. Never mind, let her swoon, let her faint!
   She has been carried here from a distant land, therefore she is fainting!

6. Then spoke up the older bestman:
   My dear aunt, the bride is swooning!

7. Never mind, let her swoon, let her faint!
   She has been carried here from a distant land, therefore she is fainting!

8. For the third time the bridegroom himself spoke up:
   My dear mother, the bride has died!

9. Coachman, my coachman, put the horse to the coach,
   Invite her mother to her daughter's wedding feast!

10. But you must not tell her to come to her wedding feast,
    Nay, you must tell her to come to her burial feast!

11. Where I am walking, even the trees are weeping,
    Leaves are falling from their tender twigs.

242

12. Fall, leaves, hide me,
    For the curse has been fulfilled on my only child!

13. Dawn's fire is kindled at the door of each bride
    But to my own daughter the bells are tolled three times.

Lelesz (Zemplén county), performed by a group of girls. Kodály = Ethn.1907, 111.
(Factory girls of Lelesz acquired the ballad in the vicinity of Szolnok.)
Dawn's fire = When the guests are coming back to eat up the remains of the
wedding feast, they kindle a bunch of straw in front of the wedded couple's door.

Although the ballad's contours are vague, the gist of the story is clearly set:
the widow does not want to give away her daughter in marriage, mostly because she
is too young to marry and sometimes because the mother does not want to stay by
herself; yet the girl marries, the mother lays curse on her and the girl dies during the
wedding procession.

Divergences: The beginning formula of Text No. 48 gives the essence of the
content in two lines, which enjoy a general validity. Characteristically enough, no
personal names are mentioned, only the phrase "a little girl", or equivalents
thereof, refers to the heroine. In the initial dialogue the mother contradicts her
daughter because she does not want to remain alone; in six cases, however, she
thinks the girl is too young to marry. "Don't marry, daughter, don't marry, because
you are not yet prepared for that!". Or: "You cannot cook a dish." In some
instances, she says simply: "You have time enough yet . . ." In the gradated scene of
dying, mainly the bestmen's or women's cries are heard to announce that the bride is
growing pale, and the answer "She is not ill., only tired" is generally omitted. Apart
from this, the representation of the story is fairly sketchy, which is made good for by
details borrowed from other ballads or lyrical songs. Thus, for instance, the scene of
the bride's dying is replaced by the motif of the bridegroom's sending on wilde-
goose chase, what is more, even the formula "May my blood flow in one stream
with yours" is taken over sometimes from the ballad of "The Disgraced Girl", or
the lines "My flowers, my flowers, fall down upon the ground!" from the ballad of
"The Bride Found Dead". Stanzas 12 and 13 originate from a brief lyrical song
about a girl who became pregnant, while Stanza 14 from a generally known lyrical
song. The manyfold attempt at complementing the story shows that the singing
community did not feel satisfactory the content of the ballad. At the same time, the
common nucleus of the ballad is presented in a rather sketchy, one should say,
excerpt form by most of the variants.

In its present form the text seems to be a recent development; nevertheless it is
not precluded that we deal with a revival of fragments of an ancient, mediaeval
ballad.

Earliest provenience: between 1891 and 1919, in the legacy of Kálmány; possibly 1903.

Dissemination: I. Zala county (Búcsúszentlászló, Kiskomárom, Letenye, Magyarszerdahely,
Miklósfa, Pórszombat, Rédics, Zajk), Somogy county (Bonnya, Kőröshegy), Baranya county
(Hegyszentmárton), Fehér county (Seregélyes), Veszprém county (Pusztamiske, Rigács), Győr county
(Nagybaráthegy); total: 15. II. Nyitra county (Zsére 2), Hont county (Lukanénye, Nagyréde),

Esztergom county (Nagysáp), Nógrád county (Ecseg, Rimóc), Heves county (Bélapátfalva, Bükkszék, Bükkszenterzsébet, Eger, Fedémes 2, Füzesabony, Ostoros), Borsod county (Mezőkövesd), Abaúj county (Cekeháza 2, Csenyéte, Kéked 3, Pányok), Zemplén county (Gesztely, Karcsa, Lelesz, Ricse 4, Sárospatak, Tarcal, Tiszakarád), Bereg county (Izsnyéte, Lónya, Fornos), Máramaros county (Hosszúmező, Técső); total: 38. III. Pest county (Isaszeg), Hajdú county (Hajdúnánás), Bács-Bodrog county (Bátya), Torontál county (Szaján), Csongrád county (Nagymágocs, Szeged region), Arad county (Gyorok), Békés county (Békés, Gyula, Mezőgyán, Vésztő), Bihar county (Nagyszalonta 4), Szabolcs county (Gégény, Nyíregyháza, Nyírtura, Tiszaágtelek, Vaja); total: 20. IV. Hunyad county (Vajdahunyad), Maros-Torda county (Jobbágytelke); total: 2. Total recordings from all-hungarian-speaking areas: 75. Seemingly the point of gravity of dissemination falls onto the northeastern corner of the language area.

Textual relationships with other ballads: Most conspicuous relationship exists with certain portions of the ballad about "The Girl Dying during the Wedding Procession", these forming the common nucleus of the two ballads. Further agreements: **65., 83.** Occasional adaptations found in **26., 10.,** and **12.;** "my coachman, my coachman..." **2.**

Tunes: 1 = 47, 2 = 48. More or less iambic variants of the two tunes and derivative forms occur in 19 cases. As concerns the further variants, No. 3 has 6, No. 5 and 4, while Nos 7 and 11 have 2 variants.

14.

15.

Variants in languages other than Hungarian:

ITALIAN: *1–6. Nigra* 23/A–F. *7. Ferraro* 1870, 27. *8–9. Idem* 1877, 59 9 and 88 4. *10. Idem* 1888 7. *11. Bernoni* 1877 Punt. IX/4. *12. Bolza* 55. *13. Pergoli*, 6 3. *14. Marcoaldi*, 170 15. *15. Widter* 94. *16. Barbi*, 25 and 26.

Partial variants:

FRENCH: *17. Arbaud* II, 166.
BULGARIAN: *18. Stoin* 1928 1023. *19–23. Idem* 1931 1159–1163.
DUTCH: *24. D. Vlr.* 52 = *Blyau–Tasseel** 13.
ENGLISH: *25. Child* 216, and the variants quoted in connection with Type **13**.

Literature: Nigra, Ferraro 1870 and *Barbi* refer to the Provençal piece of *Arbaud* which is incomplete but contains the nucleus of the story, and therefore they consider it French in origin. D. Vlr. II/2, 273–278 (Note to No. 52) gives a lengthy discussion of the Italian ballad in connection with the Verhängnissvolle Heirat, more precisely with the only extant Dutch variant. He does not decide the question of origin.

The Italian ballad is built in a fairly uniform pattern and disregarding certain minor divergences of details shows a rather even construction. A knight comes to see a widow (sometimes three knights or the son of the French king himself, or three sailors, asking the woman where they could put up for the night). They ask the girl in marriage, but the woman refuses them, saying the girl is too young. The girl's brother, however, would marry his sister to the suitor. The girl finally goes away with the suitor, whereupon the mother lays curse on them (in other instances forecasts) that they would drown in the sea. When they reach the shore the girl begins to tremble, because she remembers her mother's words. The horse casts off the girl who swims holding the bridle till she gets exhausted and drowns; or they take a boat that sinks with them. The bridegroom tries to save the bride, but all in vain, because she recalls her mother's words which come true in the end.

The beginning of the Dutch text quoted by the German summary edition bears some resemblance to the story of the ballad under discussion. A captain drops in the lodgings of a married couple. During supper it comes to light that he wants to marry their daughter. He is refused with the excuse that she is too young: he may sue for more successfully after seven years have lapsed. Here the ballad follows the development of a different ballad: that of the seven-year-old daughter of a Markgraf. The girl of the count is ridden from the pains of birth by heavenly powers. Anyway, nothing is common with the dénouement of the other ballad, except that the girl dies in both.

The essential feature of the plot is missing in the southern French text quoted by the Italians, but there is an agreement with the French and the Italian versions in the last stanzas where the husband wants to have his wife's body fished out by fishermen. This agreement gave rise to thought that the Italian song used to be known to the Provençals and even to the northern French population. Whether the Bulgarian texts belong here is highly doubtful. *20.* The girl announces that she will be betrothed by the time her flowers begin to bud and married when they are in full blossoming. Whereupon the mother curses her daughter that she may get sick when the flowers bud and lie on the bier when they are blossoming. All this comes true in the third, and final stanza of the ballad: the girl is laid out on a white sheet, with cold forehead. In *23.* the mother beats her daughter because she has pledged herself to a man. The girl is rocking her little brother in the cradle, while so doing she curses him: let he die of small-pox. But the mother hears her saying the curse, and lays her own curse on the girl: "No sooner shall you behold your dear baby than you hear fish singing, stones playing music and the white Danube speaking!" The girl makes her garland and goes to the bank of the Danube where in vain does she wait for the curious conditions to realize, fish do not sing, stones do not play music and the white Danube does not speak a word. She sends words to her bridegroom and to her father and finds her death in the river. In some more remote texts the mother curses her daughter for different reasons.

The Hungarian version contains certain elements which are obviously identical with some elements of the Italian ballad. First of all should be mentioned the principal motif: the widow does not want to hear about her daughter's marriage because she is too young. The reluctant girl marries and evokes her mother's curse. The girl dies while on the way to her lover's home, remembering her mother's curse. At the same time there are considerable differences, too. With the Italians the girl finds her death by drowning in the sea, and there is no trace whatever of the usual gradation in dying. With the Hungarians precisely this gradation offers the essential feature of the ballad, and the formulation of the scene is not unlike the parallel scenes of "The Bride Dying during the Wedding Procession". Another circumstance that may give food for thought is that the ballad as a whole seems to be rather sketchy marked by many details of a narrative character, its ending becomes vague and blurred so that the whole of the story raises the impression of an abstract, with the exception of one or two stanzas describing the bride dying during the wedding procession. One cannot but suppose that this ballad is a fairly recent derivative of "The Bride Dying during the Wedding Procession"; in a way, perhaps, as the neighbouring peoples have found some other cause for the bride's death, for instance the curse—though not the mother's. This innovation resulted, instead of partially different variants—in the development of an entirely new and uniform type of ballad. Consequently, solely on the ground of the Hungarian material, the ballad of "The Mother's Curse" may be interpreted as a modern ramification of "The Bride Dying during the Wedding Procession".

Yet, the question why the plot of the Hungarian ballad shows so marked agreement with that of the Italian remains unanswered. The description of dying through gradation, which is missing in the Italian, appears in the English ballad about the "Cruel Brother" (*Child* 216), and only there in the whole of the western popular balladry. The point of origin of the English ballad—that is the brother's vengeance for his having been ignored in the process of the marriage contract— might perhaps be brought into correlation with the story that survived with the Italians: one of the family members is for, another against the marriage, the brother being involved in both cases, only in an opposite sense. With a cast in the opposite the theme occurs in *25.*, in which the mother frustrated in her attempts at detaining her son from visiting his sweetheart curses him to the effect that he should drown in the river. The maternal curse comes true, and the girl learning her lover's fatal accident, dies of sorrow for him. This kind of parts turned into the reverse comes up rather frequently in borrowings. The balladry of the two nations mentioned shows further similarity in that the betrothed couple—or the whole of the bridal procession—make the journey on horse-back, while in the Hungarian ballads the bride is carried by a coach. (It is interesting to note that the German version of "The Bride Dying during the Wedding Procession" offers examples of both solutions.) But one may also imagine that the motif of the girl drowning in consequence of a curse and that of the girl who dies because she has been forced to marry against her will had run parallel with each other even in the western regions from the earliest times, and that the two have combined only in the Hungarian language areas where the notion of sea is less familiar with the populace. And there is still another possibility: the ancient motif of maternal curse, more appropriately the ballad based on it, had gone into oblivion, tradition preserved only blurred remains, from which the ballad revived in an innovated form—like many other ballads—and it is in this procedure that the narrative of the revived ballad incorporated in its middle section the scene of the other ballad that was currently known and thought to be well-fitting in the body of the new construction.

The fact seems to be substantiated by the spread of the two ballads mutually complementing each other: the same portions of text have merged into the "mother's curse" in a major area, but remain at the same time in their original formulation at two opposite "fringes" of the same area: i.e. with the western Palots and the population of the Szeged region.

But whether directly, or through the other type, indirectly, the Hungarian ballad is connected with close ties to the ballads of the western nations.

17. THE TWO CAPTIVES

49.

Parlando ♪ = 350

1. Já - nos Györgynek két gyer - me-két El - rab-lot - ták a ta - tá - rok,

Já- nos Györgynek két gyer-me-két El-rab - lot-ták a ta- tá - rok.

ossia:

Lacs-csa fel a ku-tya le- ve-se - det! Ég-je meg a tűz gyenge gyócs in - ge - det!

1. The two children of János György
   Were taken away by the Tartars.
   The two children of János György
   Were taken away by the Tartars.

2. A handsome son of his, and a beautiful daughter of his,
   A handsome son of his, and a beautiful daughter of his,
   Alas, they are carried away as prisoners,
   Alas, they are carried away as prisoners.

3. Alas, they locked up her young brother,
   Alas, they locked up her young brother.
   Her young brother begged her,
   Her young brother begged her:

4. Sister, sister, Lady Erzsók,
   Get hold of the key to the prison,
   And let me out,

5. Get hold of the key of the prison,
   And let me out.
   And let us set off for our home,
   Let us set off for our home!

248

6. Let us go to Újfalu in Barassó,
   Let us go to Újfalu in Barassó!
   She got hold of the key to the prison,
   She got hold of the key to the prison.

7. She let out her young brother,
   She let out her young brother.
   They set off for their home,
   They set off for their home.

8. They went to Újfalu in Barassó,
   They went to Újfalu in Barassó.
   When they reached there:
   Sister, sister, Lady Erzsók,

9. Go into the house and ask for lodging!
   Mother, mother, my dear mother,
   Give lodging for the night,
   Give lodging for the night,

10. To your handsome son and beautiful girl,
    To your handsome son and beautiful girl,
    Your released bird,
    Your released bird!

11. Go away, go away, you fancy dame,
    Do not distress my soul!
    Go away, go away, you fancy dame,
    Do not distress my soul!

12. I have just buried my little one,
    And you have reminded me of it!
    I have just buried my little one,
    And you have reminded me of it!

13. Mother, mother, my dear mother,
    At least in the shed of the sheep!
    See them out, you little servant,
    Give them lodging in the shed of the sheep!

14. But see that they lie by the door,
    But see that they lie by the door.
    Sister, sister, Lady Erzsók,
    Sister, sister, Lady Erzsók,

15. Go out and see
    If the morning star has risen...
    Daughter, daughter, my dear daughter,
    Why did you not tell me in the evening,

16. Daughter, daughter, my dear daughter,
    Why did you not tell me in the evening?
    I should have made you a soup with cumin,
    I should have made you a soup with cumin,

17. I should have put soft linen shirt on him,
    I should have put soft linen shirt on him.

18. Let dogs lick up your soup,
    Let dogs lick up your soup,
    Let fire burn your soft linen shirt,
    Let fire burn your soft linen shirt!

Gyergyóújfalu (Csík county), Antal Molnár = MF 1502/a.

50.

a. 1. El - fo - gá -nak két szép ra - bot: E-gyik szép rab Bi - ró Já - nos,

Má - sik szép rab Bi - ró Ka - ta, Má - sik szép rab Bi - ró Ka - ta

b. Mi- kor mennek va-la , Aty-ja ka- pu- já - nál, Szó-val igy fe-le - le: Menj be édes hugom!

c. Most jö-vünk Török-or-szág-búl, Egy bátyámmal vagyok,jó bátyámmal vagyok itten, I - gen megvagdal-ták.

1. Two fine captives were taken:
a. One fine captive was József Bíró,
   The other fine captive was Kata Bíró,
   The other fine captive was Kata Bíró...

2. Look back, dear sister,
a. Are not the Turks coming?
   Are not the Turks coming,
   The Turks and the Tartars?

3. Are not the Turks coming,
a. Are not the Tatars coming?
   They will cut me to pieces here,
   They will carry you away!

4. Get down, little sister, into the gully,
a. Pray to God there,
   Pray to God there
   That He may give victory to my two arms!

5. Victory to my two arms,
a. And strength to my shield.
   Victory to my two arms,
   And strength to my shield...

250

6. God helped him,
a. And only one man was left to bring home tidings.
   God helped him,
   And only one man was left to bring home tidings.

7. Come up, little sister, out of the gully,
a. Let us go home!
   Come up, little sister, out of the gully,
   Let us ho home!

8. When they reached the gate of their father's house,
b. He said: Go in, dear little sister!

9. Go in, little sister, go into our father's house
b. Ask for lodging for the two of us, if only for the night!

10. Lady, lady, my noble lady,
b. Give lodging for the two of us, if only for the night!
    If only for the night, if only by the door!

11. We have just come from Turkey,
c. I am here with my only brother,
   I am here with my kind brother
   Who has been badly wounded with the sword.

12. Go away, beggar, go away, for I cannot bear,
b. I cannot bear the stench of a beggar!

13. So the poor girl ran out,
b. She found her father in the yard.

14. My goodman, my goodman, my noble goodman,
b. Give lodging for the two of us, if only for the night!
    If only for the night, even if only in the stable!

15. We have just come from Turkey,
c. I am here with my only brother,
   I am here with my kind brother
   Who has been badly wounded with the sword!

16. May be, may be, poor prisoner girl,
b. May be, may be, poor prisoner girl...

17. Sister, my dear little sister, listen to me:
b. At the first cock-crow I shall fall ill;

18. At the first cock-crow I shall fall ill,
b. At the second cock-crow my inwards will be shaken,

19. At the second cock-crow my inwards will be shaken,
b. At the third cock-crow I shall part with this world.

20. Brother, my dear brother, my dearest-kindest brother!
b. Is it not to be regretted that we have been taken all over Turkey,
    Yet returned to out father's house.

21. Yet we returned to our father's house,
b. But when we asked our dear mother for lodging,

22. She replied: Go away, beggar, go away,
b. For I cannot bear the stench of a beggar!

23. The first serving-lad overhears this by the door.
b. He says to his mistress: My noble lady,
   I have heard lamenting enough in my life, though it is the first time I hear

24. A beggar lamenting so bitterly over the dead body of another beggar,
b. A beggar lamenting so bitterly over the dead body of another beggar!

25. Brother, my dear brother, my dearest-kindest brother!
b. Is it not to be regretted that we have been taken all over Turkey,
   Yet returned to our father's house.

26. Yet we returned to our father's house,
b. But when we asked our dear mother for lodging

27. She replied: Go away, beggar, go away,
b. For I cannot bear the stench of a beggar!

28. Then the noble lady got up and ran swiftly
b. To open the door, saying:

29. Had I known that you were my own son and daughter
b. I would not only have given you a better lodging than the one by the door,

30. I would not only have given you a better lodging than the one by the door,
b. But I would have clasped you both to my breast!
   With that she embraced her, and died a sudden death.

Csíkmadaras (Csík county), Bodon—Bartók = Ethn 1908, 43

51.

Good day to you, good day, mayor's wife of Szeged!
My dear brother has sent me to ask you
If you were so kind as to give him a slice of bread.
Go, servant maid, cut a slice of the dogs' bread
5. The servant maid took pity on her and gave her a slice of the servants' bread.
The mayor's wife of Szeged said to her:
Get out of my house, temptress of my servant,
Whore of my soldier!
The little girl goes home crying loudly:
10. Imagine, the mayor's wife of Szeged said to me:
Get out of my house, temptress of my servant, whore of my soldier!
Go, dear sister, go and ask her
To give me a piece of linen, only a piece of linen,
15. Perhaps she will give me one, because I need a shroud.
But be careful and do not betray yourself by your words!

252

Good day to you, good day, mayor's wife of Szeged!
My dear brother has sent me to ask you
If you were so kind as to give him a piece of linen.
20. Go, servant maid, cut a piece of the horse-rug!
The servant maid took pity on her and cut a piece of linen.
For the second time the mayor's wife of Szeged says to her:
Get out of my house, temptress of my servant,
Temptress of my servant, whore of my soldier!
25. The little girl goes home crying loudly:
Imagine, the mayor's wife of Szeged said to me:
Get out of my house, temptress of my servant,
Temptress of my servant, whore of my soldier!
Go, dear sister, ask her at least
30. For a piece of deal, for a piece of deal,
Perhaps she will give me one, if only for a coffin!
But be careful and do not betray you by your words!
Good day to you, good day, mayor's wife of Szeged!
My dear brother has sent me to ask you
35. If you were so kind as to give him a piece of deal
A piece of deal, if only for a coffin!
Go, servant maid, give her a piece of rotten stable-floor!
The servant maid took pity on hear and gave her a good deal.
For the third time the mayor's wife of Szeged says to her:
40. Get out of my house, temptress of my servant,
Temptress of my servant, whore of my soldier!
The little girl goes home crying loudly:
Imagine, our dear mother said to me:
Get out of my house, temptress of my servant,
45. Temptress of my servant, whore of my soldier!
Go, dear sister, go and tell my dear mother:
It is her own dear son that asks her
To come at last, if only for my burial.
Good day to you, good day, my brother asks you,
50. My dear brother who is your own offspring,
And who has been a soldier, your dear son:
To come and see him, because his end is nearing,
Come then for his burial!
When the mother reached the place,
55. His soul was just about to leave.
She took him into her arms and so took him home,
She laid him in bed and covered him with a quilt.
But when she laid him in bed, his life was ended.

Szaján (Torontál county) = Kálmány 1882, No. 2.

Divergences: Apart from the reference texts, there exist recorded variants of
the ballad from the Moldavian population, which show very considerable

differences as compared not only with the above-quoted variants but also with the entire Hungarian balladry, as well as with the general European style of ballads. As regards their length, they far exceed the longest Hungarian specimens of the genre. This fact is due to a tendency to indulging in details and repetitions—and these repetitions have nothing to do with the stylistic devices coming under this heading but rather to a practice of recapitulation (for instance, the servant reiterates lengthily what he has heard from the brothers (sisters)—and also in verbose manner of performance that enables the singer to include unimportant, trivial elements at will, to expatiate on certain details or to contract others with such liberty which, as a matter of course, spoils the poetic value of the text. In fact, this kind of presentation mars the style of the genre. We know several recordings in which the informant performed the same ballad on several occasions diluting the story each time in different degrees. Thus, for instance, No. 88 of *Kallós* 1970 contains 47 stanzas, at another time the same singer expanded the ballad to 59 stanzas; another woman performer, also of Lészped, produced first 61 and on the second occasion 68 stanzas. But the singer of Kallós 1970, No. 89 excels all the other preformers by incorporating so many details in the ballad, cramming it with so many improvised events as to raise the impression of an unsurpassable achievement in this line. First she sang 67 stanzas, then she performed the same ballad in another variant of 78 stanzas. It will be instructive to quote parts of her performance here.

1. János Bíró, Bíró, Katalina Bíró
   Both were taken by Turkish marauders.
2. They were carried to a foreign place and forced to work hard.
   They were forced to work in a mine, in a dark mine.
3. There they were made to work, and they worked amidst great pains.
   Katalin stayed at home, waiting for János to come home.
4. She was sitting in the window sewing with black silk,
   She made her embroidery with . . . . silk.
5. She was stitching, stitching, dropping her tears,
   Mourning for her brother, lamenting her place of birth.
6. And she kept mourning: My God, my God,
   Put an end to all this, put an end to our life!
7. It would be better for us to die than to draw our life
   Amidst so many pains, so many tormenting pains
8. I am sorry for my country, my father and mother,
   My father and mother and my place of birth.
9. For I cannot see them any longer, I can only see
   The pains of my suffering brother, my suffering brother.
10. He is not given time even to sleep, he is always kept at work.
    He is robbed of his soul, so hard has he to work.
11. Her brother comes home and sees his sister's tears.

   Why are you weeping, sister, do not cry so long as I am with you!

The narrative proceeds like this till in Stanza 20 the two captives decide to set out for home. This part is entirely missing from the printed variant, which in turn relates in much detail how they prepare to escape, how the girl is baking cakes, how she wakes her brother at dawn, and so on. Let us see now how the ballad ends, after the brother has died:

54. She was very much frightened and she dropped the dish,
   Then she ran to her master: Master, kind master

55. One of the beggars has died and the other is mourning him,
   And she keeps mourning: János Bíró, Bíró,

56. János Bíró, Bíró, Katalina Bíró,
   Who have been taken by the marauder Turks.

57. When they arrived in their country they were not admitted,
   They were not admitted in their rooms but in the cold stable.

58. Their mother heard this and fell down upon the ground.
   Their father jumped up like a mad dog.

59. Like a mad dog he ran to the stable;
   But Kati is lamenting her brother leaning over his body.

60. My Kati, my dear daughter, Why did not you tell me
   Why did you not tell me that you were my children?

61. He looked at his son, and his heart was broken.
   His heart was broken, and he died on the spot.

62. There comes the mother, but Kati is still lamenting
   When she heard her voice, she clasped her round the waist,

63. She clasped her round the waist and pressed her against her own body.
   She was kissing her dress though she could not speak a word.

64. She could not speak a word. They both fell down upon the ground,
   They both fell down upon the ground, and they both died.

65. The little servant goes and sees a great wonder in the stable:
   The father clasped his son, the mother her daughter.

66. All four have died. And what did he make of it?
   My God, my God, give me to die as well!

67. What can I do now, after my master has gone
   How can I bear this great heart-ache!

68. He took them into the clean room.
   He placed the father beside the mother, daughter beside the son.

69. My God, my God, I am going to the church,
   I am going to the church, because I have to toll the bells.

70. He tolled the four bells.
   People began to run about, they began to run to and and fro.

71. All were asking what the matter was?
   For it was not customary to toll all four bells for no reason!

72. They all asked him what the matter was?
   And little servant János explained them heartily:

72/a. They are dead, my master and my mistress.
   Their children have returned, and lo, they have...
   (At this point the tape had to be changed. The informant continued in a different strain)

73. The little servant said, he said to all the world:
    A great thing happened, indeed, my master and the whole of his family have died!
74. They have returned to their country, so did their children.
    And they all died, so that I have four dead bodies
75. Then all the world came to see the great wonder.
    They saw the great wonder and they all took pity on them.
76. Little servant János buried them.
    Little servant János stayed in the house.
77. He stayed in the house, and he was the master.
    But he was not glad of it at all, for his heart ached.
78. His heart ached, for their cruel death.
    He was always thinking of the death they had died.

Here we have, then, something, from the likeness of which attempts had been made earlier to deduce the ballad style, marked—as they thought—by stamps of improvisation. But it is quite obvious for us that the ballad style is not one of extemporization of casual texts, on the contrary, it is featured by a very distinct, finalized and selective formulation of details. On the other hand, it has to be admitted that the predilection to narrate of the Csángó performers is a phenomenon not to be found elsewhere. One is simply caught by the feeling, that the informant does not want to stop singing, and that she is looking for more and more details to extend the happy moments of singing. At the same time it should be added that the informant is an outstanding representative of the "old style" performance, that is the melismatic style. One cannot but wonder how an instinctive artist, as she is, has no sense for the textual part of the performance. Since she is not an exception with her diluted manner of performance—for the population of the most backward Moldavian villages (Lészped, Rácsila and Pusztina) practise the same narrative style—we have to think this mannerism an ancient Moldavian peculiarity which betokens that the oldest layers of the Moldavian populations have not assimilated the true ballad style, have not undergone the "revolution" of the genre as a whole, and that they prefer to recite all their stories of more or less versified or rather sung form, interwoven with trivial moments of their life, as if they were imparting some interesting news to each other, or relating an event that has just taken place in actual reality.

Earliest provenience: 1882, "Szeged" variant.
Dissemination: Torontál county (Szaján), Csík county (Csíkmadaras, Gyergyóalfalu), Moldavia (Lészped 8, one of which is a prose tale, three times by the same informant, two different recordings, Pusztina, Rácsila). Total: 13.
Textual relationships with other ballads: (only the three published, crystallized texts being considered). The "beggar" motif together with the asking for lodging and rejection included: Type 7. (Other complications arising from the fact that the person's identity is not recognized: Types 22, 41, 42, 43). The report of the servant about the conversation that took place in the stable, the scene of recognition and also the curse: Type 22. Escape by means of the key to the prison which the girl acquires, fight with the persecutors while the girl stays in a hiding place: Type 33. (The brother and sister are attacked on their way home: the brother is wounded while defending his sister, and dies: Type 18.)

(+ 4), 4.:

Cf. Leader 307.

Version in languages other than Hungarian:

FRENCH: *1–7. Millien* 164–169 A, A var., B, C, C var.

SLOVAK: *8.* Sl. Sp. I. 149 399 = *Horák* 28. *9. Kolečány* 6. *10.* SL'P II 476 (fragment). *11. Kollár* 57. *12. Medveczky* 1905 3.* *13. Valaštan* 86.* *14.* EA 3659, 2 (Hungarian translation) Liptó county. *15–16. Bartók* 1959 33 and 153. (Burlasova 11a.)

MORAVIAN–POLISH and UKRAINIAN: *17. Sušil* 2339 plus var. *19. Kolberg* Piesni 33. *19. Golovacky* II, 701 3, Carpathian Ukraine.

    The Hungarian ballad is a rare type, proceeding towards final extinction. The variants of the similarly rare French ballad are, with one single exception, identical in content. A young man and his sister return from the wars, or sometimes from the garrison. The girl sings a song about Napoleon. In one variant, however, a young man has his sister dressed as a page, and is on his way home with her from the barracks, after the war. These incongruous, incomprehensible elements, the barracks, the page, and the girl reveal that we are dealing with a recent modernization of an old story. "Sister, dear sister,—says the young man—Lower your voice and your beautiful song: your voice will be heard from ten miles around! Here in the midst of the forest there are many robbers. If they hear you, sister, they will carry you off." Hardly has he said these words before they enter the wood and see the robbers. There are thirty of them sitting on the greensward. Their chief demands the pretty girl for the night. The young man will not allow it and gets a dagger in his side. "Sister, dear sister, give me your kerchief, bind up my side. My love for you costs me my life." When they reach the valley, they stop at their father's house and ask for lodging like two poor strangers. Their mother replies: "O, no, children, we cannot give anyone lodging, for the whole house is full. Go on down into the village, you will get lodging there. The elder sister says: "Mother, give these poor people lodging, someone of yours is wandering about the fields, and you cannot know who will give them lodging!" "If you were not my daughter going to be married today, I would hit you in the face to stop you speaking. You have reminded me of my sorrow and anguish!" Six variants finish at this point, indeed. The seventh variant, half sung, half spoken, carries the thread of events further, after slightly different preliminaries: "The mother finally agrees to give them lodging in the stable", writes the collector of the version. The boy dies at once, the sister laments: "Where shall I get a shroud, shall I wrap him in my apron? O, if only I were in my home, there are many fine linen sheets in my chest, and I would cover my dear brother Andin."—The mother overhears this and recognizes her children.

    The agreement is complete in the end where the girl returns home with her wounded brother. At the same time, only hazy details of the French correspond to the beginning of the Hungarian ballad. Yet there, too, it appears that there must have been some escape spoken of in connection with warfare and soldiers in the original formulation, something we have in the Hungarian ballad. (The mentioning of the page clearly refers to mediaeval or sixteenth-century conditions at latest.) As to the meeting with the robbers and the loud singing of the girl, these motifs are to be found in another Hungarian ballad which will be dealt with in the next chapter Type **18**.

Among the Slovaks and the Moravians the beginning of the story has been amplified. The brother and sister are kidnapped on Whit Saturday. The girl is carried off in a carriage while the boy is tied behind the coach. She is treated well, but he is thrown into prison. He asks his sister not to forget him, but for seven years she does not think of him, then she remembers him and goes to release him. The Moravian version amplifies the episode: twice she fails to find him, but suceeds at the third attempt. His legs are buried in the earth up to the knee, and mice make their home in his hair. They set off for home. In this version, however, the battle and the wounding are missing. Here, too, the mother gives them no lodging, not even in the barn, nor yet bread or water. In one text the boy dies at the first cock-crow. The girl laments him, why did he not die on Turkish soil instead of in his mother's place. This is heard by the woman's little son (in the Slovak text) or by the neighbour's wife (in the Moravian). The ballad ends with the mother's lament in the Slovak–Moravian version as well.

Remarkably enough, both in the Slovak and the Moravian ballads the motifs of battle and wounding are missing; they trie to account for the boy's death, unmotivated otherwise, by recounting the girl's happy fate and the young man's long sufferings in the prison. (After all, the girl survives.) In this connection, the Hungarian version may well have served as an example, because in it the brother is set free by the sister. But it is highly characteristic, on the other hand, that the Slovaks and the Moravians go into more and more detail of the preliminary story, so much so that eventually they ignore the principal story: the Slovak version (*11.*) consisting of thirty alexandrines and the Ukrainian version (*19.*) finish with the girl calling a priest to her brother dying in the prison. Transformations of this kind are rather frequent in borrowings, and the presence of one in the Slav versions would be sufficient to prove, even without the French parallel, that they were taken over from the Hungarians. The assumption is confirmed by the tune of the Moravian variant: in it, reduced to three melodic sections, a widespread old-style Hungarian tune can be recognized (B. 165; cf. *Vargyas* 1959).

We obtain further proofs of the fact of borrowing by analyzing the next type which took its origin similarly from the French ballad discussed in the foregoing.

Literature: *Vargyas* 1960, 1967. *Putilov* 1965, 182–184, on the Slav versions (not quoting the Hungarian and the French versions). On this and other ballads dealing with the fate of captives he writes as follows: "The figure of captives in ballads are representing one of the most significant creations of Slav poetry. The captive as a poetic character belongs certainly to the whole of the Slav folklore as a common property, and therefore it is not too easy to demonstrate the creative contribution in the case of an individual nation."

As to the latter statement, the question would have been simpler if the folk poetry of non-Slavonic and western European nations had been taken into consideration as well.

18. THE KNIGHT AND THE LADY

52.

1. El - in - dult a Vi - téz,   Vi - téz a Ke -gyes - sel,

A ré - gi járt ú   ton,   Nagy ren - ge - teg er - dőn,

Nagy ren - ge - teg er - dőn.

1. The Knight set out,
   The Knight with the Lady,
   On an old, long-trodden way,
   In a vast forest,
   In a vast forest.

2. The Knight says, the Knight says
   To the Lady:
   Aye, my Lady, aye, my Lady,
   Sing a song to me,
   Sing a song to me!

3. I will not sing, I will not sing,
   I have a loud singing voice,
   It will be heard, it will be heard
   By the ten robbers,
   By the ten robbers.

4. They will carry me away,
   They will carry me away,
   And they will kill you,
   And they will kill you,
   And they will kill you.

5. The knight turned
   And slapped her face at once.
   The Lady began to sing
   Her plaintive song,
   Her plaintive song.

6. Her singing was heard, her singing was heard
   By the ten thieves.

Says the youngest:
Fellows, fellows,
Faithful fellows!

7. I know not what I heard,
Was it a voice singing,
A trumpet blown,
Or a fiddle played
Or a fiddle played?

8. Come on, let us bar the way,
Come on, let us bar the way!
They barred the way at once,
They carried away the Lady
And killed the Knight.

9. Then spoke up, then spoke up
The youngest thief:
I say, Lady, I say, Lady,
Are you sorry, are you sad
For the Knight who is dead?

10. I am neither sorry nor sad,
Yet I feel like mourning for him!
His loose-sleeved linen shirt
Is stained with blood,
Is stained with blood.

11. Then spoke up, then spoke up
The youngest thief:
I say, Lady, I say, Lady,
When you were still a maid
Whose girl were you?

12. In a county, you know,
I was the King's daughter.
And if you were his daughter,
I was his son,
I was his son.

13. From the pocket of my father
I stole out a hundred gold coins.
My father gave me a thrashing,
Therefore I joined the thieves,
Therefore I joined the thieves.

14. But even though you arrive at home,
Do not tell my father,
Do not tell my father
That you met with me,
That you met with me!

15. Because he will pass letters
    All over the towns,
    All over the villages;—
    But all in vain,
    But all in vain.

Magyardécse (Szolnok-Doboka county). Performed by female singers of 52 and 77 years of age, respectively. Kerényi 1943 = Éneklő Ifjúság (Singing Youth), March 1944.

The collector remarked that the text was longer originally but people can faintly recall the end of the song. (It may be of some interest to learn that the Hungarian word for Lady is *"kegyes"* in this text, meaning mistress (sweetheart) in mediaeval Hungarian records.)

Dissemination: in the wake of *Kerényi*'s publication, the collaborators of the Kolozsvár Folklore Institute took five more recordings of the ballad, one of which was published by Faragó (1965). Nevertheless, no substantial difference can be discovered between the two publications. But there are a few data at hand to show that the ballad used to be widespread in former times. For one thing, the peculiar quality of the "singing voice" comes up, though in a different context, in a fragment about "The Fair Anna of Arad" or Fair Anna Anador which has been collected among Székely people who first emigrated to Bukovina, then partly repatriated to Hertelendyfalva (Torontál county, Yugoslavia), partly to Lengyel (Transdanubia), and which survives in meaningless fragments or is included in other ballad types:

1. Meg-un-ta két lá-bam tömlec fődjit nyomni, Karcsu de-re-kam a rab-szi-jat vi-sel-ni,

Kar-csu de-re-kam a rab-szi-jat vi-sel-ni, Két vi-rág-sze-mem-vel vas-ros-tán ki-néz-ni.

1. Stanza: Prisoner's song.
The first stanza is followed by:

    Fair Anna of Arad, sing a song
    About the poor prisoners, poor Hungarians.
    I will not sing, I will not sing, my noble Lady,
    For my singing voice is very loud and my song is very sorrowful.
    You see, even now it was heard as far as the banks of the Danube,
    As far as the banks of the Danube, the coast of the Red Sea.

(From the continuation it appears that the girl was sold to the Turkish emperor, although essentially the story runs parallel with the ballad of "The Brigand's Wife".)
    Other details appear in the following medley of ballad motifs and lyrical stanzas (AP 6017/a)

1. Fúdd el szép nótá-dot A-na-dor szép Anna A szëgén ra-bokról, ár-va ma-gya-rok-ról.

Nem fuvom, nem fu-vom, nagy u-rak, asz-szonyok; Most ez az én nó-tám tën-gë-rën túl haj-lik!

Sing your beautiful song, Fair Anna Anador!
Sing about the poor prisoners, poor Hungarians!
I will not sing, I will not sing, dear my Lords and noble Ladies,
For my song will reach over the sea!

(Followed by several lyrical stanzas.)

The brother and sister are attacked while on the way; the sister is wounded in defence of her brother: Type **17**.

Versions in languages other than Hungarian:

FRENCH: *1–7.* See under The Two Captives (Type **17**.).

ROMANIAN: *8. Marienescu,* 12. *9. Alexics* 79 (bilingual publication). *10. Tocilescu* I/2 1247. *11. Teodorescu,* 633. *12. Alecsandri,* 97. *13. Amzulescu* 286.

BULGARIAN: *14. Stoin* 1931 373. *15. Dozon* 1875 34. *16. Miladinovi,* 167. *17. Stoilov* 1916–18 461. *18. Idem* 462. *19. Shapkarev* III 336. *20. Idem,* IV 1259. *21. Idem* 853. *22. Stoin* 1939 324. *23. Idem* 1934 78. *24.* SbNU 14, 80 No. 11. *25. Chekhlarov* SbNU 26 99. *26.* SbNU 41, 406. *27. Vatev* SbNU 43, 84 No. 31. *28. Ibidem* 306 140. *29. Ivanov* SbNU 44, 153 No. 150. *30. Tsitselkova* SbNU 46/I, 119, No. 204. *31.* Izv. Ethn. Muz. IV/89 No. 2. *32–33. Ivanov* SbNU 42 Nos 53–55.

SERBO-CROAT: *35. Prodanović* 170. *36. Žganec* 1950 No. 375. *37–38. Idem* 375, Note (plus reference to Variant 4 from the territory of Croatia). *39. Poljanin* I/69, XXV, *40. Vujičić* 29 = *Vuk*.

Partial variants:

CARPATHIAN-UKRAINIAN: *41–42. Golovatsky* II/599, No. 35 and 700 No. 2. *43. Lintur* 1959, 20. *44. Idem* 1963, 14–15; *Idem* 1968, 70 and Note 19 (listing the Russian variants).

RUSSIAN: *45–47. Balashov,* 124 1–3. *48–49. Chernyshev* 31–32.

The text quoted apparently also includes other portions, distorted in a different manner or obscured, of the French parallel of "The Two Captives" (Type **17**). (The French parallelism is discussed there.) One of the essential modifications is that the story speaks about two lovers instead of a brother and a sister. The sister and brother relation has been transposed—secondarily—into the relation of the robber and the girl, and consequently the story was given a different trend of development. As against this, it is beyond doubt that the motif of singing in a loud voice and the relevant notice are identical, although a further modification enters at this point inasmuch as it is not the young man who warns the girl. It is the girl who warns the Knight and because he feels slighted by the fact, the Knight treats the girl in such an exceptionally rude manner; further similarity is in the motif of meeting with the robbers in consequence of the girl's singing; but the ending is different because the Knight is not only wounded but he also dies.

Among the neighbouring peoples the story exists with the same modifications, though not in a fragmentary form but in uniform and complete tales, related with epic details. In the versions found among all three nations mentioned as neighbours the story begins with the husband wanting to visit his parent-in-law, for the first time after their marriage (although there occur such variants, too, with each of the neighbouring peoples in which the young couple are having a walk together). It is during this that the request is made for a song, and the woman is reluctant, not merely because of the robbers, but mainly because of their leader, her former sweetheart, who had asked in vain for her hand in marriage. (It should be noticed that in the French ballad, too, the robber knew the refugees and calls the young man by his name.) "Sing, Vida, do not fear, Shakoed Captain is my name, and you shall see the might of my weapon!"—says the hero of one of the Romanian variants. The song here, which is extraordinary anyway, assumes fantastic dimensions: "If I start to sing The great forests will echo, The slender trees will bow,

262

Streams will be troubled and meadows dry up." Among the southern Slavs the woman sings with "two voices from one mouth". The robbers prick up their ears as in the Hungarian, saying: "Fellows, is that the drum beating? Or is it the music of a violin?" . . . "Is it not the beating of a drum, nor yet the sound of music; it is Vida's sweet voice." Here comes the scene of fight with the robbers, in which several versions have developed. The two antagonists find themselves evenly matched, and the woman's help decides the outcome. She helps either the robber, who has persuaded her by his promises to intervene, or the husband. If the case be the former, but the husband succeeds in escaping in the end, he punishes the faithless wife, in many instance by burning her as in the Hungarian version of The Unfaithful Wife Burnt to Death.

The Balkan peoples have preserved the story in the form of a lengthy epic poem with considerable details. In comparison, the Hungarian ballad, with its threadbare story and word-for-word agreement here and there seems at first sight to be a borrowing. Nevertheless, the French ballad puts the matter into a different light. There can be no question of an independent development among the French and the eastern European peoples of such a peculiar motif as the conceptually unreal and stylized singing in the forest, and the anxiety and finally the actual meeting with the robbers. With the French, the singing voice of the Lady is heard within ten miles around in the forest, the Hungarian ballads mention only "loud" singing, of which the robbers are not quite sure whether it is the music of a violin or the sound of a trumpet. With the Romanians the whole nature is upset by the song. One of the characters is afraid in each of the variants of the robbers who may hear the loud singing and bewrong them. The occurrence of such peculiar features with various nations cannot be the matter of chance agreement; therefore we must think of borrowings. The only question is simply in what order should we picture the borrowing. Did the ballad come to Hungary with French mediaeval settlers and then split into two, the larger part remaining in The Two Captives while the smaller, altered yet characteristic elements entered into the Knight and the Lady; and did these two separate ballads then go on further, one to the north, the other southwards? Or did the reverse happen: was there one tale in the Balkans and another among the Slovaks and Moravians? Did the Hungarians take over these two distant plots, and did the French settlers acquire them from the Hungarians to unite them into one tale and return it to their former country, France? The latter picture does not seem likely at all: there is no example to show that something should have been restored to French from Eastern Europe. This is precluded by the consideration that the French used to be the people that dictated manners and they were the donors of fashionable songs as can be inferred from the examination of the history of borrowings throughout the whole Europe. At the same time, the adoption by the Slovaks and Moravians of the Hungarian version is clearly evidenced by the route of spread and the way of transformation of the ballad. Consequently, the French–Hungarian–Balkan agreement can be imagined only if a French–Hungarian–Balkan trend of dissemination is accepted: but the more archaic tradition of the southern neighbours of the Hungarians has preserved the original elements for a longer period than had the donor nations (that is the French as primary and the Hungarian as secondary donors).

The ending of the Hungarian ballad, fragmentary as it is, maintains relationship with another ballad, represented by the Ukrainian variants given above. The sons of a woman become robbers in a forest. Her only daughter marries in a distant land. When the young wife and her husband go to see the mother, they are attacked by robbers who kill the husband and rape the woman. The youngest robber asks the young woman toward midnight who her father and mother were, and so it comes to their knowledge that they have lied with their own sister, and killed their own brother-in-law. This ballad in known only in the Ukrainian and Russian language areas, disregarding the mentioned Hungarian fragment. The incorporation may have been due to the obvious similarity in the couple's travelling through the forest and the intervention of the robbers. The place where the Hungarian ballad was found is populated by Hungarians and Romanians, among whom the Russian–Ukrainian ballad is completely unknown. Its unexpected provenience in the region remains unexplained for the time being.

The Hungarian ballad under discussion belongs among the fourteenth-century borrowings of French origin.

Literature: Vargyas 1960 and 1967.

19. THE GIRL WHO SET OUT WITH THE SOLDIERS

53.

Parlando

1. Igy i - szik, úgy i - szik Há-rom haj - du le-gény
Bi - ró Zsig-mondné - nak Kö-tött ka-pu - já - ba.
Me - ző- deb-re - ce - ni s aj bé ba - ras - sa - i.

1. Three heyducks are drinking wine, drinking wine
   In front of mistress Zsigmond Bíró's gate.

2. Fair Anna Bíró walked out to see them:
   Where is your home country, three heyducks?
   It is in Meződebrecen and in Barassó.

3. Do you not know Benedök Hajdu,
   Benedök Hajdu, my sweentheart?

4. Well, we know him as one of our dearest pals.
   Will you not mind if I went along with you?
   We would like it and hold it a great honour for us.

5. Fair Anna Bíró walked in without wasting time:
   Mother, my dear mother, dearest-kindest mother,

6. Three heyducks are drinking wine, drinking wine
   In front of mistress Zsigmond Bíró's gate.

7. I have asked them, I have asked them where their home country was.
   It is in Meződebrecen and in Barassó.

8. Do you not know Benedök Hajdu,
   Benedök Hajdu, my sweetheart?

9. Well, they know him as one of their dearest pals.
   Would you mind if I went with you?
   They would like it and hold it a great honour for them.

10. Do not go away with them, my beautiful flower:
    If he loves you, he will certainly come to see you!

11. Fair Anna Bíró gave the following reply:
    Mother, my dear mother, I will go with them!
    And Fair Anna Bíró set out with them.

12. They were going, they were going along the old broad road,
    Along the old broad road, through the vast mountain covered with snow.

13. Then the eldest heyduck spoke up:
    Let us kill Fair Anna Bíró!

14. The second heyduck spoke up:
    I have nothing against it, for we should gain by it.

15. But the youngest heyduck spoke up:
    Let's not kill her, the poor soul, let her come with us!
    If you refuse to kill her, we shall kill you!

16. Then Fair Anna Bíró spoke up:
    In my right pocket you will find three hundred florins
    Which I give you if you do not kill me.

17. Then the second heyduck spoke up:
    We have your money, and we have you as well!

18. Then Fair Anna Bíró spoke up:
    In my left-hand pocket you will find four hundred florins,
    All this I give you if you do not kill me.

19. The second heyduck spoke up:
    Let us kill, let us kill Fair Anna Bíró!

20. They were going, they were going along the old broad road,
    Along the old broad road, through the vast mountains covered with snow.

21. When they reached the Brook of Lemon,
    Alas, they killed Fair Anna Bíró, the three of them.

22. They forgot to take away her many precious pearls,
    Her many precious pearles, and her rich shirt of fine linen.

23. Go back, go, youngest heyduck!
    Go and fetch me, fetch me her precious pearls,
    Her precious pearls and her rich shirt of fine linen!

24. When he reached the Brook of Lemon
    Alas, Fair Anna Bíró was still alive.

25. Don't you be afraid of me, don't you be afraid, Fair Anna Bíró!
    What words shall you send by me to Benedök Hajdu?

26. Tell Benedök Hajdu, and these are the words I send him,
    He must not perish for a vile girl that I am,
    For I have perished for Benedök Hajdu!

27. Then Benedök Hajdu goes to see them:
    Where did you get all this, three heyducks,
    Where did you get, three heyducks, all this rich clothes?

28. The eldest heyduck spoke up:
    We have bought it to make profit of it, we have bought it to make profit of it.

29. The second heyduck spoke up:
    One of our sisters has died, and she left all this to us.

30. Then the youngest heyduck spoke up:
    No sister of ours has died,
    And we did not take her money,
    Aye, we killed Fair Anna Bíró, the three of us!

31. Come with me, come, youngest heyduck,
    Show me, aye, show me Fair Anna Bíró,
    Aye, Fair Anna Bíró, my sweetheart!

32. For I will give you my grey palfrey,
    My grey palfrey and all my valuables!

33. They are going, they are going along the old broad way,
    Along the old broad way, through the vast mountains covered with snow.

34. When they reached the Brook of Lemon,
    He took his sharp dagger and leant on it:
    You have died for me, I die for you!

Lengyelfalva (Udvarhely county), female performer, Vikár, 1902 = SzNd. 66.

54.

They stop, they stop, the three heyducks
At the gate of mistress János Bíró.
They sat there, and who comes there to see them
But Fair Anna Bíró, and she spoke up:
5. Where is your home country, three heyducks?
The eldest heyduck spoke up:
Aye, we are come from Meződebrecen!
Well, then do you know Benedök Hajdu,
My sweetheart?
10. The eldest heyduck spoke up:
We know him, we know him, he is one of our best pals.
Fair Anna Bíró spoke up:
Wait a little, let me go you
To my sweetheart Benedök Hajdu!
15. With that Fair Anna Bíró walked in damask
And she fastened her skirt round her neck,
She bound up her silk apron before that,
She tied her black veil on her head,
And she put on two, fine red boots.
20. She put three hundred gold coins in her right-hand pocket,
And she put three hundred thalers in her left pocket,
She put on ten gold rings on her fingers,
And her mother spoke up:
Do not go away, do not go away, my dear beautiful daughter,

25. For the three heyducks will kill you!
O, I will go to see my dear sweetheart,
Benedök Hajdu, my dear sweetheart!
And Fair Anna Bíró set out with them.
They are going, they are going, the three heyducks
30. On forlorn paths, on forlorn paths.
As they were passing through a beautiful meadow,
Although there was no wind blowing and nothing to hold it up,
Her silk apron split in two.
My God, my God, my beloved God!
35. My mother's words will come true today,
For the three heyducks will certainly kill me!
Aye, Fair Anna Bíró spoke up:
Let us sit down, let us sit down, three heyducks!
The eldest heyduck spoke up:
40. Let's not sit down, let's not sit down, Fair Anna Bíró,
Not far from here there is a briar,
Let us have a rest in its shade!
They sat down there, they sat down there.
The eldest heyduck spoke up:
45. Let's kill, let's kill Fair Anna Bíró!
They youngest heyduck spoke up:
Let her come with us to see her sweetheart,
Benedök Hajdu!
The eldest heyduck spoke up:
50. If we don't kill her, we shall kill you!
Do not kill me and do not kill her either!
The eldest heyduck spoke up:
We certainly will kill her, we certainly will kill her,
We kill Fair Anna Bíró, Fair Anna Bíró!
55. Fair Anna Bíró spoke up:
I have my black veil on my head,
I have my shoed red long boots on my feet,
I have ten golden rings on my then fingers,
I have three hundred golden coins in my right-hand pocket,
60. I have three hundred thalers in my left-hand pocket,
All this I give to you, if only you don't kill me!
The eldest heyduck spoke up:
We have enough rings and we have enough money,
But we shall kill you, we shall kill you!
65. Fair Anna Bíró spoke up:
Do not foul me, do not stain me,
Let me die a sudden death by one blow!
The eldest heyduck hit her on the head,
And Fair Anna Bíró died a sudden death.

70. They robbed her of her many beautiful clothes,
     They covered her body with handfuls of herbage and under a bush.
     They are going, they are going, the three heyducks
     Till they arrived at an inn;
     They went into it, they went into it.
75. The eldest heyduck spoke up:
     Don't spare wine, don't spare win, pretty wife of innkeeper;
     If you want clothes, we have some to give you, and if you want money, we
     have some to give you!
     The pretty wife of the innkeeper spoke up:
     Where did you get those beautiful clothes?
80. The eldest heyduck spoke up:
     I had a beautiful young sister who died, and these were her clothes.
     Then spoke up the youngest heyduck:
     Alas, they killed, they killed Fair Anna Bíró,
     These are her clothes, these are her clothes.
85. At once Benedök Hajdu sprang forth:
     Where did you kill, where did you kill
     My sweetheart, aye, Fair Anna Bíró?
     He took hold of two heyducks:
     Come with me, come and show the place
90. Where you killed my sweetheart,
     Aye, Fair Anna Bíró, my sweetheart?!
     They set out and they went on the way
     Until they reached the place not very far away.
     Benedök Hajdu spoke up:
95. You have died for me, and now I die for you!
     With this he leant on his sharp sword,
     And at once he died a sudden death.

Székelyföld, Kriza = MNGY III, 22.

Cf. 284–6.

Divergences: several interesting traits survive in a fragment that has been
dissolved into prose:

     She tied her silk kerchief round her head,
     She put on her silk gown, too.
     Mother, my dear mother, draw my ten golden rings,
     My ten golden rings on my fingers,
 5. Put your ten silver pengős in my pocket!
     There was no wind blowing, no branch to seize it,
     Yet her silk apron was cleft in two.
     Mother, my dear mother, what shall I make of it?
     There was no wind blowing, no branch seizing it,
10. Yet my apron was cleft in two.
     My daughter, my daughter, don't you go away, don't you go away,

Don't you go away from home with the heyducks!
For these are evil omens to show that they will kill you,
In the large forest, in the thickest of the vast woods.
15. The heyduck spoke up: I am going to kill you,
Take off your rings, all your ten rings!
I give you all my ten rings,
If only you spare my life, brave heyduck!
Nontheless I will kill you.
20. I give you my ten silver pengős,
I give them to you as well, if you spare my life!
Nontheless I will kill you.

(Continued in prose): "He buried her and went home to meet his comrades. One of the lads recognized the rings, as having belonged to his sweetheart. He asked the heyduck to take him to the place where the girl was buried. When they reached there, he asked the murderer to kill himself, too."

May my blood flow in one stream with yours,
May my bones rest in one grave with yours,
25. May my soul lead a blessed life with yours in the kingdom of Heaven!

Vajdakamarás (Kolozs county). Kallós 1970. No. 65.

In one of the variants, the lover says after the discovery:"Come to the judge...", and they are sentenced. The "Brook of Lemon" occurring in several variants is a love symbol (cf. Look at the Lemon-tree (cypress-tree) with its many leaves and branches, "Sweetheart, must we part with each other?"), just like the briar, or wild-rose. It betokens what can anyway be guessed from the words of the heyducks: "Your money is ours as you yourself are ours, too!" It should be noted, further, that one of the variants places the scene under a poplar which reminds us of the tree foreboding love and life-danger in the ballad of Anna Molnár. (Cf. Chapter 3: poplar as a symbol of world-tree is rather general in Siberian songs.)
One of the variants begins with the formula: "She is sitting and sewing in the window...

Earliest provenience: 1863.
Dissemination: Kolozs county (Vajdakamarás), Maros-Torda county (Jobbágytelke, Karácsonfalva), Udvarhely county (Lengyelfalva, Kadicsfalva, and a further three *sine loco*). Total: 8.
Textual relationships with other ballads: **53.** "Show me the place!", etc. and the promise of giving him the horse and the clothes; Type: **9.** suicide over the sweetheart's body with the usual formula: Types **10., (11.?), 21., 38.** She is sewing at the window: **12., 14., 21.**
Tunes: apart from the published **53.,** a fragment was recorded by *Bartók.*

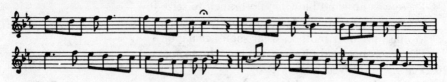

270

Versions in languages other than Hungarian:
FRENCH: *1. Wallonia* 1895, 47. *2. Rolland* III 184. *3–7. Millien* 1906, 248 53A–E. *8–10. Rossat* 1917 5A–C. *11. Smith* Romania 10,205. *12. D'Harcourt* 23. *13. Barbeau* 1962, 371. *14. Arbaud* I, 120.
ITALIAN: *15–21. Nigra* 12A–G. *22. Ferraro* 1870 13.
DANISH (SWEDISH): *23–55.* DgF 338 (*Jonsson* 338 and further references to Norwegian, Swedish, Icelandic and Faroe variants).

The French variants relate the story almost uniformly. There are three young man coming from Spain where they were engaged in warfare (sometimes they are officers or robbers). They catch glimpse of a pretty brunette not far away walking at her pleasure. "Where are you going to spend the night, pretty brunette? You should not go by yourself through this forest!" "Young man, do not lay a hand on my body and I shall give you my golden ring." "We want both your golden ring and your false heart; you will perish in this forest." The youngest of the three says: "Let's not do that, for we shall be punished severely, her blood cries for vengeance to Heaven, and we suffer every pain for it!" To this there is no answer, and the continuation speaks about a debate between the murderers about the question where to bury the girl's body. "Well, let's bury it among the fragrant violets!" Another debate follows where to go to lunch, and they go to an inn which has the murdered girl's father as the owner. "I say, innkeeper, will you give lodgings for three decent young man?" "My Dear, why should I deny you the lodging if I give it to all?" When it comes to settling the bill, the girl's golden ring rolls out of the youngest man's purse. The innkeeper does not hesitate to pick it up. Recognizing it, at once he asks where they got the ring. According to the eldest man, they found it in front of the church. The father demands that they give back his daughter, dead or alive, to him. The youngest man says: "Your daughter is lying not far away, covered nicely with leaves in the green wood." Then they are thrown into prison and executed amidst the choicest torments.

There is a seemingly slight difference at the beginning of the Hungarian ballad, in which the girl does not happen to meet with the murderers by chance but she asks them to escort her to her sweetheart whom she wants to see. But this circumstance deepens the psychological motivation of the ballad, i. e. the catastrophe. Accordingly, also the ending had to be changed: it is not the girl's father, but her lover that recognizes the girl's belongings, and he dies by the dead body of his sweetheart, in compliance with the requirements of the ballad genre. Apart from these deviations, there is a perfect agreement in the details: three soldiers here, and three heyducks there; the girl offers her valuables to the murderers before she is killed, whereupon identical replies are given in both versions. The youngest murderer takes pity on the girl, although to no avail. The dead body of the girl is covered with plants which are symbols of love in both cases, or sometimes she is buried under a bush or a tree of similar significance (briar, rose-tree, violets, poplar, etc. are mentioned). She is nicely covered with leaves of trees, which indicates that the case of murder is not a plain one, as can be inferred anyway from the words of the French young men. The girl's belongings—in one of the Hungarian variants a golden ring, just as in the French ballad—are recognized and identified in both cases in an inn. And finally, in both versions the elder young man denies while the youngest one owns up to everything and also shows the place where the murder was done.

The last-mentioned motif is apt to be used as a means to show the exact place of the Hungarian text between the French and the Italian formulations of the ballad. Namely, the merciful behaviour of the youngest man is emphatically stressed both in the French and the Hungarian versions. As against this, in half of the Italian texts it is the youngest fellow that commits the murder, while the rest of the variants seem to know nothing about the differing opinion. In every other respect the Italian variants are true reflections of the French ones. But on the basis of the mentioned significant motif, the Hungarian ballad can be brought into correlation not with the Italian, which is a secondary development, but with the original French.

Therefore the relationship is obvious between the French and the Hungarian texts: the donor party is undoubtedly the French nation, in this case, too. All their variants show a perfect agreement in connection with the ring motif applied as a means of recognition, while the Hungarians have it in one single case. Another uniform feature in the French variants is that the act of murder is detected by the innkeeper. In the Hungarian ballad only one variant speaks about the scene in the inn where the wife of the innkeeper and the girl's lover act together as discoverers of the murder. In other instances the three murderers meet with the girl's sweetheart on the way, and the *corpus delicti* is recognized without the involvement of the innkeeper. It is not likely at all that the uniform and clearcut French formulation should have come into existence by amalgamation of two rare and threadbare motifs. At the same time we often find the process in the reverse: the borrowing party modifies the ready-made material without being able to completely detach from it, and in result the element borrowed with the original and left unexploited in the borrowing area lingers as a senseless and eroded survival in the reshaped plot.

The Danish version is very instructive also from the Hungarian point of view. Three girls fail to attend the mass, then they put on their best clothes embroidered with gold and silver, adorn their hands with golden rings and set out for a walk. They meet with three robbers. "You will either make love with us or you will die!" They kill the girls, take off their rich clothes and valuables, and proceed on their way—to ask for lodging in the house of the girl's father for the night. The husband goes to sleep while the robbers approach his wife. She is shown the clothes—in variant D, the jewels—and the woman recognizes the things. She wakes up her husband, the robbers are taken and put to death. (In some of the variants it comes to light in the end that the three robbers are the three sons of the married couple who had got away from home while they were yet schoolboys. The father makes attempts at saving them from death, but they want to pay with blood for blood; in point of fact, they raped their own sisters and killed their own sisters. This solution relates the ballad with another type known from *Child* 14 under the name Babylon.) Surprisingly enough, the role of the youngest robber is distinguished in various ways: he either seeks refuge in the forest or receives special mention in the course of execution; sometimes he is buried in "Christian field" while the other two are not. In contrast, the preliminary part of the story contains no hint whatever to the effect that he should have wanted to act differently from his comrades. Thus the distinction is unmotivated in this case; it can be accounted for only as a surviving motif of the original that had lost its function in the transformed text. Another interesting observation is that the texts in which the robbers' being brothers is markedly emphasized, the role of the third (youngest) robber is not distinguished in any way; this motif had been blurred in them by the very fact of the fraternal relationship.

The inconsistent methods of transformation come into play in the Danish ballad—even though in different elements—just like in the Hungarian ballad. At the same time, the adoption by the Italians, Danes and Hungarians indicates the main trends of dissemination of the French ballads.

The Hungarian version belongs among the earliest fourteenth-century borrowings of French origin.

Literature: Ortutay 1936, without comparative analysis. *Solymossy* 1937 lists the ballad along with the eighteenth-century brigand-stories: "...it can be seen... that the bloody action has been deliberately embellished in an attempt at increasing the sensational effect, which betokens the tastes of a more recent, already decadent epoch in the oral traditions of the singing genre." *Dános* 1938: "We have no knowledge of foreign parallels. It must have developed in Hungary during the seventeenth century." *Csanádi and Vargyas* 1954, without comparative analysis. *Vargyas* 1959–62; *idem* 1964/I–II; *idem* 1967: French origin.

20. THE BRIGAND'S WIFE

55.

Let every mother consider it thoroughly
To whom she is going to sell her beautiful maiden daughter!
For I have been sold by my mother
To a highwayman, a murderer of people,
5. Who every night slips away from my side
To waylay, to murder people;
Every midnight he brings to me,
He brings to me the blood-stained clothes:
Spouse, my dear spouse, take these clothes
10. Down to the dark cave, to the running brook,
But mind, you must go down
With them so that no-one may see it,
So that not even the bird may let it out!
You must wash them, you must wash them so that the noise of your beater may not be heard,
The noise of your beater may not be heard, and the drops of water may not be seen!
15. Spouse, my dear spouse, have you been crying?
I have not been crying, I have not been crying, my husband, my husband.
The smoke of oak-tree has hurt my sloe-blue eyes,
Its flame has slapped to my red cheeks.
Spouse, my dear spouse, why did you cry, why did you cry?
20. I have got word from father that I should go to wedding,
My young brother is getting married, my young sister is getting married.
Spouse, my dear spouse, what gift will you bring to them?
Husband, my dear husband, I bring a pair of wax-candles.
It is a custom with us: should a girl marry,
25. Should a young man marry, they are given wax-candles.
Spouse, my dear spouse, how is it, how is it;
The birds do not sing in your father's woods?
Husband, my dear husband, it is a custom with us:
When a girl marries, the birds do not sing.
30. Spouse, my dear spouse, how is it, how is it;
People are not ploughing in your father's field?
Husband, my dear husband, it is a custom with us:
When a girl marries, they do neither sow nor plough.
Spouse, my dear spouse, how is it, how is it:
35. The bells are not tolled in your father's town.
Husband, my dear husband, it is a custom with us:

When a girl marries, the bells are not tolled.
Spouse, my dear spouse, how is it, how is it:
I see a great deal of people in your father's court.
40. Husband, my dear husband, it is a custom with us:
When a girl marries, many people gather together.
Spouse, my dear spouse, how is it, how is it:
I hear sounds of loud bewailing in your father's court.
Husband, my dear husband, it is a custom with us:
45. When a girl marries, people lament her with loud bewailing.
Seize him and throw him into the deepest prison:
He killed my father, he killed my mother!
Seize him and throw him into the deepest prison,
He killed my young brother, he killed my young sister!

Kánya (Tolna county) = MNGY VIII, 184.

56.

1. I thank for my mother's having raised me with tender care,
Although I cannot thank her for her having given me in marriage.

2. For she has given me to a highwayman,
To a highwayman, to a brigand in the forest.

3. For he is sleeping throughout the day and goes out killing at night,
For he is sleeping throughout the day and goes out killing at night.

Mánfa (Baranya county) 1949. Performed by a man of 77. Lajos Kiss.

57.

1. My Juli, my dear Juli,
   My dear wife,
   Do you know, my Juli,
   This blood-stainted piece of robe?

2. Sorry, I do not know it,
   For I have never seen it before.
   Sorry, I do not know it,
   For I have never seen it before.

3. Husband, my dear husband,
   My dear wedded spouse,
   My father has sent me a letter
   To go to the ball.

4. What shall we take to the ball,
   What shall we take to the ball,
   What shall we take to the ball,
   What shall we take to the ball?

5. Nothing is wanted there
   But a pair of vax candles.
   Nothing is wanted there
   But a pair of vax candles.

6. Juli, my dear Juli,
   My dear wife,
   What is the reason,
   What is the reason,

7. That in this woods
   Not even a bird sings?
   That in this woods
   Not even a bird sings?

8. But they are singing,
   But they are singing:
   Settled on the top of trees
   They are twittering.

9. My Juli, my dear Juli,
   My dear wife!
   In your father's field
   Not even a plough is seen at work!

10. Surely they are ploughing,
    Surely they are ploughing!
    Only the many farm-hands
    Are away to give the horses to drink.

11. My Juli, my dear Juli,
    My dear wife,

276

In your father's village
Bells are tolled loudly!

12. O they are not tolling the bells,
    Rather they are playing music.
    O they are not tolling the bells,
    Rather they are playing music.

13. My Juli, my dear Juli,
    My dear wife,
    In your father's kitchen
    I see smoke arising!

14. Many guests are coming,
    They are frying and cooking dishes.
    Many guests are coming,
    They are frying and cooking dishes.

15. My Juli, my dear Juli,
    My dear wife,
    In your father's yard
    They are busy at drilling and carving wood.

16. Many guets are coming,
    They are making many tables.
    Many guests are coming,
    They are making many tables.

17. My heyducks, my heyducks,
    All the twelve of you,
    All the twelve of you
    Shall line in front of me!

18. Take him, take him,
    Throw him into the deepest dungeon!
    Take him, take him,
    Throw him into the deepest dungeon!

19. My Juli, my dear Juli,
    My dear wife,
    Redeem me from death,
    From the hangman's hand!

20. And I shall not redeem you,
    Not even for a farthing!
    And I shall not redeem you,
    Not even for a farthing!

21. My Juli, my dear Juli,
    My dear wife.
    Had I known
    Had I known,

22. Had I known
    How false in your heart you were,
    In that big forest
    I should have killed you.

23. In your beautiful red blood
    I should have bathed.
    In your beautiful red blood
    I should have bathed.

Berzence (Somogy county), performed by an informant of 69. Seemayer 1932 = MF 3232/a.

The following explanation was added by the informant: "A landlord had two beautiful daughters. The bandit forced the father to marry one of them to him. He loved the younger one, yet he got the older. He breathes revenge: as the younger sister was engaged, he enticed her to go to the forest. He stabbed her to death in her bride's clothes. Then he showed the bloody veil and wreath to his wife, determined to kill her as well in case she would recognize the things. The wife noticed his intention, but pretended to be unaware of her sister's fate. Also breathing revenge, she had the bandit to leave the forest for her father's place, where he was caught by the heyducks (armed servants).

58.

1. My God, my God, make the water flood,
   Let it take me to my father's gate.
   From my father's gate to my mother's table (or: door),
   So that she may learn at last to whom she has given me in marriage.

2. For he is a pompous soldier, a renowned thief,
   Just now he is on waylaying,
   He is on waylaying, killing the orthodox priest,
   Shedding red blood for a coin or two.

3. I am not used to, I am not used to get up at dawn,
   Before crimson dawn breaks, to go down to the creek.
   To go down to the creek, washing bloody clothes,
   Soaking them with my shedding tears, beating them amidst loud words of wail.

278

4. The renowned thief overhears through the door
   How his wife is lamenting herself.
   Open up the door, open up the door, you tender Servian wife!
   Why did you weep, why did you weep, you tender Servian wife?

5. I am not weeping, I am not weeping, my dear kind husband!
   I have been busy in the kitchen, burning the wood of oak,
   Burning the wood of oak, rocking my child,
   And the smoke of oak has brought out my tears.

6. Prepare, Servian wife to go to the meadow of blood!
   Place your child in the middle of the yard!
   There wind will blow to rock it,
   There a neighbour's wife will lift it up.

Csíkvacsárcsi (Csík county) Bartók 1907 = MF 1016/a II. = Ethn. 1908, 106.

59.

1. Mother, my dear mother, Why did you give me away
   Up to the high, cold snow-covered mountain, to be wife to a renowned thief?

2. To a renowned thief, a highwayman,
   A highwayman, a robber of people,

3. Who goes out at every dawn to kill people,
   For one coin or two to shed blood mercilessly,

4. For an onion to perish a soul,
   For an onion to perish a soul,

5. I am not used to, I am not used to wash bloody kerchiefs!
   Which I have been washing with my tears dropping, beating amidst words of
   bewail.

6. At that her murderous husband reached the house:
   Why are you weeping, wife, why are you weeping? I shall take your life at
   once!

7. I am not weeping, I am not weeping, I am burning oak,
   I am burning oak, I am rocking the child.

8. The smoke of oak has brought out my tears,
   The smoke of oak has brought out my tears.

9. He took her down into the cellar and cut her throat.
Father, my dear father, where is my dear mother?

10. Hold your tongue, son, hold you tongue, your mother will come sooner or later,
Your mother will come by lunch time!

11. Father, my dear father, it is lunch time now,
It is lunch time now, yet mother has not come!

12. He took him down into the cellar and cut his throat
He cut his throat: Here is your dear mother!

Csíkszenttamás (Csík county) Bartók 1907. Female performer. Bartók = MP 1024b.

60.

Parlando ♩ = 103

1. Is - te-nem, is- te -nem, Á - raszd meg a vi - zet,

Hogy vi-gyen el en - gem A - pám ka - pu - já - ba!

1. My God, my God, make the water flood,
Let it carry me to my father's gate!

2. From my father's gate to my mother's door,
Let them know at last to whom they have given me in marriage!

3. He is a husband having eight oxen, he is pompous soldier (or: a renowned mountain thief)
I wish I had been married to a swineherd!

4. For I am tired of getting up early in the morning,
To get up early in the morning, to walk down to the brook.

5. To wash bloody clothes, to beat amidst loud bewail,
To beat amidst loud bewail, to soak with my tears.

6. For just now he is on waylaying at the cross-road,
Waylaying at the cross-road, killing the Armenian priest.

7. For one coin or two he is ready to shed blood,
For one coin or two he is ready to shed blood.

8. Her bewail was overheard by the renowned mountain thief,
He kicked at the door, he kicked at the door.

9. Let me in, let me in, you renowned whore!
Let me in, let me in, you renowned whore!

280

10. Wait a little, wait a little, my kind-hearted husband!
    Let me fasten my veil reaching to the ground to my hair,

11. Let me put on my shoed red long boots!
    Let me put on my shoed red long boots!

12. Upon her second word he kicked the door in,
    Upon her second word he kicked the door in.

13. Why are you weeping, why are you weeping, you renowned whore?
    Why are you weeping, why are you weeping, you renowned whore?

14. I am not weeping, I am not weeping, my kind-hearted husband.
    I am not weeping, I am not weeping, my kind-hearted husband!

15. I have been burning oak, I have been rocking the child,
    It is the smoke of oak that brought out my tears.

16. Prepare, wife, prepare to go to the corn-field,
    To the corn-field, to the scaffold where your head will be taken!

17. My little János, my little János, my long-haired servant,
    Draw out the coach and harness my six horses!

18. Take me to the cornfield,
    To the scaffold where my head will be taken.

19. Where my head will be taken wash my heart and my liver
    In wormwood wine, wrap them in soft linen,

20. Place them on a plate of brass and take them to Barassó,
    Take them to Barassó so that they may fasten them to the town-gate!

21. Let every father and mother take an example by me
    How they should give away their daughter in marriage in the cold mountain covered with snow.

22. To a husband having eight oxen, to a pompous soldier,
    Rather should they marry their daughter to a swineherd.

23. Hush, baby, hush pretty Péter Ráduj,
    Your mummy is coming soon, bringing you the teats,

24. Bringing you the teats, bringing me cakes.
    Bringing you the teats, bringing me cakes.

25. This was overheard by the renowned mountain thief,
    His heart broke, his child remained.

Lészped (Moldavia). Performed by a woman of 56. = Faragó–Jagamas 12a.

Cf. Leader, 273–78.

Divergences:
Gönczi 1948 publishes a fragmentary variant of 55–57. (pp. 263–64):

1. My dearest, my wife, what is this matter?
   That there are no ploughs to plow the field of Lemon?
   Never mind, my husband, they are celebrating a feast,
   They are attending the mass.

2. My dearest, my wife, what is this matter?
   Carpenters are carving and drilling in your father's yard.
   Never mind, my husband, they hired carpenters,
   They are making abodes.

3. Never mind, my husband, we shall go to my father,
   We too shall take a look at the carpenters.
   Bar, servant, bar the gates of my father,
   Kill and slay my murderer!

4. My dearest, my wife, had I known of it
   I would have killed you in the wild forest,
   I would have hung your fine, white flesh on a branch,
   I would have given your fine, red blood to the earth,
   Black ravens would have picked your two black eyes.
   (Radamos, Zala county)

Lajos Schneider collected another variant in 1953.

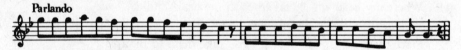

Pá-rom, é-dës pá-rom Mi an-nak az o - ka: Atyád or-szá-gá-ba Na-gyon haran- goz- nak?

1. Spouse, my dear spouse, what is the reason,
   In your father's country the bells are tolled so loud?

2. Spouse, my dear spouse, it is a custom with us:
   When a girl is married, they toll the bells loud.

3. Spouse, my dear spouse, if I only knew that,
   I certainly should have killed you in the green forest!

4. May my blood flow in one stream with yours,
   May my body rest in one grave with yours!

"She heard it as a girl on the Zdravica estate." (Verőce county, Slavonia.)
Mohács (Baranya county). Performed by a woman of 72.

The beginning formula "My God, my God, make the water flood" enjoys widest spread, since eighteen texts have it as incipit. Next the formula "Come, Danube, come with shower and rain" comes up in nine variants, the aim being again to have the flood carry the daughter to their parents. In some of the Moldavian variants the motive suffers alteration: "Little bird, little bird, do not stir up the water, Let me drink of it, and let me write a letter to my mother..." (six variants). The other formula that frequently opens the ballad is one of reproach: "Mother, my

282

dear mother, why did you give me away in marriage?" (and variants thereof), occurring in fourteen cases; "I have begged father and mother not to give me away... (or: I have told them in advance, I have told them...), in six variants. Sometimes the sentence is voiced at the beginning: "May God deal heavily with the father and mother...", or: "Cursed be the father, and cursed be the mother..." in five instances. The intense complaint is sometimes borrowed from texts of lyrical songs, as can be observed in several Moldavian variants: "Mother, my dear mother, when you were bathing me..." (or: "When you gave birth to me", and the like), also in six variants. The second part of the complaint serves as an incipit formula, too: "I am not used to, I am not used to", or: "I have got tired of getting up at dawn").

The scene of the husband who stands at the door listening, or shouting to his wife, occasionally kicking the door in, and the ensuing evasive replies of the wife comes up in its appropriate place in this ballad as well. In twenty-two cases the wife tries to delay opening the door on pretext of tidying her dress; in thirteen instances this scene is not given in detail, though the formulas: "Open the door, open the door, my wedded wife" and "The renowned thief was listening at the door", and so on, indicate the situation unmistakably. This is followed by the man's calling to answer his wife: Why did you weep, why did you weep...?; in seventeen instances, however, only this question remains in the utterly abridged texts in which only the most important details have been retained.

Two Transylvanian and twelve Moldavian texts preserve only the wife's plaintive words, without presenting the continuation of the story.

The formula in 60. (and in three other texts): "Wash my heart and liver in wormwood wine" is replaced in most of the variants by references to the head: "Take up my head, Put it in your bag, Put it in your bag And take it to Moldavia, Place it on the table of Márton Móduai! Let me stay on his table Both at dinner and supper. Early in the morning Place me in the gate! Let every father and mother Take an example of me, So that they should not give away their child In marriage up in the snow-covered, cold mountains!" In twenty-eight cases the passage is strongly curtailed. In two instances the severed head is thrown in the Danube to be carried off to the table of the wife's parents.

Instead of "They should not give her daughter in marriage up to snow-covered cold mountains..." we have sometimes the explicit demand: "Curse on him... who gives his daughter in marriage in a distant land" or "foreign country".

The following lyrical plaintive song (known as an independent construction in Transylvania (as well as in Moldavia) occurs as a beginning formula in certain Moldavian texts:

Mother, my dear mother, who nursed me kindly!
When you were bathing me in lukewarm water,
When you were bathing me in lookwarm water,
I wish you had been bathing me in boiling hot water!
When you were wrapping me in soft linen cloth,
I wish you had been wrapping me in live coal!
When you were rocking me in my little cradle,
I wish you had rocked me down to the deep earth!

Then you would not have given me away up to snow-covered, cold mountains,
To the snow-covered, cold mountains, to be the wife of a renowned thief!

The usual complaints are complemented in the Moldavian texts with the following motif:

I am not used to, I am not used to wash bloody clothes...

contrasted with pictures of by-gone days:

For I was not used, while in my father's home,
To go down to the river to wash bloody clothes,
Mingling water with my tears, make my beater heavy with my bewails.
But I was used to go to bed in the evening,
Go to bed in the evening, get up early in the morning,
Go to do a work and sing to my liking.

Earliest provenience: 1843. (*Ince Petrás,* Klézse.)
Dissemination: Zala county (Radamos), Somogy county (Berzence), Tolna county (Kánya), Baranya county (Mánfa, Mohács = Zdravica, Verőce county, Slavonia); Kolozs county (Vajdakamarás), Maros-Torda county (Marosvásárhely, Marosmagyaró), Udvarhely county (Alsórákos, "Udvarhelyszék", "Udvarhely county, Zajzon), Kadicsfalva, Lengyelfalva, Oláhfalu, Rugonfalva), Csík county (Borszék, Szárhegy, Tekerőpatak, Gyergyócsomafalva, Ditró 2, Gyergyóalfalu 2, Csíkvacsárcsi 2, Csíkmadaras, Csíkjenőfalva, Csíkszenttamás, Kászonimpér, Gyimesfelsőlok), Háromszék county ("Háromszék", "Erdővidék", Zágon 2), "Székelyföld", "A székely havasokon", Bukovina (Hertelendyfalva–Andrásfalva, Andrásfalva 5, Hadikfalva, Istensegíts, Fogadjisten, "Bukovina" 2), Moldavia (Bogdánfalva 3, Diószén, Gerlén 3, Kickófalva, Klézse 6, Lábnik 2, Lészped 11, Luizikalagor 4, Pusztina 3, Rácsila 2, Trunk). Total: 87. Transdanubia (plus Slavonia): 5 (of which 3 are fragments). Transylvania: 32, Bukovina: 11, Moldavia: 39.

Textual relationships with other ballads: Thematic correlations: Types **11–14.** Blocs of text: "Open up the door..." Types **1, 21, 78;** "Prepare, wife, prepare for to go to the scaffold..." Type **21;** "Take out my heart...": Types **6, 25, 31, 57;** "Dear father, where is my dear mother...?": Type **2;** "... Bring forth the coach...": Type **2, 39;** "Cursed be the father, a thousand times the mother...": Type **26.** Portions adopted from other ballads and applied in certain variants: "If you find him asleep...": Type **10;** "Which one will you choose of the three deaths...?": Types **1, 28** (together with the motif of combustion); "May my blood flow in one stream with yours...": chiefly Type **10;** "There will come winds..." = "There will be warm rains...": Types **2, 4, 5.**
Tunes: 1. = No. 56. 2 = No. 57, also from Moldavia with cadences 5 (4) b -flat, 3 = No. 58 (3 variants), 4 = Nos 59 and 60 (plus 7), 6. (plus 1), 14.: NB. Transposed a second lower by Bartalus. 16. (plus 1), 17. (plus 9), 18. (plus 2), 22. (plus 1), 29. (plus 1), 30. (plus 1).

285

286

Versions in languages other than Hungarian:

MORAVIAN: *1–3. Sušil* 288–289 (288 complemented with additional variants). *4–5. Bartoš–Janáček* 1901 70–71, *6. Bartoš–Janáček* 1953 186.

SLOVAK: *7–8. Bartók* 1959 332b, 337. *9–12. Slov.* sp. I 255 and 285, II 555, III 253. *13–15.* SL'P II 374, III 829 and 927. *16–17. Kolečány* 49–50. *18. Medveczky* 1906 252. *19. Kollár* 51 (= *Szeberényi* 425, in Hungarian translation). (*Burlasova* 16abc.)

CARPATHIAN-UKRAINIAN: *20. Golovatsky* III/1 7. Nagylucska (in the vicinity of Munkács). *21.* Lintur, 109.

RUSSIAN: *22–24. Balasov,* 128–131, Nos 1–3. *25–26. Chernyshev* 101–102.

ROMANIAN: *27. Amzulescu* 294 (plus 4 variants, all from the territory of prewars Hungary).

POLISH: *28. Kolberg* 1857 37a. *29–30. Czernik* 251 and 256.

CROAT-SLOVENIAN: *31.* HNP V, 151. *32–49. Dodaţak* (= complements to) HNP V, 530 151. *50–55. Štrekelj* I 99–100, 209–213. *56. Kurelac* 453 (Csemba, north-western Transdanubia). *57. Prodanović* 263. *58. Grün* 24. *Kumer* 419.

BULGARIAN: *60.* A–V 48. *61–70. Stoin* 1928 478, 1058, 1218, 1219, 1747 (1748), 2538, 2539, (2540), 2541. *71–74. Idem* 1931 345–348. *75–78. Idem* 1939 394–397. *79–81. Idem* 1934 102–104. *82.* SbNU 27 *Jankov* 175. *83. Stoilov* 26. *84. Miladinovi* 229. *85.* SbNU 8, 135. *86–90.* SbNU 43, *Vatev* 127, 379–382. *91.* SbNU 44, *Ivanov* 187. *92.* SbNU 26 178. *93–94.* SbNU 46/I, *Tsitselkova* 33–34.

Partial variants:

GERMAN: *95–100. Hauffen* 124 = D. Vlr. 107, *Gottschee.*

DANISH (SWEDISH): *101–109.* DgF 47 (*Jonsson* 47).

FRENCH: *110–189. Doncieux* 7 (enumerates 59 variants, while *Barbeau* 90; as for myself, I succeeded in listing 80).

(For the motif "Take out my heart..." etc. see Note to Type **57**.)

As regards the closing part, this ballad shows a differentiation in two distinct territorial branches. In the Transdanubian region there exists two single variant and three fragments to preserve the old tradition and the wife's vengeance. In Transylvania and Moldavia numerous variants survive of the other version in which the woman falls victim to the cruel man. Both start with the wife's complaint, from which we learn that the man pursues a criminal trade. In both versions the man overhears the wife's complaint and calls her to answer. The Transylvanian branch is cut short at this point and receives a sudden tragic ending: the suspicious husband does not give credit to the evasive replies and kills the wife. An orphan child is left back. According to the Transdanubian version, she succeeds in deceiving him; in this case the situation is made more intense by the circumstance that the wife knows her relatives had been killed by her husband. Although this particular is disclosed at the end of the ballad, the ballad is not lacking in dramatic force, on the contrary, by this fact the effect of bad omens and the woman's revenge is powerfully enhanced.

The same duality, and sometimes the contamination of the two different solutions appear also in the ballads of the neighbouring nations. Let us begin the survey in the northwestern Moravian parts and proceed from them around the borderlines of the Hungarian language area.

5. (Each line twice.) I know a castle beyond the Morava; seven lords, seven brothers with one sister in it. She has been married to the robber Yanichka. Yanichek is a real robber, he knows all the paths in the hills and all the ways to town. He goes out at night and returns during the night, never going to bed at home. He has brought home a bundle of white clothes all stained with blood. He told me to wash them with soap, though he forbade me to unwrap them. I washed and unwrapped the bundle, and a white hand rolled out of it. Wait a minute, my husband, this is my brother's hand. The hand of my youngest brother who is handsomest of all.—Katerinka, my wife, for heaven's sake, do not betray me!—O, what sort of wife should they call me if I betrayed my husband! O, what sort of sister should they call me, if I remained silent in my brother's case! Without any delay Katerinka imparted the fact to the judge: "Judge, lords, according to the law, he is my husband and also a murderer. He has killed my brother and gravely bereaved me." "Waste no time, Kachenko, go home to entertain him!" Without delay Katerinka ran home and prepared the breakfast. She kept him at home. Pandours came and arrested Yanichka. "Where are you taking me? Wife, Katerinka, this is not what you promised me!" He was taken and bound and put on a cart. "Come, Kachenka, get in the coach and take leave of one another!" "Go, Yanichka, go on your way, for I remain a good sister, without a husband I can live as a widow!"

By and large 6. has a similar construction, with the difference that the husband tries to find excuses: "It was dark, and I could not see clear enough, wind was blowing, I could not hear well enough." There is a different introduction to 1; Under the green maple-tree, the girl is ploughing with a black ox. She has hardly ploughed a furrow when her mother called out: Come home, daughter, for I have you given away in marriage, I don't know to whom; I gave you to Yanichka, the biggest robber in the world.—Yanichka, you are a real robber, you know all the ways in the hills...and so on. 2–4. contain fragments of these formulations.

Slovak 7. (Every line repeated.) The mother is rocking her child, singing: Hush, hush, my baby (it is interesting to note that the lulleby begins with the words *Csicsi, beli*, borrowed Hungarian words; cf. *8., 17.,* embedded in the text in 19.), do not be like your father. For your father is a great robber, he knows all the ways in the hills. And not only the ways but also the paths on which young women (or merchants) walk down to town. (*19.* If you were like your father, I should cut you to pieces and give you to the ravens.) He goes out at night and comes home during the night, bringing bloody clothes with him. I have to wash them, though I am not allowed to unfold them. Once I unfolded them and became very sad. I found a sleeve of a coat in it, and a white hand in the sleeve. (*14.* ends with this.) There was a golden ring on the white hand and a gem in the ring: it was my brother's hand. (*8.* ends with this.) Yanik, Yanik, why did you kill my brother!—There was a fog and I could not see well, wind was blowing and I could not hear well. (*10., 16.,* and *18.* end with this.) Tell me, my Terka, what you were singing while rocking the child! My dear husband, I was not singing, I was just rocking my child.—Pick up, Terka, your belongings, for we are going on hunting to that green grove, under the broad-leaved cherry-tree. Kneel down, Terka, let me cut off your head!—Give me my pretty son, let me kiss his face! She kissed one of his cheeks and bit the other: This is to remember you that your father killed your mother!

Other variants begin like this: The girl is ploughing with the ox, her mother calls out: Come home, daughter, I married you, but I don't know to whom!—You have married me to Yanichko, the famous robber! (*15.*) This formula agrees with that of the Moravian ballad. In other instances, however, the two parts of the statement are not separated according to persons but the continuation reads as if it were spoken also by the mother; I gave you to Yanik, the great robber. Yanik, Yanik, he is a real robber, he knows all the ways in the hills. . ., and so on. (Cf. *16.*) This opening formula comes up in six variants. (*9., 12., 13., 15., 16.* and *18.* In *15.,* the rocking of the child follows the opening lines.)

It cannot be disputed that the solution in which the preliminaries are made known by the complaining song of the woman suits better the requirements of the genre than the other one presenting the fact in the form of an introductory scene. The secondary nature of the latter solution can be clearly made out from the circumstances that the words of complaint are not put in the mouth of the proper character, or it is not made clear who says them.

A third method of starting the story is when the wife begins to complain, addressing her words to her husband: Yanko, Yanko, you are a robber who knows every road in the hills . . . This is immediately followed by the man's excuses, by which the ballad comes to a sudden end. That is to say, the Slovaks, considering the question and answer a real duologue, represented the development of the story as an accident which they felt satisfactory for motivating the ballad. (*10.*) In another instance (*19.*) other motifs follow in an irregular sequence, and the ballad ends with the woman's words of excuse.

There are three main types of resolving the conflict: (A) the ballad ends with the man's words of excuse (*10., 16., 18.*), (B) the husband is punished in three cases: he is taken in *9.* but the text begins to falter and change over into a lyrical song; *12.* "What sort of wife were you if you betrayed me?—asks the man. "What sort of sister should I be, if I kept silent in my brother's case!" Here the song is ended, with a hint to a final solution not unlike that of the Moravian variant. *13.* The husband accounts for the blood dropping from his sword in a way that he has killed a turtle-dove that was flitting in an oak, cooing day and night, not letting him sleep. After this he looks out of the window and beholds the gallows. (C) In four cases the solution is the same we have seen in the quoted text above: the man calls to answer the wife for her complaint, then after an awkward excuse on the woman's part, kills her. (*7., 11., 15., 17.*) I would like to note finally that *12.* names the husband "a mountain robber" *(horovému zbojniku),* just like some of the Hungarian variants.

The Ukrainian texts also apply the picture of the girl ploughing with the oxen as a beginning formula. The mother calls her home because she has given her in marriage to a robber—here the mother describes unambiguously the character of the man as one who goes out at night and comes back in the night, and so on. After this introduction the woman warns her child not to follow in his father's wake; she would rather than that, cut him to pieces and cast his body to the ravens to feed on. Immediately the man's voice is heard: What have you been singing? then comes the denial, followed by the command: Kneel down! The mother says: Remember, son, your father killed your mother!—The same beginning formula assumes a realistic appearance in *21.*: The girl called home by her mother bows low in front of the robber who asks her to sit on his knees and questions if she loves him. "Did I not love you, I should not have bowed before you." Then he takes home the wife and starts to beat her. It is only this scene that is followed by the complaint about the robber bringing home bloody clothes, uttered by the woman rocking her child, again with the lullaby words *beli-beli.* She warns the baby not to follow in the footstep of his father. Indeed, all the motifs known from the Slav versions mentioned so far are included in the Ukrainian, only in more detail than in *20.*

With the Russians the beginning scene is somewhat different, and closer to the Hungarian: The girl is washing in a brook or in the Danube, reciting her words of complaint about the many suitors whom she had missed and the robber to whom she has been forced to marry. Although there exists such a Kossack version in which she asks her parent not to give her to the prince or the bojar, but to the brave young mountain robber. When she realizes that he had killed her brother, mother, father, and so on, the robber apologizes by referring to the night having been dark and the wind blowing loud. In some variants he also refers to the rule that a robber must kill the one with whom he first meets. (According to collectors, this form of excuse is typical and traditional of robbers.) What is more, the robber gave sign by the hand to his brother-in-law, which he failed to understand and got first in his way, so that the robber had no other choice but to kill him, too. With the Russians the majority of the variants end with the motif of excuse.

Among the Polish all details appear which occur in the various Slovak variants, only they are arranged in a different mosaic pattern. Even the unique excuse of having killed a "turtle-dove" is involved, with the difference that the oak is replaced by a pine, rustling incessantly under his window and not letting him sleep for a moment—rendering, of course, the presence of the blood stain unbelievable. (Anyway, this motif has infiltrated the Polish areas from the East-German territories, from the ballad of the Mädchenmörder.) After this she recognizes the ringed hand, then she speaks to her mother, sings a lullaby to her child assuring him that she would sooner throw him to the ravens than to know him follow in the wake of his father. The ballad ends with the man inviting his wife to take a walk and killing her in the usual way. The identical motifs, on the other hand, show a word-for-word agreement with the Slovak variants. It have no doubt that the point of origin must have been in Slovakia or Moravia in this case, the Polish, Ukrainian and the Russian variants having disseminated from that point.

The Romanian ballad, too, begins with the words of the woman. "May the devil take you, cursed mother, why did you marry your girl to a forest robber who cannot do anything but go on waylaying. I have not been taught to sit behind closed doors, wash bloody clothes, shirts torn off others' bodies, whet knives and rusty broad-sword." The husband overhears her and says: "Wife, last night you cursed your mother and shed tears of your eyes." "I did not curse her, I was kindling the fire, the wood was smoking, therefore my eyes shed tears." "Wife, my wedded wife, if you are longing for your mother, don't weep but let me know about it, and we shall go and see her." No sooner did he pronounce these words than they set out to see his mother-in-law. They had hardly gone half-way, he cut his wife's head and thrust it into his bag. "Open the door, mother-in-law!" "Let your wife open it, she knows it well how to do that!" "My wife is in the valley of evil and her head in my bag."—Thereupon the mother-in-law begins to bewail that her daughter had been sued for by many in the village, yet she has given her to a man in a *foreign land*. As can be seen, the motif of identification of the murdered relatives is missing, as well as the recognition of the hand with the ring; only the complaint formulated in the Transylvanian manner remains, together with the robber's revenge.

The Croatian texts similarly speak about the robber who "walks in the hills, starting out at midnight and returning at midnight, bringing home a bloody sword and head of man." (*45.*) "He is sleeping in the day-time and goes on marauding in the night-time" (*43., 47., 56.*), and in addition the girl was married to a mountain robber *(za gorskog hajduka)*, (*58., 59.*). In the Croatian version all this is narrated sometimes in the third person singular first, then repeated by the woman's mouth; nevertheless, there are such variants too in which start is made with the complaint of the wife. But there is a considerable difference for all that: having recognized the severed head of her brother and the cut hair of her sister, the woman curses her mother because she forced her to marry such a brigand, while a messenger comes from home to invite her to the wedding feast of her brother and sister (who had been murdered!). She sets out with him. On the way home she sees bad omens, as in the Transdanubian ballad of the Hungarians: they are not ploughing, not hoeing, roses are not blossoming (*56.*), drums are not beaten, flutes are not blown, only carpenters' broad axes are heard clapping. (*33., 38., 44.*) Why are the birds not singing? (*56., 57.*), why are the bells tolled in the castle? (*51.*) It seems as if they were tolling the bells for a brother! (*56.*) Appeasing words are not lacking, as they are not lacking in the Hungarian variants, but in the Croatian texts they are deprived of authenticity, because the woman knew in advance that her brother and sister had been killed. Therefore the solution that she dies a sudden death at the sight of her dead kins is an obvious corruption.

This contradiction is resolved by those variants in which the motif of the wife married to a robber is omitted, together with the connected motifs of the murder of the relatives and the discovery of the fact, and the whole plot is reduced in a way that the woman married to a stranger in foreign land is called on by a messenger who asks her to go home to her brothers' (sisters') wedding; she sees the foreboding omens, hears the evasive replies, learns finally, when already at home, of the death case and dies, in many instances, after her relatives. Another definitive solution of the story can be found among the Slovenes: The mother visits her married daughters, one after the other; two of them she finds in happy conditions but the third complains about her husband who goes out at nights, leading the life of a highwayman. Obviously this cannot be regarded as a point of departure.

We cannot avoid dropping a few remarks on the abridged variant, in which there is no speaking about robbing, the whole story being restricted to the motif of calling home the wife. Starting out from the similarly abridged Gottschee text variant, *Seemann* considers this the origin of the whole theme (D. Vlr. 107). According to him, it is only this variant in which the evasive replies given in order to divert the wife's thoughts from the bad omens make some sense. At the same time, he seems to be aware of the fact that the other variant is superior to this—which he regards as a contamination with the ballad of "The Brigand's Wife". "Die kontaminierte Form der Ballade ist geschlossener und ereignisträchtiger, als die einfache. Während bei letzterer der Tod der Geschwister ein unbegründeter Verhängniss darstellt, ist er in der kontaminierten Form die Folge eines Mordanschlags des Schwagers, so dass, ... gewisse Fassungen am Schluss auf die Geschehnisse zu Beginn der Handlung zurückblenden können. Hingegen verliert bei der Kontaminationsform das Motiv der Beschönigungen an Glaubwürdigkeit..." (D. Vlr. V/2, 203.)

Admittedly so, but only in the southern Slav variants!—in which the by-characters try to conceal the facts that had been made known to the woman in advance. At the same time, the motif of "Beschönigung" does not lose of force but rather gains impetus in the Hungarian version, in which it is the wife that invites the husband to the wedding (who perhaps is unaware of whom he had murdered), and it is the man whom the wife baffles.

The Bulgarians, too, begin the ballad with the complaints of the wife. She has been given in marriage to a robber living beyond nine villages, nine mountains and nine rivers. He keeps his door closed in the day-time, unlocks it at night-time and goes on marauding, and so on. On an occasion he returns with the right arm of a dead body, and the ring has the name of her brother. Most of the variants end here. One or two texts contain attempts at diverse exceptional ending: "Why did you kill my brother?—Hold your tongue for I cut your head!" (*60.*) A merchant overhears the woman's words stating that her husband kills and robs merchants. He asks her if her complaint contained the truth. (*79–80.*) After the complaint, the woman is turned into a dove by God, flies home to her mother (*59., 82., 85., 88.,* and *91.*). Beholding the severed arm, she goes home, finds her brother without his right arm dying, and she also dies a sudden death (*86.*).

In the knowledge of the variants of the neighbouring nations, we are in a position to provide a better explanation of the Hungarian ballad. First of all, it is made clear that today the Hungarian tradition is incomplete in one respect: the recognition of the ring on the severed hand of the wife's brother is missing in it. The motif survives with congruent text parts in the formulations of both the northern and the southern neighbours, a correspondence like this can only be imagined if the motif had existed once in the intermediary territory as well, that is, among the Hungarians. The ballad in word is unknown to the Austrian populations; as to the

Romanians, they accepted the eastern Hungarian solution without the motif discussed. The connecting bridge between northern and southern regions must have been Transdanubia in respect of this variant of the ballad; indeed, the Transdanubian variant is so constructed that it may readily incorporate the missing motif, being composed of formulas not unlike the southern Slav texts. There is nothing to be wondered at a once existing motif having been lost from the only complete Hungarian text: when a traditional form reaches its final stage of development, such phenomena are not exceptional at all. And what is more, in the case of the Hungarian ballad the omission makes sense, too, because the ominous signs and the clumsy replies prepare the final dénouement with an appealing intensity if the listeners discover only at the end what had happened and what the woman had been out for. In this instance, therefore, even the corruption took place in the spirit of the genre. Besides, the motif also survived, in an obscured form, in Stanzas 1–2. of the Hungarian No. 57.

As against this, the Transylvanian–Moldavian formulation may be regarded as having preserved the original form the quondam east-Hungarian tradition without omission. With the neighbouring peoples we come across such variants, even though not very frequently, in which the woman's complaint refers to the trade of the murderer, to the bloody clothes, severed heads, but does not mention relatives who had been killed (and consequently the husband overhears a complaint without this motif). The uniformity of the numerous east-Hungarian variants also bear to the fact that this form must have been prevailing at a time when the tradition was fully flourishing. Two kinds of solutions for one and the same conflict rather frequently offers themselves for ending the ballad. By way of illustration it is enough to recall the two-fold solution of "The Wife Taken by Her Word" (Type **21.**) in the case of which the performers side now with the husband, now with the wife and lover, lending either a tragic atmosphere or giving a milder turn to the catharsis. Such duality occurs in the ballads of other European nations as well. The second type of solution, that is the eastern type, may have been known not only in Transylvania but also in other Hungarian-inhabited areas, for otherwise the Slovaks would not have been able to incorporate it in their version that goes back to the Transdanubian solution (to wit, the Slovaks had never have direct connections with the Transylvanian populations). On the other hand, the eastern Hungarians must have been acquainted only with the second-type solution; the tradition of the fringe-areas has preserved this in many variants, while the quondam universal Hungarian formulation has been restricted to two "complete" and three fragmentary texts.

The route the ballad followed in the course of its spread can be clearly drawn on the basis of the survey of the variants that surround, in the form of an unbroken semicircle, the Hungarian language area, from the northern to the southern Austrian frontiers.

Such a high degree of similarity in details of formulation precludes the possibility of texts existing independently of one another. Considering the internal contradictions of the southern Slav solution, we should regard it as a borrowing of the Transdanubian—possibly all-Hungarian—formulation. Proceeding from them towards the East, the story underwent a process of gradual abridgement till it reached the Bulgarians. As to the northern Slavs, there is not a single variant that would not mitigate in one way or another the original conflict, sometimes to the point of its final elimination. Most conspicuous is the innovation when the husband excuses by making mention of darkness of the night and blowing of the wind. Once he feels guilty and tries to apologize, the relentless revenge, the execution of his wife, is devoid of all psychological credit. That is, perhaps, why the singers feeling the weak point of the narrative, chose to end the ballad with the motif of apologizing in certain variants. These are not simple fragments, since the Ukrainians and the Russians mainly apply this solution. Another difficulty that gives food for thought is the innovation applied at the beginning of the ballad, where the mother calls her daughter to come home, letting it out at once that she had married her to a robber, or in other instances leaves us at a loss where the mother's words end, and where the girl's complaint begins. Some of the variants unmistakably put the words of complaint into the mother's mouth, though she is to know the husband's vicious occupation only at a later point of time. Another characteristic feature is that with them the woman's revenge, that would best pass with the motif of the discovery of relatives killed by the husband, can be met with in vague and strongly modified forms only. The Moravians have preserved the motif in a relatively close form: the woman hurries to the judge and the man is executed. There is only one Slovak text to point at this solution, another two contains only obscure hints to the punishment in store for the brigand. Obviously, the other solution gained the upper hand, in which the man takes his revenge on the wife whose complaints are openly telling about her sentiments in regard to him. Since the contamination did not prove a successful one the singers began to look for plots. In result, there developed three main variants. Nevertheless, the dramatic conflict is missing in six variants, i. e. half of the total material, which fact cannot be accounted for by their fragmentary nature. In the wake of the Slovak ballads, the Polish, Ukrainian and Russian borrowers had either to accept or modify these contradictions in their national versions.

Only two of the thirteen Slovak variants are free from contradiction in the beginning as well as the ending parts of the ballad. Strikingly enough, it is just these variants that show closest resemblance to the Hungarian wording.

11. (The second line of the stanza is always repeated.): Sleep, my little son, don't be like your father. Your father is a famous robber, who knows all the ways in the mountains. He goes out in the night-time and comes home in the day-time, bringing nothing to me, except a blood-stained sword and a torn shirt.—Maris, Maris, white Maris, what were you singing when you were rocking your child?—I was not singing anything, I only scolded the nurse because she forgot to wash the baby's napkin.—Maris, Maris, white Maris, put on white clothes and let's take a walk! We have been living together for three years, yet we have never taken a walk.—And we may spend three more years together, still we shall not take a walk.—Maris, Maris, white Maris, kiss your son! She kissed him on one of his cheeks and bit on the other: this shall remember you, son, that your father killed your mother. (Liptó county.)

17. There was a young lady, she was rocking her babe: *Csicsi, beli* (hush, sleep), my little son, don't be like your father! Your father is a big robber, he knows

every road, every road and every path in the mountains on which the merchants walk to town. He always returns with bloody clothes which I, unfortunate as I am, have to wash. One day I was washing, and burst out in crying. I found a sleeve among the clothes, a white hand in the sleeve, and a golden ring on the white hand which was worth five hundred pieces of gold. There was an ornament on the golden ring, by which I knew the ring belonged to my young brother, my youngest brother who was a rich merchant.—Her husband was standing in the yard and overheard the woman's singing complaint.—Tell me, my Terka, what you were singing!—I was rocking the little child.—Tell me, honest maid, what the lady was singing about!—I have not heard anything . . .—Put, coachman, the four horses to the cart, let's go, let's go and have a walk under the tall cherry tree! Go, Terka, go to the table (scaffold) and sing me your song!—But I was not singing, I was rocking my child.—Lean, my Terka, onto the table so that I may cut off your head!—Give me my son, I want to kiss his face!—She kissed one of her cheeks and bit the other: Let this remember you, my son, that your father killed your mother! *(Fiš.)*

The Romanian formulation seems to know nothing of identification by the ringed hand or the woman taking her revenge. It is in full agreement with the east Hungarian–Transylvanian—variant. There is only one motif to remind us of the Slovak–Ukrainian version: the man invites the woman to pay a visit and kills her on the way. This, however, is connected with one particular Hungarian motif both in the Slovak–Ukrainian and the Romanian versions: the robber has his coachman to take his wife to the place of execution as is the case in many a Hungarian ballad. Slovak *17.* preserves clear traces of the motif of inviting the wife for a walk, and the visit paid to the mother-in-law in the Romanian ballad can be derived from the same motif.

By arranging the corresponding motifs in the geographical order, we are able to shed more light on the question of transmissions. The Moravians living northwest of Hungary must have been acquainted with the Transdanubian variant; indeed, they clearly stick to the Transdanubian solution. (Although they borrowed other forms of solution from the Slovaks, too.) The Slovaks' language areas being adjacent to the Hungarian borders from west to east may well have combined the western and eastern Hungarian solutions; and it is the contaminated form that they spread further to the north and northeast. The Romanians are in contact with the eastern Hungarians, therefore their tradition has preserved the eastern Hungarian solution. The Croats and the Slovenes being neighbours to the Transdanubian Hungarians have adopted the Transdanubian form, which they forwarded to the southern regions. It cannot be contested that the ballad had developed in the centrally situated Hungarian territory, and that it disseminated from there towards the surrounding language areas in every direction, except Austria.

With the western nations the story is not known in its entirety as a theme. Yet there is one thread that leads us to the west; the scrupulous questions and the evasive answers seem to have been based on western ideas. Even their formulations bear evidence of this. A classical specimen of the French ballads, that of Roi Renaud (118.) is a mere explication of this single motif. The husband arrives at home wounded to death, but his death is concealed from the wife who is about to give birth to a child. The woman's suspicion is roused by various visible and audible signs: why are they hammering outdoors, what sobbing is heard, why is she to put on black clothes, and so on. Evasive replies are duly delivered to all her questions. For instance: It is customary to clothe in black after the woman gave birth to a child... Finally she learns the real fact and dies of heartbreak. The motif found, apparently, a similar application in East Europe, and strongly transformed, it appears in the Danish territory as well. (DgF 47.) In the Danish ballad the bride going to her own wedding approaches the house of her bridegroom, who is dead.

> As they went as far as the outskirts of the town,
> Every new bell was ringing.
> The bride observed this at once,
> And her heart filled with sorrow.
> Why have they to toll every bell?
> I can see nobody lying dead!
> It is the custom of this country
> To ring the bells when a flower is approaching.
> It is the custom on this island
> To ring the bells when a bride is approaching...

Erich Seemann wrote a study about the dissemination of this motif (without knowing about the existence of the Hungarian version), in which he attributed its dissemination to professional ballad writers. Accordingly, we should be faced with a wandering motif. But I think it is never the motifs but always the ballads that wander. The borrowing nations may take over certain parts of the wandering ballad, while the whole of it sinks into oblivion. The same happened in connection with the ballad under discussion: the Hungarian ballad had adopted an idea of western origin, most probably a French ballad-motif that preceded the extant Roi Renaud, and placed it in a different context.

What we mean by "different context" is actually unfolding of a similarly extant basic idea. The reluctant girl's horror of being married to a stranger in a foreign land may have given the idea that her would-be spouse should be described so as to provide an astonishing parable on the consequences of marriages of convenience of this kind: the husband practicing the meanest possible mode of money-making destroys if not the whole of his wife's family, his wife in any case. It is not by chance either that the Transdanubian ballad of "The Bride Forced to Marry against Her Will" ("The Bride Dragged to Death") echoes many times the complaint: "Why did you give me to him, to the murderer?!" At the same time this congruence is indicative of the fact that the ballad of the "Brigand's Wife" used to be widespread in the Hungarian language area. The correlation is clearly expressed by the complaints of the Hungarian heroine. (Similarly in the Bulgarian, southern Slav, and Romanian texts.) Consequently, the Hungarian ballad is correlated by two links with the ballad tradition of the West, although in its present form it is an independent and original composition.

In all likelihood, the ballad is contemporaneous with the earliest French borrowings, that is to say, it originates from the fourteenth century.

It was after I closed the manuscript that the fragment treated below has turned up in the bequest of Kodály which he had fixed on his own cylinder and in his own notation and which has not been incorporated in the MNT (Collection of Hungarian Folk Music).

1. Mother, my dear mother, Mistress János Bódizsár,
   Let me go to the banks of the Danube!
   Should I let you go, my dear, beautiful daughter,
   The fiery thieves would stand in your way.

2. I kneel down and turn to God,
   I kneel on the ground
   I lay all my hope in God.
   Oh, my dear God, why have you dealt so heavily with me?!
   For what sin of mine have you punished me?

Andrásfalva (Bukovina). Female performer of 61, Kodály 1914 = F 231 = AP 6008/b.

This is continued by the following text-fragment: "My daughter, my sweet, beautiful daughter, I should let you to the middle of the sea", then by two lines crossed by Kodály's hand: "The flooding foams of the swift sea Will wash away, I see, my gay looks." But there is no reference made as to whether the lines are continuation or variants of Lines 3–4 of Stanza 1.

We know nothing about the further content of this fragment. The first stanza can be brought into correlation with three ballads. The girl's asking leave for an

297

obviously long journey and the mother's reply, which perhaps imply warning of danger, are reminiscent of the beginning of "The Girl Setting Out with the Heyducks" (19.). The mentioning of "fiery thieves" recall the character of "The Brigand's Wife" and also the "Knight and the Lady" (18.), in which the girl's way is blocked—only not by "fiery thieves" but by "ten thieves". All this, however, represents a kindred trait; the plot of the ballad must have been different from that of any of the three ballads mentioned, as can be made clear from the fragment, which may have been some transitional form as tend to come up in ever larger numbers in more recent collections (cf. 14., 31., 41., 49–50., 61–62., and 67.)

21. THE WIFE TAKEN AT HER WORD

61.

Parlando

1. Asz-tal mel-lett ü - le   Gyönge Judit   asz-szony, Lábá-val rön-get -   te kinn fut-ko-só   fi - át.

1. Gentle wife Judit was sitting at the table,
   She was rocking with her foot her little son running about.

2. Hush, my son, hush, my son running about,
   For your father is not the man called Boldizsár Bátori

3. But your father is the captain of Erdély,
   Who gave you this golden rocking cradle,

4. This golden rocking cradle, your high fur-cap of Pozsony,
   Your high fur-cap of Pozsony and your waving linen shirt.

5. Standing at the door, Boldizsár Bátori overheard this:
   Don't deny, wife, the words you have just said!

6. I don't deny, my husband: I have been scolding the maids,
   They have picked my finest budding flowers,

7. They made wreath of them and presented young men with them.
   Prepare, wife, prepare your coach of six,

8. Your coach of six, and your handsomest young servant,
   For to go to the town of Pozsony, to a big wedding feast!

9. Prepare, wife, prepare, tomorrow at noon!
   They started out and arrived there.

10. The captain of Erdély began to dance.
    The captain of Erdély had the gentle wife Judit

11. Turn round twice, and kissed her twice.
    Boldizsár Bátori kept an eye on them.

12. Prepare, wife, prepare, tomorrow at noon,
    Tomorrow at noon, to go to place of execution.

13. Since you put up your head for play, your head will be taken!
    Thereupon the captain of Erdély drew his sword out of the sheath,

14. He drew his sword out of the sheath and fell on it:
    You have died for me, and I shall die for you!

Rugonfalva (Udvarhely county). Female informant of 55, B. Vikár. 1902 = Sz. Nd. 84.

62.

Gentle wife Judit was sitting at the table,
Rocking the beautiful golden cradle with her foot:
Hush, my son, hush, my nice son running about!
For your father is not the one called Boldizsár Bátori,
5. You see, your father is the captain of Erdély.
Who gave you this beautiful golden cradle,
With four golden pretzels in its four horns,
He also gave you the long fur-cap of Pozsony to cover your head with...
Aye, standing by the door, Boldizsár Bátori overheard all this.
10. Don't deny, wife, the words you have just said!
Why should I deny them, my dearest-kindest husband:
I have been scolding the maids, those naughty maids:
Who have picked my finest budding flowers,
They made wreath of them and presented young men with them.
15. You have denied your words, wife!
Open the door, open the door, my wedded wife!
I shall open it anon, my dearest-kindest husband!
Just let me put on my crimson long boots,
Just let me put on my skirt inwrought with gold.
20. He could not wait so long, he kicked the door in:
Prepare, wife, prepare, for tomorrow right at noon
You must go to the rose-market, to the place of execution!
Come, my dear servant, my best postilion!
Prepare my coach and harness my six horses!
25. They prepared and set out,
They set out and arrived at the place.
Wait a little, wait a little, you black hangman!
For they toll the bell three times for the dead,
But they do not ring a bell for my poor head!
30. At this moment the captain of Erdély arrived.
He turned her once, kissing her twice,
He turned her twice, kissing her a hundred times:
You are mine, nobody else's, dearest lady!

"Udvarhelyszék", Kriza = MNGY XI, 3.

63.

Parlando ♩ = 112-118

1. Csúj bĕ-láj, csuj bĕ-láj Pa-lo-ta-ji Pa-li!   i

Něm az a tě *ja-pád* ki pa-lo-tán sé-tál!   n

·Něm az .a tě *ja-pád*, ki pa-lo-tán sé-tál,   ə

Csak az a tě *ja-pád*, ki pej-pa-ri-pán jár.

1. Hush, hush, hush, hush, Pali Palotai!
   Your father is not the one walking in the palace.
   Your father is not the one walking in the palace,
   Nay, your father is he who rides on back of the bay.

2. Máriska, Máriska, my dear wife:
   Sing me the song you have been lulling just before!
   I will not sing it, I cannot sing it, for I forget it!
   I was scolding the servant maid, because she did not wash the child's napkin!

3. Máriska, Máriska, my dear wife:
   Which one will you choose: going on a long way,
   Going on a long way, climbing a tall tree,
   Or keeping burning candle at the golden table,
   Or perhaps listening to the crack of a gun?

4. Good morning, good morning, you murderer of my aunt-in-law!
   Welcome, welcome, you whoremonger of my wife!
   May my blood flow in one stream with yours,
   May my body rest in one grave with yours!
   May your bastard son be devoured by the pigs!

Szirénfalva (= Ptruska, Ung County). Male performer of 63. Tibor Ág and Lajos Kiss, 1958 = AP 2346.

Cf. Leader 240.

The epithet "running about" applied to the child occurs in several Transylvanian and Moldavian ballads with reference not to the child's actual state—it is being rocked in the cradle—but denotes a standing feature of the baby who can already walk and run without grownups' assistance.

Divergences: Diverse dénouements are to be found in the different versions of the ballad. In the one, the woman is saved by her lover, in the other the same words which indicate a flight turn into detecting symbols, and the story ends with a double death, which is more usual in the variants. Apart from this divergence, their formulation is very similar. The interpretation of the case of adultery may vary, taking sides now with this, now with that party, although the rather eroded texts are laconically telling about condemnation or sympathy. The two variants mentioning the chief justice of Derzs clearly speak for a case of love, the woman undertaking even death for what she feels her inalienable right. An unparalleled intensity and impartiality characterizes the variant collected in Ung county (*63.*) in which the final formula (May my blood flow in one stream with yours...), expressing the sacrifice of the loving couple, is followed by the curse of the cheated husband. Here we present one of its fragmentary texts:

> Mistress János Monusi was sitting at the window of her bower,
> Working on her embroidery sewn with black silk;
> Where she was short of silk, she made good for it with her tears.
> Hush, my son, hush, Samuka Monusi!
> If the Lord God send you to reach the grown-up age:
> Never believe János Monusi to be your father,
> But believe the chief justice of Derzs to be your father!
> At this, good János Monusi called in:
> I leave your life, my treasure, my wife,
> If you do not mention the chief justice of Derzs again.
> But I will mention him; and I shall never forget him!...
> May my head fall into one pit with yours,
> May my soul stand before God with yours!

MNGY I, 233. Samu Szabó. "Székelyföld".

Similar is the text published by *Kriza* (MNGY III, 17) in which the woman working over her embroidery is rocking "her *little* child running about" with her foot, and the chief justice is also "of Derzs". At the end of this ballad, we read a complementary part that does not seem authentical:

> and János Mónusi grew into a passion,
> At once he sent word to the chief justice of Derzs to come,
> And when the chief justice of Derzs arrived,
> He made them both fall, on their knees,
> And had the heads of both cut off,
> And had both heads put in the same pit.

The elaborate rhymes and the detailed representation of the plot which is only hinted at by the other variants, further the use of "filling words" to complete the rhythmic pattern—all this point to the interference on the part of the contributor of the text. In a notation of Lengyelfalva (Udvarhely county) by Vikár, the woman tries to delay the opening of the door with the same words as are known from the ballad of "The Unfaithful Wife Burnt to Death". (**1.**) This circumstance can be explained by the similar situation. At the same time she writes a letter to her lover, who is a chancery officer. At the execution the woman here again recites the commonplace formula: "Wait a little, wait a little, My dear, kind husband! For they toll the bells three times for the dead, But they do not ring a bell for me!" The lover urges his coachman to ride swifter, just as in the ballad of "The Walled-up Wife": Drive, coachman, drive, coachman, Drive as swift as possible! The horses are the dogs', The road is the Lord's, And the coach is mine!'" After this, the performer adds in prose: "And then the woman was taken away, and they did not know by whom." A song of twenty-nine stanzas from Hertelendyfalva (Torontál county), recorded from Székely settlers from Bukovina, combines the motifs of "The Bride Married against Her Will to a Foreigner" with those of "The Brigand's Wife" and the ballad under discussion, with the difference that the woman sends a letter to her "brother", who then commits suicide on her grave. (NB. "brother" may mean lover in old usage.) In addition, other ballads' motifs also come up in the variant, exemplifying a clear endeavour to jam sundry elements, hoarded from sundry places together, in one story.

Earliest provenience: 1862.
Dissemination: Ung county (Szirénfalva), Udvarhely county (Lengyelfalva, Rugonfalva, further most likely those marked "Székelyföld"), Csík county (Gyimesfelsőlok, Görbepatak—Gyimesvölgye), Bukovina (Andrásfalva—Hertelendyfalva, the latter in Torontál county), Moldavia (Lészped). Total: 10 variants.
Textual relationship with other ballads:
20. Choice between different ways of execution: **1.** "Coachman, harness the horses... The horsees are the dogs'": **2., 9, 10., 13., 16. (21, 27), 39** "Sitting at the window, she was sewing...": **12, 14, 31, (43) 49.** Attempt at delaying the opening of the door: **1., 20., 78.** "You have died for me..." (falling on his sword): **10, 19, 38 (40).;** "May my blood flow in one stream with yours": **10.**
Tunes: In addition to the published *61.* and *63.* see Examples 3–6. (5: 2 variants).

The tune of the variant collected in Ung county (63.) is a twelve-syllable melody widespread both in the Great Plain and East Hungary, generally sung to the texts beginning with the lines: "Kiszáradt a tóbul mind a sár mind a víz" (Mud and water are all dried up in the pond) and "Amerre én járok, még a fák is sírnak" (Even trees are weeping where I walk).

The story of the ballad under discussion is not known to us from any other country. In spite of this fact, it is connected with the western types on account of its theme, construction as well as the commonplace formulas occurring in it. Remarkably enough, the formula "You have died for me" is either replaced by "May my blood flow in one stream with yours", or the two are used one after the other, while in this ballad only the formula of western origin occurs. Therefore the ballad can be determined as original Hungarian, developed in the wake of western examples contemporaneously with the earliest Hungarian borrowings from the French.

303

22. THE RICH WOMAN'S MOTHER

64.

1. A woman had three beautiful daughters,
   All three she gave in marriage in three countries.
   She gave the youngest one to a man in Turkey,
   She heard news of her: she is very rich and takes no pity on the poor.

2. My husband, my dear husband, I would like to ask you
   To let me go to Turkey,
   Where I should like to visit my youngest daughter,
   Where I should like to visit my youngest daughter!

3. Go, coachman, go and put horses to the coach,
   And take your goodwife to Turkey,
   Where she wants to visit her youngest daughter! . . .
   Where she wants to visit her youngest daughter! . . .

4. They set out on the way to Turkey,
   To visit her youngest daughter.
   At the outskirts of the town the woman got out of the coach:
   Well, coachman, go back, go back to your country!

5. After three months are over, come and take me back,
   After three months are over, come and take me back!

The woman clad in beggar's rags,
And so she walked to the gate of her daughter.

6. Then she began to sing, and her voice was full of sorrow:
   Give me a piece of bread! Give me a glass of water!
   The servant heard it, and in he went to his mistress.
   Mistress, mistress, my noble mistress,

7. Upon my life, upon my death,
   There is a poor beggar woman outside, singing:
   Give me a piece of bread, give me a glass of water!
   Give me a piece of bread, give me a glass of water!
   Get out of here, because I have much to do!
   Get out of here because I have much to do!

8. But the poor beggar woman kept on singing:
   The servant heard it, and in he went to his mistress.
   Mistress, mistress, my noble mistress,
   Upon my life, upon my death.

9. There is a beggar woman out, singing:
   Give me a piece of bread, give me a glass of water!
   My servant, my servant maids, my hound and my dogs,
   Go and throw her into the dark prison!

10. The poor beggar woman kept on singing in the prison.
    Bring up, mother, bring up your daughter,
    Let your red blood spill out of your body,
    Let your sweet milk be sucked out of your body:
    So as to deserve to be thrown into a prison,
    So as to deserve to be thrown into a prison!

11. The servant heard this, and in he went to his mistress.
    Mistress, mistress, my noble mistress,
    Upon my life, upon my death,
    The poor beggar woman keeps on singing:

12. Bring up, mother, bring up your daughter,
    Let you red blood spill out of your body,
    Let your sweet milk be sucked out of your body,
    So as to deserve to be thrown into a prison!

13. Get out of here, because I have much to do,
    She cannot be my dear mother, because she does not come to see me!
    The poor beggar woman kept on singing,
    The servant heard it, and in he went to his mistress.

14. Mistress, mistress, my noble mistress,
    Upon my life, upon my death,
    The poor beggar woman keeps on singing the same strain,
    The poor beggar woman keeps on singing the same strain!

15. Show me the way, servant, let me follow you,
    Let me see what sort of a beggar woman she is!
    He opened the door, she beheld her mother,
    And casting herself on her breast, she said bewailing:

16. Mother, my dear mother, why did you not let me know,
    So that I should not have done this to you!
    Come now, dear mother, to my bower,
    And take a glass of my best wine!

17. May the wind of Hell overthrow your bower!
    May the wind of Hell spill your glass of your best wine!
    For I am not come to be treated by you:
    I have come to see what sort of a woman you are!

Ditró (Csík county). Female performant of 65. Kodály 1910 = SzNd. 28.

65.

1. U - ram, é - des u-ram, Nagy Bi - kal Pét' u - ram,

E - resz-szen el en-gem bé Tö - rök - or-szág-ba,

Bé Tö-rök - or-szág-ba, Kons-tan-ci - ná - poly- ba,

Küs - sebb le - á-nyom-nak lá - to - ga - tá - sá - ra!

1. Husband, my dear husband, my husband Péter Nagy Bihal,
   Let me go to Turkey,
   To Turkey, to Constantinople,
   Where I would like to see my youngest daughter!

2. For I have heard that she does not give alms to the poor,
   She does not give alms to the poor, she does not take pity on the poor.
   She clad in a beggar's rags
   And set out on the road to Turkey.

3. When she was passing by her gate,
   She saw the youngest table-servant standing in the gate.
   Little servant, Little servant, little servant, kind lad,
   Will you go in and ask your mistress to give me a glass of water!
   Will you go in and ask your mistress to give me a glass of water!
   And ask her for a piece of bread to eat before drinking a glass of water!

4. I would sooner pour that glass of water onto the ground,
   I would sooner cast that piece of bread to my dog.
   Go, little servant, little servant, my young lad,
   Go and take that beggar woman and throw her into the prison!
   Take that beggar woman and throw her into the prison,
   Throw her into the prison, into the deepest hole of it!

5. My God, my beloved God!
   Seven years and three days have passed
   Since I last saw the sun shine,
   Not even a beam of moonlight have I seen since!
   Standing by the door, the youngest table-servant overheard this,
   At once he ran in and said to his mistress:

6. Mistress, mistress, my noble mistress!
   Bewails I have heard enough, but never the like of it,
   Bewails I have heard enough, but never the like of it;
   For the poor beggar woman laments herself like this:

7. My God, my God, my beloved God!
   Seven years and three days have passed
   Since I last saw the sun shine!
   Not even a beam of moonlight have I seen since!

8. Little servant, little servant, my young lad,
   Take that beggar woman out of the prison,
   Take her out of the prison, out of the deepest hole!
   Let me ask her where is she come from?

9. Poor beggar woman, where are you come from?
   Where is your country, poor beggar woman?
   If my memory does not fail me, I used to be wife to Péter Nagy Bihal,
   I used to be the dear wedded spouse of Péter Nagy Bihal.

10. Well, then you have been my mother, who kindly nursed me.
    Well, then you have been my mother, who kindly nursed me.
    Come in, come in, dearest heart, kind mother!
    For I cook fine broths for you!
    Don't cook you fine broths for me, noble mistress,
    Don't cook you for me, may the devil tear you to pieces!

11. Come in, come in, dearest heart, kind mother,
    For I shall heal your limbs gnawed at by frogs,
    For I shall heal your limbs gnawed at by frogs,
    Gnawed at by frogs and bit by snakes!
    You shall not heal me, you noble mistress,
    You shall not heal me, may the devil tear you to pieces!

12. Come in, come in, my dearest heart, kind mother!
    For I shall give you my glassy coach,
    My glassy coach and my six bay palfreys,

My glassy coach and my six bay palfreys.
May your six bay palfreys be killed by pest,
May your glassy coach be eaten away by rust!

Csíkmadaras (Csík county), Bartók (after the notation of Pál Bodon) = Ethn. 1908, 51.

66.

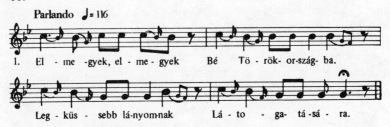

Parlando ♩=116

1. El - me -gyek, el - me - gyek   Bé Tö - rök- or-szág- ba.

Leg - küs - sebb lá-nyom-nak   Lá - to - ga- tá -sá - ra.

1. I shall go, I shall go
   To Turkey,
   My youngest daughter
   For to see there.

2. I have heard news of her
   Telling that she has no pity on the poor.
   I wish to walk to her gate,
   And sit on the beam of the bridge there.

3. There advanced, there advanced
   Her youngest table-servant.
   Go, table-servant,
   And tell your mistress

4. To give me a glass of water,
   A piece of bread,
   To a glass of water
   A bit of bread!

5. Mistress, mistress,
   My noble mistress,
   A poor beggar woman
   Keeps on saying:

6. Give me a glass of water,
   A piece of bread,
   To a glass of water
   A bit of bread!

7. Go, table servant,
   Carry in that beggar woman
   And throw her into the cellar,
   Into the deep hole of the cellar!

308

8. So that snakes and frogs
   Should gnaw and bite at her,
   So that snakes and frogs
   Should gnaw and bite at her!

9. My glass of water
   Shall be poured onto the ground,
   My bit of bread
   Shall be cast to the dogs!

10. I have come, I have come
    To Turkey,
    My youngest daughter
    For to see there.

11. I have heard news of her
    Telling that she has no pity on the poor.
    I have heard news of her
    Telling that she has no pity on the poor.

12. That her glass of water
    Is sooner poured onto the ground,
    That her bit of bread
    Is sooner cast to the dogs.

13. My noble mistress,
    The poor beggar woman,
    The poor beggar woman
    Keeps on singing:

14. I have come, I have come
    To Turkey
    My youngest daughter
    For to see there.

15. I have heard news of her
    Telling that she has no pity on the poor,
    I wish to go to her gate,
    And sit on the beam of the bridge there.

16. Her glass of water
    Is poured onto the ground,
    Her bit of bread
    Is cast to the dogs.

17. Go, table servant,
    Take in that woman,
    Let's ask her
    Where she is come form?

18. Where are you come from,
    Poor beggar woman?

I am come from the village called Bíboros,
My noble mistress.

19. I am Péter Bíboros's
Wedded wife.
And where are you come from,
Noble mistress?

20. I am come from the village of Bíboros,
Poor beggar wife,
I am Péter Bíboros's
Youngest daughter.

21. Mother, dear mother,
I give you now
My six bay palfreys,
On top of my six bay palfreys
My coach made of sheet iron.

22. May the heaves kill
Your six bay palfreys,
May the rust eat
Your coach of iron sheet!

23. If I had not been good enough
To deserve your glass of water,
If I had not been good enough
To deserve your bit of bread!

Gyimesvölgye-Rónapataka (Csík county). Performed by a girl of fourteen = Kallós 1970, No. 106.

Divergences:

There is a variant in which the story starts *in medias res:*

"The poor prisoner woman is lamenting herself:
It is three years and full three days to-day
That I fell into captivity, into this terrible, long captivity.
Where I reached my flesh, I ate it,
Where I could not reach it, snakes and frogs ate it.
Where I reached my veins, I drank my blood,
Many a time from my arms and from my legs I was sucking my blood.
He who would give me the crust of his bread,
Would see the glory of the Kingdom of Heaven.
He who would give me a glass of water,
Would taste the bliss of the Kingdom of Heaven..."

(*Kriza,* slightly transcribed, although parts of the ballad occur in other variants as well.)

Another variant in the *Kriza* collection has the following ending:

"Let dogs eat your soup of cumin,
Let your shirt of fine linen be flown away by stormy winds,
Let your painted palace be burnt by fire,
Let your polished coach be eaten by rust,
Let your fine six bay palfreys be killed by pest!
There is nothing you can give me, not even you are dear to me,
Stay by yourself, beautiful noble mistress!"

In a text from Etéd the mother having said her curse:

"Turned round and cast herself down upon the ground,
She cast herself down upon the ground and died a sudden death."

In a variant of Kibéd, it is the girl whose heart breaks, just as that of the little son of the wife walled up in the ballad of the Mason Kelemen:

"Her heart broke, as the earth under her feet,
And the woman's youngest daughter fell into the crevice."

One of the texts accounts for the heartlessness of the daughter in the following way:

"There was a *poor* woman who had a daughter
Whom she had carried on her two arms, nursed with her two arms,
Fed her with the saliva of frogs and vapour of snakes."

(The images got into the opening part of the ballad obviously from the scenes of sufferings in the prison. Compare a variant from Gyimesfelsőlok: "For three years, and for round three days, I have been kept in my youngest daughter's prison. The backs of snakes and frogs are my table, The eyes of snakes and frogs are my light."—as in the prisoners' songs of later times.)

Earliest provenience: 1864.

Dissemination: Maros-Torda county (Kibéd), Udvarhely county (Etéd, Székelyudvarhely, Szombatfa, "Udvarhely" 2), Csík county (Csíkmadaras, Ditró, Gyimesfelsőlok-Rónapataka 3, Gyimesfelsőlok-Sántatelek). Total: 12.

Textual relationships with other ballads: content elements (non-recognition, testing): **17** (7., **41.**), **42., (43., 69, 75.)**; portions of text: **33** (bewailing in the prison), **17., 42.,** (recognizing by the woman's song), **46.** (curse) **118.** (gnawed at by snakes and frogs); occasional borrowing: **2.** ("Her heart cleft and also the earth under her feet opened").

Tunes: No. 66 of the published melodies occur in three variants. Further:

NB. Parts of 65 are inversed: 3—4, 1—2.

Failure to recognize provides the nucleus of many ballads' plot in Hungarian as well as other language areas; putting to test and heartless attitude in respect of the non-recognized relative plays a similar role in balladry. The basic idea, however, of the mother clad in beggars' rags and so testing her rich daughter is not known elsewhere. Stylistic features and construction list this specimen among the best representatives of mediaeval ballads.

23. THE UNMARRIED MOTHER WHO KILLED HER CHILD

67.

Poco rubato ♩ = 108

1. Sze - gény Sza - bó Er - zsi Mind el - vesz-té ma - gát,

poco rit.

Mind el - vesz - té ma - gát Az asz - ta - gos ker - be.

1. Poor Erzsi Szabó
   Ruined herself miserably,
   She ruined herself miserably
   In the rick-field.

2. Her new-born babe
   She chopped up to small pieces,
   She chopped it up to small pieces
   And hid it among the nettles.

3. She hid it among the nettles,
   And threw it to the pigs.
   She hid it in the nettles
   And threw it to the pigs.

4. The son of Lord Lieutenant
   Saw with his two eyes
   And heard with his two ears
   How she tormented his babe.

5. The son of the Lord Lieutenant
   Also sat in the court,
   He also sat in the court
   And said the following sentence:

6. Soul is demanded for a soul,
   Death is demanded for death.
   Soul is demanded for soul,
   Death is demanded for death.

7. Poor Erzsi Szabó
   Was put into fetters up to the knees,
   She was put to fetters up to the knees,
   And so she was thrown into the prison.

312

8. Poor Erzsi Szabó
   Had a dream one night,
   And she saw in her dream,
   She saw in her dream:

9. Two black ravens
   Floating above her head
   With two ells of silken string
   Hanging from their claws.

10. There came, there came
    Her dear mother.
    Mother, my dear mother,
    Ransom me from here!

11. Child, Erzsi Szabó,
    I should ransom you
    If only you could be ransomed,
    If only you could be ransomed.

12. Mother, my dear mother,
    Last night I had a dream,
    And I saw in my dream,
    I saw in my dream

13. Two black ravens
    Floating above my head
    With two ells of silken string
    Hanging from their claws.

14. Child, Erzsi Szabó,
    Those two black ravens
    Will be your hangmen,
    Will be your hangmen.

15. The two ells of silken string
    Will be your hanging rope,
    The two ells of silken string
    Will be your hanging rope.

Lészped (Moldavia). Female performer of 33, Júlia Szegő, 1950–1953 = Faragó and Jagamas 16A.

Divergences:
In the Bukovinian variants the infanticide takes place not before the eyes of the son of the Chief Lieutenant or Prince, and sometimes it is not his child that is killed:

"Cursed István Szőcs
Was listening at the edge of the garden,
He sent word, he sent word

313

> To the village magistrate,
> To the village magistrate,
> And to the gail-keeper."

Other variants of destroying the child:

> "She chopped up her little babe
> Into small pieces,
> She put it into a walnut-tree.
> She chopped it up into small pieces
> And put it into a walnut-tree,
> But later she took it out
> And threw it into the *Tisza* river."

> "She chopped up her little baby
> Into small pieces *(bis.)*
> And threw it into the nettle-bed.
> She did not leave it there
> But threw it to the *hounds.*"
> (In two variants.)

A fuller form of the dream can be found in another variant from Bukovina:

> "Mother, my dear mother,
>   What did I see in my dream?
>   Three black ravens
>   Were floating above my head,
>   And small beads of red perl
>   Falling into my lap.
>   Small beads of red perl
>   Falling into my lap.
>   Mother, my dear mother,
>   What does this mean? . . .
>   Daughter, my daughter,
>   This is not a good dream!
>   Three black ravens:
>   Are your hangmen.
>   Small red beads of perl:
>   Are your red blood. . . ."

The theme finds application combined with several other ballads in Bukovina: for instance, with the motif of the shortening skirt borrowed from the ballad of "The Disgraced Girl" (one var.), or the diction of "The Girl Found Dead": My roses, my roses, Blossom beautifully, And when they take me out, All of you wither away!", and variants thereof; a local variant of the bride forced to marry against her will is also merged with the ballad (Fair Anna Aradon); not infrequently with the Brigand's Wife in the Moldavian and Bukovinian variants, in which case the whole of the story is performed embedded in the ballad, and many variants give to the mother's lips the farewell speech known from several lyrical songs: ". . . My sweet,

314

beautiful daughter, Will you ever return to me? I shall return, mother, I shall return, When one grain of grape When one grain of grape will yield A hundred barrels of wine. And you know, mother, that such a thing will never occur! ... When one single grain of wheat Will yield A hundred stocks... When the wild-geese will all talk Greek...So you must not wait for me to return!"

The motif of redeeming the girl—that is bribing the judges—comes up only in a few Moldavian variants. An interesting variant reads as follows:"

"My Erzsi, my dear Erzsi,
Don't grieve all the time!
I shall go to the King
And tell him
To let you free
And put me in your stead!
Don't you go, father,
Don't you take a step, dear father!
I killed my baby,
I had no more sense;
But death is due for death,
Father, my dear father!"

In several variants father, mother, sister and brother visit the girl one after the other, all proposing the same act of kindness; the formulation is also the same in each instance. Among the Moldavians, the ballad is usually amplified by describing the events so minuteously as is unknown elsewhere. One and the same singer may perform the ballad in a shorter form as well as extending it to as many as thirty or forty stanzas. In order to give an inkling of the style of swelling up the text, I quote a few passages from one of the longest variants consisting of eighty-six stanzas:

1. Erzsi, Erzsi Szabó
   Was a young girl,
   She was a young girl,
   And she was deceived.

2. Her father and mother
   Knew nothing about it,
   And she had a sweetheart,
   And it was a great secret.

3. Her lover said to her:
   Don't be sorry, Erzsi,
   God will grant it,
   And the child will come forth!

4. I shall go to the soldiers
   And spend three years with them,
   But what is three years?
   They will soon be over.

5. Her father and mother
   Set out and went away,
   They went away
   To the other village,

6. To the other village,
   To see their friends.
   Erzsi stayed at home,
   At home, all by herself.

7. Erzsi, Erzsi
   Gave birth to a baby.
   Erzsi, Erzsi Szabó
   O, she held a bad counsel with herself!

8. Her little baby
   She would cut to pieces,
   She would chop up her baby
   To small pieces.

9. She would throw it into the nettle-bed,
   Cast it to the swines.
   Young master King István
   Stood at the window and saw everything...

After this long introduction, the text of the ballad proper begins. And now let us see a few stanzas of the closing part:

79. Her dear mother
    Was weeping bitterly,
    Because her own daughter
    Was carried away on the bier.

80. Daughter, my daughter,
    Poor Erzsi Szabó;
    She has ruined herself
    As well as her baby!

81. You girls, you girls,
    Let it be an example to you
    And mind that you never have
    A lover in secret!

82. My daughter, my daughter,
    Poor Erzsi Szabó,
    You have brought a great sorrow
    To our bereived heart, indeed!

83. You were unfortunate
    When you came to life,
    And still more unfortunate was
    Your little baby,

316

84. Because you did not take pity on it,
    Because you chopped it up!
    You girls, you girls,
    You must never do that!

85. Don't do that what my daughter
    Chose to do!
    You girls, you girls,
    You beautiful girls!

86. How I wish
    I had a daughter!
    Alas, she had a lover
    In secret!"

Earliest provenience: 1914 (partially: between 1891 and 1919).

Dissemination: The Szeged region (fragment of the ill-omened dream occurs among the lines, similarly fragmentary, of the ballad about "The Disgraced Girl" in the legacy of *Kálmány*), Bukovina (Fogadjisten 3, Hadikfalva 2, Istensegíts 4, Józseffalva 2), Moldavia (Lészped 8). Total: 20.

Textual relationships with other ballads: (disregarding the amalgamations with other ballads) **24., 51., 59.** (the scene of dream).

Tunes: 1. the melody of the published No. 67. occurs in three variants. 2. has eight, 3. has two variants. 3. and 6. were performed by one and the same woman to the same text, although at different dates.; 7. also occurs in two variants.

For a comparative analysis of the ballad see the study of the next Type.

24. THE UNMARRIED MOTHER WHO KILLED HER THREE CHILDREN

68.

1. Sza-bó Vil-ma ki-ment az er-dő-be, Le-fe-küdt a di-ó-fa tö-vi-be,

O-da-men-tem, ki-ál-tot-tam ne-ki: Kelj fel Vil-ma, mer meg-lát va-la-ki!

1. Vilma Szabó went into the forest,
   And lay under an walnut-tree.
   I went to her, calling:
   Get up, Vilma, or someone will see you!

2. But Vilma was not a girl to be trifled with,
   She dashed off to the next inn,
   And ordered the innkeeper's daughter
   To place ten pints of wine on the table.

3. She had not yet drunk her wine
   When the corporal of gendarmes opened the door.
   The corporal of gendarmes shouted:
   Boys, let us arrest Vilma!

4. Vilma Szabó is escorted by six gendarmes.
   Her lover is watching her from behind the window.
   Don't watch, my sweetheart, how my life is spoiled!
   It is for you that I suffer all this.

5. Six gendarmes are grilling Vilma Szabó,
   Her lover is listening outside the door.
   Confess, Vilma, all your crimes:
   What have you done with your three children?

6. One I buried under the walnut-tree,
   One I threw into the river.
   And I myself became the murderer of the third,
   For which I suffer eternal imprisonment.

Csíkmenaság (Csík county), performed by a man of 41. = Imets 1970, 105.

69.

Tempo giusto

1. Sza-bó Vil-ma ki-ment a kis ker-be,
szö-lő -be,
Le - fe - küdt a di - ó - fa tö- vé- be.

1. Vilma Szabó went into the flower garden (or: vineyard)
   And lay under the walnut-tree.

2. I called to her once or twice:
   Get up, Vilma, or someone will see you!

3. But Vilma was not a girl to be trifled with,
   She dashed off to the inn of Becsárd.

4. She ordered the innkeeper's daughter
   To place ten pints of wine on the table.

5. As Vilma was drinking the wine,
   Nine gendarmes opened the door.

6. Well, Vilma, you must confess your crime:
   What have you done with your three children?

7. One I buried under the walnut-tree,
   The other I threw into the deep water of the Sajó.

8. And I myself am the murderer of the third.
   Alas, my God, I am a great sinner, indeed!
   (Some of the informants ended the ballad at this point.)

9. As Vilma was escorted by the gendarmes,
   Her lover was watching her from behind the window.

10. Don't be watching, sweetheart, my mournful life,
    For I suffer all this on your account!

11. The red ribbon of Vilma Szabó!
    She will never tie it in her locks.

12. Put it away, Vilma, in a drawer of the chest,
    It will do for your daughter's hair.

Áj (Abaúj county). Middle-aged men and women. Vargyas 1940–41 = Vargyas 1960, 19.

Divergences:

Names: Vilma Szabó (175), Vilma Csáki (17), Vilma Csáti (1), Vilma Sági (3), Vilma Kovács (1), Julcsa Szabó (1), Örzse Szabó (1), Náni Bereg (31), Náni Belez (1), Náni Berec (2), Náni Török (2), Mári Görög (in Bukovina: 8), Mari Utra (in Transylvania, more recent: 9), Mari Hornyák (6). Other than Vilma Szabó: 83.

Earliest of all the names is Vilma Szabó (also early Transylvanian recordings).

The ballad usually begins with the following formula: She went out to the *woods* (125), or to the small (flower) garden (74), or the vineyard (23) and lies under the walnut-tree (83), cedar (cypress)-tree (32), oak (35), linden, poplar (19–19), rose-tree (11), briar (1), on bed of rose-leaves (3), other places determined in five different ways (1–3). This formula may be preceded by another one (which, however, may find its place elsewhere as well): Over down there the sky is red (or: it thunders), Vilma Szabó is like a tomato. The tomato does not taste good, which Vilma Szabó has chosen for herself. (18). Another beginning formula: "Vilma Szabó was not born by her mother, But she was grown on top of a cedar-tree", or: "There is a rose-(fig, walnut,) tree in the woods" (10). Instead of the phrase "I shouted to her once or twice" we have sometimes "I was walking there" or "her mother shouted" (3), "Her former sweetheart was walking there", "Three gendarmes happened to pass by", or the warning is not tied up with one definite person, that is, it is voiced impersonally.

A peculiar variation is found in a few texts: she lies not under a tree but on the rails (before a steam-engine, train or fast-train) and the engine whistles three times to warn her to get up (in which case the idea of suicide is involved, although in the original conception she gives birth to her child whom she kills). The reference to "shouting" is sometimes disregarded completely, and the development takes a sudden turn towards the dénouement: "Náni Bereg noticed at once That she was surrounded by three gendarmes."

The generally used formula "Vilma Szabó was not a girl to be trifled with, She dashed off and into the inn" is sometimes modified—obviously under the impact of the so-called "highwayman" ballads—in a way that she rides on back of a horse to the inn: "She did not take it as a jest, But mounted her grey mare And galloped right to the inn." (9 variants of the formula are known.) Similarly widespread is the formula of ordering wine 10 to 100 litres, sometimes with the intention of bribing the gendarmes: "Nine gendarmes followed in her wake . . . Let the poor gendarmes drink a little wine"—recalling the highwaymen's style of bribing the gendarmes. Another general motif is the following: "The corporal of gendarmes shouts: Well, boys, seize (or: we have cornered) Vilma."

The sequence of the following motifs is highly variable: "Vilma Szabó is escorted by six gendarmes, Her lover (mother) is watching from behind the window" . . . "Don't be watching at my wretched life!"; "Vilma Szabó is interrogated by six gendarmes, Her sweetheart (mother) is listening at the door"; "Confess, Vilma your crime . . ."; the triple or quadruple infanticide: one she buried under the walnut-tree, the other she threw into the deep river Tisza (Danube, Rába), and "she just became the murderer of another one" which she sometimes kills by stabbing so that "its blood spurted out like a partridge's"—a formula borrowed from local ballads; the quadruple infanticide results from the variant in which she throws two children into the Tisza, without mention made to the third case; sometimes the murder under the walnut-tree is added as fourth. The motif: "Come, Vilma, does not it break your heart That you killed your three children? Alas, it does, and I shall die of a broken heart! I shall rattle my fetters till I die"— also come up in certain variants of the ballad. Even the motif of the red ribbon which would find its proper place towards the end of the story tend to intervene at the beginning of the song. The skirt's catching by the door of the prison is a motif that mainly occurs in the ending stanza where it fits best, indeed.

Thus the sequence of the motifs show a rather variable picture. In addition, portions of lyrical songs are added and certain motifs omitted at random. It follows that the closing formula is also interchangeable: the ballad is sometimes ended with the lines: "Alas, it does, and perhaps I die of heartbreak, Or I shall rattle my fetters to the day of my death!", or—after the confession of the triple infanticide has been made—even with the painful reproach: "It is for you that I suffer all this!"

Particular elements are the following: "The physician of the county recognized her as the girl who murdered her three children" (in 17 cases); "Náni Bereg walked to the market-place (village fair), She squeezed three rolls (three pretzels) in her hands, She broke the three rolls to nine pieces: Here you have, gendarme, this has been bought by Náni Bereg!" The scene being a display of corporeal strength has similarly been borrowed from highwayman balladry, as well as the other one in which "Vilma Szabó sends word to her mother: Send me, mother, a pillow to lay my head on!" But her mother returns the message: Let her use her knot of hair as a pillow!

Earliest provenience: 1872.

Dissemination:

I. Sopron county (Bősárkány) Vas county (Csepreg, Csörötnek 2, "Őrség", Szatta), Zala county (Búcsúszentlászló, Dergecs, "Göcsej" 2, Hegyesd, Kapolcs, Korpavár, Mihályfa, Nemessándorháza 2, Rédics, Zalakoppány), Somogy county (Alsok, Beleg, Csoma, Darány, Igal, Nemesdéd 3, Ságvár, Somogyszentmiklós, Szenna, Toponár), Verőce county (Haraszti), Baranya county (Csoboka, Hegyszentmárton, Kopács, Magyaregregy, Mohács 3, Püspökbogád), Tolna county (Decs, Értény, Lápafő, Ozora, Regöly, Sióagárd), Fejér county (Csákberény), Veszprém county (Badacsonytomaj, Bakonyszentlászló, Hánta, Réde, Veszprémfajsz—German people in Hungarian—, Zirc), Komárom county (Ács, Császár, Csilizradvány 2, Kamocsa, Kocs 2, Naszvad), Győr county (Győr, Rábakapi), "Dunántúl". I.: 64.

II. Pozsony county (Sárfenyősziget, Taksonyfalva), Nyitra county (Ghymes, Zsére), Hont county (Ipolybalog 2, Ipolyszög, Perőcsény 2) "Hont? Nógrád", Nógrád county (Becske, Bercel 2, Dejtár, Kisbárkány, Mindszent, Nógrádmegyer, Szanda, Szandaváralja), Heves county (Andornaktállya, Bükkszenterzsébet, Eger 2, "Egervidéke", Fedémes, Felsőtárkány, Füzesabony, Mezőtárkány, Parád, Tarnalelesz, Tiszanána, Verpelét), Borsod county (Borsodnádasd, Keresztespüspöki, Kisgyőr, Sajókaza, Sajólád, Sály, "Sáta-vidék", Szilvásvárad), Gömör county (Egyházasbást, Szilice), Abaúj county (Abaújvár, Áj, Beret, Cekeháza, Nagyszalánc, Pusztafalu), Zemplén county (Mályinka, Ricse 3, Sárospatak 4, Szerencs), "Ugocsa m.", Máramaros county (Hosszúmező). II.: 59.

III. Pest county (Ágasegyháza, Cegléd 2, Izsák, Kecel, Kecskemét, Kiskunhalas 4, Kiskunfélegyháza 2, Letkés, Városföldpuszta), Jász-Nagykun–Szolnok county (Jánoshida, Jászladány, Nagykörű, Tiszaföldvár, Túrkeve 2), Bács-Bodrog county (Rém, Zenta), Torontál county (Csóka, Egyházaskér, Hertelendyfalva 2, Szaján), Délalföld = Southern Great Plain *s.l.* 1, Csongrád county (Csongrád 2, Hódmezővásárhely 3, Orosháza, Tápé), Békés county (Békés 3, Doboz 4, Geszt), Arad county (Pécska), Bihar county (Biharugra 2, Hosszúhát, Körösnagyharsány 2, Nagyszalonta 6), Hajdú county (Egyek Poroszló), Szabolcs county (Biri, Érpatak 3, Rakamaz, Rétközberencs, Tiszakarád,

Tiszapolgár, Nyírbátor, Nyírlugos 2, Nyírtura, "Szabolcs m.", Vaja), Szatmár county (Csenger 3, Győrtelek, Kérsemlyén, Nagyecsed, Sárosmagyarberkesz, Tyukod), Szilágy county (Diósad). III. : 80.

IV. Hunyad county (Déva), Kolozs county (Bánffyhunyad, Magyarpalatka, Méra 2, Vajdakamarás 2, Válaszút 3, Visa, Zentelke), Szolnok–Doboka county (Árpástó), Maros-Torda county (Kibéd, "Marosszék", Marosvásárhely, Séllye, Székelycsóka), Torda-Aranyos county (Torda, Sinfalva, Várfalva), Alsó-Fehér county (Lőrincréve 2), Nagyküküllő county (Alsórákos 2), Udvarhely county (Bencéd, Korond, Lengyelfalva, Medesér, Nagykede, Rugonfalva, Szentgerince, Székelykeresztúr, Székelyzsombor, Vargyas), Brassó county (Pürkerec 2), Csík county (Csíkmenaság, Gyergyóalfalu, Gyergyócsomafalva, Gyergyóditró, Gyergyóújfalu, Gyimesfelsőlok 2, Gyimesközéplok, Gyimesvölgye), Háromszék county (Bardoc, Nyújtód, Sepsiköröspatak, Sepsiszentgyörgy, Uzon), Bukovina (Andrásfalva, "Bukovina" 2, Józseffalva 4, Hadikfalva 2), Moldavia (Frumosza, Klézse). IV. : 62. I–III total: 203, IV total 62, s.l.l; sum total: 266.

Textual relationships with other ballads: **23**; contaminated with the highwayman-motif: **108**.

Tunes: 1 = No. 68 (44 variants), 2 = No 69, 4 (12 variants), 5 (2), 6 (3), 7 (3), 13 (4), 14 (3), 16 (2), 20 (2), 21 (2), 27 (3).

324

Versions in languages other than Hungarian:

FRENCH: *1–2. Puymaigre* 1865 67–68. *3–5. Millien* 1906, 257–62, 1–3. *6–8. Rossat* 1917 3A–C. *9–11.* Romania 10, 202–3. *12. Smith* Romania 4. 112. *13. Bujeaud* II, 240. *14. Rolland* I 65. *15. Bladé* 1879 30.

BRETON: *16. Villemarqué* 38.

ITALIAN: *17–19. Nigra* 10A–C. *20. Widter* 87. *21. Marcoaldi* 173. *22. Ferraro* 1877, 111/25. (*Nigra* also quotes a variant from the environment of Venice.)

ENGLISH: *23–35. Child* 20A–M. *36. Greig* 11. *37–92. Bronson* 20. (Partial variant: Child 21.)

DANISH: *93–98.* DgF 529.

SLOVAK: *99. Horák* 1958, 58. *100. Idem* 57 = Sb. Mat. Sl. II, 35b* = *Medveczky* 1923, 16.* *101. Kolečány* 9. *102. Černík* 190.

MORAVIAN: *103–112. Sušil* 158/331–6 plus 4 variants, 158/331 = *Bartoš* 1953 180. *113–116.* Bartoš 1901, 40–42. (*Erben* 1852–1856, 34 quoted by *Horák* 1958.)

POLISH: *117–144. Kolberg* 1857, 12a–c (a, i, s = *Czernik* 149–155). *145. Kolberg* 1871–1884, 12,223/429.

UKRAINIAN: *146. Lintur* 1959, 88.

Partial variants:

GERMAN: *147–152.* E–B 213. *153–154. Parisius* 30 and 102. *155. Hauffen* 79. *156.* Ethn 1892/35 Orczyfalva, the Banate. (Only a few readily available variants are referred to from the field of the rather widespread German ballad.)

WEND: *157.Haupt–Schmaler* 202.

SLOVENE: *158–169. Štrekelj* 171–181. *Kumer* 421, 424–425.

CROAT: *169–171. Žganec* 1950–1952 349, 483, 728. *172. Kurelac* 451.

MORAVIAN–CZECH: *173. Sušil* 20/55. *174. Holas** II,1.

POLISH: *175. Kolberg* 1871–1884 4/22 = *Czernik* 213. *176–178.* Ibid. 6/387, 12/612, 17/17. *179.* Ibid. 18/346 = *Czernik* 21. *180–184. Kolberg* 1885 II 352–355 and IV 434.

UKRAINIAN: *185—189. Golovatsky* II, 727, 13, III/1, 225 95, I, 54 13, III/1, 26 15 and III/1, 245 122.

LITHUANIAN: Cf. summary, *Seemann* 1951, 71.

As has been shown, the Trans-Carpathian ballad of infanticide Erzsi Szabó does not stand alone: it is paralleled by a fairly widespread Hungarian ballad speaking about the triple infanticide in a new tone. The two ballads bear comparison not only on account of their thematic correlation, but also because the family name of the heroine is most generally Szabó in booth. It appears from the foreign versions as well that the pieces in word are correlated variants of one and the same ballad-theme. Therefore we chose to compare the two taken together with their international relations. It will be profitable to go through the individual motifs of the two ballads, and then to survey, in the sequence of the motifs, the French texts bearing closest relationship with the Hungarian ones.

1. Erzsi Szabó goes to her *flower-garden* (in Moldavia, to rig-field) where she "chops up" her baby, while Vilma Szabó goes into the small(flower)-garden or the forest, lies under a walnut-tree, an oak or a cedar.

2. Erzsi Szabó throws the chopped-up body into the nettle-bed (that is among bush and leaves); in some variants still more details are added: "she chopped it up and put it in the walnut-tree"; "threw it into the Tisza"; and sometimes she threw it to the hounds or pigs; Vilma Szabó confesses the triple murder of children: one she buried under the walnut-tree, the other (or two more) she threw into the Tisza or some other river.

3. A man figures as eye-witness to the act (sometimes it is the father of the baby, or the neighbour in rare instances); in more recent variants of the song there

have developed analogical scenes: "I shouted once or twice to her" and variants thereof (nine gendarmes happened to walk there; her former lover passed by; her mother called to her, etc.).

3a. There are such variants of the ballad of Vilma Szabó in which a physician is involved to state that the girl had given birth to three children.

4. Then the Moldavian texts continue with arresting the girl. The Bukovinian variants have a foreboding dream instead. Here Vilma Szabó dashes off to the inn to be caught there.

5. In the Moldavian story the girl's mother or father goes to the king, or to the daughter, and a dialogue follows; in the new ballad the scene of interrogation follows, overheard by the mother or the girl's sweetheart standing by the door; at this point it is made clear that murder has been committed. It is only in the Moldavian versions that attempts are made by the girl's mother (father) at ransoming the prisoner, sometimes right upon the girl's request. The attempt, however, remains unsuccesful.

6. The girl repents her sin: in one of the texts Erzsi Szabó herself declares that she deserves to be executed for what she had done. Instead of this, the new ballad speaks about the red ribbon of Vilma Szabó, which would be left to her daughter.

Let us now survey the individual elements of the French version.

1. A girl goes into the woods to pick *violets* (sometimes the youngest of three sisters), sits down on the lawn and gives birth to a child. A variant says that she had been made pregnant by three young men. She buries the baby by the road. (*13.*)

2. In certain variants she shrieks, her mother hears her shrieking and advises her what to do next with the child. Misunderstanding her mother's words, she kills the baby, mainly by throwing it into a river (once into a precipice), more often she buries it under a vinestock or covers the corpse with leaves in the corner of the vineyard.

3. While so doing she is seen by someone; either three gendarmes, or three workmen happen to pass by, or three sailors accost her; rarely "members of the court" approach. She is imprisoned.

4. After this, her sweetheart, or three young men come and ask what has happened. They want to see her. The answer is that they can see her the next day when she will be taken to the scaffold by a priest and the hangman.

5. The mother arrives, too. The daughter asks: "Doesn't it hurt your heart that the one you have brought up is to be executed?" In some variants the mother asks the daughter whether it did not hurt her heart that she had brought such sorrow on her mother.

6. Then the mother tries to bribe the judges to secure her daughter's release. But the daughter rejects the attempt, saying that one committing such a crazy thing deserves to be punished.

7. She advises her mother to hang her clothes in front of their house to serve an example to all girls; she bids her not to let her younger sister go to balls overdecorated. It is in this context that the *ribbon* and the lace is mentioned as signs of vanity. ("Quand elle aura de beaux rubans, De belles coiffures, Demandez-lui d'où elles sont venues." (*14.*)

326

In another type of text we find the following motifs:

1. The girl gives birth to a child without anyone knowing about it. In one case she kills two babies, that is twins. In one instance, here too, she throws them into the river; elsewhere it becomes clear only later that she had killed them.

2. Only the neighbour knows about the crime and it is he that reports her to the magistrate.

3. Her mother tries to bribe the magistrate. She meets with a flat refusal, her daughter is given over to the hangman the next day.

4. The girl's words pointing to the moral of the story close the action. Here, too, sometimes the words are heard: "Cursed be the ribbon and the lace!" (4.)

Beside these, there is a third type of text in which the buried corpse of the baby is dragged out by dogs. All the girls are called before the doctor for examination: the guilty person is discovered and executed. This seems to be a new transformation of the story, but preserves elements which show obvious agreement with the Hungarian ballad (cf. "she threw it to the hounds).

The motifs listed side by side show fairly close agreement even without special examination. The *small* (i.e. *flower*) garden obviously came into the Hungarian as the counterpart of the violet-picking, and is used similarly as a love symbol. But in the majority of the Hungarian variants the heroine goes into the forest, and also the motif of concealment in the vineyard is rather tenaciously preserved in the Hungarian areas. The part about calling once or twice, too, may have originated in the French mother's shouting to her daughter, although the sailors and the rest also call to the girl something like "well done, girl, well done, little girl, we have seen you", or "well, you will pay for it". ("Tout beau! tout beau! la jeune fille, Nous vous regardons, ma petite!" (3). "Paix, paix! ma belle fille, tu t'en repentiras..." (4).)

The part played by the lover or the mother as they hear the questioning of the girl through the door does not require further explanation. The admission that she has committed three murders deviates from the French—although the Moldavians speak about one murder only—but on the other hand the methods of carrying out the infanticide (throwing into the water or burying under a tree or vinestock) agree with the ways which appear separately in the French variants, and in the Hungarian it is always these two ways which appear. (Of the third as much is heard that "I have just become its murderer".) In the French variants sometimes the birth of twins occurs, which may well have played a part in the spread of the Hungarian corresponding motif, while the triple infanticide may be attributed to a Hungarian predilection to build up in three parts, although even this last motif may have some antecedent in the French ballad in which *three* lovers, or pregnancy by three young men are often mentioned.

There is a word-for-word agreement as regards the phrase: "Doesn't it break your heart?" More vaguely, but undoubtedly, there is connection with the French in the mention of the ribbon, which has, even in the obscured Hungarian, some moral echo. Finally, there is a complete agreement in respect of the scene where attempt is made at bribing. What is more, even the daughter's part rejecting the attempt is the same in both the French and the Hungarian ballad. This motif, however, is altogether missing in the ballad of Vilma Szabó. The hounds and swines coming up in the Moldavian variants may well stand comparison with the French scene in which the corpse of the murdered child is dragged out by the dogs. This occurs in two French variants. Furthermore, the medical examination also occurs in both language areas' ballads. This may be regarded as one of the agreements, too, for it would be difficult to imagine so similar developments in a similar story independently one of the other.

On the basis of these correspondences it is justified that *there existed an old-style Hungarian ballad* which *contained details of the French story*. Fragmentary, though *still old-style remains* of the old Hungarian ballad have been preserved in the Trans-Carpathian Hungarian settlements; but in Hungary proper, under the influence of the highwayman ballads, a new form evolved; it spread in this recast form in recent times throughout the country, while among the separated Hungarians in Romania it was unable to displace the old one.

Now let us cast a cursory glance at the other relationships of the French and Hungarian ballad, in order to clarify the position of the Hungarian ballad in Europe.

On the basis of experiences gathered hitherto we find it only natural that the ballad should appear among the Italians, too. Nevertheless, differences are to be found there, too, which help to distinguish it from the Hungarian. One of these is that in some of the variants the story we have been dealing with is merged with another French child-murder ballad, in which the girl gives birth while haymaking, throws the baby into the river, and the baby calls back to her, reproaching her with her crime, and also announcing that angels taught it these words. The mother frightened and repentant tries to save the child, but it is too late. Obviously it is the throwing into the river that facilitated the merging of the two stories. There are variants, in which the child visits the mother seven years later in the prison, and reproaches her for her actions. But even where the story broadly agrees with the course of the French ballad, there are still marked differences, for example that the girl's mother refuses to ransom her, for which the girl reproaches her, saying: "How cruel a mother your are, letting your only daughter die!" At the same time elements are missing, without which one could not imagine the corresponding Hungarian elements. For instance, the question: "Doesn't it break your heart?", the hiding of the baby in the vineyard or under a tree, or the words referring to the ribbon. Thus again in the northern Italian area we encounter with a more or less accurate French tradition, but the emanation of the French original this time again proves to be so incomplete as not to permit us to originate the Hungarian version from the Italian one.

The connection with the English ballad is different. This ballad has hitherto been associated by Hungarian researchers with the ballad of "The Heartless Mother" (4.), although it obviously speaks not about a mother leaving behind her children in her desperate flight, but about an unmarried mother killing her baby. The heroine goes out into the woods, leaning her back against an oak or against a briar, and gives birth to twins. She ties them up with her ribbon and stabs them to death, and then buries them under a stone beneath the tree; having done all this, she believes she can return maintaining the appearance of a maid. But either when she returns, or years later, she sees two children whom she addresses, saying: "If you were mine, I would dress you in velvet", whereat they throw in her face that they are her murdered children, and promise punishment for her in Hell. The story is faithfully followed by the Danish version, in which the heroine also goes to the woods, accompanied by her two maids, but apart from this the development proceeds in the same way. She lays down her hooked gown upon the ground and gives birth to twins. She conceals them under the turf of a stone and then follows the way home. In another variant she lies on a blue cushion, gives birth to her twins, takes them to the graveyard and buries them. The children ask God after eight years have passed to let them go down to the Earth, where they wish to see their mother. At night they knock at her door: "I have not agreed upon an appointment with anyone", says the woman, using the common formula. Then the mother swears that she had never given birth to twins, whereupon the children repeat the story word for word. She promises to give them gold if they stay with her, and in other variants she takes them in her lap soaking their faces with her tears. "It is better for us to be in Heaven while you stay in Hell", say the children, who have to leave at the first crow of the cock.

The beginning of these ballads undoubtedly comes from the French ballad, but the rest of the story may be regarded as a peculiar autonomous development.

Even further removed is the German story of the child murder. A shepherd guarding his herd beside a wood hears a child's crying, the voice comes from the hollow of a tree. It appears that his mother had already drowned one of her children in the river, buried the next one under a tree, and is just celebrating her wedding with a wreath of myrtle on her forehead. The child drops in and detects his mother's crime. The bride denies all: "Let the Devil take me away if this is true!" And the Devil appears, indeed, and carries her to Hell. The skeletal frame of the two tales is entirely different, there is only one point of agreement between the two, notably that of the triple murder, further the methods of killing the children (drowning in the river and burying under a tree). Characteristically enough, the third manner of execution of the child is also here described with uncertain contours. Maybe, the market-singers are responsible for introducing the motif into this song from a story different in construction but related in theme.

A close connection can be seen between the German formulation and a similar ballad from a part of the Slav language area. In the Croat-Slovene version clear traces of the German transmission are visible. Details of the same version, often mixed up with the story of the girl who did not go to Mass and was therefore taken to Hell turn up in the Czech, Moravian, Polish and Lithuanian texts. Here we often find again that the story itself is quite different, only the triple infanticide is mentioned with a few words, this being the only similarity with the original ballad.

Formulations entirely separate from these, however found among the Slovaks, the Moravians and the Carpathian Ukrainians living near the Hungarian frontiers, are closer again to the Hungarian version. Katuša stands on the bank of the Danube (or some other stretch of water), and throws in her new-born baby, saying: "Swim, swim, my baby, and I shall be a maid again!" This is overheard by an old woman or three women, who report her to the magistrate. In the prison she is told to look out of the window, for her father, mother (or brother) is coming. "Let the hangman come, not them!" she cries, and in 99. she adds: "I have killed three children, not one! Therefore I deserve to die." With the common elements there are, in the Slovak variants, new ones as well: the hangman wants the girl to be her lover, but she rejects him, with the same words as before. This motif appears among the Slovenes, too (Kumer 424–425). With the Moravians the three girls who witness the deed, or who happen to pass that way, rescue the child, and the action is further complicated. This takes us farther away from the common French—Hungarian formulation, although the connection with it remains still clear. The connection can, however, be imagined only with the former, prerenovation form, for the highwayman details and elements of the new version are completely lacking in it. The Slovak—Moravian version also indicates that there was, distributed throughout Hungary, some old text similar to the ballad of Erzsi Szabó, containing more of the French ballad's action than the present Bukovinian—Moldavian fragments. On the other hand, the Moravian—Slovak variants have, in spite of their old-fashioned form, preserved fewer common elements from the French ballad than the remodelled and heavily transformed Hungarian one. That is to say, they developed from the (early) Hungarian formulation.

To sum up, the Moldavian—Bukovinian ballad of Erzsi Szabó was borrowed from the French in the fourteenth century; on the other hand, the ballad of the triple infanticide (Vilma Szabó), developed from the old French borrowing and assumed its actual form during the nineteenth century.

Literature: Child 20, 1882, speaking about the connections of the English, Danish, German and Wendish ballads; Dános 1938: Type 24., derived from the German ballad in the nineteenth century; Solymossy 1937: discusses Type 24. without comparative notes; Seemann 1951: correlations between the English—German—Danish versions, on the one hand, and the east-European versions related with the German, on the other; Csanádi and Vargyas 1954: Type 24. originates from the German, Type 23. discussed without comparative analysis; Vargyas 1960: French origin, the triple child-murder in the German refers to Hungarian origin; Siuts 1962: detailed examination of five related German Types, rejects Vargyas 1960 on account of plot-construction; Vargyas 1967 = 1960, defending his standpoint against Siuts by referring to the practice of borrowing motifs within related thematic spheres.

25.THE GIRL WHO MADE LOVE WITH THE SERVANT

10.

Mihály Sárosi and János Betlen
Were sitting at table,
Eating and drinking together,
Having talk together.
5. Mihály Sárosi spoke up, saying:
Listen to me, dear friend,
Won't you discipline your young sister
So that she should not go
To the stable at nights!
10. She is making love with my coachman,
Not letting my faithful palfrey to have a quiet sleep!
Listen to me, dear friend,
My young sister is an honest girl!
Mihály Sárosi spoke up, saying:
15. And I shall show you how honest she is,
I shall show it by the strength of my two arms,
By the edge of my bright sword!
He hears the gate creak,
He hears the high heels of shoed boots patter,
20. And he hears the silken skirt rustle.
At once he goes to the stable,
To the door of the stable.
He spoke up and said to the coachman:
Open, coachman, open the door!
25. I cannot open it, my dear master,
Because my faithful palfrey is untethered
And if I open the door, it will run away,
And I know I shall never take it.
He kicked the door in with such force
30. That it fall apart immediately,—
Aye, there he found Anna Betlen!
He struck at her with his sword:
The silken skirt was torn,
Her red blood spurted out.—
35. Anna Betlen went home
And went to bed.
In the morning her aunt came to see her:
What is the matter, what is the matter, Anna Betlen?
O, there is nothing the matter, dear aunt!

40. I was stepping over the stone wall of my flower garden:
And I was caught by a rose-bush,
My silken skirt was torn,
And my blood spurted out at once.
And now I am lying in clotted blood,
45. And I am near to die...
Listen to me, Anna Betlen,
Go and stand out in the courtyard,
Pray to the Lord God and ask Him
To forgive you your sins!
50. Aunt, my aunt, my dear aunt—
Wash me with wormwood wine,
Wrap me in fine linen,
Have my body sent to Kolozsvár:
Let everybody see in my example
55. How an orphan girl fares in this world!...

Székelyföld, Kriza = MNGY III, 18.

Cf. Leader 223.

Divergences: There are two variants recorded in Maros-Torda county in which the scene of the girl praying upon her knees in the courtyard is described; the neighbour who had detected her appears and cuts her head. The request, then, heard from the severed head, is aimed at wrapping the head in fine linen, and so on. Anyway, the variants show a high degree of similarity, which is natural, since they have been collected in a relatively narrow area.

Earliest provenience: 1882.
Dissemination: Udvarhely county 2 (one of the variants originates from Kadicsfalva), Maros-Torda county (Szabéd, Csókfalva). Total: 4.
Textual relationship with other ballads: The coachman's words uttered in an attempt to hold up the following event and the kicking in of the door occur in **1., 20.,** and **21.** The girl's plaintive words towards the end of the ballad, asking people to wrap her heart in fine linen, etc. come up in **6., 20.** and **31.** **(38) 57.** (and are, in the final analysis, of French origin).
Tune: missing.

The beginning formula with the men drinking wine and having a discourse at the table is reminiscent of some English and Danish ballads with similar starting scenes (*Child* 246, to a lesser degree 268—, DgF 224), in which one of the men swears that he is able to entice any woman while the other refers to his bride, or some other maid or wife, who would resist all temptations. Apart from this, the western stories proceed in completely different ways. As to the French origin of the motif: "Let me wash in wormwood wine...", etc. see Notes to Type **57.** Disregarding the two mentioned motifs, the rest of the plot is unknown outside the Hungarian language area. In all likelihood, we are dealing with an autonomous Hungarian development that had come about under the influence of western examples. It is as old as the early French borrowings in Hungarian balladry.

26. THE GIRL DANCED TO DEATH

71.

1. Jó na-pot, jó na-pot Sá-ri bí - ró - né - nak

Sá - ri bí - ró-né - nak, A Ka-ti lá-nyá - nak!

1. Good day, good day
   To Mistress Sári the magistrate's wife,
   To Mistress Sári the magistrate's wife,
   And to her daughter Kati!

2. Come in, daughter Kati,
   Young men have come to invite you
   To the town Sári
   Where a wedding will be held.

3. I will not go, mother, I will not go,
   For I know it will not turn out well;
   János Árvadi is going now
   To feast his wedding day.

4. Put on, daughter Kati,
   Your fine silk skirt,
   Put on and wear on your feet,
   Put on your crimson boots!

5. Take your ten pairs of golden rings
   And put them all on your fingers;
   Let them break the heart
   Of your sweetheart!

6. Good evening, good evening
   To János Árvadi!
   I have arrived, among others,
   To the wedding feast.

7. Come and dance with me,
   Come and entertain yourself for a short while!

I will not go with you,
Because your sleeves are greasy!

8. Come and dance with me,
   Come and entertain yourself for a short while!
   And I will now go with you,
   Because your sleeves are no longer greasy!

9. Play, gipsy, till noon,
   From noon till evening,
   From evening to dawn,
   Till bright daybreak is shining!

10. Let me got to rest,
    For I am near to die!
    My fine silk skirt
    Has stuck to my body

11. I don't mind if you die,
    Nor if you depart from this world;
    If you did not become mine,
    You shall not become anyone else's!

12. Play, gipsy, till noon,
    From noon till evening,
    From evening to dawn,
    Till bright daybreak is shining!

13. Let me go to rest,
    For I am near to die,
    The ten pairs of golden rings
    Are tight on my fingers!

14. I don't mind if you die,
    Nor if you depart from this world;
    If you did not become mine,
    You shall not become anyone else's.

15. Let me go to rest,
    For I am near to die,
    The shanks of my boots
    Are full of clotted blood!

16. I don't mind if you die,
    Nor if you depart from this world;
    If you did not become mine,
    You shall not become anyone else's.

17. Play, gipsy, till noon,
    From noon till evening,
    From evening to dawn,
    Till she is laid out on the bier!

18. Take me, coachman, take me,
    Let's go home quickly!
    Open, mother, open
    Your painted gate,

19. Make, mother, make
    Your quilted bed,
    Let me give a rest
    To my wearied limbs!

20. Good day, good day
    To Mistress Sári the magistrate's wife,
    To Mistress Sári the magistrate's wife,
    And to her daughter Kati!

21. Well, dear mother,
    How does Kati fare now?
    Well, dear mother,
    How does Kati fare now?

22. Kati fares well enough already,
    And there is nothing the matter with her,
    She is laid out
    In the middle of the house.

23. Are you going to order
    A coffin of walnut-wood to be made for her?
    I am going, mother, to order
    A coffin of marble to be made for her.

24. Are you going to order
    The triple bells to be tolled?
    I am going, mother to order
    All the sixteen to be tolled.

25. Are you going to order
    Her body to be taken out to some pit?
    I am going, mother, to order
    Her body to be taken to the mournful graveyard.

26. Are you going to order
    A beggar to carry her out?
    I am going, mother, to order
    Sixteen gendarmes to carry her out.

27. Cursed be the father,
    Seven times cursed the mother,
    Who let their only daughter
    Go to the ball.

28. She let her go in the evening,
    She did not look for her in the morning,

And finally, on the third day,
She saw her brought home dead!

Tápiószele (Pest county), performed by a group of girls. Bartók 1906 = Bartók 176a.

72.

1. Jó es - tét, jó es - tét Csá - ti bi - ró - né asz-szony!

Ta - lán al - szik is már A ked -ves ga - lam - bom?

1. Good evening, good evening
   Mistress Csáti the magistrate's wife!
   No doubt, my dear sweetheart
   Is already asleep?

2. Wake up, wake her up,
   And send her to the ball,
   Let her put on
   A silk skirt blue as the blue sky!

3. Let her tie a silk kerchief
   Red as the red flame round her neck!
   Let her put ten pairs of golden rings
   On her fingers!

4. Let her put ten pairs of golden rings
   On her fingers,
   Let her put on
   Her boots of cordovan leather!

5. Let her put on
   Her boots of cordovan leather,
   And so send her to me,
   To pass the time in the ball till morning!

6. Good evening, good evening!
   Why did you send for me?
   Come and sit beside me, have a drink!
   And you will soon learn all about it.

7. Play, gipsies,
   From evening till morning,
   Till [the magistrate's wife] Mistress Csáti's,
   Daughter goes asleep!

8. Let me go out, let me go out,
   Let me go to rest,

Let me pour the blood
Out of my cordovan boots!

9. You cannot, you cannot,
   It's no time for you to go out,
   For the musician
   Is hired to play till morning!

10. Cursed, cursed
    The dear mother,
    Who lets her daughter
    To go to the ball in the evening.

11. She lets her go in the evening,
    She does not see her till morning,
    And at eight in the morning
    She sees her brought home dead.

12. Good morning, good morning,
    Mistress Csáti magistrate's wife!
    No doubt, my dear sweetheart
    Has already died?

13. She has died, she has died,
    And she has been buried, too.
    Although her name
    Is not forgotten.

14. Although her name
    Is not forgotten.
    You shall suffer, you scoundrel, for her,
    To the end of your life in prison!

Szilvásvárad (Heves county), performed by a man of 59. Sárosi, 1953.

Divergences: Number 71. is a rarer variant with details more elaborated, while No. 72. represents the more usual formulation, although the latter also contains less frequent formulas, for instance the motif of the sixth stanza, in which the girl is invited to a drink. This detail occurs only in some four or five texts.

As regards the names, Mistress Sági, the magistrate's wife comes up most frequently—practically in the whole of the Transdanubia and half the northern territory; beside Csáti and Sári, also Csáki is frequent. In Transylvania, Mistress Tollasi and Mistress Szőllősi are mentioned. Names of lower ratio of frequency are Katica Szegvári or Székvári, Kata Sallári, and in the oldest texts sometimes Rózsika Szalai or Katica Szalai are found to alternate, or the variants of these. The name of the young man is not usually given; but if it is still mentioned, then Kelemen Darvas Kis, Tamás Csomortányi or their corrupt variants will come up, or some other less conventional names.

Instead of the formula of greeting, sometimes the meeting of the lovers is described in the introductory stanzas; in other instances, the young man sends words to the girl from the tavern ("They are dancing, they are dancing in the tavern of Sári"). Sometimes the girl refuses to go to dance while at home, in which case the request is repeated twice. There are examples in which the young man is scorned by the girl in the girl's home, and in certain texts she talks in an abusive language: "Your mantle is ragged, your trousers are full of lice!". When so, the young man goes home to put on his sunday clothes: "Mother, my dear mother, . . . bring me my black trousers, My black trousers, My little red waistcoat; Fill its pockets With Gold and silver, With gold and silver, With white silver coins!" It is after such antecedent that the young man announces while dancing with the girl: "You have been scornful to me, and now it is my turn to scorn you!" But we have something different as a solution for the formula: "If you have not become mine...": "And I will not let you rest! I have asked you to marry me seven times, If you have not been given to me, you shall not be given to anyone else!" In certain variants the young man is blaming the girl at an earlier stage: "I have been suing for you, Rózsika Szalai, And it was not on one, not on two but on twelve occasions." What is more, he blames the girl as well: "It is you and no one else that promised me with a great oath Not to love anyone else beside me. But you have been false to me, you have cheated me, You have turned towards someone else for a few false kisses." The fact of unfaithfulness is sometimes only marked by calling the girl a "famous bride" in the course of invitation to the ball. Elsewhere the question is put like this: "Where is your daughter who is actually a bride?" Anyway, wedding is rarely mentioned in the texts, in their overwhelming majority only a ball is spoken of. Therefore it sounds rather queer when the girl is asked for in marriage: "Good day, good day, My rich aunt, the magistrate s mistress! Will you give your daughter in marriage to János Földvári?" Whereupon the mother answers: "I won't give you my daughter in marriage, Though you may have a dance with her." Then she encourages her daughter: Go, my child, go out, The young men are waiting for you outdoors!" I will not go, mother, I will not go out, Because nothing good will turn out of it! They are just having the wedding feast of János Földvári.—Put on your shoes of silk and velvet, Let they make the heart of János Földvári ache!" (*Kálmány*, 1878.)

Another motivation of the girl's being danced to death is that she loves two young men. Therefore many a variant speaks about two suitors—especially in the Transylvanian variants—: "Then the two young men tip the gipsy a wink", and in the end the lesson is often drawn: "Girls, girls, Let this be warning you Not to make love with two young men at a time!" The same moral is also formulated in prose: "This girl was courted by two young men and the girl was not able to make her choice... The young men made up their minds to invite her to the ball and break her there so that she may not marry either of the two..."

There are such variants—merely a few—in which the Devil is made responsible for dancing the girl to death. But such explanations are mainly given in prose by the performers complementing the sung variants which are fragmentary; if not so, there is an obvious discrepancy between the parts in verse and the parts in prose. For example, in one and the same village a collector made the following field note: "One informant states that the young man was in love with the girl, and since the girl's parents opposed their marriage...he danced her until... The other opinion holds that the young man dancing Ilona was the Devil who assumed the shape of Ilona's lover. The Devil kept apart Ilona's true lover during the entertainment. This they seek to support by noticing that no man of flesh and blood would be able to dance a girl to death . . . (in the end) it is not the Devil but the real lover that is speaking. The Devil has disappeared. Ilona's lover goes now to the ball to find the girl; failing to meet her there, he walks to her home where he is to learn the dreary news, and at the same time he has to hear the words accusing him for what has happened. This is obviously nonsensical. Similar is another variant: The daughter of magistrate Csáki announced that there was no-one to surpass her at dancing; but the Devil appeared in the likeness of her sweetheart and danced her to death. When she was dead, her true sweetheart came and asked the magistrate Csáki's wife to let her go to the ball,—and from this turn onwards, the song begins *anew and proceeds through the whole story of dancing to death!* (There are six texts to mention the Devil in one form or another.)

The vengeance of the lover is emphasized by such ending formulas in which the young man dies after her sweetheart. After the inquiry and the news of death one of the texts adds: "Then Kelemen Darvas Kis fall down upon the corpse of Fair Kata Sallai and so he died." A similar conception is underlying the formula— misfitting otherwise in the context—"May my blood flow in one stream with yours . . .". On the other hand, there is a text of seemingly old origin in which the young man's search for vengeance finds expression even in the closing stanza: "You will lay your quilted bed in vain, For I shall no longer knock at your leaden window-pane!" (NB., leaden window-panes were in general use in mediaeval times.) When the text did not refer to the young man's having been refused, the fatal dance found explanation by involvement of robbers: "According to the informant, robber danced the girl to death, as can be made out from the last line but one: "She lets her go in the evening, she does not see her till morning, She leaves her at the mercy of twelve brigands." Of course, the attribute "brigand" *(betyár)* in a sense approaching that of "outlaw" used to be a milder attribute, and probably referred to two young men in the beginning; the circumstance may well have been responsible for the misunderstanding of the situation.

A similar misinterpretation of the motif of dancing to death can be met with in variants from Vas county in which the young man stabs the girl in the heart and so she dies at the ball.

Apart from the formula "May my blood flow in one stream with yours . . ." also the motif of sending the young man on wild-goose chase is borrowed from Type 10. into the text of the ballad when the young man is making inquiry after the girl. Even the motif of "The Speaking Corpse" (65.) is fitted in sometimes (as can be seen in the stanzas beginning with the question: "Are you going to have . . . made for her?"). In a like way occasional details are borrowed from "The Mother's Curse" (16.) and "The Murdered Spinning Girl" (129.). (Cf. the motif of dying in scenes of gradation, further that of "Then the sky turned gloomy above her".) A variant contaminates the story with that of "The Bride Dragged to Death", as has been pointed out in connection with that ballad. There is a remote reminiscence of the tavern scene in "The Girl who Set Out with the Soldiers" in the young man's addressing the musicians like this: "If you want gold, I pay with gold, If you want silver, I pay with silver." The two texts given by way of exemplification do not include such final motifs like this: "To other beautiful girls They play music at dawn, But to the daughter of magistrate Sági They make a coffin."

Earliest provenience: 1846.
Dissemination:

I. Moson county (Mosonmagyaróvár), Sopron county (Bősárkány, Felsőpulya, Kismarton, Középbük, Középpulya, "Rábaköz" 2, Vitnyéd, Zsira), Vas county (Bejcegyertyános, Bélbaltavár, Bő, Csepreg 3, Csönge, Katafa, Kemenessömjén 2, Kisunyom 2, Olaszfa, Oszló 2, "Őrség", Pankasz, Pecől 2, Szatta 2, Várkesző, Velem, Viszák 2), Zala county (Alsónemesapáti, Andráshida, Bezeréd, Bókaháza, Búcsúszentlászló 2, Csup, Galambok, Kapolcs, Kékkút, Kiskomárom 2, Kustánszeg, Látrány, Monostorapáti, Murakeresztúr, Nagykanizsa, Nagylengyel, Nemesapáti, Nemeshetés, Nemessándorháza, Oltárc, Orosztony, Öreglak, Pálfiszeg, Pölöske, Rédics 2, Zalagalsa, "Zala c." 2), Somogy county (Alsok, Ádánd, Balatonlelle, Balatonszemes 2, Beleg, Bolhás, Bonnya, Büssü, Csoma, Csököly 3, Kaposfüred, Karád, Kereki, Kéthely, Kőröshegy, Lengyeltóti, Mosdós, Nagyberény, Ságvár, Somogyszob, Somogyszentmiklós, Szenna, Szőllősgyörök, Zsibót), Verőce county (Szentlászló 3), Szerém county (Kórogy 2), Pozsega county (Daruvár), Baranya county (Abaliget, Bános, Hegyszentmárton, Helesfa, Karácodfa 2, Kistótfalu, Kopács 2, Magyarürög, Mohács, Püspökszenterzsébet, Szilágy), Tolna county (Báta, Felsőireg 3, Koppánszántó 2, Kisszékely, Madocsa, Ozora, Öcsény 3, Püspökbogád, "Tolna c."), Fejér county (Csősz, Ercsi, Érd, Pákozd, Vereb), Veszprém county (Bakonyszentlászló, Csesznek, Csögle, Dég 3, Káptalantóti, Kup, Nemesvámos, Nyárád, Ősi, Pápa, Réde, Rigács, Szilasbalhás, Somlószőllős, Zalavár), Esztergom county (Tokod), Komárom county (Császár, Csilizradvány, Gutai quarters, Martos, Oroszlány, Tata 2), Győr county (Kóny, Ság). I. = 157.

II. Pozsony county (Felsőszeli, Nádszeg, Pered, Zsigárd), Nyitra county ("Nyitra c.", Pográny 2, Vágfarkasd, Zsére 2), Hont county (Garamsalló, Ipolybalog, Kemence), Nógrád county (Bárna, Becske, Bercel 2, Diósjenő, Gács, Hugyag, "Karancsalja", Márkháza, Mihálygerge 2, Nagybátony, Nagylóc, "Salgóvidék", Szanda, Szandaváralja 4), Heves county (Átány, Bélapátfalva, Bükkszék, Bükkszenterzsébet, Eger 3, Erdőkövesd, Erdőtelek, Fedémes 2, Felsőtárkány 2, Füzesabony, Gyöngyöspata, Nagyvisnyó, Parád, Pásztó, Recsk, Szilvásvárad, Tarnaméra, Tarnaörs, Tiszaigar 2), Borsod county (Bogács, "Borsod c.", Csincse, Domaháza, Felsőnyárád, Kisgyőr, Mezőkövesd 2, Szentistván, Tardona), Gömör county (Hanva, Kiskovácsvágása, Lucska 2, Szilice), Abaúj county (Áj, Cekeháza, Fáj, Kéked 2, Nagyszalánc), Zemplén county (Cigánd, Ricse 2, Sárospatak 3, Szerencs, Vajdácska), Bereg county (Dercen, Fornos, Lónya), Ung county (Nagydobrony, Nagygejőc, Ungvár), II. = 91.

III. Pest county (Galambospuszta, Kecskemét, Kiskunfélegyháza, Kiskunhalas 4, Perkáta, Tápióság, Tápiószele 2, Tura 2, Újszász 2), Jász-Nagykun-Szolnok county (Csököl, Jánoshida, Jászfényszaru, Jásztelek, Nagykörü, Túrkeve, Vezseny), Bács-Bodrog county (Dávod, Gombos, Homokmégy, Kunbaja, Rém, Székkutas, Zenta), Torontál county (Egyházaskér, Nagyszentmiklós, Páde, Rábé, Szaján, Szőreg), Csongrád county (Algyő, Ásotthalom, Csongrád 2, Domaszék, Hódmezővásárhely 5, Homokpuszta, Sándorfalva, Szeged 2, Szegvár, Tápé 4), Csanád county (Apáca, Magyarbánhegyes), Délalföld *s.l.*, Békés county (Doboz 4, Endrőd, Geszt, Gyopárosi-Kerektó, Gyula, Körösladány, Mezőgyán, Orosháza 2, Újkígyós, Vésztő 3), Arad county (Nagyzerind), Bihar county (Bagamér, Biharugra 3, Köröstárkány, Nagyszalonta 9), Szilágy county (Szilágysámson), Hajdú county ("Hortobágy"), Szabolcs county (Gégény, Lövőpetri, Nyírlugos, Nyírtelek 2, Nyírtura 2, Rétközberencs, Vaja 2), Szatmár county (Avasújváros, Kérsemjén 3, Ura 2, Vállaj). III. = 107.

IV. Kolozs county (Válaszút, Visa, Zentelke 2), Szolnok-Doboka county (Búza, Magyardécse, Szék), Maros-Torda county (Jobbágytelke, Kibéd, Marosvásárhely 2, Mikháza, "Nyárád riverine", Nyárádremete, Szováta), Torda-Aranyos county (Torda 2), Udvarhely county (Etéd 3, Enlaka 2, Homoródszentpál, Korond 3, Medesér, Siklód, "Udvarhely c." Zetelaka 2), Brassó county (Pürkerec), Csík county (Csatószeg, Csíkjenőfalva, Csíkmenaság 2, Csíkrákos 2, Csíkszentsimon, Gyergyócsomafalva 2, Gyergyóditró, Gyergyóteker őpatak, Gyimesközéplok, Gyimesfelsőlok 2, Magyarcsügés, Szépvíz-Kostelek), Háromszék county (Bardóc, Nagyajta, Sepsikőröspatak, Sepsiszentgyörgy, Székelytamásfalva), "Székelyföld" 2, Bukovina (Andrásfalva 3, Fogadjisten 2, Istensegíts, Józseffalva 4), Moldava (Esztufuj, Klézse, Lészped 5, "Moldava", Rácsila, Trunk). IV. = 75. I—III. 355. Sum total: 430.

Textual relationship with other ballads:
10., 16., 65. (19. and rarely **12., 13., 14., 29., 49.** "My flowers, my flowers...").

Tunes:
1. = *No.* 71. This melodic construction featured by (4) as a main cadence is unique. The principal forms are the following:

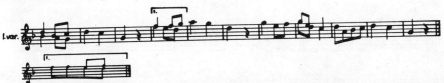

Var. 1. is disseminated throughout the whole of Area I., in the western part of Area II, and sporadically also in the other areas. There are 96 variants about the daughter of Mistress Sági, the magistrate's wife, coupled in general with sound although sketchy texts of more recent origin. 2. = No. 72. From the eastern part of Area II, from the middle of Area III, and sporadically also from elsewhere, some 81 variants have been collected. Most of the complete texts and most of the ancient elements are coupled with this variant. Main divergences:

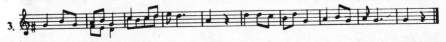

Var. 2. 3. = 46 variants from the eastern part of Area III. and from Areas IV and V. 3.

Var. 1–3. are various solutions of the same melodic idea. 4–22. 4. (10 variants), 5. (3 variants), 6. (7 variants), 7–9. (variants of the same tune; Róza or Rózsika Szalai is the girl's name, associated with archaic text elements. 10. (21 variants), Simonffy's popular composition. Often only the half-tune is sung. 12. (4 variants), 15. (2 variants).

342

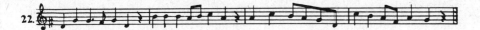

22.

Versions is languages other than Hungarian:

FRENCH: *1.* MS Liège, *2. Libiez* III, 33 plus Note on page 92, *3. Ampère* 250, *4. Beaurepaire* 144 = *Weckerlin,* 1887,4. = *Haupt* 1, *5. Davenson* 19 (second-hand publication, of which the original I have been unable to trace up), *6. Choleau* 223,* 7. Smith, Romania 7, 82, *8. Beauquier,* 81, *9. Buchon* 31, *10. D'Harcourt* 99. *11. Mélusine* 1878, 189,* *12–17. Millien,* 1906 137A–E plus variants, *18–20. Rossat,* 1917 6A–C, *21. Udry,* 63, *22. Canteloube* III, 168, *23. Canteloube* I, 52, *24. Arbaud* II, 139, *25. Tiersot,* 1931, 263,* *26. Tiersot* 1903, 113. (*Doncieux* 29 = inferred prototype: quotes 20 variants, many of which were not available to me.)

ITALIAN: *27–29. Nigra* 20A–C, *30. Ferraro,* 1870, 8 (fragment).

ENGLISH: *30–38. Child* 73. *39–69. Sharp-K* 19, *70–81. Belden* 37 (enumerates some one hundred variants that came to light after *Child,* Sharp included), *82–196. Bronson* 73 (disregarding 31 variants published by *Sharp-K* and one by *Belden,* he presents 147 variants).

GERMAN: *Hauffen* 71–72, and 79. Gottschee (Irrelevant are D. Vlr 68 = ? E–B, *Child* 64 and the corresponding Scandinavian variants.)

The French parallel of this ballad is a fairly uniform and widespread song known under the title "Les tristes noces". The story of the French ballad is the following.

The couple have been secret lovers for seven years when the young man is forced by his father to marry another girl. (This introduction to the plot is often missing in the texts.) The young man comes to tell his sweetheart that he is to marry someone else at his father's wish. "Is she more beautiful than I?", asks the girl. "No, only richer." Then the young man asks her to come to the wedding. "I will not come to the wedding, but only to the dance." He asks her to dress in fine clothes; in many cases he lists what she is to wear, for example: "In any case, when you come put on your finest clothes; put on the grey satin dress and your nice bonnet of rose colour!" (*10.*) Sometimes he himself buys her the clothes: "I shall buy you three dresses of different colours: one will be green, the other orange and the third fine velvet, which is most beautiful of all." (*23.*) Often, however, the listing comes when the girl is dressing or has the three kinds of dresses made. One or two variants add: she dresses like this in order to show her noble origin. On her arrival everyone thinks she is the bride. "Here is the new wife!—But I am not the wife, I am the forsaken one." The young man offers her to eat and to drink, but she says:" I did not come for that, but I came to dance with my sweetheart." In some rare instances the young man sees the girl approach and calls her to drink from afar. The answer is the same: "Young man, I did not come to eat and to drink, but I came to have a dance!" (*22.*) Then the fresh husband takes her by her soft, white hand: "Come, sweetheart, let's have a dance!" (*12.*) In some of the variants be calls to the musicians "Brave French musician, you know how to play a dance tune, O, do play one for us, so that my sweetheart should fully comprehend it!" (*5.*) "Play, fiddlers, play, play, play the dance tune!" (*23–24.*) A large number of variants include the motif of the girl changing her dress after each dance. ("Tout en dansant un premier tour, elle change de robe. Tout en dansant au second tour, en met encore une autre, Tout en dansant au troisième tour, la belle tomba mort.") (*9.* cf. *8., 12., 13.* and *20.*) In case the motif of changing dresses has been eroded, the girl dies after the first dance, and the young man dies after her either immediately, or after the third (or fourth) dance. In some variants they both die at a time: one of them falls to the right, the other to the left. Sometimes he stabs himself in the heart over the girl's dead body with the words familiar in the Hungarian ballads as well: "You have died for me, and I will die for you." "Si mourez pour m'amour, moi, je meurs pour le votre" (5.) "Puisqu'elle est morte pour moi, je veux mourir pour elle." (7.) The bells tolled for the dead also appear in rare cases: "Marguillier, beau marguillier, Toi qui sonn' bien les cloches, Sonn' les pitieusement!" (12. cf. 8.) Finally the invited guests mourn for the lovers and blame the father who, they say, has committed a great sin by preventing their union in marriage. "Le père a eu grand tort de n'pas l'avoir donnée." Sometimes even the young man is blamed for not having eloped with the girl!: "L' galant eut plus grand tort de n' pas l'avoir enl' vée!" (23.) "O, what a pity that these two lovers had to die because of their love!" (25.) And the guests who assembled there said one to the other: "This is the common fate of lovers who marry someone else!" (9.) And they began to bewail: "My God, my God, What a mournful wedding! To see two lovers who have died for each other!" (12.) Finally, in a few variants we have the grave-flowers that grow out of their dust to meet in a true lovers' knot. (4–5.)

As can be seen, there is hardly a motif in the French which is not represented in the Hungarian, even though in a different order sometimes. In the Hungarian there is no mention made of the seven-year secret love—perhaps the announcement "Seven times I have asked for your hand" answers this motif—, missing is further the young man's words telling the girl that he is to marry someone else. In an indirect way, however, this is expressed in No. 71., in which the daughter is reluctant to accept the invitation because it is János Árvai—the girl's lover—that is going to marry. But these motifs are missing sometimes from the French versions as well. Their complete absence accounts for the vagueness of the motivation of "dancing to death" in the Hungarian ballad. Less consequential is the absence of the other two motifs mentioned above, namely that the girl is held to be the bride because of her fine clothes and of the grave-flowers ending the story.

Looked at from the Hungarian side, every main motif is connected with the French counterparts in a way or other. The motif of invitation to the ball has apparently developed from the French girl's recurrent statement that she does not go to the wedding but to the *dance*. Devoid of meaning though, but still recognizable relic of this motif is to be found in one of the Hungarian variants, in which the mother says: "I do not give my girl to you in marriage, But I let her go to dance." On the other hand, the girl is invited to a wedding in several other variants as well—so in 71—and in the majority of cases it is the girl's sweetheart that conveys the invitation. Both nations agree consistently in that the young man prescribes what the girl is to wear at the dance, or in some way describes her gorgeous attire. Identical, though rare, are among both peoples the motif of offering food and drink to the girl and that of the rejection on her part. Calling the musicians to play is inevitable in the Hungarian, and is not infrequent in the French either. The girl's thrice-uttered request for a pause to rest, because her dress is sticking to her body, must be an idea originating from the French ballad in which the girl changes her clothes three times during the dance. But in the French the object is to show the pride of the poor girl, while in the Hungarian it is to bring out gradually her agony.

To wit, it is at this point that the Hungarians seized the tragic plot, developing a mowing drama out of the touching story of the parted lovers who died for each other. The words "Cursed be the father" etc. are identical in function with the general closing moralization of the French ballad. Finally, the anouncement of the death case by tolling the bells are also identical in the French and the Hungarian version. True to say, the grave-flowers are left out from this Hungarian story, but the double death is present in traces in some of the Hungarian variants.

Although the Hungarian is practically more powerful and effective, particularly as regards the "dancing-to-death-scene" and in several other details of the text, its structure is undeniably looser and its plot is not uniform. As against this, the French is a logical story from the beginning to the end. And so is it in each variant. Therefore it must be considered the original. Nevertheless, there is a sort of necessity seen at work in the Hungarian ballad's starting point from which the motif of the young man forced to leave the girl is regularly omitted: had it not been so, there would be no motivation for the young man dancing the girl to death. And precisely for this reason the contrast of the rich and poor had to be turned the other way round: in several variants the young man has his revenge on the rich girl who scorns him for his poverty. For this, too, the French may have given inspiration with its detailed description of the girl's rich dresses.

Some variants of the French ballad appeared in the Piedmont region, too, where we also find, so to say, word for word copies, disregarding a few omissions and alterations. It is particularly significant in these that the girl says what dress she will be wearing so that her sweetheart may recognize her—which is obviously secondary, depriving the plot of its original point. There are other motifs missing in the Piedmontese version: the offering of wine, and the reply "I did not come..." etc., the change of clothing, the remarks by the guests drawing conclusions from the story, as well as the calling of the bell-ringer. All these motifs have been applied by the Hungarians. It is evident, therefore, that the Hungarian ballad did not originate in the Italian, but in the French.

The English story takes us even more further. It is still connected to the French by recognizable threads, although its relationship to the Hungarian is already unrecognizable without the knowledge of the French ballad. Here, too, the young man invites his sweetheart to his wedding with another girl, and in one or two cases he asks her to put on fine clothes, but mostly it is the girl that does this on her own accord. There is strong emphasis on her beauty and its effect, of which the bride is jealous, there is an exchange of words between the two women, and the bride stabs the other, at which the bridegroom stabs her dead, and then himself.

In Gottschee, a German-speaking area in Slovenia, we find details of the Hungarian formulation in an almost word-for-word borrowing. Since I have no knowledge of an existing Slovene variant, I have to assume that the German speakers of Gottschee have borrowed the ballad directly from the Hungarians. In former times harvest workers and other seasonal workers used to go from what was then part of Austria over to Transdanubia. This circumstance may well be responsible for the adoption.

Literature: The Hungarian ballad is not listed in foreign publications, although *Child* quotes it in connection with No. *64.,* wrongly. *Gragger* 1926, 191 quotes Gottschee variants, and in his wake also *Ortutay*[3]. *Dános* quotes *Child* erroneously. *Solymossy* connects it with a recent local happening. *Dömötör* 1954: derives it from an event that took place at Ság or Bük in Vas county. *Csanádi* and *Vargyas* 1954: the Gottschee German version originates from the Hungarian. *Vargyas* 1960: French origin, thorough comparative analysis. *Ildikó Kriza* 1967: detailed analysis based on the Hungarian variants solely, leaving the comparative results out of consideration. *Vargyas* 1967 = 1960; *Leader* 1967: quotes Vargyas 1960, referring to Danish ballads in connection with the boots filled with clotted blood.

346

27. THE SISTER OF THE MAN CONDEMNED TO DEATH

73.

Parlando

1. Fe - hér Lász-ló lo - vat lo - pott A Fe - ke - të ha - lom a - latt.

Na - gyot pat -tant az os - to - ra, Meg -hal - lot - ta Gönc vá - ro - sa.

1. László Fehér stole a horse
   At the foot of the Black-hill.
   His whip cracked so loud
   That its sound was heard by all in the town of Gönc.

2. He was taken to merry Eger,
   He was thrown into the jail of merry Eger.
   Anna Fehér got news
   About her brother having been taken prisoner.

3. At once Anna Fehér went
   To the rail of the jail.
   Brother, my brother, László Fehér,
   Are you alive or are you dead?
   I am neither alive nor dead,
   I am always thinking of you.

4. Brother, my brother, László Fehér,
   Who is the judge here?
   Miklós Török is the judge here,
   And he is a man worthy of the gallows!

5. Then she went to the judge,
   Right to the desk of the judge.
   Judge, judge, honourable judge,
   Pray, set free my brother.
   I shall measure gold by the bowl,
   And silver coins by the bushel.

6. I do not want your bowl of gold,
   Nor your bushel of silver coins.
   Spend a night in bed with me
   And I shall let him free in a month.

7. Anna Fehér did not listen to him any longer,
   She ran down to the door of the cell.
   Brother, my brother, László Fehér,

347

The judge said:
If I spend a night in bed with him,
You will be let free in a month.

8. László Fehér replied:
Don't you spend a night with him in bed!
He will take your maidenhood,
Yet he will have your brother killed.

9. Anna Fehér did not listen to him any longer,
She spent a night with him in bed.
At a time around midnight
She heard loud noice of something rattling in the courtyard.

10. Judge, judge, honourable judge,
What's that rattling in the courtyard?
They are taking my horse to drink at the well,
The bit is rattling in its mouth.

11. Anna Fehér did not listen to him any longer,
She ran down to the door of the cell.
Brother, my brother, László Fehér,
Are you alive or are you dead?

12. The jailer spoke up and said:
Don't look for your brother in this place,
Sooner you'll find him at the edge of the wood, in the plain meadow,
On top of the gallows-tree.

13. Judge, judge, you false and faithless judge,
May the righteous Lord be heavy on you!
You have robbed me of my maidenhood,
Yet you had my brother killed!

14. May your washing water turn into blood,
May your towel burst into flames,
May the Lord deny you His grace,
May the Lord deny you His grace!

Kiskovácsvágása (Gömör county). Two female performers of 84 and 68, respectively.
Vargyas 1940.

74.

Parlando

1. Hej Fe-hér Lász-ló lo-vat-lo-pott A Fe-ke-te ha-lom a-latt. Hej
Ha-tot fo-gott su-ho-gó-ra Görc vá-ro-sa cso-dá-já-ra.

348

1. László Fehér stole horses
   At the foot of the Black-hill.
   He caught six of them in one raid,
   And it was a great wonder in the town of Görc.

2. Go at him, go at him, town of Görc,
   László Fehér has been taken.
   Let us throw him into fetters, the son of a dog,
   Shackle his right hand and left foot!

3. Surrender, you dog of a brigand,
   And tell us what your name is!
   Surrender, you dog of a brigand,
   Or tell us what your name is!

4. You know my horse with the white stocking,
   And you know my sister, Anna Fehér.
   We are not asking you about your horse,
   Nor about your haughty sister.

5. You dog of a brigand, surrender,
   And tell us what your name is!
   You dog of a brigand, surrender,
   And tell us what your name is!

6. You know my horse with the white stocking,
   And you know my sister, Anna Fehér.
   Let us throw him into fetters, the son of a dog,
   Shackle his right hand and his left foot!

7. And he was taken far away,
   And he was thrown into a deep and dark dungeon.
   And he was taken far away,
   And he was thrown into a deep and dark dungeon.

8. Anna Fehér heard news
   That his brother had been taken prisoner.
   She ordered her coachman:
   My coachman, harness my six horses!

9. My coachman, harness six horses,
   Put a bushel of gold on the coach,
   Put a bushel of gold on the coach,
   With which I shall redeem my brother.

10. Anna Fehér had no rest
    Until she reached at the iron gate:
    Brother, my brother, László Fehér,
    Are you asleep, are you resting?

11. I am not asleep and I am not resting,
    Sister, I am always thinking of you.

I am not asleep, and I am not resting,
Sister, I am always thinking of you.

12. Anna Fehér had no rest
    Until she reached at the iron gate:
    Brother, my brother, László Fehér,
    What is the judge's name here?

13. This judge is called the judge Horvát,
    And he is ripe for the gallows.
    This judge is called the judge Horvát,
    And he is ripe for the gallows.

14. At once Anna Fehér started
    And walked to the window of the judge Horvát.
    Judge, judge, judge Horvát,
    Will you set free my brother?

15. Will you set free my brother?
    I shall give you a bushel of gold.
    I don't want your bushel of gold,
    But I want you to spend a night in bed with me.

16. Anna Fehér had no rest
    Until she reached at the iron gate:
    Brother, my brother, László Fehér,
    This is what the judge said to me:

17. Your brother will be let free today
    If you spend a night in bed with me.
    Your brother will be set free today,
    If you spend a night in bed with me.

18. Sister, my sister, Anna Fehér,
    Don't you spend a night in bed with him!
    He will rob you of your maidenhood,
    And yet he will have your brother beheaded.

19. Anna Fehér had no rest,
    Until she arrived at the judge's house.
    O, she spent a night in bed with him,
    In his golden couch.

20. At a time about midnight
    There was some rattling heard from the courtyard.
    Judge, judge, judge Horvát,
    What rattling is that in your courtyard?

21. My coachman is giving his horse to drink,
    And its bit is rattling.
    My coachman is giving his horse to drink,
    And its bit is rattling.

22. Anna Fehér had no rest
    Till she arrived at the iron gate:
    Brother, my brother, László Fehér,
    Are you asleep, are you resting?

23. Pretty girl, Anna Fehér,
    Don't look for your brother in this place!
    You will find him in the green woods, in the green meadow,
    On top of the gallows-tree.

24. Then Anna Fehér started at once
    And she walked to the judge's window:
    Judge, judge, judge Horvát,
    May your horse's feet slip,

25. May your horse's feet slip,
    And may you be thrown down upon the ground!
    May your horse's feet slip,
    And may you be thrown upon the ground!

26. Thirteen cart-loads of straw
    May rot in your bed,
    For thirteen years
    May you be glued to the deal of your bed!

27. May thirteen doctors' hands
    Get tired of healing your wounds,
    May thirteen chemists' shops
    Be cleared of all the drugs for you.

28. Well, judge, that's what I wish you:
    May your water for washing turn into blood,
    May your towel burst into flames,
    May the Lord deny you His grace!

Vésztő (Békés county). Performed by a girl of 18. Bartók 1918 = Bartók No. 29.

75.

1. László Fehér stole horses
   At the foot of the Black-hill.
   His whip cracked so loud
   That it was heard by the county magistrates.

2. Take that brigand
   Who is ripe for the gallows!
   Take that brigand
   Who is ripe for the gallows!

3. Anna Fehér heard tidings
   That her brother had been taken prisoner.
   Harness, coachman, my six horses,
   Servants, put a bowl of gold in the coach,
   A bowl of gold, a bowl of diamond,
   With which I shall redeem my brother!

4. László Fehér, my dear brother,
   Are you alive, are you dying, or are you dead?
   I am neither alive, nor am I dying,
   But I am always thinking of you.
   I am neither alive, nor am I dying,
   But I am always thinking of you.

5. Judge, judge, judge Horvát,
   I shall give you a bowl of gold,
   I shall give you a bowl of diamond
   If you set free my brother.

6. Anna, Anna, Anna Fehér:
   I don't want your bowl of gold,
   Your bowl of gold, your bowl of diamond,
   I only want you to spend a night in bed with me!

7. László Fehér, my dear brother,
   He does not want my bowl of gold,
   My bowl of gold, my bowl of diamond,
   He only wants to spend a night in bed with me.

8. Anna, Anna, Anna Fehér,
   Don't you spend a night in bed with him!
   He will rob you of your maidenhood,
   And yet he will have me hanged on the gallows.

9. Anna Fehér did not pay heed to his words,
   But she spent a night in bed with the judge.
   It's three past midnight,
   Yet Anna Fehér has not fallen asleep.
   It's three past midnight,
   Yet Anna Fehér has not fallen asleep.

10. Judge, judge, judge Horvát!
    What rattling is heard in your courtyard?
    My horse is being taken to the well,
    And its bit is rattling.
    My horse is being taken to the well,
    And its bit is rattling.

11. Anna Fehér paid no heed to his words,
    But she ran to the door of the jail;
    László Fehér, my dear brother,
    Are you alive, are you dying, or are you dead?

12. The other prisoners spoke up, saying:
    Anna, Anna, Anna Fehér,
    This is not the place to find your brother in.
    You shall sooner find him in the green woods, in the plain meadow,
    On top of the gallows-tree.
    You shall sooner find him in the green woods, in the plain meadow,
    On top of the gallows-tree.

13. Judge, judge, judge Horvát,
    May your water for washing turn into blood,
    May your ploughland never yield a crop,
    May it never be reaped what you sow!
    May your ploughland never yield a crop,
    (*a*) May it never be reaped what you sow!
    (*b*) May the good Lord be heavy on you!

Nyírvasvári (Szabolcs county). Performed by a woman of 72. Vargyas 1968 = AP 7347/f. (a) and (b) refer to tune variants.

  Divergences: This ballad shows a remarkably uniform spread even the names in it being exceptionally stable. (For instance, it is a unique occurrence that the name of the town Gönc is mistaken in No. *74.*, and Görc is said instead.) Deviations may be found in the formulation of minor details, some of the variants may be more fragmentary than the others, one or another motif may be omitted. In most of the variants a "bowlful of silver" is placed on the coach, in addition to a bowlful of gold. Sometimes the following formulas of greeting are exchanged between Anna Fehér and the judge: "Good morning, Sir lieutenant! May God grant one, my perl of a bird!" The girl's coming to and fro is indicated by formulas as follows: "Anna Fehér does not answer a word, She walks to the corridor, She walks from corridor to corridor (or: from room to room) . . . And so she arrives at the gate of the jail." In some variants the following discourse takes place at night: "The clock has struck twelve. Are you asleep, Anna Fehér?" "No, I am not asleep, I cannot rest. . ." Whereupon the judge tries to appease th girl: "O, sleep in rest, It's my horse they are taking to the well . . ." In other instances, the judge speaks the plain truth: "Your brother has been finished with", and his words are immediately followed by the curse of the girl. Sometimes the judge applies attributes of art-poetic origin to the girl: "Sleep, Anna Fehér, My dearest treasure, my beautiful Diana!" Typical turns of the curse, apart from those contained in the sample texts are: "May the mire spurt up in front of you, May the water flood in front of you!" or: "May your bread turn into stone", "May your own knife turn against your heart!"

Earliest provenience: 1846 (It should be noted, however, that the story came up in a letter in Latin from 1547 and in the collection of sermons of Péter Bornemisza in 1578.)

S.1.: 1881 (Limbay) and 1914 (a Budapest publication) 2.

I. "Sopron and Vas counties", Sopron county (Rábaköz), Vas county (Alsóőr-Austria, Katafa, Mikosszéplak, Olaszfa), Zala county (Becsvölgye, Bezeréd, Bocfölde, Boncodföld, Csömödér, Csup, Galambok, Hahót, Jánosmajor, Kerkakutas, Kisgörbő, Kiskomárom 2, Komáromváros, Nemesnép, Pölöskefő, Rédics), Somogy county (Balatonberény, Berzence, Csoknya, Hetes 3, Kaposfüred, Kaposmérő, Karád 3, Kéthely, Kiliti, Nagyatád, Nemesdéd, Öreglak, Sándorpuszta, Somogyaszó, Somogyegres, Somogyszob, Szenna, Törökkoppány 4), Szerém county (Kórogy 3), Verőce county (Szentlászló 2), Baranya county (Csányoszró, Drávafok, Katádfa, Mánfa, Mohács, Püspökszenterzsébet 2, Ranódfa-puszta 2, Vásárosdombó 3), Tolna county (Báta 3, Bedeg, Gerjen 4, Öcsény 6, Bogyiszló 2), Fejér county (Dunapentele), Veszprém county (Bakonyszentlászló, Borzavár, Pápa, Réde, Tihany), Győr county (Rémsziget), Komárom county (Komárom, Naszvad). I.: 90.

II. Pozsony county (?"Csallóköz", Diószeg), Nyitra county (Ghymes 3, Vágkirályfa, Zsére 6), Bars county (Tild), Hont county (Inám, Dolinka, Ipolybalog 2, Ipolyszög, Perőcsény, Tésa), Esztergom county (Bajna), Nógrád county (Bercel, Bernecebaráti, Buják, Dejtár 2, Érsekvadkert, Márkháza, Nógrádmarcal, Romhány, "Salgóvidék", Szanda 2, Szátok, Vanyarc), Heves county (Andornaktállya, Atkár, Bekölce 2, Bélapátfalva 2, Besenyőtelek 2, Bodony, Bükkszenterzsébet, Bükkszentmárton, Erdőkövesd, Erdőtelke 3, Fedémes 6, Felnémet 2, Felsőtárkány 3, Füzesabony, Gyöngyöspata 2, Gyöngyösvisonta, "Heves county", Littke, Markaz, Mikófalva, Nagyréde, Ostoros, Parád, Pétervására, Poroszló 2, Sirok, Tarnalelesz, Tarnaméra, Tarnaörs, Tarnaszentmária, Visznek), Borsod county (Bogács, Center, Cserépváralja, Csincse, Disznóshorvát, Domaháza, Emőd, Felsőábrány, Kécs, Mályinka 2, Mezőkeresztes, Mezőkövesd 3, Sály 2, Szentistván 2, Szentistvánbaksa, Tard), Gömör county (Almágy 2, Alsófalu, Egyházasbást, Gesztete 2, Kiskovácsvágása 2, Nagybalog, Páskaháza, Péterfala 2, Szilice), Abaúj county (Cekeháza, Göncruszka, Kéked, Mogyoróska, Tornyosnémeti), Zemplén county (Bodrogmező, Cigánd, Karcsa 4, Olaszliszka, Ricse 4, Sárospatak, Szerencs), Bereg county (Dercen 2, Rafajnaújfalu 2, Tarpa, Tiszaszalka 2), Ung county (Nagydobrony 2, Szirénfalva 2), Máramaros county (Hosszúmező). II.: 144.

Pest county (Akasztó 3, Bugac 2, Bugacmonostor, Cegléd, Hetényháza, Izsák 2, Kartal, Kecskemét, Kiskunhalas, Kiskunmajsa, Lajosmizse, Lakitelek, Perkáta, Tura 2, Zsámbok), Jász-Nagykun-Szolnok county (Csépa, Jászszentandrás, Jásztelek, Karcag 3, Karcag-Berekfürdő, Kungyalu, Kunmadaras 2, Poroszló, Pusztamizse, Tiszapüspöki 2, Tiszaszentimre 2, Zagyvarékas 2), Bács-Bodrog county (Baja, Ókanizsa, Rém, Szeremle), Torontál county (Hertelendyfalva-Vojlovica 4, Törökbecse), Csongrád county (Csongrád, Hódmezővásárhely 2, Sándorfalva 2, Szegvár), Békés county (Békéscsaba 2, Dévaványa, Doboz 6, Pusztaföldvár, Sarkadkeresztúr, Szecső, Szeghalom, Vésztő 3), Arad county (Nagyzerind, Pécska, Vadász 3), Délalföld *s.1.* 3, Bihar county (Bályok, Cserekert, Csökmő, Kónyár, Köröstárkány, Nagyszalonta 5, Sáránd 3), Hajdu county (Balmazújváros, Hajdúböszörmény, Hajdúsámson, "Hortobágy", Nádudvar, Nagyléta-Cserekert, Pocsaj, Püspökladány, Sámson, Tiszacsege 2), Szabolcs county (Érpatak, Kállósemjén, Mezőladány, Nagykálló, Nyíradony, Nyírbátor 2, Nyírlugos 4, Nyírtelek-Dózsaszőllő 2, Nyírvasvári 2, Penészlek, Petneháza, Piricse, Rohod, Újszentmargita, Vaja 3), Szatmár county (Kérsemlyén 5, Kisar, Kocsord, Nagydobos, Nagyecsed, Szamosszeg, Tyukod, Ura). III.: 136.

IV. Kolozs county (Bogártelke, Kide 4, Méra, Sztána, Türe 2, Válaszút 2, Zentelke 2, Zsobok), Szolnok-Doboka county (Búza, Feketelak 2, Magyardécse, Szék, Szépkenyerűszentmárton 2, Vajdakamarás), Beszterce-Naszód county (Tacs), Torda-Aranyos county (Torda 2), Alsó-Fehér county (Lőrincréve, Marosújvár), Kisküküllő county (Küküllődombó), Nagyküküllő county (Mihályfalva), Maros-Torda county (Kibéd), Udvarhely county ("Erdővidék", Kápolnásfalu 2, Kénos, Rugonfalva,

354

"Udvarhely c."), Csík county (Csíkmenaság 3, Csíkrákos, Csíkvacsárcsi, Gyergyóalfalu, Gyergyócsomafalva, Gyergyóremete, Gyergyóújfalu, Gyimesfelsőlok, Gyimesközéplok 3, Gyimesvölgye-Gáborpataka, Kászonaltíz, Kászonjakabfalva, Szépvíz-Kostelek, Tekerőpatak), Háromszék county (Dálnok, Kézdivásárhely, Kisborosnyó, Magyarhermány, Sepsiszentgyörgy), Bukovina (Andrásfalva 5, Fogadjisten, Hadikfalva 2, Istensegíts 3), Moldavia (Bergyila, Lészped 2). IV.: 73.

I–III.: 372, IV.: 73. Sum total: 445.

Textual relationships with other ballads: "Are you alive..." **9., 10.,** "Harness, coachman, the horses..." **2., 9., 10., 13., 16., 21., 27.** and **39.**

Tunes: 1. = No. 73 (43 variants), 2. = No. 74 (10 vars), 3. = No. 75 (= var. of No. 74), 6. (6 vars), 7. (69), 8. (37), 10. (14), 12. (2), 13. (34), 16. (6), 19. (2), 20. (13), 22. (5), 24. (2), 27. (2), 31. (occasional adaptation), 33. (2), 35. (8), 36. (2), 37. (4), 39. (2), 43. (4), 44. (4), 53. (2), 54. (2), 58. (2), 60. (3), 65. (3), 66. (2), 67. (2), 71. (4).

357

358

361

Variants in languages other than Hungarian:

ITALIAN: *1–7. Nigra* 3A–E plus 2 variants (enumerates a further 9 variants), *8. Pergoli* 18, No. 11, *9. Bernoni* 1872 Punt. V. 7, *10. Bolza* 50, *11. Ferraro,* 1870, 21, *12. Idem,* 1877, 108, No. 22, *13.* Giannini 1889, 166 13, *14. Gianandrea, 2* 64 3, *15. Widter* 85. (*Pasolini* 2., *Vettori* 205–207.)

CATALAN: *16. Wolf* 157, 21.

DANISH: *17–22.* DgF 247.

Partial variants:

FRENCH: *23–24. Paris,* 1882, 97 and 103, *25. Idem,* 1883, 115, *26. Decombe* LXXXIX.

The story of beguiled Anna Fehér belongs among the widest-spread classical ballads of the Hungarian language area which at the same time preserves splendid marks of the old ballad style. Its unique popularity and living tradition are responsible for the ballad's having an exceptionally uniform plot all over the language area: the variants may be shorter or longer, complete or fragmentary, but the basic story is fully identical everywhere. Indeed, it is so strongly constructed that it would be difficult to introduce any change into its context.

The core of the story was first mentioned in a letter which József Macarius sent from Vienna to Sárvár (Western Hungary) in 1547 to György Pernezith. He relates that "a new story began to spread in the city: A citizen of Milan killed someone in a brawl and was therefore imprisoned. His wife begged the chief judge to spare his life, but the judge wanted to have the woman in exchange. She was reluctant to make the sacrifice, but the relatives urged her to yield. Finally the judge had his pleasure with the woman. However, the next day her husband was beheaded. The fresh widow applied to Duke Gonzaga with her complaint; the Duke ordered the judge to marry the woman and deposit at the same time 3,000 florins on her account, and then had the false judge beheaded."

The same story can be read in one of the Postillae of Péter Bornemisza, dated from 1578. "Gonzaga was a man of supreme authority in Mediolanum. His officer who had arrested a noble man was asked by the latter's wife to give back her husband; the officer promised her to comply with her wish, provided she would yield to him; the woman yielded in order to save her husband. But the officer had her husband executed and surrendered only the dead body of the man to the wife. The woman reported the thing to Gonzaga who in turn made the officer marry the woman. When the wedding was over and the oaths sworn, Gonzaga had the officer executed and surrendered all his wealth to the woman."

The literary adaptations of the theme have been thoroughly surveyed in the Hungarian topical literature. In one of the tales of Giambattista Geraldi Cinthio's Hecatomithi Ovvero Cento Novelle (1565) there figures a "sister" who pleas for mercy in behalf of her brother who has been condemned to death. The story found its way into various collections of tales in Latin, French and English. Shakespeare worked up the theme in his Measure for Measure. It is worthy of mention that both he and one of his sources place the plot into the Hungary of King Matthias Corvinus (the scene being in the city of Julio that may correspond, perhaps, to the name of *Gyula*).

The adaptations must have been developed after the popular ballad had become widespread: in all likelihood it was the ballad form that played the mediating role. To wit, the above-mentioned letter in Latin speaks of the story as of a widely-known one in 1547, that is eighteen years before the novella of Cinthio was published. It also weighs in the scale that both the literary adaptations and the "news" spreading the rumour assign the story to those two particular areas in which the ballad was really extant, namely to Italy and Hungary. Apart from Hungary, the story enjoys a general and traditional currency only in the Italian-speaking territories. "La povera Cecilia" is mourning for her husband who had been imprisoned and condemned to death. "Be quiet, Cecilia, there is still one way of rescuing him: whichever of us, two captains, you happen to choose as a mate for a night, he will release your husband." "Let me go into the jail so that I may tell about it to my husband and ask for his consent; I shall return in the evening." "My husband, it is my wish to sleep with the captain in order to save your life!" "Go away, Cecilia, go away, for this is no business of mine. Whatever honour you may receive in the captains room will be your share for the whole of your life." In the evening she walks to the captain's home. At midnight she begins to sigh. "What ails you, Cecilia, why does dream shun your eyes? My heart aches and the pain foretells my death. Sleep, sleep, Cecilia, for you have no reason to sigh so bitterly." As the woman wakes up in the morning and steps out of the captains room, she beholds her husband's severed head on the peak of a pole. She turns back from the balcony, saying: "O, you vile captain, you have deprived me both of my honour and of my husband!" "But there is one more possibility for you to escape: whichever you may choose of the two of us he will marry you."—"I don't want either of you. Let me lead a lonely life from hence, keep on telling my beads, so the boatmen may sing a song about my story to the generations to come."

The story appears without any significant difference, one should say almost uniformly in all the variants. What may be taken as a considerable deviation in them is that the woman dies in some cases and flowers grow out of their graves. At the same time, there is a close agreement with the Hungarian ballad, including the tiniest details. The woman walks down to the jail also in the Italian version to ask her husband, she begins to sigh at midnight, the judge appeases her, and finally she utters nearly the same curse as the Hungarian girl; there can no doubt as to their common origin. Of course, there are also differences: the Italian version has a wife instead of the prisoner's sister, the husband's consent instead of the brother's protest, the nocturnal discourse is not elicited by the rattling noise of chains, and the curse of the Hungarian heroine is replaced by a proposition of marriage. All these, however, cannot blur the view of a high-degree of agreement.

How can we explain the interrelationship? The literature so far has not attempted to solve the riddle; it rested content by stating the fact of agreement. As long as the Italian version had been known exclusively—the ballad being widespread throughout the entire northern Italy—one might reasonably suspect that Hungarian soldiers laying in Milan and other Italian towns could have brought it into Hungary. On this ground it may well have been of a more recent—eighteenth-century—origin, in which case both its unfading popularity and the involvement of the highwayman motif might be soundly explained.

But the rub is that in the eighteenth century a new type of highwayman balladry sprung up that had nothing to do with such a specimen carrying all the typical features of a classical mediaeval ballad. Another possibility would be that the story received a wider currency in the wake of the sermons held by Bornemisza and subsequent preachers. This supposition, however, would fail to account for the common traits in the Hungarian and the Italian versions, which anyway are not parts of Bornemisza's postilla.

Considering the correlations opened up in connection with the ballads discussed so far, to wit, French ballads have been found to be penetrating English, Italian, Danish and German territories, and in the case of a no longer extant French version the French origin has been demonstrated precisely by this trend of dissemination, now one might suppose that in the present instance the other links of chain have been lost, and solely the Italian survives—that is to say, the French origin will account in this case too for the similarities in the two nations' ballads.

This supposition received further support in the course of investigation. Earlier research mentioned a Catalonian version as well, quoted in the form of abstract in the Hungarian literature. As I got acquainted with this text (*16*.) I was surprised to find details of formulation typical of the Hungarian version. "Everyone had fled from the great city of Reus, except a noble lady whose husband had been thrown into prison there. She went up to Madrid to see the Commander.—Good morning, Commander, won't you release my husband?—Aye, noble lady, are you shedding tears for your husband and for his love?—Yes, indeed, Commander, I am shedding my tears for my husband and my love.—Don't worry, my noble lady, tomorrow the man will certainly appear to you." (Here something must have been omitted, as can be inferred from the following lines.) Standing by the window, she beholds her husband as he is escorted to the gallows tree. "Hold your tongue, Commander, for you will rue for what you have done! *You have robbed me of my honour, and you have hanged my husband!*—I have three sons in my army, choose whichever you like or else I myself shall be your husband." This announcement is followed by eight lines: coming from the service, the woman meets the Commander who pleas for mercy (?) but the woman reminds him that he had not shown mercy when hanging her husband, and shoots him dead with a revolver. A solution like this betrays a subsequent modification, a secondary development.

Various other elements appear in the story of a Portuguese ballad (*Wolf* 89, No. 3, Der gefangene Graf): A count rapes a girl while on a journey. He is taken; the girl is shown up to the King's court. Sentence is proclaimed: first the girl is married to the count, then the count is beheaded.

The French origin became doubtless in my eyes when I got acquainted with the Danish ballads which also include some of the important details of the plot. Notably, in principle, the story might have made its way from the Italians to the Catalonians—although for the most part their ballads are French in origin—but a route from Italy to Denmark cannot be imagined as feasible; the more cases are known of direct borrowing by the Danes from the French. Let us see, therefore, the Danish version.

247/A. The introductory part mentions three brothers of a girl, but later her fiancée is involved, still later her husband, whom the King has thrown into prison. The girl or wife goes up to the King's court, and asks him to release her man. "Tovelil, are you going to love me and spend the night in bed with me?" "I have a man so brave and noble that I must speak to him first." She walks into the jail and asks him if he allows her to spend the night with the King in order to save him. The man flies into a passion: One single night, but no more! And when you go to the King, do not put on your golden jewels!" The woman puts on her finest attire, in spite of the warning, and so she lies with the King. Next morning she receives the "morning present" due to her for the night—a commonplace in Danish ballads—including various estates and her husband's freedom in the bargain. In the second variant, she impresses the King not with her beauty but with her entreaties, and acquires her bridegroom's freedom without sacrificing her honour. Solutions camouflaging the real conflict, as in the present case, are rather common in Danish ballads which have been preserved not by folk tradition but in manuscripts of song collections. Nevertheless, even the distorted formulation betrays the ballad having been derived from the common European theme.

As the Danish version, in a like way also the French fragments of the ballad under discussion had been unknown to Hungarian researchers. The latter preserve only few elements of the story, yet they reveal very interesting partial reminiscences bearing on the *formulation* of the Hungarian version. Also the French begins with mentioning the horses (for instance in No. *26.*). The noble lady of Bois-de-Vaux, the one who has so beautiful horses! When they march along the pavement the whole of the town is trembling. It is not for the weight of their bodies, but for the gold and silver they are carrying. They carry them to her first-born son who is imprisoned in Rennes. But they did not carry enough of gold and silver. Therefore the son has been detained. (C'est la dame du Bois-De Vaux. C'est laqu'elle a de beaux chevaux. Quand ils marchaient sur le pavé, Toute la ville elle en tremblait. C'est point la pesanteur qu'ils ont; C'est l'or et l'argent qu'ils avont, Qu'ils portaient à leur fils ainé, Qui est à Rennes emprisonné. Ils n'en ont point porté assez; Le fils ainé est demeuré.") At this point the story changes into that of Roi Renaud. However, those three or four variants which start like this are completely different from the usual beginning of the Roi Renaud ballad; and what is more, the initial scene described above does not always match with the continuation of the story. (Namely, the husband is kept in jail, and rumours of his burial are heard by his wife who stays at home.) Apparently the beginning formula got from some other ballad into the most popular French ballad text. But the source, the "other ballad" remains unknown, at least to me, and it is only the incorporated portions that maintain memories of its one-time existence.

Another fragment (*23.*) runs like this: Jean Renaud, the King's cousin, O my Lord, how beautiful his horses are! He has been seen to got to Bordeaux with them, taking gold and silver to his imprisoned *brother*. Cheer up, brother, for you are no longer a prisoner! How can you ask me to cheer up when I see death in front of my couch! ("Le cousin du Roi, Jean Renaud, Mon Dieu! Qu'il a de beaux chevaux! Le cousin du Roi, Jean Renaud, On l'a vu passer à Bordeaux. De l'or, de l'argent a porté A son frère Louis emprisonné. Réjouis-toi, mon frère ainé, Car tu n'es plus emprisonné! Comment veux-tu que je m'réjouis'? Je vois la mort au pied d'mon lit...").

The next fragmentary text has been welded into *24.* They say that Madame du Clos has got beautiful horses. As they march along the pavement, the whole of the town is trembling. It is not because of the shoe-nails, but because of the gold and silver they are carrying in order to release her son who is prisoner in Paris. My son, what is the matter with you, *who keeps you here as a prisoner?* Alas, it is on account of the objects of state I have robbed from the Cathedral. Cheer up, my son, for your wife gave birth to a son yesterday... ("Chez Madame du Clos Lourmeau On dit qu'il y a de beaux chevaux; Quand ils marchaient sur ces pavés, Toute la ville elle en tremblait. Ne sont pas les clous qui font ça, C'est l'or et l'argent que li a, Pour délivrer son fils Léouis Qu'est dans les prisons de Paris. Mon fils Léouis, que s'y a ti? *Qui vous tient renfermé-z ici?* Hélas, ce sont les ornements Que j'ai dérobés au saint sacrement. Mon fils, Léouis, réjouis-toi; Ta femme a eu un fils hier au soi.")—but the rest belongs to the story of Roi Renaud, in which the husband just returning home is received with these words.

Similar is the opening formula of *25*. The lady of Vaux is arriving with her big horses. When they enter the city of Rennes, the pavement is trembling. Also the houses are shaking as they are galloping, and it is because of the gold and silver they carry with them to ransom the lady's eldest son who is prisoner in Rennes. But they did not take enough gold and silver, and the son was condemned to death. ("C'est la dame du bois des Vaux, Qui vient avec ses grands chevaux. Dans Rennes quand ils sont entrés, Tous les pavés en ont tremblés. Les maisons tremblent quand ils trottent Du poids de tout l'argent qu'ils portent Pour délivrer le fils ainé. Qui est à Rennes emprisonné. N'en ont point core assez porté, Le fils a été condamné...")

The correlation of the Hungarian ballad with these beginning formulas can be clearly discovered: the mentioning of horses and robbery gave rise to the idea of horse raiding, the great noise made by horses has been transformed into sounds of crackings with the whip that is heard throughout the town; completely identical is the motif of conveying gold and silver by cart for the purpose of redeeming the prisoner, further the addressing of the prisoner—in some instances it is her brother—, and also the question appears: who keeps him in jail? (in the Hungarian: Who is the judge here?). It seems as if the beginning part of the no longer extant French counterpart of the Hungarian ballad survived in these incorporated portions of texts: and obviously, we are dealing with the beginning lines of the French ballad, the one-time existence of which is well indicated by the occurrence of fairly uniform versious (Italian, Catalonian, Danish, and Hungarian) surrounding the French-speaking area. The original French may have had now a wife, now a sister as heroine, a duality of cast known also from the ballad about The Test of Faithfulness **(43.).** This is the reason why one people retained the one, the other people another solution. The details of the original formulation have been preserved, it seems, in the most intact forms by the Hungarian version in this instance. Admittedly, substantial transformations had been made in the course of adaptation. It appears, indeed, as if the individual words had been suggesting novel ideas for the development of a transformed story.

The ballad, which is mediaeval in origin may have been extant in the central parts of the Hungarian-speaking area as late as the end of the eighteenth century. Subsequently, when highwayman balladry developed in the decades of the "highwayman world", the story about the prisoner left at the mercy of cruel judges, who levied blackmail on his sister immediately took the imaginative force of the population, and once more the ballad was felt to be timely. Maybe, the motif of horse stealing got into the Hungarian version at that time, although it is not precluded either that the change had been made much earlier, in mediaeval times, since the Hungarian audience must have preferred the motif of horse raiding—considered to be less condemnable and also more accustomed to—to that of the crime mentioned in one of the quoted French fragments. If so, the story was the more adaptable to the popular idiosynchrasies in the eighteenth and early nineteenth centuries. One thing is beyond doubt: the flourishing dissemination and popularity of the ballad had gone hand in hand with those of the so-called highwayman songs and shepherds' songs. Even their tunes are mostly the same. Sometimes one and the same singer performs, without interruption, various highwayman ballads, highwayman songs, shepherds' songs, together with the song of László Fehér to one and the same tune. Evidently, the ballad has penetrated Transylvania in recent times; it is performed there mainly with tunes originating from Hungary proper. All this unequivocally betrays a revival of the transformed mediaeval ballad, which became a vogue-song, owing to its highwayman affinities. At the same time, its international connections speak uniformly of a western and mediaeval origin.

The ballad belongs to the oldest class of Hungarian borrowings from the French, originating in the fourteenth century.

Literature: Ortutay 1936–48 cites studies of *Béla Zolnai* (Irodalomtörténet 1917, 405 and 560): Italian origin, from there taken over in novellas Latin, English, as well as French; *Solymossy* 1937: Italian origin, based on real event; *Csanádi* and *Vargyas:* the theme is of Italian origin supplemented with outlaw-motifs in the 18th century.

28. THE CRUEL MOTHER-IN-LAW

76.

Once upon a time there was a very beautiful girl. She was also a very poor girl. She was pasturing geese at the end of the village. Since she was realy very beautiful, she was named Fair Damsel Katica. One a day the King's son passed there, and cast his eyes on her. He fell in love with her, and made up his mind to marry the girl. And so he told the girl. And the little girl went away with him. He took her into his palace. As he entered his palace, he went to his mother and spoke up, saying:

Tempo giusto ♩ . c. 70

1. Jó na - pot, jó na - pot Ked-ves é - dös - a - nyám!
Mek - hosz - tam én né - köm Ka - ti - ca szép lë-jánt.

Good morning, good morning, dearest, kindest mother!
I have brought here Fair Damsel Katica to be my wife.

Well, his mother was not pleased with the girl, because she was poor. She did not like her, although she did not dare to show signs of her dislike, for fear of her son. Well, time was passing on. The son had to go to the war. It's time for me, thought his mother, to make good of the opportunity. While her son was staying away, she planned to perish the Fair Damsel Katica. And she ordered her servants to grasp Fair Damsel Katica and throw her into the water. The order was fulfilled. They took the girl and threw her into the water. She was drowned. Well, the Prince returned from the war and asked immediately where his wife was. He begged his mother to tell him what had happened to his wife, and why she was not waiting and receiving him. His mother replied like this:

I have sent her, I have sent her into the long cellar,
To fetch you red wine, to fetch you red wine.

He went down into the cellar. He looked for her and called her name, but could not find her. As he was looking for her, a hoop came off a barrel. He heard the cracking noise and thought someone was there, and he exclaimed:

Why do you hide from me, Fair Damsel Katica?
Why do you hide from me, Fair Damsel Katica?

Alas, he did not find Fair Damsel Katica there. Therefore he went to his mother once again, asking her to bring forth his wife. What was then to be done? The mother had to tell him the truth. And she said:

I sent her, I sent her to the river, a long way away,
They ducked her, they ducked her, until they drowned her.
The Prince was very sad to hear the news. He set up and went to the fishermen:
Good morning, good morning, my fishermen friends
Spread, spread your silver nets!
Catch, catch all sorts of fish!
And also catch out the fish that is dearest to my heart!

The fishermen cast their nets, but all in vain, for Fair Damsel Katica was not in the haul. So he went to the next group of fishermen:

Good morning, good morning, my fishermen friends
Spread, spread your golden nets!
Catch me, catch me all sorts of fish!
And also catch out the fish that is dearest to my heart!

The fishermen cast their nets, but alas, they could not haul up Fair Damsel Katica. He went on until he met the third group of fishermen:

Good morning, good morning, my fishermen friends!
Spread, spread your diamond nets!
Catch me, catch me all sorts of fish,
And also catch out the fish that is dearest to my heart!

They cast their nets, and lo, they fished out Fair Damsel Katica. Then he said:

You have caught, you have caught all sorts of fish,
And you have also caught the fish that is dearest to my heart!

With this, his heart broke. Then they were buried in one grave. Then two stalks of lilies grew out of their grave. But the Prince's mother came and broke off the lilies, so angry she was with them.

Báta (Tolna county). Performed by a woman of 41. Rónai 1964 = Ethn 1965, 446.

77.

1. Durica, Durica, Fair Damsel Durica,
   Who bought you that skirt?
   Your son bought it, your son, your lordly son master Antal Nagy!
   Do not mention my son, for you must die for him!

2. Master Antal Nagy went over seven lands,
   And he went to the national fair.
   When he came home from the fair
   He could not find Durica anywhere.

3. Mother, mother, mother, my dear lady mother!
   Where did you hide, where did you hide Fair Damsel Durica?
   I sent her, I sent her down into the flower garden,
   To weed the flower beds.

4. Master Antal Nagy went down to the garden,
   But he could not find Fair Damsel Durica there.
   Mother, mother, mother, my dear lady mother!
   I cannot find Fair Damsel Durica!

5. I sent her, I sent her down to the little flowing well,
   And I went after her, and pushed her in and so I killed her.
   Then master Antal Nagy went down
   And he went to the little flowing well.

6. May my blood flow in one stream with yours,
   May my soul worship one God with yours,
   May my body be buried in one grave with yours,
   May two rosemaries grow out of our grave,
   So that they may show how we loved each other!

Mihálygerge (Nógrád county). Báró A. Nyári = Ethn 1910, 340.

78.

Parlando rubato ♩=kb. 69

1. O - lá - hul Me - ri - ka, Ma - gya - rul Mar - git - ka

Száz ka - to - na kö - zül Me - li - ket sze - re - tem?

1. 2. 3.
Ö - reg Rá   Fe - jér ász - lót e - me - li   Azt meg nem en - ged - he - tem

4.
Hon - nat fo - gom — e te - ker - ni,   Lá - bad - tól, vaj fe - jed - től?

5. 6.
Ugy el - é - get - te, Ott van az ö Me - ri - ká - ja

7. 8.
Az a - rany bü - tyű ké - se - met   Me - ri - ká - mat te - mes - sék

Le - sza - kasz - tot - ta ő - ket, Ke - ze kö - zött meg - hir - vasz - tot - ta.

Mind e két vi - rá - gocs-kát. Mind e két vi - rá-gocs-kát.

1. Merika in Romanian,
   Margitka in Hungarian,
   There are a hundred soldiers here,
   Which one of them do you love?

2. Is it the Moon or the Sun,
   Or is it the bright star?
   I love the Moon,
   And I love the Sun as well.

3. But it is the bright star
   That I love most of all.
   Merika in Romanian,
   Margitka in Hungarian:

4. The light of this sun
   Is the old voivod Ráduj,
   The light of the Moon
   Is the wife of old voivod Ráduj.

5. The sparkling bright star
   Is young Péter Ráduj.
   The sparkling bright star
   Is young Péter Ráduj.

6. Merika in Romanian,
   Margitka in Hungarian,
   I have to go to fight
   Like the others in the wars.

7. I have to fight in the wars,
   To return with happy news,
   To return with happy news,
   To lift high the white flag.

8. Mother, my dear mother,
   Will you look after her well,
   Will you look after her well,
   Look after my Merika!

9. Will you look after her well,
   Look after my Merika!
   Merika in Romanian,
   Margitka in Hungarian:

10. Will you allow me
    To use you where I chop wood,
    To use you where I chop wood
    As my chopping block?

11. That I cannot allow you,[3]
    My dearest heart, mother,
    And I cannot be your chopping block.
    Merika in Romanian,
    Margitka in Hungarian:

12. Will you allow me
    To spit you,
    To spit you,
    And to roast you by the flame of fire?

13. That I cannot allow you,
    My dearest heart, mother.
    Merika in Romanian,
    Margitka in Hungarian:

14. Will you allow me
    To wrap you all over
    In waxed linen,
    In waxed linen?

15. That I may allow you,
    My dearest heart, mother.
    Where shall I begin wrapping?
    Shall it be at your feet or at your head?[4]

16. Begin at my head
    And continue to my feet.
    Merika in Romanian,
    Margitka in Hungarian:

17. Shall I kindle it at your feet?
    Kindle it at my head,
    Kindle it at my head,
    And burn it down to my sole!

18. Mother, my dear mother,
    Is it dawning already?
    It is not dawning yet, it is not dawning yet,
    It is just midnight.

19. Merika in Romanian,
    Margitka in Hungarian.
    Mother, my dear mother,
    Is it dawning already?

20. It is not dawning yet, it is not dawning yet,
    It is just two o'clock.

Then her heart
Broke.

21. She burnt her[5]
    Like a singed stem.
    Then she took her up and carried her out
    Into the flower garden.

22. Merika in Romanian,
    Margitka in Hungarian:
    Open your gates,
    Open your gates!

23. His mother speeded out
    And opened the gates.
    Mother, you need not have come
    To open the gates!

24. Mother, my dear mother,
    Where is my Merika?
    She has gone, and she has gone
    To the rose garden.

25. She has gone to the rose garden
    To pick roses.
    He also went
    To the rose garden.

26. He was looking for her but did not find her,
    So he returned.
    Merika in Romanian,
    Margitka in Hungarian:

27. Open your gates!
    Open your gates!
    His mother speeded out,
    His mother speeded out.

28. Mother, you need not have come
    To open the gates.
    Where is my Merika,
    Where is my Merika?

29. She has gone and she has gone out
    To the corn field,
    To the corn field,
    To reap corn (wheat).

30. He was looking for her, but did not find her,
    She did not answer his calls.
    He returned,
    He returned,

31. Merika in Romanian,
    Margitka in Hungarian:
    Open my gates,
    Open my gates!

32. His mother speeded out.
    Mother, you need not have come,
    Mother, you need not have come,
    To open the gates!

33. She is gone
    And she is in the rose garden.
    White rosebush
    Is bearing red blossoms.

34. Red rosebush
    Is bearing white blossoms.
    He went at once
    To the flower garden.

35. At once he went
    To the flower garden.
    He found her Merika there,[6]
    And she was like a singed stem.

36. Mother, my dear mother,
    Do fetch me
    My knife with the golden handle[7]
    My knife with the golden handle.

37. Mother, my dear mother,
    Let me be buried
    Before the altar,
    Before the altar!

38. Mother, my dear mother,
    Let my Merika be buried[8]
    Beside the altar,
    Beside the altar!

39. And they grew up there,
    As beautiful flowers.
    And they grew up there,
    As beautiful flowers.

40. They knitted together,
    They knitted together.
    But their cursed ill-wisher
    Went to their grave.

41. She plucked them off,[9]
    And she withered them in her hands,

Both these two little flowers,
Both these two little flowers.

Somoska (Moldavia). Performed by a woman of seventy. Veress, 1930 = NÉ 1941, 163 = MF 2458/b.

Cf. Leader 313.

Divergences: The ballad of Merika–Margitka is a fairly uniformly developed type in Moldavia, showing no signs of extemporization and the concomitant expansion and modification of the text (a feature not uncommon anyway in Moldavian ballads). The power and cruelty of the mother-in-law, who was in a position to kill her daughter-in-law unpunished seems to be so strange to present-day singers that they insert various motivations in certain variants. One refers to the pride of the young woman by words known from the formulation of the ballad on the Haughty Wife: "Come, daughter-in-law, come, For I have brought you a silken veil! I don't want it, mother, I don't want it, For I have got one." (Each line repeated.) In the same manner, the mother-in-law offers a silk shirt, and a silk skirt, all in vain. After such preliminaries the daughter-in-law has to make her choice between the various kinds of deaths. Elsewhere social differences are involved, the motif being borrowed from The Two Chapel Flowers: "Pieter Ráduly junior, My son, you shall marry! You shall marry, son, one of the lords' daughters! Mother, my dear mother, instead of marrying one of them, I shall sooner marry my serf's daughter, Marinka in Romanian, Margitka in Hungarian." A solution indicating quite recent origin is when the young man goes to work instead of going to wars: "He left her to his mother; He left her to his mother, And went to work; And when he returned home in the evening..." In such case, justice is also done according to the taste of modern times: "He took his mother by the neck, He took his mother by the neck, And he took her the place where Marinka was laid, And he burnt her mother, too..." In mediaeval texts the son never punishes his mother, rather he kills himself for sorrow. There are several variants of deaths between which the young wife can make her choice: "Shall I shoot you in the head, shall I knock you at the head, Or will you serve as a candlestick throughout the night? I shall serve, I shall serve as a candlestick" "Shall you give light to my table guests?" The young man's return is also motivated in some of the variants: first he asks three soldiers about his sweetheart, "But his *magic steed* begins to speak: "Master, my dear master, don't you beat me, don't you spoil me! Your Marinka is at home, and you will find her in the rose garden, Under the rosebush..." Memory of this motif may return in another text: "Turn back turn back, my steed, So that we may go Right to the rose field..." Before the young man commits suicide in a Moldavian variant, he utters the formula known throughout Europe: "If you have died so terrible a death for my sake, Let me die an even more terrible death for you sake!" A variant of the grave flower motif is also interesting to note here: "They were growing, growing, until they rose above the altar. They knitted together their heads. Whenever their father and mother went into the church, Both of them lowered their heads. When their father and mother left the church, They rose their heads at once. You did not take pity on us while we were alive, Don't pity us now that we are dead. Forget us for ever! May God give such father, Such father and such mother Who do not hate their child, But let him marry the one he loves!" (By the way, the presence of the grave flower motif can be traced up in the Palots variant as well.)

Earliest provenience: 1841–42. *Petrás,* Klézse.

Dissemination: Tolna county (Báta), Nógrád county (Mihálygerge), Moldavia (Bogdánfalva 2, Gajcsána, Klézse 9, Nagypatak, Somoska 2, Trunk, Újfalu). Total: 19.

Textual relationships with other ballads: Choice between the kinds of death: **1.**; grave flower: **9., 10., (37.), 38., 48. (68.)**; the lover commits suicide: **10.**; occasional insertions: **9., 66.**; addressing the fishermen: **29.** sending away the husband: **10., 12.**

Tunes: 1. = No. 76, 2. = No. 78, seven variants; of the examples given below, 4. occurs in four, 5. in two variants.

Variants in languages other than Hungarian:

FRENCH: *1. Davenson* 4. *2. Legrand,* Romania 10, 369. *3–4. Barbeau* 1962, 119 and 123. *5–12. Millien* 1906 195A–F + 2 variants. *13. Smith,* Romania I, 355. *14. Bujeaud* II, 215. *15. Smith,* Romania 10, 584. *16. Smith,* Romania 7, 64 (contaminated). *17. Arbaud* I, 91. *18. Tiersot* 1903, 100–102. *19.* Mélusine 1896, 69. *20.* Rev. Trad, Pop. 1897, 294. *20/a Puymaigre,* 47.

BRETON: *21. Villemarqué* 19.

FLEMISH: *22.* Lootens-Feys 38 = D. Vlr. 76/1. *23.* D. Vlr. 76/2.

DANISH: *24–41.* DgF 342. *42.* DgF 343.

CATALAN: *43. Wolf* 14.

SPANISH: *44–47. Cossio–Solano* 104–107. *48. Cossio* 18. According to *Armisted,* it is known in Castile, Catalonia as well as among the Spanish Jews of Morocco and Yugoslavia.

ITALIAN: *49–53. Nigra* 55A–C + 2 variants. *54. Ferraro* 1870 37.

GREEK: *55. Lübke* 229, D. Vlr. 76, enumerating 136 variants. See further, *Baud-Bovy* 1936, 236–9.

ALBANIAN: *56.* Deutsches Jahrb. f. Vkde 1958, 564 = *Stockmann–Fiedler–Stockmann* 25.

ROMANIAN: *57. Marinescu* 17. *58. Ţiplea* 15. *59. Papahagi* 1925, 389. *60–61. Alexics* 289 and 362. *62. Pompiliu* 50. *63. Teodorescu,* 623. *64. Sevastos,* 248. *65. Şezatoarea* 1893, 7. *66. Tocilescu* I/II 1067. *67. Vasiliu* 33. *68. Amzulescu* 306 (enumerating twenty-two variants, including those mentioned before).

GERMAN: *69.* D. Vlr. 77/1 (Transylvanian Saxon variant).

BULGARIAN: *70. Arnaudov* 1913, 112.

SERBO-CROAT: *71. Kuhač* III, 243, Notes to 1053. *72–76. Žganec* 1950–1952 197b, 198a–c. *77. Žganec* 1950 352. *78. Kačić–Miošić,* 118†. *79. Nikolić,* 86†. *80. Štrekelj* I 51.

SLOVAK–MORAVIAN: *81.* Sl. Sp. III, 592 = *Horák* 1958 13 (enumerating a further four variants). *82. Šreznevski* 7. *83. Kolečány* 13. *84. Medveczky* 1906, 253 = *Medveczky* 1923 14*. *85.* Sl. Pohl. 1897, 497. *86–87.* Slov. Sp. II. 476 and III. 310. *88. Sušil* 92/193. *89–90. Bartoš–Janáček* 1901 39a–b. (*Burlasova* 9abcd)

POLISH: *91. Kolberg* 1857, 11c. *92. Kolberg* 1871–84 101. *93. Kolberg* 1885, I 170.

RUSSIAN: *94. Hilferding* I 299. *95–96.* Rev. Et. Slaves 1932, 215. *97.* Sov. Folkl. 1936, 142–151. *98–103. Astakhova* I 31, II. 190, 195, 197, 204, 219. *104. Chernyshev* 244. *105. Kolberg* 1882–1889 II. 117. *106–107. Golovatsky* I 30–31. *108. Sokolov* 263. *109–110. Balashov,* 54 and 57. *111. Lintur* 1959, 63 (D. Vlr. enumerating seventy-one variants).

LITHUANIAN: see the five variants listed by D. Vlr.

It can be readily recognized that the ballad under discussion is closely related to one of the most beautiful and oldest French ballads, that of Porcheronne. The story of Variant *11.* runs as follows. Monsieur de Beauvoire married young. His bride was so young that she could not even dress by herself. He had been tending her only for three days when he received a letter to say that he must go to the wars. "O, accursed letter, accursed writer! My mother is too cruel, she will send my young wife to guard the animals grazing on the pasture.—Mother, here is my wife, look after her well, see that she does nothing but eat, drink and go to Mass properly." Sieur Beauvoire had hardly gone to the wars before his wife was made to herd swines. She fed the swines for seven years but never laughed or sang. At the end of the seventh year she began to sing. "Stop, my page, stop for Heaven's sake, I hear a voice singing like the voice of my sweetheart!" "Go along this road and you will find her." He goes, and does in fact find the poor girl who does not recognize him, and from a long talk between the two it transpires that she has not slept in a bed for seven years, she has not eaten anything else but oatsbread, she has not washed, and in some of the variants her mother-in-law even offers her to the distinguished stranger for the night. And it is not until she, calling for her absent husband to help her, ready to throw herself from the window, that the knight reveals his identity and upbraids his mother.

The Italian variant (*49.*) closely follows the French: The handsome young man marries and soon he leaves for the wars. "Mother, I entrust my wife to your care", says he, asking her at the same time not to send her wife to work but to let her sit embroidering in her room. No sooner does he leave the home than his mother make the young wife herd swines and forces her to cut wood. She performs her duties for seven years, without laughing or singing; when first she begins to sing, her husband appears, asking whom the herd of pigs belongs to. "To my mother-in-law, and I wish God may call her away!" He invites her to dine with him, but she does not dare to, because she has not cut enough wood. The man goes to his mother, who fails to recognize him; he asks her for her daughter-in-law and she offers him her own daughter. In the end, the man makes his mother servant-maid to his wife.

The story of the Danish variant (DgF 342) may be summed up as follows. The man marries a girl whom his mother hates to death: "Even though I am to live till summer or autumn, I shall see that you have a changed voice." The man goes to the wars and entrusts his wife to his mother's care. The woman grows ill. But in vain does she ask her mother-in-law for water to drink or for a cup of wine. She sends a page home, who finds her mother, who comes and ask about her daughter. "She has died and is buried." The mother-in-law pretends not to know where the young woman's grave is. The girl's mother goes to the graveyard and hears her daughter's voice arising from the earth. She has her warriors dig up the dead body, takes it home and has her girl's mother-in-law burnt. The only variant of *343.* introduces some slight change into the story inasmuch as it states that the girl is not yet married to her would-be spouse, and when her bridegroom is about to join the army, he admonishes her not to go to his mother; the girl forgets about it and goes to visit her mother-in-law, thus giving rise to her tragedy. (Anyway the story is the same, even the beginning formula is identical with the words of the girl's would-be mother-in-law who promises to spoil the girl's voice even at the cost of her life.) This is a casual ramification of the main plot, in which the story receives—curiously enough though in a manner not alien to Danish balladry—a happy ending: the girl dug up from her grave becomes wife to the Prince.

The beginning of the French and Italian ballad is undoubtedly identical with the Transdanubian and Moldavian ballad (and the Palots variant can also be recognized as one mediated from the French or Italians). The difference lies in the intensification of the mother-in-law's cruelty in the Hungarian ballad to the point where she actually kills the wife. In Moldavia, the corresponding scene had been borrowed from the ballad of the Unfaithful Wife (1.)—the motif of burning alive— which once applied, the rest of the story could not further follow the line of the French pattern; this is the reason why some suitable formulas had to be resorted to in order to supply the ballad with a proper ending (in the given instance, with that of The Disgraced Girl type 10.) The East-European versions deriving from the Hungarian have long been collated with the French Porcheronne (D. Vlr. 77.) which is another indication of the fact that two kinds of solutions are recognizably connected with each other.

The East-European versions—except for two Southern Slav variant—apply by and large the same modifications in the text as the Hungarian. Such familiar motifs are to be found in them as are the murder of the young wife, sending the husband on wide-goose chase, and what is even more revealing, several northern and southern Slav variants include the element typical of Hungarian balladry: the young wife is with child who dies with her, and the husband accuses his mother with triple murder before committing suicide. This motif is known from numerous variants of the Disgraced Girl. It seems therefore that the neighbouring nations' texts have combined two different Hungarian ballads.

On the other hand, the Greeks preserved the original French form: the mother-in-law makes the young wife to guard the livestock, and the returning husband finds her alive. The story is, of course, amplified by several details, for instance, she is told to stay with the herd till it reaches a certain size, and when this happens by a marvel, and she drives the herd home, she encounters her husband; another amplification is that the dénouement takes place at a great feast. The Greeks must have acquired the story during the period in the forteenth and fifteenth centuries when Cyprus was ruled by French kings; at that time several French texts and melodies spread among the Greeks, as demonstrated by *Baud-Bovy* (1956). Consequently, the Greek form has to be distinguished from the other eastern European forms.

The Albanians have abridged the Greek ballad to become quite a brief story. The husband goes to the wars. No sooner does he step out of the door than the mother-in-law cuts off the young wife's braid and sends her to mind the flock of sheep. The young man returns and asks his mother about his wife. "She has died"—

answers the mother, and when the man wants to see the grave, she pretends that it had been washed away by flood. At this moment the young wife appears in the door and relates her story.

In the Slovak and Moravian-speaking areas the heroine is a maid-servant instead of a wife, whom the young prince leaves pregnant when he goes to the wars, and afterwards his mother, the princess, has her killed. Apart from this motif, there are also other traits to connect the ballad to the Hungarian version; for instance, the prince receives warning from his horse about the trouble at home (81.)—which occurs here and there also with the Russians (104.); the returning young man learns that his wife had died when the gate is opened; the sending of the husband on fool's errands follows, and finally the closing formula of the ballad of the Disgraced Girl also appears with the usual desire: "May my body rest together with yours!"

The Hungarian ballad spread, via the Ukrainians, toward the north-east, reached the eastern Poles, Russians and Lithuanians, and proceeded as far as Archangel, everywhere in the Hungarian form, with the wife tortured to death, and other amplifications or omissions. One of the omissions is that the husband does not go to the wars but simply "rides off" (something similar is found in the Palots fragment); among the amplifications we find the justification of the mother-in-law's cruelty by reference to the fact that her son married the girl without her previous consent; in certain variants this plot is mixed up with the stories of other ballads (cf. D. Vlr. 4, 156–8). The Lithuanian version has developed from the Russian.

The Romanian is also connected with the Hungarian version. The complete German edition (D. Vlr.) quotes only No. 59. with reference to the French form, because in it the husband finds the imprisoned and starving wife still alive in the end. A survey of the variants, however, convinces us that it is not the French plot that is here involved, for there the husband returning from the war first meets his wife, unrecognized, in the fields, and goes back with her to his mother, who also fails to recognize him, and therefore does not deny her to him. As against this, the Romanian text has, just as the Hungarian, that the returning husband goes first to his mother, because his wife is nowhere to be found; after several evasive answers, the mother sends the young man hither and thither, but he eventually finds her. Variations on the basic theme are the following: the mother says the young wife is dead and refuses to give information about the place where she had been buried, and eventually he finds her dead (57.); the mother says the young wife is dead (without being asked about the grave) and sends her son to various places where the woman had allegedly died, they both die and grave-flowers grow out of their dead bodies (64.); there is no mention of either death or grave, but the man seeks and finds her at once in the prison, and the ballad is ended with the terse statement that they both died (58.); she says her daughter-in-law is dead, but she is not willing to show him the grave and there is no meeting at the end (60–61.); she says her daughter-in-law is dead, refusing to show her grave, yet the husband finds her alive (59., 62., and 63.); finally, there is no mention of death, the husband goes straight to the prison to find his wife alive (66. and 67.). This vacillation in the death motif and the concomitant variability of the dénouement is a much safer sign of a Hungarian origin than it would be if all the Romanian variants followed the Hungarian plot

380

terminating with death. (After all, such a solution may occur to anyone in any nation.) But such a circular motion round a motif-nucleus, with minor or major divergences, can show only one thing: a start from, and increasing variations of the motifs have to be assumed, in which the various developments were able—or unable—to free themselves from the model. The trend of variations is shown also by the fact that the overwhelming majority of the Romanian variants have come up from areas that used to belong to Hungary. (Eighteen of the 22 variants published by *Amzulescu* originate from there, and the nineteenth from the Tatros valley situated between lands inhabited by Csángós and Székelys.)

Among the southern Slavs, it is also the Hungarian form that appears, with differing embellishments and omissions. Sometimes the mother-in-law does away with the young wife with poison made from a snake's head, a motif borrowed from the "Schwester Giftmischerin" type of ballads (cf. D. Vlr. IV, 156). *72.* is so much eroded that even the farewell scene is omitted, in which the husband leaves his wife to the care of his mother. The heroine's name: *Kata, Katica* betrays anyway the fact of borrowing, these forms of petnames for Catherine being used only in Hungarian. Since my first study was published, the Hungarian-Transdanubian variant has been successfully hunted up, and indeed, the heroine in it is also called *Fair Damsel Katica.*

There are, however, three Croat variants which preserve the French, more precisely the Greek form: the young wife is sent to look after the flock, and that is how she meets her husband again. Of two of them (*78–79.*) D. Vlr. states that they preserve a relationship with the Cypriot or the general Greek form through the miraculous growth of the flock and the closing feast scene. To these we may add *71.* Considering all, we have to think of the Greek tradition infiltrating the Croat area via emigrant Greeks, or else we have to suppose a literary transmission, since the text of *78.* is a counterfeat of the "collector", as I have been advised through the courtesy of *Stojan Vujičić.*

The eastern European variants—except the Greek and Albanian ones— originate from the Hungarian, which fact is indicated by several signs. But apart from this consideration, the mutually independent western and eastern groups can be linked only through the mediating role of French settlers in Hungary in this instance as well as in so many other. It is only the Italian version that raises some difficulty in this respect. To wit, the Italians have got the French form, too, while the Hungarian material is so eroded that the extant fragmentary texts with their scanty French elements cannot be distinctly separated from the Italian formulation. Furthermore, since the ballad occurs outside the Piedmontese Region, too, it is not fully precluded that the Hungarians had acquired the ballad through Italian transmission. (Italians also settled in Hungary in mediaeval times.)

For this time, therefore, we would be faced with the question of an isolated case of a Hungarian ballad having been borrowed from the Italians. Nevertheless, there is not a single sign indicating an Italian origin of the ballad type as a whole. On the contrary, we have a strong argument against such a supposition: there is no trace of the Italian formulation to be found among the southern Slavs; they had borrowed the theme from the Hungarians (sporadically from the Greeks). Therefore it can be assumed with a higher degree of certainty that this ballad had passed, together with numerous other ballads, from the French to the Hungarians, only in this instance we are not able to demonstrate the French priority against the Italian in so clearcut a form as in the other cases.

Literature: Zhdanov 1889; surveys the Russian variants; *Baud-Bovy* 1936, 236–239; the Greek variant probably originates from the Italian—French and Iberian parallels; *Seemann* 1951: lists the northern Slav and Lithuanian variants; *Csanádi* and *Vargyas* 1954: discuss the Hungarian without entering into comparative analysis; *Horálek* and *Horálkova* 1958: treats the subject together with the themes of the returning soldier; *Vargyas* 1960: French origin; *Stein* 1960: Transylvanian Saxon originates from the Romanian; *Rónai* 1965a, b: publishes a Transdanubian variant; *Mitruly* 1965: the Romanian originates from the French, the Hungarian from the Romanian; *Vargyas* 1965b: refutes Mitruly; *Vargyas* 1967: French origin. *Stein, H.* 1979: rejects my results without yielding acceptable ones instead.

29. THE GIRL ABDUCTED BY THE TURKS

79.

The water of the Tisza and the Duna is flowing downwards,
On it floats, on it floats a beautiful golden galley,
In the galley, in the galley is a hideous Turkish voivod.
That way, that way walks the fair maid of Komárom,
5. With two pitchers on her arms, she walks down to the Danube.
Give me some water, give me some water, fair maid of Komárom!
How can I give you water, you hideous Turkish voivod?
You are in the middle of the Danube, and I am at the bank of the Danube!
She extends her pitcher: he takes her by her white arm
10. And drags her onto the galley, on board of the galley.
Come and embrace me, fair girl of Komárom!
May the Fiend from Hell embrace you!
Come and kiss me, fair maid of Komárom!
May a wild lion from the desert kiss you!
15. Come and lie beside me, fair maid of Komárom!
May the Hungarians' weapon lie beside you!
He hit her in the face with his iron gauntlet so that crimson blood flowed from her
nose and mouth.

The bed of the Danube is the bottom of my coffin,
The two banks of the Danube are the two sides of my coffin,
The waves of the Danube are my winding-sheet,
20. The fish of the Danube are my coffin-nails,
The tiny fish of the Danube are my mourners,
The birds of the sky are my choir.
Fishermen, fishermen, fishermen of the Danube:
By Thursday noon you shall fish me out,
25. You shall fish me out and you shall bury me as well!
My clothes, my clothes, my finest clothes,
You shall fall off the peg, you shall shoulder each other,
So may my mother learn that you are lamenting for me!
She plunged into the middle of the Danube,
30. Fishermen caught her corpse by Thursday noon.
Her finest clothes fell off the peg,
They fell off the peg, and they shouldered each other.
So her mother learned that her daughter had died.
Magyarszentmihály (Torontál county). Kálmány = Ethn. 1914, 36.

Cf. Leader 266.
Known from one single extant variant.

Textual relationships with other ballads: A similar beginning formula is to be found in Type **30.** The words addressed to the clothes are a commonplace occurring also in Type **12.** (The Bride Found Dead), further in the variants of Types **11., 13., 15.** and **31.;** and the words addressed to the fishermen can be met with in the Transdanubian variants of Type **28.** (This correspondence between the mentioned Types must be of rather old origin, because both groups of variants maintained relics of long extinct ballads isolated from each other, and in their extant forms no interaction can be imagined between them.) The self-lament of the girl recurs in Types **52.** and **118.**

Tune: Quite exceptionally, *Kálmány* had sent the melody of this ballad to the editorial office of *Ethnographia* where it wast lost somehow.

Versions in languages other than Hungarian:

FRENCH: *1.Smith* Romania 7, 68 (contaminated). *2. Decombe* 104.

Partial variant: 3. Doncieux 42 (enumerating 28 variants). *4. Champfleury–Weckerlin* 214 (contaminated). *5–12. Rossat* 8a-h. *13. Fleury* 247. *14. Puymaigre* 1865, 106. *15. Bladé* 36. *16–17. Millien* 143–145 (mutilated). *18–23. Canteloube* I, 157, II, 381, III, 197, IV, 62, 115, 326 (without mentioning the suicide), 306 (contaminated with French 100). *24. Weckerlin* 1887 41 = *Beaurepaire* 151–152. *25. Beauquier* 124. *26. Gagnon* 38, *27–29. Rolland* II, 4p-s. *30. Legrand* XII, *31–34. Smith* VII, 68–70. *35. Benoist* III, *36. Decombe* I (contaminated). *37. Simon* 186. *38. Barbeau* 1937 51. *39–40. Idem* 1962 391 and 384.

ITALIAN: *41–45. Nigra* 14.

BRETON: *46–47. Rolland* III 186ab. *48–49. Canteloube* IV, 391 and 384.

ROMANIAN: *50. Alexics,* 279. *51–53. Papahagi* 1925 362, 367 and 408. *54–56. Bibicescu* 261, 267, 271. *57. Teodorescu,* 635. *58–59. Vulcanu,* 8 = *Marinescu,* 45 and 28. *60–61. Tocilescu* I/1, 35, I/2, 1248. *62. Sevastos,* 311. *63. Vasiliu* 26. *64.* Balade 88. *65a. Brăiloiu* 98. *65b. Moldován,* 48. *66. Amzulescu* 70 (partial variant). *Amzulescu* lists 54 variants under No. 54, and publishes No. 57.

Partial variants:

BULGARIAN: *67.* A–V 143. *68–70. Arnaudov* 1913 84–86. *71.* SbNU 11, 36, No. 6. *72. Stoin* 1928 2740. *73–74. Idem* 1934 174 and 340.

SERBO-CROAT: *75–76. Vuk* I 721–722. *77.* HNP 7 No. 358.* *78. Rajković* 221.*

SLOVAK: *79–81.* Sl. Sp. I 418 (= *Horák* 1958 29), II 797, III 513. *82.* SL' P' II 602. *83. Kolečány* 7. *84. Medveczky* 1906, 253. *85–86. Kollár* II 6–7. *87. Nemcova* 13, 59.* *88. Václavík,* 304.* *89. Medveczky* 1923. 4.* *90. Bartók* 1959, 186a.

MORAVIAN: *91–95. Sušil* 147/310–313 + variants. *96–98. Bartoš* 1901 17, 19, 20, *99.* Idem 1889 41.*

DANISH: *100–114.* DgF 241.

GREEK: cf. *Baud-Bovy* 1936, 258–262 ("La fille voyageuse") and *Bojatzides.**

In western European material the theme is not to be met with, apart from a Breton song relating a tale in the Breton epic style, that is in a marvel-fantasy form of much detail. The story runs as follows: the Anglo-Saxons raid the harbour of Dourduff and carry off a girl. They take her aboard their ship, while she sobs and sobs. To calm her, the captain says that her life is not endangered, only her honour, whereupon the girl prays to the Holy Virgin, for she would die a hundred times than sin once, and throws herself into the sea. One variant says that she is swallowed by a white fish, and taken to the shore, to her parents; in another variant two fish with a white cross on their backs, carry her ashore on their backs, but there are also texts in which she simply drowns in the sea, and the whole village laments her as she is buried.

In general, the texts of ballad character in the Breton tradition are of French origin. It seems to be granted that this song, too, originates from a shorter and more ballad-like French text, which is no longer extant. To wit, the French have eight different variants of the ballad type dealing with the fate of the girl abducted by soldiers. (Cf. French 10., 11., 25., 42., 50., 53. and 129.) In seven of these variants the

384

girl makes desperate efforts to escape disgrace, mostly by death, in one case by sham-death, and in another case by a magical change into a bird. In No. 2. it is not the soldiers but the lord of the manor that abducts her on horseback: fleeing from him, she throws herself into the *river*, but first she similarly prays to the Holy Virgin. But among the eight types there is one even closer to the Breton: the sailors' song beguiles the girl into going aboard the ship, and she is taken out to sea; when she is asked to undress, she takes the knife of one of the sailors with the pretext that she wants to cut her apron string, and stabs herself with it. It is this very wide-spread song (*3–45.*) that may represent a recent and transformed shape of a no longer existing French ballad, the story of which survives only among the Bretons nowadays. One of the variants has preserved, indeed, details of the original, though in a corrupted and contaminated form (*1.*): instead of the suicide with the knife, the young man throws the wailing girl into the *sea,* to the accompaniment of the following words: "Chantez, chantez, grenouilles, vous avez de quoi chanter, Vous avez de l'eau à boire et ma mie à manger". Here we have part of the ballad worn down till it is meaningless, referring to *frogs* in the *sea*! This is obviously a secondary development, which has none the less preserved the memory of the river water, together with the fragment of the girl's words—put into the man's mouth. Further evidence is offered by the Greek and the Danish versions. The Greeks know the story of the girl beguiled into going aboard the ship, and they mainly relate it with the suicide committed with the knife in the end; but parallel with this, they also have the scene of the Breton ballad: the girl throws herself into the water, her body is cast ashore by the waves and buried amidst much wailing. The Danish ballad runs almost like this, only the ending is different: A woman goes to the sea shore and sees a ship nearing. She sells her wine to the sailor, who makes her drunk, so he rapes her, and then sails off in stealth. The woman wakes up and cries for her sons and daughters whom she had closed up in her home. The sailor assures her that she may not return home before she has a son big enough to row and a daughter big enough to sew. Upon this, the woman lowers her hair and jumps into the sea. She is swimming night and day until she reaches the shore and her father's house. Since the Greeks and the Danes borrowed their ballads from the French in a direct way, we have every reason to suppose that the lost French song must have been similar to the Breton story.

On the basis of all this, the outlines of a French ballad can be discerned, in which the girl carried away and taken onto the ship is threatened by rape, and, after praying to the Holy Virgin, and appealing to the fish and frogs, jumps into the river. That the Bretons should have taken the swallowing by fish literally and transformed it into a miraculous escape is quite in keeping with the nature of their poetry of marvels and fantasy. Notwithstanding this, they have kept the plot of the original ballad; the two French variants have preserved a fragment of its wording each, and the Hungarian ballad has preserved it all.

The Hungarian re-modelled version spread out in every direction to the neighbouring countries, although for the most part the most striking motif had been retained by the borrowers: the girl's appeal to the fish and her jumping into the water.

The Romanian variants are nearest to the Hungarian. The main motif of the latter can be discerned in the former. Sandru's daughter Ilincuta goes to fetch water. She is to marry the son of the Turkish sultan. When now she reaches the well—sometimes the Danube or the sea—she sees the Turks. In some variants she beholds them from the window of her home, or as she sweeps the yard. She runs into the house and asks her mother to hide her. The mother says her daughter is dead, and even shows her grave to the Turks. But a cunning old Turk discovers her hiding place. She is carried away. (So far the plot is reminding us of the story of the girl married against her will.) When they reach the water's edge, she asks them to let her drink, or wash her face, which granted she throws herself into the water with the words: I would be food for fish and crayfish (or frogs) rather than the Turk's wife!" (There are variants in which these words recur in a form deprived of any meaning: "I would rather be a reaper than belong to you—I would scythe more than has ever been seen before...I would be a servant and go to serve gentlemen...", and the like. (53.)) There is even one (65.), which continues in a strain that resembles the Breton song: "There happened to be a pike there which swallowed the girl. So what did the Turk do? He sent for fishermen. They bought a net and caught many fish. Sure enough, they caught the pike, cut it open and took Ilonka out. She was dead, yet she was taken to the Pasha. And she was so beautiful that they always kept her on their hands while carrying her". In folk poetry similar to the Breton in spirit the ballad thus goes through a similar change! Links to the Hungarian are the formula of appeal to the fish, the Turk as kidnapper, and the meeting at the water-drawing; elements that separate it are the episode of the attempt to hide her and the demands for the girl, and finally the fact that the girl escapes not from a ship but from a coach. (The latter being elements of the ballad of The Bride Dying during the Wedding Procession.) At the same time, it differs from the Breton in precisely these points.

In the countries to the north of Hungary—with the Slovaks and the Ukrainians, who are neighbours to the Romanian as well—the words of the girl jumping into the water has been similarly incorporated into the story of "The Bride Dying during the Wedding Procession". With them it is not for sorrow that the bride dies, but when reaching the Danube she asks for something to eat and jumps into the water, saying: "Swallow me, tiny fish, so that I may not be a friend to the Turks", much in the same way as in the Romanian variant. According to the variant collected by *Kollár* (85.) "It is more pleasant to be in the Danube than to live in the Turkish *harem*. Christian death is more beautiful than pagan life." Ballads never speak about *harems*, and in them the Turks always have wives. Apparently, deliberate literary intervention is responsible for the introduction of these concepts alien to the world of ballads. (Cf. *Horálek* 1959.)

Still more remote and obscure are the textual relationships between the Hungarian and the southern neighbours' ballads. For among them the leap into the water is inserted into a number of different plots. One of the Bulgarian tales speaking of White Jána (Queen Isabella of Hungary) incorporated the motif in a way that after the capture of Buda she is carried off as a slave by the Turks. On reaching the Danube, she asks them to untie her hands so that she may wash her face. There is no mention of fish or crayfish: she only appeals to the Danube to take her rather than let the Turks have her. (*67.* and *71.*) In *69.* and *70.* she meets her lover at the spring, but finally the Turk still carries her off to be his wife; on the way she throws herself into the Danube, and the Turk shouts after her that the fish and crayfish will eat her, to which she replies she would rather they than the Turk ate her. In the same story she sometimes kills herself with a dagger. (*68.*) In *Vuk*'s Serbian text the girl flees from her elder brother and an incestuous marriage into the watery grave; here the characteristic appeal is addressed to the fish of the sea. Neither here not in the Croatian texts, and the Serbian texts from the Bácska does she escape from the ship. (*77–78.*) But in the latter, fleeing from the Turk, she wishes to become food for the fish.

The nations neighbouring the Hungarian to the north, east and south all put into the girl's mouth the formula: "I had rather belong to the fish than to the Turk!" This sentence must have been included in the text of the Hungarian ballad as well. Otherwise it could not have passed from one people to another by jumping over Hungarian territories (even if it were not of Hungarian origin). Anyway, the formula comes up in one of the variants of Type **31.**: "Instead of becoming soldiers' prisoner, I shall rather become supper for frogs, supper for frogs, dinner for fish." The only extant Hungarian variant, notwithstanding all its poetic beauty, seems to be fairly eroded, and we cannot be certain that it has preserved every detail of the general concept. In any case, it did preserve the main traits of the western ballad, which cannot be stated with reference to the neighbouring peoples' balladry. In spite of this, the latter are unmistakably connected with the Hungarian, and show at the same time divergences between themselves as regards the frame of the plot and certain details. From all this it can be concluded that the Hungarian ballad is an adaptation of a French (possibly Breton) ballad, whose details had proceeded from Hungary as a focal point towards the neighbouring peoples. Since it is rare with both the French and the Hungarians, it may well belong to the earliest group of borrowings, probably originating from the early fourteenth century.

Literature: Kálmány 1914, 37: compares with Romanian *65.* (in company of other, erroneous agreements); *Csanádi* and *Vargyas* 1954: accepts Romanian parallelism stated by *Kálmány; Manga* 1956: Slovak and Hungarian variants came into existence owing to similar historical conditions; *Vargyas* 1960: French origin; *Mitruly* 1962: demonstrating Romanian influence in texts which are, in my opinion, irrelevant to the point; *Putilov* 1965: since it is widerspread in Slav territories, the French–Hungarian origin is not likely; *Vargyas* 1967 = 1960; *Sirovátka* 1966–67 and 1968 II: in Czech and Moravian territories its spread is mainly restricted to Moravia, showing the highest degree of frequency in the neighbourhood of the Hungarian frontiers; the Turkish character is a secondary development.

30. THE GIRL ESCAPED FROM THE TURKS

80.

The water of the bonny Danube is softly flowing, flowing,
Fair Pink Örzsébet washes in it.
She is washing her two white beautiful arms,
Her two white beautiful legs, her fair crimson cheeks.
5. At once the chief Turkish pasha caught her.
They are going, they are going towards Turkey,
As they are going, the chief Turkish pasha asks:
Fair Pink Örzsébet, do you love me?
Did not love you, you could not have taken me!
10. They are going, they are going towards Turkey,
The chief Turkish pasha asks her once more:
Fair Pink Örzsébet, do you love me?
Did I not love you, you could not have taken me;
They are going, they are going towards Turkey,
15. The chief Turkish pasha asks her once more:
Fair Pink Örzsébet, do you love me?
Did I not love you, you could not have taken me!
There is a great feast with the chief Turks,
We are going to drink dream-wine as well, Fair Pink Örzsébet.
20. But you must not drink of it, if you love me,
For if you drink of it, you will go to sleep for good!
The others drank of it, but she did not.
She returned, she returned and went home.
25. She went home, and she went to her mother's home.
Open, mother, open your railed gates,
Open, mother, open your painted door,
For those fiends will soon reach me here.

As soon as the mother let her daughter in, the Turks arrived.

Go away, you fiend, go away, and do not tempt me!
30. For I have no daughter: I am fishing for her in the Danube!
Nine weeks have passed since I began to search her!
I have sent twelve divers to search for her in the Danube.

She hid her daughter, the Turks could not find her and finally went away.

Pádé (Torontál county) = *Kálmány 1891,* 4.

Neither *text variants* nor *tune* are known.

The beginning scene, in which the girl is caught by the Turks, agrees with that of the previous ballad. The scene of seduction and the subsequent motifs of escape and persecution, as well as that of the Turks returning without having achieved their goal, show a fair agreement with the parallel scenes and motifs of **5.** But the motif of the girl assuring the Turk of her love, and of the subsequent escape relates the ballad, to a certain extent, with the ballad of The Enticed Wife **(3.).** (The words about the "dream-wine" may refer, perhaps, to indulging in a hashish-like drug.) "Go away, fiend . . ." said by the mother to the Turk, is adressed to the daughter in **5.** These ballads from the Szeged region have been preserved in the tradition of Hungarians that lived isolated in the period of Turkish occupation and point back to mediaeval times as their origin. There is a strong interconnection between them, and in spite of their fragmentary appearance, they have maintained a common traditional pattern—sometimes the fragmentary portions are completed with elements borrowed from folk tales (cf. the motif of persecution in the present ballad and that of the saliva speaking in human voice in **5.**).

We are dealing here with an eroded variant of a mediaeval ballad that must have originated in times before the Turkish occupation.

31. THE GIRL KIDNAPPED BY SOLDIERS

81.

1. Fudd el jó szél, fudd el   Bú-mats bá - na - ti - mat!

Fudd el   jó szél, fudd el   Bú-mat s bá-na - ti-mat!

1. Blow away, good wind, blow away
   My grief and my sorrows!
   Blow away, good wind, blow away
   My grief and my sorrows!

2. Mother, my dear mother,
   Hide me!
   Turks are coming
   To take me away.

3. The flag has been set up
   On my gatepost,
   The drum has been beaten
   To grieve my heart.

4. Child, my dear daughter,
   Where could I hide you,
   Where could I hide you
   So that I may save you?

5. Go into the pantry,
   Hide there in the big chest!
   At that moment they dashed in,
   And they dashed into the house.

6. They streamed into the house,
   Seventy-seven soldiers,
   Seventy-seven soldiers,
   The whole company.

7. My old dear mother,
   Where is your daughter?
   I don't know, I don't know,
   Where she has gone.

390

8. My old dear mother,
   Surrender your daughter,
   Surrender your daughter,
   For we shall take you away!

9. We shall take you away
   And we shall cut your head off,
   And then we shall cut off
   Her head as well.

10. Go into the pantry,
    There you will find her in a chest.
    Go into the pantry,
    There you will find her in a chest.

11. They take out from the chest,
    The poor soul, her daughter.
    She began to bewail,
    Lamenting with loud words of bewail:

12. My clothes, my clothes,
    My beautiful, finely woven clothes!
    When I am being beheaded,
    Fall down upon the ground!

13. Fall down upon the ground
    And mourn for me!
    Fall down upon the ground
    And mourn for me!

14. Mother, my dear mother,
    Stay in peace,
    Extend your right hand
    So that I may kiss it once more!

15. So that I may kiss it once more,
    Once and last this time it will be,
    Once and last this time it will be,
    And this is our last farewell.

16. At once and at the place where she was standing
    She fell down upon the ground,
    She fell down upon the ground,
    Down fell her dear mother.

17. She said lamenting,
    She said with loud words of bewail:
    My God, my God,
    My beloved God!

18. Why did you create me
    To be a mother on the earth,

Why did you not create me
To be a tree in the forest!

19. Once more she asked her mother,
Her dear mother:
Mother, my dear mother,
I ask you a favour:

20. After they had taken my head,
Put it into a copper plate,
Put in into a copper plate,
My poor head!

21. Send it to Kolozsvár,
Let it be fixed on the gate of the castle,
So that everybody may see
How a kidnapped girl fares.

22. Well, my dear mother,
Stay in peace,
This is the last time
We say farewell to each other.

23. And they made her poor daughter,
Her grievous daughter start on the way.
Loudly crying,
The poor mother stayed back.

24. From above downwards,
A brook is flowing.
With lamenting words, he is looking for me,
Lamenting, my dear sweetheart.

25. You are looking for me in vain, my sweetheart,
For I have been hidden,
Under the dry leaves of oak
I have been buried.

Lészped (Moldavia). Thirty-year-old female performer. Kallós 1956 = MSZ 6277.

82.

1. Ab - lak - ba ül va - la Sze - gény Ká - dár Ka - ta,

Var - ja va - la in - git Fe - ke - te se - lem - mel.

1. Sitting in her window,
Poor Kata Kádár

392

Is sewing her shirt
With black silk.

2. She is stiching with her needle
   Threaded with pure gay silken thread,
   She is knitting the holes,
   Filling them with her pouring tears.

3. She looked down the slope,
   Onto the corn-field:
   Aye, there are coming
   Seventy-seven soldiers.

4. Seventy-seven soldiers,
   The whole company.
   They all streamed to the door
   And called in.

5. Mother, my dear mother,
   Hide me!
   Soldiers are coming
   To take me away.

6. Child, my dear child,
   Where could I hide you?
   Go into the pantry
   And hide in the chest!

7. But they streamed into the house,
   Seventy-seven soldier,
   Seventy-seven soldiers,
   The whole company.

8. Where is your daughter?
   Give her in my hand!
   Then her dear mother
   Began to lament her:

9. Go into the pantry,
   She is hiding in a chest.
   Go into the pantry,
   She is hiding in a chest.

10. Wait a moment,
    'Seventy-seven soldiers,
    Let me speak a word or three
    And take leave of her!

11. For every dead body
    The bells are tolled three times.
    The first two chimes are broken,
    But the third is tolled to the end.

393

12. But for my daughter
    Not a single bell is tolled.
    She is not yet dead,
    Yet I must lament her.

13. The flag has been set up
    On my gatepole,
    The drum has been beaten
    To grieve my heart.

14. I am going to serve the emperor,
    But I am not proud of it.
    It is only my bereaved heart
    That makes me say this.

15. Soldiers' horses!
    Do not carry me,
    Do not carry me
    As a bride!

16. Do not carry me
    As a bride is carried,
    But carry me
    As a dead body is carried!

*Lészped (Moldavia). Sixty-seven-year-old female performer. Kallós 1959 = Kallós
1970 No. 95.*

Divergences: Sometimes the mother pretends her daughter is dead:

My daughter is not here,
She has died, and I have buried her,
She has died and I have buried her
Under the double window,
She is buried deep, she is buried deep.

There are two variants in which elements of The Girl Abducted by the Turks are
incorporated: the girl, reaching the edge of the river Tisza, jumps into the water,
saying:

Instead of becoming
Soldiers' prisoner,
Instead of becoming
Soldiers' prisoner,
I shall become
Frogs' supper,
I shall become
Frogs' supper,
I shall become
Frogs' supper,
Frogs' supper,

394

And fish's dinner,
Frogs' supper,
And fish's dinner.

Another variant changes, by means of the formula "Tisza did not take him in" into the ballad of The Speaking Corpse only to continue, after some two stanzas with motif known from The Test of Faithfulness. In some variants the girl curses her mother for having betrayed her, while in two texts the mother hides her son before he is taken to the soldiers, or to prison. In some cases the girl bids farewell to her mother with the following words:

Mother, my dear mother, stay with peace!
May God reward you for all your kindness!
You have brought me up to this day and saved me from all troubles,
From danger of fire, water and all troubles.

And then she curses the soldiers.

Earliest provenience: 1954.
Dissemination: Moldavia (Gerlén 3, Lészped 8, Pusztina, Rácsila 2). Total: 14.
Textual relationships with other ballads: "Place my head (Take out My Heart)": **6., 20., 25.**; "My flowers, my flowers...": **10., 11., 12., 13., 15., 29., 31.**; "She is sitting in her window...": **12., 14., 21., 31., 43., 49.** (Occasional mergers in certain variants are left out of consideration.)
Tunes: 1. = 81 (four variants), 2. = No. 82. No. 7. occurs in two variants.

No direct correspondence of this ballad can be found in European balladry. The French have six different stories to relate the fate of the girl abducted by soldiers, and such stories are to be found in the Iberian Peninsula as well (for the former see the list of French variants in the chapter on The Girl Abducted by the Turks, Type **29.**; while for the Iberian ballad, see *Armistead* and *Silverman* 1971, 266). But the Hungarian text cannot be brought into any correlation with these. At the same time, a certain degree of similarity can be discovered in the Romanian counterpart of The Girl Abducted by the Turks, in which the Turks are looking for Ilinkuţa in the house, and the mother tries to make them believe that her daughter is dead; further, the scene of suicide and the speech addressed to the fish, occurring in two Hungarian variants, can also be met with in the Romanian version. The Csángó ballads often show a vaguely defined formulation, relating only the mere narrative of the story, mainly in such instances when (1) they are not bound to a strictly formulated Hungarian ballad-pattern; (2) a no longer extant ballad-story is involved, of which only some blurred vistas of certain motifs linger now in the memory; (3) fresh adaptations are remodelled and the texts have not yet been adequately assimilated to local folklore tradition. Considering all this, the ballad under discussion may well be a recent adaptation of the Romanian ballad of Ilinkuţa—that is to say, it may be a re-adaptation of a ballad of Hungarian origin— but it may equally be a Hungarian ballad that has reached the verge of final extinction, the fragmentary portions of which are rounded off by attempts at inclusion of various alien texts. Finally, it may be regarded to be a fragmentary relic of the Hungarian ballad of The Girl Abducted by the Turks. If the latter case be true, then the address to frogs and fish does not indicate a borrowing from the Romanians but a survival of an old Hungarian ballad. The question will perhaps be settled at a later date when further, so far latent, variants are discovered.

32. THE MOUNTAIN SHEPHERD MURDERED BY ROBBERS

83.

Parlando rubato

1.Szép fe-hér pe - ku-lár e - zer bá-rány - ká - ja,

E - zer bá-rány-ká - ja, nincs-te-len sok ju - ha,

Ud më-nen, ud 3 më - nen há - rom disz -no fur - kár:

Jó na - pot, jó na - pot szép fe-hér pe - ku-lár.

1. The handsome, white-skinned shepherd has a thousand lambs,
   A thousand lambs and numberless sheep.
   There arrive, there arrive three swineherds:
   Good morning, good morning, handsome, white-skinned shepherd!

2. Welcome to you, three swineherds,
   And I know, I know that you take my head.
   When you have taken my head, bury me,
   Bury me by the gate of my sheep-pen.

3. Put my longer pipe beside my head,
   When wind comes and blows it, blows is softly,
   People listening to it will say:
   The handsome, white-skinned shepherd is lamenting himself.

4. Put my shorter pipe beside my feet.
   When wind comes and blows it, blows it softly,
   People listening to it will say:
   The handsome, white-skinned shepherd is lamenting himself.

5. When you first reach a small, smoky house,
   You will find my old mother in it.
   She is washing a large woolen cloth, mourning for me,
   I know it well, I know it well, she will ask you about me.

6. When you first reach a flower garden,
   You will find my two maiden sisters in it.

They are setting flowers, mourning for me,
I know it well, I know it well, they will ask you about me.

7. They will ask you if I had married.
   Tell them that I had married
   The offspring of Earth, the sister of Sun,
   The offspring of Earth, the sister of Sun.

Somoska (Moldavia). Seventy-year-old female performer. S. Veress 1930 = M.H. 2458/a and M.H. 2457.

Divergences: Instead of three swineherds sometimes we have "fiery thieves", sometimes "renowned thieves" and rarely "three wicked Tartars".

Earliest provenience: 1843 (recorded by *Ince Petrás*).

Dissemination: "Transylvania", Háromszék county (Polyán), Moldavia (Klézse 5, Külsőrekecsin, Somoska 2, Trunk 3); 2 Transylvanian variants, 12 Moldavian. Total: 14.

Textual relationships with other ballads: certain phrases can be demonstrated from other ballads: "fiery thieves": **20.** "For the dead three chimes are tolled...", which may come up in any ballad.

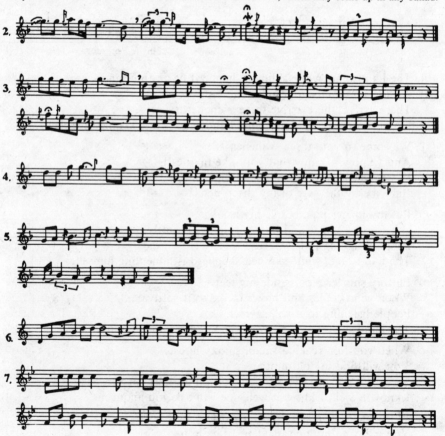

8.

Tunes: 1. the published plus one variant, 2–8.: all from Moldavia.
Cf. Leader 341.
Versions in languages other than Hungarian:
ROMANIAN: *Amzulescu* 196 (listing published variants), Fochi (publishes texts of 825 variants and a tune), *Armistead* kindly drew my attention to a Spanish manuscript ballad: "La Muerte del pastor", the text of which shows a surprising agreement with this ballad (preserved in the Menéndez Pidal Archive).

This story is an adaptation of the most wide-spread Romanian ballad; Miorița ("Little Lamb"). Three or sometimes nine shepherds are descending from the mountain, driving their sheep down to the valley. They plan to kill one of their fellows whom they envy because of his rich stock of sheep, and also because of his handsome face. (Variants: the murder is committed by servants.) A miraculous lamb warns the shepherd of the impending danger. The shepherd imparts to it his last wish; he should be buried in the corner of the sheepfold, his flute should be put by his head or into his hand (sometimes a trumpet or a mountain horn is mentioned), so that their sound raised by the wind may remind the sheep of their master. In certain Moldavian and Muntanian variants the ballad continues in the strain of another song (23.), in which the shepherd asks people not to tell his mother and his sweetheart that he is dead but tell them, that he had stayed at a place from which there is no returning, that is he had united, figuratively, with nature. In the Transylvanian variants, which are rather in the nature of shepherds' colindas (Romanian Christmas carol), the plan of the murder is usually prepared by cousins of the shepherd who send the "strange man" to fetch water, or to turn back the flock of sheep. The divination of the miraculous sheep is often missing from the Transylvanian variants. The variant published by Alexandri contains the following lines: "When my mother asks you where I am, tell her that I have married a princess, but you must not tell her that a star fell down while I was feasting myself at my wedding, that my bestmen were the fir-trees, my wedding priests were the high mountains, my musicians were the birds, a thousand of birds, and stars served as torches."

The ballad is mainly known among the Csángós of Moldavia, although it has spread sporadically in the Hungarian population of Transylvania, too: it has been recorded among the eastern Székely settlements. Its dissemination among the Hungarians may have been due to its poetic beauty, to the touching words with which the state of mind of the shepherd is depicted, and also to the fact that the attitude of the bequeathing shepherd shows a certain degree of similarity to some Hungarian motifs of ballads. The Hungarians adopted the Transylvanian variant in which the motif of the lamb's warning is omitted. At the same time, they borrowed from the Moldavian and Muntanian variants the motif of sending word to the mother and the sweetheart, telling them that he had married representatives of natural forces (Sun, Earth), that is, a motif of figurative description of annihilation.

Literature: Faragó 1961; Fochi 1964; Vrabie 1966; Kriza 1969.

33. THE YOUNG LORDS ESCAPED FROM THE EMPEROR'S PRISON

84.

Comrade, my comrade, my best comrade!
It is seven years that we had been taken prisoners,
Cast into the jail of the emperor, for two grapes of vine;
Since that time we have not seen the go of the Sun
5. Nor the changing turn of the Moon and stars!
This was overheard by the beautiful daughter of the emperor standing outside the door.
Do you hear what I say, two Hungarian young lords,
Young masters escaped from my father's prison?
10. Will you give me your words that if I get you out of here
You will take me to Hungary?
Brave Miklós Szilágyi answers her words:
We give our words, to be sure, beautiful daughter of the emperor!
At once the beautiful daughter of the emperor
15. Started out and went to his father's house.
She took in her hand the key to the prison,
She put into her pocket her few golden coins,
And she made speed to open up their door.
And they started, and left the place speedily.
20. As they were going on their way,
The beautiful daughter of the emperor looked back several times.
Listen to my words, two Hungarian young lords!
Young masters escaped from my father's prison:
Look there, and see my father's troup nearing;
25. Alas! As soon as they reach us, they will cut you into pieces,
And they will take me home.
Don't be afraid, don't be afraid, beautiful daughter of the emperor!
If this sword of mine does not break, they will not cut us to pieces,
Nor will they take you home, if God help us!
30. Comrade, my comrade, mind the young lady,
And I shall take care of the rest!
He reached the troup and entered into struggle with them.
On his way forward he cut a footpath,
And on his way back he cut a cart-track;
35. Of the whole big troup he left only one man alive
To go and bring tidings to those at home.
With this done, they continued their way.
László Hagymási spoke up, saying:
Comrade, my comrade, let's test each other

40. And see which of us shall have the beautiful daughter of the emperor!
Listen to my words, two Hungarian young lords,
Young masters escaped from my father's prison!
You must not cut each other on my account:
Rather I fall on my knees so that you may take my head.

45. Thereupon brave Miklós Szilágyi spoke up, saying:
Comrade, my comrade, my best comrade,
I am ready to leave the beautiful daughter of the emperor to you,
For I have a betrothed bride at home;
Whom I promised to marry as my wedded wife!

50. After these words, the beautiful daughter of the emperor
Remained to stay with László Hagymási.
Brave Miklós Szilágyi started for home.
László Hagymási married the young lady.

"Székelyföld", Samu Szabó = MNGY I, 160.

85.

As the two Hungarian young lords had been kept prisoners
In the emperor's prison, for two grapes of vine,
And they had been there, forgotten, for seven years,
In the emperor's prison, these two Hungarian young lords,

5. Grew very sad, and began to sing,
And they sang a song about their captivity:
My God, my beloved God!
Don't let us be kept in this dark prison any longer.
For it is seven years now that we have been here!

10. Since that time we have not know anything about the world outside,
We cannot see the go of the Sun,
We cannot see the changing turns of the stars.
The emperor's beautiful daughter overheard this standing by the door.
She addressed the two Hungarian young lords, saying:

15. Listen to my words, two Hungarian young lords,
Young masters who have been living in my father's prison for a long time!
Will you give me your word that if I get you out of this place,
You will take me to Hungary?
To her words the two Hungarian young lords answered:

20. Emperor's beautiful daughter, we give our words to you, to be sure.
The emperor's beautiful daughter started out
And went quickly to her bower,
She took what little change she had,
And she put her three hundred golden coins into her pocket.

25. Then she went up to her father's house.
She took in her hand the key to the prison;
She speeded then to the horses' stable;
And singling out her father's best palfreys,
She led out three saddled horses.

30. On each of the three she placed a sharp sword.
She went to the gate of the prison,
And open its cracking lock quickly.
She called in loud words: Two Hungarian young lords!

35. Come out and see the light of the world,
The bright go of the beautiful shining sun,
And the changing turn of the stars!
The three of them set on a palfrey each,
And they started out on a broad, old way.
As they were going on their way, by the first blush of dawn,

40. The emperor's beautiful daughter looked back.
She beholds from afar a big host,
She beholds her father's cruel troup nearing.
With loud words she says to the two Hungarian young lords:
Lo, my father's cruel troup is nearing,

45. They will cut you to pieces and take me back,
They will stain the earth with your crimson blood at this place.
Upon her words, the two Hungarian young lords answer:
They will not take you back, if God help us,
Nor will they cut us in pieces, if the sword does not break.

50. Anon the strong troup of the emperor arrived,
And they addressed the two Hungarian young lords:
Good morning, good morning, two Hungarian young lords!
Upon these words, the two Hungarian young lords answered:

55. Welcome to you, strong troup of the emperor!
Next the emperor's soldier spoke up, saying:
We have come to have a fight with you.
Upon these words, brave Miklós Szilágyi answered:
I don't mind, I don't mind if we want a fight.

60. On his way forward he cut a footpath,
And on his way back, he cut a cart-track.
Of all the big troup he left only one man
To bring tidings to the emperor.

"Csíkszék". Collected by Károly Szabó. Source: a rural manuscript = MNGY I, 158.

Cf. *Leader* 257.

The ballad is known to be extant in the two variants published here.

The two texts published are not the *first recordings* of the ballad. A long time before these, preceding indeed all Hungarian ballad publications, it had been heralded by an abstract whose authenticity thus cannot be doubted. Speaking about the Hungarian settlements in Moldavia *Elek Gegő* (1838, p. 80) mentions a narrative by an old man, called Csáki, of the village Kománfalva (Komineshte), who related how two good comrades—brave Miklós Szilágyi and brave László Hagymási—had been taken prisoners by the Turks for two grapes of vine; how they were released by the emperor's beautiful daughter, supplying them with gold, change and horses and oats for the way to Hungary where she also wished to flee. His informant continued relating how the emperor sent soldiers after them, emphasizing that brave Miklós Szilágyi did the great feat during the fight: "On his way forward he cut a footpath, On his way back he cut a cart-track"; how the two Hungarian young lords, reaching the borders of their country in the end, wanted to fight with sword for the emperor's girl, to whose entreaties Miklós Szilágyi left his sword unsheathed, remarking that she had had a betrothed bride at home. Gyulai adds to these in his note to the ballad saying: "Travelling about my birthplace, Transylvania, in 1845, as a student, I also heard a few fragmentary lines of the ballad sung by an old slightly drunk Székely in Oláhfalu. I made a notation of it on the spot, which I lost on the way (MNGY I, 557). As appears from these data, the ballad was more widespread at that time. What is more, also a Slovak variant is known from the sixteenth century.

Textual relationships with other ballads: The formula used to characterize the hero's power to fight: "On his way forward he cut a footpath, And on his way back he cut a cart-track" occurs in the ballad of "The Hero Who Fell in Defence of His Household" (**34.**). Reference to the song of the prisoners: **118., 22.;** fight with the persecutors during which the girl hides: **17.;** "It is seven years and three days today": **39., 43.**

Tune was not recorded.

Historical and international versions of the story: The story itself is much older than its first recording from folk tradition. There are two extant variants of the sixteenth-century manuscript poem written by the anonymous poet of Szendrő who worked up the same theme. He dates one of his narrative in verse to 1561, the other to 1571. For comparison's sake, I publish here the variant from 1561 (omitting stanzas 9–25; these, being absent in the other version, are probably secondary developments).

1. I would like to remember a beautiful old story, if you listened to me,
   And I am sure you have never heard a story like this
   About the emperor's beautiful daughter, which is worth-while to be wondered at.

2. In former time two young warriors of noble origin fell in captivity,
   And they were carried away and given over to the Turkish emperor in Istanbul,
   And the emperor had them cast into prison.

3. Not far away from the emperor's residence, lo, there stood the prison,
   In which the the two young, noble warriors were thrown,
   One of them was called Mihály Szilágyi, the other László Hagymási.

4. At a time as they reached at the day of Whitsun,
   Mihály Szilágyi happened to be looking out of the prison's rails,
   Holding his lute in his hands, he sounded it to the tune of a plaintive song.

5. Filled with grief and sorrow, he began to sing a song:
   Today last year I entertained a merry company at my home
   With my father, my aged mother and young sister.

6. The emperor's daughter was sitting in the window of her bower,
   Listening to the young man's wistful song,
   And she took a great liking in the stature of Szilágyi.

7. Soon after, on a day the emperor's daughter went to see them in stealth,
   And to comfort Mihály's sad heart,
   The emperor's daughter said the following words in her sweet voice:

8. Noble young warrior! Had you promised me upon your true faith
   To take me to your home-land in Hungary,
   And to marry me, I should answer your kindness.

26. In a day or two I should release you from the prison of my father,
    In a way or other I should release you from the pains of prison,
    But first you must swear to me upon your true faith.

27. As Mihály Szilágyi heard this, he answered:
    Release us, and I swear upon my true faith,
    Emperor's daughter, that I shall marry you and take you to my home-land.

28. Then the girl agreed with the keeper of the jail,
    And she had the young warriors taken out at midnight;
    And took them to the stable of her father's horses.

29. The girl gave two gilt sables to the noble young men,
    With which they took the heads of both the chief stableman and his grooms,
    And they saddled three-year-old horses without any delay.

30. They dressed in fine, dear clothes,
    Set the emperor's daughter on back of one of the palfreys,
    And cut the necks of all the rest of the horses.

31. Next morning the servants reported to the emperor
    That the young noblemen had run away from the prison
    And that they had taken the heads of the chiefs stableman and his grooms.

32. They asked the customs officers at ferries as to what way the refugees followed:
    They tried their fortune on the wolves' paths towards Nagyszombat,
    And if God granted luck to them, they will reach that place.

33. Therefore the emperor ordered his brave warriors,
    And his chief voivods to gather together, and bade them
    To follow in their wake without any delay, and to lead the warriors before him.

34. At the customs houses and ferry places the voivods gave orders:
    If people of such description happened to come this way, you must arrest them at once,
    And you must take them at once to the Turkish emperor in Istanbul.

35. As the young warriors reached the customs houses,
    The customs officers attacked them, according to orders,
    There followed a big fight, but the young warriors succeeded in passing over.

36. The customs officers reported the event to the emperors man,
    The voivods reached them at a beautiful island, and they began to fight face to face,
    And God so willed it that all the voivods should be killed at the fight.

37. Before the fight, however, they sent the emperor's daughter over the island,
    For fear she would be hurt and lost in the fight;
    So they sent her away and carried the fight to an end.

38. As they were looking for the emperor's daughter,
    Szilágyi, the brave warrior, heard the tender lamenting voice of the girl: ·
    The emperor's daughter was lamenting the brave warrior Szilágyi.

39. The emperor's daughter said in her tender lamenting voice:
    Gracious God! I have escaped with the young warriors,
    Alas, where shall I go with all my sorrows in this wild forest?

40. I am sorry for my own sake, but much more sorry I am for the young noble warriors,
    For they had been cut down cruelly by the swords of the voivods, the poor souls,
    Therefore I must die a horrible death anon.

41. This wild forest shall be my burying place,
    Beasts, birds and wolves shall be my mourners,
    And now I offer my soul to your grace, my dear God!

42. Mihály Szilágyi run to her with great speed,
    And the girl was very glad to see her darling alive.
    He took the girl by the hand and took her out of the island.

43. They started out and hurried towards Hungary,
    And as they crossed the border, Hagymási spoke up, saying:
    Let's fight the two of us for the possession of this girl!

44. Mihály Szilágyi answered to László Hagymási:
    My beloved comrade, upon the name of the great Lord I ask you:
    Leave her to me, for you have one, as is known to all.

45. The emperor's daughter entreats the warriors, saying:
    I am not worth of being fought for by such warriors,
    Put me to the sword instead of running such a risk!

46. László Hagymási would not agree to renouncing the girl,
    So they drew swords and began to fight, and while fighting
    Mihály Szilágyi chopped off Hagymási's hand at the wrist.

47. Brave Hagymási then spoke up and said to Mihály Szilágyi:
    My beloved companion, I beg you on the name of the great Lord,
    Forgive me, for this is how a sinner is punished.

48. I have two beautiful little sons and a kind spouse,
    The great Lord has punished me for my great sin,
    Be in good health and forgive me, my beloved companion.

49. Then the two noble youngmen parted with each other with many a kind word,
    And as Mihály Szilágyi and the emperor's daughter arrived,
    Brave Szilágyi married the emperor's daughter.

50. In fifteen hundred and sixty-one
    A young man wrote this to while away time in the castle of Szendrő,
    He put the story into verse after a poet, to banish his sad mood.

The folk ballad presents the story in a much shorter form and in a different style. *János Horváth* (1957) stated that the ballad cannot be derived from the sixteenth-century poem. This statement, however, holds true only for the formulation of the story, which is otherwise identical to the minutest detail. And what is most conspicuous: even the names are identical. Only Szilágyi's Christian name had changed from Mihály into Miklós in the popular ballad and their role in the duel had been reversed. To wit, it is really Mihály Szilágyi involved, uncle of King Matthias Corvinus of Hungary, who was one of the defenders of Belgrade (Nándorfehérvár in those days). He is one of the main heroes of southern Slav epic poetry. He is said to have been imprisoned by the Turks on two occasions, first he was redeemed, but the second time the Sultan had him beheaded. László Hagymási was a feudal lord having estates in Szilágyi's neighbourhood. János Thury has brought to light a data, according to which a member of the Sultan's family fled to Hungary during the reign of King Matthias; the daughter of this refugee was baptized and received the name Katalin Császár (Catherine Emperor). She married one of the partisans of the Hunyadis. This would be the "historical background" of the ballad.

János Honti (1930), however, refutes this explanation, because "it does not agree with the historical facts". "Katalin Császár came to Hungary in 1430 or so, and Szilágyi was first made prisoner in 1448." (Nevertheless we have to remark that these dates originate from oral transmission rather than from historical sources.) In *Honti*'s opinion, therefore, Mihály Szilágyi could not marry the Sultan's female relative. But must we suppose that the writers of epic songs had been so much insisting on accurate historical data and that what little is given had not been sufficient to provide a "historical background" for an epic verse to link these characters with a well-proved epic tradition, replacing the former names with new ones? Indeed, the Anonymous author of Szendrő remarked that he had written his verse after the composition of an earlier poet who, according to literary opinion, had written it in Latin. Thus the adaptation may well have taken place in the years of King Matthias. And even though we cannot accept the view shared also by *János Horváth,* according to which it was King Matthias that had a poem written in praise of his uncle in order to support his political aspiration: his claim to the throne against the Sultan, yet we do not think it precluded that we are dealing with a chance survival of Hungarian epic poetry from the times of the Hunyadis in this case. *Bertalan Korompay* is certainly right in this respect.

Is it, then, this poem that had given rise to a ballad among the rural population? A direct adaptation does not seem to be likely. Unfortunately, it cannot be now established to what extent the earlier sixteenth-century epic song may have been closer to folk tradition than the other song originating from the late sixteenth century; but one thing is certain: the popular text variants have preserved such turns of style which can be reduced to much earlier practice. It cannot be ascertained for certain, either, whether or not the King's court-singers had availed temselves of these turns (if the question were to be answered in the affirmative, then the anonymous writer of Szendrő is to blame for the ommission of these from the composition of his predecessor). For the sake of closer approach of the question, I recall the formula with which the hero's exceptional power is characterized in both text variants of the ballad under discussion (and also in **34.** about Izsák Kerekes, the hero who fell in defence of his household): "On his way forward he cut a footpath, And on his way back he cut a cart-track. Of all the big troup, he left only one man alive." Commonplaces like these are only found in the Turkic and Mongolian epic songs of Inner Asia and in Russian bilinas. "On their way forward they killed sixty men, on their way back they killed seventy men, they killed the whole bloody army, leaving only three warriors alive." (*Radloff* II, No. 9, lines 836–841, from the Abakhan region.) In the sketchy abstracts of *Potanin* (No. 182, p. 621), we find a yet more closer formulation: "Against this army the father stood up with his son. The two of them, on their way forward, cut seventy men, *they made a street* for them; on their way back, they cut sixty men. In six days' time they cut down the whole army." Sometimes the formula occurs in connection with hunting scenes (No. 183): "On his way forward he killed seven (beasts), On his way back he killed six." In his utterly abridged sketchy notations, *Verbitsky* thinks it important to include the formula, too—another proof of the tenacity with which the lines in question attracted the collectors' attention who rendered it verbatim: "Tas-Altyn led his army against Er Kulataj; the latter offered a bold resistance. He cut forward with his sword, and the heads of sixty men fell down, turning back, he cut again and the heads of fifty men rolled down. Thus he killed the whole army."

The following variants can be found in the Russian *bilina*s. "Where they passed, they left streets behind, Where they turned, lanes." (*Speranskij* I, 288; *Vasilij* pp. 305–6.) "He goes on the one side, and he makes a street, he turns on other side, and he makes a lane." (*Ibid.* 43.; Dobrynya and Vasilij Kazimirovich, line 310.) "Where he gives a flick, streets open, where he flicks backward, lanes." (*Ibid.* 184; Ilya i razboyniki, line 55.) "As he flicks forward, a street opens, and as he flicks backward, a lane." (*Ibid.* 214; Michail Danilovich, lines 195–6.) "Suhmantyushka gives a flick: a street opens; he flicks backward, a pass. He stretches his hand forward again, and a lane opens." (*Ibid.* 192; Suhman lines 99–101.) "As they flick forward, it is as if they were walking in a street, as they flick backward, in lane." (*Ibid.* 399; The Battle of Kama, line 311.) "Where he strikes, a street opens; where he hits, a pass." (Kaman line 292; Vasilij Buslaevich p. 248. Quoted on the basis of Rybnikov, 2nd ed. Moscow 1910, II, line 169.) "Where he flicks, a street opens, And if he flicks backward, lanes open." (*Ibid.* Ilya i razboyniki, pp. 153–4. Quoted on the basis of Hilferding III, No. 257.)

The *bilina* texts are closer to the Hungarian in so far as they mention narrow and wide streets. At the same time, they are farther, since the parallelism of moving forward and backward is missing or blurred in them, replaced by formulas more or less distinct reference to proceeding forward or sideways. Furthermore, the concluding part, common in Hungarian and Central Asian poems: "He cut down the whole army, leaving but one man to bring tidings" is absent in the *bilina*s. The Hungarian formulation seems to be most reasonable: proceeding forward, the hero cuts a narrow path, returning, he makes it broader. Anyway, the texts from Central Asia agree with the Russian inasmuch as they suggest lower numbers as the hero turns back (narrow street).

This formula could certainly not have appeared in the *bilina*s before the Kiev cycle arose in the thirteenth century. But no territorial connection with the Hungarians can be demonstrated from that time. With the Central Asiatic regions, however, the possibility of a genetic connection is given. At the same time, it may be readily surmised that the Russians got acquainted with the formula in question while engaged in warfares with the Tartars. It is a well-known fact that warfare does not mean complete separation between the enemies. Pretenders to the throne of Russia had often tried to meet their aims through the aid of Tartar military forces. Similarly, Hungarian scribes and even singers often appeared as employees of Turkish pashas in the time of Hungarian–Turkish wars, as well as their Turkish counterparts in the courts of Hungarian lords; not to mention those who had fallen into captivity of the one or the other party. Thus, the adoption of stylistic devices can be explained.

It seems as if the Hungarian ballads had preserved some earlier formulation of these Central Asiatic epic commonplaces. Maybe, they have attained a more explicit and mature form of the expression in Hungarian practice. Be it as it may, I have not found anything like this in European balladry (apart from the Hungarian). But in the Hungarian material, the formula shows a vigorous tenacity: it occurs in more recent folk poetry as well. *Domokos* (1931, 104) publishes a legendary

407

recollection of a Hungarian hussar's feat who in one of the battles of the War of Independence of 1848–49 "cut a path with his sword both on his way forward and on his way back". In a more eroded form, Sándor Rózsa, the famous Hungarian highwayman of the last century, escaped from the ring of his enemies in a way that he stroke at them with his whip (horseherd's long whip) where their lines were not so thick. "And at once a lane was open, so that he was able to escape through it." (*Dömötör*, 1930, 100.—My attention has been drawn to the last-mentioned two data through the courtesy of *Imre Katona*.)

The song of the young captives is another feature worthy of mention in this ballad type. "It is seven years since we had been made prisoners. . . . From that time forth we saw neither the go of the Sun, Nor the changing turns of the Moon and the stars." The same complaint is put into the mouths of the imprisoned heroes in the French, Portuguese and Italian ballads: "Sept ans y a bien resté sans voir soleil ni lune" (*Smith:* Romania 7, 66; for further variants, see *Canteloube* II, 17, 102, 158 and 271, *Millien* 257A). Portuguese: "Manda-a metter n'uma torre, Que nem lua via . . . Ao cabo de sete annos Viu a torre . . ." (*Braga I,* 449; for further variants, see *ibidem* I, 183, 456, 460, 482, 494, 498, 508, 511, 526 and 541). Italian: "E l'e stata la set' ani Senza veder sol ne luna". (*Bernoni* 1874, No. 2; for further variants, see *Nigra* 50A–G). It is interesting to note that the Hungarian *'bella istoria'* does not apply either of the formulas that point to international connections.

There can be no doubt raised as to the close correlation of these partial agreements of formulations. So closely related agreements of texts cannot come about independently of one another, in so remote areas. Another thing is the question of major interconnections viewed from the side of the content, in which immediate connection cannot be demonstrated, in spite of all the efforts of literary historians and folklorists who have tried to establish relationships between the Hungarian song and various literary and folklore compositions of other nations. So far all the parallelisms referred to partial agreements but never to the whole of the story of the Szilágyi and Hagymási theme. This is the reason why we have not presented a list of versions in other language areas in connection with this Hungarian ballad type. We had to content ourselves by referring to comparative studies in this instance. In the following we propose to expatiate on these for some while.

Honti traces back the story to the German mediaeval song in Latin entitled *Waltharius manu fortis* (The Strong-armed Walter). In that song, however, it is not the daughter of the lord, who keeps the prisoners in captivity, that sets free a warrior, but the hostage Walter escapes, together with a German girl, also a hostage, from the court of Attila, the king of the Huns. The duel does not take place between two friends not do they fight the army of prosecutors, but with the host of the German prince coming to meet the refugee in his homeland, and with a friend who had fled home at an earlier time. In addition, the fight is not for the girl, but because Walter had killed one of his friend's relatives in the course of some warfare. Therefore *Honti*'s comparative procedure is not accurate: he gathers together a common skeletal story from various songs and prose narratives (e. g. Gypsy tales), which does not agree with the Hungarian plot, nor can it be found in its entirety in any of the exploited songs and tales, one or another important element being always missing in them.

In any case, with the motif of escaping which enjoys widest popularity: a prisoner released by the daughter of a monarch—Turkish, Arab or other fabulous countries being mentioned usually—a ready-made pattern of numerous ballads or epic songs are given. (In fact, we know two French songs in which the jail-keeper's daughter releases the prisoner (38., and 108.). But the plots of all these stories continue in a different way. For comparison's sake, I adduce some of the examples. In a popular English ballad (*Child* 53B) the daughter of the king of the Moors falls in love with Beicham who is a prisoner in her father's jail. She releases him against his promise to marry her, now in three, now in seven years. The young man forgets of his promise and is just celebrating his wedding with another bride, when his earlier sweetheart arrives. After a scene of recognition, the actual bride is sent away and the redeemer maried instead.

In the Slovenian songs about King Matthias (cf. *Horálek* 1964 II and Korompay) we see also a prisoner escaping from captivity. *Korompay* publishes a typical specimen of this cycle. King Matthias is taken prisoner by the Turks, the Sultan's daughter sets him free and asks him to marry her. Matthias says honestly that he cannot marry her because he has a wife at home. But he promises to marry her to one of his three sons. After such preliminaries the scene of escape follows, then that of the persecution, both embellished with fabulous details. The king's wife is not glad to receive a rival in her household, but the plot is solved by marrying the girl to a son called Matthias (in some variants replaced by the king's younger brother or brother-in-law).

A type of the cycle about Prince Marko resolves the plot in a still different manner. (This time I quote No. 24 on p. 69 of *Vatev*.) In the Bulgarian version, Marko is released by an Arab girl from her father's prison against the prisoner's promise to marry her. Arriving in his country, Marko notices that the girl's face is black. Therefore he cuts her head. Similar solution is found in *Child* 9, in which the young man, arriving at home, dismisses his redeemer, saying that he had had already a wife and that he only needed the girl's assistance while he was a prisoner.

Apart from the different continuation, a considerable divergence is that in these songs we find only one hero, that is, there is no possibility for the friends to quarrel over the girl. On the other hand, the latter motif can be met with disconnected with the motif of escape. Horálek (1964 II) mentions the southern Slav type of songs in which two brothers ask for the hand of one and the same girl. The girl suggests a contest to settle the debate, and the two brothers collapse dead before the goal, whereupon the girl also does away with herself.

Szegedy (1915) quotes another type: Two brothers have a rest before they continue hunting, and a fairy appears. One of the brothers wants to marry her, but the other one, who is married already, also claims her, and kills his unmarried brother. *Szegedy* states that the southern Slav ballads contain all essential motifs of the Hungarian legend of Szilágyi and Hagymási—which are widespread on the international plane—but nowhere can be found the correlation of the various motifs as they are linked up in the Hungarian ballad and 'bella istoria'. In this achievement he also sees Hungarian tradition at work.

These related themes may be survivals of forms that used to be predecessors of the epic songs of the age of the Hunyadis, and they may be their remote relatives as well, which are swarming around the central theme without having been reunited with it. In any case, the motif of escape with the help of the girl in whose father's prison the warrior was kept may have existed before the Hungarian story had developed. At the same time, the international relationship is not so strong in this instance as in the other cases, and no such relationship can be made responsible for the coming into existence of the Hungarian ballad under dicussion. Consequently, in this example the Hungarian popular formulation cannot enjoy priority over the literary composition; in all probability it had originally been a composition of a court singer, from whose practice it was mediated to the rural population through the agency of some class of singers that used to preserve traditional Central Asiatic forms of performance. In this manner we can explain the development of the Székely ballad that represents the heroic song of the vocational singers of yore in an almost perfectly crystallized ballad style. To sum up, we are faced here with a rare case in the sphere of Hungarian balladry (such one is the song about Izsák Kerekes mentioned before), a case when literary antecedents can be directly demonstrated from written tradition of quondam epic singers—"poets"—whose compositions turned into traditional popular ballads in the course of time.

Literature: EMU I, 67.69, 1887: publishes a Transylvanian Saxon song, together with Romanian and Gipsy variants and other parallels; *Thury* 1893: historical data on the 'bella istoria'; *Szegedy* 1911 and 1915: southern Slav parallels, the 'bella istoria' originates from the southern Slavs; *Gragger* 1926: the folk ballad developed from two variants of 'bella istoria', with a reconciling dénouement which is well in accord with the spirit of folk poetry (?); *Honti* 1930: originates from the *Waltharius manu fortis* song, the southern Slav versions mentioned by *Szegedy* do not belong here; *Ortutay* 1936–1948: accepts *Honti's* theory as well as those authors who used to derive the ballad from international folklore parallels; *Korompay* 1953: quotes Slovenian parallels, rejects *Honti,* and proclaims the theory of an international folklore theme (*Child* 9, 53, etc.), the 'bella istoria' formulation of the story is survival of an epic song from the time of King Matthias; *Horváth* 1957, 227–231: the Székely popular ballads cannot be directly derived from the 'bella istoria', although the latter shows a sort of transition into the ballad style; *Horálek* 1964 I–II: mentions the Hungarian ballad in connection with southern Slav parallels; *Csanda* 1961: examines the relationship between Hungarian and Slovak variants of the 'bella istoria', the Slovak variant is a translation from Hungarian.

34. THE HERO WHO FELL IN DEFENCE OF HIS HOUSEHOLD

86.

Have you heard the fame of famous Szeben,
Of famous Szeben and famous Moha,
Of Péter Kerekes, living at Moha,
And of Izsák Kerekes, his grown-up son?
5. He once went drunk into the stable,
And lay down there in the horses' manger.
Then his father went out to the porch
And from there scanned the region.
Aye, a big black host is approaching.
10. It seems in the far distance like a dark cloud,
They know not what it may be, the Prince's or the Emperor's troup,
Although they think: they are Serbians from Szeben.
Then Izsák's father went down
To the horses' manger, and spoke up, saying:
15. Get up, my son, get up, bold Izsák Kerekes,
For it seems a big black host is approaching,
It looks in the far distance like a dark cloud,
We know not what they are, Prince's or Emperor's troup,
Although we think: they are Serbians from Szeben.
20. Then he turned in his first sleep,
Yet he did not rise from the horses' manger.
The second time his mother went out,
And she was eager to wake him up, saying:
Get up, my son, get up, brave Izsák Kerekes!
25. Aye, a big black host is approaching,
It seems in the far distance like a dark cloud,
We know not what they are, Prince's or Emperor's troup,
Although we think: they are Serbians from Szeben.
Then he turned in his second sleep,
30. Yet he did not rise from the horses' manger.
The third time his beautiful betrothed went out,
She went to the porch and looked down at the field.
Aye, the enemy is quickly approaching!
She ran down to the horses' manger
35. And began to speak to his dear man:
Get up, sweetheart, get up, for the enemy is here!
We know not what they are, the Prince's or Emperor's troup,
Although we think: they are Serbians from Szeben.
And then up jumped bold Izsák Kerekes.

40. They brought out his horse very swiftly,
    He girded his sword at once,
    And neatly mounted his good bay,
    And looked back, and spoke up, saying:
    I shall spill my blood for my father and mother,
45. I shall get killed for my beautiful betrothed bride,
    I shall die for my Hungarian nation before the day is over!
    After these words, he spurred his horse,
    Driving it boldly towards the enemy.
    Aye, the Serbians are coming and he standing in front of them.
50. Brandishing his blade, he rushes at them with terrible wrath.
    Surrender, surrender, bold Izsák Kerekes!
    The Serbians shout to him from afar.
    We see that you are a brave warrior, but you are by yourself,
    And there is no hope whatever left for you,
    For no matter how skilful you are, you are in our hands!
55. What if I am by myself, it is no business of yours!
    Sword does not pierce me, cut me as you may!
    Thus spoke Izsák Kerekes, striking to the right and to the left,
    And the Serbians fell before his sword one after the other.
    On his way forward he cut a footpath,
60. On his way back he cut a cart-track,
    But then his horse's foot stumbled,
    And he fell off his horse down upon the ground.
    This is how bold Izsák Kerekes fared with his horse,
    And the Serbians dashed at him with sword and pike,
65. Cutting and killing him, and he fighting
    To the last kick, to the last breath.
    This is how they perished bold Izsák Kerekes,
    Who cut down many Serbians with his sword.

Székelyföld, Kriza = MNGY III, 4.

87.

Have you heard the fame of Kis Cserepes,
Of Kis Cserepes and St. Margita,
Of Pál Veres, the shepherd who lives at St. Margita,
And of his son Jóska Veres?
5. The one who drank at the Skull Inn till dawn for seven nights,
Danced for seven days and ate seven lambs,
And then went to hide and sleep [= in trance] for a full week.
While asleep, he had gathered strength enough for seven.
When sleeping, he had strength of seven,
10. But when he woke up from his trance, he had strength of seventy-seven,
He had all the courage of seven hearts!
Living Jóska Veres was sleeping as though he were dead.

412

His father woke him: Get up, son, Jóska,
There is a wind blowing from the Inta, and a big black cloud,
15. A flood of wolves circling the flock of sheep,
Some sort of enemy, Tartars or their like.
Jóska woke up for a moment at these words,
Then went to sleep again, and his sleep was even more heavy,
He hid even more deeper, in a trance deeper than before.
20. And his father could not wake him whatever he said.
Then his mother, his own dear mother went to him
To tell about the coming evil.
She woke him, saying: Get up, son, Jóska,
But he only half woke up, then fell back asleep.
25. Then his betrothed sweetheart went to him:
There is a wind blowing from the Inta, and a big black cloud,
It must be some enemy, Tartars or their like,
A flood of wolves are circling the flock of sheep.
At the words of his sweetheart, at the news of disaster,
30. Jóska jumped on his horse at once.
And raising his sword and praying aloud
He charged the huge heathen army.
Aye, God in Heaven, look down on my end!
I shall die for my country, for my beloved sweetheart,
35. For my Hungarian nation, my father and mother,
My good name and my Jesus Christ!
With these words he cut a path on his way forward,
And he cut a cart-track on his way back.
But then his horse fell under him,
40. A javelin pierced his heart, and a Tartar's arrow went into his head.
He died, as he had said, for his country,
For his father, mother and for our Hungarian nation,
His wedded spouse, our Jesus Christ,
And he is buried here in the Red Hill.

*Nagyiván (Heves county). Performed by 93-year-old József Kiss, László K. Kovács,
1951.= Ethn. 1960, 511–512.*

No more variants are known to be extant.

Earliest provenience: 1864.

Dissemination: "Székelyföld" (probably Udvarhely county) and Hajdú county.

Textual relationships with other ballads: The formula depicting the fight: "On his way forward he cut a footpath..." can be found in an identical wording in both variants of the ballad of "The Young Lords Escaped from the Emperor's Prison" **(33.)** *Tune* has not been recorded with any of the variants.

Versions in languages other than Hungarian:

KARAKIRGHIZ: *1. Radloff* V, No. II.
VOGUL: *2–9.* VNGY II/1, 38–40, 227, 245–6, 306, 308, IV, 141–42, 152–155.

The drunkenness mentioned seemingly without sufficient motivation at the beginning of the song about Izsák Kerekes is apparently a survival of some significant motif for otherwise it would not have been included in the text at all, or would have been fully omitted from it. The second song, speaking about Jóska Veres of the Trans-Tisza Region, is more complete and suggests that a sort of magic drunkenness, magic sleeping is involved, consequently the hero possesses supernatural abilitites. The motif—and other elements of the two Hungarian songs—can be found in one of the lengthiest Siberian epic songs, in that of Joloi Khan. The Karakirghiz hero is outstanding in his capacity for eating and drinking: with this his superhuman strength is indicated. But precisely because of this superhuman power he gets drunk at every entertainment or feast, and in the heroic poem about him all the great dangers arise from this habit of his. The Karakirghiz song begins with the following scene: Joloi Khan lies drunk in his tent while the enemy attacks and kills his people. For three days, his wife tries in vain to wake him. Finally, on the forth day, she plunges his sword into his heart, whereupon, as though at an insect's bite, he jumps up and onto his horse, and crushes the enemy. Then, after many adventures, he falls into the hands of the enemy, and is kept, half dead, in a pit. The poem contains many long adventures, among others his escape from the dungeon: a wild-goose with an injured wing falls down to him; he heals it, writes a letter on its wing in blood from his finger, and lets it fly away: the message is received and he gets free. Other parts of the epic song tell of the adventures of the Khan and his son, that is, the story of two generations. The Uzbek Alpamysh epic poem relates the same story.

This type of song must represent some old tradition that used to be widespread over a wide area, for its characteristic motifs also appear in the Vogul epic poems. In *Munkácsi's* collection (VNGY IV, 155a, lines 191 and ff.) we may read the following description: "When he reached home he lay down. He says to his wife: You are not strong enough to wake me if you hear some little noise, so stick a knife in my hip. He sleeps for a time, long or short, and suddenly an enemy force approaches. His wife is unable to wake him, and weeps. Suddenly he feels he is lying in water, and waking up he finds that his wife is weeping and that he is lying in her tears. What are you doing?—An enemy force is approaching. He gets up and turns against the approaching enemy, and scatters them as one scatterns a thick cloud of mosquitoes. Then he says: I am going to die, and after ten winters and ten summers I shall rise again. He dies and is buried . . . ."

The same Vogul poem contains also other portions of the epic song about Joloi Khan: while fighting the enemy, he falls into a seven-fathom-deep pit. A chip of wood falls into the pit, and he makes a tambura out of it. He enchants a wide-goose with the sound of his tambura, so that it lights down in the pit. He writes on the fowl's wing a message to his magic horse, and he is rescued. Then his son gets drunk at a feast. His adventures are not unlike his father's: he is cast into a pit and locked up, together with his horse, in a threefold iron cage. He also makes a tambura out of a shaving, sends message written on the goose-feather and escapes as his father did.

But the motif of the long waking is still more characteristic of the Vogul epic songs. In VNGY II/1, from line 300 on, we have the following: "Having sat for a long time or for a short time, the woman took a knife from his side, and stuck it into the armpit of her sleeping man. He wakes and says: After the guests arrived, could you not have wakened me earlier?..." (The same can be read on page 306 of Chapter 17, on page 308 of Chapter 19, pages 38–40 of Chapter 1, Volume II, and pages 245–6 of Volume 1.) The epic songs about the chieftains of the Konda lowlands (II, 227) show an even more obvious similarity to the ballad-song of the Székelys: "The young chieftain-hero's wife came out, went back, and said: It looks as though some army were coming towards us, some sort of visitors coming towards us, and they advance like one end of a lopped forest. The younger chieftain-hero dressed and put on his armour and sword, and went out, and lo! the armies were beginning to arrive." In an Oborsk Samoyed song (IV, 141–142), the wife tries to wake her husband twice, because his younger brother is coming with an army.

These details probably got into the Vogul folk poetry from the epic tradition of the Turkic peoples, and other motifs of the "Altai-type" heroic songs also appear among the Voguls. One of the motifs relates to the method of communicating through the "smoke-hole" between the various regions of earth and heaven: "Through this opening from the lower part of the black earth they rose above the face of the earth, and thus came to their relatives, seven men living in the nether world..." (Page 230, Volume II). In the "Song about the Upbringing of the Man Guarding the World" (ibid. 112–13), the infant hero receives his armour. See also the motif of head-searching before the wrestling, discussed above, in connection with the ballad on Anna Molnár. We cannot decide on the basis of our present-day knowledge whether the Voguls had received these elements from the neighbouring Tartars or from some other people with whom they had/come into contact at a much earlier date. In any case, we have to suppose survivals of some archaic Turkic tradition which can still be demonstrated in the more or less eroded Hungarian and Vogul texts. In the Hungarian songs, we find motifs, like the repeated attempts at waking the drunken hero, while the enemy is nearing, the failure of the first two attempts and the wife's success on the third occasion, then the struggle and the death—even perhaps the final words—of the hero foreseeing his end; indeed, all these show a striking resemblance to the adventures of Joloi Khan, and to their counterparts in the Vogul epic songs, even though the comparable plot nuclei are rather scanty. But they are not scantier than what usually remains in the form of survivals of lengthy epic songs in ballad materials in similar cases.

Of course, the mentioning of the Szeben Serbians, which has formerly been considered as being relevant to the origin of the ballad (at the period of the Rákóczi War of Independence), has no greater significance than that the Serbs were the most recent enemy to whom the old story was related. That is, it was not a record of the origin or genesis but of the most recent association with current events. It may well have been the case that the association originally took place outside the sphere of folk poetry. To wit, both songs bear imprints of obvious art-poetic interferences—perhaps those of cantors. Such are, for instance, the enjambments used in lines 7–8, 13–14, 31–32 and 65–66, which are not typical of folk poetry. Further evidence of this is the use of certain epic formulas, e.g. the question: "Have you heard the fame of...?", or the formula known from later historical lays: "I shall spill my blood... I shall die today for my Hungarian nation." But the most obvious sign is the detailing style of delivery, which is completely alien to the ballad style, for instance in lines 46–66. And the song about Jóska Veres shows the same style at its utter corruption, indeed, it is a semi-popular, cantorial representation of the story. To sum up, this song may have really preserved elements of epic poems in the form of traditional epic songs, possibly to the most recent times and at a level of art songs of the István Kádár's lay type, from which it has descended lately to the popular layers, where it continued to maintain its earlier traits at a stage of verging into a true popular ballad.

The song must have developed between the fourteenth and eighteenth centuries.

Literature: Vargyas 1962, 1967.

416

35. THE PRINCE'S SOLDIER

88.

Poco rubato, lento

1. Meg - öl-ték   a   Ba - sa Pis-tát   Fe - je-de - lem   ka - to-ná   - ját,

Út szé-lén hó   tan ta - lál-ták,   Len-gyel-or-szág-nak ha-tá - rán:

1. They killed Pista Basa,
   The Prince's soldier.
   He was found dead on the wayside,
   On the border of Poland.

2. On the border of Poland,
   During the time of Rákóczi's exile.
   Pista Basa was taken there,
   And there his life was extinguished.

3. His gilt, embroidered pelisse
   Was tainted with his spilt blood.
   Alas, my God, alas, Holy Virgin,
   That I have come into exile!

4. I sacrificed my life,
   I defended my generals;
   I stood the ground on the frontier of my country,
   I entered into a fight against the murderers.

5. Julis Fehér is waiting for him to come home
   Every night, for supper.
   Don't wait for him, Julis, don't wait for him, Julis
   . . .

Diósad (Szilágy county). Female performer, 1914, Lajtha = SzNd No. 50.

A fragment, known from one single variant. No textual interrelationship with other ballads can be demonstrated.

Bóta makes attempts at deducing the entire song from what memory has preserved in connection with a certain István Basa. Earlier opinion maintained that the story of the ballad referred to the disastrous military expedition of György Rákóczi II in Poland in 1657 (not to be mistaken for Francis Rákóczi II, the great Prince of the War of Independence in the early eighteenth century). *Bóta*, however, proved that the only person known by the name of István Basa was hanged by the Transylvanian Prince Gábor Bethlen near Kéménd, on one of his campaigns to the Highlands (Northern Hungary, now Slovakia), because Basa proved to be guilty of sacking the soil-bound peasantry, "Mantles of poor people having been found with him", as János Kemény put it in his autobiography. Therefore Pista Basa cannot be regarded as the Great Prince Ferenc Rákóczi's warrior. Neither does the line "I have defended my generals" pass to him, because he had contrived a conspiracy against Gábor Báthori, for which he was condemned to death *in contumatiam* by the National Assembly of Beszterce, and later on he was also involved in similar conspiracies against Gábor Bethlen. The latter Prince forgave him for what Basa committed against him, though he had him executed for his having plundered the poor.

Bóta bases his theory attributing the whole story to this sinner István Basa on two statements of the song. From the line "He was found dead on the wayside" it follows that he had been executed instead of being killed in a battle, as the words ". . . taken there, And there his life was extinguished" may apply to a hanged man sooner than to a brave soldier. At the same time, he cannot explain how the lines "On the border of Poland, During the time of Rákóczi's exile" . . . "His guilt, embroidered pelisse Was tainted with his spilt blood. . ." and the stanza "I sacrificed my life, I defended my generals, I stood the ground on the frontier of my country, I entered into a *fight against the murderers"* got into the ballad. From these, as well as other similar places of the ballad we can infer references to an act of heroic resistance and death in warfare. Insisting upon the identity of the historical name with the name of the ballad's hero, that is the connection between the ballad and the historical facts, *Bóta* presumes that István Basa may have participated in the campaign of György Rákóczi I, a general of Gábor Bethlen, against Homonnai's troups invading Hungary from the Polish side. Had it been so, the story would have been subjected to certain modifications all the same, as a matter of course.

Contradiction only prevails if we stick to the conception that name and historical person are always in full agreement in folk poetry. In this instance, it is just *Bóta's* data that bear evidence of the fact that the name of a ballad's hero may be distinctly detached from the story in which it comes up. One thing is important: the name must have been in wide currency, known from some renowned family's history. The family Basa used to be landowners near the place where the ballad was collected, in the vicinity of Dés, Transylvania. That much is enough for the people to include their name into a narrative. But had it been so as *Bóta* has concluded, to wit, that the executed brigand's song had amalgamated with some other song about a historical event, we should still have the same result: people forget the real names of historical persons as well as the factual background of historical events, and transforming the tradition they maintain only as much of it as is necessary to meet the points of poetic fantasy, a poetic representation.

In any case, the point of origin of this ballad may have been provided by a seventeenth-century historical song; nevertheless, the method of line-repetition and the technique of presenting the story in singular first person and reflecting to the significance of the hero's moral courage are typical of ballad-like thinking; still

418

more so is the closing stanza, fragmentary as it is, in which the spouse left on her own appears, elevating the death in action to the rank of a ballad theme preoccupied with the contingencies of human fate, and of human psychic conditions.

Literature: Lajtha 1928: the ballad is connected with the Polish campaign of György Rákóczi II; *Ortutay* 1936–48: accepts Lajtha; *Csanádi* and *Vargyas* 1954: accepts *Lajtha; Bóta* 1972: demonstrates historical facts connected with István Basa's execution; the story contaminated with motifs of other ballads.

36. THE BANQUET OF THE PASHA OF VÁRAD

89.

1. Püs - pök vá - ro - sá - ba Hogy bé - men - tem va - la,

Nem so - kad ma - gam-mal, Csak szá - zad ma - gam-mal.

1. When the Bishop's town
   I walked in,
   There were not too many of us,
   We were a hundred altogether.

2. The Pasha of Várad
   Called me to a banquet;
   And I was not late a moment,
   I went to see him without delay.

3. As I entered
   The gate of the town,
   As I entered
   The gate of the town,

4. The Pasha stood on my side,
   Holding my right arm,
   And on the other side the pagan folks
   Were binding my body.

5. What does this mean, warriors,
   That you are binding me?
   What does this mean, warriors,
   That you are binding me?

6. Perhaps you still think of me
   As of one who is not a prisoner.
   Alas, if only you knew
   That I am kept in schackles up to the knees.

7. Drums were beaten
   In the middle of the market-place,
   Pipes were blown
   On top of the tower.

8. Pride of lordly people,
   Sámuel Rákóczy!
   Your former lordly dignity
   Has now been reduced to servitude.

9. Pride of lordly people,
   Sámuel Rákóczy!
   Your body that used to be cared for tenderly
   Is lying now in shackles up to the knees.

10. Were the water of the sea
    To turn into pure ink.
    Were every blade of grass
    To turn into a pen each,

11. Still they could not write down
    The plenty of his pains,
    With which they are perishing
    The poor soul, His Highness.

PHÁ No. 250, before 1813.

László Rákóczi, cousin of the Transylvanian Prince György Rákóczi I, and a friend of the poet and general Miklós Zrínyi fell in action against the Turks at the gate of the castle of Várad in 1662 or 1664, according to the testimony of chronicles. Accompanied by an insignificant number of Heyduck warriors, the named László Rákóczi penetrated the town in order to recapture it by a stratagem. He plotted to execute the plan at a time when market was held in the city, and he went in probably in disguise. Unfortunately, his Heyducks began to sack the market people, set fire on the tents, and therefore the Turks noticed their presence. The assailants were killed and their leader was taken prisoner. The story had been known from several sources even before *Ádám Pálóczi Horváth* published his text variant which shows a considerable influence of the ballad style while the tune associated with it is a clearly discernible variant of the old-style epic folksongs. It seems that the story had been disseminating also in oral tradition to some extent, subjected, of course, to modifications. For comparison's sake, I publish here one of the recorded texts which may be closest to the original as an undoubtedly art-poetic composition.

1. As I entered the Bishop's town,
   I had the trumpets blown to my splendid army.
   I called the Pasha of Várad to a banquet,
   Which I had to rue later with bitter tears.

2. Calling the Pasha of Várad to a banquet,
   And wishing to overcome him with three hundred men,
   I was about to cross the gate of the castle,
   When they began to put to sword my men.

3. To think of it, my God, that my men are being killed,
   That I shall never see my wife again,
   That I shall never see my beautiful children once more;
   On the one side the Pasha is holding my arm,
   On the other side the Turks are binding my body.

4. What does this mean, warriors, that you are binding me?
   I have never in my life committed a sin against you!
   Although you always ruin the army of my Emperor;
   And I have never sinned against my Hungarian nation.

5. It is my own army that acted as traitors to me.
   And you, pagan Turks, why are you my traitors?
   Will hearts and souls not take pity on my fate?
   Consider, I have fallen into your hands through the treason of my own army!

6. Alas, they proclaim that I walk free!
   Alas, can I walk about free? O, I am a prisoner!
   My tenderly cherished face has withered,
   My body attended upon so tenderly has become feeble.

7. My lordly status has changed into servitude,
   My former pleasures have forsaken me for good,
   My former gaiety has departed for good,
   And also my heart is clouded with sorrow.

8. Youngest offspring of the clan Rákóczi:
   Handsom Ferenc Rákóczi, and all my sons:
   Farewell to you, my beautiful little ones!
   My dear children, you will never see me again.

9. My fame filled the whole of Hungary,
   My name was Handsom László Rákóczi.
   But my own flock had betrayed me!
   O, how I was betrayed by my best general!

10. In sixteen hundred and sixty-seven,
    In the third week of the month of our Blessed Virgin,
    I composed these verses in my bitter sorrow,
    In the depth of the dungeon of the Pasha of Várad.

Miklós Jankovich: Nemzeti Dalok Gyűjteménye (Collection of National Songs). Ki. OSZK. Quart. Hung. 173. Vol. VIII, p. 10a = *Thaly:* Vitézi Énekek (Warriors' Songs), Vol. I, 171. (Published after Thaly.) The dating in the poem is probably erroneous, owing to the copyst's mistake: *seven* is written instead of *two*.

It appears from this late eighteenth-century notation that the story was associated with the Great Prince Ferenc Rákóczi; this is the reason why the phrase "I was betrayed by my best general" got into the verse. This statement may have been released from subsequent copyists by the already incorporated phrase "It is my own army that betrayed me"; although it must have referred to the undisciplined conduct of the heyducks in the original. *Thaly* takes it verbatim that the prisoner wrote the poem while a captive, whereas it was obviously composed by his court poet who attributed the verse to the hero himself, just as the poet of the lay of István Kádár put the words of his verse into the hero's mouth, while he stayed under the cloak of anonymity.

The art-poetic variant was written apparently in 1662, that is immediately after the event took place; by the time *Ádám Pálóczi* put the song to paper it must have acquired its colouring of a popular ballad.

37. THE KING'S SON AND A KING'S DAUGHTER

90.

Lento (Rubato)

1. Hal - lod e te, ki - rály fi - a, Gye - re hez-zám gu - zsa - lyas-ba! Nem me - gyek, mert se -tét va- gyon, Se - tét va-gyon i - gen na - gyon.

1. I say, you king's son
   Will you come to keep me company in the spinning house?
   I will not go because it is dark,
   Sure, it is very dark,

2. And I shall fall into the sea,
   Right in the middle of the sea;
   I shall fall into the sea,
   Just at the place where it is deepest.

3. I shall kindle my candle of gold,
   And you may come by its light;
   I shall kindle my candle of gold,
   And you may come by its light.

4. The king's son started out
   To the spinning house late at night;
   He fell into the sea,
   Right in the middle of the sea.

5. He fell into the sea,
   Right in the middle of the sea,
   Just at the place where it is deepest.
   Just at the place where it is deepest.

6. The king's daughter is weeping, weeping,
   She is near to pine away;
   The king's daughter is weeping, weeping,
   She is near to pine away.

7. Her mother spoke up, saying:
   Why are you weeping, why are you weeping, my dear daughter?
   Alas, mother, I cannot but weep
   For I lost my pearly head-dress;

8. It fell into the sea,
   Right in the middle of the sea,
   It fell into the sea,
   Just at the place where it is deepest.

9. Don't you weep, don't you weep, my dear daughter,
   For I shall give you my own one!
   But I don't want the one you have,
   I only want my own one!

10. They hired a diver
    And set out in search of it.
    And they did not fish out the pearly head-dress,
    But they fished out the son of a king.

11. The queen spoke up, saying:
    Draw him onto the shore;
    Take him into the palace,
    And place him into the laid bed!

12. Let us have a stone coffin made,
    Let us have the bells tolled;
    See him out to the crypt,
    Drop three drops of tear on him!

Homoród (Udvarhely county) = Bartalus II, No. 5.

91.

I say, you son of a king,
Will you come to the spinning house in the evening?
I cannot go, you daughter of the king,
How could I get across the Danube?

5. It will grow dark late in the evening,
   And I shall fall into the Danube.
   O, I have a torch
   And I shall place it on my porch,
   And I shall kindle it as soon as needed,

10. By its light you may come across.
    The son of a king,
    The prince started out
    To the spinning house late in the evening;
    And he fell into the Danube,
    Right in the middle of the Danube.

15. The daughter of the king is weeping, weeping,
    The daughter of the king, little Júlia.
    Her mother spoke up, saying:
    Why are you weeping, child, little Júlia?
    Alas, mother, I cannot but weep

20. For I lost my pearly head-dress,
    It fell into the Danube,
    Right in the middle of the Danube.
    But I have a pearly head-dress
    And I give it to you at once.
25. I don't want anyone's head-dress,
    I only want my own one!
    But I say, mother,
    Let us send for Jankó Bíró,
    Jankó Bíró, the diver!
30. Tell him to fish out my pearly head-dress.
    I say, you Jankó Bíró,
    Fish out my pearly head-dress!
    But I do not find a head-dress,
    What I found is the son of a king.
31. That's what I want, that's what I want, Jankó Bíró,
    Jankó Bíró, the diver,
    Bring him up into my palace,
    Place him here in my bed!
    The king's daughter is weeping, weeping,
40. The king's daughter, little Júlia.
    Her heart broke with sorrow,
    And she died a terrible death.
    For the one they had
    A coffin of white marble made,
45. For the other they had
    A coffin of red marble made.
    They buried them in the flower garden,
    They placed them side by side,
    They planted
50. A white streaky tulip on the one,
    And they planted
    A pure red tulip on the other.
    The souls of the lovers
    Turned into living tulips,
55. And they grew, and they grew,
    Until they embraced each other.

"Udvarhelyszék", Sándor Gálfi, 1830 = MNGY I, 183.

Only two published variants are known. (The third one published in MNGY III, p. 61 suffered so much alteration that it cannot be regarded as an authentic variant.)

Earliest provenience: 1830.
Dissemination: Udvarhely county, "Udvarhelyszék".

426

Textual relationships with other ballads: The hiring of divers: **9.**; the fishing out of the lovers drowned in the water occurs in **28.** "Let us have a stone coffin made..." etc. is related with the corresponding motif of **65.** The grave-flower comes up in **9., 10., 28.,** and **38.** The closing lines clarifying the meaning of this motif ("The souls of the lovers Turned into living tulips") is obviously the collector's insertion, since no such "explanation" can be found in other ballads.

Parallels in languages other than Hungarian:

FRENCH: *1–3. Rolland* 187B–C, E. *4. D'Harcourt* 5. *5. Millien* 113. *6. Beauquier,* 312. *7–8. Rossat* 2A–D. *11. Delzangles* 26 (*Doncieux* 22: inferred text. *Idem:* 17 variants quoted), see also *Davenson* 17.

ITALIAN: *12. Nigra* 7.

SPANISH: *13–14. Armistead–Silverman* 1971, 44 and 70, B3 and C2 (recorded exclusively from Iberian Jews settled in the Balkans). *Idem* 1978/IV.

CATALAN: *15. Wolf* 137.

DUTCH-FLEMISH: *16. Willems* 142. *17. Lootens-Feys* 82* (translated by *Rolland*). *18.* JbfVf III, 198. *19. Lambrechts* 160.

GERMAN: *20–337.* D. Vlr 20 (316 variants, resp. notes, and 2 divergent variants from Gottschee; I have made direct use of several of the variants).

DANISH: *338–340. Berggreen* 75a–c. *341.* Dal 53 (English translation).

SWEDISH: *342. Arwidson* III/198* (translated by *Rolland*).

FINNISH: *343. Haavio* 167 (a few fragments and a variant that can be regarded as complete).

WENDISH: *344. Haupt–Schmaler* II/13.

MORAVIAN: *345–346. Sušil* 395–396.

UKRAINIAN: *347. Čubinsky* 609, 643 (French translation).

SLOVENIAN: *348. Štrekelj* 291.

Partial variants: 349–365. Kolberg 9a–5. (*Child* 216 being irrelevant.)

The prototype of European adaptations is to be looked for in the ancient legend of Hero and Leander known from the fourth-century elaboration by Musaeus. One of the priestesses of Aphrodite is closed up in a tower so that she may not be raped by men. She falls in love with a young man whom she happens to meet at a festival; soon they agree that the young man will swim across the sea and meets the maid. However, the torch she sets to show the direction is extinguished by the wind, and the young man drowns in the sea. As the girl catches glimpse of her darling, she jumps from the cliff to meet him in the water.

The theme has been remodelled in several European languages. In France it first appears in a Provençal poem of the eleventh century, in the Netherlands it was first worked up by Dirck Potter in the fifteenth century, and in Germany by Hans Sachs in the sixteenth century. As to the Hungarian versions, István Völcsei Tóth wrote a 'bella istoria' of the story, which was lost, although we know about its one-time existence from a reference of Gyöngyösi's work János Kemény (1693).

In the French ballad, the girl is locked up in a tower by her father who wishes to keep her aloof from her sweetheart. They agree that the girl will set a torch whenever the young man visits her. As he reaches the foot of the tower, he falls into the sea. In other variants he is carried away by stormy waves. According to a Canadian version, he falls into the depth of the sea ("au fond de la mer"). Next morning the girl is looking high and looking low, finally she beholds her darling's dead body floating in the sea. She is lamenting him: Had I got scissors, I should cut my veins and revive my sweetheart with my own blood. (In certain variants the last sentence has that she is lamenting her sweetheart but not her parents.)

The German ballad which shows a wider spread and spans over a longer period of time has a closer affinity with the early literary tradition. The lovers are separated by a broad sea, or by two waters (or by two mountains with water between them) so that they cannot meet. The girl asks her sweetheart (sometimes by way of a letter) to swim over to her, promising him to place a burning candle to show the proper direction. However, the candle is blown out by a wicked woman (a nun), who had overheard their talk. The young man drowns. Next morning the girl entreats her mother to let her go on a walk, pretending headache (or saying that she would go to the mass). The mother refuses to let her out by herself, and orders the girl's younger brother or sister to guard her. The girl raises excuses: the brother will shoot the birds, and the girl will pick all the flowers in the way. Eventually she reaches the shore by herself, meets a fisherman whom she asks to fish out the prince (king's son). He succeeds in hauling the young man's body at first attempt (or he catches him by his angle). The girl kisses him, rewards the fisherman with her crown or her ring, and leaps into the sea to meet her death there.

As can be seen, both formulations deviate in substantial details from the Hungarian. The latter's common feature with the French is that there is no mention of the sea to be crossed by swimming, but the young man falls into the water; but the deviation is that the girl beholds the corpse of her sweetheart floating in the water, looking down from the tower in which she is kept prisoner, this sort of captivity being similarly absent in the Hungarian. Further, the reference to the scissors is also unknown in the Hungarian version. But the mentioning of the two princely offspring—zwei Königskinder—relates the Hungarian with the German, as well as the fishing out of the drowned sweetheart, which is effectuated by the aid of fishermen in the German, and of divers in the Hungarian. At the same time, the Hungarian dispenses with the following motifs, which are to be found in the German: the blowing out of the candle, the girl's lengthy duologue with the mother about the walk outdoors, the suicide in the sea, the rewarding of the fisherman, furthermore the girl is not separated by force from the young man, but she simply calls him to to come and see her at night, and the young man is afraid of falling into the water.

The differences are conspicuous, and at the same time there are no such particular similarities of formulation which should indicate a common origin. It seems, therefore, that in all three distinct language areas the ballad had developed independently of each other from such literary antecedents which may or may not survive among the nations involved. In any case, the ancient formulation of the story must have undergone considerable simplifications in the course of literary mediation.

The German formulation is followed almost word for word, although with the usual omissions, by the Dutch, as well as the Danish versions, amplified, of course, with the aristocratic features typical of these nations' balladry. Apparently, they have borrowed the theme from the German. The same refers to the strongly transformed Wendish version. On the other hand, the Moravian and Slovenian versions have nothing in common with the German: in the Moravians there is no mention made of water separating the lovers, instead we see them standing on the banks of the Danube, the girl washing her feet and the young man giving his horse to drink, while a conversation is going on between the two. The girl invites the young man, promising him to burn a candle to show the way. But it is not put out by anyone; the young man drowns in the river. True to say, the girl has him hauled by fishermen, but they are told to catch fish for her; first fish are caught, and the girl says: "It is not the sort of fish I would like to have", with the second hauling the young man's dead body is caught out, at whose sight the girl says: "This is the sort of fish that's my heart loves dearly". That is to say, the whole of the scene shows a word-for-word agreement with the Hungarian ballad entitled "Fair Damsel Katica" (Nos 28/76). Further textual relationships with the Hungarian version are that the young man is afraid of the dark night, for fear of falling into the water; the ballad ends with a double death: the girl has two knives, with the one she digs a grave for her sweetheart, with the other she stabs herself in the heart. In another variant, however, she asks her mother to let her go on a walk outdoors, since she has lost her ring which she would like to recover. The mother wants to hold her back, but the girl escapes—and at this point the ballad bears resemblance to the German. Can it be surmised that the ballad reached the Moravian population from two opposite directions? *Seemann* (1951, No. 66) states that although the German motif of blowing out of the candle is absent in the Slav material, still there are certain motifs to relate them with the German.

The Slovenian version, too, contains only the motifs of drowning and lightening of the candle, while the elements characteristic of the German are missing. Consequently, the peoples neighbouring have retained as much of the plot as has the Hungarian ballad.

We may accept the theory, according to which the Slav versions have been mediated from two source areas. And this circumstance is another proof of the Hungarian ballad having developed independently of the German. Otherwise the Slavs would have received their ballads from the Germans exclusively, and the Hungarians should have borrowed them from the Slavs.

The Italian ballad is similar to the French: the girl is locked up in a tower. But the Italians have preserved the original name of the hero: Leandro. A new trait is included, however, inasmuch as the Italian young man happens to fall asleep at the foot of the tower, and by the time he wakes up, the tower has been set aflame. In a dispair, he commits suicide, and the girl does away with herself. Undoubtedly, the ballad could not have spread from the Italians towards the Eastern European regions (I know only one variant from Piedmont). As to the Polish version, it is an abridged variant of the German (if it belongs at all to the Type under discussion), beginning immediately with the scene in which the girl is looking for her sweetheart; also the motif of asking leave of her mother occurs, but as a whole the plot proper is missing.

The Hungarian ballad is undisputedly old, although the point of time of its origin can be dated to anywhere between the fourteenth and the seventeenth centuries.

Literature: Gulyás 1940: about a lost bella istoria; *Ortutay* 1936–48: international relations; *Seemann* 1951: German, Lithuanian and Slav connections; *Haavio* 1955: detailed documentation of ancient antecedents, the French originates from these, the Finnish follows the Swedish. In regard of the Hungarian, he cannot decide on the basis of the scanty available material if accidental similarities are involved or the Hungarian represents a formulation of the theme older than the German.

38. THE PAGAN KING'S DAUGHTER

92.

Fair Julia, my beautiful daughter,
My tulip that sprang in my flower garden,
Don't you love your serf!
I don't love the serf,
5. I only love the young man,
The handsome young man, my dearest one!
O, the old king went out
And had the young man caught,
He had him locked up in the tower,
10. On the top of the tower.
O, Fair Julia went out,
And the young man caught sight of her:
O, my Julia, my Fair Julia,
My beautiful violet that sprang in the garden,
15. Go to your father,
Fall on your knees before him,
Entreat him with words like these:
Father, my father, old king,
Have the young man removed
20. From the top of the tower;
Don't let him beat by the rain,
Don't let him blown at by the wind,
Don't let him burnt by the sun!
O, Fair Julia went in
25. And falling on her knees before him,
She said, entreating him with words like these:
Father, my father, old king,
Have the young man removed
From the top of the tower,
30. Don't let him beat by the rain,
Don't let him blown at by the wind,
Don't let him burnt by the sun!
O, the old king went out
And had the young man removed
35. From the top of the tower,
Had him taken out into the field,
Right into the middle of the field.
There he had him killed at once,
And had his heart and liver taken out,

40. And sent them to Julia's bower.
   As Fair Julia saw
   That the young man was killed,
   She lowered her head down to the ground
   And surrendered herself to death.

45. As the old king saw
   Her Julia dying:
   O, my Julia, my beautiful daughter,
   My tulip that sprang in my garden,
   Had I foreseen this,

50. Surely I should not have killed him,
   I should have owned him my son instead,
   And my kingdom, and my land
   I should have all endowed to him...

Székelyföld, Kriza = MNGY III, No. 4.

93.

1. The daughter of the pagan king
   Is walking in the street with much grace,
   A handsome young man is keeping her company,
   A handsome young man is keeping her company.

2. As the pagan king beheld them walking,
   He had the young man caught
   And had him taken up to the bulwark of his fortress.
   There he had him blown at by the cold wind,
   There he had him beat by the rain.

3. There went little Lilia,
   Fairly grown fair violet:
   What are you doing there, handsome young man?
   O, I am like an orphan
   Separated from his mate.

4. Little Lilia went home,
   Fairly grown fair violet:
   Father, my king, I would say a word
   If you did not deny it to me:

5. The handsome young man begs you, and I am his tounge,
   Do let him remove from the bulwark of the fortress,
   Don't let him blow at by the cold wind,
   Don't let him beat by the rain.

6. The pagan king turned round,
   And he kicked her daughter
   So that her red skirt was cleft,
   Her red blood spurted out,
   And she died a terrible death on the spot.

7. The bells began to be tolled,
   And the handsome young man heard the chime:
   O, how beautifully the bells are chiming,
   Is it perhaps because of my Fair Lilia?

8. O, if she has died for my sake,
   I shall die for her sake!
   He turned down from the bulwark of the fortress
   And died a terrible death on the spot.

Tordátfalva (Udvarhely county). Female performer, B. Vikár, 1902 = SzNd No. 70 = Ethn. 1915, 309.

Divergences: The other variant published by *Kriza* agrees with the variant from Tordátfalva, with the difference that in it the young man is first cast into a deep dungeon, in which he is "torn by frogs and sucked by snakes". The girl asks her father to have him taken out of the dungeon, where "O, how his lean flesh is torn, O, how his red blood is sucked!" It is only then that the king has him placed on the bulwark of the fortress. The continuation agrees with the published variant. At the end, however, the motif of the grave-flower appears:

   The pagan king had him taken out of the dungeon,
   And he had them placed side by side.
   For the one he ordered to make
   A coffin of white marble,
   For the other he ordered to make
   A coffin of red marble.
   The one he ordered to be buried
   In front of the altar,
   The other he ordered to be buried
   Behind the altar.
   Out of the one's body there sprang
   A white lily of marble,
   Out of the other's body there sprang
   A red lily of marble.
   They grew and grew
   Until they combined in a knot.
   The pagan king walked to them,

432

Wishing to tear them off.
His daughter spoke up, saying:
Father, my father, my dear father,
You did not let us have peace while we were alive,
Do let us in peace now that we are dead!

László Vikár recorded two stanzas of the ballad in 1963 together with a variant of the tune published here, but since the informant was an antitrinitarian priest, there is every reason to think of a possibility of a secondary revival from printed matter.

Dissemination: Udvarhely county (the texts of *Kriza* published *sine loco* are also originating from that county, in all probability). Total: 4 variants.

Textual relationships with other ballads: The deep dungeon inhabited with snakes and frogs is a commonplace known from the the the so-called outlaw ballads, too **(118.)**; "The red skirt was cleft . . ." etc.: **25.**; the grave flower: **9., 10., 28., 37.**; the motif of cutting out of the liver and heart occurs in **6., 20., 25.,** and **57.**

Parallels in languages other than Hungarian:
ENGLISH: *1–5.* Child 269. *6–7.* Greig 90.
DANISH (SWEDISH): *8–63.* DgF. 305 (*ibid.* Jonsson)
GERMAN–DUTCH: *64–74.* D. Vlr. 16 (9 are old recordings from the mid-sixteenth century onwards, 1 being from Gottschee).
ITALIAN: *75.* Pergoli 12. No. 6. *76.* Widter 93. *77.* Bernoni 1875 39 (in prose).
Partial variants:
DANISH: *78–79.* DgF 94.
Dubious: ROMANIAN: *80.* Amzulescu No. 217 (plus 6 variants enumerated).

Only one of the ballads belonging to the type discussed has preserved the central motif of the internationally known theme: the heart of the executed lover is placed on a tray and so furnished to the girl, who dies either because of the sight of it, or because she ate of it. Apparently, at a more advanced stage of development people thought too cruel the original idea to be credible and contented themselves with referring to the tragic fate of the lovers who died in consequence of the social differences separating them. In this form the theme was meaningful enough to express the original idea of love breaking through social barriers. The spread of the ballad is restricted to western Europe and to Hungary. The German summary edition (D. Vlr 16.) states that the motif of the lover's heart offered as a dish to the surviving sweetheart first presented itself as a theme in France, from where it spread to Italy, England, the German areas and Scandinavian territories. In its older form, the theme appears as a tragedy of married spouses (cf. Boccaccio, Novella 9 of the fourth day); a more recent application is the one attached to a father and his daughter (cf. Boccaccio, Novella 1 of the same day). According to German scholars, the latter form is only known in the English (Scottish)-speaking territories (D. Vlr. fails to mention the Hungarian version). At the same time, the other form is allotted by the D. Vlr. exclusively to the French and the Germans. It states further that the Scandinavian ballads contain both forms. An adaptation of the theme is known from the oeuvre of Konrad von Würzburg; on the turn of the thirteenth—fourteenth centuries, it was connected with the name of Brennberger, possibly the Minnesänger. After such preliminaries, let us see what the national versions have to say to us.

The English ballad also speaks about love breaking through social barriers. The father of the girl—or a wandering ghost—discovers his daughter's pregnancy (cf. Var. C: Her petticoat grew short before), and asks her if the child is by a lord or a nobleman at least. Learning that it is by a kitchen boy, he has the young man executed, cuts out his heart and sends it in a golden cup to her daughter. The girl washes it with her tears and dies with the following words: "Since he's died for me, I'll die for him". The King curses his men for not having prevented him from committing the bloody deed.

The Danish version shows in part a closer, in part a more distant relationship with the Hungarian. The king's daughter is picking flower in the garden. His father is looking at her from the windows, and calls her to him: Whom do you pick those flowers to?—To Prince Frydenborg.—Have you not yet cast him out of your mind? He has him brought up from the prison, and orders him to be tied to a tree. Then he has him cut down as peasants cut the cattle, has him roasted on spit as peasants have the fish, has his heart take out and serve up to his daughter. "What a terrible dish this is!" "This is the heart of Prince Frydenborg." "Then this is my last supper. Bring wine in a silver jug!" In three variants she drinks poison and dies. The king receiving tidings, says: "Had I known they loved each other so much, I should not have done that!" They are buried side by side, and white and blue lilies grow out of their bodies. In this instance there is no social obstacle involved, but the lover is first cast into the dungeon, the king sees his daughter pick flowers—in the Hungarian ballad he sees her walking with the young man—and in the end the king repents his deed, which is in agreement with the Hungarian, and so are the flowers in one of the Hungarian variants. DgF 94 goes even further: the characters are husband and wife, and in the end the wife has her lover revived by the aid of the water of life, the young man takes vengeance on the husband by cutting off his head, after which there is no obstacle to the lovers' union. Of course, this version has nothing to do with the Hungarian ballad. The Dutch formulation also carries us away from the Hungarian: the wife of a man makes a wreath for a knight. She is betrayed to the husband, who has the knight thrown into prison. He spends seven miserable years in the prison, and his hair and beard become white; the woman rides over to him and assures him of her love and faithfulness. The scene is repeated when the knight is being taken to the gallows. His heart is cut out and is served, peppered, to the woman. "What dish has it been? It did taste me good!" Learning the truth, she asks for wine and dies. Thus neither the Dutch ballad's plot is based on social difference. In the German version we do not know by whom the young man was imprisoned after he had spent a night with his sweetheart. Kept for three years in prison, he is finally placed on a table and cut up as a fish; they take out his heart—sometimes cut it to pieces—and serve it to the woman. As she learns what she has eaten, she asks for wine and her heart breaks with the first drop of wine.

Also the Italian version speaks about a king who keeps his daughter under strict surveillance. She is seen to the school by twelve servants, with one of whom she falls in love. His fellows tell about it to the king. He is cast into prison and kept there without anything to eat or drink. On the third day he is killed, his heart taken out and served to his sweetheart. "Frontida, will you accept this act of kindness! This is the heart of Giasmond." A fierce debate ensues between the father and the daughter. She poisons herself and dies. The names are not unlike those in the Boccaccian story.

General opinion holds that the ballad can be reduced to the Boccaccian novella. (This is seemingly corroborated by the identical names in the Italian ballad.) In connection with the Hungarian ballad literary historians spread the opinion that it did not originate directly from *Boccaccio* but indirectly, through the mediation of *György Enyedi's* 'bella istoria', entitled Guiscardus and Guismonda (1577). This opinion is supported by the fact that *Enyedi* was an antitrinitarian bishop of Transylvania from 1592 onward, and the ballad was also recorded in Transylvania. But an international survey of the ballad type reveals some difficulties of these suppositions. First of all, both the Italian original and the Hungarian adaptation of the story consist of very long texts in prose or verse, focussed around an academic debate about the condemnation of social antagonisms and the assertion of the principle of equal rights to love. The Hungarian verse was first published in 1574, when it comprised 242 lines, the second time it was published in 310 lines in 1582. As against this, the ballads are characterized by briefness of formulation, this story presented in verse, having no textual relationships with either the short story or the romance. (Also their rhythmic patterns are different: the 'bella istoria' is written in eleven-syllable lines while the ballad constructs in lines of eight syllables.) Therefore it is out of question that the ballad should be a variant abridged by omissions of the romance; it is a completely new formulation of the theme. Can it reasonably be imagined that the various peoples should have made excerpts of literary compositions in so uniform a way? On the basis of names, such a thing might be thought of in connection with the Italian ballad, but a supposed spread of the same cannot solve the question either. The nearest neighbouring people, the German, does not even mention the name of the character responsible for the execution of the young man, the Dutch ballad knows about a husband and a wife, and there is no common trait in the formulation of the texts of the two nations. In the same way, different is the English version, too, having the theme of pregnancy in the centre of the epic plot. And the Hungarian shows further deviation with the young man pining away in the tower and the girl pleading for mercy on his behalf. Anyway, it is the Hungarian version that proceeds farthest from the Boccaccian story. At the same time, the same Hungarian ballad shows a certain degree of affinity with the Danish ballad, at least the figure of the repenting king and the motif of the grave-flowers seem to suggest so, while the formula "You have died for me, And I shall die for you" links the ballad to the similar commonplace of the English version. *Archer Taylor* (1964) refers to "mediaeval short stories", which also *Child* mentioned with reference to *Boccaccio*, as ones that might serve as starting points for the English ballad. And we cannot reject the idea, according to which the theme had found its origin in the French *antecedents* of *Boccaccio*, perhaps in times before or parallel with the Italian elaboration of the story. The motif of cutting out of the lover's heart and serving it as a dish to the woman is so old as to be traceable back to a twelfth-century adaptation of the theme of Tristan, in which Isolde sings a chanson about a husband who treats his wife's lover much in the same way. Even later French elaborations follow in the wake of this prototype, as stated by D. Vlr. In the notes of the same place in D. Vlr. (I, 169) mention is made of the Hungarian version as of one that may have been shaped after the Provençal model.

Even though we do not know about the existence of a *ballad* framed out of the story in the French areas, the area of dissemination does not fail this time either to support such a consideration, the more so since the Hungarian ballad this while again seems to have closest connections with the English and the Danish versions, and least of all with the German. Also, the "Pagan" king comes up in the character of a "Heathen King" or a "Heathen Prince" in English and Danish ballads (*Child* 104). ans what is more, DgF 71 speaks about the hero marrying just the daughter of the heathen king—hedens konge datter—another commonplace of western balladry that connects the Hungarian version with the West and separates it from the Boccaccian novella. But apart from all this, the *Boccaccio* story is abounding in detailed descriptions—think of the meetings of the two lovers, the incidental discovery of the father, the wife's lengthy tirade about the lover's descent and the rights of carnal love—that is to say, it is so elaborately presented that it precludes almost every possibility of its having served as a model to a ballad, a genre that is typically based on "one single theme", in sharp contrast to the over-minuteously detailed literary composition. Neither does the Italian ballad show any closer resemblance to the Boccaccian story—and the names they have in common can be well explained by a process of secondary adaptation through the agency of broadside literature.

But whether or not the ballads of the various peoples had been originating from *Boccaccio,* or from a French romance contemporaneous with or earlier than the Boccaccian novella, in the last analysis it is beyond doubt that there must have existed a common ballad "ancestor" which had fully revaluated the theme in the true spirit of the new genre, making use of its internationally recognized clichés. In either case, the Hungarian ballad is linked with the European formulation of the theme, and it can by no means be derived from the '*bella istoria*' composed by *Enyedi* at a relatively late period, for if we were to accept the latter contingency, we could not account for the similarities existing between the Hungarian ballad and its western counterparts.

The motif of the heart cut out and served as a meal is missing from the Romanian ballad as well as from the Hungarian variants, and without this we cannot establish a connection between the Romanian and the western (European and Hungarian) ballad themes. The sire imprisons his daughter's lover or wife because he has eloped his daughter, or because he falls victim to court intrigues of jealous rivals, who accuse him of cherishing usurping ambitions. The girl curses her father, or commits suicide at the sight of her lover's dead body. Trees grow out of their graves to unite in a lovers' knot.

Literature: Gragger 1923: refers to Enyedi and Brennberger; D. Vlr. 16 1953 *(J. Meier); Ortutay* 1936–48: refers to *Boccaccio* and *Child*; Taylor 1964.

39. THE WIFE KICKED TO DEATH

94.

It is seven years and three full days
That we have been together, that we have been together,
Yet we have not eaten a bit of bread together,
Yet we have not drunk a glass of water together.
5. My God, my God, what is the reason of it,
What is the reason of it, brave János Egri?
You know it quite well, you know it quite well, Zsófika Kálnoki,
The reason is that I have never loved you,
Nor will I ever love you.
10. Then he kicked her, than he kicked her,
And he kicked her right from the table to the door,
He kicked her right from the table to the door.
Then Zsófika Kálnoki spoke up, saying:
Stop it, stop it at last, brave János Egri!
15. On my left side the sun has shone in,
On my right side my blood has spilled out.
Then brave János Egri spoke up, saying:
Hey, my foot-page, my dear foot-page, my first foot-page,
Lift her up and put her into her bed!
20 My foot-page, my dear foot-page, my first foot-page,
Let us go out shooting hare, shooting hare, and hunting.
Then Zsófika Kálnoki spoke up, saying:
My foot-page, my dear foot-page, my little foot-page,
Bring out, bring out my mournful coach!
25. Harness, harness my fastest horses to it!
The coach for the fire, the horses for the dogs,
Drive, drive on as fast as you can,
To my dear mother's place, to Mistress Pál Kálnoki!
Good morning, good morning, my dearest heart, mother!
30. Welcome, child, my dearest heart, my daughter!
I have not come to have a good time, but I have come to die.
Hey, my foot-page, my dear foot-page, my first foot-page:
Climb this tree and see if you can see a light!
I cannot see any light, except the one at the noble Lady's house.
35. Then come along, come along to my mother-in-law's house!
Good evening, good evening, dear mother-in-law!
Welcome, my son, my dear son-in-law!
How did you, how did you leave my daughter?
I left her, I left her in good health.

40. Upon this, she went in her little bower,
    Into her private chamber,
    And cut a slice of bread from her table,
    And poured out a glass of water from her jug:
    Eat that, my son, my dear son-in-law
    As if it were my daughter's flesh,
    Drink that, my son, my dear son-in-law
    As if it were my daughter's blood!

Szabéd (Maros-Torda county). Ferenc Kanyaró = Ortutay 1955. No. 16.

Cf. *Leader* 181.

Neither variants nor tune of the ballad are known to be extant. The picture that shows the curious huge wound on the woman's waist has come up in other ballads from Moldavia as a secondary development in them; in any case, the occurrence of the motif there indicates that the ballad had been widespread in former times. A text recorded at Klézse is a mixture of three ballads, beginning with the story of The Bride Given in Marriage to Poland **(14.),** then turning into the narrative of The Haughty Wife **(66.),** finally it changes over to the formulation of The Brigand's Wife **(20.).** From the point of view of the present discussion, it is interesting that the description of the wife-beating scene of this ballad from Klézse includes the lines referring to the wound on the woman's waist:

Then he took his Tartar's scourge
And started to lash her across her slender waist.
Enough of that, enough, enough, my dear husband!
The sun has shone into one of my sides,
The moonlight has shone out of the other!

Another variant of the same Moldavian text describes the scene in the following manner:

Your cheeks were like two beautiful peonies,
Now they are like two pale cloths...
. . .
Out of my right side the sunlight has shone out,
Into my left side the moonlight has shone in.

Textual relationships with other ballads:
The formula "seven years and three days" occurs in Types **33** and **43;** the urging of the coachman
in **2, 10, 13** and **21.**
Parallels in languages other than Hungarian:
FRENCH: *1. Bladé* II, 51. *2. Delzangles* 71.
Partial variants:
PORTUGUESE: *3–5. Braga* 42, 209–211 (209 = *Geibel–Schack* No. 18).
CROAT: *6. Kuhač* 649 (?).
SPANISH: *7–8. Catalan* III, 110; III/21, Nos 26 and 27. (*Goyri* and *Menéndez–Pidál* III, Note 26, p. 110, refers to a Bosnian Sefardi variant.)

The peculiar picture exaggerating the size of the wounds on the broken waist of the woman offers points of approach for comparison (the sunlight and the moonlight shining in and out, respectively). In a Portuguese ballad of a different plot the size of the wounds is indicated in a similar manner, although with a different connotation, when describing the corpse of the hero that fell in an action: "In one of his wounds the sun was seen, in the other the moon, and in the third one a beautiful dice." (3.) "Through one of them the sun went in, through the other the moon, while through the smallest one an eagle flew in." (4.) "Through one of them the sun went in, through the other the moon, while through the smallest one a royal eagle flew in with spread wings, without getting blood on him." (5.) Thus, instead of the stylized picture of the opening between the ribs we have the excessive exaggeration of the size of the wound. Between the Portuguese formulas and the Hungarian texts a link is provided by a French fragment with a plot faintly reminiscent of the Hungarian ballad, and the formula too can be found in it in hazy outlines. In a text from Gascony three cavaliers make remarks about favours they claim to have received from a married wife. The husband of the woman overhears them and beats her so severely that "On one side the rib was broken, and on the other her daughter's head." (That is to say, she was pregnant.) Before she dies, she makes her will: her husband shall be hanged, her mother burnt to death and the ashes of her body scattered from the beautiful bridge in Lyons. As the mother's role cannot be discerned from the obscure text, obviously the full story has not been preserved in it. In a text from Auvergne we find it even vaguer (2.): At the first blow he gave her, three of her ribs broke, at the second, she fell ill. And here we have more about the hostile *mother-in-law,* yet not enough for us to be able to make out her real function in the story. Although it is enigmatic, and therefore fragmentary, the collector describes it as a popular song of drovers and workmen. In northern France, its true home, the full form of the ballad must have existed once, and it must have been closer to the Hungarian. Thus what we actually have at hand is the last fragment of a song that used to be widespread in its original, complete form. The surviving formula being the most impressing portion of the text may well have started a separate life of its own, and so it had been adapted by the Csángós in a quite different context; the same happened to it among the Portuguese. The process of fading had been a matter of course with the French; the picture has assumed a semi-realistic meaning also in the Hungarian ballad: "On one of my sides the sun shone in, and on my right side *my blood has run out."* The transformation of the original image has been fully carried out with the French, under the pressure of an ever more prevailing rationalistic trend.

In the Croat song, Asagana is walking with his wife who is pregnant, and beholds the lovely daughter of Demir. He wants to go over to her, which brings about a quarrel between the husband and his wife; he kicks her so brutally at the heart that her blood starts to flow, and she gives birth to a still-born son. Her mother tends her, and before the wife dies she says what she will leave to her mother, sister, brother, husband and rival. Four years after her death the husband marries the beautiful girl.

Here again we have , perhaps, the common nucleus in the framework of a different story, in which even the characteristic description of the wounds have

439

completely disappeared. At the same time, there is an agreement with the Hungarian ballad in that the wife is kicked to death, while the scene of the dying woman telling her last will reminds us of the French. The woman's mother also in this text takes sides with her daughter, in a sharp contrast with the hostile mother-in-law figuring in the French fragment.

The songs of the two nations living side by side in the territory of prewar Hungary have preserved various elements of the old French–Portuguese ballads; the Hungarian versions have maintained a larger number of survivals which are more characteristic at the same time than the elements preserved by the scanty Croatian material. As the Croat version belongs to the type here discussed, we have to suppose that it came about under the influence of the Hungarian version, incorporating further elements into the story. (In the French, the woman's alleged perfidy gave rise to the tragedy, in the Hungarian the woman's complaint about her husband's unkindness, while in the Croat version the husband casts his eyes on another woman.) Both the French and the Hungarian had exposed the traditional story at a stage of final erosion, before it was utterly extinct. It belongs to the oldest French borrowings in Hungarian balladry.

40. THE BROTHER PURSUING HIS SISTER'S BETROTHED

95.

My husband, my husband, my dear goodman,
I have served you for a year,
For a year and a half.
Will you give me what you had promised to give;
5. Your beautiful daughter Kata Bíró!
Let's go away, my dear betrothed,
For your father has promised you to me.
They arrive in a big forest.
Sit down, sit down, my dear betrothed,
10. Look in my head for a little while!
She was sitting, she was sitting, and she looked his head,
He went asleep in her lap.
Kata Bító looked in the direction where her home stood.
Aye, her brave brother is coming.
15. Her brave brother Mózes Bíró.
Get up, get up, my dear betrothed,
For my brother is coming there.
But he did not wake up, he did not wake up.
Her brave brother arrived there,
20. Her brave brother Mózes Bíró.
He drew out his bright sword
And cut the lover's white neck.
Let's go, my dear sister.
Wait a minute, wait a minute, my dear brother!
25. Let me pick up his white shirt,
Let me wipe up his red blood!
Maybe, you are sorry for him, my dear sister!?
No, no, I am not sorry for him, my brave brother,
No, no, but I am sorry for his white shirt,
30. Which is foaming with blood so red.
She picked his shirt and wiped up his blood.
They are going, they are going towards their home.
I am very thirsty, my brave brother!
Well, come on, my dear sister,
35. I know a river water flowing nearby.
I don't want to go to the river,
For I know a well of stone nearby.
She went over to the well of stone.
There she found a beautiful green twig.

40. She hanged her head-dress on it:
    If he died for me, it is not pity for me either!
    And she sank into the well.
    Her brave brother was waiting for her to return,
    Waiting for her, but she did not come back.
45. He went over to the well of stone,
    And there he saw her head-dress hanging.
    My God, my God,
    I have perished two souls,
    And the third will be mine.
50. He drew out his bright sword
    And lent on it.

Faragó 1957 = Faragó 1965, 174.

The tune of the ballad was not noted down. No variant of the ballad is known to be extant.

    Textual relationships with other ballads: "Searching in the head" occurs in the ballad of The Enticed Wife (**3.**), The Enticed Wife Forsaking her Child (**5.**) and The Wife Longing to Go Home (**41.**). The closing motif agrees with the solutions of The Disgraced Girl (**10.**), The Cruel Mother-in-Law (**28.**). Serving for the hand of the master's daughter also comes up in **55.**
    Parallels in languages other than Hungarian:
ENGLISH: *1–6. Child* 7. *7–47. Bronson* 7.
DANISH (SWEDISH): *48–74.* DgF 82. (ibid. *Jonsson*).
GERMAN: *75.* D. Vlr. 44.
ROMANIAN: *76. Amzulescu* 320. (13 variants enumerated).

    The nucleus of the theme, namely that the brother is chasing the girl and her sweetheart—in some cases as many as seven brothers are involved—is remarkably common in the West, supplying the basis for such much discussed ballads as are the English "Earl Brand" and the Danish "Ribold og Guldborg". The story, however, is different inasmuch as in the western ballads the lover kills all the girl's brothers, while he himself is wounded to death. The girl dies too. The German version maintains a closer relationship with the Hungarian in some other respect: the bridegroom kills the three brothers who are out to take them, whereupon the girl announces that she does not love him so much after what has happened. Then the bridegroom stabs her to death and he himself drives his sword into his body. The Hungarian version resembles only in its outlines the western ballads, and seems to be an amalgamation of several commonplaces, having a different ending than those known from the foreign parallels. In any case, it is built up from western elements, although we cannot establish a direct connection between the Hungarian and the western forms on the basis of this single survival whose text fails to provide any fix point of orientation.

442

It is likely that either the extant version or some lost variants thereof had supplied an example for the Romanian ballad mentioned among the parallels. A girl escapes with her lover and is very much frightened by the thought that her brothers might set out to chase them. The brothers, indeed, reach them and pass sentence on the girl. Nevertheless, the youngest brother tries to appease his elder brothers: the girls lot is similar to that of the apples, which are hanging on the branch while they are little but fall down as soon as they grow big. With this the story ends. Thus the conflict in the plot has been eliminated.

41. THE WIFE LONGING TO GO HOME

96.

Tempo giusto ♩ = 85

1. Ё - hĕn gyün, ё - hĕn gyün Két bá - na - tos fī - jú.

Is - te - nĕm, te - rem-tőm, Gyógyíts mёg en - gё - met!

1. There are coming, there are coming
Two sad young men.
My Lord, my Creator,
Heal me!

2. So that I may erect
A splendid church,
So that I may engage
Spiritual teachers in it.

3. In one (of the windows)
Fair Ilona Horvát is weeping,
In the other, on his elbow,
The pagan Turkish emperor is leaning.

4. Fair Ilona Horvát,
Why are you weeping?
Don't you love me,
Don't you love me?

5. I am not weeping
Because I don't love you,
But I have just thought of
My dear mother who gave me birth, (to the 3rd section)
And my dear Hungarian country.

6. My coachman, my coachman,
Put the horses to the coach,
Turn the shaft-bar
Of my gilt coach.

7. Take her
To little Hungary,
To her father's court,
To her mother's home!

444

8. Good evening, good evening,
   My dear mother who gave me birth!
   If only for this one night
   You could afford to give me lodging!

9. That I cannot afford to give,
   That I cannot afford to give,
   Because I am waiting for guests to come,
   Because I am waiting for guests to come.

10. And who is going to be
    Your welcome guest?
    Fair Ilona Horvát
    And the pagan Turkish emperor.

11. But see, then, I am
    Your welcome guest!
    But see, then, I am
    Your welcome guest!

12. And I will not believe it,
    Before I see him in front of me,
    Before I see him in front of me,
    The pagan Turkish emperor!

13. Upon this word
    The pagan Turkish emperor sprang forth.
    Fair Ilona Horvát
    Died a terrible death at once.

14. Her silver and her gold
    She left to her father,
    Her diamond and her ruby
    She left to her mother.

15. Her six horses fed on oats
    She left to her coachman,
    Her wedded spouse
    She left to the devil.

The informant learned the ballad while a small girl, from her father. The pagan Turkish emperor was, in point of fact, the devil himself. Therefore he was able to appear all of a sudden. Once he asked Ilona "to look in his head". Then Ilona saw that he had horns, that is to say, that he was the devil, therefore she began to weep. (Cf. Stanza 3.)
Bajna (Esztergom county), 87-year-old female informant. 1955, Schnöller.

The story is so obscure and fragmentary that it cannot be put to use for comparative purposes. The testament in the end of the ballad is a commonplace known all over Europe. (Cf. János Who Was Poisoned, **60.** and the related ballads.) The motif of the daughter whom the mother fails to recognize comes up rather frequently in ballads. The motif of "searching in the head" is known from the Type of "The Enticed Young Wife". The "devil" occurs in several ballads in which obscure elements cannot meet a plausible explanation. (Cf. The Girl Danced to Death, The Bride Dragged to Death.) Stanzas 3 and 4 = Stanzas 2 and 3 of No. 11/36, even the name is identical! In the case of Type 11, however, the figuring of the wife would seem to be inconsistent, because all the other texts speak about a suitor-bridegroom rejected by the bride. It is not impossible that the motif got into Type 11 from this ballad.

In any case, the ballad seems to be a survival of some mediaeval European ballad theme. In its actual form it is threadbare and confused beyond recognition.

42. THE MOTHER KIDNAPPED BY THE SON

97.

Once, when there was a war, people were torn apart from one another, and the little baby was left in the cradle. The Turks took pity on the pretty creature and took it away with them. The mother also got there and was made to work as a charwoman. When the young man married, he did not know that he had his own mother in his house. She was nursing her grandson, lulling the following song to him:

Rubato, parlando

1. Csi - ja   bu - ja   ba - ba, Böl - cső - be - li   ba - ba!

Ne-kem is volt   o - lyan Böl - cső - be - li   ba - bám.

2. De el - vit - ték a tö - rö - kök,   Mi - kor Bé - cset bir - ták.

Most is   meg-is - mer - ném, Hogy-ha meg - lát - hat - nám.

3. Két fe - ke - te sze - mölcs Két szép fe - hér kar - ján.

Most is   meg - is - mer - ném, Hogyha meg- lát - hat - nám.

1. Rock-a-bye, hush-hush,
   Rock-a-bye, baby in the cradle,
   I used to have
   Such a baby in the cradle.

2. But he had been taken by the Turks
   When they were lording it over Vienna.
   Even now I could recognize him
   If I saw him.

3. Two black warts
   Were on his two white arms.
   I should recognize him
   If I saw him.

This song was overheard by her son. He turned up his sleeves, and lo, there were the two warts on his arms.

4. Hal-lod   e - te, ö - reg,   U - gyan mit du - dol - gatsz?
   Nem   dú - dol - ga - tok   én,   Gye - re - ket   rin - ga - tok.

4. I say, old woman,
   What song are you humming there?
   I am not humming a song,
   But I am lulling-rocking a child.

5. Rock-a-bye, hush-hush,
   Rock-a-bye, baby in the cradle,
   I also used to have
   Such a baby in the cradle.

6. But he had been taken by the Turks
   When they were lording it over Vienna.
   Even now I could recognize him
   If I saw him.

7. Two black warts
   Were on his two white arms.
   I should recognize him
   If I saw him.

Then the son went over to her, turned up both sleeves of his shirt. Then they recognized each other, and from that time on she was not kept as a nurse in the house. They were crying with joy.

Cered (Nógrád county), 70-year-old female informant Mistress Andor Szabó. 1956 = AP 1522/b.

98.

Long-long ago, when the Turks were ruling the major part of Hungary, the following story took place.

As they ransacked the towns and the castles, they carried away all people they could lay hold on, men, women and children alike, far-far away, to the shore of the sea.

448

With the rest of the prisoners, a small child got into the household of a great Turkish lord. As he grew up, he rose high in the ranks of the world and became a pasha.

As a child was born to him, a nurse was needed. A fatigued old woman happened to walk there. Well, he took her to the household as a nurse. But the pasha told her that he would break her body in a mortar is she failed to tend the child carefully, protecting it even from the blowing wind.

The poor woman nursed the child as if it had been her own son.

On one day, the little child grew sick, and indeed there must have been something the matter with it, for it was always crying.

What can ail this little innocent creature?—The old woman thought to herself musingly. If the pasha happens to hear it crying, what comes on me? Don't you cry, baby...Alas, what am I to do with you? ...Thus the old woman burst out. Then she began to sing, overcome with sorrow:

> Rock-a-bye, hush-hush,
> You beautiful Turkish child!
> I also used to have
> A beautiful little child.
>
> But he was taken by the Turks
> When they ransacked the castle
> At a beautiful crimson dawn,
> At day-break.
>
> But even now I should recognize him,
> Should he stand in front of me.
> I should tell him by the white skin of his arms,
> By the white warts on his arms.

The noise of her crying-weeping was heard by the wife of the pasha. She entered her husband's room, saying: Do you hear, my husband, do you hear, what that captive woman is saying?

Then she told him what the old woman was lulling over the small child to rock him to sleep.

Well, to cut short the story, the pasha showed his left arm to the nurse to see if she can notice anything on it.

It appeared that the pasha was the son of the poor old woman. This was how the captive woman found her son whom she had lost many years before.

Kiskundorozsma (Csongrád county) = Nyr VIII. 1879, 180–82.

99.

There was once a woman who had a son and a daughter. Her daughter was called Ilona, her son was called Albert. She branded them both. Then the Turks carried away Albert as well as Ilona. They were raised in a foreign country. They did not know that they were sister and brother, and they were married to each other. Later on, Albert invaded Great Hungary in order to rape people. And he raped an old woman who was his own mother. But he did not know that she was his own mother, nor did the old woman know that he was her son. As he took her mother, tied her to his horse and so he tormented her. The old woman asked him not to tie her to the horse but let her walk free; she begged the Turk not to torment her so cruelly, but the Turk replied:

1. Swim in the same blood in which my horse swims,
   Eat the same hay which my horse eats,
   Drink the same water which my horse drinks!

As they arrived at home, the Turk's wife asked whom he had brought? He answered that he could not find anybody except an old woman.—Spare her life, she may well do as a nurse to our child! She was ordered to nurse the child. So they lived until the old woman happened to see the Turk and his wife undressed: she saw the marks she had branded on them... The old woman grew very sad; she knew that they both were her children; and she was very sad to learn that she had been tormented by her own son. Then the old woman began to sing:

2. Rock-a-bye, hush-hush, you beautiful Turkish child,
   My own son's handsome son, my own daughter's offspring,
   My own daughter's offspring, my own grandson!

3. It is nine years since they were robbed by the Turks,
   After nine years, I myself was robbed,
   After nine years I myself was robbed.

4. The Turks carried away my son Albert,
   My son Albert and my daughter Ilona,
   Then I was carried away, tied to a horse!

5. Swim the same blood which my horse swims,
   Eat the same hay which my horse eats,
   Drink the same water which my horse drinks!

A maid-servant overheard her and called the Turk. Then also the Turk overheard her song... The Turk thus learned that the woman was his own mother! But he still made a try, saying: Shall I believe that the child is your grandson? Then the old woman told him:

Take off your shirt and look at the warts!

They took a look at the warts on the wife and on the husband alike, and lo, they were quite the same! Then the Turk embraced his mother, took her into his room and treated her as her own, dear mother afterwards...

Deszk (Torontál county) = Kálmány 1881–1891 III, 198.

100.

The son of a woman was robbed by the Turks. He was carried to Turkey. The mother went after him, she wandered from village to village in search of her son. At last she got to Turkey. There she served as a nurse in the house of a rich Turk. When she was rocking the Turk's son to sleep, she always sang the same song:

Rock-a-bye, hush-hush, you little Turkish child,
I also used to have such a beautiful Hungarian little child.
But when the Turks occupied the town,
They carried away my little Hungarian son together with his cradle.
Even now I should recognize him, if he stood in front of me,
Even now I should recognize him, if he stood in front of me:
On his right shoulder and on his right thigh
There are moles of the size of a plum-stone,
On his left shoulder and on his left thigh
There are moles of the form of an apricot-stone.

One day as she was singing, the Turk overheard her song. He entered the door, the same Turk, asking her: Recite your song once more, mother! Then she began to sing, crying:
Rock-a-bye, hush-hush, you little Turkish child... As she finished singing, the Turk said to her: Should you recognize it, mother, if you were allowed to see it? ... The young man undressed, saying: I am the Hungarian child that used to be taken prisoner! Then they embraced each other, and he gave order to the whole of the family to honour the old woman not as a nurse but as his own dear mother... By the time the old woman found her son he had become a great lord... God led the mother to the place because she loved her son so dearly that she went after him, wandering from village to village, from town to town...
Tornya (Torontál county) = Kálmány 1954, 143.

101.

Well, it so happened that once upon a day the dog-headed Tartars came over the Tisza. But sooner than they had got out of the river they started to shout: Kata, Panna, Roza! The dog-headed Tartars have gone away. Then they caught all they were able to reach, and they took away those they were able to catch. They shouted in through the windows as well: Come out, Kata, Panna! The dog-headed Tartars have gone away! A brother and a sister tried to hide, digging themselves in the dunghill. Yet they were discovered and carried away by the dog-headed Tartars. They were living as captives, but they did not recognize each other. After a while they got married to each other. Then they returned home to their mother's place, but by that time they had had their small baby. The newly married couple went into the kitchen to cook a dish of dumplings, while their mother was singing:

Daughter of my daughter, son of my son:
Son of my son, daughter of my daughter,
My own grandson.

The young ones came in and asked: Mother, why did you sing that song?—Well, I am afraid to tell you, for fear of you parting with each other, perhaps. Yet she told them in the end: This has been brought on you by the dog-headed Tartars. You are my son and my daughter.—Hearing this, they looked at each other, frightened to death.—Well, you must put up with what had taken place, since you were in so great danger that you could not know you were brother and sister. And you have been away for such a long time.—Therefore the mother did not want to tell them why she was singing her song.

Tápé (Csongrád county). 57-year-old female performer. Imre Katona, 1943.

Divergences: A fragment of six lines (*Kálmány* 1891, 197) has preserved the song about the "two little orphan boys" only. Another fragment recorded after 1891 gives more information about the mother's *only* child who had a white wart on his arm. "Finally it appeared that he was the son of the captive woman." (Unknown provenience, *Kálmány* 1954 3A/2). According to a data recorded by *Kálmány* after 1891 at Békéssámson, the woman was carried away together with other prisoners and made later a nurse. She recalls memories of her own little one, singing: On his left hand and foot there were moles of the form of an apricot-stone. The Turk asks her why she is weeping. "I am crying for my son who had been thrown into the ditch." The Turk sends people to find the child and restores him to the mother. The latest-recorded variant is completely eroded. (*Katona* and *Tripolyszky,* Zenta.) The son had a warp on his breast. The mother is looking for him but cannot find him. On a day Turks are marching by, and a Turkish officer asks the woman for a cup of water. While drinking, he opens his shirt and his mother recognizes him by the black wart. The son does not believe her and goes away. Later on, when he is dying, it occurs to him that the woman might have been his mother indeed.

Earliest provenience: 1879.
Dissemination: Counties Csongrád, Csanád, Torontál and Békés, that is the area that used to receive populations emigrating from Szeged, and there is an additional data from the environment of Balassagyarmat (Nógrád county). Total: 9.
Textual relationships with other ballads: Relatives failing to recognize each other learn the factual reality from a song: **17.** and **22.**
Tune: Only the variant from Cered has been recorded with a tune.
Parallels in languages other than Hungarian:
SPANISH: *1. Wolf* and *Hofmann* No. 130. *2–3. Menéndez* and *Pidal* 1885, 122–24, Nos 19 and 20.
PORTUGUESE: *4–7. Braga* II, 128, 131, 136 and 144. *8. Geibel* and *Schack,* 334.
CATALAN: *9–10. Amades* 2324 and 3028. *11. Wolf* 75 (partial variant).
MORAVIAN: *12–17. Sirovátka* 1963. *18–25. Rychnová* 1–6 and B1–2.
UKRAINIAN: *26–30. Golovatsky* I, 42, Nos 4 and 44, No. 5, III/I, 15, No. 2, and 22, No. 10, 23, No. 11. *31. Kolberg* 1882–1889 II, 225, No. 416.
RUSSIAN: *32–44. Putilov* and *Dobrovolsky* 24–38.
POLISH: *45. Czernik* 71.
SOUTHERN SLAV: *46.* HNP VI, No. 30. *47. Vuk* 1966, No. 144.
MACEDONIAN: *48. Vasiljević* II, No. 326.
BULGARIAN: *49. Stoilov* 30. *50–51.* A–V 148 and 161. *52–53. Arnaudov* 1913 59A–B. *54. Stoin* 1939, No. 126. *55. Verković* 141. *56. Miladinovi* 110. *57–58. Shapkarev* 301 and 319. *59.* SbNU X, 70,

452

No. 1. *60–61. Ivanov* 1936, No. 84. *62. Idem* 1949, No. 128. *63.* SbNU 26, No. 35. *64.* Izv. Etn Mus. III,
49. *65. Burmov* 109. *66.* SbNU 42, *Kepov* 221–22. *67. Stoin* 1931, No. 161 (partial variant).

Indirectly related variants:
ENGLISH: *68–70.* Child 62. *78–84.* Bronson 62.
DANISH: *85–163.* DgF 258.
GERMAN–DUTCH: *164–168.* D. Vlr. 74.

Of the nine Hungarian texts, two speak about a case of incest; one fragment
mentions two brothers without telling anything about their story; six fragments
refer to one son only, and one of them refers to a baby thrown into the ditch at the
capture of the town which was subsequently carried away by the Turk who, however,
was not son to the mother; this latter fragment is indoubtedly an eroded variant.
With this left out of consideration, we have five sound stories in which son and
mother are the main characters, two stories with a marriage plot, and a fragment
about two brothers. As a matter of course, points of quantity in themselves cannot
decide the question of origin: rare motifs preserved in a few texts may be older and
closer to the original; at the same time, the numerical excess may be indicative of a
general form, in relation of which a rarer trait is resulting from subsequent
insertion. What is more important: incestuous marriage between sister and brother
seems to be meaningless to the singers: in the first published text, which is the
completest, it has no implication whatever for the psychological dénouement of the
plot; the point of the story concerns the reunion of mother and child. The performer
of the variant recorded from Tápé seems to be conscious of the "vicious" nature of
the story—and this is some rational, modern colouring in the narrative of a woman
who has already broken with the original naive approach to the tradition, and who
tries to carry to the end the train of thought that used to be irrelevant to singers of
former times spelled only by the plot—but since she does not see the fact
consequential for the solution of the plot, she chooses to leave it as it is, saying:
"Well, you have to put up with it." Further, it is conspicuous that the sister-wife has
no role at all in the run of the story: it is the son that speaks to his mother about the
fact of recognition in this tale, as well as in the other legends of this kind. All this
points to the circumstance that the motif of incest is a secondary development, an
inorganic insertion in the body of this ballad.

It is worth-while to examine the texts of the neighbouring language areas
from this point of view. Among the Moravians only one ballad survives which is
performed throughout as a singing piece (*12.*), the rest of their stories are prose
narratives with inserts of verse, similar to the Hungarian version; in some instances
only the inserted song survives in the form of a lullaby (*13–17.*). As to their content,
they are rather uniform. The Turks kidnap a young cattle-herd, the only son of a
widow. The woman looks in vain for her child. In some years, also the widow is
carried away by the Turks (*12.*). She is mostly taken prisoner by her own son (*18.,
19.* and *21.*) or in other cases she follows the Turkish army on her own accord (*20.,
24–25.*), and offers her services as a nurse to the Turk, that is her son. She is singing a
lullaby, in which she calls the little child her grandson, and relates the story of her
imprisonment. Upon the query of the Turk, she tells that she had recognized him by
a wart (mole) on his arm (shoulder or side). The janissary gladly embraces his
mother.

453

No marriage of a sister and a brother occurs in the Moravian stories, and the partial agreements supply sufficient evidence of the two versions, that is the Moravian and the Hungarian, being closely related with each other. (Even the name of the son Albert is identical in *24*. and *25*.) On the basis of the agreements between the ballads of the two neighbour nations it can be surmised that the conflict between mother and son is the original nucleus of the story.

A similar story is current among the Russians, Ukrainians and the Polish, also without the motif of incest involved. Both the Cis- and Trans-Carpatian Ukrainians' texts show a number of interesting features, some of which remind us of the Hungarian version. People are taken by the Tartars. The latter start to share the prey.

A girl gets in the possession of a young man, while the mother-in-law in that of her son-in-law. He dragged the wife tied to his horse. The horse ran through thorn and briar, the woman's feet were bleeding, a black raven flew there to drink up the blood. The Tartar carries her home to serve as a prisoner to his wife. He orders her to do three kinds of work: to guard the herd with her eyes, to spin with her hands and to rock the cradle with her feet. She is singing a cradle-song: Hush-hush, little Tartar, son of my daughter . . .etc. A servant overhears her song, reports about it to his lady who speeds to her, asking: By what can you tell me your daughter? I can tell you my daughter by your cut finger! The daughter embraces her and dresses her in fine clothes. "Do you wish to stay here as a lady or would you prefer to go home?" The woman wants to go home, and the daughter sends her home by a coach. (*26*.) Another short song (*27*.) has a different incipit: Why are the hens so silent, and why don't we hear people stirring? The Turks have raided the village, carried away all the people, including two sisters. They were driven on the way, stones hurt their feet, and their black blood was drunk up by a black raven. One of the sisters says to the other: Sister, ask your Turkish husband to cut off my blond hair and send it to my mother so that she may not prepare a wreath for me, because I have lost my maidenhood under the green maple, lying there with a young Turk.

The next story (*28*.) is not quite clear. The Turk goes to the market, buys a Russian girl and takes her home. They are playing at cards. The girl relates, in answer to the Turk's queries, that she had four brothers: one of them turned Turk, the other vent to Moscow, the third is roaming in the wide world, and the fourth brother left home without taking leave of his mother and father, and nobody knows what befell to him, and lo, she had to live to see the day when her brother failed to recognize his sister. (The text of the song keeps silent on how the girl discovered her brother in the Turk.) Even more confused is the narrative in the next two songs (*29*. and *30*.) A widow gives birth to two children whom she puts on the water of the Danube to be drifted away by the waves. Later on they meet again. The mother marries one of her children, and her daughter (born in the meanwhile?) marries the other son. Thus it came about that brother and sister did not recognize each other. The story has no more to say about the relation of the mother and her son, consequently it should be regarded as a secondary development in this case. But the Hungarian ballad's motif recurs in *31*. At the first raid, the Turk carried away the son. At the second raid, he carried away a woman to serve as a nurse to his son. The

Turk dragged the woman, tied to the tail of his horse, through thorn and briar; her blood was drunk up by a black raven. "I have brought a woman to serve here as a prisoner to the end of her life. After lengthy details, here again she is ordered to perform three kinds of jobs. Then follows the lullaby: Hush-hush, little Tartar, son of my daughter!" The maid-servants report on the turn to their lady. "What are you singing, prisoner woman?" She repeats her song. "By what have you recognized me?" "When I was bathing you, a spark got into your right eye-ball." They make cheer, the daughter gives honey and wine to her mother, but the woman wants to go home. "Bring her a horse and let her go home!"

When all is said and considered, details of the Hungarian legend from the Szeged region can be identified in the northern Slav version (cf. the Turk dragging her mother tied to his horse and saying: "Swim the same blood...etc."). Also the motif of the imprisoned of two sisters occurs, and it can be made out, though not quite distinctly, that one of them had already married the Turk. The reference to mother's and daughter's falling into captivity together is similarly indistinct; what we have in a fairly explicit form is the mother's being taken a prisoner and a slave to her own daughter. This latter solution passed over to the Russians and the Poles. The motif they all have in common is that the Tartars are dividing the prey between themselves, and one of them receives the elder woman. She is taken to the Tartar's house where the usual triple work is allotted to her. Finally the relationship is discovered, and mother and daughter are glad to be reunited. The scene of recognition is, of course, preceded by the mother singing her berceuse, calling the little Tartar her own grandson. In some of the details, the following deviations can be ascertained: the beginning of the song makes it clear that the mother-in-law gets into the possession of her own son-in-law (*32–35., 37., 38., 43.* and *44.*); the Tartars carry away the girl, and later also the mother of the girl is taken into captivity; the girl gets into the possession of her brother while the mother into that of her son-in-law (*39.*—no intermarriage between brother and sister is mentioned in the continuation of the song); mother and daughter fall into captivity together, but later on the mother is surrendered as a slave to her daughter, much in the same way as in the rest of the variants (*40.*). A beautiful girl goes to fetch water, falls into the hands of Tartars and made wife to one of them; an old woman is taken prisoner subsequently (*42., 43.*) an eagle is telling a story to a falcon about how war was fought against the Tartars, how they carried away the prisoners, how a *brother* let his *sister* go home to Sainted Russia, and how the son-in-law made his mother-in-law a prisoner; then the usual narrative follows; although discernible traces of some other connection can also be discovered, the lullaby contains the sign by which the mother recognizes her daughter: a mole or wart is seen on her right cheek, or under her right teat, or one of the fingers of her left foot is missing of the young woman who had been carried away seven years before, or as a girl of seven; also the closing parts contain minor divergences: the mother wants to go home unconditionally (*32., 33.* and *44.*), or on the contrary, it is the daughter that would have her go home although the mother is willing to stay with her (*34–37.*); the daughter sends her mother home while she remains with her child since it has been so willed by God (*39.*); in other variants they mount their horses and ride home to make cheer with the relatives (*38.*); the rest of the texts end with the motif of recognition and

455

rejoicing; in general, Tartars are spoken of, and only one of the variants mentions Turks (44.); the Ukrainian songs mostly mention Turks, and only in a few instances do they speak about Tartars and even in these they appear in combination with the Turks; as the bilinas speak consistently of Tartars, looking back to times of Russian–Tartar wars, the replacement of Turks by Tartars can be well explained; in the Hungarian and Moravian areas, however, only the Turks can be logically involved; should the Hungarian ballad have Tartars originally, then the substitution of Turks would be completely ununderstandable, precisely on account of what has been said in connection with the bilinas and the historical background.

The only Polish text known to me (45.) starts with the formula of the Ukrainian 27., asking why the hens are silent and the noise of people is not heard? The village is raided by the Turks. A widow is carried away. Three kinds of jobs are appointed to her, and while rocking the child she is singing her cradle-song. How can you recognize me, asks her daughter. The mother says she has recognized her by the sign on her arm. Then the mother is clothed in precious dresses, and there is an end to the story.

The nations neighbouring Hungary in the North do not build their story on the motif of intermarriage between sister and brother, although reminiscences of a brother and a sister taken prisoners together haunt in certain obscure parts or fragments of their songs. Different is the picture with the southern neighbours: the Bulgarians have the incestuous marriage of brother and sister as their basic theme for the song. The two Southern Slav stories are certainly divergent: in 40. the Turks find "a Turkish youth" when they ransack the region of Szerémség (Syrmia). They carry away thirty girls, and Andelia is one of them. "What the Turk said when drunk did when sober", says the hazy text. Then we have the beginning of the story word for word. When it comes to meting out the prisoners, Andelia gets into the possession of Smailu, who asks the girl if she has living relatives. It appears then that she is his own sister. Upon his question by what she could recognize her brother the girl mentions his wound which he had received falling down from the stairs as a small child. Hearing this, the young man gives the girl in marriage to another Turk. The other story (41.) speaks about the simultaneous captivity of two sisters.

There are many variants of the song among the Bulgarians. These can be divided into two groups. In the one group, the voivode Mihály invading Bulgaria carries away a woman together with her daughter; his mother and sister. He marries the girl who gives birth to a child. Nursing the child, the grandmother sings the cradle-song as usual, mentioning the phrase "son of my son and my daughter" known from the Hungarian version. But it fails to tell us how the mother had learned the secret, and when, and why she has refrained from letting it out earlier, perhaps at the time when they were taken prisoners. What is even more conspicuous, no allusion is made to the fact that the voivode Mihály had been kidnapped (since he figures as the prince of his country in the song). With these left out of consideration, the song continues: the voivode overhears the singing woman and wants her to repeat the cradle-song. For fear of being killed, the woman asks him to make a solemn oath: may his arm wither if he did any harm to the woman. Then the song is heard again. The voivode draws his sword to kill the woman, but his arm withers, or in any case falls down, before he can carry out his will. Thus he understands that the woman is really his own mother and he entreats her to forgive him (52., 53., 59–61., 63. and 65.).

The other type has Janka and Jankula (a sister and a brother whose names may vary) as the hero and heroine of the story. (50., 51., 54–58., 62., 64. and 66.) The Turk kidnaps a mother and two children whom he separates from one another later; not knowing each other, the brother marries his sister who gives birth to a son. (One of the variants—64.—emphasizes the motif of incest by stating that the child is unlike other normal babies, because he is like a snake.) The woman sends her husband to go to the bazar and buy a nurse to tend her son. He buys his own mother. In this case, too, the old woman sings a lullaby from which they learn that she is nursing her own grandson, born of her own children. I have come across one single text to inform about a mole on the body of her son and daughter, respectively, by which she has recognized them. All other variants tell only about the circumstances of their imprisonment. Under the impact of the incest motif, the story meets various endings: they decide to kill their child, possibly themselves as well, or they retire in a monastery or convent. A Macedonian text reiterates the story in an identical formulation (48.).

The Bulgarian songs are unanimously based on the incest motif. At the same time, they show an indisputable correlation with the Hungarian and the Moravian songs, especially in the middle portion, in which the cradle-song over the grandchild forms a close connection between the various solutions. In all the variants this scene represents the summit and the key to the interpretation. At the same time, none of the Bulgarian variants can be regarded as the prototype of the set of variants: the songs about the voivode Mihály are uniform inasmuch as they always present the motif of recognition without any motivation added, that is in an incomplete form; another fault with this version of the story is that it also fails to give an account of the acts of kidnapping at different times (if the voivode had not been taken prisoner as a child, the whole of the plot remains senseless). The other type gives a logically built narrative in which only one essential and characteristic element is missing, to wit, that of recognition by a sign on the body, which anyway prevails throughout the entire area of examination, and what is more, constitutes a connecting link with still farther territories, as will be shown later. But the fact that here and there this motif comes up also in the Bulgarian tradition indicates that it did reach the Bulgarians in some form, only the singers failed to attach importance to it. One cannot think of erosion or sinking into oblivion of the motif, because it is precisely the Bulgarian area from which the highest number of sound variants have been recorded. From this circumstances it follows that, unlike the Hungarians, the Bulgarians have preserved a living tradition. But apart from this, recognition by a mole is a widespread motif in European balladry which will be given further consideration below in connection with the examination of the remaining members of the type.

On the basis of what has been stated so far it seems as if the Bulgarians had borrowed the ballad from their northern neighbours, that is from the Hungarians. Only the motif of incest comes into conflict with this supposition. Although it can well be imagined that this motif made its way into the southern Hungarian variants through the mediation of Southern Slavs, possibly of Bulgarians. The view of the mixed population of the southern part of prewars Hungary does not preclude such a possibility. But it is seriously contradicted by the fact that the ballad is hardly demonstrable from the Southern Slav traditions, and if it occurs sporadically in their areas, it is always in a very fragmentary form and without the motif of incest included, furthermore, it was only most recently that isolated Bulgarian ethnic groups appeared in the region of Bánság (Banate). Finally, the greatest obstacle is to be found in the composition of the Hungarian ballad which bears no resemblance to the plot of the Bulgarian Janka and a Jankula type or to that of the voivode Mihály. In spite of its fragmentary nature, the Hungarian type has preserved the common nucleus of the plot in a fuller and more consistent form.

Obviously, it is the motif of incest that primarily influenced the researchers in stating the point of origin. *Horálek* derives the story from the Southern Slavs (having no nowledge of the Hungarian version). But even in the knowledge of the Hungarian texts, *Putilov* maintains that the theme of this, as well as other Hungarian ballads referring to the Turkish period (such as The Girl Abducted by the Turks, The Two Captives, The Bride Dying in the Bridal Procession), had been originally a common inheritance of the Slavs, the motif of incest having been an ancient folklore theme with them, from which the Hungarian version tended to become increasingly detached. He goes yet farther by stating that all the songs about Turkish imprisonment used to be the exclusive property not of one single Slav nation, but of all the Slavs taken together, and that these songs had been moulded in a sometimes surprisingly identical form by identical historical conditions.

Of course, "identical" historical conditions prevailed in Hungary as well, where the theme survives, and in Romania, too, where the theme is absent. To continue the examples, such historical conditions prevailed with the Moravians to a rather negligible extent and at a relatively late time: according to *Rychnová,* Turkish raids reached Moravia from Hungarian territories between 1605 and 1701 (the second date being somewhat dubious since after the liberation of Buda in 1686 the Turks were soon swept out of the Hungarian areas, and very little chance were left for them to invade Moravia once more). As against this, the Hungarians had been engaged in a life-struggle with the Turks since the early fifteenth century, and the northern boundary of the Turkish-ruled areas stretched through the body of Hungary from 1541 to 1690. Such conditions, of course, involved incessant warfare even in relatively "peaceful" periods as well. Consequently, if the theme of the mother kidnapped by her son is an expression of a given historical situation in the folklore of all nations concerned, then the Hungarians can hardly be overlooked in the panorama. Nor can they be left out of consideration even if a Slavonic origin is accepted: even with such a possibility granted, the theme should have wandered through Hungarian-inhabited areas from north to south or conversely, from south to north! Neither the Austrians nor the Romanians have acquired the theme of the ballad under discussion, although these two nations with the Hungarians in between occupy a wide stretch of land that separates the Northern and the Southern Slavs. The theme could have formed a common property of the Slavs only in case it had developed in times before the Great Hungarian Conquest took place, that is prior to 896, from which time on considerable numbers of Hungarian population had wedged in between the Northern and Southern Slavs. But from that date it took a long time indeed till those "common historical conditions" or the "pathos of the struggle against the Turkish or Tartar yoke" or the "relatively identical level of popular conscience", that is to say, the social-historical forces whose typological implications *Putilov* chose to demonstrate throughout his book (1966) could emerge and take shape at all.

Anyway, the very concept of typological agreement is fully unadaptable to this ballad type. Admittedly, identical conditions may bring about such themes as are "captivity", "liberation from imprisonment", "reunion of detached relatives" and the like, but they cannot provide explanation for such series of plot-elements as are repeated kidnapping from one and the same family, the singing of a lullaby at the cradle of the son of a formerly kidnapped relative, recognition by signs on some part of the body, and agreeing names of the characters. All this viewed as a whole must have taken its origin at a certain definite place, and must have wandered from one place to another. It cannot be contested that the motif of incest should have been a common Slavonic motif in times before balladry developed; yet, why has this same motif been disregarded in the ballads of the Moravians, Ukrainians and Russians who are Slavs indeed! Let alone the fact that the incest problem, mainly love between sister and brother, is just as much the theme of the Germanic peoples than of the Slavs. (In the survey of the ballads: DgF 437–439, and 458; *Child* 14–16, and 51; and as a possibility D. Vlr. 72 are enough to exemplify the fact.) And as to the focus of dissemination, the quantitative factor has to be handled with utmost caution in the case of areas with traditions of different strength.

But is the intermarriage of sister and borther a really important and original constituent of this ballad theme? A survey of the ballads outside the Eastern European areas seems to convince us of the contrary. Let us examine first the Spanish, Portuguese and Catalonian texts which include all the characteristic elements of the Hungarian story, only the persons involved being somewhat differing.

The common essence of the Iberian variants can be summed up as follows. The Queen of the Moors wants to have a white female slave so that she may talk to someone, says one of the variants; in another one, she would like to converse with somebody coming from her own country. In general, however, only the command is expressed: "Bring me a female slave!" The flotilla or a troop of soldiers start out to find one. They meet a count returning from his pilgrimage. The count is killed and his wife taken prisoner and made housekeeper to the Queen. The two women give birth to children at a time, and the nurses, out of fun, exchange the babies. The slave-mother is singing over the cradle of the exchanged, that is the Queen's, child: If we were in my home, I should baptize you after the name of my sister Blanca Flor whom the Moors had robbed long ago. Hearing this, the Queen asks her what song she was singing and if she could recognize her sister. The woman then tells her about the distinctive marks by which she would know her sister: a black mole under her breast (in three variants), a crescent-shaped mole on her back or right shoulder (in two variants), a red cross between her two teats or a red spot on her breast (in two variants); there are two variants in which she simply tells the name of her family or that of her sister, or she describes the scene and the circumstances of the robbery.

459

The Queen shows her the same signs of her body, and they recognize each other. This is where *5.* and *9.* end. In *1., 4.* and *10.* they both escape and go home (collecting first all the valuables, as is usual in tales); in *2.* and *3., 6.* and *7.* the Queen or the King himself gives permission to the sister to go home alone, and in *6.* the King allows also his wife to leave for home. Nevertheless, in *3.* the Queen sends her sister home saying that she herself would fain go, only she cannot because she is a renegade,—a motif which is apparently a later development. One of the Portuguese songs (*6.*) relates, by way of introduction, how a girl had been robbed by the Moors; the young girl here takes leave of "the French soil"; later on the Moors wishing to acquire more female slaves, send out a troop of soldiers to *France* for the purpose.

All the Iberian variants contain the motif of the exchange of babies born at the same time. Yet, this motif does not belong to the plot organically, because it is inconsequential for the further development of the story (except that the slave woman will sing the cradle song not over her own child but over that of the woman who had been kidnapped earlier). It seems as if the role of the housekeeper had replaced here the original function of the nurse. In order to save the central scene, in which the second woman slave sings her lullaby at the cradle of the first-robbed one's child, recourse had to be made to this episode superfluous and inconsistent otherwise. Namely, in this case the role of the nurse is more solidly embedded in the story than in the Hungarian version. In the Iberian narrative it is explicitly expressed that the new white woman slave was kidnapped upon the request of the queen. As against this, the motif comes up in the Hungarian version in a form that the husband starts out the second time to find someone, and the female he happens to acquire nurses the child; on the other hand, in the Bulgarian songs the husband starts out—not to rob but to the bazar—to buy a nurse for the wife's baby. In spite of the differences, the agreement of this motif in the folklore of peoples living so wide apart suggests the idea that originally the wife that gave birth to a child wanted to have a woman slave to nurse her child; and while this woman slave turns out to be the sister of the wife in the Iberian version, according to the Hungarian and the named Eastern European versions she is the mother of the son, or son and daughter, that had been kidnapped earlier. Otherwise the agreement is clear and convincing in all other details: there are repeated kidnappings, the second-robbed woman is singing over the cradle, and it appears from her song that they are relatives, and the fact receives verification through discovery of corporal signs, and finally the relatives are glad to be reunited. And the last-mentioned moment is the essential point: the dénouement always emphasizes the happy recognition. This feature is brought out in the Iberian songs when the "kind enemy" lets the relative go home. Happiness of reunited relatives constitutes the main point also in the Hungarian, Moravian, as well as in most of the Russian texts, in which the Moorish or Turkish character of the robber is washed away towards the end of the songs, although this character of the kidnapper is emphasized by *Putilov* as the carrier of his theory.

Thus a knowledge of the Iberian variants enables us to lend a different meaning to the basic elements of the skeletal story. The series of motifs which are undoubtedly correlated may be used in connection with children and their mother, and may be referred to sister and sister (or brother) as well. At this point I have to recall the story of the two sisters, or the threadbare traces thereof, existing in isolation among the Ukrainians and Southern Slavs, further the motif of sister-brother-mother incestuous relationship in the Hungarian and Bulgarian legends: are not these survivals of the ancient story of the two sisters that used to arrive in the eastern regions from the West? As the plot is unknown with the Moravians, the transformation should have taken place in Hungarian territories: the borrowers wishing to enhance the tragical effect replaced the relation of the slave-keeping sister and the slave sister by another relation, that of mother and child. Nevertheless, in certain instances they were unable to get rid of the original solution, therefore we find that they retained the motif of the kidnapped sisters, adding to it the motif of the kidnapped mother (and son), from which the intermarriage of close relatives developed without the characters being aware of the incestuous relation, or else the numerous variety of sister plus sister (brother) arose; accordingly, two basic patterns can be distinguished in Eastern European folklore: (1) the mother kidnapped by her son, and (2) the mother-in-law robbed by her son-in-law; one or the other variant of these had come to prevail in the areas concerned although the traces of the original plot with the sister plus sister solution could not be altogether eliminated. It is not impossible that first the modification involved daughter plus mother relation, and later on the role of the daughter was replaced by that of the son, obviously because thus the parable was made stronger by the cruel scenes in which the mother was kidnapped and tormented by her own son. In this way we can reasonably explain the Hungarian version, and the Ukrainian songs developed from the former, including such scenes.

The originality of the sister plus sister motif is corroborated by evidence of a set of remotely related western ballads. The English, Scandinavian, German and Dutch ballads (78–168.) are based on the following common plot: A girl is kidnapped by robbers (with the Danes, sold to a lord), and the girl becomes concubine to a noble man and gives birth to seven of his children. Then the nobleman announces that he will marry a girl of a foreign country. The essential point in this ballad is the description of the psychic condition of the concubine mother who tries to receive her rival with utmost kindness. (In the Danish version, the nobleman makes her enumerate all the presents she is going to give to the bride.) The scene of reception and the bridal is minuteously detailed in both the Danish and the English ballads; following this, the bride asks the concubine about her descent and learns that they are sisters. And what is even more important, in variants E, F, I and J of *Child* the concubine staying in the next room when the bride is led to bed begins to sing a song, from which the young wife learns her origin and sorrowful fate. Thus the motif of recognition by singing occurs also in the northern sphere! After this the bride returns home with her maidenhood left intact, and the nobleman marries his former mistress.

According to another German ballad (D. Vlr. 72 = DgF 378) a knight putting up in an inn beholds a beautiful girl, and asks the hostess to let him have the girl for the night. (In some of the variants he recognizes his sister by a ring, in others the knight has a long inquisitive talk with the hostess about the girl's origin.) The girl goes weeping up to the knight's quarter and prays to God to save her chastity. The knight questions her why she is so sad and who her parents were. Upon this the girl relates how she had been kidnapped by a merchant who had brought her in a

461

basket to the inn where the hostess bought her. This is how the knight discovers that the girl is his own sister (in a few variants, however, he recognizes her by the mole on the girl's neck). The next morning the knight punishes the hostess and goes home with his long-sought-for sister whom the whole family is glad to see again. And this ballad theme has a very wide relationship in both the Northern and the Southern Slav areas!

As can be seen, there is no enemy involved either in the German or in the English–Scandinavian versions. In comparison with the Iberian versions, the only difference is that the roles of the woman slave and wife are exchanged: in the northern ballads the first-kidnapped girl will be kept as a woman slave and the second girl will be the prospected wife, who returns to her country, and who is not robbed but simply brought from the foreign country, that is kidnapping does not occur on two occasions. At the same time, the fact is that the same man receives woman on two occasions, and that the two females are sisters, one of whom returns to her country. The identification, however, mostly takes place not in consequence of a song or the discovery of some corporal sign, but through the narration of the girl's descent, rarely by a ring. In any case we are dealing with ramifications of one common ancient theme from which both the Iberian and the Eastern European songs took their origin.

The common ancestor has to be looked for in French territories. This can be seen in the Portuguese song, and the English–Scandinavian type has already been brought in connection with the French *Lai de la Freisne*. What degree of relationship can be established between this *lai* and the ballad stories examined above?

A noble lady gives birth to twin-daughters. She places one of them in front of a nunnery, wrapped in a valuable cloth and with a precious ring (bracelet) on her arm. The girl is brought up in the nunnery. A knight falls in love with her and she elopes with him. (We have elopement here instead of kidnapping.) The knight lives with her as a paramour, until he is persuaded, for the sake of a lawful heir, to marry a young lady matching him in rank. The knight asks for the other twin-girl's hand in marriage. Her sister tries her best to show all kindness to her rival and spreads the cloth she had received in heritage over the bride's bed to make it look cosier. The mother of the twins comes and sees the cloth, and upon her inquiry also the bracelet is shown. Thus light is cast on the preliminaries. The knight marries his paramour while the bride returns home as a maid.

We have to suppose that there existed a French ballad that transformed the theme of the *Lai de la Freisne* in a way that the girl kidnapped became the wife of the robber, then her sister is taken into captivity to the same robber's place, and the second sister having been identifed is returned home. Recognition took place by some bodily sign (the motif is widely popular with folklore stories), and the fact received expression in the form of a berceuse which the slaver overheard. Without the supposition of a one-time ballad of this kind we cannot create connection between the Spanish–Portuguese and the Hungarian–East-European texts. On the other hand, with such a link of chain the close agreement can be readily substantiated between the stocks of ballads. It is this French ballad, long extinct already, that the southern neighbours in the Iberian peninsula had adopted, transforming it by addition of the motifs of double birth and the exchange of the new-born babies. And the same ballad had been imported by French-Walloon settlers into Hungary where it was transformed differently: the role of the sisters was replaced by that of mother and son, or mother and daughter; in certain cases the two motifs merged in a way that the sister and brother were taken prisoners together and subsequently married so that the mother might find the children side by side. Each of these solutions are represented in the form of survivals in Hungarian balladry, and each of them had been passed over to one or another of the neighbouring nations: the son–mother solution reached the Moravians, the daughter plus mother had wandered over to the Polish, Ukrainians and Russians, while the theme of marriage between sister and brother migrated to the Bulgarians to become there a puzzling source of further contradictions.

The ballad belongs among the earliest pieces of mediaeval origin.

Literature: Child 1885: besides the English ballads, refers to Scandinavian (German) and Portuguese parallels, as well as to the French Lai de la Freisne; *Rychnová* 1953: publishes legend-variants from Moravia together with their Ukrainian, Russian and Bulgarian parallels; *Csanádi* and *Vargyas* 1954: recapitulation of Hungarian variants without comparative material added; *Putilov* and *Dobrovolsky* 1960: Russian variants interpreted as relics of Russian–Tartar wars in the thirteenth to fifteenth centuries, together with Slav parallels; *Horálek* 1963: comparative analysis of the Slav material, the Northern Slav variants are of Southern Slav origin; *Sirovátka* 1963: extant Moravian version and Slav–Hungarian parallels; the Moravian shows a closer affinity to the Hungarian than to the Russian; *Balashov* 1963, 133: "Brother marries his sister" motif proceeded from the Ukrainians towards the Russians; *Putilov* 1964: the Hungarian legend used to be a folk ballad and a connecting link between the various Slav types, it separated gradually from the incest theme; *Putilov* 1965: Slav and Hungarian versions discussed together with other themes of "Turkish imprisonment"; the incest motif was the oldest, the Turkish imprisonment is a common theme of the Slav peoples, reference to historical-typological analogies; the story is secondary with the Hungarians, since it is much more deeply rooted in the Slav tradition.

43. THE TEST OF FAITHFULNESS

102.

1. Hogyan ne - vel - ke - dék   Körül foj-ta tö - vét   Gyenge gyo- pár vi - rág.
   Egy a - rany al - ma - fa,

1. As it was growing and growing,
   That golden apple-tree there,
   There grew by its root
   A tender edelweiss flower.

2. And sitting under it,
   A poor orphan girl
   Is twining a garland for her hair,
   And she is bemoaning her fate.

3. I have neither father nor mother,
   Nor anyone else to take care of me.
   From the gate, she was overheard
   By a proud soldier.

4. Why are you weeping, why are you weeping (why are you weeping),
   You poor orphan girl?
   I shall be your father, your mother,
   And I shall take care of you.

5. I do not want you to be that,
   You proud soldier,
   For I have already
   My betrothed one, my betrothed one.

6. And I shall be waiting for him
   For seven years,
   And I shall be waiting for him
   For three full days.

7. And I shall be waiting for him
   For seven years,
   And if he does not come by that time,
   I myself shall go.

8. And while I am alive
I shall find my God,
And when I die,
I shall stand before God.

Tordátfalva (Udvarhely county). Female singer. Vikár 1900 = MF 106/b.

103.

Behold, there has grown
A golden apple-tree,
And by its root there has grown
A tender edelweiss flower.
5. And under it there sits
A poor orphan girl,
Twining a garland for her hair,
And bemoaning her fate:
I have neither father nor mother,
10. Nor anyone else to take care of me.
From the gate, she was overheard
By a proud soldier:
Don't weep, don't be sad,
You poor orphan girl,
15. I shall be your father and mother,
And I shall take care of you.
I don't want you to be that,
You proud soldier,
For I have already
20. My betrothed one who is pledged to me.
For whom I have been waiting
For seven years,
For seven years
And three days at that.
25. But I shall be waiting for him
For another seven years,
For another seven years,
And for three days.
And if he is not come by that time,
30. I shall go
To the nuns,
To the land of the nuns,
And as long as I am living there
I shall serve God,
35. And when I die,
I shall stand before God.

"Székelyföld". Kriza = MNGY III, No. 15

104.

1. Behold, there has grown a sweet apple-tree,
   And a yellow edelweiss flower has grown under it.
   A poor orphan girl is sitting under it,
   Twining a garland for her hair.

2. And where she is short of edelweiss flower, she puts in white pearls,
   And she puts in white pearls, and embroiders it with gold thread.
   And she is singing songs she had learned,
   And she is drying her bitter tears.

3. My God, my God, my beloved God!
   Without father and mother how can I live?
   Without kinfolks, and without a wedded spouse
   What am I to do alone in my life?

4. At the door a stranger spoke up, saying:
   Don't weep, don't be sad,—thus he spoke.
   For I shall be father and mother and kin to you,
   And instead of a wedded spouse I shall be a wedded spouse to you.

5. Do not beguile me, you proud stranger,
   For I have a betrothd sweetheart,
   A betrothed one, pledged with a ring to be my handsome bridegroom,
   He is to be my father and mother while I am alive.

6. He who is away at the wars to fight the enemy,
   To fight the enemy, to bear the standard.
   But maybe, tomorrow morning he will bring good news,
   At dawn I shall go to meet him.

Klézse, (Moldavia). I. Petrás, 1841–42 = Erdélyi I, No. 421.

Cf. *Leader* 332.

In one of the texts of the ballad "The Brigand's Wife" (*Faragó* and *Jagamas* 12/c) a few lines of "The Test of Faithfulness" come up: "...Why did you give me away To be wife to a famous thief... Who is away ...At the wars to fight the enemy", and then in Stanza 5: "At the doorway there spoke up A proud soldier: Let me in...". On evidence of all other variants it can be stated that these lines do not belong organically to the text of "The Brigand's Wife" but are borrowings from the ballad discussed here.

Earliest provenience: 1841–42, *Petrás*, Klézse.

Dissemination: Udvarhely county (Tordátfalva and the designation "Székelyföld" probably refer to this county), further Klézse and Trunk, Moldavia.

Textual relationships with other ballads: The lover returning home is not recognized: related to the motif of relatives who are not recognized, **17., 22.,** and **41.** tests take place in **22.** and **69.,** and also the test of faithfulness occurs in **75.** The image of the girl binding her wreath is reminiscent of the starting lines of "The Girl Taken to Heaven" (**8.**), and is related at the same time with the formula "She is sewing in the window" (**12.**, **14.**, **21.**, and **49.**) "Instead of your spouse I shall be your spouse": **44.** "For seven years and three days": **33.**, and **39.**

Tune: only the published one is recorded.

Versions in languages other than Hungarian:

FRENCH: *1. Millien* 1906 II, 178A + var.† *2.* Ibid. 168† (*Piguet* enumerates a further 5 variants.)

PORTUGUESE: *3–17. Braga* I, 33 (= *Geibel* and *Schack* 371), 36, 39, 42, 45–48, 50, 52, 57, 59, 62, 64, 67.

SPANISH: *18. Wolf* and *Hoffmann* 156. (= *Geibel* and *Schack* 375.) *19–20.* Ibid. II. 155 and 217. *21–30. Cossio* and *Solano* 108–117. *31–32. Menéndez–Pidál* 1885, No. 35. *33. Romero*, 68–73 together with the full bibliography of the Spanish–American material on pages 72–73. *34–35. Armistead* and *Silverman*, 46 and 75 B/6 and C/7.

CATALAN: *36. Milá* 202† = *Wolf* 67. *37.* Ibid. var. *38. Amades*, 417, No. 2307.

ITALIAN: *39–42. Nigra* 54A–D. *43. Ferraro* 1888, No. 35. *44. Idem* 1870 41. *45. Gianandrea*, 270, No. 7. *46. Widter* and *Wolf* 91, *47. Babudri*, 176, No. 12.† *48. Giannini* 1889, 154, No. 8. *49. Marcoaldi*, 151. *50. Bolza* 53. *51. Pergoli* 23. *52–53. Bernoni* 1872 Punt. V, No. 6 and IX, No. 1. *54–55. Ferraro* 1877, 14, No. 2 and 105, No. 18 (*Nigra* and DVA refer to further variants from the regions of Florence, Faenza, Lombardy and Trentino.)

DUTCH: *56.* Horae. b. No. 26. *57. Lootens* and *Feys* 48 *58–59.* Souterliedekens 7–8.

ENGLISH: *60. Child* 263. *61.* JAF 1909, 379.† *62. Mackenzie* I, 63A.†

GERMAN: Of the numerous German variants, we mention the following ones by way of exemplification: *63–68.* E–B 67a–f. *69–70. Hauffen* 55, 55a. *71. Mittler*, 56. *72. Meinert*, 243.

WENDISH: *73. Haupt* and *Schmaler* 43. *74. Kuhač* 974. (DVA mentions a further 7 variants.)

SOUTHERN SLAV: *75–79. Kuhač* 104–5, Nos 238, 973 and variants. *80–102. Štrekelj* 773–194. (*Kumer* 400–402.)

CZECH—MORAVIAN: *103–104. Sušil* 114/245–246. *105–110. Bartoš* 1901, 103a–f. (DVA mentions 12 more variants.)

SLOVAK: *111. Horák* 1958, 22 = Sl. Sp. II 63. *112.* Sl. Sp. III 308. *113–114.* SL'P 158 and 365. *115. Černik* 219. *116. Kollár* II, 382. *117–119. Bartók* 1959 349a–c.

DANISH (SWEDISH): *120–261.* DgF 254 (71 variants), 252 (32 variants), 253 (10 variants), and 250 (29 variants). The Swedish variants are listed by *Jonsson* beside DgF 252.)

GREEK: *262. Lübke* 227 (Cf. *Baud-Bovy* 1936, 228–232 and D. Vlr. IV, 145, Note to No. 76.)

Partial variants:

POLISH: *263–269. Kolberg* 1857, 24a–g.

The ballad is known all over the West-European ballad area. It is most widespread with the Germans, the nearest western neighbours of the Hungarians. The opening motif is that of the branchy linden-tree that stands in a valley, under which a young man is taking leave of her sweetheart: he is either starting on travels for seven years or he is going to war, promising to return by summer. Sometimes he gives a ring to his sweetheart as a pledge. When the appointed time comes, he does not return. The girl goes to meet him in the forest. (There are such variants in which a garden is mentioned at this point, yet later she goes to walk in the woods.) While walking, she meets a knight, who asks her what she is doing there, has she perhaps a secret lover? The girl answers that she is waiting for the return of her sweetheart. "I saw him in the next town", says the knight, "and he is just getting married to another girl." His sweetheart still gives him her blessing, at which the knight—the returning lover—makes himself known, and draws the moral: "Had you cursed me, I would have left you for ever." The story, by and large in the same form, with the opening scene under the linden-tree, is found in a broadside dated 1592. Some variants also originating from the reading matter of the same century, leave out the farewell scene, giving only the scene where they meet again, yet the essentials of the ballad's motifs are the same from the beginning onward. Thus here the returning lover does not try to entice the girl, but puts her love to the test with the story of his own unfaithfulness.

Among the Dutch, we find a very similar text, with more or less deviations. Here the lover tries to entice his sweetheart after giving news of his own unfaithfulness, and here too, there is neither the beginning scene of leave-taking, nor the ending scene with the moral drawn. In other things, the Dutch version resembles the German, above all in having the girl bless her lover in spite of her infidelity, and the knight makes an attempt at enticing. This form represents a transition between the German ballad and the southern texts to be dealt with in the following.

By and large, the Italian formulations are uniform. The ballad begins with an impersonal address: "Sing, little girl, sing, until you get married!" "I have no wish to sing or to laugh, my heart aches, because my sweetheart went to the wars seven years ago and has not yet returned." (Remember: in the Hungarian she sang the songs she had learned!) After this she goes into the woods and meets the young man. She asks him if she had seen her sweetheart. The young man, in turn, asks her, how he was dressed, and replies that he has seen him being buried. At this the sorrowful girl sinks down upon the ground, and her lover makes himself known, although in some variants she believes him only when he shows the ring she gave him. This ballad is widespread throughout the whole of Northern Italy.

The Spanish–Portuguese versions have a married woman in place of a girl. She, however, is sitting in her garden, as in the Hungarian, and what is more, in an orchard, as appears from the continuation, when a stranger, in this case a captain just come frome the sea, steps to her, giving an opportunity to the woman to ask about her husband. Here again she has to describe him, and the sailor replies that he saw him fall in battle. (Here follows the motif, familiar in other ballads, of the three great wounds, which we discussed earlier in another context.) The woman bewails her fate, and the sailor asks her what she would give him if he could restore her husband to her. The woman runs through the list of her treasures in increasing order of value, promising first her orange-trees, then her gold and finally her three daughters (cf. "The Song of the Ferrymen"). The man announces that he wants the woman herself. Angered, the woman calls her servants; then the husband discloses his identity, by showing the incredulous woman the ring she had given him. His demand has been only a test of faithfulness.

Further details come up in the Catalan versions. The husband has gone to France, and the wife is waiting for him in the harbour. He returns, and his wife, not recognizing him, makes inquiry after her husband. The stranger pretends that he had met him, and that he has brought his command to her to marry someone else, as he himself has married the French king's daughter. The wife then calls for a blessing on him, and curses only the father-in-law. After this, she continues: "I have been waiting for him as a happy bride for seven years, and I shall be waiting for him for another seven years as a forsaken widow; if he does not return by that time, I shall be a nun." The scene of recognition ends this version.

There is another Catalan text, less distinct and more eroded, whose beginning, however, is closer to the Hungarian–German–Portuguese form. For it

468

begins with the beautiful woman sleeping under a fir-tree, when a knight appears. He does not want to wake her, and puts a garland of violets on her breast. (Cf. the Hungarian motif: She is twining her garland for her hair.) On waking up, the woman asks what news there is in the land he has come from. The reply is that a pilgrim has died, and describes his appearance. The woman recognizes that he is her husband. She wants to see him once more, starts out to go there, in spite of the stranger's warning of the great distance and the life-dangers. Finally, he makes himself known.

On the whole, the Spanish version is similar to the Portuguese, apart from some elements borrowed from other ballads (e.g. the three big wounds, the woman's promises of what she would give to get back her husband). There are other divergences on the other hand, which seem to be subsequent insertions: the husband does not divulge his identity that same day, only the following day, when he finds his wife dressed in mourning for her husband's death. But we do find that element of the Hungarian, according to which the wife hearing of her husband's death intends to become a nun.

The Danish ballads speak in four variants about the test of the wife's fidelity. The first-mentioned one (DgF 254) seems to bear closest resemblance to the German formulation, although direct connection can be demonstrated only in the motif of the lovers' meeting in a rose-garden. The other three versions explicate the basic theme in a new and independent plot, with the unidentified husband or lover trying to entice the sweetheart.

The Greeks also sing about a wife and a returning husband. The content of their ballad can be summed up, after *Baud-Bovy*, in the following manner: The scene more often than not begins at a spring in which the woman is washing her underwears or from which she is drawing water. A knight appears and asks for water to drink. The woman begins to weep at his sight, because he is like her husband. The stranger pretends that her husband is dead, and that he himself has buried him. Upon his proposal to substitute for her husband, the woman shrinks back in a horror. Thus reassured of her fidelity, the husband makes himself known to the woman. In *Lübke's* variant we have a nunnery, too: she has already been waiting for twelve years for her husband to return, and she is going to wait three years more, after which she will retire to the nunnery. D. Vlr. quotes similar details from the coasts of the Black Sea. These show signs of various contaminations. *Baud-Bovy* derives the Greek variants from the southern isles where they spread during the reign of the "Franks". The theory of mediation by Neo-Latin nations seems to be corroborated by the fact that whenever the ballad appears in combination with another theme, the latter is always the French song "Les métamorphoses", of which we gave account at another place.

For the time being, we propose to leave out of consideration the other East-European versions, since they appear to be variants of either the Hungarian or the German ballad. The survey convinces us that the German version contains most such details which do not come up in other nations' balladry. For instance, the farewell scene right at the beginning; the Portuguese, Catalan, Spanish, Italian, Greek and Hungarian versions start the story with the scene of return, and the preliminaries are made clear in them subsequently from the duologues. This, being more in harmony with the ballad style, can be considered to be more original a trait. The encounter in the Iberian and the Hungarian texts takes place in a way that a stranger enters the garden in which the woman is sitting. The Italian and the German girls go off to meet the sweetheart. Reference to such a solution can be found also in the Hungarian when the girl says that she would go the next day to meet him. This probably had been the original form, and the Germans and the Italians had transformed the allusion into a real encounter. The meeting in the garden can be explained only in this way; and that this might have been the original scene of encounter is brought out by the circumstance that garden is mentioned in such ballads in which the actual encounter takes place in a wood or a valley. (There occur fourteen such variants in the DVA material with the Germans.) Another proof of this is that even in such instances the meeting is thought to take place under a tree. (Cf. the German and Catalan versions.) The Hungarian girl is singing in the garden, the Italian is addressed impersonally and so asked to sing—this latter obviously being a result of erosion.

The next scene is the one in which the woman (girl) makes inquiry after her sweetheart, whom she has to describe; following this, she hears about his having died, and is plunged into sorrow and despair. Essentially, this scene is identical in both the Italian and the Iberian versions, and may therefore be regarded as having been the original form. At the same time, it is fully absent in the Hungarian and has assumed quite a unique shape in the German: in the latter it is not the girl that asks questions about her sweetheart, but the stranger who then imparts to her not tidings of his death but of his marrying to another woman (this is what comes up in the Catalan version, too), and also the dénouement deviates from the other ballads accordingly: the husband puts to test not the wife's fidelity but her kindheartedness. The Italian contents itself with the news of death told, while the Spanish, Portuguese, Greek and Hungarian ballads incorporate attempts at enticing the woman. Most likely, the tidings of death and the subsequent proposal on the part of the stranger used to form part of the original story. Similarly, the sentence about the girl's entering the nunnery is original as it comes up in the Spanish, Portuguese, Greek and Hungarian versions.

The sequence of events is broken in the Hungarian at the point where the tempter is refused; this scene must have been followed by one of recognition, according to the evidence of other nations' versions. The involvement of the ring at the recognition may have also been an original trait, at least this can be inferred from the German, Spanish, Portuguese and Italian ballads.

To sum up the conclusions we may state the following. Several essential details are absent in the Hungarian ballad from the middle of the plot to the end, which can be explained by its being a fragment; at the same time, all details which are included can be demonstrated from other versions, that is to say, they are original motifs. The German formulation, containing most elements unknown in other countries, deviates most from the general form, including the Hungarian. At the same time, most of the Hungarian elements are common with the Spanish–Portuguese–Catalan texts, in spite of all the marked differences between them. Less common features are seen in the Italian, and least in the German. The Italian and the Iberian versions include the greatest number of common elements, yet their secondary nature is more than obvious. A clear indication of this fact is the inserted short ballad "What would you give if...", a question, the answers to which are really misfitted in between the tidings of death of the husband and the love proposal of the stranger; similar is the case with the detail about the three deep wounds, which is also a secondary development. As regards the Spanish ballad, the double encounter before recognition takes place is undramatic and against the nature of the genre. With the Italians it is the blurred outlines of the incipit that goes against the ballad style. Obviously, the scene in which the girl is singing songs bemoaning her forsakenness is more in the nature of the ballad genre, because it is naturally followed by the appearance of the stranger or enticer, than is the impersonal address, asking the woman to sing, after which she gives a realistic answer, and goes to meet her sweetheart. The Hungarian version has preserved only portions of the original, but fragmentary as it is, what it contains is original and well in line with ballad traditions. And while it markedly differs from the ballad of the nearest neighbour nation (the German) it shows striking analogies (sometimes world-for-world agreements) with the ballads of the remote Iberian and Greek nations, in which again sharp differences and secondary features come into prominence. All this leads inevitably to the supposition of the one-time existence of a French ballad that had been adopted by all neighbouring peoples, as well as by the Greeks and the Hungarians, and that the agreements between the Iberian and Hungarian versions undoubtedly point to a common source of origin.

Transformed survivals of this French original can be detected in the *pastourelles*. After she had been waiting for two years in vain, the girl—with her child on her arm—starts out to be a shepherdess. As such, she is met by a soldier, who brings news of her lover's death, as in the ballad. When the girl filled with despair runs to drown herself in the water, he discovers his identity by producing the ring in which the girl's name is engraved (1.). In another song the soldier returns after six years had elapsed, and wants to seduce the girl; meeting a flat refusal, he makes himself known (2.). All this is said and told in the tone of eighteenth-century pastourelles. Texts of similar intonation and of decidedly broadside prehistory can be found in English and American territories. Even though these have undergone a process of modernization, the traits of the old song can be discovered in them. The lover goes to the army for two or six years (the motif of joining the soldiers, only the customary seven years have been replaced by six, according to modern concepts). It is a new idea, however, that the girl as a shepherdess meets the stranger. This scene may be a survival of the Porcheronne—The Cruel Mother-in-Law, given new life by the vogue of pastoral poetry. It should be noted in this connection that *Piquet* quotes a variant of Germine, the later version of the Porcheronne, in which the woman is found by the returning and unrecognized husband *in a garden* where she is *picking flowers*. It is obvious that the returning soldier husband and the returning soldier sweetheart often cross one another's paths in the stories. (In Germine, too, the husband tries to seduce his wife, and the faithful wife also asks for a sign, which the husband gives in the form of a ring.) For this reason *Piquet* always quotes the two models of the story side by side, when giving the contents of the variants: He puts to test the shepherd girl's fidelity, who is his wife (bride), pretending that her husband (bridegroom) is dead. This intertwining is also seen in the versions of the

471

peoples neighbouring the French language area: in the Italian, German (Hungarian), the heroine is a girl, and in the Spanish, Portuguese, Catalan and Greek, a wife.

This dualism also appears in the methods used in the test. The news of death and the attempt to seduce are side by side in the French, while the neighbouring nations apply sometimes the one or the other and it is only the Iberian version in which the two co-exist. There may have been a similar duality in the old French texts, too. The other motifs are completely identical with those we have met so far, and only in their modern formulation do they differ—the meeting, the girl's question about her sweetheart, the despair at the news of his death, followed by the recognition by the ring. Only the nunnery is not mentioned, which is not to be wondered at, considering the spirit of pastourelles. And the new song agrees with the old—unlike the German version—in that the story begins with the scene of encounter, that is to say, the plot is built on one single scene.

The German construction deviating from the generally accepted form by the different application of the farewell and encounter scenes has found wide outlet in the Czech-Moravian and Slovak territories. Among the Yugoslavs, however, another arrangement prevails, also uniformly: the girl is planting flower in the garden, when a young soldier approaches and asks for a *garland*. "For nine years I have given a garland to no one, since my sweetheart went to the wars." "Your sweetheart is dead, take me instead." "I don't want anybody else, I love my first love." And in one variant (94.) she adds: "I will wait another seven years, and if my sweetheart is not back by that time, I shall go to a nunnery." After what has been said of the Hungarian version, it is unnecessary to give proofs that this variant is an adaptation of the Hungarian formulation.

To these has to be added the Greek ballad, which like the Hungarian, took its origin directly from the French. Thus the East-European nations adopted the story from three different sources: the French, the Germans and the Hungarians.

The ballad is of mediaeval origin, probably from the fourteenth century.

Literature: Abafi 1876c: Hungarian—German comparison: *Piguet* [+]1927: on the French variants; *Baud–Bovy* 1936: the Greek variants originate from the Neo-Latin; *Dános* 1938: Catalan, Dutch, German and (erroneous) Scottish correspondences to Hungarian variants; *Ortutay* 1948: accepts *Dános; Csanádi* and *Vargyas* 1954: accept *Dános;* D. Vlr. IV, 145, 1957: Black-Sea Greek variants listed with reference to The Cruel Mother-in-Law; *Vargyas* 1960 and 1967: the above survey and conclusions, without reference to the Danish version.

44. THE TURTLE-DOVE THAT LOST HER MATE

105.

A sad turtle-dove cooing sadly
Has lost her dear mate.
She flew into the green woods,
Yet she did not light on a green bough,
5. But she lighted on a dry bough;
Rapping on the dry bough,
She is lamenting her dear mate:
My mate, my mate, my dear mate!
I shall never have a dear mate
10. Like you, my dear mate!
The sad turtle-dove cooing sadly
Flew off to a distant land,
To a distant land and into a green corn-field.
Yet she did not light in the green corn-field,
15. But she lighted on a dry corn-cockle;
Rapping on the dry corn-cockle,
She is lamenting her dear mate:
My mate, my mate, my dear mate,
I shall never have a dear mate
20. Like you, my dear mate!
The sad turtle-dove cooing sadly
Flew off to a distant land,
To a distant land and to a river,
But she does not drink pure water,
25. Even if she drank a drop, she stirs up the water first,
And so is she lamenting her dear mate:
My mate, my mate, my dear mate!
I shall never have a dear mate
Like you, my dear mate!

Kolozsvár, 1872. Pál Gyulai = MNGY I, 179.

106.

Parlando

1. Küc ge - ri - ce   pa - tak mar - tyán   Csat-tog-tas - sa   szár-nyocs-ká-ját.

473

1. On the bank of the brook a little turtle-dove
   Is flapping her tiny wings,

2. Yet she does not get back her little mate,
   Yet she does not get back her little mate.

3. The big bird lights by her side:
   Why are you weeping, why are you weeping, little turtle-dove?

4. I cannot but weep, I cannot but cry,
   Because I am robbed of my dear mate,

5. Also my nest has been ruined.
   Don't weep, don't cry, little turtle-dove,

6. For I shall be a mate in place of your mate.
   But I don't want anyone else's mate,

7. Anyone else's mate, anyone else's curse,
   I only want my own true mate,
   I only want my own true mate.

8. She took on her wings and flew off,
   And she flew into the green woods.

9. Yet even there she did not light on a green bough,
   But even there she lighted on a dry bough.

10. She took on her wings again and flew off,
    And she flew into the green corn-field.

11. Yet even there she did not light in the green corn-field,
    But even there she lighted on a corn-cockle.

12. She took on her wings again and flew off,
    And she flew to the green meadow.

13. But even there she did not light on the nice green grass,
    But even there she lighted on the dry grass.

Gaiceana-Unguri (Moldavia). Young girls and women. 1934 = Domokos, No. 1.

Divergences: The first example (*105.*) had been followed by an analogus recording, similarly from Transylvania; our second example, in which the enticing bird appears, is parelleled by other songs, all from Moldavia, in which the other bird tries to approach the turtle-dove that has lost her mate. Remarkably enough, there are three variants speaking about a "big bird", the seducer, expelling the turtle-dove's mate. Instead of a "big bird" some texts mention a *nightingale*.

Earliest provenience: 1841–42 (Ince Petrás).

Dissemination: Transylvania, without closer specification of the provenience; Kolozs county (Kolozsvár), Csík county (Tekerőpatak); Moldavia (Dioszén 2, Forrófalva, Gajcsána, Klézse 3, Luizikalagor, Magyarfalu). Total 12.

Textual relationship with other ballads: "I shall be a mate in place of your mate"; **43.** (Attempt at seducing: **43.**; the bird as symbol of a lover: **45.**)

Tunes: 1. Tune published, plus a variant thereof;

Versions in languages other than Hungarian:

SPANISH: 1–6. Asensio, 234–235 Nos 1–4., 259, 260. 7. Geibel-Schack 414.

ROMANIAN: 8. Alexandri 264, No. XXXIII (Hungarian translation in Ethn. 1897, 187); 9–10. Teodorescu, 347–348 (in Hungarian, see Moldován 86).

Partial variants:

GERMAN: 11–14. E-B 67a-b, 681, 702.

DANISH (SWEDISH): 15. DgF 475 (Stanza 132, cf. Jonsson).

GREEK: 16. Firmenrich, 49.

FRENCH: 17. Gerold, 40 No. XXIX = Paris, 69 No. LXXI (from a MS of 1597).

Dubious analogies:

RUSSIAN: 18. Lintur 1968, 74–75.

It is after Physiologus's mediaeval *Natural History* that the belief according to which the turtle-dove that lost her first mate will never choose another and will never light on a green bough but mourns throughout her life, had spread all over Europe. True, originally a crow was mentioned in his work, but it was replaced by a turtle-dove in subsequent adaptations. As concerns Hungary, the theme can be traced from the publication of the sermons of Pelbárt Temesvári (*Aureum Rosarium*, 1504): "cum fuerit viduata de cetero non copulatur, siccis ramis arborum insidet semper tristis sicut et palumba". As a commonplace, it occurs in the poems of Balassi as well: "I am living as a widowed turtle-dove", and also in the verses of Rimay: "also the bird sees sorrows after its mate is died and lost; it has no more joys, and flying to and fro it looks for dry boughs in the green trees on which to light down..." (sixteenth century). In the seventeenth-century *Vásárhelyi Song-Book* the sorrowful turtle-dove comes up several times, although without reference to dry bough. But again in a gest of Poncianus (1653) we have the following: "I shall be like the turtle-dove which having lost its mate will never seek another one to live with, and will never light on a green bough, but always on a dry bough, because of its great sorrow."

The image of dry bough had been seconded by that of stirred-up water as late as the eighteenth century. A collection of songs entitled *Szíveket újító bokréta* (A bunch of flowers to enliven the hearts) contains the following lines: "Like a mournful turtle-dove whose heart is full of sorrow will wander from place to place to hide, having no hope whatever, the poor soul. It will not drink pure water, And it will always light on a dry bough, never on a green bough. So it wanders and laments to death, filled with pain." The same collection includes two more songs in which the motif of turtle-dove lighting on dry boughs occurs. Accordingly, this motif may be taken for the most typical trait of this literary commonplace—being at the same time the only mentioned characteristic feature of the earliest sources. The motif of stirred-up water is a secondary development. The only motif that I have failed to trace up in Hungarian literature is that of the nightingale assuming the role of the seducer, that is the love scene depicted by the aid of bird-symbols, which does occur in the Moldavian folklore texts.

It seems to be a promising venture to search the spread of the motif of the sorrowful turtle-dove in the field of European folklore anyway. The German texts use it as a simile to characterize the state of the bereaved lover. Stanzas 3–4 of "Die Trauernde" (E–B 702) read as follows: "Drum will ich mir kaufen ein aschergraues Kleid, Darunter will ich tragen gross Herzeleid, Gross Herzeleid und getreuen Muth, Wie es das Turteltäubchen auch tut. Das Turteltäubelein so hubsch und so fein, Es ruht nie auf einem grünen Zweigelein, Es trinkt auch niemanden das Wasser rein, Es schlägt erst mit beiden Flügelein drein." Similarly, in the variants of The Test of Faithfulness the heroine, upon advise by a stranger telling about her sweetheart's getting married to another girl, wants to mourn like a turtle-dove: "Es setzt sich auf ein dürren Ast, Das irret weder Laub noch Gras, Und meidet das Brümlein Und trinket das Wasser trübe" (E–B 67a, Stanza 13, much like E–B 67b, Stanza 12). It should be noted, however, that with the Germans a manuscript and a broadside variant of a folksong survive from the mid-sixteenth century: "Nu will jch senckenn meinenn moet, gleich wie die torteltaube thuet, wann sie jrenn gaden verlieret und nummer kheinen andern widder erkieset. Sie ensinget och nummer so süeßen sanck, sie endrincket auch nummer so lauteren dranck, sie floemet jnnen mit den foeßen ..." (JbfVf III = Liederhandschr. Minderscheidt, Stanzas 6 and 7.) This is fairly well paralleled by the stanzas of "The Test of Faithfulness", in which we have the following lines: "Ich führe jetzt ein betrüben muth gleich wie das Turteltäublen thut das seinen Bulen verloren hat so sitzt es auf ein dürren Ast. Sie trinckt das Wasser trübe das geschicht auß lauter lieb vnd güte sie betrübts mit jren füssen..." (Mid-sixteenth-century broadside E–B 67, Stanzas 10 and 11.)

The picture of the disturbed water here brings us nearer to the Hungarian, although the love scene of the two birds does not occur in these stanzas either. With the Danes the theme comes up in the form of a quotation embedded in the text of a different ballad type. DgF 475, Stanza 132: Throughout my life I shall sorrow like a turtle-dove. It never lights on a green but on a barren bough, and its legs are never tired: it never drinks clear water, but stirs it up with its legs.—As can be seen, the image of the stirred water comes up everywhere in folk poetry, whereas it does not occur in Hungarian literary texts before the eighteenth century.

Finally, the motif occurs included in an independent symbolic bird-story in the Spanish language area much in the same form as in the Csángó song of Moldavia: "Fresh fountain, nice and clear, every bird of the woods go there to appease its heart, except the turtle-dove that leads the life of a mournful widow. The traitor nightingale flies to her, and his speech is full of cheat and deception: Madam, will you please take me as your sweetheart!—Go away, your hateful beguiler, for I shall never rest on a green bough, nor in a flowery meadow. Where I find pure water, first I stir it up, and only then do I drink of it. I don't want to have anyone for a husband, nor do I want to have a child any longer. I don't want to be comforted in my mourn; I shall never have a lover, let alone a husband!" (7.)

According to *Asensio* (p. 235), the nightingale playing the role of a beguiler is a widespread motif in France, although it is not known in Spain. By emphasizing this circumstance he suggests that the song is of French origin. And indeed, traces of it can be found in the French folk poetry; two variants of the song about "The Two Princely Children" contain the concluding picture of the girl lamenting like this: "Je m'en irois parmi le bois, faire comme la tourterelle: Quand el a perdu son ami, Sur la branche s'en va mourir." (*Doncieux* 22). "Je m'en irai dedans le bois Faire comme la tourterelle, Lorsqu' elle a perdu son ami, Sur la plus haut' branch' du bois S'en mourir." (*Rolland* 187/c.)

Of course, also *Asensio* derives the motif of the sad turtle-dove from Physiologus as ultimate source.

This derivation should be certainly interpreted in a way that the motif had been commonly known by the learned circles as well as the populace, owing to mediaeval literary preliminaries. In addition, *Sándor Eckhardt* supposes that the popular song represents "a descended cultural element", that is to say, it is a reflection of some poetic composition. His idea, however, does not seem to be satisfactorily supported by literary texts. For one thing, and this is the main point, the figures of the two lovers symbolized by birds are fully absent in them; another thing is that the motif is consistently referred to as a commonplace taken for granted, and the situation is never explicated in full. Consequently, such allusions could never have given rise to a ballad in a direct way. Of course, it can be imagined that a popular song should have come into being from such allusions incidentally, that is in a circuitous way, but in this case also the Hungarian song ought to have been a chance work, with the nightingale as the central figure, like in the Spanish song. Such a coincidence, however, is hard to surmise. But what can be much more safely supposed is that the song—in the genre of a short symbolic story—had developed, perhaps from literary antecedents, among the French, from whom it had set out on its wanderings from people to people, just as the "scholarly tradition" did its wanderings among the learned circles of the various European nations. It is at this place that while working on the translation *Imre Gombos* called my attention to the following: "Chaucer's poem entitled *The Assembly of Fowls* includes a brief characterization of the turtle-dove as the symbol of faithful love, faithful to his lost mate to death, and of the owl as the representative of less lofty love, together with other birds, waterfowls, goose etc. *D. Laing Purves* refers to the French *fabliaus* as sources of the Chaucerian poem. These fabliaus most probably have their antecedents in Provençal courtly farces introducing characters masked as birds who represented the love affairs of the court." Accordingly, both may have got their own formulations. From the available data it may be inferred that it is the popular form that gave rise to the image of the turtle-dove sorrowing on the dry bough, by adding the motif of stirring up the water before drinking, either with her wings or her legs; this supposition seems the more plausible since the motif survives among peoples living far away from one another—Hungarian, Spanish, German and Danish—and since the motif is known from a mid-sixteenth-century folksong, whereas no literary data are known from before the late eighteenth century—not at least in Hungary— and even then it is suggestive of a folklore quotation. (The same can be well supposed in connection with the earlier literary sources, such as the stanzas quoted from Balassi or Rimay.) As against this, literature mainly passes down the "natural history" description of Physiologus, without unfolding the theme into a scene.

The song occurs in the Romanian language area in nearly the same form as in the Hungarian. I think it instructive to refer here to the version of Alexandri: "The sad turtle-dove cooing so sadly Alas, woe to her, poor soul! She has been left orphan, with no one to live with, Poor soul, alas, woe to her! She flies sadly to the wilderness, Alas, poor soul, woe to her! She is half dead, the poor creature, Having no rest, not a single happy moment, She does not want to take another one's lover as her mate. If she flies into the green woods, she does not care how green it may be, In a swoon she flies on and on, But she never lights on a green bough. If she stops flying sometimes, she lights on a dry bough, Or she sits on a rock, Hungry and thirsty as she is! If she comes by a cool fountain, She stirs up its stream, And if she meets with a hunter, She makes herself a prey to him." (It should be noted that the touch of Alexandri's literary taste is to be felt on the transcription.)

Also this song lacks the scene of temptation, this outstanding feature of the Hungarian version that links it up with the Spanish. Its form has some connection solely with the Hungarian version recorded by *Gyulay* (*105.*), which was first known to literature. Considering the geographical situation, the Romanians could hardly obtained the ballad from sources other than Hungarian.

A more remote parallel is offered by the Russian song described by *Lintur*. A couple of doves are sitting in an oak-tree, cuddling and kissing each other. A hunter or an eagle comes and kills the male. The couple are torn apart from one another. In vain does the hunter (eagle) try to comfort her, in vain does he offer her corn to eat and clear water to drink, for the dove does not eat and drink; she is lamenting all the time. And in vain does the hunter bring her other doves by the hundred, asking her to have her choice among them, she refuses all of them, and dies of sorrow in the end.

To sum up, the Hungarians have preserved a mediaeval, probably French theme, also in this song, supposedly in a form that bears much resemblance to the original. This is well brought out by the fact that the German–Danish version survives in the form of quotation embedded in other stories, while the distant Spanish song conforms in every respect to the Hungarian formulation. And traces of the motif can be detected in mediaeval French songs: *17.*, and the other listed pieces.

Literature: Eckhardt, S.: Középkori természetszemlélet a magyar költészetben (Mediaeval approach to Nature in Hungarian poetry). EPhK 1929, 81–99. *Ortutay* 1936–48 quotes *Eckhardt:* mediaeval origin; showing influence of literary flower-songs; *Csanádi* and *Vargyas* 1954: mediaeval origin, a popular belief was turned into ballad.

45. THE LITTLE OWL-WOMAN

107.

1. Pusz - ta ma-lom - ba Pusz - ta ma-lom - ba

Csër - fa gë - rën - da, Csër - fa gë - rën - da

1. In a desolate mill,
   In a desolate mill,
   There is a beam of oak,
   There is a beam of oak.

2. There is sitting on it,
   There is sitting on it,
   An owl-woman,
   An owl-woman.

3. Why do you weep, why do you grieve,
   Why do you weep, why do you grieve,
   You owl-woman,
   You owl-woman?

4. Alas, I have reason to weep,
   Alas, I have reason to weep,
   I have reason to grieve,
   I have reason to grieve.

5. For I left at home,
   For I left at home
   My painted bed,
   My painted bed.

6. I left in it,
   I left in it
   My husband János,
   My husband János.

7. I left by his side,
   I left by his side
   My rocking cradle,
   My rocking cradle.

8. I left in it,
   I left in it
   My son Imre,
   My son Imre.

9. I left by his side,
   I left by his side
   My tinned chest,
   My tinned chest.

10. I left in it,
    I left in it
    My chignon,
    My chignon.

11. Had I it about me,
    Had I it about me,
    I should leap
    As a steed.

12. Had I it about me,
    Had I it about me,
    I should turn
    Like a wheel.

Ghymes (Nyitra county). Three young girls (17 to 19 years old). Kodály 1916.

108.

In a desolate mill
There is a beam of oak,
There is walking on it
A little owl-woman.
5. After her is walking
A white turtle-dove.
Why are you weeping, why are you weeping,
Little owl-woman?
I have reason to weep,
10. You white turtle-dove:
I have left at home
My rocking cradle,
I have left in it
My crying baby!
15. Alas, alas, my baby,
My crying baby.
Why are you weeping, why are you weeping,
You white turtle-dove?
I have reason to weep,

20. You little owl-woman,
    For I left at home
    My locked chest,
    I left in it
    My pearled head-dress.
25. Alas, my pearled head-dress,
    My beautiful head-dress!

Udvarhelyszék, 1853. Kriza = MNGY XI. No. 267.

(When singing this song, the young will stand in a circle, in whose middle a young man, standing with a cushion in his hands, is looking around until he chooses a girl from the circle; he puts the cushion before her and kneels on it; the girl, too, has to kneel on the same cushion and accept the young man's kiss. Then she will stand in the middle of the circle occupying the place of the young man, and the play continues by her looking round in the above-described manner, to choose one of the young men.)

The meaning of the text is obscure. The forsaken cradle, husband, head-dress or bride's wreath may suggest some amorous, perhaps adulterous story, which often found expression by animal symbols in mediaeval times. In this respect the verse stands near the song of The Sad Turtle-Dove That Lost Her Mate (No. **44.**).

Divergences:

Stork-woman may replace the owl-woman; in one of the texts, owl-woman and Hungarian woman come up alternately, who are addressed by "a proud soldier walking there". The woman amswers: "Alas, I have reason to weep, You proud soldier..." (These variants have all been recorded from the Zobor Region.) In Veszprém county the "little owl-woman" is interrogated by a "gnat-woman". In three Transylvanian variants we have two birds asking questions: the nightingale and the tomtit put questions to the white turtle-dove.

Earliest provenience: 1853.

Dissemination: Veszprém county (Csetény), Nyitra county (Gerencsér, Ghymes 3, Zsére), Bars county (Lédec), Maros-Torda county (Marosvásárhely = Nagykálló, recorded in Szabolcs county, the informant having learned the song from his grandfather), Beszterce-Naszód county (Tacs 2), Udvarhely county ("Udvarhelyszék"). Total 11.

Textual relationships with other ballads: For the symbolic representation of two birds see Type **44.** (Perhaps the birds represent lovers.)

Tunes: 1. = 107. + 3.

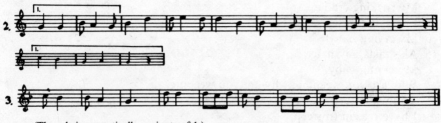

(These being practically variants of 1.)

482

Analogies are not known from other language areas. On the basis of the style and obscure symbolism of the text, the Type may well belong to the class of old (mediaeval) Hungarian ballads.

Here again holds *Imre Gombos's* previous reference (p. 477–8) namely that "the owl in this ballad may well have borrowed its character from the French fabliaus, perhaps from the Provençal courtly farces, as the symbol of enticer. Hence the character of the owl in this ballad and in certain lyrical songs (e.g. It can be easily told who is a whore, She goes to the well late in the evening; She can be recognized by her carriage, refr. As the owl by her call;" *L. Kiss,* Hódmezővásárhely).

46. THE RICH OLD HUSBAND

109.

Why do you weep, why do you moun, my dear wife?
I have got riches, a great deal of wealth,
A great deal of wealth, beautiful arables,
Beautiful arables, well-yielding vineyards,
5. Well-yielding vineyards, three herds of cattle,
Three herds of cattle, four nice horses to put to the coach,
Four nice horses to put to the coach, a castle built of stone,
A castle built of stone, and a beautiful daughter of the marrying age...
May God lay curse upon your great deal of wealth,
10. May the flood wash away your beautiful arables,
May the hail destroy your well-yielding vineyards,
May the lightning kill your four nice horses to put to the coach,
May plague destroy your three herds of cattle,
May your castle built of stone fall on you,
15. May I myself not see the sun tomorrow,
If you have no more of youthful strength.

Nagydém (Veszprém county). Káldy 1906 = MNGY VIII, 182.

The ballad is known to exist in three variants. The second variant ends with a lyrical folksong, which is also telling about the complaint of a woman whose marriage has gone wrong. The third variant has been reduced to seven lines, but even so it contains the entire problem and all the essential features of the other variants.

Earliest provenience: 1872.
Dissemination: Veszprém county (Nagydém, Tés), Tolna county (Ireg), Total 3.
Textual relationships with other ballads: for the content, cf. Type **131;** for the motif of curse, and practically the formulation of the entire duologue, Type **22;** displaying richness: Type **83.**
No tune has been recorded.

Regarding its theme, the manner of presentation in the form of duologue, and the style, the piece well fits into the stock of old ballads. A similar theme occurs among the French ballads (cf. 31.) and the Spanish balladry (cf. *Jona,* Note 4 to 64–65). Since however the composition lacks a plot, no analogies can be determined. For the time being, we must consider it to be a mediaeval ballad of Hungarian origin.

47. THE LOVER RETURNING AT HIS SWEETHEART'S WEDDING

110.

♩ = 132

1. A kert fe - ne - ki - be egy kör - te - fa a - latt

Ott van I - lo - nacs - ka, Györ - gyi - ké - vel sir - nak.

György te - le kö - nyü - vel, I - lo - ná - nak mond-ja:

1. Down by the garden, under a pear-tree,
   There is little Ilona, and she is weeping, together with little György.
   His eyes full of tears, György says to Ilona:
   His eyes full of tears, György says to Ilona:

2. I must tell you, little Ilona, that tomorrow I leave here,
   I leave here to join the army, to be a soldier.
   But it will not be a long time, only three years,
   But it will not be a long time, only three years.

3. Do you hear, little Ilona, what I tell you?
   I tell you to wait for me for three years!
   Swear by your little heart
   That you will be waiting for me for three years!

4. After all, three years are not so long a time,
   And a true sweatheart can wait until that in peace.
   But if you do not wait for me, little Ilona,
   May God grant me when I return home

5. That I can see your round courtyard tidy and clean,
   That I can see your body in the coffin in your courtyard!
   Let your father and your brothers lament over you,
   And let the banquet-table be laid before your gate!

6. Do you know what I have about that, my György?
   Three years are a long time to wait.
   But hurry, my György, hurry, and don't curse me!
   Hurry, my György, hurry, for I shall be yours.

7. Young György has gone to join the soldiers
   Little Ilona, alas, she has stayed back to marry another man.
   But not long after that György returned home,
   And asked his mother where little Ilona was.

8. They are gone, they are gone, and they are in the church,
   She is standing in front of the altar, and the priest is taking her oath.
   Poor György started, and a sad man he was.
   To see Ilona once more in the church.

9. When little Ilona saw György,
   Her heart broke with grief, and she died on the spot.
   György hurries to her, he hurries to see Ilona,
   His heart broke, and also he died.

10. But it was no sooner than he had died that he spoke up, saying:
    May the Lord deal heavily and may He not grant peace
    To those who separate two loving hearts from one another!
    To those who separate two loving hearts from one another!

Lészped (Moldavia). 19-year-old girl, 1955. Kallós = MSz 6280.

Apart from the detailed formulation of the Moldavian recordings, the motifs are identical and there is hardly any difference between the variants.

Earliest provenience: 1934 (fragment).
Dissemination: Moldavia (Bogdánfalva, Lészped 6, Rácsila, Trunk 4). Total 13.
Textual relationships with other ballads: For the farewell scene in the garden cf. **43.**, the death-curse, **59.**

Tunes: cf. the melody of No. 110, which is associated with 11 variants of this ballad. See further:

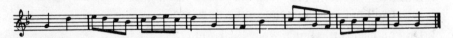

The recorded tune of one of the variants has not yet been published.

Versions in languages other than Hungarian:
FRENCH: *1–10. Millien* 173–176A–B plus 8 variants; *11. Puymaigre* 1865, 27.
ITALIAN: *12. Nigra* 28A.
GERMAN: *13–34.* D. Vlr. 102.
SPANISH-PORTUGUESE: Catalan IV, 15–19*, *Goyri* and *Menéndez–Pidal* IV, 15–19
(3 Spanish and 1 Portuguese variants).

The French ballad has the following plot: A girl encounters with a young man (sometimes with three), who (or one of them) accosts her: eventually he engages her. As the girl is too young to marry, the young man goes to the soldiers—or returns to the soldiers in case he had served with the army earlier. Later on, the father forces his daughter to marry an old man. Upon the wedding, the young man returns, and the girl dies in his arms. Then also the young man dies of sorrow. While dying, he sends word to his own father, telling that he had died with the soldiers (cf. the French Type 113). The Italian version has much the same story as the French. With the Germans the only difference is that when the young man returns on the day of his sweetheart's wedding, he appears at the feast and takes a seat at the table. During the feast he makes himself known to his bride. She asks her mother what to do but the young man, sooner than the answer could reach him, mounts his horse and gallops back to the army. (It is not impossible that two French ballads of the "returning" type have been combined in this plot, to wit, No. 113 and No. 115.)

After I had first published this ballad in 1960, *József Faragó* informed me in a letter that the theme has been worked up in a Romanian poem, and that in all likelihood the Csángó texts have derived from it. So far, however, I have been unable to acquire the Romanian text. Nevertheless, considering the international dissemination of the song, further the fairly uniform and rich tradition of the Csángó ballad, we may suppose with a high degree of certainty that it is the old Hungarian borrowing of the French ballad that survives among the Csángós of Moldavia to this date.

48. LÁZÁR, THE SON OF THE HUNGARIAN EMPEROR

111.

1. Ma - gya - ri csá - szár - nak Lá - zár fi - a va - la,

Mes - te - re Má- nó -nak És egy lá - nya va - la.

1. The Hungarian emperor
   Had a son called Lázár,
   Master Mánó
   Also had a daughter,

2. But their fathers did not let them
   Love each other,
   They did not even let them
   Have a talk together.

3. But they could not live without each other
   And whenever they met,
   Whenever they met,
   They had a talk.

4. The Hungarian emperor
   Had a son called Lázár,
   Who went to see
   Master Mánó's place.

5. Good day to you, good day to you,
   My unknown mother!
   Welcome, welcome
   My unknown son.

6. O, where can I find, where can I find
   My beautiful bride Erzsébet?
   She has gone, she has gone
   To the rose-field.

7. She has gone to the rose-field
   To gather roses,
   To gather roses,
   And to make a wreath from them.

8. And he went
   To the rose-field,
   But he could not find
   His bride Erzsébet there.

9. And he went back
   To Master Mánó's place.
   Good day to you, good day to you,
   My unknown mother!

10. Welcome, welcome,
    My unknown son!
    The second time I ask you,
    O, where can I find her, where can I find her?

11. Where can I find, where can I find
    My beautiful bride Erzsébet?
    She has gone, she has gone
    To the inn.

12. She has gone, she has gone,
    To the inn,
    To the inn,
    Where she is washing dish.

13. And he went
    To the inn.
    But even there he could not find
    His bride Erzsébet.

14. From there he went back
    To Master Mánó's place.
    Good day to you, good day to you,
    My unknown mother!

15. Welcome, welcome,
    My unknown son!
    The third time I ask you,
    Where can I find, o, where can I find her?

16. O, where can I find, where can I find
    My beautiful bride Erzsébet?
    Why should I deny,
    I have to own up to it in the end:

17. In the inner chamber,
    She is lying in her bed.
    And he entered
    The inner chamber.

18. And he entered
    The inner chamber.

And there he found
His bride Erzsébet.

19. May your body lie with my body
    In one common grave,
    May your blood flow with my blood
    In one common ditch.

20. May it flow in one common ditch,
    May it work a mill,
    And may that mill have
    Three stones.

21. May the first stone
    Drop small coins,
    May the second stone
    Grind love.

22. May the third stone
    Grind only sorrow!
    And they stayed there
    Until they died.

*Klézse (Moldavia). Female performer of 33 years of age. 1966, Kallós = Kallós
1970, No. 5.*

112.

1. The Hungarian Emperor
   Had a son called Lázár,
   Master Mánó
   Had a daughter called Erzsébet.

2. Their fathers did not let them
   Love each other,
   They did not even let them
   Have a talk together.

3. But they could not live without each other,
   And whenever they met,
   Whenever they met
   They had a talk.

4. But they had to die
   For each other's sake,
   For each other's sake,
   For their secret love.

5. For one of them they made
   A coffin of marble,
   For the other they also made
   A coffin of marble.

6. They buried one of them
   By on side of the road,
   And they buried the other
   By the other side of the road.

7. From one of them there grew
   A red rose-bush,
   From the other also grew
   A white rose-bush.

8. They were growing
   For three years,
   For three years
   They were in blossom.

9. The red rose-bush
   Brought beautiful white flowers,
   The white rose-bush
   Brought red flowers.

10. And they took delight in each other,
    And they were very glad,
    Because they bent together
    And began to talk.

11. But when their fathers and mothers
    Went to the place,
    They were so much bereaved
    That they withered down to their roots.

12. By the end of the third year
    They were cut out from the root,
    They were cut out from the root,
    And they were thrown on the fire-place.

13. Even their ashes
    Were blown away by the wind,
    And not even the memory survives
    Of their love.

Klézse (Moldavia). A 16-year-old girl, 1955. Kallós = MSz 6284.

Earliest provenience: 1955.

Dissemination: Moldavia (Klézse 6, Lészped). Total 7.

Textual relationships with other ballads: **9.,** "Let my blood flow with yours..." **10.,** "The Miraculous Mill" **68.**

Tunes: No. 111 occurs in two variants, No. 112, in three. (NB. The performer of 111 sang the text to both tune variants on different occasions.)

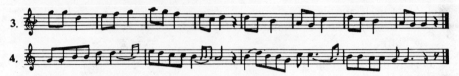

Versions in languages other than Hungarian:

ROMANIAN: *Amzulescu* No. 246. The story runs as follows: A lad and a young girl have been in love with each other from their early childhood. Their parents did not allow them to marry each other. Therefore they committed suicide by drowning themselves in water. The parents have the fishermen haul them, and bury the young man in the middle, the girl by the side of the field. Out of the young man's body there grew a tall pine, and out of the girl's body, a vinestock. The bypassers curse the parents who separated the lovers. (In some of the variants the flowers embrace each other.)

This ballad is a variant, one might even say, the extract of "The Two Chapel Flowers" **(9).** In a similar way, the Romanian song is an abridged variety of the theme of "The Two Chapel Flowers" which exists in a fuller form also in the Romanian language area. We have to consider two possible course of derivation in connection with this ballad. First, the two "abstracts" have developed one from the other, in which case the Romanian should be taken for the original since the ballad is known only by the Moldavian Csángós of the Hungarian language area. The second, both nations constructed a new version from a more detailed ballad story which they possessed on their own. This latter supposition seems to be corroborated by the fact that this time the Moldavian Csángós do not perform the story in their usual extemporized, lengthy and rather blurred formulation, but they follow the method of strict, strophic construction, selecting the portions of the song from various motifs of three Hungarian, that is Transylvanian ballads. The close agreements with the three Hungarian ballads suggest at the same time a very strong relationship between the Csángó "Abstract" and the Hungarian tradition. The only element that points to a Romanian origin is the name Master Mánó (Mestere Manó), which corresponds to the name of the hero known from the Romanian version of "The Walled-up Wife". But a single name used in isolation from other borrowed elements may well be regarded as an occasional adoption, which is the less significant since it does not come up in the parallel Romanian story. That is to say, the Csángó performers should have taken it from somewhere else in any case. (In this context we have to note that eight variants of those enumerated by *Amzulescu* have been recorded from territories inside the Carpathian Basin, and only two from outside—and none of them from Moldavia.) As a result of more recent investigations, this ballad increases the number of the so-called "transitional types".

492

49. FAIR ILONA LANGOS

113.

1. I - lo - nám, I - lo - nám, Lan-gos szép I - lo - nám,

I - lo - nám, I - lo - nám Lan - gos szép I - lo - nám.

1. My Ilona, my Ilona,
   My Fair Ilona Langos
   My Ilona, my Ilona,
   My Fair Ilona Langos.

2. She was sewing by the window
   With nice blue silk,
   She was sewing by the window
   With nice blue silk.

3. She adorned it
   With pure gold thread,
   She adorned it
   With pure gold thread.

4. Once she looked out of
   Her large window-pane,
   Once she looked out of
   Her large window-pane.

5. My brother, my dear brother,
   My brother, my dear brother,
   There they are coming, brother,
   There they are coming, brother!

6. You are mistaken, sister,
   You are mistaken, sister.
   My brother, my dear brother,
   My brother, my dear brother.

7. There they are coming, brother,
   There they are coming, brother,
   With five coaches
   And sixty soldiers.

8. My sister, my dear sister,
My sister, my dear sister,
Go into the chamber,
Go into the chamber.

9. Hide in the painted chest,
Hide in the painted chest.
And they arrived,
And they arrived.

10. With six horses and coaches,
And sixty soldiers.
With six horses and coaches,
And sixty soldiers.

11. With sixty soldiers,
And with a big, shabby man.
With sixty soldiers,
And with a big, shabby man.

12. And that big, shabby man,
Was her would-be mate,
And that big shabby man
Was her would-be mate.

Bogdánfalva (Moldavia). 59-year-old female performer, 1965. Kallós = AP 6283/a.

114.

1. S úgy var, úgy var va - la   Lan - gos szép I - lo - na,

Úgy var,   úgy var va - la, Ab - lak - ba var   va - la.

1. O, she was sewing, o, she was sewing,
Fair Ilona Langos,
O she was sewing, o, she was sewing,
Sitting by her window.

2. She embroidered it, she embroidered it
With rich silk thread,
And she filled the holes in it
With her flooding tears.

3. Why are you weeping, why are you moaning,
Fair Ilona Langos?
Alas, I have reason to weep,
I have reason to moan!

494

4. I have been my mother's
   Denied child,
   Who has lived in this world
   Without seeing a lucky day.

5. I have seen
   Only sadness and sorrow,
   Only sadness and sorrow,
   And this black mourn.

6. Wrapped full in black mourn
   Is this very year,
   In which my heart
   Finds no reason to rejoice.

7. Don't weep, don't moan,
   Fair Ilona Langos!
   For we shall look for
   The key to the green chest.

8. And we shall look for
   The happiness of your heart,
   And we shall look for
   The happiness of your heart.

9. My brother, my brother,
   I am very much afraid of
   The roaring green woods,
   The cracking guns.

10. Don't be afraid, sister, don't be afraid,
    For I can do something to stop
    The roaring of the woods,
    The cracking of guns.

11. As they took pains in coming here,
    In the same way they will return broken down,
    As they took pains in coming here
    In the same way they will return broken down.

"I don't know what she was afraid of."

Klézse (Moldavia). 61-year-old female performer. 1956. Kallós = Kallós 1970, No. 94.

The story is continued in other variants like this. The girl hides in a chest but is found and she takes leave of her mother: "Mother, my dear mother, This is the time for you to lament me!" The plot is not clear. Perhaps, it bears relationship with that of the ballad about "The Girl Forced to Marry against Her Will"—in which case the arrival of the "fine" procession would be understandable (cf. Types **11–15**). But in this version, then, the role of the brother would have been altered, because it is

495

not he that forces the girl to marry but on the contrary, he helps her hide. At the same time it is not precluded either that the ballad speaks about "The Girl Kidnapped by Soldiers" (cf. No. **31**), since in that story, as in the present one, the girl hides, or is hidden by her mother, in vain in the chest, because the visitors detect her hiding place.

Earliest provenience: 1955.

Dissemination: Moldavia (Bogdánfalva 3, Klézse, Külsőrekecsin (fragment), Lészped (fragment)). Total 6.

Textual relationships with other ballads: **11.–16., 31.,** for the opening formula, cf. **11.–14., 21., 31., (43.)** and **49.;** for the procession coming for the girl, cf. **14.**

Tunes: all the rest are essentially variants of the two melodies published here.

In all probability, this ballad has developed from Type **14,** with motifs borrowed from Type **31.** In principle, it may represent an old transitional form as well as the result of recent variation. In the Moldavian parts, even a modern variation may bear marks of the old style.

50. THE TWO CAPTIVE LASSES

115.

1. A tö-rö-kök s a ta-tá-rok két szép le-ányt el-rab-lá-nak,
Az e-gyik lányt, Bi-ró An-nát, s a má-si-kat, Bi-ró É-vát.

1. The Turks and the Tartars
   Had kidnapped two beautiful girls.
   One of them was called Anna Bíró,
   The other was called Éva Bíró.

2. Anna Bíró and Éva Bíró
   Had been kidnapped by the Turks.
   They chained their hands,
   And so they took them out of the village.

3. The girls were weeping
   Because they had to start for the long way,
   Their parents were weeping,
   Because they would never see them again.

4. Punish, Lord, punish the heathen folk,
   Who take away the Székely girls,
   To the grief of their parents,
   To the pleasure of the Turks.

5. In the inner part of Transylvania
   Nine small castles have been built.
   Nine bailiffs in the nine castles
   Have been put in iron by the Turks.

Csíkrákos (Csík county). 57-year-old man, 1957. Kallós = Vörös Zászló (Marosvásárhely), 11 August 1957 = AP 6586/b, Sárosi 1967.

116.

1. A tö-rö-kök, s a ta-tá-rok Mó-du-vá-ba ki-ha-tá-nak.

Mó - du - vá - nak sok tér - sé - ge Ve - ress vér - vel bé - precs - kel - ve.

1. The Turks and the Tartars
   Made a raid upon Moldavia.
   Many a place in Moldavia
   Has been spoiled with red blood.

2. The Turks and the Tartars
   Carried away two beautiful captives:
   One of them was the Fair Captive Erzsi Szabó,
   The other was the Fair Captive Kata Szabó.

3. As thirty-three years had elapsed,
   They returned to their village,
   They returned to their village,
   And to the gate of their father.

4. Let us in for the night,
   For we are fatigued to the last.
   For three days we have been walking,
   For three days we have not eaten a bit.

5. Go away from my gate,
   For we are having an entertainment in the house!
   Servant, chase them away,
   So that I may not see them again here!

6. Go wherever you may,
   For I don't want to receive beggars.
   My dear goodman, allow us
   To spend the night in the stable at least!

7. Servant, let them in the stable,
   Let them sleep in the manger!
   They went to the stable,
   And Erzsi Szabó soon died.

8. Kata began to lament:
   Sister, my sister, Erzsi Szabó,
   After thirty-three years
   We have returned to our father's estate.

9. And they did not want to let us in,
   And lo, here we are in the stable!
   O, why did we come back?
   O, why did we not stay there!

10. Noise of entertainment is heard from the house,
    Noise of lamenting from the stable.

Alas, my dear sister, kind sister,
Why did you leave me by myself?!

11. We had set out to seek joy,
And we arrived here to find grief.
But could we have thought of them
Not taking us in?

12. János Szabó, our dear father,
Come here, and you too, our dear mother
To see how Erzsi Szabó has died
To the great wonder of the whole world!

13. My goodwife was walking out,
And heard the wailing words of Kata.
Make speed, man, and come at once,
Because my two beautiful daughters have come home!

14. She took up Erzsi Szabó,
Kissing her face and her hands.
My dear child, my kind daughter!
My dear child, my kind daughter!

15. Sooner than her father arrived
Kata Szabó died, too.
The whole world gathered together there
To take a look at the two bodies.

16. Erzsi Szabó, Kata Szabó,
They have come home to meet their deaths.
Their dear father and their dear mother
Are lamenting them bitterly.

17. And they may lament them, they may mourn for them,
Now that both of them are dead!
They cannot revive them for a moment,
Why did they not let them in!?

*Lészped (Moldavia). 67-year-old female performer. Kallós 1959 = Utunk XXIV,
No. 44 (1006). 31 October 1969, 7.*

Apart from the figures of the two sisters and a word-for-word agreement of
one of the stanzas announcing their having been taken prisoners, the two ballads
have hardly a trait in common. The second ballad relates the story of Type 17. (The
Two Captives) in a Moldavian styling: the sisters, not recognized, fail to be
admitted in their parent's house, and recognition takes place only after one of them
has died. As against this, the motifs of struggle, wounding, etc. are omitted, which is
only natural in the case of girls. (This story occurs much in the same form in another
variant from Lészped.) The first ballad, No. 115, on the other hand, knows nothing
about the girls' return, but preserves such details which may perhaps be considered
as fragmentary survivals of some other story. It is not impossible that from such a

no longer extant ballad-story, and from that of the Moldavian story about The Two Captives, a new version has developed in the Moldavian region. In any case, the two ballads under discussion provide examples for transition variants between fully crystallized types. Considering this, we may well regard the ballads as recent developments, although it is not precluded either that they preserve survivals of some very old tradition. This refers in particular to No. *115*. The tune of the third variant is the following:

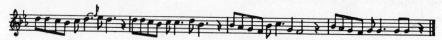

51. THE YOUNG LORD OF MEZŐBÁND

117.

Have you heard the fame of famous Barassó?
In it they had a wasting prison made,
And the young lord of Mezőbánd was thrown in it.
At a time, the young lord of Mezőbánd spoke:
5. I wish I had a scribe
And a trustworthy man:
Then I would have a letter written by my scribe,
And would have it delivered by my trustworthy man.
At that very instance his mother dropped in.
10. Mother, mother mother, my dear soul, my mother!
I had a dream last night:
Two ells of red thread around my neck,
And two black ravens above my head!
The devil take your dream, son!
15. The two ells of red thread mean your red blood,
The two black ravens mean your hangman.
Mother, mother, mother,
I wish you had born a stone when giving birth to me,
And when you were washing me in lukewarm water,
20. I wish, you had been washing me in boiling water!
And when you were wrapping me in soft linen,
I wish you had wrapped me in living coal!

"Marosszék" = *MNGY I, 188.*

This ballad recorded without a tune survives in this single variant.

Textual relationship with other ballads: The opening formula constitutes a much-favoured turn of recent Hungarian prisoners' songs. For the dream, cf. Type **23,** and for the self-curse of the young man, Type **20** (and a great number of lyrical songs). This ballad is distinguished from the next Type **(52)** by the absence of the motif of ransom, furthermore, and this is more important, by the circumstance that here there is no mention of Turkish imprisonment, and that the hero is not a war-prisoner but a victim of the feudal times, possibly a convict. As it is, this ballad represents a link connecting old-type Hungarian ballads with the more recent outlaw ballads.

52. THE LITTLE NOBLE LAD

118.

In big Turkey, a little noble lad,
Innocent and blameless as he is, the poor soul, is being kept in prison.
He shouts with loud words: Mother, my dear mother,
You have got three castles built of stone, do ransom me by one of them!
5. I shall not ransom you, I shall not ransom you, my dearest heart, my son,
For the Lord will grant me a son instead of a son,
But the Lord will not grant me a castle of stone instead of a castle of stone!
Then I don't mind, mother, dearest heart, I don't mind,
The two coasts of the sea will be my coffin,
10. The thick foam of the sea will be my shroud,
The roaring of the sea will be my chiming.
I shall be buried by the fish of the sea,
I shall be lamented by the birds of the sky,
By the birds of the sky, and by the beasts of the woods.

"Székelyföld", Kriza = MNGY III, No. 28.

The ballad exists in one single tuneless recording.

Textual relationships with other ballads: The Lord grants me a son instead of a son: **4** and **69**; for the self-lament of the prisoner, cf. Type **29**.

The thematic build of the ballad has close relationship with the story of The Heartless Mother, and well fits into the general conception of mediaeval ballads. Memories of the Turkish occupation survive in the motifs of castles made of stone and the redeeming of the son who is a prisoner abroad. The situation in which a young prisoner asks his mother to ransom him comes up fairly frequently in Hungarian prisoners' songs, and this text element is a connecting link between these and the more recent outlaw ballads. No foreign parallels are known to exist. It may be a mediaeval as well as a recent development.

53. THREE YOUNG THIEVES

119.

There they are going, there they are going,
The three young thieves,
There they are going, there they are going,
Through vast forests.
5. In the vast forests
They hit upon a Greek merchant,
The Greek merchant they killed,
And they looted his cart.
There they are going, there they are going,
10. The three young thieves.
They hit upon a tavern,
And they entered it.
They began to ask at once:
Hey, landlady!
15. Is there any good wine to be had here?
I have got good wine,
And I also have got a nice girl,
Although I myself am a merry dame.
There they are eating, there they are drinking,
20. The three young thieves.
Although the youngest one
Does neither eat nor drink,
He does neither eat nor drink.
He is full of sorrow:
25. May the Lord had granted
That my rocking cradle
Should have been my coffin,
My swaddling clothes
Alas, should have been my shroud,
30. And my swaddling band
The rope with which my body would have been sunk into the grave!

Transylvania. Kriza = MNGY III, No. 17.

The ballad survives in one single recording.

Textual relationships with other ballads: The motif of the three brigands with the youngest one who rues the day he was born, and the construction with the landlady involved, bear resemblance to Type **19**; the complaint in the end, to Type **20**.

503

The French too have such ballad-like texts in which the robber repents his misfeats, complaining about his way of life and the crimes he had committed (cf. 134–135). Nevertheless, we cannot establish a direct connection between these and the Hungarian ballad that may have developed at a time when old French ballads made their way into Hungarian folklore. Perhaps it is contemporaneous with Type **19.**

54. THE OUTCAST

120.

1. Over Bodok, there is a thick grove,
   And poor Dávid Dáncsuj is moaning in it.
   It is not safe, it is not safe for you to walk about here,
   For how can you escape if someone happens to detect you?

2. If I cannot find peace here, then where shall I go?
   Where can I find a little place of safety at last?
   Where the gendarmes are not always at my heels,
   And where I need not always tremble for my life?

3. Were it that the black earth would cleave in two,
   Poor Dávid Dáncsuj would certainly sink in it.
   But the black earth cannot cleave in two,
   And poor Dávid Dáncsuj cannot sink in it.

4. My lord, my Lord, where is my sweetheart
   To say a consoling word to me?
   You have promised me, sweetheart, to come on wings to see me,
   But if you cannot come on wings, you might come by foot at least.

5. I have become, darling, like a dry stalk
   Left behind by the sickle after harvest.
   You might come to see me, darling,
   For I am lying here in line with the dead.

6. Son, my dear son, do not mourn over your fate,
   For we shall put right your case somehow.
   Come home at last and surrender,
   So that the gendarmes may not trace you all the time.

7. I do not go, but I thank you,
   Dear, kind mother and dear kind father,
   That you have raised a brave son to serve the emperor,
   To serve the emperor and to deserve the gallows.

Sepsiszentgyörgy (Háromszék county). A pupil of F. Kanyaró = Ethn 1906, 237.

Divergences: The variants of this ballad have retained only the motifs of lyrical complaint and the imagined address of the robber; regarding its theme, the song belongs to the group of the outlaw ballads, while the intonation recalls the style of old ballads. It must have developed in recent times under the influence of old-style ballads and prisoners' songs. Allegedly, it has as its hero a Romanian outlaw who lived in the mid-nineteenth century.

Earliest provenience: 1882.

Dissemination: "Erdély" (Transylvania) without any closer reference, Háromszék county (Sepsiszentgyörgy, Dálnok, Málnás), Total: 7.

Textual relationships with other ballads: The complaints of the outcast resemble in more than one respect those of "The Brigand's Wife". At the same time, they show a fair agreement with a number of lyrical plaintive songs.

Tunes:

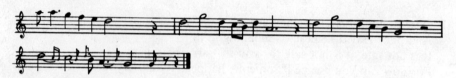

In two variants.
No foreign parallels have been found.

55. EMPEROR FÜLÖP

121.

Quasi rubato ♩= cca 100

1. Szolgálj in-gem, szolgálj, Szolgálj in-gem, szolgálj

Gaz-dag Fü - löp csá-szár, gaz-dag Fü-löp csá - szár!

Mert ién né-ked a-dom, Mert ién né - ked a-dom.

1. Serve me, serve me,
   Serve me, serve me,
   Rich emperor Philip,
   Rich emperor Philip!
   For I'll give you,
   For I give you

2. Fair Black Kata,
   Fair Black Kata.
   It has been useless,
   It has been useless
   For me to get up so early in the morning,
   To get up so early in the morning.

3. Because they did not give me,
   Because they did not give me
   Fair Black Kata,
   Fair Black Kata...

Trunk (Moldavia). 36-year-old man. Veress 1930 = MF 2491a.

There exists one more text mixed with lyrical elements of this ballad type:

1. Mother, my dear mother,
   It has been useless for me
   To get up early in the morning,
   To go to bed late at night,

2. To drive the cart with the six oxen,
   To plough the long field;
   For they did not give me
   Black Kata Rén.

3. For they did not give me
   Black Kata Rén,
   Black Kata Rén,
   Our serf's daughter.

4. Mother, my dear mother,
   I wish I were river water,
   So that I might not see sorrow...
   (etc. in seven stanzas.)

Earliest provenience: 1930.
Dissemination: Moldavia (Klézse, Somoska, Trunk). Total: 3.
Textual relationships with other ballads: **9? 40? 73?**
Tunes: apart from the published No. 121, see the following ones:

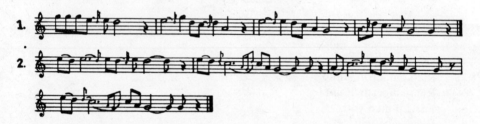

Versions in languages other than Hungarian: The two fragments at hand contain so very few elements of the original story as to make any comparison with other ballads impossible. The motif of doing service in order to deserve the hand of a lord's daughter occurs in the beginning of Type **40,** as well as in many of the European ballads. It is also a beginning formula in the English ballads. See, for instance, *Child* 17, Hind Horn D/2: "Seven long years he served the king. An it's a' for the sake of his daughter Jean." F/2: "Seven long years he served the king, For the love of his daughter Jean." The motifs of serving the king and of love developing between the hero and the king's daughter come up in *Child* 99, 101.

In all likelihood, the fragment is an eroded survival of a mediaeval ballad.

56. FAIRY ILONA

122.

Poco rubato ♩= cca 96

1. Ho - va mensz, ho - va mensz Te. ke - vil ka - ta -na?

Itt e - lé, s itt e - lé, Te - ker - gős pa - tok - ra.

1. Where are you going, where are you going
   You proud soldier?
   Going ahead, going ahead
   Onto the winding brook.

2. Onto the winding brook,
   And to Fairy Ilona.
   Fairy Ilona's
   Gate is ivied.

3. Her gate is ivied,
   Her door is creaking,
   Her door is creaking,
   Her ceiling is all ribbons.

4. She has four glass windows,
   And her cross-beam is spun of strings.
   Her floor is covered with marble,
   And her ingle-nook is full of flower.

5. Her table is made of marble,
   Her table-cloth is woven from laurel...

Klézse (Moldavia). 39-year-old female performer. 1950–53 = Faragó-Jagamas No. 15.

This fragment survives in one single variant. The beginning stanza bears a certain degree of semblance to the incipit of Type **76** (The Suitor of the Faulty Girl). Anyway, neither the relationship of the theme nor the time of its origin can be ascertained.

57. TAKE OUT MY WEARY HEART...

123.

Poco rubato ♪ = 156

1. Meg - be- te - gült Sza - bó Ka - ta a di - ós - ba.

A di - ós - ba, a di - ós - ba, mo-gyo-rós - ba.

1. Kata Szabó grew sick in the nut-tree grove.
   In the nut-tree grove, in the nut-tree grove, in the hazelnut grove.

2. Her mother asks her what ails her?
   It is neither heart-ache, neither heart-ache, nor head-ache,

3. It is neither heart-ache, neither heart-ache, nor head-ache,
   It is because I have fallen in love.

4. Mother dear, let my speaking heart be taken out,
   My speaking heart, my speaking heart, my light gaiety!

5. Let it be taken out, let it be placed in a new chest,
   So take it, so take it to the new shop.

6. If people ask you, if people as you what you are selling:
   You are selling Kata Szabó's speaking heart, and her light gaiety!

Ghymes (Nyitra county). 70-year-old female performer. T. Ág, 1960 = M. Sz. 6771.

Nut and hazelnut are often used as love-symbols. (Cf. the texts related to the custom of fire-kindling on midsummer nights, MNT II, 260–68.) Fragment recorded in one single variant.

Textual relationships with other ballads: Cf. the text of Type **68.** from Nyitra county: "It is neither heart ache nor head-ache..." etc. "Let my speaking heart be taken out...", etc., in Types **6., 20., 25.** and **31.;** further the motif of taking out the heart really in Type **38.**

Versions in languages other than Hungarian:

FRENCH: *1. Wallonia* I, 36, 1893. *2. Bujeaud* II, 213. *3. Libiez* III, No. 21. *4. Canteloube* IV, 157. *5–6. Puymaigre* 1865, 171, and Notes to 172–3. *7. Barbeau* 1962, 421. *8. Udry,* 196; *9. Choleau,* 153. *10. Seignolle,* 155.

ITALIAN: *11–14. Nigra* 27A–D (E and G: lacking this motif; F: unidentifiable).

Partial variants:

FRENCH: *15. Meyrac* 263. *16. Tarbé* III, 57. *17–18. Canteloube* III, 111 and IV, 134. *19. Puymaigre* 1865, 390. *20–22. Rolland* I 50a–b and II 50a–b.

The figure of the girl suffering from love, together with the nut-symbol, occurs in a French ballad as well (83, cf. partial variants). The girl had eaten three nuts in her father's orchard and fell ill in the ninth month. She wants to see her lover again, and when he arrives, she begins to feel better. (In other context but still as a love-symbol the motif comes up with the English: *Child* 41/B, Stanza 1.) On the basis of the more detailed Hungarian ballads enumerated above, the motif of the girl's wish to have her heart be taken out and locked up in a chest, etc. can be fairly well recognized in another French ballad, in 123. The story runs like this: a young man goes to the soldiers. He beholds his sweetheart's ring on the finger of his officer. A duel takes place, and the young man kills the officer. Before his execution he says the following words: "Que l'on mette mon coeur Dans un' serviette blanche, Qu'on le porte a mà mie, Qui demeure au pays En disant: c'est le coeur De votre serviteur." (*2., 3.*). "On env'loppra mon coeur Dans un' serviette blanche..." (*4., 8.*). "Coupez mon coeur en quatre, Envoyez-le à Paris, A Paris chez ma mie, Quand elle verra, Elle s'en repentira." (*5.*) And finally: "Qu'on le porte a Paris A mamzelle Julie, Qu'elle me fasse l'honneur de recevoir mon coeur. Elle prit son coeur, Le mit dans une *cantine, Dans cantine d'eau-de-vie*... (*6.*) At this point, however, the French text seems to be obviously corrupt, since it must have been originally the soldier who said the last sentence, because then it goes on: "Soldats de mon pays, Ne l'dit's pas à ma mère..." It was probably originally: Qu'elle prit mon coeur..." etc.

As can be seen, the French version shows a perfect agreement with the formulas found in old-style Hungarian ballads: "Take out my heart, Take out my liver, Put them into a brass plate, Wash them in wormwood wine, Wrap them in fine linen, Send them to Moldavia, To the gate of my father, From his gate to his table..." (Type **6,** The Three Orphans And what is more, a recently discovered Moldavian variant adds: "Cut it into five or six, Wash it in wormwood wine". In other variants, the youngest orphan's heart is placed in a chest or a coffin instead of a brass plate.

The French song is new in its intonation; the motif of taking out the heart and sending it to the sweetheart is mediaeval of origin (cf. Type **38**). In the French version in which the grieving lover wants his sweetheart to remember him may well be equally of mediaeval origin, otherwise we could not find such a close agreement between the French and the Hungarian details. Also the Italians know the French song, although they have preserved no more than "Take my heart and bring it to my sweetheart"; that is to say, missing are the wrapping in a kerchief, the washing in wormwood wine or spirit,—all such details that are apt to connect the Hungarian formulation with the French. With the French, the old texts must have undergone a transformation in recent times, while with the Hungarians there survives only one fragment which seems to preserve an original context, on the one hand, and as a separately fitting motif in four different stories on the other. Its antiquity is indicated also by the circumstance that it is once again the distant areas of Transylvania, Moldavia and the Zobor region in County Nyitra that have maintained the motif in a form similar to the French. Both the fragment and the details of the other ballads originate in the period of French–Hungarian contacts of the fourteenth century.

With the French, this formula always occurs in the same ballad, and constitutes an organic part of the story. With the Hungarians, however, this formula—although seemingly more complete and frequent—finds application in several stories of different plot-schemes, and does not form an essential part of the narrative. That is to say, it is a formula-like element torn out of its original environment and fitted into the story as a secondary development. Consequently, this Hungarian fragment is a merger of two French ballads whose elements have been welded into one.

All this seems to indicate that the Hungarian version is a borrowing which has preserved an earlier formulation than the French did in its original place of birth where it was subjected to strong subsequent changes.

Literature: Vargyas 1960, 1967; *Leader* 1967.

58. SITTING BY MY NEW DISTAFF

124.

1. Új gu-zsa-lyam mel-lett   Pus-ka rop-pa-ná-sa,

Po-gány vér-vel   fes-tett,   Ab-lam vil-lám-lá-sa

1. Sitting by my new distaff
   I heard the crack of a gun,
   And I saw the flash
   Of a sable painted with pagan blood.

2. O, you beautiful girls,
   What are you smiling at?
   I can see with my two eyes
   That you are laughing at me.

3. Instead of laughing at me,
   You had better give me to eat,
   From your brass cup
   You had better give me to drink.

4. There go seven girls,
   And all the seven are wearing a head-dress,
   They are followed by seven young men,
   And all the seven are wearing spurs.

5. Your skirts are long,
   You stir much dust,
   Your hair is long,
   Your brain is short.

Klézse (Moldavia). 17-year-old girl. Kallós = Kallós 1958, N. 11.

The ballad is a fragment recorded in one single variant. It is not quite sure if it is a ballad at all, only its duologue form lends the scene a ballad-like appearance. Otherwise, it permits of no inference regarding its content or origin.

59. FAREWELL TO THE SWEETHEART

125.

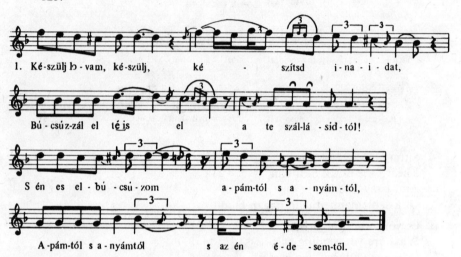

1. Ké-szülj ló-vam, ké-szülj, ké - szítsd i - na - i - dat,

Bú - csúz-zál el té is el a te szál-lá - sid-tól!

S én es el - bú - csú - zom a - pám-tól s a - nyám - tól,

A -pám-tól s a - nyámtól s az én é - de - sem-től.

1. Prepare, my steed, prepare, and make ready your legs,
   Bid farewell to your lodgings, you too!
   For I bid farewell to my father and mother,
   To my father and mother, and to my sweetheart.

2. To my sweetheart, my only love in this wide world.
   To my sweetheart, my only love in this wide world.
   Give me a kiss, sweetheart, before I start on my long journey!
   The Lord brings me back, and then I give you a hundred kisses.

3. You may depart or sit by my side,
   For my heart breaks at your sight!
   May the Lord grant me that, when I return,
   When I return on the paths of love,

4. I should find your creaking gate open at last,
   I should find your creaking gate open at last,
   I should find your courtyard properly cleaned,
   I should find your coffin placed in front of your door!

5. I should find your father and mother bent over your coffin,
   I should find all your relatives standing round it!
   And I do not want your death, sweetheart,
   Because I am bored of your earthly life,

514

6. I only want your death, sweetheart,
   Because you cannot pass your days with me;
   And I do not want you to seek pleasure in someone else's arms,
   And I do not want you to seek pleasure in someone else's arms!
   Rosemary stalk grown in the mountain of Lévános,
   Precious drops of dew pour on each of its branches. (To lines 3 and 4.)

Ketris (Moldavia). 63-year-old female performer. Veress 1930 = NÉ 1941, 165.

126.

Early on Friday morning
I had a dream:
Early on Sunday morning
It came true to me.
5. I went up to my garden,
And I looked down from the garden:
My finest rose-tree
Lowered one of its branches.
From the place the sun rises
10. It spread to the place where the sun sets.
Then my heart
Was wrapped in black mourn.
My sweetheart came to me,
And she asked me:
15. Why do you weep, sweetheart?
O, my heart is aching,
And I don't really know for whom,
And I don't really know for what;
Is it perhaps for me?
20. You are right, sweetheart.
When I walk down
On the street of love,
May I find your mournful coffin
In front of your door.
25. May I see in it
Your beautiful, white body,
And may I see the priest and the cantor
Standing at your head,
And all your kind relatives may I see
30. Standing around you!
But I do not wish, sweetheart,
That you should die
Because I have been tired
Of living with you.

35. But if you have not found
    Your pleasure with me,
    You must not have another one
    To give pleasure to you!

Csíkrákos (Csík county). Mailand 1905 = MNGY VII, 11.

The story is presented in a rather vague outline. The third text completes the sentences referring to the burial like this: "If you have been tired, sweetheart, Of living with me, Have a coffin made And me buried in it! Write on my cross That an orphan is lying there Who has died of love."

Earliest provenience: 1905.
Dissemination: Csík county: (Csíkrákos), Moldavia (Ketris, Klézse), Total 3.
Textual relationships with other ballads: The wish of death as a curse appears in **47** as well. The first four lines of 126 occur in **23**.
Tunes: 1. = No. 125; 2:

We have no data referring to the existence of any foreign parallels. It may be regarded as a special motif which has not yet been rounded into a complete story; but it may be a portion of some other ballad that begins to start a separate life.

60. JÁNOS WHO WAS POISONED

127.

1. Where have you been, my dearest heart János?
   Alas, I have been at my sister-in-law, dear mother!
   Oh, my heart aches, aches, lay my bed!

2. What did they give you to eat, my dearest heart János?
   They gave me four-legged crab, dear mother!
   Alas, my heart aches, aches, lay my bed!

3. In what plate did they serve it, my dearest heart János?
   They served it in a polished plate, dear mother!
   Alas, my heart aches, aches, lay my bed!

4. Maybe, that dish made you sick, my dearest heart János.
   It will take me deep into the earth, dear mother!
   Alas, my heart aches, aches, lay my bed!

5. And what do you leave to your father, my dearest heart János?
   My good ironed cart, dearest heart mother!
   Alas, my heart aches, aches, lay my bed!

6. And what do you leave to your elder brother, my dearest heart János?
   My four good oxen, dearest heart mother!
   Alas, my heart aches, aches, lay my bed!

7. And what do you leave to your younger brother, my dearest heart János?
   My four fine harnessed steeds, dearest heart mother!
   Alas, my heart aches, aches, lay my bed!

8. And what do you leave to your young sister, my dearest heart János?
   My household movables, dearest heart mother!
   Alas, my heart aches, aches, lay my bed!

9. And what do you leave to your sister-in-law, my dearest heart János?
   Eternal damnation, dearest heart mother!
   Alas, my heart aches, aches, lay my bed!

10. And what do you leave to your mother, my dearest heart János?
    Grief and sorrow, dearest heart mother!
    Alas, my heart aches, aches, lay my bed!

Székelyföld, Kriza 1882 = MNGY III, Stanza 3.

128.

1. Where have you been, where have you been, my dear son János?
   Alas, I have been at my sister-in-law, alas, I have been at my sister-in-law.
   Oh, lay my bed soon, dear mother!

2. And what dish were you given by your sister-in-law, my dear son János?
   Alas, stuffed chicken, alas, a festive cake.
   Oh, lay my bed soon, dear mother!

3. And what dish were you given by your sweetheart my dear son János?
   Alas, head of the hatchet(?), alas, spotted loach.
   Oh, lay my bed soon, dear mother!

4. And what do you leave to your sweetheart, my dear son János?
   Alas, heart-ache, alas, a great illness.
   Oh, lay my bed soon, dear mother!

5. And what do you leave to your sister-in-law, my dear son János?
   Alas, six oxen, alas, an ironed cart.
   Oh, lay my bed soon, dear mother!

6. And what do you leave to your father, my dear son János?
   Alas, sickness, alas, poverty.
   Oh, lay my bed soon, dear mother!

7. And what do you leave to your mother, my dear son János?
   Alas, blindness, alas, begging from door to door.
   Oh, why did you not lay my bed?

"Felső Marosvölgy" (Maros-Torda county). A girl informant. Meltzl 1880.

129.

1. Hol vol - tál az es - te, szü-vem, Já - no - som?   A szom - széd - ba vó - tam,
é - des - a - nyám asz-szony. Jaj jaj szü - vem fáj,   Vesd az á - gyat most!

Where were you last night, my bonny son János?
At the neighbour's, my dear mother.
Alas, alas, my heart aches, lay my bed soon!

Udvarhely county, 1871–72 = Bartalus VI. No. 2.

Kriza notes that "the four-legged crab should be interpreted, according to the informants as paddock, that is poison". The "spotted loach" mentioned in Stanza 3 was taken by *Meltzl* for a sort of vermicelli, whereas it definitely refers to loach and

518

its colour. Anyway, this variant is rather eroded and corrupt, and nothing is known about the notator. As far as it can be judged from the last stanza, the piece was taken down not after a singing performance but from the mouth of a reciter. (*Translator's note:* the "head of the hatchet?" =*fejszefokot* is obviously a corrupt expression, due either to lapse of memory or to faulty notation, instead of *vejsze-fogott*= "fishweir-caught". This seems the more likely since some English variants also refer to mud, and the 'loach' lives in mud.)

Earliest provenience: during the winter of 1871–72, the period in which *Bartalus* made his collection. Published in 1895.

Dissemination: Udvarhely and Maros-Torda counties (without any reference to the community, 3 vars).

Textual relationships with other ballads: For content and formulation, see **61.** and **62.;** see further **41.** and **79.** for the stanzas about the bequest.

Tune: solely given in connection with No. 129.

Versions in languages other than Hungarian:

ENGLISH: *1–48. Child* 12, plus I, 499–501, IV, 449–450, V, 208–209. *49–149. Bronson* 12. *150–163. Belden* 25A–D. (D. Vlr. 79 lists a further 52 variants.)

ITALIAN: *154–155. Bernoni* 1874 No. 1 plus variant. *156. Bolza* No. 49. *157. Giannini,* 199 No. 27. *158. Pergoli,* 17 No. 10. *159–161. Nigra* 26A–C.

GERMAN: *162–192.* D. Vlr. 79 (I have been given an opportunity to study the unpublished variants in original notation).

DANISH (SWEDISH): *193–195.* DgF 341, plus X, 791 *(ibid. Jonsson).*

SLOVAK: *96. Horák* 1958, 43 No. 4. = *Kollár* II, 35/46. *197–198.* Slov. sp. III, Nos 362 and 568. *199.* EMU I, 89–90. *200. Kolečány,* 35 No. 10. *201–203.* SL'P I, No. 287, II, No. 378, III, No. 566. *204–206. Bartók* 1971, 464c, 623c, 625a. (D. Vlr. lists a further 7 variants. See also *Burlashova* 18ab:)

CROAT (CARPATHIAN-UKRAINIAN): *207. Žganec* 1946, 109.

Dubious relationships:

ROMANIAN: *208. Brăiloiu,* 83. *209–210.* Ethn 1897, 284 and 285. *211. Pompiliu,* 27.

This ballad, as many other Hungarian ballads, represents an easternmost type of a very extensive European family and shows a striking similarity to the formulations of distant western nations: over a vast field it enjoys a spread in the same repetitive strophic construction with refrains. Also the content is invariably the same: the returning son or daughter is interrogated by the mother (father), and from the answers it appears gradually that he (she) has been poisoned.

The row of variants ranges from the English (-American) language areas, through Scandinavia and Germany, to the Slovaks and the Italians (even a Polish provenience in one single copy is available). The number of variants in English amounts to 205 (according to the 1959 summary German edition). Of these, I have been able to study 153 variants, in addition to the 31 listed German and 2 Danish ones. Most of the Slovak variants have come to my hand, but of the 50 Italian listed texts, only 8 have been accessible to me. Since, however, the Italian formulation is uniform practically with no essential divergences, no surprisingly new type is likely to occur among them. Certain Romanian and Slovakian texts have been disregarded in my survey, although they are mentioned in the German summary edition. My reason for this have been that the Romanian ballad has nothing in common with the otherwise fairly uniform European tradition, apart from the fact that a case of some poison applied occurs in them; the Slovenian ballad, on the other hand, will be discussed below, along with the members of the type of "The Bewitched Son".

519

It seems most appropriate to begin the examination of the national formulations with the German version, since the Germans are neighbours of the Hungarians. The following text was recorded among the Transylvanian Saxons. (*Schuster* 62, No. 58.)

1. Më käinjt, wat hout dëch trôfen?
   më käinjt sô mer mî!
   Ach fuoter! mëinj härz wäl zes'präinjen,
   o wî! o wî!
2. Më käinjt, wat huoszt ta gieszen?...
   E fäschken af kîle gebrôden...
3. Më käinjt, wier huot dert gebrôden...,
   De moter huot mer't gebrôden...
4. Më käinjt, wo huot se't gefangen?...
   Am podel häinjder dem guorten,...
5. Më käinjt, dat wor ned e fäschken,...
   Dat wor jo gäftich noter...
6. Wat wäinjscht ta na deinjem fuoter?...
   En gäldäne stal äm hemel.
7. Wat wäinjscht ta na deinjer moter?
   me käinjt, sô mer mî!
   En glanije stal än der häl,
   o wî! o wî!

(Mülbach)

(What ails you, my son, tell me! O, father, my heart is near breaking, o wee, o wee! What have you eaten, my son, tell me! A fried fish, o wee, o wee! Who fried it, my son... Mother has fried it to me, etc. Where did they catch it, my son... Down by the garden... Son, it was not a fish... It was poison... What do you wish to your father?... A golden chair in Heaven... What do you wish to your mother?... Fiery iron in Hell...)

As appears, the ballad lacks the main characteristics of the Hungarian version, to wit the refrain, together with the reference to the heart-ache and the making of the bed. Although the first stanza speaks about the young man's heart about to break, but no refrain-like continuation follows. Even less does the refrain-construction characterize the rest of the German variants, in which, as a rule, the refrain, if any, consists of words of bewail, as in the present text. At the same time, the verse consists of simple questions and answers: "Kind, wo bist du denn henne west?"—"In juerm S(ch)esters Huse!"—"Wat hett se dy do denn giwen?" etc. Only two isolated variants of the 31 texts contain a refrain similar to the Hungarian, one of them originates from the region of Schleswig-Holstein bordering on the Danish frontier, the other from Pomeranian areas situated somewhat more to the South. "Johann, main lieber Sohn, wo warst du denn so lange? Bei meiner jüngsten Schwester, Herzmutter mein. Wie weh thut mir mein Herze, Mach sie mein Bettelein!" But even though this motif shows a certain affinity with the Hungarian, the rest of the ballad differs the more from it: the hero has been visiting his sister,

520

and the questions as to what he has eaten and drunk are followed by a simple inquiry: "Where do you want to be buried?" The refrain appears in a still more threadbare form in a Silesian variant: "Woe to my young heart, make my bed!" These ballads, however, are different from the average German variants, in which the main character is mostly a girl, or a person of unspecified sex (Kind), and very often the father puts the questions. Such a solution is not to be found in the other nations' balladry. In two German variants, the young man has been visiting his sweetheart's place (Schleswig-Holstein and Potsdam)—much in the same way as in the English and Italian versions (and apparently in two Hungarian texts here published); in the rest of the texts, his young sister, his aunt or step-mother, and not infrequently even the school, are mentioned. As against this, there occurs in them another motif also typical of the English and Italian versions, namely that of the young man's dog which is also killed with the poison. The scene of bequeathing mainly starts with the formula "What is your wish", a variety of which implies questions concerning the kind of grave and the place of burial.

The Italian ballad brings us nearer to the Hungarian version. The refrain is general in it, speaking about heart-ache: "Signora Mama, mio core sta mal!" And here also the question is closer to the Hungarian: "Dove si sta jersira", or "ersera a veglia", that is, where were you last night? On the other hand, the Italian version knows nothing about the bed-making.

The parallel of the full Hungarian refrain comes up in the English variants, and does so as a *typical feature*.

Oh where have you been, Johnny Randall, my son?
. . . .
I've been with my true love, oh make my bed soon,
I've pain in my heart and want to lie down.

Or:
For I'm sick at the heart and fain would lie down.

But further similarities offer themselves for comparison. In the English version it appears with an increasing force that the dish with which the hero was poisoned was not fish. The place where it was caught is a ditch, or a spot near the garden's gate, or a thorny hedge, sometimes, heath-covered slope, and the tool with which it was taken is a stick; its colour figures as a constant motif: it is mostly green, spotted or streaky, and even the *spotty, speckled back* of the animal is often mentioned. Finally it becomes quite evident that *paddock* is understood (*Bronson* 97). And what is even more to our surprise, the quaint circumscription of the Hungarian text's "four-footed crab" occurs almost literally in three English variants in the following wording: "four-footed fish" (*Child* 12), "a wee fishie wi four wee feeties" (*Child* V, 209, 12X), "fower-fitted fish" (*Bronson* 12/103). Consequently, this must be a very ancient element of the ballad, which, however, seems to be completely missing from the German and Italian formulations. Probably, they have never applied it. Had they ever known this curious feature, than at least the colour of the fish should be referred to in them, as a sort of survival. But even in this form it cannot be traced in the mentioned two language areas. In contrast, this peculiar trait of the English, beside the refrain, creates a close affinity with the Hungarian ballad. In addition, the whole construction of the two versions shows a high degree of similarity, beginning with the hero's name mentioned, with the involvement of a love affair, the refrains containing the formulas of bequeathing, and concluding with the duologue presentation of the entire story. (NB., in both versions the duologue takes place between mother and son!) Finally, the mentioning of the four-footed crab cannot be imagined as a chance agreement. Such a queer partial agreement—let alone the paddock used as poison, and the particular description of the animal—can by no means be interpreted in a way that it had developed independently of each other in the two ballad types. And there are further minor similarities to corroborate the interdependence of the typical parallelisms, such as the mentioning of the plate in which the poisoned dish was served. (The image of a rusty vessel lingers in the German version as a vague reminiscence of this motif.) Therefore, the Hungarian ballad must have had some definite Western connection, however remote it may have been.

This supposition is also supported by the fact that no genetic correlation with the neighbouring German formulation can be reasonably imagined. What the Hungarian and the German ballads have in common can be found in every nations' texts, and that is the framework of the story. At the same time, it is the German version that most deviates from the Hungarian. In the former, the father is the interrogator, a girl the main character who has received the poison at her sister's, aunt's or step-mother's place. (Such solutions come up with the English, although very rarely.) Furthermore, in the German ballads the refrain is restricted, with the exception of three isolated texts, to words of bewail. And what seems to be an even more important evidence, the ballad is completely unknown in such German-speaking neighbour areas as Austria, Bavaria and Switzerland. As to the two German variants that have been collected in pre-wars Hungarian territories (Transylvania)—showing features strongly opposing to the Hungarian formulation—they have to be regarded not as the easternmost specimens of the German version, but as isolated pieces, probably imported by settlers from distant regions. All this is enough to prove that the Hungarians did not acquire this ballad from the Germans.

The Slovak version well exemplifies how the ballad should have been formulated if borrowed from the Germans. In the Slovak, similarly a girl is poisoned, and she returns from a wedding feast or a dancing party. She complains about head-ache (instead of heart-ache), and there is no refrain construction to make the fact of poisoning known to the reader. In three texts, she ate unsalted fish, and therefore she became ill. No further details are added. Finally, the scene of bequeathing is utterly missing, in place of this, sometimes the mother asks the daughter what she wants her to give her, whereupon the daughter answers that she wants a burial place, or nothing at all. More frequently, however, the mother asks her daughter where she wants to be buried; and receives the answer that she wants to buried beside the church. German influence, or mediation, can be inferred from the Danish version too, because there are two Danish fragments in which the girl complains about having a head-ache although no mention is made of the bed-making in the refrain. (Anyway, also No. 204 may have been mediated by

Transcarpathian Ukrainian settlers from the Slovak borders since apart from this neither the Croats nor the Carpathian-Ukrainians know this ballad.)

Would it follow, then, that the Hungarians had acquired this ballad from the English? Such a proposition, however, cannot be supported by historical considerations. Further, there are such minor details which are missing from the English version but which occur in the Italian; such are the mentioning of the evening and the punishment of the mother required by the hero.

Thus the story may have been mediated from some region neighbouring the English area which maintained direct connections with Italian and German territories, that is from France. And although the type does not exist, to the best of my present knowledge in the French-speaking areas, the range of dissemination surrounding France as the centre—namely in Italian, German, English and the more remote Hungarian environment—seems to indicate a one-time existence of a similar French plot that made its way from there in every direction, and went into oblivion in later times.

Literature: Child 1882: Italian, German, Dutch, Swedish, Danish, Hungarian (1) and Wendish versions (as well as other stories about poisoning) surveyed in addition to the English group; *Ortutay* 1936–48: following *Child,* surveys the European parallels of No. 127; perhaps the Hungarian ballad is a fake, since it has no variants (?): *Dános* 1938: accepts *Ortutay; Csanádi* and *Vargyas* 1954: known all over Europe, the Hungarian version stands nearest to the English.

61. THE MURDERED SISTER

130.

1. Where have you been, where have you been, my son Hermán?
With the neighbour's, with my sister, my dear mother, O!

2. What did you do there, what did you do there, my son Hermán?
I rocked two small children to sleep, my dear mother, O!

3. And what did you eat there, what did you eat there, my son Hermán?
I was gnawing away a little bone, my dear mother, O!

4. And what drink did you take, what drink did you take, my son Hermán?
Cold water from a jug, my dear mother, O!

5. And what did you see there, what did you see there, my son Hermán?
My murdered sister, my dear mother, O!

6. And what do you wish to your sister, my son Hermán?
A quiet rest and bliss, my dear mother, O!

7. And what do you wish to your mother, my son Hermán?
To you I wish the pains of Hell, my dear mother, O!

Bereg county, 1882–89. Péter Szini = MTA, Incr. 595/52, fasc. III, p. 174. No. 424.

Known from a single text without tune.

This ballad shows an almost perfect agreement in all its details with the former one about the poisoned lover. The mother asks her son much in the same way about where he has been and what he has eaten and drunk (the motif of potion is present also in the German and Slovak versions, and even in some English texts, and the combination is natural); further the son's answers and testament are also similar in both types. As a new element appears, however, the rocking of the child. But the English variants offer examples even for this: *Bronson* 12/95 relates that the son has visited his grandmother, and to the questions as to what he has been doing there, he answers: I tended the small child and washed up the dishes. Finally, he wishes a piece of rope to his grandmother who has poisoned him. Another novel element is the murdered sister; but the most conspicuous divergence is that the son sends his mother to Hell and that, and this is perhaps the most significant, the motif of poisoning is missing. All these differences make the ballad similar to the English Edward-type (*Child* 13); true, in the Hungarian version it is not made clear that the murder has been committed by the son, but the curse he lays on his mother suggests accompliccity, bringing the ballad in connection with one of the English variants (NB., *A. Taylor* a monographer of the type does not hold this feature an original English trait!). On the other hand, this ballad is unknown in Hungarian tradition, and so it is in the whole of Central European folklore.

Nor can we ascertain whether we are dealing with a contamination of two types or with a transitional form that sprang from the text of the ballad of János Who Was Poisoned. It is not precluded that what we have at hand is a text in the primitive stage of transformation far from attaining the rank of an independent type, although it seems to be more likely that the name *Hermán,* quite unusual in Hungarian, and the story itself, are some fresh borrowings from a foreign-language community. At the same time we have to emphasize that names in ballads offer doubtful evidence since they can migrate independently of the texts.

As long as more information is not received from Hungarian or foreign sources, the single text should be regarded a transitional form vaguely linking the mentioned types together.

62. THE BEWITCHED SON

131.

1. Hol hál - tál az éj - jel fi - am, ár - vám? Csip-ke-bo-kor a - latt hál-tam, én é- des-a - nyám.

1. Where have you slept last night, my poor son?
   I have slept under the briar, my dear mother.

2. What vision did you have last night, my poor son?
   Three witches were haunting me, my dear mother.

3. Who was the first, my poor son?
   The first was my sister, my dear mother.

4. Who was the second, my poor son?
   The second was my sister-in-law, my dear mother.

5. Who was the third, my poor son?
   You yourself were the third, my dear mother.

6. What did the first do, my poor son?
   She was praying over my head, my dear mother.

7. What did the second do, my poor son?
   She was sucking my red blood, my dear mother.

8. And what did the third do, my poor son?
   She was cracking my tender bones, my dear mother.

9. What do you wish to your sister, my poor son?
   The bliss of the world beyond, my dear mother.

10. What do you wish to your sister-in-law, my poor son?
    The evil of the world beyond, my dear mother.

11. What do you wish to your mother, my poor son?
    The fiery hell of the world beyond, my dear mother.

Érd (Fehér county). 18-year-old girl. Mrs. Kodály 1917.

The ballad is known to exist in this single variant.

Textual relationships with other ballads: **60., 61., 41., 79.**
Versions in languages other than Hungarian:
SOUTHERN SLAV: *1–11. Štrekelj 159–169. 12–20. Bošković-Štulli 1–9. 21–32. Kuhač V, Nos 376–382 plus 5 variants, on pages 426–27 and 430. (Slovenske ljudske pesmi No. 23. Fifteen variants.)*

GERMAN: *33*. D. Vlr. 80. *Gottschee.*

SLOVAK: (?) *34*. Fővárosi Lapok 1867. No. 198 (Hungarian translation) = EMU I, 89–90, 1987 (German translation).

This is the second ballad type which is closely related with the text of János Who Was Poisoned. Once again, the story starts with the mother's questions, and the dramatic situation develops from the duologue. Some fatal trick has been played to the boy in both ballads: he is poisoned in the one, and bewitched in the other. Here again we have the formulas of beqeathing with the traditional questions "What do you wish to this and that" well known from the foreign texts of the type of the poisoned son. Thus, in the final issue, the main difference is that here the young man is killed not by poisoning but by bewitching. The murder is invariably committed by relatives. A minor difference is that one of the relatives stands for the young man, and that he wishes good to that relative. This turn, however, may owe its occurrence to the circumstance that the dying son in the other ballad wishes good to every relative except his own mother (or the one found guilty). It is obvious, therefore, that this time again we are dealing with the ramification of a *known* and *definitely outlined* type, that is with a transitional form, just as in the preceding chapter.

Up to 1969, this text had been unknown to me as well as to all other Hungarian researchers of balladry. Even to No. 80 of the German comprehensive publication I gave the information that the theme was unknown in Hungarian folklore. (Cf. D. Vlr. IV, 220, Note 3.) While surveying the vast material of collection heaped up at the Folk Music Research Group of the Hungarian Academy of Sciences, I happened to hit upon this variant which Mrs. Kodály had taken down from the lips of her housemaid, text and tune together in 1917. Thus, the piece having been unknown until recently, I made notes on certain variants in the material of Štrekelj as distant parallels of János Who Was Poisoned, when I was assembling the European relations of the Hungarian ballads. It is a fortunate circumstance that the D. Vlr. No. 80 discusses the entire family and the full dissemination of the ballad type, including some 83 Southern Slav texts. And the article by Mrs Bošković-Štulli publishes nine complete texts and all the typical form-variants thereof. Consequently, I still had had an opportunity to compare the versions in detail.

In spite of this, it is not easy to follow the path of the type's development. Seeing the immense numbers of Slovenian, Croat, Serbian variants that form a wide arch around the southern borders of the Hungarian language area—and considering at the same time that the ballad is unknown with other nations (no closer data are available on the Slovak version)—we are inclined to suppose that this single Hungarian text has been adopted from the Southern Slavs by the Hungarians, and the supposition seems the more plausible because among the inhabitants of Érd, from where the text originates, Serbians live mixed with the Hungarians. In the same way, *Erich Seemann* established in the German comprehensive edition that the only Gottschee variant had been borrowed from the Slovenians. Notably, it is a general trait in Southern Slav popular beliefs that the *vilas* will take out the victims' hearts, and this feature comes up, in company with the Slavic name of the hero, also in the German text, while the related belief itself is otherwise not known among the German populations.

Such a connection, however, cannot be established with regard to the Hungarian ballad. The fact that in most of the Southern Slav texts a typically Southern Slav belief is embodied can be interpreted only in a way that every nation tends to resolve the riddle of the bewitching motif within the scope of its own related traditions. Direct borrowing can only be suspected of if a belief characteristic of a nation appears in the text of some other nation, as is the case with the German-Slovenian parallelism.

On the other hand, the two formulations: that is the Hungarian and certain Southern Slav variants, are featured by so many common traits that their interconnection cannot be doubted. But here we are faced with the first serious difficulty. Namely, this similar formulation shows just the same close agreement with the text of János Who Was Poisoned. Can it be reasonably imagined that the two Hungarian ballads have developed independently of each other? At the same time, the Southern Slav tradition does not know the theme of János Who Was Poisoned, nor of the wider European type of Randall. It would be very difficult to explain how this Southern Slav ballad came into existence independently of the all-European tradition, yet showing so great degree of similarity with it; and yet more incredible would it seem that the Hungarians should have borrowed a ballad from the Southern neighbours which bears a perfect affinity to another Hungarian ballad which, however, is completely unknown to the Southern Slavs.

By a closer examination of the Southern Slav variants, we can eastablish that they show a conspicuous dissimilarity at more than one point. For one thing, only some of the texts start with the mother's questions: What have you eaten and drunk?, and the like. Other starting formulas prevail in the majority of them: the mother gets up in the morning, prepares breakfast, then wakes her son and sends him to work which the son either performs or pretends to have already performed, or in some instances states that he is unable to do a work because the vilas have taken out his heart. In other texts, the son goes to the field to work, there he meets with the three vilas, and we learn from the continuation what had happened between them; finally the questions are asked by the mother. But several texts have the following incipit: The sky is decorated with stars, the field with sheep, and the shepherd boy has gone to sleep beside them . . . then follows the narrative, although not related by the young man. In a like way, different solutions are found to explain the method of the vilas' bewitching the boy. In most instances, they take out his heart and eat it, but sometimes they bite him at the throat (and the young man's words of wail reach up to the sky—and there is an end to the story). "Let us eat it" say the vilas, whereupon the young man's sweetheart pleads to them, offering the young man's horse for food instead of him, and begging them to let him live at least till his name's day. Another difference between the variants is that not all of them apply the formula of bequeathing. And a striking divergence as compared with the Hungarian ballad is that the Southern Slav texts are not built up from rhythmically recurring strophic elements, like the Hungarian repetitive constructions, but are more of the epic-narrative nature, presenting the story in the chronological order of events. All this brings the Slav ballad far away from the Hungarian type of János

Who Was Poisoned or its English counterpart, Lord Randall. The difference is obvious as regards their construction and formulations.

It follows from what has been said that if this ballad is examined in its context with the Western version, with all the apparent textual agreement between them, then a possibility of Hungarian transmission towards the Southern Slavs seems to be likely: in this case, the find of Érd should be regarded as the last survival of an extinct ballad, a "pièce de résistance". At the same time, the Southern Slav tradition may have preserved a larger number of the borrowed story—and the instance should not stand unparalleled at all.

63. THE BAD WIFE

132.

1. Jöj - jön ha - za   é - des - a - nyám,   Azt ü - zen - te   é - des - a - pám!

Várj fi - am   egy ki - csit,   Had tán - col - jak   egy pi - cint! Mind -jár   ha - za - me - nek.

1. Come home, mother dear,
   For father is asking you!
   Wait, child, a moment,
   Let me dance for a while!
   I shall be home at once.

2. Come home, mother dear,
   For father is very ill!
   Wait, child, a moment,
   Let me dance for a while!
   I shall be home at once.

3. Come home, mother dear,
   Father has died already!
   Wait, child, a moment,
   Let me dance for a while!
   I shall be home at once.

4. Come home, mother dear,
   We have buried father!
   Wait, child, a moment,
   Let me dance for a while!
   I shall be home at once.

5. Come home, mother dear,
   Suitors have come to see me!
   Let me go, lads!
   For I don't want to have more dance with you,
   Now I am going home!

Nyirád (Veszprém county). 46-year-old female performer. Kerényi–Mrs. Lévai, 1956 = AP 1483/b.

530

133.

Poco parlando ♩=100-108   Giusto

1. Jöj-jön ha-za é-děs-a-nyám,   Vár lá-nyom ëgy ki-csit. Hadd tán-có-jak
   Mert be-teg az é-děs-a-pám!

ëgy ki-csît, Minnyár én is mě-nyěk, É-gyet-ket-tőt for-du-lok,Minnyár otthon lë-szëk.

6. str.

i Jaj jaj le-pe-dőm,Szép fehér le-pe-dőm! (m) Mer én u-rat még ka-pok,

De le-pë-dőt nem sza-bok,, Mer én fon-ni něm tu-dok, Le-pë-dőt sěm csi-ná-lok.

1. Come home, mother dear,
   For my dear father is ill!
   Wait, daughter, wait a little,
   Let me dance a little,
   And I shall go at once.
   Just one or two more turns,
   And I shall be home at once.

2. Come home, mother dear,
   Salve my dear father!
   Wait, daughter, wait a little,
   Let me dance a little
   And I shall go at once.
   Just one or two more turns,
   And I shall be home at once.

3. Come home, mother dear,
   Let's call a priest to confess my dear father!
   Wait, daughter, wait a little,
   Let me dance a little,
   And I shall go home at once,
   Just one or two more turns,
   And I shall be home at once.

4. Come home, mother dear,
   For my dear father has died!
   Wait, daughter, wait a little,
   Let me dance a little,

And I shall go at once.
Just one or two more turns,
And I shall be home at once.

5. Come home, mother dear,
   Let's bury my dear father!
   Tell those who carry him
   Not to take him past the fence,
   For his arm is hooked,
   It will catch in the paling,
   And he will come back to pester me.

6. Come home, mother dear,
   For my dear father has been buried!
   Alas, alas, my sheet,
   My fine, white sheet!
   For I may get another man,
   But I cannot make another sheet.
   For I cannot spin
   And I cannot make a sheet!

Kászonújfalu (Csík county). 60-year-old female performer. Kodály 1912 = SzND. No. 14.

Divergences: In four instances a father is called home from the dancing party, but this variation, which may well be a recent development, occurs only in notations recorded in Hungary proper (exclusive of Transylvania). It is interesting to note that in Ghymes (Nyitra county) a mother figured in the ballad in 1906 when Kodály made collection there, but at the same place the villagers sang about a father in 1966 to László Vikár. The motif of complaining about the buried sheet comes up in a fragment of Zala county: "I am sorry for my sheet rather than for my husband's death, For I may get a man, but I cannot make a sheet for my husband's death." Another fragment from Szatmár county: "Let the devil dance any longer, I am sorry for my sheet, Now I may go home." Ten variants are known from Transylvania and Moldavia. For instance: "What have you wrapped him in, child? In a white sheet. My sheet, my sheet, My fine, white sheet! For I can get a man somehow But I cannot make a sheet . . ." A variant of Klézse adds: "For I have not got the money for that." Disregarding certain minor divergences, three more variants from Csík county bear a close semblance to No. 133. Apart from these, there is a Transylvanian variant that contains the typical motif: "Do not take him past the garden For his leg is crooked, It will catch in the fence, And he will come back to pester me. Alas, my dearest heart husband, my dear husband, Why did you die!" In a text from Szalafő, even the following wording can be found in a short fragment: "Take him, take him, but do not take him past the fence, For he will catch in the paling And run back to me!" Mock-laments may also be referred to in demonstration of the extensive use of the motif of grieving for the lost sheet in the Transdanubian counties; such mock-laments come up in verse form almost the same as the ballad's commonplace, indicating the source from where the parody

532

originates. Volume V of MNT (p. 1094) quotes 2 data from Somogy and 2 from Zala. And another variant from Zala county applies the story of The Old Husband (131) as introduction to the ballad of The Bad Wife. At Szandaváralja, people usually perform it in the spinning-room when they get sleepy or feel cold their legs: at such parties a singer will present the calling lines, the others present the responsive choir part, and while the performance is going on, they will raise their legs and knock them against on another to the rhythm of the melody. The suitor occurs in the concluding formula of two more variants, and we find only reference to him in yet two more texts: "You have got a father again". In variants having the father as the central character—and in many a text with the mother being called— we find no deviation whatever towards the end of the text, the response in the refrain form is performed throughout unchanged. The ending lines of a variant calling the father reads like this: "My poor wife has died, My greatest enemy, So that now I can go home." And it has been noted down from the performance of a female singer in the following wording: "Play the fiddle merrily, For all that and all that, Let him lie under the sod, So that I can go home in the end!"

Earliest provenience: end of the eighteenth century (manuscript, whose last private owner introduced the date 1824 in it).

Dissemination: Sine loco: late eighteenth century, from before 1824; Erdélyi III, No. 281, 1848; Sopron county (Vitnyéd); Vas county (Szalafő); Zala county (Balatonederics, Bezeréd, Kiskomárom, Nagylengyel, Rédics); Baranya county (Boda); Veszprém county (Lovászpatona, Nyirád); Győr county (Kóny); Nyitra county (Ghymes 2); Hont county (Kemence); Nógrád county (Szandaváralja); Borsod county (Kisgyőr, Szentistván); Pest county (Galgahévíz, Szentgyörgypuszta); Torontál county (Szaján, Tiszahegyes); Csongrád county (Szeged-Felsőváros); Bihar county (Bályok, Nagyszalonta); Szatmár county (Szamosszeg); Kolozs county (Györgyfalva); Szolnok-Doboka county (Kendilona); Maros-Torda county (Kibéd, Nyárádszentanna); Udvarhely county (Énlaka, Sepsiköröspatak); Csík county (Csíkkarcfalva, Gyergyóremete, Kászonimpér 3, Kászonújfalu); Bukovina (Andrásfalva-Hertelendfalva 3, Andrásfalva-Apar, Tolna county Józseffalva-Bátaszék); Moldavia (Bogdánfalva, Klézse). Total: 46. I–III: 27, IV–V: 19.

Textual relationships with other ballads: similar to Type 64, with reversed cast.

Tunes: 1 = No. 132; 2 = No. 133 (in four variants) from among 3–29, Nos 7, 10 and 21 occur in two variants each. In compliance with the calling words of the daughter and the refrain-like answers the melodic pattern assumes a two-part construction form: mostly a slower portion is followed by a quicker rhythm, a parlando-rubato by a giusto; in many instances, however, we have only a change in the rhythm without tempo differences. This rhythmic change is reminiscent of the so-called "proportio" in mediaeval and renaissance dance music: the same tune performed first in paired then in unpaired bars and with modified tempo; such is, for instance, No. 5 (with 3/4~ 2/4 bars alternating), and perhaps Nos 132 and 10, in which the original mazurka-rhythm of No. 5 has been changed by the introduction of a pause, or by extenuation of the tone; and such one is, perhaps, No 12, in which 5/8 alternates with 2/4; different is the use of proportio in 18, 24 and 27 their tripodal metres alternating with bipodal ones. True, it is not the entire melody that receives now the one, now the other kind of rhythm, but the two moieties of the same tune are distinguished from one another by the proportio. Since, however, the text speaks about dancing, it would be natural to suppose the influence of such a dance music feature. The rhythmic and tempo changes are sometimes underlined by a change of minor-major keys, for example in No. 22.

Parlando, lento   Giusto, vivace

3.

534

Versions in languages other than Hungarian:

GERMAN: *1–4.* E–B 910a–d. *5. Köhler–Meier* 209 (with a list of the printed variants). *6. Marriage* 196. *7. Schuster,* 139. No. 72. *8–48.* Manuscript variants reported on from all German-speaking areas (from Brazil to the Volga-German groups) in the DVA).

DUTCH: *48.* Lootens-Feys 91. *49.* Manuscript in DVA.

GREEK: *50. Lübke,* 45.

AROMUN: *51. Weigand* II, 56–57.

BULGARIAN: SbNU 10, 108 No. 2.

Partial variants:

FRENCH: *53.* Manuscript, Belgium. *54. Rolland I,* No. 31a (1724). *55. Recueil des chansons galantes, badines et à boire* (1739) III, pp 423–8.* *56–58. Rolland I* 31b–d. *59. Libiez* III 15. *60–62. Canteloube* III, 165 and 332; IV, 335 = *Udry,* 137. *63. Fleury* 359/1. *64–65. De la Gruyère,* No. 16 (4 variants). *68. Beauquier,* 125. *69–71. Bujeaud,* 67 (3 variants). *72–73. Decombe* 46. *74. Tiersot* (s.a./II) 40. (Further a ms. from Liège)

ITALIAN: *75–77. Nigra* 84A–B and No. 107. *78. Bernoni* 1872 Punt. XI, No. 3. *79–80. Giannini* 1889, 197 No. 26 plus variant.

PORTUGUESE: *81. Braga* II, 257; IV, No. 18. (Through courtesy of *Seemann* I have been informed of the existence of a Danish version, too, which, however, I have had no opportunity to examine as yet.)

In the German texts, too, we have the solution that the woman returns home only after the arrival of the suitors had been announced. The similarity is so marked that in southern German songs even the two tempos are found much in the same arrangement as in the Hungarian: the daughter calling in a dragging rubato, and the mother replying in a brisk dance tempo play their parts alternately, as in every Hungarian variant recorded with tunes. But apart from this, the two wordings show so great degree of agreement that they can be almost considered as translations of each other. One example of the many will suffice to be quoted here: "Frau, du sollst nachheime gehn, dein Mann der ist krank. Ess e krank, Gott sei Dank. Gott sei Dank! Komm, lieber Franz, noch einen Tanz, Noch einen Tanz, Noch ist nicht Zeit zum Heimgehn . . . ist schlecht . . . Geschieht em Recht . . . Dein Mann der liegt in den letzten Zügn. En de letzte Zügen, lass en nur liegn . . . Ess e tod, Gnad ihm Gott ::: dein Mann wird begrabn . . . will ich mich labn . . . Ein Freund ist im Haus. Jstr im Haus, schmeisst en raus! . . . Ein Freier ist im Haus. Jstr im Haus, lasst ihn nicht raus . . . Main lieber Franz, den letzten Tanz, denn ist es Zeit zum Haimgehn."

Two important elements of the Hungarian version are absent in the German texts: one is the sheet-bewailing, and the other "don't carry him by the fence . . ." motif. But the bewailing of the sheet occurs in a French and an Italian ballad, respectively, with a nearly identical content, which however, in spite of all the similarity shows a different pattern of construction. The husband is ill, asks for something to eat, or a doctor to be called. His wife is away from Easter to St Denis. When she returns she hears the death-knell and renders thanks to God. On entering the house she finds that her husband is wrapped in six ells of linen. She then bewails the loss of the linen; sometimes this bewailing is left out, and instead we see the woman seize her scissors and cut the linen off the body. When she comes to his mouth, she is afraid he will bite her, and when she reaches his arms, she fears he will strike her. She laughs and mocks at the burial, then, in some variants takes the cleric to bed, in others re-marries at once.

The many varieties of expression: "Je regrettais bien ma toile et mon peloton de fil", "Je ne regrette que la toile Qu'il ma emporté pourri", "Je me suis mis à pleurer Mais ce n'état pas pour li. C'état pour mes deux aunes de toile Qui étaient autour de li", and so on, and even more clearly in the Italian: "a filare ci vuol pena, dei mariti ce n'e cosi" indicate without a doubt a connection with the Hungarian. As far as the German language area is concerned, the feature is absolutely absent. Similarly unknown are in them such portions as "Don't carry him by the fence, Because his hands are crooked, they might be caught by the pale, and he would come back to pester me!" For an echo to the Hungarian detail we should turn to the Portuguese text: Call the grave-diggers; Let us take him on a direct way to get there as soon as possible!" And even the fear of the French wife that he would bite her and beat her seem to be faintly reflecting the Hungarian counterparts.

The bewailing of the sheet is general in the French; the numerous variants are built up on this as the point of the story. But in the Hungarian it appears in only some of the variants, and the story is effective even without it. It is obvious, therefore, that the Hungarians must have taken it over, and not the other way round. Here, too, we find the Italian parallels over an extraordinarily small and distant area: there are only two records from the vicinity of Turino. It cannot have reached the Hungarians from there. The only question is how to explain the extensive agreement between the German and the Hungarian ballads.

The Hungarian ballad is strikingly uniform in having the wife (sometimes the husband) refusing to go home from the *dance*. This feature is missing in the great majority of the German texts and appears in the Austrian, Czech and Bavarian territories, and further in the riverine of the Rhein, that is to say, in the vicinity of the borders between French—Hungarian language areas. The Hungarian is uniform further in that it is invariably the daughter that calls home her mother. In a few German variants from the Rhein region this trait also occurs, but in every other case the woman is called to go home impersonally, most frequently with the term

"Madame". We also find here and there the exchange of roles between wife and husband in German and Dutch areas.

It is striking further that, as in the Hungarian, it is from the *dance* that the wife is called home in the Greek, Aromun and the only south-Bulgarian text. For example, the Greek story runs like this: Kind wife, Mariora, your husband is hungry. Let him starve, Let us have a turn in the dance, Let my boots be torn, No sooner will I stop dancing! There is plenty of bread in the chest, He can take it out if he wishes to... Your husband is thirsty... and so on. Your husband is dying... The incense is there wrapped in paper, and there is the candle, too... Your husband has died... Let the women lament him, Let the priest bury him in the grave!

In the Aromun and Bulgarian texts the woman is called to her dying child, but she does not stop dancing in spite of repeated entreaties. The existence of these isolated southern texts cannot be explained either from the Hungarian or the German versions, while the Greek can be explained from the French. At the same time, the Piedmont region has got an Italian song—which is not a counterpart of the French with the motif of sheet-bewailing—and a girl is called—instead of the mother—to go to see various members of her family. Nevertheless, the strophic-repetitive construction revealing the mercilessness of the girl who refuses to stop dancing for the sake of her dying relatives clearly indicates that the basic idea of the story is identical with that of the Hungarian, Greek and German ballads. Thus the Italians have both motifs: the sheet-bewailing one known from the French, as well as the calling home from the dance. This latter feature, however, deviates from the uniform solution of the dissemination area, consequently it must be a secondary development. And if it cannot be taken for the original, then we have to suspect a French origin, considering the great number of French borrowings among the Italian songs.

Another striking circumstance is that the Hungarians merged the sheet-bewailing to indubitable French origin just into this particular song. If the ballad were of German origin, it would be hard to imagine an element borrowed from another nation being embedded in it: on the other hand, the history of ballads shows that the acquirer often has merged elements of two songs borrowed from the same people.

Considering all what has been said, we must regard both the loss of the dance scene and the impersonalized call as attrition in the German ballads. The motif of *dance* figures in every nations balladry, including the German (in some variants). This is indicated by the melodic pattern, with the slow rhythm of the call followed by the faster reply in a dance-rhythm; and this is not missing in the German variants, either. Yet those variants preponderate among them in which the call is impersonal, and in which it is not made quite clear from where the woman does not want to go home. On evidence of the German material we may conclude, therefore, that the ballad spread, gradually loosing its original meaning, from the French and Hungarian borders over the German language areas.

Putting all this together reinforces our conviction that here, too, we are dealing with a lost, ballad-like French text which the Hungarians merged in places with an element of another related French text, and that this ballad, too, spread over into the German territories from two sides in just the same way as the "Three Orphans" discussed before.

Literature Köhler–Meier 1896: refers to Hungarian, Greek and Aromun versions in connection with the German; *Ortutay* 1936–48: refers to the German versions of E–B 910; *Dános* 1938: quotes *Ortutay* and accepts his data; *Csanádi* and *Vargyas* 1954: German origin on the basis of E–B 910; *Vargyas* 1960 and 1967: French origin.

64. THE INCREDULOUS HUSBAND

134.

1. Dá-vid fe-le-sé-ge Be-teg-ség-be e-sett, Dá-vid még-sem hitt ne-ki.

Kelj fel He-lé-nám, Ked-ves fe-le-sé-gem, Nem fáj ne-ked sem-mi sem!

1. Dávid's wife
   Fell sick,
   Yet Dávid did not believe her.
   Get up, my Heléna,
   My dear wife,
   For no limb of yours is aching!

2. Dávid's wife was taken to a doctor,
   Yet Dávid did not believe her.
   Get up, my Heléna,
   My dear wife,
   For no limb of yours is aching!

3. Dávid's wife
   Was put in bed,
   Yet Dávid did not believe her.
   Get up, my Heléna,
   My dear wife,
   For no limb of yours is aching.

4. Dávid's wife
   Was laid out,
   Yet Dávid did not believe her.
   Get up, my Heléna,
   My dear wife,
   For no limb of yours is aching!

5. Dávid's wife
   Was put into the coffin,
   Yet Dávid did not believe her.
   Get up, my Heléna,
   My dear wife,
   For no limb of yours is aching!

6. Dávid's wife
   Was taken to the cemetery,
   Yet Dávid did not believe her.
   Get up, my Heléna,
   My dear wife,
   For no limb of yours is aching!

7. Dávid's wife
   Was put into the grave,
   Yet Dávid did not believe her.
   Get up, my Heléna,
   My dear wife,
   For no limb of yours is aching!

8. When David's wife
   Was buried in earth,
   Dávid began to believe her.
   Rest in peace, my Heléna,
   My dear wife,
   And may God grant you a quiet rest!

Beregújfalu (Bereg county). Árpád Színi = Ethn. 1915, 142.

Divergences: In a few Great-Plain variants the story speaks about a shepherd and his wife, but the hero is usually Dávid, in one instance he is called Berger, and in Transylvania has the name János. Sometimes the husband says in the last stanza: "I know every limb of yours is aching, or "This ought to have occurred long ago!"

Earliets provenience: between 1872 and 1919 or 1906.

Dissemination: Borsod county (Mezőkövesd, Szirma); Zemplén county (Ricse 2); Bereg county (Beregújfalu 2); Pest county (Újszász); Jász-Nagykun-Szolnok county (Karcag); Szeged region; Békés county (Gyula, Körösladány, Vésztő); Bihar county (Körös-Nagyharsány); Szabolcs county (Kisvárda); Szatmár county (Tunyog); Szolnok-Doboka county (Mezőveresegyháza); Alsó-Fehér county (Lőrincréve); Udvarhely county (Bözöd). Total: 18.

Textual relationships with other ballads: Type **63** with reversed characters.

Tunes: 1 = No. 134 (nine variants); the cadence in the fourth melodic section shows a great variety in the variants; the cadence of the third line may be 1 or 5 occasionally. Further melody in three variants:

2.

Versions in languages other than Hungarian:
   SLOVAK: *1. Kodály* 1915, 305, Darázs (Nyitra county) = *Bartók* 1971, 671b. *2. Ibid:* 306 Zsemlér (Bars county) = *Bartók* 1971, 675c. *3. Bartoš* 1901, No. 958, Slovakia.
   MORAVIAN: *4–5. Sušil* 169/356–357; *1.* collected by *Bartók, 2.* by *Kodály.* In the one, the husband is called Janko, in the other Dutko. In other respects, they show a close agreement with the Hungarian both as regards content and presentation. The same can be said of Nos 3–5. The melody of *2.* is a widespread Hungarian folksong tune (cf. *Kodály* 1954, 18 = *Kodály* 1971, 24).

No other foreign parallels are known to have come up so far. The area and the frequency of dissemination are indicative of a Hungarian origin. As to the date of origin, it cannot be stated: the ballad may have developed at any time between the fourteenth and the nineteenth centuries.

Literature: Kodály 1915: publishes Slovak and Hungarian tunes, and compares one of the Slovak tunes with a sixteenth-century psalm melody.

65. THE SPEAKING CORPSE

135.

(Parlando)

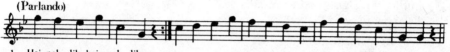

1. Haj-nal - lik, haj - nal - lik,
   De nem jól haj-nal - lik.
   A vaj - dá - csi le - gé - nyekről Nem jó hír hal - lat - szik.

1. The dawn is breaking, the dawn is breaking,
   Although it is not breaking to bring good news.
   Of the lads of Vajdácska
   Sad tidings are heard.

2. A lad has been murdered
   For his seven hundred florins,
   And he was thrown into the Tisza
   For his bay.

3. He was not taken in by the Tisza,
   For it cast him up on the bank,
   A ferryman passed that way
   And took him into his net.

4. His mother went up to him.
   She tries to wake him, but all in vain:
   Get up, my son, my dear son,
   Come home with me!

5. I would get up if only I could,
   But I am dead.
   My yellow boots with the spurs of brass
   Are frozen on my legs.

6. His father went up to him.
   He tries to wake him, but all in vain:
   Get up, my son, my dear son,
   Come home with me.

7. I would get up if I could,
   But I am dead.
   My blond hair reaching down to my shoulders
   Are frozen in my neck.

8. His sweetheart goes up to him.
   She tries to wake him, and not in vain:
   She embraces his neck, crying,
   And kisses his mouth.

9. Wake, my dear sweetheart,
   Let me take you home!
   For three days, or for four days
   Rest in my bower!

10. I cannot wake
    Because I am dead!
    But let three girls and three lads
    Take me to your bower!

11. Will you lament me
    In the presence of three lads?
    I shall lament you, dear sweetheart,
    In the presence of the whole world!

12. Will you have
    A walnut coffin made for me?
    I shall have, dear sweetheart,
    A marble coffin made for you!

13. After you have buried me,
    You must not forget me;
    And set rosemary-flower
    On my grave!

14. And the girls must water it,
    So that it may not wither away,
    So that your heart, dear sweetheart,
    May not break with sorrow!

Vajdácska (Zemplén county). 21-year-old male performer. Lajtha 1921 = MF 2519/b.

136.

1. Meg - öl - tek   egy   le - gényt Hat - van fo - rint - já - ért,
   Be   is   dob - ták   a Ti - szá - ba Szür - ke pej - lo - vá - ért.
   Be - ve - tet - ték

1. A lad was killed
   For his sixty florins,
   He was thrown into the Tisza
   For his grey steed.

544

2. He was not taken in by the Tisza,
   It cast him up on its bank.
   A ferryman came on that way,
   He was not late to report the case.

3. His father came up to him,
   He calls him, but the does not hear him.
   His yellow boots with the spurs
   Are frozen on his legs.

4. His mother comes up to him,
   She calls him, but he does not hear her.
   His chestnut-colour brown hair
   Is frozen in his neck.

5. His sweetheart comes up to him,
   She calls him, and he hears her:
   Get up, my dear sweetheart,
   Place your head on my bosom.

6. Place your head on my bosom,
   I shall take you home.
   You will lie for three days
   In my bed covered with quilt.

7. Will you lay me out
   On some cheap canvas?
   O, I shall lay you out, sweetheart,
   On a double velvet sheet!

8. Will you have
   Some cheap coffin made for me?
   O, I shall have, sweetheart,
   A marble coffin made for you.

9. Will you have it studded
   With iron nails?
   I shall have it studded, sweetheart,
   With golden and silver nails.

10. Will you have, then,
    The triple bell tolled?
    O, I shall have, sweetheart,
    Tolled all the six bells in Buda...

11. Will you see me out, then,
    To the ditch of the cemetery?
    O, I shall see you out, sweetheart,
    To the eternal home!

Áj (Abaúj county). 16-year-old female performer. Vargyas 1939 = MF 4314.

Divergences: Only such divergences occur in this very uniform ballad text which do not alter the development of the plot. The victim my be occasionally a horseman, a cowboy, a shepherd, a hussar, a bailiff, a Jew or a gendarme, sometimes a Gipsy boy and even a small girl. In Transylvania also the name of Bátori occurs in one ballad, obviously under the influence of historical names coming up in old-style ballads. Several variants melt it with the ballad of Imre Bogár, the outlaw, even with its tune. The combination can be accounted for by the similar metric construction of the two ballads: with 6, 6, 8 and 6 syllabic patterns. In such contaminations the text starts with Imre Bogár confessing his misfeat: "I have killed a lad . . .". Characteristically enough, the name of Imre Bogár occurs even in a Moldavian ballad, together with the name of the river Tisza. (At the same time, it is worth-while to mention that there is only one Moldavian text which changes over into the story of The Test of Faithfulness, and in this one ballad the incipit is borrowed from a foreign song.) Of the Moldavian variant mentioned, sometimes only the following transformation is found: "I have murdered a lad . . .", and the dead body answers in two texts from Háromszék county like this: "I cannot get up . . . because Sándor Rózsa has driven His sharp knife into my heart!"

The motif of throwing the corpse into the water can occasionally be replaced by other ones. "Do you hear, girls, what has happened at Szolnok? Dani, the poor soul, has died, On the roadside." "On the slope of the Mátra There stands a lonely tree; Under it a lad is lying, And he is frozen in his blood." "In the castle of Hollókő There is a little room, In it a brown lad is lying, And perhaps he is dead already." "On the store of the Balaton A young man was fishing, And he caught in his net A red-brown little girl." "The foot of the Leshegy is slippery, And there is no green grass on it. What can the herd of horses Find to graze on it during the night? The horseman was killed . . ." "The young lad is not allowed To go and see the brown girl. His mother forbids him to go there, But the lad does not pay heed to her. He is walking around the girl's place, And finally he stays there dead", Or: he has been killed "because of his beautiful sweetheart." And a Moldavian variant starts with the following lines: "Lo, there is a little lad in the pit. We have to go to the pit, and we have to take him out of it!"

The answer the corpse gives sometimes says: "I am not dead", or occasionally: "I have withered away", or "swooned" or "feel faint", but then there follows invariably the duologue about the coffin to be made, the mourning, etc. Only one or two fragments conclude with restoring to life: "I get up, sweetheart, I am not dead."

The triple visit of father, mother and sweetheart is sometimes swollen into a multiplicity of relatives seeing the dead body (aunt, daughter-in-law, sister, etc.), and in some Moldavian variants even the brother, elder sister, brother-in-law, friend or other relatives are enumerated before the sweetheart appears.

Earliest provenience: 1846.
Dissemination: Six variants have been published without specification of places.
I. Sopron county (Bősárkány, Sopronkövesd); Vas county (Felsőőr); Zala county (Búcsúszentlászló, Dergecs, Kiskomárom, Kustánszeg, Lövőpetri, Mumor, Rédics, Szentgyörgyvölgy, Szentmargitfalva, Zalaújlak 2); Somogy county (Balatonszentgyörgy, Berzence, Kaposújlak, Karád,

Nemespátró, "Somogy m.", Somogyszob, Szigliget, Szőllősgyörök); Baranya county (Hegyszent-márton, Kisbodolya, Mohács, Nagybaracska, "Ormányság" data, Szebény, Szilágy); Tolna county (Felsőireg, Gerjen, Madocsa, Öcsény 2), Fejér county (Csákvár, Dunapentele, Mány, Pákozd, Perkáta), Veszprém county (Szilasbalhás, Várpalota); Pest county (Páty); Komárom county (Csep, Kocs 2, Martos, Tárkány, Udvard); Győr county (Ság). I. total: 50.

II. Nyitra county (Pográny), Bars county (Tild); Hont county (Lukanénye, Perőcsény); Esztergom county (Kisújfalu); Nógrád county (Bárna 2, Nagybátony, Szirák, Rimóc); Heves county (Bekölce, Bükkszenterzsébet, Erdőkövesd, Erdőtelek, Felsőtárkány, Füzesabony, Gyöngyös, Mátra-balla, Mátraderecske, Mátraszentimre 2, Pély, Pétervására, Poroszló 3, Recsk, Terpes, Visznek); Borsod county (Harsány, Mezőkövesd, Muhi, Parasznya); Gömör county (Almágy, Abaúj, Áj 2, Bodvalenke, Boldogkőfalu, Boldogkőváralja, Cekeháza 3, Csenyéte, Gibárt, Göncruszka, Kéked 2, Mogyoróska); Zemplén county (Bodroshalom, "Bodrogregion", Cséke, Karcsa, Karos, Mezőzombor, Sárospatak 5, Ricse 6, Tiszakarád 2, Vajdácska 2); Bereg county ("Bereg c.", Beregszász, Gulács, Lónya, Tiszaszalka, Vári); Ugocsa county ("Ugocsa c."); Ung county (Nagybodrony). II. total: 77.

III. Pest county (Ágasegyháza, Dunapataj, Kiskunfélegyháza 3, Kunszentmiklós 2, Mogyoród, Nagytarcsa, Szigetmonostor, Valkó); Jász-Nagykun-Szolnok county (Alattyán, Jászalsószentgyörgy, Jászladány, Jásztelek, Tiszafüred 2, Tiszapolgár, Túrkeve); Bács-Bodrog county (Felsőerek, Gombos, Homokmégy, Jánoshalma 2, Rém, Zenta 3); Torontál county (Hertelendyfalva 2, Magyarszentmihály, Nagybecskerek 2, Szaján, Tiszahegyes); Csongrád county (Ásotthalom, "Csongrád c.", Csongrád, Hódmezővásárhely 3, Homokpuszta, Sándorfalva, Szeged, Szegvár, Tápé); Csanád county (Makó); Békés county (Békés, Bélmegyer, Endrőd 3, Geszt, Orosháza, Mezőberény, Mezőgyán 2, Vésztő); Arad county (Arad, "Arad environment"); Bihar county (Biharugra, Furta, Körösladány, Körösnagyhar-sány, Köröstárkány, Nagyszalonta 7); Hajdú county ("Hortobágy" 3, Tiszacsege 2); Szabolcs county (Ajak, Beszterce, Császárszállás, Demecser, Dombrád, Érpatak, Kiskálló, Kisvárda, Lövőpetri, Matolcs, Mezőladány 2, Nyírábrány, Nyírcsaholy, Nyírkáta, Nyírlugos 3, Nyírtelek, Nyírtura, Nyírvasvári 3, Pócspetri, Polgár, Rakamaz, "Szabolcs" 1846, Újfehértó 2, Vaja 2); Szatmár county (Botpalád, Csegöld, Jármi, Kántorjánosi, Kérsemjén 4, Kisar, Nagydobos, Nagyecsed, Szamosszeg 3, Tiszakonyár, Tyukod); Szilágy county (Diósad). III. total: 125.

IV–V. "Erdély", with no closer specification of the place: 1. Kolozs county (Bánffyhunyad, Gyalu, Körösfő 3, Mákófalva, Türe, Válaszút, Zentelke 2); Szolnok-Doboka county (Melegföldvár 2, Szék); Maros-Torda county (Gernyeszeg, Iszló, Kibéd, Maros-Séllye "Marosszék-Sóvidék", Marosvásárhely 2, Szabéd, Székelyvaja); Torda-Aranyos county (Torda, Tordatúr); Nagyküküllő county (Alsórákos, Mihályfalva) Alsó-Fehér county (Lőrincréve 2); Udvarhely county (Felsőboldogasszonyfalva, Firtosváralja, Homoródalmás, Sepsiköröspatak, Székelykeresztúr, Szentegyházasoláhfalu); Brassó county (Hosszúfalu, Pürkerec, Tatrang 3); Csík county (Csíkkarcfalva, Csíkmenaság 2, Csíkrákos, Csíkszentmihály, Gyergyóalfalu, Gyergyócsomafalva, Gyergyótekerőpa-tak, Gyimesfelsőlok 2, Gyimesközéplok); Háromszék county (Bölön, Dálnok, Erdőfüle, Kilyén, Komolló); "Székely-land", Bukovina (Hadikfalva 2, Istensegíts 2, Józseffalva); Moldavia (Bogdánfalva, Diószeg, Forrófalva, Gerlén, Klézse, Lábnik, Nagypatak, Pusztina); IV–V. total: 70. I–III. total: 252 (plus 6). Total: 328.

Textual relationships with other ballads: Type **6**: the dead body is speaking; recent incorporation in this ballad: introduction of No. **101**; the motif of coffin-making (Will you have a walnut coffin made for me? . . .) taken over into **12., 16., 26.** and **37.**

Tunes: 1. = Nos 135–136 in 74 variants. In the northeastern part of the language area this tune enjoys an almost exclusive prevalence; anyway, the centre of dissemination of this ballad also falls in this region. In counties Szabolcs and Szatmár, this tune is also played to the dance called *csárdás*. The other tunes of the ballad are:

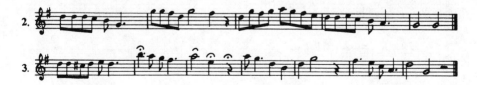

548

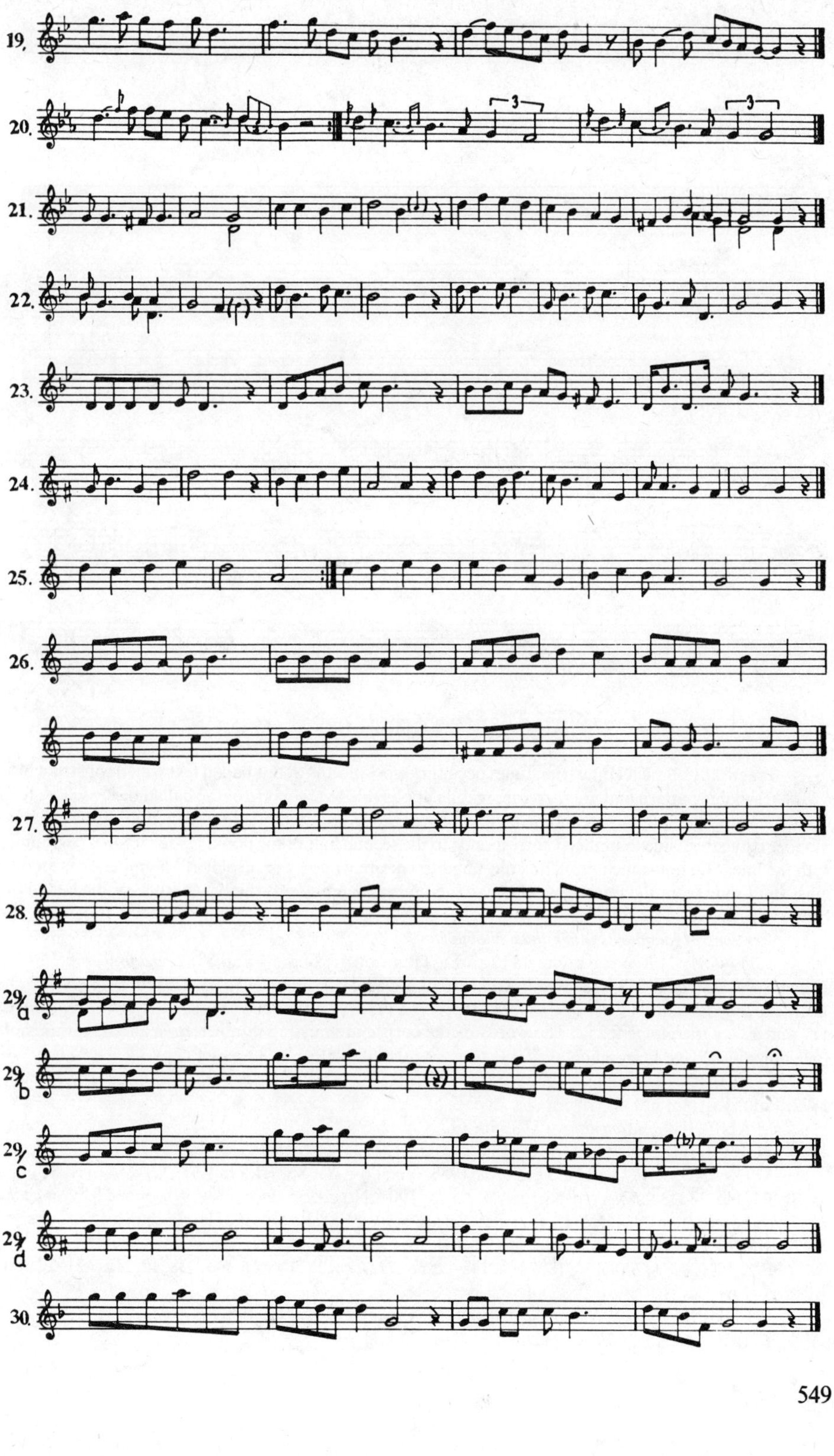
19.
20.
21.
22.
23.
24.
25.
26.
27.
28.
29/a
29/b
29/c
29/d
30.

6. (19 variants), 8–9. (2), 10. (14), 18. (16), 21. (8), 22. (13), 24. (3), 25. (2), 29. (24), 33. (2), 34. (2), 35. (2).

Practically all such Hungarian tunes occur in association with this ballad text which construct in a 6, 6, 8, 6 syllabic pattern and are therefore readily applicable to the metre of the ballad discussed. A few isometric tunes (6, 6, 6, 6), if combined with this text, have been modified by reduction of the syllabic number in the third line. Number 7 corresponds to the second half of the popular song Pt 437, beginning with the line: "O, how much rain and cold I had to endure while I was a soldier." Number 15 is an old music-hall song from the time of World War I. Number 22 represents the typical tune of the ballad of Imre Bogár.

Versions in languages other than Hungarian:

FRENCH: *1. Libiez* III, No. 18. *2–3. La Tradition* 1896, p. 64 and 58. *4. Beaurepaire,* 146 = *Haupt,* 86. *5. Barbeau* 1962, 411. *6–8. Rossat* 1917 21a, c, and j. *9. Canteloube* III, 127. *10. Beauquier,* 323. *11–12. D'Indy* 108 and 113. *13. Seignolle,* 140*, *14. Udry,* 207. *15. Canteloube* I, 127. *16–17. Tiersot* 1903, 117 and 127. *17/a. Ampère* 252. The words of the corpse are missing in nineteen Walloon variants of Belgium which have been made available to me—together with No. 13—in a copy by R. *Pinon.*

ITALIAN: *18–23. Nigra* 17A–F. *24. Ferraro* 1888, No. 2. *25. Idem* 1877, No. 39. *26. Bernoni* 1872, Punt. IX. No. 6.

SPANISH: *27. Menéndez–Pidál* No. 61.

PORTUGUESE: *28. Braga* I, 615. *29. ibid,* II, 122. *30. Geibel–Schack,* 354 II.

SLOVAK–MORAVIAN: *31. Horák* 1958, No. 47 = Sl. Sp. III, No. 565. *32. Kolečány* No. 33. *33.* SL'P I, No. 184. *34. Kolečány* No. 55. *35. Bartoš* 1901, No. 51. *36. Idem* 1882, No. 366. *37–39. Bartók* 1959 297abc. *40. Idem* 1934, No. 13. (See also *Bartoš–Janáček* 51. Its tune is of Hungarian origin. See also *Burlashova* 12.)

POLISH: *41–67. Kolberg* 1857 No. 14a–cc. *68–71. Idem* 1871–84, 6, No. 338, 12, Nos 421–22 and 16, No. 479.

WENDISH: *72–74. Haupt–Schmaler* I, Nos 6 and 55, II, No. 105.

LITHUANIAN: CF; *Seemann* 1951, Nos 72 and 76.

BULGARIAN: (dubious relationship): *75 Shapkarev* No. 1256. *76. Stoin* 1939, No. 905. *77–84. Idem* 1928, Nos 1494–1503. *85.* SbNU 9, 54, No. 4. *86. ibid.* 60, No. 2. *87.* A–V, No. 68. *88–90. Tsitselkova* 75, 79 and 81.

The theme of the speaking sweetheart who is dead is to be found among the French, only with reversed characters: it is the young man that wishes to wake the girl. The story begins with a scene in which the young man learns from a nightingale that his sweetheart has died. He makes speed to arrive at her house. (Less frequently, in more recent texts, he asks for leave with the soldiers to visit the girl whom he finds to be dead.) After greeting the sweetheart's father, mother, and sometimes even her brothers and sisters, he learns from them what has happened. He walks to the grave, talks to the girl and she answers. In order to give an idea of the French text's similarity to the Hungarian, I think it expedient to quote the following passages: "Relève-toi, ma mie Françoise, Ma mie, de grace, lève-toi!— Comment veux-tu que je me lève, Il y a sept (p) ans que je suis là. J'ai les yeux tout remplis de terre, Mais les tiens, ils sont si brillants!" (*9.*)—J'ai tant pleuré, versé des larmes, Que ma mie s'est réveillée. Réveille-toi, bouche riante, Réveille-toi et parle-moi! Comment veux-tu que je te parle? Je n'ose plus te regarder, Mon visage est couvert de terre, Le tien est frais comme un bouquet." (*16.*)—"Bonjour chère Nanette, voudrais-tu me parler? Du profond de ton âme voudrais-tu m'embrasser? Nanette lui répond: J'ai ma bouch' plein' de terre, Ma bouche plein', Ma bouche plein' de terre et la tienn' plein d'amour." (*6.*)—"Oh ma mie, ma tant douce amie, Pourquoi vous laissez mourir? Comment vouliez-vous que je vive? Vous étiez si loin de moi. Oh ma mie ma tant douce amie, Baisons-nous encore une fois!—O ma bouche sent la terre, La votre le vin d'Arbois." (*8.*)—"Qui est donc là, dessus ma tombe, A pleurer sur moi tant et tant?—Ah c'est ton bon ami, la belle, Ton ami qui veut te parler!—Comment veeux-tu que je te parle? J'ai sept pans de terre sur moi!" (*15.*)—"Est-ce bien toi ma mignonne? Embrasse-moi encore un'fois.—Comment vous embrasserais-je? Vous êtes si loin de moi." (*10.*)—"Ah bonjour! ma Jeanett', Réponds ancor'un' fois, Si tu connais les larm's Que j'ai verse's pour toi. Jeanette lui répond: Ma bouch' est plein' de terre. Ma bouch'est plein' de terre, La tienn' est plein'd' amour." (*1.*)

After this, the girl speaks about the ring which is still on the young man's finger, and about the belt he had received from her. Then a word or two are dropped about how she wants him to lament her. In most instances she asks him to give her ring to someone else who would pray for her. More detailed is the following scene: "Prenez tout et donnez-le à qui priera dieu pour moi. Faites-en dire trois messes, un' pour vous et deux pour moi. N'allez plus aux assemblées, danser, rire et vous ivrer. Ne conduisez plus le filles..." (*4.*)—"Je batirai un ermitage, Et là je finirai mes jours..." (*15.*) As appears, the details show a fair degree of agreement as regards content with the passages of the Hungarian: "Will you have a walnut coffin made for me?"—"Are you going to mourn for me... Will you have the triple bell tolled for me?...; and so on.

The Hungarian text with its ballad-formulas and strophe-repetitions is uniformly built and clear in outline. At first sight the French ballad seems to be vague, corrupt and lacking in uniformity. On closer examination, however, the

French proves to be more uniform and consistent. To begin with, all that is left in the Hungarian of the corpse's actual speech is the replacement of the formula "...tries to wake him, and he does not hear" by "...tries to wake him, and he hears", followed by the series of questions and answers, now quite mechanical: "Will you have a wooden coffin made?" "I shall have a marble coffin made!", and so on. In the French, however, we find everywhere a real conversation with the dead person, the essence of the ballad. In the second place, the triple build-up of the Hungarian, with the father's, the mother's, and finally the sweetheart's pleading, cannot be original, in spite of its effective character. For the formula "...tries to wake him (her)", is preserved in those variants only where the dead body replies to his father, mother, and finally his sweetheart. It is obvious that this triple build-up is not organically connected with the original structure, and was only developed subsequently in Hungary as a formula from the parts played by the father and mother. Another innovation is that the roles are exchanged: the man is the corpse, the girl the questioner; and further that instead of burial, we have throwing into the water, so it is not his mouth that is filled with earth but his hair frozen onto his shoulders, his boots onto his legs.

The uniform spread of this form, together with its modern wording lacking all archaic turns, furthermore its popularity among young people, too, all this taken together indicates that the ballad has been revived lately, and transformed so as to suit modern tastes. This is also brought out by the occurrence of such elements with the neighbouring peoples as well as the more remote East-European nations which stand nearer to the French formulation, being at the same time farther off from it if the whole of the poem is considered. Among the Slovaks we also find the modern Hungarian form turning up accurately, word for word and with the same metre (lines of 6, 6, 8, 6 syllables), obviously taken over together with the melody (34.); and there is a Moravian fragment (35.) that has been borrowed from the Hungarians, text and tune together. The other texts are, however, more archaic, and the further they diverge from the modern Hungarian, the closer they are to the French. Here again it is a man looking for his sweetheart; three girls in the forest tell him that she is in the grave. He circles the graveyard three times, and finds the grave: "Who is walking round my grave disturbing my sleep?" "It is I, your sweetheart...", and then follows the long dialogue about the presents they had given one another, including the ring: has he still it, and she gives it, or cannot give it, back to him. Missing, moreover, is the characteristic part: "I cannot kiss you for my mouth (face) is covered with earth", "How can you ask me to rise, seven boards cover me" (French)—"I cannot rise for I am dead" (Hungarian). There are known, however, scattered occurrences of a similar detail ("my mouth is full of sand") from the Wends and the Lithuanians. Otherwise the northern Slav and Baltic plots are even more distant, and are embellished with epic preliminaries. Among the Poles, the young man serves seven years for the girl, then goes to be a soldier, and his darling dies while he is away. When he returns, there is a long dialogue between them about the gifts. Then the girl asks him to have the organ played for her, and he promises to have the big bell rung for her.

These Northern Slav variants provide a key to the riddle what elements the Hungarian ballad may have included before it had been transformed. It is doubtless that also it had the man as the surviving party, as in the French, as well as in the entire East-European group. He must have come home and looked for his sweetheart as his French and Slovak counterparts, only it was not three girls but the sweetheart's father, mother, from whom he learned the truth, as in the French. Otherwise the Hungarian texts would not have so consistently the father, mother and lover as *dramatis personae*. The Hungarian formulation of the answers following the girl's questions render a reliable point of orientation: "I cannot rise because I am dead", and the sporadic northern formula: "my mouth is full of sand". It is after this that the ring may have been mentioned (Slovak), and the manner of lamenting discussed (Hungarian), and naturally enough, also the bells involved (Hungarian and Polish).

Since in the Slovak many elements are missing which were preserved in the Hungarian either as direct borrowings or in an altered form, and are still to be found in the Northern Slav area, it may be established in this case, too, that the ballad spread from the Hungarians, after having been borrowed from the French.

The French ballad is also known in the Piedmont region and in the Iberian Peninsula. The Italian version contains the French motifs in a sketchy form, but some of the variants lack the dialogue with the corpse about his rising or inability to rise because the earth is pressing him down, and so on. All the two lovers speak about is the ring. Nor do we find the detailed description of the mourning which we saw in the French, and which forms such a large part of the Hungarian ballad. But as far as we know, it does not appear in other Italian-speaking areas. Therefore the Hungarian ballad cannot be derived from the Italian. Even less from the Portuguese–Spanish, in which the essentials of the original story are hardly recognizable—if indeed they have any connection with it. A long preliminary story tells how the young man goes into exile, because he is not allowed to marry the girl he loves, and while he is away the girl dies. He returns and goes to her grave to mourn her. The dead girl speaks to him: "You must go on living, my darling, my arms, which used to embrace you, have lost their strength, my mouth, which kissed you, is without life. You must return to life." But the young man cannot do this without his sweetheart; whereupon she actually rises, and the ballad closes with the reassuring sentence: "Let him have her darling, because he deserves it, for he has brought her back to life!"

All things considered, the ballad reached Hungary from the French and from Hungary it made its way to the neighbouring countries.

Literature: Gragger 1926: without comparative notes; *Dános* 1938: undoubtedly Hungarian origin, new style; *Ortutay* 1948: accepts *Dános; Seemann* 1951, Nos 72 and 76: discusses the Lithuanian and Slav material in parallel with the German, without mentioning the French, Hungarian, Slovak and Moravian versions; *Csanádi* and *Vargyas* 1954: not even remote parallels are known; *Vargyas* 1960 and 1967: *French* origin.

66. THE HAUGHTY WIFE

137.

1. Sze - gény le - gény vol - tam, gazdag lányt vet - tem el

Hm hm hm hm hm   Ha ha ha ha ha

1. I was a poor lad
   And married a rich girl.
   O, o, o, o,
   Aye, aye, aye, aye.

2. First I went
   To the market of Palm Sunday.
   O, etc.

3. From there I brought her
   A pink skirt.
   O, etc.

4. Taking it home,
   I placed it on the table.
   O, etc.

5. But she did not even deign to look at it,
   Nor did she take a glance at it.
   O, etc.

6. I went the second time
   To the market of Palm Sunday.
   O, etc.

7. From there I brought her
   A pair of high-heeled boots.
   O, etc.

8. Taking them home,
   I placed them on the table.
   O, etc.

9. But she did not even deign to look at it,
   Nor did she take a glance at it.
   O, etc.

10. The third time I went
    To the market of Palm Sunday.
    O, etc.

554

11. From there I brought her
    A scourge of eight tails.
    O, etc.

12. But she did not even deign to look at it,
    Nor did she take a glance at it.
    O, etc.

13. Then I took it in my hand
    And lashed her with it in the neck.
    O, etc.

14. Then she embraced me,
    And kissed me, and had a liking for me.
    O, etc.

Drávapalkonya (Baranya county). 73-year-old male performer. Kerényi 1935.

138.

1. I went to the fair
   And bought a silken kerchief.
   When I arrived at home,
   I tied it round her neck.

2. My dear wife,
   Do you love me?
   I don't love you, dear soul,
   You are no husband to me.

3. I went to the fair
   And bought a pair of crimson boots.
   When I arrived at home,
   I placed them before her.

4. My dear wife,
   Do you love me?
   I don't love you, dear soul,
   You are no husband to me.

5. I went to the fair
   And bought a cudgel.
   When I arrived at home,
   A gave her a thrash on the back.

6. Well, my wife,
   Do you now love me?
   O, now I do love you, dear soul,
   And you are a husband to me from now on!

Bogács (Borsod county). 72-year-old female performer. Vig 1958 = AP 1988/c.

139.

1. Szë - gény le - gény vol - tam,   Gaz-da(g) le - jánt vet - tem.
A   gaz-da(g) le - ány - nak   Ked - vit nem lel - het - tem.

1. I was a poor lad,
   And married a rich girl.
   For this rich girl
   I could not do a thing to please.

2. My wife, darling,
   Will you call me your husband!
   Not I, never and never, to be sure,
   Never in my life.

3. For in father's house
   Lords bigger than you have been guests,
   Yet I did not respect them,
   Nor will I respect you.

4. I went to town
   And bought a tasselled kerchief.
   Taking it home,
   I put it in her hands.

5. My wife, darling,
   Will you call me your husband!
   Not I, never and never, to be sure,
   Never in my life.

6. For in father's house
   Lords bigger than you have been guests,
   Yet I did not respect them,
   Nor will I respect you.

7. I went to the fair
   And bought a pair of crimson boots.
   Taking them home,
   I put them on the table.

556

8. My wife, darling,
   Will you call me your husband!
   Not I, never and never, to be sure,
   Never in my life.

9. For in father's house
   Lords bigger than you have been guests,
   Yet I did not respect them,
   Nor will I respect you.

10. I went to the woods
    And cut a wand of dogwood.
    Taking it home,
    I put it under the table.

11. My wife, darling,
    Will you call me your husband!
    Not I, never and never, to be sure,
    Never in my life.

12. For in father's house
    Lords bigger than you have been guests,
    Yet I did not respect them,
    Nor will I respect you!

13. With this I took the wand all of a sudden
    And began to beat her on the back.
    Oh, you are my husband, you are my husband,
    My dear hubby to the day of my death!

Kecsetkisfalud (Udvarhely county). Performed by three men between 19 and 26 years of age. Lajtha 1940 = Gr 77b.

Divergences: A variant from Csákvár ends with the following lines: "Then I beat her once with my whip (refr.). Then she sprang at me, catching at my hair (refr.). I beat her the second time, and she fell down upon the ground (refr.) ...I beat her the third time, So that I myself felt pity for her... Nowhere in this big world can you find a wife better than she... Coins are good if counted, Wives are good if beaten." The contrast of rich and poor characters have been omitted in nine variants from Hungary proper and one from Moldavia. (of. No. 138). Nevertheless, one of such variants bear the collector's note: "Side-husband, that is, a poor man who married into a rich family." At the beginning of Kálmány's notation from Arad we find a detail *borrowed* from a different song chiding the drunkard husband. This is apparently a novel modification, for otherwise the Transylvanian— Moldavian variants are fairly uniform of wording. As against this, there are two texts from Klézse in which motifs of The Bride Given in Marriage to Poland, The Wife Kicked to Death and The Brigand's Wife have been contaminated.

Earliest provenience: an 18th-century manuscript.

Dissemination: Transdanubia(?), an 18th-century manuscript without specifying the proven-
ience; Baranya county (Drávapalkonya); Fejér county (Csákvár), Somogy county (Csurgó); Veszprém
county (Szilasbalhás); Borsod county (Bogács); Zemplén county ("Bodrogköz", Ricse), Arad county
(Arad, Pécska), Békés county (Csorvás); Udvarhely county (Énlaka, Kecsetkisfalud); Csík county
(Gyimesközéplok-Jávordipatak); Háromszék county ("Erdővidék"); Moldavia (Diószén, Gerlén,
Klézse 3, Kickófalva, Lábnik, Lészped 2, Ploszkucén). Total: 24. (Hungary proper 11, Transylvania—
Moldavia 13).

Textual relationships with other ballads: **67.**

Tunes: 1. = No. 137; 2. = No. 138; 3. = 139; 4–12. (10. and 12. in two variants each):

Versions in languages other than Hungarian:
ENGLISH: *1–7. Child* 277.

The story of the "taming of the shrew" coming from the ranks of the nobility can be read in the ballad quoted from *Child*. With the English, the husband beats his wife not precisely because she refuses to call him her husband but because she shuns all kinds of household work for fear of dirtying her hand. The thrashing also takes place somewhat differently: the husband hangs the skin of a ram onto the wife's shoulders and delivers the strokes through it, saying: "It is not you that I am beating, I only dust this hide." Obviously, this motif derives from the tale-type of "The Lazy Cat" (AaTh 1370) in which the husband orders the cat to do the wife's work, which failing, he beats the cat, although on the back of the lazy wife. The Hungarian ballad has no connection whatever with this tale-type. Nevertheless, there is one point which still relates the English to the Hungarian version, to wit, the husband seeks to find excuse in case the wife would raise complaint in her family. In the final issue, the two themes are correlated in some way, even though there is not a single feature they have in common on the basis of which a direct connection could be documented between the two.

This ballad is Hungarian in origin. As to the time of its generation, we may well suspect, on the basis of the variants which occur in areas separated by great distances and which are not too numerous at the same time, that the text itself is contemporaneous with other classical mediaeval Hungarian ballads.

67. THE LAZY WIFE

140.

1. Jó bor, jó e-gész-ség, Szíp asz-szony fe-le-ség.

Mi hasz-na, ha szép vagy, Ö-rö-ké be-teg vagy.

1. Good wine, good health,
   A nice woman for wife.
   But what use is your beauty,
   If you are always ill.

2. On Friday you are ill,
   On Saturday you are better,
   On Sunday you are a dove,
   On Sunday you are a dove.

3. At Monday dawn
   You are deadly sick.
   Prepare, wife, prepare,
   Prepare to get up and out of your bed!

4. We are going to the field
   To turn up furrows,
   To turn up furrows,
   To make new hay.

5. I cannot, I cannot,
   My kind, gentle husband,
   For my back aches me so much
   That I cannot even speak a word.

6. Prepare, wife, prepare,
   For we are going to the ball.
   Just bring me here
   My pair of little red shoes.

7. I get up at once,
   Soon I put on my dress,
   And prepare to go to the ball,
   To have a good round of csárdás.

560

8. They went to the ball,
   And they had a good round of csárdás.
   Then they went home,
   And the wife went to bed.

9. Prepare, wife, prepare,
   Prepare to get up and out of your bed!
   We are going
   To turn up furrows!

10. To turn up furrows,
    To make new hay.
    I cannot, I cannot,
    My kind, gentle husband!

11. My bones ache me so much
    That I am near dying.
    What is the matter with you, wife?
    Are you ill when it comes to work?

12. But if it comes to go to the ball,
    You are better at once?
    Out of the house I went
    And went down to the garden

13. I cut a wand of cornel-wood
    And put it behind the door.
    Prepare, wife, prepare,
    Get up and out of your bed!

14. We are going to the field
    To turn up furrows!
    I don't go, I don't go,
    Because I am very ill.

15. Never mind, never mind,
    I shall fetch a doctor.
    Behind the door
    I have a doctor.

16. And I took
    My wand of cornel-wood.
    And I began to beat and thrash
    My tender wife.

17. Stop it, stop it,
    My kind, gentle husband!
    For such a doctor
    Is no good to me!

18. And I do not feel any longer
    Alas, my back ache,
    Let's go to the field
    To turn up furrows!

19. To turn up furrows,
    And to make new hay!
    Never in my life shall I feel
    My tender back ache!

Lészped (Moldavia). 55-year-old female performer. Kallós 1957 = Kallós 1970, No. 129.

Textual relationship with other ballad: 66.

The plot-theme of teaching a lesson to the haughty wife is applied here to the case of the lazy wife; therefore a close resemblance prevails between the two ballads. Maybe, the story of the lazy wife has developed at a very late time, and this is why its wording is so hazy, although similar haziness is often met with among old-style Moldavian ballads as well, whenever they are swelled by adding extemporized portions to the old text. We have no knowledge of a similar song in foreign balladry. It may well have come into existence in recent days.

Known from one single recording.

68. THE MARVELLOUS CORPSE

141.

Tempo giusto, poco rubato ♩ = 80

1. Fi - am, fi - am, Bá - lint vi - téz, Szi - ved- i, fáj, fe - jed - i fáj?

Sëm szi - vem fáj, sëm fe - jem fáj; Mëg - ha - lok szép I - lo - na - é(r).
I - lo - ná - nak szép - se - ge - é(r), Sár - ga bo - dor gyöngy haja - é(r).

ül - te - tett be - le

1. My son, my son, warrior Bálind,
   Does your heart ache, does your head ache?
   Neither my heart nor my head aches,
   But I shall die for fair Ilona,
   For Ilona's beauty,
   For her yellow-crispy, beautiful hair.

2. My son, my son, warrior Bálind,
   Do not die for fair Ilona!
   For Ilona's beauty,
   For her yellow-crispy, beautiful hair.

3. I shall have a garden with stone walls built,
   So that you may plant flowers in it.
   And all the fair girls will come,
   All the fair girls and all the handsome young men,
   And fair Ilona will be among them.

4. She had a garden with stone walls built,
   He planted flowers in it.
   And all the fair girls came,
   All the fair girls and all the handsome young men,
   But fair Ilona was not among them.

5. My son, my son, warrior Bálind,
   Does your heart ache, does your head ache?
   Neither my heart nor my head aches,
   But I shall die for fair Ilona,

For Ilona's beauty,
For her yellow-crispy, beautiful hair.

6. My son, my son, warrior Bálind,
Do not die for fair Ilona,
For Ilona's beauty,
For her yellow-crispy, beautiful hair.

7. I shall have a gold mill built,
So that you may mill nice little pearls,
And all the fair girls will come,
All the fair girls and all the handsome young men,
And fair Ilona will be among them.

8. She had a gold mill built,
And he had nice little pearls milled.
And all the fair girls came,
All the fair girls and all the handsome young men,
But fair Ilona was not among them.

9. My son, my son, warrior Bálind,
Does your heart ache, does your head ache?
Neither my heart nor my head aches,
But I shall die for fair Ilona,
For Ilona's beauty,
For her yellow-crispy, beautiful hair!

10. I have a bell made to toll your death-knell,
So that you may have it tolled at your death,
And all the fair girls will come,
All the fair girls and all the handsome young men,
And fair Ilona will be among them.

11. She had a bell made to toll his death-knell,
And he had it tolled at his death.
And all the fair girls came,
All the fair girls and all the handsome young men,
And fair Ilona was among them.

12. Girls, girls, my girl-mates,
My dear friends that have grown up with me,
I have never seen such a marvellous corpse
As the corpse of warrior Bálind!

Zsére (Nyitra county). Performed by a girl of 17. Manga 1938 = MF 3829.

142.

A widow had a daughter called Ilona. Well, a young man used to visit her. He was called the warrior Bálány. But the young man's mother did not want him to court the girl. Therefore she tried to keep him away by many tricks; he made a

marvellous flower-garden, and planted marvellous flowers in it. And many girls
came and his Ilona was not among them. And he sang a song:

I have made a marvellous flower-garden,
And I have planted marvellous flowers in it.
Many girls come to see it,
Yet my Ilona is not among them.
I have to die for my Ilona,
For her softly walking feet,
And for her eyes that are sadly looking at me!

He had a marvellous mill built, and he had a marvellous miller to work it.
Many girls came to see it, but his Ilona was not among them. And then he continued
his song:

I had a marvellous mill built,
And I had a marvellous miller to work it.
Many girls came to see it,
Yet my Ilona is not among them.

I have to die for Ilona,
For her softly walking feet,
And for her eyes that are sadly looking at me!

Then he pretended to be dead. He was thought dead, so he was laid out. As
the bells were tolled for him, the girl said to her stepmother: Mother, he has died,
warrior Bálány is dead!—Well, daughter, if he is dead, take the two jugs and go to
fetch water and take a look at him and see how he has been laid out!—The girl
started and placed the two jugs into the oven, and then she went in to see how the
young man was laid out. And as she finished lamenting over him and was just about
to kiss him, the young man caught him by the waist . . . and the young man died, his
heart cleft from joy, and the girl's heart cleft from sorrow. Both of them died. The
stepmother even then forbade them to be buried in a common grave. Instead, the
young girl was buried on one side of the Catholic church, and the young man on the
other. And two lilies . . . a stalk of lily from one grave, and another stalk of lily from
the other grave, arose, and they twined over the top of the high tower of the church.
Finally they were united!

*Nyírvasvári (Szabolcs county). Performed by a woman of 67. Vargyas 1968 = AP
7346/i.*

143.

1. I am going to die,
   Mother, my dear mother,
   For Ilona Görög,
   For her slender waist,

2. For her slender waist,
   For her rosebud mouth,
   For her rosebud mouth,
   For her rosy cheeks.

3. Don't die, son, don't die,
   László Bertelaki!
   For I shall have
   A marvellous mill built for you,

4. Whose one stone
   Shall throw out white pearls,
   And the other stone
   Shall throw out coins

5. And there come to see it
   Maidens, beautiful girls,
   And also your dear one will come,
   Who is Fair Ilona Görög.

6. Let me go, mother,
   My mother, my dear mother,
   To take a look at the marvellous mill,
   To take a look at the marvellous mill!

7. Don't go, daughter, don't go,
   Fair Ilona Görög,
   For they cast a net
   To catch the barbel!

8. I am going to die,
   Mother, my dear mother,
   For Ilona Görög,
   For her slender waist,

9. For her slender waist,
   For her rosebud lips,
   For her rosebud lips,
   For her rosy cheeks.

10. Don't die, son, don't die,
    László Bertelaki!
    For I shall have
    A marvellous tower built for you,

11. Whose height
    Will reach up to the sky,

And whose breadth will reach
The bank of the Tisza!

12. And there come to see it
    Maidens, beautiful girls,
    And also your dear one will come,
    Who is Fair Ilona Görög.

13. Let me go, mother,
    My mother, my dear mother,
    To take a look at the marvellous tower,
    To take a look at the marvellous tower!

14. Whose height
    Reaches up to the sky,
    And whose breadth reaches
    The bank of the Tisza!

15. Don't go, daughter, don't go,
    Fair Ilona Görög,
    For they cast a net
    To catch the barbel!

16. I am going to die,
    Mother, my dear mother,
    For Ilona Görög,
    For her slender waist,

17. For her slender waist,
    For her rosebud lips,
    For her rosebud lips,
    For her rosy cheeks.

18. Do die, son, do die,
    László Bertelaki!
    For then they will come
    To see a marvellous corpse.

19. And also your dear one will come,
    Fair Ilona Görög.
    And also your dear one will come,
    Fair Ilona Görög.

20. Let me go, mother,
    My mother, my dear mother,
    To take a look at a marvellous corpse,
    To take a look at a marvellous corpse!
    Who has died for my sake,
    Who has given himself over to death!

21. I will not let you go, daughter,
    My daughter, my dear daughter.

At that, she slipped
Into her dressing bower.

22. And she put on
    Her unplaited skirt,
    And over it she put
    Her white apron,
    And she drew on to her feet
    Her crimson, iron-tipped long boots.

23. Get up, son, get up,
    László Bertelaki,
    For I see coming through the field
    Fair Ilona Görög,
    For whom you have died,
    For whom you have given yourself over to death!

24. Get up, my son, get up,
    For I see standing at your feet
    The one for whom you have died,
    For whom you have given yourself over to death!

25. I have seen dead bodies,
    But I have never seen the like of this,
    Whose feet
    Are ready to jump up,

26. Whose arms
    Are ready to embrace,
    Whose mouth
    Is ready to kiss!
    With this, he sprang to his feet,
    So did László Bertelaki!

*Rugonfalva (Udvarhely county). Performed by a woman of 55. Vikár 1902 = SzNd
No. 97 = MF 346/c.*

Divergences: While collecting at Zsére in 1915, *Kodály* recorded some 10
stanzas of the ballad as follows:
    1. Mother, my mother, my dear mother, I am going to die for Fair Ilona, For
Ilona's beauty, For her yellow-crispy, beautiful hair! 2. My son, my son, warrior
Bálind, Do not die for Fair Ilona, For Ilona's beauty, For her yellow-crispy,
beautiful hair! 3. I shall have a golden bridge made, Fair girls will come to see it,
Fair girls and handsome young men, And Fair Ilona will be among them, too.
(Stanzas 1 and 2 repeated.) 6. I shall have a gold mill built, Fair girls will come to see
it, Fair girls and handsome young men, And Fair Ilona will be among them, too.
(Stanzas 1 and 2 repeated.) 9. I shall have a bell made to toll your death-knell, Fair
girls will come to mourn you, Fair girls and handsome young men, And Fair Ilona
will be among them, too. (*By that time the girl* really arrived.) 10. Bálind, Bálind, my
sweetheart. (At that, the text was broken and left a fragment.) In the nineteen forties

Zagiba also recorded the ballad. (Cf. *Zagiba* 71.) He published its first two lines together with the content and a wrongly noted down tune. The lines of text are identical with the first two lines of No. 141.

The hero of the ballad is usually called Bálint Mónár, in two instances Handsome (!) Antal Pálbeli; the heroine is named Fair Ilona in 17 cases. In the incipit, she is mostly mentioned as Ilona (I must die for *Ilona*); in 9 texts Ilona Görög, in 1 Ilona Varga occur. In the other variants the means of cajoling are as follows: silver and gold mill (plus death); gold and diamond mill (plus death); silver, copper, and gold mill (plus death); marvellous mill, golden staff with a silver spindle (plus death); copper mill and death; marvellous mill with one stone grinding white pearls, with the second throwing sweet kisses and with the third throwing small coins,—then a string iron bridge and death; there are two Moldavian texts which have only a "marvellous tiny mill" plus the sham death, and finally one Moldavian variant starts with the motif of luring by death, though the ballad consists as many as 88 lines.

Sometimes the girl asks the neighbours: for whom the bells are tolled. The concluding part of one of the texts begins like this: "Fair Ilona *starts lamenting:* I have never seen such a dead body Whose feet are ready to move to walk..." and so on. In another variant the ballad ends with the following lines: "Bálint Mónár was not late to spring up, He embraced Fair Ilona Never to let her free again." A Moldavian variant expands the scene into a duologue, in which the girl asks the young man to let her go home but the young man will not let her free for the rest of her life. A text from Lészped, presented anyway in the usual repetitive form and with the customary details of formulation, ends like this: "And Bálint Molnár sprang up at once, Kissing and embracing her; He said to her: Fair Ilona, you shall not go home! You cannot go home Because I am dead. But all this has been arranged in order that I may take you, And you can never go home. Fair Ilona answered, crying with tears: Let me go, Bálint Molnár! Because my dear mother is a cruel woman! You cannot go, you cannot go, Fair Ilona. And your mother may do what she will, She may even burst, But you shall never go home. And a glad man Bálint Molnár was, indeed. He was looking at her as if at a flower, He could hardly believe that it was Fair Ilona. Every now and then he asked her: Is it you really that I have here, Fair Ilona?" Of course, this finale is the performer's personal addition to the story.

Earliest provenience: 1872
Dissemination: Nyitra county (Zsére 3), Szabolcs county (Nyírvasvári), Udvarhely county (Rugonfalva 4), Csík county (Borszék, Csíkmenaság, Gyergyóalfalu), "Székelyföld" 2, Bukovina (Józseffalva 7), Moldavia (Klézse 3, Lészped 5, Trunk). Total: 29.
Textual relationships with other ballads: The motif of the marvellous mill occurs also in No. **48;** the line Neither my heart nor my head aches' occurs in No. **57;** the motif of acquiring a lover gradually, in Nos **70, 72–73** and **77.**
Tunes: 1. = Nr. 141. 2. = No. 143. (4 in 7 variants, all from Józseffalva; 8 in three variants.)

Versions in languages other than Hungarian:

FRENCH: I. *1. Arbaud* II, 123. *2. Barbeau* 1962, 397. II. (L'enlèvement au Couvent). *3.* La Tradition X, 54, 1896. *4–5. Beauquier,* 149–151 A–B. *6–8. Millien* 1906, 236A–C (according to Notes, he recorded 30 variants). *9. Rossat* 1917 II, 201. *10. Simon* 1926, 524. *11. Barbillat-Tourain* 4, 73† *12. Seignolle,* 151.* *13. Tiersot* 1903, 145. *14. Van Gennep,* Mercure de France 1, IX, 1910, 45* *14/a. Puymaigre* 1865 35. *14/b. Smith* Romania VII, 73. (*3.*, *12.* and *14.* are known to me from copies I have received through courtesy of *R. Pinon.*)

ENGLISH: *15–19. Child* 25A–E. *20. Bronson* 25/2 (the rest being identical with those in *Child*).

DANISH: *21–63.* DgF 409 and 408.

DUTCH: *64.* Souterliedekens No. 10 = D. Vlr. 58.

BULGARIAN: *65–67. Stoin* 1928 Nos 2398, 3676–3677. *68–71. Miladinovi* Nos 117, 185–187. *72.* SbNU 16/7, 100. *73. Stoilov* 1916–1918 No. 324. *74. Shapkarev* 797. *75–78. Stoin* 1931 Nos 831–833, 2022. *79–85. Stoin* 1939, Nos 709–715. *86. Idem* 1934 No. 325. *87.* SbNU 40, 399 No. 33. *88. Ivanov* 1949, 257–307. *89. Tsitselkova* 233. *90. Verković* 304. *91.* SbNU 38 *Ivanov* 5. *92. Ibidem Burmov* 161. *93–94. Ivanov* 1936 Nos 92–93.

SERBO–CROAT: *95–96. Vuk* I 580 and 737. *97. Osvetnik* 23. *98. Djordjević* 1928 No. 367. *99. Stojanović-Vitezica,* 696 = *Marjanović** I 25. *100. Prodanović* 78. *101–102. Žganec* 1950 Nos 209 and 405. *103. Poljanin* II, 15 No. XI. *104.* HNP VI No. 39. *105. Kurelac* 447.

SLOVENE: *106–107. Štrekelj* 112–113. *108. Grün,* 36. *109.* EPhK 1887, 700. + *Kumer* 76–77.

GERMAN: *110. Hauffen* 63–63a Gottschee = D. Vlr. 58/14–15.

ITALIAN: *111–118. Nigra* 41A–H. *119. Ferraro* 1870. No. 40 (see further the occurrences quoted in D. Vlr. from the regions of Emilia and the Abruzzos, and Vidossi 25A from Istria.)

GREEK: *120. Baud-Bovy* 1936, 208.

SLOVAK: *121. Horák* 1958 No. 11. *122. Kolečány* 34.

UKRAINIAN: *123. Chubinsky* V. No. 249.† *Golovatsky* II, 710 No. 13. (According to *Lintur,* the ballad is known in the Sub-Carpathian Ukraine.)

ROMANIAN: *125. Amzulescu* 266 (1 variant from Maramureș.)

Partial variants, Group I: The Marvellous Mill.

FRENCH: *126. Tarbé* II, 127–129. *127. Fleury,* 356. *128. Decombe,* 221. *129. Beauquier,* 203. *130. Canteloube* III, 322. *131. Rolland* I. 128g. *132. Bladé* 1881–1882 III No. 101. *133. Poueigh,* 268.

ITALIAN: *134. Nigra* 68. *135. Widter-Wolf* 69. Giannini 1889, 186.

PORTUGUESE–SPANISH–CATALAN: (cf. the variants listed in the Chapter dealing with the Test of Faithfulness, further *Armistead-Silvermann* 1971, 51, Note 33.)

Partial variants, Group II:

ITALIAN: (Elopement from nunnery without the motif of sham death involved, yet closely related to the story of the French ballad): *137–152. Nigra* 80A–K plus 5 variants.

Partial variants, Group III:

GERMAN (Gottschee): *153.* D. Vlr. 110B (cajoling by building a tavern, mill, church, further by showing sham death, and finally the double death case as concluding motif).

The European dissemination area can be divided into two distinct regions. The northwestern group includes Scottish, Scandinavian and the French texts that apply the motif of sham death as the only means of luring. (Sometimes, however, only illness is mentioned.) The southeastern branch covers the Italian, Southern Slav, Hungarian, Slovak, Ukrainian and Romanian variants, presenting the motif of luring by a development of gradation, as in the Hungarian. According to *Seemann,* the entire southern group originates from a Bulgarian or a Southern Slav formulation, including the Gottschee German, the Italian as well as the Hungarian and the further northern variants, failing, however, to explain how the two separate groups are related to each other. In order to arrive at a correct answer, we propose to survey the formulations of the two distinct areas.

The Scottish ballad begins much in the same way as the Hungarian: "O Willie my son, what makes you so sad? . . . I lye sarely sick for the love of a maid". Then the mother counsels his son to pretend to be dead, to have the death-bell chimed, and so to allure his love. The girl hears the chime and learns that her lover is dead. She asks her father to let her go to see her dead sweetheart. The father wants the girl's brothers to accompany her, but the girl manages to start alone. The young man makes her pregnant in order to force her to marry him.

The Danish variants build up the plot in a similar way. The young man turns to his mother for counsel immediately at the beginning of the ballad: would she recommend a stratagem with which he could win his sweetheart? The mother advises him to lie on a bier, have the death-knell tolled, and take care that people should not suspect he is alive. The girl is called to wake. She asks for leave of her mother. "I neither deny you it, nor say yes, for they (the young man and his mother) are sly and will cheat you. The girl puts on her best garments and enters the young man's house. Standing first at the head, then at the foot of the bed, she recites her prayers and confesses that she has always been loving him. She is lamenting for him. Suddenly the young man stirs and embraces the horrified girl. "Tomorrow I will stand before the priest with my young bride!" In certain variants the young man asks for a piece of advice to know how he would be able to redeem his sweetheart from the nunnery, and the plot changes accordingly: the girl arrives right from the nunnery to wake over the body of the young man. At the same time we encounter with such variants as well (G) in which the girl has to be cheated out of the nunnery, yet she asks for leave of her mother, just as in the variants without the motif of the nunnery involved. The contamination is due to the influence of another Danish ballad–DgF 408–which shows a close resemblance to the ballad under discussion. A young man is in love with a poor girl, but his parents disapprove of their marriage. The young man is sent over the seas, while the girl to a nunnery. The former returns home and discusses the stratagem with his brothers: clad as a dead body, he will lie on the bier while his brother goes to the nunnery to announce the death. The girl asks for leave to see the corpse, the prioress warns her to take heed of "Mortens who is so very shrewd", yet she enters the church, walks to the bier, sheds her tears confessing her love of him. Hearing this, the sham-dead man springs up and lifting the girl on back of his horse, gallops away. The nuns think the girl was carried away by an angel (and are not unwilling to be eloped in a like way). But this type survives only in manuscripts of the aristocratic circles, the only extant broadside copy of the ballad having been recorded from oral tradition on one occasion. It is obvious that the solution of this plot has influenced the other ballad's dénouement, which in turn must have been of earlier origin, otherwise the motif of the nunnery could not have entered it, not even in the above-described incomplete combination.

Versions of the story with the motif of elopement from nunnery is not unknown in the French-speaking areas either, but the texts are rather modern developments. In order to separate the heroine and the young man, her parents send her to a closter, while the young man is either abroad or thought to be dead. Returning home (from the soldiers), the young man searches for his sweetheart, first in the girl's home, then in the nunnery; the nuns do not give her out, therefore the young man pretends to be dead and elopes the girl when she arrives to lament over him. This story can be read in six different collections, in one of which as many as thirty variants of it are to be found. The same story is known to exist in even more modern forms: the young man intrudes in a nunnery under the cloak of a gardener and so he succeeds in winning his sweetheart, without being in need of simulating death.

But already the first variant referring to a nunnery may have been transformed from an earlier story in which the young man cheated out his sweetheart not from a closter but from her home. The two texts quoted under I— one of them coming from Provence, the other being a variant brought by French settlers to Canada—begin with the young man's feigned illness with which he tries to decoy the girl to see him. (Remember, the Danish mother sometimes tells her son to simulate illness and lie on the bier!) She asks her father if she may go, but he warns her that she runs the risk of seduction. The girl goes in spite of the warning, and while she is talking to the young man, her boat is cast off. When she wants to go home, he tells her that she is far from her father, and that there is no returning home. She wails, saying her father was right, but he assures her that she will be not a seduced girl but his truly beloved one. This southern French text and its Canadian variant originating from northern France, from where it had been brought to Canada, can be complemented with data derived from a Dutch manuscript from between 1385 and 1400, in which the scene can be read in the form of a prelude to a play (Cf. *Creizenach*). In it there is a scene in which a rich youth tries to gain the affections of a poor girl, but money does not bring him success. Then his mother advises him to feign illness, and the girl is sent for. The girl thus seduced goes through all sorts of adventures which are entirely literary in character. Research has established that this piece and similar ones were assembled mosaic-like from various narrative motifs, even from cycles of epics. And it would seem, judged by the above scene, that even folk ballads may have come into the play. Consequently, there must have existed, from southern France right up to Holland, a story of this sort before the modernization with the introduction of the escape from the nunnery took place. This seems to be corroborated by the fact that the theme had occurred— as *Baud-Bovy* pointed out—in the Greek territories as well. And if the motif of eloping from the convent comes up in sixteenth-century Danish manuscripts, then the solution that shows a close agreement with the Hungarian ballad must have been of a much earlier origin: the girl leaves her home in order to see, and wake over, the dead body—and this formulation is typical of the Scottish ballads, and can be discovered among the Danes as well.

But the motif of the marvellous mill is known to the French as well, and this is to show the way how the ballad arrived at the eastern territories. This motif comes up in a different type in French balladry, and formed a favourite part of earlier collections. The ballad bears the title "Le joli tambour". Here a young drummer wants to marry a princess, and to pave his way he exaggerates his riches by saying that he has three mills: one turns out gold, another silver, and the third his sweetheart's love. (In some of the variants boats are mentioned, one of which is laden with gold, another with silver, while the third is for rescuing his sweetheart.) If now we consider that in one of the Transylvanian variants one stone of the marvellous mill grinds out pearls, the second coins, and the third kisses, the correspondence becomes almost complete. This image also appears, though rarely and very blurred, in the areas bordering on the French-speaking parts: in a seventeenth-century Dutch ballad the young man tempts the girl with seven mills which grind gold and silver. Among the Germans, these mills will grind sugar, nutmeg, and cloves; among the Portuguese there are three mills for spices; while with the Italians we merely find mills that grind white and yellow flour. Thus the Hungarian image may have come directly from the French, and it can be readily supposed that the Hungarians merged this French motif into the likewise French story of the lover who used his feigned death as a decoy, and that it was they that amplified it into the triple build-up. This assumption is further supported by the fact that there are two motifs which are always present in the Hungarian variants: (1) the marvellous mill, and (2) the feigned death; the third motif may vary: now a marvellous tower, now a garden with stone walls or a little flower-garden come up, on other occasions a strong iron bridge, or nothing at all, except the mills supplying gold, silver and diamond in gradation, while the marvellous mill and the marvellous corpse are never left out.

And if the texts of the nations living in the neighbourhood of the Hungarians are examined, it will appear that the new solution had spread from the Hungarians.

In Gottschee, for example, in that group of German-speakers wedged among the Slovenes, reference is only made to the mill, and to a church to which young people go for milling or to Mass. This realistic—and precisely for that reason unrealistic—idea, putting up a real church to decoy the girl, is anything but ballad-like. The ballad favours stylized symbols, a marvellous mill, a marvellous tower, and the further we get from these, the deeper we plunge into incredible reality. This text, incidentally, agrees in its other details almost word for word with the Hungarian. For instance: "Mother, my heart aches for that beautiful girl I saw at the market." "Never mind, my son, we will build a white mill. When people come to have milling, the pretty girl will come, too." And everybody came to have milling, except the pretty girl.—And the ending: "What a marvellous corpse it is: its legs jump up, its eyes open, and its arms rise!" etc. And in the text mentioned in Group III of the partial variants, the story merges with that of the young boy buried alive, with the hero when grown up behaving much in the same manner as described in the scenes of cajoling (cf. No. 142, with which text agrees even in the motif of the double death).

Similar texts are found among the Slovenes, but the mill disappears to be replaced by a well and a temple (or in the reverse order). In some variants (106.) even a vintage scene is added as a third step; the change is obviously in the direction of realism. (What is more, in the more recent variants the girl does not go to see the "corpse". Kumer 76–77.) It goes further in Italian areas: a bridge, a golden well, a flower-garden, a dance, in one case a church and a Mass figure in a multi-coloured jumble and in various order; generally with a four-part gradation, but without a mill. It would be absurd to suppose that the spread had taken place in the reverse direction: to imagine that the construction without the mill spread from the Italians to the Slovenes and the people of Gottschee, that they put in the real mill, and that the Hungarians adopted this construction and turned it into one of a marvellous mill of precisely the same sort as we find in the French ballad. We can only suppose the opposite: a French concept, framed in the ballad style, disseminated from the Hungarian area, becoming gradually vaguer in the process. It is also remarkable that this ballad is found in the northern Italian districts except Piedmont, so that the absorption from the Slovenes is easily imaginable. In this respect, too, the case differs from those in which the Italians took over French variants, for such have been recorded for the most part only in Piedmont and its surroundings.

As we proceed southwards in the Southern Slav and Bulgarian area, the ballad-like characteristics tend to disappear, gradually giving way to the epic method of relating the story. As against this, the international (western) distribution of the story appears in an explicit ballad form, a fact that clearly marks the latter's priority in time. In other words, the loss of ballad-like characteristics argues against a derivation from the Southern Slavs.

Throughout the Bulgarian language area the story is rendered in the strophe-repetitive structure, although this style of construction does never prevail consistently in the poems; in the course of incremental repetition, now this, now that part is left out—the mother's words, the son's pleas, or the formula "then all the fair girls came...", and the story is amplified, occasionally shortened in the narrative style. There is a variant in which the mother gives all the suggestions taken together—well, garden, church, feigned death—and the young man, too, carries them out together. All this indicates that the function of the form was not clearly felt. Yet, some extant details plainly show the routes followed in the diffusion. For if we found in the Bulgarian an exclusively epic delivery of what is in Hungarian a fully stanza-repeating poem, then either nation might in theory have been the recipient, and might have changed it into its own familiar form. If, on the other hand, it is found that fragments and misunderstood versions of the general Hungarian form are preserved in the Bulgarian tradition, then it can only be assumed that it was the Bulgarians that had taken the plot over from the Hungarians. Support for this is also provided by such corruptions in the Bulgarian as the one in which the mother tries to dissuade her son from building the decoys—the well, the church—and he nevertheless carries out the plan (65.). The entire body of the related European variants, including an isolated fourteenth-century Duch drama, witness that the original form is that in which the mother gives her son advice concerning the method of decoying to be followed. And the striving for realism is shown in the Bulgarian by such details as that in which the mother urges her son to hire masons and build a church, or even to fill his pockets with gold for the building operations (66. and 72).

If we examine all the Serbo-Croat material, we find a great variety in the stories. In regions distant from Hungary the curtailed plot assumes an epic form, and either preserves only the idea of the feigned death (95., 97., and 101.)—and even then it contains some element or other of the Hungarian stanza-repetition, such as, for instance, "what sort of corpse is that? ..." etc., so that there can be no doubt as to its relevance here—or it merges with some other story. An example of such contamination is where the feigned death preceded by several gradations, is insufficient to decoy the girl, and finally the young man disguised as a girl lays hold of his sweetheart (99., 101.). Another example: the girl decoyed by the feigned death alone chooses imprisonment rather than the young man's love. In other cases hardly anything remains of the original story: the girl humiliates the young man (telling him to go home to his pregnant sister), then, at her mother's urging, and regretting her behaviour, goes to see him, now ill, but she goes dressed as a man, i.e. disguised. She asks him what he would do with the girl if he got hold of her; the reply is that he would seduce her and then leave her. At this, she discloses her identity. But in addition to these special formations, there are variants—in Croat areas near the Hungarian border—in which we also find both the stanza-repeating structure and the original plot; the gradation takes place by means of four elements in these variants, just as in the Bulgarian and the Italian ones: church, two kinds of well, work done in common, and feigned death, or the feigned death without any preliminaries, and all this occurring in a medley. But in no variant do we find the *marvellous mill* in the whole of the Balkan tradition. Beyond the frontiers of Hungary, all we find of this ballad-image is a real mill in Gottschee. Considering all this, we have to reject a possible derivation from the Balkan peoples.

Seemann holds that the Southern Slav origin of the Hungarian ballad is supported by the fact that it is found only in the southeastern parts of Hungary, furthermore, he regards as a decisive proof that the name Ilona *Görög* (= Greek) is a family name in Hungarian, while in Bulgarian it is a common word. The former argument falls to the ground in the face of the Nyitra examples, and of the prose-variants collected from Szabolcs county; apart from this, also the number of variants is considerable. As to the name *Görög, Tibor Klaniczay* has pointed out conclusively that it is of literary origin with the Hungarian people. On the basis of a Hungarian story of Troy, very popular in the Middle Ages but now known only by inference, the Anonymous of Léva published in 1570 the story in verse of Paris and Helen. In the incipit, this has the expression "Görög Szép Ilona"—Fair Greek Helen—but later refers to the heroine by the phrase "Szép Ilona"—fair Helen. Subsequently, this literary text may have reached people as a broadside, and may well have lent to the phrase "Szép Ilona" the adjective "Görög".

The variants which were isolated at an early date, those known from Nyitra and those collected in Bukovina, know only the name "Fair Helen". But in Transylvania and in Moldavia, this ballad comes up now with the name of "Szép Ilona", now with that of "Görög Ilona". The Magyars of Bukovina emigrated there after 1764, from Transylvania. It was after this, that the broadside variant may have influenced the Transylvanian and Moldavian tradition, although not even from these regions was it able to oust utterly the original version of "Szép Ilona".

The two Slovak variants follow the Hungarian ballad in their construction. Here too the young man is ready to die for the shepherdess, but asks advice from his *father* (and this motif appears only here in the whole area of the ballad's dissemination), but the marvellous mill here too has degenerated into a church, a bridge or an inn. Finally the girl appears at the death-knell and is surprised much as in the Hungarian: "My goodness, what sort of corpse is this? Its eyes smile, its face is pink!" In the Ukrainian texts the decoy is similarly a church and an inn (and in one case a bridge), but here we cannot tell from the corrupt text whether the girl came to see or not, and in *124.* the feigned death is replaced by a real death—and a double one at that—with the motif of the grave-flower introduced to close the story, as in the Hungarian No. 142. Apparently, all these East-European forms are borrowings from the Hungarians.

576

This ballad belongs among the earliest Hungarian borrowings from the French

Literature: *Child* 25, 1882: survey of Scottish, Scandinavian, Italian, Slovene and Hungarian versions; *Creizenach* 1893: discussing fourteenth-century Dutch literary texts; Hauffen 1895: the Hungarians took it over from the Slovenes; *Köhler* 1900, 219: on the motif of the marvellous mill; *Gragger* 1926: refers to German, Danish, Swedish, Scottish, Italian, Albanian and Slovenian versions without mentioning their provenience; *Ortutay* 1936–1948 and *Dános* 1938: accept *Gragger; Csanádi* and *Vargyas* 1954: discern between northern and southern groups, the Slovenian—German version originates from the Hungarian; D. Vlr. 58 *(Seemann)* 1953; surrvey of the whole European dissemination area, the Hungarian originates from the Bulgarian; *Vargyas* 1960: French origin; *Horálek* 1963, 100: Southern Slav origin, reached Ukraine through Hungarian mediation; *Vargyas* 1967 = *Vargyas* 1960.

69. THE TEST OF LOVE

144.

1. Ke - be - lem - be bú - vék egy nagy ás - pis - ki - gyó.

Vedd ki, a - pám, vedd ki! Bi - zony, nem ve-szem én.

E - redj az a - nyád-hoz, majd ta - lán ki - ve - szi.

Vedd ki a - nyám, vedd ki! Bi-zony nem ve - szem én.

1. A big asp has crept into my bosom,
   Take it out, father, take it out! I will not take it out,
   Go to your mother, perhaps she will take it out;
   Take it out, mother, take it out! I will not take it out,

2. Go to your brother, perhaps he will take it out;
   Take it out, brother, take it out! I will not take it out;
   Go to your sister-in-law, perhaps she will take it out;
   Take it out, sister-in-law, take it out! I will not take it out;

3. Go to your brother-in-law, perhaps he will take it out;
   Take it out, brother-in-law, take it out! I will not take it out;
   Go to your sister, perhaps she will take it out;
   Take it out, sister, take it out! I will not take it out;

4. Go to your betrothed one, perhaps he will take it out;
   Take it out, my betrothed, take it out! I will certainly take it out.
   A big asp has crept into my bosom,
   Take it out, betrothed, take it out! I will certainly take it out!

Transdanubia (?), prior to 1813. Ádám Pálóczi Horváth, No. 292.

145.

1. Od a - lá szol-gál - tam, Szol - ga le - gin vó - tam.

Le - haj - tot - tam fe - jem Csip - ke - bu - kor a - lá.

1. I was serving over down there,
   And I was a poor servant lad.
   I rested my head
   Under a brier.

2. Into my bosom
   There crept a big asp.
   It is squeezing my heart,
   It is sucking my red blood.

3. Take out, father, take out
   The big asp!
   It is squeezing my heart,
   It is sucking my red blood.

4. I will not take it out,
   For I am afraid of it.
   Take it to your mother,
   Perhaps she will take it out.

5. Take out, mother, take out
   The big asp!
   It is squeezing my heart,
   It is sucking my red blood.

6. I will not take it out,
   For I am afraid of it.
   Take it to your sister,
   Perhaps she will take it out.

7. Take out, sister, take out
   The big asp!
   It is squeezing my heart,
   It is sucking my red blood.

8. I will not take it out,
   For I am afraid of it.
   Take it to your brother,
   Perhaps he will take it out.

9. Take out, brother, take out
   The big asp!
   It is squeezing my heart,
   It is sucking my red blood.

10. I will not take it out,
    For I am afraid of it.
    Take it to your sister-in-law,
    Perhaps she will take it out.

56*/II

11. Take out, sister-in-law, take out
    The big asp!
    It is squeezing my heart,
    It is sucking my red blood.

12. I will not take it out,
    For I am afraid of it.
    Take it to your betrothed,
    Perhaps he will take it out.

13. Take out, my betrothed, take out
    The big asp!
    It is squeezing my heart,
    It is sucking my red blood.

14. Wait, betrothed, wait!
    I shall go to the tailor,
    I shall go to the tailor,
    And I shall have a pair of gloves cut.

(By way of explanation the singer added that the girl did not have an asp in her bosom but she found a heap of gold coins, and she wanted to test her relatives. Eventually she did not let anyone share her coins, except her fiancée.)

Ghymes (Nyitra county). Performed by a woman of seventy. Kodály 1906 = Ethn 1907, 112.

146.

1. El - a - lud -tam va - la   Sár-pa - tak - ja   mel - lett.

El - a - lud - tam va-la   Sár - pa - tak - ja   mel - lett.

1. I fell asleep
   By the brook of Sár.
   I fell asleep
   By the brook of Sár.

2. Into my bosom
   There crept a snake of yellow belly.
   Into my bosom
   There crept a snake of yellow belly.

3. Take it out, my gracious
   Kind father.
   Take it out, my gracious
   Kind father.

4. Instead of living without my hand,
   I shall live without my daugher.
   Instead of living without my hand,
   I shall live without my daughter.

5. Take it out, my gracious
   Kind mother,
   Take it out, my gracious
   Kind mother.

6. Instead of living without my hand,
   I shall live without my daughter.
   Instead of living without my hand,
   I shall live without my daughter.

7. Take it out, my gracious
   Kind, dear (elder) brother,
   Take it out, my gracious
   Kind, dear (elder) brother.

8. Instead of living without my hand,
   I shall live without my sister.
   Instead of living without my hand,
   I shall live without my sister.

9. Take it out, my gracious
   Kind, dear (younger) sister,
   Take it out, my gracious
   Kind, dear (younger) sister.

10. Instead of living without my hand,
    I shall live without my sister.
    Instead of living without my hand,
    I shall live without my sister.

11. Take it out, my gracious
    Kind, dear (younger) brother,
    Take it out, my gracious,
    Kind, dear (younger) brother.

12. Instead of living without my hand,
    I shall live without my sister.
    Instead of living without my hand,
    I shall live without my sister.

13. Take it out, my gracious
    Kind, dear betrothed,
    Take it out, my gracious
    Kind, dear betrothed.

14. Instead of living without my betrothed,
    I shall live without my hand,

Instead of living without my betrothed,
I shall live without my hand!

The performer adds:
"She had a good deal of money in her bosom. Her betrothed was given a lot of money. She tested everyone of them."

Gajdár (Moldavia). Performed by a woman of 47. Jagamas and Kallós, 1951 = Faragó and Jagamas 6/B.

Divergences: As to the main character, in one or two cases it cannot be made clear whether a young man or a girl should be understood (mostly a young man). In Transylvania, the heroine is a girl in three cases, and a young married woman in six cases. In general, she is grazing oxen, sometimes colts, in other instances only a "shepherd lad" is mentioned. In twelve variants, brier is mentioned as a resting place, in one case a white rose-tree, and in another text an "ash-bush" figures on the "Ash-hill" in the first lines of the song. The snake is usually yellow, sometimes an "asp, a poisonous snake", a dragon, and in Moldavia a "yellow asp" (all these with a certain degree of corruption). In some variants the young woman is warned against walking in the bush or shrub covered with dry leaves because "There lurks the snake that bites you in the *likeness of love!"* The members of the family put to test are sometimes father, mother, elder sister, elder brother (younger brother), sister-in-law, coming in the row one after the other. Sometimes the lover has a pair of gloves cut with which he takes the snake out. In other cases he wraps "his tender hand in cloth, And so he removes the snake with the yellow belly from her bosom". But a number of the variants conclude the story by introducing the contrast: "I shall rather live without one of my hands Than without my sweetheart." Half the variants maintain that "The snake with the yellow belly was a golden apple", "He thrusted his hand in her bosom, Well, a golden apple got into his hand", or simply gold, a bag of money, and the like are mentioned. The singers add such remarks in prose form. *Kálmány* recorded a variant in which the parents reproach their son for not having advised them about the gold: "Why did you not tell us so?" This addition, however, carries the narrative beyond the point. In one of the variants the following lesson is drawn: "There is no heart in father, In mother and brother, Nor in my sister, Only in my sweetheart". Or: "I am not sorry for my father, since he was not sorry for me. ...(mother and brother are mentioned)... I am sorry for my sweetheart, because he was sorry for me...". Then a passage in prose follows telling about the girl's testing her family by putting gold in her bosom. A text from Gerlén and another from Lészped insert stanzas borrowed from The Speaking Corpse (Type **65.**); according to two variants of Lészped, the girl dies when the snake is removed.

Earliest provenience: 1813.
Dissemination: Transdanubia (without specification), Zala county (Zajk), Tolna county (Szakcs), Nyitra county (Ghymes 2), Nógrád county (Lapujtő), Csongrád county (?), the Szeged region (without specification). Torontál county (Csóka, Morotva, Szaján 2), Csanád county (Apáca, Meződombegyháza), Arad county (Pécska), Maros-Torda county (Mezőbánd), Udvarhely county?

582

(without specification), Nagyküküllő county (Alsórákos), Csík county (Csíkgyimes, Csíkmadaras, Csíkrákos 3, Gyergyószárhegy), Bukovina (Józseffalva-Hertelendyfalva, Torontál county), Moldavia (Bogdánfalva, Forrófalva, Gajdár, Gerlén, Klézse 2, Lészped 5, Máriafalva, Szketura, Trunk). Total: 37. (I–III: 14, IV: 10, V: 13.)

Textual relationships with other ballads: "For instead of a son God grants me a son": **4., 52.** Testing of a member of the family: **22.,** of the sweetheart: **43., 75.;** similarity with The Speaking Corpse **(65.)** in the following order: His father went there, His mother went there... and with the circumstance that the corpse answers only his sweetheart's entreaty may well explain the presence of this motif in this ballad.

Tunes: 1. = 144, 2. = 145, 3. = 146.

Tune examples: 4. (2 variants), 10. (2 variants), 11. (2 variants), 12. (2 variants), 15. (3 variants), 19. (2 variants).

Versions in languages other than Hungarian:

ENGLISH: *1–9. Child* 95. *10–77. Bronson* 95.

GERMAN: *78–82.* E–B 78. *83–85. Parisius* 16, 90, 748. *86. Hauffen* 65 (plus Pohl 66 variants elaborated).

DANISH: *87–99.* DgF 486.

ITALIAN: *100–101. Giannini* 25, plus variant.

SOUTHERN SLAV: *102.* HNP VII No. 234. *103. Blažinčić,* 80. *104–112. Kuhač* 106, 142, 1060, plus 6 variants. *113. Djordjević* 1920, No. 17. *114–115. Idem* 1931 Nos 252 and 491: *116–118.* VuK I, Nos 212–214, 289–291. *119–120. Vasilević* I, 196 and 350. *121–123. Žganec* 1950 Nos 27–28, and 214. *124–125. Milojević†* 284 and 302. *126. Petranović* I No. 20†. *127. Grün,* 30. (*Kumer* 72–73? bees instead of human beings.)

BULGARIAN: *128.* A–V 54. *129–138. Stoin* 1928 Nos 63–68 and 529–532. *139. Idem* 1931 No. 2189. *140. Idem* 1934 No 613. *141. Miladinovi* 495. *142–143.* SbNU 16/17 Materialy, 57, Nos 3–4.

144–145. Vatev 185 and 343. *146–148. Tsitselkova* 230–232. *149–150. Ivanov* 1949 Nos 279–280. *151–152. Idem* 1936 Nos 323–324. *153–154. Dozon* 3 and 61. *155. Stoilov* 177.

AROMUN: *156. Weigand* II No. 90.

ROMANIAN: *157. Amzulescu* 242. *158. Teodorescu* 682. *159. Brăiloiu*, 75. *160. Vasiliu* 32. *161. Tocilescu*, 29. *162. Giuglea-Vâlsan*, 189. *163. Frâncu-Candrea*, 226. *164. Pompiliu*, 41 (Hungarian translation by *Moldovan*, 161). *165. Vulcanu*, 27 (Hungarian translation). *166–167.* Ethn 1897, 281 (bilingual), 2 variants.

UKRAINIAN: *168–178. Golovatsky* I, 46, No. 7, 48, No. 8, 50, No. 11, 114, No. 27, II, 80, No. 14,149, No. 10, 161, No. 15, 245, No. 7, 596, No. 33, 726, No. 11, III/1, 64, No. 4, *179–180. Kolberg* 1882–1889 II, 226, No. 418 and 227, No. 420.

SLOVAK: *181–184.* Slov. sp. I, 208 and 369, III, 222 and 601. *185–186. Kolečány* 35–36. *187. Kollár* II, 13 (= *Szeberényi*, Hungarian translation).

MORAVIAN: *188–189. Bartoš* 1901 Nos 122 and 1696.

POLISH: *190–191. Kolberg* 1871–1884 XII, 78–79 No. 157.

SPANISH: *192. Attias* 51 (cf. *Long, Bronzini's* survey).

CATALAN: (cf. *Armistead-Silvermann* 1962, 73 note 56.)

TURKISH: *193. Namik*, 87–95.

GIPSY: *194.* EMU I (1887), 40–41.

Indirectly related:

ROMANIAN: *195. Amzulescu* 243.

Considering the widespread of this ballad, there is nothing to be wondered at its having entered the scope of ballad research at a relatively early date. Apart from the theme of The Enticed Wife, no other ballad has been dealt with in so many papers in both the European and the American expert literature. Most recently, *Eleanor Long* dedicated a full monograph to it (University of California publication). In spite of her great input of efforts, she has not been successful in clarifying in a reassuring way the questions connected with the origin and the dissemination of the ballad, and I am of the opinion that for a long time nobody will be able to boast of a greater success in this respect. But let us see, for the time being, the facts.

With the English, the hero, sometimes heroine, has to be redeemed from the hands of the hangman. The German version speaks about a girl whom her parents and brothers and sisters refuse to release from the hands of the corsairs. The same story is current among the Scandinavians. Somewhat more complicated is the situation in the Italian variants: some of them contain the story of the girl kidnapped by corsairs, but at least as many texts speak about imprisonment in a jail. Among the enumerated nations, the story is fairly uniform as regards representation and the use of strophe repetition and what is more, even the trend of dissemination can be inferred on the basis of certain partial textual agreements between the different versions. In any case, the affinity is fairly obvious in the northern group; problems arise, however, in connection with the Italian variants, in which some minor partial agreements go crosswise the universal relationship and frustrate our attempt at drawing conclusions. In Spain a preliminary story is attached to the ballad inasmuch as the girl is cajoled by sailors who promise to give her silk on the boat; indeed, only one variant introduces the girl's entreaties to her relatives. The literature before *E. Long* considered now the northern, now the southern, Italian group as original. One thing has been made clear already, in any case, to wit, the basic idea is rooted in Greek antiquity. The legend of Alcestis is involved; Admetus, the husband of Alcestis, is to die for he had failed to offer a wedding sacrifice. *Snakes* appear wriggling in his room, but through the intervention of Apollo he is granted the favour of escaping death, provided somebody is willing do die in his stead. Neither his father nor his mother, only his wife is ready to bring the sacrifice. Alcestis, however, is sent back by Persephone from Hades, or according to another version of the legend, is rescued by Hercules from the messenger of Hades. Thus the story comes to a happy ending.

Tales related to this legend are extant in eastern, African and East-European traditions. At the birth of a child it is divined that he should die at his wedding feast either in consequence of a snake's bite or by drowning in water. Through the intervention of somebody, occasionally a servant, the verdict is modified so that he can escape if one of his relatives will be willing to incur death in his place. In other instances, the relative should surrender his or her remaining years of life to the convict. His father and mother, occasionally other relatives refuse to undertake the sacrifice, but his bride does not. Finally, the bride escapes, also in a miraculous way. (*Megas* 1933). This story is related, among other sources, by a thirteenth-century Turkish collection of short-stories, the Kitab-i Dede Quorquud (*193.*). In the fifth story God forbids the hero who is engaged in desperate struggle against Azrail, saying that he might survive if someone is willing to die in his place. The hero turns first to his father and mother, but neither of them are inclined to make the sacrifice. Then he takes leave of his sweetheart who learns the reason of his departure and offers her life to rescue him without delay. God is pleased with her magnanimity and forgives both of them.

All this would seem to provide sufficient explanation for the development of the Hungarian version, as well as for that of several neighbourning nations' ballads: in which the relatives are put to test by means of the snake. Nevertheless, certain contradictions arise here again. So far, Hungarian folk tales have failed to present any trace of the variant in which snake-bite is foretold for a young man when he is sitting at his marriage feast. Accordingly, some of the southern neighbour nations should be taken into consideration. On the grounds of different reasoning, *Long* arrives at the same conclusion. She considers the motif of redemption from prison to be the starting point. Therefore we have to examine the interconnections between the East-European versions in order to assess the value this possible of approach, too, and to acquire a deeper insight into the complicated question of the spread of this ballad.

As regards the northern neighbours, it is the Ukrainians whose variants are available to me in highest numbers, therefore I propose to begin with them. According to one of the stories, a young Cossack sends a letter from the prison to his father, mother, brother and sister, asking them to redeem him. They ask him, in turn, how much they are supposed to pay for him. Receiving the specification of the items (varying by relatives), they answer they are unable to pay that much. But the sweetheart (wife) is ready to pay the sum. (*176., 179–180.*); in *169.*, the mother (in this variant the only relative contrasted with the sweetheart) exclaims: "May you perish!". In *168.*, however, the relatives' answers are followed by a few lines indicating that the young man has been left in the prison after all. By way of gradation, in one of the variants the girl kept prisoner by a Turk in an inn, begs him not to kill her for her father will soon come and pay the ransom. The father arrives without the ransom. The girl is sobbing with tears. The scene is repeated with the arrival of the mother. Finally the ransom is brought by the girl's lover. "A sweetheart is better than the bloodkins", the lesson is drawn in *169.* and *175.* Another frequent variation of the basic idea is that the hero, a Cossack in *171.,* is drowning in a river without receiving help from his father, mother, brother and sister who have neither a boat nor oars; nevertheless, his sweetheart rescues him. The relatives say: "You may perish as well!" while the sweetheart says: "You must not perish!" The same plot takes place with a *girl as heroine* in *172.* and *177.*; the father and mother in the latter curse their daughter: "May you perish, because you have not been a good child to me!" According to *174,* a corrupt variant, the girl drifted away by water refuses to accept her brother's help who extends his hand towards her, similarly she swims farther from her sister, though she draws near to her sweetheart only to be lost from sight in an utterly confused text. A third solution is when the young man mowing grass or selecting goods to be sold at the market calls to the members of his family asking them to bring him water to drink; they refuse to do the favour (*173.*), and what is more, the text even motivates their refusal by referring to certain jobs they have to do, until finally his sweetheart brings him "honey and a little good wine" (*178.*).

With the Slovaks we encounter somewhat vaguer formulations. In *181.* the girl, having lost her cow in the oak-woods, misses her way home. "O, how I wish my father would come, he would find the cow!" The father comes but fails to find the animal. Her brother and sister are not successful either. Finally the sweetheart finds the cow and takes the girl out of the hills. Similarly a cow turns up, though with a different role, in *187.* While a *young boy* is guarding the beast in the field, it tramples to death the landlord's peacock, and the boy is therefore imprisoned by the lord. He writes letters to his relatives, but only his sweetheart helps him, just as in the Ukrainian version. The Slovaks too know the solution with the girl swimming in the water: the relatives similarly refuse to help the girl drifted away by the calm Danube, saying "May God drown her because she was not an obedient girl!" Only her sweetheart encourages her to swim ashore, extending his hands to rescue her. "The sweetheart is kinder than all the relatives are!" (*186.*) The testing of relatives by the *young man* asking for water to drink shows a further agreement with the Ukrainian: under the pretext of being occupied in several ways, the relatives refuse to comply with his wish (mother, sister are working on some embroidery), and finally he receives water to drink from his sweetheart. "She is better than the relatives." (*185.*) The same version of the story is known among the Moravians (*188–189.*), who, however, have another variant in which the girl immediately turns to the sweetheart for help and meets with a flat refusal on his part, just as on her father's (*184.*). Farthest lying from the basic scheme (if pertaining to it at all) seems to be the solution in *182–183*: "I ask you, little mother, if I may live with you any longer?" "O, daughter, instead of me, rather with the one you have chosen for yourself." The question is repeated and answered by father, brother and sister, and finally the conclusion is formulated: "I have chosen a pretty husband. Good-bye to you, father, mother, brother, sister," etc. The stanza-repeating form mentions the members of her family one after the other, contrasting them with the sweetheart— thus much the story has in common with the ballads discussed above, only the motif of the test of love is missing from it. A similarly extreme example is found in the Polish texts: the husband is beating his wife who calls her father, mother and sister to help her; finally her brother arrives with a sword in hand, and standing on the threshold gives a thorough scolding to the husband, until the latter begs his wife for pardon. In this formulation the husband—sweetheart cannot play a nobler part than the relatives, therefore the point is utterly lost.

The Romanian variants contain practically none of the several Slav solutions. With them exclusively the Hungarian-type is known: a snake must be removed from the young man's bosom. The strophe-repetition prevails throughout the ballad, sometimes somewhat variegated though, and always in an ampler formulation than with the Hungarians. It will be instructive to publish here a verbatim translation of a Romanian variants. (*159.*)

"Three leaves of bramble, hey! Milea calls out from the hills, from the deep valleys. It is three days since he has been calling. His father heard Milea calling, and asked him: Milea, Milea, your father's dear Milea, Have you lost the sheep, have you worn your clothes, have you lost your money, or perhaps someone has beaten you? I have not lost my sheep, I have not worn my clothes, I have not dropped what little of money I have, nor have I been beaten by anyone. I only had a short sleep under the tall round apple-tree which is in full blossom. And I have had a beautiful dream: rain was falling on me, it was falling on the blossoms, and a dragon-snake crept into my bosom. It is a dragon-snake with golden scales. Father, please, wrap your hand in cloth and thrust it into my bosom, under my waistcoat, and remove the dragon-snake! As it is stretching itself, it surrounds my body, as it is contracting, it will kill me, it will cleave my tender heart! Milea, Milea, my dear son! Rather than remain without a hand, I shall live without you. As he heard this, tears flooded his eyes. He turned to his mother. Mother dear, my dear mother, you nursed me when I was a baby, now that I am big, wrap your hand in your headsquare, thrust it into my bosom, under my waistcoat, take out the snake, for it is a veritable dragon-snake with golden scales! Your mother's dearest Milea, rather than remain without a hand I shall remain without you. For I have another son like you. As he heard this, his eyes filled with tears. Turning to his brother, he said: Brother, my dear elder brother! Both of us are sons of one and the same father and have been brought up in the same wild forest. Wrap your hand in cloth, brother, and take the snake out of my bosom! Milea, Milea, dear brother to your brother, Instead of remaining without a hand, I prefer to live without you. For I have mates as brave a you are. As Milea heard this, his eyes filled with tears and he turned to his sister. Sister, my pretty sister, we are born of the same mother, like two trees that have grown from one root. Wrap your hand in cloth, thrust it into my bosom, under my waistcoat, Remove the snake from there. For it stretches out, embraces me, and if it contracts, it will kill me! Milea, Milea, your sister's beloved one, instead of remaining without a hand, alas, I shall remain without you. For there are other young men as brave as you. As Milea heard this, his eyes filled with tears. He started upwards on the bank of the Danube. He called for Lina. Lina, my little Lina, my dear little wife! Wrap your hand in cloth, thrust it into my bosom, under my waistcoat, and take out the snake! For it is going to eat up my tender heart! As Lina heard this, she did not even wrap her hand in cloth, but thrust it into his bosom, and lo, she removed a purse full of gold. Then Milea spoke up: Rather a bit of pity than a father and a mother. For even a stranger will take pity on you, and lend you a helping hand! Rather a bit of pity than a brother and a sister! For even though a stranger, only she shows compassion and pity. There is no pity and sympathy in your brother, and there is not pity and sympathy in your father and mother, but there is in your kind-hearted wife."

As can be seen, what we have here is not a kind of stanza-repetition but rather variations on a stanza. We have texts ampler and more variable than this at hand, although we have also shorter ones marked by a somewhat more stable structural pattern.

There exists another type among the Romanian ballads which is partially relevant: there is no testing of relatives in it. The father, mother and other relatives of an imprisoned young man came in turn to redeem him, but the "lord" who keeps him prisoner does not let him go. Finally the sweetheart arrives, upon whose entreaties the landlord sets him free (*195*.)

Before reviewing the Southern Slav texts of the Balkan peninsula, let us be acquainted with the only Gipsy version available for us in print. It is the more interesting for our point of view because it was recorded in the territory of pre-wars Hungary. It should be noted, however, that the Gipsy version reads as a sort of prose tale instead of a song. Four sisters are living together, and the eldest puts the question: whom do they think love them best and would sacrifice his life for them in case of necessity? One of the sisters says, it is their father, the other, their mother, the third one, their brother. The eldest sister is laughing at their answers, asking them to make a test: let each of them hide and call for the person she has named, asking him (or her) to remove a snake from her bosom. All three girls are left in the lurch; finally the eldest sister calls her sweetheart who is willing, indeed, to take out the snake.

A more recent manuscript collection contains a sung variant of the story: the Gipsy variant recorded by the *Csenki brothers* (*Imre Csenki* and *Sándor Csenki*, 1938) at Püspökladány (Great Hungarian Plain, Hajdú county). The content of the song-text can be summed up as follows: A little red snake has crept into the young man's bosom. He asks first his mother, then his father, his sister and finally his sweetheart to take it out. His blood-relatives all deny him, saying: It is better for me to live without my son (brother) than to live without my hand. Finally his sweetheart wraps her hand in a silk kerchief in order to remove the snake, and she finds treasure instead of it. The stanza-repetition prevails throughout the construction. It is more than obvious that the Gipsy song closely follows the structure of the Hungarian ballad. Particularly interesting is the mentioning of the snake's colour, a trait typical of the Hungarian version (yellow, or yellow-bellied snake occurs in the variants), and so is the circumstance that the girl wraps her hand in a kerchief. Also the melody of the song shows a marked affinity with the old-style Hungarian tune types. (By courtesy of *Imre Csenki*.)

South of the Romanian language area, among the Bulgarians, the snake motif also appears, and what is more, it does so in texts which are related to the Hungarian on account of similarities of formulation (besides, their concise construction also speaks of a Hungarian rather than a Romanian relationship). The young man calls from the hills: (*140., 142., 148.* and *155.*) or the girl (*147*): a snake has crept into his (her) bosom. The mother, father, sister, and so on, are requested one after the other to remove the snake. The wording is sometimes rather close to the Hungarian: "Woe to me, I am done with, mother, a snake has crept into my bosom, and the cursed creature is going to eat my heart!" (*142.*) "Son, I am so very sorry for you that even the leaves of trees are falling, even the sun has stopped in the sky" and the like; every answer contains reference to a different miraculous occurrence. One of the texts contains the same answer as the Hungarian: "Son, I can live without you, but I can't without my hand". (*142.*) Finally the Bulgarian sweetheart removes gold, pearl, coins or jewels instead of a snake. The same terse and pointed story receives sometimes a lengthy introduction, in which case the whole life-story of the hero is related, not in a stanza-repetitive form, and it is only after this that the song proper is performed in the repetitive construction. (*144., 139.*) It should be noted that a portion of the latter song (*139.*) shows a yet closer resemblance to the Hungarian: the snake is sucking the blood of the young man's heart. In certain instances the song is shortened to such an extent that only one step of the gradation remains: the mother is immediately followed by the loving mate (*151.* and *152.*). The effect is weakened by such solutions in which the texts lay out in advance that the shepherd wants to put to test his relatives by hiding gold, silver in his bosom (*129.*), or in which the calling of the young man is not followed by the appearance of reluctant relatives and their role can only be inferred from the last phase where the sweetheart removes the snake (*143.*). A stage of final erosion can be seen in *133.*: a kind of preliminary story, which is incomplete, speaks about an eagle that breaks its flight in the sky and falls down in the court of the young man's mother, crying: Take out, take out, dear mother, the poisonous snake that has crept into my bosom to suck out the blood of my heart! —and there is an end to the song. A similar erosion of the snake-motif is when a dragon in the form of a fish has crept into the bosom of a *girl*.

As another solution, the Bulgarian performers apply the motif of falling into the water. In the general formulation, the *girl* is washing clothes in the Danube and while so doing, but sometimes even without any mention of the act, falls into the river. Her father, mother and sisters and brothers encourage her to swim ashore so that they may lend her a helping hand, but she cannot because a stem of some tree or other water-plant holds her up by the hair. Nevertheless, her sweetheart, without any summon to the effect, swims in and rescues the girl (*128., 136., 150., 154.*). The first-mentioned ballad represents the story in a rather detailed manner: we have a realistic description of how the young man takes hold of a branch of tree with one of his hands while he is dragging the girl with the other; and sometimes we can hear about what they were talking of between themselves while walking home after the successful escape. On the other hand, the next text is shortened and corrupted so much so that only the brother's encouraging words are heard together with the girl's answer telling her brother that she is unable to swim ashore. (*135.*) The other group of the contrasted elements are missing in *137.* inasmuch as the village is so far that no one can hear the girl's cry, except her lover, who comes to rescue her from the river. (The story is even more truncated in *130., 131.* and *134.*, in which we have only a few fragmentary lines from the beginning of the story.) In *149.* the girl not rescued by her father and mother is saved by a Turk (?).

Further solutions: *132.* relates a long story about a *young man* who has to be redeemed from imprisonment. He is confident of his mother who has three castles, but she calls to him: I can live without my son but I cannot live without my three castles. There is no contrasted situation. In *141.* and *145.* cold wind is blowing and the *girl* would like to warm herself, but she is sent away by her father and the rest of her family; finally she is admitted by her sweetheart, or he comes to warm her.

The snake-motif appears, together with many other solutions, among the Southern Slavs as well, although somewhat less frequently than with the Bulgarians. Furthermore, we find signs of corruption in their texts in nearly every case. As regards both formulation and plot, *119.* shows closest resemblance to the Hungarian as well as certain Bulgarian variants, only the order of answers is altered (whether intentionally or incidentally) by the performer. "Stojan is playing the flute: I am going to die, mother, come and put your hand in my armpit and take out this poisonous snake! The poisonous snake torments me so terribly, mother!—I can live without my hand, son, but I cannot live without you." And so it goes on with the father, then the sister, until finally the man calls his wife, who says: "Without you, my man, I can live, but I cannot live without my hand." This solution in the reverse cannot be attributed to chance work and cannot be incidental in *124.*, in which the relatives show some pity towards the snake-bitten young man (the leaves of trees are falling, as in the Bulgarian ballad), yet refuse to help him, while the sweetheart does not hesitate to throw in the teeth of the victim that she can find a young man like him. A correct content and a sound order of answers characterize *125.*, although it is not presented in a strophe-repetitive structure but in a continuous narrative form. The same is the case in the *Vuk* variant (*116.*) formulated in the ten-syllabic lines of the epic songs (deseterac). It should be mentioned in this context, however, that the point of the story is made known in advance: while grazing the herd, the boy finds pearls, which he hides in his bosom in order to test his relatives. This same solution comes up several times in the strophe-repetitive structures as well: the hero either buys pearls or a golden apple is turned out by the coulter while he is ploughing, and either the one or the other he pretends to be a snake (*102.*, *103.* and *126.*) In such cases a preliminary story of variable length is added to the song. (For example, in *102.*, and especially in *103.*, in which the young man plants straw-berry with which to lure the girl to visit him, but by the time she arrives the season of straw-berry is over. It is only after this that he finds the golden apple while he is ploughing.) In *113.*, on the other hand, the relatives, who refuse to remove the snake from the young man's breast, are followed by the sweetheart, but we never know with what result, because the story is broken at this point.

The motif of redemption from captivity is not unknown in the Southern Slav language areas either where the relatives refuse to pay the ransom, which they find to be too high, and finally the hero is rescued by his sweetheart. (*105.*, *121.*, *122.*—a letter is sent from the prison—and *127.*). In *123.* and *124.* I found the case of the girl who fell into the water: the question is who is to bring a boat to rescue the girl. The beginning of *124.* bears some resemblance to the Hungarian version's first lines:

"O, thorny little wood, cold little water, A girl is swimming in it . . ." and so on. Interestingly enough, the relatives here not only deny help but also throw stones at the drowning girl, shouting: "Drown in the water, you devil, because you have never been kind to me!" A transformation of the motif of falling into the water is when the girl is picking pearls in the pond, asking her relatives to bring a boat and take the pearls out of the pond. (*109., 115.* and *117.*)

The figure of the young man calling for water occurs in this language area as well (*106.–108.* and *114.*). Only his sweetheart is willing to bring him water. And an utterly eroded form of the basic idea occurs in *110., 111.* and *112.* telling about a girl sharing out the golden apple found by the young man; here the question is if she keeps the better half for herself or yields it over to the young man. In *118.* the girl is picking flowers on the hill-side, offers them to her relatives, but only the sweetheart accepts her present (*118.*). And finally she wants to creep as a flower into the bosom of one of her relatives, but only the sweetheart is willing to comply with her strange wish (*120.*).

The Greek songs have it that the relatives must sacrifice part of their lives, half of it, or many more years. The difference is so apparent in relation of all the Balkan and West-European versions that the Greek cannot be considered as point of origin. At the same time, it can be accepted as a surviving form of the ancient Greek tradition.

Many varieties of the corrupted forms of the basic idea may be discovered in the multifarious solutions of East-European balladry. Most conspicuous is among them the formulation in which the main idea is lost from sight: even the sweetheart does not help his (her) mate (*119., 125., 184., 190.* and *191.*). But the point may be lost in other ways as well: there is no conclusion to the story, or there is no-one to help (*113., 132., 133., 135., 137.* and *143.*—in the latter case there is no confrontation—*149., 168.,* and *184.*). The point is weakened when the dénouement is laid out in advance (*102–103., 116., 126.* and *129.*). A similar weakening occurs when the test of love does not involve life danger. It is in this respect that the most conspicuous deviations from the basic idea, and also the most numerous ones, occur. Here included is the case of redemption from imprisonment without explicit life danger (*105., 106–112., 114., 115., 117., 118., 120–122., 127., 132., 141., 145., 168–170., 173., 174., 176., 178–183.,* and *187–191.*). We may consider secondary developments those variants which do not present the story in a stanza-repetitive form (*116., 125., 128., 132., 133., 135.* and *137.*). To wit, this form prevails in the West as well as in Hungary, and comes up also with the eastern neighbours of the Hungarians in a very similar construction; that is to say, this form apparently belonged to the ballad from the very beginning. Thus, its disappearance should be regarded as a consequence of wear and tear. Erosion like this is the process in which a long preliminary story in an epic form is added to the plot laid out in the stanza-repetition form (*102., 103., 139.* and *144.*). A case of partial erosion is represented by the change of the text when it tries to alleviate the indifferent attitudes of the relatives in a way, say, that they take pity on the drowning girl, calling her to swim ashore, only they are afraid to plunge into the water to rescue her (*128., 135., 146., 148., 149.* and *154.*). We qualify as a similar corruption the case when the relatives behave in the opposite manner: they leave her in the lurch and call her names, expressing a kind of hatred that leads far beyond the scope of the original plot (*104.,* *177.* and *186.*).

And if we accept *E. Long*, according to whom the genuine hero was a man— provided the starting point is to be sought for in the legend of Alcestis—then all the versions that have a female as central character should be taken for corrupt forms. Were it so, then the Hungarian would stand nearest the original, because out of 39 cases only 9 speak about a female while the rest about a male main character. As against this, the East-European and the English conception seems to be secondary, since the ratio of male and female is fifty to fifty. Erosion has gone farthest in the German ballads, and in their derivates, which employ exclusively female characters.

Nor is it accidental that many East-European versions have a solution similar to that of the German. By a closer consideration, the two most frequent Eastern versions occurring among both the northern and the southern neighbours of Hungary, that is redemption from prison and rescuing from water, may be taken for variations of the German *Losgekaufte* story, in which the girl has to be redeemed from corsairs and the relatives think the ransom abnormally high; in any case, the conception of boat may well have associated with that of water.

In connection with the question of origin of the Slav variants *Megaș* and *Pohl* raise the idea of a possible contamination with the ballad "Edelmann und Schäfer" which itself shows a certain degree of contamination with elements of the "Losgekaufte" in some variants. The content of this ballad is the following: A nobleman meets a shepherd who is clad in silk and velvet. The nobleman throws him into prison because of his lordly attire and haughty replies. The young man's father offers various prices to redeem him, and in some of the variants the relatives come and do the same, and finally he is released. The variants of this ballad and of the "Losgekaufte" may have spread by the hundred among both the northern and southern Slavs, giving rise to the development of further variants with the motif of redemption from prison. The outlines of this second-mentioned German ballad can be discerned very clearly in the Slovak solution, according to which the cowboy is thrown into prison because his cow has trampled the landlord's peacock. It can be readily imagined that the Hungarian version with the snake motif, further the German motif of redemption from the boat and the "Edelmann und Schäfer" had exercised a combined effect, with all their variants overlapping each other, upon the eastern as well as southern Slav areas, initiating a process of variation and resulting ultimately in the medley of varieties found among the neighbouring nations. (At the same time we have to reject *Pohl*'s opinion, according to which the Slavs obtained the ballad from the Germans through Lithuanian mediation, because it clearly appears from the profound study of *Seemann* (1951) that the spread of the ballad invariably shows a trend from Slavs to Lithuanians.)

These motifs could not reach the Romanians since the Hungarian language area separates them from the German. Thus only the motif of "asking for water" remains problematic: there is no answer as yet to the question why it occurs in the northern as well as southern Slav areas. The rest of the types may well be ascribed to the performers' propensity to produce variants or to their misinterpreting the theme.

All this said and done, the questions relating to the spread of a part of the East-European versions have been solved. Only the version with the "snake motif" would stay unclarified. It enjoys an exclusive prevalence in the Hungarian and Romanian versions (if the partially relevant *195* is left out of consideration), and occurs rather frequently in the Bulgarian and Serbian areas, but is completely missing in the nations north of Hungary. This solution is always associated with a clear, strophic form of incremental repetition, further it occurs always in an uncorrupted form bearing traces of the strophic-repetitive construction in the Romanian, and is found, corrupted in many ways, in strophic form in Bulgarian (or in an eroded strophic construction). This constellation induces us to suppose a trend of dissemination starting out from the Hungarian territory. The characteristics of the melodies coupled with the ballads seem to support this idea. With the southern neighbours of Hungary, the text is never sung to strophic tunes, and with them the individual lines of the stanzas are not linked to a definite melodic section which is bound to recur in the same association from stanza to stanza. The Bulgarians will sing the text to one melodic section which is repeated stichically; the Romanians' ballad tunes are composed of variable sections and form units larger than the West-European strophes, and in their case the stanzas of the text part are not associated consistently to the strophic parts of the melody, that is to say, a given line should not be linked to a given melodic section of the composition. Such constructions are the usual frames of epic songs in which variation is a common element of the style. It is natural that under the influence of epic tradition the performers will apply the strophic repetition technique in a somewhat looser way when this technique arrives at them, and it is also natural that they tend to transform it according to their taste—which results, of course, in an erosion of the original strictly strophic construction.

When it comes to the clarification of questions connected with the origin and spread of this theme, decisive importance should be attached to a particular property of the Southern Slav folk poetry: a tenacity of traditions relating to the organization of the extended family in which brothers and sisters enjoy priority over a bride or a wife. *Horálek* (1964 II, p. 33) writes in this connection: "Für die südslawische Volksdichtung sind diejenigen Volkslieder charakteristischer, in denen ein Mädchen oder eine Frau den Bruder höher schätzt als den Geliebten (den Gemahl)", referring at the same time to certain pieces in the collections of *Vuk, Žganec, Štrekelj* and *Delorko*. Vielleicht beruht das Motif "Bruder über Geliebten" auf einer alten balkanischen Tradition. It is clear enough that in an area where people are possessed with such innate ideas there is little chance for a theme diagonally opposed to them to strike root in their folk poetry.

All things considered, it seems that the version with the "snake motif" spread from Hungarian territories towards the southern neighbours. Nevertheless, two questions are still left unsolved: how did the ancient legend get into the western balladry, and how the ballad spread from West to Hungary?

After all, it can be hardly doubted that similarly to most of the ballads, and the strophe-repetition technique itself, this theme also wandered from West to East. And if we do not conduct our examination solely along the thread of dissemination of one or another motif but consider genre and poetic solution in their full context,

594

then we have to acknowledge that the "test of love" is a typically western ballad-subject, and that the basic concept that love conquers all sorts of ties arising from kindredship is also a typically western idea. This taken for granted, a route that would run counterwise the usual West–East trend cannot be substantiated by the relative data. The conception of *E. Long* is not supported by detailed analytical examinations of the variants. Diversity of a high number of variants can demonstrate deep-rootedness of a theme only in case it has been formulated in several, properly outlined, clear types. In this ballad, however, variations tend to dissolve the *same* formulation. Therefore the eastern versions could not have provided points of origin for the western songs, whether their form or their content is considered.

Still less can we accept the role of Gipsies as mediators. One of the records coming from them represents an extreme example as regards both form and content. The other builds in strophe-repetitive structure, but is a variant of the Hungarian version with the snake motif, of which no trace can be discovered in the West. Anyway, our recent knowledge of Gipsy folklore bears out a surprising fact: rhymed stanzas are hardly known in genuine Gipsy tradition; even in their texts borrowed from Hungarians the rhymes are mostly spoiled and the original fixed form dissolved. Consequently, it is absolutely out of question that a song as elaborate in form as The Test of Love should have been disseminated by Gipsies. Apart from this, it can be sifted out from experiences gathered from the full East-European territory that while Gipsy tradition is saturated with poetic elements of the host nation—some of the host nation's poetic branches are sometimes cultivated by them—they never enrich the folklore of the society in which they live by passing over elements of their own folklore, precisely because of their particular social status. It would be similarly difficult to explain why only the solution with redemption from the prison should have spread from East to West—provided this route could be proved—while the other ones, including the most attractive and most complete version with the snak-motif, solely represented among the Gipsy songs, had failed to follow the same route.

If priority is lent to the western version, a case of literary mediation between the ancient legend and mediaeval folk poetry may be imagined let us say, through the agency of mediaeval literature and semi-popular channels. But the question of "where" still remains unanswered. Constrasting literary results have so far mutually refuted the possibility of a trend from North as well as from South, and for the present we cannot adopt a safe standpoint in this respect either. It is really surprising how easily *Pohl* proclaimed the theory of a Mediterranean origin, and that on the basis of the most variable element: to wit, he made departure from the ethnic names Moor and Turk applied as attributes to the kidnappers, although these occur only in the Italian–Spanish and the Scandinavian formulations; while framing his theory, he disregards the fact that the Italian–Spanish tradition combines this motif with other stories as secondary forms. In any case, it is a rather peculiar circumstance—which took also *Pohl* by surprise—that the French language area keeps silent in respect of this problem. The French taciturnity in questions of balladry and mediaeval literature alike raise problems indeed, because the theme presents itself with fairly identical solution in a broad stretch of land surrounding France. Yet, a story of a vague affinity can be found in French literature: according to an episode of the mediaeval "Livre de Caradoc" the hero is beguiled into putting his hand in a box in which a snake has been hidden. The snake winds on his arm. He is rescued by his sweetheart in a way that while the young man is put into a barrel full of vinegar the girl sinks into another one full of milk. The girl offers her teat to the snake which leaving the young man bites off the girl's nipple. Her brother, however, heals her by means of the magic knob of his shield.

On the basis of what we know about the process of transformation of themes it may well be imagined that we are dealing with some kind of literary adaptation of a popular (folklore) theme that may have resembled another tale extant in the eastern Mediterranean parts. Even though in a different situation, the interrelation between the characters, and the form of the narrative betray a degree of similarity inasmuch as a young man is saved by his sweetheart while also her brother is made to play a role in the tale. But the rub again is that there is no trace of such a variant either in French or the surrounding areas. Thus, the snake-motif occurring in the Hungarian and neighbouring solutions are not linked by any ties to the western forms.

Yet there is something to connect them: if not the snake-motif, the occurrence of briar relates the Hungarian story, not with the French but with the English version. The Hungarian hero always rests his head under a briar, and it is there that the snake creeps into his bosom. Briar is a love symbol of folklore (let us recall such phrases of our ballad as "...the snake will bite you in the semblance of love"), and at the same time, thorn indicates impending trouble or danger, possibly also failure. The English refrains have "prickly bush", "briery bush" or "broom" as love symbols, which occur with a remarkable tenacity among the variants, and always in an identical formulation. (*Child C, Bronson* 4, 8, 17, 20, 49, 51 and 55.) And they do so with no reasonable relevance to the story. After the father, mother, etc. announce that they are not willing to pay the ransom but will look at the act of hanging, the refrain follows: "O the briery bush. That pricks my heart sore! If I once get out of the briery bush, I'll never get in any more"; "...Now I've got out of the briery bush, I'll never get in any more." *Sharp* 1905–1909, 121 = *Bronson* 49.

Thus, from evidence offered by the dissemination area, certain vague traces come up to indicate a western origin for this ballad. Nevertheless, it is out of question that a German, Italian, or English ballad should be taken for source of origin. The dissemination area in both East Europe and in the western territories surrounding France, and what is more, even the process of dissemination, show a fair agreement with those cases in which a ballad arrived at Hungary by French mediation, and the fact can be proved or at least considered probable. In the present instance, however, gaps and divergences are so great between the Hungarian and the various western formulations that we should run risks by launching any kind of conclusion to the effect. At the same time, a possible origin from a tale is not precluded, particularly since *Megaş* (1933) demonstrated the relation of the ancient tale with folklore themes. If he be right in his supposition, then both the western ballad and the East-European snake motifs may well have originated directly from the same source. Let it suffice for the present that we are faced with question marks, and the situation will last as long as further data will have arisen to settle the thorny problem in the one or the other direction.

Literature: Child 1886: Scandinavian, German, Russian, Wendish and Slovenian versions aligned with the English; Hermann, A. EMU 1887: Romanian, Bulgarian, Gipsy and African versions paralleled with the Hungarian; Gragger 1926: complements Child and Hermann by listing Italian, Catalan and Czech parallels; Megaș 1932: northern origin, reminiscent of Norman raids in the period of heathendom, the Slav forms have contaminated the story with that of "Edelmann und Schäfer", and according to him the Hungarian is secondary development; Idem 1933: connections between the Alcestis legend and the tale; Pohl 1934: originating from a Mediterranean epic poem, the story proceeded from South to North, the Scandinavian and Baltic versions derive from the German, the Slave merged the German version with the story of "Edelmann and Schäfer", the Hungarian is outstanding, originating perhaps from some epic material of pre-ballad times; Ortutay 1934–1948: quotes the above-mentioned authors inclusive of Pohl (Megaș omitted), perhaps a social game is involved, the structure being related with that of Izsák Kerekes (34.); Dános 1938: refers to the above-mentioned authors, considering the tune it may have been a dance-tune or a social game; Seemann 1951: lists Lithuanian parallels, further ballads and strophe-repetitive lyrical songs to prove how widespread this form is among the Lithuanians; Long 1971: the story can be traced back to the antiquity and to folklore, redemption from prison seems to be primordial, this version had been disseminated by Gipsies in the West. (He fails to refer to the Hungarian version.)

70. CRYING JÁNOS

147.

Giusto ♩=110

1. A ka-pu-ba csak sir-do gál Jan-csi.

Kér-di tő-le gaz-da-szo-nya: mi lelt, szi-vem Jan-csi?

Gaz-dasz-szo-nyom meg-en-ged-né, hogy a ház-ba be-me-het-nék!

Sza-bad, szi-vem Jan-csi, Le-het, szi-vem, Jan-csi.

1. Jancsi is crying at the gate.
   His goodwife asks him:
   What's the matter with you, my heart Jancsi?
   If only my goodwife allowed me
   To enter the house...
   You are free to come in, my heart Jancsi,
   You may come in, my heart Jancsi!

2. Jancsi continues crying even within the house.
   His goodwife asks him:
   What's the matter with you, my heart Jancsi?
   If only my goodwife allowed me
   To sit on the bench...
   You are free to do it, my heart Jancsi,
   You may sit on it, my heart Jancsi!

3. Jancsi continues crying even on the bench.
   His goodwife asks him:
   What's the matter with you, my heart Jancsi?
   If only my goodwife allowed me
   To lie on the bed...
   You are free to do it, my heart Jancsi,
   You may lie on it, my heart Jancsi!

4. Jancsi continues crying even on the bed.
   His goodwife asks him:
   What's the matter with you, my heart Jancsi?
   If only my goodwife allowed me
   To lie on your daughter...
   You are free to do it, my heart Jancsi,
   Confound you, Jancsi!

Dercen (Bereg county). Performed by a girl of fourteen. Bartók 1912 = MF 1642/b.

148.

1. János is walking, crying, outside the gate.
   His goodwife asks him:
   What's the matter with you, János?
   If only my goodwife allowed me
   To get inside the gate...
   You may do that, my heart János!

2. János is walking, crying, inside the gate.
   His goodwife asks him:
   What's still the matter, János?
   If only my goodwife allowed me
   To walk before the house...
   You may do that, my heart János!

3. János is walking, crying, before the house.
   His goodwife asks him:
   What's still the matter, János?
   If only my goodwife allowed me
   To walk to the porch ...
   You may do that, my heart János!

4. János is walking, crying, in the porch.
   His goodwife asks him:
   What's still the matter, János?
   If only my goodwife allowed me
   To walk into the inner room...
   You may do that, my heart János!

5. János is walking, crying, in the inner room.
   His goodwife asks him:
   What's still the matter, János?
   If only my goodwife allowed me
   To lie on the bed...
   You may do that, my heart János!

6. János is lying, still crying, on the bed.
   His goodwife asks him:
   What's still the matter, János

599

If only my goodwife allowed me
To cuddle her ...
You may do that, my heart János!
...And János was not crying any longer.

"Csongrád county" = MNGY II, 18.

Divergences:
This ballad is based on the humorous contrast between the young man's seemingly awkward but really deliberate entreaties and the woman's yielding answers which are no less deliberate. The Hungarian variants end the story with a remarkable multiplicity of points: most of them emphasize the successful arrival. In other instances a gradual deviation is described. A variation of the same is when a so far yielding woman appears to be reluctant at the last moment. Some of the texts have a Miss instead of a Mistress.

Earliest provenience: 1872.
Dissemination: Fejér county (Érd), Borsod county (Borsodszentiván, Mezőkövesd), Zemplén county (Karos), Bereg county (Dercen), Máramaros county (Hosszúmező), Csongrád county (Szeged, "Csongrád megye"), Beszterce-Naszód county (Tacs), Udvarhely county (Betlenfalva), Csík county (Gyimesközéplok), Háromszék county (Uzon), Bukovina (Hertelendyfalva = Torontál county). Total: 13.
Textual relationships with other ballads: **71.**; winning the favour of the woman, step by step; **68., 72., 73., 77.**
Tunes: 1. = tune published under 147; 2. (four variants), 3–6.

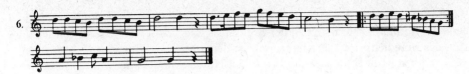

Versions in languages other than Hungarian:

FRENCH: *1–4. Rossat* 15A–D. *5. Beauquier*, 266. *6. Rolland* II, 104, No. 70. *7. Rolland* I, 149A. *8. Idem* 150–151B, collection dating from 1724. *9. Chevais* 64. *10.* Mélusine 1888/9, 354. A prose anecdote from the seventeenth century (plus *"Exemplum de monacho"*, a parrallel story in Latin from the twelfth century).

BRETON: *11.* Mélusine 1878(I), 550–551.

POLISH: *12. Kolberg* 1885 I, 86, No. 18. *13. Steffen* II, Nos 42 and 35,* *14. Kolberg* 1871–1884 21, 13 No. 25. *15., Kolberg* 1885 III, 303 No. 445. *16. Kamienski*, 115.†

LITHUANIAN: cf. *Seemann* 1951, 150–151.

YAKUT: *17. Potanin*, 632, No. 186.

GERMAN: *18.* E–B 668 *Göttingen?. 19.* DVA A 170249 Baden 3. DVA A 155184 *Hannover.*

DANISH: *20. Kristensen*, Dyrefabler, 198* = Mélusine 1888/9, 354 (in French translation).

Outside the Hungarian frontiers this ballad survives in the most intact form with the French, among whom it also enjoys the widest spread. According to a Swiss version, the text (translated from vernacular into literary French) reads as follows: "Carême-entrant qui est derrière chez nous, Qui pleure, qui pleure! Carême-entrant qui est derrière chez nous, Qui pleure son sort! Bien volontiers j'irais chez vous, mais je n'ose, mais je n'ose, Bien volontiers j'irais chez vous, mais je n'ose, je n'oserais. Viens-y donc bien hardiment, Carême-entrant, oh!" Variable portions in the repeated stanzas are the following: "je déboucherais votre poêlon...je prendrais une fourchette...je prendrais le boudin...je vous embrasserais... je coucherais avec vous...and finally: Bien volontiers je vous le ferais—Faites-le donc bien hardiment, Carême-entrant ho!" In certain variants, the young man asks for the favour of the woman's daughter, in others he asks her to allow him to re-commence the thing, which the woman does not deny him. There is a text in which the point is that the woman frightens the lover by telling him about the sudden return of her husband who was thought to have been away. Even such variants occur which include a scene of the young man's departure without settling the bill (the partner being an innkeeper's wife). The hero of the Breton songs goes as far as blackmailing the woman by telling her he would let out the secret to her husband. The young man is crying or entreating, as a rule, and he is laughing on one single occasion only (7.).

The story survives in the form of a seventeenth-century anecdote and occurs in a somewhat altered version in a monastic work of the twelfth century (in Latin): a woman is asking a monk to admit her entrance, but when she comes to the last proposition, the monk expels her. Obviously, the story based on the folksong version, was transcribed with a view to provide a moral lesson, although the transcriber as well as the listeners must have found pleasure in the narrative.

It follows from what has been stated in the foregoing that a similar story must have been current among the French in the Middle Ages.

One of the three German texts, No. *18,* reads as follows: "Hermann auf der Treppe sass, Hermann weinte sehr. Sprach zu ihm das Mädglein roth: Hermann, was ist deine Not? O du goldner Hermann! Dass ich möchte sitzen In dem Stübchen

601

dein! Sprach zu ihm das Mädglein fein: Hermann, das kann auch wohl sein. O du goldner Hermann! Hermann in der Stube sass, Hermann weinte sehr. Sprach zu ihm das Mägdlein roth: Hermann, was ist deine Not? . . . Das ich möchte küssen deine rothen Mund. Küss du unsern Pudel-Hund Von dem Schwanz bis auf den Mund, O du dummer Hermann!"

This version goes contrary to the solution of other areas; the girl refuses and derides the young man. As against this, in the two other variants a Jew appears grinning and successful, after four steps taken, in winning what both of them wanted to have. The Jew as the hero of the story is rather frequent with the Polish and the Lithuanians, too, and it is not precluded that the German version had taken over this character from either of them. Nevertheless, this version is not uniform in its relatively few variants. In any case, laughing occurs in one single variant among the French, the Lithuanian and Polish tempters are crying like the Hungarians.

The problems connected with this ballad cannot be properly examined without a parallel consideration of the next type entitled The Coward Lover. To wit, these two ballads of related themes have merged with the German into one pointless, vaguely defined construction which enjoys general spread over the whole of the German-speaking areas. But even this form lacks the essence of Crying János and the humour of The Coward Lover; the invitation of the persistent girl, the awkward excuses of the lad, and the dénouement, that is the girl's driving away the young man, have been simplified into a sort of dialogue, in which the young man's timid questions are answered by the girl's spicy counsels until finally the goal is attained. A similar merger may be responsible for the ending of 18., a variant in which the young man is expelled as in the other story (where it is more reasonable a point than in 18.).

There are a few variants that have preserved the basic idea in a fairly distinct form, but they have come up in the westernmost fringes of the German-speaking area—two in the North and one in the South—, far away from the Hungarian borders. We find in between the great mass of the diluted and contracted formulations, also known to the German-speaking populations living around and inside the pre-wars Hungary. (Cf. the listing in the next chapter.) Therefore the Hungarians could not have received this ballad from the Germans. The ballad reached Hungary through French mediation.

More closer affinity can be discovered between the Polish and the Hungarian versions, whether the former received theirs from the Hungarians or from French settlers as direct mediators. The Polish have retained the original idea, as well as the gradual development thereof: the crying lover approaches step by step towards his goal. The only innovation is that the comic character is represented by a Jew. How widespread this ballad may have been with the Poles can be judged from the fact that it reached, either through Russian mediation or directly from Polish exiles the Yakut people of Siberia: one of their best known heroic songs returns the story as an incorporated alien body that has nothing to do with the rest of the song. After a number of adventures, the hero arrives at the place of the female character, a girl besieged by hosts of suitors. He enters her house as a crippled young man clad in rags and relates stories about a brave warrior, that is about himself. Then he begins to cry. The girl asks for explanation. He says, he is cold and tired. The girl puts him

602

in her own bed, and confesses that she would be willing to marry the hero of the narrative. Upon this, the young man resumes his original shape and discloses the purpose of his arrival. Then he starts weeping again because the girl cannot be his wife. She answers: it depends solely on you; you may have your chance against nine suitors. The hero begins to cry anew, pretending to be cold. The girl embraces him, trying to warm him. The young man continues to weep. Then the girl asks him to lie over her body; so he does and the girl cuddles him with her legs to warm his body; the hero cries and cries on, until, fortunately, his magic horse calls in warning him that it is time to break flirting since the rivals are waiting for him outside. Thus the hero returns into the normal course of the story. (17.)

It is interesting to note that the story is associated with the winter-solstice plays of village boys among the Poles, followed by dancing. Considering that the French version had had a close connection with the Carnival festivals, we may suppose that in older times the song was part of some sort of farcical play, precisely because of the obscene point; and also the sequence of the comic gradation may have given rise to inclusion of this song into such popular dramatic performances.

On the other hand, the Danish version follows the Hungarian form step by step. As the young man arrives at the door, he is crying, shaking his hand, shedding bitter tears. The fine Miss asks him: What's the matter with you, my boy O, I would like to enter your room, Miss, only I dare not to! Come in, boy, and don't cry any longer! When already within the room, he continues: . . . I would like to take a seat at the end of the table . . . lie in your bed . . . rest in your arms . . . win your pleasure. Obviously, the Danes acquired the ballad directly from the French.

The song dates in the fourteenth century.

71. THE COWARD LOVER

149.

Parlando

1. Vár-lak ró-zsám va-cso-rá - ra, Ap-ró mé - zes po- gá - csá - ra. Be-jö-hetsz szívem bát- ran.

Még sem me -rek én be - men - ni, Oh , jaj é - des   an - gya - lom.
Az aj - tó - tok csi - kor - gá - sán Esz - re vesz - nek, vi - rá - gom.

1. I am waiting you for a good supper, sweetheart,
   Won't you come in, then?
   For tiny, little honey-cakes,
   You may come in, sweetheart, safely,
   Safely you may come to me,
   And you may lie on my bed.

2. Oh, I am afraid to enter,
   My dear, sweet angel.
   The dogs going to bark,
   And people will notice me, flower.
   Cast a bone to the dog,
   And it will stop barking!
   You may come in safely, sweetheart,
   Safely you may come to me,
   My bed is laid, you may lie on it.

3. Oh, I am afraid to enter,
   My dear, sweet angel.
   My boots are going pit-a-pat,
   And people will notice me, flower.
   Wrap the heels of your boots in rags,
   So that they may not go pit-a-pat!
   You may come in safely, sweetheart,
   Safely you may come to me,
   My bed is laid, you may lie on it!

4. Oh, I am afraid to enter,
   My dear, sweet angel.

The door will be creaking,
And people will notice me, flower.
I have smeared its hinge with fat,
People cannot hear it creaking!
You may come in safely, sweetheart,
Safely you may come to me,
My bed is laid, you may lie on it!

5. Oh, I am afraid to enter,
My dear, sweet angel.
The candle will be lighting,
And people will notice me, flower.
Cast a farthing to the old hag,
And she will put out the candle-light!
You may come in safely, sweetheart,
Safely you may come to me,
My bed is laid, you may lie on it!

6. Oh, I am afraid to enter,
My dear, sweet angel.
Mice will be squeaking,
And people will notice me, flower.
Alas, you are a brave man indeed, a good-for-nothing,
Dreading even the mice!
You may go away as well, I don't want you any longer,
You are not dear to me!

Resznek (Zala county). Vikár, B. = MF 2210/b = Ethn 1910, 204.

MF 631/c contains certain deviations from the printed text-publication, but it is recorded with one stanza only. As long as the full text is not discovered in the manuscript legacy of *Vikár*, we have to rely on the published version.

Divergences: "Alas, how can I enter your room, my sweet, beautiful love!"—"I am invited to a supper, Made of meal and curd and poppy-seeds, I should go in, but I don't dare to..."—"I should like to go to your place..."—"But they will notice me by the trampling of my horse...Give oats (hay) to it... "By the cackling of the geese...Give them corn... "By the creaking of my boots...Take off your boots..."—"By the mewing of the cat...I shall give milk to the cat..."—"By the light of your mother's candle, People would notice me!...Blow out that burning candle Kiss my mother's hand..."—"Catch mice for the cat, And it will stop mewing"...—"By the smack of our kisses...O, you bold man, what is your worth If you are afraid to exchange kisses."

Earliest provenience: 1848.
Dissemination: Zala county (Balatonederics, Resznek, Szombatfa), Somogy county (Berzence), Baranya county (Magyaregregy, Mohács), Fejér county ? (without specification), Abaúj county

(Hegyalja, Bodrogköz), Békés county (Pusztaföldvár); without specification: the dissemination area of Szeged, Bihar county (Nagyszalonta), Udvarhely county (Korond, Lengyelfalva, Farkaslaka). Total 21.

Thirteen of the notations are recorded with tunes, of which four are actually latent. Vikár recorded the ballad also at Felsőtárkány (Heves county), but this variant is similarly latent.

Textual relationships with other ballads: The basic idea is the same as that of "Crying János" **(70).** and of **77.**

Tunes: The text is sung to the published tune everywhere where it is performed. This melody seems to be an art song composed in the German style of the early nineteenth century. As far as rhythm and structure are concerned, the following variant may stand closest to the original:

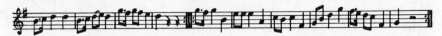

The variants of the tune are brought about by the varying structure of the stanzas which must preserve, in all likelihood, mediaeval patterns, or the simplified varieties, of the following syllabic divisions: $8+6, 8+6, 8+8+6, 8+8+6$, or $8+7, 8+7, 8+8+7$.

Versions in languages other than Hungarian:

FRENCH: *1. Lambert* I, 371 (partially relevant).

SPANISH: *2.–3. Cossio-Solano* I, 233, 235. Nos 132. and 133.

DUTCH: *4.* Horae belgicae II 154, *Van Duyse* (?)

GERMAN: A) (partially relevant) *5.* E–B 460 = print 1621 = Wunderhorn II, 413 = *Uhland*. Similar melodic incipit from 1540 and from the late sixteenth century; Flugblatt, *idem* from 1602. *6.* E–B 460b Cologne = *Mittler*, 915 (Stanza 1 = E–B). *7. Meinert*, 112 = *Mittler*, 916 Kuhländchen B). *8–39.* DVACod. Heidelb. No. 38, Rheinland 2, Lorraine, Württemberg, Hannover, Kurhessen 2, Sachsen-Oberfranken, Thuringia 4, Upper Silesia, Pomerania 3, Egerland, Nassau 3, Allgäu (Bavarian-Swabian), Switzerland, Bohemia 3, Körmöcbánya, Schönhengst (Slovakia) 3, Pennsylvania. (A different formulation is to be found in Gottschee.)

SLOVENIAN: *40. Kuhač* 576, from Hungary. *41. Kurelac*, 48 No. 241, from Hungary.

CROAT: *42.* HNP VI, No. 114. *43.* HNP VII, 317 No. 507. *44. Žganec* 1950, 189–190 Nos 220–221 (fragments). *45–47. Štrekelj* II Nos 1713–1715.

SERBIAN: *48. Tordinac*, 47 No. 37.

SLOVAK: *49. Mišik* 19.† *50.* Sl. sp. II, 151. No. 408 (fragment).

MORAVIAN: *51. Sušil* 812/2075.

POLISH: *52–54. Kolberg* 1871–84 I, No. 178, V, No. 246, XII, No. 386. *55. Idem* 1885, III, No. 370. *56. Pauli* 124, No. 29.†

UKRAINIAN: *57. Hvilya* 189.† *58. Chubinsky* V, 193 No. 390.

Seemann considers this ballad to be identical with the former one, although it certainly has a different basic idea: in the one a timid, weeping young man asks for admission to the woman and attains his aim gradually; in the other, it is the girl that invites the young man who raises all sorts of excuses for fear of being discovered, and indeed, fails to get him in. The German variants, however, merge the two themes in a way that the basic idea is lost, which is the comic contrast, in other words, creations of stylized characters.

5. A.

Tiny girl, where can I find your father's home?
Walk along this street and you will find my father's home at the end of it.
Refr. Hush, keep silent and stop asking questions.
But, tiny girl, your little dog will be barking!
Call for the night-watch in a low voice, And the dog will stop barking.
Well, but your little door will be creaking...

Lay your hand on its hinge, and it will turn smoothly...
The fire will be flashing...
Pour a little water on it, and the fire will stop flashing...
But where can I find your little bower?...
Go through the kitchen keeping always to the right by the wall...
And what shall I do in the morning?...
Put on your clothes and leave the place, that's what you must do in the morning...

6. B. (= Parisius No. 264).

What way may I reach your father's (my father-in-law's) house, to my beloved little girl?
Walk to the end of this street and enter the fourth house. *Refr.*
How can I get at the door of your bower?
Open the door slowly, Then father will think it is a mouse.
(Or: Press the latch silently, and father will think it is the wind.)
How can I get upstairs?
Take off your shoes and walk slowly,
And father will think it is a mouse.
Finally: How can I get into your bed?

These texts are hardly more than simple dialogues of a loving couple in which the young man asks how he can get into the room of his sweetheart; the girl describes the way, from step to step. Some of the variants preserve traces of the young man's worries and the girl's reassuring answers, yet it is obvious that the genuine solution had long fallen into oblivion.

The original idea can be detected clearly in the Spanish texts. In them, the first words of the song are heard from the husband's mouth: I got up in the morning, put on my waistcoat and began to play the guitar when I heard someone ringing at Mariana's door.—Actually, the plot begins at this point, and the husband acts as an outside listener: My child is in my arms, my husband in my bed—says the woman.—Throw away the child!—My maid is a bloody gossip always letting out secrets.—Give her a waistcoat and she will leave the house.—I have a little dog which will be barking if it noses you.—Cast a bit of bread to it, and then it will keep silent.—My door is creaking.—Pour water on it! After this, the husband speaks up again: What is that, Marianita?—It is the widow's cat chasing our cat.—Is it not the widow's son chasing you?—He is going to see you in the middle of the market-place, standing on top of a cartload of wood blown by the wind of Galicia so that it may burn better!—No, husband, he is going to see you lying in the middle of a room, and your legs will be all yellow, and you will be colourless, and the parson singing over you, and I mourning over you, so that people will say: What a deep sorrow this Mariana has been plunged in.

As can be seen, the Spanish present the plot in a blanket formula—which must be a secondary development—and the solution built up of worrying questions and assuring answers is formulated with characters acting in the reverse, although almost in the same way as in the Hungarian parallel, as far at least as this part of the

607

story is concerned. Since in general the Spanish versions can be deduced from the French, it is apparent also in this instance that the French link, which is no longer extant, can be inferred from the further developed Spanish formulation.

This missing link can be found partially in a south-French text originating from Languedoc.

Would you admit a pilgrim, Madono, madono?
Would you admit a pilgrim, for God's sake?
Well, come and rest inside the gate, you poor man.
Well, come and rest inside the gate, you poor man.
But the dogs will bite me . . .
Well, come and rest on the stairs . . .
But when they sweep, I get dirty . . .
Well, come and rest inside the house . . .
But when the servants see me, they will laugh at me . . .
Well, come and rest at the fire-place . . .
But when they kindle the fire, I shall be burnt . . .
Well then, come and rest in my bed . . .
Have you slept well during the night? . . .
All the flees were biting me . . .
Well then, come and let's have a fuck . . .

And all this is recited to the tune of the eighth psalm. The story once again has been merged from the motifs of the coward lover's excuses and the weeping lover's gradual advance, only the excuses are aimed at forcing out admission. At the same time, however, the "weeping" type exists with the French in a clear-cut formulation, as has been shown above, and therefore this obscure southern variant is apt to demonstrate that the excuses of the coward lover had not been unknown to French tradition.

The dissemination area of the thirty-four German variants cover the entire German-speaking territory, including the German settlement in Hungary. The Hungarians could not have borrowed their two ballads from the Germans, since they have preserved, in contrast to the Germans, both versions in their original clarity. These same two clear forms survive among the East-European nations, this time with the southern as well as all the northern neighbours of Hungary. That is to say, it has a more uniform spread than the ballad of "Crying János".

It can be made out from the relics that survive that the western—French-form used to be similarly uncontaminated. Their clear presentation is separated from the equally clear eastern formulations by a bloc of merged German variants. The two poles can again be spanned by the theory of mediaeval French—Hungarian contacts. The national mosaic-like fragments provide evidence for this. It is a convincing sign of spreading from Hungary towards the East that the Polish and White Russians have preserved even the motif of fear of the squeaking mice as the point at which the girl finally expels the young man. But there are other details to show further agreements: the dog barks—give it bread; the door creaks—smear it with fat. The same formulas occur also in the Croatian version mixed with further ones (give tobacco to my father!), in the latter the point is mostly lost, that is to say, the girl is not usually disappointed at seeing the coward behaviour of her lover. This ballad too is mediaeval in origin.

Literature: *Gragger* 1926: German, Dutch (*Van Duyse* 276–277) and Danish (Kristensen 46–47) versions; *Seemann* 1951: the ballad is identical with the former one, reviews the Slav—Lithuanian variants; *Csanádi* and *Vargyas* 1954: in the wake of *Gragger*, refer to German, Dutch and Danish versions, the Hungarians have changed the form into a comic story.

72. THE SONG OF THE FERRYMEN

150.

Poco rubato

1. Haj ré - vész, ré - vész, Ma - gyar if - ju ré - vész, Vigy ál - tal a ha - jón.

Ne - ked a - dom ne-ked, Bi - zony ne-ked a - dom Szép se - lem ken - dő - met.
Nem köll kedvem-nck, Én sze - rel - mem-nek, Bá - na - ta szí - vem - nek.

1. Hey, ferryman, ferryman,
   Young Hungarian ferryman!
   Take me over by boat!
   And I shall give you, I give you,
   Well, I give you
   My fine silk kerchief.
   It is not a thing to rejoice me,
   It does not relieve my love,
   It makes my heart sad.

2. Hey, ferryman, ferryman,
   Young Hungarian ferryman!
   Take me over by boat!
   And I shall give you, I give to you
   My fine pearly head-dress,
   My fine pearly head-dress.
   It is not a thing to rejoice me,
   It does not relieve my love,
   It makes my heart sad.

3. Hey, ferryman, ferryman,
   Young Hungarian ferryman!
   Take me over by boat!
   And I shall give you, I give to you
   My fine maidenhood,
   My fine maidenhood.
   Well, it is the thing to rejoice me,
   It does relieve my love,
   It makes my heart glad!

Kolon (Nyitra country). Performed by a woman of 64. Vikár, L. 1956 = AP 1685/f.

Divergences: In some variants it is a man that wants to cross the river and succeeds only when he offers one of his two daughters to the ferryman. In southern Transdanubia the names of Rákóci and Bercsényi occur in the text. The songs from Nyitra county are embedded in bridal farewell tunes. In a text from Magyarszentmárton, the character bears the name of Mistress Rákóci; this song is completed with a story in prose: she has the fishermen to milk the herd of horses and cows which she has promised to give them; upon her advice they bathe in the milk so gained, and they all burn and shrink to the size of cracklings. Thus the woman escapes. (The tale motif is eastern in origin.)

Earliest provenience: 1891.

Dissemination: Somogy county (Bonnya, Szenna); Baranya county (Bánfa, Mohács 3, Szaporca, Tarcsapuszta); Tolna county (Felsőireg); Nyitra county (Béd, Kolon 2, Ghymes, Menyhe 4); Bars county (Lédec 2); Bács-Bodrog county (Dávod, Gombos 2); Torontál county (Csóka, Magyarszentmárton, Szőreg, Vrbica); Csongrád county (Fábiánsebestyén). Total: 26.

Textual relationships with other ballads: 73.; gradually gaining the swetheart's favour: **68., 70., 73., 77.** and **131.**

Tunes: 1. = tune published in connection with 72. Further: 2. in three variants; 3. in four variants; 4. in three variants; 5. in two variants; and the rest occur in one variant each.

Versions in languages other than Hungarian:
FRENCH: *1. Smith* VII, 60. *2–3. Canteloube* II, 77 and III, 257. *4. Decombe* XV.
PORTUGUESE: *5–19. Braga* I, 33, 36, 39, 40, 42, 45, 48, 52, 55, 57, 59, 62, 64 and 67.
SPANISH: *20. Geibel–Schack*, 371.
DANISH: *21–29. DgF* 263.
GREEK: *30. Lübke*, 75.
GERMAN: *31–33. E–B* 2063–2065.
ROMANIAN: *34. Pompiliu* 24.
Partial variants:
POLISH: *35. Steffen* 26.†

The gist of the Hungarian song is that a woman proceeds to promise more and more to a man in order to obtain her goal, the point always being that she has finally to offer her own self. This situation of the Hungarian song develops in relation of a woman wishing to cross a river and a ferryman. The same plot practically with the same point can be found in many places in Europe, although rarely with a ferryman and a woman as characters.

Among the French the story survives in a fairly eroded form and even so very rarely. A prince hears a peasant girl singing or perceives her from his window. He asks her to sing a song. The girl is unwilling to do so because she has lately buried her dear relatives. The prince offers her first his page, then his brother, and finally himself as husband. The girl accepts his last offer. The idea of gradual enhancement of the value of the person offered had been certainly included as a subsequent development, for there occur several variants of the story which are round and complete even without this motif added: the prince meets the beautiful peasant girl and marries her. (*Canteloube* II, 335, III, 175, *Gagnon,* 97. *Bladé* II, 110); while in *4.* the girl refuses to accept the offer stating that she has got a lover already.

Similarly as a later insertion the motif is found in a Portuguese story that originally must have had nothing to do with it. In all the variants of the ballad type mentioned in connection with The Test of Faithfulness we find the portion in which the man arriving from a foreign country asks the wife what she would give him if he gave her back her husband. The woman offers first gold, then orange trees, then her house, three mills that grind spices, finally her three daughters, but the man insists that he wants the woman herself; at this point the woman hurt to death in her honour calls her servants and her dogs. The insertion as it is awkward beyond doubt, for the stranger previously had described in detail how he had found the wife's husband dead, bleeding with many wounds. The secondary nature of the motif, therefore, is obvious, in spite of its presence in all variants of the mentioned type.

The story is known to the Danes as well. The son of the king asks the girl to dance: he promises silken shirt, silver shoes, golden ring, a knife studded with silver nails, and the like, depending on variants; the girl answers invariably that such things are to be found in her home as well. Finally, the prince offers her his fidelity and honour, and gains the girl. Yet the story is not finished with this. The girl gives birth to a child, or becomes pregnant, and so she is seen by a suitor—her former lover. The suitor asks by whom she became pregnant and what she had got in reward for her honour. Thereupon the girl repeats the story known from the beginning of the ballad; the prince comes and says he is the father of the child, and the loving couple unite in marriage. Here again we have an addition which did not originally form part of the story based on gradually strengthening amatory proposition; to wit, this motif can be found without any introduction in several other stories as well (DgF 245, 278–280).

This ballad can be found among the Greeks with the ferry-scene much in the same form as among the Hungarians. The girl asks the son of the "Frank" (i. e. French or Italian) to take her over the water. She offers a bracelet, a ring, a pair of ear-rings, her stockings, but the ferryman always demands something more valuable. The girl proposes to kiss and embrace him on the further bank; the ferryman accepts this offer and takes the girl over the water. But the story is not ended with this here either: ever further places are proposed by the girl where to fulfil her promise; finally they enter her house; she calls her mother, and the two women deride the ferryman. This story is a well-known French gay ballad: L'occasion manqué. (English version: The Baffled Knight, *Child* 112). Thus, here we find the scene, which stands separately in the Hungarian, incorporated into another story. Since, however, it is linked with a different story everywhere, and always with such one which exists independently, without this scene, the secondary nature of the amalgamation is doubtless even with the French. The Portuguese as well as the Greek obviously merged it with a ballad of French origin, which in itself is evidence of our ballad's French descent. Also the dissemination area indicates this: the ballad comes up in disconnected geographical points at great distances, where otherwise strong French connections can be demonstrated (Danish, Portuguese, Greek—and Hungarian). The oldest French solution must have been similar to the Hungarian; some light amatory dialogue, with a point in the end, takes place between the woman and the ferryman; were it not so, we could not find the plot of the story among the Greek. The current French form is eroded, merged with a fable conceived after the fashion of pastoral poetry much in vogue in subsequent times. This fact betrays its secondary formulation.

Perhaps it is a christianized transformation of the original what we find in the German version: this speaks about the wandering of Mary. The Holy Virgin arrives at the sea and asks the sailor to take her in his boat. The sailor, in turn, asks for her favour either in the form of a mild proposition or a sacred marriage, but he meets with her flat refusal. The Holy Virgin walks through the sea, and by the time she reaches as far as the middle, the bells are tolled, which makes the sailor's heart break. The placing of the motif in a sacred environment explains reasonably why the humorous proposition proceeding by grades is omitted, although the point— interpreted as a sinful wish—remains. The original situation prevails with the gradual proposition omitted. In the Romanian version the young woman tries to escape from her husband; running with her child on her arm, she asks the ferrymen to take her over the river Maros against a fee of twenty kreutzers. "No sooner than you kiss us all one after the other shall you find a hearing on our part." The dialogue continues, the ferrymen tease the woman until she jumps into the water.

In the Polish version (*35.*) the landlord breaks the green jug of a girl. The girl is crying over the broken jug, the landlord tries to console her, promising thalers, ducats, a horse, etc. to the girl, who however does not accept the presents but insists upon her green jug. Finally he recovers it by offering his own self.

The strophe-repetitive structure prevails to various extent in the Danish, Portuguese and Greek versions. All this indicates that the Hungarian song has preserved the one-time French chanson in its original form.

In all likelihood, the ballad developed in the fourteenth century.

73. THE SERVANT AND MY GOODWIFE

151.

My golden star, my goodwife, pay me off!
My servant, my servant, don't leave me,
I shall give you, I shall give you my herd of cattle...
I don't want, I don't want your herd of cattle,
5. The year is over, pay me off!
My servant, my servant, don't leave me,
I shall give you, I shall give you my chest of treasure...
I don't want, I dont want your chest of treasure,
The year is over, pay me off!
10. My servant, my servant, don't leave me,
I shall give you, I shall give you my maiden daughter...
I don't want, I don't want your maiden daughter,
The year is over, pay me off!
My servant, my servant, don't leave me,
15. I shall give you, I shall give you...I offer you my own self...
My golden star, my goodwife, that's what I have been waiting for all the time!

Kánya (Tolna county). 1900 = MNGY VIII, 191.

Recorded in one single variant without a tune.

Textual relationships with other ballads:
72.; winning the lover gradually: **68., 70., 73., 77.** and **131.**
Versions in languages other than Hungarian:
GERMAN: *1–24.* D. Vlr. 34.
GREEK: *25. Lübke,* 34.
CROAT: *26–27. Žganec* 1950–1952 Nos 150a–b. *28.* Istarske II, No. 39.

At first sight this text raises the idea that it may have developed in Hungary from The Song of the Ferrymen, only the characters have been changed. Nevertheless, a similar change can be found among the Greeks and the Germans; this again indicates that the song had been existing in France, and that if changes ensued in nations living at a long distance one from the other then they must have been effectuated independently of one another.

With the Germans, the basic idea is embedded in an enlarged frame, in which the gradual propositions become ever more shorter, and are, indeed, missing from most of the variants. The sire and his servant (page) ride together; the sire would have his servant climb a tree and bring down a bird, but the servant does not dare to undertake the risk, therefore the lord climbs, and falls down and is dying. The servant asks how he is going to receive his dues after things have turned out so badly; the sire offers his weapons, his horse, but the servant is not content with these; finally he offers his wife (sometimes his daughter), which satisfies the servant, now becoming lord himself. In certain variants it is not the wife that counts but the estate. In one of the variants he rejects his master's offer because he wants to get into Paradise together with his lord.

The Greek version, again, has a close relationship with the Hungarian. An orphan lad has been serving in the house of a widow for twelve years without ever having seen her. Once still he happens to catch a glimpse of her, and then he asks her to pay him off because he has been called to go home and get married. At this, the woman offers him a choice among her three daughters. The song presents a detailed description of all three damsels. But the young man refuses all of them, and insists upon having the woman herself, whose beauty is depicted in the closing lines of the poem. As can be seen, this version shows a fair agreement with the Hungarian, except for the strophe-repetitive structure which is missing in the Greek. (Provided, the only one available translation can offer sufficient ground for this conclusion.) It seems that we have to deal with, as in the previous case, a French borrowing which has reached the neighbouring Croats as well. In the Croatian versse, the landlord is dying and wants to settle his account with the servant: he promises him first the estate (hills and plains), then his horses, his eldest and his next daughter, but the lad keeps saying that he had not been serving to be paid with such things. Finally he is offered to receive the master's youngest daughter with whom the servant is satisfied. In *28.* the goodwife pays off the servant, offering him lambs, goats, cows, and the like; the young man answers that he has got all these thing. Finally, the woman offers her own self which meets the servant's pleasure because her love is dear to his heart. In this version also the strophic construction remains, as well as certain details of formulation showing a fair agreement with the Hungarian. At the same time, the geographical situation suggests the only possibility that the Croatian developed from the Hungarian.

In all likelihood, a no longer extant French ballad has been retained by the only Transdanubian recording whose age agrees with that of other fourteenth-century French borrowings.

74. THE TWO KINDS OF BRIDE

152.

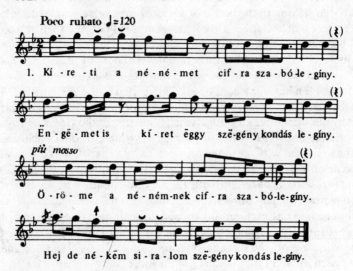

Poco rubato ♩=120

1. Kí - re - ti   a   né - né - met   cif - ra sza - bó -le - gíny.

Én - gĕ - met is   kí - ret   ĕggy   szĕ - gény kondás le - gíny.

più mosso

Ö - rö - me   a   né - ném-nek cif - ra   sza - bó - le - gíny.

Hej de né - kĕm si - ra - lom szĕ-gény kondás le - gíny.

1. My sister has been sued for
   By a pompous tailor,
   And I have been sued for
   By a poor swineherd.
   It is a great joy for my sister
   To have a pompous tailor,
   But, oh, it is a great sorrow for me
   To have a poor swineherd.

2. My sister is escorted
   To the tune of loud music,
   And I am escorted
   To the tune of squeaking mice.
   It is a great joy for my sister
   To have a pompous tailor,
   But, oh, it is a great sorrow for me
   To have a poor swineherd.

3. My sister's hair is put up
   With a frilly head-dress,
   And my hair is put up
   With a swine's bladder.
   It is a great joy for my sister
   To have a pompous tailor,

618

But, oh, it is a great sorrow for me
To have a poor swineherd.

4. My sister is seated
   At a golden table,
   And I am seated
   At the trough of swines.
   It is a great joy for my sister
   To have a pompous tailor,
   But, oh, it is a great sorrow for me
   To have a poor swineherd.

5. My sister is given
   Almond cakes to eat,
   And I am given
   Ash-cakes to eat.
   It is a great joy for my sister
   To have a pompous tailor,
   But, oh, it is a great sorrow for me
   To have a poor swineherd.

6. My sister's meal is served
   In a golden plate,
   And my meal is served
   In the trough of swines.
   It is a great joy for my sister
   To have a pompous tailor,
   But, oh, it is a great sorrow for me
   To have a poor swineherd.

7. My sister is given to drink
   From a crystal glass,
   And I am given to drink
   From the trough of swines.
   It is a great joy for my sister
   To have a pompous tailour,
   But, oh, it is a great sorrow for me
   To have a poor swineherd.

8. My sister is placed
   In a golden coach,
   And I am placed
   In a cart drawn by a donkey.
   It is a great joy for my sister
   To have a pompous tailor,
   But, oh, it is a great sorrow for me
   To have a poor swineherd.

9. My sister is laid
   In a towered couch,

And I am laid
In the den of swines.
It is a great joy for my sister
To have a pompous tailor,
But, oh, it is a great sorrow for me
To have a poor swineherd.

10. My sister is waked up
With a scourge of eight tails,
And I am waked up
With sweet morning kisses.
It is a great sorrow for my sister
To have a pompous tailor,
But, oh, it is a great joy for me
To have a poor swineherd!

Nagyszalonta (Bihar county). Performed by a girl of 21 and a woman of 76. Kodály 1916 = MNGY XIV, 31.

Divergences: In some of the variants the contrast between the fates of the sisters is not reversed but the parallelism remains unchanged to the end. Even so the difference is sharpened, only the painful contradiction between the experiences of the sisters is left unsolved. In certain cases the contrast is depicted with irrealistic details, carried away to far-fetched extremes. Sometimes a mother and her daughter are involved.

Earliest provenience: 1846.
Dissemination: Vas county (Nagyrákos, Pankasz, Velem); Zala county (Búcsúszentlászló 2, Kiskomárom, Mumor, Nemeshetés 2, Resznek, Rédics, Zalacsány); Somogy county (Perdócpuszta); Baranya county (Boda, Kopács, Mánfa); Tolna county (Gerjen); Fejér county (Érd); Veszprém county (Kis-Berzseny); Komárom county (Nagymegyer, Naszvad); Győr county (Győr? Hédervár); Nyitra county (Zsére); Heves county (Erdőtelek); Bereg county (Dercen, Lónya); Csongrád county (Hódmezővásárhely, Szeged-Alsóváros); Torontál county (Szaján); Békés county (Mezőgyán); Arad county (Pécska); Bihar county (Nagyszalonta, Nagyzomlinpuszta); Szilágy county (Kárásztelek 3); Szatmár county (Tunyog); Kolozs county (Válaszút); Udvarhely county ("Udvarhelyszék"); without further specification (Dunántúl?). Total: 41.
Textual relationships with other ballads: none.
Tunes: 1. = the tune published in connection with 152., 2 variants; further, 2–14. A 2. and 13 in 2 variants, 3. in four, 5. in 2.

Versions in languages other than Hungarian: none.

As to its origin, the ballad may have come into existence at any date from the fourteenth to the early nineteenth century.

75. THE PRINCE PREPARING TO MARRY

153.

Tempo giusto ♩= 96 - 100

1. E-gy-szer egy ki -rály-fi Mit -gon-dol ma-gá - ba? Felöl - tö-zött, fe-löl-tö - zött Csi -kó-si ru- há-ba.

1. Once upon a time a prince,
— Look what he found out! —
He put on, he put on
A horseherd's robes.

2. He went over to the neighbour's,
To see the rich mayor's daughter,
Ihhajnáré, fikafiné
To see the rich mayor's daughter.

3. Good morning to you,
Rich mayor's daughter,
Ihhajnáré, fikafiné
Rich mayor's daughter.

4. Come on, come on
And take a seat on the chair,
Ihhajnáré, fikafiné
Take a seat on the chair!

5. I did not come here
To take a seat in your house,
Ihhajnáré, fikafiné
To take a seat in your house.

6. But I have come to ask you
If you are willing to marry me,
Ihhajnáré, fikafiné,
If you are willing to marry me.

7. I cannot marry you,
I cannot marry you, horseherd,
Ihhajnáré, fikafiné,
I cannot marry you, horseherd.

8. He went over to the neighbour's
To see the poor man's daughter,
Ihhajnáré, fikafiné
To see the poor man's daughter.

623

9. Good morning to you,
   Poor man's daughter,
   Ihhajnáré, fikafiné
   Poor man's daughter.

10. Come on, come on
    And take a seat on the chair,
    Ihhajnáré, fikafiné
    Take a seat! on the chair!

11. I did not come here
    To take a seat in your house,
    Ihhajnáré, fikafiné
    To take a seat in your house.

12. But I have come to ask you
    If you are willing to marry me,
    Ihhajnáré, fikafiné
    If you are willing to marry me.

13. O, I am willing to marry you,
    To marry you, horseherd,
    Ihhajnáré, fikafiné
    I am willing to marry you, horseherd.

14. Once again the prince
    — Look, what he found out! —
    He put on, he put on
    A princely robe.

15. He went over to the neighbour's
    To see the rich mayor's daughter,
    Ihhajnáré, fikafiné
    To see the rich mayor's daughter.

16. Good morning to you,
    Rich mayor's daughter,
    Ihhajnáré, fikafiné
    Rich mayor's daughter.

17. Welcome to you,
    Welcome, young prince,
    Ihhajnáré, fikafiné
    Welcome, young prince.

18. Come on, come on
    And take a seat on the sofa,
    Ihhajnáré, fikafiné
    Take a seat on the sofa!

19. I did not come here
    To take a seat in your house,
    Ihhajnáré, fikafiné
    To take a seat in your house.

20. But I have come to ask you
    If you are willing to marry me,
    Ihhajnáré, fikafiné
    If you are willing to marry me.

21. Oh, I am willing to marry you,
    To marry you, young prince,
    Ihhajnáré, fikafiné
    To marry you, young prince.

22. I don't want you any longer,
    You bloody bitch,
    Why did you refuse me, why did you refuse me
    When I came as a horseman?

23. He went over to the neighbour's,
    To see the poor man's daughter,
    Ihhajnáré, fikafiné
    The poor man's daughter.

24. Good morning to you,
    Poor man's daughter,
    Ihhajnáré, fikafiné
    Poor man's daughter.

25. Welcome to you,
    Welcome, young prince,
    Ihhajnáré, fikafiné
    Welcome, young prince.

26. Come on, come on
    And take a seat on the chair,
    Ihhajnáré, fikafiné
    Take a seat on the chair.

27. I did not come here
    To take a seat in your house,
    Ihhajnáré, fikafiné
    To take a seat in your house,

28. But I have come to ask you
    If you are willing to marry me,
    Ihhajnáré, fikafiné
    If you are willing to marry me.

29. But I cannot marry you,
    I cannot marry you, young prince,
    Ihhajnáré, fikafiné
    I cannot marry you, young prince.

30. For I have just been engaged
    To a young horseman,
    Ihhajnáré, fikafiné
    To a young horse-man.

31. I am the same man and nobody else,
    Let's embrace each other!
    Ihhajnáré, fikafiné
    Let's embrace each other!

Szomod (Komárom county). Performed by a man of 72. Kodály 1922 = MSz. 1506.

Divergences: The prince mostly is disguised as a coachman, and the poor man's daughter has a basket-maker as father; sometimes the rich girl's father is a county sheriff. Occasionally, the pride of the rich is expressed more pronouncedly in the words of the mayor's daughter: "You can find a poor orphan girl in the next house *(refr.),* I am a rich girl and I am not supposed to marry a poor man". In other instances, we have the reverse opinion put in the mouth of the poor girl: "I am a poor girl not supposed to marry a rich man." Sometimes the story of "The Two Kinds of Bride" is added **(74.)** only with a reversed cast. Not infrequently the prince applies rough attributes to the yielding rich girl when refusing her offer to marry him. There is only one single variant which ends with marriage between the prince and the rich girl. The performer explained the case by adding the following comment in prose: "Then the prince married the daughter of the county sheriff. For it is becoming that every young man should find his match, a rich girl if he is rich, for a poor one can never fit into a princely house." Obviously, the parable found a personal interpretation in this instance. The ballad occurs in fragmentary forms in Moldavia: only the saluting formulas can be recognized, and even these embedded in lyrical stanzas. Only one variant from Lészped presents the whole of the story. Further divergences are extant in deficient, fragmentary or corrupt forms.

Earliest provenience: 1809 (cf. *Stoll,* and *Faragó* 1972).

Dissemination: Without specification of the place: 1859–60; Sopron county (Rábaszovát); Vas county ("Vas c.", Pankasz 2); Zala county (Nemessándorháza, Nemesszentandrás, Pölöske, Resznek, Szentgyörgyvölgye, Zalagalsa); Somogy county ("The Balaton Region", Csoknya, Kéthely, Somogy-szob); Baranya county (Kopács, Magyaregregy, Mánfa 2, Mohács, Püspökszenterzsébet, Szaporca); Tolna county (Dombovár, Fornád, Paks, Sárpilis, Szekszárd); Veszprém county (Veszprém, "Veszprém c."); Komárom county (Ógyalla, Szomod); Győr county (Szemere); Nyitra county (Farkasd, Tardoskedd, Zsére); Bars county (Léva); Nógrád county (Bercel 2): Heves county (Eger, Fedémes, Mezőtárkány, Parád); Borsod county (Domaháza, Tard); Gömör county (Lucska); Abaúj county (Áj); Zemplén county (Bodrogköz ?, Karcsa, Mezőzombor, Szerencs); Pest county (Újszász 2); Jász-Nagykun-Szolnok county (Jászberény, Túrkeve); Bács-Bodrog county (Rém); Torontál county (Egyházaskér, Padé); Csongrád county ("Csongrád c." 2, Hódmezővásárhely, Szentes); Békés county (Pusztaföldvár, Szarvas); Bihar county (Körösnagyharsány 2, Nagyszalonta 6); Szatmár county (Kérsemlyén, Nagybánya); "Alföld", Udvarhely county (Székelyudvarhely); Csík county (Csíkmenaság, Kászonújfalu); Háromszék county (Kézdialbis 1809), "Székelyföld", Bukovina (Józseffalva); Moldavia (Bogdánfalva, Klézse 2, Külsőrekecsin, Lészped). Total: 86. (I–III: 75; IV–V: 11.)

Textual relationships with other ballads: **74.** (in certain variants); testing the faithfulness of a lover or a relative: **22., 43.,** and **69.**

Tunes: 1. = 153; 2. (2 variants); 7. (17 variants); 9. (3 variants); 14. (2 variants); 15. (4 variants); 16. (5 variants).

The ballad has no foreign parallels. There is a Danish ballad (DgF 372) to show a somewhat similar exposition of the problem: at a dancing party the girl puts up to shame her dancing partner saying his clothes are dirty. The young man answers in excuse that he has just arrived from the battle-field, but the girl continues in the former haughty tune; when the young man asks her in marriage, she mocks him. Soon she learns, however, that the young man is the crown-prince of England (the intimation comes from her maid). At once she asks him to meet under the linden-tree in her father's garden. This time it is she that meets with a flat refusal on the part of the prince.

In spite of the similarity, this story is still different: we cannot discover in it the contrast of rich and poor characters, neither the motif of double proposition to marry; let alone textual agreements which are not detectable even in traces.

The Hungarian formulation resorts to a technique of stylization enhanced to such a degree which far exceeds the customary ballad frame, displaying a sketchy character rather familiar in folk tales. On the basis of certain indications, the ballad may well be of recent origin. For one thing, it is hardly known in Transylvania; furthermore, it is worded in a fairly modern style and its melody in a functional major mode refers to foreign taste. All these, however, can be found, though not together, in such Hungarian ballads whose mediaeval origin cannot be called into doubt. Consequently, no safe conclusion can be drawn for the present. The ballad may have developed at any time between the fourteenth and the mid-eighteenth centuries. In any case, it seems to be a genuine Hungarian ballad.

76. THE SUITOR OF THE FAULTY GIRL

54.

1. Ho - va mensz, ho-va mensz Te ke-vé ka - to - na? Ho-va mensz,ho-va mensz Te ke-vé ka - to-na?

1. Where are you going, where are you going
   You bold soldier?
   Where are you going, where are you going
   You bold soldier?

2. Not too far, not too far,
   I am just going to Anna's street.
   Not too far, not too far,
   I am just going to Anna's street.

3. Don't go there, don't go there,
   Don't go to that girl!
   Don't go there, don't go there,
   Don't go to that girl!

4. For that girl has
   Three faults.
   For that girl has
   Three faults.

5. Her first fault is
   That she is a drunkard.
   Her first fault is
   That she is a drunkard.

6. It does not matter, it does not matter,
   I don't care a pin.
   It does not matter, it does not matter,
   I don't care a pin.

7. There is wine in the cellar,
   Let her drink of it.
   There is wine in the cellar,
   Let her drink of it.

8. Her second fault is
   That she is lame.
   Her second fault is
   That she is lame.

9. It does not matter, it does not matter,
   I don't care a pin.
   It does not matter, it does not matter,
   I don't care a pin.

10. I am going to town
    And buy her the things she needs,
    I am going to town
    And buy her the things she needs.

11. I buy her such a short skirt
    And also a pair of high-heeled boots.
    I buy her such a short skirt
    And also a pair of high-heeled boots.

12. Her third fault is
    That she is always angry.
    Her third fault is
    That she is always angry.

13. It does not matter, it does not matter,
    I don't care a pin.
    It does not matter, it does not matter,
    I don't care a pin.

14. Whenever she is angry, whenever she is angry,
    I stand out of her way.
    Whenever she is angry, whenever she is angry,
    I stand out of her way.

15. Whenever she is angry, whenever she is angry,
    I take a scourge.
    Whenever she is angry, whenever she is angry,
    I take a scourge.

16. I take a scourge,
    And I whip her soundly.
    I take a scourge,
    And I whip her soundly.

Pokolpatak (Moldavia)—Egyházaskozár, (Baranya county). Performed by a man of 52. 1953 = Domokos and Rajeczky No. 25.

Divergences: "...The girl is also lame.—I don't mind, I don't mind, I shall have such a skirt made for her which will reach down to the ground, so that it may hide her lameness." "There are three faults in that girl. First of all, she is lazy, never doing a thing. I don't mind, I don't mind, I don't care a pin. I don't care a pin, For I have money enough in my pocket. I may have a work done with it. ...Secondly, that girl, that girl is a drunkard. I don't mind...I have wine enough in my cellar, I have wine enough in my cellar, And she may drink of it. Thirdly, The girl is sort of a whore. I don't mind . . . I have faithful servants, I have faithful servants, And I shall have them beat her."

Practically the same simple form is repeated in all the variants, with the exception of two found in the transcribed collection of Benedek-Sebesi, which presents a "sophisticated" re-formulation of the story thought otherwise "meagre". In point of fact, we are not dealing with a story but with genre-painting.

"Don't spur your steed, János Ugron, For if you chase it further this way, It will be devoured by dogs! The horse is mine, and I may spur it, and it is no business of yours! I am going to lunch with Mistress Torma at Keresztúr! Don't go there, János Ugron, For the daughter of Mistress Torma is both a drunkard and an angry female, Besides she is lame in the left leg. If she is a drunkard, she may drink as much as she can; if she is angry, she may quarrel with my servants. And if she be lame, Let her put on long-legged boots. A pair of red, high-heeled boots On her lame leg! You shall see the day on which you would spur and drive your bay, János Ugron, to get aloof, hey, from your wedded spouse! . . . My Dear Lord! Have I not lost all my wits when married this lame strumpet, this burden on my back! Her fair complexion, her poisonous mouth have robbed me of my wit; Her false soul and her wickedness Have restored it to me!"

Medősér? (Udvarhely county). = MNGY III, 55.

"Where are you riding in such a hurry, Proud János Ugron? I am going to town, to Szilás Keresztúr, to see the young damsel Panna Torma. Don't go there, don't go there, Proud János Ugron! For that damsel has great faults. She has three great faults. I don't mind if she has thirty-three faults! Her first fault is that she is lame! I don't mind, I don't mind, she may be lame as well! I shall have a pair of high-heeled boots made for her, And also a long silken skirt; the one side will be lengthened, while the other will hide the lameness of her leg. Her second fault is that she is angry. She is always in a rage. Once she flies into a passion, she will chase away your two unraised motherless children from the house. I don't mind if she is angry, I am not afraid of her, and my unraised children will stand out of her way. Her third fault is that she is always tipsy. She starts drinking at dawn and ends drinking after supper, Pots and plates alike suffer from her drunken moods. I don't mind, I don't mind, The cellar is full of wine, And if she has had her fill, she may pour out the remains. And János Ugron went on, and he went to see the beautiful girl. Where are you riding in such a hurry, Proud János Ugron? Don't call me Proud János Ugron any longer! My lame wife has chased me out of my home. And now I am going to roam in the world, unless my unraised children allow me to live with them!"

Rugonfalva (?) (Udvarhely county) = MNGY III, 53.

Apparently we are dealing with a "literary" composition; style and manner of thinking bear sufficient evidence of the fact. Besides, the Hungarian originals of these two pieces resist any attempt at breaking it up into stanzas so as to match a strophic tune; therefore it could never have been in popular use as a folklore product.

Earliest provenience: 1872.

Dissemination: Kolozs county (Kolozsvár); Maros-Torda county (Mezőbánd); Udvarhely county ("Udvarhelyszék"); Bukovina (Józseffalva); Moldavia (Pokolpatak). Total: 5.

Textual relationship with other ballad: 56. (opening formula).

Tunes: 1. = 154.;

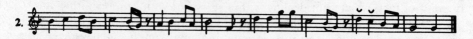

This ballad is only known by the Hungarians. As to the time of its origin, we have no data whatever to rely on.

77. WHERE HAVE YOU SLEPT LAST NIGHT, TOMTIT?

155.

1. Hol-jár-tál az éj-jel ci-në-ge-ma-dár? A ka-pud-ba hál-tam, szi-vem asz-szony-kám.

Mér bej-jebb nëm jöt-tél ci-në-ge-ma-dár? U-rad-tól nëm mer-tem, szi-vem asz-szony-kám.

1. Where have you slept last night, tomtit?
   At your gate, darling, pretty wife.
   Why did you not come inner, tomtit?
   I was afraid of your man, darling, pretty wife.

2. My man is not at home, tomtit.
   He is at the swift brook, making a new bridge.
   He has good horses and comes home very often,
   He has good horses and comes home very often.

3. Where have you slept last night, tomtit?
   In your window, darling, pretty wife.
   Why did you not come inner, tomtit?
   I was afraid of your man, darling, pretty wife.

4. My man is not at home, tomtit,
   He is at the swift brook, making a new bridge.
   He has good horses and comes home very often,
   He has good horses and comes home very often.

5. Where have you slept last night, tomtit?
   In your bed, darling, pretty wife.
   Why did you not come inner, tomtit?
   I was afraid of your man, darling, pretty wife.

6. My man is not at home, tomtit,
   He is at the swift brook, making a new bridge.
   He has good horses and comes home very often,
   He has good horses and comes home very often.

7. Where have you slept last night, tomtit?
   On your belly, darling, pretty wife.
   Why did you not come inner, tomtit?
   I was afraid of your man, darling, pretty wife.

8. My man is not at home, tomtit,
   He is at the swift brook, making a new bridge.
   He has good horses and comes home very often,
   He has good horses and comes home very often.

9. Where have you slept last night, tomtit?
   On your peg, darling, pretty wife.
   Why did you not come inner, tomtit?
   I was afraid of your man, darling, pretty wife.

10. My man is not at home, tomtit,
    He is at the swift brook, making a new bridge.
    He has good horses and comes home very often,
    He has good horses and comes home very often.

Felsőiregh (Tolna county). Performed by a female. Bartók 1907 = Bartók 305 (abridged text) = MF 998/b.

Divergences:
Actually this song exists in variants of one-three stanzas, and can hardly be formed a ballad, much sooner a lyrical song. Earlier, tuneless recordings, however, have preserved the original story in detail, in a strophic construction proceeding towards a usually obscene point. For instance:

1. Where have you slept last night, tomtit?
   In my sweetheart's window, tender violet.
   Why did you not come in, tomtit?
   I was afraid of your man, tender violet.
2. My man is not at home, tomtit.
   He is making bridges in the woods of Litvaj.
   He has good horses and comes home soon,
   I shall rue it, my rose, if he finds me with you.
3. Where have you slept last night, tomtit?
   At my sweetheart's door, tender violet.
   Why did you not come in, tomtit?
   I was afraid of your man, tender violet.
4. My man is not at home, tomtit.
   He is making bridges in the woods of Litvaj.
   He has good horses and comes home soon,
   I shall rue it, my rose, if he finds me with you.
5. Where have you slept last night, tomtit?
   In front of my sweetheart's bed, my tender violet,
   Why did you not come in, tomtit?
   I was afraid of your man, my tender violet.
6. My man is not at home, tomtit.
   He is making bridges in the woods of Litvaj.
   If you are so timid, what do you live for, tomtit?
   Let me alone, for I have another one to sleep with!

Hosszúhát (Jász-Nagykun-Szolnok county). Kálmány = Kálmány 1891. 5.

In this example we meet with the solution known from The Coward Lover (71.) The same refers to the ending portion of the text in the Csákvár manuscript. A contrary solution is found in the next piece which resembles the ballad of Crying János (70.).

Where have you slept, where have you been, tomtit?
In front of your gate, on the lawn, darling pretty wife.
Where have you slept, where have you been, tomtit?
I have been walking in your yard, darling pretty wife.
Where have you slept, where have you been, tomtit?
I have been bouncing in your window, darling pretty wife.
Where have you slept, where have you been, tomtit?
I have been warming myself on your peg, darling pretty wife.
Where have you slept, where have you been, tomtit?
In the thicket between your thighs, darling pretty wife.

Supposedly from a manuscript written in Transylvania in the eighteenth century. Ethn 1907, 249. (OSZK Ms. Oct. Hung. 640.)

The supposition of a Transylvanian origin is based on dialectal phrases. If credit can be given to this assumption, this recording, oldest of all, offers indication of the text having been extant outside the boundaries of Southern Transdanubia as well.

Earliest provenience: eighteenth century (towards the end?).

Dissemination: I. Vas county (Hosszúpereszteg); Zala county (Dergecs, Felsőzsid, Galambok, Garabonc, Kiskomárom 3, Komárváros 2, Nemeshetés 2, Rezi, Resznek); Somogy county (Attala, Beleg, Belezna, Bolhás 2, Buzsák 4, Csákány, Csoma, Fonyód, Igal 2, Karád 2, Kisbárapáti 3, Nagybajom 2, Öreglak, Somodor, Somogyszentpál 2, Szabás, Szenna, Tapsony, Telki, Vízvár); Verőce county (Haraszti 2, Rétfalu 2, Szentlászló 7); Szerém county (Kórógy); Pozsega county (Antunovác); Baranya county (Csányoszró 2, Dunafalva, Dunaszekcső 2, Hosszúhetény, Kákics, Katádfa, Mohács 2, Nagyváty, Ocsárd, Püspökbogád, Szebény, Szilágy 2, Szilvás, Várdaróc, Zaláta); Tolna county (Báta 2, Decs 7, Felsőireg, Madocsa 2, Nagydorog, Öcsény, Sárpilis, Sióagárd); Pest county (Bogyiszló 4, Szeremle); Fejér county (Csákvár); II. Jász-Nagykun-Szolnok county (Hosszúhát); Bács-Bodrog county (Bátmonostor, Dávod 4, Gombos, Nagybaracska); Szabolcs county (Nyíradony); IV. "Transylvania"? without specification. Total: 108.

Textual relationships with other ballads: 70., 71.; (to win the sweetheart by gradation: 68., 72., and 73., 131.).

Tunes: 1. = No. 155 (7 variants). However, 2. represents the most typical tune of this song:

in 75 variants. (Instrumental performances being left out of consideration.) 1. is known in Vas and Zala counties, 2. is a widespread living tune often played to dance in a narrow, contiguous area, notably in Somogy county and the Hungarian-inhabited villages of the Drava riverine in Slavonia, further in Baranya and Tolna counties and in some villages situated beyond the Danube in Bács county. (Cf. Type 1 in *Corpus Musicae Popularis Hungaricae* Vol. VI).

Rezi (Zala county), recorded on one occasion only. The other variants originating from places outside the focal area of dissemination have been recorded without tunes. It is a fairly rare occurrence that a text is so closely associated with an old Hungarian melody (if No. 155 is also considered, then with two melodies); this fact provides also evidence of the text's antiquity. (The other tune—No. 155—is an old foreign melody, although it may be even more important for the origin of the ballad.)

Foreign variants are not published. According to a note *Bartók* appended to No. 305 in 1924, "The text has many parallels in Slovak language".

The song is Hungarian, possibly originating from mediaeval times.

78. THE CLEVER ADULTERESS

156.

1. The tender Servian young wife was standing at the window,
   Lo, young Gyurka Barber was walking by.
   Come in, come in, young Gyurka Barber,
   Come in, come in, young Gyurka Barber!

2. I have good beer and I also have good wine,
   To you I give to drink for nothing, although to other people I give for money.
   Nobody is at home, only I am at home.
   Nobody is at home, only I am at home.

3. My man is in town to buy a pair of red boots,
   My father is in the woods to cut cornel-sticks,
   My mother is at the mill to grind white flour,
   My mother is at the mill to grind white flour.

4. She was luring young Gyurka Barber
   Until she lured her into the house.
   All at once her wedded man returned home.
   All at once her wedded man returned home.

5. Wife, darling, let me in,
   I have been to town and brought a pair of red boots.
   I have brought a pair of red boots, fine they are, as fine as can be had.
   I have brought a pair of red boots, fine they are, as fine as can be had.

6. Anon I shall let you in, my dearest treasure, my man,
   Only wait till I put on my skirt bought at Kővár,
   Still her dear man asked her to let him in,
   Still her dear man asked her to let him in.

7. Wife, darling, let me in,
   I have been to town and brought a pair of red boots,
   I have brought a pair of red boots, fine they are, as fine as can be had,
   I have brought a pair of red boots, fine they are, as fine as can be had.

8. Anon I shall let you in, my dearest treasure, my man,
   Only wait till I put on my slippers bought at Kővár.
   Still her dear man asked her to let him in,
   Still her dear man asked her to let him in.

9. Wife, darling, let me in,
   I have been to town and brought a pair of red boots,
   I have brought a pair of red boots, fine they are, as fine as can be had,
   I have brought a pair of red boots, fine they are, as fine as can be had.

10. Anon I shall let you in, my dearest treasure, my man,
    Only wait till I gird up my black apron.
    Still her dear man asked her to let him in,
    Still her dear man asked her to let him in.

11. Wife, darling, let me in,
    I have been to town and brought a pair of red boots.
    Then she let her dear man in,
    And under her right arm, let Gyurka out.

"Udvarhelyszék" Kriza 1863 = MNGY XI, 27, No. 9.

157.

1. In the window, bent over her fancy sewing,
   The tender Servian young wife was sitting.
   In the window, bent over her fancy sewing,
   The tender Servian young wife was sitting.

2. She was embroidering it
   With black silk yarn.
   She was embroidering it
   With black silk yarn.

3. She finished it, she made it complete,
   With white beads of pearl,
   She finished it, she made it complete,
   With white beads of pearl.

4. And where she was short of pearls,
   She filled it with her thick tears.
   And where she was short of pearls,
   She filled it with her thick tears.

5. Young Gyurka Barber
   Was walking up and down there.
   Young Gyurka Barber
   Was walking up and down there.

6. Come in, come in,
   Young Gyurka Barber.
   Come in, come in,
   Young Gyurka Barber.

638

7. I don't go in, I don't go in,
   Tender Servian young wife.
   I don't go in, I don't go in,
   Tender Servian young wife.

8. For your father is at home,
   Also your mother is at home.
   For your father is at home,
   Also your mother is at home.
   (Even your husband is at home.)

9. Come in, come in,
   Young Gyurka Barber.
   Come in, come in,
   Young Gyurka Barber.

10. For I have good wine,
    And I have also brandy.
    For I have good wine,
    And I have also brandy.

11. I give you to drink for nothing,
    To other people for money.
    I give you to drink for nothing,
    To other people for money.

12. To you I give to drink from a tin-cup,
    To other people from a wooden cup.
    To you I give to drink from a tin-cup,
    To other people from a wooden cup.

13. To you I give to drink at my table,
    To other people at the fire-place.
    To you I give to drink at my table,
    To other people at the fire-place.

14. She was luring him,
    Till she lured him in.
    She was luring him,
    Till she lured him in.

15. I don't go in, I don't go in,
    Tender Servian young wife!
    I don't go in, I don't go in,
    Tender Servian young wife.

16. For your father is at home,
    Also your mother is at home,
    Your mother is at home,
    And also your husband is at home.

17. My father has gone to the mill,
    My mother has gone to the neighbour's,
    My father has gone to the mill,
    To grind white flour.

18. My mother has gone to the neighbour's
    For to fetch a sieve,
    My mother has gone to the neighbour's
    For to fetch a sieve.

19. My man has gone to the woods
    To cut faggots,
    My man has gone to the woods
    To cut faggots.

20. She was luring him,
    Till she lured him in.
    She was luring him,
    Till she lured him in.

21. At once her kind husband
    Spoke up at the door,
    At once her kind husband
    Spoke up at the door:

22. Let me in, let me in,
    My tender wife!
    Let me in, let me in,
    My tender wife!

23. Wait a little, wait a little,
    Till I put on,
    Wait a little, wait a little,
    Till I put on,

24. Till I put on
    My slippers brough from Lyánta,
    Till I put on my shoulders
    My fur-coat brought from Lyánta.

25. Young Gyurka Barber:
    Is he to break through the window?
    Is he to break through the window,
    Or to escape through the funnel?

26. Young Gyurka, Barber,
    You need not break through the window,
    You need not break through the window,
    Nor need you escape through the funnel.

27. For I shall let you out
    Under my right arm-pit,

While I shall let him in
Under my left arm-pit.

28. But he forced her tender wife
Down upon her knees,
But he forced her tender wife
Down upon her knees.

29. He drew his sword from its scabbard,
And cut her neck,
He drew his sword from its scabbard
And cut her neck.

Gajcsán (Moldavia)—Egyházaskozár (Baranya county). Performed by a woman of 40. 1950 = Gr. 144/A = Domokos and Rajeczky 15/a

Divergences: The tragic turn at the end of 157. is the performer's occasional addition; the rest of the Moldavian variants finish the song with the statement expressed in Stanza 26.

Earliest provenience: 1863.

Dissemination: Maros-Torda county (?); Udvarhely county ("Udvarhelyszék"); Moldavia (Gajcsána 2, Lábnik = all the variants, Egyházaskozár in Baranya county). Total: 5.

Textual relationships with other ballads: The returning husband's repeated command to open the door and the delaying replies of the wife caught *in flagranti* agree with the corresponding places in the ballad of The Unfaithful Wife Burnt to Death **(1.).** Further, with portions of **20.** and **21.** These parallelisms and the similarity of the situation render the present ballad a counterpart, so to say, a parody of the former one. It often occurs also in English and Danish ballads that a tragic story is transformed into a merry narrative, by introducing comic elements into the plot, alleviating the conflict. The ballad about The Clever Adulteress is also comic in nature, in so far as it represents a possible form of typifying not alien to balladry, even though it cannot boast of any particular poetic merit. It is noteworthy, in any case, that one of the Moldavian variants was turned into a tragic story; it seems the comic ending was not felt satisfactory to the public. The Type may be fairly recent of origin.

Tunes: the melody of 157. is known from two more recordings. Further tune variants are:

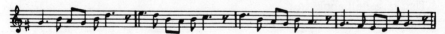

Versions in languages other than Hungarian: none.

79. THE GIRL WHO SOLVES RIDDLES

158.

1. Ifju Mátyás kerál Olyan álmot látott:

Éveg ablak alatt Nagy, hosszú almafa.

1. Young King Mátyás
   Saw a dream:
   Under the glass-window
   There stood a tall apple-tree.

2. The large, tall apple-tree
   Had twelve beautiful branches,
   Three hundred leaves,
   Sixty-six blossoms.

3. There came to the place
   A very old man.
   Look here, old father,
   I have seen a dream:

4. Under the glass-window
   There stood a large, tall apple-tree,
   That large tall apple-tree
   Had twelve beautiful branches,

5. Three hundred leaves,
   Sixty-six blossoms.
   If you cannot tell me
   What all this means,

6. What all this means,
   I shall have your head taken at once.
   He went home.
   Crying bitterly.

7. His beautiful young daughter
   Saw him weeping.
   Why are you weeping, father, why are you weeping,
   What made you grieve so bitterly?

8. I have reason to weep, I have,
   I have reason to grieve,
   Young King Mátyás
   Saw a dream:

9. Under the glass-window
   There stood a large, tall apple-tree,
   That large, tall apple-tree
   Had twelve beautiful branches,

10. Three hundred leaves,
    Sixty-six blossoms.
    , You must not be sad for that,
    My dear old father.

11. Go and tell him,
    Go and tell him:
    The large, tall tree means
    A long, good year,

12. Its twelve beautiful branches mean
    Twelve beautiful months,
    Its three hundred leaves mean
    Three hundred work-days,

13. Its sixty-six blossoms mean
    Sixty-six Sundays.
    And he went indeed
    And said what he was told to say.

14. He took in his hands
    One or two hemp-stalks.
    Take this, father, take this, father,
    Take it home to your daughter.

15. Tell her to make of this
    A cloth large enough to cover a tent,
    A towel,
    And a table-cloth.

16. He went home,
    Crying bitterly.
    His beautiful young daughter
    Saw him weeping.

17. Why are you weeping, father, why are you weeping?
    What made you grieve so bitterly this time?
    I have reason to weep, I have,
    I have reason to grieve.

18. Look, what young King Mátyás
    Commanded you to do:

Of this, you must make for him
A cloth large enough to cover a tent,

19. A towel,
And a table-cloth.
His beautiful young daughter
Walked to the chopping block,

20. She took in her hands
Two tiny chips of shavings.
Take this, father, take this,
And take this to him.

21. Tell him to make of this
A weaving-loom and a bobbin,
And this is to tell him plainly
What I need for the weaving.

22. He took the chips
And handed them over to him:
Take this, take this,
Young King Mátyás.

23. Make of this for her
A weaving-loom and a bobbin,
And this is to tell you plainly
What she needs for the weaving.

24. I don't want, I don't want
The cloth to cover the tent,
Nor the towel
And the table-cloth.

25. I only want, I only want
Your beautiful young daughter.
He went home,
Crying bitterly.

26. His beautiful young daughter
Saw him weeping.
Why are you weeping, father, why are you weeping?
What made you grieve so bitterly this time?

27. I have reason to weep, I have,
I have reason to grieve.
Look, what young King Mátyás
Told me to tell you.

28. He does not want, he does not want
The cloth to cover the tent,
Nor the towel
And the table-cloth.

644

29. He only wants you,
    My beautiful young daughter.
    Don't weep, father, don't weep,
    Don't grieve this time.

30. For God will grant me
    At first cock-crow,
    At first cock-crow
    A light disease.

31. At second cock-crow,
    A heavy disease,
    At third cock-crow,
    Departure from this world.

32. At fourth cock-crow,
    Being closed in the coffin,
    At fifth cock-crow,
    A merry party to amuse myself.

Klézse (Moldavia). Performed by a woman of 43. Kallós 1953.

Divergences: Two variants end with the King's words: "I don't want, I don't want the towel, Neither the towel, or the cloth to cover the tent, Nor the table-cloth, I only want you!" This is a happy ending to the story. The majority of the variants, however, turn into tragedy with the death of the girl who does not want to be a queen. One of the texts ends after the last riddle is puzzled out like this: "No sooner did she say this Than she met her end."

Earliest provenience: 1950 (Stanzas 1 and 2 were published in 1902 by *Mózes Rubinyi* in the Nyelvőr.)
Dissemination: Moldavia (Klézse 7). Total 7.
Textual relationships with other ballads: the girl desirous to die: **12., 8.**
Tunes: 1. = 158. published above (two variants). 3. has three variants.

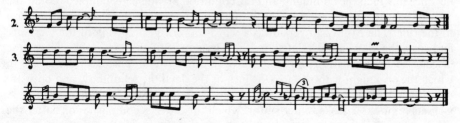

Versions in languages other than Hungarian:
(partially relevant):
ENGLISH: *Child* 45 and 1–2.
GERMAN: E–B, Nos 1090–1094.
DANISH: DgF 18.
FINNISH: *Haavio*, 143.
POLISH: *Kolberg* 1871–1884, 6 No. 296.

LITHUANIAN: *Seemann* 1951, No. 94.
MORAVIAN: *Sušil* 815 (2080).
SLOVENE: *Štrekelj* 193.
ROMANIAN: *Marinescu*, 1 = Hungarian translation. *Vulcanu* 13.

The theme of this ballad based on the girl's apposite answers to the King's questions, occurs, outside the Hungarian language area, solely among the English ballads, notably in two variants of "King John and the Bishop". The difference that in the English version it is the bishop's brother, a shepherd, that solves the task while in the Hungarian the serf's daughter, does not alter the fact that the two stories are identical. In spite of this, the two formulation cannot be brought into correlation with one onother. For one thing, the English is a broadside story, the wording of which shows no similarity with that of the Hungarian folk ballad. Secondly, in the English the task is to answer three questions while in the Hungarian the puzzling out of the riddle is followed by stating of unsolvable tasks rejected by similarly unsolvable conditions on the girl's part. The latter form, in turn, occurs in other songs among the Germans, Danes, Polish, and two other English types mentioned in the list of foreign parallels above. In these, however, there is no question of puzzling out a riddle, consequently they cannot be paralleled with the Hungarian ballad's corresponding portions. A comparison is not primarily precluded by the circumstances that the unfeasible tasks and countertasks are of a different nature—which is only natural since in such instances every nation makes recourse to its own inventive spirit—but mainly because the Hungarian ballad is constructed in a logically built up form: the counter-task being always a precondition of implementing the first-set task. (For instance: a golden shirt is to be woven from hundred-years-old hemp—the precondition being: a weaving-loom should be prepared from a hundred-years-old hedge. (As against this, many German variants contain wishes that have nothing to do with each other, the essence in them being to invent some absurd requirement with which to rebuff the rival. Such are, for example, the following absurdities: to weave silk from straw of oats—to tailor a dress from a linden leaf; to bear seven babies and remain maiden at the same time—to prepare seven cradles without a cut. There is only one single instance in which the command and the condition are logically coupled: count the stars of heaven—make a ladder that reaches up to the sky! But this is an exception to the rule. The Moravian version is a word-for-word borrowing of the German, and also the Slovene is related to the German. Still less resemblance can be discovered between the Hungarian and the other two English stories (*1.–2.*), in which the elf-knight wants to win the girl, or the devil the schoolboy, and both are outwitted. A yet greater distance can be seen in relation of the Romanian version. A girl sets impossible tasks to her suitor, which the latter accomplishes one after the other; when the last and most absurd task is uttered, namely that the man should shoot down the evening star, he shoots his arrow into the girl's body, to punish her. Thus we cannot find connections between the Romanian and Hungarian formulations.

Both the discussed elements (the puzzling out of the riddle in the presence of the king, and the achievements of unfeasible tasks) occur in the realm of folktales, and by and large in the same form with every European nation (AaTh 875.). This is the reason why *Taylor* (1964) includes this ballad type in his list presenting connections between folk ballads and folktales. Even the characters are identical in the Hungarian folktale: King Matthias and the clever girl; therefore there can be no doubt that the Hungarian ballad derives from the folktale. It is remarkable, however, that the king is told to be young, which attribute does not occur in the Hungarian legends connected with Matthias. At the same time, in the rich Southern Slav tradition relating to King Matthias, he is often called young, and so even in lyrical songs. (Cf. *Žganec,* 1950–52, No. 110: "kralj Matejuš mladi".) The tasks in the Hungarian ballad show a close agreement with those of the folktales, Hungarian and other European alike. (In this place I express my gratitude to *Ágnes Kovács* who allowed me insight into the relevant part of her catalogue of folktales.) On the other hand, the tree representing the year does not come up either in folktales or in songs as listed above. Therefore this motif is an innovation of the Hungarian ballad. Further agreement with the folktale: the king wants to marry the young girl; in turn, it is again a typically ballad motif that the girl seeks refuge in death in more than one variant. In conclusion, the Hungarian ballad is a rare example of how a tale—though by no means a fairy tale—provides subject-matter for a ballad theme. As to the generation of the ballad, any date may be suspected from the fourteenth to the nineteenth century.

Literature: Child 2 notes to 2 and 45; *Seemann* 1951, No. 94; *Haavio* 1955: Finnish originating from Swedish, and the latter from Danish; songs of this kind are derivates of tales or frame-stories containing riddles of eastern collections; *Taylor* 1964; *Á. Kovács:* Hungarian Folktale Catalogue.

80. THE SOLDIER GIRL

159.

Parlando ♪=200

1. Az ö-reg Dan-ci - a ma-gát si-rat - gas-sa:

Is - te - nem, is-te-nem, ki-lenc lá-nyom kö-zül,

Ki - lenc lá-nyom kö-zül még egy fi-am sin - csen!

Is-te-nem, is - te - nem, ki vált-son fel in-gem,
Ki vált-son fel in-gem ka-to - na-rab-ság - ból?

1. Old Dancia bewails his fate:
   My God, my God, among my nine daughters,
   Among my nine daughters, I have not a single son.
   My God, my God, who is to release me,
   Who is to release me from my military duties?

2. His youngest daughter overhears all this through the door.
   Father, my dear father,
   Let us cut my hair like a soldier's,
   Let us tailor my coat like a hussar's.

3. And she mounted her grey steed.
   When she reached the banks of the Danube,
   She set off to do the military service.

4. My God, my God, who can this be,
   A knight or a lady?
   Her riding posture is like a man's,
   But her mien is like a woman's.

5. Let us put up to show fine distaffs,
   Let us put up to show fine distaffs and muskets;
   For a knight will choose a musket,
   But a lady will choose a distaff.

648

6. She did not even look at the distaff, she picked one of the muskets,
   Thus they could not find out whether she was a soldier or a lady.
   Let us put up to show fine stacks,
   Let us place fine rosemary beneath the stacks.

7. For a knight will choose from the top,
   But a lady will choose from the bottom.
   She did not even look beneath but she picked from the top,
   Thus again they could not find out whether she was a soldier or a lady.

8. Let us go to the splendid stable (hall),
   Let us prepare a hot bath in the splendid stable.
   And then we shall learn whether this is a knight or a lady.
   My servants, my servants, when I take off,

9. When I take off my boots with the Polish spurs,
   You must shout out: Rise, my lord, rise,
   Rise, my lord, rise, emperor Jóska Ferenc,
   For your realm is put to the fire, and your people carried off!
   Thus again they could not find out whether she was a knight or a lady.

10. My God, my God, for nine years,
    For nine years and full three days
    We have drunk and eaten together, sitting at the same table,
    And still have not found out whether this is a knight or a lady!

11. I am, I am the daughter of old Dancia,
    The daughter of old Dancia, his youngest daughter.
    Among his nine daughters he had not a single son
    To release him from the military duties.

Pusztina (Moldavia). Performed by a forty-seven-year-old blind man. Z. Kallós, 1951.

The introduction, which is missing in our ballad, states in the foreign parallels that the country is threatened by war and the ruler calls his knights to arms; he who cannot join the army himself must send his son instead of him. In the seventh stanza the order of tests is changed: she picks from the top, that is if she picks the rosemary, then a girl, and if from the bottom, a young man is revealed. Even the end of the ballad is eroded to the utmost: we fail to have the part in which the ruler, upon receiving her letter, permits Dancia's daughter to avoid the bathing scene, allowing her at the same time to speed home to defend her family's estate. In the versions completed with this motif, the girl calls to the soldiers from afar on her way home that she is a girl. (The contrast between *vitéz* (Knight) and *kegyes* (Damsel) refers, as in Type **18,** to mediaeval usage, that survived up to the end of the sixteenth century.)

Divergences: A variant recorded with tune is worthy of our attention from the fifth stanza on:

5. On hearing this,
   His youngest daughter

Stood before him,
And spoke up with loud words:

6. Father, my dear father,
Gracious King Dancia,
Pass orders to dress me
In a knight's garments.

7. Let my hair cut
After young men's fashion,
Have your own bright sword
Girt on my waist!

8. I am going to redeem you
From the military duties
Place at my disposal
Your fine steed,

9. And so it was,
And so she went away.
His daughter started out
And went to foreign lands.

10. His daughter started out
And went to foreign lands,
To release her father
From the military duties.

11. How could we find out
Who this might be?
How can one display
So much bravery?

12. King Dancia
Has got only daughters.
Who this might be,
How could we find it out?

13. Let us put up to show
Fine stacks,
Fine, tiny stacks,
And tiny distaffs.

14. For a damsel will choose
A distaff,
But a knight will choose
From the stacks.

15. She made her horse prance,
This daughter of Dancia,
As a true knight
With the sword on her waist.

650

16. She made her horse prance
    And picked from the stacks.
    She did not even look
    At the distaffs.

17. How could we find out
    Who this might be?
    How can one display
    So much bravery?

18. King Dancia
    Has got only daughters.
    Who this might be,
    How could we find it out?

19. Let us arrange
    Lordly baths for the day.
    Perhaps she will come
    And have a bath!

20. Let us arrange
    Lordly baths for the day.
    Lordly baths
    And lady's spinning day.

21. If this be a damsel
    She will take a distaff,
    But if a knight,
    He will go to have a bath.

22. Dancia's daughter
    Made her horse prance,
    As a true knight
    With the sword girt on her waist.

23. She did not look at the distaffs,
    She went to the bath.
    She uttered a loud cry
    So that all may hear it:

24. Your country is being ransacked,
    Your people is being killed!
    All of them ran away,
    And nobody looked at her.

25. Then Dancia's daughter
    Had a fine bath,
    She had a fine bath
    And then returned.

26. They could not find out
    That she was a damsel,
    That she was a damsel,
    Only that she was a brave knight.

As can be seen, the tests are mixed up, the middle one is completely disregarded, and even the final test turns out in a different way: the girl follows a different path of escape. It will be shown below that the solution found in the former text is more general while the present formulation is only an altered variant of the same; all considered, this text is even more corrupt than the first.

Still the text is interesting because it has preserved traces of the strophe-repetitive construction. (The portions beginning with stanzas 11 and 16 contain word-for-word repetitions.) The name King Dancia also refers to the early years of balladry, and so do several other linguistic features.

Earliest provenience:
1951. A literary transcription by the Anonymous Poet of Sempte originates from 1570, bearing the title "Bella Istoria on King Béla and the Daughter of Bankó" (cf. *Barta* and *Klaniczay* 1951, 399), and containing thirty-eight stanzas of four lines, each consisting of twelve syllables; altogether 152 lines.
Dissemination: Moldavia (Lészped, Pusztina 2). Total 3.
Textual relationships with other ballads: no direct connections can be established; the hero (heroine)(s) not recognized and putting up to tests: **7., 17., 22., 41., 42., 43.,** and **69.**
A partially published text (*Kallós* 1970, No. 124) is associated with the following tune:

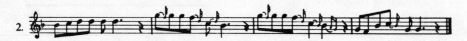

The tune of the fragmentary variant (= *Faragó* and *Jagamas*, No. 18):

The bella istoria begins the story with the usual literary formula meant to provoke interest among the audience:

1. Listen to me for I am going to relate an old story,
   Speaking about the times of King Béla
   And speaking about the daughter of old Bankó,
   Which I expose to you for remembrance's sake.
2. It was ordered by King Béla
   That all the barons under his rule,
   A hundred and seventy-seven sacred knights
   Should make speed and gather together at court.
3. Tidings of this was brought to Knight Bankó
   Who was plunged in sorrow because of his advanced age.
   He had no male offspring
   To be sent up to the King's court.
4. He had *nine* unmarried beautiful daughters,
   Among whom the youngest was the most beautiful
   But her carriage was like a man's,
   She spoke up, saying to her father:
5. *My beloved father, let my hair shaved,*
   Let my garb tailored after the hussars' style,
   And place your fine steeds at my disposal,
   And tell your brave men to escort me.

With all these done and granted, she goes to Buda where she attracts the King's attention:

8. How young you are, I admire you indeed,
   Your nice mien is like that of a girl,
   Though your carriage is like a man's.
   It is my wish to understand all this.

The King tries to unveil the secret, and orders to make the first test:

10. The King commands all his chief nobles
    . . . . . .
    To assemble at the market-place of Buda,
    And to take there spindles and distaffs.
11. He says: If this young knight is a girl,
    She will regard the spindle and the distaff.
    But if it is a man, he leaves them unnoticed,
    And casts her eyes upon the bright weapons.
12. Seventy-seven and fifty-one knights marched out,
    And gathered together to entertain themselves at the market-place of Buda.
    She did not show interest in spindles and distaffs,
    But she cast her eyes on the fine, bright weapons.
13. The young knight took up an arched bow,
    She put a fine, long arrow to the string;
    With two fingers she spanned the arrow;
    And she did all this in the eyes of the knights.
14. Again the knights spoke up in accord:
    Come and shoot at the target for a pledge, all of us!
    The knights shot at the target, all of them,
    But none of them was able to hit the target.
15. Old Bankó's daughter was the last to shoot,
    And she hit right into the middle of the target.
    At once she won the pledge of the knights.
    And the knights said at once:
16. Listen, young knight, let us cast stones.

But the girl conquered all of them even in the stone-casting competition. Then a race was arranged, in which again she came out victorious; after this, a drinking-bout followed, and the girl stayed sober among the drunk knights. Thus defeated, the knights went to the King, reporting that the young knight was not a girl but a man. Reconsidering the things, the King orders all his knights to go to bath.

25. Old Bankó's daughter does not want to have a bath;
    The King, sitting himself in the bath, says:
    Why do you not have a bath with us, old Bankó's daughter?
    He commands her to bathe with them.

At this point, the poet gives the epithet "Bankó's daughter", used so far only in the narrative parts of the composition, into the King's mouth.

26. Old Bankó's daughter answered to the King:
    You powerful King! It amazes me to learn
    That you pretend not to know about my grieves and sorrows:
    Don't you know how I worry for my old father?
27. Take a look at the letter in my hand,
    In which he writes about his great distress:
    Turks and Tartars layed siege on all my castles,
    Putting to fire and the sword all my provinces.

And the King allows her to go home, saying:

29. Make speed, son, and go home to defend your lands,
    Your beautiful castles, your fine legacy.

The girl goes aboard a galley and when already in the middle of the river, she unbuttons her dolman to show her breast to the King, shouting: 32. Tell me, King, if all your realm, all your beautiful gardens Can bear such precious apples As these ones in my own garden, that have been before you? 33. I have brought these two precious apples up to Buda, But you could not, King, pick these apples! ...After this, the King follows in her wake, shouting to her that he would marry her. But he cannot reach her. At home, the girl relates her adventures to her father, who accompanies the story with loud roars of laughter. Finally, we have the author's concluding lines:

37. This has been lately translated from Croatian into Hungarian,
    In the town of Sempte on the swift Vág...
38. When people wrote the number of years
    Fifteen hundred and seventy,
    In the first week of the Holy Virgin's month,
    May the Lord be praised in the high Heavens.

Versions in languages other than Hungarian:

FRENCH: *1. Poueigh,* 225, at the Atlantic end of the Pyrennees. *2. Puymaigre* 1874, 96 = *Puymaigre,* Folklore 94, VI.

PORTUGUESE: *3–16. Braga* I, 95–144 (95 = *Hardung,* 93, 131 = *Hardung,* 88 = *Geibel-Schack,* 400 = *Wolf* 12.; 136 = *Hardung,* 96). *Pires de Lima* lists 50 Portuguese variants.

CATALAN: *17–21. Milá* 245A–E.†

SPANISH: *22–29. Cossio-Solano* II, Nos 64–66. *30. Menéndez–Pidál* 1885, No. 50. *31–32. Armistead–Silverman* 1971, 53 and 85, Nos B/14 and C/17. *Pires de Lima* knows about 100 Spanish variants.

ITALIAN: *33–37. Nigra* 48A–E. *38. Widter–Wolf,* 79. *39. Ferraro* 1870, No. 38. *40. Idem* 1888, No. 25. *41. Gianandrea,* 280. *42. Bernoni* XI, No. 5. *43. Ferraro* 1877, 89, No. 5. *44–45. Giannini,* 145, No. 5 and variant. *46. Pergoli* 22. *47. Barbi,* 57.† *48. Ferraro* 1890, 268.† *49. Giannini* 1892, 158,† fragment. *Giannini* also mentions tale-versions from Northern- and Central Italian collections.

GERMAN: *50. Hauffen* 77, *Gottschee* (Slovenia) = D. Vlr. 95.

SOUTHERN SLAV: *51–52.* manuscripts† from Slovenia (preserved at Glasbeno-narodopisni Inst., Ljubljana). *53–54. Štrekelj* I, Nos 56–57. *55. Kurelac* 483. *56–57. Žganec* 1950, Nos 163–164. *58. Blažinčić* 25.† *59–61. Poljanin* Nos 2, 8 and 17. (Hungarian abstract, Szegedy). *62.* Istarske 6,† *63. Bogišić* 96. 1758 = Hungarian abstract by *Szegedy. 64.* HNP II, No. 36 = Hungarian abstract by *Pável. 65–67.* HNP II, Nos 406–407 (supplement to No. 36). *68.* HNP VI, No. 16 (other variants also mentioned). *69. Vuk* III, No. 40 = Tommaseo's translation in Italian = Hungarian abstract by *Szegedy* 1913. *70. Stojanović-Vitezica,* 607. *71. Jasztrebov,* 135.† *Nikolić* 55.† *73. Kačić-Miošić* 6. (Slovenske ljudske pesme 8. 6 var.)

BULGARIAN: *74. Chekhlarov* 8 = A–V, No. 45. *75–76. Verković* 11 and 250. *77–79. Miladinovi* 103 and 201. *80–82. Shapkarev* 374, 404 and 461. *83, Arnaudov* 1913 138. *84. Stoilov* 1916–18, No. 439. *85. Mihailov* 234.† *86. Bonchev* 51.† *87. Kachanovsky,* 50. *88. Cholakov* 76* = Bulgarian abstract A–V, No. 45. *89. Stoin* 1939, No. 346. *90. Idem* 1931, No. 231. *91–95. Idem* 1928, Nos 543 and 1550–1553. *96. Idem* 1934, No. 82. *97–101.* SbNU 5, No. 21 and 16 No. 3.; 13, 43, No. 3; 15, 24; 40, 385, No 8; 40, 388, No. 13. *102–103. Vatev,* 308, No. 141 and 310, No. 142. *104–105. Ivanov* 191, No. 203 and 193, No. 205. *106–107. Tsitselkova* I, 16, No. 17 and II, 137, No. 169. *108–109.* SbNU 5, 16, No. 3 and 6, 58 No. 4. *110.* Izv. Etn. Muz. VII, 123. *111–114.* SbNU I, 269 No. 231 53, No. 31; 42 *Kepov,* 209 and *Ivanov,* 84, No. 2; 38 *Burmov,* 27, No. 3. I have been unable to get hold of SbNU 2, Nos 95 and 126 (what I know about these is owing to Mr. *Seemann's* courtesy).

ROMANIAN: *115. Brăiloiu,* 52, *116. Negoescu,* 7* = *Antologie,* 360. *117–118. Tocilescu,* 126 and 128. *119. Popovici,* 73.† *120. Giuglea,* 88. *121. Sandu* T., 174.† *122–124.* Institutul de Folclor manuscript 4536†, 8406,† 14524.† Reference to a variant No. 13899.* (Cf. *Amzulescu* No. 19.)

CZECH: *125. Waldau* 352. *126. Bartoš-Janáček* 1953, No. 193.

MORAVIAN: *127–129. Sušil* 109/232–234. *130. Bartoš–Janáček* 1901, No. 82. *131–132. Bartoš* 1882 No. 171 and 292.

SLOVAK: *133. Horák* 1958, No. 24 = *Kollár* II, 6, No. 4. = *Medveczky* 1923, No. 1. *134. Kolečány* 39. *135.* EA 3659, 5, Hungarian translation, from Liptó county. *136–139. Bartók* 1959, No. 248ab, d, f. *Kollár* lists a further six variants.

654

POLISH: *140. Kolberg* 1871–84, Vol. 19, 159, No. 478 = *Czernik*, 275.

UKRAINIAN–WHITE RUSSIAN: *141–142. Chernyshev* 6 and variant in the Notes. According to Lintur, the ballad is current among the Trans-Carpathian Ukrainians as well.

ALBANIAN: *143. Lambretz*, 145,* narrative in prose. *144. Hahn* 101, narrative in prose.

GREEK: *145. Tommaseo* III, 78, fragment. *146. Hahn* 10. narrative in prose.

Partial variants

DANISH: *147–148.* DgF 119 (from the Faroese Islands, further the French types 34, 43, 47 110 and a Russian type Hilferding No. 151).

The Hungarian "bella istoria" is the earliest representative of the ballad story throughout its dissemination area. True to say, it is a literary product; but the author of the poem declaires that he had translated it from Croatian, and indeed, some portions of the Southern Slav versions agree with it. At the same time, we have no knowledge of a Southern Slav literary elaboration of the theme. Thus, in spite of its Hungarian rendering, it should be regarded as one of the first recordings of the Southern Slav variants. As demonstrated below it also should be considered the first recorded document of the Hungarian popular variants. In any case, it is a proof of the internationally spread ballad from 1570. (The earliest Portuguese reference originates from 1619.)

What we have at hand from the French area is a fragment recorded from southern France in two variants. (*1–2.*) War has broken out. Down in Ossau, in the coastal area, there is a nobleman who has three daughters. He goes to the first: "Child, will you go to the army?" "No, father, I shall not go to the wars." He turns to the youngest: "Will you go, my child?" "O yes, father, I shall go to fight. Give me a war-horse and the weapons you had got from the king, and give me a page who will be faithful to me. (Jeanne, the soldier, collects her troops and scatters the enemy.) The part put in brackets is missing from the recorded version of the last century.

It is usually observed that the French ballads make their way to the English and the Danes. This time, however, we experience a rather extensive dissemination in the South. Although the northern areas also preserve some traces of the theme. Later French formulations (*34., 43., 47.*, and *110.*) appeared in English broadsides: the girl clad in man's garb joins the soldiers to follow her sweetheart who has been separated from her; in òther variants, she has her hair cut and so she joins the army to fight the enemy or to kill her unfaithful lover in a duel. (Cf. *Roberts, W. E.* and *Laws*, 205–208.)

In the Danish area it is not the theme but some of its details of formulation that come up, nevertheless this is the more eloquent proof of an immediate connection. "The war has broken out, the Swedes are about to invade Denmark. The king orders every man to go to the battle-field. Sire Peter is supposed to bear the banners. He has no sons to send to the war, therefore he asks his daughter to represent his colours." In the rest of the story, a different course is followed (cf. DgF 119, stanzas 19–22).

In the Portuguese area the story is complete, and a very large number of variants are extant. War broke out, usually between France and Aragon, more rarely in the domains of the elderly noble. The father curses his wife because he has seven daughters but no sons to send to the army. His eldest (sometimes youngest)

655

daughter undertakes to go, asking for weapons and a horse. Her father hesitates, saying they might recognize her. "Your hair is fair".—"Give me scissors to cut it off."—"You have sparkling eyes"—"I shall keep them cast down."—"Your bosom is round."—"The armour will flatten it."—"Your hands are fine."—"The wind will coarsen them."—"Your feet are small."—"I shall wear big boots."— "Your step is short."—"Before men I shall step out". Then follows the recognition. "Mother, I am dying for Don Martinho's eyes", moans the young prince. "His body is the body of a man but his eyes the eyes of a woman". His mother advises various tests by which her son can find out whether the knight is a girl: he must invite the knight to dinner; if he is a man, he will sit on a high seat, if a woman, on a low; take him to the market-place: a man will reach for the swords, a woman for ribbons; let them go to bed together (but the girl says she is bound by an oath not to take off her underhose when she goes to sleep)—and finally let them go to the bath together. The number of tests is often four; the last test occurs in all the fourteen Portuguese ballads though often in an eroded form, or in a different place of sequence. The general version, which is also found in the Hungarian, is that when it comes to undressing, the girl's page initiated into the plot brings a letter to the effect that she must hurry home because her father (or mother) is dying. Indeed, in three instances we find the formula used in the Hungarian ballad: when she starts to take off her boots, the news is brought to her (*4., 7., 8.*). As she leaves, she calls back to the young man from a distance: "I have served for seven years, I came as a virgin, and as a virgin I return to my home."Sometimes the young man accompanies her, sometimes the story ends in marriage; elsewhere the girl boasts to her father about her experiences.

The Spanish and Catalan variants offer nothing new, only make the story, through various losses, vaguer and more hazy in comparison to the Portuguese. For example, the young man recognizing the heroine says that she resembles his wife, yet finally asks her to marry him. The tests, too, are less and less comprehensible; they must go to a mill, and there she does not touch the flour but goes fishing; or they go to pull flax, and the girl pulls a large quantity, or they go toward the flax (probably to the retting pit), and she stops on the bank; in the garden she chooses an apple instead of an almond, and in the end she is given in marriage to the prince hurrying after her, provided he can recognize her among the seven sisters. Here too, the heroine cuts of her hair in two versions. Sometimes three girls figure in the song, sometimes seven, but even then only three are asked to go to the army. It is interesting that one of the variants *(9.)* calls the heroine a "Portuguese maiden".

In the Catalan variants we find among the tests already listed the motif of the competition at the drinking-bout; here the test at the bath turns into one of swimming. Anyway, it is characteristic of the entire Iberian area that the father curses his seven daughters or his wife because he has no sons. Sketchier but more uniform are the Italian texts which are found all over northern Italy. Here the father's troubles are inferred from his daughter's questions and her offers. "Why do you weep, father? I shall go to the war in your stead!"; and there is always one daughter spoken of, and not a single text mentions sisters. In one variant we still find the father being afraid lest she should be discovered, but in general only the requests follow: he must give her weapons, a horse, and clothing. The *hair-cutting* motif is altogether missing though there are nine instances in which she asks for a page (sometimes a servant) to serve her faithfully. The tests here seem to be rather secondary; the first, second and third tests occur in one text each, at the same time there are eight texts with four tests, and one has even six. In ten instances we encounter the test at the market-place, although the test of choosing between crop and blossom is reduced to a mere flower-picking. In any case, the test-scenes show a great degree of variation and dispersion. The bathing test too is completely altered: here it is consistently replaced by a test of swimming in a river, in any case, by crossing a water. The rescue message brought by a letter is general, but only in one single Piedmont variant is it bound up with the moment when the boots are taken off.

As against these, it is an entirely new element that in four variants the girl replaces not her father but her brother in the army; in one variant, to be precise, she goes to take her father's place but bids farewell to her brother. By this the girl's undertaking is deprived of all sense since she is not bound to go to the war because her father has no son. The introductory part announcing this circumstance is missing from the Italian text, this is the reason that makes the corruption understandable. And finally, we also find the general ending of the Portuguese and Spanish ballads: I came as a virgin, and as a virgin I go home.

The only Gottschee German text similarly knows about one daughter who takes the place of her aged father, and asks him for man's clothing and advice as to how she should behave in the army. The father's advice is that she should not take off her headgear because she would be discovered by her red, braided hair, further, that she should not sing when rubbing her horse down, and the like. And if she should be asked why she not sing, she must say "it is the custom in our part". She serves in the army for seven years, the text makes no reference to the test for her detection, and when she goes home she mocks her comrades for not having discovered her being a girl.

In the rich Southern Slav material the call to the wars is often given by letter (ferman), or by a messenger. Instead of the aged father, the girl has to replace her brother in three cases. The fact of substitution is often not motivated by reference to the father's advanced age, and in one instance the father is described as a *young ensign*. These are signs of deterioration, although the motif of the father too old for the wars occurs fairly frequently and in detail in the Southern Slav texts. The number of daughters vary from one to nine. There is no mention made of a page, but in two instances a servant accompanies the girl. The motif of hair-cutting is completely missing, except for one single Bosnian text; where hair is mentioned, it is for quite a different reason: either she is to hide it under her headgear or, sometimes, she shows it to the warriors, when she opens also her mantle to show her bosom. In many a text we hear the suspicious young man say: "Her carriage is like a man's but her look like a woman's". The tests here too show a wide dispersion, although we cannot meet among them the motif of choosing between crop and flower. Tests of strength often come up in them: casting stones, jumping, running, throwing away muskets, and the like. The bath is found three times in its original form (in eastern Bosnian texts), on twelve occasions she has to cross a river, and the aim is not to have her undress but to put to test her strength and dexterity. Accordingly, it is not the last test in every case, and the rescue under the pretext of the letter occurs in connection with three bathing scenes, but not at the moment when the girl has to take off her boots but when she walks to the bath or unbuttons her mantle. Also the number of tests vary from one to four. It has to be mentioned finally that in the variants of Istria and Slovenia, the girl has to swim across the *Danube,* at a place from which that river flows the farthest, while no mention is made of the sea, or the rivers Drava or Sava, situated much nearer.

The endings also take a different form: from the further bank of the river she shows her breast and hair to the pursuers to mock them, (sometimes a button is torn off from her mantle during the tests and so her bosom is seen). Other forms of ending are: she relates her adventures to her parents; on the further bank of the river she announces that she had been serving for seven years yet nobody recognized her; they pursue her to her home and finally a marriage ensues; and we have one text in which the girl coming out victorious of the tests is allowed to leave the army and go home.

The material collected by the Bulgarians is very rich, and the most striking thing is that we find in it twelve occurrences of the name *Bankó,* the name of the hero of the Hungarian *bella istoria,* which does not come up in the Yugoslav variants; moreover, the Bulgarian material, owing to erosion and corruption, shows further losses and in part closer correspondences with the distant western and Hungarian ballads. The number of girls is usually nine, rarely three, if mentioned at all. The father is mostly seen bemouning his fate for having been called to the army, and sometimes he curses his daughters. The girl here too asks for clothes, weapons (sometimes, strikingly enough, for buffalloes put to cart). The more detailed requirements are again mentioned as they are fulfilled, and thereby this part becomes the longest in the story. There is no mention of a page, although in some of the variants she goes to the wars with a strong retinue, sometimes under the escort of her cousins. As in the Portuguese and the Hungarian stories, the heroine has her hair cut in seven texts. An individual feature is the way of discovery, in which the queen dreams there is a girl in the army, or the girl sings in the stable on the feast of St. Lazarus, and the queen hears her. The tests take on forms showing they have been sung "to destruction". Their numbers, varying from one to five, are fairly evenly distributed among the variants. At the bazaar she is offered choice between a distaff and something else: weapons on two occasions, a flute, a drum or an apple occur as counterparts in other instances. Sometimes she does not even choose a thing. Choice between flowers and crops does not occur at all. Sometimes the question is simply if she is going to pick one wreath of flowers or two. The bath-test in its original form appears ten times, but the erosion is to be felt very strongly here too: in many cases it is not the point of the story, the rescue by means of a letter is omitted and so is the boot-removal. The solutions are confused: a herald announces before the bathing-scene takes place: "she that is a girl must give word of it", whereupon she makes a bow before the emperor; in other instances she unbuttons her gown on the shore and so she gives herself away. Other solutions are that she goes on in front and does in fact bathe, or she frightens the soldiers out of bathing with talk of illness, or she herself shaves the members of the army before bathing, etc. In any case it is obvious that this part has lost its original meaning or

658

point. The closing part is similarly corrupt. In many cases the girl is discovered before the story meets its point. A fabulous turn is when she is transfigurated into the shape of a bird and so she flies away to light on her father's knee, from where, again she is taken to the Tsar, and when waking up in his lap, she dies a sudden death.

While we find mutilated stories and fragments with the Bulgarians, the Romanians have further developed the tale, in a folktale fashion, so that it has become very long. The most striking novelty is that before reaching the army, the girl is put to various tests by her own father assuming the appearance of a bear, a wolf or a dragon. Her two elder sisters do not stand the tests set by the father, but she succeeds in overcoming the obstacles by the help of her magic horse. In the Romanian version the tests of sex bear no resemblance whatever to the solutions of other nations, however fragmentary or eroded they may be. (For example, there is a hip-measuring incident in the barracks, and she cuts her own flesh off her hips; when she has to choose between a fork and a mace, she throws her mace up so high in the air that it does not fall back for nine hours.) As in the Hungarian version, she has her hair cut, and she has to make her choice between the distaff and the musket. On the basis of all this, we have to consider the Romanian version to be a faded survival of the original, common series of versions, developed into a fantastic tale.

Among the Greeks, apart from a verse fragment, the story survives in a prose version—to my knowledge—which is close to the general content, although towards the end it is further developed in fable style. Here the aged father has three daughters as in the French; the two elder daughters refuse to take his place in the army, leaving him with abuse. The youngest goes and returns victorious, and then she is subjected to tests by a foreign prince (she has to sleep on the grass, and the grass stays fresh under her,—it fails to show the shape of her body?). In the rest of the tale, we have the tale motif of the dumb woman who speaks at the wedding feast. The Albanians have taken this over in part, together with the Greek heroine's name Theodora; further, we also meet with the three tests known from the Romanian version, too: the father subjecting his three daughters to various tests, turns first into a river, then changes into a monster to frighten them; other tale-elements are also found: when the heroine breathes on a hair, a magic dog appears before her and helps her stand the tests.

Among the northern neighbours of the Hungarians we find again the ballad-form disseminated. According to the Slovak version, the father has three daughters, but only the youngest undertakes to go to fight, asking for weapon and garb. Her father advises her to stay in the rear at battle, but the girl does not obey, goes to the forefront and cuts down everybody. Seeing this, or perhaps even sooner, the king takes a liking to her, and would ask her to marry him if she were a girl; she reveals herself, and the song meets a sudden end, closed down by a few more lines. So here the tests must necessarily be omitted since the story develops differently. According to the Slovak formulation, the preliminaries occupy the major part of the story, describing how the father asks her three daughters to replace him in the army. This conception, sometimes with a word-for-word agreement, now with one daughter, now with three mentioned, spread from the Slovaks towards the Czechs, and via the Poles, to the Russians.

To our great surprise, the story abridged by the Slovaks has come up most recently, in a rather literary Hungarian formulation, at a Transylvanian village. It is betrayed by the forced technique of rhyming, the use of attributes and phrases— part of which has been distorted by the singer, that the song must have been written by some rural versificator who may have translated it from Slovak. In any case, the Transylvanian counterfeit follows closely the plot of the Slovak–Moravian version. Here are some portions of the text:

> The bloody sword
> Is carried over the country.
> I must go to the wars
> To fight the Turks and Tartars...
> I cannot, I cannot
> Ride a horse,
> How could I, how could I
> Chase the Turks!
> My daughter, my dear daughter,
> My eldest daughter,
> Go to the battle-field in my place,
> Take pity on your father!
> I will not go, father,
> How could I go there?
> The many Turks
> Would frighten me to death!
> ......
> Give me, give me
> A golden-haired steed,
> Give me, give me
> Your silvered sword,
> Give me a diamond rosette
> To adorn my mantle,
> A saddle to put on my steed,
> A bright, embroidered caparison.
> Her buoyant fair hair
> She had cut to the root,
> Not even a drop of tears
> Did she shed after her golden hair...
> She stroked her brave steed,
> And she stroked it,
> While riding in a gallop
> Out of the village... (and so on).

This text was sung to the tunes of a very old, and widely spread folk-melody by a seventy-eight-year-old female performer of the village of Csíkkarcfalva (as late as 1971!). In spite of the merits of the performance, we have to omit the song from the data referring to the dissemination of the ballad.

660

By reviewing the versions of the various nations it is easy to establish the place of origin and the route taken in the course of distribution. The single fragmentary French text cannot represent the complete ancient French tradition. Perhaps subsequent transformations had ousted it from the realm of French folklore (cf. the related French types *34, 43, 47* and *110*). The mentioned versions testify the popularity of the theme of The Soldier Girl among the French. On the other hand, the fragment referred to above allows us to draw the conclusion that the versions occurring in the neighbouring areas had developed from the French. For example, the words of the Italian version in the scene where the girl asks for a page show a complete agreement with those of the corresponding part of the French fragment, while in other language areas they are either absent or exist in traces only (retinue, cousins, or a servant to follow the girl). So we have one point at least to connect the two formulations. At the same time, it appears clearly from the French text, fragmentary as it is, that the Italian cannot be taken for original. Namely, the former, as far as it goes, is more detailed than the latter, in which there is no mention of the father having been called to military service, nor of the essential turns of the dialogue between father and daughter, which form unalienable parts of the story, by the evidence of the whole dissemination area. Therefore only the Italians could be the borrowers and the French the donors. The break of the French version may be attributed to later erosion. The French text mentions three daughters, the youngest willing to replace her father. Apart from this, the motif in question occurs among the Greek and the Slovaks (who live in the territory of pre-wars Hungary); that is to say, its occurrence among them can be well accounted for by the mediating role of French settlers. Consequently, the figuring of one single girl in the Italian text must be a secondary development. All this becomes yet clearer when the Hungarian is compared with the other national versions. To wit, there exists a motif which is common in the Portuguese–Spanish, in the Hungarian, further in the Bulgarian and Romanian traditions, although missing from the Italian: the cutting off of the girl's hair. Now then, this connection cannot be imagined by leaping over the Italian link. The motif must have formed part of the original French, from which it has been omitted through wear and tear. This motif had been mediated by mediaeval French settlers to the Hungarians, who in turn had passed it over to other nations. One might say that the motif of hair-cutting is so natural that it may arise among the various peoples independently as well. Nevertheless, it is not so naturally applied, because in the Southern Slav formulation it is not only missing, but on the contrary: the girl shows just her hair (and her breast) to the outwitted soldiers; according to the Germans of Gottschee, the girl's father advises his daughter not to take off her chako lest she should be discovered. From the Italian it is simply omitted, although not so from the Iberian texts, in which the motif occurs abundantly. Perhaps this can explain—namely, the sequence broken with the Italians—why the Southern Slavs and the Germans living among them resort to a different style of formulation: they could not hit by themselves upon this "natural thing". The motif appears again in the national versions after it has been transferred to their areas in a ready-made form: among the French settlers in Hungary, then among the neighbouring peoples who adopted the Hungarian formulation.

The Southern Slav version displays one more Italian trait: the girl replaces her brother or takes leave of her brother. At the same time, a number of variants among the Southern Slavs also preserve the Hungarian–French solution: the girl has to take her father's place in the army. With them, therefore, we have to consider two trends: a stronger Hungarian and a weaker Italian.

It is through the French mediation that the scene of boot-removal occurs much in the same formulation in the Portuguese (thrice), in the Italian (once), and in the Hungarian versions. Precisely at this scene the servant has to appear with the letter! Since this motif is completely absent in the Southern Slav variants, it "should have leapt over" a wide stretch of land in its route to Hungary. But the one-time presence of French–Walloon settlers in Hungary fills the gap. Furthermore, there are such motifs which come up in a clear-cut form only in the Portuguese and the Hungarian ballads, and, in an aroded form, among the Italians and Southern Slavs: the choice between fruit (crops) and flowers.

The evidence of these details clearly shows that the ballad did not reach the Hungarians from the southern nations. Nor could it come from the northern peoples, because their versions have uniformly left out the tests; and it is out of question that the Hungarians should have found them out on their own. Besides, there arise further difficulties from geographical considerations: the French–Iberian and the Slovak–Moravian–Polish–Russian areas would be completely isolated from one another if the Hungarian area were not taken into account. Therefore the only solution is to suppose a trend of dissemination starting from the French, proceeding towards Hungary, and from there to the neighbouring nations. The influence in Hungary of the French girl-soldier is shown by the Slovaks' three daughters' scene, too. The fact that it is missing from the single Moldavian variant does not necessarily mean that it was missing from the old Hungarian tradition, too. Territorial differences must have existed, as shown by the dual form of the old knight's name: the Moldavian texts speak about Dancia, while the sixteenth-century *bella istoria* and the Bulgarian version mention Bankó. The latter must have been used by the old Hungarian folk-texts, at least by part of them, otherwise the Bulgarians could not have taken it over; to wit, the name Bankó has left no trace in the Southern Slav, from which the author of the *bella istoria* made his "translation".

The role of France as a radiating centre is further brought out by the condition of the Portuguese–Spanish ballad which is "sung apart" (zersungen). The process has gone farther among the Spanish. French ballads may have spread in the Iberian peninsula during the French reign in Portugal and Catalonia. Subsequently they reached the Spanish. It is characteristic enough that in the former-mentioned two countries we find no historical epic poetry but we do find ballads, while in Spain, a country that has never been exposed to any stronger French influence, comparatively few ballads can be found although there are many historical lays. To remain with our ballad, it cannot be attributed to mere chance that one of the Spanish variants mention the heroine under the name "Portuguese Maid". (According to *Armistead,* however, the Spanish ballad is more original than the Portuguese one.)

From the French the ballad made its way to the Greeks (in the years of the Frank rule in Cyprus) as well as to the Hungarians, and from them to the other Eastern nations. In demonstration of the close textual relationships, we refer—in addition to the above-mentioned parts—to the following details: Portuguese: "O corpo tenia de hombre, Os olhos de mulher são" = Her body shows a man, Her eyes are like a woman's (*3.*). Hungarian: Sits the horse like a man, but looks like a woman; Southern Slav: "Na skoku je kano i delija, Na pogledu kano i divojka" = By her carriage she looks like a knight, by her mien, like girl (*57.*); the Hungarian *bella istoria*: "Your pretty mien is that of a girl, your carriage that of a man"; Bulgarian: Pogleda i je devochki, Pofatta i je junachka = Her mien is like a girl's, her carriage, a knight's (*87.*). And only thus can we understand the agreement between the Iberian and the Bulgarian versions, in which the father curses his wife or the daughters with nearly the same phrases.

There remains the connection between the *bella istoria* and the folk tradition to be clarified. Its author's admission about the translation from Croat is confirmed in particular by two elements: the showing of the breasts and the trials of strength. This connection, however, is not enough to fully explain the text of the *bella istoria*. Notably, there remain such parts which cannot be inferred from the Southern Slav version. For one thing, we mention the name of *Bankó*. The author of the *bella istoria* could not have made his translation from Bulgarian, since he definitely mentions Croat, which fact finds adequate support in the one-time existence of Croats around the fortress of Sempte, further in the composition of the garrisons in the forts of the borders. But the main reason is that from the Bulgarian texts we could not deduce the details typical of the Croat, let alone the Hungarian ones. Anyway, the name Bankó is an old Hungarian personal name (quoted by the Etymological Dictionary of Gombocz and Melich "Bancone comite", 1222, and Benedicto Banco, 1483). Perhaps the Moldavian Dancia is a dialectal sibilant variant of Dancs (Danch) quoted from 1478 by the mentioned Dictionary, provided with a diminutive suffix. A further evidence is the bath-scene, which is described by the author much in the same way as the Hungarian folk ballad has it, that is differently from the Croat form of crossing the river by swimming. The three variants recorded from Bosnia, showing an exceptional similarity to the Hungarian in this respect, are far apart from the Hungarian language area, and still farther from the lines of Turkish–Hungarian warfares, and from the border-fortress of Sempte in Nyitra county. There are portions in the *bella istoria* which certainly indicate that the author made use of the Hungarian ballad, only he incorporated certain Southern Slav details which aroused his interest. For example, Stanza 5 of the *bella istoria* shows a very close resemblance to the Moldavian ballad—if it is compared to Stanza 2 of No. 159, or to Stanzas 6–8 of the two other mentioned texts. That a subsequent "insertion" of text parts took place clearly appears from the description of the tests. The first and the last are set by the king himself, and this circumstance recalls the concise style of representation in balladry. (Stanzas 10–12—Stanzas 5–6 of the ballad.) Following this, the build-up of the story shows a sudden change: in the course of setting the tests no inherent rhythmic repetition is found, and it is not the king that orders the tests to be arranged: instead, the warriors instigate their companion for ever new competitions, and these four tests are described in a flow, not unlike the style of short-stories. No sooner than the bath-test takes place does the story return to the original rut, this last test being set by the king again. The curious order of the tests $(1+4+1)$, as well as the sudden change in the style of presentation is revealing enough. In the same way, revealing is the evidence of those few details which bear a very close resemblance to the Hungarian ballads' correspondig parts on account of their presentation more concise than the rest of the poem. At these points, it seems, the author could not altogether get rid of the ballad's influence. The other parts betray the hand of a court poet. In my opinion, the author must have known the Hungarian version of the ballad, too, but he found the theme worthy of elaboration only after he was acquainted with the Croat version with all its soldierly contests and the gallant detail of breast-display in the end. The expression "has translated" may well cover as much as this, for in the "naive" poetry the phrases like "has composed" or "has translated" do not yet convey any precisely delimited concepts. (Mihály Kecskeméti Vég, for instance, the author of the sixteenth-century text of the Psalmus Hungaricus, designates his work as his own "composition" though it was a simple paraphrase of a psalm text.)

Finally, let us cast a glance on the broader relationships of the ballad under discussion. The principal turns of the ballad (namely, the girl dressed in male's clothing and the trials devised for her undressing) appear also embedded in other stories and other types of narration: folktales, mediaeval legends and stories. However, in these the change of dress turns out to be a real change of sex in the end; when it comes to the bathing-scene, she miraculously changes into a man. (Such legends were mentioned by *Veselovsky* 1881, and *György* wrote about their later descendents (1941, 289, and *idem.* 1911)). Sometimes the outwitted demon curses her, and therefore she changes into a man, as in the folktales. (Cf. *Aarne-Thompson* 614, *Bolte-Polivka* III, 57, *Anderson, Istvánovits.*) The most striking is that in the wealth of tales in the Balkans and Georgia the sex-change motif merges with the Albanian version of the Soldier Girl: of the three girls put to the test by their father, the youngest changes into a young man. Istvánovits regards these Georgian fables as borrowings from the Balkans, because the girl soldier is not known specifically in any other form, nor is the sex-change, only the combination of the two precisely in the form found in the Balkans. The question is further complicated by the fact that more recently *Meletinsky* published a similar solution from the tradition of the Altai-Turks; in the heroic songs of Central Asia the youngest girl goes to the wars instead of her father, while her two sisters stay at home, discouraged by their father in the shape of a fox. Finally the girl receives a hero's name and changes into a man. Still more striking is the similarity which links this ballad with an old Chinese song. In the Song of Mu-lan (cf. *Tőkei* 1959, 80) it is not the father but the daughter that complains, because her father is being called to the wars by the *kagan*: "My father has no sons, and poor Mu-lan has no brother at all. I shall go to the market to buy a horse and a saddle, and go to fight instead of my father." Then the song goes on to tell how she gets the things she needs at the market, how she gallops from battle to battle, hears the "barbarian hoof-beats of the *hu*-horses", how she acquires distinction before the kagan, and returns to her joyful parents. And when she appears, now dressed in a girl's clothing, before her soldier comrades who have accompanied her home, they cry astonished: "For twelve years you have been a warrior among us, and now we see a young lady!" The poem is from a collection completed in the tenth century, but it may well originate from the fourth or fifth centuries. According to *Tőkei,* the poem is possibly connected in some way with the folklore of some "hu" (barbarian) people. This can be inferred at least from the mentioning of the title kagan. Since the text shows very close similarity to the ballad discussed, it is difficult to imagine that they had developed independently of one another; therefore we do not think it impossible that the basic story of the soldier girl reached Europe with the waves of the Great Migrations, and here acquired (perhaps from the tale) the amplification of the sex-tests (which occur separately in tales: cf. Aa-Th 884, Motif-Index H 1578), and thus developed on French soil into a ballad. Nevertheless, the European ballads constitute a closely related text-group whose trend of dissemination can only be imagined on the grounds discussed above. This wide range of dissemination refers to immense antiquity, and so does the rarity and fragmentary nature of the French version.

All things considered, the ballad on The Soldier Girl belongs to the earliest fourteenth-century French borrowings in Hungarian balladry.

Literature: Nigra 1958*: southern French origin; *Veselovsky,* Ateneo Italiano, 15th April 1886: criticizes *Nigra; Szilády* 1879: two Southern Slav variants parallel with the Hungarian *bella istoria* in verse: *Veselovsky* 1881: discussion of variants in the sex-change, Southern Slav ballad of The Soldier Girl from the Italian; *Nigra* 1884, 178: southern French origin; *Sozonovič* 1886: Italian from Southern Slavs; *Veselovsky* 1887: criticizes *Sozonović; Nigra 2* 1888: *Portuguese–French–Greek–Slav distribution, to the Latin peoples from the southern French; *György* 1911: international distribution; *Szegedy* 1913: Southern Slav *57–59., 61.* and *67.* as sources of the *bella istoria: Pável* 1913 adds *62.,* and *Bajza* 1934 adds *53.; Entwistle* 1939: Portuguese–Southern Slav–Albanian–Greek–Romanian–Czech–Ukrainian distribution without bibliographical support, French origin (because the basic idea is French in character); *György* 1941: international dissemination; *Faragó* 1956: the Moldavian Hungarian from the Romanian Mizil Crai; *Istvánovits* 1959: sex-change plot distributed over the area extending from Georgia to France, Romanian–Georgian variant type of Balkan origin; *Pires de Lima* 1958; fifty Portuguese and a hundred Spanish variants; *Anderson* 1961; French origin of the theme, spread through the Spanish to the Portuguese; *Meletinsky* 1963, 336–37: the version with the sex-change (Balkan–Georgian) and Central Asian parallels. D. Vlr. 95. 1967. German variant from Gottschee of Slav origin.

For more details see *Vargyas* 1960 and 1967.

81. THE GIRL WITH THE GANDER

160.

1. Fël-mën-tëm a ma-gas-domb-ra Szé-pën szó-ló, szé-pën já-ró
Gan-gos gu-na-ram-mal. Gan-gos gu-na-ram-mal.

1. I went up the high ridge
   With my fair-spoken, nicely walking
   Stately gander.

2. The mayor's son passed that way
   With his golden mace,
   With his golden mace.

3. He struck my goosey dead,
   My fair-spoken, nicely walking
   Stately gander,
   Stately gander.

4. I am going to report, I am going to report
   My complaint,
   My complaint.

5. Good morning, mayor!
   Welcome, Fair Ilona!
   What is your complaint?
   What is your complaint?

6. I went up the high ridge
   With my fair-spoken, nicely walking
   Stately gander.

7. The mayor's son passed that way
   With his golden mace,
   With his golden mace.

8. He struck my goosey dead
   My fair-spoken, nicely walking
   Stately gander,
   Stately gander.

666

9. What do you want, Fair Ilona,
   For your fair-spoken, nicely walking
   Stately gander,
   Stately gander?

10. For its head, for its head
    A beautiful golden apple,
    A beautiful golden apple

11. For its eyes, for its eyes
    Golden eyeglasses,
    Golden eyeglasses.

12. For its feet, for its feet
    A golden wand,
    A golden wand.

13. For its wings, for its wings
    A golden fan,
    A golden fan.

14. For its feather, for its feather
    A nice eider pillow,
    And the mayor's son into the bargain!

Balatonederics (Zala county). Forty-nine-year-old female performer, Seemayer 1922.

161.

1. Ki - haj - tott-tam   a   li - bá - mat   Sej   haj   a   pást - ra.

Ar - ra jött   a   bi - ró   fi - a,   Meg - ha - jin -gál - ta.

Hát   még   az   ma - ga   meny-nyit   ér!

1. I turned out my goosey
   Hey-ho, to grass.
   The mayor's son came that way
   And he struck it dead.

2. Don't strike it dead, mayor's son,
   Don't strike my grey gander dead!
   For I go and tell your father
   All of my complaint.

3. Good morning, mayor,
   Hey-ho, good morning!
   Welcome, dear daughter,
   What's your complaint?

4. Your son has struck
   My grey gander dead.
   What do you demand for it, dear daughter?
   I will give it to you.

5. For its head, for its feet
   Two bushels of wheat.
   For its gizzard, for its liver
   Two golden apples.

6. And to think of its spotted, greyish tail,
   How much it alone was worth!
   Marry me, mayor's son,
   And I don't ask for other compensation!

Áj (Abaúj county). Performed by young people. Vargyas 1940 = Csanádi and Vargyas, 115.

162.

1. Is - ten jó nap, bi - ró gaz-da A kend há-zá - ban!

Fo - gadj is - ten, szép I - lo - na Az én há - zam-ban!

1. Good morning, mayor,
   To all your household!
   Welcome, Fair Ilona
   In my household!

2. What's the reason you have come, Fair Ilona,
   To see my household?
   I have come, mayor,
   To see your household:

3. Because I turned out my geese
   To grass in the green meadow.
   The mayor's son passed that way,
   And drove in the midst of them.

4. The mayor's son struck
   My stately gander dead.
   The mayor's son struck
   My stately gander dead...

5. What do you want, then, Fair Ilona,
   For your stately gander?
   I want, mayor,
   For my stately gander:

6. For each of its feathers
   As many coins of gold,
   For its wings that spread so nicely
   A bowl of gold,

7. For its nicely walking feet
   A spoon of gold,
   For its dawn-heralding throat
   A trumpet of gold...

8. There is no end to the wishes
   Of Fair Ilona.
   Therefore the gallows is the due
   Of the mayor's son.

9. Go, then, mayor's son,
   And hang yourself,
   On Fair Ilona's two arms
   You must hang yourself!

10. May your gallows be like
    A newly sprung rose,
    Her two feet, her two arms
    Shall be your gallows!

Sárospatak (Zemplén county). Before 1789 = Bartha 29.

At the bottom of the playfully intoned song we find a love symbol. The goose, in point of fact, symbolizes the girl, in a like way as a young man is often symbolized by his horse or ox. If the mayor's son has struck the goose dead—and with his "golden mace" at that—for which the girl demands compensation, it is clear that she wants the young man to make good the act of love that took place between them, by forcing out the marriage.

Divergences: In certain variants we have the following opening formulas: "If I turn out"... or "If she turns out...". In seven variants the mayor's son strikes the goose dead by a "golden mace", in one variant by a "poker", and in another one he "beheads" it. In five variants (and two fragments) it is not made clear whether or not the girl wants the mayor's son. On the other hand, one of the variants formulates her demand in the following manner: "I want every night the mayor's son to come in my bed!" (The continuation is a stanza borrowed from some other goose-song.) Sometimes they include two names, in which case the song is performed as a coupling song (tune singing together marrying couples). When the song is dramatized and performed with "casts", we encounter a recent custom spreading from village schools. In one instance the "son of a shepherd" is involved, but in all other variants the "mayor's" son is mentioned. There are closing formulas differing from the widespread 161, as well as from other published variants: "I give you my son, He may be yours! That's I want, mayor, And I don't want anything else!" and "There is no end to the wishes of Fair Ilona. Therefore the gallows is the due of the mayor's son!—May the gallows be like A newly sprung rose, My two arms shall be her two beautiful bow-rests, His gallows!"

Earliest provenience: 1789.

Dissemination: Four recordings originate from 1789, without specification of the site; two from the end of the eighteenth century, from the college-melodiary of Sárospatak (cf. Bartha 29). The songs of the melodiary may have resulted from the treasure of songs brought together from the most different places of the country by students learning at Sárospatak. Further, the variant published in *Hasznos Mulatságok* (Useful Entertainments), 1834, which agrees word for word with Erdélyi I, 175, recorded in Szatmár county; Zala county (Balatonederics, Gutorfölde, Zalagalsa); Baranya county (Boda, Hosszúhetény, Katádfa 2); Tolna county (Felsőireg); Komárom county (Nagymegyer); Győr county (Ménfőcsanak); Nógrád county (Bercel, Diósjenő, Ipolytölgyes); Heves county (Fedémes, Gyöngyöspata, Hevesaranyos); Borsod county (Mályinka, Szentistván 3); Gömör county (Péterfa); Abaúj county (Áj, Kéked, Újdiósgyőr); Zemplén county (Sárospatak 4); Ung county (Veskóc); Jász-Nagykun-Szolnok county (Jászárokszállás); Csanád county (Csanádapátfalva); Csongrád county ("Csongrád county"); Bihar county (Biharkeresztes, Körösnagyharsány 2); Szabolcs county ((Kótaj, Nyíregyháza, Nyírlugos, Nyírvasvári 3, Rétközberencs, "Szabolcs county" 1846); Udvarhely county (Bethlenfalva, Lengyelfalva); "Székely". Total 48.

Textual relationships with other ballads: none.

Tunes: 1. = No. 160, 2. = No. 161 (21 variants), 3. = No. 162. 4. and 6. = in three variants.

Versions in languages other than Hungarian (partial variants):

FRENCH: *1–92. Barbeau* 1947: on the basis of 92 Canadian variants he reconstructed a "critical text". *93–99. Rolland* I, 126a–f, II 126. *100. Tiersot, s. a.* II, 11. *101. Simon* 242. *102–105. Canteloube* III, 81, 215, IV, 218, 351. *106. Barbeau-Sapir* 118. *107. Beaurepaire* 163. *108. Ampère* 262 ("much in use at harvest times"). *109. Barbeau* 1937, 151.

ITALIAN: *110–114. Nigra* 61. *115. Marcoaldi,* 152, No. 2. *116. Ferraro* 1870, 92, No. 69.

DANISH: *117. DgF* 216.

We have no knowledge about the existence of any real correspondence. Something similar can be found in a French song about three nice ducks. Its opening motif is the following: "There is a nice pond behind our house..."; the indication of the place customary in love-songs betrays that a girl is involved. (Cf. "In my father's apple-garden; In the garden behind our house..." and the like.) In the pond three ducks are swimming. The prince is out hunting and shoots one of them with his *silver gun*. "O, prince, what have you done to me, you are hard-hearted indeed!" And there follows an enumeration of details, mentioning that blood is flowing from under the wing of the white duck, wheat is dropping from its tail, diamond from its two eyes, and gold and silver from its beak. (All this recalls the Hungarian heroine giving a list of her valuable parts.) Its feathers are scattered by wind; three ladies gather it and make a feather-bed in the field, so that those passing by may lie in it.

The Italian version stands much farther. Three swallows are coming from the sea. The most beautiful of them lights to bathe in the water, then sits on an oak to dry its feather. There comes a hunter who take the swallow for a blackbird and shoots it. The "beautiful one"—"la bella" begins to weep: "I am to die!".—"Don't weep so bitterly, beautiful girl, I have two brothers in France, one of them is a physician, the other a barber, and they will cure you and you will feel no pain."— "Next time we shall fly so as to shun the hunter", say the swallows.

The Danish story resembles the Hungarian in a different way. The queen invites Kirsten for a game of dice; the latter complains that a knight slighted her. The queen orders the knight to appear and wants to have him flayed. The knight entreating for mercy offers various presents in exchange for his life. The enumeration occupies eight stanzas. In the ninth he declares that he has run out all of his valuables and has nothing more to offer. At that, the queen thanks him for the presents and asks which one of her maids the knight wants to marry. "Kirsten", sounds the answer. They lay a silk-cloth down upon the ground, have the wedding feast arranged, and the lovers are happy.

As appears from the framing of these stories, there can be no agreement between them; at most a playful love-story is found in the songs with a similarly inspired formulation. Nevertheless, the bird-symbols of the French song and one or two typical motifs (golden mace, silver gun, connected with an apparent love affair) suggest a certain degree of interrelation. There are some Hungarian song fragments which seem to bring even more closer the two ballad types to one another. A Hungarian coupling song (MNT IV, Nos 104–105) with a foreign tune has the following text: "In the pond of Gyimes a golden duch is bathing. Comrade, take that gun and shoot that duck! You will have its feather, I shall have its red legs." (Each line repeated.) Number 104 runs the same, with lesser deviations; and No. 103 is also interesting for its words: "At a swiftly running brook There are three little birds. They are conversing: Where should they fly? One of them flew to Italy, The other flew to France." (Each line sung twice.) The mentioning of Italy and France may be reminiscent of mediaeval settlers in Hungary from those countries. Both songs preserve survivals of some ancient love-symbol. It is not impossible that we are dealing with the remains of a common ancient source from which also The Girl with the Gander has derived, through transformations.

On the basis of our present knowledge, all this is unsupported: a common origin cannot be demonstrated for lack of similarities. One thing is certain, however, and that concerns the strong intellectual relationship between the songs of the two nations.

Literature: *Dános* 1938: undoubtedly Hungarian in origin, "...not exempt from certain Slav influence", considering its foreign tune. (?)

82. THE EVENING IN THE SPINNING-HOUSE

163.

1. On one evening I went to the spinning-house,
   And began to play with the miller's lad.

2. O, I wish the bright morning star would not come up,
   So that there should be no ending to the pleasures of love.

3. Finally I still had to go home from the spinning-house,
   But mother also got up from her bed.

4. She took a twig of birch, and quick she was
   To slash it at my slender waist.

5. Even though the miller's lad were made of pure diamond,
   I should never go to the spinning-house.

"Udvarhelyszék". Kriza = MNGY XI, No. 12.

164.

Rubato ♪=108

1. He - gyen-föl - dön   já - ro - ga - tok va - la   Vi - rá - gecs-kát sze - de - ge - tek va - la.

Csin-csecs-kék-be   csin-csel - ge - tem va - la.   Bok-ré - tá - ba   kö - tö - ge - tem va - la.

1. I was roaming over hills and dales,
   Picking tiny flowers.
   Binding them into nice bunches,
   Making a wreath from them.

2. Girls, girls, my good girl-friends,
   Come to see me in the spinning-room at night,
   I give you my sister's wreath,
   Do bind a wreath for me!

3. Bind it from twigs, buds, white lilies,
   And from pure-pure roses.
   Let its flowers fall into my lap,
   Let its smell reach my heart!

4. Let it reach me, let it reach me and comfort me,
   May the good Lord not forsake me.
   And in the evening I went to the spinning-room
   And I met my sweetheart Jancsi.

5. He placed his right hand on my left shoulder,
   And he placed his left hand on my right shoulder.
   I told him all my grieves and sorrows,
   I told him all my grieves and sorrows.

6. Late in the evening I went home from the spinning-room,
   And lay down in my soft bed.
   Father took his slender cane
   And thrashed my slender waist thoroughly.

7. I walked out and into the stable,
   Turned out my slender bay,
   Harnessed it with the curved saddle,
   And started on the long way.

8. I started on the long way,
   The twilight fell on me in a hunting wood.
   I laid bed for me and my horse,
   For myself from leaves of oak,

9. For myself from leaves of oak,
   For my horse from its twigs and buds.
   I fall asleep with my first dream,
   I woke at beautiful, crimson dawn.

10. I looked up and looked at the branch above my head:
    Lo, there was a little turtle-dove!
    It held a slip of paper in its clutches,
    Into which my sweetheart wrote his will.

11. With its nails it scraped it,
    With its mouth it smiled.
    You would deserve, my kind father,
    You would deserve to be put to the yoke.

12. To be given nettle-stalk to eat,
    To be made to draw blocks of oak,
    Rather than to forbid me all these thing,
    You should rather allow me to keep a lover.

*Somoska (Moldavia). Performed by a sixty-seven-year-old man. 1960 = Kallós
1970, No. 117.*

While the briefer formulation of the theme (No. 163), and the rest of the more
concise variants, speak in favour of the righteous parents, although do so in a nicely
joking manner, the longer variants voice the revolt of lovers in the face of tyrannical

parents. The former concept is represented by five short Transylvanian texts (the shortest one contains both motifs), and the latter by the other Moldavian texts, which are longer.

Divergences: One of the variants gives a long lyrical confession into the girl's mouth, after the tête-à-tête with the miller's lad:

"All the mills
That can be found in this wide world,
Even though all their wheels
Were made of pure gold,
Even though their inner wheels
Were made of white silver
Grinding pure pearl,
Dropping precious coins,
I should not change for them
The miller's lad!
If the depths of the sea
Were an inkwell,
The waves of the sea
Were all ink,
If all the grass in the world
Were as many pens
All the stars of Heaven
Were scribes,
They could not describe
My love of the miller's lad and his love of me.

Earliest provenience: 1863?

Dissemination: Szolnok-Doboka county (Ördöngösfüzes); Maros-Torda county (Mezőbánd, "Sóvidék"); Udvarhely county ("Udvarhelyszék" 2); Moldavia (Klézse 2, Luizikalagor 3, Pokolpatak, Somoska 2). Total: 13.

Textual relationship with other ballads: 68. (The Marvellous Mill.)

Tunes: 1. = No. 164 in three variants.

The ballad has no foreign parallel. However, the love affair with the miller's lad represents a connecting link with mediaeval western folk poetry. The miller's figure occurs in several French love songs and jocular-erotic texts. (Cf. *Simon* 28, *Bladé* 1881–1882 III, 17 and 161.) Anyway, the central role of mills in peasant life is reflected by numerous old folk-texts.

Original Hungarian ballad, come down perhaps from mediaeval times.

83. THE BRIDE BROUGHT BACK

165.

1. Ma - gya - ró - si Ta - más, Mi - re há - za - so - dál?

Vaj - da el - föld - jé - re, Vaj - da le - á - nyá - ra.

1. Tamás Magyarósi, what did you marry on?
   On the voivod's plain, I married the voivod's daughter!

2. On the voivod's plain, I married the voivod's daughter,
   The voivod's daughter, Ilona Voivod!

3. As they were passing through a big forest,
   As the coach was going, the girl was weeping.

4. The youngest bridesmaid spoke up:
   Had she not been distressed, she would certainly not weep,
   But since she is distressed, believe me, she is weeping...

5. The coach was going on, the girl was weeping.
   The eldest bridesmaid spoke up:

6. I say, I say, Tamás Magyarósi,
   Give me, give me your fine linen shirt.

7. Your fine linen shirt for baby's cloth,
   Your silken handkerchief for navel bandage!

8. My servant, my dear servant, turn back my horses,
   Turn back my horses and my numberless wedding-guests.

9. As they reached the voivod's gate:
   Are you in, are you in, father voivod?
   I am in, I am in, my son Magyarósi!

10. What we took away, the same we have brought back,
    If you have taught her like this, you have to make use of her like this!

Csíkmadaras (Csík county). Bodon 1907 = SzNd No. 121.

Cf. Leader 263.
Divergence: The other variant (MNGY III, No. 7) contains interesting
details.

676

Where did you marry from, Tamás Magyarósi?
I married from Barassó.
I married old Mistress János Vajda's beautiful grown-up daughter,
Ilona Vajda!
The coach is going on, the girl is weeping,
Tamás Magyarósi is looking back at her.
Why are you weeping, why are you moaning, my beautiful betrothed bride?
Perhaps you think that I have not got
Twelve strong oxen and a strong ironed cart?
I don't think that, for I know that you have.
The eldest bridesmaid spoke up:
Give me, give me, Tamás Magyarósi,
Your fine linen shirt to make baby's cloth!
I don't give, I don't give my fine linen shirt
To make baby's cloth to this bloody whore!
The coach is going, the girl is weeping...
Perhaps you think that I have not got
A good herd of war-horses, a good flock of sheep?

The scene of the previous passage follows, after which the bride is brought back.

Textual relationships with other ballads: The situation of the bride nearing the moment of giving birth to a baby in the bridal procession is described in similar details as her dying in **13.** and **16.** "Perhaps you think that I have not got...": **46.**

The plot of this ballad is not to be found outside the Hungarian language area, although one of its features, notably the bridegroom's response to the father when returning the bride can be likened to the words of the Spanish ballad's Beguiled Husband who similarly brings back his wife to his father-in-law: "La ha cogido de la mano y a su padre la llavó. Ahi tiene usted a su hija, ensénela usted mejor." (In nine texts.) Or: "A su madre se la entrego; aqui tiene usté a su hija, eduquela usté mejor." (One variant.) (*Cossio-Solano* I, 215–227/120–129. "Taking by the hand, he led her to her father, viz. mother, saying: If you have brought her up like this, you should have taught her better!")

In point of fact, the ballad contains nothing new except this basic scene, which is preceded by the main scene of The Bride Dying in the Wedding Procession, with the difference that the wedding-guests report not on the bride dying but on her giving birth to a child.

The scornful wording—which presents a typical figure mocking it at the same time—is unmistakably aimed at making a laughing stock of the conventional marriages of the rich.

It seems that we are once again dealing with a ballad built up from western elements (perhaps with the contraction of two French ballad plots). As to its development, we have to think of the time when the Hungarians got acquainted with the French ballads, that is, of the fourteenth century.

BALLAD-LIKE OLD SONGS
Types 84–92.

84. THE WIFE WHO WAS SOLD AWAY

166.

1. Sze - gény le - gény vó-tam, s én meg-há- za - sod - tam, Jaj már gyer-meke- im nem vót mi - vel tart-sam.

El kell va - la vi - gyem   a fe - le - sé - ge - met
Jaj már a pi - ac - ra,   el-fog-jam á - rul - ni.

1. I was a poor lad, and got married.
   Alas, I had nothing to sustain my children with.
   I had to take my wife,
   Alas, and sell her at the market.

2. Alas, there came a rich boyar;
   Good morning, good morning, alas, poor man.
   Welcome, you rich boyar.
   Tell me what are you selling.

3. I am selling my wife.
   I have too many children to sustain.
   I have too many children to sustain.
   I have many children and I cannot give them to eat.

4. Then the boyar asked him:
   Tell me how much do you ask for her.
   A thousand, a thousand, and a hundred besides.
   Then the boyar counted down the money.

5. He says to the wife: come with me,
   I shall marry you as my wedded wife!
   He took her, he took her into his calm home,
   And he seated her at his drinking table.

6. Take a seat, take a seat at my table,
   Tell me, what name you have got,
   By what name shall I address you?
   I got the name Anna, daughter of Dán.

7. I was born in Transylvania.
   Then you must know that you are my sister.
   Then you must know that you are my sister.
   For I am Péter, son of Dán.

8. If this be the case, I will not marry you.
   Make speed and go home to your man.
   Make speed and go home to your children,
   So that you may raise them!

9. Brother, my dear brother, I would you take me
   To town and sell me again,
   Rather than take me back into that great poverty!
   I would rather be sold!

10. Sister, my dear sister, you shall go back,
    For I give you as much money as I have given your husband,
    So that you may raise your children.
    And indeed, her brother started back with her.

11. Alas, her man was walking in the courtyard,
    And his little son asked him every now and then:
    Father, dear father, where is my dear mother?
    At once the boyar appeared and greeted them.

12. Good morning, good morning, alas, poor man.
    I have brought back your wife.
    Alas, she is my sister, and I cannot keep her
    As a wife in my home.

13. I have no money, says the poor man,
    To restore you what you had given me.
    I don't want any money, for I give you as much again;
    I give you as much again as I had given you before.

14. Then the children embraced
    And kissed their mother with many kisses,
    And they rejoiced to have a dear mother again,
    To have a dear mother to take care of them.

"Well, you know, many years ago it was customary to sell away wives for money."

Lészped (Moldavia). Performed by a woman of fifty-five. Kallós 1957.
   Boyar = landlord.
   This ballad has been recorded in one variant.

Textual relationship with other ballad: none.
Versions in languages other than Hungarian:
ROMANIAN: *1. Amzulescu* 287. *2. Bud* 8. *3. Țiplea* 17. *4. Brăiloiu* 102 (in Hungarian: *Moldovan, 3* and *Vulcanu,* 17).
   SOUTHERN SLAV: *5. Vuk* I, No. 725. *6–7. HNP* VI, Nos 28–29. *8. HNP* X, 162, No. 15. *9. Kuba* 195. *10. Žganec* 1950, No. 259. *11. Prodanović* 221.
   BULGARIAN: *12–14. Tsitselkova* 219–221. *15. Ivanov* 229. *16. Vatev* 189. *17–18. SbNU* 16–17 *Materialy,* 92, No. 9 and 98, No. 1.
   GREEK: *19. Lüdecke–Megaş* 76. Cf. *Baud–Bovy* 1936, 242.

682

The story of the indebted husband who sells his wife to his brother-in-law is known throughout the Balkan peninsula. The Southern Slav variants which may come into consideration differ in two points from the Hungarian: first, the uniform beginning motif, according to which the man is owner of nine vineyards, secondly, he first wants to sell his mother, and only at the instigation of the latter is he willing to part with his wife; these have been omitted from the Hungarian variant. Since only one single Moldavian Csángó text has occurred in the Hungarian language area, the story is borrowed, beyond doubt, from the Romanians.

Literature: Putilov 1965, 114–120, unreasonably draws the song into the sphere of "captive" and "Turk" themes as a historical ballad.

85. THE DEAD BRIDEGROOM

167.

A young girl's sweetheart, who was a soldier, fell in the battle-field. The girl would have liked to see her sweetheart once more. Therefore she went to a witch to ask for advice. This said to her: "On Good-Friday's night walk out, daughter, to the cemetery and find your sweetheart's grave, break a small piece of wood from his cross and boil it in smash at about eleven o'clock. When the smash begins to bubble, your sweetheart will appear." The girl did what she was told to. The smash was bubbling, and someone was tapping at the door:

1. E - ressz be már I - lo - nám, Én I - lo - nám, szép ró - zsám!
Nem e - reszt - lek, nem én! Nem vagy az én ró - zsám.

1. Let me in, my Ilona,
   My Ilona, my beautiful rose!
   I will not let you in, not I,
   For you are not my sweetheart!
Still she let him in in the end.

2. Prepare a dish for supper, my Ilona,
   My Ilona, my beautiful rose!
   I will not prepare a dish, not I,
   For you are not my sweetheart!
Still she prepared it in the end.

3. Lay the table, my Ilona,
   My Ilona, my beautiful rose!
   I will not lay the table, not I,
   For you are not my sweetheart!
Still she laid the table in the end.

4. Give me to eat, my Ilona,
   My Ilona, my beautiful rose!
   I will not give you to eat, not I,
   For you are not my sweetheart!
Still she gave him to eat in the end.

684

5. Take a seat beside me, my Ilona,
   My Ilona, my beautiful rose!
   I will not take a seat, not I,
   For you are not my sweetheart!

Still she sat beside him in the end.

6. Kiss me, my Ilona,
   My Ilona, my beautiful rose!
   I will not kiss you, not I,
   For you are not my sweetheart!

Still she kissed him in the end.

7. Come with me, my Ilona,
   My Ilona, my beautiful rose!
   I will not go with you, not I,
   For you are not my sweetheart!

Still she started out with him in the end. But as they were leaving the room, Ilona looked at the feet of his sweetheart and saw that he had cloven hooves. She was very much frightened and began to sing:

8. Oh, cocks, crow,
   Angels, blow your horns!
   For I am ill,
   And I am perhaps dying!

The devil said: "You did well to call the angels, otherwise I would have torn you apart at once."
     To wit, it was the devil that took on the form of her sweetheart.
     Performed by an aged wine-dresser's wife.
Szekszárd (Tolna county). Ethn 1908, 297.

168.

Once upon a time there was a girl who had a bridegroom. But the bridegroom soon died. The girl was lamenting him bitterly. She stood in the gateway, and there she was lamenting him. A wise-woman passing by asked the girl why she was crying. She told her that her sweetheart had died, and she could not converse with him any longer. "You must not be sorry for that—says the wise-woman. Go to the cemetery and bring a cross from there. And you must boil it in a big kettle under the funnel at midnight. The girl did as she was told to. At midnight, her bridegroom appeared indeed on back of St. Michael horse (bier). He told the girl to see him out to the cemetery. And the girl saw him out. On the way, the young man spoke up:

   Aye, how beautifully the moon shines,
   And here walks a live body with a dead one.
   Are you afraid of me, my sweet rose?
   I am not afraid at all in your company.

They were going on, they were walking near the cemetery, when the young man spoke up once more:

> Aye, how beautifully the moon shines,
> And here walks a live body with a dead one.
> Are you afraid of me, my sweet rose?
> I am not afraid at all in your company.

By that time they walked inside the cemetery. The young man sank into the grave, and to make sure that the girl should not escape, he fastened his belt to the girl's hand. At that time the girl was already in a fright. She tied the string to the cross and ran away as swiftly as she could. She ran into a house, in which a dead body was laid out under the table. The girl hid beside the dead body. But the young man in the grave was pulling at the string all in vain, because the girl did not go in after him. Finally he pulled down the cross. The young man was very angry finding that the girl had escaped. He ran after her. The girl was just crossing the door. When the young man reached the house, he called in through the window: "Dead brother-in-law, give me the live body!" Alas, my God! The girl was very much frightened, and began to pray wholeheartedly, so that she would not be given out by the dead body. The dead body answered: "I would fein give her out, only I cannot stir." The girl prayed and prayed, so that she may not be given out by the dead body. Once more the young man called in: "Dead brother-in-law, give out the live body!" The dead body once more answered: "I would fein give her out, only I cannot stir." The clock of the tower was just striking one. The young man once more called in: "Dead body, give out the live body!" Now the dead body did not answer at all. Then the young man called in once again: "It is well to you, girl, that my hour is over, otherwise you would already be lying by my side!"

Jászfényszaru (Jász-Nagykun-Szolnok county). Zoltán Velsinszky = Ethn 1928, 5.

Divergences: When the bridegroom calls in to the dead body, asking for the girl, the former shivers at the first word, sits up at the second, and opens the door at the third; the girl is only saved by the cock-crow.

Apart from 167., all the variants have only three lines of verse:

> The moon shines beautifully,
> The live body is riding together with the dead,
> Are you not afraid, my sweet rose?

These lines are variegated in the different texts. No more than this verse fragment is published by *Kálmány* from Egyházaskér and MNGY I from Csurgó.

Earliest provenience: 1865.
Dissemination: Somogy county (Csurgó); Tolna county (Szekszárd); Veszprém county (Somló region); Nógrád county? (Palots Folk Poems); Jász-Nagykun-Szolnok county (Jászfényszaru); the Szeged region. Total: 6.
Textual relationships with other ballads: none.
Tune: Only 167. was recorded with tune, and even that probably erroneously.
Versions in languages other than Hungarian:
GERMAN: *A.* (all variants are in verse): *1.* E–B 197. *2. Hruschka–Toischer*, 93, No. 5. *3.* Ethn 1892, 35, Banate (Yugoslavia). *4. Hauffen* 54. *B.* (stories in prose with verse insets): *5. Schlosser* 13

(Unter-Steiermark). *6–9. Vernaleken*, 76–79; Nos 6–8, from Lower-Austria, No. 9 from Moravia. *10–12. Schmidt* 1902, 226 (the environment of Linz). *13.* EMU 1898, 341 (Old-Buda).

POLISH: *14. Kolberg* Lud 14 (1881), No. 41. *15. Treichel*, 144. *16. Wollner* quotes *Zamarski*, 121.

UKRAINIAN: *17–20. Wollner* quotes *Chubinsky,* 119 and 121, and two texts from *Dragomanov.*

CZECH–MORAVIAN: *21–22. Wollner* quotes two texts from Erben. *23–24. Šusil* 112/242 and Nova zbirka 14/2337.

SLOVAK: *25–26.* Slov. Sp. II, 285, and III, 278 (fargment). *27.* SL'P II, No. 605.

SOUTHERN SLAV: *28–30. Štrekelj* 61–63. *31. Žganec* 1952, 84. *Kuhač* 506. (Sung variants). *33. Wollner*, 256 (prose tale). (*Kumer* 389 sung var.).

ENGLISH: *34. Child* 272.

DANISH: *35.* DgF 90.

FRENCH: *36. Sébillot* 1881, 197.

Ever since *Bürger* wrote his world-famous ballad of Lenore, the story has been known to exist in three versions in the German-speaking areas: (a) a version in verse from which the riding scene of the dead body is missing; (b) another version in verse which includes the riding scene, this being the true formulation of the Lenore theme (cf. *4.*); (c) a prose tale with insets in verse (cf. *5–13.*). This latter has Austria and Slovakia as its dissemination area, and this is the form that exists exclusively in the Hungarian language area. Closest relationship can be discovered with the Austrian version. The degree of similarity is well demonstrated by the following Austrian tale.

In the village of Pettauerfeld there lived once a young man and a girl who loved each other dearly. The lad had to join the army, and it was hard for them to part with each other. They make an oath that not even death can separate them. The one that will have to die first will let the other know about it.

Soon war broke out, and the young man was taken to a distant land. The girl heard no tidings of him for a long time. She thought he must have fallen in action. One day she exclaimed: "I should like to see him once more, whether he is alive or dead, just once more I should like to see him!" That night she heard someone knocking at her window. When she opened the window, she saw a white knight sitting on a white steed. He extended his arms, saying: "Here am I. Bind your valuables in a bundle and come with me!" The girl thought it was her sweetheart that came home and followed him at once. The young man seated her on back of his grey horse, and swift as wind they ran away. As they were passing through the village, the young man asked:

The moon, the moon shines bright,
The dead body, the dead body rides fast.
My dearest, are you afraid?

He put the same question in the next village, and also in the third. Finally they reached a cemetery. The gate opened by itself before them. The rider went to a grave which was open, and told the girl to throw her bundle into it and descend. The girl was reluctant, saying she was a stranger in the region and cannot know her way about, and asked the young man to lead the way. The dead body agreed, whereupon the girl jumped off the horse and ran fast as she could out of the cemetery and into the next house. She barred the door and hid herself in the farthest nook behind the stove. But the house was the mortuary of the graveyard. The girl looking round beheld a corpse on the bier. At that moment there was a knocking at the door, and the girl heard her sweetheart's voice: "Dead body, give me out the live body!" Upon this, the corpse extended one of his arms. Once again the sweetheart exclaimed: "Dead body, give me out the live one!" Upon this, the corpse sat up. At the sweetheart's third request, the corpse stood up and snatched at the girl. In that very moment the clock struck twelve and the cock crowed. The corpse at once returned to the bier. At the second crow he sat down, and at the third it was dumb and dead again. Immediately the admonition was heard from outside: "This has been a lesson to teach you that the dead must be let alone in peace. If the cock did not crow, I should have torn you to pieces!" Then everything sank into silence.

For a long time the girl could not stir for fear. Finally she crawled out of her hiding nook and staggered out of the mortuary. The land and the people were strange to her. Although the ride did not seem to take a long time, she found herself in a strange country, where her sweetheart was killed. Trembling in all her parts, she lay down in a rye-field, and soon she died.

The story follows the same strict order of arrangement in *7., 9–10, 12–13*. The last-mentioned variant stands the nearer to the Hungarian because it lays out a brief folk-text in authentic vernacular phrases, instead of a mere summary of the content. Even the shortest Hungarian variants have their exact correspondences in the Austrian material. (Cf. *6., 8.,* and *11.*)

The Slav versions are much farther from the Hungarian. The deviation is greatest in relation with the Ukrainian variants which swell the story enormously and present the German and Hungarian plot deprived of their formula-like turns. Thus the motif of the very important passage about the question set in the moonlight is dissolved into a dialogue in a scene burdened with the figures of dancing corpses: "Why do you think that I am afraid?" "Is your country still far?" "There you can see its chimneys." "O they are only tombstones!"—and so on. In one of the variants the sweetheart does not appear knocking at the girl's window but the girl mourning him in the cemetery arouses him from his grave; still they ride, after such preliminaries, to the *cemetery,* and the next day the girl finds herself in her own village. Another example: the formula of "Dead body, give out the live one to me!" sounds like this: "Hey, comrade, I say, give the woman to me, because I have brought her from a seven hundred verst distance to this place!" Or: "Good evening, how are you..." is the opening phrase of the bargain. In other instances we find three corpses quarrelling with the bridegroom about the girl. In another, the bridegroom catches the girl by the foot and tears her apart.

According to the Polish version, the girl begins to tremble with fear during the dialogue already. The detail in verse reads as follows: "People and cocks are sleeping, while the dead bodies ride with the live ones round the world." In this case the girl is not asked directly if she is afraid, instead the narrative intimates to us that the girl is half-dead for fear. The girl throws pearls of her headgear at the corpse rising in the house, to make the corpse fall back on the bier, and says to her sweetheart that stones are falling on the forehead of the corpse. In other tales, the girl flying in the air tears herself out of the arms of her sweetheart and falls into a chimney; in this case the bridegroom does not ask the corpse for help, but applies to inanimate objects, a broomstick or a bunch of hemp, etc. Another solution is that the girl flees into a hospital where she finds a dead "dziad" (a student, clerk, or precentor) waked over by two live bodies, and when the dead "dziad" wants to rise at request by the bridegroom, the live bodies order him to recline.

The Moravian and Slovak verse variants belong to the German types *1–3*. and have no connection whatever with the Hungarian. The same holds for most of the Southern Slav variants. (Cf. *28–32*.) Only the prose tale with insets in verse (*33*.) shows some similarity to the Hungarian and Austrian versions, containing many corresponding details. As against these, there is an important difference inasmuch as the dead lying on the bier answers the bridegroom's request by the following warning: "Dead body, leave the live ones in peace!"—that is to say, it offers protection to the girl.

The English "Suffolk Miracle" with all its broadside formulation, further the Danish and the French superstitious stories are so distant from the Hungarian ballad-like story as to frustrate any attempt at comparison.

As appears from the foregoing, the Hungarian texts are closely related with the Austrian and Hungarian–German texts. As a rule, a prose tale with verse insets should be regarded as a dissolution in prose of a one-time fully verse composition. If, therefore, we can find a language area in which the purely versified form occurs parallel with the mixed forms, this should be taken for the original country of the story. Accordingly, the German formulation provided the point of origin and by no means the Slav versions which ramify in many directions. As to the Hungarian version, undoubtedly a German descent has to be reckoned with, and in this case probably through the intermediary of the German-speaking population of Hungary. Since the narrative has spread throughout Hungary in the form of a superstitious tale in prose with verse insets, it is very likely—in spite of the fact that one of the variants has been recorded together with a tune—that a full verse form has never lived in the Hungarian language area. Consequently, we cannot take it for a true ballad in the body of Hungarian balladry.

Literature: Vargyas 1964.

86. THE DEAD BROTHER

169.

Parlando ♩= 88

1. Egy asz - szony-nak ki - lenc fi - a, Ki - lenc fi - a, egy le - á - nya.

Egy asz - szony-nak ki - lenc fi - a, Ki - lenc fi - a, egy le - á - nya.

1. A woman had nine sons,
   Nine sons and one daughter.
   A woman had nine sons,
   Nine sons and one daughter.

2. She married away her nine sons,
   And she sold away her only daughter.
   She married away her nine sons,
   And sold away her only daughter.

3. The day was come,
   People came to ask for her daughter's hand.
   The day was come,
   People came to ask for her daughter's hand.

4. They came from a foreign land,
   She went to her eldest son.
   They came from a foreign land,
   She went to her eldest son.

5. My son, my son, my dear son,
   People came to ask for my daughter's hand.
   My son, my son, my dear son,
   People came to ask for my daughter's hand.

6. They came from a foreign land,
   Shall we give her to them, or shall we not?
   They came from a foreign land,
   Shall we give her to them, or shall we not?

7. Shall we give her, or shall we not?
   We may not see her again.
   Shall we give her, or shall we not?
   We shall not see her again.

690

8. Alas, we shall not give her, dear mother,
   We shall not see her again.
   Alas, we shall not give her, dear mother,
   We shall not see her again.

9. She went to her middle son,
   My son, my son, my dear son
   She went to her middle son,
   My son, my son, my dear son.

10. People came to ask for my daughter's hand.
    They came from a foreign land.
    People came to ask my daughter's hand,
    They came from a foreign land.

11. Shall we give her, my dear son?
    Shall we give her, or shall we not?
    Shall we give her, my dear son?
    Shall we give her, or shall we not?

12. Alas, we shall not give her, my dear mother,
    We shall never see her again.
    Alas, we shall not give her, my dear mother,
    We shall never see her again.

13. She went to her youngest son,
    My son, my son, my dear son.
    She went to her youngest son,
    My son, my son, my dear son.

14. People came to ask for my daughter's hand,
    They came from a foreign land.
    People came to ask for my daughters hand,
    They came from a foreign land.

15. Shall we give her, or shall we not.
    We shall not see her again.
    Shall we give her, or shall we not,
    We shall not see her again.

16. Let us give her, my dear mother,
    We shall give her, my dear mother.
    Let us give her, my dear mother,
    We shall give her, my dear mother.

17. A big cloud came
    And lifted her daughter.
    A big cloud came
    And lifted her daughter.

18. She was taken away, she was taken away
    Never to be seen again.

She was taken away, she was taken away
Never to be seen again.

19. The mother laid a curse
    On her youngest son.
    The mother laid a curse
    On her youngest son.

20. May God work it, son,
    That not even the earth shall take you in.
    May God work it, son,
    That not even the earth shall take you in.

21. The day was come
    When her youngest son died.
    The day was come
    When her youngest son died.

22. They took him to the cemetery,
    Not even the earth did take him in.
    They took him to the cemetery,
    Not even the earth did take him in.

23. The dead body started out on the way,
    The dead body started out on the way.
    The dead body started out on the way,
    The dead body started out on the way.

24. He was going, he was going,
    Wandering over fields and woods,
    He was going, he was going,
    Wandering over fields and woods,

25. Until he arrived at a big house.
    That house was turning round and round.
    He arrived at a big house,
    That house was turning round and round.

26. No door was seen on it,
    Neither a door, nor a window.
    No door was seen on it,
    Neither a door, nor a window.

27. His sister beheld him;
    The palace was turning round and round.
    His sister beheld him;
    The palace was turning round and round.

28. What are you looking for?
    They will take your head.
    What are you looking for?
    They will take your head.

29. Come home with me.
    He lifted her on his back.
    Come home with me,
    He lifted her on his back.

30. They started back,
    They are going, they are going,
    They had started back,
    They are going, they are going.

31. Over big woods, over large fields,
    Over big woods, over large fields,
    Over big woods, over large fields,
    Over big woods, over large fields.

32. And the birds all say:
    Look, how a dead body carries a live body.
    And the birds all say:
    Look, how the dead body carries a live body.

33. Look, how the dead body carries a live body,
    Look, how the dead body carries a live body.
    Look, how the dead body carries a live body,
    Look, how the dead body carries a live body.

34. What do the birds say?
    Don't listen to them.
    What do the birds say?
    Don't listen to them.

35. Don't listen to the little birds,
    For it is not true what they say.
    Don't listen to the little birds,
    For it is not true what they say.

36. He went to his old mother's house,
    He took home his sister.
    He went to his old mother's house,
    He took home his sister.

37. When they arrived home,
    He went to the cemetery.
    When they arrived home,
    He went to the cemetery.

38. And the earth did now take him in,
    And the earth did now take him in,
    And the earth did now take him in,
    And the earth did now take him in.

Magyarfalu (Moldavia). Performed by a woman of forty-four. Faragó and Jagamas, 1954, No. 17.

A single Moldavian Csángó recording of the story is known to exist from 1954.

Versions in languages other than Hungarian:
ROMANIAN: *1. Amzulescu* 26. (lists 21 variants from the Romanian language area). *2. Tocilescu,* 139. *3. Corcea,* 41. *4. Ţiplea,* 15. *5. Giuglea,* 253. (In Hungarian translation by *Kádár,* 39.)
SOUTHERN SLAV: *6. Vuk* II, No. 9. (Hungarian translation by *Csuka* 41.) *7–8.* HNP I, 29–30 (plus variants and abstracts in Dodatak, pp. 514–17). French translation: *Dozon,* 321.
ALBANIAN: *31. Dozon,* 327 (in French translation).
BULGARIAN: *32.* A–V, No. 67. *33.* SbNU 38. *Arnaudov* 2. *34. Khachanovsky* 48. *35.* SbNU 42 (1936), No. 144. *36–112.* SbNU 13–15, *Smirnov* (77 variants). *113.* Izv. na Etnogr. Muz. VI, 117. *114–118. Stoin* 1928, 554, Nos 1580–81 and 3629–30. *119–121. Bukoreshliev* 198, 362, 441. *122.* SbNU 41, No. 407. *123. Stoilov* I–II, 25. (French translation: *Dozon,* 319.)
GREEK: *124. Baud-Bovy* 1936, 162–68; *Lübke,* 254 (= Firmenrich 53, *Dozon,* 324.)

The theme of this ballad enjoys a wide popularity in the whole of the Balkans, being Greek in origin according to scholarly opinions. The Csángó text shows a fair agreement with the Romanian formulation which has the following content in *Amzulescu*'s summary account: A woman has nine sons and a daughter. Suitors arrive, but the mother does not want to let her daughter to be taken away. She gives her consent only when her eldest son promises to bring home the daughter every year. Epidemic carries away all her sons. The mother, in utter despair, invokes her eldest son who persuaded her to marry the girl. The son comes out of the grave and, riding on his coffin, carries home his sister in the dead hours of the night. No sooner than he disappears can the girl understand what has happened to her; the brother goes back to the grave. Upon the girl's entreaties, the mother allows her to enter the house. Recognition follows, and both mother and daughter die.

The Csángó texts incorporate certain fabulous elements, such as the motif of the turning castle well known from Hungarian folk tales, further some details of "The Dead Bridegroom" (The dead body carries the live one).

Since this ballad is extant in Hungarian only among the Csángós, there can be no doubt regarding its Romanian origin. It must be a recent borrowing.

Literature: Baud-Bovy 1936, 162–68; *Entwistle* 1939, 86: Greek, Romanian, Bulgarian and Serbian versions; the English Suffolk miracle derives from the Greek version; *Vrabie* 1966, 108–43.

87. THE GIRL AND THE RIDER

170.

On the ridge of a mountain
A girl and a young man are going.
The young man is riding a horse,
But the girl is going by foot.
5. Picking flowers here and there,
Now a small one, now a big one,
The girl says to the young man:
Put me on back of the horse,
For if I have to walk long
10. I grow tired and I shall die.
But the young man says:
I cannot put you on back of the horse,
For my horse is of a small kind,
I myself can hardly sit on it.
15. The girl says to him, weeping:
If you forsake me, sweetheart,
May the Lord be heavy on you!
Bring to an end what you have thought out,
Deceiving me like this!
20. I did not do anything else,
Only I cut a tress of your hair
And putting it into the water,
I said the following curse:
As your hair is drifted by the water,
25. So your heart shall burn for me.
I have had enough of your falsehood,
May the Holy Trinity be heavy on you!
On top of this mountain,
Sitting in the saddle on your horse,
30. Where your passage is roughest,
May your blood flow in streams,
May your horse stumble,
May it cast you down upon the ground!

Lozsád (Hunyad county). Performed by a 76-year-old female. Faragó 1965 I, 388.

A single, tuneless recording is known of this ballad-like verse.

Versions in languages other than Hungarian: Amzulescu 245.

This piece is an occasional borrowing from the Romanians. It has the following plot: A soldier is harnessing his horse for a ride. The girl asks him to take her on the ride, promising him to be a faithful companion and a loving sweetheart. The soldier refuses the girl, and she lays a curse on him. The oath is effective.

The formulation of the Hungarian text shows that the verse is a translation not yet fully adapted to the traditional ballad style. This circumstance is also brought out by its isolated standing. It is a recent borrowing.

Literature: Faragó 1969.

88. KING ISTVÁN OF HUNGARY

171.

1. Ma - gyar Ist - ván ki - rály, Or - szá - gunk is - táp - ja

Fel - kö - té a kard - ját, Vé-ve trom-bi - tá - ját.

1. King István of Hungary,
   The patron of our country,
   Girded on his sword,
   And took his trumpet.

2. He went to the gate,
   Stepped out into the courtyard,
   And proclaimed, turning towards the East,
   That by sunset

3. All should gather together,
   All his sons,
   All his sons,
   All his brave warriors.

4. And they gathered together,
   And he equipped them with weapons.
   And so he started to the battle-field,
   To meet the enemy.

"I forget where he had gone and what he did. Whom he fought, I forget. It is a long time since I heard this, I was a small child then. They sang it in the spinning-house. Those women have all died since."

Luizikalagor (Moldavia). Performed by a man of 71 who was blind and illiterate. 1958. Kallós = Kallós 1958, No. 1.

Divergences: Another variant of twenty stanzas seems to be a complete story, although it does not present a round story about "King István". Its extemporized formulation, as shown below, bears little resemblance to the verse recorded from Luizikalagor.

1. King István has gone
   To the wars,
   He has gone to face the Turks
   In the wars.

2. King István's foot
   Has been shot.
   Therefore he has gone home,
   Into his calm country.

After this, he asks his mother to let him in, because the Turks are nearing, but first the mother does not recognize him; and when she does, she sends her son back to the wars, for "Alas, in the interest of our country You must suffer death!" The king gathers together his soldiers and cuts the Turks to the last man so that blood-streams are flooding. Once more he asks his mother for admission. His wife "plays him round", but his mother lets him in. Then he puts on his best attire and goes to church.

19. Then the bells
    Were tolled with loud roar:
    Roar, you bells,
    Bow, you flags!
20. Oh, King István
    Is coming to church!
    To him, all the flags
    Bowed low.

The collector adds that the ballad speaks about Stefan cel Mare (Steven the Great), Prince of Moldavia. The old informant stated that she had translated the verse from Romanian, although she did not speak Romanian well, and at the request of the collector she was unable to recite one single Romanian stanza correctly, she only recalled threadbare fragments in prose. Nevertheless, the apparently improvised, somewhat obscure text shows no agreement with No. 171. On the other side, the published fragment seems to be more well-formed, suggesting an earlier life in tradition. On account of the identity of names, the phrase "patron of our country" had been borrowed from the song about "King St. István" of Hungary; this circumstance also refers to some earlier traditional life of the song.

Earliest provenience: 1958.
   Dissemination: Moldavia (Luizikalagor, Lészped). Total: 2.
   Textual relationship with other ballads: The improvised text recorded at Lészped includes scenes known from plots based on the motif of non-recognition of relatives; of. first of all Type **30**.
   Tunes: See the tune of the other text.

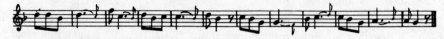

Borrowed from Romanian folklore or popular layer of songs, probably in recent time.

89. THE RIVALRY OF FLOWERS

172.

1. Ké - szek ve - sze - ked - ni   Szép bu - za - me - ző - be

Há - rom- fé - le   vi - rág,   Há - rom - fé -le   vi - rág.

1. Lo, they are ready to contest
   In the beautiful corn-field.
   Three kinds of flowers they are,
   Three kinds of flowers they are.

2. Lo, they are ready to contest
   In the beautiful corn-field,
   In the beautiful corn-field,
   Three kinds of flowers they are.

3. The first to begin was
   The beautiful corn-flower:
   I am the most beautiful, the most beautiful
   Among all of you.

4. For people pick me,
   They place me on the altar
   As the sainted body of Jesus Christ,
   And there they adore me.

5. The second to begin was
   The beautiful vine-flower:
   I am the most beautiful, the most beautiful
   Among all of you.

6. For people pick me,
   Place me on the altar
   As the sainted blood of Jesus Christ,
   And there they adore me.

7. The third to begin was
   The beautiful rose-flower:

I am the lovliest
Among all of you.

8. For people pick me,
   Make a wreath of me,
   Young men and young girls
   Give me as present to their sweethearts.

Bogyiszló (Pest county). Performed by a male singer of sixty. Lajtha 1922 = MF 2632.

173.

1. In the corn-field
   There are three kinds of flower.
   The first flower is
   The beautiful corn-flower.

2. The second flower is
   The beautiful vine-flower.
   The third flower is
   The beautiful pink-flower.

3. There spoke up
   The beautiful corn-flower:
   I am the most beautiful, I am the kindest
   Among all of you,

4. For people will take me
   To the altar,
   And there they name me
   Sainted body of Jesus Christ.

5. There spoke up
   The beautiful vine-flower:
   I am the most beautiful, I am the kindest
   Among all of you,

6. For people will take me
   To the corner of the altar,
   And there they name me
   Sainted blood of Jesus Christ.

700

7. There spoke up
   The beautiful pink-flower:
   I am the most beautiful, I am the kindest
   Among all of you,

8. For people will pick me,
   Make a wreath of me,
   Young men and young girls
   Put me by their hats.
   They wear me proudly,
   They are thrown into Hell.

(The last two lines are rarely added.)
Kászonújfalu (Csík county). Performed by a woman of sixty. Kodály 1912 = Sz.Nd. 36.

Divergences: The variants of Nyitra county surviving in largest numbers are all connected to the "fire-leaping feast", customarily practised on mid-summer nights. We present below the earliest complete text published, together with the description of the custom as observed at Kolon, by Kubinyi and Vahot III, 1854, p. 29 (cf. MNT II, p. 255).

Three kinds of flower are contesting.

> My flower, I shall go with you,
> My flower, I shall not part with you!

The one kind of flower is the beautiful vine-flower.
Do not contest with me, beautiful corn-flower.
For all this wide world lives on me!

> My flower, I shall go with you,
> My flower, I shall not part with you!

There spoke up the beautiful corn-flower:
Do not contest with me, beautiful rose-flower,
For people will serve a mass with me!

> My flower, I shall go with you,
> My flower, I shall not part with you!

Do not contest with me, beautiful violet-flower,
For the girls adorn themselves with me!

> My flower, I shall go with you,
> My flower, I shall not part with you!

(The majority of the Nyitra variants are available under Nos 254–259 of MNT II.)

Earliest provenience: 1848.
Dissemination: Nyitra county (Ghymes 7, Kolon 4); Pest county (Bogyiszló); Maros-Torda county ("Marosszék"); Csík county (Gyergyócsomafalva, Kászonújfalu); Brassó county (Krizba 2). Total: 17.

Textual relationship with other ballads: none.

Tunes: 1. = No. 172; 2. = No. 173 (two variants); 3. has been recorded in seven variants (**Example** 1. in MNT II, Nos 254–259); 4–6. occur in one single recording each.

Partially relevant versions in languages other than Hungarian:
GERMAN: *1–15.* E.–B 1066–1080.
UKRAINIAN: *16–17. Golovatsky* III/2, 3, Nos 1–2.
ROMANIAN: *18–23. Viciu* 137–152. *24–25. Bartók* 1923, Nos 15–16 (all colindas).
SOUTHERN SLAV: *26. Kuhač* 440. *27–28.* Ist.pj. II, Nos 32 and 134. *29. Geseman* 7. *30. Vuk* I, No. 619.
BULGARIAN: *31. Vatev* 414. *32. Stoin* 1928, No. 2081.
SPANISH: (recorded exclusively from Spanish Jews re-settled in the Balkans; translation from Greek). *33. Armistead–Silvermann* 1968, No. 395.

This song, which can be termed only with reservation as a ballad, represents a folk-version of the mediaeval genre called *certamen. Sándor Eckhardt* referred to Aristophanes (Clouds) as to the first literary provenience of the theme. The Romans called the type of song by the name *comparatio,* and in mediaeval Latin it occurred under the denominations of *certamen, conflictus* and *disputatio.* Provençal, French and Italian literature also produced specimens of this song. The dispute of the flowers found its first formulation in the verse of fifty hexametres by the ninth-century Irish monk Sedulius Scottus, who wrote about the contest of the rose and the lily, and Spring as a benevolent arbiter between the two. The theme reverberated in thirteenth-century rhymed *vagans* poems, composed by students, about the contest of the violet and the rose, the latter being placed on tables of kings, or on the altars of cathedrals, and seen in children's hands or at the caps of young men. In the *vagans* songs, it is again an arbiter that makes peace between the contesting parties. We are also indebted to *S. Eckhardt* for his having pointed to similar debates occurring in French folklore in the form of songs about the rivalry of wine and water, the like of which came up in Hungarian students' poems of the seventeenth and eighteenth centuries. He takes it for certain that in Hungary the theme of contesting flowers had disseminated through the mediation of Latin *vagans* poems. This supposition seems to be corroborated by the evidence of Romanian colindas (winter-solstice greeting-songs) which are formulated in a similar manner (as emphasized also by *Eckhardt*). He provided the text of *19.*, which in English translation reads as follows.

"Dear sun has risen, shining over all lands, roads and ways. There above, in the heavenly court, there is a nice custom, originating from Jesus Christ himself, for there are broad tables and burning candles. There are arm-chairs placed round the tables. Laid across the tables, there are three small flowers, three blades of grass. They are slighting each other: Which one is worthiest of them? The good Lord sitting in Heaven is looking at them, and speaks to them.—The corn-flower speaks well, saying with much confidence: Next to God, I am the greatest one, because where I am not found there is no cake on the table, nor repletion on the house.—The vine-flower speaks well, saying with much confidence: Next to God, I am the greatest one, because where I am not found, there is no joy, neither happiness.—The olive-flower speaks well, saying with much confidence: Next to God, I am the greatest one, because where I am not found, there is no baptizing.—The good Lord is sitting in Heaven, looking at them and speaks to them: why are you contesting, three little flowers, three tiny blades of grass? I say, you all are mine. The corn-flower speaks well, because it is my body. The vine-flower speaks well, because it is my blood, and of all the world. The olive-flower speaks well, because it is my baptism, and of all the world, and by it the pagans are made Christians. Kind people, I wish you splendid health!"

The shortest text *(18.)* lays out the theme as follows: "The corn-flower says: Flowers, you are all flowers indeed, but I am the flower of corn, and I am the body of our Lord. The vine-flower speaks: Flowers, you are all flowers indeed, but I am the flower of vine, and I am the blood of our Lord. The olive-flower speaks: Flowers, you are all flowers indeed, but I am the flower of olive, and I anoint people and christen them to become faithful Christians."

All the Romanian variants referred to and quoted by me originate from the pre-wars territory of Hungary (Máramaros county and Middle-Transylvania inhabited by mixed Hungarian and Romanian population) In the opinion of *Eckhardt,* the Hungarian and the Romanian songs stem from the same root, from Latin texts, independently of each other. Namely, the Romanian maintains an element of the mediaeval Latin literary formulations inasmuch as in them the "judge" intervenes and settles the debate to the contentment of each interested party, while the Hungarian preserved another mediaeval element, to wit, that of the introduction of a rose or a violet, instead of the olive-flower, thus adding a secular point to the story, in the style of the *vagans* songs.

The similar songs of other nations fail to display such a close resemblance to the Hungarian texts. The German versions speak about the rivalry of summer and winter, water and wine, burgher and peasant, various trees, and so on, of which perhaps the last-mentioned antagonists bear some degree of likeness to the Hungarian, being plants involved in this case as well. The debate is going on between the ever-green and the willow. They argue about the worth of the products made of them, and their rivalry is represented in the form of alternating stanzas. Finally the willow puts forward the argument that it keeps springs cool so as to refresh the thirsty loving couples. At this, the ever-green admist its inferiority. This solution is kindred as regards its spirit with the Hungarian, but in all other respects the composition differs from the Hungarian version. The German text displays other ideas and elements of formulation.

The Ukrainian songs are telling about the debate of the Sun, Moon and Shower; the Southern Slav versions about the rivalry of Apple, Orange and other flowers, eventually the young man and the young girl, each refuting the other party by anouncing simply: I am more beautiful than you, and you have no reason for being proud at all. All these are independent continuations of the mediaeval basic idea. What surprises us is that the contest of the flowers only survives in the Hungarian folklore and with the south-eastern neighbours of the Hungarian people. In any case, the songs look back upon some mediaeval students' song as their antecedent; this supposition supports the song's reference to the mass, as well as its concluding motif of worldly love.

Literature: Eckhardt 1930: connection of the Hungarian song with the mediaeval *certamen* and the Romanian version; *Ortutay* 1936–48: quotes Eckhardt; *Armistead–Silvermann* 1968: mediaeval *certamen*, Balkanian Shephard formulation, paralleled by Greek, Aroumun, Bulgarian, Serbo-Croat and Hungarian versions.

90. THE HOLY VIRGIN SEARCHING FOR HER SON

174.

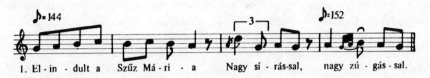

1. El - in - dult a   Szűz Má - ri - a   Nagy sí - rás-sal,   nagy zú - gás - sal.

1. The Holy Virgin set out
   Crying bitterly, and wailing loudly,

2. To look for her sainted son,
   And she met with a Jewish girl.

3. Good morning, Jewish girl.
   Welcome, Holy Virgin.

4. Have you not seen my sainted son?
   I don't know, I have not seen him...

5. The Holy Virgin went on,
   And she arrived at Betlehem.

6. Good morning, Betlen man,
   Welcome, Holy Virgin.

7. Have you not seen my sainted son?
   What colour is your sainted son?

8. What colour my sainted son is?
   He has golden teeth and chesnut hair.

9. Go on, go on, Holy Virgin,
   Go on, go on, and make speed!

10. Just now they are crowning his sainted head,
    Just now they are nailing his sainted hands.

11. Just now they are piercing through his sainted flank,
    They are spurting out his red blood.

Szépkenyerűszentmárton (Szolnok-Doboka county). Performed by a woman of seventy. Lajtha 1941 = MNT II, No. 25.
    Cf. *Leader 328.*

Versions in languages other than Hungarian:
GERMAN: *1–7.* E–B Nos 2056–2062.
DANISH (SWEDISH): *8–10.* DgF 97 *(ibid. Jonsson).*

The first stanza of the German song was recorded as early as 1349, its full text in 1591. Thus it is deeply rooted in German tradition, and is known from several recordings from German language areas. In Hungary, it turned up in one single recording, from Transylvania. Undoubtedly, it is a borrowing from the Germans (so is the Danish version), judged by the contracted, excerpt-like character of the song. In spite of this, a new element is interwoven in the texture of the song, and that is the encounter with the Jewess, which is certainly a secondary development derived from Hungarian charms. The Hungarian charm-texts speak about the Holy Virgin walking with the Holy Infant in her arms and meeting with three Jewesses. They look at the child with admiration, meanwhile they also cast a spell on him. Mary cures him by means of a special method, setting an example to cure people by the same spell. This is the very popular and widespread superstitious text that had supplied the first scene of the Hungarian song, which proves to be superfluous at the same time, because the Holy Virgin continues her wandering, and it is only later that the plot proper develops. The tune of the Hungarian song agrees with those of the Romanian colindas, as well as with one of the E–B tunes (2058 "Andere Melodie"), which circumstance is another evidence of the song having originated from the German. It is probably a recent borrowing in Hungary.

Literature: *Lajtha* 1947; first publication, the text compared with those of Hungarian charms; *Vargyas* 1964: German origin; *Hilmar* 1966: 177 German variants, further Danish, Estonian, Polish, Slovak, Wendish, Spanish, Portuguese and Italian texts, 439 in all, surveyed. The Hungarian variant and the relating article by the present author ignored.

91. THE CRICKET'S WEDDING

175.

1. Szë - gin le - gin a prü-csök, Ké - szül há - za- sod - ni.

Ö - le - ge - ti a le - gyet, Mëg-a - kar - ja kér - ni.

"Ő - ne- ki se ő - se, Ő - ne- ki se ő - se."

1. The cricket, a poor lad,
   He is about to marry,
   He is cuddling the fly,
   He wants to propose to her.

2. The little fly is licking-tonguing
   The cricket's mouth.
   The cricket takes hold
   Of the little fly's leg.

3. The hamster snoars up,
   He wants to be the bridesman.
   A souslik sprang beside him,
   He wants to be a bridesman as well.

4. The two bridesmen pleased
   The little bridegroom,
   He told them at once
   To go and look for a bestman.

5. A pig was made the best man,
   He tied them together:
   . . . .
   . . . .
   (Onomatopoetic sounds imitating the pig's grunt)

6. The wolf was made the butcher,
   He slaughtered a good steer,
   And besides
   He throttled two young pigs.

7. The vixen was made the cook,
   She is preparing the dish of chitterlings.
   The harehound is washing the sausage skin
   Which the dog fills.

8. The owl is a famous brigand,
   Keeping an eye on his portion of sausage,
   . . . . . .
   . . . . . .

9. The louse grows angry,
   It takes the nit
   And gives it a box on the ear, the poor soul,
   Pulling it by the hair.

10. The little fly made a quarrel
    With the humming wasp,
    They are figting on the ground,
    And wicked enemies they are indeed!

11. A monkey passes by,
    He wants to be the judge,
    . . . .
    . . . . . .

12. The monkey draws into the dance
    The hidious turkey.
    And the monkey is dancing eagerly,
    Letting out loud farts.

Fogadjisten (Bukovina). Performed by a woman of thirty-eight. Kodály 1914 = Sz. Nd. 5.

Divergences: The formula occurs rather often: "I would like to marry you, little fly, If only you were not so small. I would marry you, cricket, If only you were not so crooked."

One of the marrying couple is always a cricket (with one exception), while the other is always a fly (with two exceptions). One of the texts has: "The cricket is going to marry, He is proposing to the gnat's daughter." An exceptional fragment collected at Jobbágytelke speaks about the marriage of a mouse and a bat. The additional characters show a striking medley: gnat (8), stork (8), wolf (7), bear (6), frog (6), hamster (5), souslik (4), stinking beetle (4), mouse (3), heron (3), dog (3) louse (2) flee (2) spider (2), maybeetle (2), fox (vixen) (2), donkey (2), turkey (2), cat (2), and the following come up on one occasion each: crab, skunk, hare, rat, hen, long-horned beetle, pelican, owl, ox, monkey, goose, wasp, and also the devil, further "mouse-bat" and objects used at weddings, e. g. oven-peel and broom; many of the variants describe the musicians: prime fiddler (usually stork), second fiddler (frog), flutist (gnat), and so on. The zoological names are often made to alliterate (*"Nagyot herkent a hörcsög"; "Büdös bogár a bőgős"; "Tetű sógor sótörő"*, and so on).

708

There is another variant ending with the strife-scene. Unfortunately, this, the Pécska variant, has been recorded without tune. Very frequently bawdy, obscene details are included.

Earliest provenience: between 1705–1710 in the songbook Szentsey, 13.
Dissemination:
I. Sopron county (Vitnyéd); Zala county (Kerkakutas); Verőce county (Lászlófalva); Tolna county (Felsőireg); Komárom county (Ete).
II. Heves county (Bodony); Gömör county (Felsőrás).
III. Pest county (Kiskunhalas); Bács-Bodrog county (Homokmégy); Arad county (Pécska); Bihar county (Köröstárkány); Szabolcs county (Fülöp).
IV. Maros-Torda county (Jobbágytelke, Marosvásárhely); Csík county (Gyimesfelsőlok, Gyimesközéplok); Bukovina (Andrásfalva 3, Fogadjisten). Total: 20.
Textual relationship with other ballads: none.
Tunes: 1. = No. 175.

(2., 4., and 12. occurring in two variants.)

Versions in languages other than Hungarian:

FRENCH: *1. Barbillat–Touraine* 109. *2–4. Poueigh* 146–49. *5. Arbaud* II, 189. (Several variants in Rev. Trad. Pop. 1890 and Mélusine 1878.)

SPANISH: *6–7. Romero* 119–121. (*Armistead:* known on the entire language area.)

ITALIAN: *8–9. Ferraro* 1877, 26, No. 14 and 113, No. 28. *10. Idem* 1870, No. 97. *11. Idem* 1888, No. 40. *12. Pergoli* No. 40. *13. Widter–Wolf* 102. *14. Gianandrea,* 257.

GERMAN: *15–27.* E–B 163a–g, 164a–d, 165a–b.

DANISH: *28–29.* Dal 38–39.

SLOVENE: *30–56. Štrekelj* I, Nos 972–997. (*Kumer*) 117.

CROAT: *57. Žganec* 1924, No. 51. *58. Idem* 1950, No. 108. *59. Idem* 1950–52 No. 146.

SERBIAN: *60. Stojanović-Vitezica,* 565.

BULGARIAN: *61. Stoilov* 943.

SLOVAK: *62. Bartók* 1959 259c. Slov. sp. I, No. 505 and II, No. 588.

MORAVIAN: *65. Bartoš* 1953, No. 159.

UKRAINIAN: *66–72. Golovatsky* II, 503, No. 2, 505, No. 4, 507, No. 5, 564, No. 5, 732, No. 17. III, 494, No. 1, 502, No. 6.

RUSSIAN: *73–80. Chernyshev* 301–305 and 307–309.

In this instance we cannot detect any closer connection between the Hungarian and the French versions. Although the latter has also beetles (louse, flee), and other zoological characters, it describes a birds' wedding with finch and lark as spouses. But the story is presented in the form of the "chanson énumerative": "but we have no bread, where can we get some", and one of the animals appears carrying bread on its back. "Now we have bread though we have no wine..."—and so on. The brawl-scene of the Hungarian is rather tersely formulated in the French: one of the musicians, a rat attracts the attention of a cat in the nook, the latter jumps and takes the former, which in turn calls for help.

The pattern of the "chanson énumerative" is followed by the Catalan–Spanish and sometimes even by the Italian formulations. Instead of the louse and flee and the bird characters of the French and Iberian versions, the Italian one has cricket and ant as marrying couple, which resembles the Hungarian story. But as regards the content, most of the texts stand wide apart from the Hungarian: in point of fact, there is no mention of a wedding with zoological characters, only a dialogue and the exchange of rings refer to marriage; the cricket slips and breaks its limbs, the ant calls a doctor, but by the time the doctor arrives the cricket is dead.

The German versions tell a story about a birds' wedding and another about a beetle's wedding. What is more, some of the north-German texts speak about animals' wedding, which, however, leads us into the realm of the lying tales. The two main types do not mix up the animal characters, and even their formulations are distinct from one another. In *Imre Gombos*'s plausible supposition the birds' wedding is a low-life parody of the Provençal love plays with bird characters. The birds' wedding is essentially a rhyming game: a moment of the wedding feast is attached, by means of rhyming words, to each bird's name. This type of text survives in a 1530 broadside and in a lute-book printed in 1603. These two variants have the longest texts in this type. Subsequently developed specimens recorded from oral tradition are briefer, but still characterized by the original tendency to produce a rhyming game. The German beetles' wedding has actually the same, or wellnigh the same characters as the Hungarian, although the plot and the formulation are completely different. In every case, a "beetle" not mentioned by name proposes to a fly. A short dialogue takes place between them, the gist of which is worded like this: "I should be a fool if I married you." Still the fly starts to assemble seven bridemaids. Finally she asks where her maid-servant, the gnat, is to be found? While dancing at the wedding feast, the guests trample down the fly, the beetle mourns it in black clothing, then a cock jumps and swallows the beetle. Here we have neither a bridegroom nor a bride.

Among the nations neighbouring the Hungarian we find birds' wedding (Moravian, Slovak, Ukrainian, Russian and Croat—the latter speak about a nightingale), alternating with the wedding of a gnat and a fly—as in the Hungarian—and with other animals. With the Russians only a gnat-burial occurs.

Not even the nearest neighbouring people's (Slovak) version can be regarded as an immediate relative of the Hungarian: the gnat marries the fly, but the wine is supplied by the nightingale. They get drunk and slay the gnat. The fly laments the gnat. As against the Slovak song consisting of a few lines, the Serbian formulation goes into much detail. The Slovenes produce the greatest medley of all: apart from bear, fox, thrush and pigeon, also the gnat is involved in the marriage scene. a more surprising agreement offers itself in the Danish versions, which treat again separately the birds' wedding and the beetles' wedding. The former is marked by details characteristic of art poetry as opposed to folklore. In the latter, a gnat proposes to the "little fly"; a short dialogue is followed by the wedding feast; although only beetles are involved, the gnat drags the fly on the ground by its hair; the fly bursts out in tears, saying that the gnat's promise had been different. Eventually excisemen appear, and the song is concluded with a scene of general brawl. (The tax-collectors are represented by bees and wasps.)

The above survey does not allow us to infer any correlation between the various national solutions. Thus we are at a loss as to the questions of origin and trend of dissemination. Certain similarities shine through fully dissimilar elements which have no relation to one another in the least degree, and which appear in a rather whimsical mosaic pattern throughhout the examined areas. Considering the two German types which are well discernible from one another, one of them occurring in the written source of the mid-sixteenth century as mentioned earlier, a German origin might be perhaps forwarded. The rest of the versions amalgamated these two types, hence the confused solutions to be found nearly everywhere. The supposition receives further support from the type of *Schwankballade,* a farce-like ballad much favoured throughout the German language area. On the other hand, it is impossible to infer any consistency in the medley of solutions from the possible contacts. *Seemann* states in connection with the Lithuanian variants that they cannot be brought into correlation with the German types, much more plausibly with the Slav versions—by which he virtually separates the latter from the versions of his own language area.

In conclusion, we are prone to believe that for this ballad it is perhaps the rhythmical possibilities of the various zoological names that suggested the various solutions. The basic idea—the queer cast of animals to represent human relations— has been exploited by the sundry nations according to their own tastes. Thus a mosaic pattern baffles the researcher, from which no conclusion regarding the possible trend of dissemination can be drawn, not at least for the while being. However, the Hungarian version is nearer to the German than to the French one.

Literature: Bolte 1902: mainly Italian and French variants completed with enumeration of English, Scandinavian, Greek and a few Eastern European data; *Seemann* 1951: surveying the Slav versions in connection with the Lithuanian variants.

92. LAMENT-LIKE BALLADS (CORONACH)

176.

I, U - ti Mis-ka mit gon - dol - tál, Mi - kor ha -ról el - in - dul - tál?

Mi - kor ha - zól el - in - dul - tál?

1. Miska Uti, what did you have in your mind
   When you started out of your home,
   When you started out of your home?

2. What I had in my mind was
   That I set out on an unlucky way,
   That I set out on an unlucky way.

3. My body fell in the bush,
   My blood spurted in the dust,
   My blood spurted in the dust.

4. There came birds flittering about.
   They waked over me singing songs,
   They waked over me singing songs.

5. My master heard them,
   He put his horses to the cart,
   He put his horses to the cart.

6. Master, master, my dear master,
   Put me on your cart,
   Put me on your cart.

7. Carry me to my home,
   To the town of Nyilvánfalu,
   To the town of Nyilvánfalu.

8. Open, mother, open your gate,
   Here is your handsome son brought home dead,
   Prepare the bier for him!

9. Give me shirt and pants,
   For this is the last time you can give me a thing,
   For this is the last time you can give me a thing.

10. Mourn for me, girls,
    For I do know that you are sorry for me,
    For I do know that you are sorry for me.

11. This is my last word to all:
    No-one should fell tree on a feast morn,
    No-one should fell tree on a feast morn.

12. For I felled on a feast morn,
    And I set out on an unlucky way,
    And I set out on an unlucky way.

Gyergyótekerőpatak (Csík county). Bartók 1907 = MF 1029/b.

177.

1. Far - kas Már - ton mit - gon - dol-tál,   Mi - kor ha - zól el - in - dul - tál?

Én   e - gye - bet nem-gon - dol - tam, Bá - na - tos ut - ra   in - dul - tam.

1. Márton Farkas, what did you have in your mind
   When you started out of your home?
   What I had in my mind was
   That I started on a sad way.

2. I went along the sad way,
   And death was my companion:
   Mózsi Paizs was waiting for me,
   And he stabbed me in the back.

3. My blood was spilt in the dust,
   I fell face ahead on the ground.
   And the sun was shining bright
   When he killed me.

4. Two of my comrades came,
   Two of my friends carried me home.
   Márton Farkas, open your gate,
   They are bringing home your handsome son.

5. When I was taken to the soldiers,
   I told them not to mourn me.
   You must mourn me now, and you must not leave it to others,
   For this is the last time you can mourn me!

6. Mózsi Paizs, cast into the prison,
   May rattle the iron shackles to the end of his life.
   You are living, you did not die,
   But you are deprived of freedom.

Gyergyóújfalu (Csík county). Bartók 1907 = M.Sz. 1099/b = Ethn 1908, 111.

Divergences: To No. 177 the informants added the following lyrical song which is not pertaining to the lament ballad but stands on its own as a separate song:

"My youthful moods like a bird *(falcon)*, Merry they are as long as they are free to flitter where they want to. Oh, woe to me, poor soul, For my heart has given up all hope of freedom. Had I a girl's heart, I should soak a hundred handkerchiefs with my tears."

The ballad prospers in numerous mature variants in Transylvania and Moldavia. So far the researchers have not known about its provenience outside the Transylvanian areas. Therefore I restrict my observation on the type-areas IV and V. The extraneous variants will be surveyed later.

Essentially we cannot speak of a ballad in the true sense of the term. The type discussed includes narratives about death-cases, narratives which have local traditions of formulation. It is these formal peculiarities that provide the framework for the diverse content elements. Two main features characterize the style of this group of songs. First, in general, the narrative is heard from the lips of the victim who relates the circumstances of his death. Secondly, a peculiar questioning formula is used to start the story: ". . . what·did you have in your mind when . . . you started?" and the question is followed by a similarly formula-like reply: "What I had in my mind was . . ." (In certain cases the pattern is completed: "János Bibilók, what did you have in your mind, What did you dream on Monday night?")

In spite of the two preponderating features, differences occur in the variants. For one thing, not all of the stories start with the question formula. Sometimes the formula occurs in the middle of the story, addressed not to the victim but to the murderer: "Mózsi Firtos, this has been my name, And I lived forty-eight years . . . Áron Péter, what did you have in your mind When you started out of your home?" (Székelyudvarhely); in certain cases, it is the victim that puts the question to the murderer: "I had my home in Magyarós, For two months I lived there, In the third, I started out. As I was passing by a wood, Demeter stood up in front of me. O Demeter, what did you have in your mind When you started out of your home? I had nothing in my mind But that I gave my soul to murdering . . ." (Torda). There is a text from Marosludas, in which neither the questioning formula nor the exclusive prevalence of the narration in singular first can be detected, being the whole plot based on the dialogue between the deceased daughter and her mother. "O, if you knew, mother, Where my last hour struck! It was at Torda by the Aranyos. There I finished my life. So it was ordered That I should die in the deep water. Why did you go there, my violet? To wash my face, dear mother . . ." And the narrative ends with the following lines: "I had written to you, mother: Do come to see me once more, Bend over my grave, And God best blessing be with you!"

In some examples the murderer is questioned right at the beginning of the song; this type then has the murderer to relate the story which ends with his imprisonment (Borszék). Not infrequently the moral of the story is put into the dead body's mouth.

Let us quote some further turns. "I had nothing in my mind" is followed by the phrase "I started out on the sad way", or "I set out on an unlucky way", or "I met with the man who murdered me". Before the narrative proper, the sentences "I passed along the way, And death was my companion", or "Death came to meet me" are sounded several times. The murder is mainly accomplished with a knife. "My blood poured in the dust, My body was thrown into the bush", or "I fell down upon the road" are natural consequences of the action. Similarly: "I shall perish in the spilt blood Like a small fish in the sea". When the murder takes place by drowning in the water: "The depth of the water is greater Than the strength of my two arms" are the customary phrases. The concluding formula: "Mistress György Farkas, open your gate, They are bringing home your handsome dead son" seems to have an overall prevalence. So is the one read in the published variant: "Mourn me, mother, don't leave it to others, For this is the last time you can lament for me!"

Let us now survey the variants recorded from areas outside Transylvania. *Dömötör* (1930, 22) published the text of a song about a murderer who was executed at Mohács. This song-text was submitted to *János Erdélyi,* therefore this is the earliest provenience of the formula: "Pista Bence, what did you have in your mind When you started out to shed blood?" In this case the murderer is questioned instead of the victim. The rest of the song is also addressed to him. But in one stanza the hanged man (or the man to be hanged?) announces: "Oh, you girls of Bisse, I wish good health to you! Not to everyone of you, but to one, To my dearest sweetheart!" In a text recorded from Felsőireg we hear the question at the end of the narrative: "Oh, Maráci, what did you have in your mind when you started out robbing? My God, I had in mind..." In another variant from Felsőireg the question is addressed to the victim right at the beginning: "Oh, you gendarme, what did you think When you stood up in the window? Did you not think of your life, Only of the cook, your sweetheart?" (To wit, he was thought to be a robber and shot.) At Dunapentele, the report on Maráci is begun with the question: "Oh, Maráci, what did you have in your mind When you started to rob?" In one of the two songs recorded in Pest county this formula occurs at the beginning, in the other, at the end of the story.

At Kishartyán (Palots region) also the usual answer appears: "Comrade János, what did you have in your mind When you were walking in the corn-field? I did not think anything But that I should slay my wife." Similarly in Borsod county: "Erzsi Balog, what did you have in your mind When you began to teach me how to steal? I did not think anything But that I had never followed the right way." (Sometimes the formula is applied in other context, too, as in Hódmezővásárhely: "Tell me, Jóska, what did you have in your mind When you had a large overcoat made?") The other formula of the Transylvanian variants also comes up at Tass: "Gábor Szabó, what did you dream On Thursday night? Look, by Friday night Your heart will be pierced by a knife." (The continuation relates a murder story in the Transylvanian fashion, only not through the mouth of the dead body.)

Nevertheless, the account of the dead body in singular first person is not altogether unknown in areas I–III either. In a story recorded at Kákics, for instance, the murdered wife relates the event like this: "...I started to visit my mother's home. By mere chance I fell into the net of death. For a murderer crossed my way; I left behind two unraised children who are now orphan." At Felsőireg, the narration in singular first is known as well as the opening question: "On the twenty-seventh of February When I parted with you, sweetheart, I did not think that I should wake on a morn like that, On which I perished in the field of Bányos..." Another example from the same place: "...When the gun cracked I was frightened; I knew at once that I was given over to death..." In Veszprém county: "József Vámi is my name, And I committed such a murder... In 1864 on an isle of Brusa, It was the twelfth of May, I parted with life on top of a big dry tree..." Finally, an example from the legacy of Kálmány, recorded from Csongrád and Torontál counties: "Emanuel Dékány is my name, I spent my twenty-second year of age... Had I not leaned to a strumpet's word, I should not have died at Vásárhely." (This ballad speaks about a man who was hanged.) "My God, my God, I committed a great sin inded When I entered the gate of Matyi Hódi... He runs into the kitchen Then into the room, Taking a big knife in his hand, He thrusts it in my breast..." (about a man who was murdered). A text from Tiszapolgár includes the self-lament of the dead body together with the questioning formula, though addressed to the murderer: "...My good mates who loved me dearly, My ruined body that you will put in the grave, Write on the lid of my coffin, Lord, deal heavily with the murderer for ever!... Hey, Lajos Nagy, what did you have in your mind on the day When you took the knife in your hand? I thought...".

As has been shown, the same turns and features characterize the variants both in Transylvania–Moldavia and in areas I–III. The type may have, therefore, been widespread throughout the whole of the country in former times.

Earliest provenience: before 1846.
Dissemination:
I. Baranya county (Kákics, Mohács); Tolna county (Felsőireg 4); Fejér county (Dunapentele); Veszprém county).
II. Nógrád county (Kishartyán); Borsod county (Szentistván).
III. Pest county (Akasztó, Keserűtelek, Tass); Torontál county (Magyarszentmárton); Csongrád county (Derekegyháza, Hódmezővásárhely); Szabolcs county (Polgár); I–III: 17.
IV. Kolozs county (Kide); Maros-Torda county (Kibéd, Marosvásárhely, Szentgerice); Torda-Aranyos county (Marosludas, Torda 3); Alsó-Fehér county (Vízakna); Kisküküllő county (Ádámos, Dicsőszentmárton, "Küküllő county"); Udvarhely county (Árvátfalva, Bágy, Bözöd, Csekefalva, Énlaka, Farkasfalva, Kadicsfalva, Lengyelfalva, Medesér 2, Rugonfalva, Siklód, Szentegyházasoláhfalu, Székelyudvarhely 2, "Udvarhelyszék" 2); Csík county (Borszék, Csíkmadaras, Csíkmenaság 2, Csíkrákos, Csíkszentkirály, "Csíkszék", Gyergyótekerőpatak 2, Gyergyőszentmiklós, Gyergyóújfalu 2, Gyimes, Gyimesbükk 3, Gyimesfelsőlok 4, Gyimesközéplok 6, Hidegség); Háromszék county (Árkos, Bükkszád, "Erdővidék", Nagybacon, Nagykadácsi, Nyujtód, Sepsiszentgyörgy, Uzon 2); "Székelyland" 3, s. l. from the Székely region 5, "Transylvania" 2, Bukovina (Hadikfalva 2). IV: 77.
V. Moldavia (Gerlén 2, Lészped 10, Pusztina 2, Trunk); V: 15. IV–V: 91. Total: 109.
Textual relationship with other ballads: none.
Tunes: almost exclusively associated with old-type Hungarian folksong melodies. In Transylvania and Moldavia they represent the best examples of the old-style, ornamented performance. Since no international connection are involved, and the tunes have no import over and above what has been stated before, we omit the publication of all relating melodies.

No similar song is known outside the borders of the Hungarian language area. (At most one single Moravian song (Sušil 99/208) reports on a similar death-case, and one Slovak cantorial valedictory (Slov. sp. II, No. 420) contains such a singular first-person performance.) Nevertheless, something has to be told about the historical background of the type.

Farewell songs given into the mouth of the deceased body is a widespread tradition among the Hungarian populations. To the latest date, it has been an essential part of the cantorial valedictory that it said farewell to those left behind with the words of the dead body. That is to say, in singular first person. Not only the words addressed to the relatives constituted parts of the valedictory, but also the details of the death-case and circumstances and events of the life of the deceased person entered the scope of such songs. The populace has had enough opportunity to listen to such products of clerical service, and in the absence of a parson or a cantor, the customary songs were made by one or another member of the community. Folk-style valedictories have been recorded from more than one place, for instance 2 from Etéd, Hunyad county, 2 from Sepsiköröspatak, 1 from Homoródalmás (Háromszék county) and another 1 from Szentlászló (Verőce county). At the last-mentioned village even a fixed text has been used for the purpose, which reads like this:

1. I have now to part with you,
   Alas, I have no other choice,
   I must leave you, my good relatives;
   May God bless you for all your kindness
   Now and for ever!
   May the Lord grant us a reunion in Heaven,
   In the name of God!

2. It is difficult to part with you,
   As I have been brought up in this place,
   Here I was toiling, here I was suffering.
   I leave you my best wishes
   Now and for ever.
   May the Lord grant us a reunion in Heaven,
   In the name of God.

3. My heart and all my limbs ache
   That I cannot stay here any longer,
   I cannot stay with you, my beloved ones.
   I must go to my grave,
   My soul goes to Heaven.
   May the Lord grant us a reunion in Heaven,
   In the name of God.

4. You will forget me
   After I am taken away from here
   Into the gloomy realm of the cemetery,
   Where, among the dead ones,
   I shall be slumbering.
   May the Lord grant us a reunion in Heaven,
   In the name of God!

"This is what my dear daddy used to say standing at the feet of the dead body, right before it was taken out of the mourning house."

718

Szentlászló (Verőce county). Performed by a woman of seventy-six. L. Kiss, 1957 =
AP 1826/b.

This "cantorial valedictory" looks back upon a remarkable literary example of the farewell speech in singular first person in Csokonai's poem entitled *"A lélek halhatatlansága"* (The Soul's Immortality). For the members of the family of the Count Rhédey obviously the farewell speech constituted the most important part of the poem. Examples of lesser literary merits are also known from written sources: we may refer here to the laments composed in remembrance of renowned warriors who fell in actions in the Turkish wars—these having mostly been written by their scribes—and even more so to the description of the circumstances in which the death took place. Let it suffice here to recall the famous song about the death of István Kádár, a song that survives in folk-tradition as well. In this, the deceased warrior bids farewell to his relatives and comrades, the incipit of the poem being: "One of the brave warriors have left us today".

Since the practice has lived long and in broad social strata, we may suppose that we are dealing with a deep-rooted, ancient tradition. In this connection a discovery of *Emil Jakubovich* should be mentioned: early Hungarian chroniclers state that the chieftains in the years of the Hungarian Conquest wanted to perpetuate "their earthly glory" by "songs made by themselves". He points out that the chroniclers misinterpreted the manner of presentation in singular first person, which is to be met with rather frequently in similar Siberian heroic songs. The best known example of the practice is found in the Old-Turkic inscription of Orkhon, in which Kagan Bilge is speaking in first person about his deeds; further examples can be adduced from the stock of Vogul and Ostyak heroic epics. Nevertheless, such "enumerations" may have other people than famous warriors as their heroes: let us remember the Ob-Ugrian "songs of destiny", in which a man or a woman relates the story of his or her life. Although personal sorrows and events are laid out in these songs in singular first, yet since they represent universal troubles and strives of life, they are akin to the genre of the lamenting ballads. Recalling the deeds of a prominent hero after death in the hero's own words shows very little difference as compared with the tone of a "song of destiny", only the person involved is more significant. The method of song-composition referred to by the chroniclers must be a survival of the widespread Siberian tradition, as well as the later "historical lays" and the cantorial valedictory performed in the name of the deceased should be considered continuations of the same practice. Similarly, the folk ballad in the form of laments is nothing else than an offshoot of the same tradition.

Regarding its ancient standing, the genre discussed may be ranked with the earliest types of ballads; there are common features of formulation and stylistic traits showing a tendency to poetic stylization that relate the genre with the ballads. Still, they cannot be named true ballads because essentially they are occasional recitals in verse of some local events.

Literature: Kodály 1933, Note 1: comparing the valedictory in singular first with the corresponding portions of chronicles.

BROADSIDE BALLADS FROM THE EIGHTEENTH AND NINETEENTH (TWENTIETH) CENTURIES

Types 93–100.

93. THE GIRL WITH THE PEACOCK

178.

1. Egy le - ány a he- gyek kö-zött Csak e - gye - dül pá - vát őr - zött.

Jöt - tek hoz - zá jö - ve - vé - nyek, Há-rom if - jú szép le - gé - nyek.

1. All by herself in the hills
   A girl guarded a peacock.
   Strange people came to see her,
   Three hadsome young men.

2. They said: Beautiful maid, we ask you
   To come and walk in the wood with us.
   To walk there as good friends,
   Having a nice entertainment.

3. If I go along with you,
   Where am I to put my peacock?
   Drive your peacock to the spring,
   For you must not trust it to anyone's care!

4. For if it went astray and were lost,
   My heart would break with sorrow.
   You can find it there,
   And you must not walk long, you will see.

5. As they reached the forest,
   They lay down in the grass.
   Since she was tired, the maid lay down to rest
   And she fell asleep.

6. Seeing this, the young men
   Examined the sleeping girl.
   They gave her kisses on the lips
   In order to comfort her heart.

7. The maid woke up by night
   When nightingales were singing.
   Seeing that she was lonely and forsaken,
   She broke in tears, saying:

8. Oh, Great Lord, who lives
   In Heaven and watches over us,
   Punish them with thy scourge,
   With thy flame falling down from the sky!

Mindszenty MS, No. 20. 1831.

179.

1. A he - gyek közt, A völ - gyek közt,   A he - gyek közt, a völ - gyek közt,

Egy szü - zecs - ke pá - vát őr - zött,   Egy szü - zecs - ke pá - vát őr - zött.

1. In the hills and in the dales,
   In the hills and in the dales,
   A little maid was guarding a peacock,
   A little maid was guarding a peacock.

2. Strange people go and pass by,
   Well-grown, smart young men,
   Two handsome young men,
   Two handsome young men.

3. Well, beautiful maid, we ask you,
   Well, beautiful maid, we ask you
   To come with us to the green woods,
   To come with us to the green woods.

4. If I go with you,
   If I go with you,
   Who is going to guard my peacock?
   Who is going to guard my peacock?

5. Drive it to a spring,
   Drive it to a spring,
   For you cannot trust it to other's care,
   For you cannot trust it to other's care.

6. They went into the green woods,
   They went into the green woods.
   They prepared a resting place for the beautiful maid,
   They prepared a resting place for the beautiful maid.

7. The maid woke up by night,
   The maid woke up by night,
   At the singing of the nightingale,
   At the singing of the nightingale.

8. Alas, my God, what am I to do,
   Alas, my God, what am I to do?
   I have to doff my maiden head-dress,
   I have to doff my maiden head-dress.

9. I have to don the head-kerchief,
   I have to don the head-kerchief.
   Although there is no-one to stand by me wearing it,
   Although there is no-one to stand by me wearing it!

Kisgyőr (Borsod county). Performed by a man of sixty-one. Lajtha 1929 = MF 2391/b.

Divergences: The first manuscript and another two early manuscript versions continue, after the curse, with a moral lesson extending to six stanzas; girls should not give credit to young men before they are wedded by the parson, and sometimes not even after that. The concluding part of a manuscript of 1854 reads like this:

> I have withered my maiden head-dress,
> I shall rue it while I am alive.
> Don't weep, sweetheart, don't grieve!
> I shall pick new flowers in place of your head-dress.
> You may well pick them every day and every night,
> Yet I shall never be a maid again.
> I have lost my maiden head-dress,
> I have buried it under my apron.

This seems to be a borrowing from some other song. Otherwise, the variants show a close agreement which is surprising enough, considering the non-folklore turns of the text and its dissemination over a rather wide area. Is it that people felt the song so strange as to spare the pains of removing its strange by-taste in the course of variation? Even the rhymes remain the same in most cases. At the end of a manuscript of 1852, lyrical stanzas in the eighteenth-century style are found, completing the scene in which the girl falls asleep. According to one single variant, the girl herds her peacock not in the hills but by a pond. The first recording and certain early variants add: "When she started out in your company, She was not a merry girl, but she was very sad. I definitely feel threatened, For you will leave me by myself." We find refrains like "Alas, my daughter, alas", or "Alas, alas, alas, alas, oh" in some of the variants collected at Homoród.

Earliest provenience: 1789 (from the manuscript collection of Miklós Jankovich).
Dissemination: Without specification: 7 (MS. 1789, 2 broadsides from the turn of the eighteenth and seventeenth centuries; MS. from the early nineteenth century, MS. from 1827; Mindszenty MS. from 1831; MS. from 1854.); Sopron county (Csepreg); Vas county (Alsóság); Somogy county (Szenna); Tolna county (Decs 2); Veszprém county (Bakonybél); Győr county (Győr, MS. from 1852); Nyitra county (Muzsla 1834); Esztergom county (Nagysáp, Pilismarót); Hont county (Perőcsény); Nógrád county (Ecseg, Kisterenye); Heves county (Fedémes); Borsod county (Disznóshorvát, Kisgyőr); Zemplén county ("Bodrogköz" region, Tarcal 1834?); Ung county ("Ung county" 1834?, Ungvár); Máramaros county (Técső 2); Pest county (Tura); Bihar county (Biharderecske, Nagyszal-

725

onta = Arany MS. 1874); Kolozs county (Bánffyhunyad, Szucsák); Szolnok-Doboka county (Bálványosváralja); Maros-Torda county (Jobbágytelke, Mezőbánd); Udvarhely county (Homoródalmás, Homoródszentpéter, "Homoród region", Kénos); Csík county (Kászonfeltíz). Total: 41. (I–III = 31; IV = 10)

Textual relationships with other ballads: None.

Tunes: 1. = No. 178 (3 variants), 2. = No. 179, 6. (5 variants), 10. (2 variants).

Versions in languages other than Hungarian:
SLOVAK: *1. Bartók* 1959, 253a. *2. Slov. sp.* I, No. 140.

In connection with No. 205, *Bartók* stated in 1924 that it was associated with a Slovak melody. (The variant being that of Tura.) At the same time, the text of the ballad under discussion has been collected, except for the two Slovak variants, from Hungarian language areas. Even of the two Slovak texts, *2.* is a fragment, and *1.* a brief excerpt. Thus it is out of question that the Hungarian should have derived from the Slovak, the more so since the melody of *2.* is a new-style Hungarian tune. On the other hand, a Hungarian origin seems the more plausible because the ballad can be demonstrated from Hungarian territories from the late eighteenth century as a broadside (Cf. *Pogány* Nos 25 and 44), further the first MS. dates back to 1789, from which year onwards many MSS and broadside variants turned up. The only folk-text published here occurs in a series of recordings from the late eighteenth to the late nineteenth century. It was heard on the stage as well in 1853 recited in Act 2 of the popular play "The Tsigan" (Gipsy) of Szigligeti. Obviously, the song owed its sudden success to the agency of broadside literature. The foreign character of its text and melody, too, can be ascribed to broadside origin rather than to borrowing from some other nation.

But there is one thing that gives food for consideration. The peacock as a symbol of virginity occurs in several songs with the northern Slavs. Driving away of the peacock in their narrative verses or lyrical dialogues of a different character always indicates that something wrong is going to happen to the girl's maidenhood. (Cf. *Slov. sp.* II, No. 48; III, No. 300; *Bartoš* 1901, 71 No. 92; *Kolberg* 1871–84, 12 Nos 32–33, and 72–74, As this motif cannot be demonstrated in Hungarian folklore material, in which the peacock always heralds liberation, as a symbol derivable from mediaeval associations with sun, i.e. Jesus Christ, we are prone to think that the onetime broadside poet may have taken it over from Slav tradition when composing his new verse. Thus the song is of recent origin, contemporaneous probably with the manuscript variants.

Literature: Ortutay 1936–48: reminiscent of the Hungarian ballad "Fair Anna Bíró" (cf. No. 29.). *Dános:* 1938: quotes Ortutay; *Pogány* 1959; chronological order of early broadsides and MSS.

94. THREE GIRLS PICKING BERRIES

180.

1. El - in - du - la há - rom ár - va   A há - rom kis csi - por - ká - val
Az er - dő - be e - pör szed - ni,   Az er - dő - be e - pör szed - ni.

1. Three orphans started out,
   Each carrying a little cup,
   To pick berries in the woods,
   To pick berries in the woods.

2. Their dear little mummy
   Left them lots of precious pearls;
   They were quarrelling about them on their way,
   They were quarrelling about them on their way.

3. The three orphans came to an agreement:
   The pearls will belong to the one
   Who first fills,
   Who first fills her little cup.

4. Little Pendzsóka was first to fill it,
   Therefore her two sisters killed her.
   They hid her in the hole of a tall tree,
   And went home with great speed.

5. Their father asks them:
   Where his youngest daughter stayed back,
   His youngest daughter, little Pendzsóka?
   You went three and come two.
   Why does my youngest daughter tarry,
   Why does my youngest daughter tarry?

(to lines 3 and 4)

6. Alas, my God, where shall I go,
   Where shall I go, what shall I do?
   Where shall I look for her, where shall I go?
   Where shall I look for her, where shall I go?

7. He travelled to the woods,
   For to seek his little orphan.
   He looks at the hole of a tree,
   Lo, there is a fiddle.

8. He is looking at it long, and takes it in his hands.
   He is pondering what to do,
   Is music becoming in his sorrow?
   Finally he still sounds the fiddle:
   And the little fiddle sounds beautiful, (to lines 3 and 4)
   The little fiddle sounds beautiful.

9. Play on, play on, my royal father,
   My dearest one who raised me!
   My sisters killed me,
   They hid me in the hole of the tree.

10. He went home, and they played the fiddle.
    This song they played on the fiddle:
    Play on, play on, my dear sister,
    My dear murderer who killed me!

11. I used to be a princess,
    A princess, called little Pendzsóka.
    Now I am a little fiddle,
    My sisters killed me,
    They hid me in the hole of the tree. (to line 4)

Lengyelfalva (Udvarhely county). Performed by a woman of forty-five. Béla Vikár 1902/3 = MF 361/b.

Divergences:
Different incipit (beginning in prose): "A king had three beautiful daughters, the youngest one, called Erzsa, they loved dearly. Their mother promised to give a silken gown to the one who would first fill her jug." (Continued in verse.)

Erzsa was very intent
To gather berries.
Her sister took revenge
And they robbed her of her life.
They took her body
And placed it in the hole of a decaying tree.
A man was passing by the decaying tree.
What a great wonder surprises him:
From the hole of the decaying tree, a fiddle
Together with its bow came out!
The poor man took it in his hands,
And played a song in his great wonder...

The rest of the story agrees with the variant presented above, as well as with the corresponding details of the other variants.

729

The main difference among the variants is seen in the message of the fiddle: "Don't play on me any longer, dear mother! Can you pay no more heed to me? I used to be the royal Erzsa, But see what became of me! I filled my jug, And these wicked murderers killed me." The formula is applied to each member of the family. When it comes to the girls, the fiddle says: "Don't play on me, you bigger murderer! . . . I filled my jug, And you killed me, you murderers. You did not take pity on my blood, You took away my life, So that you may get my pearls!" Another variant adds in prose the following remark: "The king had his two daughters executed and kept the violin." Otherwise, most of the sung variants preserved the above details in fragmentary forms. The part published by Vikár in the 1903 volume of the Vasárnapi Újság, and which was republished by Faragó, 1965 No. 101, shows no full agreement with any of the text notations preserved in the Ethnological Archives of the Ethnographical Museum of Budapest; yet each of the details of the Vikár text recurs in some of the variants. Probably, the great collector amalgamated several variants to form a complete whole, which in turn can be read, unfortunately without tune, in two recordings of Nándor Tilesch, one noted down in Udvarhely county, the other in Háromszék county.

The story of this ballad is well known from Hungarian folktales as well. (AaTh 780, Berze Nagy 780.) Also the Tale of the Maple speaks about three princesses, but the body of the murdered girl turns into a maple-tree. A shepherd lad makes a flute of the tree's twig, which when sounded relates the murderous story. The Hungarian tale version presents only the account of the flute in verse, which however resembles the turns of the ballad: "Blow, blow, my sepherd . . . my royal father . . . my murderer! I used to be a princess. And now I am a little maple, A little flute made of maple-tree." But there is a variant recorded from Maros-Torda county, in which the severed head of the youngest princess is left in a cart rut where it changes into a violin, precisely as in the ballad shown above. Yet the beginning and the ending parts of the tale is different: the king sets various tasks to his daughters which the youngest can solve best, thus provoking the jealousy of her sisters. At the end the sister who murdered the girl listens to the revealing sounds of the flute and casts the instrument down upon the ground; and the murdered sister jumps alive out of the broken violin. The murderers are punished and the youngest sister will be lording it over the country.

Earliest provenience: 1902–03.

Dissemination: Udvarhely county (Dobó-Vágás, Lengyelfalva 3, "Several communities in Udvarhely county"); Háromszék county (Zágon). Total: 6.

Textual relationships with other ballads: none.

Tunes:

1. = 180 (in two variants, for one of them see Bartók 1924, No. 186), and the following:

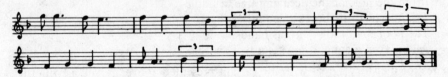

Versions in languages other than Hungarian:

DANISH: *1–10.* DgF 95 (enumerating further Swedish, Norwegian, Faroe and Icelandic variants, F = *Dal* 7).

ENGLISH: *11–37.* Child 10. *38–134.* Bronson 10. *135–137.* Belden 20–23 C, D, F.

SPANISH: *138.* Romero*, 150.

GERMAN: *139.* Hauffen 53. Gottschee. *140.* E–B 8.

SLOVENE: *141.* cf. *Seemann* 1951, No. 176.

LITHUANIAN: *142. ibid.*

RUSSIAN: *143–144. Chernyshev* 334 (and note).

CZECH: see *Sirovátka* 1965.

The Danish ballad is not known from old manuscripts, only recent variants of it have come up from folklore tradition. The story runs as follows. Suitors come to see the two sisters, one of whom is a splendid fair girl, the other "black". The young men all want to marry the fair one. Her sister grows jealous, calls her fair sister, who is younger than she, to go to the coast to wash. She drowns her sister in the sea. In vain does the fair girl call for help, in vain does she offer all her valuables to the other girl, her sister refuses to draw her to the coast. Two minstrels appear and haul the corpse; they make a harp, the fingers of the girl are the keys and her hair the strings. At a wedding feast in town the musical instrument reveals the murder. The cruel sister is burnt at the stake.

The English version agrees in detail with the Scandinavian variants. Similarly, the elder, ugly sister is jealous of the younger sister; she calls her to go to the coast to see the arrival of their father's boats, and thrusts her into the water. A miller hauls the corpse—which motif does not fit well into the maritime environment, rather would it pass with a river. A harper or a fiddler turns up and strings his musical instrument with the girl's hair. In some of the variants he makes various component parts from her body. When sounded, the instrument here again discloses the fate of the girl. The questions connected with the origin and the interrelationships of the English and Scandinavian ballads have been long discussed by researchers. There is a general agreement that the English formulation is the secondary development, the Scandinavian–Norwegian being the original. More complicated is the interconnection of the East-European versions.

Solymossy 1920 goes into details of the theme. Mapping its places of provenience, he concludes that in contrast to the West-European (English and Scottish) versions which construct in verse form, tales in prose are prevalent in all the East-European language areas. On this ground he considers the tale form original, from which the sung ballad was framed by minstrels (poets who composed music to their verse).

But Solymossy failed to provide a comprehensive survey. Sung variants in verse occur also in East Europe, even though in a low number. Seemann informs us that the Lithuanians have a song-version of the theme with the following plot. A fisherman lives on the coast of the sea. He has several daughters. One of them has been engaged to a young man. The eldest sister thrusts her into the sea while walking on the shore. Fishermen haul the corpse and make a zither from her bones and strings from her hair. The sound of the zither is heard in the house of her father-in-law; Listen, sister, what the zither says: you are not happy but I am content in my grave. (It can be inferred that the murderous sister became wife to the young man.

Seemann 1951, No. 176.) He cannot bring into correlation with this ballad the German variant of Gottschee which shows a closer affinity to the western story than does the rather eroded Lithuanian song. The Gottschee text has the following plot. A king has two daughters. While they are washing on the sea-shore, the elder thrusts the younger into the water. At home she pretends that her sister had been taken away by suitors who arrived in a boat. Fiddlers are walking on the shore and become attentive of a female's voice saying: "Take my silken hair and use it as strings, my finger as keys, and play your violin before the king's door: The king had two daughters; the elder thrust the younger into the sea." The King exclaims: Oh, wicked daughter, what have you done?

Seemann has made an attempt at discovering the preliminaries of the Gottschee text in the Slovenian material; with Štrekelj he has not found anything, except perhaps a distantly related fragment published in a collection inaccessible to me, which has the following story: A girl stabs her younger sister in the heart and throws her into a lake, because she wants to acquire her sister's share of heritage. A fisherman fishes the corpse out and makes a bow from her hand, keys from her fingers and strings from her hair. Then he goes to play music in the castle. At the first sound of the violin the king's daughter bursts out in tears, and that is the end to the song.

Seemann explains the Lithuanian text from the Scandinavian. Also the Russian developed from the Swedish, according to Chernyshev, with the decisive scene omitted: the Russian does not contain the motif of discovery by the sounds of the musical instrument. Anyway, also the Russian speaks about two girls, the elder being black as night, the younger white as sunlight. The elder sister calls the younger to take a walk by the sea and thrusts her into the water. The poor girl makes efforts to reach the shore, but all in vain, for the elder sister calls out to her: "All labour is lost for you can never step on the shore". At night a fisherman nets the dead body of the Tsar's daughter, and the story is ended with this. (The notes provide information on some further Russian variants.)

The revealing portion of the text is always an inserted verse in the East-European tales, and sometimes it is even performed in singing voice. In general, this practice is typical of ballad themes dissolved into a tale. All this seems to indicate that we have succeeded in discovering the original ballad form of the prose tale, which supposition is corroborated by verse variants coming up here and there isolated one from the other.

But the rub is that these variants are hard to be brought into connection with each other. True, *Seemann* explains the Lithuanian from Scandinavian preliminaries, from which also the Russian is derived. At the same time, Seemann does not even try to clarify the origin of the Slovene–German (Gottschee) version. He simply supposes a Slovenian derivation of the Gottschee text. By suggesting a possible existence of a mediaeval Hungarian ballad we could solve the riddle, but unfortunately the Hungarian texts do not allow us such a speculation. The Hungarian formulations are very casual, clumsy and burdened with marks of recent development. It appears at first sight that the rhymster made desperate efforts to "keep the lines in rhythm" even at the expense of grammatical errors. The patchwork with all its modernized setting of the theme (the violin is found in the hole of a decaying tree, which is nothing else but a sophisticated substitution for the flower grown out of the dust of the buried body) is unmistakably due to an attempt at forgery. At the same time, the typical turns of the verse show so close aggreement with those of the prose-tale as to render it doubtless that the former developed from the latter (we think here of the motifs of "the three princesses", "the fiddle", "the revealing sound of the fiddle or flute"). In all probability, the tale had been transformed into verse by a broadside vendor visiting village fairs, and in this form it was spread in a narrower area of two Székely counties neighbouring each other. But it seems that the piece soon fell in oblivion, for recent collectors have failed to trace it anywhere. The scattered Slovenian variants may be similarly occasional transcriptions of the prose-tale into verse, or else they are survivals of so far unknown and blurred parallels, inextricable in any case for the time being.

Literature: Child 1882: discussing the sung (verse) variants and the European dissemination of the tale; *Solymossy* 1920: surveying the dissemination and discussing the origin; *Seemann* 1951, No. 58: Gottschee-German from the Slovenian, Lithuanian from the Scandinavian, reference to data of European dissemination (without mentioning the Hungarian verse-variants); *Brewster* 1953: trend of dissemination from Norway to Great Britain; *Wilgus* 1959, 306–308: a critical survey of the research results concerning the English and Scandinavian versions; *Siuts* 1962: German data and bibliography; *Taylor* 1964, 106: "The concluding incident in the tale—the bones or hair of the dead sister speak—is found only in Scandinavian versions of the ballad and is lacking elsewhere". This statement obviously refers to areas outside the British (although the motif is also missing from the numerous more recent English–American variants); states the full agreement of the tale and ballad as regards their content, an agreement which is a very rare occurrence even in his opinion.

95. THE GIRL WHO SHIRKS GOING TO CHURCH

181.

1. A mor - va - ji kis le - jány Nem mënt el a mi - sé - re,
mi - sé - re. Nem mënt el a mi - sé - re.

1. The little girl of Morva
   Did not go to the mass, to the mass,
   She did not go to the mass.

2. She went down to the rose-garden,
   To her little rose-garden, rose-garden,
   To her little rose-garden

3. She made three wreathes,
   She made three wreathes, she made the one after the other,
   And she made the third one as well.

4. When she was making the first,
   The priest just began, just began the mass,
   The priest began the mass.

5. When she was making the second,
   The priest came to the elevation,
   The priest came to the elevation.

6. When she was making the third,
   The priest finished the mass,
   The priest finished the mass.

7. In the shape of her sweetheart
   Three devils came to carry her away, to carry her away,
   Three devils to carry her away.

8. Is there anyone here from Morva,
   From the great city of my father, Morva,
   From my great city of Morva?

9. I would like to send words to my father,
   Through father to mother, to my mother,
   Through father to my mother.

734

10. So that she should instruct her sons and daughters,
    She should send them to the sacred mass, send them to the mass,
    She should send them to the sacred mass!

Mánfa (Baranya county). Performed by a woman of fifty-three. L. Kiss, 1958 = AP 2147.

The incipit mentioning the little girl of Morva occurs in three variants; in the rest, the wife of the mayor of Karád plays the mother's part, the text beginning with the statement that "On Sunday morn the tiny sun appeared".

Earliest provenience: 1900.
Dissemination: Somogy county (Karád, Köttse, Tengőd); Baranya county (Boda, Mánfa 2); Nyitra county (Menyhe). Total: 7.
Textual relationships with other ballads: none.
Tunes: The published tune is known in another variant, the other tunes (2–5) exist in one each.

Versions in languages other than Hungarian:
MORAVIAN: *1–6. Sušil* 20/50–56 (with indications of further variants). *7–10. Bartoš* 1901, 3a–c, No. 2054. *11. Waldau* CXXXVI.
UKRAINIAN: *12. Golovatsky* I, No. 36.

The Hungarian texts seem to represent a stage in which they had hardly reached the folklore level. Most probably they are products of village-market singers. Both the text and the tune agrees with the words and melody of the Moravian version, as was pointed out by *Kodály* in 1962. Even the text contains reference to Moravian origin (Little girl of Morva). For comparison's sake, we present here two Moravian tunes:

The fact that the song is a recent borrowing is shown, among other things, also by the circumstance that it comes up sporadically, and only in the western part of Hungary. (Kodály calls attention to an archival record, according to which Northern Slavs settled in the region in the course of the eighteenth century.)

Literature: Kodály 1962.

735

96. THE INNKEEPER'S FAMILY THAT WAS MASSACRED

182.

Rubato

1. Jaj de szé-les, jaj de hosz-szú az az út, A-kin az a ki-lenc be-tyár el-in-dult!

A-kin az a ki-lenc be-tyár el-in-dult, Pá-pa-i úr ud-va-rá-ba be-for-dult.

1. Alas, it is a broad, alas, it is a long way
   On which nine brigands started off,
   On which nine brigands started off,
   And reached the courtyard of Esquire Pápai.

2. Mistress Pápai, may the Lord grant you a good evening!
   May the Lord grant good luck to the gentlemen!
   Don't you wish us good luck!
   Before this night is over, the long knife will pierce your heart.

3. Mistress Pápai went out and stood in front of the house,
   She raised her eyes up to the blue, starry sky:
   My Dear, take me up to the blue sky,
   So that my red blood may not be spilt on the ground!

4. Come, Kati, hold this light,
   Till I finish with your wicked stepmother!
   But Kati's heart was plunged into mourn,
   Because by that time she was standing in blood reaching up to her ankle.

5. Dear Sir, my godfather, pray,
   Don't kill my kind stepmother!
   I don't spare your life for the very reason
   That you called me by my name.

6. The clock struck one after midnight
   When the coachman of Esquire Pápai arrived.
   My Dear, something has gone wrong here:
   I find all the doors and windows flung open.

7. He peeped in the furthermost room,
   And lo, Esquire Pápai was lying there in bed.
   His arms bound down with yellow chain,
   The thalers picked out of his left pocket.

8. The main street of Szolnok is plunged into mourn,
   Esquire Pápai's dead body is being carried along it.
   He is carried along it with six members of his family,
   Among them his dear, wedded spouse.

Derzstomaj (Jász-Nagykun-Szolnok county). Performed by a man of eighty-two.
Vargyas 1939 = Vargyas 1943, No. 93.

The event related in this song has the following factual background (Ethn 1918, p. 245): "...some of the relatives of the extirpated family survived the massacre, and they remembered details of the bloody story. The following have been made clear from their account.

"South of Szolnok, at the Vezseny bend of the river Tisza, where the railway going to Szentes touches upon the bank of the Tisza in our days, there stood the inn of Hajlat (today a railway watchman's hut is standing there). The tenant of the inn was Mihály Pápai in the fifties. He and his family were killed in 1859, when it was dawning on Assention Day. According to the witness relatives, the following members of the family had been murdered: the innkeeper Mihály Pápai and his wife Katalin Darvas, further their children: Franciska and Katalin; furthermore, a mechanic of Kunszentmárton, his wife, and the coachman who spent the night in the inn, their names being unknown. Two of the children of the innkeeper escaped, namely Rozália and Gyula, who looked over the murderous act from the nook of the oven. Allegedly, they recognized the murderer as well, who was a fellow of the innkeeper and godfather to his children. The surname of the murderer was Kasza Kovács (his Christian name is not known). His assistants are not known by name. The murder was committed out of vengeance, as far as we know."

Let us quote some of the variants of the song, presented in their chronological order.

(a)

1. There is a nice inn at the bend of the Tisza,
   In the year of eighteen hundred it was plunged into deep mourn;
   On the day of Holy Thursday
   Esquire Pápai met his death there.

2. First the mechanic was murdered;
   Seeing this, Esquire Pápai begged them:
   Dear friends, how can you do such a thing?
   How can you kill an innocent man?

3. Fányi, daughter of Esquire Pápai spoke up:
   I say, men, how can you do such a thing,
   I say, men, how can you do such a thing?
   To kill my innocent father!

4. Hush, you bitch, for we kill you as well.
   We lay you in your blood, face down to earth!
   But her heart was already plunged into mourn
   For she was standing in blood up to her ankle.

5. I say, comrade, whet your knife sharp,
   So that I can cut Fányi's neck at once.
   I don't want to do a dirty work at her neck,
   Why should I cause the doctor trouble with her.

6. Hearing this, the wife of Esquire Pápai
   Folds her hands round her head:
   Alas, my God, I would never have thought to see the day
   When my husband meets such a terrible end!

7. The coachman also came home late at dawn,
   Lo, both the door and the window are open,
   Lo, both the door and the window are open,
   Esquire Pápai is lying dead in the room.

8. The coachman runs down to the manor.
   Get up, Sir, for a wicked thing has happened,
   Get up, Sir, for a cruel thing has happened,
   Esquire Pápai is lying dead in the room!

9. Go, coachman, don't tell me such a lie!
   I was there at eight last night,
   I was there at eight last night,
   And Esquire Pápai was having a high time at table then!

10. The main street of Szolnok is plunged into deep mourn,
    Esquire Pápai will not be walking along it any more;
    The graveyard of Szolnok is plunged into deep mourn,
    Esquire Pápai is lying in it in the first grave.
    Engraved on his cross can be read:
    Esquire Pápai and his daughter are buried here.

Visk (Hont county). 1875.

(b)

1. At the bend of the Tisza there is an inn,
   In which Pápai met his death.
   His hands they tied with yellow wire on his back,
   So they picked his money out of his left pocket.

2. First thing to do is to kill Esquire Pápai—
   So the brigands started speaking.
   Good friend, how can you do such a thing,
   How can you kill an innocent man?

3. Sir, my godfather, pray,
   You may take all my riches,
   My riches, and my red wines I am willing to give to you,
   But I would be sorry to part with my life.

4. The hostess instantly placed flasks of wine before them.
   But the brigand answered:
   First we shed his red blood,
   Then we drink your red wine.

5. The brigands did not spare his life,
   They shed his blood.
   As his wife saw this,
   She clasped her hands round her head.

6. My Dear, I should never have thought
   That my man should meet such a cruel end!
   Fáni then went out and stood in front of the inn,
   She looked up and prayed to the starry skies:

7. My dear Lord, to your grace I offer my soul,
   For these murderers are going to kill me!
   Sister Katyi, rock your brother in the cradle
   For before the night is over a knife will pierce your heart.

8. Sir outlaw, raise your eyes up to the sky,
   Or look at those two orphan children.
   Well, comrade, let us be kind to the two infants,
   For who is to tend to them till morning?

9. The lesser one they threw into the cradle,
   The bigger one was weeping beside it.
   Kasza Kovács, Józsi Doktor, these were the names of those
   Who killed those two innocent creatures.

10. The main street of Szolnok was plunged into deep mourn,
    When Kasza Kovács walked along it.
    Three big bells were tolled, and surly was their chime,
    Three white pigeons were tolling them.
    His hands and legs are cast in iron,
    His comrade is lamenting him bitterly.

Pécska (Arad county) = *Kálmány 1877, 46.*

(c)

1. In the bend of the Tisza there is an inn,
   Which was plunged in full mourn in fifty-nine.
   On Ascension Day
   Esquire Pápai met his end.

2. Marsócki was the first to lay a murderous hand on him.
   Esquire Pápai broke out in entreating words:
   Good friends, how can you do such a thing,
   How can you kill a good man?

3. Pepi, the daughter of Esquire Pápai spoke up:
   Good men, how can you do such a thing?
   Hold your tongue, bitch, for we do the same to you,
   You will be laid in your own blood with face to the ground.

4. Then Pepi ran out of the house
   And looked up at the starry sky:
   My God, take my soul in your grace,
   Take me up to the high Heaven!

5. As the coachman ran into the inn,
   He found the doors flung open.
   He found the doors flung open,
   And he saw Esquire Pápai lying at the door.

6. His hands were tied up with yellow wire to his back,
   Even his moustache was torn out.
   Then the coachman ran out to the farmstead,
   Esquire! come out and to the inn!

7. I have found all the doors open,
   I have found Esquire Pápai at the door.
   His hands are tied back with yellow wire,
   Even his moustache is torn out.

8. It is not true what you say, Károly,
   For at eight last night I was there,
   At eight last night I was there,
   Esquire Pápai was having a high time at table.

9. The cemetery of Szolnok is plunged into mourn,
   Esquire Pápai is the first to be buried there.
   Esquire Pápai is taken there together with his four men,
   And her beautiful, kind wife.

Apáca (Csanád county) = *Kálmány 1878, 74.*

   (d)

1. What happened in the inn at the Tisza bend?
   On Ascension Day six souls were murdered there.
   On Ascension Day six souls were murdered there,
   Also Lovasi was painted with red blood.

2. Lovasi set out with good luck,
   He went right to Pápai's inn.
   He ordered a pint of wine to be brought to him
   But the robbers did not let him drink it.

3. They tied up his hands with yellow wire on his back,
   They picked his money out of his left pocket.
   I don't mind if you take my money,
   Only spare my life!

740

4. Pápai's wife then spoke up:
   Alas, my God, to live to see the day,
   Alas, my God, to live to see the day
   On which an innocent man is killed!

5. Come, Kati, hold the candle,
   Let me cut your mother's neck.
   For if we have killed these six people,
   You yourself will be thrown into red blood.

6. Go, Pali, whet the knife sharp,
   Let me cut Kati's neck at once!
   And he cut it, and cut her to pieces,
   So that she may not be a doctor's sweetheart.

7. Come, Julcsa, rock your brother to sleep,
   If you don't want this knife to pierce your heart.
   For if we had known that you could speak,
   We would have done the same to you as well.

8. Then Julcsa ran out, and a frightened girl she was,
   Looking up at the sky with tears in her eyes:
   Alas, my God, take me into your mercy,
   Take my soul into your Heaven!

9. The coachman went home at dawn,
   He found all the doors flung open.
   Alas, my God, what is the matter here,
   That I find all doors flung open?

10. The coachman lights a candle in the kitchen,
    So he beheld his master.
    But the coachman ran out into the manor,
    Tenant, there is a great disaster in the inn!

"Békés" county. Bartók, 1906. = M.Sz. 1.

(e)

1. Alas, very broad, alas, very long is the way
   On which the nine outlaws set out!
   The nine outlaws rode in nine directions,
   And they met in the inn of Mistress Pápai.
   The nine outlaws rode in nine directions,
   And they met in the inn of Mistress Pápai.

2. Good evening, Mistress Pápai!
   Welcome, you nine outlaws!
   Don't wish luck to us, Mistress Pápai,
   Because a knife will pierce your heart before the night is over!
   Don't wish luck to us, Mistress Pápai,
   Because a knife will pierce your heart before the night is over!

3. As Mistress Pápai hears this,
   She clasps her two hands round her head:
   Alas, my God, that I have to see the day
   On which I must leave back nine orphans!
   Alas, my God, that I have to see the day,
   On which I must leave back nine orphans!

4. Daughter Trézi, run down to the cellar,
   And fetch wine in the golden cup!
   I don't need your wine, nor do I need you,
   I want you to place your heart on the table!
   I don't need your wine, nor do I need you,
   I want you to place your heart on the table!

5. Pray, my honoured godfather,
   Don't shoot my dear mother!
   Hold your tongue, rock your little brother,
   Your heart will be pierced by knife before this night is over!
   Hold your tongue, rock your little brother,
   Your heart will be pierced by knife before this night is over!

6. The clock struck one after midnight,
   The coachman of Mistress Pápai arrived at home.
   Alas, my God, something has gone wrong here,
   Because I find the doors and windows open!
   Alas, my God, something has gone wrong here,
   Because I find the doors and windows open!

7. He entered the house of Mistress Pápai,
   He found Mistress Pápai dead in her bed.
   Her hands tied with yellow chain,
   The banknotes taken out of her left pocket.
   Her hands tied with yellow chain,
   The banknotes taken out of her left pocket.

Majláthfalva (Temes county).—Ercsi (Fejér county). Performed by a man of fifty-five. Sztanó 1958 = AP 2165/g.

The development of the song can be well traced in the variants presented. It is instructive to note how detailed the recordings taken soon after the event are. Obviously they are still strongly affected by the singers of the village fairs who were eager to pick up all such bloody sensational stories together with all their minutest details. (Cf. *L. Takács.*) Later the overdetailed parts are omitted and only the psychologically valuable ones retained, and even unfolded. The early notations begin with mentioning the place-name, as usual in broadsides; the guest that was killed together with the innkeeper is also mentioned by name, and other details, like the dialogue of the coachman and the tenant are given. In the later variants all these are absent; the beginning lines that tied the event to a definite place are generally replaced by Stanza 1 of No. 122, and this incipit conquered the majority of the dissemination area. Thus the polishing effect of the process of "folklorization" began to render the piece "more abstract".

Still the story has failed to develop into a real ballad, because it does not contain any psychological conflict, only a bloody deed is related. Nevertheless, what can be sifted out from the variants may be instructive for the method of folklore creation.

Earliest provenience: 1875.

Dissemination: Without mentioning the place: 2.

I. Sopron county ("Rábaköz region"); Vas county ("Őrség region"); Zala county (Bazsi, Dergecs, Kávás, Kiskomárom 2, Lesenceistvánd, Lövőpetri, Nemessándorháza, Rédics, Resznek, Zalagalsa); Somogy county (Csököly, Darány, Karád, Nagyatád, Ságvár 2, Somogyszob 2, Taszár, Zamárdi, Zselickisfalud); Szerém county (Kórógy); Verőce county (Lászlófalva, Szentlászló 2); Baranya county (Becefa, Csoboka, Hosszúhetény, Kákics 2, Szentkatalin, "Ormánság" region) Tolna county (Felsőireg, Nagydorog, Sárpilis); Fejér county (Csákvár); Veszprém county (Gyenesdiás, Nagyesztergár, Pápa, Pápasalamon); Pest county (Tinnye); Esztergom county (Szölgyén); Komárom county (Ács 2, Izsa, Kocs, Nagylég, Naszvad); Győr county (Gyömöre, Győr, Kóny, Nyalka, Szemere, Táp). I: 58.

II. Pozsony county (Galánta 2); Nyitra county (Felsőkirályi); Bars county (Lédec); Hont county (Ipolybalog, Lukanénye, Perőcsény, Visk); Nógrád county (Buják, Ipolytölgyes, Nagybátony, Nógrádmegyer, Szanda, Szandaváralja 2, Szarvasgede); Heves county (Bükkszenterzsébet 3, Fedémes 4, Feldebrő, Maklár, Mátraszentimre, Mikófalva, Tarnalelesz, Tiszanána); Borsod county (Abod, Bács, "Southern part of Borsod county", Borsodnádasd, Bükkaranyos, Hernádkércs, Mezőkeresztes, Mezőkövesd, Putnok, Sály); Gömör county (Almágy 2, Egyházasbást 3); Abaúj county (Cekeháza, Csenyéte, Felsőméra, Felsődobsza, Göncruzska, Kéked); Zemplén county (Ricse 6, Sárospatak 5, Taktanador); Bereg county (Lónya); Ung county ("Tisza—Latorca Interfluve"). II: 64.

III. Pest county (Alpár, Bugacmonostor, Dány, Galambospuszta, Kecskemét, Kiskunhalas 6, Pilis, Tápiószele, Tóalmás, Tura 2); Jász-Nagykun-Szolnok county (Alattyán, Derzstomaj, Jászapáti, Jászárokszállás, Jásztelek, Kisújszállás); "Szolnok county" (Tiszaföldvár 3, Tiszaszalka, Tiszaszentimre); Bács-Bodrog county (Bátya, Borota, Dávod, Gombos, Pacsér, Rém 3); Temes county (Majláthfalva, Székelykeve); Torontál county (Csóka, Hertelendyfalva, Szaján, Szőreg); Southern Great Plain without specification; Csongrád county (Csongrád, Domaszék, Hódmezővásárhely 2, Horgos, Kiskundorozsma, Mindszent, Szeged, Szeged-Királyhalom, Szegvár, Székkutas); Békés county ("Békés c.", Doboz 4, Endrőd 2, Mezőberény, Mezőgyán, Vésztő); Csanád county (Apáca); Arad county (Simonyifalva); Bihar county (Nagyszalonta 3, Torda); Hajdú county ("Hortobágy" 2); Szabolcs county (Gégény, Kenézlő, Lövőpetri, Nagyhalász, Nagykálló, Nyírábrány Nyíradony 2, Piricse, Tiszapolgár, Rétközberencs); Szatmár county (Gebe, Kérsemjén, Kisar, Tyukod, Vállaj). III: 88.

IV. Kolozs county (Kolozsvár, Mákófalva, Méra, Válaszút, Visa; Torda-Aranyos county (Sínfalva); Udvarhely county (Bencéd, "Udvarhely c."); Brassó county (Pürkerec); Csík county (Csíkvacsárcsi 2, Szárhegy); Háromszék county (Dálnok, Sepsikörőspatak); Bukovina (Andrásfalva 5, Istensegíts 2). IV: 21.

Total: 233.

Textual relationships with other ballads: opening formula **124**.

Tunes: 1. = No. 182 in 22 variants; 2. (4), 5. (2), 6. (2), 8. (2), 9. (2), 10. (6), 13. (4), 15. (3), 18. (2), 23. (2), 24. (2), 29. (6), 30. (3), 34. (2) 35. (3), 36. (2), 38. (2).

746

A great variety of melodies has been associated with the text, but the great majority of these tunes were performed on one single occasion only, or at most in some neighbouring villages, sometimes in one and the same village at repeated recordings. Apparently, the text passes with any melody with a division of eleven syllabic lines. Nevertheless, the main tune type preponderating in number shows an even distribution along the middle and lower stretches of the Tisza. Since the event took place at the middle course of the Tisza, the focal point of dissemination can be logically supposed in that region. The main tune is at the same time linked with the earliest text-variants. Probably this was the melody with which the village-fair singers began to popularize their "compositions".

Some of the other tunes associated with the verse belong to the old-style melodies (2., 3., 7., 8., 9., 11., 13., 14., 15., 16., 18., 19.), or the category of art-songs (4., 5., 6., 12.? 17.? 23.? 24.?), or new-style tunes showing more or less urban influence; well-shaped, new-style tunes occur relatively seldom in this association (28., 29., 38). All these are, however, occasional associations, varying from village to village.

The song developed from the creation of some village-market singer after 1859 and followed a course of gradual assimilation into the folklore stock.

97. THE COUNT AND THE NUN

183.

1. A - mott egy hegy- te - tő - rül Egy völgy-be néz - tem át.

Ott lát - tam há - rom gró - fot. Egy csó - na-kon ha- lász.

- lász.

1. There is a hill-top over there,
   From which I looked down into the valley.
   I saw three counts fishing,
   Standing in a boat.

2. The youngest count
   Who stood by the side of the boat,
   Held a golden chalice in his hand,
   Offering the girl a drink of his good wine.

3. Why do you offer me your wine,
   Look, I cannot drink of if,
   For I am a poor little girl,
   But you are a rich count.

4. Then the young count
   Handed over a ring to the girl.
   Take this, my love,
   As a token of my heart.

5. Why do you offer me your ring,
   Look, I cannot wear it.
   For I am a poor little girl,
   But you are a rich count.

6. If you are a poor girl,
   Having no money and wealth,
   Think of the bright flame
   That flares in your heart.

7. I don't want to think of such things,
   Look, I don't need a man.
   Rather I go to the nunnery
   To be covered by the nuns' hood.

8. Next day someone appeared before the nunnery,
   He pressed the ring.
   Where is the new nun
   That came here yesterday?

9. Nobody came here,
   Nor could anybody leave the place.
   I shall set the convent on fire
   If you refuse to let her out.

10. At this, the nun steps out,
    Clad all in white, stands there.
    Her hair is cut short,
    Look, she is an ordained nun already.

11. He took a golden ring
    From his finger.
    Take it, my love,
    As a token of my heart.

12. Why do you offer me your ring,
    Look, I cannot wear it.
    I must die in the convent,
    I know it for certain.

13. The count felt at his belt,
    And drew a pistol.
    He shot the girl dead.
    Then he shot himself dead.

Áj (Abaúj county). Performed by a man of forty-eight. Vargyas 1940.

Divergences: The story and its formulation show a fair agreement in the variants, even the linguistic absurdities are much the same in them. At most certain omissions, and misunderstandings of the melodic and rhythmic pattern give rise to differences. Rarely the count becomes a priest in the end (instead of shooting himself).

Earliest provenience: 1923.
Dissemination:
I. Sopron county (Felsőpulya); Vas county (Sorkifalud); Zala county (Muraszemere, Rédics); Somogy county (Gyugy); Baranya county (Alsómocsolád); Veszprém county (Veszprémfajsz, data: the German inhabitants of the village perform the song in Hungarian).
II. Nyitra county (Bodok, Zsére); Hont county (Ipolyszög); Abaúj county (Áj); Zemplén county (Ricse).

III. Jász-Nagykun-Szolnok county (Jánoshida); Bács-Bodrog county (Zombor); Bihar county (Biharugra, Körösnagyharsány); Hajdú county (Poroszló); Szabolcs county (Nyírlugos, Nyírtura). Total: 19.

Textual relationships with other ballads: none.

Tunes: All variants are nearly related to the published 183. (10 notations.)

The relatively low number of notations is due to the circumstance that the collectors did not always think the ballad worthy of notations, partly because of the strange tune associated with the un-Hungarian text that sounds exceptionally strange in Hungarian folklore. Nevertheless, the song occurs in every part of the Hungarian language area. The grammatical errors appear in the same form at diagonally opposed points of the country. The tune is always beginning with up-beat, and has three-four rhythmic patterns; in counties Bihar and Szabolcs it is a waltz-melody. Since the Hungarian peasants are altogether unfamiliar with the use of upbeats and iambic rhythm, they confuse the rhythmic flow of the tune, leaving the idea of the melodic structure unrealized; what is more, even lines are omitted, owing to uncertainty of performance sometimes. Blurred and unstable variations are brought out by such remarks of collectors which refer to "changing the tune from stanza to stanza as if improvising it". All this is indicative of the ballad having been disseminated by village-fair singers and by broadside in comparatively recent times. Short-lived tradition has not yet transformed the song into a real folklore piece.

The same subject-matter occurs among the Germans and the Dutch as well, as a long-known and rather widespread ballad theme.

Versions in languages other than Hungarian:

GERMAN: *1–6.* E–B 89a–F. *7–21. Parisius* 18, 187, 249, 347–8, 417, 436, 524–5, 537, 687–9, 735 and 739. *22. Hruschka-Toischer,* No. 14b. (Only a few examples are mentioned, without any pretence of completeness. The numbers of *Parisius* give an idea of the dissemination: even a restricted area can offer so many variants!)

DUTCH: *23. Van Duyse* 3 (1544). Another reference to tune demonstrates the existence of the ballad among the Dutch in the fifteenth century.

The Hungarian texts are closest to *22.,* originating from Czech–German territory. The story of it runs as follows: Once I was standing on a high hill, I looked down into the valley, and saw a little boat swimming with three counts in it. The youngest of the three was sitting in the middle, and offered me wine to drink from his bottle. What do you think he drew off his finger? A golden ring! "Keep this, my beautiful betrothed, I give it as a souvenir to you!" "What shall I do with this ring if I cannot wear it on my finger? I am a poor maid, without any money or riches." "Even though you are a poor maid without any money or land, still think of our love which tied us together!" "I don't think of love, I don't think of a man, I only think of the Great Lord who alone can help me. I go to the nuns, I want to live in the convent." "If you want to be a nun and live in the convent, I travel round the world, and I shall be travelling as long as I return to you." He said to his servant: "Harness my horse, we shall travel round the world for this girl is worth the pains of it." As he reached the convent again, he knocked softly at the door: "Give me the most beautiful nun who came here yesterday!" "Nobody came here yesterday, and nobody is allowed to go out of this house!" "Then I set the convent on fire, together with all the nuns in it." "If you want to set this convent on fire together with all the nuns in it, then we tell the nun to come out to you." The girl, clad all in white, moved out swiftly, her hair was cut short since she had already been ordained. What do you think she held in her hand? A silver jug. She offered the young gentleman to drink, and he died of heart-break. And the girl dug a grave with the young man's dagger, and buried the corpse with her own white hands. Whith her tender fingers she pulled the rope of the bell, and in her low voice she sang a lament for the dead body.

More than one place of the Hungarian appears to be translation if compared to this text. It seems that Czech–Moravian or Czeh–German singers visiting Hungarian fairs had spread the ballad in Hungary, probably in the last decades of the Austro–Hungarian Monarchy, at the turn of the century. (According to the verbal intimation of Professor Wiora, the tune is not a German one.)

Literature: Vargyas 1964. Originating from German broadside.

98. THE MAN WHO KILLED HIS SWEETHEART AND COMMITTED SUICIDE

184.

1.Sza-bolcs me-gye,nyi-regy-há - zi   nagy er - dő.   Vér - rel van ott be - csö-pögve a me - ző.

Fúj - ja /a szél, min - den-fe - le   len - ge - ti,   Jaj is - te- nem de so - kat kell szen-ved-ni!

1. Szabolcs county, the big forest of Nyíregyháza,
   You find in it a field sprinkled with blood.
   Wind spreads it abroad in every direction:
   Alas, my God, one has to suffer in this life!

2. Gyula Szabó loves Jolán Horvát
   But Jolán's mother does not tolerate it.
   Well, Jolán, if they don't let me love you,
   You will see what I am going to do!

3. On a Sunday afternoon, Gyula Szabó
   Met Jolánka in the street.
   He took her to walk in the woods,
   To pick flowers, that's what he said.

4. But as they entered the woods,
   And sat under a rose-tree, he said:
   I did not come here to pick flowers,
   But to kill you in this instance.

5. The young girl kneeled before him,
   Begging him not to kill her in the woods.
   The wicked murderer did not pay heed to her,
   He threw her down to the ground and trampled on her neck.

6. He chopped up her hands and feet,
   Severed her head from her neck,
   Carved out her heart with his sharp knife,
   So he sent her soul to the world beyond.

7. Twelve balls are in my bright revolver!
   Three of them will do for me!
   The two corpses are lying there, one above the other,
   The whole world go there to see the wonder.

8. On the thirteenth of March
Many young girls put on their mourning dresses.
They put pearly head-dress on their pows,
So they saw Jolánka to the cemetery.

9. Fathers, mothers, learn the lesson of all this,
Behold, what came out of their true love!
Don't turn your mind towards great riches,
Rather turn your mind towards true happiness!

Mátraderecske (Heves county). Performed by a woman of thirty-nine. Kerényi 1957 = AP 2436/f.

Divergences: insignificant if any: the formulation betrays a uniform village-fair origin.

Earliest provenience: 1932.
Dissemination: Zala county (Aranyod, Gyürüs, Hahót, Zalacsány); Veszprém county (Jásd); Komárom county (Martos); Nyitra county (Tardoskedd, Vágfarkasd); Nógrád county (Abasár, Apácapuszta, Derecske, Mátraballa, Váraszó); Borsod county (Abod, Ónod); Gömör county (Egyházasbást); Abaúj county (Kéked, Pányok); Zemplén county (Bodroshalom); Bács-Bodrog county (Zenta); Hajdú county (Mikepércs); Szabolcs county (Nyírlugos 2, Nyírvasvári, Piricse); Kolozs county (Méra 2, Vajdakamarás, Válaszút 2); Szolnok-Doboka county (Feketelak); Alsó-Fehér county (Lőrincréve); Udvarhely county (Vargyas); Csík county (Csíkmenaság, Gyimesközéplok 2, Gyimesvölgye 2). Total: 38.
Textual relationship with other ballads: none.
Tunes: 1. = No. 184, in 13 variants; 2. (6 variants), 5. (2 variants), 8. (3 variants), 13. (3 variants). 15. (2 variants).

Semipopular ballad developed recently and spread undoubtedly through the mediary of market-singers. In distant parts of the country its text is the same; no marks of any conspicuous folklorization can be discovered in it. Also the tunes support the recent origin: in Transylvania, several new-style tunes also appear in association with the text, but the most frequent two tune-types of the song are not belonging to the new style. These are recorded from the territory of Hungary. All this indicates that the ballad began to spread from the central parts of the country about the middle of the last century.

99. THE FORSAKEN SWEETHEART WHO COMMITTED SUICIDE

184.

1. Mi tör-tént a Hont me-gye - i   ha-tár - ba!   Bi - ró Fe-renc Mar-git ne-vü le - á - nya.

Bi - ró Fe - renc Margit ne-vü   le - á - nya   Ki - nek az el - ső ti- zed-be nincs pár-ja.

1. What happened in the province of Hont county?
   Ferenc Bíró has a daughter, called Margit,
   Ferenc Bíró has a daughter, called Margit,
   And no-one can match her among the girls.

2. Margit has been cajoled by many young men,
   But Imre Kis has been most determined to entice her.
   Don't be afraid, Margit, pearl of my heart, I love you,
   Next autumn will bring the day on which I marry you!

3. But Imre had another girl in his mind,
   He sent word to the Cserép's
   That he would see them one evening,
   And that he would marry their daughter Zsuzsi.

4. He went there, indeed, on a Saturday night,
   Zsuzsi Cserép was waiting for him at the gate.
   She gave a few kind words and also a few hearty kisses to the lad,
   She seated her sweetheart at table.

5. Dear daughter, you must go to the parson,
   Have your names entered into the big book!
   For if Margit Bíró hears of this,
   She will lay an eternal curse on my daughter Zsuzsi.

6. The clock struck one after midnight,
   Margit Bíró set out to fetch water from the well.
   At the well she heard news, and sad it was,
   So that she could hardly walk home.

7. No sooner than she put down her jug,
   She set out and went to Imre Kis's house.
   She did not step in, only she knocked at the door:
   You false scoundrel, come out and hear a word of mine!

756

8. Imre Kis walked to the gate,
Margit Bíró received him with these words:
Is it true, Imre, that you have married,
Bringing such a great sorrow onto my heart?
It is true, indeed, Margit Bíró, I love another one!
For it's a long time since we have been in love with each other.

9. My dear sweetheart, give me your hand,
Let me wish you a happy life!
For three years and thirty-six months
Shall you, sweetheart, be confined to your bed.

10. You shall use the drugs of nine doctors,
You shall not meet rest anywhere!
Neither heaven nor earth shall take you in,
May your grave throw you out on the left side!

11. The clock struck two after midnight.
Margit Bíró set out on the long way.
She did not return greetings on her way,
She went home and hanged herself.

12. Girls, girls, let this be an example to you,
Do not keep a lover whom you love with all your heart!
For I loved my sweetheart with all my heart,
And my love took me to my grave too soon!

Ipoly Tölgyes (Hont county). Performed by a girl of sixteen. László Vikár.

Divergences: insignificant; the variants are all marked by the same village-fair style.

Earliest provenience: 1957.

Dissemination: Zala county (Alsószenterzsébet); Baranya county (Kopács); Nyitra county (Kolon); Hont county (Perőcsény, Ipolytölgyes), Heves county (Mátraballa, Váraszó); Bács-Bodrog county (Zenta); Arad county (Simonyifalva); Szabolcs county (Biri, Demecser). Total: 11.
The ballad certainly lives in many variants, considerably more than what have been collected so far.

Textual relationship with other ballads: none.

Tunes: 1. = No. 184, in 2 variants; 2. (in six variants, from which 3 are half-tunes, and one strongly corrupted).

Recently developed broadside.

100. THE HUNTER AND HIS DAUGHTER

186.

♩=112

1. Ec - cör ëgy szép bar - na lány ki - mönt az er - dő - be, ki - mönt az er - dő - be.

U - tá - na ment az ap - ja va - dász - öl - tö - zet - be, va - dász - öl - tö - zet - be.

Jó rög - get, tě szép lě - ány, igy szó - lal az úr.

Jó rög - get tě szép lě - ány! Mit ke - re - söl ij ko - rán

Eb - be j az er - dő - be, eb - be j a sű - rű - be?

1. Once upon a time, a beautiful brown girl
   Walked out and went into the woods, into the woods.
   Her father clothed in hunters' suit followed her,
   He followed her in hunters' suit.
   Good morning, beautiful girl, said the lord.
   Good morning, beautiful girl, What are you
   Looking for so early in the morning
   In this wood, in this thicket?

2. I have come to pick berries and I am waiting (to line 3)
   For my sweetheart to come here
   In this wood, in this thicket.

3. Come nearer, handsome hunter, said the girl, (to line 2)
   Come nearer, handsome hunter, (to line 3)
   I shall kiss you, if you come
   In this wood, in this thicket. (to line 4)

4. I cannot go with my horse, (to line 3 and 4)
   Nor can I be your sweetheart
   In this wood, in this thicket.

5. Tie your horse to a tree, and come, hunter, to your sweetheart
   In this wood, in this thicket.

759

6. I cannot go with my dog,
   Nor can I be your sweetheart
   In this wood, in this thicket.

7. Let your dog bark and come to make cheers with me
   In this wood, in this thicket.

8. I see, daughter, that you are blind,
   Can't you see that you are my own daughter
   In this wood, in this thicket?

9. If you had known that you were my father,
   Why did you not tell me so sooner
   In this wood, in this thicket?

10. Take your gun and aim it at your daughter,
    Shoot her right in the heart
    In this wood, in this thicket.

11. Gun-shot is heard,
    The hunter's daughter is dying
    In this wood, in this thicket.

Kiskunhalas (Pest county). Performed by a girl of sixteen. Szomjas, 1934.

Divergences: It does not appear at the beginning of most of the variants that the hunter is father to the girl. Their relationship is disclosed at the end of the song, which begins with the dialogue at once. More usually, the hunter kills the girl without being asked to do so by the latter.

Earliest provenience: between 1872 and 1911, possibly 1900.

Dissemination: Vas county (Hegyszentmárton, Katafa); Zala county (Kerkakutas, Rédics, Rezi); Somogy county (Nagyberki); Tolna county (Szekszárd); Fejér county (Csór); Győr county (Halászi, Táp); Nyitra county (Zsére); Hont county ("Hont c.", Perőcsény); Nógrád county (Bercel, Bükkszenterzsébet, Fedémes); Borsod county (Mezőkövesd); Zemplén county (Ricse); Pest county (Galambospuszta, Isaszeg, Kiskunfélegyháza, Kiskunhalas, Miske); Southern Great Plain without further specification: Hajdú county (Hajdúböszörmény); Szabolcs county (Nyírbátor); Maros-Torda county (Nyárádmagyarós); Torda-Aranyos county (Torda); Udvarhely county (Erdővidék, Miklósfalva, Vargyas, Zetelaka); Bukovina (Andrásfalva). Total: 33.

(The low number of variants reported is due to indifference on the part of the collectors. Mainly amateur collectors have paid attention to this song, whose tune and words are anything but a folklore product.)

Textual relationship with other ballads: none.

Tunes: all are variants of the published No. 100.

The strange stanza-pattern and the foreign melody of this song both point to broadside origin. In vain have I been looking for German or Czech–Moravian parallels in this case, but to my great surprise, the Danish material includes a version of it, recorded from oral tradition (DgF 435). The text runs like this.

"Listen to me, O Sir Peder, and hear what I say: Will you spend the night with me in bed?—I cannot spend the night with so fine a young lady, because of my horse.—You may tie your horse in the stable and spend the night with me. I cannot lie with you, because of my saddle. You may hang it on a peg.—I cannot, because of my gloves.—You may take them off and put them aside.—I cannot, because of my suit.—You may put it on the bench.—Sir Peder unfolded his white robe and there he stood in his fine linen underwear.—Listen, Sir Peder, what I say: Who sewed your fine linen underwear?—My little sister, Kirsten, she sewed my fine linen underwear.—Oh, little Kirsten, your sister sewed it! Then you must be my brother!—Sir Peder drew his bright dagger and drove it into little Kirsten's bosom. And this was a pity, because twins were playing in the mother's womb."

It was after the manuscript of my book was closed that in the texts of Vol. VII of the D. Vlr. I found nineteenth-century broadsides (Bd. VII/1 B in the manuscript then under preparation) whose build-up shows a very close aggreement with the Hungarian version, and which provide evidence of the latter's having originated from recent German broadsides.

OUTLAW BALLADS
Types 101–120.

101. IMRE BOGÁR

187.

1.Za - va - ros a Ti - sza, Nem a - kar hig - gad - ni.

Az a hí - res Bo - gár Im - re Ál - tal a - kar men-ni.

1. The Tisza is troubled,
   It does not want to settle.
   Famous Imre Bogár
   Wants to cross it.

2. He wants to cross it,
   He wants to steal a colt.
   At the green market of Kecskemét
   He wants to make money.

3. He wants to make money,
   To buy a cradle;
   He wants to marry
   That famous Marcsa Duli.

4. My hostess, I say,
   Can you give me something to eat for supper?
   I can give you a supper, I have prepared paprika meat
   For guests to come.

5. My hostess, I say,
   Will you give me a hundred pints of wine!
   I shall offer a drink to the county's men,
   So that I may not be their prisoner.

6. But the county's men know better than that,
   They don't drink of the wine.
   For poor Imre Bogár
   Has fallen now in their hands.

7. Chain the brigand,
   Shackles on his hands and feet!
   Marcsa Duli is waiting in vain
   For her sweetheart to come.

8. Look out, Marcsa, look out
Of your curtained window!
Imre Bogár is escorted,
And his steed is of golden colour.

9. Its bit is made of silver,
Its bridle is made of gold.
Famous Imre Bogár
Is the master of that horse!

10. The bells are tolled for noon,
It's half past eleven.
Imre Bogár is escorted
To the gallows.

11. The Tisza has settled down,
Only its mud remains.
Poor Imre Bogár is dead,
Only his fame remains.

S. l. (probably from Heves county). = Bartalus II 1875, 12, No. 11.

188.

1. The Tisza is troubled,
It does not want to settle.
Famous Imre Bogár
Wants to cross it.

2. He wants to cross it,
He wants to steal a colt.
At the green market of Kecskemét
He wants to make money.

3. He wants to make money,
To buy a cradle;
He wants to marry
That famous Marcsa Duli.

4. My hostess, I say,
Can you give me something to eat for supper?
I have paprika meat in the cauldron,
Cooked for guests to come.

5. My hostess, I say,
   Will you bring me a hundred pints of wine!
   I shall offer a drink to the county's men,
   So that I may not become their prisoner.

6. But the county's men know better than that,
   They don't drink of the wine.
   That famous Imre Bogár
   Has fallen now in their hands.

7. Open, sweetheart, open
   Your curtained window!
   Imre Bogár is being escorted,
   And his steed is a dark bay.

8. Its bit is gold,
   Its bridle is silver.
   The nice young girls of Kecskemét
   Are looking after him all in a wonder.

9. The bells are tolled for noon,
   It's half past eleven.
   That famous Imre Bogár
   Shall stand up on the chair.

10. He stood up on the chair,
    He looked up at the sky:
    My Dear, all my numerous robberies
    Come to my mind now!

11. Mother, you were my mother,
    Why did you not teach me better?
    I was a twig of a living tree,
    Why did you not bend me?

12. The Tisza has settled,
    Only its mud remains.
    Poor Imre Bogár is dead,
    Only his fame remains.

Bugacmonostor (Pest county). Performed by a woman of twenty-nine and a male informant. Zoltán Vásárhelyi, 1933.

Note: The green market of Kecskemét offered occasion to sell away stolen animals.—The verse of stanza 11 of the second text occurs only in this variant. Stanzas 4 and 5 of the published texts refer to representatives of the county gendarmerie who were on guard to take the outlaw at the roadside inn.

Divergences:
Let us see a few stanzas of a Hortobágy variant:

1. The Tisza is troubled,
   It does not want to settle.
   Famous Imre Bogár
   Wants to cross it.

2. He wants to cross it,
   He wants to steal a horse.
   At the green market of Debrecen
   He wants to sell it.
3. He wants to sell it,
   He wants to buy a fur-coat
   In which he can wrap
   His sweetheart.
4. My hostess, I say!
   Have you a well-laid bed?
   I have a well-laid bed, and also a nice girl
   To meet the pleasure of outlaws.
5. My hostess, I say!
   Will you give me a hundred pints of wine?
   I shall offer a drink to the county's men,
   So that I may not be their prisoner.
6. The county's men know better than that,
   They don't drink of the wine.
   For poor Imre Bogár
   Has fallen now in their hands.
7. The county's men are rascals,
   And so is the sheriff.
   Put to his coach, put to his landau
   Is seen the stolen colt...
10. The bells are tolled at noon,
    It's half past eleven.
    That famous Imre Bogár
    Is going to the gallows.
11. The bells are tolled at noon,
    It's sharp twelve.
    The hangman says: Imre Bogár,
    Stand up on the chair!
12. He stood up on the chair,
    He looked up at the sky:
    Alas, my God, my numerous robberies
    Come now to my mind!
13. The Tisza is calm,
    Only its waves remain.
    Poor Imre Bogár is dead,
    Only his fame remains.

In the rest of the variants we find hardly any divergence from the published ones: one or two stanzas may be missing in them, sometimes they are fragmentary. Occasionally a variant changes into the ballad of The Speaking Corpse. In such instances the performance begins with the closing scene of Imre Bogár: he stands up

on the stool and says: "I have killed a lad...", and then follows the other ballad.
The merger is possible obviously because of identical metre and similar tune
structure.

Earliest provenience: 1870–71.
   Dissemination:
S. 1.: 3.
   I. Sopron county (Bágyog, Osli); Vas county (Csepreg, Felsőőr, Katafa); Zala county
(Andráshida, Béc, Búcsúszentlászló, Dergecs, Jánosmajor, Kiskomárom 6, Oltárc, Zalaújlak,
Zöldhalom); Somogy county (Felső-Ágazás-tanya, Kisbárapáti, Koppánymegyer, Nemesdéd);
Baranya county (Belvárd, Berkesd, Boda, Csányoszró, Kopács, Mohács, Ranódfapuszta); Tolna
county (Nagydorog, Pusztahencse, Tüskepuszta); Fejér county (Csákvár, Dunapentele, Gárdony,
Soponya); Veszprém county (Réde, Somlószőllős, Szigliget, Tés); Komárom county (Guta, Izsa,
Martos, Naszvad, "Tata region"); Győr county (Győr, Kisbér). I.: 48.
   II. Nyitra county (Kolon); Hont county (Bajta, Perőcsény); Pest county (Váchartyán 2); Nógrád
county (Bercel 3, Szanda); Heves county (Besenyőtelek, Eger 3, Mátraderecske, Nagyréde, Pély,
Poroszló, Tiszaigar); Borsod county (Gesztely, Szakácsi, Mezőkövesd); Gömör county (Szilice); Abaúj
county (Áj 2, Beret, Cekeháza, Pányok); Zemplén county (Karcsa, Karos, Mikóháza, Ricse 2,
Tiszakarád); Bereg county (Lónya); Ung county (Palágy). II.: 35.
   III. Pest county (Bankfalva, Bugacmonostor, Galambospuszta, Izsák, Kalocsa, Kecskemét,
Kiskunfélegyháza 3, Kiskunhalas 4, Nagykőrös, Pálmonostor, Perkáta); Jász-Nagykun-Szolnok
county (Jásztelek, Mesterszállás); Bács-Bodrog county (Gombos 2); Torontál county (Nagybecskerek,
Szaján); Csongrád county (Csongrád 2, "Csongrád c.", Hódmezővásárhely, Szegvár, Tápé 3,
Tömörkény); Békés county (Endrőd, Mezőberény); Bihar county (Ártánd, Derecske, Nagyszalonta 7);
Szabolcs county (Biri, Kisvárda, Lövőpetri, Nyírbátor, Nyírtelek, Vaja); Szatmár county (Szamosszeg).
III.: 50.
   IV. Kolozs county (Gyalu, Válaszút); Maros-Torda county (Szováta); Torda-Aranyos county
(Aranyosgerend, Felvinc, Tordatúr); Alsó-Fehér county (Nagyenyed); Udvarhely county (Bencéd,
Felsőboldogasszonyfalva, Medesér, Nagygalambfalva, Rugonfalva'2, Siklód, Szentgerice, Vargyas);
Brassó county (Hosszúfalu); Csík county (Csíkkarcfalva, Gyergyóújfalu, Gyimesbükk,
Gyimesfelsőlok, Gyimesközéplok, Szépvíz); Háromszék county (Erdőfüle, Felsődoboly); Bukovina
(Andrásfalva 4, Istensegits 2, Józseffalva); Moldavia (Klézse). IV–V.: 33. Total: 169.
   Textual relationship with other ballads: none.
   Tunes: 1. = Nos 187–188 (39 variants). NB., *Bartalus* noted down the tune of No. 187 in the so-
called choriambic rhythm (— ∪ ∪ —), which had been thought to be the most typical Hungarian
rhythmic pattern. This I have transcribed into the usual rhythm of the other variants. 5. (6 var.) 9. (2
variants), 16. (2), 20. (2), 25. (2), 26. (2), 31. (3), 34. (2), 35. (2), 37. (3).

22. 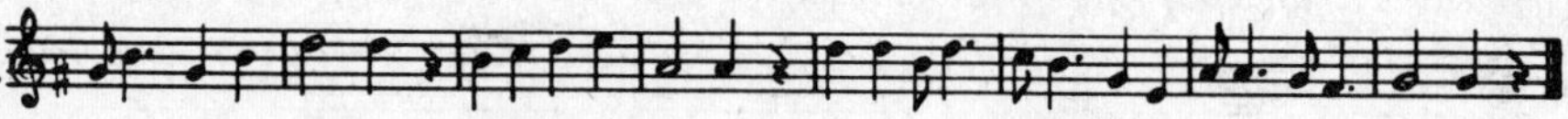

23. 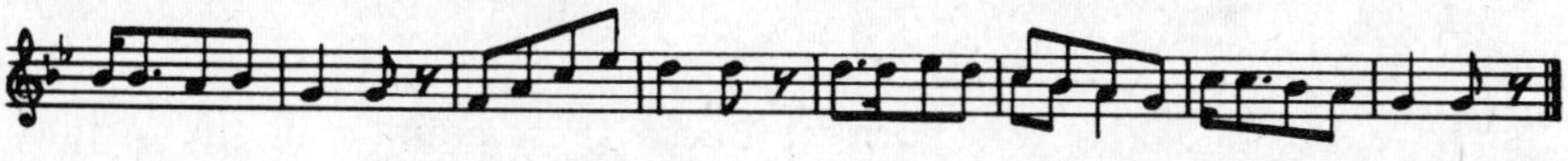

24. 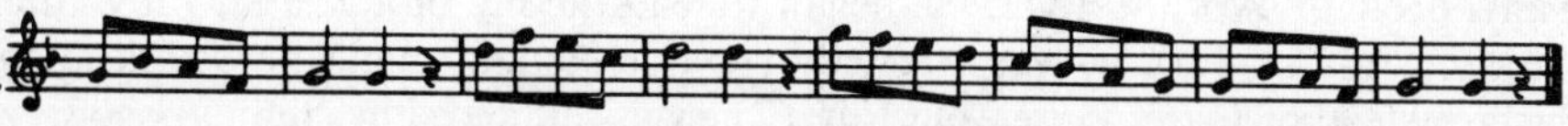

25. 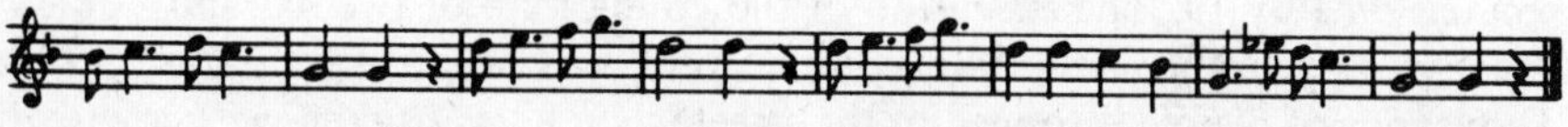

26. 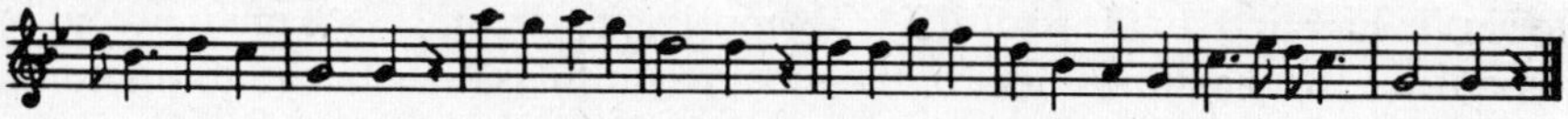

27. 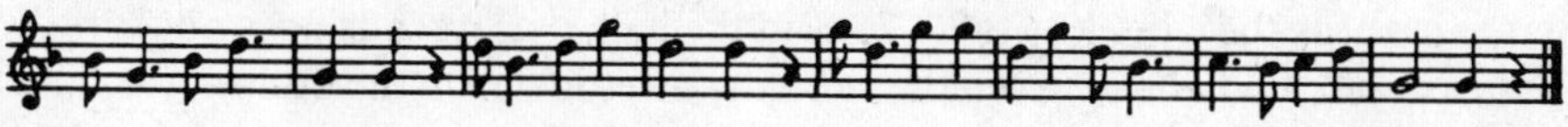

28. 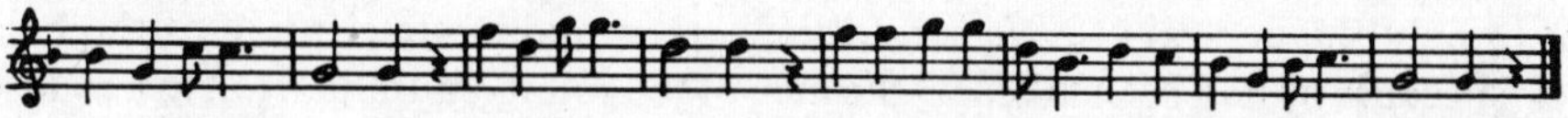

29. 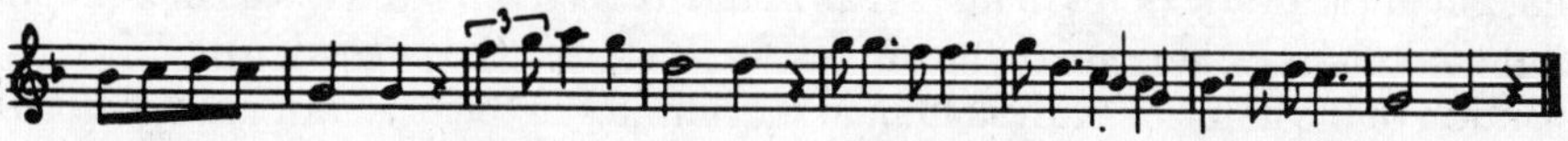

30. 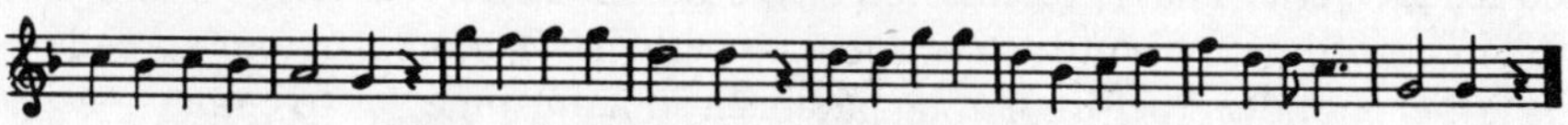

31. 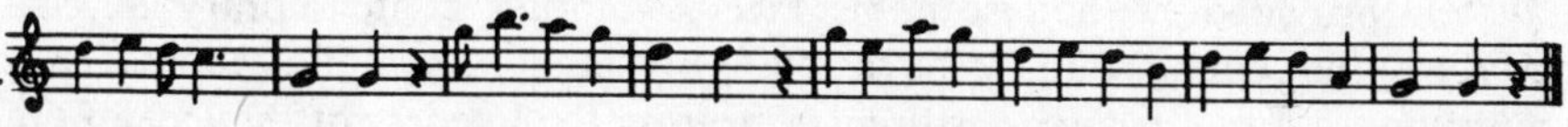

32. 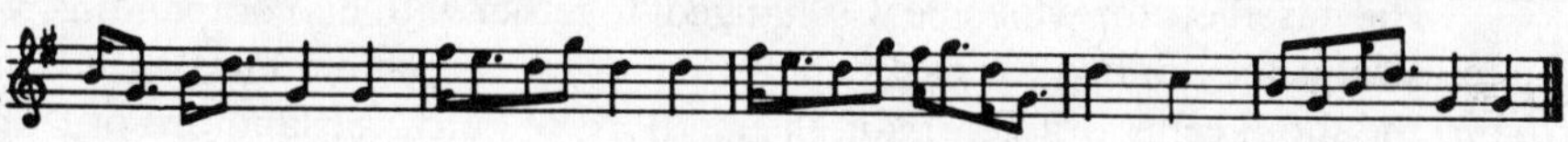

33. 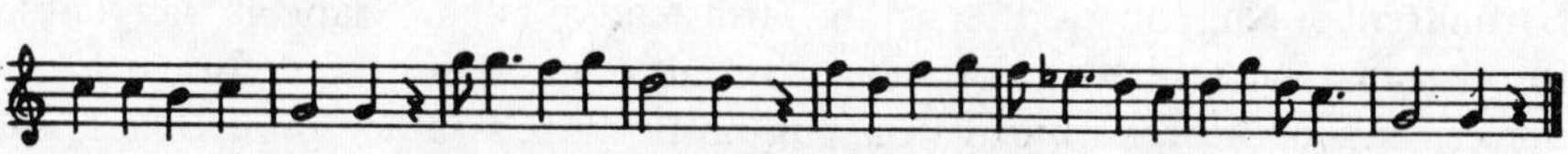

34. 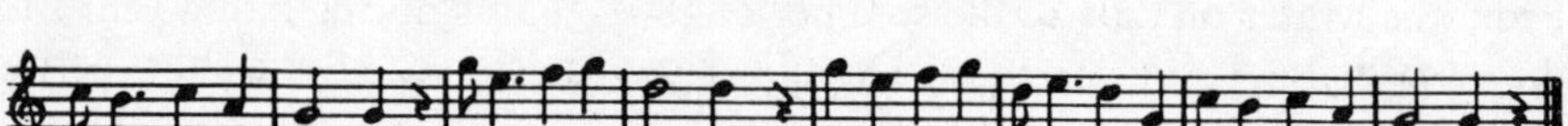

35. 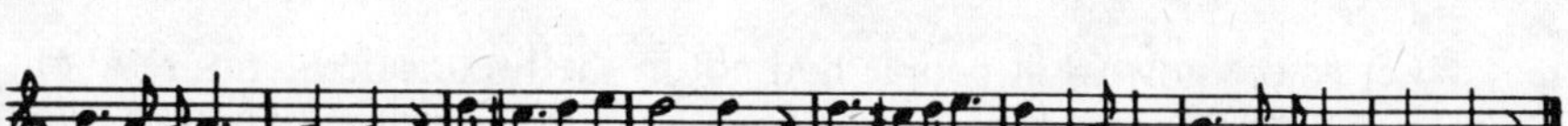

36. 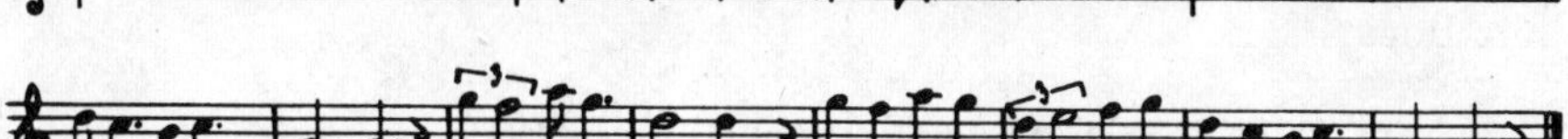

37. 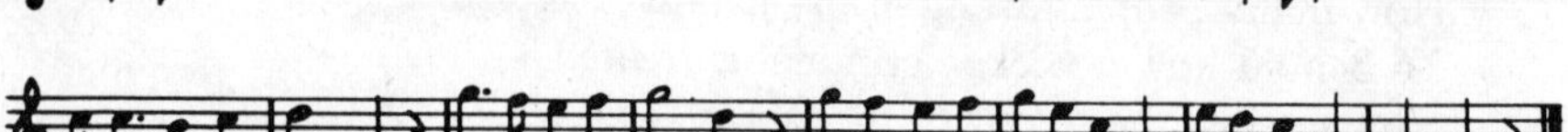

Imre Bogár Szabó was born at Bócsa (Pest county, in the vicinity of Nagykőrös) on April 6, 1842. He began to lead the life of an outlaw in winter of 1861. On July 11, 1862 he was arrested by two lieutenants while he was sleeping at the farmstead of József Pintér. On July 17 he was sentenced by summary court and executed on July 19. The execution of the young man of twenty, and "of a very attractive appearance and fair complexion" was a great sensation in Pest. "Thousands of people thronged in the street when he was taken, with a wreath of flowers in his hand, to the scaffold". Obviously, the circumstance of his execution is responsible for the attachment of the most beautiful outlaw ballad to his name. It developed comparatively quickly, because *Bartalus* was able to note down a variant of it as early as the winter of 1870–71. But the ballad as it reads does not agree with the facts presented above. Even the circumstances in which the outlaw was arrested are described differently; perhaps the arrest of another member of the group, that of Mihály Bogár Szabó, gave rise to the corresponding description of the ballad text, because he had been taken by the men of the county, although not in a roadside inn, but at the house of his maitress called mistress István Ruzsa, wife of a shepherd of the Jászlajos estate, where the outlaw was shot dead by a gendarme. There is no mention of the name of Marcsa Duli in the minutes of the trial, nor in the records of the gendarmerie. The representation of the gallant outlaw clad in gold and silver is well in accord with his attractive appearance; what is more, rumour spread about his father shot dead before that he had been so handsome "as to embarrass even a Lavater, provided he had seen his face". Another contemporary newspaper describes the young outlaw as a man of "a stately build, almost puerile youthfulness, a real beauty—with mien bearing the likeness of the face of God".

The mischiefs for which he was hanged, together with his companions, were the following: they raided the cartmen of Baja at the December fair of 1861; they robbed the shopkeeper of Újhartyán, the landlord of Páhy, the landlord of Dabas, Baron Rédl of Nagybócsa; they set the farmstead of István Szabó at Nagybócsa on fire, because he refused to provide them accommodation and forage for their horses, and because he killed in a gun-battle Imre's father Imre Bogár Szabó. From the winter of 1861 to the summer of 1862, that is during half a year's time, they were flying to and fro in the Danube-Tisza Interfluve. After a short period of brigandry, there followed the fall.

Let us see now what people had got in the broadside literature about the story. Here is a passage of a broadside from 1881, presenting the farewell speech of Imre Bogár.

1. How many people see me out to my early grave,
   How many people throng at my gallows,
   To behold how a wicked criminal is treated,
   How terrible the rigour of the law is!

772

2. They throw bunches of flowers at my sinful feet,
   Oh, how I resembled once these flowers,
   Before I lost my innocence,
   Before I became a criminal, a robber...

3. Alas, as a child I turned into a criminal,
   For what could I learn from my dear father?
   They never sent me to school,
   They never sent me to church!...

22. Good-bye, world, people who are sorry for me.
    Take an example from my mournful death,
    Tell my fate to these who listen to you some time
    That this is how every criminal fares in the end.

23. Good-bye, my dear spiritual father
    Who spent so much care on me.
    May you save me from devil's power,
    May you pass my soul into the hand of Our Father.

24. Good-bye, my righteous judges!
    Who sentenced me to mend the world.
    Thank you for the lesson you taught me,
    God knows your sentence is justified!

25. And now, my kind hangman, finish my life,
    So that I may surrender my soul to God.
    Oh, Heavenly Father, you are Almighty,
    Show me mercy, poor criminal as I am!

As can be seen, people framed a different conception about the event and a different opinion about the life of the outlaws. The pious lines of the broadside had no effect whatever on them. The peasant communities voiced their own opinion, and that in the genuine tone of poetry. And this is what they do in their songs even today.

Literature: Ferenc Szabó, 1964, 115. Békés, 202–220.

102. WHAT THOUGH SIX COUNTIES COME ON ME!

189.

1. Ku - tya - ko - po - nya - i csár - da,   Zsan - dár - ral van kö - rül - áll --va.

Kö - rű - kö - rű, kör - nyes - kö - rű,   Csak Vid - róc - kit fog - ták kö - rű.

1. The inn of Dog's Scull
   Is surrounded by gendarmes.
   Round, round, all round,
   They have surrounded Vidrócki, no-one else.

2. Well, Vidrócki, come out if you are a man!
   Six counties are waiting for you outside!
   What though six counties come on me,
   Let twelve come here!

3. They shot in through the window.
   Red blood spurted through his lips.
   His sweetheart's handkerchief
   Turned crimson with his blood.

4. His father is weeping, his mother is crying,
   Both his brothers are weeping.
   Don't weep, father, don't cry, mother,
   I shan't play the outlaw any longer!
   Twenty years have been enough of it,
   Now I shall be wrapped in mourn by the cemetery.

5. The bells are tolled, the bells are tolled,
   Is it perhaps because of Vidrócki?
   It is certainly because of Vidrócki,
   Because of that famous outlaw.

Pétervására (Heves county). Performed by a man of fifty-three. László Tary, 1958 =
László Tary: Heves-megyei népdalok (Folksongs from Heves County), 22.

Divergences:
In the more remote areas the name of the hero is changed to Miklóci,
Mitrovszki and Játrócki. Otherwise the hero is, rather surprisingly, always
Vidrócki. Several variants start with the formula: "There is a watery moon, The

name of Vidrócki is great. His fame flows As the water of the running brook", or "As the swift water of the Danube". Very seldom the song about Vidrócki's herd of swine is incorporated in the ballad, mostly one stanza of the song, which is sung separately as a rule. The completest form reads like this:

1. The famous herd of swine of Vidrócki
   Is roaring and grumbling in the Mátra.
   It is roaring and grumbling in the Mátra,
   Because it does not find Vidrócki anywhere.

2. Bring out, sweetheart, my felt-coat and my hatchet,
   Let me go after my herd of swine!
   For they. will cut down my boar,
   They will cut down my barrow with the white stocking.

3. The sun is setting, soon it will grow dark,
   I should like to ask for lodgings, only there is no-one to be asked,
   My lodgings is in the thick woods,
   My flat is in the briar.

Szuha (Heves county). Kodály.

In Szabolcs-Szatmár county, far away from the area of the outlaw's "activity", only the fully developed, or almost fully developed, ballad is extant.

Earliest provenience: before 1919 (*Kálmány* MSS).
Dissemination:
(A) the ballad:
Fejér county (Jánk); Nógrád county (Bárna, Etes, Mátraszele, Somoskő, Szanda, Tereske); Heves county (Bekölce, Bélapátfalva, Bükkszék, Bükkszenterzsébet, Egerbocs, Fedémes, Felsőtárkány 3, Hevesaranyos, Istenmezeje, Mikófalva, Parád, 3, Pétervására 2, Tar, Tarnalelesz); Borsod county (Abod, Bőcs, Kissikátor, Mezőkövesd, Sajómercse); Gömör county (Borzova, Pelsőc, Tornagörgő); Abaúj county (Cekeháza, Pányok); Zemplén county (Karos, Kistárkány, Sárospatak); Bereg county (Lónya); Jász-Nagykun-Szolnok county (Tiszaszalka); Southern Great Plain without closer specification; Bihar county (Nagyvárad); Hajdú county ("Hortobágy", Nyírábrány); Szabolcs county (Érpatak, Gyulaháza, Kállósemjén, Kisvárda, Mándok, Nyírbogdány, Nyírlugos, Nyírtura, Paszab, Vaja 3); Szatmár county (Nagyecsed, Piricse, Szamosszeg, Tornyospálca)? without specification (Eastern Great Plain?); Szolnok-Doboka county (Árpástó). Total: 63.
(B) "The famous herd of swine of Vidrócki": Nógrád county (Etes, Maconka 2); Heves county (Fedémes, Mátramindszent, Szuha 2, Tar, Tarnalelesz); Borsod county (Borsodnádasd, Csokvaomány, Tardona); Gömör (Nemesradnót, Sajótiba).
(C) "Have you heard the great fame of Vidrócki?" Nógrád (Szanda); Heves county (Parád); Gömör (Zabar).
Textual relationship with other ballads: none.
Tunes: 1. = No. 189. (15 variants); 2. (3), this is the tune usually sung with the texts summed up under (B); 3. (5).

The researches of Bodgál provide valuable information on the ballad's hero. His data throw light also on the birth of folklore composition.

Marci Vidróczki was born at Mónosbél (Borsod county) on November 12, 1837. His father was a shepherd, his mother was called Panna Kormos. His death occurred in a different manner than related in the ballad. Local papers report on his death on February 8, 1873 like this: "...In a similar way they visited the community of Bodony on eighth of the current month, where they enjoyed themselves throughout the whole day, paying no heed to the fact that the gendarmerie commissar, living in the next village of Maconka, stayed at home at that time. The wine-cellar of Mr. Edmond Almásy also lived in that village; Mr. Bogyó, bailiff and vine-dresser to the landlord, was decanting wine from one barrel to the other, assisted by the mayor of the village who sought refuge from the robbers in the cellar. They were just talking about the outlaws having a good time in the other village, when a man appeared, approaching to the cellar, gun in his hand with drawn-up cock: "Is there anything like a commissar or a lieutenant? For I would like to converse with them." The bailiff reassured that there was nobody of the said description there, and invited him for a glass of wine which the man accepted. Then he asked for a gallon of wine for his comrades. The vine-dresser complying with the command took the wine out of the cellar, but found, to not little surprise of his, five men standing in front of the cellar and aiming their guns at the door ready to use them in case of necessity. At a sign of Vidrovszky they put aside their arms and before drinking of the wine the bailiff offered them, they made the bailiff taste it, only after this did they begin to consume the wine, without saying anything. Meanwhile Vidrovszki and Mr. Bogyó retired in the vine-dresser's room to discuss some matter. One of the outlaws came in, saluted Vidrovszky in a soldierly manner, asking him to put right one of the fellows outdoors who—he said—was jumping on and off his horse with his gun in his hand, and thus there was a danger of his shooting either himself or his horse. Vidrovszky went out and gave the man a thorough scold, ending with the threat of shooting him dead at once if he did not behave properly. At the same time he warned his men not to get drunk because he planned to see, together with his band, the landlord Edmond Almásy and ask him to account why he had made his swineherd pay 240 florins for the eight pigs that had been driven away. "We cannot abide such a heartlessness!" With this, he turned to the bailiff asking him to tell his master to receive them as guests at eight at night.

Threatened by the adverse news, the houshold people and some others who came over from the next village were waiting for the arrival of the unwanted-for guest. In the meanwhile, the lady of the house went to see the commissar in the village, who however could not appear in person, being ill, nor were his lieutenants at hand, thus was unable to provide the help which the landlord asked for in a letter brought by the lady. In such a distressed state they passed the time till half past seven, when a gun-shot was heard from a distance. They thought it was the beginning of what should follow next; they waited intently till nine. Then a courageous farmhand decided to learn what the shot was for. He walked out, accompanied by a few men, and soon returned with the discovery that there is someone moaning and whispering near the manor-house. Afterwards the people in the house waked till morning. Then the farmhands reported that they had found a corpse at the bridge by the highway, whose face was distorted beyond recognition by many cuts, shot at the left arm; the bailiff still could tell by its face that it was the corpse of Vidrovszki."

Later his arrested comrades related the following story: "Led before the above-mentioned magistrate, the men owned that they were Vidrovszki's accomplices, namely István Pintér and Antal Rácz. Pintér's confession, as we referred to it in our last issue, made it clear that they were really toping in the cellar of Almásy, from where three of them, Vidrovszky, István Pintér and András Rácz set out at twilight to rob Mr. Almásy, while two of them left for the woods of Bátony, under Vidrovszky command to this effect. On the way I told Vidrovszky that I did not want to go to rob Mr. Almásy and that there was no means to change my decision. But at that very moment Vidrovszky drew his revolver, and aiming it at my breast announced that he would shoot me if I refused to obey him. I was aware of how cruel Vidrovszki was, and followed him frightened. So we walked the three of us, to the bridge of the Zagyva, where Vidrovszki was leading the way; we followed him. I asked Antal Rácz to hand me his hatchet, thinking that if I did not slay him he would shoot me. Therefore I hit him in the head from behind with the hatchet. He fell down on the ground, and I gave him two more hits on the head, shot him with my gun: his coat caught fire from the shot, but I stifled it so that people may recognize him later. We picked his weapons and threw them, together with ours, into the water of the river Zagyva. On the spot we came to an agreement that abandoning our former course of life, we should report on the case at the court . . ." The worthy county ordered at once the corpse to be transported to Eger so that the corpse should be identified by the outlaw's mates and parents already in custody. As appeared subsequently, he was identified." (*Bodgál,* 82–83.)

It is interesting to note that the real facts concerning the circumstances of the death-case has been entered into the words of a folksong as well:

Have you heard the great fame of Vidrócki?
How Pista Pintér cut off his head?
Pista Pintér cut it at one stroke
So that Vidrócki fell down upon the ground immediately.

(Cf. Kodály: Mátrai képek—Scenes from the Mátra). The original notation was made at Zabar, Gömör county.)

Furthermore, the prose traditions published by Bodgál and the legends collected by Ujváry contain particulars of the actual facts of the death-case. Still the fate of the outlaw was commemorated in the above ballad by the village communities, and the story spread in that form.

The sympathetic presentation finds its explanation in the popularity of the hero which transpires from contemporary newspaper accounts. Not long before the fatal assault, Vidrócki visited one of the villages. "On 23 January of the current year, the mayor of the village Szilvás, István Köz Varró celebrating the wedding of his son, held an entertainment. After the guests segregated about midnight, also the gipsy musicians, specially brought from Csermely for the occasion, prepared to retire when Mihály Bak, a pandoor not long before, appeared on the spot and forced the gipsies to follow him.

Their way led right to the inn, where Vidrócki and an unknown companion of his were waiting for them.

The table of the drinking room was laid with bottles of wine, the entertainment was begun to the tune of violins, and the three rascals kept on drinking the liquid produced from the cellar till six in the morning. Then Vidrócki, wishing to drink some coffee, visited the district physician, but in vain, therefore returned, accompanied by the gipsy band, to the inn.

The morning procession and the music roused the village and the young people, mainly young wives and girls clad in their best dresses filled the drinking hall in a minute.

Vidrócki declared the festivity opened with the following words: "Long live Vidrócki!" The self-greeting evoked loud response. After a short interlude the women formed a choir and began to sing the following song, which had become since a favourite item of the repertoire of the singers at Szilvás and Apátfalva. After the singing of this song was finished, Vidrócki presented some of the women with silver coins worth ten crown each. He said it would be souvenir of the day.

THE SONG OF MARCI VIDRÓCKI

Have you heard the fame of Vidrócki?
When the pandoors were looking for him here?
Suddenly he escaped through the window and off the hillside;
Come here, you dog of a pandoor, to meet your death here!

My lodgings is in the fir-wood of Fegyvernek
Sweetheart, come and see me there!
You will see my abode of golden wand,
My slender, tall Lombardy poplar.

778

Sweet angel, if you come to my place to-night,
Put red apples in your little handkerchief!
Give them to the commissar,
For not even the pandoors are enemies to me.

If the commissar asks who has sent him the apples,
Tell him: it is that famous Vidrócki.
If the commissar asks who has sent him the apples,
It is that renowned, famous Vidrócki.

We can see three fires in the distance,
Let's go, comrade, perhaps it will be worth-wile to go there.
Let's go, comrade, let's walk round the herd,
Let's drive away a few head of cattle!

A bay colt is grazing there alone,
Its legs are tied with a hundred shackles.
Go, comrade, turn that colt,
So that I can cut the shackles off its feet.

Once we took off the shackles,
We can manage the rest with ease.
We shall take it from west to east,
Next morning we drink shiller wine for the money it brings to us.

As can be seen, at that stage the song about "the local hero" absorbed generally known lyrical songs and outlaw songs, only here and there did it refer to the actual situation. "The dance lasted until noon. The revellers consumed much brandy and two barrels of wine, leaving the account to be settled by the "big bell" (that is, unsettled), and to make things worth, they broke all the glass-wares of the inn-keeper.

The invitation of the villagers for dinner caused some difficulty, because everybody wanted to share his feast. Finally János Kasza's home was found most worthy for the distinction... "However, Vidrócki fall asleep by the table, the gipsies stole away and also the participants of the drinking bout disappeared one after the other. Waking up from his stupor Vidrócki saw only one attendent about, Miska Bak who watched faithfully over him in his unguarded condition against a possible surprise by the gendarmes.

There is another proof of the fact that Vidrócki was not too much afraid of such an assault: when the gendarmes charged with his prosecution appeared at Apátfalva, he did not even try to escape, but went to sleep in the bed of a rich peasant, dreaming about his Eldorado of Szilvás." (*Bodgál* 81–82.)

It should be mentioned that the birth-place of Vidrócki was not lacking in revolutionary traditions. In connection with Bélapátfalva, a neighbouring village of Mónosbél considered by some to have been the place where Vidrócki was born, the Pallas Encyclopaedia writes the following: "Together with some other communities, Apátfalva refused to yield the quit-rent in 1750, and some four hundred serfs assembled to offer resistance to the armed forces and order was not restored until a

779

mounted regiment did not appear on the scene, casting into iron thirty-four of the rebels and hanging some of them."

This is another instance to show that when creating a ballad, the villagers do not insist on representing details but want to express what is thought to be of general significance. A song can acquire recognition in a wider circle only if it succeeds in grasping something of this nature.

Literature: Újváry 1961: legends in prose, birth certificate; *Békés* 1966: confronts the ballad and the data of *Újvári* in his account: "The career of an unknown outlaw in art"; *Bodgál* 1971, publishing contemporary newspaper articles.

103. THE SOLDIER WHO DESERTED FROM THE GERMANS

190.

Rubato

1. En - gem hiv - nak Fá - bi - ján Pis - tá - nak   Ki is   ál - lok hu - szon-négy zsan - dár-nak.

Ki is   ál - lok   hu - szon-négy zsan-dár-nak.   Még-mu - ta - tom kit hív-nak be - tyár - nak!

1. I am called Pista Fábián,
   And I can stand up against twenty-four gendarmes,
   I can stand up against twenty-four gendarmes,
   Showing them who is worth the name of an outlaw.

2. Good-bye, town of Szalonta,
   I shan't be a dweller of you any longer.
   The words of that famous Medidrászki
   Penetrated into the heart of Pista Fábián.

3. Son Pista, put down your weapon!
   You will see that I leave your life.
   If I put it down, I know, I shall be cast in iron,
   And thrown into prison before this night is over.

4. The apricot-tree blossoms at spring,
   Pista Fábián is prancing his steed.
   Prance, my steed, prance for the last time,
   Tomorrow I shall be taken to the gallows.

5. This is the farmstead of the famous Mistress Bajó
   That was plunged into mourn yesterday at dawn.
   Pista Fábián was taken, he was taken,
   And he was hanged on the gallows-tree.

Nagyszalonta (Bihar county). Performed by a woman of seventy-nine. Imre Fábián, 1970 = Művelődés 1970. July, 43.

(The above text was published without tune by the collector, but all the other variants recorded at Nagyszalonta were sung to the given melody.)

191.

1. I am called Pista Fábián.
   I can stand up against twenty-four gendarmes.
   Flee, gendarmes, Pista Fábián is coming,
   Don't you hear the thumping of his horse's feet?

2. Black earth grows good wheat,
   Thick forest raises the outlaw.
   Hostesses take care of him,
   Hostesses take care of him.

3. I don't wear a grey mantle,
   Nor do I eat the soldiers' bread.
   Rather I choose death
   But I don't be a soldier of the Germans.

4. The gendarmes are coming from all directions.
   Bullets are flying over my head.
   Poor Pista is standing by himself,
   Turning round and round with his weapon.

5. Alas, my God, what shall I do?
   Shall I surrender to the gendarme?
   If I surrender, I shall be cast in iron from neck to heel,
   My life of a gay lad will be finished.

6. Fábiány likes to dance,
   He is rattling the chain on the way to Várad.
   Oh, how nicely his spurs are clinking!
   The county had them made for him.

7. There is a gallows-tree by Várad,
   Three outlaws found rest on it.
   Two of them could not speak a word,
   But Fábiány was saying his farewell speech:

8. Good-bye, town of Szalonta,
   I shall not be your dweller any longer.
   The fen may bring green grass,
   My horse will not trample it any longer.
   I am not sorry that my outlaw's life is over,
   I am only sorry for my sweetheart.

Pusztaföldvár (Békés county) = *Kálmány 1878, 70.*

Divergences: Kálmány noted down, without the tune, a similar text, which reads as follows:

I am called Pista Fábiány,
Deserted soldier of the Germans.
I don't wear their grey mantle,
I don't eat the Germans' bread.
Black earth grows good wheat,
Thick forest raises the outlaw.
Hostesses take care of him,
The Great Lord sees to his troubles.
The breeze comes from Szeged,

782

Gendarmes are coming like shower.
Poor Fábiány stands all by himself,
Offering resistance with his weapon.
My brave heart, I enter into the fight,
Answering my Hungarian speech.
Alas, my God, alas, great is my sin,
Because I shot the officer of the gendarmes!
Alas, my God, either I must suffer death,
Or live in life-long captivity.
Beyond Szeged, there stands the gallows,
Oh, my last walk leads to it!
German grey-hounds will bury me,
Beasts of the forest will lament me.
I shall be feed for the eagles
Rather than a soldier to the Germans.
Good-bye, town of Szalonta,
I shan't be your outlaw any longer.
The fen may bring green grass,
The steed of Fábiány will not graze on it any longer.

Apáca (Csanád county).

"Germans" mean here the army of the Austrian Emperor.

Local compositions of various length exist in the environment of Nagyszalonta which relate details of the seizure and the life-story of the outlaw, mingled with passages of the folklore texts. Let us see portions of these as well.

"I was listed to the soldiers,
But I fled to become an outlaw.
I did not like to serve the Germans,
I preferred to be an outlaw.
My first dwelling was in Erdőgyarak,
Matyi Zuh was my first good comrade,
János Kenyeres asked him
To betray me, and then he would be released.
But as I learned this,
I shot comrade Matyi in the head.
Alas, my God, I am left alone,
Alas, I have lost the only man I trusted in!
János Cege was next to be listed,
He was ready to be an outlaw too.
Mihály Pásztor, and comrade Jóska Rocskás,
Well, the four of us were a gang of outlaws."

These are followed by three stanzas of the folk ballad. Then the composition reads on like this:

"The famous farmstead of Mistress Bajó
Was plunged into mourn at seven on Tuesday,

783

Because the many fair words of Mezidrácky
Touched the heart of Pista Fábián.
Mezidrácky and eleven of his men
Swore by the Trinity:
Son Pista, put down your weapon!
I say, I spare your life.
As Pista arrived at Kajla (= name of an inn)
He looked up at the gallows:
Then he said to Mezidrácky:
Lieutenant, you are going to hang me.
Mezidrácky answered:
Don't be afraid, Pista, it has not been erected for you.
An able man I was, strong of hand and foot when I was brought home,
At home I was bound with strong chain.
They tethered me on the porch.
Looking around whom did I see:
Mihály Pásztor, Jóska Rocskás, my comrades.
Well, what's news did you hear at Várad?
There is no news at Várad, except
That István Fábiján will be hanged.
Sister Erzsi, my kind sister Sári,
Ask the gentlemen with fair-spoken words,
Ask them, if they forbore
Not to rob me of my mournful life.
Sándor Nagy was my school mate,
He came to see me at hour of my death.
Wipe your black eyes,
Let me not see how you shed tears for me!

Two stanzas of farewell follow, then the ending one:
"Beyond the *Kajla* there stands the gallows,
Three outlaws met their rest on it.
Mihály Pásztor, comrade Jóska Rocskás,
Look, what fate has been in store for the three of us!

But there is a still longer text collected at Nagyszalonta, consisting of forty-seven stanzas (of four lines of eleven syllables each), apparently a broadside coloured with local folklore additions. The first three stanzas seem to be such local composition:

In the year of eighteen hundred and fifty-four
I fell in the heavy hands of the Germans.
Decision was passed on me in the letter
That I should be taken prisoner and to the redout.

2. Working hungry and thirsty day by day,
I grew tired of dancing to German tune.
I was always turning in my mind
To get once more to my country.

784

3. I would show the German world
   That I am not a man to be jerked by the nose!
   My wish has been fulfilled,
   This was the reason why I became an outlaw.

These had been the preliminaries of the variant still extant at Nagyszalonta—No. 190, and the texts closely related to it. Nevertheless, the large-scale collection of 1918 at Nagyszalonta includes a more ballad-like variant that has preserved memories of the factual background of the story.

1. I am called Pista Fábiján,
   And I stand up against thirty-four gendarmes.
   My steed is swift at ride and calm at pace,
   Also my coachman seeks my pleasure.

2. The apricot-tree has red blossoms,
   Pista Fábiján is whirling like a wheel.
   Don't forget, Pista, you will soon be taken,
   You will be drawn high on the gallows-tree.

3. If I am taken, bound in chains,
   My life as an outlaw will be ended.
   I shall be buried by the beasts of the fields,
   I shall be mourned for by the singing birds of the sky.

4. Here we are at the good old inn of Kajla,
   Stop, comrade, let's have a last drink!
   The black crow has laid three eggs,
   The hostess's daughter loves me dearly.

5. Cold blows the wind from the direction of Sarkad.
   The tune it blows says that I am to die today.
   The heavens don't allow me
   To live with you, sweetheart.

6. Megyedrászky and ten of his men
   Swore by the Holy Trinity:
   Son Pista, put down your weapon,
   I shall certainly spare your life!

7. Sister Sára, my kind sister Júccsa,
   Ask the lords with fair-spoke words,
   Ask them to let me go home
   And spare the life of an outlaw this time.

8. Here is the Kajla, the inn I shan't visit any longer.
   Stop and let me have a last drink!
   There stands a gallows-tree beyond the Kajla,
   Three outlaws met their rest on it.

9. Mihály Pásztor did not say a word,
   István Fábján encouraged him like this:
   Don't be scared, comrade, we have one life and one death,
   The bold outlaw must die in the end!

This song represents, by and large, the final folk text. In any case, the variants of it which are less folklorized hit upon the true ballad tone at least in the closing stanzas containing the farewell speech, as shown by No. 191 and the closely related variant of Pusztaföldvár. These two have become the prototype of the ballad spread over the country, and the other folk variants, too, fragmentary though they are, can be derived from them. Sometimes they consist of only two or rarely three stanzas.

The facts can be made out from the local researches of *Imre Fábián*. István Fábián began to lead the life of an outlaw after 1849 when he was rope-listed (taken forcibly) by the county bailiff János Kenyeres and transported to the company of refractory soldiers at Komárom. As early as that, the young man promised to take his vengeance for his forceful enlisting. And really, soon tiding spread that István Fábián, together with Miska Zuh, was hiding in the forest of Erdőgyarak, Feketetót and Csegőd, in the Szalonta region. János Kenyeres dared not step out of the Szalonta area unless under escort of a troup of gendarmes for fear of encountering Pista Fábján.

He used to be one of the outlaws who did not commit misdeeds excessively if let at peace. He only wanted to acquire his food. But if he was betrayed he turned into a dangerous man, as can be seen from the example of the innkeeper of Árpád who had dealings with the gendarmes. The outlaws, making a raid upon his inn, left the innkeeper in his blood. Pista wanted to give the hostess's jewels to his sweetheart Julcsa Berecki, but Miska Zuh also wanted to have his share of the prey. A quarrel followed in which Pista proved quicker and shot Zuh. His prosecution began after another murder that was not committed by him in point of fact. The county sent out Medidráczki to arrest him, who succeeded in seizing him: during the prosecution Fábján was cornered in a shed from where there was no escape.

Earliest provenience: 1872.

Dissemination: (complete variants are marked by asterisk(*))

Zala county (Zalaújlak, Orosztony); Tolna county (Őcsény); Borsod county (Radostyán 2); Zemplén county (Perbenyik); Pest county (Tura, Kiskunfélegyháza, Kiskunhalas 2); Jász-Nagykun-Szolnok county (Jászárokszállás, Kisújszállás); Csongrád county ("Csongrád c." 2, one of them*); Csanád county (Apáca*); Békés county (Doboz 5, Geszt, Gyulavári, Pusztaföldvár*, Sarkadkeresztur); Bihar county (Ártánd, Nagyszalonta 15, 8*); Hajdú county (Nádudvar, "Hortobágy" 3); Maros-Torda county (Kibéd); Udvarhely county (Tordátfalva). Total: 46.

Textual relationship with other ballads: **118, 111.**

Tunes: 1. = No. 190 (fifteen variants).

The development of the ballad took place according to the methods of folklore creation: occasional, personal details are gradually omitted, while the general parable-like moments are retained, and refined. The text of No. 191 and the variant published after it show the final formulation: the characterization of the outlaw has assumed the form of an abstraction, a pattern from which all factual details have been dropped. The variants noted down in any part of the language area represent stanzas of either of the two texts; these having become generally adopted. At the same time, many local variants sprang up in the vicinity of the outlaw's birth-place. But of these, no genuine folk-compositions have turned out up to this date.

Literature: Imre Fábián 1970: six variants from Nagyszalonta and contemporary accounts of the story.

104. HAVE I NOT TOLD YOU, BANDI ANGYAL?

192.

1. Lám meg mond-tam, An - gyal Ban - di, Ne menj az Al-föld - re,

Csi - kó - sok - nak, gu - lyá - sok - nak Kö - zi - be, kö - zi - be.

1. Have I not told you, Bandi Angyal, not to go to the lowland,
   To live amidst horseherds and cattleherds?!

2. For the first thing you can learn there is to steal horses,
   For which you'll get into the hands of the county's men.

3. As Bandi Angyal begins to saddle his steed,
   To harness it with the gorgeous horseherd's bridle,

4. He has his fur-cap put nicely on his head,
   He wears white veil around his neck.

5. His embroidered coat covers his shoulders,
   The fringe of it reaches down to his legs.

6. He has on his pants tasselled with gold,
   Made of Silesian linen.

7. His forehead is like alabaster, finer than marble,
   His beautiful black eyebrows are like rainbow.

8. As Bandi Angyal rode to the farmstead,
   To feast on that tender veil prepared for supper,

9. The town of Gönc raided on him and caught him,
   They bound his two hands with rope,

10. Then Bandi Angyal began to stare,
    Changing in colour.

11. Bandi Angyal was bound with rope,
    So he was escorted up to Kassa by armed men.

12. A pint of water and a pound of bread to Bandi Angyal,
    Iron of thirty-three pounds on his hands and feet.

Limbay 1882, 526. = MNT IV, No. 190.

The text agrees word for word, apart from certain phonetic dissimilarities, with the manscript of *S. Almási* (1834, II, No. 41) and *J. Erdélyi's* (1846) No. 236. Also the tune is the same as that of Almási.

The earliest recorded text includes the following lines (1807):

St. 3.Bandi Angyal is prancing his steed,
   Training it on the plain of Hortobágy.

St. 5.Sometimes he strolls out to the Hortobágy with a halter,
   Carrying a bridle and a gnarled staff.

St. 8.He is eyeing only the horses' necks,
   He either steals them or exchanges them.

These lines never recurred afterwards. At the same time, the first recording does not contain certain lines which turn up in later broadsides and folk-texts (for instance, "His forehead is like alabaster, finer than marble, His beautiful eyebrows are like rainbow"). The feast of veil is not mentioned in the text of 1807. In texts of later origin we are informed of "Two daughters of the hostess of the inn of Hortobágy Inviting Bandi to lie with them at night". And a still earlier variant, probably of 1810, adds: "That little girl is looking at him, In such a sorrow that she is near to piss." But this stanza cannot be found elsewhere either in the folk- or the broadside variants.

Anyway, the folklore variants do not add new moments to the story; only mix it with details of other songs, epic or lyrical; more often they omit certain stanzas. More or less complete are the texts of three variants from Gömör county, three from Abaúj county and one from the Banate. The opening formula and some other motifs can be detected in several folklore variants of the other texts: so, for example, in those recorded in counties Tolna (1), Komárom (1), Pozsony (1), Nógrád (1), Borsod (2), Abaúj (4), Bereg (1), and Bihar (1). Many folksongs have preserved only the first stanza, adding the folksong beginning with the line "The horseherds and cattleherds wear short jackets", on account of similarity of the text. This form prevails exclusively in county Szabolcs-Szatmár (eight variants), and also in Nógrád (3), Borsod (3), Bihar (2) and even in Bukovina (1). A song from Veszprém mentions the name of Angyal, but in quite a different context. As can be seen, tradition has been closely linked with the north-eastern regions where the outlaw was active and caught. The song bears traces of gradual erosion in folk tradition.

Earliest provenience: Pál Kiss, Világi nóták (Secular songs), MS. Debrecen 1807. Dömötör (1971) publishes it after G. Otrokocsi Nagy (1942). The MS. and published variants preceding the ones collected from folk-tradition are also worth-while listing here: 2) Antal Szirmay MS. (1812), O.Sz.K. 225., 122 fol. Published by Schram 1959, 141. Cf. Stoll 633, 3). Broadside from c. 1810, cf. Pogány Nos 26 and 98. Published by Békés 1840. 4) broadside from 1817. O.Sz.K. L. No. 744, V. 15. 5. 5) Almási MS. (1834) with tune. 6) Erdélyi J. No. 236 (1846). 7) Broadside (1860) published by Schram (1959), 140–41. 8) Bartalus 1876 (collection from 1871–72), with tune. 9) Limbay 1882, with tune (published above).
   Dissemination:
   I. Tolna county (Lápafő); Veszprém county (Réde); Komárom county (Csicsó) I.: 3.
   II. Pozsony county (Vásárút); Nógrád county (Borsodberény, Nógrádmegyer, Kosd, Szanda); Borsod county (Bőcs, Szentistván, Kisgyőr, Mezőkeresztes, Szirma, Tiszakeszi); Gömör county (Bátka, Licce 2, Szilice); Abaúj county (Cekeháza, Göncruszka, Kéked 2, Nyíri, Pányok); Bereg county (Dercen). II.: 23.
   III. Banate (on the Romanian side: Zsigmondháza); Bihar county (Nagyszalonta 3); Szabolcs county (Biri, Bököny, Érpatak, Nyíradony, Nyírlugos, Nyírtelek, Nyírvaja, Nyírvasvári); Szatmár county (Kérsemjén, Kocsord, Tyukod 2). III.: 16.
   IV. Bukovina (Hadikfalva).
   Total: 43 plus 9 early notation.
   Textual relationship with other ballads: none.
   Tunes:
   The published tune is extant in nine different recordings. All early notations of the text are coupled with this particular tune. Further, two variants from Abaúj county, two from Borsod, one from

Bereg were sung by villagers to this melody, and a text from Bukovina to a farther variant of the same tune. Distant ramifications of the main tune are represented by the other tunes (1. and 2–3., the two last ones being known from two variants). Tune 4 was recorded four times (in counties Nógrád and Gömör). Nos 5–9 are isolated variants. Tunes of fragmentary variants are sung in county Szabolcs-Szatmár, as shown by the one single stanza presented in association with No. 10. This is actually the shepherd's song (Horsemen and cattleherds wear short waistcoats...), occurring in twelve variants (one from county Ung and another from Abaúj).

Bandi Angyal—András Ónodi by his name—was born of a well-to-do gentry family at Sajószentpéter (county Borsod), 1759, and died at the same place on 19 November 1806. He was first sentenced on May, 21 1788 to eight years'

imprisonment aggravated with forced labour. He was charged with stealing twelve horses (three cases proven!), which he had committed with the help of a soldier deserter. Later the punishment was considerably mitigated, and finally suspended on petition for mercy. Next time he was condemned for two years imprisonment, in 1799, but in a process of court-appeals the case was delayed until 1804 when his period of imprisonment was raised to four years. But by that time he was not to be found anywhere. The warrant of apprehension contains the following: "Description of person of András Ónody—who calls himself sometimes by the name of Bandi Angyal—condemned to four years' imprisonment in the Gaol of Szeged: he is tall of stature, eight inches above five feet, and stout of body, broad shouldered, deep chested, his legs are strong and his cheeks of a nice red complexion; his hair is cut short, not thick, getting bald at the forehead, his moustache is bushy, but twisted up occasionally; as regards his age, his is forty-five or so. As concern his garments: he wears a Hungarian gown, sometimes only Hungarian pants, always a Hungarian shirt, a pair of long-legged boots with broad silver, but mainly iron spurs; a belt with a big brass buckle sometimes under and sometimes over his shirt, and to complete his costume, a good fur overcoat as is usual with shepherds. He can speak Hungarian, Latin, a little German and Slovak." Miskolc, July 12, 1805.

Beside the warrant of apprehension, pinned on the advertisement board was seen his authentical portrait showing the outlaw sitting in the costume described above on a richly harnessed steed. (For the picture see *Dömötör*.)

In spite of the warrant of apprehension and the sentence, he died of some illness at home.

On the basis of the minutes of the trial and with reference to the rather complete variant of 1807 published by *Gábor O. Nagy, Dömötör* considers the poem a literary product expressing inimical feelings against Bandi Angyal. According to her, the peasants had a critical opinion of the horse-stealer nobleman; this seems to be supported by the fact that peasants of Zsujta (Abaúj county) detected and disarmed two horse-thieves, defending themselves bravely with their cudgels; so the thieves were arrested. Earlier opinions, on the other hand, regarded the poem as a panegyric of the handsome mounted outlaw.

The question is not as simple as that: one can adduce arguments to prove the people's sympathy or antipathy in respect of an outlaw, as well as pros and cons concerning the folklore origin of the poem. True, outlaws of peasant origin were taken not infrequently by villagers (for instance, Marci Zöld and Sándor Rózsa whom they had hidden for years formerly). Thus a similar attitude of the populace does not offer an argument against Bandi Angyal as a horse-thief and a nobleman at the same time. But in some eroded variants from Szabolcs-Szatmár county we have: "Don't cross the ways of horsemen and cattleherds!" and in a Bukovinian variant probably deriving from the former the passage "Bandi Angyal was bound with rope, So he was escorted to Kassa" had been changed into: "You will be caught by horsemen and their hands. Once you are taken, you will be bound by rope and so escorted under arms to Eger." Nevertheless, here we find a case of final erosion which cannot reasonably be regarded as a true reflection of traditional features. Nor can we rely in this case on the analysis of formal and content elements. The form with its repetitive line endigs seems to be an art composition at first sight.

791

But this is rather usual with Hungarian folksongs of ten-syllabic lines. By doubling the first four-syllable bars of the lines a rare variant of the widespread rhythmic pattern called "swineherds' dance" has been developed. Anyway, the genuine folklore composition of the ballad of Imre Bogár is also a strange form of 6, 6, 8, 6 syllabic lines, even its melody is foreign—Slovak—of origin, although not so strange as the earliest-recorded Angyal Bandi tune. More conspicuous than this is the over-refined technique of rhyming.

The depicting of the gorgeous robe of the outlaw had been taken for another proof of the popular origin of the song. Bandi Angyal is clothed in gold and silk, just as Imre Bogár appears on back of a bay harnessed with silver bridle and golden bit. But the description of Bandi Angyal's garment is overdetailed, in a sharp contrast to that of Imre Bogár which is fable-like, stylized and terse, casting just a cursory glimpse on the stately outlaw's figure; as against this, the song of Bandi Angyal follows—from point to point—the description of the person as offered by the warrant of apprehension. This is too much for a true ballad or folksong! Some later variants, therefore, omitted these details or preserved them abridged to one or two stanzas only.

More consideration should be given to the content side: this text is not yet a ballad because there is no real tragic conflict in it; rather a sort of content and approval can be read out of the lines, indeed. But the earliest known outlaw ballad, that of Péter Barna, is not a ballad in the true sense of the word, only a series of low-life scenes, and also the later popular outlaw stories are lacking in any genuine tragic features, although their manner of construction invariably follows, essentially, the same pattern as that of Bandi Angyal's ballad: the figure of the outlaw turns up dauntingly in all his glory, only to fall in the end. Truly tragic tone can only be found in the latest-developed outlaw ballads, namely of Imre Bogár, Vidrócki and Pista Fábián. For this, two generations' development was needed.

Dömötör attributes a great significance to the first-recorded text, details of which include information typical of the activity of Angyal, details that must have originated from the pen of a well-informed man. This circumstance may settle the debate in favour of the urban conception. But the weakness of this argument lies in that the details involved never occur in subsequent formulations, not even in the earliest broadside versions, although broadsides are inclined to indulge in similar details. If they had been included in the first literary text, the prototype of all later variants, then they should have turn up here and there in the derivates. It is worth-wile to survey the folk variants and establish the scale of frequency in which portions of the earliest and largely uniform variants come up in the thirty-seven folklore variants. Following the order of stanzas in the published variant, we see the following distribution: St. 1 occurs 36 times, on three occasions the line "To live amidst horseherds and cattleherds" is omitted, and in eight cases the phrase "don't cross their ways" is entered; St. 2: 14; St. 3: 8; St. 4: 3; St. 5: 6; St. 7: 7; St. 8: 3; St. 9: 7; St. 10: 5; St. 11: 10; St. 12: turning up 9 times. In the basic text we do not find the lines of the variant recorded in 1810 "Two daughters of the hostess of the inn of Hortobágy Inviting Bandi to lie with them at night", though the folk versions have them in three instances. Only the strange lines of the first-recorded text of 1807 do not come up again. Although the MS. involved was not written by the "author" for it is a subsequent notation of the song which was spreading in the countryside by that time. And if we start from the consideration that the composition of some poet was disseminated by the broadside literature—a spread by MS copies being precluded—then we should find traces of the mentioned strange lines in the broadsides. As minor alterations got here and there into the folk as well as written variants, we may well suppose a subsequent insertion into the text of Debrecen, the strange portions having been details gathered from hearsay. In any case, we should be cautious in regard of what is called "earliest notation" which is not always the most authoritative in the flow of folk tradition.

All things considered, I am prone to take the song for the text of a broadside that succeeded in hitting upon a tone fairly agreeing with that of folklore compositions; obviously, it was written under the inspiration of the first arrest of the outlaw and not later than the nobleman, after sundry adventures, had died at home of some illness that confined him to bed. In conclusion: Bandi Angyal is not a hero of the peasantry and his song is not yet a folk ballad. It is a ballad-like—more precisely a narrative-song interspersed with dramatic details, which did not refine in the course of time but on the contrary, it has undergone a process of erosion to a stage where only the name and the appended admonition survive, the latter in the nature of a proverb.

Developed between 1788 and 1807.
Literature: Gábor O. Nagy 1942; *Pogány* 1959, No. 26 and p. 166, No. 98; *Békés* 1966, 35–41; *Dömötör* 1971.

105. MY GREY HORSE WAS A GOOD ONE

193.

Parlando ♩•61

1.Szë - gény Bar - na Pé - tĕr   a lo - vát   i - tat - ja.

Ro - má - né két   lá - nya   Jó   e - béd - re   vár - ja.

1. Poor Péter Barna
   Gives his horse to drink.
   The two daughters of Mistress Román
   Are waiting for him to come and have a good dinner.

2. They are waiting for him to eat cabbage
   And drink honeyed brandy.
   Drink, Péter Barna,
   Have your revenge on the world!

3. Poor Péter Barna
   Took off his mantle.
   The two daughters of Mistress Román
   Took it in their hands only too eagerly.

4. The horses of the county
   Are fattened with oats.
   When chasing Péter Barna
   They often are made to run swift.

5. Oh, when they run swift,
   They might tumble and fall on the earth!
   So that poor Péter Barna
   May not be reached in his flight.

6. Blow off, breeze, blow off
   The dust of the long way,
   So that no one should be able
   To trace the hoofprints of my horse.

7. Hold tight in your hand
   The red bridle,
   The county is upon you,
   You must not surrender!

8. The roaring of the green woods,
   The cooing of turtle-doves
   Are like the smile
   Of poor Péter Barna.

9. There, down by Árpád,
   There is a little grove.
   Poor Péter Barna
   Is roaming about.

10. Comrade Pista, it is not well,
    It is not well to stay here.
    Poor reckless fellows
    Are usually taken here.

11. Comrade Péter Barna,
    We ought to go to Gyula,
    We ought to raid colts,
    We ought to sell them there.

12. My grey horse was a good one,
    And a good horse foaled it,
    May God bless him
    Who raised it!

13. It had often circled
    The environs of Győr county.
    Poor Péter Barna
    Oh, he had stolen many horses indeed.

14. The peacock has lit
    On top of the county's house.
    Péter Barna is being taken
    Into its courtyard.

15. The gate of the county's house
    Is not open in vain.
    Poor Péter Barna is being taken
    Into the condemned cell.

16. He is tied to the gallows tree
    With long, strong chains.
    The two daughters of Mistress Román
    Mourn for him at a distance.

17. I have told you, my dear Mariska,
    Not to fall in love with me!
    My heart is double-dealing,
    It will deceive you.

18. May the radish perish
    In its black soil!

May the two daughters of Mistress Román
Have perished in their mother's womb!

19. With us for a dead body
Bells are tolled three times.
But to poor Péter Barna
Not even one chime is sounded.

*Valkonya (Zala county). Performed by a man of seventy-one. Seemayer 1932 = Nz.
Cs. 1151.*

194.

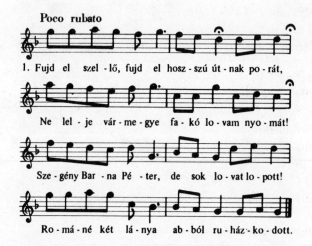

Poco rubato

1. Fujd el szel-lő, fujd el hosz-szú út-nak po-rát,

Ne lel-je vár-me-gye fa-kó lo-vam nyo-mát!

Sze-gény Bar-na Pé-ter, de sok lo-vat lo-pott!

Ro-má-né két lá-nya ab-ból ru-ház-ko-dott.

1. Blow off, breeze, blow off the long way's dust
So that the county should not trace my horse!
Poor Péter Barna has stolen many horses,
The two daughters of Mistress Román clothed from them.

2. May the black radish perish in the soil,
May the two daughters of Mistress Román perish in their mother's womb!
Then the inn of the roadside would not be thrown into mourn,
Poor Péter Barna would not be thrown into prison.

3. In the plain of Tarcsa there is a two-branched tree,
It is going to serve as the resting place for Péter Barna.
Open, skies, hide me,
For the black earth cannot take me in!

4. With us, to the dead bodies the bells are tolled three times,
But to Péter Barna not even a chime is sounded.
On St. John's Day, poor Péter Barna
Was seen to the paling of Tarcsa where he was put to death.

5. It would be a pity for me to dry on the tree,
   To have my waving linen pants be blown by the wind,
   To have my beautiful spurred long-legged boots be beaten together by the wind,
   To have ravens pick my two black eyes.

Kisgyarmat (Hont county). Performed by an aged woman. Kodály 1912.

Divergences: The completest variant of the ballad is represented by a broadside which, according to the statement of *Péter Pogány,* sprang forth in the second decade of the last century.

1. The linen shirt and pants of Pista Sallai
   And all his bodily clothings are blossoming blood.
   Poor Péter Barna is giving his horse to drink,
   The two daughters of Mistress Román have prepared a good supper for him.

2. They have prepared cabbage and honeyed brandy,
   Drink, Péter Barna, and take your vengeance on the world!
   Poor Péter Barna has stolen many horses,
   The two daughters of Mistress Román clothed from them.

3. As Péter Barna bought the dresses
   The two daughters of Mistress Román were rejoicing.
   The horses of the county are fattened with oats.
   And often made to run swiftly after Péter Barna.

4. Oh, would they tumble over the ground as they run!
   So that poor Péter Barna might escape!
   Blow off, good wind, blow off the dust of the long way,
   So that the county may not trace my grey horse.

5. You have not blown off, good wind, the dust of the long way,
   The county has traced up the hoofprints of my grey horse.
   Hold tight its red bridle,
   The county is about you, don't surrender!

6. The roaring of the green woods and the cooing of turtle-doves
   Are like the smile of poor Péter Barna.
   Down by Ártánd there is a small thick grove,
   Poor Péter Barna is roaming about it.

7. It is not a good soil, comrade, to live on.
   For outlaws are usually caught here.
   We ought to go to Gyula to raid colts,
   Comrade Péter Barna, it would be good to sell them.

8. May God bless the feet of my grey steed,
   It has often rode the environs of the town of Gönc!
   My grey steed was a good horse foaled by a good mare,
   May God bless the one who reared it.

9. The shoes have fallen off my horse's hoofs,
   Only one remains and even that one is loose.
   The inn by the roadside is plunged into sorrow,
   Poor Péter Barna has been taken prisoner.

10. The gate of the county's house does not open in vain,
    Poor Péter Barna is being taken into its courtyard.
    The peacock has lit on top of the county's house,
    To herald the release of poor Péter Barna.

11. Open, skies, hide me,
    For the black earth does not take me in!
    Poor Péter Barna was escorted to meet his death
    In the field of Tarcsa, on Saint John's day.

12. He is tied to the gallows with strong chains,
    The two daughters of Mistress Román mourn him at a distance.
    May the radish have perished in the black soil,
    May the two daughters of Mistress Román have perished in the womb of
    their mother!

13. I have told you, my Mariska, not to love me,
    My heart is double-dealing, it will deceive you.
    There is a two-branched tree in the plain of Acsád,
    This will serve as a resting place for Péter Barna.

14. It would be a pity for me to dry on the tree,
    To have my waving linen pants be blown by the wind,
    To have my beautiful spurred long-legged boots be beaten together by the
    wind,
    To have ravens pick my two black eyes.

15. With us three bells are tolled to the dead body,
    But to Péter Barna not even a chime is sounded.
    I was not sick, still I had to die,
    I am resting in the plain of Acsád.

16. Roses will grow by my grave,
    Lads and women-folk will come to pick them.
    Pick them, sweetheart, pick them into your handkerchief,
    In defy of the town and in token of grief the girls mourn for me!

Certain later notations have preserved this text either unchanged or slightly changed; such are: a text from the legacy of *Abafi,* perhaps the broadside itself, another publication by *Erdélyi* from 1846, which also *Bartalus* took over, furthermore, a notation by *Kálmány* from 1891, from Temes county. The early recordings are closer to the original broadside, the later ones have retained portions of it. The variants without exception survive in the fringe areas of old traditional folklore around the centre of the language area. There is only one single variant to show novel features against the other ones, and it has been collected among the Székelys of Bukovina resettled in Hertelendyfalva; it seems, however, that this variant did not belong to their old store of knowledge but developed in the new surroundings, that is in Torontál county.

1. As Péter Barna was giving his horse to drink,
   The two daughters of Mistress Román were inviting him for a big dinner.

2. I heard a voice: Mount your horse,
   Mount your horse and start on your way.

3. The six horses of the county are fed on oats,
   And often driven in the wake of Péter Barna.

4. May the radish have perished in its black soil,
   The two daughters of Mistress Román in the womb of their mother.

5. May the horses tumble over while running,
   So that Péter Barna might escape.

6. As he was roaming to and fro he hit upon an inn,
   Let me in, my darling hostess!

7. I won't let you in for I don't know who you are.
   I am, I am a poor horseherd.

8. My legs are cold, my mantle is soaked with rain.
   My fine bay is uneasy down by the garden.

9. The grey horse was a good horse, may it remain so!
   May God bless him who raised it.

10. The horses of the county could not reach it,
    Poor Péter Barna won space with it.

11. I am sorry, sorry, very sorry
    For the two daughters of Mistress Román, oh, how sorry I am for them!

12. For I owe my life to them.
    I have killed many gentlemen and saved many poor people.

13. God is my witness that I have not committed a sin in all my life,
    For they killed many poor people with their heavy taxes.

14. In the big lords'houses they often entertain themselves,
    The lords are merry-making, while the poor are weeping.

15. Only God knows how I could fare,
    A man forced to be an outlaw, like me.

(Repetition): God forgive me, if He created me to be one!
God forgive me, if He created me to be one!

Hertelendyfalva (Torontál county). Performed by a woman of sixty-eight. Ernő Király 1955.

Earliest provenience: between 1810 and 1820.
Dissemination: Without specification: 5 (broadside 1810–20, the legacy of Abafi 2, Erdélyi J. No. 383, III, No. 278).

Zala county (Dergecs, Murarátka, Valkonya, Zalakaros) Szerém county (Kórógy); Baranya county (Mohács), Hont county (Kisgyarmat) Nógrád county (Romhány); Bács-Bodrog county (Gombos); Temes county (Monostor); Torontál county (Hertelendyfalva 5); Hajdú county ("Hortobágy", Tiszacsege); Hunyad county (Lózsád); Maros-Torda county (Székelyvaja); Alsó-Fehér county (Csombord); Csík county (Gyergyószentmiklós, Mádéfalva); Bukovina (Istensegíts 3); Total: 30.

Textual relationship with other ballads: **101.**, incidental insertion, **118.** (The motifs of the latter occurring in the present ballad: 1., 7. (2 variants), 8–9. (6 variants), 28. (5 variants), 81. (4 variants), 18. and 81. appear as broadsides as early as 1810–20.

Tunes: 1. = No. 193 (3 variants); 2 = No. 194 (2 variants); 4 = (5 variants).

Nothing is known about the person after whom the hero of the ballad was named. As the song was fully developed by the end of the first decade of the last century, it must have originated from the eighteenth century. In the first half of the eighteenth century an outlaw called Péter Barna was hanged (1736) at Makó. But the date seems to be too early and the place of execution was other than mentioned in the texts. One thing is certain: the ballad must have existed in the late eighteenth century. Accordingly, its typical prisoners' song motifs had been generally known by that time. ("It would be a pity for me to dry on the tree . . ."; "The peacock has lit on top of the county's house . . .", etc.).

Literature: Dömötör 1930; *Pogány* 1959, listing the broadsides; *Békés* 1966, 66–74.

106. MARCI ZÖLD

195.

1. Ad - dig vár - lak még Már - to - nom, Mig ezt a szöszt le nem fo - nom.

S ha el nem jön ak - ko - rá - ra, Mást kö - tök fel a rok - ká - ra.

1. I shall be waiting for you, dear Márton,
   Till I shall have spun this tow.
   If you don't arrive by that time,
   I shall bind some more on the spinning-wheel.

2. The last spindleful is soon finished,
   And my heart is still waiting for your heart to come.
   The cock crows at dawn,
   Come to my house's window!

3. Who is tapping at my door?
   Perhaps he has heard my voice?
   Come, Marci, I let you in,
   And oh, you receive a hearty welcome.

4. Forgive me, my beautiful angel,
   It makes me grieve as well
   That I could not come earlier,
   But it is not my fault.

5. An enemy of mine attacked me,
   And I was nearly lost.
   I thank it to the speed of my horse
   That I was able to come and see you.
   The poor soul, it was foaming with blood (to lines 3 and 4)
   Till it reached here.

6. But what to recall this for?
   Be gay while beside me!
   Let's feast and drink, and when we have enough of it,
   We still have time to sleep till dawn.

7. I see the sky clouded,
   A heavy cloud is threatening.
   The wind blows from Fegyvernek,
   I am trembling for fear of lightning.

8. I asked Marci by heavens
   Not to go to Fegyvernek!
   But he did not pay heed to me,
   Leaving sorrow in my heart.

9. When bidding his last farewell
   He pressed his lips on my lips,
   He kissed me the last time then,
   And so he mounted his grey steed.

10. His horse returned three times,
    It carried him about to and fro.
    As if it had felt how much we loved each other,
    How our fate was fulfilled.

11. He is gone, and I know, in the future
    He will not wrap me in his fur-coat.
    Where shall I rest my sad head,
    Who is going to warm me?

12. If my sweetheart is to die,
    Carry me away, death!
    Let me perish, for this life
    Is punishment without him about me.

Gyergyóújfalu (Csík county). Bartók 1907.

   Divergences:
   The style of formulation and the technique of rhyming betray that the song is an art composition, and really a variant of it can be discovered among the broadsides of the nineteenth century.

The Song of Marci Zöld's Sweetheart:

1. Cold wind blows from the north,
   My soul is shivering with cold in me.
   Come and lie under my beautiful cotton
   Quilt, my sweetheart Márton.

2. Becskereki, Becskereki,
   Perhaps you betrayed him?
   If I thought you a traitor,
   I should lay an eternal curse on you!

3. But you are not an ill-wisher of mine,
   I know a different soul in you.
   Someone else must have betrayed me,
   Or my sweetheart must have been caught.

4. I shall be waiting for you, dear Márton,
   Till I shall have spun this tow.
   If you do not come by that time
   I shall put some more on the spinning-wheel.

5. The last spindleful is soon finished,
   And my heart is still waiting for your heart to come.
   The cock crows at dawn,
   Come on my house's window!
6. Who is tapping at my door?
   Perhaps he has heard my voice?
   Come, Marci, I let you in,
   And oh, you receive a hearty welcome!

Marci Zöld answers:

1. Forgive me, my beautiful angel,
   It makes me grieve as well
   That I could not come earlier,
   But it is not my fault.
2. An enemy of mine attacked me,
   And I nearly lost my last chance
   To see you again,
   My dearest heart.
3. I thank it to the speed of my horse
   That I was able to come and see you.
   The poor soul, it was foaming with blood,
   Till it brought me here.
4. But what use to recall this?
   Be gay while beside me!
   Let's feast and drink, and when we had our fill
   There will be still time to sleep till dawn.

The sweetheart answers:

1. I see the sky getting cloudy,
   A heavy cloud is threatening.
   Its wind blows from Fegyvernek,
   I am trembling for fear of lightning.
2. I asked Marci by heavens
   Not to go to Fegyvernek.
   But he paid no heed to me,
   Leaving sorrow in my heart.
3. When bidding his last farewell
   He pressed his lips on my lips,
   Then he kissed me the last time,
   And so he mounted his grey steed.
4. Oh, pure token of love,
   How hot his embrace was!
   Oh, you guardian angel of my heart,
   Your throat was like pure honey!
5. His horse returned three times,
   It carried him about to and fro.

As if it had felt how dearly we loved each other,
And how our fate was fulfilled.

6. He is gone, and I know, in the future
He will not wrap me in his fur-coat.
Where shall I rest my sad head?
Who is going to warm me?

7. If my Marci Zöld is to die,
Carry me away, death!
Let me perish, for this life
Is punishment without him about me!

Mostly associated with old tunes, this typical broadside verse survives in folk tradition; the rest of the composition burdened with sham-pious laments for the outlaws in general had left untouched the folksong. Still there are some bookish texts which contain other details than known from the broadside and what can be read in the minutes of the trial.

1. I grew sleepy on the bank of a brook,
Rain came, and I ran away
To have a sleep in a sheep-pen.
There I met a man wrapped in a fur-coat.

2. I asked him in the darkness,
Who he was.
He andwered: I am Palatinszki,
And I want to steal a few horses.

3. If I succeed in getting a few horses,
I shall ride off and cover a long way.
When it dawns
I shall have left the boundary behind me.

4. After these words
He addressed me in a lower tone:
Who should I honour in your person?
I told him boldly, I was Marci Zöld.

5. He expressed his contentment upon this,
And shaking hands with me,
Answered: I am very glad
To have met with an expert companion.

6. He left the sheep-pen,
Took off his fur-coat,
Blew his whistle,
And renounced friendship.

7. As I looked out of the sheep-pen,
I beheld nine gendarmes standing around.
The tenth opened the door
And chained my hands.

8. As long as I did not say the truth
   I had been leading a happy life.
   Now I said truth, and bound in chains
   I am escorted to Szamosújvár.

This text, abridged and somewhat folklorized, was current in several variants. It is interesting to read the Arad-county variant, in which the bookish verse is seen at an early stage of transformation in the folk style, intermingled with motifs of prisoners' songs and genuine outlaw songs.

1. Cold wind blows from every direction,
   My soul is shivering with cold in me.
   Come, my dear Veronka, and embrace me,
   And God's best blessing be with you!
2. I am laden with sorrow
   Like a sour apple-tree.
   Two or three ripen on the branches,
   While the ground is covered with them underneath.
3. At dawn on Thursday
   I sat on the boat of sleep.
   At ten I went to bed,
   And had a short slumber.
4. As I opened my eyes,
   I saw three heyducks standing by me.
   I asked them what they were looking for,
   And if they had come to take me?
5. We have come to take you, and we bind you
   And escort you into the county's house,
   Cast you into its deep dungeon,
   Into its deepest floor.
6. Becskereki, Palatinszki,
   Has someone betrayed me?
   If only I knew that it is Veronka,
   Her blood would run in one flow with mine.
7. I sent word to the judge
   Not to be glad of our imprisonment.
   But the judge thought differently,
   He sentenced the three of us.
8. Marci Zöld and Becskereki,
   His affectionate friend Palatinszki,
   On the flat plain of Fegyvernek
   They are hanging from the gallows-tree.

As can be seen, hardly anything remains of the original composition in this song. The first stanza bears some reminiscene of it, further, stanzas 6 and 8 have retained certain elements, although strongly transformed, except for one single line. Otherwise the text raises the impression of a genuine folksong.

Earliest provenience: probably 1817; soon after the execution a broadside was published, as was usual.

Dissemination: Without specification of the place: print. Somogy county (Kutas); Szerém county (Kórógy); Arad county (Varjas); Southern Great Plain, without further specification; Csongrád county (Tápé); Békés county (Pusztaföldvár); Szatmár county (Botpalád, Fehérgyarmat); Kolozs county (Méra); Csík county (Csíkkarcfalva, Csíkrákos, Gyergyóújfalu). Total: 13.

Tunes: 1. = No. 195 (two variants).

Marci Zöld was born at Berettyóújfalu (Bihar county) around 1790. "Because of his deeds as a rioter without any hope of improvement, the judges of the community gave Marci Zöld over to the regiment of Prince Hessen-Homburg lying at Nagyvárad. He fled together with one of his comrades around Christmas of 1815...from hence he found refuge, as a deserter, in the ranks of the brigands."

806

(*Békés,* 42.) A typical outlaw-story spread the following data: "Marci Zöld and Palatinszki arrested a company of gentry-folk of twenty-one members starting to vintage. One of the landlors, old Farkas Szúnyog, a descent of a famous Szabolcs family, entreated Marci Zöld laying out a proposal for patronizing him with the vice-bailiff of the county if they leave the company at peace. The outlaw, allegedly, kissed the old gentleman's hand, saying to Palatinszki: Well, Peti, mount your horse, we are not doing anything this time! At that, Palatinszki broke out in loud swears, murmuring: "Is it all that you called me here for? Do you give credence to the words of all bloody rascals?" (*Ibid* 43.) Finally his fall was caused by treason indeed: a cattleherd of Gyula reported on Marci Zöld while he was hiding at a farmstead of Öcsöd; five cattleherds raided on him, armed with hay-making forks, caught him and escorted him to Tiszaföldvár, where Palatinszki had already been jailed (the latter was called Becskereki among the outlaws). The two of them and Miska Kapus were hanged in 1816. Nevertheless, this account of his fall is not the same as that known from the semi-folklore variant presented above.

Petőfi wrote a poem about Marci Zöld, and *Vörösmarty* about Becskereki. Yet, the people did not commemorate their fame in a genuine folksong.

107. PANDOOR, PUT ASIDE YOUR WEAPON!

196.

Köszönhetem bajaimat, A bogáti tiszttartónak.

Mikor nála juhász voltam, Juhok mellett elaludtam.

1. I owe all my troubles
   To the farm-bailiff of Bogát.
   When I was engaged as a shepherd by him,
   I fell asleep by the flock of sheep.

2. My sheep went astray,
   And they went into the lucerne-field.
   Thirty-three of them swelled,
   So I became a dismissed man.

3. But he did not give me a proper letter of dismissal,
   Nobody wanted to engage me.
   Still I did not become an outlaw.
   I only began to buy and sell pigs.

4. Three times I was fortunate in my deals,
   But the fourth time I found myself at a loss.
   The red mayor of Osztopán,
   That veritable gallows-bird,

5. The red mayor of Osztopán,
   That veritable gallows-bird
   Stood up in my way
   Driving off my pigs.

6. Driving off my pigs,
   He reported my case at Kaposvár.
   The pandoors came out at once,
   Black they were like eagles.

7. I was looking at them from afar,
   From the edge of the woods of Fiad.
   Yet I did not become an outlaw
   Until I acquired six comrades.

8. I acquired six good companions,
   Then we went on robbing on a large scale.
   We started towards west,
   Towards the inn of Nyíres.

9. No sooner stepped I in the room
   Than I was asked about my name.
   András Juhász is my name,
   Pandoor, what's the matter between us?

10. There is nothing the matter between us,
    I only ask your name.
    Put aside, pandoor, your weapons,
    Don't be scared for life this time!

11. Put aside, pandoor, your weapon,
    Don't be scared for life this time.
    Feast and drink and have a good time!
    After all, you took pains to meet me.

12. My hostess, pearly violet,
    Have you got fat geese properly dressed?
    I have some, András, though not properly dressed,
    But they will soon be roasted.

13. Roast them without any delay,
    Let's have enough of roasted geese!
    Drink, lads, let's have a good time,
    Since we are together with the pandoors!

14. It's about midnight,
    Lads, we must go.
    Having had a good time here,
    We may leave the pandoors behind.

Szenna (Somogy county). Performed by a man of seventy-six. B. Rónai 1963 = AP 4874/a.

Divergences:
In general, the song begins with the following stanza:

   My name is Andris Juhász,

   Zala and Somogy cannot defeat me.

   Zala and Somogy will not hurt me,

   For I have not caused damage to burghers.

or: ...will not hurt me

   Since they know a kind man.

   The number of swollen sheep varies from one to thirty-three. The majority of the texts present the story of how András Juhász became an outlaw, and keep silent on the encounter with the pandoors. Instead, the story is finished with motifs of prisoners' songs. Another song speaks about the outlaw's revenge on the bailiff of Osztopán, mainly by inclusion of turns of other well-known ballads (96. 124.). One of the texts of Szenna reads as follows:

1. Well, lads, we are together, all the six of us,
   Let's go right to Osztopán.
   Now we leave here for Osztopán,
   We shall visit the house of the red mayor of Osztopán.

2. Red mayor, good evening, good evening!
   May God grant you luck, gentlemen!
   I don't know if it be luck or death,
   That will meet you in your bed.

3. András Juhász lit the light,
   The red mayor lies weeping in his bed.
   Get up, dog, kneel down upon the ground,
   Why did you cross the way of András Juhász?

4. András Juhász shot him in the head,
   Ferkó Ruzsin in the chest.
   This serves you well, dog, they will dig you in the earth,
   Why did you cross the way of a highwayman?

5. András Juhász has his pants made from sixteen fathoms,
   He spreads it on his horse he had acquired at Inke.
   Wash, sweetheart, my shirt and my pants white,
   Tomorrow I appear before the high judge.

6. Sir High Judge, may the Lord grant you a good day!
   Welcome, son András, what's the matter with you?
   Sir High Judge, I want to report now
   That I shot the mayor of Osztopán in the head.

7. Son András, why did you do that?
   Why did you not take pity on his three children?
   There's his estate he has left behind,
   And his wife to raise the orphans.

In one or two variants the outlaw speaks like this: "We have robbed the rich gentlemen To make rich the poor." or: "They did not rob the peasants, Only the rich lords."

Earliest provenience: 1907.
Dissemination: Zala county (Bókháza, Boncodfölde, Murakeresztúr); Somogy county (Attala 2, Balatonlelle, Bélavár, Karád 4, Riticspuszta, Somogyaszaló, Szenna 3, Toponár, Zimány); Baranya county (Bánfa, Boda, Katádfa 2); Tolna county (Felsőireg); Veszprém county (Pusztamiske); Győr county (Dunaremete, Kisbajcs). Total: 26.

Textual relationship with other ballads: **96., 126., 118.**

11.

Fine   D.C. al Fine

Tunes 9–11 belong to a separate song about the murder of the mayor of Osztopán.

The "début" of András Juhász, an outlaw in Somogy county, fell in the year of 1867. The government commissioner of the county was appointed, at the county's request, on his account, and when the better part of the outlaw's gang was annihilated, and the county applied for the liquidation of the commissionary's office, the Minister of Interior rejected the petition with the following motivation: "...as the chief of the robbers may succeed in gathering together a new gang in a county where the populace makes a hero of the chief robber, spreading his name and fame by means of verses recited by villagers, it is not unjustified in the least that the part of the population which does not show any understanding of the sins committed against the society should realize, at least from the pecuniary aspect, the weight of that extraordinary measure which had to be taken precisely on account of its peccable indolence." Later the leader was slain at the farmstead of a peasant of Karos. As he wished to hide, solitarily, in the peasant's shed, the latter refused him, fearing of the consequences. A quarrel followed, then the peasant called some people who raided on the outlaw and cut him. Covered with wounds, he was put on a cart and so he died on the way. The case was published in the December 8, 1868 issue of the Somogy newspaper, after the account of a juryman. Characteristic of the time is the introductory part of the communication: "Being convinced that the broad public has developed a deep interest in the fate of the chief robber...I regard it as my duty to report—true to facts—the circumstances of his exit ...to the general public."

Apart from the murder of the mayor of Osztopán, András Juhász did not kill people, except when he was engaged in struggle with the pandoors and military forces. He committed his robberies without applying force or torture. It is held that once he met with his former farm-bailiff who had dismissed him. The latter offered his purse to the outlaw, whereupon the outlaw said to him: "I don't need your money. I acknowledge that I was not faultless. But you may wait for me and two of my comrades for supper." After supper, the outlaw took leave by hand-shake of the bailiff. This may well be a legend, for the bailiff moved into the city of Pécs for fear of Juhász. The outlaws did not dare to penetrate the town. Be it as it may, one thing is certain: the benefits of Juhász had been extolled among the people, because he protected the poor against the rich.

Yet his ballad never became a true folklore composition: whether written by himself or by someone else, it is hardly more than a diary. True-to-fact details, reality, but not poetry. Only the part describing the encounter and entertainment with the pandoors is raised above the level of a simple report. This, however, occurs in a few variants only, although it seems as if this novel insertion began to spread in ever wider circles recently.

Literature: Gönczi 1944, pp. 168–171 and 327–348.

108. HIS STEED STUMBLED...

197.

1. Kocs-má-ros - né, cit - ro-mos bort hoz-zon kend! Szol-gá - ló - ját strá/sá -ra ál -lít - sa kend!

Szol-gá - ló - ját strá - zsá - ra ál - lit - sa kend! Ha zsan-dár jön, hír -a - dás-sal le - gyen kend!

1. My hostess, bring me wine with lemon,
   Let your maid-servant stand out and watch!
   Let your maid-servant stand out and watch,
   If gendarmes come, let us know of it!

2. Once the maid runs in frightened,
   Nine gendarmes are approaching with arms.
   Pista Csehek did not made a trifle of it,
   But mounted his steed called Velvet,

3. Mounted his steed called Velvet,
   Rode off to the plain of Csongorád.
   His steed stumbled in a pit,
   So Pista was suppressed lying in it.

4. I humbly ask my Sir Commissar
   Not to shoot off my horse from under me!
   Look, look, this devil of an outlaw,
   Is not sorry for his own life but for that of his horse!

5. Pista Csehek is bound on the coach.
   He asks where his horse called Velvet is.
   You need not a Velvet horse any longer, you wretched outlaw,
   Soon your necktie will be a string!

Alpár (Pest county). Performed by a man of fifty. Zoltán Vásárhelyi, 1934.

Divergences: Variations on the first stanza:
"My hostess, fry fish for me, Serve wine with lemon with it, Let your maid-servant stand out on watch..." and so on. Another beginning: "It is raining, drops of rain are falling mildly, Pista Csali sits in the inn, and he is not a gay man. Hostess, bring wine onto the table, Let your most beautiful maid stand out on watch!" More rarely: "There you can see a thin fence of deal. Wild colt's neighing is heard there. Pista Cseri is saddling his Velvet horse..." and so on. "My hostess, good day to

813

you! When were here mounted gendarmes for the last time?" The second stanza sometimes reads: "My hostess walks into the room And leans on Jóska Geszti's shoulder..."

The third stanza has sometimes the following lines: "His horse Velvet took him a long distance, Right to the edge of the Bakony forest. His steed stumbled at a fir-tree. So Pista Csehó was caught there for good." The outlaw asking about his horse receives the following answer from the captain of the gendarmes: "Proudly the captain of the gendarmes answers: You wretched outlaw, you will not ride a steed any longer!" Several variants end with the following lines: "I have sent word to my wife To take care of my two children! She must not give them to shepherds, nor to horsemen, Rather should they be trained to become outlaws like their father was."

Here again the motif of bribing the judges appears: "I humbly ask my Sir Corporal of gendarmes Not to engross my case. I shall steal ram-lambs six for you If you let me go free." (Kiskunhalas.) "I ask you, commissary gentlemen To give me back my horse called Szikra. I shall steal, if I have it, oxen, young bulls and cows Enough to share them with the gentlemen." (Nyírlugos.) In some variants the following stanza is given in reply to the maid-servant's reporting: "Corporal of gendarmes, put aside your weapon, For dogs will lick up your blood! I will show you soon: I put you deep in the womb of the earth!" And there is an end to the plot, too. Obviously, this motif has been borrowed from the ballad of András Juhász.

This song cannot be linked definitely to any of the outlaws known by names to us, for the names occur in them in a great variety: Pista Csali (52 times, and if the variants are also added: Sali (3), Sajó (12), Sahalj, Saló, Saljó, Saju, Csaló-Csalló (4), Csala, Csahó, Csehó (15), Csehi (2), Csehoj (2) Csehol (2), Csehö, Csehöj, Csihó, Csehej, Cserely, Cseji, Csejó, Csehek, Csani, Sanyi), then a number of 108 results. It must be an invented name. Further ones are (the outlaws' names known from sources are italicized): *Sándor Rózsa* (29, mainly occurring in Transylvania), *Imre Bogár* (27), Jóska Geszten (Geszter, Gesztej, Geszti, 6), *Savanyu* (5), Jóska Cseri (Bandi Cseri, Pista Cseri, 4), Miska or Bandi Szökfü (4), *Pista Patkó* (3), Miska Kisvég (2), Uncle Pista (2), Jóska Albert, *Bandi Angyal,* Sándor Borsos, Pista Deli, *Gábor Dobos,* Imre Dombi, István Hódi, Mihály Kis, Pista Magyar, Jóska Mező, *Pista Séta, Pista Sisa,* Pali Szabó, Pista Szabó. In thirteen instances the simple denominations "an outlaw", "this outlaw", "famous, poor, outlaw", "young outlaw" or "outlaw lad" are substituted for the names. Apparently, this variety of names in itself indicates that the ballad was not made in commemoration of one person. In one case the hero is referred to as "robbers' chief", and in fifteen examples, mainly fragmentary, he is not named at all.

Earliest provenience: around 1860, MS.
Dissemination: Without specification: 5.
I. Moson county (Öttevény); Sopron county (Bősárkány, Kisfalud, Kismarton); Vas county (Búcsú, Csörötnek 2, Gersekarát, Nagyrákos, Rábakovácsi), Zala county (Alsópáhok, Bezeréd, Búcsúszentlászló, Dergecs 2, Kapolcs, Letenye, Kiskomárom, Nemessándorháza, Oltárc, Rédics, Resznek, Rigyác, Szilvád, Zalaapáti, Zalaegerszeg); Somogy cnunty (Almamellék, Balatonlelle, Kéthely, Kisbárapáti, Ságvár, "Somogy c." Somogyszentmiklósfa, Tászár 2, Zamárdi, Zselickisfalud,

Szerém county (Kórógy 2); Verőce county (Szentlászló); Baranya county (Csoboka 2, Hosszúhetény, Kémes, Kopács 3, Mánfa, Nagyváty, Püspökszenterzsébet); Tolna county (Bedeg?, Sárpilis, Sióagárd); Fejér county (Dunapentele, Pusztaforna); Veszprém county (Alsópáhok, Bakonyszentlászló, Berhida, Dég 2, Hegyesd 2, Nemesbük, Szilasbalhás, Tés, Várpalota); Komárom county (Ács, Kocs, Naszvad, Szentgyörgypuszta); Győr county (Győrság, Győrsziget); I.: 72.

II. Hont county ("Hont c."); Nógrád county (Bercel, Kishartyán, Magyargéc, Salgóvidék, Szandaváralja); Heves county (Adács, Bükkszenterzsébet 2, Eger, Erdőtelke, Fedémes 4, Felsőtárkány, Gyöngyöshalász, Mátraderecske, Mátraszentistván, Mezőtárkány, Nagyiván, Tiszanána, Pálosveresmart, Pétervására); Borsod county (Borsodnádasd, Bükkaranyos, Mezőcsát, Mezőkeresztes, Mezőkövesd, Szilvásvárad, Várkony); Gömör county (Egyházasbást 2, Hét, Péterfa); Abaúj county (Áj, Tornagörgő, Tornyosnémeti); Zemplén county (Ricse 2, Sárospatak 3, Szerencs). II.: 44.

III. Pest county (Alpár 2, Bugacmonostor, Bugacpuszta, Csillaghegy, Csolyospuszta, Galambospuszta 2, Irsa, Izsák, Kiskunfélegyháza 4, Kiskunhalas 10, Lakitelek, Pusztaapát, Tápiószele); Jász-Nagykun-Szolnok county (Alattyán, Jászkisér, Kisújszállás, Kungyalu); Bács-Bodrog county (Bajsa, Domoszló, Mélykút, Rém, Zenta); Torontál county (Egyházaskér, Hertelendyfalva, Majdán, Nagybecskerek); Csongrád county (Csongrád, Hódmezővásárhely 5, Horgos, Makó, Szegedalsóváros, Szegedfelsőváros, Szentes); Csanád county (Magyarbánhegyes); Arad county (Pécska); Southern Great Plain without further specification 3; "Great Plain"; Békés county (Bélmegyer, Doboz 3, Ecsegfalva, Endrőd 2, Geszt, Gyula, Mezőgyán, Szarvas 2, Vésztő 3); Bihar county (Csegőd, Derecske, Nagyszalonta); Hajdú county (Kismarja 2, Hajdúhadház, Hajdúnánás 2, "Hortobágy"); Szabolcs county (Balsa, Biri, Kótaj, Nyírbátor, Nyírlugos, Nyírtura, Vaja); Szatmár county (Garbolc). III.: 89.

IV. Kolozs county (Györgyfalva, Zentelke); Szolnok-Doboka county (Árpástó, Búza, Feketelak); Maros-Torda county (Kibéd); Udvarhely county (Kápolnásfalu, Kénos, Kőrispatak, Olasztelek, Rugonfalva); Brassó county (Tatrang); Csík county (Csíkvacsárcsi, Gyergyócsomafalva, Tekerőpatak); Háromszék county (Dálnok, Sepsiszentkirály); Bukovina (Andrásfalva, Istensegíts 2). IV.: 19. Total: 229.

Textual relationship with other ballads: **107.**

Tunes: 1. = No. 197 (8 variants). Closely related variants are 2. (6 variants), 3. (2 variants), and 4. However, most typical is 5. (49 variants), 7. (2 variants), 13. (2 variants), 19. (2 variants), 20. (2 variants), 22. (3 variants).

816

Developed in the mid-nineteenth century, the ballad is not connected with factual events, place or person; it provides an invented picture of the outlaws as they live in people's imagination.

109. THE OUTLAW'S PASSPORT

198.

Parlando

1. Něm lop - tam én é - le - těm - be, Csak ěgy csi - kót Deb - re - cěn - be.

Csak ěgy csi - kót měg hat ti - nót, Mind a hat da - ru - sző - rű vót.

1. I did not steal in all my life,
   Except a colt in Debrecen.
   Only a colt and six young bulls,
   All the six were grey like cranes.

2. I drove them to the fair,
   They asked me about their price.
   I sold the stolen beasts
   And bought honest ones for their price.

3. I shall give one to the notary
   So that he may not write my name in the register.
   I give three to the judge
   So that he may verify my paper.

4. I left the fair,
   And fortunate was my leave.
   At the inn of Becsali at Kondoros
   Nine gendarmes stood up in my way.

5. They asked my name,
   And where my passport was.
   Wait a minute, I shall show it,
   Only I unbutton my waistcoat.

6. I felt at my inner pocket,
   Well, a pistol got in my hand,
   One or two of them I shot in the head,
   That's my passport!

7. Alas, my God, what am I to do now?
   Shall I run away or shall I stay?
   If I run away, they shoot me in the head,
   If I stay, they will cast me into irons.

818

8. The gate of the prison is banged,
   Is it perhaps the county bailiff?
   He is examining my chains,
   Adding years to my imprisonment.

*Földeák (Csanád county). Performed by a man of twenty-three. Pécely 1942 = M.
Sz. 4370.*

Divergences: Other incipit: "I fell asleep on the bank of the Tisza, Alas, I
dreamt a sad dream. The meaning of my dream was That I shall not be yours,
sweetheart. (The stanza which lives as a separate folksong, obviously got into the
ballad as a subsequent insertion.) "As I woke up at last, Nine gendarmes were
standing at my head..." Or:"At dawn on Thursday I hit upon a fieldguard's hut. As
soon as I fell asleep, Nine gendarmes appeared, standing up around me..." This
latter beginning formula occurs in 88 instances, while the published one in 36; a
further 31 starts immediately with the scene of encounter, which mostly takes place
at an inn. Sometimes the song begins with motifs of prisoners' songs, the encounter
with the gendarmes being narrated afterwards. More frequently, however, the
prisoners' motifs are presented towards the end of the ballad: that is, after various
adventures are given, current motifs of prisoners' songs are added to the story (in 18
variants). Rather often (in 15 instances) the stanza "This wild colt is not up to sale,
Nor is it fitting under a gendarme, For if a gendarme mounted it, Even the birds
would be made prisoners."

The songs end partly with the motif of bold defiance ("That's my passport!"),
partly with a more realistic close ("Alas, my God, what shall I do?"); and in certain
cases with a still more realistic description of some scene of prisoners' lives. There
are only a few variants to solve the venture by telling about the outlaw escaping and
seeking his sweetheart (in which case a different folksong is inserted to this end).
The phrase "Alas, my God, what shall I do..." is sometimes followed by "I have
thought I should turn And re-fill my gun... I answered to the other five men:
That's my passport!" Occasionally, the outlaw rejoices over his escape, there is no
obstacle of his running off to the plains.

It is worth-while to examine a few more less frequent details. After shooting
the gendarmes, the outlaw gives the following counsel to his pal: "Don't you steal
geese, lambs or chickens, If you want to escape the deep dungeon! Steal horses,
good palfreys, Wild young oxen that had not yet been yoked! Let the lords have
their share of them, And they will release you!" The standing phrase "If I stay I shall
be bound..." is followed by "So they escort me to Debrecen, Before the court. My
little hat is swimming in blood, My horse is in the hands of the gendarmes' corporal.
My horse in the hands of the gendarmes' corporal, While I am in the county's house.
They call me to the court now and again, Standing before the court I can see the pen
scribbling, I can see false witnesses accusing me. Heigh, witnesses, don't accuse me,
For you don't know what you bring on your heads! As you treat me, So I shall serve
you!" Finally, in order to obtain a knowledge of the method with which motifs of
prisoners's songs and outlaw ballads are amalgamated, I present here a text from
Hajdúszoboszló (Hajdú county), whose first four stanzas follow, by and large,
those of the type text; then the story continues like this:

Run, my dear horse! Outlaw!
Don't stop before you reach the Hortobágy!
I knock at the door:
Will you give me, sweetheart, a tender voice!
They pressed me against the river Körös,
Driving me from noon till nightfall.
I swam across the Körös,
But I could not sleep a wink:
As I opened my blue eyes,
I saw gendarmes standing by.
What are you going to do here, gentlemen?
Do you want to chain me, perhaps?
If you chain me,
Even the birds will mourn for me!
The saddle and the harness of my horse are tasselled,
My little bay is muddy.
Tomorrow at eight o'clock
I am taken up to the court.
In the great hall of Arad
Twelve lords are sitting at court.
Twelve lords are passing sentence over me,
All being ready to perish me.
Winking in my eyes they ask me:
Does the bay colt not occur to you?
Only a grey one occurs to me,
And the six bullocks of Debrecen.
That's why I was put into iron,
By the storied-house of Arad.
May the storied-house be set on flame,
May the shackles fall off my limbs.
If once the shackles fall off my limbs,
I shall see the gendarme that can close me up again!

And let us see a strange incipit; borrowed from an outlaw song:

Looking out of the big inn of Marócsa
I see how it is snowing.
Like a black flock of eagles
Gendarmes are coming for to catch me.
At the inn of Marócsa
Nine gendarmes stand up in front of me...

Earliest provenience: 1878.
Dissemination: Without specification: 3.
Zala county (Csonkahegyhát, Lendvahosszúfalu, Pálfiszeg); Somogy county (Attala 2, Babony, Kutas); Baranya county (Csányoszró 2, Csoboka, Dunafalva, Felsőlegéncsepuszta, Kákics, Kisbodolya, Mohács, Szaporca); Fejér county (Inota 2); Veszprém county (Hegyesd, Réde); Komárom county (Csilizradvány, Naszvad, Örtény-Guta); Győr county (Pér); Hont county (the region of

Ipolyság); Nógrád county (Bárna, Borsosberény, Szécsény, Szandaváralja, Tardoskedd); Heves county (Bodony, Derecske, Mátraszentimre, Mezőtárkány, Poroszló); Borsod county (Bogács, Csincse, Disznóshorvát, Felsőnyárád, Mezőkövesd 2, Sály 2); Gömör county (Beje, Nagybalog); Abaúj county (Boldogkőújfalu, Cekeháza, Tornagörgő); Zemplén county ("Bodrogköz region", Erdőbénye, Megyaszó, Nagyrozvány 2, Nagytárkány, Ricse, Sárospatak 4, Taktanador, Zalkod); Bereg county (Lónya, Tarpa, "Tiszahát region"); Máramaros county (Hosszúmező); Pest county (Bugac, Kalocsa, Kecel, Keserűtelek, Kiskunhalas 4, Kiskunmajsa, Monostorfalva, Ráckeve, Tura, Újszász, Városföld-puszta); Jász-Nagykun-Szolnok county (Jánoshida, Jászalsószentgyörgy, Jászárokszállás, Jászkarajenő, Kisújszállás 2, Ladánybene, Nagyrév); Bács-Bodrog county (Bátya, Gombos 4); Torontál county (Csóka, Hertelendyfalva 2, Rém, Torda); Csongrád county (Csongrád, Hódmezővásárhely, Kiskundorozsma, Mindszent, Sándorfalva 2, Szeged); Csanád county (Apátfalva, Földeák 2); Arad county (Pécska, Simonyifalva, Vadász); Békés county (Békés, Doboz, Újkígyós); Bihar county (Bályok, Biharugra, Körösnagyharsány, Nagyszalonta 2); Hajdú county (Hajdúszoboszló, Hortobágy, Nyírábrány); Szabolcs county (Kisvárda, Nyírlugos, Nyírmada, Tiszapolgár); Szatmár county (Kérsemjén, Vámosoroszi); Szilágy county (Szilágyperecsen); Kolozs county (Mákófalva); Szolnok-Doboka county (Búza, Pusztakamarás?); Maros-Torda county (Kibéd 2, Szabéd); Udvarhely county (Bethlenfalva, Bögöz, Bözöd, Etéd, Homoródszentpál, Korond, Tarcsafalva, Vargyas); Csík county (Gyimesbükk, Gyimesközéplok); Háromszék county (Dálnok, Sepsiköröspatak); Bukovina (Andrásfalva, Hadikfalva, Istensegíts); Moldavia (Bogdánfalva 2, Lészped, Luizikalagor). Total: 155.

    Textual relationship with other ballads: **115, 118** (including the following motifs: 2., 3. (5 variants) 11. (7), 12., 14., 16. (2), 17. (2), 21., 22., 34. (5), 35., 43., 49., 57. (5), 74. (2), 76. (2), 98. (5), 100.

    Tunes: 1. = No. 198 (11 variants), 2. (2), 3. (5), 6. (7), 8. (3), 10. (2), 16. (14), 18. (3), 20. (8), 21. (15), 22. (2), 24. (2), 25. (2).

823

This story formulated in singular first person without any mentioning the hero's name presents, so to say, the abstract picture of the outlaw. Although vaguely, the general contours of the usual course of the outlaw ballads can be still discovered: the way of life of outlaws, their bold resistance, and their fall. Originating from the late nineteenth century.

110. WORD IS SENT TO THE GENDARMES...

199.

Ná - di Jan-csi Fe - nék - be van, Pan - du - rok - nak ü - zen - ve van,

Hogy jöj - je - nek ha - mar - já - ba: Ná - di Jan - csi a csár - dá - ba!

1. Jancsi Nádi is at Fenék,
   Word is sent to the pandoors
   To make speed and come,
   For Jancsi Nádi is at the inn!

2. The pandoors make speed and arrive
   With their double-charged weapons.
   Standing at the door:
   Prepare, Jancsi, for your death!

3. He utters a terrible oath,
   Grasps his weapon,
   But the pandoors answer:
   It is too late, poor Jancsi!

4. He orders the inn-keeper
   To lower the curtains of the window.
   Sooner than he could realize
   A ball pierced his heart.

5. The red blood of Jancsi Nádi
   Was spilt on the ground at Fenék.
   Treszka Kálmán, his sweetheart,
   Gathered it in a white plate.

*Vörs (Somogy county). Performed by a man of seventy-five. János Bartók 1952 =
AP 639/a.*

Divergences: The following text was published, without tune, by *Gyula
Sebestyén* from Pölöskefő:

1. Jancsi Nádi staying in the inn
   Gives orders to the inn-keeper:
   Lower the window curtains,
   I want to have a spree!

2. Jancsi Nádi is staying at Fenék,
   Word is sent to the gendarmes,
   Make speed and come without delay,
   For Jancsi Nádi is in the inn!
3. A pint of wine is still in store for me,
   Were it not that my time is over,
   My time is over:
   Six gendarmes are standing by the door.
4. The gendarmes came without delay
   With double-charged weapons
   Will you die, Jancsi?
   Or else you must surrender!
5. Jancsi took up his weapon,
   Uttered a terrible oath,
   Sooner than he could realize
   The ball pierced his heart.
6. The white body of Jancsi Nádi
   Is buried at Fenék.
   In the cemetery of Fenék
   He rests in the black earth.

Another variant of the beginning: "That Jancsi Nád is a famous outlaw, Who walks at Fenék by daylight. You can tell him by his carriage, By his chesnut-brown hair. Oh, János, what did you have in your mind When you started to Fenék? Letter has been sent to the pandoors ..." This addressing formula, implying the lesson of the story, is used as incipit in several variants (anyway, it is known already from Type **92**). For instance: Jancsi Nádi, what did you have in your mind When you started to Fenék? Did not you think That you might be caught at Fenék?" Or: "... You had yourself shot dead, You made your comrade a prisoner."

Earliest provenience: 1898.
Dissemination:
Zala county (Alsópáhok, Dergecs, Keszthely, Pölöskefő, Rigyác, Szigliget); Somogy county (Bolhás, Böhönye, Büssü, Sòmogyszob, Vörs); Veszprém county (Monostorapáti). Total: 12.

Textual relationship with other ballads: **92.**
Tunes: the published tune in 9 variants.

Since we do not know about an outlaw called Jancsi Nádi, it is not impossible that we are dealing with one of the pseudonyms of Jancsi Patkó, who indeed was buried at Fenék by Keszthely. The ballad developed uniformly in a narrow area by the Lake Balaton. The scene it describes resembles to that of the ballad on Vidrócki: the outlaw having a binge in the inn and proudly defying the gendarmes is shot dead from outside, through the window. But no textual correlation can be established between the two ballads.

The song was composed, in all likelihood, in the last decades of the last century.

111. I AM A FAMOUS OUTLAW...

200.

1. I am a famous outlaw,
   My name being Patkó,
   Thirteen counties have long been
   Tracing after me.

2. Over hills and valleys
   In vain do they stroll,
   For they will never can lay a hand
   On an outlaw.

3. Although I appear
   Where they least think I should.
   My famous steed
   Is admired everywhere.

4. If I spur it,
   I jump over ten frontiers,
   But pandoors will never
   Lay a hand on me.

5. The Bakony is my country,
   This vast forest,
   Which if I leave
   My heart grows almost sick.

6. Heigh, to think of the many outlaws
   That used to live in it!
   Were I in their company I would not be afraid
   Of any man's weapon!

7. My dearest-kindest sweetheart,
   Let me rest my head,
   Let me hide my sorrowful soul
   In your lap.

8. Wake over me
   While I am sleeping in a slumber.
   And if people came to worry me,
   Wake me, sweetheart!

9. Loud noise of horses is heard
   From the distant woods.
   Don't sleep, darling,
   Be on the alert for a while!

10. Also the noise of guns are heard,
    They are looking for you.
    I shall die for you
    If you are taken away.

11. Don't be scared, sweetheart,
    Mount my horse,
    I shall take care of you
    Just as of myself!

12. I fire my gun,
    Let them know I have been here.
    Let them know that I have kissed
    Your pretty lips a hundred times!

*Kisbárapáti (Somogy county). Performed by a man of seventy-five. Lajtha 1923 =
MF 2580/a.*

Divergences: A text from Zselickisfalud may give an idea of the variants:

1. I am a famous outlaw, my name being Patkó,
   The whole of the county is in search of me.
   They roam over hills and valleys,
   Yet they cannot find the outlaw anywhere.
2. Although he is to be found where they least suspect,
   All people admire him riding his dark bay.
   If I give it a spur, I jumps over the Tisza,
   But I do not let it get into the hands of gendarmes.
3. Bakony is my country, this vast forest,
   If I leave it, my heart breaks.
   My Bözsi, darling, let me lay my head
   In your tiny lap, to sleep a little.
4. Weapons are cracking, they are looking for you.
   Alas, where am I to go if you are taken away?
   Where I go you will go with me,
   If I get wounded, you will dress my wounds.
5. Yellow is my steed, yellow, and if I mount it,
   I don't care if all the gendarmes of the county follow upon my heels.
   If I give it a spur, I jump over the Tisza,
   But I shan't give myself into the hands of the gendarmes!

A variant adds motifs of prisoners' songs to the ballad, without any apparent reason. (7 plus 18.) A variant from Borsod county applies to Vidrócki the first and second stanzas of the above ballad, then enumerates prisoners' motifs through eight stanzas, obviously induced by the tune (6.). (The motifs are: $4+6+13+39+1$.)

Earliest provenience: between 1892 and 1900. *(Vikár.)*
Dissemination:
Zala county (Béc, Rigyác); Somogy county (Csurgó, Hetes, Igal, Kisbárapáti, Sándorpuszta, Simonfa, Szenna, Szilvásszentmárton, Zselickisfalud, Zselickislak 2); Tolna county (Felsőnyék); Hont county (Bernecebaráti); Nógrád county ("Nógrád c."); Heves county (Gyöngyöshalász); Borsod county (Hernádkércs, Mezőkövesd); Pest county (Újszász, Lakitelek); Hajdú county ("Hortobágy"). Total: 22.
Textual relationship with other ballads: **106.**
Tunes: 1. = No. 200, 2. (7 variants), 4. (4).

Apparently, the ballad is a semi-folklore composition, with many details borrowed from the broadside of Marci Zöld. It has nothing to do with the real facts known in connection with the activity of Patkó and his gang. Neither Patkó nor the other Transdanubian outlaws were mounted men; their shelter was offered by the forest where a horse would have impeded their move. The true country of mounted outlaws had been the Great Hungarian Plain. The versificator composed his verse obviously under the influence of the general concept of the figure of an outlaw. The poem enjoyed a certain degree of popularity within the narrower region where Patkó and his men used to live, that is in Somogy county. It has been folklorized to some extent. The ballad had been transplanted into counties Heves and Borsod by seasonal agricultural workers employed in the Transdanubian part, in all probability.

829

112. THE LANDLORD JUMPING OUT OF THE WINDOW

201.

1. Sándor Patkó did not come from the gentry stock,
   He does not need a silken quilt.
   He does not wear, heigh-ho, anybody's worn clothes,
   He is content with his pants made of linen of sixteen ells' length.

2. Sándor Patkó walks into the woods,
   His double-barrelled pistol is charged with cut iron.
   He shoots, heigh-ho, the charge of cut iron one after the other,
   The pandoor is running into the inn of Somogy.

3. Sándor Patkó writes a letter to Sitke:
   Prepare nine thousand florins, beforehand!
   Imre Illés, heigh-ho, endorses the letter:
   Also supper must be prepared for nine men!

4. The young shepherd served the supper outside the house,
   Sándor Patkó was standing under a branchy oak-tree.
   He asks the young lad: Heigh-ho, what news have we from Sándor Nagy?
   His words are: Oh, Sándor Patkó is a big lord, indeed!

5. Sándor Patkó was tapping at the door,
   Sándor Nagy woke up with a start,
   Golden glass, heigh-ho, was glittering in moonshine,
   Sándor Nagy jumped out of the window.

Rábaköz region (Western Hungary). Miska Polák = EA 3551, 36 = Csanádi and Vargyas No. 175.

Divergences: The story is sometimes linked to the name of Jóska Savanyú. The real names of the brothers Patkó come up rather rarely, Pista is found in some variants, while János occurs only in one from the Szerémség region. The name Bandi owes its spread to a broadside. The name Sándor had been introduced, in all probability, for the sake of rhyming to the name of the landlord Sándor Nagy, who in other cases is called Kálmán Hácki; or Bogyay jumps out of the window while the host Kálmán Hácki hands over the money to the outlaws. The original topographical name Sitke had been changed to Csitke, Csipke and the like in the course of variation. Beside the golden glass, sometimes also silver spoon occurs.

Sándor Nagy was just sitting at supper,
He threw away his silver spoon at once.
Golden cup, silver spoon glittered,
Sándor Nagy jumped out through the window.

830

Several variants are telling about the outlaw who asks the landlord for "the price of the wool" and the latter makes desperate efforts to escape at a lower price:

> Sándor Nagy paid eight thousand florens,
> But Sándor Patkó was not content with it.
> The bailiff Renkli, heigh-ho, added five thousand,
> Sándor Patkó was content with it.

Some of the variants describe a veritable war-scene:

> Sándor Patkó blew the trumpet,
> Collecting all his nine comrades.
> He collected, heigh-ho, all his nine comrades,
> And surrounded the castle of Sándor Nagy.

Nevertheless, most of the variants have preserved only those stanzas which have some point in them: that is, the landlord's escape by jumping out of the window.

Earliest provenience: before 1900.

Dissemination: Without specification: 2 (probably from Transdanubia). "Rábaköz region" 2; Vas county (Pecöl, Kisrákos?); Zala county (Andráshida, Dergecs, Kapolcs, Monostorapáti 2, Nemesszentandrás, Nova, Pölöske, Sümeg); Somogy county ("Somogy c."; Taszár); Verőce county (Szentlászló); Fejér county (Pusztaforna); Veszprém county (Pápa); Komárom county (Ács, Kocs); Heves county (Besenyőtelek, "Mátra Piedmont"); Jász-Nagykun-Szolnok county (Jászkarajenő). Total: 25.

Textual relationship with other ballads: none
Tunes: 1. = 3 variants, 2. = 3 variants.

6.

János Patkó and Pista Patkó (by their original names János Tóth and István Tóth) were born at Vásárosbéc (Somogy county) in 1825, and 1827, respectively. The elder, Jancsi was more famous than his younger brother who segregated from the former's gang to become an independent chief. János was enlisted for twelve years to serve with the soldiers in Italy, and it was after his returning, when he was thirty-five, that he began to lead the life of outlaws. He was a literate, sometimes leaving message in writing behind. After each of his robbery he sent word to the county bailiff not to look after the culprit, because it was he. He is said to have shot dead anyone that committed robbery in his name. In 1861, an entire squadron was sent out to chase him up, and what is more, a battalion of rifles was mobilized from Pécs to the Drava riverine to arrest him. A thousand florens were set as blood-money for his head. He was wounded in a fire-battle in 1862. His comrades took him with them. Since, however, the wound began to sphacelate, he was shot dead at his own request. He was buried at Fenék.

His brother Pista was active separately in northern Somogy. It is he that committed the robbery of Sitke. Also he died in 1862: taken wounded, he died soon, in the hands of his enemies.

Their ballad is rather incomplete, it could not be rounded off into a folklore story. But there is a hit in it: when the outlaw makes the landlord jump out of the window amidst the glitter of his gold and silver vessels. This is a moment, fascinating with its contrast, which people retained everywhere with more or less self-satisfaction.

Literature: Gönczi, 271–300; Békés, 160–202.

113. THE OUTLAW DRESSED AS A GIRL

202.

1. E - ger fe - le ve - zet egy út, Ki - re Já - ger Jós - ka in - dul. Be - ér E - ger vá - ro - sá - ba, Vé -gig megy az ut - cá - já - ba.

1. There is a road leading to Eger.
   On which Jóska Jáger has set out.
   He arrives in the city of Eger,
   And walks along its street.

2. Clad in silk and velvet, Jóska Jáger
   Walks through the city.
   In his skirt reaching down to his knees
   He enters one shop after the other.

3. He is having his choice among the silk materials,
   There are finer than fine things among them.
   He writes on the door of the shop:
   That famous outlaw Jóska Jáger has bought things here.

4. As he enters a ladies' outfitter's shop,
   In his skirt reaching down to his knees,
   The shopkeeper greets him like this:
   Welcome, pretty Miss.

5. Welcome, pretty Miss,
   Will you take a seat on the sofa here!
   I cannot take a seat here, my dear sir,
   For I have to walk downway.

6. Night is falling already,
   The woods of Lelesz is glowing like blood.
   Jóska Sipkás has kindled a fire,
   Jóska Jáger sprang at him.

7. I say, you wretched shepherd:
   Have you any bread and bacon?
   I have both cheese and curd,
   And I have both bread and bacon.

8. Here you have your curd, milk, bacon and bread:
   Have your fill, outlaw, eat as much as you can hold!
   And when you have made your fill,
   I shall give you my bright hatchet.

9. I raised my hand,
   Praying to God:
   Holy angel of the Living Lord,
   Grant strength to my arms!
   So that I may brandish my hatchet
   And cut down Jóska Jáger!

10. I raised my arms,
    I brandished my hatchet,
    I delivered oner or two blows,
    I slew Jóska Jáger.

11. I slew Jóska Jáger,
    I drew him into a pit.
    I drew him into a pit,
    I covered him with dry leaves under an oak-tree.

12. Well, you outlaw, here you may have a rest,
    Until the coach arrives.
    When the coach arrives,
    We shall make our way towards Eger.

13. And without haste I dropped in
    Csucs first, than Bot.
    Sir mayor, Jóska Pukér:
    Jóska Jáger is lying dead!

14. You dog of a Sipkás, what have you done?
    How could you fight an outlaw?
    Oh, he was asking for my felt overcoat and for my boots,
    And I gave him a blow on the head with my hatchet.
    He was just pulling my boots, (to lines 3 and 4)
    When I chopped his head in two.

Bekölce (Heves county). Performed by a man of 68. L. Gulyás and P. Sztanó, 1954.

Divergences: Another incipit reads like this:

Night is falling, it is getting dark,
The thick woods is plunged into darkness.
There is a famous outlaw in it
Who is bold enough to face a hundred men.
Pista Völner is walking ahead,
Jóska Jáger is following him.

Don't shoot me dead, Jóska Jáger,
I give you my bay horse.
I don't want your bay horse,
I can find one in every stable!
I don't want your bay horse,
I only want to take the man who enticed my sweetheart.

Here is a variant in which a more detailed description of the fight with the shepherd can be found:

The young swineherd set a fire.
Jóska Jáger sprang at him:
Good evening, swineherd!
Have you any fried bacon and bread?
Have your fill, brother, eat as much as you are able to take in!
As Jóska finished the supper,
He lent his back to the oak-tree:
Give me your felt overcoat and your whip,
Your boots with the spurns!

I cannot give you my felt overcoat, nor my boots,
Before I have closed my herd in the pen.
After I have closed my herd in the pen,
I give you my felt overcoat and my boots.

Pista went to turn his herd,
And he prayed to God.
Jesus Christ, son of my God,
Lend strength to my arms!

Lend strength to my arms,
So that I can brandish my hatchet,
So that I can brandish my hatchet,
And slay Jóska Jáger!

Bold Pista did not waste time,
But gave him a blow on the nape.
He gave him a blow on the nape.
Jóska Jáger fell face down to ground.

The scene in which the outlaw plays round the shopkeeper, finds continuation in one of the variants like this:

O you guard at the gate,
Tell me what toll I have to pay?
Tell me without delay, for I am in a hurry,
I am bound to a foreign country.

I don't want you to pay me the toll,
But you must tell me your true name!
My true name is Jóska Geszten,
And my abode is among the hillocks of the Nyírség.

As appears from this variant, beside the name of Jóska Jáger, also Jóska Geszten, and sometimes Jóska Veszpri occur, although with a much lower frequency. Some of the variants seem to know something about the way Jóska Jáger was buried:

Jóska Jáger was a man of fame,
So that he did not even have a coffin.
He is resting deep in the earth's womb,
Wrapped in a black furcoat.

Earliest provenience: 1870–1 (Bartalus).
Dissemination:
Zala county (Dergecs); Fejér county (Bodajk); Veszprém county (Csesznek); Komárom county (Kiskeszi); Győr county (Ság); Nógrád county (Nógrádmegyer, Palotás, Sóshartyán, Zagyvapálfalva); Heves county (Bekölce 2, Egerszalók, Felsőtárkány 3, Mátraszentimre 2, Mátraszentistván, Pétervására); Borsod county (Csincse, Keresztespüspöki, Mezőkövesd, Sály); Gömör county (Felsővály); Zemplén county (Mikóháza, Perbenyik); Máramaros county (Hosszúmező); Jász-Nagykun-Szolnok county (Jászárokszállás, Mezőtúr); Békés county (Békésszentandrás, Doboz 2, Gyula); Bihar county (Érbogyoszló, Nagyszalonta); Hajdú county (Debrecen); Szabolcs county (Nyíregyháza); Szatmár county (Csenger, Gacsály); Alsó-Fehér county (Nagyenyed); Udvarhely county (Homoródszentpál, Kénos); Bukovina (Andrásfalva—Lengyel, Tolna c.). Total: 43.

Textual relationships with other ballads: none.

Tunes: 1. = No. 202 (9 variants), 2 (2), 3. (2). 6. (2), 7. (6).

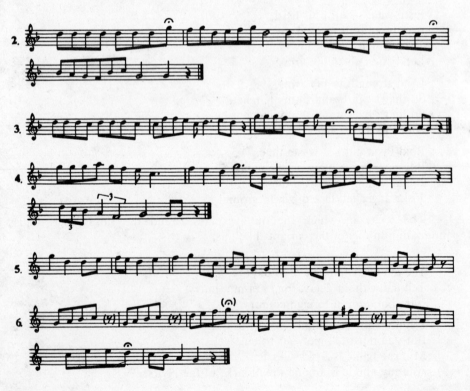

This is the only outlaw song in Hungarian folklore to face a shepherd with an outlaw. In this case, the outlaw is not sympathetically represented. (The statement does not refer to the scene in the shop with the outlaw entering clad in a girl's attire, which provides sometimes the sole subject-matter of the song.) As can be inferred from the dissemination, the hero of the song may have been born somewhere in the Palots Region, and was in all likelihood a forester or son of a forester (Jáger meaning a forester in the vernacular). No actual reports on his adventures have been discovered so far.

114. I WILL NEITHER STEP OUT, NOR SHALL I SURRENDER

203.

Nem messze van i - de Kis-mar-gi - ta.   Kör-nyeskörül foly-ja jazt a Ti - sza.

Kö - ze - pi - be Ko-po-nya - si   csár-da,   Ab-ba j i - szik egy betyár ma - gá - ba.

1. Kismargita is not lying far from here.
   The River Tisza flows it round.
   In its middle there stands the inn of Koponya,
   An outlaw is drinking wine in it all by himself.

2. There come the gendarmes, and eight they are
   Hey, their shakos shine bright!
   They are headed by the corporal
   Who leads them right to the inn of Koponya.

3. May God grant you a good evening, hostess!
   Can you tell me whom this palfrey belongs to?
   The owner of it is drinking good wine,
   He has arrived here within this last half of an hour.

4. Well, send out, then, the owner of it!
   We shan't do any harm to him if he surrenders.
   I will neither step out, nor shall I surrender,
   Whosoever wishes may take off my horse.

5. I don't really mind my horse,
   I am more sorry for the saddle and harness.
   My purse is in the sweat-cloth,
   With a hundred thousand florens in it.

6. I have spent a hundred for my palfrey,
   Another hundred for the harness,
   A third one hundred for a beautiful brown girl,
   And a fourth one hundred for the night I spent with her.

7. The fifth one hundred for a cask of good wine,
   A six one hundred for the pleasure of bibing it,
   A seventh one hundred I have put aside
   For to offer a drink to the gendarmes in case they happened to appear.

Tiszacsege (Hajdú county). Performed by a man of 31. Péter Balla 1937 = Gr 1/B/b.
Noted down by Béla Bartók.

838

Divergences: Most of the variants have the following closing lines: "The third one hundred for a beautiful brown girl, Whom I should not change for the whole world." Apart from this and some other minor deviations (for instance: Whom does this nice bay steed belong to?), the ballad is fairly evenly formulated throughout the language area, only incorporations of parts of other songs give rise to certain differences.

Earliest provenience: 1891 *(Kálmány).*

Dissemination:

I. Sopron county (Bősárkány, Kapuvár); Vas county (Balozsameggyes, Csipkerek, Gencs, Hosszúpereszteg 2, Salköveskút, Sorkifalud, Sziget-Őrsziget, Vasszilvágy); Zala county (Badacsony, Balatongyörök, Balatonmagyaród 2, Bezeréd, Búcsúszentlászló, Jakabfa, Kapolcs, Kiskomárom 2, Komáromváros, Letenye, Murakeresztúr, Nemessándorháza, Nova 2, Oltárc, Orosztony 2, Pölöskefő, Rédics, Rigyác, Szentgyörgyvölgy, Vindornyaszöllős, Zalabér, Zalavár 2, "Zala c."); Somogy county (Almamellék, Bábony, Balatonberény, Balatonszemes, Bárdudvarnok, Csákány, Csoma, Csurgó, Kálmáncsa, Kaposvár, Karád, Kercseliget, Kereki, Kisbárapáti, Kisbonnya, Köröshegy, Kutas, Nagybajom, Ordacsehi, Őrtilos, Somogyegres, Somogysámson, Somogyszentmiklósfa, Szenyér, Szilvásszentmárton, Taszár 2, Zics, Zselickisfalud); Verőce county (Szentlászló); Baranya county (Bánfa, Bános, Becefa, Berkesd, Bogád, Botyka, Csoboka, Dunaszekcső, Kákics, Kemse, Kopács 2, Mánfa, Mohács 5, Pécsarányos, Püspökszenterzsébet, Szebény, Szentkatalin, Szilágy, Szőke, Vásárosdombó); Tolna county (Decs, Felsőireg, Madocsa, Őcsény 2, Pincehely, Regöly, Sárpilis 2, Szekszárd); Fejér county (Baracs, Csór, Érd, Jenő); Veszprém county (Berhida, Dég, Hárságy, Káptalantóti, Kővágóörs, Nyirád, Pápa, Réde, Szilasbalhás); Komárom county (Császár, Martos, Naszály, Naszvad, Tata, Udvard); Győr county (Hollómajor, Kóny, Mezőörs, Ság, Vének). I: 127.

II. Pozsony county (Galánta); Nyitra county (Béd, Farkasd); Bars county (Lédec); Hont county ("Hont", Perőcsény); Nógrád county (Becske, Bercel 2, Borsosberény, Nógrádmegyer, Rimóc 2, Szanda, Szandaváralja 2, Szécsény); Heves county (Átány 3, Besenyőtelek, Bükkszenterzsébet, Fedémes 2, Füzesabony 2, Gyöngyös, Gyöngyösoroszi, Jákóhalma, Mátraballa, Mátraszentimre, Mikófalva, Nagyiván, Poroszló 3, Tar, Tarnaszentmária 2, Tiszaigar 2, Tiszanána, Tiszapély, Váraszó); Borsod county (Borsodnádasd, Kisgyőr, Mezőkövesd, Sajómercse, Sály, Szentistván 2, Szegilong 2); Gömör county (Alsóbalog, Szilice); Abaúj county (Áj 2, Boldogkőújfalu, Cekeháza, Debrőd, Nagyhalász, Tornyosnémeti); Zemplén county (Nagykapos, Ricse 4, Sárospatak, Vajdácska); Bereg county ("Bereg" county, Beregszász, Gát, Lónya); Máramaros county (Hosszúmező 2). II: 75.

III. Pest county (Alpár, Bugac 2, Bugacmonostor 2, Csillaghegy, Fülöpszállás, Galambospuszta, Galgahéviz, Izsák 3, Kecel 5, Kiskunfélegyháza 5, Kiskunhalas 2, Kóka, Orgovány, Pálosmonostor 2, Szakmár, Tura); Jász-Nagykun-Szolnok county (Derzstomaj 3, Dévaványa, Jánoshida 4, Jászalsószentgyörgy, Jászárokszállás, Jászberény 3, Karcag 2, Kisújszállás, Kőtelek, Kunmadaras 2, Mesterszállás, Mezőcsát, Tiszafüred, Tiszapolgár, Tiszaszentimre, Túrkeve); Bács-Bodrog county (Bácsalmás, Bátya 2, Gombos 2, Kisfái, Rém); Sztára Torina?, Torontál county (Hertelendyfalva, Majdán, Nagybecskerek); Csongrád county (Ásotthalom, Csongrád 4, "Csongrád county", Domaszék, Hódmezővásárhely 5, Horgos, Kiskundorozsma, Szeged 3, Szentes 2, Tápé 2, Tömörkény, Újszeged); Csanád county (Alberti, Apátfalva); Arad county (Arad); Southern Great Plain s. 1. 2, Békés county (Doboz 3, Ecseg, Endrőd 4, the Vinyards of Fényes, Gyula, Pusztaföldvár, Sarkadkeresztúr); Bihar county (Furta, Konyár, Körösnagyharsány, Nagyszalonta 6, Nagyvárad, Pardi, Pocsaj, Sáránd 2, Újiráz); Hajdú county (Hajdúböszörmény, Hajdúhadház, "Hortobágy", Tiszacsege); Szabolcs county (Érpatak 2, Kenézlő, Nyírábrány, Nyírlugos 3, Nyírmada, Nyírtelek, Nyírtura 2, Mezőladány, Tornyospálca, Újfehértó, Vaja); Szatmár county (Darnó, Jármi 2, Kérsemjén 2, Kocsord, Piricse, Szamosszeg); Szilágy county (Szilágyperecsen). III: 146.

IV. Kolozs county (Inaktelke, Mákófalva 3, Sárvásár 2, Türe, Válaszút); Szolnok-Doboka county (Szamosújvár, Szék); Maros-Torda county (Kibéd, Nyárádmagyaros); Udvarhely county (Kápolnásfalu, Vargyas); Csík county (Gyimesfelsőlok, Gyimesközéplok, Csíkmenaság, Csíkvacsárcsi); Bukovina (Andrásfalva, Hadikfalva, Istensegíts, Józseffalva-Józsefszállás). IV: 22.

Total: 370.

Textual relationships with other ballads: none.

Tunes: 1. = No. 203 in 103 variants. Of these, 38 continues, after the first melodic section, with a major third instead of a sixth, by which circumstance both the tone and the melodic construction deteriorate, so that various solutions are resorted to in order to shape it in a sensible way. Another wide-spread tune is No. 2, recorded in 72 variants, 39 of which is contaminated with No. 1, starting with the first section of the latter and resuming a different melodic pattern only in the rest of the strophe. By this, the melody gives up its recurring construction.

No. 3 has been noted down in 8, No. 4 in 7, No. 7 in 4, No. 8 in 7, No. 16 in 3 variants. The rest of the associated melodies are adaptations.

841

Impersonal outlaw song, changing into a lyrical tone towards the end. A transitory form can be observed here between the outlaw ballads and the lyrical low-life scenes. The song as it is now obviously originates from the final period of the flourishing of outlaw ballads. This is indicated also by the fact that *Lajos Kálmány,* an excellent collector of the folklore tradition in the Great Plain, published one single specimen of the ballad, and that in last volume, Vol. III of *Szeged Népe* [The People of Szeged]. The same statement is further supported by the high number of rather uniformly shaped variants. Supposedly, it originated in the Middle Tisza Region about 1880. The most complete texts and tunes are found in this region.

115. MY BOLTER IS NOT UP TO SALE

204.

1. Csü - tör - tö - kön vi - ra - dó - ra   Ta - lál - tam egy pej - csi - kó - ra.

Majd éj - fé - lig   te - rel - get - tem,   Még-is fel - kö - tő - fé - kez - tem.

1. As it was dawning on Thursday
   I hit upon a bay colt.
   I was after it almost till midnight,
   And I succeeded in bridling it in the end.

2. I mounted it,
   And so I went to Fejérvár.
   From Fejérvár to Szengyörvár,
   To the fair of Szengyörvár.

3. They asked me at what price I would sell the colt.
   But the colt is not up to sale,
   But the colt is not up to sale,
   Nor would it be fitting under a gendarme.

4. For if a gendarme mounted it,
   Even birds would be made prisoners.
   For if a gendarme mounted it,
   Even birds would be made prisoners.

*Alsok (Somogy county). Performed by a male singer. Vikár 1899 = MF 43/a =
MNGY VI, 159.*

205.

Poco rubato ♪=cca 200

1. Csü - tör - tö - kön vi - ra - dó - ra   Ta - lál - tam egy   pej - csi - kó - ra.

Én azt   ad - dig ke - rül - get - tem,   Míg fel nem kö - tő - fi - kez - tem.

1. As it was dawning on Thursday
   I hit upon a bay colt.
   I kept walking round it
   Until I succeeded in bridling it.

2. As I bridled it,
   I rode towards Debrecen.
   They asked me to sell it for bank-notes,
   Worth three hundred thousand forints.

3. This colt is not up to sale,
   Nor does it fit under a gendarmerie commissar.
   For if a gendarme mounted it,
   Even birds would be made prisoners.

4. Máramaros is a country of hills and valleys.
   I am looked after by the county.
   At eight o'clock tomorrow
   I shall be taken to the prison.

5. They wink me into the eyes:
   How many bay colts can I remember?
   I can remember only a sorrel,
   Which I rode while driving the six young bulls.
   I rode it while driving the six young bulls, (to lines 3 and 4)
   All six were grey as cranes. (to lines 3 and 4)

Nádudvar (Hajdú county). Performed by a man of 59. J. Papp, 1961 = AP 6399/a.

Divergences:

Variants on the incipit:

As it was dawning on Thursday
I entered a field-ward's hut.
No sooner did I fall asleep
Than nine gendarmes stood up around me.

Another one:

I feel asleep on the bank of the Tisza (or a Ditch), etc.

Still another:

When I was a cowboy,
I fell asleep by my herd . . . (By the way, this beginning is known from a separate pastoral song of the lyrical kind.) Special beginnings are the following.

As I was sixteen years of age,
I learned how to steal horse.
I have stolen thirty-three horses,
Light chesnut bay steeds they were all.

Yellow colt by the road
Is grazing up the grass.
Feed, yellow steed, for you are not orphan,
I shall ride on your back to the inn.

These incipits are followed by continuations in the other beginning stanzas.
The point that best expresses the basic idea of the song is gradation.

For if it were mounted by a gendarme,
Even free birds would be made prisoners.

The beginning lines of this song show a fair agreement with those of the
ballad about "The Outlaw's Passport" (Type **109**). This circumstance gives rise
to frequent contamination of the two types. Sometimes Type **109** comes first,
followed—quite illogically—by the present ballad, in other instances the picture is
in the reverse, in which case a well founded story develops, ending with the motif of
the gendarmes' being shot dead. For example:

...Even birds would be made prisoners.
Tell me, scoundrel, what is your name!
Do you have a passport?
Wait a minute, sir gendarmes,
I have to unbutton my coat.
I unbuttoned my coat,
I drew my revolver,
And I shot one or two of them in the head:
Here you have my passport!

This motif is sometimes interwoven in the other stanzas of the ballad under
discussion. The two types are so much intertwined that the only criteria of
differentiating between them had been given by the characteristic beginning lines;
those songs starting with the motif of "passport" have been listed with Type **109,**
and those which mention the "bolter" at the beginning, with the present one.

A merger with other outlaw songs' texts can be demonstrated by the
following variant:

I have a horse, a light chestnut bay it is,
It has white stockings on all its four legs.
For twenty-four hours
It was able to keep abreast with an engine.
They asked me to sell my horse at a high price,
They offered fifteen hundred new forints for it.
But my horse is not up to sale,
Nor would it be fitting under a lieutenant.
For if a lieutenant mounted it,
Every outlaw would be made prisoner.
As it was dawning on Thursday,
I hit upon a field-ward's but.
No sooner did I fall asleep
Than I found the men of the county surrounding me.

845

I humbly ask the men of the county
Not to treat the outlaws unkindly.
I have not stolen anything, nor did I kill anybody,
I only wanted to see my sweetheart.
But the men of the county kept on querying:
Where is my passport?
Hey, I show it to you anon,
Only wait till I unbutton my waistcoat.
I unbuttoned my waistcoat,
I shot two of them in the head at once.
Here you have my passport!
Gendarmes are coming from every direction.
They are pressing me to the Tisza.
The water of Tisza will be my graveyard,
Unless my colt Breeze takes me over!
I crossed the water of Tisza swimming,
And I thanked God gratefully.
While my saddle and overcoat were drying,
I was sleeping for an hour.

The song also contaminates with prisoners' complaints. For instance:

1. I fell asleep on the bank of the Tisza,
I had very beautiful dreams.
About midnight I woke,
Lo, nine gendarmes are standing by me!

2. Sir gendarmes! What do you want of me?
Are you going perhaps to cast me into iron?
We do not want to cast you into iron,
But we are looking for a bolter.

3. My bolter is not up to sale,
Nor is it fitting under a gendarme.
For if it were mounted by a gendarme,
Even free birds would be made prisoners.

4. Then they asked me:
Where my passport was.
Wait a minute, gendarme,
Until I unbutton my blue waistcoat.

5. I unbuttoned my blue waistcoat,
I drew out my pistol.
Two of them I shot in the head at once,
Here you have my passport!

6. Alas, my God! What am I to do now?
Shall I run or shall I stay.
If I take to run, they will shoot me,
If I stay here, they will rope me.

846

7. As I was taken to Kanizsa,
   My hands and feet were put in iron.
   Girls were weeping around,
   As they saw me cast in iron.

8. I shall be free again,
   I shall not be a prisoner for all my life.
   I shall be free again,
   I shall not be a prisoner for all my life.

9. You are like a free bird, sweetheart,
   Still you rarely come to see me.
   Were I as free as you,
   I should see you every night!

   (Osztorony, Zala county.)

There is a characteristic ending to the story:
We have not come to drive away a colt,
We have come to put you into iron.
Outlaw, hold out your hands,
The bloody Lord of your soul of a scoundrel!

I hold out my hands,
Don't rob me of my life!
I did not kill anybody, I did not murder a man,
I only robbed the rich lords.

Earliest provenience: 1846.
Dissemination:

I. Sopron county (Középpulya); Vas county (Balozsamedgyes, Mikosszéplak); Zala county (Andráshida, Csörnyeföld, Dergecs, Kiskomárom 4, Monostorapáti, Nagygörbő, Orosztony); Somogy county (Alsok 2, Bedegkér, Erdőcsoknya, Hetes, Kaposújlak, Karád 3, Sándorpuszta, Somogy-szentmiklósfa, Szaplényosakol); Verőce county (Zdravicapuszta); Baranya county (Kölked, Nagyba-racska, Vásárosdombó); Tolna county (Decs, Gerjen, Pusztakenese); Fejér county (Pusztaforna); Veszprém county (Dudar, Pápa); Pest county (Tök); Komárom county (Kocs, Udvard); Győr county (Győr, Ság).

II. Pozsony county (Felsőszeli); Nógrád county (Bárna, Dejtár, Kisbárkány, Nógrádmegyer, Rimóc 2, Romhány, Szécsény); Heves county (Besenyőtelek, Derecske, Fedémes, Gyöngyösoroszi, Mátraszentistván); Borsod county (Kisgyőr, "Sajó Valley", Szilvásvárad 2); Gömör county (Alsóbalog, Beje 2, Szilice); Abaúj county (Beret, Boldogkőújfalu, Cekeháza, Füzérkomlós, Kéked); Zemplén county (Pácin); Bereg county ("Bereg county", Fornos 2).

III. Pest county (Bugacmonostor, Galambospuszta, Izsák, Jászberény, Kecskemét, Kiskunfélegyháza 2, Kiskunhalas 3, Orgovány, Sáp, Tura 2); Jász-Nagykun-Szolnok county (Tiszapüspöki); Bács-Bodrog county (Gombos, Horgos, Mélykút); Csongrád county (Ásotthalom, Csongrád 2, Hódmezővásárhely 2, Kiskundorozsma, Szeged); Bihar county (Nagyszalonta); Hajdú county (Debrecen, Hajdúböszörmény, "Hortobágy" 3, Nádudvar); Szabolcs county (Szabolcs, "Szabolcs county", Timár); Szatmár county (Darnó, Kálmánd, Kérsemlyén).

IV. Udvarhely county (Bözöd, Vargyas); Csík county (Gyimesvölgye); Háromszék county (Magyarhermány); Bukovina (Hadikfalva). Total: 115.

Textual relationship with other ballads: **109, 118.**
Tunes: 1. = No. 204 (8 variants, also with main cadence 5), 2. = No. 205 (8 variants, also with main cadence $\flat$3, or the cadence of the third section is $\flat$3), 4. (6 variants, also with main cadence 4), 5. (4), 7. (3), 9. (3 variants, also with main cadence 4), 10. (9), 11. (2), 13. (4), 14. (3), 15. (4), 16. (3).

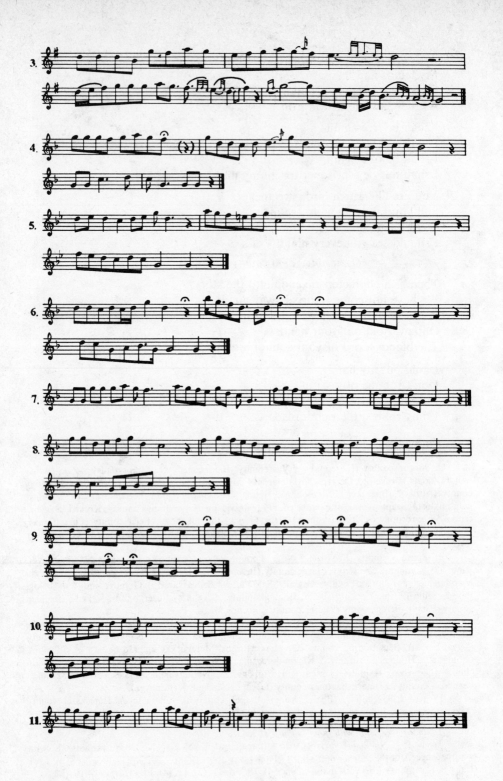

848

Apparently the ballad has not developed to any special tune, but it has been associated with several new-style melodies.

It hardly has a plot of its own; being built on one single thought, it can rather be regarded as a lyrical song. Nevertheless, considering its form characterized by the use of dialogue, further the scene, as well as its interrelations with other outlaw and prisoners' songs, we have relegated this composition to the borderline of outlaw ballads.

116. MY BELL-WETHER DOES NOT WANT TO GRAZE

206.

1. Nem a-kar a ve-zé-rö-rüm le-gel-ni. Réz-per-gő-jit ha-ra-go-san per-ge-ti.

I-de-gen sza-got é-rez a pusz-tá-ba Hát-ra né-zek jön hét zsan-dár u-tán-nam.

1. My bell-whether does not want to graze.
   It is ringing its brazen bell angrily.
   It smells a stranger in the field.
   Looking back, I see seven gendarmes approaching.

2. And one of them steps to me directly,
   Striking at me with his scourge of three tails.
   Hard was the blow on the head of the poor shepherd lad:
   He fell on the ground before his donkey.

3. Well, that was not a thing to be trifled with,
   The shepherd lad took up his crook and laid it on his shoulder:
   Sir gendarme, don't try to give me another blow!
   Upon my faith, I shall knock you on the head!

4. Then the gendarme asked him:
   Where were you born, you shepherd lad?
   My country is Ternótörökszentmiklós,
   Where I was raised as an orphan by my dear mother.

5. I say, shepherd lad, pack your thing upon your donkey!
   We are going to bind your hands and feet at once!
   Seven gendarmes, have no power enough
   To sever me from my flock of sheep.

6. I cannot leave my flock
   Before giving account to my head-shepherd.
   Only three wethers are missing which I have slain
   So that they might not mar my flock.

7. My head-shepherd has come from town.
   And I take leave of my silken-fleeced flock.
   Good-bye, my silken-fleeced flock, I must go now.
   I shall either die or I shall live with my sweetheart!

Hortobágy (Hajdú county). Performed by a male singer. Ecsedi = Ecsedi 72, No. 2.

Divergences:

"Harness, shepherd, harness your donkey!
To-night I put iron on your hands and feet!
Six gendarmes have not power enough
To sever me from my flock.
He has a cat-of-nine-tails in his hand,
He delivers a blow right on the head of the shepherd.
But the shepherd was not a man to be trifled with,
He flag his sheep-hook on his shoulder,
He hit the head of the gendarme with his crook
So that the gendarme fell down upon the ground before his little bay."

"The corporal of the gendarmes was not a man to be trifled with,
He delivered a sound blow on the shepherd's crispy head.
Sir gendarme, don't give me another blow!
Upon my faith, I knock you down at once!
He hit the corporal on the head
So that he fell on the ground in front of the shepherd's little bay."

"Upon this word the corporal asked him:
Were were you born, shepherd lad?
The famous land of the Cumans, Kecskemét is my country,
My dear mother gave me birth there.
I was born in the hilly land of Kecskemét,
I had no mother, yet I was raised.
I grew up as mushrooms in the woods.
I stole horses in my tenth year of age."

Earliest provenience: between 1892 and 1900 *(Vikár).*
Dissemination:
Moson county (Mosonszentmiklós); Vas county (Csönge, Kisrákos); Zala county (Alsópáhok 2, Andráshida, Csonkahegyhát, Felsőszemenye, Kiskomárom, Nemeshetés); Somogy county (Darány, Gerézdpuszta, Hetes, Juta, Kaposfüred, Somogyhárságy, Zselickisfalud); Baranya county (Csoboka, Kölked, Magyaregregy, Vajszló); Tolna county (Őcsény, Sárpilis); Veszprém county (Borzavár, Hegyesd 2, Réde, Zirc); Komárom county (Kocs, Tata); Győr county (Felpéc, Nagybaráthegy); Nógrád county (Nógrádmegyer, Szandaváralja); Heves county (Parád); Borsod county (Bogács, Domaháza, Kissikátor, Sajómercse); Abaúj county (Cekeháza, Tarnagörgő); Zemplén county (Mikóháza, Sárospatak); Ung county (Nagygejőc); Pest county (Bugac 2, Csernamiske, Hetényegyháza, Izsák, Kecel, Kiskunhalas 8, Szabadszállás, Tura); Jász-Nagykun-Szolnok county (Cibakháza, Jászapáti, Jászberény 2, Jászfényszaru, Jászkisér, Kunhegyes, Nagykörű, Tiszaszentimre); Bács-Bodrog county (Bajsa); Torontál county (Egyházaskér); Southern Great Plain s. 1. 2, Csongrád county (Csongrád 3, Röszke, Szeged-Alsóváros); Békés county (Békés, Pusztaföldvár); Bihar county (Körösnagyharsány 2, Nagyszalonta); Hajdú county (Hajdúböszörmény, Hajdúnánás 2, "Hortobágy"); Szabolcs county (Biri, Lövőpetri, Vaja 2); Szatmár county (Nábrád); Torda-Aranyos county (Torda, Újtorda); Kolozs county (Felsőzsuk); Csík county (Gyimesvölgye, Gyimesfelsőlok). Total: 97.

Textual relationships with other ballads: none.
Tunes: 1. = No. 206 (18 variants), 2. (3), 6. (2), 13. (2), 14. (2), 16. (4).

852

An outlaw story developed at the end of the last century without any pretence to
constructing in the ballad form.

117. TO HORSE, HORSEMEN, TO HORSE, THE STUD HAS BOLTED!

207.

Rubato ♩ = 72

1. Ló - ra csi - kós, ló - ra, El - sza - ladt a mé - nös, El - sza - ladt a mé - nös!

Csak e - gye - dül ma - radt A pány-ván a nyer - gös.

1. To horse, horse-herd, to horse,
   The stud has run away,
   The stud has run away!
   Only the saddle-horse has stayed
   Because it has been tethered.

2. Saddle then, boys,
   This reddish-brown bay horse,
   This reddish-brown bay horse!
   So that I can leap over
   The muddy river Maros.

3. The muddy River Maros
   I shall leap over by myself,
   I shall leap over by myself.
   With the cattle-herd of Bánát
   I shall eat a good dish of paprika meat.

4. Drink and eat, comrade!
   This is a good feast, indeed,
   This is a good feast, indeed!
   And we shall have another one
   When you drive cattle here.

5. Sure, I shall drive cattle here,
   Thirty-six cows,
   Thirty-six cows,
   For which the butcher
   Will pay well in bank-notes.

6. Cold blows the wind
   From the direction of Rimaszombat,
   From the direction of Rimaszombat.
   The gendarmes are gathering,
   Sweetheart, from every direction.

855

7. The keys of shackles are rattling,
   The keys of shackles are clapping, in his pocket,
   The keys of shackles are clapping in his pocket.
   Thirty-three mounted gendarmes
   Are escorting me to the jail.

8. Have you ever heard the fame
   Of that famous Tokeró,
   Of that famous Tokeró?
   And of the cells
   Which are to be found in it?

9. I have not only heard of it
   But I have also suffered in it,
   I have also suffered in it
   May God punish the man
   Who had built it!

10. Don't wonder, sweetheart,
    At my yellow-pale skin,
    At my yellow-pale skin:
    For nine years
    I have been a prisoner.

11. I am spending the tenth
    In the castle of Buda,
    In the castle of Buda.
    Many buckets of water have I brought
    For the prisoners!

12. There is no bread more bitter
    Than that of the prisoners,
    Than that of the prisoners:
    Pouring their tears, the poor men,
    Eat their bread.

Kiskunhalas (Pest country). Performed by a man of 37. Szomjas 1933.

Divergences: The ballad proper ends with the fifth stanza; most of the variants run out with it. The first five stanzas show but little variations. Sometimes, however the usual beginning formula is preceded by the first stanza of another shepherds' song, beginning with the lines: "Mist is rising from the hills of Mátra, It looks like rain...". The description of the feast sometimes finds a more detailed formulation: "The cowherd of Bánát Slaughtered a fine young bull, From which my teeth chewed a good dish of meat for supper. (Sometimes put in the present-tense.) Variations on the cattle-herd's address are like these: "On returning, We shall meet again"," or: "This is the last time That I drove stolen cattle here." The last statement in the fifth stanza reads sometimes like this: "For which the county Is looking for me night and day."

There are, however, at least as many variants to continue the song by adding prisoners' motifs to it. The occurring motifs are as follows (According to the number of motifs enumerated in the note to No. **118**):

1. Occurring six times; 4–5. (25); 9–10. (5); 18. (7, always in the same form: The bird has brought water for the prisoners. Drink, prisoners . . . etc.); 28. (2); 31. (5); 32., 33., 37. (2); 38. (4); 41., 52., 55. (3); 80., 98. No. 31 presents clearest transition between the scenes of outlaw life and the motifs of prison (cf. Stanza 6 of the text published above): it indicates the impending danger. In this case, and in certain other solutions, the two different elements have been merged into an organic whole. In other instances, the two kinds of elements are put together in an incoherent way, the only connecting link between the two being the contrast between the outlaw's style of life and the inevitable consequences of the same. Originally the common tune may have given rise to the combination: many examples show that the singers considered them as two different songs sung to the same tune. (In such cases the prisoner song was performed first followed by the outlaw song, or one of them was sung by the one, the other by the other informant. Such recordings have not been included into the list of variants.) Practice has shown, however, that the two kinds of song fit each other, and incidentally the different elements coagulated.

Earliest provenience: between 1892 and 1900 (collected by *Vikár*).
Dissemination:

I. Zala county (Zalalövő); Somogy county (Kadarkút, Zics); Baranya county (Csányoszró, Dunafalva, Kákics, Zaláta); Tolna county (Báta, Decs, Sárpilis); Pest county (Bogyiszló).

II. Nógrád county (Buják); Heves county (Bekölce, Füzesabony, Parád); Borsod county (Abod, Sály 2); Abaúj county (Cekeháza); Ung county (Latorca).

III. Pest county (Ágasegyháza, Akasztó, Bócsa, Bugac, Bugac-Alsómonostor 2, Bugacpuszta, Csikva, Csornamiske, Galambospuszta 2, Homokmégy, Izsák 2, Jászberény, Jászkarajenő, Kalocsa, Kecel 4, Kecskemét 3, Kiskunfélegyháza 3, Kiskunhalas 4, Kiskunmajsa, Lajosmizse, Orgovány, Sükösd, Szabadszállás, Tura); Jász-Nagykun-Szolnok county (Alattyán, Karcag, Rákóczifalva); Bács-Bodrog county (Bácsborsod, Bajaszentistván, Báty 2, Felsőerek, Rém 3); Csongrád county (Csongrád 5, Horgos, Szegvár); Csanád county (Apátfalva); Békés county (Dévaványa, Gyula); Hajdú county (Hajdúszoboszló, Hortobágy 2, Nádudvar, Tiszacsege); Szabolcs county (Beszterec, Fülöp, Nyírbátor).

IV. Csík county (Gyergyószentmiklós). Total: 86.

Textual relationships with other ballads: **118., 105.** (in one single Transylvanian variant).

Tunes: 1. = No. 207 (71 variants, seven of which are composed of four-lined stanzas; in two cases the third in five cases the second line has been omitted). The rest of the tunes have been coupled with the text in result of occasional combination.

As appears from its dissemination, the song was generated in the Danube–Tisza Interfluve towards the end of the last century. (*Kálmány* had not yet recorded it.) Impersonal, rather abstract presentation of scenes of the life of outlaws; by including the additional prisoner motifs, it realizes the same construction pattern as are characteristic of the best specimens of the outlaw ballads: after glorius feats, the fall and punishment follows inevitably.

118. PRISONERS' SONGS

208.

1. (Ej)Hal - lot - tad - e hí - rét Za - la - e - gër - szëg - nek?

(Ej) Od vët - ték fël az én Ra - bi é - le - të - met.

1. Have you heard the fame
   Of Zalaegerszeg?
   There I have been sentenced
   To pass my years of a prisoner.

2. I saw the lords sitting there,
   Twenty-four they were,
   All the twenty-four
   Sat together to sentence me.

3. As they produced
   The black book,
   They read out of it
   My life of a prisoner.

4. I am a prisoner, I am a prisoner,
   I am cast in iron up to my knees.
   I am cast in iron up to my knees,
   In shackles up to my elbows.

5. I am cast in iron up to my knees,
   In shackles up to my elbows,
   My eyes are going to run dry
   In this great darkness.

6. The deepest dungeon of the jail
   Is my laid bed,
   Its two walls
   Are my sleeping companions.

7. Nine iron fetters a pound each
   I have worn to pieces,
   Even the tenth
   I have made thin already.

8. The rose will wither
   On top of the hill,
   I also shall wither
   In the deep dungeon.

9. Light, peacock, light
   On the county's house,
   So that the many outlaws
   May get free.

10. Fly, bird, fly
    Over the county,
    Tell a word or two to my sweetheart
    Who is all by herself.

11. If she asks you where I am,
    Tell her that I am a prisoner,
    In the catle of Egerszeg
    I am cast in iron up to my knees.

12. Mother, my dear mother,
    What did the lords say?
    They said, the lords,
    That they were going to hang you.

13. Mother, my dear mother,
    It would be a pity to hang me!
    To have my nice, crispy hair
    Blown by the winds!

Murakeresztúr (Zala county). Performed by a man of 63. Seemayer 1932 = MF 3201/c.

209.

1. El-her-vadt cid-rus-fa   A ma-gos hegy-te-tőn.

Én is el-her-vad-tam   A bör-tön fe-ne-kén.

1. The cypress-tree has withered
   On the top of the high hill.
   I myself have withered
   In the deep dungeon.

2. Eight shackles, nine pounds each,
   I have torn to pieces already.

Even the ninth
I have made thin enough.

3. Mother, my dear mother,
Ask them to give out my paper,
Ask them to give out my paper,
To give me back my free life!

4. Mother, my dear mother,
What did the lords say?
The lords said
They are going to hang you.

5. O, mother dear,
It would be a pity to hang me,
To have my nice, crispy hair
Blown by the wind!

6. For nothing else, for nothing else,
But for two grey colts,
And for the decorated harness
Belonging to them.

Balatonberény (Somogy county). Bartók 1906 = Bartók 1924, 33/a.

210.

1. Jaj de na-gyon szé-lös Az a-csa-i be-rök!
Szö-gény Bo-gár Pé-tör Ab-ba-he-ve-ré-szött.

1. Alas, very wide is
The grove of Acsa!
Poor Péter Bogár
Was having a rest in it.

2. Blow away, breeze, blow away
The dust of the high way,
So that the gendarmes
May not see the hoof-prints of my bay horse.

3. From the direction of Rimaszombat
A light breeze is coming.
Aye, bad are the tidings
I have heard about my own fate!

4. They have spread on me
   The net to take me,
   They have taken me
   As a highwayman.

5. They escorted me
   To Rimaszombathel,
   In Rimaszombathel
   To the dark prison.

6. I can see the lords,
   Twelve they are,
   All the twelve
   Are thinking about me.

7. One of them says:
   He must be sent to the gallows,
   The next one says:
   Twenty years' imprisonment.

8. Fly, bird, fly
   Over the woods,
   Fly to my sweetheart's place,
   Where she is all by herself!

9. If she asks you, where I am,
   Tell her: I am a prisoner,
   In Rimaszobathel
   I am the first lad.

10. I am cast in iron up to my knees,
    In shackles up to my elbows.
    I am going to wither, sweetheart,
    Down in the darkness.

11. Of iron-fetters, nine pounds each,
    I have worn three to pieces already,
    And even the fourth
    I have made thin enough.

12. Wither, rose, wither
    On top of the hill there!
    I am going to die here,
    In the deepest cell of the prison.

Szenna (Somogy county). Performed by a man of 67. Olsvai 1963.

211.

Parlando rubato ♩ = cca 98

1. Hal-lot-ták - e hi-rét Za-la - e - ger-szeg-nek, Za-la - e - ger - szeg - nek?

Hát a ben-ne-le-vő Ösz-szes bör-tö-nök-nek?

1. Have you heard the fame
   Of Zalaegerszeg?
   Of Zalaegerszeg,
   Or the many cells of the prison
   That have been built in it?

2. I have heard of it, I have heard of it,
   And I have also suffered in it.
   I have also suffered in it.
   May the Lord deal heavily with the one
   For whom I have suffered!

3. Its outer walls
   Are washed by the river Mura,
   They are washed by the river Mura.
   Its inner walls
   Are inhabited by snakes and toads.

4. The eyes of snakes and toads
   Serve me as torches,
   They serve me as torches.
   The rattling of the keys of my cell
   Is my morning chime.

5. I have seen the lords,
   They have been thirty-two,
   They have been thirty-two.
   All the thirty-two of them
   Were busy at sentencing me.

6. They opened before me
   The black book,
   The big black book,
   From which they read out
   All my sins.

7. Do your hear, mother, do you hear,
   What the lords are saying,
   What the lords are saying?

The lords are saying
That they will hang me.

8. It would be a pity to hang me,
   To rob me of my life,
   To rob me of my life.
   To have my nice crispy hair
   Blown by the winds.

9. I am a prisoner, I am a prisoner,
   I am a prisoner of the state,
   I am a prisoner of the state.
   But I have no idea
   Of when I shall be released.

10. No sooner shall I have
    A nice, free flow of life,
    A nice, free flow of life
    Than a grain of wheat
    Will yield a hundred stooks.

11. Although I know it will never
    Yield as much as that.
    It will never yield as much as that.
    Therefore, sweetheart darling,
    Don't wait for my return.

Dunafalva (Baranya county). Performed by a man of 70. Andrásfalvy, Martin and R. Pesovár 1961 = AP 6329/c.

212.

1. Hal-lot-tad-e hi-rit   A Ri-ma-vi-zi-nek,   A Ri-ma vi-zi-nek?

Hát an-nak a   hí-res Mis-kol-ci töm-löc-nek?

1. Have you heard the fame
   Of the water of Rima,
   Of the water of Rima?
   Or the fame of the renowned
   Prison of Miskolc?

2. I have heard of it, I have heard of it,
   And I have also suffered in it,
   And I have also suffered in it.

864

My the Lord punish the one
Who had it built.

3. There are two young men in it,
   Two strange young men,
   Two strange young men.
   They spend their days and nights there,
   Without having enough to eat and drink, the poor souls.

4. They are cast in iron up to the knee,
   In blood up to the elbow,
   In blood up to the elbow.
   They have wept their eyes blind
   In the great darkness.

5. Brothers, kinsfolk,
   How faithless you are,
   How faithless you are!
   From this long imprisonment of mine
   You would not redeem me!

6. I shall go home,
   I shall not remain a prisoner for ever,
   I shall not remain a prisoner for ever.
   For all your kindness
   I shall make quit with you.

7. There is a big house there,
   Court of law, so they name it,
   Court of law, so they name it.
   Bitter is the stew
   They cook in it!

8. There is a table in it
   Covered with sorrow,
   Covered with sorrow.
   There are two glasses on it,
   Filled with poison.

9. Whosoever has filled
   That glass to the brim,
   That glass to the brim,
   I wish he would be carried away
   By a black bird!

10. Or if the glass filled to the brim
    Were mine,
    If it were mine,
    The redeming death
    Would drift me away at once.

11. Flow, swallow,
    Over the county of Heves,
    Over the county of Borsod,
    Take this sad tidings
    To my sweetheart!

12. If she asks you where I am,
    Tell her, that I am a prisoner,
    Tell her that I am sick,
    I am withering away
    On the iron bed of the jail of Miskolc.

Bekölce (Heves county). Performed by a man of 25. Mathia 1953 = NzCs 2023.

213.

1. Have you heard the fame
   Of the red triangle,
   Of the red triangle?
   Or that of the renowned
   Prison of Miskolc?

2. I have heard it, I have heard it,
   And I have also suffered in it,
   And I have also suffered in it.
   May the Lord deal heavily with the one
   Who had it built!

3. Even now it is closed,
   A young man of twenty,
   A young man of twenty
   Is spending his days in it,
   Without having enough to eat and drink, the poor soul.

4. He is cast in iron down to the heels,
   In blood up to the elbow,
   In blood up to the elbow.
   His eyes are sunk
   Because of the great darkness.

5. The ceiling of the arched cell
Serves me as my eiderdown,
It serves me as my eiderdown
The eyes of snakes and toads
Serve me as my lighting candles.

6. I have written to my mother,
Asking her to send me clean clothes,
Asking her to send me clean clothes.
But she wrote me in answer
That she had nothing to do with me.

7. There is a big house there,
Court of law, so they name it,
Court of law, so they name it.
The rooms in it are filled
With judges.

8. I saw the lords sitting there,
Twenty-four they were,
Twenty-four they were.
All the twenty-four of them
Pass sentence on me.

9. The twenty-ninth
Is writing the letter,
Is writing the letter.
A brown young woman
Dictates him my name.

10. Don't miss my name,
You brown young woman,
You brown young woman!
Look up to the sky
And rescue my life!

11. They spread before me
The black book,
The black book.
It is from that book
That they sentenced me as an outlaw.

12. I shall leave this place once,
I shall not stay a prisoner for life,
I shall not stay a prisoner for life!
For all the kindness of my kinsfolk
I shall make quit with them!

Tarnalelesz (Heves county). Performed by a man of 60. Maácz 1958 = NzCs 2030.

214.

Parlando rubato

1. Mi - kor men-tem Bu - da - pest - re, Bu - da - pes- ti - tör - vény -szék - be,

Lá - tom az u - ra - kat ír - ni, Rám te - kin - tett va - la - meny - nyi.

1. As I arrived in Budapest,
   At the court of law of Budapest,
   I saw the lords writing,
   All of them were looking at me.

2. They sentenced me for three years.
   I would fain get free, but it is not possible.
   I wrote a letter to my mother
   Asking her to send me clean clothes.

3. My civilian clothes were sent to me.
   Mother threw herself into my arms.
   You may weep now, mother, you may wail as well:
   You have had one son, and even that became a prisoner.

4. Arched is my cell,
   Not even the moonlight shines on me!
   How could I hope, then, that the bright sun-beam
   Should shine on my pale cheeks!

5. The iron door is rattling and cracking.
   Perhaps the jail-keeper is coming!
   He is holding two candles in his hands,
   He is counting the days I have spent here.

6. Mother, mother, my dear mother,
   Come and see my cell!
   Two deals serve me as bed.
   I am going to die here, my dear mother!

Áj (Abaúj county). Performed by a man of 48. Vargyas 1940 = Vargyas 1960, 4/a.

215.

1. The net of the world has been spread on me.
   I have been fished out like a true orphan.
   I have been thrown into a dark cell.
   They told me I should perish there!

2. I was caught by the county of Torontál,
   And my person was cast into a dark cell.
   My laid bed is the floor of the jail,
   My conversing mate is the ceiling of the jail.

3. Snakes and toads are my light candles,
   The opening of the door is my morning chime.
   The court consists of fifteen men,
   All the fifteen of them are counselling on me.

4. The sixteenth is writing my document,
   The seventeenth is dictating him my name.
   You false traitor, don't dictate my name,
   For all know how mournful my life has been!

5. Brothers, brothers, how faithless you are
   Not to see me in such a distressed condition!
   I shall go home again, and I shall behave properly,
   For your brotherly kindness I shall be grateful to you.

6. The road of Becskerek is covered with asphalt,
   Many kind mothers are walking on it, weeping.
   Don't weep, dear mother, it had to be like this,
   For my bad deeds I must pay like this!

7. His mother, his dear mother asks him:
   When do you come home again?
   I go home again
   When one grain of wheat yields a hundred stooks.

8. For the key of my jail has been lost already.
   And I shall never be released from here!
   Aye, but the key of my prison will be recovered one day,
   And I shall be released from here some day!

Magyarszentmárton (Torontál county). = Kálmány 1954, 22/a.

216.

Poco rubato

1. Ü - tik az a - ra - di do - bot, Ki - sé - rik a sze - gény ra - bot.

Ra - bot, ra - bot rab - sá - gá - ért, En - gem a be - tyár - sá - go - mért.

1. They are beating the drums in Arad,
   They are escorting the poor prisoner.
   The prisoner is taken for his robbery,
   I have been taken for my having been an outlaw.

2. They sentenced me for a few years.
   I would fain get free, but it is not possible.
   I wrote a letter to mother at home,
   To send clean clothes to her prisoner son.

3. So my mother came to see me,
   Weeping and crying she embraced me.
   You may well weep now, mother, and you may cry as well,
   You have had but one son, and lo, he has become a prisoner.

4. The iron door is rattling and clattering.
   Now the jail-keeper is coming.
   He examines the head of my bed
   Curious to know if I am not digging through the wall of my cell.

5. I told the jail-keeper
   Not to be glad of my being a prisoner.
   For if he is glad of my being a prisoner
   There will be a knife turning round in his heart!

6. For I am going to get free,
   I shall not be a prisoner for good.
   The way one treats me
   So I shall treat one then!

7. As I was walking home,
   The sky opened in the east.
   The stars were shining on me,
   They knew that I had been released.

Hernádkércs (Borsod county). Performed by a man of 48. L. Vikár, 1957.

217.

1. Down there mounted people are coming,
   They are swarming like eagles.
   Aye, outlaws, aye, outlaws,
   Why are your pants painted with blood?

2. Welcome, good day, my dear friend!
   Well, how are you? As I can see...
   Welcome, sir gendarme!
   I can't say, I am very well now!

3. Alas, my God, alas, my dear!
   I am made a prisoner now!
   Father and mother are mourning for me,
   My dearest sweetheart is mourning for me.

4. Don't mourn for me, don't be so scared,
   I have not yet been taken to be shot.
   You may mourn for me, you may be scared
   When I am being taken to be shot.

5. Light here, my sweet swallow,
   Take my letter on your wing!
   Take it to my father's window,
   Spread it on his table!

6. From it he will learn where his son is:
   In the great prison of Gyula!
   In the great prison of Gyula
   My sad heart has been closed down!

7. The iron door is rattling and clanging,
   Lo, the jail-keeper is coming.
   He examines the head of my bed,
   Curious to know if I am not digging the wall.

8. I have not got an embroidered pillow,
   I am lying on the wing of my fur-coat.
   I lean my sad head on it,
   Pouring my tears.

9. I shall not be a prisoner all the time,
   I shall be released from here.
   The way they treat me
   So I shall serve them!

10. The iron door is rattling and clanking,
    Lo, the jail-keeper is coming.
    Take up your things, you poor orphan,
    I am releasing you from here.

Apáca (Csanád county). = Kálmány 1878, 151.

Divergences: The class of prisoners' songs do not constitute a coherently developed type with a fixed plot pattern: rather do they include a number of motifs, of which a new series is shaped on every occasion. By way of exemplification we may refer here to a string of beads: pearls of various colours are arranged in a different order on the string in most of the instances. Therefore the sample pieces fail to represent a general form which could be supplemented with the variants showing more or less marked deviations. The texts published can give an inkling of the method with which the possible motifs can be assembled. In addition to these, we have to show the multitude of motifs and poetic ideas the Hungarian people has invented to describe the painful lot of prisoners in folksongs. At the same time, we may have an opportunity to peep into the method of folklore creation as well.

Below, the motifs will be introduced in their order of frequency, by and large, with the insignificant variations disregarded, as a matter of course; the number of all variants will be given according to their territorial distribution. The variants known from other ballads are referred to by numbers in brackets, since these data are also characteristic of their dissemination. By means of the serial numbers here applied, the areal survey of the content of the individual variants will be facilitated.

1. I see the lords..., cf. No. 208, St. 2; No. 210, St. 6; No. 211, St. 5; No. 213, Stanzas 8–10; No. 215, Stanzas 3–4. Another beginning formula: The lords of .... are twenty-four... Sometimes the following lines are inserted after the third stanza: "But the famous dame did not pay heed to my words. Tomorrow I shall be taken to the gallows". 86 variants. I: 25; II: 35; III: 22; IV: 4. (8).

2. As I was going ..... to the court of law..., cf. No. 214, St. 1. Divergence: "I must go to the court..." or I was taken to the court. There we were astonished a little, Seeing the many lords writing..." In line 4: "...there I shall be sentenced." 50 variants. I: 7; II: 22; III: 15; IV: 5; s. l.: 1.

3. In the court of .... Twenty-four lords are sitting by the desk. They are winking in my eyes, asking How many colts I can remember. I cannot remember more Than a black and a grey colt..." or: "No more than for what I have been thrown into prison." 12 variants. I: 1; II: 2; III: 9. (5).

4. Have you heard the fame of..., cf. No. 208, St. 1; No. 212, St. 1; No. 216, St. 1. 73 variants. I: 19; II: 27; III: 26; IV: 1. (25).

5. I have heard it..., cf. No. 211, St. 2; No. 212, St. 2; No. 213, St. 2; 54 variants. I: 12; II: 19; III: 23. (25).

6. There is a young man in it..., cf. No. 212, St. 3; No. 213, St. 3. 28 variants. I: 2; II: 14; III: 12.

7. Fly, bird..., cf. No. 208, St. 10; No. 210, St. 8; No. 212, St. 11; No. 217, St. 5. Divergence: "Fly, peacock, fly", or (more rarely): "Light, raven, light, Light on my window, Let me write a letter on both of your wings... To my father, my mother, and my betrothed one." (This is adaptation of an old prisoner lyric song.) 62 variants. I: 8; II: 30; III: 12; IV: 11. (these being archaic, related to the Turks); S.l. 1. (2).

8. "A black cloud is rising there A black raven is pluming in it. Fly, raven fly, Take my letter to my father, mother, and my betrothed one." A lyrical song that can be traced back as far as the period of the Turkish occupation. 9 variants. I: 1; III: 5; IV: 3. (1).

9. If they ask you where I am ..., cf. No. 208, St. 11; No. 210, St. 9; No. 212, St. 12. 66 variants. I: 8; II: 28; III: 15; IV: 14; s.l. 1. (6).

10. I am cast in iron up to my knees..., cf. No. 208, St. 11; No. 210, St. 10; No. 212, St. 4; No. 213, St. 4. 58 variants. I: 10; II: 23; III: 19; IV: 5; s.l. 1. (5).

11. The iron door is rattling and clattering ..., cf. No. 214, St. 5; No. 216, St. 4; No. 217, St. 7. Divergence: "He examines my shackles. They are glad of my being a prisoner"; "In the evening the jail-keeper is walking round. The iron door is rattling angrily. Candles are carried in front of him, He is examining the outlaw", or: "the sinful prisoner". 66 variants. I: 18; II: 17; III: 14.

12. ...take up your things ..., cf. No. 217, St. 10. 7 variants. I: 2; II: 2; III: 3. (1).

13. The ceiling of my arched cell serves me as my eiderdown ...., cf. No. 208, St. 6; No. 213, St. 5; No. 215, St. 2. Variant: "The head of my bed Is a piece of brick, My eiderdown is the ceiling of the prison"; "The ceiling of the prison Is my shroud, The rattling of iron shackles Is my chiming bell, The eyes of snakes are my lamps." 41 variants. I: 10; II: 14; III: 11; IV: 6.

872

14. They sentenced me to ... years ..., cf. N. 214, St. 2., No. 216 St. 2. Lines 3 and 4 sometimes read: "You may well cry with bewailing words, mother, You had but one son, end even he became a prisoner." 41 variants. I: 1; II: 21; III: 13; IV: 5; s.l. 1. (1).

15. They have sent, or: They have brought the civilian clothes..., cf. No. 214, St. 3. 39 variants. I: 2; II: 17; III: 14; IV: 4; s.l.: 1.

16. Mother... come and see my cell ..., cf. No. 214, St. 6. 32 variants. I: 1; II: 19; III: 10; IV: 1; s.l.: 1 (2).

17. Mother, send me clothes ..., cf. No. 214, St. 2, Lines 3–4; No. 213, St. 6 (which is very rare). 39. variants. I: 3; II: 16; III: 13; IV: 6; s.l.: 1.

18. The peacock lighted down ..., cf. No. 208, St. 9. Different formulations: "The peacock has lighted upon ..."; "Fly, peacock, fly away..."; "Fly, peacock, fly...", and the continuation may be: "It has brought water in its peak for the prisoners. Drink, you prisoners..." or: "Wash, you prisoners". 36 variants. I: 26; III: 18; IV: 2 (13, appeared in the first broadside publications in 1810–20).

19. Cf. No. 208, St. 4; No. 211, St. 9. The general form is as follows: "I am a prisoner, I am a prisoner, I am looking forward to being released. Only God knows When I shall be released." 35 variants. I: 23; II: 1; III: 4; IV: 7.

20. Brothers, you are faithless, indeed..., cf. No. 212, St. 5; No. 215, St. 5. 15 variants. II: 6; III: 9.

21. I shall be released and I shall treat you as you have treated me..., cf. No. 212, St. 6; No. 213, St. 12; No. 215, St. 5, Lines 3–4; No. 216, St. 6, 217 St. 9. 40 variants. I: 5; II: 16; III: 15, IV: 4. (1).

22. My cell is arched..., cf. No. 214, St. 4. Variants: "My room is iron-gated...", and in one text: "My palace is made of stone...". A rare variant for lines 3–4: "The head of my bed is made of stone, It wears away my crispy hair." 28 variants. I: 7; II: 5; III: 7; IV: 9. (1).

23. There is a big house there..., cf. No. 212, St. 7; No. 213, St. 7. 26 variants. II: 16; III: 4; IV: 6.

24. In the house...there is a table ..., cf. No. 212, St. 8. 28 variants. I: 3; II: 13; III: 4; IV: 8.

25. Whosoever may have filled That glass ..., I wish the redeeming death Would come and take me away. ..., cf. No. 212, Stanzas 9–10 (somewhat modified). 18 variants. II: 10; III: 2; IV: 6.

26. Mother...ask them for my letter ..., cf. No. 208, St. 12; No. 209, St. 3. 17 variants. I: 12; II: 3; III: 1; IV: 1.

27. What did the lords say?, cf. No. 208, St. 13; No. 209, St. 4; No. 211, St. 7. 19 variants. I: 16; II: 1; III: 1, IV: 1.

28. It would be a pity to do so ..., cf. No. 208, St. 14; No. 209, Stanzas 5–6; No. 211, St. 8. 27 variants. I: 15; II: 4; III: 6; IV: 1. (7).

29. The rose is withering on top of the hill..., cf. No. 208, St. 8; No. 209, St. 1, No. 210, St. 12. 17 variants. I: 15; II: 1; III: 1.

30. I have worn ... Iron shackles nine pounds..., cf. No. 208, St. 7; No. 209, St. 2; No. 210, St. 11. 19 variants. I: 18; III: 1.

31. The breeze is blowing . . . , cf. No. 210, St. 3; 20 variants. I: 10; II: 5; III: 5. (5). It is to be noted that "Rimaszombat" (Gömör county) occurs, without exception, in this motif, which enjoys widest spread in Transdanubia.

32. Don't wonder, sweetheart . . . , or: Don't wonder, darling, that I am yellow . . . , or: Don't stare at me Because I am pale, For I have been a prisoner For nine years. 26 variants. I: 15; II: 1; III: 9; IV: 1.

33. The tenth (year) I spent in the castle of Arad; Aye, many buckets of water have I brought for the prisoners! 4 variants. III. (1).

34. He who is glad of my being a prisoner . . . , cf. No. 216, St. 5. 24 variants. I: 2; II: 6; III: 6; IV: 9; s.l.: 1. (5).

35. When it was dawning on Thursday, I hit upon a field-ward's hut. No sooner did I fall asleep Than I saw nine gendarmes standing about me. Or: At the edge of the Tisza I fell asleep, Alas, I had a dreadful dream . . . . A more remote variant: On Thursday night I found myself . . . Cast into iron at the inn of . . . The motif represents a transition from outlaw ballads to prisoners' songs. 29 variants. I: 9; II: 2; III: 11; IV: 6. (1).

36. Sir gendarmes, what do you want? Or: Well, you dogs, what do you want? Will you perhaps cast me in iron? 17 variants. I: 3; II: 3; III: 7; IV: 4.

37. Don't weep, dear mother, It had to turn out like this: There must be a wicked one In every clan! Or: For my many wicked deeds I have to pay like this . . . , cf. No. 215, St. 6, Lines 3–4; 20 variants. I: 2; II: 1; III: 12; IV: 5. (4).

38. Cf. No. 215, St. 6, Lines 1–2. More frequently: "The jail of . . . is made of stone, Many kind mothers are walking beneath it, pouring their tears." 17 variants. I: 1; II: 1; III: 12; IV: 3. (4).

39. They lay out the black book before me . . . , cf. No. 208, St. 3; No. 209, St. 6; No. 213, St. 11. Variant: "They lay out the big black book before me, From it they read out the deeds I have committed as an outlaw." 15 variants. I: 10; II: 3; III: 2.

40. No sooner shall I be freed Than . . . , cf. No. 211, Stanzas 10–11; No. 215, St. 7. 11 variants. I: 3; II: 3; III: 5.

41. Cf. No. 210, St. 7. The general form is: "One of them says: He should be hanged. The other says: It would be a pity to do harm to him!" 10 variants. I: 1; II: 3; III: 6. (1).

42. We shall cast you in iron, we shall bind you, We shall escort you to Szeged. 11 variants. I: 1; II: 1; III: 7; IV: 1; s.l.: 1.

43. As I am taken to Vác, I look back to my beautiful country. I see my brothers and sisters, They are lamenting me.—Other variant: "As I am taken to Nagyvárad, My hands and feet are cast in iron. My sisters are weeping they see me cast in iron." 10 variants. I: 7; II: 2; IV: 1. (1).

44. If I am freed, I shall make a vow: Three times a day I shall go to church. But I am not going to pray there for the deceased believers, Rather shall I pray for those many prisoners. 9 variants. All from Region I.

45. Cf. No. 217, St. 8. Or: I have no eiderdown, I have no pillow, I am lying on the county's bed . . . The door of the jail is frosty, Wuthering wind comes in, And I have no eiderdown . . . etc. 11 variants. I: 1; III: 4; IV: 6.

46. I would never have believed That the walls of the jail should be pressing my sides, Wearing down my crispy hair, Withering my red face. Or: You did not believe, mother: My bed is laid on two deals. I can't see the starry sky, nor the moonlight, Even the sun does not shine on me. 8 variants. I: 4; II: 1; III: 3.

47. Once I am released, Many people will rue the day! Here a yoke, there a halter Will be sheltered in the loft! 8 variants. I: 4; II: 1; III: 2; IV: 1.

48. The net was cast..., cf. No. 210, St. 4; No. 215, St. 1. 8 variants. I: 5; III: 3.

49. If I die, Who is going to lament me? Or: All my clothes should be put on me.—My dear mother will be lamenting for me, She who has been tending to me. 10 variants. II: 3; III: 5; IV: 22. (1).

50. Heyduck, heyduck, old heyduck, So far I have not known What sorrow was. Until I was walking free, I had friends everywhere. But now that I have fallen prisoner, I have not a single friend anywhere. Or: "... Tell me what grief is. For I cannot grieve. I am sure I shall be released." 6 variants. II: 1; III: 2; IV: 2; s.l.: 1.

51. They are beating the drum in Kassa..., cf. No. 216, St. 1. 7 variants. I: 3; II: 4.

52. There is no bread more bitter Than that of the poor prisoner, For the prisoner's bread is meted out by the pound.—5 variants. I: 2; II: 3. (1).

54. Sun and three kinds of star, Alas, I have been robbed of their sight!—4 variants. I: 3; III: 1.

55. On the grated window a little bird is singing, Whistling to my sweetheart: A sad day has dawned on me! ...is playing the fiddle. Fly to my darling, She is alone. 4 variants. I: 2; II: 2. (3).

56. Snakes and toads Are my lighting candles, The creaking of the door (or: the clattering of my shackles) Is my morning chime. Cf. No. 215, St. 3, Lines 1–2. 4 variants. I: 3; III: 1.

57. As I was going to Komárom, With my hands and feet in shackles, The girls were weeping To see me cast in iron.—4 variants. I: 1; II: 1; III: 1; IV: 1. (5).

58. As I was going to ... |: I looked back to my beautiful country :|, My tears were falling onto my shoulders. III: 1.

59. Open, you skies and earth! Let me complain to you! I tell my complaints to the earth, Because it does not let them out to anyone.—My mouth is full of complaint, But I have no-one to complain to.—I have neither a father nor a mother To tell my complaints to. etc. 5 variants. I: 4; III: 1.

60. Tap, sweetheart, The grates of my window! I also rattle The shackles on my feet. (Or: The iron of the county). 4 variants. I: 3; IV: 1.

61. On Thursday ... I am cast in iron. My sweetheart goes there, She is lamenting me with much bewail. Well, I have reason to lament for you, When I see you cast in iron! 6 variants. I: 4; III: 1; IV: 1.

62. You know, darling, what you have promised me under oath When you placed your hand in mine: You would be my care-taker In case I happened to become a prisoner. IV: 4.

63. The beasts of the woods Will bury me, And they will also lament me. Or: The birds of the sky will lament me.—6 variants. III. It is interesting that this motif is sung as part of plaintive songs in Transylvania, still it is not in

Transylvania that it found its way into the prisoners' songs but in the Great Plain, where, in turn, it does not come up in any other connection.

64. Avoid, comrade, avoid The hand of the county, So that you may not rue The day you taste its bitter bread!—I have tried to avoid it, comrade... 4 variants. I: 1; II: 1; III: 2.

65. Bring it as a news to my sweetheart: I have become in colour like the dead– and a possible continuation: What I eat does not taste good to me, All my food and drink is bitter. 3 variants. II: 1; III: 2.

66. The stars were shining ..., cf. No. 216. St. 7. In other contexts: For they knew that I was free. 3 variants. I: 1; II: 2.

67. Hand over, sweetheart, hand over Your white handkerchief, Let me wipe down My pouring tears. 3 variants. I: 2; II: 1.

68. My window is iron-gated. Extend your arm, my little angel! Let me touch it for the last time! For I am going to take leave soon. 4 variants, all from III.

69. ...let me perish for ever..., cf. No. 215, St. 1, Lines 3–4. 3 variants. III.

70. ...May the Lord deal heavily with him Who cast on me this! May He deal heavily, heavily with him, May He not leave him unpunished, For his having ordered me To be cast in these heavy shackles! 2 variants. I: 1; III: 1.

71. Woods, woods, round woods. There is a prisoners' burial place in the middle of it. There is a death-bird in the middle of it, Flying from one grave to another. 2 variants. I: 1; III: 1.

72. Its outer walls Are washed by the waters of the Mura..., cf. No. 211, St. 3. I: 2.

73. My little bay has grazed up All the grass by the road. Its master has been taken prisoner, There is nobody to take care of it. I: 2.

74. My horse eats oats and hay, I eat the food that I get from the county. My horse is given in rent, I am in the castle of Lipolt. 3 variants. I: 1; III: 2.

75. I am escorted down into the single-man cell, I am all by myself in it (cast in iron). I would like to complain, But there is no-one to complain to. Thus I don't say a word. I: 2.

76. As I was taken towards Arad, The sky parted in two. The bright starts were weeping, They saw that I was a poor prisoner (or: an innocent prisoner). III: 3. (2).

77. They put heavy iron shackles On my tender hands, Iron shackles of nine pounds On my tender feet. I: 2.

78. The clanging of my shackles (or: keys) Is my morning chime. I: 2.

79. Whoever could have devised this, That I should spend twenty years in prison? One year would be quite enough To make me ponder over things! I: 3.

80. Only sorrow has been sown to me In the confines of Miskolc (or: the storeyed building of Komárom). I wish that never a bird Whistling beautifully should light on it! (The little bird keeps crying: Let's leave this place, comrade, And return to our old dwelling.) 4 variants. II: 1; II: 3. (1).

81. Let's leave this place, comrade, For it is not good to stay here! For the county will Often frequent this place. Lo, it has appeared already! And it has taken me! It had thrown me Into its dark dungeon.—2 variants. II: 1; III: 1 appeared in the first broadside publication in 1810–20).

82. Thanks to the county For its kindness to have my place whitewashed, So that I may sit confortably alone.—II: 2.

83. Nine years I have spent in the jail of Szeged, And twenty-one in the jail of Rima.—III: 2.

84. The two long sides of the jail of Rima are yellow. There are three hundred and six doors on each side of it. There are also windows in it: six hundred and twenty-three. Mournful I am peeping out of their Thick grates. III: 2.

85. May the Lord have granted Not to see you in my life ||: Not to hear your name and fame:||, Perhaps I could have lived a few more years.—III: 2.

86. Don't lament me with so much bewailing as yet..., cf. No. 217, St. 4. III: 2.

87. They take my horse to Gyula, And myself, cast in iron, after it. III: 2.

88. I sent word to the mayor: Let he have my two arms released from the bondage. Yet the mayor did not do that, he had me roped even tighter. III: 2.

89. Wait and see, heyduck, you will rue the day On which you began to maltreat the prisoners! I shall cut a strap out of your back, And make you dance the fox-dance! IV: 2.

90. My Lord, my country, Where am I going to meet my death? Is it in wood, or in field, or in the vast desert? 3 variants. II: 1; III: 2.

Most of the other motifs are known from one notation each, therefore they should be regarded as "individual" inventions. Nevertheless, they are marked by soundness of form and a high motivic power, thus we may suppose that a more comprehensive collecting work could have produced their variants as well. (Only the motifs occurring in more than one variant are indicated.)

91. I ask the lords Not to cut my throat. But the pandour answers: It's a business of law. IV.

92. My Lord, My dear God, Whom shall I go to complaint to? When nowhere in this world Can you find a true man. III.

93. You son of a whore, son of a bitch! Don't scold me like a dog! I am not accustomed to it! I am used to nice words! I.

94. At the foot of the high stone-wall of Arad I am cast in shackles. III.

95. It is not good to be a prisoner at Ilova, For one has to sit in single-man cell. I shall be standing at the corner, I shall be watched there as well. II 2.

96. There is the black book, bound in black cover,
A dame is sitting by it, Enumerating my sins.... I.

97. They light the candle, And put it in my hand. They are not going to toll The bells of the village to me. III: 2.

98. Don't weep, mother, Because I am cast in iron. Pray to God And I shall be released one day! III: (6).

99. The swan flies high in the air. The outlaw has been taken prisoner. His name is Jóska Albert. His hands and feet are put in cross-shackles. III: 2.

100. They are driving my horse to Gyula, I myself am walking after it. Don't drive it so quickly, For I am not going to be in iron very long. III: 3. (1).

101. My sweetheart is a nice little brown girl, She would like to converse with me. I ask the lords to allow me To see my sweetheart! But the lords answered: The court of law forbade it! III.

102. I have spent my years of imprisonment |: Fortunately, they have sent me away :|. But all the same, they have made me a poor man. III.

103. I am clanging the iron-shackles on my hands and feet. My sweetheart's tender heart is near to break with grief for me. I.

104. The jail of Kaposvár Is not a church, Rather is it a place Where prisoners are murdered. I.

105. I was made a great prisoner, My wife was made a whore, My children were made orphan, My wealth was made to perish. I.

106. The county's house of Fejérvár: I have been wrapped in mourn in it. Well, I may well be wrapped in mourn, Since my hands are put in shackles I.

107. It is nine years Since I was made a prisoner. ||: Since I did not see The run of the sun in the sky :|| The run of the sun, the turn of the moon. II.

108. My door is iron-grated. Every now and then the jail-keeper appears. They are rattling my shackles, They don't mind my troubles at all. II.

109. The prison of Illava ||: Is full of prisoners : ||, Minor or major they may be. In one of the prisons They are thirty-two. In the other prison, They are thirty-three. II.

110. I have been walking in the courtyard of the county's hall. I have not heard else but words of wail there. II.

111. Sun, moon, stars, be plunged into mourn now! I am living as a desolate prisoner. II.

112. The gendarme has bound me. The shackles cut my flesh to the bones. I am rattling my shackles and my chains mournfully, Alas, my God, my free life is ended! III.

113. I am escorted to the jail of Szeged. There were neither beds nor pillows in it. I lay down with face to the hard deal. Hard deal is ruining my sides. III.

114. If I began to count my days: How many nights am I going to spend here. I count them in the evening, in the morning and at noon, And my heart is always in dispair. III.

115. My name is Gyura Angyal. The county is out to take me. My pockets are full of bank-notes. My stable is full of stolen horses. III.

116. The county has taken me, It has placed my body . . ., cf. No. 215, St. 2, Lines 1–2. III: 2.

117. For the key of the prison has been lost . . ., cf. No. 215. St. 8, lines 1–2. III.

118. I see the pen scribbling, I see false witnesses standing by. III (1).

119. My darling, whom I acquired with much pain, Whom shall you be left to? I shall be left to God, And to kind-hearted people. III.

120. The floor of the prison of Ilova Is paved with marble. Its door is covered with iron. It lays heavily on the hearts of the prisoners. III.

121. Don't weep, mother dear! I shall return home in the autumn. I shall plough your land with your rusty plough-share. III.

122. In the court of Gyula Twelve judges have gathered together, They are examining the black book To make it out how many thefts I have committed. III.

123. Sir commissar encourages me To steal six bay horses for him. If I drive them into his courtyard, I shall have supper with him. III.

124. They have taken me, They have put me in iron. They have thrown me into the deep dungeon Of the jail of Szeged. (cf. No. 116.) II: 1; III: 1.

125. That storeyed building should be set aflame, The iron-shackles should fall off me. The iron-shackles have fallen off me, It needs a good gendarme to close me up again! III (1).

126. As long as I fared well, I had friends everywhere. But since I am a prisoner, I have not a single friend. III.

Of these motifs a series hardly repeats itself. A geographical survey of the variants shows that full arrangements of the motifs are very rare, if not altogether missing. What we see is a restless whirl of quickly changing elements; sometimes the same motifs are altered by a slight change of the order or words, or replacement of one word with another. Yet a certain degree of constancy can be observed here and there. The motivic order of No. 214 (2 + 14 + 17 + 15 + 22 + 11 + 16) is repeated sometimes with certain omissions, and in one or two occasions without any change in the eastern parts of areas II and III. In a similar way the material of No. 209 also shows an identical arrangement (29–30–26–27–28) in territory II. More or less coherent blocs are composed of motifs 7 + 9 + 10 (in older texts 8 + 9 + 10). A particularly rare example of motivic consolidation has been recorded from Nagykörü (Jász-Nagykun-Szolnok county, area III) where collectors found the same, unaltered text in 1901, between 1906 and 1910, and in 1956. A picture in the reverse has been observed at Nagyszalonta (Bihar county, III) from where twelve utterly different motivic orders or a song of one single motif have been collected during a thorough field-work.

There are longer motifs, the related parts of which are distinctly indicated, because not all of them occur in every composition. Since parts of these come up separately as well, they provide instructive examples of variable application: 4 + 5 + 6 + , 7 + 9 + 10. 20 + 21, 23 + 24 + 25, 26 + 27 + 28.

The great variety is enhanced by "individual" ideas (indicated by the letter "e" in the list of series). This refers sometimes to a complete, long verse, in other instances only a short stanza. Both in the former and the latter cases texts of high poetic value occur. For example after 8 + 9 + 10:

Father, dear mother, why did you not kill me
When I was being tended by you!
But you thought you would find pleasure in me
When I am grown, and that I would be your delight.
I would like to learn the will of the lords,
I would have them to tell me about their intention,
For if I grow angry, I shall make a try:
I shall dig out the wall of the prison.
I shall be roaming over hills and dales,
As long as I can see a star in the sky.
Death will meet me somewhere,
Putting an end to my life with his sharp spear.

(Egyházaskér (Torontál county).

879

(The sharp spear of death must be literary reminiscence, pointing to cantorial mediation.)

In other instances individual transformation of a well developed text, or portion of text, can be encountered, in which the "individual" contribution may mean a higher degree of variation only.

> In the prison of Pécs my body is ruined by the dungeon.
> I live among walls of stone. I know, sweetheart, that I am going to die.
> My room is built of plain marble, my bed is made of eight rows of brick.
> My bed is made of eight rows of brick. My weak body must wither on it.

The next piece shows how an individual tone may be added to generally known motifs, interweaving them by no means commonplace ideas of a particular mood.

1. May God bless the legs of my little dog,
   For it has turned back the herd of cattle of Hunyady many times.

2. The gendarmes are coming, to take me away, as I have been told.
   For my few misdeeds they take me into great imprisonment.

3. They are escorting me before the lords,
   My old comrades are going to make confession against me in my eyes.

4. They then see me down to the dark jail.
   My God, I don't know what comes on me.

5. Mother, mother dear, ask the lords
   To tell you what they want to do with me.

6. Son, my dear son, the lords have decided
   To take your head within twenty-four hours.

7. Mother, mother dear, it would be a pity to do so,
   To take my head by the hands of a hangman.

8. To expose my spurs of brass to the breathing wind,
   To have my pants blown by the wind.

9. To have my beautiful crispy hair curled by the wind,
   To expose my beautiful red face to the burning sun.

10. My wonderful cattle, thirteen you are,
    All thirteen of you are of a nice white colour.

11. The thirteenth has been carried away by the big eagle,
    It has painted the earth with its beautiful red blood.

12. The place where I give my beasts to drink is bubbling with blood,
    The place where I give my beasts to eat is turned upward down.

13. So this is to be my last hour.
    My dear mother, God bless you now!

Juta (Somogy county). Tune: 1.

Made up of outlaw and prisoner motifs, the following song shows a sound construction:

1. When I was a small boy,
   I was a young cowherd.
   I lay on the green mound,
   From where I could see my herd.

2. But when I was a grown-up man,
   I became a false-hearted fellow.
   Once I looked backward,
   Lo, the country's men are coming.

3. I dashed towards my horse,
   Towards my light-chesnut bay with the white stockings.
   But as I mounted my horse,
   Two gendarmes stood by me.

4. Stop, outlaw, you must stop,
   You must not run off.
   Alas, my God, what am I to do,
   Shall I run off, or shall I stop?
   If I run off, they will shoot me,
   If I stop, they will rope me.

5. They tied my arms back,
   So they knocked out my teeth.
   Alas, I swooned many times!
   It' a wonder that I stayed alive!

6. My wife does not even know
   That I have been taken by this dog.
   How I wish there were someone
   To send word by to her.

7. My dearest, kindest wife,
   Gather together my washings,
   For I am going on a long way,
   And you must not wait for me to come home again.

8. Tell the commissar
   Not to be glad of my imprisonment!
   For if he is glad of my imprisonment,
   A knife will be turned round in his heart!

9. I shall not stay a prisoner for ever,
   I shall be free again!
   As one has treated me
   One will be treated in a like way by me then!

Jázova (Torontál county) = *Kálmány 1882, 179.*

The next song is practically a variant of No. 217.

1. There is a round wood down there,
   Twelve outlaws are living in it.
   They come every now and then to the edge of the wood,
   Waiting for evil to fall on their heads.

2. There are mounted people coming down there,
   They are black as eagles.
   If they are outlaws, then they are good friends,
   If they are gendarmes, I have to run off.

3. Good day, friend!
   Well, how are you, if I may ask?
   Welcome, sir gendarme,
   I cannot say I fell well when I am like this.

4. Alas, my God, alas, my Dear!
   I must be a prisoner now!
   Father and mother are lamenting me,
   My sweetheart is lamenting for me.

5. You need not lament me as yet,
   They are not taking me to be shot.
   You may lament me
   When I am being taken to be shot.

6. They are putting me in iron,
   They escort me to Kalocsa.
   He ties his horse to my horse,
   Myself to the coach.
   My horse is eating fine hay,
   I am eating the food of the county.

7. At the big court of Kalocsa,
   Twelve lords are sitting.
   They are looking in my eyes:
   How many colts can I remember?

8. I cannot remember more than the one
   I have sold in Debrecen.
   The one whose price I have drunk up, the one whose price I have eaten up,
   The one whose price I spent on my sweetheart.
   Her skirt cost a lot of money,
   The price of three young bullocks went into it.

9. First I stole these four young bullocks,
   All four were grey as cranes.
   Then I stole a bay colt:
   All four legs of it had white stockings.

882

10. Then I stole six oxen,
   All six went to the lords:
   I gave two to the judge,
   Another two to the commissar,
   Still another two to the county bailiff,
   So that not a single one remained to me.

Monostor (Torontál county).

Earliest provenience: 1782 (*Stoll* 1962).
   The old manuscript has preserved the following text with combined motifs of known prisoners'
songs applied in an individual way and mixed with fragments of folksongs—just as they are found today
in folk tradition.

   1. The hog is hiding together with her nine pigs,
      The swineherd walks after it with his empty bag.
      He is blowing his bagpipe, and sad is his song:
      I should have better go beyond the Tisza,
      To eat the bitter bread of the soldiers,
      To avoid the kitchen of János Almási.
   2. O my dear mother, go to the lords, Ask them when I am set free?
      My dearest child, my first-born son, You will be set free
      When the top of your gate will grow green leaves,
      When it will be budding red and blossoming white.
   3. Alas, lords, big lords of Gyöngyös,
      It would be a pity for me to go to the gallows,
      To have my beautiful crispy hair blown by the wind,
      To have my red cheeks be withered by the sun,
      To have the ravens pick my two black eyes,
      To have my handsome, tender skin be dried to the bone,
      For who has ever heard of hanging a man for a hog?
      To send such an orphan lad to die and go out of this world?
   4. O my dear mother, I take now leave of you,
      O you false world, your abode is liable to be cheated.
      Unlucky was the hour when I was born,
      Damned is the wood from where I got here,
      To taste the bread of János Almási.
      God be with you, people of Gyöngyös!
      You will not see me in the prison any longer,
      You will see me hanging on the gallows-tree with my grey hair.

Dissemination:
   In the list to follow I complement the numbers of motifs with various symbols: b = element of
outlaw songs; e = individual addition about prisoners' fate; nd = folksong; m = other than prisoner
motif added as an individual device. The question mark (?) means a distant variant.
   I. Sopron county (Szovát 4+5+6+13+56+1, Vitnyéd 1); Vas county (Kisrákos 35+11,
Pankasz 18+9, "Vas c." b+13+56+67); Zala county (Almás 19+30+b?+1+26+27+28+m,
Alsónemesapáti b+1+26+27+28+29+30, Bocska 48+77+30+b, Bunnya farmstead 1+26+27+
30+29+39, Hottó 29+32+30+26+27+28+18, Jakabfa 32+19, ib. 73+74+75+59, Keszthely 2+
17+16+71+m, Kiskomárom 19+44, ib. 18+19, ib. 11+e+14+17+15+43+2, Murakeresztúr 4+
1+10+19+10+13+30+29+18+7+9+26+27+28, ib. 4+5+1+28, Murarátka 59+11+e+2+
e, Nova 26+27+28, ib. 2+17?+15+11?+34, Resznek 29+32+30+26+27+1, Rigyác 31+4+5,
Szilvágy 11+54+22, Zalakaros m+35+46+43+11+m); Somogy county (Alsok 61, Attala 18+60+
32+1+39, Bajcsa b+4+48+29?+24, Badacsony 29+32+30+26, Balatonberény 29+30+26+
27+28, Berzence 18+19+3, Csoknya b+48+77?+m+29+13, Csurgó 31+4+5+1+39+19+30+

29 + 60, ib. 35 + 54 + 12? + m, ib. 18 + 19 + 1 + 39, Gerszdpuszta 1 + 39, Hencse 37 + 32 + 4 + 1 + 5 + 38 + 37, Henész 22 + 11?, Hetes 43 + 75 + 59, ib. 61, Juta e + 27? + 28 + m, ib. 7 + 9 + 56, ib. 4 + 1 + 7 + 9 + 10 + 18 + 19 + nd + 32 + 30 + 29 + 13, ib. 35 + 36 + e, ib. 1 + e + 18, Kaposújlak 18, Karád 4 + 5 + 37 + 18, Nagyatád 31 + 32 + e, Nagybajom 1, ib. 1, 39 + e + 32 + 30 + 4, ib. 12 + 35 + b, Nagyberki 4 + 10 + 70 + 52, ib. 4 + 6 + e + 55 + 7 + 9 + 10 + 70 + 103, ib. 35 + 36 + 2 + e, Pödöripuszta nd + e + 30 + 10 + 60 + 30? + 19? + nd + 18, Rinyaújlak 31 + 4 + 5 + e + 26 + 27 + 28, Sándorpuszta 31 + 4 + 5 + 1 + 27 + 28, Somogyszob nd + 46, Surd 19 + 7, Szenna b + 31 + 48 + e + 1 + 41? + 4 + 9 + 10 + 30 + 29, ib. 52 + 32? + e, ib. 31 + 48 + e + 7 + 9 + 10 + 30 + 29?, Szőllősgyörök e + 104 + 24 + 18 + 26? + 27 + 28, Vörs 4 + e + 32 + 30 + 29, Zselickisfalud b + 24 + 1 + 39 + 19 + 32 + 18, ib. 18); Verőce county (Haraszti b + 19 + 1 + 18 + 44, ib. e + 18 + 19 + 44 + nd, ib. 18 + 19 + 44, Szentlászló 18 + 44 + 19 + 44); Szerém county (Kórógy 19 + 18 + m, ib. 18, ib. 18 + 19 + 44, ib. 73 + 11? ib. 11?, ib. 8 + 40 + 19 + 44); Baranya county (Alsóegerszeg 57 + 43 + 21 + 11, Boda 35 + 42 + 2 + 1 + 43 + 22 + 67? + nd, Csányoszró nd + 4 + 5 + 31, Dunafalva 4 + 5 + 72 + 13 + 78 + 1 + 39 + 27 + 28 + 19 + 40, Kákics b + e + 79 + 22 + 45 + 11 + 47 + 18 + e + 66, Katádfa e + 11 + e + 79, Kölked 43 + 11 + 34 + 11 + b + 21, Mánfa 4 + 5 + 72 + 13 + 27 + 28, Mohács 19 + 44, ib. 18 + 32 + 30 + 19 + 44, Püspökszenterzsébet 11? + 1 + 39, Sumongy 31? + 32 + 30 + 39 + 64?, Zaláta 46 + 22? + 105 + 47 + 59?); Tolna (Decs nd + 18 + 55 + 9 + 10 + 39 + 96, Gerjen e + 13, Lápafő 61, Szedres 4 + 5 + 72 + 13 + 78 + 39 + 27 + 28 + 40), Fejér county (Csákvár 46 + 22 + nd, ib. b + 36 + e + 2 + e + nd, Csór 35 + 36 + 3 + b, Pusztaforna 61 + 1 + 51 + 19, ib. 106 + e + 22 + 21 + 47 + b, ib. e + 35 + 54 + 11? + e + 93); Veszprém county (Bodorfa 29 + 32 + 26 + 27 + 28, Réde 18 + 19 + nd); Pest county (Páty 11 + 21 + 47 + e), Esztergom county (Barót 18? + 1?); Komárom county (Naszvad 7? + 9? + 21?), I.: 104.

II. Pozsony county (Albár nd + b + 1 + 7 + 9); Nyitra county (Béd 1?, Ghymes 55 + 19, ib. 32 + 107, ib. 55 + 7 + 10 + 26 + 27 + 28 + 29, Kolon 11 + 34 + 17 + 15 + 16, Nyitracsehi 31 + 1); Bars county (Csitár 22? + 67? + 108, Lédec* 2 + 14 + 16 + 49); Hont county (Hidvég 31 + 46? + 11); Nógrád county (Bocsárlapujtő m + 23 + 24 + 25 + nd, Nógrádberce 7 + 9 + 10 + 1, Nógrádmegyer 7 + 9 + 10 + 23 + 24 + 25, Palotás 7 + 9? + 10 + 1 + 20 + 21, Rimóc m + 2 + 14 + 17 + nd, Somoskő 7 + 9 + 10, Szuha 7 + 9 + 10 + 1, Tardoskedd 107 + 1, Utaspuszta 20 + 21 + 38 + 37 + 7 + 9 + 10 + 13?); Heves county (Bekölce 4 + 5 + 6 + 10 + 20 + 21 + 23 + 24 + 25 + 7 + 9, Besenyőtelek 22 + 11 + 16? + 65, Deménd 4 + 5, Ecséd 1 + 20 + 21 + 40, Eger m + 2 + 14 + 15 + 16 + 49, Egerfarmos 7 + 9 + 10, Egerszalók 22 + 12?, Fedémes 4 + 23 + 6 + 10 + 7 + 9 + 21, ib. 4 + 23 + 6, Füzesabony 4 + 5, ib. 7 + 9 + 10 + 1, ib. 7 + 5, ib. 11, ib. 110, Gyöngyös 1782 nd + e + 26? + 40 + 28 + m, Heves 4 + 5 + 1, Hevesaranyos m + 1, ib. 23 + 24 + 25, Ivád 23 + 6 + 13 + 7 + 9 + 24 + 25, "Heves c." 35 + 111 + 21 + m, Mátraballa 2 + 14 + 16, Mátraszentimre 7 + 9 + 10 + 1, ib. 2 + 14 + 17 + 16, ib. 1, Mezőszemere 4 + 6, Mikófalva 2 + 14 + 17 + 15 + 16, Nagyréde 7 + 9 + 10 + 13 + 1 + 15 + 20 + 21, Pétervására 23 + 1, Szihalom 11 + m, Tarnalelesz 23 + 24 + 25, ib. 4 + 5 + 6 + 10 + 13 + 15 + 23 + 1 + 39 + 21, ib. 2 + 14 + 17 + 15 + 16, ib. 23 + 24); Borsod county (Alsóábrány 7 + 9 + 6 + 13, Bogács nd + 7 + 9 + 10 + 13 + 1, ib. 7 + 1, Borsodivánka 2 + 3, Bőcs 4 + 5, Cserépváralja 7 + 9 + 10 + 1, Csincsetanya 2? + 3 + b, Csoknya 4 + 5 + 1, Győr 90 + 4 + 5, Hernádkércs b + 4 + 6 + 13 + 39 + 1, ib. 51 + 14 + 11 + 34 + 21 + 66, Kacs nd + 4 + 5 + 7 + 9 + 10 + 1, Mezőkövesd 7 + 9, Radostyán 4 + 5, Sajókazinc 80 + 81 + e + 13?, ib. 11, Sály 4 + 5 + 1, ib. 2 + 14 + 17 + 15 + 16, ib. 31 + 1, ib. 4 + 5, ib. 36 + 11 + 34, Sáta 23 + 24 + 7 + 9 + 10, Szentistván 4 + 5, ib. 11 + 50 + 21, Szentistvánbaksa nd + 1, Tard 4 + 5 + 1 + 7 + 9); Gömör county (Almágy 23 + 24 + 25 + 1, ib. 23 + 24 + 25 + 9 + 10, Egyházasbást 2 + 14 + 17 + 15, Gesztete 23 + 24 + 25 + 6 + 7 + 9 + 10 + 13, Hárskút 2 + 14 + 17 + 15, Kiskovácsvágása 23 + 24 + 25, Nagykövesd 2 + 14 + 17 + 15 + 16 + 49, Sajószárnya 23 + 7 + 9); Abaúj county (Áj 11 + 34, ib. 2 + 14 + 17 + 15 + 22 + 11 + 16, ib. 22 + 21, Cekeháza 4 + 5 + 1 + 41 + 7 + 9 + 20 + 21, ib. 4, Kéked 10 + 1 + 21, Kisléh 4 + 5 + 64 + 7 + 9 + 13, Nagyszalánc 4 + 5 + 1 + 41 + 1?, ib. 4 + 6 + 1, ib. 51 + 11, Nyíri 4 + 6 + 1, Tarnagörgő 51 + 2 + 17 + 15 + 1 + 11? + 21 + 12 + e + 44); Zemplén county (Bodrogszentes 31 + e + 124 + 17 + 26 + 28 + 1 + 4 + 6 + 13, Mikóháza 31 + 1 + 82 + 21, Nagykövesd 2 + 14 + 17, Nagyrozvány 1 + 41 + 28, Rábaköz 7 + 9 + 13 + 24, Ricse 2 + 14, ib. 2 + 14 + 17 + 15 + 16 + m + 12, ib. 4 + 5 + 6 + 13 + 10?, ib. 95 + 92, ib. 16 + 14 + 17 + 15, Sárospatak 57 + 21 + 47 + 11? + 34, ib. 2 + 14 + 17 + 15 + 16, ib. 2 + 14 + 17 + 15 + 16, ib. 2 + 14 + 16 + 15); Ung county (Nagydobrony 35 + 36 + 42? + 51 + 95 + 16 + 66, Szirénfalva 11 + 40, "Ung m." 2 + 14 + 15 + 16). II.: 114.

Pest county (Akasztó 31 + 32 + 83 + 84 + 18, Alpár nd + 3 + 11, Bugacmonostor 112 + 113 + 11?, Dunavecse 4 + 5 + 1 + 6 + 10 + 13, Kalocsa 1 + 37? + 38, Kecel 4 + 5 + 18, ib. 126 + 1, Kecskemét 18 + 5 + 24, ib. 11 + 34 + 11 + 21 + 50 + m, ib. 4 + 5, Kiskőrös 31 + 32 + 83 + 84, Kiskunhalas 115 + 76 + 11 + 102 + nd, Monor 22 + 16 + 58, Tápiószele 23 + 24, Tura 11, ib. 2 + 14 + 17 + 15 + 16 + 68, ib. 4 + 5, ib. e), Jász-Nagykun-Szolnok county (Alattyán 19 + 30 + 8, Csataszög 7 + 9 + 10 + 1, Jászapáti 18 + 1 + 97 + m, Jászárokszállás 2 + 14 + 17 + 15 + 16 + 68, Jászkarajenő 2 + 16 + 11, Nagykörü 4 + 5 + 38 + 37 + 1, ib.

4 + 5 + 38 + 37 + 1, ib. 4 + 5 + 38 + 37 + 1, Tiszavárkony 2 + 14 + 17 + 15 + 16 + 11 + nd); Bács-Bodrog county (Bátmonostor 4 + 5, Rém 4 + 5 + 80); Torontál county (Egyházaskér 8 + 9 + 10 + e!, ib. 4 + 6 + e + nd + 40 + e + 63, Lőrincfalva e + m + nd, ib. e + 32 + 33 + m + 8 + 9 + 10 + e + 38 + 37, ib. e, Magyarszentmárton m + 38 + 37 + 32 + 33 + m, ib. 48 + 69 + 116 + 13? + 56 + 1 + 20 + 21 + 38 + 37 + 40 + 117, ib. 99 + 100 + 34 + 21 + 46 + 101 + m, ib. 48 + 69 + 13? + 56 + 20 + 21 + 38 + 37, Monostor b + 86 + 42 + 74 + 3, Nagybecskerek 35 + 3 + b + 42 + 1 + 11, ib. e, ib. 59 + 11 + 118 + e, Padé e + 28 + 1 + 18, Rábé 8 + 9 + 19 + 10 + 13 + 38 + 37 + e + 1 + 39 + 41 + 28 + e, Szaján 23 + 24 + e + 41 + 28 + 40 + e + 63, ib. 23 + 24 + 25 + e, Torda b + 3, ib. b + 35 + 36 + 42 + 65 + 3 + 45 + e, Törökbecse e + 35 + 36 + 42 + 3 + 11 + 34 + b + 65 + 17 + b, ib. 22 + 11 + e + 68 + e, ib. 8! + 9 + 10 + 28 + e + nd; South Great Plain, without precise indication of locality b + 35 + 36 + 42 + 22 + 11, ib. 46 + 45 + 119, ib. 4 + 6 + 40 + m + 63, ib. 35 + 54 + 11 + 3); Csongrád county (Csongrád 25.+ 9 + 70, Hódmezővásárhely 61 + m, ib. 29 + m, ib. 29 + m, Mohol 2 + 17 + 15 + 16 + nd + 71, Sándorfalva nd + 74 + 11, ib. 4 + 5 + 32 + 33 + 7 + 9, Szegvár 18 + 19 + 52 + 19, Tömörkény 2 + 14 + 17 + 15 + 16 + 120, Üllés 1); Csanád county (Apáca b + 86 + 7? + e + 11 + 45 + 21 + 12, Apátfalva 11 + 21, Makó m + 37 + 6 + 32 + 19 + 18 + 19); Békés county (Békésszentandrás 7 + 9 + 4 + 5 + 1 + e, Doboz 18 + 38 + 98 + 1 + 26 + 27, ib. 122 + b + 22 + nd + 12,ib. 4 + 6 + 31 + 32 + 33, Szarvas 2 + 14 + 15 + 16); Arad county (Pécska b + e + 87 + 21 + 50, ib. 31? + 1 + 85, ib. 76 + e + b + e, ib. nd + 35 + 36 + 42 + 88 + 3 + 123?), Bihar county (Bagamér 2 + 14 + 15 + e + 16, ib. 7 + 9 + 10 + e, Csökmő 31 + 80 + 124 + 10 + 1 + 39 + 20 + 21, Esztár 48 + 69 + 20? + 21?, Nagyszalonta m + 87 + 34, ib. 45 + e + nd + 21, ib. 100 + 47, ib. 46 + 68 + 76, ib. nd + 1 + 97? + e, ib. e, ib. e + 90 + 63 + e, ib. nd + 116 + 13 + 18 + 19 + nd, ib. 80, ib. 38 + 37, ib. e + 6 + e, ib. 99 + b, Pocsaj 4 + 6 + 10 + 13, ib. 4 + 6 + 5 + 7 + 9, Sáránd nd + 4 + 5 + 32 + 6? + 10 + 13 + 7 + e + 121); Hajdú county (Balmazújváros 4 + 5 + 1 + 20 + 21 + 40, Cserekert 4 + 5 + 6 + 10 + 21 + 7 + 9 + 20 + 21 + 38 + 37, Hajdúhadház 43 + 21 + 47 + 11 + e + 12, ib. 57 + 43 + 21, "Hortobágy" b + 35 + e + b + 125, ib. e + 100 + 34, ib. 4 + 5 + 52 + 64 + 20 + 21, Nagyléta-Cserekert 4 + 5 + 6 + 10 + 13, Püspökladány 4 + 5 + 1 + 41 + 28, Tiszacsege nd + m + 92 + 41 + 92 + 20 + 21 + 52 + 64 + 4 + 5, Tetétlen 2 + 15? + 17 + 15 + 49?, Vámospércs 2 + 17 + 15 + 14 + 49); Szabolcs county (Balsa 2 + 14 + 17 + 15 + 16 + 49, Fülöp 4 + 5? + 1 + b, ib. 4 + 5 + 7 + 9 + 10, ib. 2 + 14 + 17 + 15 + 49, Kállósemjén 35 + 36 + 34 + b, Nagykálló 7 + 9 + 10 + 1, Nyírábrány 23 + 24, Nyírbogdány 4 + e + 7 + 9 + 10 + 13, Nyírlugos nd + 2 + 14 + 17 + 15, Nyírparasznya 2 + 14 + 17 + 15 + 49, Rábaköz nd + 35 + 36 + 42 + 88, Szamosszeg 2 + 14 + 17 + 15, Vaja nd + 81? + 1 + 41 + 28); Szatmár county (Kérsemjén 18 + 41 + 28, Kispalád 4 + 5 + 22 + 6 + 10? + 9 + 7, Nábrád 90 + 63 + e, ib. e, Szamostatárfalva 35 + 36 + 94 + e, Ura e + 22). III.: 126.

IV. Kolozs county (Inaktelke 7 + 9 + 10, Magyarszovát 11 + 21, Visa 8 + 2? + 9?, Zentelke 7 + 9, ib. 18); Szolnok-Doboka county (Búza 2 + 14 + 17 + 15 + 11, Feketelak 2 + 14 + 17 + 15 + 11 + 49); Beszterce-Naszód county (Tacs 2 + 14 + 17 + 15 + 11 + 49), Maros-Torda county ("Marosszék" 8 + m, Nyárádszentanna 4 + 38 + 37 + 19 + 1), Nagyküküllő county (Székelyszáldobos 22 + 45 + 11 + 36 + b + e + 34 + 21); Udvarhely county (Etéd 7 + 9 + 10, Lengyelfalva 7 + 9, Oroszhegy 23 + 24 + 19, ib. 19? + 7 + 9 + e + 23 + 24 + 25, Rugonfalva 61, Szentegyházasoláhfalu 7 + 9 + 13?, ib. nd + 7 + 9? + 13?, Szentgerice 37 + 19 + 1 + nd, ib. 37 + 19 + 1 + nd, Tarcsafalva 7 + 9 + 10 + 7 + 23 + 24 + 25, "Udvarhelyszék" 7 + 9 + 13 + 24 + 25, Zetelaka 22, ib. 22, ib. 57 + 21 + 64? + 11 + 34); Brassó county ("Hétfalu" 8); Csík county (Ajnád b + e, Csíkmadaras 7 + 9 + 10, Csíkmenaság 2 + 91 + 43 + nd, Csíkszék e + 9 + e + 9 + e + 23 + 24 + 25? + nd + 9, Csíkszentdomokos m + 13 + 60 + 23? + 24? + 25? + m, Csíkvacsárcsi 22, Gyergyóújfalu m + 22 + 16? + nd, Gyimesbükk nd + 11 + 62 + 34? + 35? + b + nd, Gyimesfelsőlok b + 35 + 50 + 89, ib. 23 + 24 + nd, ib. 35? + 36? + nd, ib. 34? + 62 + 11 + 45?, Gyimesközéplok 22 + nd, ib. 2? + 14? + 17 + 15 + m, ib. 11 + 45 + e + 17 + 34, Gyimesvölgye b + 35 + 50 + 89, ib. 38? + 37 + nd + 1 + 7 + 9?); Háromszék county (Magyarhermány 22 + 11 + 36 + b + e + 3); Bukovina (Andrásfalva 6? + 3 + 11 + nd, Hadikfalva 6? + 13 + 24 + 25, ib. 18 + nd, Istensegíts 11 + e + nd + 47); Moldavia (Diószén 35? + 36? + m, Gajcsána 38 + 37 + 20 + 21 + e, Klézse 19? + nd + 28?, ib. 32? + 13? + nd, ib. 7? + 9? + 10? + nd, Lészped 22 + 45? + 11 + 62 + 34?, ib. nd + 35? + 42? + e + 11 + 45? + 34?, ib. 22? + 45? + 11 + 62 + 34?, ib. 26? + 27? + nd + 28), IV.: 57.

S.l.: 2 + 14 + 17 + 15 + 16, 35 + 42 + 50 + 34, b + 7 + 9 + 10. S.l.: 3.

Total: 403.

Textual relationships with other ballads:

33. (We see neither the sun nor the moon). **13., 14, 20., 49.** (When I have free life again? When one grain of wheat yields a hundred stacks, etc.); **51.** (Have you heard the fame of the prison of . . .?, Mother, when you gave birth to me.); **52.** (I shall be buried by the beasts of the woods); **105., 109., 117.** (frequent occurrence of prisoners' motifs.)

A variant of the Zobor region (Nyitra county, II) offers an example of the survival of motif 33: Don't wonder, sweetheart, that I am yellow: It is nine years since I have been living in prison. It is nine years since I have been living in prison, Since I have not seen the sun moving in the sky, Neither the sun, nor the moon growing and waning. ("Yet I know what day is today..." and the text changes into a Whitsuntide song.) It is characteristic that in this instance, as in many others, a motif known only from the southeastern Székelys has been preserved also in the Zobor region. Both places may be suspected of having maintained the motif from a common ancient Hungarian tradition. This motif has been further developed by 22., 46., and 54. motives of the prisoners' songs all in a new formulation.

A similarly old folklore formula is the one which has the beasts of woods and birds of the sky give the obsequies to the man who dies in exile. This motif well known from earlier collections in Transylvania is fairly well represented also in the Great Plain collections, thanks to the zeal of *Lajos Kálmány* who had been fortunate to find the oldest Great Plain folklore pieces in the one-time dissemination area of Szeged in the 70s and 80s of the last century, before the new style had ousted them from memory. A high number of archaic songs have come from Torontál county in particular. Motif 8 survives there in greatest number and in soundest form, which is another proof of surviving old folklore tradition. Let us show a beautiful example:

> A black cloud is rising there,
> A yellow-legged raven is pluming in it.
> Light, raven, light on the window of the jail,
> Fly, raven, fly from there to the door of the jail!
> Take word of me to father and mother,
> To my betrothed one!
> Light, raven, light on the foreign land,
> Let me write my letter
> On your dry breast!
> Take it to my mother, to my betrothed one!
> If she asks you about me, tell her that I am a prisoner!

(I am a prisoner, I am a prisoner, Waiting to be let free...etc., and in the continuation we encounter the known turns.)

Rábé (Torontál county).

Tunes:

1. = Nos 208 and 209 (17 variants); 2. = No. 210 (4 variants); 3. = Nos 211–13 (89 variants); 4. = No. 214; 5. = No. 216 (20 variants), 6. = (6 variants); 7. (5 variants); 9. = (7 variants); 14. (9 variants); 15. (3 variants); 18. (2); 29 (2); 34 (4); 35. (5); 36. (3); 38. (15, 3 variants have only half-tunes); 39. (5); 40. (2); 41. (2); 42. (2); 45. (3); 46. (2); 47. (2); 50. (2); 55. (3); 61. (4); 90 (2).

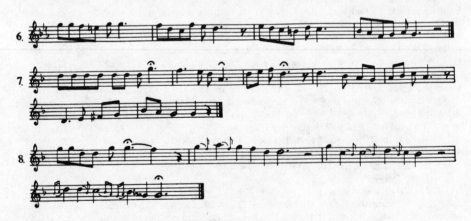

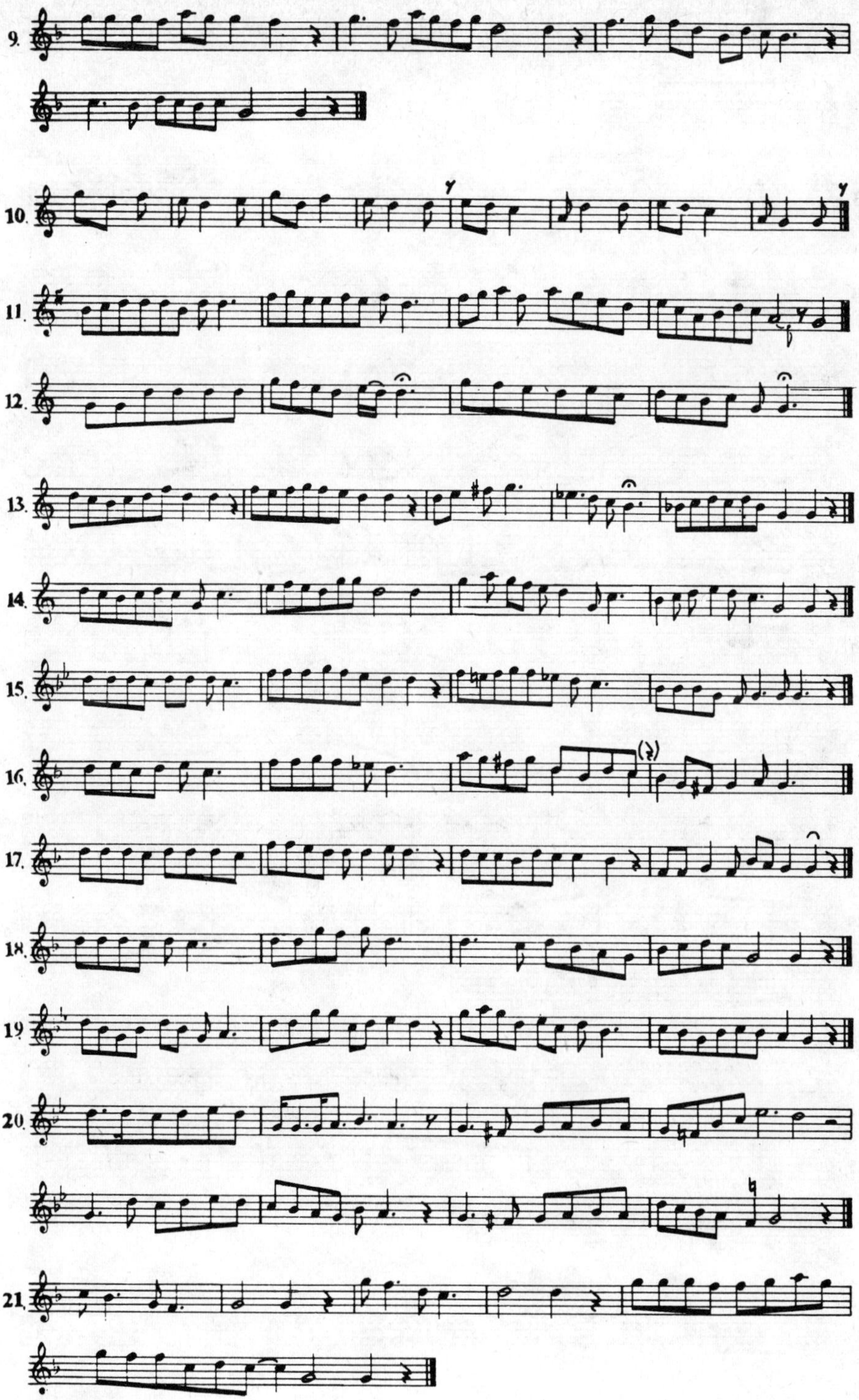
9.
10.
11.
12.
13.
14.
15.
16.
17.
18.
19.
20.
21.

888

889

This kind of poetry, unknown outside the Hungarian language area, is a product of fermenting nineteenth-century Hungarian peasantry, more closely, of the outlaw period. It is a great poetry, covering a broad spectrum of human sufferings, despair, defiant revolt, as well as of tendency to reveal the corrupt representatives of states power, and the final shaking of man's heart in front of inevitable death. The pictures of the prisoners' tormenting fate here again finds expression in a stylized yet realistic presentation so characteristic of folk poetry.

In this respect it has a close connection with the ballad genre. At the same time it differs from it inasmuch as no plot can be found in it. This feature, however, organically ensues from the passive experiences of imprisonment. We may speak of a low-life scene, some traits of psychic state may be described in them, presented in the form of soliloquies and dialogues; occasionally the latter may develop into minor dramatic scenes, still this type of songs never has a plot. There is no real *story* in it. Attempt at such can be discovered in those variants which start with an outlaw feat, a criminal act, followed logically by the hero's being taken prisoner, descriptions of redemption or execution (cf. No. 217). In any case, the two main methods of folklore creation can be touched upon in these pieces: on the one hand, there stands a medley of individual ideas coming to life independently of one another, and on the other, the assembling work of those who try to give them a structure, to a coherent series of them.

Such a variety of poetic inventions could born within the sphere of crime and punishment only in case the whole body of the peasantry backed the development. Obviously, most of the songs were not composed by those who fell victim of the severe judges. But the great mass of poems speaking in a tone of sympathetic compassion about outlaws cast into prison betrays that people considered the fate of prisoners a common disaster on which they felt it necessary to pass their judgement. (Typically enough, a real criminal standpoint is expressed only by one single text (No. 115), and even the stubborn defiant attitude thirsting for revenge is another, similarly solitary specimen, No. 47.)

No prisoners' poetry of such a broad scale can develop where the broad masses do not defy the justice of the ruling order.

The tunes are equal matches for the poetic text. The peasants had selected the tunes associated with these songs from the oldest store of their melodic traditions. Thus, although developed in a relatively recent period, the Hungarian prisoners' songs represent the noblest style of folksongs in Hungary. In general, they had sprung forth between the 20s and 70s of the last century, and mainly in the Great Plain and Transdanubia, further the Palots region bordering on the former area.

Transsylvania was not a country for outlaws in this sense, therefore the variants seeped there in recent times. This is well brought out by the stylistic features, the manner of formulation and the sparsity of variants which in Transylvania show only a vague relationship with the motifs listed above, containing at the same time a number of old elements, such as the portions connected with Turkish imprisonment.

In the central part of the language area, this type of songs had developed by recent social movements, along with the development of the outlaw ballads. Once more and perhaps the last time, flashes of the poetic beauties of ancient Hungarian folk-poetry can be seen in them.

119. THE GERMANS' GENDARMES

218.

1. Had I been warned by God
   Not to step out of the inn!
   It would have been much better for me to go to bed and sleep
   Than to go out to the farmstead of Bozó!

2. The branches of the acacia-tree bent in two directions.
   I have also been a gendarme to the Germans.
   I have also been a gendarme to the Germans,
   But the ball did not allow me to continue long.

3. I send word to the other gendarmes
   Not to dash blindly at the outlaws.
   For the outlaws will have them placed in coffin,
   And their dead bodies taken to the cemetery.

4. Alas, my Dear, I was quite a young man
   When Lajos Dinom placed me into a coffin.
   He robbed me of my life too soon.
   I would never have thought of this before!

5. The main street of Mindszent has plunged in mourn,
   Gendarme Jani is seen along it.
   The cemetery of Mindszent is in blossom.
   Gendarme Jani is lying in the front line of it.

Kiskunhalas (Pest county). Imre László, 1900 = EA 3658, 16.

This ballad stands alone, having no variants and neither tunes associated with it. Still we may accept it as a "type", owing to the folklore style, the clever basic idea, and the skilful execution of the story. Self-lament and recital in singular first person belong to the archaic tradition of Hungarian folk poetry. (Cf. Type **92**.) Similar scornful application of the tone is to be found in the so-called Kuruts (Rákóczi's soldiers') poetry; the lesson drawn from a serious defeat of the Labants army (that of the Emperor) is put into the mouth of a Labants general called Ricsány.

120. THE GALLANTS OF KECSKEMÉT

219.

Parlando

1. Kecs - ke - mé - ti ga - val - lé - rok, Ö - ten vó - tak nagy hun -cu - tok:

Var - ga Sán - dor, Ko-csi An - tal, Ko-vács Pis-ta, Lö-csös Mi-hály, Ö-tö - dik vót a Csu - to ra.

1. The gallants of Kecskemét
   Five they were, mischievous fellows:
   Sándor Varga, Antal Kocsi,
   Pista Kovács, Miska Lőcsös,
   The fifth was Csutora.

2. They set out on the way to Vác
   To rob a felt-coat tailor.
   In the pasturing field of Létom
   They dropped in an inn.

3. They ordered the tapster
   To bring wine for the guests.
   Hail! Friends! Csutora!
   Let every lad have his turn in drinking!

4. My hostess, dear angel,
   Antal Kocsis speaks up, and harsh is his voice,
   Take care of the supper and see
   That each poor lad has a dish.

5. My hostess is determined
   Not to prepare supper.
   They are looking high and low:
   Meat is needed to the wine.

6. But Csutora speaks up:
   Get all of you in the coach!
   There over a shepherd is grazing his flock of sheep,
   Blowing the pipe as shepherds are wont to.

7. Sándor Varga swears, spitting in his palm,
   That he will drive away the whole flock.
   But Csutora says:
   It must be done in a different way!

8. As the shepherd was grazing his flock,
   Blowing the pipe as shepherds are wont to,
   They dashed at the shepherd
   And shed his blood cruelly.

9. Do not shed my blood!
   For I am willing to give you a few sheep.
   The two orphan children of my wife!
   O, what fate is waiting for them afterwards!

Doboz (Békés county). Performed by a male informant. Bartók 1906.

From the second strophe onwards, the melodic portion in square brackets has been omitted.

Divergences:

As they are going, going ahead,
They saw a flock of sheep approach.
Half the flock they drove away,
Pressing them towards Debrecen.
As they were going, going ahead,
They saw the men of the county approach.

The men of the county had all of them taken,
All the four thrown into prison.

Northerly wind is blowing,
Pista Kovács is now having a good time.
He is clicking the heels of his fine boots,
He is waving his ample pants.

Ravens come to pick his eyes,
Birds come to eat up his body.
Ravens come to pick his eyes,
Birds come to eat up his body.

The third variant expires with the following stanza:

There are still three hours back,
Prepare, comrade, for your death!
We have one life in this world,
We have to pass one death!

Earliest provenience: between 1891 and 1919, or 1906.
Dissemination:
    Zala county (Dergecs); Békés county (Doboz); Arad county (Pécska).
Textual relationships with other ballads: **118., 121.**
Tunes: Solely the tune of the published variant has been noted down.

This story of individual formulations has hardly got through the stage of folklorization. Still it is worth-while publishing it: the fact that variants of this song have been recorded at great distances from one another indicates a certain degree of dissemination; at the same time, the transformation of the text is instructive from the point of view of how folk poetry develops: in the process of transformation, metaphors of general validity replace detailed description; for example, the stanzas about hanged outlaws have been incorporated as representatives of old traditions of Hungarian folk poetry.

NEW BALLADS
Types 121–134.

121. THE BARON'S DAUGHTER AND THE SHEPHERD

220.

1. O - da a - lá a szed - re - i ha - tár - ba Ki - vi - rág -zott egy nagy hársfa bu - já - ba

Ki - vi - rág -zott egy nagy hársfa bu - já - ba. Ju - hász le - gény fu-ru-lyáz az al - já - ba.

1. Down there in the land of Szedrő
   A tall poplar burst into blossom for grief.
   A tall poplar burst into blossom for grief.
   The young shepherd is blowing his pipe under it.

2. The clock has struck one after midnight,
   And the pipe is still blown sweet in tune.
   The sound of the pipe is heard in the mansion:
   Little baroness Mariska Szedri, are you awake?

3. The window of the bed-room is open,
   Little Mariska is looking out of it, weeping.
   Little Mariska is breathing with heavy sighs:
   Why was I born to be daughter to baron Szedri!

4. Why was I born to be daughter to baron Szedri,
   Why can I not be the poor shepherd's sweetheart?!
   Little Mariska is no match for a poor shepherd,
   The thorns of the stubble-field would hurt her tender feet!

5. Baron Szedri has saddled his horse
   And rides round the fields of Szedervár.
   He asks his eldest shepherd
   If he had seen little baroness Mariska Szedri.

6. Baron Szedri, I have not seen your daughter,
   Nor have I seen my young shepherd for three days.
   Your honour's daughter must be with him,
   They must have hidden in the fields of Szedrő.

7. Beyond the Tisza they are carving the beam
   On which the poor shepherd will be hanged.
   The wind is blowing his black, crispy hair,
   Another man will cuddle little baroness Mariska Szedri.

Tárkány (Komárom county). Performed by a woman of 33. Schnöller 1958 = AP 2132/j.

Divergences:

> Far away in the field of Endrőd
> There stands a lonely, tall poplar just breaking into leaf.
> The poplar of baron Endresz has burst into blossom,
> A young shepherd often goes to it to give vent to his sorrow.
> The young shepherd's heart is very sad.
> He takes his pipe and blows it.
> The sound of the pipe is heard behind a window:
> Wake, young lady!
> One of the windows of the mansion opens,
> The little baroness with eyes black as sloe looks out of it.

Sometimes the old shepherd answers like this: "...Examine my hut: My embroidered felt-coat and brass hatchet are in it; My meershaum pipe and my flute are in it."—Some of the variants have the following ending formulas:

> The baron Szendre sends a carriage and four for to bring home his daughter
> And nine gendarmes for to fetch the young shepherd.
> For you, daughter, there stands the mansion,
> Young shepherd, prepare for the gallows-tree!
> . . . .
> His shirt of fine linen, his pants of fine linen are blown by the wind,
> Why did he make love with the baron's daughter?
>
> Or: My Dear, why did I make love with the baroness!

Several variants add:

> The tent of the Gipsy woman stands at the end of the village,
> Many young girls go there to have her tell fortune.
> I also go there to learn my future:
> Shall I ever be my unhappy lover's sweetheart?
> I dare not walk through the village for fear
> They should see I am wearing mourn in black.
> Black mourn, my handkerchief is snow-white.
> My first lover was a young shepherd.

There are variants fused with the following ballad, the merger being explainable by similarities of the two plots.

> 1. There stands a tall, lonely poplar.
>   The young shepherd is blowing his pipe under it.
>   The sound of the pipe is heard in the farmstead;
>   Wake, wake up, daughter of baron Szendre!
> 2. She woke up and she opened her window.
>   A brown girl with eyes black as sloe looks out of it.
>   Aye, shepherd, you blow your pipe sweet in tune!
>   I can hear it in my mirrored room.

3. The landlord's *herd of cattle* is grazing calmly,
   The miss is walking in its wake.
   From afar she calls to the *shepherd*:
   Sweetheart, shepherd, lay down your fine furcoat!
4. I cannot lay down my fur-coat this time,
   Lest they should drive away this flock of sheep.
   Never mind your sheep, sweetheart shepherd!
   For my father will redeem your flock, upon my word.
5. Next morning baron Szendre, now a sad man,
   Walks out to the plain of Nagyharaszt.
   He asks the husband of his shepherds,
   Have you not seen my daughter with eyes black as sloe?
6. I have not seen her, sir baron, upon my word,
   One of my young shepherds has not come home for three days.
   For three days one of my young shepherds has been away.
   Maybe, the miss is with him.
7. Daughter, daughter, I don't even call you my daughter,
   If you want to marry a shepherd.
   I don't care, father, you may deny me,
   Yet, my heart breaks with grief for the shepherd.
8. Alas, the beam has been carved nicely,
   On which the young shepherd will be hanged.
   Wind is blowing his black, crispy hair.
   Why did he make love with the baron's daughter!?

Szentivánbaksa (Borsod county).

In most instances the merger has not been as successful as this. Still the intention to create a more complete plot by contraction of the two related themes can be detected. This attempt finds the sole justification in the similarity of the two texts; otherwise, the tunes are utterly different.

Earliest provenience: 1857 (1872)
Dissemination:
S.l.: 1
   I. "Transdanubia", Sopron county (Bősárkány, Jakabháza, "Danube-Rába Interfluve"), Vas county (Kemenessömjén, Kisrákos, Pankasz, Sárfimizdó, Táp, Várkesző, Velemér); Zala county (Csömödér, Kisgörbő, Kiskanizsa, Komárváros, Letenye, Monostorapáti, Nagygörbő, Nemeshetés, Oltárc, Rédics 2, Szombatfa, Zalacsány); Somogy county (Andocs, "Balaton Region", Csákány, Csurgó, Inke, Őrtilos, Ságvár, Somogyszob, Szenna, Szilvásszentmárton, Zamárdi); Verőce county (Szentlászló 2); Baranya county (Alsómocsolád, Becefa, Berkesd, Kisbodolya, Kopács, Mohács 2, "Ormányság", Téseny, Zsibót); Pest county (Bogyiszló); Fejér county (Seregélyes 2, Pusztaapát); Veszprém county (Bakonyoszlop, Csököl, Devecser, Dég, Dudar, Hegyesd, Olaszfalu, Réde, Veszprémfajsz — Germans in Hungarian); Komárom county (Mocsa, Tata, Tárkány); Győr county (Alsóság, Felpéc, Hollómajor, Nagybaráthegy, Rábcakapi). I.: 69.
   II. Hont county ("Hont", Ipolybalog 2, Kemence, Perőcsény 2); Nógrád county (Becske 2, Bercel 3, Litke, Márkháza, Mátraverebély, Nagybátony, Nógrádmegyer, Rimóc 3, Szandaváralja, Szécsény, Szuha); Heves county (Bükkszenterzsébet 2, Fedémes 3, Füzesabony, Gyöngyöshalász, Heves, Markaz, Mátraderecske, Mátraszentistván, Poroszló, Szihalom, Tiszapély); Borsod county

905

(Bogács, Kisgyőr, Mályinka, Sály, Sárazsadány, Szegi, Szentistvánbaksa, Szilvásvárad); Gömör county (Egyházasbást, Nagybalog, Pelsőc); Abaúj county (Boldogkőújfalu, Cekeháza, Felsőméra, Kéked, Pusztafalu, Tornyosnémeti); Zemplén county (Alsóregmec, Gesztely, Mezőzombor 2, Pácin, Ricse 5, Szerencs, Sárospatak 8, Tolcsva); Bereg county ("Bereg", Beregszász, Fornos 2, Lónya, Nagybereg, Vári), II.: 80.

III. Pest county (Bánkháza, Bugac 2, Bugacmonostor, Cegléd 2, Dunakeszi, Galambospuszta, Galgahévíz, Homokszentlőrinc, Izsák, Kecel 2, Kecskemét, Keserűtelek, Kiskunfélegyháza 2, Kiskunhalas 3, Lajosmizse, Törtel, Tura); Jász-Nagykun-Szolnok county (Derzstomaj, Jászalsószentgyörgy, Jászberény 4, Karcag, Kisújszállás, Rákóczifalva, Tiszabő); Bács-Bodrog county (Bácsalmás, Homokmégy, Katymár, Mélykút, Miske, Rém, Zenta, Zombor); Csongrád county (Csongrád 4, "Csongrád c.", Hódmezővásárhely 2, Kistelek, environs of Szentes, Tápé 2); South Great Plain, without precise indication of locality 4; Békés county ("Békés", Békés 2, Endrőd 4, Geszt, Mezőgyán, Sarkadkeresztúr, Vésztő 2); Bihar county (Nagyszalonta 4, Gyulavári, Körösnagyharsány); Arad county (Arad); Szilágy county (Désháza); Hajdú county (Balmazújváros, Hajdúböszörmény, Hajdúnánás 2, Hajdúszoboszló, "Hortobágy", Porod 2, Tiszacsege); Szabolcs county (Bököny, Érpatak, Gégény, Nyírmada, Nyírparasznya, Nyírvasvári, Piricse, Tiszadada, Vaja 2); Szatmár county (Kérsemjén, Kocsord 2, Nagyecsed, Szamosszeg); Szilágy county (Kraszna), III.: 101.

IV. Kolozs county (Türe 2, Válaszút); Maros-Torda county (Rabosnya); Csík county (Csíkkarcfalva, Csíkmenaság, Gyimesközéplok, Szépvíz, Ugrapataka); Háromszék county (Angyalos, Bardoc); Bukovina (Istensegíts-Nagyvejke, Tolna c.). IV.: 12. Total: 263.

Textual relationships with other ballads: **122., 118.**

Tunes: 1. = No. 219 (27 variants); 2. (53); 3. (12); 11. (2).

Tunes 1 and 2 really belong to this ballad: the first being more widespread in Transdanubia, the latter known exclusively in the Great Plain. Perhaps the third tune can also be related to the ballad, but all the rest are occasional associations.

A transcribed variant of this ballad was published as his own composition by Gusztáv Magyari Kossa in 1857 (cf. Mihály Boros: *Kalauz* (Guide), No. 16), and in 1858 it was repeatedly published in his *Magyari költeményi,* (Magyari's Poems), p. 58. In the same year, however, József Berki also published it as his own verse in his *Költeményei* (Poems). p. 37. A debate of plagiarism ensued on the pages of the *Vasárnapi Újság* (Sunday Paper), No. 51, 1891 and Nos 1–2, 1892, which was closed with the editorial statement: " . . . both have been borrowed from a common source, that is the body of folksongs." This statement is obviously correct. The ballad has stemmed from the popular mind, and its having originated from higher circles is absolutely precluded. Within the given time limits, no likelihood of an "experience" of a landlord hanging a shepherd philandering with his daughter is admitted! Consequently, the plot is a heritage passed down from earlier times, together with the tragic tenor of old ballads. The metaphor of the shirt and hair blown by wind has been borrowed from the prisoners' ballads; nevertheless, it became an unalienable element of the ballad, representing, so to say, the essence of the story; the same motif penetrated into other ballads, too, including the next type which is related with the present one.

The debate of plagiarism is revealing in any case that the ballad was already extant at that time. Therefore, it may be originated from the twenties or thirties of the last century.

122. THE BARONESS AND THE COWHERD

221.

1. Szé - pen le - gel a kis-asz -szony gu - já - ja. A kis - asz-szony maga sé - tál u - tán - na.

Még mesz-szi-rül ki - ált - ja ¡a gu - jás - nak: Szi-vem,Jancsi te-ritsd lë a su - bá - dat!

1. The Miss's herd of cattle is grazing with calm and ease.
   The Miss is following in its wake.
   From afar she calls to the cattle-herd:
   Sweetheart Jancsi, spread your fine fur-coat.

2. This is not the place to spread my fur-coat,
   The corn-field is near, and they will drive in my herd.
   Well, sweetheart Jancsi, never mind your herd!
   My mother is going to redeem it, upon my word.

3. Mother dear, will you redeem my herd of cattle!
   I have spent the night with the cattle-herd.
   Daughter, daughter, I will not call you my daughter
   If you marry a cattle-herd.
   I don't care, mother dear, deny me,
   Still my heart breaks with grief for the cattle-herd.

Szirénfalva (Ung county). Performed by a woman of 61. L. Kiss 1958 = AP 2339/g.

Divergences:

"The baroness's herd of cattle is grazing with calm and ease (or: The herd of cattle of the Baron Orczy). The young baroness is walking in its wake." Sometimes stanzas borrowed from the field of art-songs introduce the ballad: "Calm is the evening that lights on the plain. The ring of the steer is silent. Alone the pipe is weeping. The Miss is listening at her window to its sound. In the plain I live as a cattleherd's hand. A thousand horses and a thousand cattle I am in charge of. When the Miss comes to walk in the plain, She looks smiling at the young cowherd." But in most instances, the story is rounded off with portions of the previous type (The Baroness and the Shepherd). This is owing to the similarity existing between the two songs, although briefness of the plot is also conducive to supplementation. Mostly the closing lines are taken over, showing the shepherd's shirt and pants blown by wind on the gallows-tree. In other cases the beginning stanzas are incorporated.

Here and there, however, only the dialogue of the baroness and the shepherd is
inserted to form the middle part of the song. In the material elaborated, twenty-six
variants include portions of the other ballad. Next an example of merger is given.

Alas, they have carved the beam nicely
On which the cattle-herd's hand will be hanged.
Wind is blowing his black, crispy hair,
He will never again cuddle the baron's daughter.
I dare not walk along the main street
For fear they should say I am wearing black mourn.
Black mourn, snow-white is my fancy kerchief.
A young shepherd was my first lover.
The Gipsy woman's tent stands at the end of the village,
Many young girls walk there every day.
I shall go, too, and ask her to tell me my fortune:
Am I going to find a sweetheart faithful to life.

Earliest provenience: 1864.
Dissemination:
I. Vas county (Nagykölked, Pankasz, Semjénháza), Zala county (Komárváros, Letenye,
Zalacsány); Somogy county (Hetes, Karád, "Sármellék", Somogyszentpál, Szentmihályhegy, Szenna,
Szilvásszentmárton); Baranya county (Csányoszró, Csoboka, Diósviszló, Dunaszekcső, Jagónak,
Kopács, Vásárosdombó); Tolna county (Madocsa, Sárpilis); Fejér county (Sárbogárd, Sárszentmihály,
Seregélyes, Úrhida, Vereb); Veszprém county (Dég, Hárságy, Ősi, environs of Szilasbalhás, Zirc);
Esztergom county (Pilismarót); Komárom county (Ács, Kocs, Naszvad), Győr county (Szemere). I.: 37.
II. Nyitra county (Negyed, Tardoskedd, Vága, Vágfarkasd); Hont county (Ipolybél,
Lukanénye); Nógrád county (Mihálygerge, "Nógrád c.", Nógrádmegyer, Nőtincs, Salgóvidék, Szanda,
Szandaváralja 2, Tolmács); Heves county (Átány, Bükkszenterzsébet, Egerbocs, Erdőtelke, Fedémes 3,
Füzesabony, Mátraderecske, Tarnalelesz, Tiszaigar, Tiszanána, Tiszaörs); Borsod county (Csincse,
Nagyvisnyó, Sajónémeti 2, Sály 3, Szakácsi); Gömör county (Bánréve, Hidaspuszta, Kövecser, Pelsőc,
Sajótila); Abaúj county (Beret, Felsőméra, Nagytárkány); Zemplén county ("Bodrogköz", Mikóháza,
Ricse 2, Sárospatak, Tolcsva, Vajdácska); Ung county (Szirénfalva 2); Bereg county (Beregszász);
Ugocsa county ("Ugocsa") II.: 55.
III. Pest county (Cegléd, Csíkvár, Jászkarajenő, Jászszentgyörgy, Kiskunfélegyháza 2,
Kiskunhalas 7, Pálmonostor, "Pest county" 2, Pilis); Jász-Nagykun-Szolnok county (Ballatelep,
Jákóhalma, Jászalsószentgyörgy, Kisújszállás, Mesterszállás 2, Nagykörü, Tiszaigar); Bács-Bodrog
county (Bajmok, Katymár, Mélykút); Csongrád county (Ásotthalom, Csongrád, Domaszék 2,
Forráskút, Hódmezővásárhely 2, Homokpuszta 3, Horgosi Királyhalom, Kistelek 2, Ruzsa,
Sándorfalva, environs of Szentes, Tömörkény 2, Üllés); Arad county (Arad, Vadász); Békés county
(Geszt, Kondoros, Köröstarcsa, Szeghalom); Bihar county (Biharugra 4, Esztár, Körösnagyharsány 2,
Nagyszalonta 8, Sáránd, Újiráz); Hajdú county ("Hortobágy", Hosszúpályi, Tiszacsege); Szabolcs
county (Kisvárda, Nyírbátor, Nyíregyháza, Nyírlugos 2, Nyírtura, Nyírvasvári, Rakamaz,
Tornyospálca, Vaja); Szatmár county (Csengöld, Kérsemjén 3, Szamosszeg 2, Szatmárökörító,
Turricse, Vállaj). III.: 92.
IV. Kolozs county (Kolozsvár, Mákófalva 2, Vajdakamarás); Torda-Aranyos county
(Torockó); Szolnok-Doboka county (Bálványosváralja, Feketelak, Mezőveresegyháza, Szék); Maros-
Torda county (Szabéd); Nagyküküllő county (Egerbegy); Udvarhely county (Kápolnásoláhfalu,
Medesér, Tordátfalva); Csík county (Szárhegy); Háromszék county (Sepsiköröspatak); Bukovina
(Istensegíts). IV.: 16.
Total: 200.
Textual relationships with other ballads: **121.**
Tunes: 1. = No. 221, 4. (3 variants), 5. (13), 6. (2), 7. (2), 11. (7), 12. (2), 13. (4), 15. (15), 16. (2), 17.
(8), 21. (4).

910

A fairly recent text which probably originates from the first half of the last century. Reminiscences of urban influence are to be felt in the formulation. Also the tunes associated are of the art-song type (13., 15.). Representing a border-case of ballad poetry, the song has hardly any plot in it.

123. THE SPINNING GIRL WHO WAS MURDERED

222.

„Csendes, siralmas"- Lento, doloroso

1. Es-te van, es-te van, hét-re jár az ó-ra.
Minden e-la-dó-lyány ké-szül a fo-nó-ba.

Sze-gény Szűcs Ma-ris is o-da-in-dult vol-na,
Ha az ég fe-let-te bé nem bo-rult vol-na.

1. It is evening, it is evening, the clock soon strikes seven.
   All marriageable girls prepare for the spinning house.
   Poor Maris Szűcs would have started there, too,
   If only the sky had not turned gloomy above her.

2. It has turned gloomy, it has turned gloomy, it has drown dark,
   A gloomy night has settled on poor Maris Szűcs.
   She went to the spinning house and set on the bench.
   A young man asks her to go out for a minute.

3. Come, girls, come and help me!
   Alas, I shall never again come to the spinning house with you!
   They went out and laid her on the ground,
   Her blood painted the ground red.

4. My hostess asks: whose daughter this be?
   A young man jumps up: She is my darling!
   Girls, girls, girls, take an example from me:
   You must never make friends with jealous lads!

5. Girls, girls, girls, take an example from me:
   If you go to the spinning house, don't take a distaff with you!
   For if you take a distaff with you, you will share the same fate:
   At Monday dawn your words will stop for ever.

Bodrogköz (Tisza-Bodrog Interfluve). 1864 = Szini 74, No. 53.

Divergences: For the main divergences and the development of the song, see vol 1. Merger often takes place with The Disgraced Girl (10.) and The Prince Preparing to Marry (75.). The modern recordings are fragmentary, the old ones more detailed.

914

Earliest provenience: 1831 *(Mindszenty)*
Dissemination: S. 1.: 3.

I. Sopron county ("Danube-Rába Interfluve"); Zala county (Dergecs 2, Szombatfa); Somogy county (Csákány, Somogyszob); Szerém county (Kórógy); Verőce county (Haraszti?); Baranya county (Püspökszenterzsébet, Vásárosdombó); Tolna county (Miszla, Öcsény); Veszprém county (Dég, "Somló region"); Komárom county (Tárkány); Győr county (Abda, "Győr region", Nyúl 2, Tényő) I.: 20.

II. Pozsony county (Nagykeszi, Pográny); Bars county (Lédec); Hont county (Ipolybalog, Letkés); Esztergom county (Libád); Nógrád county (Lapujtő, "Nógrád"; Rétság), Heves county (Tiszanána); Borsod county ("Borsod"), "Borsod and Gömör"; Gömör county (Alsóbalog); Zemplén county ("Tisza-Bodrog Interfluve"?, Nagytárkány, Sárospatak) II.: 16.

III. Pest county (Fülöpszállás, Keserűtelek, Kiskunhalas, Tura); Bács-Bodrog county (Homokmégy); Torontál county (Lőrincfalva, Nagybecskerek, Szőreg); South Great Plain (without precise indication of locality) 4.; Csongrád county (Ásotthalom, Hódmezővásárhely 2, Szeged 2, Szentes); Csanád county (Mezőkovácsháza); Békés county (Endrőd); Szabolcs county (Nagykálló) III.: 21.

IV. Kolozs county (Válaszút, Visa); Maros-Torda county (Magyaró); Torda-Aranyos county (Bágyon, Sinfalva); Alsófehér county ("Alsó-Fehér c.", Magyarlapád); Kisküküllő county (Bélavásár); Nagyküküllő county (Alsórákos); Udvarhely county (Kézdiszentlélek, Medesér); Csík county (Kászonjakabfalva); Háromszék county ("Háromszék"); "Székely land", Transylvania (without precise indication of locality); Moldva (Klézse 3, Lészped) IV.: 19.

Total: 79.
Textual relationships with other ballads: **10., 75.**
Tunes: 1. = No. 222 (5 variants; this being the tune recorded together with the earliest texts); 2. (17 variants; this being the tune spread throughout the county); the rest are occasional associations.

The murder took place in 1822. A local verse-composition provided basis for the folk-variants (by more or less modification). In spite of its recent generation and quick spreading, the ballad is rather rare of occurrence nowadays. Although disseminated throughout the entire language area, the number of variants are few everywhere. They mostly turn up in a fragmentary form and in areas with old folklore tradition. Attempts at merger indicate that the plot was felt insufficient in itself. Slowly it fades from tradition.

124. THE WIFE WHO MURDERED HER HUSBAND

223.

1. Aunt Sára, what are you washing at the well?
   It's the bed-linen of my husband I am washing.
   I have dropped it in the blood of the duck,
   And I have to wash it for tomorrow, which is a festival day.

2. Aye, that duck had had really much blood,
   Even more, perhaps, than your husband had!
   Well, I have dropped it in the blood of the duck,
   And I am cleansing it for tomorrow's feast.

3. Aunt Sára, where has your husband gone?
   Is he perhaps feathering the duck in the kitchen?
   He is gone to cut wood in the woods, together with his brother,
   While I have come to wash my linen for the feast.

4. Aunt Sára keeps saying in the dungeon:
   Let her have her linen, she wants to wash it,
   She has dropped it in the blood of the duck,
   And she has to wash it for tomorrow's feast.

Nagyszalonta (Bihar county). Performed by a woman of 68. 1919 = MNGY XIV,
20.

224.

1. What are you washing, Borcsa Zsaóri, at the well?
   It is the fine linen bed-cloth of my husband, kind sister.
   I have dropped it in blood,
   I must wash it for Good Friday,
   Alas, alas, alas!

2. Black ravens are crowing in the big forest.
   Borcsa Zsaóri, there is a spot of blood in the linen!
   I have dropped it in the blood of a goose,
   I must wash it for Good Friday,
   Alas, alas, alas!

3. Black ravens are crowing above your head.
   What have you done to your elder husband?
   I have sent him to the big forest,
   I am going to marry the younger one
   Alas, alas, alas!

4. A black raven has lighted on the window of the jail.
   Borcsa Zsaóri begins again in this strain:
   I have dropped it in the blood of a goose,
   I must wash it for Good Friday.
   Alas, alas, alas!

5. I have dropped it in blood,
   I am going to marry the younger one.
   Alas, alas, alas!

Otrokócs (Gömör county). László Juhász, 1890 = Nyr 1890, 528.

Younger husband means the next brother of the husband. Only the two published texts are known. No tune has been recorded.

Textual relationships with other ballads: None.

The ballad has turned up at two places far from each other, which circumstance indicates a certain degree of dissemination. As the text has been recorded also at Nagyszalonta, it may be assumed that *János Arany (1817–1882)* had known it. Perhaps he had drawn inspiration to write his ballad entitled *Ágnes Asszony* (Wife Ágnes) from the popular form. Innuendoes, elliptical construction, refrains, awkward excuses and the description of the psychological condition refer the text to the realm of old-type ballads. (Ancient international motifs come up in it: "Why is your sword dropping with blood, Edward, Edward?—I have killed a pigeon.") But the form of construction and the formulation of the Hungarian is different. It rather raises the impression as if it were a novel development reaching back to old tradition. In a simple dialogue of four stanzas it brings forth all what is related in the twenty-six stanzas of its literary parallel. Even though a corrupt, unpretentious text is contrasted with a literary masterpiece, the comparison may be instructive for our purpose; the differences of literary and folklore methods of approach can be assessed. The poet builds a scene out of the impersonal question of the folk ballad: "The boys of the street gather together . . . The neighbour women assemble in a haste . . .". All this is redundant for the folklore composition, in which only a hint to the murder is sufficient. The innuendo can be implied in any sort of dialogue. The pattern can be applied to anybody, according to the imaginative power of the audience. With Arany, also the answer lets out more details: "My dearest star, he is sleeping in the house, Don't go in lest he should wake". At this point the folk version is more effective in its suggestion. The literary parallel turns into a narrative from Stanza 4 ("The heyduck comes: Wife Ágnes, you must come now to the prison..." down to Stanza 26 (the court scene and the detailed description of the woman's going mad); all this, approached from the side of folk composition, seems to be an over-detailed presentation more in the style of a short-story than of a ballad, since the four stanzas of the folk ballad include all the important motifs. As to the last stanzas of Arany, resplendent with poetic beauty as they are, they can be regarded, by principles of folk compositions, as extenuation of the story after its plot has been closed (the part contains the description of the aged figure of the crazy woman still washing her linen). Notably, the essential motif consists in that the woman went mad after the murder, repeating lunatically the empty excuse, and once said, this does not need to be told again. Therefore the folk creation contents itself by stating the fact, and puts an end to the story. As a matter of course, it cannot boast of so refined poetic devices as, for example: "The quivering shadow of her body is trembling on the waves, Her locks in the stray breeze..., On moonlight nights When the crests of the waves are shining bright, The far-sounding broken bangs of her beater are heard, Its flashes are seen from afar," and the like. But people are not attracted by possibilities of representing other things than the plot and the figures involved in it. They do not want to indulge in scenes, descriptions of environment and details of secondary importance: folk balladry being a homo-centric poetry does not want to carry the problem beyond the point of a satisfactory understanding. It presents the speeded-up conflict in a naked form. That is to say, there is one thing in which it surpasses all art poetry: it can produce a masterly structure, it can condense things, it feels what is essential and how much is wanted to express what is essential. Here lies the secret of folklore style.

125. THE WIFE WHO KILLED HER OLD HUSBAND

225.

Parlando ♪=160

1. El - mënt, el - mënt a vén ko - vács   If - ju Ör - zsét meg - ké - ret - ni.

Mëg - ké - ret - te a fi - á - nak,   Ha - za - vit - te ö - ma - gá - nak.

1. The old blacksmith arose and went
   To sue for the hand of young Örzse.
   He asked her to marry his son,
   And took her home for himself.

2. Young Örzse arose and went
   To enjoy herself with young men.
   The old blacksmith went after her:
   Come home, young Örzse!

3. For I did not marry you
   To see you enjoy yourself with young men,
   But I married you
   To look into my grey head!

4. To look into my grey head,
   To kiss my withered face,
   To kiss my withered face,
   To scratch my crooked back.

5. Come on, come on, you old blacksmith,
   Let's take a look at the Tisza and the Danube!
   Let's take a look at the Tisza and the Danube
   And see if they are flowing downwards or upwards?

6. Tisza, Danube, be in full bloom now!
   The old blacksmith is lying in your bed.
   Punish, God, the mother
   Who marries off her daughter to an old man!

7. If rain falls, he is shivering,
   If wind blows, he is trembling.
   If rain falls, he is shivering,
   If wind blows, he is trembling.

Mánfa (Baranya county). Performed by a woman of 71. L. Kiss 1958 = AP 2147/c.

Divergences: There is a variant in which the young wife does not utter a word before they arrive at the bank of the river. When arrived, she says:

> Stand in front of me, you old blacksmith!
> Let me take a look at your body.
> At your body, at your beauty,
> At your slim and slender waist!

Then she thrust him into the water. According to another version, the young wife goes home upon the call of her husband:

> The fresh young wife went home
> To blow into flame the sparkling fire.
> To blow into flame the sparkling fire,
> To put on a vessel of water.
> Come here, you old man,
> Bow your head in my lap,
> Bow your head in my lap,
> Let me pluck your old head!
> Come over, gossip,
> The old man is dying!
> He is bulging his eyes,
> He is moving his beard.
> Don't be afraid of him, gossip,
> Fasten a rope to his feet,
> Draw him, pull him to the bed of holyhock!

The warming of water was followed, in all likelihood, by the shaving of the beard, as appears from the next variant:

> Alas, my Lord, what a pity!
> I was shaving my husband
> And drove the razor in his neck
> Because so I wished.
> Onion, onion,
> Be sharp in my eyes,
> So that I may lament my old man,
> So that I may lament my old man!

Some of the motifs enter into other connections occasionally:

> ..... He takes her home for himself.
> The old man asks her,
> The old man asks her:
> Am I handsome, fair Ilona?
> Am I handsome, fair Ilona?
> You are handsome, you are handsome, you old man
> As a rotten block in the woods.
> If wind blows, it is shaking,
> If rain falls, it is rotting.

Fair Ilona asks him:
Am I beautiful, you old man? (Repetition as above throughout.)
You are beautiful, you are beautiful fair Ilona,
Like a rose that sprang in the garden of flowers.

A variant from Nyitra county incorporates motifs of The Enticed Wife (Type **3.**) and The Girl Abducted by the Turks (Type **29.**):

... Fair Ilona arose and went
To fetch water in copper jugs from the well.
The old man went after her:
Give me water, fair Ilona!
She passed, she passed him the copper jug.
Then he took her by her white arm...
He drew her, drew her through hills and valleys,
Through hills and valleys, and thorny thickets.
Stop, stop, you old man!
A thorn has driven in my leg.
We shall stop, fair Ilona,
We shall stop by the cut tree.
I have nine castles there,
I shall lock you up in the tenth.
Fair Ilona arose and went
To play with young girls..."

The repulsive features of the old man are sometimes exaggerated beyond belief:

But I married you
To scratch my grey head,
To scrape my grubby neck,
To lick my mucuous nose,
To suck my muddy eyes!

Earliest provenience: 1846.
Dissemination: Sopron county ("The Fertő Region"); Vas county (Nagyrákos); Zala county (Pölöske); Baranya county (Mánfa 4, Püspökszenterzsébet); Tolna county (Kánya); Nyitra county (Béd, Menyhe, Vicsápapáti); Arad county (Pécska); Southern Great Plain (s.l.); Bihar county (Nagyszalonta). Total: 15.
Textual relationships with other ballads: **3., 29.**
Tunes: 1. = No. 225 (five variants); 3. (3).

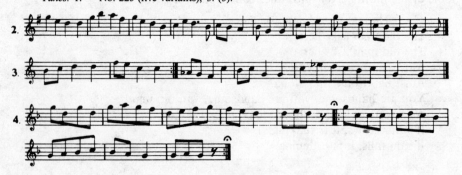

The figure of the young wife taking her vengeance on her old man to whom she had been forced to marry is not unknown with the French either. (Cf. 31.) Nevertheless, the two nations treat the theme in a different way. No direct connections can, therefore, be seen between the French and the Hungarian ballads. The gaps in the dissemination, and the variants occurring in distant tradition-preserving regions indicate that the story must have been more widespread in older times. It is not precluded that we are dealing with survivals of some old ballad. (This seems to be supported by embedded motifs of old-style ballads). Provisionally we relegated this piece to the class of new ballads on account of its modern language.

126. THE MURDERER WHO GAVE HIMSELF UP

226.

1. Bar-na Ja - nit ar - ra kér - te ba - bá - ja: É - desany-ját te - gye a más - vi - lág - ra!

Bar-na Ja - ni ki - hív - ta az er - dő - be,   É - lös ké - sét szúr-ta any - ja szí - vé - be.

1. Jani Barna was asked by his sweetheart
   To send his mother over to the world beyond.
   Jani Barna called his mother to the woods,
   He drove his sharp knife into his mother's heart.

2. Jani Barna's suit is stained with blood.
   He has no mother to clean it.
   Wash, sweetheart, whiten my shirt and my pants!
   Tomorrow I go to the gendarmes' commissar.

3. Good day, sir gendarmes' commissar!
   Welcome, Jani Barna, what's the matter with you?
   Sir commissar, my heart is heavy with grief
   For I have killed my mother upon advice of a girl.

4. Jani Barna, it is a pity to have done so,
   To kill your mother upon advice of a girl.
   Sir commissar, she has been an old enemy of mine,
   I could not marry the one I loved best.

5. The beam has been carved on the bank of the Tisza,
   On which Jani Barna will be hanged.
   Wind blows his black, crispy hair,
   Someone else is cuddling the sweetheart of Jani Barna.

Búcsú (Vas county). Performed by a woman of 36. Békefi 1965.

227.

1. Jaj, de szé - les, jaj de hosz-szú ez az út,   A - me-lyi-ken Bar-na Jan - csi el - in - dult!

Raj - ta van a fe - hér in - ge, ga - tyá - ja.   Rá - sü - tött a haj - nal-csil-lag su - gá - ra.

1. Alas, it is a broad way, alas, it is a long way
   On which Jancsi Barna has set out!
   He has his white shirt and pants on,
   The beam of the morning star lights on him.

2. Jancsi Barna goes to the woods.
   His best friend is lying at the foot of a tree.
   His best friend is lying at the foot of a tree.
   Jancsi Barna killed him as he was lying there.

3. Jancsi Barna's suit was spotted with blood.
   His sweetheart, his darling is going to clean it.
   Wash, darling, whiten my shirt and my pants,
   Tomorrow I shall go to the commissar of the gendarmes.

4. Sir commissar, may God grant us a good day!
   Welcome, Jancsi Barna! What is the matter with you?
   Sir commissar, sorrow is pressing down my heart,
   I have killed my best friend for a girl.

5. Jancsi Barna, this you have not done well,
   That you killed your best friend for a girl!
   Sir commissar, he was an old enemy of mine,
   Mari Kovács could not be my wife.

6. Alas, yellow is the gate of the Illava prison!
   Jancsi Barna has been closed up there.
   Gate of Illava prison, may you break!
   Jancsi Barna will never let be free!

Kiskunhalas (Pest county). Performed by a woman of 35. Vargyas 1939 = Vargyas 1954, 63/a.

Divergences: The development of the plot has been discussed, in the study in connection with the early variants. Anyway, there occur only minor deviations. In more recent recordings, and almost generally in the Transdanubian parts, the young man kills his own mother. It seems as if variations have proceeded towards a deeper conflict.

Earliest provenience: 1882. (There exist several earlier notations, in which, however, the text had not reached its stage of full development.)

Dissemination: Vas county (Búcsú, Ják, Kenéz, Nagymizdó, Pankasz, Pecöl, Perenye, Rábakovácsi); Zala county (Csácsbozsok, Csáford, Nemeshetés, Kanizsa, Kiskomárom, Oltárc, Rédics 2, Zalaapáti, Zalacsány, Zalakoppány); Somogy county (Csákány, Ságvár, Somogyzsitfa, Zamárdi); Baranya county (Kopács, Mohács); Tolna county (Pincehely, Szekszárd); Pest county (Bogyiszló); Fejér county (Csákvár, Dunapentele, Etyek region); Veszprém county (Bakony-Sárkány, Berhida, Hegyesd, Szentkirályszabadja); Komárom county (Császár, Csilizradvány, Kiskeszi, Nagylég, Naszvad); Győr county (Hollómajor, Nagybaráthegy, Táplánypuszta); Pozsony county (Ógelle); Nyitra county (Zsére 2, Zsitvabesenyő); Bars county (Lédec); Hont county (Ipolyszög, Perőcsény); Nógrád county (Bercel 2, Rimóc); Heves county (Bükkszenterzsébet); Borsod county (Mályinka, Sajómercse); Zemplén county ("Tisza-Bodrog Interfluve", Ricse 2, Sárospatak, Szürnyeg, Takta-nador); Pest county (Galambospuszta, Kiskunfélegyháza 2, Kiskunhalas 4); Jász-Nagykun-Szolnok county (Cibakháza, Jászberény, Nagykörű); Bács-Bodrog county (Bácsalmás, Csóka, Kunbaja, Zenta); Torontál county (Hertelendyfalva, Pádé, Szaján); Csongrád county (Átokháza, "Csongrád county" 2,

Hódmezővásárhely 5, Horgos, Mindszent, Tápé); Arad county (Pécska); South Great Plain (without precise indication of locality 2), Csanád county (Apátfalva, Makó); Békés county (Doboz, Endrőd 2, Gyula, Mezőberény, Okány, Orosháza, Szarvas); Bihar county (Körösnagyharsány, Nagyszalonta 7); Szabolcs county (Gégény, Nyírábrány, Nyírbátor, Nyírlugos 2, Nyírtura 2); Szatmár county (Ura); Szilágy county (Kraszna); Kolozs county (Méra 3); Szolnok-Doboka county (Búza 2); Maros-Torda county (Szentgerice); Udvarhely county (Tordátfalva, Zetelaka); Csík county (Csíkmenaság, Csíkszentimre, Gyimesközéplok, Gyimesbükk); Háromszék county (Dálnok, Sepsibükszád, Székelytamásfalva), "Bukovina"; Moldva (Lészped, Újfalu). Total: 138.

Textual relationships with other ballads: **96., 121.**

Tunes: 1. = No. 226. (17 variants), 2. = No. 227. (29 variants), 4. (3), 5. (2), 6. (3).

(3–10. in the geographical order; 10. Moldavian.)

This ballad which has spread most recently belongs to the favourite songs in the dissemination area. This fact is also borne out by its fairly uniform text and tune. Tunes 226 and 227 are closely related. The other melodies coupled with the text resemble the mentioned ones. The development of the text has been described on page vol. I, 148–152. It may have assumed its present form towards the en of the last century.

127. A FIGHT IS BOUND TO COME

228.

Poco rubato ♩=94

1. Ba - kony - er - dő jász - ba van, Ba - kony - er - dő jász - ba van.

Ró - zsa Sán - dor fog - va van, Ró - zsa Sán - dor fog - va van.

1. The Bakony forest is plunged into mourn,
   The Bakony forest is plunged into mourn,
   Sándor Rózsa has been taken prisoner,
   Sándor Rózsa has been taken prisoner.

2. On a Sunday afternoon,
   On a Sunday afternoon,
   He was walking merrily in the street,
   He was walking merrily in the street.

3. His kind mother follows him,
   His kind mother follows him.
   Son, Sándor, come home,
   Son, Sándor, come home!

4. I cannot go home,
   I cannot go home,
   I must go to the inn,
   I must go to the inn.

5. A fight is bound to come,
   A fight is bound to come.
   I shall bathe in blood,
   I shall bathe in blood.

6. And I know whose blood it will be,
   And I know whose blood it will be.
   I shall bathe in the commissar's blood,
   Not in the shallow water of the Tisza.

7. Mother dear, I am come home,
   Mother dear, I am come home.
   Is there a dirty shirt among my soiled clothes,
   Is there a dirty shirt among my soiled clothes?

8. If there is no dirty shirt among them,
   If there is no dirty shirt among them,
   I have brought one soiled with blood,
   I have brought one soiled with blood.

Mánfa (Baranya county). Performed by a woman of 45. K. Kiss 1949.

Divergences:

1. The fir-woods is plunged into mourn (Each line repeated),
   For an outlaw is lying dead.
2. On a Sunday afternoon
   He walked after the girls.
3. He went to the inn,
   He stood at the door.
4. Three outlaws were enjoying themselves,
   The fourth one pointed to him:
5. You dog, shun my hand,
   Because you have broken my head!
6. A copper hatchet is in my head,
   A double-edged knife in my heart!
7. Mother dear, mother dear,
   Have I a soiled shirt among the dirty clothes?
8. Take it to the Tisza,
   Wash it clean for your son who is dead.
9. Aye, girls, weep,
   Make pearly wreath and bow down at my grave!

Cigánd (Zemplén county).

Some of the texts have a different continuation after the fourth outlaw points to Sándor Rózsa: "The first outlaw rushed at him, The second kept him back, The third stood up And hit Sándor at the head." Then follows: "If you have cut my head, Shun, you dog, my hand!"

The name Sándor Rózsa has in this case nothing to do with the famous outlaw. A fairly even dissemination of the text is conspicuous, made even more emphatic by the exclusive association with the tune and the constant line-repetitive construction. Rather ommissions than variants can be spoken of.

Earliest provenience: 1871–72 *(Bartalus).*
Dissemination:
I. Moson county (Cikolasziget, Lébény); Sopron county (Bágyog, Bősárkány); Vas county (Alsóőr, Megyehid, Nagykölked, the "Őrség Region", Várkesző, Velem); Zala county (Nemessándorháza 3, Pálfiszeg, Resznek, Rédics, Sümeg, Zalahárságy, Zalavár); Somogy county (Darány, Karád, Kálmáncsa 2, Kiliti, Kőröshegy, Kutas, Mesztegnyő, Somogyzsitfa); Verőce county (Szentlászló); Baranya county (Csuza, Karácodfa, Kisbodolya, Kopács, Magyaregregy, Mánfa, Püspökszenterzsébet); Tolna county (Kánya, Koppányszántó, Madocsa); Fejér county (Csór, Érd); Veszprém county (Balatonszöllős, Csesznek, Lovászpatona, Ősi, Pápa 2, Réde, Pápasalamon, "Somló region", Tés, Várpalota 2, Veszprémfajsz—Germans in Hungarian); Komárom county (Ács, Csicsó, Csilizpata, Naszvad); Győr county (Felpéc, Győr, Kunsziget, Ménfőcsanak) I.: 62.

II. Pozsony county ("Csallóköz", Diószeg, Doborgaz); Nyitra county (Vágkirályfa, Zsére); Hont county (Bernecebaráti, Ipolybalog 3, Perőcsény, Tésa); Nógrád county (Bárna, Bercei, Csákányháza, Gács 2, Nagybátony, Patak, Romhány, Szandaváralja, Tereske); Heves county (Adács, Bodony, Bükkszenterzsébet, Dorogháza, Fedémes 2, Mátraszentistván, Nagyvisnyó, Parád); Borsod county (Borsodnádasd, Emődi, Mezőkeresztes, Szilvásvárad); Gömör county (Hanva 3, Rimaszombat); Abaúj county (Abaújvár, Cekeháza); Zemplén county ("Tisza-Bodrog Interfluve", Bodrogolaszi, Cigánd, Megyaszó, Ricse 3, Sárospatak 4, Szerencs, Tiszakarád 2). II.: 54.

III. Pest county (Bugacmonostor, Dunavecse, Kiskunfélegyháza, Nagytarcsa, Pákapuszta, Tura); Jász-Nagykun-Szolnok county (Alattyán, Jászladány 2, Jásztelek, Karcag, Kőtelek, Nagykörü, Pusztasüly, Szelevény 2); Bács-Bodrog county (Bajsa, Rém, Zenta, Zombor); Torontál county (Egyházaskér, Hertelendyfalva, Omor, Pádé, Szőreg; "Torontál county"); Csongrád county ("Csongrád c.", Hódmezővásárhely 2), South Great Plain (without precise indication of locality 2); Békés coounty (Battonya, Békés, Endrőd, Kondoros, Pusztaföldvár, Vésztő); Arad county (Arad, Pécska); Bihar county (Biharugra, Körösnagyharsány, Nagyszalonta 5, Újiráz); Szabolcs county (Kállósemjén, Ksivárda, Mátészalka, Nyírtura); Szatmár county ("Szatmár", Tunyog); Szilágy county (Kárásztelek). III.: 52.

IV. Kolozs county (Mákófalva, Pusztakamarás, Vajdakamarás); Szolnok-Doboka county (Árpástó); Torda-Aranyos county (Sínfalva 2, Torda); Alsó-Fehér county (Lőrincréve); Udvarhely county (Alsóbencéd, Kőrispatak, Székelykeresztúr, Tordátfalva); Csík county (Csíkdelne 2, Csíkrákos 2); Háromszék county (Kálnok, Sepsiköröspatak); Bukovina (Andrásfalva, Istensegíts 2); Moldavia (Nicolae Balcescu). IV–V.: 23. Total: 191.

Textual relationships with other ballads: None.

Tunes: All the variants are sung to variants of the tune published. (Cf. *Bartók* 1924, No. 85, and notes.)

The ballad is a recent development. Uniquely formulated, as it is, the text has a peculiar interconnection with the melody. The revival of the ancient technique of line-repetition in a consistent way, as in this case, is rather exceptional in recent folklore products.

128. THE GIRL WHO FELL INTO THE THRESHING MACHINE

229.

Tempo giusto

1. E - zör - nyócszáz - nyócvanha-to - dik év - be   Mi tör-tént a   kis - doz-da -ji   szü - rü - be!

Szar - vas Jul-csa föl - lé - pött a   nagy dobra,   E-gyö - ne - sen   be - le - e - sött a dob - ba.

1. What happened in the threshing field of Kisdozda
   In the year of eighteen hundred and eighty-six?
   Julcsa Szarvas mounted the big drum,
   And fell into the big drum.

2. As Pali Gazsi saw this,
   He clasped his hands on his head
   Crying: Stop the machine!
   My dear Juliska has fallen into the drum!

3. They lifted Julcsa Szarvas out of the big drum,
   And took her to the old doctor's.
   Old doctor takes a look at her, saying:
   Only the good Lord can be the doctor of Julcsa.

4. The stubble-field of barley is very broad at Kisdozda!
   A little lark sets in it, singing.
   She sings to the mother of Julcsa Szarvas:
   Your daughter has met a sudden death!

5. Open, mother, your green-painted gate;
   Let in your daughter who has been crushed.
   For her blood is flowing in streams,
   Her faithful sweetheart's heart is near to break!

6. Candles are burnt, one after the other, with the Szarvas's,
   They are waking over Julcsa Szarvas.
   Julcsa Szarvas is resting on two deals,
   Her lover, bent over her, is shedding tears.

7. In vain does he say: Open, sweetheart, your window!
   Hold out your two round arms!
   After your arms, your snow-white breast,
   Let me write my name under your heart!

8. Come, girls, let us dress in white!
   Let us take Julcsa to the graveyard!
   Come, girls, let us take her to the graveyard,
   Let us place her to rest for ever!

Hegyszentmárton (Baranya county). Performed by a woman of 29. 1934 = Berze Nagy, 236–37.

Divergences:

Sometimes the beginning stanza reads like this: "Have you heard what happened in Belegrad? . . . The mechanic misunderstanding this, Gave more steam to the engine (bis). So poor Julcsa was torn to pieces." In such variants the mechanic casts himself on the grave, cursing himself for his having caused the accident. "By the time the machine stopped, The weak voice of Julcsa Farkas also stopped." Or: "All the red blood of her body was spilt." "Her red blood flew in streams Her mother's heart broke with grief."

Earliest provenience: 1891.
Dissemination:
S.1.: 1.

I. Vas county (Búcsú, Csempeszkopács, Csörötnek, Hosszúpereszteg, Nádasd, Oszkó); Zala county (Csömödér, Kiskomárom 2, Monostorapáti, Oltárc, Rédics); Somogy county (Bedegkér, Zamárdi 2); Baranya county (Becefa, Hegyszentmárton, Kopács, "Ormányság"); Tolna county (Koppányszántó, Nova, Szekszárd); Veszprém county (Jásd, Réde); Komárom county (Komárom, Naszvad); Győr county (Győr, Ság). I.: 28.

II. Pozsony county (Taksonyfalva); Nyitra county (Zsére); Hont county (Bernecebaráti 2, Ipolybalog, Ipolyszög, Ipolyvece, Lukanénye, Perőcsény); Nógrád county (Bercel 2, Szandaváralja 2); Heves county (Bükkszenterzsébet, Eger 2, Erk, Fedémes 2, Feldebrő, Mátraderecske, Poroszló); Borsod county (Abod, Bogács, Mezőkeresztes, Szilvásvárad); Zemplén county ("Tisza-Bodrog Interfluve", Deregnyő, Ricse 2, Sárospatak 2, Szerencs); Bereg county (Lónya, Nagysárkány); Ung county (Palágy), II.: 38.

III. Pest county (Isaszeg, Kecskemét 3, Kiskunfélegyháza, Kiskunhalas 4); Jász-Nagykun-Szolnok county (Jákóhalma, Jászberény, Túrkeve 2); Bács-Bodrog county (Bácsalmás, Bajsa, Kunbaja, Pince, Rém 2, Zenta, Zsidaborota); Torontál county (Egyházaskér, Klárafalva, Majdán); South Great Plain (without precise indication of locality); Csongrád county (Hódmezővásárhely, Tápé); Békés county (Csorvás, Endrőd, Sarkadkeresztúr, Vésztő 2); Bihar county (Biharugra, Körösnagyharsány 2, Nagyszalonta 2); Szabolcs county (Gégény 2, Nyírbátor, Nyírlugos 2, Paszab, Polgár, Piricse, Tiszakarád); Szatmár county (Kérsemjén); Szilágy county (Dobra, Kárásztelek 2). III.: 50.

IV. Hunyad county (Déva); Kolozs county (Méra); Szolnok-Doboka county (Cege); Maros-Torda county (Malomfalva, Marosvásárhely 2, Póka, Szováta); Nagyküküllő county (Medgyes); Udvarhely county (Boldogasszonyfalva); Csík county (Csíkszentimre, Gyergyótekerőpatak); Háromszék county (Bardoc, Magyarhermány); Bukovina (Andrásfalva). IV.: 15. Total: 132.

The list of proveniences fails to show the entire dissemination of the ballad. With the method of questioning, the song can be found in nearly every village in areas I–III.

Textual relationships with other ballads: none.
Tunes:

Associated either with the melody of No. 229 or some other new-style folksong in areas I–III. (Few tunes have been recorded by mainly unprofessional collectors.) Other kinds of tunes are coupled with the text in the fringe areas of the Great Plain and area IV. These are as follows:

(Nos 2 and 3 are extant in two notations.)

As the harvesting machines began to spread in the 70s of the last century, the song must have developed after that decade. Nevertheless, the dates are very divergent in the texts (from 1848 to 1914). The point is to match the rhythmic pattern with the number of syllables. It seems, however, that 1886 is nearest to truth. *Kálmány* pretends to know that the event took place at Zenta. He dates the song as late as 1891. Without exception, the lines are of the eleven-syllable type of new-style folksongs. The influence of the latter is also shown by the melodies associated with the texts. The song must have developed in the eighties. Although telling about a death-case, it has not become a true ballad. No matter how many efforts are seen on the part of the informants to make it effective by introducing novel lyrical ideas, the verse remains a simple record of an accident.

I have knowledge of a single version in foreign language: SL'P III, No. 819. Three stanzas of this are verbatim translations of the Hungarian version; the tune is a generally known Hungarian melody of the new style. Thus the foreign version must be regarded as an adaptation of the Hungarian.

129. THE BEGUILED HUSBAND

230.

1. É - des- ked- ves   fe - le - sé - gem! Mi baj, no,   àn - gya - lom?

Mit ke - res - nek   itt   a   lo - vak   az   ud - va - ro - mon?

1. My dearest, sweetest wife!
   What's the matter, my dear angel?
   I see horses in the courtyard
   And I can't see the reason.

2. Look, you are a stupid man indeed,
   Who can see a horse here?
   Milking cows they are,
   I bought them at the fair.

3. Milking cows, saddled,
   Has anyone ever seen such a thing?
   Am I not a silly, beguiled
   Husband I have ever been?

4. In entered the room,
   And what was I to see?
   A pair of boots under the table,
   One, two, three pairs of them!

5. I asked: Dear wife...,
   What's the matter, my dear angel?
   I see boots under the table,
   And I can't see the reason.

6. Look, you are a stupid man indeed,
   Who can see boots here?
   Milk jugs they are,
   I bought them at the fair.

6. Milk jugs with spurs,
   Has anyone ever seen such a thing?
   Am I not a silly, beguiled
   Husband I have ever been?

8. I went still inner the room,
   And what was I to see?
   A pair of swords on the table:
   One, two, three pairs of them!

9. I asked: Dear wife...,
   What's the matter, my dear angel?
   I see swords on the table,
   And I can't see the reason.

10. Look, you are a stupid man indeed.
    Who can see swords here?
    They are knives to cut meal with,
    I bought them at the fair.

11. Knives to cut meal, and they are tasselled,
    Has anyone ever seen such a thing?
    Am I not a silly, beguiled
    Husband I have ever been?

12. I went still inner the room,
    And what was I to see?
    A pair of shakoes on the table,
    One, two, three pairs of them.

13. I asked: Dear wife...,
    What's the matter, my dear angel?
    I see shakoes on the table
    And I can't see the reason.

14. Look, you are a stupid man indeed,
    Who can see shakoes here?
    Milk pots they are,
    I bought them at the fair.

15. Milk pots with bright buttons,
    Has anyone ever seen such a thing?
    Am I not a silly, beguiled
    Husband I have ever been?

16. I went still inner the room,
    And what was I to see?
    Mantles on the pegs,
    One, two, three of them.

17. I asked: Dear wife...,
    What's the matter, my dear angel?
    I see mantles on the pegs,
    And I can't see the reason.

18. Look, you are a stupid man indeed!
    Who can see mantles here?
    It is the silken gown of my servant maid,
    Spotted with mould.

19. Silken gown with stars and frogs,
    Has anyone ever seen such a thing?
    Am I not a silly, beguiled
    Husband I have ever been?

20. I went still inner the room,
    And what was I to see?
    Soldiers in my bed,
    One, two, three of them!

21. I asked: Dear wife...,
    What's the matter, my dear angel?
    I see soldiers in my bed,
    And I can't see the reason.

22. Look, you are a stupid man indeed!
    Who can see soldiers here?
    They are grandmother's servant maids
    Who sweep the room.

23. Servant maids with red moustaches,
    Has anyone ever seen such a thing?
    Am I not a silly, beguiled
    Husband I have ever been?

24. My dearest, kindest wife!
    What's the matter, my dear angel?
    We are having a ball tonight,
    I say, and that's my wish!

25. The wife is looking here and there,
    What kind of ball are we going to have?
    Behind the door, there is the knotted rope,
    And there is also a long staff there.

Újszász (Pest county). Performed by a woman of 26. Bartók 1918.

Divergences: Only minor differences can be found, for instance: "As I go home from the fair, I see: there are three horses standing there..."; further, the "finds" are complemented with other things, too. On the whole, this is a uniformly shaped ballad.

Earliest provenience: 1832.

Dissemination:

S.l.: 3.

Sopron county ("Danube-Rába Interfluve"); Vas county (Őrség); Zala county (Rédics, Tapolca); Komárom county (Martos); Nyitra county (Ghymes 2); Nógrád county (Bercel 3, Szanda, Szandaváralja); Gömör county (Lucska); Abaúj county (Kéked, Pányok); Zemplén county (Legenye, Ricse); Pest county (Adony, Felsőerek, Fülöpszállás, Kiskunmajsa, Páhi, Tápiószele, Újszász); Bács-Bodrog county (Nagybaracska); Torontál county (Csóka); South Great Plain (without precise indication of locality 2); Csongrád county (Algyő, Csongrád, Hódmezővásárhely, Kiskundorozsma, Szentes); Békés county (Endrőd 2, Körösladány, Vésztő); Arad county (Arad, Gyorok); Bihar county (Biharugra); Szabolcs county (Lövőpetri, Nyíregyháza); Szatmár county (Avasújváros, Kérsemjén 2); Hunyad county (Lelesz); Maros-Torda county (Jobbágytelke, Kibéd, "Salt region"); Udvarhely county (Bethlenfalva); Csík county (Csíkkarcfalva, Csíkrákos, Gyergyócsomafalva, Gyimesvölgye, Kászonjakabfalva); Háromszék county (Dálnok, Kézdimárkosfalva); Bukovina (Istensegíts 3, Józseffalva); Moldavia (Lészped 2). Total: 63.

Textual relationships with other ballads: None.

Tunes: sung without exception to variants of the published tune, or to melodies related to it.

Versions in languages other than Hungarian:

GERMAN: E–B 900.

DANISH: DgF 304.

ENGLISH: *Child* 274.

FRENCH: *Canteloube* I, 68 IV, 279; *D'Harcourt* No. 96.

ITALIAN: *Nigra* 85.

SPANISH: *Geibel–Schack*, 348 and 350; *Cossio-Solano* I, 215–227 XXVII/120–129; *Cossio** No. 21, *Armistead–Silvermann* 1971/II, No. 16. (detailed bibliography in Note 11, p. 209); *Romero* 109 ("very popular in Spanish–America"), *Armistead* 1978/I 3A–B, *idem* 1978/II, 245 (refers to 5 variants).

RUSSIAN: *Chernyshev* No. 33–35.

ROMANIAN: *Amzulescu* 291 (enumerates 12 variants). See further: *Seemann* 1951 No. 88. (The national versions have been adduced for the sake of exemplification, without any pretence to full representation of the variants.)

The question of origin of this type had been solved by *Child* already; he stated in the comparative notes to the British variant: "B is a broadside version which had had an interesting history on the Continent. It was translated into German by *F. Wilh. Meyer* in 1789, in a very happy style, with a *dénouement* in which the man gives his wife a beating and explains his cuffs as caresses which her mother has sent her. *Meyer's* ballad was printed in 1790. It had a great and immediate success, was circulated as broadside, and was taken up by the people, in whose mouth it underwent the usual treatment of ballads traditionally propagated. From Germany it spread into Scandinavia and Hungary, and perhaps elsewhere."

In the knowledge of the Hungarian variants and the related tunes, we can fully endorse this opinion. Even details of the German version are followed by the Hungarian texts, further, both the tunes and the stanzaic construction are so strange as to betray at first sight the foreign origin. To prove this it will suffice to quote a German text and tune for comparison's sake.

E–B 900: "Als ich nun nach Hause kam, Da standen viele Pferde da. O weh, o weh, o weh! O liebes Weib, nun schau mir an, was sind die Pferde da? Milchkühe sind es ja, die Mutter schickt sie mir. Milchküh mit Lederzeug? O weh, o weh, o weh! Bin ein betrogner Eheman, wie viele andre sind. (Repetition.) 2. Als ich in die Küche kam, Da hingen viele Säbel da. O weh, o weh, o weh ... etc. O liebes Weib, schau mir an: Was sein für Säbel da? Bratspiesse sind es ja, Die Mutter schickt sie mir. Bratspiess mit Portepee? O weh, ... etc. 3. Stube, Mäntel, Nachtjacken, ...Nachtjacken mit Achselknöpfn? ... 4. ... Kammer... Stiefel... Milchtöpfe... Milchtöpfe mit Sporen.... 5. ...in das Bette ...lagen viele Husaren drin...Milchmädchen mit Schnurrbärten ...

The earliest Hungarian notation stands close to the variant published by *Erk-Böhme.*

Later the form was simplified in various ways, although the characteristic major tone and functional harmonies of the melody and the strange construction of the verse have been retained in every variant. Only the method of repetition shows a degree of divergence, owing to simplification.

The text follows the German original as closely as the tune. The same parallels occur in both: the palfrey—milch-cow saddled, bridled; boots—milk-jugs with spurs; mantle—with golden buttons; sword (occurring frequently in the variants)— spit (in MNGY II, 327; "portupé"!); and finally, in some twelve variants even the German husband's complaint is repeated in verbatim translation: "I am a poor silly husband, as are so many others!"

No other western sources come into consideration, since all the formulations except the German are widely differing from the Hungarian. Conspicuous are, on the other hand, the slight differences of variants. This refers to recent adaptation, supporting *Child's* statement. Even if we suppose that the earliest written specimen—in the songbook of *István Tóth*—was looking back upon some past in folk use as a popular song, the adaptation cannot be dated earlier than ten or twenty years after the German broadside was published.

Only the Romanian version allows of a possible Hungarian mediation. No other way of spreading towards the Southeast can be surmised. In this connection, a

937

weighty argument is that all the Romanian variants came up from the territories of pre-wars Hungary. The dénouement shows contamination with the story of The Unfaithful Wife Burnt to Death; thus a tragic ending has been given to a comic story; "In the absence of her husband, the wife calls his lover. The husband returns and discovers strange horses in the stable, boots under the bed, cap and sword on the peg. The faithless wife finds explanation for all this, but refuses to produce the key to the chest in which the husband wants to look for his mantle. The man breaks the side of the chest and detects the lover of the wife. He is successful in convincing the man that the woman is to blame what has happened. The husband forgives him and kills the wife." It is interesting that another "borrowing" nation, the Spanish, gives a similar twist to the song. (They had taken the song from the French.) For instance: *Romero* 109: "The wife is working on her embroidery at the window. The emperor's son Don Carlos sees her and love develops between them. The wife invites him for the night, as her husband went on hunting. As they are rejoicing in each other's love, the husband arrives. The familiar questions follow: Whose horse is this?—Yours, father gave it to you.—Whose weapons are these? Yours, father gave them to you.—Whose footsteps are those in the corridor? No more excuses are found: Kill me, my husband, I have cheated you! The two knights began to fight, one of them dies at midnight, the other at morn."

Literature: Child 1898: the Hungarian from the German; *Ortutay* 1936–48: *Child* 49 (?), E–B 689 and 900 paralleled with the Hungarian; *Dános* 1938: the Hungarian borrowed from the Slavs; *Seemann* 1951, No. 88: Lithuanian and Slav versions discussed in connection with the German; *Vargyas* 1964: German origin.

130. THE SICK WIFE

231.

1. In the environs of Léva, there over,
   There is a sick wife who does not want to get up.
   She is thirsty, but has no water,
   She would like to send someone to the well, but there is no-one at hand.

2. She has an old husband,
   She sends him to the well.
   As the husband starts to the well,
   A brown lad lies in the bed.
   As the husband returns home, (to lines 3 and 4)
   The brown lad walks to the bench.

3. Sick wife, dear angel,
   Who has lying in your bed?
   The cat was chasing mice,
   It was lying there for a long time.

4. Sick wife, my dear angel,
   Who is lying on the bench?
   A pauper of God is lying there.
   He is cold, the poor soul, and warming himself.

5. Then her husband feels in his pocket,
   And gives a coin to the pauper.
   The sick woman is laughing at seeing
   That the pauper accepts it.

"Csongrád county" = MNGY II, 45.

Divergences:

Sometimes the sick girl sends away her mother. "You are very kind to me, mother, Having brought so good water to me! You must go to fetch some many times, And you needn't hurry at all!" When a girl is spoken of, detection mostly follows: "What's the matter with your belly? Why is it so much swollen?" and so on.

Earliest provenience: 1872.
Dissemination: "Csongrád county" 2; "Szatmár county"; Csík county (Gyimesfelsőlok); Moldavia (Lészped 2). Total: 5. (The list is not complete: several recent notations with tune are known,

mostly recorded with truncated, short texts. For a long time I have not considered this song a ballad, nor did I collect its variants.) The song from Gyimesfelsőlok has a repetitive form, complemented with refrains.

Textual relationships with other ballads: none.
Tunes: 1. (2 variants).

This song is more of a low-life scene than a ballad. (The story of *Armistead–Silvermann* 1971, 81 13A resembles this song.)

131. DANCE, FRIAR, A DANCE!

232.

1.Jár -jad, pap u - ram, a tán -cot! Maj egy fal - ka lu - dat a -dok.

Nem já - rom, nem tu - dom, Pap -nak tán - cot jár - ni!
Nem il - lik, nemsza - bad

1. Dance, friar, a dance!
   I shall give you a flock of geese.
   I don't dance, I cannot dance,
   It is not becoming, it is forbidden
   For a friar to dance a dance.

2. Dance, friar, a dance!
   I shall give you a fat pig.
   I don't dance, I cannot dance,
   It is not becoming, it is forbidden
   For a friar to dance a dance!

3. Dance, friar, a dance!
   I shall give you a nice young wife.
   I will dance, I can dance,
   It is becoming, it is not forbidden
   For a friar to dance a dance!

Mohács (Baranya county). Performed by a woman of 50. Schneider 1938 = Berze Nagy 243–244.

Dissemination: County Baranya (Mohács), county Nyitra (Kolon), County Kolozs (Magyargyerőmonostor, Méra). Total: 4.
Textual relationships with other ballads: **72., 73.**

Versions in languages other than Hungarian: Songs mocking friars have a farreaching tradition. A fairly close form of this story is *Gagnon* 130: "Oh, if only this friar danced a dance! I would give him a hood! (Each line repeated.) Dance, friar, dance! You are a bad dancer, not hearing the rhythm of the mill's sound. Oh, if only this friar danced a dance! I would give him a hair-shirt...a rosary...a nice book of psalms...And had he not made a vow of poverty I would give him something else, too."

Although the point of the latter song is different, it is closely related with the Hungarian, not only as regards content but also the strophe-repetitive form. Yet no direct connection can be assumed between the two. Isolated position, new-style formulation, and the fact that songs mocking friars are reborn every now and then, never losing their timeliness, warn us to be cautious in drawing any definite conclusion.

132. THE BELATED WEDDING

233.

Tempo giusto

1. El -mënt a pap mi -sét tön - ni,   Bar - na kis-lánt es - küt-tet - ni.   Igy tëdd rá, ugy tëdd rá!

A - lig vár - ta, hogy es - küd - jön,   A templombul e - me - hes - sön. Igy tëdd rá, ugy tëdd rá!

1. The parson went to celebrate a mass,
   The wedding of a pretty brown girl took place.
   Hey-ho, whoopee, Hey-ho, whoopee!
   She could hardly wait till it was over,
   She ran away from the church.
   Hey-ho, whoopee, hey-ho, whoopee!

2. They have hardly reached the third house,
   The bride gave birth to a baby.
   Hey-ho, whoopee, hey-ho, whoopee!
   She took off her skirt,
   And wrapped the baby in it.
   Hey-ho, whoopee, hey-ho, whoopee!

3. The baby is crying in the kitchen.
   Don't cry, baby in the kitchen!
   Hey-ho, whoopee, hey-ho, whoopee!
   Your mother is dancing in the room,
   Your father is sorrowing at the table!
   Hey,-ho, whoopee, hey-ho, whoopee!

Boda (Baranya county). Performed by a woman of 63. 1935 = Berze Nagy 158–159.

Associated with a recruiting dance-tune (verbunk).

234.

Tempo giusto

1. Be - süt a   nap   a   temp-lom - ba   I - ha - ja, csu -ha -ja,

El - sőt ha - ran - goz-tat   a pap   I - ha - ja, csu - ha - ja.

943

1. The sun shines in the church,
   Here's to us, here's to us!
   The parson tolled the first chime,
   Here's to us, here's to us!

2. The parson goes in to deliver a sermon,
   Here's to us, here's to us!
   To celebrate a brown girl's wedlock,
   Here's to us, here's to us!

3. She can hardly wait till the ceremony is over,
   Here's to us, here's to us!
   Till she can leave the altar,
   Here's to us, here's to us!

4. They have hardly arrived at the third house,
   Here's to us, here's to us!
   The bride gives birth to a baby,
   Here's to us, here's to us!

5. Aunt Sári, aunt Jutka,
   Here's to us, here's to us!
   Open the little gate,
   Here's to us, here's to us!

6. We went, the two of us, and we arrived, the three of us,
   Here's to us, here's to us
   We lead a shameful life,
   Here's to us, here's to us!

Felsőireg (Tolna county). Performed by a group of girls. Bartók 1906 = MSz. 171 = Ethn. 1909, 304.

235.
1. Panna Lévaji filled with sorrow
   Went down to the big Tisza.
   Her mother walked after her:
   Come home, daughter Panna!

2. I would fain go home, only I don't dare to,
   For fear of my brother Gyurka!
   Never fear, daughter, he is not going to hurt you,
   Being your dear brother, your dear brother!

3. As they returned home,
   They walked over to the Keszeg's.
   Illés Keszeg, come on with me,
   Marry me, and I shall be your wife!

4. I would fain marry you, only I cannot,
   My dear mother does not allow me to marry you!
   Deny your mother, then,
   Together with all your kinsfolk!

5. Horses ought to be put to the cart,
   We ought to go to Kökinda,
   We ought to go to Kökinda,
   To have Panna examined by the doctor.

6. You must not arrange for the wedding feast,
   You must rather buy a cradle.
   Nor is a virgin's head-dress needed any longer,
   Sooner than that a bandage is needed.

7. She takes off her ribbons
   And places them on the knob of the cradle.
   They do not arrange for the wedding feast,
   Rather they buy a cradle with the money.

Szaján (Torontál county). = Kálmány 1882, 24.

Divergences: The variants are fairly well represented by the published texts.

Earliest provenience: 1878.
Dissemination: Zala county (Szentmargitfalva); Somogy county (Csököl); Baranya county (Boda); Tolna county (Felsőireg); Torontál county (Szaján); Arad county (Pécska). Total: 6.
Tunes: as published.

The witty, mocking texts are of recent development.

133. THE BURNT SHEEP-PEN

236.

Rubato ♩=88

1. Le - é - gett a Csi - ri - bi - ri ho - dály.   Be - le - é - gett ki-lenc juhász - boj-tár.

A ki-lenc-nek ki-lenc pár ru - há - ja,   Szá-ma - dó - nak ki-var - rott bun-dá - ja.

1. The barracks of Csiribiri has burnt down,
   Nine young shepherds have burnt in it.
   Nine pairs of clothes of the nine lads,
   Together with the embroidered fur-coat of the old shepherd.

2. The old shepherd has not lost too much,
   He can buy a new fur-coat at the Füred fair.
   But the nine young shepherds, the poor souls,
   Have been burnt with all their things in the barracks.

3. A pretty brown girl is walking round the barracks
   Asking the old shepherd about the young one.
   In vain are you looking for him,
   The one who loved you dearly has burnt in the barracks.

4. Show me, then, his grave,
   So that I can set roses on it!
   Let it grow roses instead of thistle,
   For he has been my true lover!

Bernáthegy (Heves county). Performed by a man of 52. (In the 1950s.)

Divergences: No essential differences can be observed among the variants.

Earliest provenience: 1871/72 (Bartalus)
Dissemination: S.l.: 2.
I. Vas county (Nagyrákos); Zala county (Dergecs, Keszthely); Somogy county (Zamárdi); Baranya county (Kölked, Szebény); Tolna county (Sárpilis, "Tolna c."); Fejér county (Dunapentele); Veszprém county (Rezi, Veszprém); Pest county (Tök); Komárom county (Mocsa); Győr county (Győr, Ménfőcsanak), I.: 15.
II. Nógrád county (Nagybátony 2, Szuha?); Heves county (Átány, Bernáthegy, Besenyőtelek, Fedémes 2, Füzesabony 2, "Heves c."?, Mátraszentimre 2, Mátraszentistván, Pálasveresmart, Tar, Tiszanána, Várászó); Borsod county (Kisgyőr, Sály, Szegilong); Gömör county (Almágy); Abaúj county (Boldogkőújfalu, Gagyvendégi, Tornyosnémeti 2); Zemplén county ("Tisza–Bodrog Interfluve", Bodrogszerdahely, Gesztely, Nagytárkány 2, Örös, Ricse, Sárospatak, Tiszakarád). II.: 35.

III. Pest county (Bugacmonostor, Galambospuszta, Izsák, Kiskunfélegyháza, Kiskunhalas 6, Lajosmizse, Makád, "Pest c."); Jász-Nagykun-Szolnok county (Jászapáti, Jászberény); Bács-Bodrog county (Bácsalmás, Mélykút); South Great Plain (without precise indication of locality 2); Csongrád county (Csongrád, Hódmezővásárhely 2); Békés county (Doboz); Bihar county (Nagyszalonta 2); Hajdú county (Hajdúböszörmény, Hajdúnánás 2, Hajdúszoboszló, "Hortobágy", Porod 2); Szabolcs county (Balsa, Lövőpetri, Tiszalök, Vaja); Szatmár county (Szamosszeg). III.: 37.

IV. Szolnok-Doboka county (Szék); Torda-Aranyos county (Újtorda); Szeben county, (Szeben); Udvarhely county (Olasztelek, Tordátfalva); Csík county (Csíkmenaság); Háromszék county (Kisborosnyó, Nagyajta). IV.: 8. Total: 97.

Textual relationships with other ballads: None.

Tunes: 1. = No. 236 (24 variants); 2. (7); 3. (6).

2. — the melody composed to *Petőfi*'s poem entitled *'Alku"* (first lime: "Young shepherd, poor young shepherd"). 4. — the melody of an art song beginning with the line: "Maybeetle, yellow maybeetle".

Both tunes are very widespread among the peasantry.

The song developed at the end of the last century changes the plot into a lyrical piece. It can hardly be termed a ballad.

134. COME, SWEETHEART, REDEEM ME!

237.

1. The mayor of Semjén
   Is said to have two fine horses.
   I try to steal them in the dark of the night,
   Before dawn shines on me.

2. Dawn is breaking,
   Two gendarmes are coming to put me in iron.
   They put shackles on my two tender hands,
   I am taken away today.

3. I am taken to the single-man cell,
   From the single-man cell to the two-men cell.
   Come, sweetheart, redeem me,
   Don't let me wither here.

4. I shall redeem you, never fear,
   I shall not let you wither away.
   I shall sell my yellow dancing-shoes,
   I shall redeem my sweetheart!

Kérsemjén (Szatmár county). Performed by a man of 34. Halmos 1955 = Nz 4184.

Divergences: No considerable difference can be observed among the variants.

Earliest provenience: 1906 *(Vikár).*
Dissemination: S. l.: 1.
   Zala county (Magyarszerdahely); Somogy county (Bálványos, Karád 2); Tolna county (Sárpilis); Fejér county (Pusztaforna); Veszprém county (Tata); Nógrád county (Nézsa); Heves county (Boldog, Fedémes, Mezőszemere, Pétervására); Borsod county (Alsóábrány, Felsőnyárád, Mezőkövesd, Sajókaza 3, Sajókazinc); Abaúj county (Cekeháza); Zemplén county (Erdőshorváti,

Ricse); Pest county (Bugacmonostor, Fülöpszállás, Galgamácsa, Galgahévíz, Göböljárás, Kecel, Kecskemét, Keserűtelek, Kiskunfélegyháza, Kiskunhalas 4, Kiskunmajsa, Nagykőrös); Jász-Nagykun-Szolnok county (Cibakháza, Jászszentandrás, Tiszabő, Tiszaföldvár 2, Tiszafüred, Tiszaigar, Tiszakürt, Tiszazug); Bács-Bodrog county (Doroszló), Homokmégy, Rém 2, Szakmár, Tiszakécske); Csongrád county (Algyő, Ásotthalom, Balástya, Csongrád, Domaszék, Hódmezővásárhely 3, Homokpuszta 4, Horgos, Kistelek 2, Mindszent, Mórahalom, Szeged-Felsőtanya, Tápé 3, Üllés); Békés county (Doboz 2, Ecseg, Kaszaper); Hajdú county (Darvas, Debrecen-Nyulas, Földes, Hortobágy-Halastó, Hosszúpályi); Szabolcs county, (Nyíracsád, Nyírbátor, Nyírlugos); Szatmár county (Kérsemjén 2, Szamosszeg 2). Total: 91.

Tunes: Sung almost exclusively to the published tune (in 84 recordings); in three cases it was performed with the following melody:

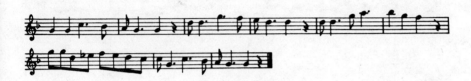

This song has developed quite recently and shows an unparalleled uniformity in all the variants. What seems to be an outlaw story at first sight is nothing else than a lyrical low-life scene. Therefore we have not listed it along with the outlaw ballads.

APPENDIX

1. WHAT HAS NOT BEEN INCLUDED IN THE PUBLICATION

The published material does not cover the entire stock of Hungarian ballad variants. In compiling them, I arrived at a point where I had to close the number of variants in order to be able to provide a conclusive study-text. After December 31, 1972 not even the newly collected ballads of the Folk Music Research Group have been taken into consideration, although collections coming in from the most diverse regions of the language area have been continually elaborated at the Group. I am convinced, however, that the ceaselessly streaming new data will not alter essentially the overall view gained so far. Mainly new-style ballads, or variants of very widespread types—for instance of The Sister of the Man Condemned to Death—turn up, or further notations of the material recorded from Moldavia, and Transylvania. (Nevertheless, exception to this rule has been made in connection with some specially important texts, variants which have been incorporated in the body of the ballad stock after the mentioned date.)

Apart from the Types enumerated here, there are texts qualified by various collectors as ballads. I have not taken every text with a plot for a ballad. The material of my study could have been perhaps doubled in size, had all the verses dealing with local events, murders, suicidal acts, and the like, been included. To wit, there is no end to the number of these. Points of dissemination have been made the standard: we have omitted all songs which occur in a single locality and its neighbourhood only, and included all those which have a nation-wide spread. (The Girl Who Fell into the Threshing Machine, No. **128.** or The Man Who Killed His Sweetheart and Committed Suicide, No. **98.**). A certain degree of the polishing interference of the community can be witnessed in such cases; and even if it cannot, dissemination in wider spheres betray something about the taste of the villagers (or the deterioration of their tastes). As against these, the local ballads are short-lived, hardly extending further than the life-span of a generation. Compared to that of the whole language community and the true folklore products, their existence is brief: one might say, they are anti-substances of folklore tradition coming to life for an evanescent moment to vanish immediately. They are "personal suggestions" rejected by the community. As such, they are apt to study the popular method of creation on them, since very often they resort to the use of "prefabricated elements", accepted turns and portions of folksongs. To study these thoroughly would blow up the frame of the present work, without bringing any appreciable results.

Special mention should be made of the "forgeries". Regrettably enough, the general European trend to create sham-ballads did not shun Hungary in the last century. Hardly did the first exquisite old Hungarian ballads appear when authors under the guise of collectors presented themselves. Most diligent of these was *Jób Sebesi* who overpoured the third volume of MNGY with his compositions. Traces of his hand can be discerned in several phases. Sometimes only a minor detail of the collected text can be attributed to him. For instance, in the case of The Walled-up Wife (No. 40 with him): "Kelemen's wife was frightened, My God, my God, Give me my little child Together with its cradle, Place it before me! God gave an ear to her request, He placed it before her, He gave a warm shower . . ." and so on. Typical is the ending part of The Two Royal Children (No. 36 with him); "They gave a splendid burial To the King's daughter. They threw back her sweetheart Into the sea. (A characteristically unballad-like conception!) The soul, of the girl, the soul of the young man Always meet in a flowery meadow. They embrace and kiss each other, They are constantly rejoicing. As midnight comes, They appear at the bed of the King. They torment him, because he did not let them marry each other, While they were alive." It is noteworthy that alone he of all the contributors of the ballad about The Marvellous Corpse refers to the girl's round bottom (beside her slender waist and knobbed lips). Here we are faced with an instance of pseudo-folkloristic attitude, for a true ballad will never enter into such ostentatious details. Anyway, most of his pieces are compositions which have nothing to do with folklore. (Cf. MNGY III, 29–35, 41, 43–47, 50, 52–56, 59, 61, 67.) Interestingly, he sometimes presents a real folklore piece, too, and even more interesting than that is that he published immediately a transcribed variant thereof. Thus, the Three Orphans (No. 42) is a regular variant known from parallels. It is followed by No. 43:

1. Three orphans set out To wander on a long way,
   Their step-mother threatened them She beat them with a log.
2. They went to the cemetery, And sat down on their mother's grave.
   Rise, rise, dear mother, Our shirts and pants are torn.
3. Go, three orphans, To the abode of your stepmother,
   Tell her what I say: I shall never forget of her vileness.
4. If I learn that you are unwell: I turn in my grave,
   I go home to suck you, I visit you by night.

It cannot be made our aim here to go into details of his falsifications, yet we have to show, by a few examples which found their way into later collections as well, how far they are from the true spirit of folk poetry. For example, the beginning of Ilona Kis (No. 44 with him) reads like this:
"The mayor of Szentmárton wanted his son to marry Sári Hajdú, Although in vain, For the young man did not want her, He did not want Péter Hajdú's daughter with her painted face. His father forced him, his mother forced him: Dear son, marry her: Meet our pleasure this time at least. All this does not help anything . . .".
In No 47 the wife sends her husband asleep by means of a drug, then she lets in her lover, and the two of them kill the wife's husband. "The brave husband's blood was spilt. They left the brave husband lying in his blood, And they packed up all the treasure. They are walking, walking in a thick forest. In the thick forest they find a tall oak-tree, With a cold spring under it. Let's stop here, wife Sári, I am thirsty and want to drink of the water of this spring. Does it taste good to you, blond lad? Alas, I am dying, wife Sári! The spring's water is throbbing with blood. It keeps saying: I am a murderer! Let's leave this place, blond lad! I don't go with you, wife Sári,

Something is buzzing in my ears, I can't bear the burden of my sin! Bend your head in my lap, blond lad, have a sleep! I cannot sleep, wife Sári, My great sin does not let me sleep. Let's go, let's go, blond lad! Never in my life! Blond lad, what has become to your mind? Is it perhaps the wine that made you dizzy? It is you, wife Sári, Your honeyed words have made me dizzy. Wife Sári, look up in the tree, And Prepare to die with me!''

As can be seen, extensive performance, individual content elements never occurring elsewhere, absence of strophic construction (a feature based on the misunderstanding of folk compositions in which sometimes a fifth and sixth line is sung to the third and fourth melodic sections), unsystematic arrangements of the lines, exaggerated folkish style; —all this renders his texts unmistakeably distinct from anything else. Even where less conspicuous pseudo-folklore tone is hit upon, his peculiar style can be certainly discovered (by the way, such creations as those about The Captive Soldier, or Máté Bíró stand quite solitary in the body of Hungarian balladry). (Nos 29 and 30.) These have made their way into anthologies of later dates (Cf. *Ortutay* and *I. Kriza,* Nos 25 and 26). Let us give a few lines of The Captive Soldier: "The peacock has lighted On the coast of the sea, From the coast of the sea To the splendid court of the Great Turkish Emperor. From there the peacock—The proud peacock—Went to the wall of the prison... "Can't you see that I am a prisoner, Cast in iron up to my knees. I was a Székely lad, I was a brave lad, Now I am nothing, Yet the guard has to report on me...". Another example is taken from the much-quoted, even staged, Máté Bíró: "There with tender hands he took off The golden saddle Of the fair daughter of the King, Of his Fair Ilona. With tender hands, he laid her On a soft bed of moss, There he embraced her, There he kissed her. With his two strong arms, He embraced softly The beautiful daughter of the King, His Fair Ilona, That famous Máté Bíró, Captain of robbers."—These are typical examples of the style of *Jób Sebesi,* marked by superfluous repetitions added to closed sentences, unparalleled in folk poetry. Similarly isolated pieces were produced by *Béla Kővári,* whose unfolkish tone has marred the Göcsej collection to such an extent that it was considered for a long time as unusable for any practical purposes. Still, recently some of the anthologies have included certain of the ballads collected by *Kővári* and first published by *Abafi* (cf. *Ortutay* 1955 74a, and in his wake: *Leader* 291), although the act of forgery cannot be called into doubt at seeing such unballad-like lines in isolated pieces as the following ones:

"The once-upon-a-time king Had a once-upon-a-son, The other king had a beautiful daughter. The handsome prince appeared in a coach and six To ask for the hand of the princess in marriage. They soon agreed, and gave the girl to him. The wedding feast lasted a week. The prince took away the girl whom he loved dearly, He took him in a coach and six, rolling on golden wheels. ... Listen, listen, your majestic princess! You can redeem yourself, and save your husband at the same time: Spend three nights in the bed of our captain. After that you can leave together with your husband and horses..." The poem reads throughout in such a lofty style. Even he who has no ear for the exaggerated rhymes and the unpopular manner of presentation of thoughts, which are themselves alien to popular thinking, might perhaps be cautious of such unsuccessful attempts at imitating the dialect style.

As a matter of course, compositions created in a spirit other than that of folksongs are sung by people in many instances. But the extensive dissemination of such creations can be proved by numberless notations and recordings of melodies. As against this, pieces originating from one author, occurring though massively on the pages of collections (invariably tuneless), but having no parallels elsewhere, are certainly such ones as had never been sung by the people. Rubbish of this kind has been due to uncritical enthusiasm of the last century, and as such must be excluded from the realm of folk compositions which are noble in their puritan simplicity.

2. CONFLICT PLOTS AND THEMES IN HUNGARIAN BALLADS

LOVE

1. Faithfulness **43. 44.**
2. Love beyond grave **9. 65. 133.**
3. Danger run for sweetheart **19. 37.**
4. Infidelity **47. 59. 91.**
5. Separation **59.**
6. Forbidden love **82. 121. 122.**
7. Separated lovers **19. 37. 44.**
   Lovers separated by death **9. 44. 65. 133.**
8. Enticement **3. 5. 68.93.**
   Enticed sweetheart forsaken **93.**
   Enticed returns **3. 5. 30.**
   Enticement (abduction) with apparent death **68.**
9. Enticer rejected **43. 44.**
10. Winning the sweetheart by degrees **68. 70. 72. 73. 77. 131.**
11. Winning the sweetheart by service **40. 55. 73.**
12. Coward lover **70. 71.**
13. Love conquers everything **89.**
14. Sorrows of love **57.**
15. Pregnant girl **10. 23. 24. 83.**
    Unmarried mother kills her babe **23. 24.**
    Pregnant girl executed **10. 23.**
    Pregnant bride taken back **83.**
16 Girl seduced by force demands marriage **81.**
17. Kidnapped girl (by enemies) **29. 30. 31.**
18. Girl defends her virtue (by suicide) **29.**
19. Girl sacrificing her virtue to rescue her brother **27.**
20. Lover kills (or wants to kill) his sweetheart **3. 26. 98. 123.**
    out of jealousy **26. 98. 123.**
    out of revenge **26.**
    Murderer of sweetheart punished **3.**
21. Rejected suitor takes revenge **11.**
22. Friends as rivals in love **33. 126.**
23. False judge extorts love from the girl **27.**
24. Asking the girl in marriage **56. 76.**
    Bad marriage **76.**

MARRIAGE (love)

25. Forced marriage **11. 12. 13. 14. 15 (49?)**
    Forced bride found dead **12.**
    Forced bride dies in the wedding procession **13.**
26. Forbidden marriage **9. 16. 48. 98. 126.**
    Mother against her daughter's marriage **16.**
27. Head of family kills lover (sweetheart), or has him (her) executed **9. 38. 40. 121.**
28. Adultery **1. 21. 77. 78. 129. 130.**
    Adultery detected **1. 21. 129.**
    Revenged (punished) adultery **1. 21.**
29. Enticed wife **3.**
30. Reunion with enticed wife **3.**
31. Husband threatens wife to death **41.**
32. Matrimonial fidelity **44.**
33. Mourning for lost spouse **44.**
34. Unloved spouse **39. 63. 64.**

FAMILY CONFLICTS

35. Husband punishes wife **66. 67.**
36. Murder of the wife's kinsfolk by husband **20.**
37. Wife takes revenge for a murdered member of her family **20.**
38. Husband kills the wife who detected him **20.**
39. Cruelty—unkindness to family member **2. 4. 5. 6. 9. 10. 16. 20. 23. 24. 25. 28. 38. 39. 52. 60. 62. 69. 94. 124. 125.** (Unrecognized) **17. 22. 42.**
40. Poisoning of relative (lover) **60.**
41. Incest (done, intended) **42. 84. 100.**
42. Wealth more important than a member of family **2. 4. 52.**
43. Lover kinder than the relatives **69.**
44. Mother forsakes her child **4. 5.**
45. Mother rejects her child **5. 41.** (Unrecognized) **17.**
46. Sacrifice for member of family **27.**
47. Rejected sacrifice for member of family **52. 69.**
48. Motherly love beyond grave **6.**
49. (Lost) member of family is not recognized **3. 17. 18. 22. 42. 84. 100.**
50. Girl married abroad returns home **41.**
51. Separation from member of family (farewell to) **8.**

SOCIAL DIFFERENCES–CONFLICTS

52. Cruelty, high-handedness with the poor (7.) 9. 17. 22. 38. 121.
53. Poor revenges himself on rich 26. 66. 74. 75.
54. Denunciation of the rich (thirst for riches) 2. 4. 7. 22. 46. 52.
55. Love breaks through class barriers 9. 25. 38. 75. 121. 122.
56. Poor and rich contrasted 26. 66. 74. 75. 133.
57. Lover believed to be poor is rich 75.

REVOLT AGAINST SOCIAL DISCRIMINATION (PROSECUTED CRIMINAL)

58. Exile 54.
59. Life and fall of outlaws 101. 102. 103. 104. 105. 106. 108. 109. 110. (111. 134.)
60. Adventures of outlaws 107. 112. 113. 119. 120.
61. The fate of solitary revolter 103.

62. Haughty outlaw resists 114. 115.
63. Outlaw falls 116.
64. Heroic resistance and fall 102. 103. 109. 110.
65. Outlaw after fall 118.

OTHER

66. Husband killed at action 34. 35.
67. Hero sacrifices his life for Leander 35.
68. Captivity (17.) 36. 50. 51. 52.
69. Escape from imprisonment 17. 33.
70. Robbery and murder 19. 32. 96.
71. Robber repents 53.
72. Sin and punishment (according to Christian faith) 95.
73. Miracle (according to Christian faith) (6.) 8.
74. Dead body returns (6.) 85. 86.
75. Lad killed at brawl 127.
76. Fatal incident 128.
77. Girl disguised as soldier 80.

3. SCENES, CHARACTERS AND DETAILS
OF FORMULATION
IN HUNGARIAN BALLADS

Animal characters: **15. 44. 45. 77. 91.**

Balcony: girl (wife) embroidering with gold on the balcony **12. 13.**
Biblical figures as characters: **7. 8. 90. 95.**
Bride: demanding at door **12. 14. 31.**
Bride dying in the wedding procession **13. 16.**
Building sacrifice: **2.**
Burning (alive): **1. 28.**

Choice among kinds of deaths: **1. 28.**
Corpse: transforms, speaks **9. 94.**
    Dialogue with corpse **6. 9. 65.**
Curse: **2. 9. 16. 17. 22. 27. 46. 47. 59. 87. 93. 99.**
    Curse upon unfaithful lover **47. 59. 87. 93. 99.**
    Self-cursing **12. 13. 20. 51.**

Dancing to death: **26.**
Death: sweetheart dies after lover **37. 38. 47. 48.** (Cf. Suicide)
Delay: cf. "Door"
Detection: sex-detecting tests **80.**
    Unsuccessful attempts at **80.**
    Detection of pregnancy by the shortening skirt **10.**
Dialogue: with animals **15.**
    with corpse: cf. "Corpse"
Disguise: **3. (17.) 22. 43. 75. 80.**
    Woman dressed as a man **80.**
Door: delay in opening the door **1. 20. 25. 31. 78.**
Dream: ill omen **2. 23. 51.**

Elopement from prison: **17. 33.**
Evasive replies: **1. 2. 3. 10. 12. 14. (16.) 20. 21. 25. 27. 28. 78. (83.) 100. 129.**

Farewell: to flowers, dresses **10. 11. 12. 13. 14. 15. 29. 31.**
    Mother takes leave of her (orphan) child **2. 4. 5. 20.**
Finding the corpse: cf. "Grave"
Flight, fight with prosecutors: **17. (18.) 33.**
Flower characters: **89.**

Girl binds wreath: **8. 43.**
Gradations: conflict revealed by degrees **60. 61. 62. 65.**
    Comic conflicts with points: **63. 64. 66. 67. 70. 71. 72. 73. 76. 77. 129. 131.**
    Gradual disappointment: **71. 77.**
Grave: showing the grave (corpse) of died lover **9. 10. 19.**
Grave (Chapel-) flower: **9. 10. 28. 37. 38. 48. (68.)**

Heavenly bridegroom: **8.**

Impossible tasks: **79.**
Indication (ill omen): **2. 9. 19. 23. 51.**
Inn: (robbers in the inn) **19. 53.**

Kinds of death: cf. "Choice among kinds of..."

Lament: self-lament of the hero **29. 52.** (in prison) **22. 33. 118.**
    Mock-lament: **63.**
Last will: **32. 41. 60. 62.**
Lifting corpse out of water: **9. 28. 37.**
Lodging-seeker (rejected): **7. 17.**
Love (erotic) symbol: **19. 24. 44. 45. 57. 81. 93.**

Man goes to the war: **28. (34. 36.) 88.**
Message through bird: **10. 118.**

Overheard speech (through door): **20. 21.**

Prisoner (condemned) randomed (refused to be randomed): **23. 27. 52. 118.**

Recognition (of relative, lover): **18. 42. 84.**
    by singing: cf. "Song"
Relative, lover is not recognized: **3. 17. 22. 30. 41. 42. (43.)**
Robbery and murder: **19. 32.**

Saliva (speaking): **30.**
Searching in the head: **3. 5. 40. 41.**
Sending astray (to baffle, gain time): **10. 12. 28.**
Solving of riddle: **79.**
Song: recognition by song **17. 22. 42.**
    Extraordinary, loud singing **18.**

Suicide: for died lover (sweetheart) **9. 10. 19. 21. 28. 38. 40. (98.)**
For unfaithful lover: **47. 99.**

Taking out of the heart (liver), cutting off the head:
6. 20. 25. 31. 38. 57.
Test: **17. 22. 43. 69. 75. 80.**
In disguise: **17. 22. 43. 75.**

Urging the coachman ("The horse belongs to dogs..."): **2. 9. 10. 16. 21. 27. 39.**

Violence: **19. (93.)**

Warrior asks girls for food and drink: **58.**
Window: (weeping) woman sewing in the window **14. 21. 31. 49.**